CONTEMPORARY RHETORICAL THEORY

A Reader

Edited by
JOHN LOUIS LUCAITES
CELESTE MICHELLE CONDIT
SALLY CAUDILL

The Guilford Press
New York   London

© 1999 The Guilford Press
A Division of Guilford Publications, Inc.
72 Spring Street, New York, NY 10012
http://www.guilford.com

Printed in the United States of America

This book is printed on acid-free paper.

Last digit is print number: 9 8 7 6 5 4 3 2 1

Library of Congress Cataloging-in-Publication Data

Contemporary rhetorical theory : a reader / edited by John Louis
   Lucaites, Celeste Michelle Condit, Sally Caudill.
     p.   cm. — (Revisioning rhetoric)
   Includes bibliographical references and index.
   ISBN 1-57230-401-4 (pbk. : alk. paper)
   1. Rhetoric.   I. Lucaites, John Louis. II. Condit, Celeste
Michelle, 1956– . III. Caudill, Sally. IV. Series.
P301.C574 1999   98-37101
808'.001–dc21   CIP

CONTEMPORARY RHETORICAL THEORY

REVISIONING RHETORIC
A Guilford Series
Karlyn Kohrs Campbell and Celeste Michelle Condit
Series Editors

Contemporary Rhetorical Theory:
A Reader
*John Louis Lucaites, Celeste Michelle Condit,
and Sally Caudill,* Editors

Reading Nietzsche Rhetorically
Douglas Thomas

At the Intersection:
Cultural Studies and Rhetorical Studies
Thomas Rosteck, Editor

Rhetoric in Postmodern America:
Conversations with Michael Calvin McGee
Carol Corbin, Editor

Analyzing Media: Communication Technologies
as Symbolic and Cognitive Systems
James W. Chesebro and Dale W. Bertelsen

The following articles are reprinted from *Communication Monographs* by permission of the National Communication Association: Bruce E. Gronbeck, "The Functions of Presidential Campaigning," vol. 25 (1978): 268–280; Walter R. Fisher, "Narrative as A Human Communication Paradigm," vol. 51 (1984): 1–22; Raymie E. McKerrow. "Critical Rhetoric: Theory and Praxis," vol. 56 (1989): 91–111.

The following articles are reprinted from *Critical Studies in Mass Communication* by permission of the National Communication Association: Barry Brummett, "Burke's Representative Anecdote as a Method of Media Criticism," vol. 1 (1984): 161–176; Celeste Michelle Condit, "The Rhetorical Limits of Polysemy," vol. 6 (1989): 103–122.

The following articles are reprinted from *Philosophy and Rhetoric* by permission of The Pennsylvania State University Press, ©1968, 1973, 1976, 1983, 1989, 1991: Lloyd Bitzer, "The Rhetorical Situation," vol. 1 (1968): 1–14; Richard E. Vatz, "The Myth of the Rhetorical Situation," vol. 6 (1973): 154–157; Barry Brummett, "Some Implications of 'Process' or 'Intersubjectivity': Postmodern Rhetoric," vol. 9 (1976): 21–51; John Poulakos, "Toward A Sophistic Definition of Rhetoric," vol. 16 (1983): 35–48; Barbara Biesecker, "Rethinking the Rhetorical Situation from within the Thematic of *Différance*," vol. 22 (1989): 110–130; Thomas Farrell, "Practicing the Arts of Rhetoric: Tradition and Invention," vol. 24 (1991): 183–212.

The following articles are reprinted from the *Quarterly Journal of Speech* by permission of the National Communication Association: Herbert W. Simons, "Requirements, Problems and Strategies: A Theory of Persuasion for Social Movements," vol. 56 (1970): 1–11; Edwin Black, "The Second Persona," vol. 56 (1970): 109–119; Karlyn Kohrs Campbell, "The Rhetoric of Women's Liberation: An Oxymoron," vol. 59 (1973): 74–86; Michael C. McGee, "In Search of 'the People': A Rhetorical Alternative," vol. 61 (1975): 235–249; Thomas Farrell, "Knowledge, Consensus, and Rhetorical Theory," vol. 62 (1976): 1–14; Michael Calvin McGee, "The 'Ideograph': A Link Between Rhetoric and Ideology," vol. 6 (1980): 1–16; Richard A. Cherwitz and James W. Hikins, "Rhetorical Perspectivism," vol. 69 (1983): 249–266; Thomas S. Frentz, "Rhetorical Conversation, Time, and Moral Action," vol. 71 (1985): 1–18; Celeste Michelle Condit, "Crafting Virtue: The Rhetorical Construction of Public Morality," vol. 73 (1987): 79–87; Janice Hocker Rushing and Thomas S. Frentz, "Integrating Ideology and Archetype in Rhetorical Criticism," vol. 77 (1991): 385–406; Carole Blair, Julie R. Brown, and Leslie A. Baxter, "Disciplining the Feminine," vol. 84 (1994): 383–409; Robert Hariman, "Status, Marginality and Rhetorical Theory," vol. 72 (1995): 2–17.

In addition, we gratefully acknowledge permission to reprint the following articles from various sources: Michael Leff, "The Habitation of Rhetoric," in *Argument and Critical Practice: Proceedings of the Fifth SCA/AFA Conference on Argumentation*. Ed. Joseph Wenzel. Annandale, VA: SCA. 1987. 1–9. Used by permission of the National Communication Association. Michael Calvin McGee, "Text, Context, and the Fragmentation of Contemporary Culture.," *Western Journal of Speech Communication* 54 (1990): 274–289. Used by permission of the Western Communication Association. Jane Sutton, "The Taming of *Polos/Polis*: Rhetoric As an Achievement Without Woman.," *Southern Communication Journal* 57 (1992): 97–119. Reprinted with permission of the Southern States Communication Association. Robert Scott, "On Viewing Rhetoric as Epistemic.," *Central States Speech Journal* 18 (1967) 9–16. Used by permission of the Central States Communication Association. Dilip Parameshwar Gaonkar, "Rhetoric and Its Double: Reflections on the Rhetorical Turn in the Human Sciences," in *The Rhetorical Turn: Invention and Persuasion in the Conduct of Inquiry*, 341–366. Ed. Herbert W. Simons. Chicago: University of Chicago Press, 1990. ©1990 by the University of Chicago. G. Thomas Goodnight, "The Personal, Technical, and Public Sphere of Argumentation: A Speculative Inquiry into the Art of Public Deliberation.," *Argumentation and Advocacy* 18 (1982): 214–227. Reproduced by permission of the American Forensic Association. Philip Wander, "The Third Persona: An ideological Turn in Rhetorical Theory.," *Communication Studies* 33 (1984): 197–216. Used by permission of the Central States Communication Association. Maurice Charland, "Rehabilitating Rhetoric: Confronting Blindspots in Discourse and Social Theory.," *Communication* 11 (1990): 253–264. Reprinted by permission of Gordon and Breach Publishers. James Arnt Aune, "Cultures of Discourse: Marxism and Rhetorical Theory," in *Argumentation Theory and the Rhetoric of Assent,*

EDITOR'S NOTE: The essays reprinted in this volume appear as they did in their original publication. The editors have regularized capitalization and italicization of foreign words and phrases throughout the volume for the purpose of stylistic consistency.

Preface

In 1972 Douglas Ehninger edited *Contemporary Rhetoric: A Reader's Coursebook*. That volume served as an introduction to the nature and scope of rhetorical studies to many of us who began our journey into the study of rhetorical theory and practice in the wake of the impact of The National Developmental Project on Rhetoric in 1970 and the subsequent publication of *The Prospects of Rhetoric* in 1971. *Contemporary Rhetoric* was very much an object of its times, looking *outward* from the work of contemporary rhetorical theorists to the connections it might make with poetry, philosophy, communication theory, social theory, composition studies, etc. One of the results of that work has been to develop a richer, more complex body of rhetorical theory from within the perspective of communication studies writ large. *Contemporary Rhetorical Theory: A Reader* picks up the story from where Ehninger left off, focusing attention *inward* to the ways in which contemporary rhetorical theorists since the early 1970s have incorporated, implicated, and contributed to the broad range of humanistic attempts to engage communication and discourse in the context of the problems and possibilities of public persuasion, identification, and representation.

True to its name, all of the essays included in this volume are written by individuals who identify themselves as rhetorical theorists, and all of the work has been produced and published within the last forty years. The volume begins with an introductory essay that situates contemporary rhetorical theory within both a larger history of rhetorical theory and practice, and the competing tensions between modernity and postmodernity that seem to be most salient in guiding the work of contemporary rhetorical theorists. The first section poses the question "What Can a Rhetoric Be?" and offers a range of contemporary answers to that question. Subsequent sections of the volume explore key topics and issues that have occupied the attention of contemporary rhetorical theorists, including rhetoric and epistemology; the character of the rhetorical situation; rhetoric, reason and public morality; the nature of the audience; the role of discourse in social change; rhetoric and the mass media; and a range of challenges to the traditions of rhetorical theory from the margins. The volume concludes with an epilogue that invites students to consider the future promise and possibilities for rhetorical theory as we approach the next millennium—an expanded and globalized, multi-cultural, postmodern world in which the need for practicing rhetoricians will be of increasing and supreme importance.

The volume has been designed as an introduction for both advanced undergraduate and graduate students. Each Part of the volume begins with an introductory statement designed to frame the key issues and problems addressed by the essays contained therein. These headnotes are written so as to provide concrete anchors for those students who are coming to the study of rhetorical theory for the very first time, and thus to make it easier for them to identify and engage the issues that have traditionally been the concern of rhetoricians. At the same time, the headnotes are written in an open-ended manner designed to invite more advanced students to engage the materials more creatively with an eye toward their own inventive and critical participation in the conversation of contemporary rhetorical theory. Each headnote concludes with a brief list of selected additional readings.

All rhetoric is a material practice, and this volume is nothing if it is not a rhetorical practice guided by our collective experiences in teaching contemporary rhetorical theory to undergraduate and graduate students over the past fifteen years. In that context, we are indebted to the many students who have helped to shape and develop our understanding of what is important in introducing new generations of rhetoricians to what is surely the most exciting, practical, and productive of the liberal arts. Beyond our students, we have been blessed with numerous other friends and colleagues who have given graciously of their time and wisdom in helping us to complete this project. Stuart Ainsworth deserves special recognition for his assistance in scanning the essays into a usable computer format; so too must we acknowledge Stephanie Houston Grey, Doyle Srader, and Marcia Tiersky for their help in the thankless task of proofreading the original computer output. James P. McDaniel did yeoman's work in preparing the index. Numerous colleagues encouraged and assisted the project with their suggestions and hard-hitting critiques, and we cannot imagine this volume without their input. In particular we would like to acknowledge James Arnt Aune, Barbara Biesecker, Karlyn Kohrs Campbell, Bruce E. Gronbeck, Robert L. Ivie, James Jasinski, Mary Kahl, William Lewis, John Sloop, Charles Alan Taylor, Robert Terrill, and Philip Wander. Additionally, two individuals who deserve special gratitude are Robert Hariman, for his guidance on the selection of issues and articles to include in this volume, and Michael Calvin McGee, for his general guidance of our thoughts and careers as rhetorical theorists. We also thank the authors and publishers of the essays included in this volume, not only for their dedication to the task of producing rhetorical theory, but also for keeping the cost of reprinting the essays within reason so that the book might be accessible to the widest possible audience.

JOHN LOUIS LUCAITES
Bloomington, IN

CELESTE MICHELLE CONDIT
Athens, GA

SALLY CAUDILL
St. Cloud, MN

Contents

Introduction

JOHN LOUIS LUCAITES
CELESTE MICHELLE CONDIT

The ability to create a sense of community, and thus the possibility of social and political life as we know it, depends upon the human capacity for communication. For thousands of years, scholars and laity alike have recognized that the complexities of human communication are linked tightly to the unique and varied forms of social interaction. Twenty-four hundred years ago, for example, Isocrates—a teacher of both Plato and Aristotle, and identified by some as perhaps the most important classical advocate of a rhetorical education—advised his students that the "art of discourse" was "that power which, of all the faculties which belong to the nature of man, is the source of most of our blessings." The reasons he gave for this became central components of what was to become known as civic humanism: "In the other powers which we possess . . . we are in no respect superior to other living creatures; nay, we are inferior to many in swiftness and in strength and in other resources; but, because there has been implanted in us the power to persuade each other and to make clear to each other whatever we desire, not only have we escaped the life of the wild beasts, but we have come together and founded cities and made laws and invented arts; and, generally speaking, there is no institution devised by man which the power of speech has not helped us establish."[1]

Given the centrality of the art of discourse to human, social, and political endeavors, it is not at all surprising that academics, preachers, politicians, entrepreneurs, and an almost incalculable host of others have all attended closely to the problems and possibilities of human communication. This breadth of attention to the power and art of discourse by groups and individuals with fundamentally different purposes and orientations has produced a wide range of approaches to the study of human communication. One of the most powerful of such approaches from antiquity to the present has operated under the rubric of "rhetoric" or "rhetorical studies." As we note in the introduction to Part 1, the definition of "rhetoric" is itself a highly contested concept and its meaning has varied widely, both across the ages and within any given time period.

1

Our goal in this essay is not to provide a history of the concept of "rhetoric" from classical times to the present, although we do strongly encourage anyone interested in the discipline or study of contemporary rhetorical theory to consult its long and interesting heritage and to consider the impact that its various pasts have had upon its present study and uses.[2] Rather, our purpose here is to provide a brief introduction to the contemporary issues and concerns that have animated the work of rhetorical theorists since the late 1960s, a time of great social, political, and intellectual change. Of course, the contemporary interest in rhetorical theory cannot be completely bracketed and divorced from the interests and concerns of the larger histories of rhetoric that rhetorical theorists have crafted for themselves as a discipline. By the same token, however, it would be difficult to understand the complexities and conceptual importance of contemporary rhetorical theory if we focused primarily on the relationship between past and present. Our approach here, then, is to contextualize the interests and concerns of contemporary rhetorical theorists *both* historically and conceptually as they have manifested themselves over the past thirty-some years. To that end we begin by offering a brief survey of some of the key conceptual assumptions made by contemporary rhetorical theorists that derive from an understanding of the theory and practice of rhetoric in classical antiquity. Following that we consider how these assumptions have been contextualized and made problematic in the work of contemporary American rhetorical theorists.

CONTEMPORARY RHETORICAL THEORY'S LINK TO THE PAST

The earliest theorists of rhetoric are typically identified in the Western, liberal-democratic tradition as residing in ancient Greece and Rome, and not so coincidentally they are equally identified with the creation of democratic and republican forms of government. In this classical tradition, the focus on rhetoric typically emphasized the *public*, *persuasive*, and *contextual* characteristics of human discourse in situations governed by the problems of *contingency*.

Contingent situations occur when decisions have to be made and acted upon, but decision makers are forced to rely upon probabilities rather than certainties. Examples of such situations typically include deciding guilt or innocence where either the evidence is purely circumstantial or one has to rely on the credibility of witnesses, or deliberating on what the best course for future action might be. In either situation one must rely upon judgments derived from the probability or likelihood of "truth," rather than on certain knowledge. Even when there is an eyewitness to an alleged crime we cannot know for *certain* what the witness saw. Some witnesses might actually lie about what they saw, while the testimony of other witnesses might be tainted—inadvertently or not—by prejudice or point of view. This is one of the reasons why our contemporary judicial system places so much importance on the cross-examination of witnesses. Judgments about guilt or innocence are always about past actions, but determinations of how one ought to act in consequence of such judgments, the goal of deliberative assemblies like the legislature, is no less problematic in its reliance upon probability as a guide to belief and action. Short of a crystal ball we can never know for *certain* what the best future course of action might be, for it has yet to happen and it is impossible to take into account the finitude of events that might intercede between making the decision and enacting it. The best we can do is to make reasoned decisions based upon our knowledge of the past and the likelihood of future possibilities.

The emphasis on *public* discourse focused attention on communicative acts that affected the entire community and were typically performed before the law courts, the legislative assemblies, and occasional celebratory gatherings of the citizenry-at-large. Public discourse was thus distinguished from technical discourse addressed to specialized or elite audiences (e.g., the discourses of astronomy or medicine) and private discourse addressed to more personal audiences that did not directly effect the social and political community-at-large (e.g., family communication, master–slave interactions). The ability to contribute to public policy debates and to affect the direction and life of the community through public discourse was taken by classical teachers of rhetoric as an essential attribute of the educated citizen and thus very highly valued.

Quite naturally, given the classical commitments to democratic and republican forms of governance, public discourse was valorized because of its capacity for *persuasion*, that is, its ability to affect belief and behavior through the power of symbolic interaction. One entailment of this commitment was the belief that the ways in which something was expressed and engaged in public discourse had an important, determining effect on meaning and behavior. This point of view stood in contrast to the position of many philosophers (and later scientists) who treated discourse as a neutral conduit for representing an otherwise objective independent "truth." From the more philosophical point of view, discourse could function to clarify or confuse meaning, to make objective and predetermined "truths" appear more or less attractive, but it could not actually affect the truth of the thing being described or discussed. Rhetoricians vehemently disputed this point of view, arguing instead that particularly in the context of social and political affairs, the manner and form of discourse was integral to the "truth" of the thing being described and played a central role in shaping and motivating collective identity and action. So, for example, rhetoricians believed that the particular words and narratives used to characterize the Athenian "people" as "courageous" and "peace-loving" in a ceremonial funeral oration were not merely neutral descriptors of these particular qualities, but central to the act of defining what it meant to be "Athenian." And in a similar fashion, they believed that the particular "reasons" that a speaker expressed for why Athens ought to go to war with Sparta were central to their effectiveness in motivating those who thought of themselves as "Athenians" to sacrifice their lives and property for their city-state. Public discourse was thus understood as potentially (perhaps even inherently) persuasive, and hence central to life in a democratic or republican polity.

Finally, the classical rhetorical perspective treated the relationship between language and meaning as *contextual*. This is to say that the meaning of a particular linguistic usage (e.g., tropes, figures of speech, narratives, examples, etc.) derived from the particular experiences and understanding of a particular audience addressed by a particular speaker at a specific moment in time. The metaphor "I have a dream" takes on a very special meaning when uttered by Reverend Martin Luther King Jr. in the presence of 250,000 black and white American citizens sitting literally in shadow of the Lincoln Memorial in the early 1960s and demanding that the U.S. Congress pass civil rights legislation. Change the circumstances and the meaning or nuance of that phrase can change correspondingly. Can you imagine, for example, Newt Gingrich uttering that phrase before a congregation of the Christian Coalition in Atlanta, Georgia, in the wake of the so-called Republican Revolution of 1994? Or Louis Farrakhan speaking those words in an interview on ABC's *Nightline* in the wake of yet another church bombing in Mississippi. Do you hear the strains of irony and sarcasm dripping from his voice? This is not to suggest that linguistic meaning is variable in all directions at all time, for language usages are also rooted in broader historical and cultural contexts. In the examples above one could not hear either Gingrich or Farrakhan without also hearing the resonance of King at the same time, and thus there will be something of a dialogic connection between the various meanings. What we do mean to suggest, however, is that the capacity for meaning in any linguistic usage is almost always subject to change and adaptation. A rhetorical perspective on the relationship between language and meaning thus stands in stark contrast to more philosophical and scientific perspectives that presume that either the meaning of linguistic usages is permanent and universal, or that it is essentially ahistorical, fundamentally unaffected by the particular, communicative contexts in which it is employed.

The classical focus on discourse as *contingent, public, persuasive*, and *contextual* has clearly influenced the ways in which contemporary rhetoricians have treated the role and significance of public communication. Of most importance has been the focus of attention on texts such as speeches and political pamphlets (and more recently mass-mediated entertainment) that address the public-at-large, rather than on private correspondences or philosophical treatises addressed to elite, intellectual audiences. The rationale here is that whatever the private goals motivating individuals to act might be, it is usually only once a public or the citizenry is persuaded to endorse and act upon communally shared goals that history moves forward (or backward) in significant ways. Thus, whereas someone uninterested in rhetoric might prefer to study the private letters of Winston Churchill in order to understand how his leadership helped England to stave off the threat of fascism posed by Adolf Hitler, a rhetorician would be inclined to focus on important speeches, such as Churchill's "War Situation I." The influence of classical rhetoric's emphasis on the public dimension of communication interaction has thus clearly been evidenced in the contemporary rhetoricians' choice of documents.

The classical rhetorical emphasis on context has also influenced the ways in which contemporary rhetoricians describe public discourse. In the speech mentioned above, Churchill found himself addressing a thoroughly demoralized British people suffering the despair of a crushing military defeat at the hands of the Nazis in the battle for Dunkirk. Churchill realized that the only chance for Britain to succeed against the overwhelming forces of totalitarianism would require an extraordinary, collective act of faith and determination. One way in which he sought to motivate his audience to persevere was to compel them to believe in the inevitability of their triumph. Focusing his listener's attention on the Mississippi River as a metaphor for the United States's eventual involvement in the war effort, he recalled the song "Ole Man River" from the hit Broadway musical *Showboat* that had been very popular in London during its recent run there. Despite the almost impossible odds that faced Britain in its battle, Churchill noted, the positive course of history and the "inexorable" triumph of good over evil was "like the Mississippi," in that it "just keeps rollin' along." A perspective that ignored the impact of the rhetorical context of its usage would probably judge this as a weak and inappropriate metaphor. River metaphors, it might be argued, are ineffective in depicting success, for rivers flow down hill, and the concept of "descent" typically connotes failure and death. Moreover, one might argue the effectiveness of Churchill's particular metaphor is potentially limited by unpredictable factors such as the listening audience's familiarity (or lack of familiarity) with the story of *Showboat*. Thus, it might be concluded, Churchill's metaphor lacked artistry and aesthetic appeal because it was insufficiently universal in its power or application.

By contrast, the rhetorician, inclined to understand the power of language within the specific context(s) of its particular usage, would in all likelihood recognize the propriety of Churchill's Mississippi River metaphor given the exigency confronting him. Churchill had a serious rhetorical problem. He needed to convince the British people that the United States would eventually enter the war, because without them, it was obvious to all that Britain could not defeat Hitler. However, he could not explicitly assert this claim, for that would have undermined delicate secret negotiations and prolonged America's neutrality; indeed, at the time there was some reason to believe that it might even have kept the United States out of the war altogether. By invoking the Mississippi River metaphor, however, Churchill was able to imply the United States's eventual involvement in the war.

Moreover, Churchill's use of this metaphor was extremely powerful precisely because it drew upon the strong emotional resonance of the Mississippi River created by Paul Robeson's forceful performance of the song "Ole Man River," a rendition of the song that would have been familiar to most of those hearing the speech. That song, with its focus on dark times and the power of human resilience in the face of apparently overwhelming forces, was an especially appropriate symbol given the situation facing Britain. Further, Churchill negated the normative sense that rivers flow downhill by describing the Mississippi River as flowing out to "broader lands and better days," a depiction consonant with the image of a river that culminates in a delta. Thus, even though Churchill's use of the Mississippi River metaphor might not have had the same effectiveness for all audiences (and in that sense would not be considered a universally appropriate metaphor for "success"), rhetoricians operating from an orientation that emphasizes the importance of rhetorical context would describe its usage as an appropriate, artistic, and exceptionally skillful rhetorical performance.

Finally, the specifically rhetorical focus on persuasiveness affects how one judges instances of human communication. A social scientific or philosophic view of this speech would more than likely condemn Churchill as a fuzzy-headed optimist who juggled literary tropes and figures and drastically misrepresented the world. It might be noted, for example, that Churchill never actually characterizes the battle of Dunkirk as the resounding military defeat that most people considered it to be. Instead, he portrays the "withdrawal" of the British Expeditionary Forces from French soil—facilitated by an armada of merchant ships and pleasure boats—as a "triumph" of the British spirit, of its resiliency and ability to prevail against all odds. Similarly, instead of admitting that Britain was making no progress against Hitler and the Nazi threat, Churchill emphasized that the nation's "offensive springs are being coiled" for later battles. Those who believe that human communication should be neutral and objective would be inclined to portray Churchill as a charlatan, a liar, and a fraud who either ignored or misrepresented the facts and constructed a fictive, self-interested interpretation of events. And yet, one must ask, what interests would have been served if Churchill had simply and accurately conveyed "the facts" of the situation to the British people in a neutral and disinterested way, even if that were a real possibility? From the rhetorical perspective, where attention focuses on the persuasive potential of public discourse, the emphasis is not on the truth or falsity of language, but on the power and effectiveness of the performance to interpret and evaluate, to envision new possibilities, to call a community together and to motivate it to act in the name of shared values and interests. Though Churchill's speech failed to represent what might be considered an "objective truth," his performance was nevertheless outstanding, and all the more significant because of it, for it was precisely his ability to persuade the British people to a faith in their cause that helped to produce the conditions that enabled the eventual triumph of the Allies in World War II.

The point we want to emphasize here is that classical rhetoricians brought a distinctive set of assumptions to the study of communication that underscored the ways in which advocates—typically public speakers or orators—actively sought to exert influence on a specific audience by strategically deploying language in the interest of an immediate and particular goal. These assumptions, however, were not uncontested, and over the centuries would prove to be precarious. To begin with, the trajectory of Western thought from Plato's Academy through the seventeenth- and eighteenth-century Enlightenment of reason and well into the scientific modernism of the present century spawned an intellectual predisposition for theories of knowledge in which the values of universality and objectivity were privileged over those of particularity, situatedness, and subjectivity or intersubjectivity. Rhetoric, with its commitment to the later cluster of values, has a minimal role to play in such a world. Ironically enough, however, even as rhetoric was being held up to contempt in the intellectual world of the Enlightenment and its modernist aftermath, its presence and significance in the everyday world was increasingly pronounced, particularly in Western Europe and the United States, where the rapid growth of the public sphere came to play an increasingly prevalent role in the realms of commerce and political decision making.

We do not mean to suggest that the study of rhetoric in the post-Enlightenment and modernist eras disappeared altogether (or that it is a uniquely Western phenomenon), but only that its significance was relegated to the margins of serious Western intellectual thought. Indeed, it was not infrequently referred to as the "Harlot of the Arts." In this context, rhetorical theorists managed to preserve some academic status for their study by conceding to a secondary or derivative role, allowing rhetoric to be cast in the role of "supplement" or "handmaiden" to more authentic modes of inquiry. The primary concession here was that rhetoric existed apart from the categories of "truth" and "knowledge" whose proper intellectual domains were science and philosophy. Once one properly discovered "truth" or "knowledge," rhetoricians might help to "dress it up" so as to communicate it more effectively to a larger, more common audience; but importantly, it was believed rhetoric played *no* role in the actual process of discovering such "truth" or "knowledge."

At the same time that rhetoric was seen as a useful supplement to the work of science and philosophy, it was also deprecated for its role in the realm of "public debate" where "truth" and "knowledge" were allegedly subordinated to the self-interested ideology of political actors. Since public rhetoric was always oriented toward the particular, and thus generated no universal or timeless truths, its study was typically of marginal interest to serious scholars, who preferred to devote their efforts to the exploration and explanation of the putative, universal beauties of art or the enduring truths of science and philosophy. Of course there were notable exceptions, but they were relatively few and far between, and on the whole the study of rhetoric in the Enlightenment and modernist eras was generally subordinated to the study of science and philosophy.

The classical assumptions about the nature and function of rhetoric that we detail above continue to be important to those who study communication from a rhetorical perspective. However, their significance has been modified by the subsequent history of rhetoric and the distinctive dialogue that has taken place in the recent past. Our primary purpose in this volume is to introduce the most recent, significant discussions and debates about contemporary rhetorical theory as they function to extend, problematize, and move beyond these assumptions. Before we proceed, however, it important that we qualify our particular understanding of the phrase "contemporary rhetorical theory."

To identify that which is contemporary is never a simple task. The word itself usually distinguishes those things that are "current" or "marked by characteristics of the present period."[3] In the present context we use it to refer to the problems of rhetorical theory currently being discussed by scholars; however, we do not mean to include everyone who is presently writing about rhetorical theory in our definition. In the twentieth century the study of rhetorical theory has generally operated within the domain of scholars in the discipline of communication studies (sometimes referred to as "speech" or "speech communication"). In recent years, however, there has been an explosion of interest in the study of rhetoric, and an increasing number of scholars from disciplines such as English and composition, philosophy, economics, law, political science, and social psychology currently identify themselves as "rhetoricians."[4] The work being produced by these scholars is interesting and important—particularly given the historical marginalization of rhetoric within the academy—and it is frequently cited and cross-referenced by rhetoricians operating out of communication studies. However, such work is also frequently motivated by interests and concerns generated by the home discipline with which it is affiliated. Our interest here is with the community of rhetorical theorists who share an identifiable disciplinary history *and* who have generated a distinctive set of issues and concerns that *start* with the common assumption that public communication matters.

What then is "contemporary rhetorical theory" as we delineate it in this volume? It is a series of problems addressed by the community of rhetoricians operating from within the discipline of communication studies since approximately the mid-1960s. As with all communities, the community of contemporary rhetorical scholars is defined and located by the discourse that has generated it. In this case, the generative discourse is not only a particular interpretation of the classical rhetorical tradition, but also the important work of a group of scholars and teachers who effected the revival of classical rhetoric in the early part of the twentieth century as they contributed to the institutionalization of communication studies as an academic discipline. In order to grasp and engage what is distinctive about contemporary rhetorical theory as we define it here, we need an understanding of its origins within twentieth-century communication studies, as well as the initial efforts to transform its study. That task is the function of the next section of this introduction.

THE REBIRTH OF RHETORIC IN
TWENTIETH-CENTURY COMMUNICATION STUDIES

What today we call "communication studies" emerged as a formal discipline of study in the United States during the early part of the twentieth century and in the specific context of Progressive-era politics. Faced with the imminent transformation to a mass democratic society, forward-looking intellectuals and educators like John Dewey were concerned about the ability of the citizenry to participate effectively in this new world and thus sought to alter the public education system accordingly. "Public speaking" was seen as essential to being an effective citizen, and thus became the central focus of the new discipline. Consequently, the initial study of rhetorical theory within twentieth-century communication studies focused on the historical examination of classical and civic humanist models of persuasion and governance. Such study served a dual function. On the one hand, it bestowed scholarly legitimacy on the new discipline by demonstrating its ancient and historical roots in the writings of respected philosophers and scholars such as Plato, Isocrates, Aristotle, Cicero, Quintilian, Longinus, Saint Augustine, and others. On the other hand, and perhaps more important to the subsequent development of the new discipline, the philosophical and technical treatises concerning rhetoric that had been written from classical antiquity through the Renaissance and well into the eighteenth and nineteenth centuries served as sources of effective strategies for teaching the art of rhetoric to college students.[5]

There is little wonder, therefore, that Aristotle's definition of rhetoric as the faculty or power "of discovering in the particular case what are the available means of persuasion" was so influential in shaping the emerging discipline's perception of both the meaning of "rhetoric" as a strategic art and the meaning of "rhetorical theory" as a history of the philosophy of communication.[6] And indeed, for nearly forty years—from the 1920s through the 1960s—rhetorical theory was treated largely as an exercise in intellectual history. At the same time, the creation of new rhetorical theory was subordinated to the pedagogical goal of creating effective speakers along the lines of fairly classical models represented most fully by Quintilian's *vir bonus*, "the good man speaking well."

THE SEEDS OF INTELLECTUAL FERMENT

By the mid- to late-1960s dissatisfaction with this approach to rhetoric began to grow. It became increasingly clear that however important the intellectual history of rhetorical theory was to our understanding of rhetoric as a discipline, the pressing need was to develop "new" rhetorical theories that would adapt our understanding of rhetoric to the changing conditions of the new era. Two independent but not unrelated phenomena were of particular importance in generating the need for such theories. The first phenomenon was the meteoric rise of television as a primary mass medium of public discourse. Television not only altered the ways in which public discourse was conducted, but it began to call increasing attention to the problem of what it might mean to be a "public," as well as to the problem of how public discourse was received and interpreted by the mass and multiple audiences that attended to it.[7] As we will see subsequently, these problems have been translated into a number of significant questions that have occupied the attention of contemporary rhetorical theorists. The second phenomenon was the emergence of significant grassroots social movements such as the civil rights movement, the student/antiwar movement, and the woman's liberation movement, all of which began to question the effectiveness of classical models of rhetoric and communication for the increasingly vocal, oppositional, and marginalized groups concerned to infiltrate and overturn what they perceived as rigid social and political hierarchies and hegemonies.[8]

The change that came about was relatively pronounced and immediate as such things go. Between 1967 and 1976 the fundamental focus of rhetorical theory shifted from a concern with intellectual histories and simple, classical models of rhetorical pedagogy, to an eager interest in understanding the relationships between rhetoric and social theory. The initial hints that a change was stirring appeared in two articles published early in 1967. In the first essay, "The Rhetoric of the Streets," Franklin Haiman recognized that "our society today is confronted with a wide range of activities unfamiliar to those accustomed to thinking of protest in terms of a Faneuil Hall rally or a Bughouse Square soapbox orator." Accordingly, Haiman issued an impassioned call for careful consideration of the ethical and legal standards by which we interpret and evaluate "the *contemporary* rhetoric of the streets."[9] Responding to the same spirit of the times, Robert L. Scott offered a more philosophical challenge to our understanding of the substance and sociopolitical significance of rhetoric in "On Viewing Rhetoric as Epistemic."[10] In this essay, which was the starting point of significant debates in the 1970s and 1980s on the role of rhetoric in the construction of truth, Scott argued that rhetoric is not simply a means of making the truth effective, but is quite literally a way of knowing, a means for the production of truth and knowledge in a world where certainty is rare and yet action must be taken. He thereby instigated the repudiation of the secondary status that had been assigned to rhetoric and which had been largely integrated into the assumptions of those who had refounded rhetoric in the twentieth century.

These two essays provided new perspectives on two of the major issues upon which this volume focuses: the character of public morality (Part 4), and the important and puzzling question of rhetoric's relationship to truth (Part 2). The following year, two additional essays by Lloyd Bitzer and Douglas Ehninger continued to push in the direction of examining and accounting for the broader social dimensions of rhetoric. Lloyd Bitzer's "The Rhetorical Situation," one of the most often cited essays in speech communication journals in the 1970s and 1980s, argued for rhetoric's status as a practical discipline by calling attention to the ways in which discourse that is rhetorical is "called into being" as a result of the relationship between three constituent elements: exigencies, audiences, and constraints.[11] Exigencies consisted of the events and social relationships that seemed to call for some sort of interpretation. Audiences were those persons who were positioned to respond to the events in productive ways. Constraints were those things that limited the possible ways in which a rhetor could propose a response to the event. In Bitzer's words, the rhetorical situation was defined as "a complex of persons, events, objects, and relations presenting an actual or potential exigence which can be completely or partially removed if discourse, introduced into the situation, can so constrain human decision or action as to bring about the significant modification of the exigence." By locating the essence of rhetoric in the broader social situation rather than in the intent of the speaker, Bitzer posed a third critical issue for contemporary rhetorical theorists (Part 3): to what extent is rhetoric bound to its context, and what is a context anyway? In "On Systems of Rhetoric," another much-cited essay of the ensuing decades, Ehninger seconded Bitzer's position in a more macroscopic way when he argued that rhetoric was a function of its culture, and thus encouraged increased attention to the multiple forms and functions of rhetorics at different times and in different places.[12]

Similar themes were being picked up by any number of other critics and theorists writing in the period. Between 1967 and 1970 almost a dozen important essays on social movements were published.[13] Collectively they raised the fourth theoretical problem addressed in this volume (Part 6): What is the relationship between rhetoric and social change? These essays also had a broader impact, shifting the attention of rhetorical studies so as to address the key problems and concerns of twentieth-century social and political theory. The implications of this work began to crystallize formally at two conferences sponsored by the National Developmental Project on Rhetoric (NDPR) in 1970 and reported in an important volume edited by Lloyd F. Bitzer and Edwin Black titled *The Prospect of Rhetoric*.[14]

In the words of the founders of the NDPR, "[Its] central objective was to outline and amplify a theory of rhetoric suitable to twentieth-century concepts and needs."[15] The debates and discussions at the Wingspread Conference in January, 1970 and the National

Conference on Rhetoric later in May were spirited and often heated. In the end, however, the conferees, consisting of over forty of the leading male scholars in rhetorical studies, combined to offer recommendations on the advancement and refinement of rhetorical criticism, the scope of rhetoric and the place of rhetorical studies in higher education, and the nature of rhetorical invention.[16] It is interesting to read the specific recommendations generated in each of these areas to get a portrait of the particular issues of the times and to see how the general culture of the 1960s affected the conception of rhetoric that was developing (and thus implicitly endorsing Ehninger's suggestion that rhetorics were a function of the particular and localized cultures in which they emerged). For our purposes, however, what is even more striking and important is the "consensus judgment" that was arrived at regarding the outline of a satisfactory contemporary theory of rhetoric. It consisted of four specific recommendations:

1. The technology of the twentieth century has created so many new channels and techniques of communication, and the problems confronting contemporary societies are so related to communicative methods and contents that it is imperative that rhetorical studies be broadened to explore communicative procedures and practices not traditionally covered.
2. Our recognition of the scope of rhetorical theory and practice should be greatly widened.
3. At the same time, a clarified and expanded concept of reason and rational decision should be worked out.
4. Rhetorical invention should be restored to a position of centrality in theory and practice.[17]

Although these recommendations were very general, they clearly resonated with the sense that rhetoric was not merely the art of teaching public speaking, but rather that to be rhetorical was a central and substantial dimension of many facets of the human social experience. To borrow a phrase that Simons would later coin to describe the increasing interest in rhetoric within the academy as a whole, "the rhetorical turn" was about to be taken in a most thorough-going fashion; no longer, at least amongst rhetoricians, would rhetoric be presumed as a mere supplement or "handmaiden" to philosophy, sociology, history, or English. Instead, it would constitute its own significant perspective on the problems and possibilities of life-in-society. As such, the commitment to the production and performance of rhetorical theory, rather than simply the study of the history of rhetorical theory, became a central part of rhetorical studies.

"RHETORIC" COMES OF AGE (AGAIN) IN A POSTMODERN ERA

It took several years for the full implications of the findings of the NDPR to be completely understood, for the impact was quite literally to call into question and revise the assumptions undergirding our understanding of rhetoric as a fundamental, social human phenomenon. But more than that, it also had implications for how we think about the relationships between theory, criticism, and practice. Only Barry Brummett, at the time a graduate student at the University of Minnesota, began to talk in terms of a "postmodern rhetoric."[18] However, the seeds for the contemporary debate between modernism and postmodernism were sown here.

The differences between modernist and postmodernist perspectives have been the focus of significant and productive debates between and among rhetorical theorists in recent years as they have addressed the specific concerns of rhetorical study, and there is every reason to believe that such debates will continue well into the twenty-first century. You will see various facets of these debates emerge in each of the subsequent eight parts of this volume as particular problems and issues are addressed. Modernism features a commitment to scientism, and objective, morally neutral, universal knowledge.[19] In the modern worldview, the universe is a relatively simple, stable, highly ordered place, describable in and reducible to absolute formulas that hold across contexts. Disagreement, in such a worldview, is treated as an unnecessary pathology that arises primarily from ignorance and irrationality. The solution or cure for social discord is therefore greater research, less passion, more rationality, and more education.

By contrast, postmodernism prefers interpretation over scientific study because it operates with the assumption that all knowledge is subjective and/or intersubjective, morally culpable, and local. In the postmodern worldview, the universe is a rapidly changing, highly complex entity. From this perspective, universally applicable formulas or "covering laws" designed for the purposes of describing and controlling the world are of minimal use, for the multiple and competing factors operating in every context override even the possibility of formulaic understanding. Each situation must be addressed in its own and often chaotic particularity. Disagreement is thus considered a rather "natural" result of different social, political, and ethnic groups, with different logics, interests, and values living together and competing for limited or scarce resources. On this view, struggle, not consensus, is the defining characteristic of social life; accordingly, social discord is not a pathology to be cured but a condition to be productively managed.

The first inklings of the tensions that would be generated by these dramatically conflicting worldviews began to emerge in a published debate in the *Quarterly Journal of Speech* in 1972 concerning critical assessments of President Richard Nixon's November 3, 1969, speech to the nation on the war in Vietnam. Forbes Hill employed a neo-Aristotelian perspective to evaluate Nixon's speech.[20] Neo-Aristotelianism was a method of rhetorical criticism heavily influenced by modernist notions of objectivity and the moral neutrality of the critic. Its primary goal was to evaluate a speech in terms of the degree to which it employed what Aristotle referred to as "the available means of persuasion" in attempting to achieve its goal. To the degree that a speech employed all of the means available to it, it was judged to be a good speech; to the degree that it failed to employ all such means it was, correspondingly, a bad speech. Importantly, the critic was to maintain objective distance from the critical object, and thus there was no space in neo-Aristotelian criticism for evaluating the morality of particular choices or the ultimate outcome of the speech. According to Hill, Nixon's speech employed all of the available means of persuasion, and thus he judged it to be a good speech

In the Forum that followed Hill's essay Karlyn Kohrs Campbell called both the method of neo-Aristotelianism and the substance of Hill's particular conclusions into question.[21] The key point of her argument was that appearances to the contrary, Hill's reliance upon an allegedly "objective" and "morally neutral" critical perspective was ultimately neither. More importantly, she argued, Hill actively ignored the important intellectual responsibility of situating his analysis as a morally culpable, theoretical practice.

Though many at the time concluded that Kohrs Campbell had made the more compelling argument, the truly significant, albeit implicit, claim this dispute evidenced was the clear need to (re)negotiate the relationship between critical and theoretical concerns. Modernist approaches to criticism and theory that presupposed the application of neutral and objective criteria to speeches (or other communication events) as a means of judging them would no longer suffice as a means of theorizing the rhetorical. Put differently, it was becoming increasingly clear that rhetoric was not a practice that culminated in "the amassing of objective knowledge or the generation of purely abstract theory," but was rather a "performance" that needed to be interpreted and evaluated in particular, interested, local contexts.[22] Rejecting the rigid modernist spirit of positivism and scientism in rhetorical studies proved to be relatively easy. Determining specifically what ought to replace it has been a much more difficult problem, and trying to solve that problem has been an issue that the discipline has visited over and again in the subsequent twenty-five years. Indeed, it is a problem that pervades many of the essays that you will find included in this volume.

One of the most important set of stimuli for the search to replace the spirit of modernism in this period of ferment were the issues raised by the burgeoning woman's movement. In 1973 Kohrs Campbell published "The Rhetoric of Women's Liberation: An Oxymoron," in the *Quarterly Journal of Speech*.[23] In this essay she argued that classical rhetorical theories failed to provide an appropriate or useful guide for the type of rhetoric that shaped women's liberation. From the perspective of classical rhetoric, she suggested, women's liberation was an oxymoron. It could not succeed because it could not appeal to audiences steeped in traditionally gendered norms; additionally, it employed alternative strategies such as small group "consciousness raising" rather than the more traditional public platform as a means of effecting persuasion. Following Kohrs Campbell's lead, a variety of scholars have continued to explore feminist issues such as the proposed Equal Rights Amendment, abortion, and women's roles, forging new critical tools from new theoretical perspectives. These inquiries have included a questioning of both the substantive and the stylistic formulae for theory construction, as evidenced in efforts such as Jane Sutton's creative essay in (Part 1) on the relationship of the construction of rhetoric and female gendering in the classical rhetorical tradition.[24] There is little agreement today on what constitutes a feminist rhetorical theory, but this body of theoretical work continually exerts pressure for broader perspectives to be taken upon the general theories of rhetoric that are most widely circulated, and this debt of the center to the margins has not been acknowledged very widely.[25] Kohrs Campbell's work is thus important, not only because it offered an important contribution to our understanding of the relationship between rhetoric and social change (Part 6) but because it also helped to spur work on the relationship between rhetoric and traditionally marginalized groups (as considered in Part 8).

The decade of rhetoric's renewal as a theoretical discipline that began around 1967 culminated in 1975 and 1976 with the publication of two essays by young scholars who would prove to be among the next generation's most important intellectual leaders. These essays by Michael C. McGee and Thomas Farrell were important not only because they embodied the renewed emphasis on rhetorical theories as a means for understanding contemporary social and political life, but also because they encouraged increased contact and conversation with the emergence (in translation) of a growing community of continental social theorists who were beginning to focus attention on discourse and communication theory. McGee's "In Search of 'the People': A Rhetorical

Alternative" (Part 5) argued that the premiere challenge facing the discipline was to recognize the significance of rhetoric as central to the constitution of collective life, not merely a matter of teaching speeches or observing their immediate effects on audiences. In McGee's words, the field should not simply be pursuing its mission by trying to "[inquire] into the effects of rhetoric or by exhorting fledgling advocates to avoid *argumentum ad populam*." Instead, rhetoricians should turn concepts like "audience" upon themselves by "recognizing the collective life as a condition of being the 'audience' of those who pretend to lead the society."[26] In other words, we should begin to explore how it is that our ability to live together as a community is made possible only to the extent that we can assent to the visions and images of ourselves created by those we select as our public leaders.

McGee's point was that rhetorical theory that took itself seriously would draw critically upon concrete instances of persuasive discourse. It would use the scholarly study of such instances to "explore the reciprocal relationship between rhetoric and social theory and to participate in the serious Hegelian and Marxist dialogues of the previous two centuries which have so greatly affected life in our own time."[27] McGee's essay was particularly important for at least two reasons. First, it encouraged us to rethink what we mean by the concept of "audience" (Part 5). Rather than to think of an audience as either the real, live beings attending to a discourse, or as a purely abstract, symbolic phenomenon, such as the statistical aggregates that are typically used to summarize "public opinion," McGee argued that we should understand audiences as rhetorically material, that is, as constituted in and through public discourse. Speakers called an audience into being, urging potential members of a collectivity to see themselves in the specific visions sketched by the rhetor. Second, and perhaps more importantly for the ongoing development of rhetorical theory, McGee's essay helped to demonstrate the potential of the discipline of rhetorical studies as a substantive perspective from which to speak to the problems and concerns of contemporary social theory, including the issues of power, ideology, leadership, and social change.[28]

The second essay, published in 1976, was Thomas Farrell's "Knowledge, Consensus, and Rhetorical Theory" (Part 2). Whereas McGee wrote with an Isocratean bias, Farrell sought to recover and reconstruct Aristotle's commitment to the combination of "[an] art of rhetoric and a generally accepted body of knowledge pertaining to matters of public concern."[29] Reading Aristotle into and through the context of American pragmatism, and drawing upon the increasingly elaborate social theory of Jürgen Habermas, Farrell developed a conception of "social knowledge" that stood in contrast to "technical knowledge." He then elaborated the functional characteristics of social knowledge, identifying it as consensual, audience-dependent, generative, and normative. As with McGee, Farrell underscored the need to rethink the ways in which we understand and employ the key components of the rhetorical process. He thus emphasized the importance of bringing classical rhetorical perspectives (Aristotle) into dialogue with contemporary U.S. philosophical perspectives (e.g., pragmatism), as well as continental philosophy and social theory (e.g., Habermas's revision of Marxist critical theory). In Farrell's own work this expansion was reflected in a broadened definition of rhetoric as "a collaborative manner of engaging others through discourse so that contingencies may be resolved, judgments rendered, action produced."[30]

Subsequent to these two essays by McGee and Farrell there was no turning back. Rhetorical studies had become substantively theoretical in its focus. The positions and perspectives McGee and Farrell exemplified would come under attack, to be sure, but even such efforts were framed by the theoretical project that joined these essays and stood as the culminating implication of the work of the previous ten years. Whereas previously theory, criticism, and history stood as starkly different dimensions of rhetorical studies, henceforth they would become increasingly implicated in and by one another (by some accounts oppressively so).[31]

PLAN OF THE VOLUME

The essays in this volume mark the course and development of rhetorical theory from 1967 to the present, though we present it less as a history, for which it would be altogether incomplete and inadequate, and more as an indication of the range of specific questions, problems, issues, and approaches that have occupied contemporary American rhetorical theorists in this period and continue to occupy them today. Indeed, in an important sense we offer the volume as an invitation to beginning scholars to become part of the community and the dialogue that is constituted by the essays and voices that are contained herein. The volume begins with a section titled "What Can a 'Rhetoric' Be?" and ends with a section titled "Challenging the Tradition of Rhetorical Theory from the Margins." The opening section demonstrates that even though there are overlapping assumptions within the mainstream about what rhetoric might be, there is no univocal consensus on how we should understand it. The closing section underscores and emphasizes the ways in which those operating outside the mainstream are actively and productively critiquing and contesting those overlapping assumptions in ways that make rhetorical studies a vital and variable, if not also very contentious, field of study and action.

The remaining six parts identify the major problems and issues that have occupied contemporary rhetorical theorists in recent years and provide a range of voices and approaches on each one. We cannot possibly provide comprehensive coverage on each topic, so we have included a brief list of additional readings in each area. Part 2 addresses the rhetoric and epistemology debates. We position this section early because it represents one of the most enduring debates in the period covered here and because the position one takes on the epistemological status of rhetoric will have much to say about the stance one takes as a rhetorical theorist.

Part 3 examines the problem of the rhetorical situation. Contemporary rhetorical theorists have conceded Bitzer's general claim that rhetoric and discourse are in some sense inherently and historically situated, rather than timeless and universal. This is not a position that has been generally conceded by continental discourse theorists, but even within American rhetorical theory there is no consensus on what we mean when we say that rhetoric is situated. The essays included in this section indicate three different ways in which we might understand context.

Part 4 focuses on the relationship between rhetoric, reason, and public morality. Throughout much of the twentieth century the concept of "reason" was rooted in Enlightenment conceptions of scientific or instrumental rationality. That concept has come under significant scrutiny in the past forty years, particularly as it relates to the problems and possibilities of deliberation where issues of moral action and public virtue are at stake. The essays in this section examine the ways in which argumentation, conversation, and narrative function in constructing conceptions of public good and public morality.

Part 5 directs attention to our understanding of the ways in which the audience is understood in the rhetorical process. In many respects, this is the key issue confronting rhetorical theory, particularly in the context of recent efforts to engage the relationship between rhetoric and cultural studies. Just as rhetoricians are agreed that rhetoric is somehow situated, so too they agree that every rhetoric is always in some ways addressed to some audience that it seeks to influence or persuade. The point of controversy is where and how we identify that audience. What is its status within the rhetorical process? What effect or influence does it have on the authorization of social or public knowledge and/or the construction of social and political identity? What is its agency? The essays in this section engage these questions in contentious and provocative ways.

Part 6 considers the broad relationship between rhetoric and social and political change. There are many ways in which such a section could be organized. We have chosen to explore the range of concerns raised when different types of social groupings are taken as the unit of analysis. The essays in this section offer studies of social change that attend to social organization at different scales, including the electoral politics of the nation-state, the organized social movement, the identity group, mass culture, society, and even "anti-society." Each social grouping elicits different ways in which rhetoric functions and has effects and influence on collective beliefs, attitudes, and behaviors. These essays provide original and telling glimpses into the varying roles of rhetoric in social change in disparate circumstances.

Part 7 concerns the relationship between rhetoric and the mass media. Rhetoric, of course, was a technology invented in the fifth century B.C.E. as a means of wielding power and influence. Since that time subsequent technological innovations from the printing press to the telegraph to radio and television to computer-mediated communications have had significant and sometimes revolutionary effects upon the ways in which the rhetorical impulse is experienced and understood. The essays included in this section address this problem in the contemporary context of the mass media and with particular attention to television and film, calling attention both to how rhetorical theory might help us better to understand the social, political, and cultural significance of these media of social interaction, and to how these media effect and influence the ways in which we might think of rhetorical theory in a mass mediated era.

Collectively, these essays represent some of the most important contributions of contemporary rhetorical theory to the larger academic discussions concerning the social and political implications of discourse. Since the mid-1960s the academic discussion on the importance and role of discourse has framed major intellectual currents in a wide range of traditional disciplines from anthropology, English, and history to sociology and political science. It has also been a significant, animating factor in what has most recently been identified as the "antidisciplines" such as cultural studies and women's studies.[32] We (tentatively) address the specific contributions of rhetorical studies to this larger academic conversation (sometimes it seems more like a "shouting match") in the Epilogue. We hope that after you engage the essays in this volume, you will begin to gain a sense of what rhetorical theory has been in the contemporary period and, more importantly, of the future contributions it might make. And in that context it is our hope that the Epilogue may actually function as the prologue to the future studies that you will produce.

To understand ourselves and the societies we create with our words is a challenging and daunting task, but we are inexorably committed to the belief that it is the richest and most rewarding of endeavors available. We offer the essays collected in this volume as both the evidence of and a contribution to that endeavor.

Notes

1. Isocrates, "Antidosis," in *Isocrates*, trans. George Norlin (Cambridge, MA: Harvard University Press, 1929), vol.2, pp. 253–255. For an important discussion of the importance of Isocrates to the rhetorical tradition, see Takis Poulakos, *Isocrates' Rhetorical Education* (Columbia: University of South Carolina Press, 1997).

2. There are numerous and quite good surveys of the history of rhetoric. The most readily available ones still in print include Thomas Conley, *Rhetoric in the European Tradition* (Chicago: University of Chicago Press, 1994); George A. Kennedy, *Classical Rhetoric and Its Christian and Secular Tradition from Ancient to Modern Times* (Chapel Hill: University of North Carolina Press, 1980); George A. Kennedy, *A New History of Classical Rhetorics* (Princeton, NJ: Princeton University Press, 1994); and Brian Vickers, *In Defense of Rhetoric* (Oxford: Clarendon Press, 1988). A very good survey that includes major excerpts from significant theoretical texts is Patricia Bizzell and Bruce Herzberg, eds., *The Rhetorical Tradition: Readings from Classical Times to the Present* (Boston: Bedford Books, 1990). A slightly dated, but nonetheless very useful, collection of bibliographical review essays on the history of rhetoric are contained in Winifred Bryan Horner, ed., *The Present State of Scholarship in Historical and Contemporary Rhetoric* (Columbia: University of Missouri Press, 1990).

3. *Merriam Webster's Tenth Collegiate Dictionary*, s.v. "contemporary."

4. Representative examples of such work include Michael Billig, *Ideology and Opinions: Studies in Rhetorical Psychology* (Newbury Park, CA: Sage, 1991); Donald N. McCloskey, *The Rhetoric of Economics* (Madison: University of Wisconsin Press, 1985); James Boyd White, *Heracles' Bow: Essays on the Rhetoric and Poetics of the Law* (Madison: University of Wisconsin Press, 1985); and John S. Nelson, *Tropes of Politics: Science, Theory, Rhetoric, Action* (Madison: University of Wisconsin Press, 1998). Two useful collections of essays include John Bender and David E. Wellbery, eds., *The Ends of Rhetoric: History, Theory, Practice* (Stanford, CA: Stanford University Press, 1990); and John S. Nelson et al., eds., *The Rhetoric of the Human Sciences: Language and Argument in Scholarship and Public Affairs* (Madison: University of Wisconsin Press, 1987).

5. The full history of the development of rhetorical theory in the discipline of communication studies has yet to be written. An important initial effort that emphasizes the early years in particular is Michael Leff and Margaret Organ Procario, "Rhetorical Theory in Speech Communication," in Thomas W. Benson, ed., *Speech Communication in the Twentieth Century* (Carbondale: Southern Illinois University Press, 1985), pp. 3–27.

6. Aristotle, *The Rhetoric of Aristotle*, 1355b26, trans. Lane Cooper (New York: Prentice-Hall, 1960), p. 7.

7. See Kathleen Hall Jamieson, *Eloquence in an Electronic Age: The Transformation of Political Speechmaking* (New York: Oxford University Press, 1988).

8. John W. Bowers and Donovan J. Ochs, *The Rhetoric of Agitation and Control* (Reading, MA: Addison-Wesley, 1971).

9. Franklin Haiman, "The Rhetoric of the Streets: Legal and Ethical Considerations," *Quarterly Journal of Speech* 53 (1967): 99, 114.

10. Robert L. Scott, "On Viewing Rhetoric as Epistemic," *Central States Speech Journal* 18 (1967): 9–16.

11. Lloyd F. Bitzer, "The Rhetorical Situation," *Philosophy and Rhetoric* 1 (1968): 1–14.

12. Douglas Ehninger, "On Systems of Rhetoric," *Philosophy and Rhetoric* 1 (1968): 131–144.

13. See Michael Osborn, "Archetypal Metaphor in Rhetoric: The Light-Dark Family," *Quarterly Journal of Speech* 53 (1967): 115–126; Parke G. Burgess, "The Rhetoric of Black Power: A Moral Demand?," *Quarterly Journal of Speech* 54 (1968): 122–133, and "The Rhetoric of Moral Conflict: Two Critical Dimensions," *Quarterly Journal of Speech* 56 (1970): 120–130; Robert L. Scott and Donald K. Smith, "The Rhetoric of Confrontation," *Quarterly Journal of Speech* 55 (1969): 9–16; Edwin Black, "The Second Persona," *Quarterly Journal of Speech* 56 (1970): 109–119; Walter R. Fisher, "A Motive View of Communication," *Quarterly Journal of Speech* 54 (1970): 131–139; and Herbert W. Simons, "Requirements, Problems, and Strategies: A Theory of Persuasion for Social Movements," *Quarterly Journal of Speech* 56 (1970): 1–11.

14. The conferences were organized by the National Developmental Project on Rhetoric (NDPR), and sponsored by the Speech Communication Association and the National Endowment for the Humanities. See Lloyd F. Bitzer and Edwin Black, eds., *The Prospect of Rhetoric: Report of the National Developmental Project* (Englewood Cliffs, NJ: Prentice-Hall, 1971).

15. Bitzer and Black, *The Prospects of Rhetoric,* p. v.

16. It is important to note that of the forty-plus rhetoricians invited to the conferences, there were *no* women. This might be accounted for, in part, by the dearth of women rhetoricians publishing in this time period. The notable omission of Marie Hochmuth Nichols, who had just completed a term as the editor of the *Quarterly Journal of Speech,* who had edited volume three of the then important *History and Criticism of Public Address,* and who had published as well an important collection of lectures on the development of a "new rhetoric," *Rhetoric and Culture* (Baton Rouge: Louisiana State University Press, 1963), is nonetheless somewhat odd. For one account, see Gerard Hauser, review of *Encyclopedia of Rhetoric and Composition,* edited by Theresa Enos, in *Quarterly Journal of Speech* 83 (1997): 243–246. The history of these conferences is just now beginning to be written, See, e.g., Theresa Enos and Richard McNabb, eds., *Making and Unmaking the Prospects of Rhetoric* (Mahwah, NJ: Earlbaum, 1997).

17. Bitzer and Black, *Prospects of Rhetoric,* pp. 238–239.

18. Barry Brummett, "Some Implications of 'Process' or 'Intersubjectivity': Postmodern Rhetoric," *Philosophy and Rhetoric* 9 (1976): 21–51.

19. The tension between modernism and postmodernism that we offer here is a grossly oversimplified rendition of a complex intellectual and philosophical dispute that we cannot hope even to begin to unpack in a few short pages. There is a voluminous and growing literature on the debates concerning the meaning of and relationships between the conditions of modernity and postmodernity and the philosophical positions of modernism and postmodernism. A useful introduction to the relevant issues is David Lyons, *Postmodernity* (Minneapolis: University of Minnesota Press, 1994). For more complex, historically situated considerations of the relationships, one might look to David Harvey's *The Condition of Postmodernity* (Cambridge, MA: Basil Blackwell, 1989) or to Barry Smart, *Modern Conditions, Postmodern Controversies* (New York: Routledge, 1992). Those interested in charting the tensions and debates through what many consider to be the primary texts of modernism and postmodernism might look to Lawrence Cahoone, ed., *From Modernism to Postmodernism: An Anthology* (Cambridge, MA: Basil Blackwell, 1996).

20. Forbes Hill, "Conventional Wisdom—Traditional Form—The President's Message of November 3, 1969," *Quarterly Journal of Speech* 58 (1972): 373–386.

21. Karlyn Kohrs Campbell, "'Conventional Wisdom—Traditional Form': A Rejoinder" and Forbes Hill, "A Response to Professor Campbell," *Quarterly Journal of Speech* 58 (1972): 452–460.

22. Leff and Procario, "Rhetorical Theory," p. 5.

23. Karlyn Kohrs Campbell, "The Rhetoric of Women's Liberation: An Oxymoron," *Quarterly Journal of Speech* 59 (1973): 74–86.

24. Jane Sutton, "The Taming of *Polos/Polis*: Rhetoric as an Achievement Without Woman," *Southern Communication Journal 57 (1992)*: 97–119.

25. For a description of feminist research in rhetorical studies in this period, see Celeste Michelle Condit, "Opposites in an Oppositional Practice: Rhetorical Criticism and Feminism," in Sheryl Perlmutter Bowen and Nancy Wyatt, eds., *Transforming Visions: Feminist Critiques in Communication Studies* (Cresskill, NJ: Hampton Press, 1993), pp. 205–230.

26. Michael C. McGee, "In Search of 'the People': A Rhetorical Alternative," *Quarterly Journal of Speech* 61 (1975): 236.

27. Ibid., p. 249.

28. For examples of McGee's own efforts in such contexts, see "'Not Men, but Measures': The Origins and Import of an Ideological Principle," *Quarterly Journal of Speech* 64 (1978): 141–155; "The 'Ideograph': A Link Between Rhetoric and Ideology," *Quarterly Journal of Speech* 66 (1980): 1–17; "The Origins of 'Liberty': A Feminization of Power,*" Communication Monographs* 47 (1980): 23–45; (with Martha Anna Martin), "Public Knowledge and Ideological Argumenta-

tion," *Communication Monographs* 50 (1983): 47–65; "Secular Humanism: A Radical Reading of 'Culture Industry' Productions," *Critical Studies in Mass Communication* 1 (1984): 1–33; and "Text, Context, and the Fragmentation of Contemporary Culture," *Western Journal of Speech Communication* 54 (1990): 274–289. See also Carol Corbin, ed., *Rhetoric in Postmodern America: Conversations with Michael Calvin McGee* (New York: Guilford Press, 1998).

29. Thomas Farrell, "Knowledge, Consensus, and Rhetorical Theory," *Quarterly Journal of Speech* 62 (1976): 1.

30. Thomas Farrell, "From the Parthenon to the Bassinet: Along the Epistemic Trail," *Quarterly Journal of Speech* 76 (1990): 83. For the fullest development of Farrell's perspective, see his *Norms of Rhetorical Culture* (New Haven, CT: Yale University Press, 1993).

31. See James Darsey, "Must We All Be Rhetorical Theorists?: An Anti-Democratic Inquiry," *Western Journal of Speech Communication* 58 (1994): 164–181.

32. See Cary Nelson and Dilip Parameshwar Gaonkar, eds., *Disciplinarity and Dissent in Cultural Studies* (New York: Routledge, 1996), pp. 1–22.

PART 1

What Can a "Rhetoric" Be?

At least since Plato's attack on rhetoric as "mere cookery," one of the enduring questions that rhetoricians have sought to answer is "What is rhetoric"? The answers have been many and varied, ranging from Aristotle's "the faculty wherein one discovers the available means of persuasion in any case whatsoever," to Francis Bacon's "the application of reason to the imagination for the better moving of the will," to Kenneth Burke's concept of "identification" which presumes that "you persuade a man only insofar as you can talk his language by speech, gesture, tonality, order, image, attitude, idea, *identifying* your ways with his," to *Group Mu*'s conception of rhetoric as stylistics. In some instances the definitions attributed to rhetoric have made it so narrow as to include little more than style and delivery within its purview; in other instances its meaning has been so broad as to colonize and include all other forms of discourse, ranging from logic to poetics. Indeed, the range of answers to this question is so varied, and the implications of each answer so significant for how we engage the practical, critical, and theoretical problematics of rhetoric, that it seems more productive to ask the more inclusive and proactive question "What can a rhetoric be?" rather than to ask the foundational and totalizing question "What is rhetoric?" Five of the essays included in this section represent a range of significant, relatively recent answers to this question, in each instance identifying the implications of the answer that it provides for the significance of rhetoric in contemporary times. One essay speaks directly to the very problematic of defining rhetoric and the political and theoretical entailments of doing so.

For the largest part of the twentieth century, the most prominent definition of rhetoric has been Aristotle's, in large measure no doubt as a result of the development of speech departments in the 1920s and the influence at that time of progressivism and pragmatism upon the public education of an American citizenry. By most accounts, Aristotle conceived of rhetoric as a practical and pragmatic doctrine, and his *Ars rhetorica* was initially appropriated in speech departments as a technical handbook for training fledgling orators to be effective public speakers. In "Practicing the Arts of Rhetoric: Tradition and Invention," Thomas Farrell rereads Aristotle to suggest that rhetoric is a higher order practice that entails "the entire process of forming, expressing, and judging public thought in real life." The implications of such a characterization are significant, for it suggests that rhetoric is an ethical practice that goes beyond simple questions of individual and utilitarian effectiveness, and is measured (Farrell's term is "redeemed") by the degree to which it achieves *phronesis*, or practical wisdom, in dealing with civic matters. Rhetoric is thus a function of prudential and communal decision making. In the second half of the essay Farrell outlines the implications of such a reconceptualization of rhetoric for rhetorical practice, rhetorical form, and rhetorical community in contemporary rhetorical culture.

Central to Farrell's notion of a revised Aristotelianism is the sense in which rhetoric is a *praxis*, in both the classical sense of combining theory and action, and in the more contemporary, Marxist, critical theoretical sense of "the concrete embodiment of existent social forces, understood as a mode of production." The tension between classical and contemporary conceptions of *praxis* has been central to a number of efforts to identify what a rhetoric might be—and how it might function—in contemporary times. In "The Habitation of Rhetoric," Michael Leff poses the problem in terms of rhetoric's "home," questioning whether rhetoric is an independent "art" that possesses its own "substance" or whether it belongs to a more substantial discipline or body of knowledge such as philosophy or political science. Leff locates the problem in the context of a forced and unnatural division between rhetoric as product and rhetoric as process that has made it difficult for us to understand how action and production are integrated in any given rhetorical context. According to Leff, the problem manifests itself most fully in the separation of persuasion, argumentation, and aesthetics (style), specifically in instances where "judgments must be rendered about specific matters of communal interest." The solution, according to Leff, is to return to a Ciceronian notion of decorum that helps us to understand the ways in which rhetoric is a unified praxis that aligns the stylistic and argumentative features of a discourse both internally as text and externally as a social force.

John Poulakos addresses the problem of *praxis* in "Toward a Sophistic Definition of Rhetoric." The Sophists were the first rhetoricians, and arguably it was in response to their power and presence in ancient Greece—and their commitment to a most radical relativism—that Plato developed his conception of philosophy and dialectic. Drawing upon the remaining fragments of sophistic treatises, Poulakos reconstructs a conception of sophistic rhetoric as "the art which seeks to capture in opportune moments that which is appropriate and attempts to suggest that which is possible." According to Poulakos, the Sophists thought of rhetoric as a *techne* (art) that operated through *logos* (the word) to produce both *pistis* (belief or proof) and *terpsis* (aesthetic pleasure). The enactment of rhetoric thus relied upon the human desire to be different or "other," and the social capacity to identify and adapt to the temporal and formal structures of the situations being addressed through the artful use of language. From this perspective, then, rhetoric is a social *praxis* that is enacted as a function of its *kairotic* (timely), aesthetic performance.

The issue of rhetoric as performance is taken up more fully in "Text, Context, and the Fragmentation of Contemporary Culture" by Michael Calvin McGee, who borrows from an Isocratean perspective that treats rhetoric as a critical form of social surgery. McGee is particularly interested in the ways in which academic rhetoricians perform their roles as critics and theorists in what he calls the postmodern condition. In particular, he believes that rhetorical theorists and critics have devoted far too much attention in recent years to the idealized study of singular texts and have ignored the need to produce material rhetorics, that is, discourses that might help the members of the polity understand how to construct powerful and compelling conceptions of collective living out of the textual fragments that constitute their contemporary culture. For McGee, then, the problem of *praxis* is not so much a hypothetical concern with unifying thought and action for a homogeneous culture or understanding rhetoric as the embodiment of text and context, but is rather a specific social force that actively engages and manages (but never totally transcends) the tensions between thought and action, and text and context, in a fragmented, heterogeneous, multicultural society.

Since classical antiquity the theoretical question of "what a rhetoric can be" has been answered primarily, if not almost exclusively, by men. This bears a certain irony when we recall that since classical antiquity rhetoric has been characterized derogatorily in female terms as "Dame Rhetoric" and "The Harlot of the Arts." Recent years have been witness to an increasingly elaborate feminist critique of rhetoric as "patriarchal," "malestream," and "phallogocentric," leading many to argue for feminist conceptions of what a rhetoric might be.

In "The Taming of *Polos/Polis*: Rhetoric as an Achievement Without Woman," Jane Sutton probes the history of rhetoric as a discourse that has been written in relationship to woman's body. Sutton argues that the meaning of rhetoric has historically been imbricated in an archetype that equates it with images of horses and woman—both represented in classical literature as uncivilized forces in need of domestication—images that have functioned to help create the conditions to justify "taming" and controlling rhetoric's potentially unruly and disruptive power. To demonstrate and subvert the logic of this definition, Sutton playfully reconstructs the relationship between rhetoric-horse-woman through a

technique of collage that metaphorically, metonymically, synecdochically, and ironically reconstitutes rhetoric's history explicitly in terms of
woman's body as a means of unleashing its power and force. The focus
on the trope of the body is a provocative one that warrants careful
consideration, for it not only emphasizes the performative dimensions
of the rhetorical (and this seems to be a thread that connects all the
conceptions of what a rhetoric might be that are discussed in this
section of the reader), but also seeks to resist and reconstruct problematic hierarchies that restrict and limit the ways in which men and women
enact the rhetorical.

The question of definitional hierarchy is taken up most fully and
provocatively by Robert Hariman in "Status, Marginality, and Rhetorical
Theory." Although Hariman offers a definition of rhetoric as "a mode
of reflection upon the sociality of language," his primary task is not so
much to answer the question "What might a rhetoric be?" as to ask
"What is at stake in posing the question in the first place?" As such, it
provides, at least conceptually, a metacommentary on the task of the
other essays in this section. Hariman notes that historically most efforts
at defining rhetoric have treated it generically by distinguishing it from
other forms of discourse, most notably philosophy, logic, and poetry.
All such efforts at definition operate in a powerful dialectic of status
and marginality that functions to empower and constrain the meaning
and force of any given discourse by "activating a pattern of thinking,"
that locates it in a social hierarchy of desirability and potency. For Plato,
the hierarchy had dialectic at the top and rhetoric at the bottom; for
the Sophists, the hierarchy was reversed. In either case, however, the
dialectic constitutes relations of dominance and subordination, and of
an authority that seeks to conceal itself. By treating the history of the
definition of rhetoric in terms of the social functions of status and
marginality, Hariman argues, we ought to be in a much better position
to deconstruct (or at least to understand) the political and ontological
implications of the ways in which any conception of rhetoric affects how
we think of and practice rhetorical theory. More importantly, perhaps,
it also calls attention to the mutability of the social meanings and
relations of discourse and of the continuing need to engage rhetorical
inquiry as a means of reflecting upon "the art of reclassification" and
of wondering "What might a rhetoric be?"

Additional Readings

Burke, Kenneth. (1945). *The Rhetoric of Motives*. Berkeley and Los Angeles:
University of California Press.
Ehninger, Douglas. (1968). "On Systems of Rhetoric." *Philosophy and Rhetoric*
1: 131–144.

Gearhart, Sally. (1979). "The Womanization of Rhetoric." *Woman's Studies International Quarterly* 2 : 195–201.

Group Mu [J. Dubois, F. Edeline, J.-M. Klinkenberg, P. Minguet, F. Pire, and H. Trinon]. (1981). *A General Rhetoric.* Translated by Paul B. Burrell and Edgar M. Slotkin. Baltimore: Johns Hopkins University Press. [Originally published in French in 1970.]

Jarrat, Susan C. (1991). *Rereading the Sophists: Classical Rhetoric Refigured.* Carbondale: Southern Illinois University Press.

McGee, Michael Calvin. (1982). "A Materialist's Conception of Rhetoric." In Ray E. McKerrow, ed., *Explorations in Rhetoric: Studies in Honor of Douglas Ehninger* (Glenview, IL: Scott, Foresman), pp. 23–48.

McGuire, Michael. (1982). "The Structural Study of Speech." In Ray E. McKerrow, ed., *Explorations in Rhetoric: Studies in Honor of Douglas Ehninger* (Glenview, IL: Scott, Foresman), pp. 1–22.

McKeon, Richard. (1971). "The Uses of Rhetoric in a Technological Age: Architectonic Productive Arts." In Lloyd F. Bitzer and Edwin F. Black, eds., *The Prospect of Rhetoric* (Englewood Cliffs, NJ: Prentice-Hall), pp. 44–63.

Scott, Robert L. (1973). "On *Not* Defining 'Rhetoric.'" *Philosophy and Rhetoric* 6: 81–96.

Sproule, Michael. (1988). "The New Managerial Rhetoric and the Old Criticism." *Quarterly Journal of Speech* 74: 401–415.

Toward a Sophistic Definition of Rhetoric

JOHN POULAKOS

When Hegel undertook to reanimate the Sophists,[1] he established with poignant observations that the message of those itinerant teachers of culture was a natural as well as a necessary link between pre-Socratic (especially Anaxagoran) and Platonic thought.[2] Thus, he endowed their views with intellectual integrity on the one hand, and gave them a place in the history of philosophy on the other. The recent plenitude of sophistic studies shows that Hegel's work was not an instance of philosophical lightning but an origin of things to come. But whereas he and others[3] after him have placed the Sophists' views historically or topically, the meaning of their rhetorical perspective has not received adequate attention.

This essay presumes that without the Sophists our picture of the rhetoric that came out of the Greek experience is incomplete. For over two millennia we have relied almost exclusively on the Platonic and Aristotelian notions of discourse while we have treated the sophistic position as an obscure but interesting historical footnote. And despite Hegel's and others' efforts to rehabilitate the Sophists, we are still bound to the directives of Plato's system of Idealism and Aristotle's system of Development. But because rhetoric came about as an activity grounded in human experience, not in philosophical reflection, we must approach it by looking at those who *practiced* it before turning to those who *reflected* about it.

In recent years the above position has been espoused by many students and teachers of rhetoric. Thus far, however, it has led mainly to studies enabling us to better understand individual Sophists. But if Greek rhetoric is indeed a trilogy, we need to concern ourselves with its first part, which to this day remains fragmentary. To do so, we must reexamine the surviving fragments of and about the Sophists and seek to articulate on probable grounds their view of rhetoric. This essay purports to do just that. More specifically, it purports to derive a "sophistic" definition of rhetoric and to discuss some of its more important implications.[4]

Although not as rigorous systematizers of thought as Plato or Aristotle, the Sophists were the first to infuse rhetoric with life. Indebted only to the poetry of their past, not to any formal rhetorical theory, they found themselves free to experiment playfully with form and style and to fashion their words in the Greek spirit of excellence. Aware of the human limitations in the acquisition of knowledge, they sought to ground the abstract notions of their predecessors[5] in the actuality of everydayness. Conscious of people's susceptibility to each others' language, they taught eloquence whose peculiar characteristic is "to show the manifold points of view existing in a thing, and to give force to those which harmonize with what appears to me to be more useful."[6] As practitioners and teachers of rhetoric, the Sophists made Greece aware of her culture and demonstrated to the rest of the world that rhetoric is an integral part of the social life of all civilized people.[7]

The definition I wish to advance is: *Rhetoric is the art which seeks to capture in opportune moments that which is appropriate and attempts to suggest that which is possible.* Very briefly, this definition intimates that rhetoric is an artistic undertaking which concerns itself with the how, the when, and the what of expression and understands the why of purpose. Further, this definition links rhetoric to a movement originating in the sphere of actuality and striving to attain a place in that of potentiality. The following discussion focuses on key notions and terms which, if seen together, constitute a coherent and defensible position on rhetoric. The example of the Sophists suggests that the notions and terms to be investigated are rhetoric as art, style as personal expression, *kairos* (the opportune moment), *to prepon* (the appropriate), and *to dynaton* (the possible).

The Sophists conceived of rhetoric primarily as a *techné*[7]* (art) whose medium is *logos* and whose double aim is *terpsis* (aesthetic pleasure) and *pistis* (belief).[8] The evidence supporting their artistic view comes from several sources. According to Philodemus, Metrodorus seems to make it clear enough that "the rhetoric of the Sophists has the status of an Art."[9] On a more specific comment, Philostratus claims that within Antiphon's forensic speeches "lies all that is derived from the art [of rhetoric]" (87 B44a). Similarly, Suidas informs us that Thrasymachus wrote, among other things, "a rhetorical art" (85 Al). In Plato's *Protagoras* (317b), Protagoras discloses that he has been many years "in the art," while Gorgias asserts in the *Gorgias* (450b) that "the rhetorical art is about words" and boasts in the same diaolgue (456b), that he often persuaded reluctant patients to submit to medical treatment "through no other art than the rhetorical." In his *Encomium to Helen* (13), Gorgias extends his conception of rhetoric by implying that if a speech is to be persuasive it must be "written with art."

Conceiving of rhetoric as art is important because on the one hand it designates the sophistic view proper[10] and on the other it helps place the controversy between Plato and the Sophists in the right light. In particular, one may argue, rhetoric as art does not admit criteria appropriate to strictly epistemological or axiological matters; nor does it call for the same considerations which rhetoric as argument does. Thus, some of the well-known Platonic charges against rhetoric become inapplicable.[11] In distinction to *episteme*, rhetoric does not strive for cognitive certitude, the affirmation of logic, or the articulation of universals. Conditioned by the people who create it, rhetoric moves beyond the domain of logic and, satisfied with probability, lends itself to the flexibility of the contingent.[12] Because the sophistic notion of rhetoric as art is a topic too large for the purposes of this essay, the following comments will be limited to the sophistic concern for the artistic aspect of discourse, or style.

---

*Editor's note: The footnote no. 7 appears twice in the original.

The story of the Sophists' preoccupation with style is too well known to be recounted here. Collectively, they were held in contempt for dealing with "the non-essentials" of rhetoric.[13] However, this preoccupation seems to have arisen from the realization, expressed later by Aristotle, that "the way a thing is said does affect its intelligibility."[14] Antiphon is quite explicit about the grave consequences of effective or ineffective style when he says: "it is as unfair that a bad choice of words should cause a man of good behavior to be put to death as it is that a good choice of words should lead to the acquittal of a criminal."[15] Of course, there is room to argue that stylistic emphasis in discourse, that is, emphasis of the how over the what, displays a preference indicative of misplaced values. But however small its value, style is an inescapable reality of speech, one which must be attended to necessarily. Aristotle himself, who insists on the primacy of facts and their proof,[16] acknowledges the reality and necessity of style when he writes: "It is not sufficient to know *what* one ought to say, but it is necessary also to know *how* one ought to say it."[17] So, to the extent that style is allowed to be seen primarily as an aesthetical issue, the question of its superiority or inferiority to content, essentially an axiological question, becomes secondary.

The evidence of the Sophists' excellence in style is plentiful. Protagoras, who on some matters held the same opinion which Diagoras, is said to have "used different words in order to avoid its extreme forcefulness" (80 A23). Philostratus reports in the *Lives of the Sophists* that Gorgias, who did for rhetoric as much as Aeschylus did for tragedy, "was an example of forcefulness to the Sophists and of marvels and inspiration and of giving utterance to great subjects in the grand style, and of detached phrases and transitions, through which speech becomes sweeter than itself and more pompous, and he also introduced poetical words for ornament and dignity" (82 Al [2]).[18] Xenophon, after re-creating the tale of Hercules' dilemma between Virtue and Vice, tells us that Prodicus, its original author, "embellished the [above] thoughts with still more magnificent words than I [have done] just now" (84 B2 [34]). Dionysius of Halicarnassus writes that Thrasymachus was "clean-cut and subtle and formidable in inventing and expressing tersely and extraordinarily that which he wants" (85 A13). According to Philostratus, Hippias "used to enchant Greece at Olympia with varied and well-heeded speeches" (86 A2 [7]). Philostratus praises Antiphon's *On Concord* by saying that it contains "brilliant and wise maxims and narrative elevated and flowered with poetical names and diffuse exposition like the smoothness of the plain" (87 B44a). Philostratus also praises the speech of Kritias for being "sweet . . . and smooth like the west breeze" (88 A1).

As the historical record indicates, the Sophists were master rhetoricians. That their excellence in the area of style has often been construed as a liability is due partly to Plato's influence on posterity and partly to the excesses of some of their successors. But if it is agreed that what is said must be said somehow, and that the how is a matter of the speaker's choice, then style betrays the speaker's unique grasp of language and becomes the peculiar expression of his personality.[19] If this is so, the Sophists need no longer be misunderstood. As some of their artifacts reveal, they were highly accomplished linguistic craftsmen with a heightened sense of the nature of *logos*, their medium.[20]

As the suggested definition of rhetoric implies, the Sophists were interested in the problem of time in relation to speaking. At least one of them, Gorgias, asserted that situations have a way of revealing themselves to man and of eliciting responses from him. As he states in his treatise *On Non-Being or On Nature*, "the external becomes the revealer of *logos*" (82 B3 [85]). But Gorgias was not alone in asserting that situations exist in time and that speech as a situational response does also. The Sophists stressed that speech must show respect to the temporal dimension of the situation it addresses, that is, it must be timely. In other words, speech must take into account and be guided by the temporality of the situation in which it occurs.

For the most part, what compels a rhetor to speak is a sense of urgency. Under normal circumstances, that is, under circumstances in which we are composed and things are "under control," there is no pressing need to speak. But during times of stress, we feel compelled to intervene and, with the power of the word, to attempt to end a crisis, redistribute justice, or restore order. In his *Defense of Palamedes* (32), Gorgias has the speaker say, following a lengthy statement of self-praise: "But [ordinarily] it is not for me to praise myself; but the present moment necessitated . . . that I defend myself in every way possible." Illustrating the same point, Thrasymachus, we are told, once addressed the Athenians by saying: "I wish, Athenians, that I had belonged to that time when silence sufficed for young people, since the state of affairs did not force them to make speeches and the older men were managing the city properly. But since our fortune has reserved us . . . misfortunes . . . one really has to speak" (85 B1).[21] In the former example it is urgent that the defendant reinstate his threatened reputation, while in the latter it is crucial that the citizens protest against the injurious practices of their civic leaders.

Both of the above examples imply that ideas have their place in time and unless they are given existence, unless they are voiced at the precise moment they are called upon, they miss their chance to satisfy situationally shared voids within a particular audience. Moreover, the two examples seem to restrict speaking to only those times calling for it, and to suggest that silence be the alternative at all other times. In fact, Gorgias praises the dead in his *Epitaphios* for having known when to speak (*legein*) and when to be silent (*sigan*) (B6).

Clearly, speaking involves a temporal choice. The choice is not whether to speak but whether to speak now; more precisely, it is whether now is the time to speak. When a rhetor speaks, he responds to a situation. But the fact that he speaks now, the fact that he has chosen this moment over another, reminds the listener that the situation is ephemeral, urgent, and, by implication, significant. But if the rhetor chooses to address the present, he also agrees to confront the contingent elements of the situation as they unfold. As such, he is taking on a risk, the risk that his timing might not coincide with the temporal needs of the situation. According to Philostratus, Gorgias, who held in contempt those who spoke about "things that had been said many times," devoted himself to what was timely (82 A24). Further, Gorgias "was the first to proclaim himself willing to take this risk . . . that he would trust to the opportune moment to speak on any subject" (82 A1a). That addressing the present requires courage and involves the taking of a risk is apparent in the compromise of extemporaneous speaking, the kind which literally occurs out of time. Prepared speech texts betray our insensitivity to and insecurity about all that is contingent in the act of speaking. Prepared texts have a designated time in the future and a prefabricated content. But by designating the time and by prefabricating the content of a speech, we are essentially setting the parameters of a situation to come and prepare ourselves in advance to treat it in its fixity. This compromise we make out of our apprehension regarding the indeterminate aspects of a situation to which we have no immediate access.[22] The example of several Sophists, most notably that of Gorgias and Hippias, suggests that an accomplished speaker has no need for notes or a text, rehearsal, or presituational practice.

The sophistic insistence that speaking be done with respect to time does not stem from a philosophical position regarding the nature of *logos* but from the observation that if what is said is timely, its timeliness renders it more sensible, more rightful, and ultimately more persuasive. Reportedly, Protagoras was the first to expound on "the power of the opportune moment" to give speech advantages it otherwise would not have (80 A1). In the anonymous sophistic treatise *Dissoi Logoi* 2 (19), the author is quite explicit about this point. Specifically, he states that "nothing is always virtuous, nor [always] disgraceful, but taking the same things the opportune moment made disgraceful and after changing [them made them] virtuous." Clearly, the notion of *kairos* points out that speech exists in time; but more important, it constitutes a prompting toward speaking and a criterion of the value of speech.[23] In short, *kairos* dictates that what is said must be said at the right time.

In conjunction with the notion of *kairos*, the Sophists gave impetus to the related concept of *to prepon* (the appropriate) apparently prescribing that what is said must conform to both audience and occasion. Illustrating *to prepon*, Gorgias praises in his *Epitaphios* the dead for having been "well-disposed toward the appropriate," while in his *Defense of Palamedes* (28) he has the defendant admit that what he is about to say is "inappropriate to one who has not been accused but suitable to one who has been accused." In the same speech, Gorgias strongly implies that the strategy of a legal defense depends largely on the speaker's audience. Specifically, he has the defendant state that while it is useful to employ appeals to pity and entreaties and the intercession of friends when the trial takes place before a mob, before noble and wise judges one must concentrate on the explanation of the truth (33).

A complement to the notion of *kairos*, *to prepon* points out that situations have formal characteristics, and demands that speaking as a response to a situation be suitable to those very characteristics. Both notions are concerned with the rhetor's response; but while the former is interested in the when, the latter is concerned with the what of speaking. *To prepon* requires that speech must take into account and be guided by the formal structure of the situation it addresses. Like *kairos*, *to prepon* constitutes not only a guide to what must be said but also a standard of the value of speech.[24] In distinction to *kairos*, which focuses on man's sense of time, *to prepon* emphasizes his sense of propriety.

Appropriateness refers to that quality which makes an expression be correlative to the formal aspects of the situation it addresses. When appropriate, speech is perfectly compatible with the audience and the occasion it affirms and simultaneously seeks to alter. An appropriate expression reveals the rhetor's rhetorical readiness and evokes the audience's gratitude; conversely, an inappropriate expression indicates a misreading on the rhetor's part and a mismeeting between rhetor and audience. If what is spoken is the result of a misreading on the part of the rhetor, it subsequently becomes obvious to us, even to him, that "this was not the right thing to say." If silence is called for and the response is speech, we have a rhetor misspeaking to an audience not ready to listen, or not ready to listen to what he has to say, or ready to listen but not to the things he is saying. If speech is needed and silence prevails instead, we have a rhetor who has misread the situation, a frustrated audience whose needs and expectations are not met, and a situation that perpetuates itself.

Both timeliness and appropriateness are rhetorical motifs whose essence cannot be apprehended strictly cognitively and whose application cannot be learnt mechanically.[25] As George Kennedy states, "The two together constitute what may be called the artistic elements in rhetorical theory as opposed to the prescribed rules."[26] Unlike rigid scientific principles, the two are more a matter of feeling. Some of the factors contributing to one's sense of the timely and the appropriate are one's discretionary powers, the cultural norms in which he participates, his reading of the situation he wishes to address, his image of his audience, and his prediction of the potential effects of his words on his listeners. Timeliness and appropriateness are similar qualities in the sense that they render an expression more persuasive. What is said, then, must be both appropriate to time, or timely, and appropriate to the audience and the occasion. Untimely and appropriate speech cannot move an audience because it is untimely; similarly, timely and inappropriate speech cannot achieve its aims because it is inappropriate. If persuasion is to occur, both qualities must be present in the spoken word. In short, the right thing must be said at the right time; inversely, the right time becomes apparent precisely because the right thing has been spoken.

As pointed out earlier, these two qualities are vague in conceptualization and elastic in application. Their observance does not "confine reality within a dogmatic scheme but allow[s] it to rage in all its contradictions, in all its tragic intensity, in all its impartiality imposed by an intelligibility which will revive the joy of truth."[27] Because the rhetorician concerns himself with the particular and the pragmatic, his way is not that of an abstract absolutism created in the spirit of *a priori* truths; rather, it is that of a relativism of concrete rhetorical situations to which situationally derived truths are the only opportune and appropriate responses. But the rhetorician is not confined to a single movement. After he captures the appropriate and places it temporally, he moves toward the suggestion of the possible. The starting point for the articulation of the possible is the ontological assumption that the main driving forces in man's life are his desires,[28] especially the desire to be other and to be elsewhere. Another relevant assumption is that the sphere of actuality always entails a lack, the absence of that which exists only in the future; more particularly, that actuality frustrates man when he dreams of being other and binds him to where he already is when he wants to be elsewhere.

Consideration of the possible affirms in man the desire to be at another place or at another time and takes him away from the world of actuality and transports him in that of potentiality. Moreover, it intensifies in him the awareness that actuality is hostile to what he wishes and, as such, denies its existence. Finally, it refines his wishes and shows him how to apply them, what to ask, and whom to reach.[29] To be sure, man walks on earth and his feet are a constant reminder of his connection to the ground. But at the same time, he looks at the horizon about him and perceives himself "not as he is, not where he is, but precisely as he is not and where he is not." Even though he functions daily in the world of actuality, he often finds himself concerned with his situation not as it is here-and-now but as it could be there-and-then. Thus, he participates at once in two worlds each of which opposes the other. For Georges Poulet, man finds himself in "two realities which simultaneously exist at a distance and which reciprocally deny each other: the reality in which one lives and that in which one does not live, the place in which one has situated one's dream and the place where with horror one sees oneself surrendered to chance and ill luck."[30]

This is where the rhetorician steps in and helps him resolve his existential dilemma. By exploiting people's proclivity to perceive themselves in the future and their readiness to thrust themselves into unknown regions, the rhetorician tells them what they could be, brings out in them futuristic versions of themselves, and sets before them both goals and the directions which lead to those goals. All this he does by creating and presenting to them that which has the potential to be, but is not. Thus it is no paradox to say that rhetoric strives to create and labors to put forth, to propose that which is not.

The rhetorician concerns himself with the possible because he refuses to keep people in their actual situation. Granted, he must initially address them as they are and where they are. The earlier discussion about *kairos* and *to prepon* established that. But subsequently he tries to lift them from the vicissitudes of custom and habit and take them into a new place where new discoveries and new conquests can be made. Gorgias hints at this notion in the *Encomium to Helen* (5) when he states that "to tell the knowing what they know has credibility but brings no delight." Gorgias is stressing here that to speak about actualities to those who are already aware of them is nearly a purposeless act[31] whose most notable defect is that it fails to please the audience. But if by relying on actualities we fall short of our rhetorical ends, where should we turn? The *Encomium to Helen* suggests that the province of rhetoric is the possible, that which has not yet occurred to the audience. Following his own example, Gorgias argues that one of the causes of Helen's abduction is the might of *logos* (a presumably novel idea not previously entertained by those familiar with her story).

A special dimension of the possible, then, is afforded by the novel,[32] the unusual, that prior to which we have no awareness, the unprecedented. As a group, the Sophists are known to have been the first to say or do a number of things. Several fragments testify to their novel claims and practices: 80 A1 (51) and (52); 82 A1 (1), A1a, A4 (4); 84 A1O; 85 A3; 86 A2. Xenophon tells us that Hippias told Socrates once: "I always try to say something new"[33] [86 A14 (6)] clarifying at the same time that he did so on matters which admit of subjective treatment (i.e., justice) and agreeing that on such subjects as arithmetic the novel has no place. Aristotle, pointing out one of the effects of the novel on audiences, refers to Prodicus, who thought that announcing that what one is about to say has never been heard before can literally awaken a drowsy audience (*Rhetoric* 1415b). Read together, the above fragments imply, as Aristotle remarks, that people are "admirers of things which are not part of their experience" (*Rhetoric* 1404b), and are drawn to them because they raise their curiosity and carry an element of surprise. New thoughts, new insights, and new ideas always attract our attention not only because we have not encountered them before but also because they offer us new ways to perceive ourselves and the world. On the other hand, things with which we are familiar condition our responses and restrict our actions.

The possible is the opposite of the actual. A derivative of the Heracleitean perspective, evoking the possible challenges the one and advances the manifold; it rejects permanence and favors change; it privileges becoming over being. Unlike the actual, the possible is not a given which can be known or verified; it exists in the future as something incomplete and dormant, something awaiting the proper conditions to be realized. Therefore, its evocation goes hand in hand with hope and modesty; hope because the speaker always awaits his listeners' contribution, which will bring the possible to completion and realization; and modesty because what the speaker says is always potentially dismissable. By voicing the possible, the rhetor discloses his vision of a new world to his listeners and invites them to join him there by honoring his disclosure and by adopting his suggestion. Essentially, he is asking them to abandon the shelter of their prudential heaven and opt for that which exists "by favor of human imagination and effort."[34] Of course, the risk always exists that the audience may decline his invitation. But this is a risk he must face if he dares stand up and offer an alternative to the mundanity, the mediocrity, or misery of those he wishes to address.

The possible is an aspect of non-actuality claiming that, given the proper chance, it can turn into something actual. And even though it opposes the actual, it always seeks to become actualized. In and through the speech of the rhetor, the seed of the possible is planted in the ground of actuality. However, its roots do not begin to form until the audience fails to see "why not," until they cannot find any reason to frustrate or repudiate it. Granted, the rhetor must show them why they ought to adopt his possible;

the tradition of rhetoric demands that propositions be justified. At the same time, he must go one step further and ask them to find reasons, their reasons, should they be inclined to say no. Thus, Gorgias asks in the *Encomium to Helen* (12): "What cause then prevents the conclusion that Helen ... might have come under the influence of speech?" This rhetorical question pits the actual belief (Helen is blameworthy as a woman with loose morals) against the possible belief (she is not to blame because she fell under the might of speech). The same approach is taken by Thrasymachus, who asks in *The Constitution* (Bl): "Why should anyone put off speaking [what] is in his mind, if [it has fallen] to him to be injured by the present situation and he thinks he is on to something that will put an end to such things?" In this instance, the possible Thrasymachus wishes to have his listeners adopt is speaking openly and with no hesitation, something which presumably will end their pain. In both cases, the rhetor is asking the audience to discover at least one reason why the conclusion suggested should not be the case. Should they fail, they ought to adopt what he says; should they succeed, they have grounds on which to reject what he advocates. In the former case, the possible is well on its way to actuality; but even in the latter, it has served a useful function: it has provided the challenge in response to which the listeners have reexamined their actual situation. That they may decide to affirm their previously held views is not that important. What is more important is that by doing so they have moved from accepting actuality uncritically, as it is and because it is, to accepting it deliberately, because it has withstood the challenge of a possible. To use Heidegger's language, they have moved closer to the realm of authenticity.

In this essay I have argued that the history of rhetoric dictates that the Sophists' views regarding the art of discourse need wider notice and further exploration. Extracting key ideas and terms from the preserved fragments of the Sophists, I have suggested a "sophistic" definition of rhetoric founded on and consistent with the notions of rhetoric as art, style as personal expression, the timely, the appropriate, and the possible. This definition posits that man is driven primarily by his desire to be other, the wish to move from the sphere of actuality to that of possibility. Moreover, it points out that as man becomes what he is not he encounters situations to which he often responds with language. It also suggests that if man's responses are to be effective, they must take into account the temporal and formal structure of the situations he addresses. As such, they must be guided by his sense of time and propriety, and must be formulated in ways consonant with himself. Finally, this definition stresses that the whole enterprise of symbolic expression falls within the region of art.

Since the time of the Sophists, the area over which this definition extends has been covered with rigor far greater than I can muster. Therefore, I do not claim to have introduced new ideas in the field of rhetorical theory. However, the contribution of this essay is threefold: (1) it establishes that the Sophists' rhetorical practices are founded upon a coherent notion of rhetoric, (2) it articulates that notion, and (3) it reinforces the often neglected idea that some of our contemporary concepts about rhetoric originated with the Sophists.

Notes

1. By "Sophists," I refer to those commonly recognized as the major figures of this group of teachers of rhetoric, i.e., Protagoras, Gorgias, Prodicus, Antiphon, Hippias, Critias, and Thrasymachus.

2. G.W.F. Hegel, *Lectures in the History of Philosophy*, trans. E. S. Haldane (New York: Humanities Press, 1963), pp. 352–354.

3. See Mario Untersteiner, *The Sophists*, trans. Kathleen Freeman (New York: Philosophical Library, 1954); Laszlo Versenyi, *Socratic Humanism* (New Haven, CT: Yale University Press, 1963); E. M. Cope, "On the Sophistical Rhetoric," *Journal of Classical and Sacred Philology* 2 (1855): 126–169, and 3 (1856): 34–80, 253–258. For a more detailed list, see W.K.C. Guthrie, *The Sophists* (London: Cambridge University Press, 1971), pp. 9–13.

4. When I say "sophistic" rhetoric, I do not mean to disregard the fact that in many cases the Sophists differed in their views on rhetoric. Rather, I mean to emphasize those common elements among them which permit us to regard them as a group.

5. Hegel, *Lectures*, p. 355.

6. Ibid., p. 358.

7. Regarding the meaning of the term *techné*, Guthrie remarks: "No English word produces exactly the same effect as the Greek *techné*. 'Art' suffers from its aesthetic associations, and also from the opposition between 'the arts' and the natural sciences. Those who know no Greek may be helped by the term itself: its incorporation in our 'technical' and 'technology' is not fortuitous. It includes every branch of human or divine (cf. Plato, *Soph.* 265e) skill, or applied intelligence, as opposed to the unaided work of nature" (*The Sophists*, p. 115, n. 3).

8. For an insightful discussion on the relationship between *pistis* and *terpsis*, see Charles P. Segal, "Gorgias and the Psychology of the Logos," *Harvard Studies in Classical Philology* 66 (1962): 119ff.

9. Philodemus, *Rhetoric*, 2.49. Cited in Hermann Diels and Walther Kranz, *Die Fragmente der Vorsokratiker* (Berlin: Weidmannsche Verlagsbuchhandlung, 1952), 85 B7a. All subsequent fragments are from this source. The translation of this fragment is by Francis E. Sparshott, in Rosamond K. Sprague, ed., *The Older Sophists* (Columbia: University of South Carolina Press, 1972). Unless otherwise specified, the translations which follow are mine. I have taken fewer liberties with the texts than have other translators and have tried to remain as faithful as possible to the Greek. As a result, the reader will note, the English in several cases is awkward.

10. In the *Gorgias* 463b, Socrates refers to rhetoric as *kolakeia* (flattery) and refutes Gorgias by saying that rhetoric is not art but *empeiria* and *tribe* ("habitude" and "knack"). On the other hand, Aristotle, although he does refer to rhetoric as art (*Rhetoric*, 1402a), conceives of it primarily as a faculty (*dynamis*); see *Rhetoric*, 1355b and 1359b.

11. For Plato's criticism of rhetoric, see the *Gorgias* and the *Phaedrus*.

12. A useful discussion of the notion of contingency is provided by Robert L. Scott, "On Viewing Rhetoric as Epistemic," *Central States Speech Journal* 15 (1967): 9–17 (reprinted in this volume).

13. Aristotle, *Rhetoric*, 1354a.

14. Ibid., 1404a. This is Rhys Roberts's translation and I have included it for syntactical purposes. A more literal translation is given by E. M. Cope: "for it makes *some* difference in the clearness of an explanation whether we speak in one way or another"; see Cope, in John E. Sandys, ed., *The Rhetoric of Aristotle* (London: Cambridge University Press, 1877).

15. J. S. Morrison's translation, in *The Older Sophists*.

16. Aristotle, *Rhetoric*, 1404a.

17. Ibid., 1403b; emphasis added.

18. With the exception of minor changes, this is George Kennedy's translation in *The Older Sophists*. On a more focused comment, Suidas writes that Gorgias "was the first to give to the rhetorical genre the verbal power and art of deliberate culture and employed tropes and metaphors and allegories and hypallage and catachreses and hyperbata and doublings of words and repetitions and apostrophes and isokola" (82 A2; Kennedy's translation with minor changes).

19. Georges Gusdorf, the phenomenologist, says that "style signifies the task given to man of becoming aware of perspective. Each of us, even the most simple of mortals, is charged with finding the expression to fit his situation. Each of us is charged with realizing himself in a language, a personal echo of the language of all which represents his contribution to the human

world. The struggle for style is the struggle for consciousness (la vie spirituelle)"; see *Speaking* (*La parole*), trans. Paul Brockelman (Evanston, IL: Northwestern University Press, 1965), p. 76.

20. Bromley Smith demonstrates how this is so in his article "Gorgias: A Study of Oratorical Style," *Quarterly Journal of Speech Education* 7 (1921): 335–359.

21. Sparshott's translation, in *The Older Sophists*.

22. For a discussion of the merits of impromptu speaking, see Alcidamas's *On Those Who Write Written Speeches or On the Sophists*. Since Alcidamas was Gorgias's student, it is not unreasonable to suppose that some of his views coincide with those of other Sophists.

23. This view is expressed by Isocrates in *Against the Sophists*, 293 (13): "for it is not possible for speeches to be good if they do not partake of the opportune moments, and the appropriate and the novel." For a treatment of the moment as a criterion of the value of speech, see Gusdorf's *Speaking*, p. 85.

24. Ibid.

25. Untersteiner stresses this point in *The Sophists*, p. 198.

26. George Kennedy, *The Art of Persuasion in Greece* (Princeton, NJ: Princeton University Press, 1963), p. 67.

27. Untersteiner, *The Sophists*, p. xvi.

28. Hegel, *Lectures*, p. 358.

29. Georges Poulet, *The Interior Distance*, trans. Elliott Coleman (Ann Arbor: University of Michigan Press, 1959), p. 239.

30. Ibid., p. 240.

31. Aristotle points out that "about those things which we know or have decided there is no further use in speaking about them"; see *Rhetoric*, 1391b.

32. See note 23, above.

33. Ibid. As if he is echoing Hippias's comment, Gusdorf writes: "The great artist avoids imitating even himself. He continually undertakes the task of remaining vigilantly aware of the world of words, a task forever unfinished because the world changes and is renewed, and living man with it" (*Speaking*, p. 75).

34. Richard Weaver, *The Ethics of Rhetoric* (Chicago: Henry Regnery, 1953), p. 20.

Status, Marginality, and Rhetorical Theory

ROBERT HARIMAN

The history of rhetorical studies includes recurrent discussion of the proper demarcating of rhetoric and dialectic, rhetoric and poetic, rhetoric and logic, and similar divisions of the verbal arts. Although such comparisons are unavoidable when defining any type of discourse, they have a special significance for rhetoric. Rhetoric as a tradition of erudition has been shaped powerfully by the debates over the relative worth of its subject, and these debates have been inseparable from the activity of categorizing the several kinds of discourse.

The story of the ruling comparisons in the history of rhetoric is well known: Plato placed heavy sanctions upon rhetoric by subordinating it to dialectic; Aristotle gave rhetoric a more generous appraisal; Cicero and Quintilian reversed Plato's order; Augustine recovered rhetoric from the censure of pagan letters by other Church Fathers; Ramus removed rhetoric from the major curriculum of European letters, and so forth. What has not been done is to ask why the arts of language were compared so aggressively, and compared with such a heavy emphasis upon their relative superiority or inferiority. We do have excellent glosses on the arguments advanced to justify the specific comparisons, but we have not considered the comparisons as means to an end.

This project of demarcating the universe of discourse is particularly intense today, when there is widespread intellectual debate regarding the "end of philosophy" and the resurrection by continental writers of such antiquities as hermeneutics and the rhetoric of tropes. Calvin Schrag has underscored the significance of this situation for rhetorical studies by pointing to the "complex phenomenon of the emergence of philosophy from rhetoric and its subsequent return"[1] and calling for a "complementary deconstruction of rhetoric"[2] that would create a "shared milieu of self and social understanding."[3] I propose to continue this process of radical reflection, considering how the arts of language are determined by some of the harsher elements in their common sociality.

This essay will suggest how arguments about genres of discourse often contain, as a crucial element, an attribution of *status*. That is, the act of comparing discourses implies both manifest definitions of substance and latent attributions of status for each genre, and the disputes about categorizing discourses often are concerned more with questions of status than of substance. Status is the determination by one's associates of one's worth relative to their worth, and includes one's rank, reputation, respect, esteem, prestige, or place. The attribution of status to genre is a device for establishing the privileges—and powers—of those discourses in the verbal sciences. By focusing upon those comparisons that attribute an inferior status to rhetoric, the particular dynamic of empowering through status can be identified: as superior status is a condition of social *privilege*, so inferior status is a condition of social *marginality*, and we empower discourses by imposing a social order upon the world that relegates words, writers, and speakers to zones of centrality or marginality.

My argument is about a question of significance. It is obvious that theorists always have ranked discourses, and that they have, while ranking, praised their preferred art and faulted others, and that they have, while praising and faulting, indulged the more temperamental side of their thinking. When philosophers (say, Plato) denounce rhetoric, or when rhetoricians (say, Cicero) ridicule philosophy, they seem to be engaging in the inevitable but trivial vanity and irascibility accompanying all human endeavor.[4] They do not seem to be revealing a fundamental characteristic of their arguments or, by extension, of our intellectual tradition. We should recognize, however, that such appraisals are grounded in the division of discourses: the text has been divided, according to a dissociation of terms, into the (real) language of argument and the (apparent) language of arguing. By dismissing the status claims, we overlook the deconstructive character of the theorists' texts: for the status claim accompanying the substantive conception of genre is precisely the manner in which the theoretical text simultaneously asserts and denies its own authority. It seems, then, that there is a possibility that a process of mystification has been at work in our thinking. Linguistic theorists, and especially rhetorical theorists, think by means of a technique that they also describe as trivial. Perhaps this paradox can be corrected by recognizing how sociality is an essential constituent of linguistic power in theoretical discourse and how marginality is a conventional condition of rhetorical studies.

This essay first will present representative examples of arguments about genre that contain attributions of status, then examine the dynamic of marginality that is the source of the attributions' power, and conclude by discussing the implications of these claims for the politics of rhetorical theory and the ontology of rhetorical discourse.

STATUS

Rhetoric will always have to answer to Plato's questioning of its merit. Moreover, Plato's investigation of rhetoric is inseparable from his relentless attack upon the status held by the Sophists in his community. Nor can we escape this fact by distinguishing between speaker (the persons he knew as Sophists) and discourse, for each serves in his dialogues as a metonym for the other. Whatever the sublimity of the Platonic dialogues, the definitions of rhetoric are marked by irony and sarcasm. Through his famous metaphor of cookery, for example, rhetoric is simultaneously defined and shamed.

This emphasis upon Plato's tone need not deny the important qualifications to his conception of rhetoric. Contemporary scholars have devoted extensive discussion to at least four counterpoints: Plato's concomitant suggestion of an ideal rhetoric; his incorporation of some elements of *mythos* into his philosophical system; his incorporation of irony, paradox, and outright contradiction in his dialogues; and the corresponding complexity and difficulty of the dialectic he offers as an alternative to rhetoric.[5] On the other hand, emphasis upon these fascinating considerations can obstruct reconsideration of the more obvious, though not less simple, facts of the original attack and, more importantly, its historical import. This paper approaches its subject by returning to the observation Edwin Black provided several decades ago: "Indeed, the only uniformity which crystallizes from this diversity of interpretation is the judgment that Plato disapproved of rhetoric, and was, in fact, rhetoric's most effective historical opponent."[6]

Unfortunately, Plato has too often escaped Cicero's observation that "what impressed me most deeply about Plato in that book was, that it was when making fun of orators that he himself seemed to me to be the consummate orator."[7] Cicero is raising a question of motive, and indicating that Plato's strategy is to denigrate rhetoric in order to elevate philosophy as a privileged subject. For example, in the *Gorgias* Socrates contrasts philosophy to public opinion—philosophy is always true and never capricious like the public—at once stating what each subject is and marking its value.[8] The *Phaedrus* contains explicit discussions of the inferiority of writing, reading, and rhetoric when they are compared to the superior acts of philosophical discussion, reasoning, and dialectic. By the time Socrates concludes by telling the boy resolutely that the lover of wisdom must "disdain" all manner of discourse other than that of philosophy, which is discriminated as the highest form of instruction of the soul on justice, honor, and goodness, Plato has created a philosophical discourse in part by ordering all discourse beneath his own, and he has delineated philosophy by contrasting it with the inferior social good of rhetoric.[9] In Samuel Ijsseling's summary, "One can even say that Platonic philosophy arose within the polemic against the orator and the sophist."[10]

Plato's attack on rhetoric demonstrates a powerful version of a common strategy: we determine what any of the arts of language is by stating how important it is. We define dialectic, or poetics, or dialogue, or investigative reporting by both saying what it is and where it is in some social order. This strategy is more than a restatement of Kenneth Burke's "paradox of substance," for the social placement is more than saying what something is by saying what it is not.[11] That attribution of status says that something is something because it is valued as something, and this reciprocity between individual substance and social position generates more than ambiguity and the possibility of semantic transformation; I argue below that it generates power.

Moreover, this authorizing of discourses by ranking them socially often is accomplished by demonstrating how the preferred art is *not* mere rhetoric. Although there is no necessary relation between these discourses, for any can be superior or inferior (as later examples will show), the arts of language often are defined as subjects of inquiry by being declared superior to rhetoric. The denouncing of rhetoric has become a convention of linguistic theory. As diverse scholars have suggested, this convention has predominated in the modern era—that is, at least since the Enlightenment.[12]

Immanuel Kant provides the clearest example of this strategy in his *Critique of Judgment*. The chapter "Comparison of the Respective Aesthetical Worth of the Beautiful Arts" begins by granting poetry "the first rank" and identifying the substance and function of that art: "It expands the mind by setting the Imagination at liberty; . . . It strengthens the mind by making it feel its faculty . . . of considering and judging nature as . . . a sort of schema for, the supersensible."[13] Kant then interrupts his ranking to contrast poetry with rhetoric, known as the "art of persuasion, i.e., of deceiving by a beautiful show."[14] Although Kant recognizes distinctions between better and worse forms of rhetoric and does not ban its practice altogether from the arts or civil society, his basic appraisal is thoroughly negative: rhetoric uses illusion not to liberate the understanding but to preclude judgment and deprive us of our freedom. Moreover, he concludes by declaring that "the art of availing oneself of the weaknesses of men for one's own designs (whether these be well meant or even actually good does not matter) is worthy of no *respect*."[15] Only after this contrast between poetry and rhetoric does Kant return to the task of identifying the other arts by ranking them in descending order from poetry. Thus, he has elaborated his aesthetic philosophy by simultaneously defining the arts, ranking them according to a hierarchy of social values, and denigrating rhetoric.

John Locke provides another example. Locke concludes the third chapter of his *Essay on Human Understanding*, "On Words," by discussing the "Imperfection" and "Abuse" of words and offering his "Remedies." Locke faults both of the Schoolmen's arts of language—rhetoric and dialectic—and offers his remedies as the means of restoring both civil discourse and philosophy. He begins by contrasting civil and philosophical communication, giving the latter the greater exactness, and then bemoans the false estimation granted the other arts of language. Rhetoric, known by the "artificial and figurative application of words," gives us "perfect cheats" and its general practice brings Locke to conclude that:

> I cannot but observe how little the preservation and improvement of truth and knowledge is the care and concern of mankind; since the arts of fallacy are endowed and preferred. It is evident how much men love to deceive and be deceived, since rhetoric, that powerful instrument of error and deceit, has its established professors, is publicly taught, and has always been had in great reputation.[16]

Locke's argument is a bit more complicated than Kant's, for he explicitly contests a received ranking, and places more emphasis upon the deceitfulness of the art. Locke's inverting of the received hierarchy into his rightful, vernacular society of plain words has the same effect as Kant's more pedantic rebuff: his discourse is found to be more honorable than another. In sum, both the rationalist and the empiricist follow the same pattern, for in each case an argument for a change in philosophical method is joined with an argument over status containing a condemnation of rhetoric.

Note also how such discourse contains a technique for concealing its inherent textuality. Kant and Locke (and Plato) are each demonstrating the dissociation of concepts: they restructure the received unity of all discourse into separate realms of appearance and reality, and thereby erase the assumption that rhetoric and philosophy are both arts of language.[17] This dissociation is activated by identifying rhetoric with "deceit" and "show," against the implicit artlessness of their discourse.

Moreover, the simultaneous association of appearance with patently social acts— e.g., one deceives others, shows to others—also conceals the inherent sociality of the superior discourse: it suggests that their ranking of discourses is itself not constituted by the approval of others. These writers succeed not only at incorporating into their texts signs of the "transtextual" quality of truthfulness, but also at defining their opponents as merely social—rather than philosophical—creatures, while they engage in the quintessentially social act of sneering.

At this point I should stress that rhetoric does not have to be the denigrated genre.

The nature of status—of any social condition—is that it exists by attribution; no praise or blame is inevitable in establishing a hierarchy. Rhetoric was the superior art in ancient Rome and throughout the Renaissance. Occasionally it has escaped mention altogether. For example, philosophy also has been aligned against poetry. Anicius Boethius begins *The Consolation of Philosophy* with a scene from his sickbed, where he is "driven by grief to shelter in sad songs."[18] The scene is conventional: author attributing his genius to the muses, whose naming will serve as his forward to the work (recall the naming of the god in *Phaedrus*). This scene is interrupted, however, by a majestic woman in ethereal garb. Her gown is hemmed with the letter Pi (for practical philosophy) at the bottom and the letter Theta (for speculative philosophy) at the top, with a ladder of steps rising from the lower to the higher letter. Again, this personification of philosophy was not strange then and remains comprehensible today. But this story takes a turn away from the conventional depictions of the harmony of the arts:

> At the sight of the Muses of Poetry at my bedside dictating words to accompany my tears, she became angry. "Who," she demanded, her piercing eyes alight with fire, "has allowed these hysterical sluts to approach this sick man's bedside? They have no medicine to ease his pains, only sweetened poisons to make them worse. These are the very women who kill the rich and fruitful harvest of Reason with the barren thorns of Passion."[19]

Again, one verbal art has been placed above another in a social hierarchy, and the substance of the art (Reason) is defined simultaneously with a depiction of its status. By portraying poetry as the discourse of sluts, Boethius epitomizes the act of ranking-by-insult. The tactic is no less an ornament than the figures of personification and metaphor in his text, but it reminds us that all this ornamentation should be read reflectively, and that the ornaments of exclusion should be included in our understanding of philosophy and of rhetoric as much as such already privileged figures of harmony as Apollo's chariot, the Symposium, or the music of the spheres.

Ranking discourses need not only privilege philosophy. Poetics has enjoyed in the twentieth century an autonomy and legitimacy previously unknown in its history. A large part of this success stems from one document—Shelley's *Defense of Poetry*, "one of the three or four greatest critical essays in the English language."[20] Shelley's essay is a response to Thomas Love Peacock's essay on "The Four Ages of Poetry," and the exchange is, start to finish, a debate about the status of poetry. Peacock's intention is to ridicule the Romantic poets already becoming renowned in his day. He proceeds by charting a cycle of four periods: of iron, gold, silver, and brass—with the Romantics then exemplifying the last. In each case he offers a perfect identification of rank and substance: for example, poetry of the iron age has, commensurate with its place in the hierarchy of human development, the subject of heroic exploits, the rhythms of oral composition, a diction of natural and supernatural images, and the social function of awakening the community to the dawn of civilization.[21] And so each rank of poetry is described, including the modern age of brass where poetry has the substance of "harmony, which is language on the rack of Procrustes; sentiment, which is canting egotism in the mask of refined feeling; passion, which is the commotion of a weak and selfish mind; pathos, which is the whining of an unmanly spirit; and sublimity, which is the inflation of an empty head."[22] Here insult piles upon insult as the moderns are condemned for their abandonment of thought and their indulgence of ornament—in sum, found unfit for the authority of "the political palm and the critical chair."[23]

Shelley's long reply takes the high road, generally eschewing insult for a sustained call to arms for his poetics, but maintains both the received fascination with status and the technique of ranking discourses. For example:

> The fame of legislators and founders of religions, so long as their institutions last, alone seems to exceed that of poets in the restricted sense; but it can scarcely be a question, whether, if we deduct the celebrity which their flattery of the gross opinions of the vulgar usually conciliates, together with that, which belonged to them in their higher character of poets, any excess will remain.[24]

Shelley's "defense" also is an attack on the neoclassical social order which valued prose over poetry and declamation over aesthetics. (Shelley's antipathy to the rhetorical training of his day is not expressed prominently in his text but was obvious to his audience.) Rather than rebuke the rhetorical tradition directly, he devotes most of his argument to evoking hierarchies—of the faculties, the historical development of the species, our personal development, the arts, and so on—that are topped by poetic properties. Each placement—for example, "Reason is to the imagination as the instrument to the agent, as the body to the spirit, as the shadow to the substance"[25]—advances the battle for poetry's status while securing the accompanying definition of its substance. Throughout the essay this social consciousness is enhanced by frequent use of such adjectives as "highest," "loftiest," "imperial," and "majestic." Finally, Shelley brings us to the greatest hierarchy of all: "Poetry is indeed something divine."[26] This universal definition of substance begins a long elaboration of the claim in Plato's *Ion* that poetry is superior to knowledge, and ends with the assertion that "poets are the unacknowledged legislators of the world."[27] The substance of poetry—inspiration—is revealed through an argument for its status, and Shelley's genius—his status—is secured through his strategy of reversing the received hierarchy of discourses by locating the power of poetry in its unacknowledgment. We must acknowledge his triumph: poetry still is presumed by many to be an autonomous art ruled wholly by its internal laws.[28]

To summarize: the previous examples suggest how attributions of status are a characteristic of arguments about discourse, and also how rhetoric—or the techniques of ornamentation typically consigned to rhetoric—often are assigned an inferior status in regard to another discourse. But why would Plato or Kant go to such trouble—why labor to debunk the subject one is not inspired to study and magnify? What is it about their inquiry—and not their individual motives, which will remain opaque to us—that draws them to this act of censure? What is it about the act of censure that contributes to their inquiry?

MARGINALITY

Status is a concomitant of socializing. Attributing status is a social act, perhaps the quintessential social act, for status cannot exist without the cooperation of other people and can exist then without any material support, consequence, or correlative. One's status is everything—people will kill for it—and nothing—other people may never acknowledge it. Status may be compared to the theatrical scrim: a cloth that can appear solid or translucent depending on how it is illuminated. Thus, in accepting that sociality is the foundation of thinking, one must accept this reversibility as a condition of one's thought. Perhaps Plato's attack upon rhetoric was an attack upon this limitation of sociality upon the powers of the mind: rhetoric was the metonym for sociality, and the status of the Sophists the surest sign of the nature of rhetoric. "At the outset Plato denied what was for Sophism the very foundation of man's humanness, his impulse to associate with his fellows within the social institution of the *polis*. He claimed that social intercourse necessarily destroys the philosophic act. Hence, solitude became a precondition for thought as he would have it understood."[29] Yet, as Cicero observed, Plato succeeds at having thought understood to be a transcendental rather than a social act because he appropriates the very qualities of thinking he advises against.

In other words, sociality is a contested characteristic of our intellectual tradition. We are social thinkers and we suppress this fact. My claim that theoretical discourse often includes as a crucial element attributions of status obviously is a reassertion of the primacy of the social qualities of our thinking. But what is the value of again stating that philosophy is not what Plato wanted it to be? The answer is that by deconstructing his case, we can uncover and study anew those varieties of thought that he suppressed.

To better understand why ranking is so powerful, we need a model of the social thinking that is active in the arguments over the status of discourses. Every society distinguishes itself not only against the surrounding welter of people, places, and things, but by discriminating more and less acceptable or coherent behaviors within its experience. Any society, that is, conceives itself as having a center, a periphery, and a beyond. And the conception of the periphery—or margin—of the society is essential to the conception of the center. Social marginality is the zone of what is recognizable as pertaining to one's identity, but is undesirable. The margin of the society contains what one is but should not be, and the disciplining of the individual to avoid the margin is the means by which one is socialized. As Emile Durkheim and others have observed, marginal behavior is an essential part of society, something that cannot be eliminated without undermining a community's morality and cohesiveness.[30]

Attribution of status activates our sensitivity to social marginality. "High" status identifies a "central" substance and "low" status identifies a "marginal" substance. The differences between a physician and a quack, or a social drinker and a drunk, or a lady and a whore, or a Brahmin and an untouchable are differences between social centrality and social marginality. In each case the marginal character is necessary for the proper identification of the central character, the images of each contain reciprocal attributions of status and identity, and these operations themselves require social validation. These dynamics are epitomized in the insult, "an act, remark, or gesture which expresses a severely negative opinion of a person or group."[31] Insult is a subversion of one's status and it works by identifying one with the signs of marginality. Plato's describing rhetoric as cookery places it in the margin of his aristocracy, and Boethius' marking the Muses of poetry as sluts places them in the margin of his civil society. And the difference between the "harlot of the arts" and her sisters is the difference between marginality and authority. In every case the insult reveals the expectations of the social order, often with more economy and force than any positive declaration. In fact, by locating marginal behavior by insult, the social order receives implicit justification: it is superior to what is scorned. This is precisely the strategy in Saint Jerome's dream of being called before the throne of heaven to hear himself denounced as a "Ciceronianus."[32] Thus, "insult is one means by which social stratification systems are both constituted and maintained."[33] And so it also is one means by which we constitute and maintain those social stratification systems that are known as theories.

Arguments about status, then, do more than "ornament" definitions of substance: the attribution of status activates a pattern of thinking. This pattern of thinking is profoundly social: it is the marking of symbols according to their centrality or marginality to the society of the thinker. And this marking gives the symbols their power within the society. For every society constitutes itself by emphasizing and deemphasizing—sanctioning and censuring—the various human potencies. Those symbols marked as central to a society draw upon those powers amplified by the society's economy, institutions, and so on. Those marked as marginal are denied those powers, but they also acquire access to those potencies suppressed by the society. That is why the argument over status is important to the arguers: they are competing for the powers of argument, the powers that they then can transfer to their own thinking. Stated otherwise, the function of placing a discourse in the condition of social marginality is to determine the conditions for power (and powerlessness) in the other, non-marginal genres of discourse. As Mary Douglas observed in her study of pollution symbolism, "granted that disorder spoils pattern; it also provides the materials of pattern. . . . its potential for patterning is indefinite. . . . It symbolizes both danger and power."[34]

The dependence of the theorist upon this pattern of thinking follows not from the accident of being socially conditioned, but from the theorist's task of discriminating and amplifying the powers of the mind. This process of selective use requires subordination of those potencies not selected. So the powers of mind are authorized by their assertion over other powers. Thus, Kant consigns to marginality the powers of appearance in order to create transcendental facts; Locke suppresses the power of social inheritance in order to create representational meanings; Boethius suppresses the power of Passion in order to create a redeeming Reason; and Shelley displaces the power of declamation in order to authorize the imagination.

Moreover, the discourse marked as marginal then acquires those powers suppressed within the society, and consequently becomes less comprehensible. Marginal discourse must be seen as essentially confused, inarticulate, flawed. This attribution of inchoateness serves the society in two ways: it is used to discipline speaking, to keep speech within the margins, and it remains a continual source of symbolic renewal, a resource for creating new hierarchies. So marginality can be understood as the internal dynamic of social thinking used to generate verbal power, and as a limitation upon the words given social sanction, and as a condition of being for those words placed in the margin. This last observation provides my point of departure for discussion of both the politics of rhetorical theory and the ontology of rhetorical discourse.

THE POLITICS OF RHETORICAL THEORY

The first implication of my argument, that status arguments create conditions of marginality that determine our understanding, is that theoretical discourse is political discourse—that is, it inevitably establishes relations of dominance and subordination. It is political not only because it is determined by the "extra-literary" or "material" conditions of its production, but also because it produces conditions of empowerment which also become conditions of knowing. If substance and status were wholly separate properties of genre, then questions of ranking, and of the anxieties and altercations of ranking, might be questions of circumstance and incident alone. The interdependence of status and substance provides a denominator for knowledge and power, however. Shelley's ranking of discourses is a *sine qua non* of his concept of the imagination and his assertion of its imperial role in the invention of discourse, and his ranking continues to dominate the division of powers between rhetoric and poetics. Plato's depicting rhetoric as dishonorable separated truth and textuality in Western culture, and his authority remains unassailable as long as his technique remains concealed.

The next implication is that theoretical discourse can be analyzed as a restatement of comprehensive conditions of authority and marginality. This claim is more than a restatement of Kenneth Burke's observation that any selection of reality is a deflection of reality, for the condition of marginality changes that which is deflected.[35] To empower discourse one must do what always is done to create power through discourse—consign someone to marginality—and this mutual defining of self and other as esteemed and marginal is a process of transformation: each individual is made into a social character. Consigning a type of discourse to marginality involves more than a subsequent inattention to the discourse: it necessitates an alternation, a change in the substance of the discourse. And given the shared sociality of the different genres, this change is matched by a change in the privileged discourse. Although the specific character given to any genre will depend upon the social nuances of its placement, the attribution of marginality is likely to follow a general disposition to identify the marginal with the incomplete, confused, or inchoate. Thus, we should avoid seeing Plato and Kant assigning the same marginality to rhetoric—just as we would avoid claiming that they adhere to an identical idealism—but we should ask if they each assign rhetoric mutually incongruous properties, such as being both capricious and confining. They do, and they can do so because rhetoric's marginal placement transforms it from a comprehensible practice to the condition of disorientation that must be corrected by the authorized practice of philosophy.

The fact that theories of discourse are in part arguments over the conditions of authority and marginality carries particular significance for rhetorical theory. Obviously, rhetoric often has been conceived as a marginal form of discourse, and this placement conditions the rationale for a rhetorical theory: if rhetorical discourse is marginal, either there is no need for a rhetorical theory, or there is need only for a rhetorical theory designed to monitor and restrain rhetorical discourse. The dispute over the extent of Plato's objection to rhetoric can be allayed if we consider that he was writing *Phaedrus* as a program for restraining the dangerous impulses of marginality.[36] Consider the image of Apollo reining in the dark horse alongside the white horse as they pull his chariot across the heavens. The horse has the sure marks of marginality, for he is flawed: "[he] is crooked of frame, a massive jumble of a creature, with thick short neck, snub nose, black skin, and grey eyes; hot-blooded, consorting with wantonness and vainglory; shaggy of ear, deaf, and hard to control with whip and goad."[37] Plato tells us that rhetoric cannot be banished entirely and can give us the power to approach the truth, but only if yoked to a superior form and properly controlled. Despite his case for an ideal rhetoric, Plato's definition of actual rhetoric unmistakably places it in the condition of being marginal in respect to another discourse.

But the first possibility remains the most debilitating: rhetorical theory is written under a particular burden—the inherited sentence that it should not be written at all. Stated otherwise, rhetorical theory is aggressively deconstructive, subverting its authority to adjudicate discourses by emphasizing its reliance upon philosophically unacceptable discourse. This interdiction of the tendency of rhetoric to account for itself has specific consequences. Although rhetoric cannot escape its history as the discourse conventionally used to establish the margin for authorizing other discourses, the history of rhetoric can be better understood as characterized by this tension between marginality and authority.

The primary implication of my thesis for rhetorical theory is that this tradition of erudition can be analyzed as a continuing reaction to the use of rhetoric as a margin by other theorists of language. Because all theories of discourse are in part prolonged arguments for the status of their subjects, and since rhetoric often is used conventionally in those arguments as the inferior discourse, rhetorical theorists usually assume the special burden of arguing that rhetoric is *not* the inferior art. Rhetorical theory begins in the zone of the philosophically unacceptable, as an asylum. This burden is one reason why so many rhetorical theories are labeled a New Rhetoric.[38] Whereas other humanists would be happy to see their work as cumulative, the rhetorician is burdened with a commitment to a perpetual revolution. Thus Paul de Man can discover that "the aporia between performative and constative language is merely a version of the aporia between trope and persuasion that both generates and paralyzes rhetoric and thus gives it the appearance of a history."[39] Stated otherwise, rhetorical theory is grounded in the contradiction of elaborating a condition of self-doubt.

It should not be surprising that many of the "innovations" in rhetorical theory are denials of the use of rhetoric as the margin for the philosophical subject. Aristotle obviously is the most significant example here: his opening declaration that "rhetoric is the counterpart of dialectic" is a patent argument about the status of rhetoric and specifically designed to dismantle the Platonic hierarchy of discourses which obstructed an appreciative investigation of rhetoric.[40] Kenneth Burke's *A Rhetoric of Motives* not only appropriates Aristotle's appraisal of rhetorical inquiry, it also ponders mightily the "spirit of hierarchy" he finds suffusing rhetorical discourse. As he has summarized his *Rhetoric*: "It concerns the relations that characterize a ladder of Mr. Bigs and Mr. Littles, all along the line, up and down, with the 'magic' of these."[41] Much of the work done by contemporary scholars on the relationship between philosophy and rhetoric also has been directed to contest their received hierarchy of discourses (and specifically the hierarchy and logic of theoretical reduction developed by the analytical and positivist philosophers in this century).[42] Richard Weaver's work consistently was directed to rehabilitate the status of the orator to that of the nineteenth-century figure who had "a peculiar sense of stature. He always talked like a big man."[43]

Perhaps the most obvious contemporary example of a theory offering a strategy for escaping the peculiar burden of rhetorical studies is Robert L. Scott's conception of "rhetoric as epistemic." Scott begins by addressing the inferior status of rhetoric: "Professing rhetoric seems always eventually to lead to embarrassment. . . . At best good men grant rhetoric a slight role but grudgingly."[44] His argument then works both to change our discrimination of the rhetorical subject from a skill to a way of knowing and to elevate the status of the subject. Notice also how Scott's essay moves from his urging that we read rhetoric as a way of knowing to his provision of the concepts of toleration, will, and responsibility as the means of knowing rhetorically. He has shifted from epistemology to an ethic—what he believes is the proper attitude for interlocutors to have if they are to come to know by communicating. Here Scott exemplifies another motive informing the struggle to overcome the received condemnation of rhetoric: his ethic is a *perfecting* of the condition of sociality that is the ground of rhetoric. Even marginal discourse follows the logic of elaboration Burke identified as the motive for perfection, and we find any rhetorical theorist will be disposed, even in appreciating the marginality of rhetoric, to elaborate it into versions of itself ever more formally satisfying, such that eventually Burke's irony would be confirmed by articulating a version of the marginal condition too elegant to still carry the perspective and powers of the margin.[45]

Scott's essay demonstrates that although this "rehabilitative" project is laudable, it does merit a caution.[46] Generally, we attempt to elevate ourselves by imitating our "superiors"; doing too much of that rarely is wise. In the case of rhetoric, the pursuit of such high-status commodities as "philosophy" or "hermeneutics" may result in losing the opportunity to explore the margins of our time. As rhetoric is marginal, it also is a reservoir of power—a zone of those potencies suppressed in our society. What philosophers label error is also knowable as desire or will or Eros or Thanatos or the ineradicable conflicts of the political unconscious and so on. This may be Stanley Deetz's intention when he claims that the function of rhetoric can be "intrinsic to the perception formation process, not in a positive manner, but through a denial, an affronting, of the forces of perceptual domination."[47] The rhetorical theorist inherits a tradition of study that contains ineradicable aporias, failed practices, and practices that were prevented from being valorized as traditions, and the excavation of these marginal discourses can never be a mere filling in of the record, for any change in their status will alter the authority of the dominant discourses. The convention of placing rhetoric in the margin should be read as a challenge, though not the challenge to secure respectability.

THE ONTOLOGY OF RHETORICAL DISCOURSE

Paolo Valesio observes that "in rhetoric more than in any other of the language sciences the metalanguage is closely interwoven with the ambiguities and conflicting connotations of the object language."[48] The reliance upon status claims is one example of how these languages partake of each other: whether a speaker claiming expert authority or a theorist dismissing another's work as partisan, rhetor and rhetorician follow a continuous pattern of ranking to activate the dynamics of marginality. At this point the politics of interpretation merges with questions about the ontology of the verbal world. I shall conclude by considering how reflecting upon the political character of rhetorical theory may lead to a better understanding of rhetorical discourse.

The division central to the conflict between philosophy and rhetoric has been that between *episteme* and *doxa*, knowledge and opinion. The relevant ontological question is, "What is the nature of *doxa*?" One answer suggested by the reciprocity of substance and status in theoretical discourse is that status is a constituent of *doxa*. More specifically, *doxa* can be understood better by identifying how it is a complex of the relations of regard, ranking, and concealment.

To the Greeks *doxa* meant not only opinion ("what seems to be the case to the person spoken of") but also reputation ("what seems to others to be the case with the person spoken of"), as well as expectation and fame. Martin Heidegger seizes upon this usage to explicate *doxa*:

> *Doxa* means aspect, regard [*Ansehen*], namely the regard in which one stands. If the regard, in keeping with what emerges in it, is a distinguished one, *doxa* means fame and glory. . . . For the Greeks glory was not something additional which one might or might not obtain; it was the mode of the highest being.[49]

Heidegger's insight exemplifies what some scholars call the "intersubjective" reality of rhetoric: that is, something that is not explained fully by the distinctions between subject and object or between fact and value.[50] The regard in which one is held is a property of (that is, changeable by) both the community and the individual, and it is both a description of one's being and one's worth. In other words, regard epitomizes the reciprocity of substance and status in the verbal world. One is what one is said to be. Although we find some speech forms, such as encomia and insults, assuming the greater burden of invoking regard, the perseverance of this motive in even our "higher" discourses, such as those discourses about discourses we label theories, suggests that regard is a part of the sociality of discourse, and therefore a means of emphasizing the patterns of social thinking.

Regard is one product of the act of ranking, as when we say, "She is held in the highest regard." The ranking of genres so prevalent in statements about the arts and sciences suggests that ranking may be an important metonym of verbal reality. If *doxa* involves an act of regard, then it can be understood as something that is meaningful in part because ranked. This provisional conceptualization accounts for the ontological ambiguity of *doxa*: on the one hand, an opinion is an assertion that something is what it is valued to be (that is, an opinion is inextricably both descriptive and normative), yet, on the other hand, anything ranked seems to possess a being prior to being ranked—there is a separation between its existence and its position—because that thing can also be present in alternative rankings. So *doxa* can exemplify the indivisibility of being and appearance, as well as their separation. This ambiguity raises the dilemma of grounding inquiry in opinion: opinion appears to be groundless yet essential for full presentation of the *logos*, the speaking being. The provisional solution seems to be to argue for the best order of discourses, which if nothing else reproduces the structure of the object of the inquiry. (Perhaps this is why rhetorical studies have traditionally been largely a continuing reproduction of typologies.)

The ambiguities inherent in regard and ranking can be managed through addition of a third concept: concealment. No one is known in one's entirety; *doxa* consists in the means by which one is known at all. Obviously, if one were known in one's exact identity—that is, only as a complex of particulars—then no ranking would be possible. Ranking occurs through a process of selecting and deflecting, revealing and concealing, our attention to the nature of a thing. Our opinion of another requires concealing as well as revealing some of what we know, and we are known through our own acts of concealment as well as disclosure. This conception of understanding as a process of concealing and revealing is paradoxical at first glance, just as is the idea that one's regard, one's radiance in the eyes of others, is the manifestation of an act of concealment.

Doxa is created by acts of concealment, and so a complete conceptualization of *doxa* must include the idea that regard is in part achieved by the concealments of rank. This interpretation repositions *doxa*: it is no longer contrasted with *episteme*, but rather with *aletheia*, truth (literally "unhiddenness"). This is not a relation of opposites, however: *doxa* and *aletheia* are different stages in the production of meaning. This dynamic of concealment and unconcealment—of authorizing and marginalizing—is the means by which we determine what we believe, what we know, and what we believe to be true. And the identification of a discourse as the manifestation of *doxa* means that it cannot be wholly laid bare, known in its entirety, without ceasing to exist. The unconcealing of the discourse does not show us what it contains—rather, it transforms it into another type of discourse (such as *aletheia*). Concealment is an act of metamorphosis, and one not comprehensible (or valuable) without awareness of its operation within the activity of ranking. Consider the analogy of our clothing: clothes create meaning by concealment, for they cover the body to disclose its intention, and in covering identify the individual in respect to the social body. They reveal only by suggestion, yet when they are removed, the "interior" or "hidden" meaning disappears, and a person's identity can be reconstructed only by reference to the "external" society.[51] So it is with *doxa*: although we can know the truth by bringing things out of unconcealment, complete disclosure would exhaust our means of knowing at all.

This reconsideration of *doxa* as the mask of meaning gives it a limitless correspondence with *episteme* but also restricts its engagement with *aletheia*. Consider the case of the status claims attending theories of discourse. They are expressions of *doxa*, assertions of regard achieved through the concealments of rank. They attend claims of *episteme* and demonstrate not only the structure but also a function of *doxa*: being a reservoir of potential meanings for epistemic claims. Yet they cannot alone suffice for the experience of truth, for they are acts of concealment that activate all the anxieties of displacement. According to one model of verbal authority, an opinion is the weak approximation of a truth; according to my understanding of the sociality common to rhetorical theory and practice, an opinion is a truth that has been changed as a necessary part of the process of determining regard, and with that, inventing values and guiding conduct. In other words, the "social knowledge" that grounds rhetorical practice and implies "certain notions of preferable public behavior" is constituted by the dynamics of regard, ranking, and concealment.[52] Rhetorical inquiry is both an account and an example of *doxa*, and this participation in the structure of *doxa* limits the inquiry's relation to truth—it necessarily is antecedent or attendant to the experience of truth. However, if rhetorical theory is grounded in opinions about rhetorical discourse, those opinions are truths concealed according to received attributions of authority and marginality. This relation between *doxa* and *aletheia* is not quite the conventional doctrine that rhetoric can only make the truth effective, however, for once the truth is construed in terms of the conditions of authority and marginality it loses its presumption of being the authentic end of thought.

CONCLUSION

This reconsideration of the rhetorical subject carries additional implications for rhetorical theory. First, the conception of *doxa* as reflecting status (and the determination of the role of status in discourse theory) suggests a contribution to the "philosophical" task of systematic ontology. A status-sensitive rhetorical theory could help create a language for the description of being in both an analytical and a constitutive manner. The analytical function of rhetoric has been summarized best by Valesio: "Rhetoric is the key to ontology because it is the most concrete and precise tool that can be used in order to show that every positive ontology is an ideological construction."[53] In other words, rhetorical analysis could situate the ontological claims within a social history of discourse and a dialectic of authority and marginality. The constitutive contribution would be to reformulate the concepts of being within the activities of the *logos* as understood through the concept of *doxa*. Heidegger provides the pertinent example of this project, as summarized by Hans-Georg Gadamer: "When he says that the truth of being is the *un*truth, that is, the concealment of being in 'error', then the decisive change in the concept of 'essence' which follows from the destruction of the Greek tradition of metaphysics can no longer be ignored. For Heidegger leaves behind him both the traditional concept of essence and that of the ground of essence."[54] Whatever the particular ontology developed, the use of status as a model of being would impel both a departure from transcendental thinking and an emphasis upon the process of being constituted by the perceptions of the other.

The final implication of focusing upon status is that this emphasis recommends a particular attitude toward the evaluation of theories in the humanities. Acceptance of the inevitability of status also must include acceptance of its mutability. Although ranking is embedded in the discourse of the humanities, no one order should be seen as foundational. This claim should be taken as a restatement, although not a doctrine, of epistemological relativism. More importantly, it offers specific direction for the task of evaluation. First, we must take seriously the question of how to begin a rhetorical theory. Second, we should accept that any rhetorical theory should begin at least with a consideration of the historical and current inhibitions of its subject. That is, one should begin by locating the subject (and its rationale) within a topography of authority. For example, any theory today would have to consider how rhetoric is understood as both an antique literary language and a suspect public practice. Third, the exploration of status should culminate in the articulation of heuristic standards rather than in the endorsement of ethical charges. This distinction does not intend to escape the reproduction of status within one's argument, only to avoid the lesser version of ranking known as moralizing. Thus, rather than concluding that rhetoric is civilizing but poetry liberating, or rhetoric authentic and philosophy alienated, and so on, we should consider how any ranking is a power move even as it serves a specific intellectual purpose.

To conclude, I have argued for an understanding of the rhetorical tradition as one burdened with justifying its subject and its inquiry within a dialectic of authority and marginality. My argument has first identified how status claims typify all arguments about the classification of discourses, then analyzed those status claims in terms of a particular conception of sociality that stresses the use of marginality in the constituting of meanings, and then elaborated several implications for the politics of rhetorical theory and the ontology of rhetorical discourse. I have not attempted to develop a method for escaping this dialectic, however; that would be a mystification. Rhetorical inquiry is better appreciated as an opportunity for engagement with, rather than escape from, the problems of authority and marginality and the methods of concealment and revelation. Rather than resist marginality, we can define rhetoric as a mode of reflection upon the sociality of language. Rather than endorse authority, we can engage in the art of reclassification.

Notes

1. Calvin O. Schrag, "Rhetoric Resituated at the End of Philosophy," *Quarterly Journal of Speech* 71 (1985): 167.

2. Ibid., p. 168.

3. Ibid., p. 170.

4. Plato rarely misses an opportunity for the attack. Illustrative examples are the comparison with cookery in the *Gorgias* 464–465 and the description of "a hunt after young men of wealth and rank" in the *Sophist* 223; see Edith Hamilton and Huntington Cairns, eds., *Plato: The Collected Dialogues*, Bollingen Series 71 (Princeton, NJ: Princeton University Press, 1961). Cicero replies in *De oratore* 3.15.58 by depicting philosophy as a diversion for idle minds, similar to gambling; see E. W. Sutton and H. Rackham, trans., *De oratore*, Loeb Classical Library (Cambridge, MA: Harvard University Press, 1942).

5. The first two qualifications are reviewed in Edwin Black, "Plato's View of Rhetoric," *Quarterly Journal of Speech* 44 (1958), reprinted in Lionel Crocker and Paul A. Carmack, eds., *Readings in Rhetoric* (Springfield, IL: Charles C. Thomas, 1965), pp. 68–88; the second also is stressed in Ernesto Grassi, *Rhetoric as Philosophy: The Humanist Tradition* (University Park: Pennsylvania State University Press, 1980), p. 28; the third is emphasized by Paolo Valesio, *Novantiqua* (Bloomington: Indiana University Press, 1980), p. 88; the fourth is featured by James Boyd White, *When Words Lose Their Meaning: Constitutions and Reconstitutions of Language, Character, and Community* (Chicago: University of Chicago Press, 1984), pp. 93–113.

6. Black, "Plato's View," p. 68.

7. *De oratore* 1.11.47.

8. *Gorgias* 481c–482c.

9. *Phaedrus* 277e–278.

10. Samuel Ijsseling, *Rhetoric and Philosophy in Conflict* (The Hague: Martinus Nijhoff, 1976), p. 14.

11. Kenneth Burke, *A Grammar of Motives* (1945; rpt., Berkeley and Los Angeles: University of California Press, 1969), pp. 21–23.

12. See C. Perelman and L. Olbrechts-Tyteca, *The New Rhetoric: A Treatise on Argumentation*, trans. John Wilkinson and Purcell Weaver (South Bend, IN: University of Notre Dame Press, 1969); Ijsseling, *Rhetoric and Philosophy*; Grassi, *Rhetoric as Philosophy* ; Valesio, *Novantiqua*; Michel Foucault, *The Order of Things: An Archaeology of the Human Sciences* (1970; rpt., New York: Vintage, 1973); Richard Rorty, *Philosophy and the Mirror of Nature* (Princeton, NJ: Princeton University Press, 1979); Alasdair MacIntyre, *After Virtue: A Study in Moral Theory* (South Bend, IN: University of Notre Dame Press, 1981); and Gerald Bruns, *Inventions: Writing, Textuality, and Understanding in Literary History* (New Haven, CT: Yale University Press, 1982).

13. Immanuel Kant, *Critique of Judgement*, 2d ed., trans. J. H. Bernard (London: Macmillan, 1931), p. 215.

14. Ibid.

15. Ibid., p. 217.

16. John Locke, *An Essay Concerning Human Understanding*, ed. Alexander Campbell Fraser (Oxford: Clarendon Press, 1894), vol. 2, p. 146. Both Kant and Locke also deal with rhetoric in more subtlety, distinguishing between better and worse rhetorics. Locke parses clearness and figuration, Kant divides eloquence and oratory, but these qualifications continue and strengthen the larger ranking of the arts. The selections from Kant and Locke also are discussed by Grassi, in *Rhetoric as Philosophy*, pp. 18–19. Locke also is quoted by Nietzsche to document the continuing disrepute of rhetoric; see Carole Blair, "Nietzsche's Lecture Notes on Rhetoric: A Translation," *Philosophy and Rhetoric* 16 (1983): 127, note.

17. Perelman and Olbrechts, *The New Rhetoric*, pp. 411–459. Dissociation includes the construction of a hierarchy of terms (p. 416) that produces an equation of "reality and value" for the privileged term (p. 417). In other words, substance and status are invented reciprocally. See also the analysis of *Phaedrus* (p. 421) and the discussion of how dissociation is used to attack rhetoric (pp. 450–459). The authors provide an excellent statement of how this attack is a motive in the invention of philosophy: "But we must not overlook that everything that promotes perception of a device—the mechanical, farfetched, abstract, codified, and formal aspects of a speech—will prompt the search for a reality that is dissociated from it" (p. 453).

18. Anicius Boethius, *The Consolation of Philosophy*, trans. V. E. Watts (New York: Penguin, 1969), p. 35.

19. Boethius, *Consolation*, p. 36.

20. Gay Wilson Allen and Harry Hayden Clark, *Literary Criticism: Pope to Croce* (1941; rpt., Detroit: Wayne State University Press, 1962), p. 296.

21. H.F.B. Brett-Smith, ed., *Peacock's "Four Ages of Poetry," Shelley's "Defense of Poetry," Browning's "Essay on Shelley"* (Boston: Houghton, Mifflin, 1921), pp. 4–6.

22. Peacock, "Four Ages, "in Brett-Smith, ed., p. 18.

23. Ibid., p. 19.

24. Percy Bysshe Shelley, *A Defense of Poetry*, in *The Harvard Classics*, ed. Charles W. Elliot (New York: P. F. Collier and Son, 1937), vol. 27, p. 333.

25. Ibid., p. 329.

26. Ibid., p. 354.

27. Ibid., p. 359.

28. See William K Wimsatt Jr. and Cleanth Brooks, *Literary Criticism: A Short History* (New York: Knopf, 1959), pp. 422–423: "When he [Shelley] talks about poetry getting at the motives for good, . . . the words are . . . part of an appeal for a vastly creative and autonomous power. There is no appeal to any other authority. . . . The honor conferred upon poetic imagination, though nebulous, is the highest possible." Wimsatt and Brooks strive throughout their book to promote the autonomy of poetry. For another important extension of Shelley's influence, see Cleanth Brooks and Robert Penn Warren, *Understanding Poetry*, 3d ed. (New York: Holt, Rinehart and Winston, 1960). For a broader analysis of sovereign aestheticism, see Allan Megill, *Prophets of Extremity: Nietzsche, Heidegger, Foucault, Derrida* (Berkeley and Los Angeles: University of California Press, 1985).

29. Larry Rosenfield, "An Autopsy of the Rhetorical Tradition," in Lloyd F. Bitzer and Edwin Black, eds., *The Prospect of Rhetoric* (Englewood Cliffs, NJ: Prentice-Hall, 1971), p. 68.

30. Emile Durkheim, *The Rules of Sociological Method*, 8th ed., trans. Sarah A. Solovay and John H. Mueller, ed. George E.G. Catlin (Glencoe, IL: Free Press, 1938), pp. 67–75. See also Kai Erikson, *Wayward Puritans: A Study in the Sociology of Deviance* (New York: John Wiley and Sons, 1966).

31. Charles P. Flynn, *Insult and Society: Patterns of Comparative Interaction* (Point Washington, WA: Kennikat Press, 1977), p. 1.

32. Jerome, Letter 23, in *Select Letters of St. Jerome*, trans. F. A. Wright, Loeb Classical Library (New York: G. P. Putnam, 1933), p. 126. The early churchmen were able strategists when discriminating their subject of Christian faith: "Cyprian, who had been a teacher of rhetoric . . . renounced profane letters completely and for the rest of his life never again quoted a pagan poet, rhetorician, or orator." The old tradition of rhetoric (representing all pagan letters) is used as the margin for the new discourse of Christian belief. The quotation is from James J. Murphy, "Saint Augustine and the Debate about a Christian Rhetoric," *Quarterly Journal of Speech* 46 (1960): 401.

33. Flynn, *Insult and Society*, p. 39.

34. Mary Douglas, *Purity and Danger: An Analysis of the Concepts of Pollution and Taboo* (1966; rpt., London: Routledge & Kegan Paul, 1969), p. 94.

35. Burke's complete statement is: "Even if any given terminology is a *reflection* of reality, by its very nature as a terminology it must be a *selection* of reality; and to this extent it must function also as a *deflection* of reality"; see *Language as Symbolic Action* (Berkeley and Los Angeles: University of California Press, 1966), p. 45.

36. For a review of this debate, see Black, "Plato's View of Rhetoric."

37. *Phaedrus* 253e.

38. Several of the many examples available are: Marie Hochmuth Nichols, "Kenneth Burke and the 'New Rhetoric,' " *Quarterly Journal of Speech* 38 (1952): 133–144; Daniel Fogarty, *Roots for a New Rhetoric* (1959; rpt., New York: Russell and Russell, 1968); Martin Steinmann Jr., *The New Rhetorics* (New York: Scribners, 1967); Perelman and Olbrechts-Tyteca, *The New Rhetoric*.

39. Paul de Man, *Allegories of Reading: Figural Language in Rousseau, Nietzsche, Rilke, and Proust* (New Haven, CT: Yale University Press, 1979), p. 131.

40. Aristotle, *Rhetoric*, trans. W. Rhys Roberts, ed. Friedrich Solmsen (New York: Random House, 1954), 1354a.

41. Kenneth Burke, *Counter-Statement* (Berkeley and Los Angeles: University of California Press, 1968), p. 218.

42. See John Lyne, "Rhetoric of Inquiry," *Quarterly Journal of Speech* 71 (1985): 65.

43. Richard Weaver, "The Spaciousness of the Old Rhetoric," *The Ethics of Rhetoric* (Chicago: Henry Regnery, 1953), p. 185. Weaver's reaction against the devaluation of rhetoric is summed

up in his essay, "Language Is Sermonic," which begins: "Our age has witnessed the decline of a number of subjects that once enjoyed prestige and esteem, but no subject, I believe, has suffered more amazingly in this respect than rhetoric"; see Richard L. Johannesen, Rennart Strickland, and Ralph T. Eubanks, eds., *Language Is Sermonic* (Baton Rouge: Louisiana State University Press, 1970), p. 201.

44. Robert L. Scott, "On Viewing Rhetoric as Epistemic," *Central States Speech Journal* 18 (1967): 9. (Reprinted in this volume.)

45. Burke, *Language as Symbolic Action*, pp. 17–18.

46. See Ijsseling, chap. 1, "The Rehabilitation of Rhetoric," and Vasile Florescu, "Rhetoric and Its Rehabilitation in Contemporary Philosophy," *Philosophy and Rhetoric* 3 (1970): 193–224.

47. Stanley Deetz, "Negation and the Political Function of Rhetoric," *Quarterly Journal of Speech* 69 (1983): 435.

48. Valesio, *Novantiqua*, p. 3.

49. Martin Heidegger, *An Introduction to Metaphysics*, trans. Ralph Manheim (New Haven, CT: Yale University Press, 1959), pp. 102–103. For further contrast with the modern temper, see Cicero: e.g., in *Brutus*, his musing on the problems of appraising status correctly (21.83–85), or the peroration to eminence (96.331–333); *Brutus*, trans. G .L. Hendrickson, Loeb Classical Library (Cambridge, MA: Harvard University Press, 1962). See also Larry Rosenfield, "The Practical Celebration of Epideictic," in Eugene E. White, ed., *Rhetoric in Transition: Studies in the Nature and Uses of Rhetoric* (University Park: Pennsylvania State University Press, 1980), pp. 131–155. Rosenfield argues that epideictic rhetoric was conceived as restoring, through an act of revelation, the oneness of being and appearance that was lost in deliberative rhetoric. His general argument surpasses my use of regard as a mode of being, although I believe he errs in identifying *doxa* entirely with deliberative rhetoric.

50. For the intersubjective perspective, see Barry Brummett, "Some Implications of 'Process' or 'Intersubjectivity': Postmodern Rhetoric," *Philosophy and Rhetoric* 9 (1976): 21–51 (reprinted in this volume), and "On Rhetorical Relativism," in "The Forum," *Quarterly Journal of Speech* 68 (1982): 425–430.

51. Kenneth Burke also has attempted to penetrate the concept of concealment in his study of rhetoric. See his chapters on Bentham on "covering devices" and on Carlyle on clothes in *A Rhetoric of Motives* (1950; rpt., Berkeley and Los Angles: University of California Press, 1969), pp. 99–100 and 119–123.

52. Thomas Farrell, "Knowledge, Consensus, and Rhetorical Theory," *Quarterly Journal of Speech* 62 (1976): 4 (reprinted in this volume). See also the exchange between Walter M. Carlton and Farrell in *Quarterly Journal of Speech* 64 (1978): 313–334.

53. Valesio, *Novantiqua*, p. 96.

54. Hans-Georg Gadamer, *Philosophical Hermeneutics*, trans. and ed. David E. Linge (Berkeley and Los Angeles: University of California Press, 1976), p. 234.

The Habitation of Rhetoric

MICHAEL LEFF

The problem I want to engage is both fundamental and ancient. When Cicero wrote his *De inventione*, it already had had a long history. Yet his comments on that history still retain a lively theoretical interest for students of rhetoric and argumentation. Consequently, they can serve as an appropriate text for introducing and locating the issues addressed in this paper.

As part of the standard *accessus* to the technical precepts of the art, Cicero considers the definition of rhetoric and its placement relative to other disciplines. One aspect of this task is to understand the material of rhetoric, by which he means "those subjects with which the art and power of rhetoric are concerned." He then explains that "some have thought that there are more and some less of these subjects. To cite one example, Gorgias of Leontini, almost the earliest teacher of oratory, held that the orator could speak better than anyone else on all subjects. Apparently he assigned to the profession a vast—and in fact infinite—material. Aristotle, on the other hand, who did much to improve and adorn this art, thought that the function of the orator was concerned with three classes of subjects, the epideictic, the deliberative, and the judicial." This commentary leads immediately to a judgment: "According to my opinion, at least, the art and faculty of the orator must be thought of as concerned with this threefold material."[1] This judgment, moreover, is consistent with Cicero's earlier definition of rhetoric as a "part of political science" (*civilis scientiae partem*).[2] That is, Cicero here assumes that the Aristotelian genres exhaust the boundaries of political discourse.

This assumption becomes more explicit in the next section of the text, where Cicero considers another aspect of the tradition. The Hellenistic rhetorician Hermagoras of Temnos divides the material of rhetoric into two types of issues, the special and the general. The former (often called the hypothesis) refers to controversies that involve specific circumstances; Cicero identifies such issues with the subjects indicated by the three Aristotelian genres. The latter (often called the thesis) refers to disputations about abstract issues unconnected with specific circumstances—such questions as "Is there any good but honor?," or "Can the senses be trusted?" Hermagoras,

Cicero argues, errs in assigning such issues to rhetoric, since "everyone understands that these questions are far removed from the business of the orator."[3] The scope of rhetoric, then, is limited to the hypothesis, which, in turn, draws its materials from the conduct of civic affairs.

This position obviously arises from a schematic and over-simplified version of the tradition. In fact, Aristotle's conception of the matter is much more complicated and ambiguous than its representation in *De inventione* suggests. And as Cicero realized in his later works, the whole issue demands careful inquiry and sophisticated reflection on the tradition rather than mere schematization.[4] Nevertheless, whatever the defects of our text, its bald simplicity has symptomatic value. The dichotomy between a "restrained rhetoric" and a "liberated rhetoric," sketched here in such consciously emphatic terms, recurs throughout the later history of rhetorical theory, normally in forms that are better disguised though no less potent. Certainly, as he embodies this dichotomy by reference to the opposition between "neo-Aristotelian" and Gorgianic (or "neo-sophistic") approaches, Cicero anticipates one of the main problems lurking just beneath the murky surface of twentieth-century rhetorical scholarship.

Before turning to these contemporary applications, however, I want to add one more note about the text. *De inventione*, consistent with most other rhetorical treatises, deals with the scope and location of the art as though these issues raised problems of strictly logical classification. But a slight adjustment of perspective might lead us to view the matter as a rhetorical operation, as an exercise in metonymy. In moving through one side of this metonymic process, the neo-Aristotelians regard rhetoric as a thing contained; it is an art domiciled within the territory of politics and domesticated by this political confinement. Moving in the opposite direction, the neo-sophists attempt to liberate rhetoric by conceiving it as a container, or, more properly, as a containing force. Unfettered by any particular subject matter, rhetoric becomes a power that ranges across the entire domain of human discourse, containing whatever matter it encounters. Since it is pure force, it is a container that constantly shifts its own configuration as it responds to circumstances, social interests, or the free play of linguistic whimsy.

In their modern incarnations, these two approaches yield results so different that their opposition seems total. Yet, viewed within a somewhat broader context, both share at least one important characteristic. While neo-Aristotelians seek to constrain the range of the rhetorical process and the neo-sophists seek to expand it, both alike center attention in process. Rhetoric is either process confined within some larger domain from which it draws substance, or it is the unbounded action of process itself. In either case, rhetoric per se is not substantive, since it is a form of action that generates or manages material without ever resting in a material embodiment. This attenuation between activity and production is obvious in respect to the neo-sophistic position, but it may seem puzzling or even paradoxical when attributed to neo-Aristotelianism, since that position is so clearly centered around the oration itself. Nevertheless, especially when the interest is dominantly critical rather than pedagogical, neo-Aristotelianism tends to bracket the oratorical text as a product with an integrity of its own. The oration simply establishes a referent for studying contexts or for locating processes which are to be gauged in terms of their extrinsic effect. The text becomes a medium or an instrument rather than a substantive product.[5] Consequently, the metonymic strategies in neo-Aristotelianism and neo-sophisticism yield diametrically opposed conceptions of the scope of rhetoric, but they both encourage a similar preoccupation with action as opposed to substance. When either of these extremes is isolated, or when the two are set in unmediated opposition, the result is to weaken or sever the connection between action and production.

Throughout most of the history of the discipline, certain forces have militated against this kind of metonymic reduction. Most obviously, there is the pedagogical tradition that links rhetorical scholarship with the teaching of composition. So long as that connection holds, the tendency of abstract definition is checked against the concrete problems involved in teaching students how to *make* discourses, and it is only in our century that rhetorical scholarship has become clearly dissociated from its pedagogical orientation. More important, however, amidst its technical clutter, the pedagogical tradition also houses a humane philosophy concerning practical discourse and its implications. This humanistic impulse traces itself in a line that moves from Isocrates to Cicero and Quintilian and from there forward to the Renaissance; its integrity consists in the effort to balance the aesthetics of production and the requirements of ethical action within the texture of practical discourse. Perhaps the key term informing this ideal is propriety, the flexible measure that unifies the elements of a discourse even as it adjusts them to the fluid ethical and political contexts in which it appears. Approached from this angle, a rhetorical discourse can be substantive, not because rhetoric commands a particular subject matter, but because the discourse commands attention as a thing made. Rhetorical discourse thus assumes an ontological solidity different in degree but not in kind from the products of the poetic art.

Humanistic rhetoric entailed a delicate balance that was always difficult to understand, let alone realize. And it always remained open to attack because of the way it blurred categories by treating them not as stable abstract entities, but as principles manifested in production and practical action. Hence, the humanistic perspective often was eclipsed by more technical conceptions of rhetoric and by more purely theoretical schemes for conceiving the placement of the arts in general. The most dramatic of these set backs occurred during the Enlightenment, when the mainstream of philosophical thought collapsed the space needed to sustain the humanistic position. The Enlightenment liberated the aesthetic from the perturbations of all other forms of experience—set it in a zone of free and autonomous experience where it was to remain innocent of any prudential or teleological concerns. From this perspective, oratory was an inherently dubious business, since it conflated the aesthetic with matters of practical interest. More generally, Ciceronian rhetorical philosophy became a pseudo-philosophy, a jumble of category errors which undermined the necessary separation among ethical judgment, the operation of the intellect, and the impulse of the artistic spirit.[6]

One of Jacques Derrida's best known principles is that erasures always leave their traces. In this instance, however, we should remember that traces are often difficult to find and that erasures are sometimes effective in removing items from cultural awareness. That is, we need to understand current rhetorical scholarship against the background of what the Enlightenment blocked from direct perception. By the dawn of this century, oratory and composition had lost respectability within the academy, and rhetoric, in so far as it existed at all, was reduced to the mechanics of elocution or the taxonomic classification of tropes and figures. The humanistic conception of rhetoric was not simply rejected; it had been forgotten, or at best, distorted through the alien lens of Enlightenment thought. It was inconceivable that substantive art could arise from local adjustments to practical circumstance. Thus, subsequent efforts to revive rhetoric proceeded without much regard for the density of rhetorical products. The ballast that had kept pre-modern rhetoric close to the ground had been jettisoned, and the way was opened for the free action of the metonymic process.

In that twentieth-century innovation called the American Department of Speech, the history of rhetorical scholarship is, in considerable measure, the story of competing metonymic perspectives. The general direction of this conflict is reasonably clear: it is a movement from the neo-Aristotelian toward the neo-sophistic pole, from rhetoric contained to rhetoric as container. The details of this story are well known, and I want to pause here only long enough to indicate how they adhere to the pattern I have just sketched. And mindful of the contemporary interest in narrative, I will try to tell the story as a story.

Once upon a time, but not very long ago, there was a poor waif named Rhetoric. Though once the ruler of the arts, he had been banished from Europe and had found an academic home only in a new and unstable fiefdom known as the American Department of Speech. The people who lived in this fiefdom were concerned to define its boundaries so that it would not be annexed by powerful neighbors. Most of all, they feared the Duchy of English, which might try to enslave Rhetoric and commandeer his sections of the public speaking course. The great lords of English, moreover, disdained Rhetoric, since they regarded his teachings as impure and his bearing as too ordinary and insufficiently handsome. And so the leaders in the fiefdom of Speech, who were later known as the neo-Aristotelians, undertook a defense of Rhetoric which celebrated his individuality and modest respectability. They did so in words that echoed the sentiments of Cicero's *De inventione*. Rhetoric, they maintained, was confined to a particular kind of discourse, the political oration, and the rhetorical perspective was "patently single." Rhetoric cared not a whit for "permanence, nor yet ... beauty." Instead, he was preoccupied "with effect" and taught us to regard a "speech as a communication to a specific audience."[7] As it turned out, the lords of English were concerned with their own squabbles and had no time to invade other territories. So the fiefdom of Speech survived and held its turf. But eventually it suffered from its own internal dissensions. A new generation of scholars arose and challenged the authority of the neo-Aristotelians. They complained that the older generation had committed the high crime of being atheoretical, and besides, it had neglected forms of discourse other than the oration. They broadcast these charges in all the journals of the fiefdom and gradually won adherents. Rhetoric was no longer viewed just as a modestly respectable actor in the political arena. He now seemed a great and powerful leader of the arts whose force had to be acknowledged in all the fiefdoms of the academy.

The point of this story is nicely summarized by comparing Donald Bryant's two well-known definitions of rhetoric. The first formulation appeared in 1953 and designated rhetoric as "the rationale of informative and suasory discourse." The amended version, published twenty years later, defined rhetoric "as the rationale of the informative and suasory in discourses."[8] The shift here is from a kind of discourse to a dimension in discourse, from an emphasis on certain products to an emphasis on a certain kind of activity. Though Bryant remained conservative in his attachment to public address, this rearrangement of priorities implicitly indicated a broader and more theoretical conception of rhetoric, and others have pushed this position in more radical directions. Much the same kind of progression has occurred within the area of argumentation. As Cox and Willard observe, "Historical-critical studies of particular orators, debates, or documents—long the dominant focus of argumentation scholars—have been gradually replaced by philosophical and theoretical examinations of the field's assumptions and methods." In the process, argument itself has come to be viewed as "a distinct form of human communication"[9]—that is, as a kind of activity that transcends any particular area of application. Moreover, this tendency in our discipline reflects the more general developments in the interdisciplinary revival of rhetoric. LaCapra, after surveying a number of apparently disparate forms of this revival, locates their common ground in "the idea that rhetoric is a dimension of all language use rather than a separable set of uses or a realm of discourse."[10]

Consistent with this orientation, the recent scholarship has centered around theories, models, and organizing conceptions that generally inform the process of arguing and persuading. The number of alternatives found here is striking—cognitive processing constructivist psychology, narrative, ideology, cultural theory, symbolic interactionism, and the like.[11] Yet all of them are informed by a common interest in conceiving rhetoric as an activity conducted at the level of discourse. This interest implies a tension between process and product, and in the earlier phases of this development that tension manifests itself rather forcefully.

Two entries in the report of the 1970 National Developmental Project on Rhetoric illustrate my point. In his essay "Rhetorical Studies for the Modern World," Samuel Becker presents a running critique of traditional scholarship in rhetoric and public address. Becker argues that "single message encounters" are an inadequate basis for drawing conclusions about how messages influence audiences. Consequently, he concludes that "our traditional concept of the message has severely limited usefulness for understanding contemporary communication. The emphasis of rhetorical studies should probably remain upon the message, but we must define message in a more fruitful way, in a way that is more descriptive of what man as receiver is exposed to, rather than what man as source creates."[12] Wayne Brockreide supports and extends this line of argument. He emphatically rejects "the idea that the most appropriate unit of rhetoric is the 'speech,' a one-shot attempt at persuasion, the idea that a rhetorical transaction is bounded by a speaker's introduction and his conclusion." In his view, Becker "argues convincingly that the speech is not an appropriate unit of analysis." Moreover, this position cannot be "assimilated as a minor modification of a traditional concept of rhetorical communication. It is revolutionary."[13]

Hence, we achieve a nearly total, a revolutionary, disjunction between the study of the rhetorical process and a serious interest in any particular rhetorical product. This sort of argument rarely appears in the more recent literature, but I suspect the reason is that the issue seems resolved. Neo-Aristotelianism is now only an historical curiosity, not a live option, and the placement of rhetoric at the abstract level of process has become a largely unconscious but well-established orthodoxy.

Yet I think that the issue calls for reconsideration. The position outlined by Brockreide and Becker has real force when applied to neo-Aristotelianism and its presupposition that rhetoric deals solely with extrinsic effect. If rhetoric concerns itself only with the way auditors process "messages," then attention to isolated "messages" has limited utility. Viewed from a broader perspective, however, the neo-Aristotelian doctrine itself appears as an aberration negatively informed by the Enlightenment's anti-rhetorical presuppositions.

In this important respect, the position described by Becker and Brockreide is not revolutionary. Rather, it reverses the focus of attention within an existing frame of reference and corrects the older position by driving its assumptions to their ultimate conclusion. The neo-Aristotelian conception of rhetoric is largely a defensive gesture which accommodates the strict dichotomy between fine and practical arts simply by yielding to its demands. Since it is a practical art, rhetoric produces nothing intrinsically interesting, and so its products offer no more than an occasion for studying a process.

In another intellectual environment, it might seem apparent that the power of a practical art would emerge from a qualitative study of its products. But the burden of the Enlightenment forces attention toward purely extrinsic standards, toward the process triggered by the product. From here it takes only a small step to bracket the product altogether. Becker's term "message" captures this reduction perfectly, since, in a way wholly consistent with the neo-Aristotelian technical psychosis, it suggests a concern for what is in and what is conveyed by a discourse without much concern for the discourse itself. A message is an abstracted thing, distanced from the voice of the speaker or the hand of the writer, embedded only at the point of its impact. Ironically, the neo-Aristotelian commitment to the particular perfects itself in the abstract study of message processing.

Brockreide clearly summarizes these tendencies when he asserts that the "speech is not an appropriate unit for analysis." On its surface, this position seems curious. Presumably, a critical study of one of Lincoln's speeches, motivated by an interest in the design of the speech per se, engages an inappropriate unit for rhetorical analysis. Imagine, if you will, a poetic theorist arguing that a Shakespearean sonnet is not an appropriate unit for poetic analysis.

Perhaps, however, the analogy makes Brockreide's point seem not so curious. Even the most ardent apologist for rhetorical art must admit that rhetoric's status as a productive discipline is much less apparent than that of poetic. The basic terminology associated with the two arts aptly illustrates the difference. In one instance, we have the terms poet, poem, and poetic, which nicely distinguish the maker, the thing made, and the process of making. In the case of rhetoric, as Bryant has observed, "we are in something of a mess."[14] The term rhetor serves as analogue for poet, as does rhetoric for poetic. But we have no word that indicates a rhetorical product in the generic sense that poem designates a poetic product. Instead, we are forced to refer to some species of rhetorical artifact—an oration, an editorial, or a pamphlet.

This lexical gap is hardly an accident. On most accounts, the distinctive feature of the rhetorical art is the way that it embeds itself in and responds to specific, public circumstances. Moreover, in accepting persuasion as its goal, rhetorical discourse strives to efface its status as a constructed thing since it calls for prudential judgments rather than judgments about its own integrity as a product. As it blends into the fabric of events and actions, such discourse seems to become a form of action, an embodiment of processes immediately connected with the referent of the discourse. By contrast, the poetic suspension of disbelief weakens this connection and focuses attention more sharply on the fabric of the discourse itself. Thus, if as McKeon has done, we group rhetoric and poetic together as practical/productive arts, they gravitate toward different margins in the category. Rhetoric emerges most clearly at the practical margin, because of its emphasis on efficient cause and on the exercise of productive powers. Poetry emerges at the productive margin, because of its emphasis on material cause and its obvious concern with the objects produced by the art "as composite wholes."[15] This contrast suggests the problematic status of rhetoric as a productive art and the difficulty involved in attaching rhetoric to distinctive products of its own making.

Consequently, the current tendency to view rhetoric as coherent only at the global level of discursive process reflects inherent problems and not just confusions associated with the recent history of the discipline. Yet current theory too often overcomes these problems simply by refusing to acknowledge their existence. Moreover, such innocence survives only through adherence to a systematic and fundamentally anti-rhetorical dichotomy between the prudential and the aesthetic. A far richer conception of rhetoric, especially with regard to its argumentative function, arises from the effort to confront the problem and grapple with the ambiguous relationships between action and production.

At this point, I hope to have shown that the placement of rhetoric is not merely an ancient *topos* but a persistent and fundamental issue. The problem initially surfaces in terms of categories that define rhetoric's place within the orbit of human arts and activities, but the latent territorial imagery involved here encourages a metonymic perspective. In turn, the metonymic process yields a dichotomy between rhetoric as an art contained within some substantive domain or rhetoric as a power that ranges over various domains. The epistemological implications of this division are relatively straight-forward. From the contained perspective of neo-Aristotelianism, rhetoric tends to become a domestic art that arranges and communicates the materials of the domain which subsumes it. From the liberated perspective of neo-sophisticism, rhetoric tends to become a generative force actively engaged in the acquisition and formation of knowledge. Both perspectives commonly stress the nature of rhetoric as process or activity and deflect attention from its relationship to finished products. Once recognized, this bias in the metonymic process leads us to a second question about the "placement" of rhetoric. We are forced to consider not just the domain of rhetoric, but the level of its manifestation. Is the habitation of rhetoric found at the level of discourse per se or at the level of a discourse? Does rhetoric exist only as an abstract activity or does it also exist in concrete embodiments? As the terms "manifestation" and "exist-ence" imply, these questions have an ontological rather than an epistemological bearing.

As I have just framed it, this ontological issue implies a departure from previous attempts to locate the "substance of rhetoric." In the familiar tradition that proceeds from Hoyt Hudson through Karl Wallace, substance is found in the argumentative or inventional aspect of the rhetorical process.[16] The alternative I am now suggesting defines rhetorical discourses as substantive in themselves. The substance of rhetoric, that is, does not arise from processes attached to the logical, ethical, or psychological co-ordinates of discourse; instead, it arises from the way such processes congeal within a particular rhetorical artifact. On this view, the essence of rhetoric becomes the constructed rhetorical thing-in-itself.

Yet, for reasons outlined above, even when we set Enlightenment prejudices to the side, the task of understanding polemic discourse as "substantive" raises some exceed-ingly difficult problems. To approach these problems, we must develop a better refined conception of how action and production interrelate in practical discourse, and to accomplish this end, we are faced with a reconception of the basic relationships among persuasion, argument, and aesthetics.

Obviously, these matters are far too complex to be resolved in this presentation, but it does seem to me that the elements needed for the reconstruction already exist in the current literature. The defect in that literature, from my perspective, is that it divides itself into two arenas—the one concerned with the linkage between persuasion and argument, and the other concerned with persuasion and aesthetics. The two remain largely unconnected with one another, and hence a full synthesis has yet to emerge. In order to illustrate this problem and to suggest a possible resolution, I now want to turn to the first study in Paul Ricoeur's important book *The Rule of Metaphor*. Despite the complexity and erudition of that study, its main argument clearly reveals the imbalance that occurs when modernist assumptions about aesthetics are corrected without reference to recent thought concerning argumentation. At the same time, however,

Ricoeur connects poetry with ontology in a way that suggests an important expansion of current thought about rhetorical argument.

In general, Ricoeur seeks to establish the ontological significance of metaphor. He does so by tracing its operation at its various levels of manifestation–the word, the sentence, and the discourse (i.e., the poem, narrative, essay, etc.) As analysis moves through each of these stages, metaphor assumes increasing potency, until, at the hermeneutic level of discourse, it becomes the prime vehicle for redescribing reality. Yet, for Ricoeur, metaphor does not come to rest at this final level, since its place, "its most intimate abode, is neither name, nor sentence, nor even discourse, but the copula of the verb to be."[17] In short, the power of metaphor consists in its capacity to align the different levels of discourse while connecting discourse itself to the contexts in which it appears. And as it effects this extraordinary negotiation, metaphor becomes the nexus between language and world that is basic to all our ontological conceptions.

His first study presents an extended analysis of this conception as it applies to Aristotle's thought. This analysis requires consideration of both the *Rhetoric* and the *Poetics*, the two loci of his theory of metaphor. On Ricoeur's account, Aristotle assigns a single operation to metaphor in both domains; it consistently works to transfer meaning. Yet it functions differently in the two arts, and the difference follows from the goals proper to each.[18] Ultimately, this distinction leads Ricoeur to affirm the ontological solidity of poetic discourse while denying a similar status to rhetorical discourse.

The goal of poetic is mimesis, and all poetic discourse must find direction from this mimetic function. Thus, all elements of the poetic art cohere in service to this single, over-arching goal. Moreover, these elements–*muthos* (plot), character, *lexis* (diction), thought, spectacle, and melody–are themselves placed in a hierarchical order, since *muthos* structures the other five in respect to their poetic operation. *Muthos*, then, is the fulcrum of the poetic act; it is the principle that organizes the other aspects of the act into a coherent internal form, while it simultaneously draws the whole apparatus towards its mimetic goal. The relationship between *muthos* and mimesis is intimate, and the complex function of *muthos* holds sense and reference together within the fabric of the poetic text. The plot, in other words, retains its integrity as a linguistic product even as it sustains reference to the world that extends beyond its self-constituted limits. As it thus wavers constructively between submission to the reality of human action and the creative action of "poetry as such," *muthos* imparts an ontological density to poetic discourse.[19] The poem, like the metaphor, both is and is not "real," and yet always remains like the real.

In the case of the *Rhetoric*, Ricoeur cannot discover any analogous principle of complex structural integrity. The goal of rhetoric is persuasion, and its proper habitat is the arena of political power. Within this space, discourse is neither free to develop its own possibilities nor is it subject to the philosophical demand for truth. Hence, in Ricoeur's view, Aristotle's purpose is to domesticate or institutionalize rhetoric,[20] and he does so by devising a means whereby philosophy can "watch over rhetoric."[21] To achieve this purpose, Aristotle constructs a theory of probable reasoning which delimits the operation of rhetorical discourse and which, through the link with dialectic, places rhetoric in some contact with first philosophy. In this way, Aristotle finds a point of equilibrium between the conflicting claims of power and truth.[22]

Yet, as Ricoeur understands the matter, this equilibrium is fragile and incapable of sustaining a coherent realm of discourse. Owing to its connection with common opinion, rhetoric cannot become a purely formal discipline, and its content sprawls throughout the entire range of human affairs. Thus, the rhetorical art seems doomed by an "overburdening content" that leaves its elements scattered and uncoordinated.[23] This problem manifests itself most obviously when Ricoeur considers the rhetorical function of metaphor.

That function is difficult to apprehend, since the connection between style and argument in the *Rhetoric* is rather tenuous. Whereas, in poetry, form and meaning blend in a way similar to sculpture, the public use of speech encourages a dissociation between style and proof. Manner in oratory appears "extrinsic" and "variable." For this reason, the devices of style in rhetoric require special adaptation to the larger purposes of the art; they cannot develop according to their own impulses, but must respond to probative ends which they do not shape. Metaphor, in this context, does not generate contact between discourse and world, but is bent in the direction of "creating the right impression." This process, Ricoeur explains, entails its own complexities, and it does involve a certain cognitive element. Metaphor and the other aspects of *lexis* enter into rhetoric as a manifestation of a kind of thought concerned not with proof alone but with proof relative to a hearer.[24] Yet Ricoeur holds that this persuasive function of metaphor exists in a state of unresolved tension with the requirements of proof, and hence rhetorical metaphor becomes something *added to* rather than *embedded within* the discursive formations of the art.

This tension reveals the divided condition of the rhetorical art as a whole and accounts for its incapacity to describe or generate discourses that preserve an independent integrity. Moreover, Ricoeur implies that this defect is inherent in rhetoric per se and not the result of Aristotle's particular construction of the art. "The lack of consistency in the link between a treatise on argumentation and a treatise on style reveals contradictions within the very project of persuasion. Set between two limits exterior to it—logic and violence—rhetoric oscillates between its two constitutive poles—proof and persuasion. When persuasion frees itself from the concern for proof, it is carried away by the desire to seduce and please; and style itself ceases to be the 'face' (figure) that expresses and reveals the body, and becomes an ornament in the cosmetic sense of the word. But this possibility was written into the origins of the rhetorical project."[25]

To sum up Ricoeur's argument, it is apparent that poetic holds an ontologically privileged status because of its capacity to connect the resources of language with our fundamental experience of life in the world. Poetic accomplishes this fusion through the mediating force of *muthos*, an element of the poetic process that simultaneously attunes the internal constituents of poetic discourse and directs them toward the final goal of mimesis. Rhetoric, however, is a divided business, since its goal—persuasion—entails the seemingly incompatible demands of objective proof and aesthetic appeal. Lacking a principle that would coordinate these elements, rhetoric fails to achieve ontological significance at the level of discourse.

The main flaw in this analysis requires little explanation before this audience. Although Ricoeur carefully distinguishes between the rhetorical and poetic functions of style, he is curiously unaware of any functional distinction between argumentation and apodeictic proof. For him, rhetorical proof is little more than formal logic *in mufti*. As a consequence, he couples a strikingly postmodern defense of metaphor and poetry with an outmoded interpretation of Aristotle's *Rhetoric*[26] and a general view of the relationship between logic and argument that slights the main developments in the scholarship over the past three decades.[27]

Nevertheless, when Ricoeur notes the tenuous connection between argument and style in Aristotle's *Rhetoric*, he certainly stands on firm ground. Moreover, the same problem persists in the recent scholarship where, as the contrast between Perelman and Group Mu indicates, the two aspects of the tradition sometimes have been severed completely from one another. Thus, I believe that Ricoeur accurately diagnoses the main obstacle to a conception of rhetorical discourse as substantive. Moreover, once we abandon his questionable distinction between proof and persuasion, his method suggests how we might resolve this problem.

Ricoeur observes that rhetorical style achieves its distinctive characteristics because of the way it is attracted to the goal of persuasion. Rhetorical *lexis*, that is, responds to the requirements of proof relative to a specific group of auditors and a specific set of public circumstances. It thus must balance the mode of expression against the occasion, the subject, and the interests of those who render judgment. In the terms of classical humanism, the point of balance is called decorum or propriety, and the flexible standard of decorum becomes the measure for assessing the rhetorical quality of expression.

Recent conceptions of argumentation exhibit a similar concern for proof in relation to specific circumstances and audiences. To cite just one example, Blair and Johnson distinguish argumentation from the logic of implication precisely because argument presupposes interlocutors, finds its end in persuasion, and develops "against the background of heterogeneity of point of view and of other arguments."[28] Conceived in this way, persuasion and proof are not antithetical, but rather persuasion is intimately and necessarily connected with one important type of proof—the proof that operates in public deliberation. Likewise, persuasion does not function in a way that is external to the subject, but as part of an adaptive mechanism vital to any reasonable understanding of public events themselves. Consequently, formal deductive logic cannot watch over or control the argumentative practice, since its abstracted principles have "little light to cast on the appropriate standards of argument."[29] Instead, these standards arise from the historically grounded context of argument and the community of interlocutors involved in the deliberative process.[30]

This flexible, socially grounded, and audience-centered conception of argumentative proof demands that arguers exercise a form of balanced judgment. In this important sense, argumentative practice seems to engage principles that are strikingly similar to the traditional notion of decorum or propriety. Yet, to my knowledge, no contemporary theorist has invoked these terms in respect to argumentation. The reason, I suspect, is that, in its contemporary usage, "decorum" has become associated exclusively with style. But this restriction is not necessary, and as Wesley Trimpi has shown, pre-modern rhetorical theory grants a much wider application for decorum— one that embraces cognitive as well as stylistic concerns.[31] The grounds for this broader conception have a strong bearing on current argumentative theory and its relation to rhetorical style in the sense that Ricoeur describes it.

Rhetorical discourse occurs in contexts where judgments must be rendered about specific matters of communal interest. Such judgments normally invoke the general principles that categorize and direct our response to public events. Yet the application of these principles is open to question, and, in their abstract state, they are insufficient to allow for an adequate decision in any given case. Moreover, these principles themselves are subject to revision in light of our concrete experience. Consequently, rhetorical judgment cannot suffer reduction to strictly formal or methodical procedures. It always engages qualitative considerations that balance the particulars of occasion and circumstance against the more general rubrics that inform our thinking.[32]

This adjustment, moreover, does not simply concern the external form of a persuasive discourse, but also enters into our very mode of understanding the subjects of such discourse. In other words, both understanding and representation entail a mediation between concrete circumstances and principles of intelligibility. Moreover, whenever discourse addresses complex circumstances and heterogeneous interests, a clear separation between expressive form and argumentative content becomes virtually impossible. Our mode of representing situations and our assessment of their nature and moral significance coalesce within the structure of rhetorical judgment. And, in fact, the most skillfully constructed rhetorical discourses blend these elements so as to render them indistinguishable. This artistic skill is neither cosmetic nor deceptive. Instead, it reflects the unity of thought and expression necessary for the comprehension and direction of life in the pluralistic space of public experience.

Decorum is the term that best describes the process of mediation and balance connected with qualitative judgment. It is the principle of decorum that allows us to comprehend a situation as a whole, to locate its meaning within a context, and to translate this understanding into a discursive form that becomes an incentive to action. As it applies to the rhetorical act, decorum orders the elements of a discourse and rounds them out into a coherent product relative to the occasion. That is, it works to align the stylistic and argumentative features of the discourse within a unified structure while adjusting the whole structure to the context from which the discourse arises and to which it responds. The locus of decorum always depends upon the particular case, and so, although it directs artistic production, it is incapable of being formulated in terms of abstract, artistic precepts. It manifests itself only as embodied in particular discourses, and it governs the integrity of the discourse as a whole. Decorum, then, is a principle of action that accounts for the adaptive power of persuasive discourse, and it also establishes a flexible standard for assessing the intrinsic merit of a rhetorical product. Thus, decorum functions as the rhetorical counterpart of poetic *muthos*, for, like *muthos*, decorum mediates between internal sense and external reference in a certain kind of discursive product, and it does so in a way that maintains a consistent link with the subjects and goals proper to the domain where it operates.

Finally, referring back to the point from which this analysis began, decorum seems a peculiarly rhetorical principle because of its ambiguous placement between action and production. Decorum has no substantive stability across situations, since it represents a constantly moving process of negotiation. It is, as Trimpi says, "an activity, rather than a possession, of the consciousness."[33] Nevertheless, the achievement of decorum in a given situation establishes a point of maximum balance and stability. At the global level, decorum is pure process, but its local manifestations are products that display a powerful solidity. So also is rhetoric a universal activity that finds its habitation only in the particular. Since it is the art of the persuasive dimension in discourse, rhetoric finds no rest at the theoretical level. Its adaptive genius cannot be circumscribed by the fixed boundaries of theoretical constructions. As a form of activity, it must retain the freedom to encounter subjects, occasions, and audiences as each situation demands. Yet, within the particular situation, this adaptive process achieves productive closure; its mobile resources of argument and expression coalesce and become embodied as they grasp the matter of an actual case. Viewed at a distance, the principle of adaptation to situations becomes a nomadic process, a constantly changing program for action. Viewed within some specific situation, this principle manifests itself as a product, as a discourse possessing the density and integrity demanded by that situation.

Notes

1. *De inventione*, 1.7, trans. H. M. Hubbell (Cambridge, MA.: Harvard University Press, 1960). All subsequent quotations from *De inventione* are taken from this translation.

2. *De inv.* 1.6.

3. *De inv.* 1.8.

4. See Wesley Trimpi, *Muses of One Mind: The Literary Analysis of Experience and Its Continuity* (Princeton, NJ: Princeton University Press, 1983), pp. 247–252.

5. For a more detailed argument concerning this point, see Michael Leff, "Textual Criticism: The Legacy of G. P. Mohrmann," *Quarterly Journal of Speech* 72 (1986): 383–385.

6. Concerning these trends in Enlightenment thought, see Hans-Georg Gadamer, *Truth and Method* (New York: Crossroads, 1984), pp. 39–73.

7. The quotations above are all from Herbert A. Wichelns, "The Literary Criticism of Oratory," in Bernard L. Brock and Robert L. Scott, eds., *Methods of Rhetorical Criticism* (Detroit, MI: Wayne State University Press, 1980), p. 67.

8. Cf. Donald Bryant, "Rhetoric: Its Functions and Its Scope," *Quarterly Journal of Speech* 39 (1953): 401–424, and "Rhetoric: Its Functions and Its Scope, 'Rediviva,'" in Bryant, *Rhetorical Dimensions in Criticism* (Baton Rouge: Louisiana State University Press, 1973), pp. 3–23.

9. J. Robert Cox and Charles A. Willard, eds., "Introduction: The Field of Argument," in *Advances in Argumentation Theory and Research* (Carbondale: Southern Illinois University Press, 1982), pp. xiii–xiv.

10. Dominick LaCapra, *History and Criticism* (Ithaca, NY, and London: Cornell University Press., 1985), p. 17.

11. Cox and Willard, "Introduction," p. xiv, enumerate some of the approaches in the literature on argumentation.

12. In Lloyd F. Bitzer and Edwin Black, eds., *The Prospect of Rhetoric: Report of the National Developmental Project* (Englewood Cliffs, NJ: Prentice-Hall, 1971), p. 31.

13. Wayne Brockreide, "Trends in the Study of Rhetoric: Toward a Blending of Criticism and Science," in Bitzer and Black, eds., *The Prospect of Rhetoric*, pp. 125–126.

14. Bryant, *Rhetorical Dimensions*, p. 3.

15. Richard McKeon, "Rhetoric and Poetic in the Philosophy of Aristotle," in Elder Olson, ed., *Aristotle's "Poetics" and English Literature: A Collection of Critical Essays* (Chicago: University of Chicago Press, 1965), pp. 207–208.

16. See, inter alia, Hoyt H. Hudson, "Can We Modernize the Study of Invention?," *Quarterly Journal of Speech* 7 (1921): 325–334, and Karl R. Wallace, "The Substance of Rhetoric: Good Reasons," *Quarterly Journal of Speech* 40 (1963): 239–249.

17. Paul Ricoeur, *The Rule of Metaphor: Multi-Disciplinary Studies of the Creation of Meaning in Language*, trans. Robert Czerny with Kathleen McLaughlin and John Costello (London: Routledge & Kegan Paul), p. 7.

18. Ibid., p. 12.

19. Ibid., p. 39.

20. Ibid., p. 10.

21. Ibid., p. 28.

22. Ibid., p. 10.

23. Ibid., p. 30.

24. Ibid., p. 31.

25. Ibid., p. 32.

26. See my review essay, "Recovering Aristotle: Rhetoric, Politics, and the Limits of Rationality," *Quarterly Journal of Speech* 71 (1985): 363, and Thomas M. Conley, "The Enthymeme in Perspective," *Quarterly Journal of Speech* 70 (1984): 168–172, and the references cited in both these papers.

27. See Cox and Willard, "Introduction," and J. Anthony Blair and Ralph H. Johnson, "Argumentation as Dialectical," *Argumentation* 1 (1987): 41–56.

28. Blair and Johnson, "Argumentation," p. 48.

29. Ibid., p. 48.

30. Ibid., pp. 51–53.

31. Trimpi, *Muses of One Mind*, pp. 87–240.

32. My argument here owes much to Ronald Beiner, *Political Judgment* (Chicago: University of Chicago Press, 1983).

33. Trimpi, *Muses of One Mind*, p. 234.

Text, Context, and the Fragmentation of Contemporary Culture

MICHAEL CALVIN McGEE

In the mid-1960s, rhetoricians were led away from their study of public address by a new way of asking questions that centered on understanding the methods rather than the substance of their academic practice. The result was a limited ability to deal effectively with new cultural conditions that require different strategies for managing the relationship between a text and its context. This essay suggests that the fragmentation of our American culture has resulted in a role reversal, making *interpretation* the primary task of speakers and writers and *text construction* the primary task of audiences, readers, and critics. (Interpretation and text construction go together like reading and writing, of course, so it is important to understand from the outset that I am not suggesting that today's critics no longer need to worry about interpretation, or that today's speakers need not make speeches. "Primary task" means "the most essential" or "crucial" operation in successful reading/listening and writing/speaking.)

CRITICISM IN COMMUNICATION STUDIES

For the past twenty-five years or so, the field has been preoccupied with the pure act of criticism. From the beginning, in such books as Thonssen's and Baird's *Speech Criticism* (1948), we have recognized that criticism is intimately connected with any analysis of discourse. We translated Greek and Roman theories of communication into a theory of criticism, implying that rhetoricians possess performative skills which permit role-playing the part of great speakers at the moment of eloquence, or even the part of great authors at the point of writing a masterpiece of literature. Our theory of criticism treated the finished discourse as a final choice from among possible arguments and arrangements, styles and media. This way of conceiving discourse presupposes that criticism is purposive and tendentious: Great oratory ought to be celebrated for its wisdom and eloquence; bad oratory should be exposed for its bombast and eristic. The *telos* of both kinds of judgment is ultimately pedagogical, the clear faith that fledgling orators can profit from studying the successes and mistakes of more experienced speakers.

Since 1965, however, a spate of books and essays redefined criticism, making it an *object* of study rather than a *vehicle* of study. That is, we translated *how* we study into *what* we study, suggesting that our practice as critics is self-justifying. In Black's words (1978, p. 4), "criticism is what critics do." It need not "lead" to other kinds of knowledge or "go" anywhere in particular. "The critic" became portrayed as an entirely independent agent, so much in charge of his or her intellectual labor that whatever is produced under the name of "criticism" should be acceptable in principle, subject only to criteria of internal consistency and a reader's tutored preference. As Gronbeck (1985) tells the story, our reorientation resulted in the "death" of public address, an academic practice killed when some of us decided that we were "critics" and others that we were "analysts" (cf. Hart, 1985). Whatever you think of Gronbeck's death metaphor, "public address" has clearly dissolved, being no longer a discrete object of study nor a necessary ground for critical judgment. But notice also that *rhetoric* has dissolved! Most obviously, in the sheer linguistics of the new terminology, rhetoric shifted from noun to qualifier, and in its new adjectival state, it remains occluded by focus on "criticism." It is now more important to be familiar with the theories of those who write about "criticism" from any field of the Academy than it is to understand the nature of the "rhetorical" in human life generally, in and out of the Academy. Though we all know better, we write as if *rhetoric* were uncontested, uninteresting, a subordinate term.

Where has rhetoric gone? The term "rhetorical criticism" invites us to Black's emphasis on critical practice. The term "critical rhetoric" (McKerrow, 1989) invites emphasis on rhetorical practice, "rhetoric is what rhetoricians do." With Black's accent, rhetoric is too easily submerged in philosophical and/or literary thinking.

WITH ACCENT ON CRITICISM

From one angle, emphasis on "criticism" dissolves rhetoric into philosophy. Nearly everyone has called Plato the "Father of Philosophy," but Richard Rorty more specifically claims that Plato "invented philosophical thinking" from the materials of rhetoric, the lore of "Sophists" (1979, pp. 156–157). Plato's criticism of rhetoric emphasizes its easy acceptance of appearance and lack of concern for truth. Rhetoricians such as Isocrates did recognize a clear tension between appearance and reality, but they described it as *opposition*, not as *contradiction*. That is, when different modes of interpretation are also at odds, each claiming to be true, rhetoricians saw a *stasis*, an impasse resolved when judges imbued with *phronesis* (practical wisdom) make decisions. Plato doubted the practical wisdom of the Athenian *polis* that usually made such judgments, claiming that decisions are often polluted by the superstition and fear of uncritical minds. He wanted a more reliable, certain criterion of truth, so he invented philosophical thinking by characterizing an opposition as more than *stasis*, as *krisis*, a contradiction that results from the imperfection of language. Words cannot capture the reality, the truth, of what they "stand for" in discourse; but some are closer to the mark than others. We must begin with the supposition that reality is hidden by appearance, truth by discourse. We search for that interpretation which most closely mirrors nature, truth for its own sake. Rhetoricians claimed that Plato made the study of *krisis*, the act of criticism, an object rather than a vehicle—discourse should "lead" somewhere beyond truth for the sake of truth, specifically to an enactment and embodiment of practical wisdom (Isocrates, 1961, pp. 329–333). For a while yet, until Rorty and his allies succeed in reshaping "mirror of nature" philosophy, there will be a place in the Platonic tradition for "the critic" whose labor goes nowhere beyond truth for the sake of truth. But this will be, as it has ever been, a place without rhetoricians, a place where rhetoric is degraded, where truth and action, theory and practice, have precious little to do with one another.

From another angle, the emphasis on "criticism" dissolves rhetoric into literary theory. As McKerrow (1989) has suggested, we might have said "critical rhetoric" instead of "rhetorical criticism," thus keeping it clear that criticism is a vehicle for doing rhetoric. When we reduced rhetoric to its adjectival state, however, we accepted the literary habit of taking the bite out of criticism by conceiving it as a kind of interpretation. Literary critics celebrate artists and worship art. "The Critic," like the high priest of antiquity, assumes the burden of making the hidden meanings of the artist/oracle manifest. Art *is presumed* to be an articulation of truth. If you can't understand the James Joyce novel, it's not because Joyce was an incompetent communicator—the fault is yours, because you haven't invested enough intellectual labor in reading it properly. When we teach performance, rhetoricians insist on bearing a burden of communication: The responsibility for any audience's failure to understand rests with the speaker or writer. Rhetoric is artful, but it is artful *as a performance*, not as an artifact. When rhetoric dissolves into literary criticism, the performative skills of the rhetorician are devalued, buried in literature's deep association with religion and the sacred text. The Bible simply presents itself, requiring interpretation because it is sacred. A clear supposition of literary criticism is that literature deserves the same regard. This is why readers are supposed to assume a burden of interpretation in the process of understanding Joyce's *Ulysses*. A muse bit Joyce and infected him with a divine madness. What he writes is not just a *message*, but a *divine message*, a revelation like the discourse of prophets. To condemn it and ignore it for its lack of clarity is vaguely sacrilegious. Rhetorical critics who valorize discourse that is "only" communicative are thus in a double-bind: If they emphasize what distinguishes them from literary critics, their mastery of *rhetoric*, they are incompetent readers of literature, because they cannot account for transcendence ("divinity") very well. If they emphasize what they have in common with literary critics, their mastery of *critical* theory and practice, they dilute their ability to deal with materiality (the everydayness of practical discourse), for they are in the position of using techniques for interpreting "divinity" on discourse distinguished by its lack of "divinity" (by the absence, or the presence in lesser degree, of "literary value").

In terms of contemporary discourse theory, the distance between rhetoric and literature, performance and artifact, is the distance between speaking and writing. Notice how important it is to those thinkers most influential on contemporary literary theory that they are dealing with *writing*. Barthes wanted to study problems of constraint and determination, so he drew a firm line of dialectical opposition between speech as "open" communication and writing as "closed anti-communication":

> All modes of writing have in common the fact of being "closed" and thus different from spoken language. writing is in no way an instrument for communication, it is not an open

route through which there passes only the intention to speak. . . . Writing is a hardened language which is self-contained and is in no way meant to deliver to its own duration a mobile series of approximations. It is on the contrary meant to impose . . . the image of a speech which had a structure even before it came into existence. What makes writing the opposite of speech is that the former always *appears* symbolical, introverted, ostensibly turned towards an occult side of language, whereas the second is nothing but a flow of empty signs, the movement of which alone is significant. The whole of speech is epitomized in this expendability of words, in this froth ceaselessly swept onwards, and speech is found only where language self-evidently functions like a devouring process which swallows only the moving crest of the words. Writing, on the contrary, is always rooted in something beyond language, it develops like a seed, not like a line, it manifests an essence and holds the threat of a secret, it is an anti-communication, it is intimidating. (Barthes, 1968, p. 19–20)

Ricoeur, whose "hermeneutics of suspicion" greatly influenced the recent "interpretive turn" in literary theory (see Mitchell, 1983), specifically excludes speaking from the meaning of the term *text*, and thus from being considered in analysis of social, political, and cultural structures, until such time as it has been *inscribed*, written down, and thus ceased to be what it is in everyday life, *spoken*:

I assume that the primary sense of the word "hermeneutics" concerns the rules required for the interpretation of the written documents of our culture. In assuming this starting point I am remaining faithful to the concept of *Auslegung* as it was stated by Wilhelm Dilthey. . . . *Auslegung* (interpretation, exegesis) implies something more specific [than understanding, comprehension]: it covers only a limited category of signs, those which are fixed by writing, including all the sorts of documents and monuments which entail a fixation similar to writing. . . . if there are specific problems which are raised by the interpretation of texts because they are texts and not spoken language, and if these problems are the ones which constitute hermeneutics as such, then the human sciences may be said to be hermeneutical (1) inasmuch as their *object* displays some of the features constitutive of a text as text, and (2) inasmuch as their *methodology* develops the same kind of procedures as those of *Auslegung* or text-interpretation. (Ricoeur, 1971, p. 529)

Derrida and the Yale school of literary theorists mark the development of writing as a decisive moment in Western civilization. "Fixing" speech in writing introduces problems of power and domination in cultural analysis, all but irretrievably disabling discourse as a vehicle or mediator of truth:

At the precisely calculated center of the dialogue [Plato's *Phaedrus*]–the reader can count the lines–the question of *logography* is raised. ["Logography" is the "writing down" of "speech," giving up one's own "speech" to be "spoken/read" by someone else.] Phaedrus reminds Socrates that the citizens of greatest influence and dignity, the men who are the most free, feel ashamed at "speechwriting." . . . They fear the judgment of posterity, which might consider them "sophists." The logographer, in the strict sense, is a *ghost writer* who composes speeches for use by litigants, speeches which he himself does not pronounce, which he does not attend, so to speak, in person, and which produce their effects in his absence. In writing what he does not speak, what he would never say and, in truth, would probably never think, the author of the written speech is already entrenched in the posture of the sophist: the man of non-presence and of non-truth. Writing is thus already on the scene. The incompatibility between the *written* and the *true* is clearly announced. (Derrida, 1981, p. 68; cf. Burke, 1961)

There are some striking ironies in literary theory's fascination with problems arising from the differences between speaking and writing. The *worshipful attitude* of the literary critic is preserved, but texts themselves are profaned: The truths they contain are hidden messages of secular exploitation and dominion, not the divine revelations of an oracle. Writing and truth are incompatible; yet the scholar's time and attention should be preoccupied with the interpretation of writing. Because it is set in such stark contrast over and against writing, speaking is almost a regulative ideal of discourse: It is open, embodied, enacted, capable where writing is not, in its capacity to bear communication and engender community. Yet, among influential writers, Karl Apel (1972) and Jürgen Habermas (1981) are virtually alone in their attempt to theorize speaking as the regulative ideal of discourse—and they are almost never encountered in approving ways in the work of literary theorists.

WITH ACCENT ON RHETORIC

I do not entirely disapprove of new literary theory or of the turn in some circles toward the deconstruction of the history of philosophy. These trends have been inspiration to many, myself included. I believe that Barthes in particular is responsible for setting in motion a revolution in the Academy that will ultimately unify science and the humanities in a common quest for control over unimaginably complex post-industrial societies and economies. A circle of negativism (decentering, deconstructing) should be broken, however. I think it is time to stop whining about the so-called "post-modern" condition and to develop realistic strategies to cope with it as a fact of human life, perhaps in the present, certainly in the not-too-distant twenty-first century. I believe that an assertion of critical rhetoric, a reappraisal of the way we associate the terms *criticism* and *rhetoric*, might lead to such strategies.

Instead of beginning with the claim that "criticism is what critics do," we might begin conceiving our academic practice by saying that *rhetoric is what rhetoricians do*. This announces that we are concerned more with speech than with writing (in the same sense that the difference between speech and writing is critical in contemporary discourse theory); and, therefore, that our focus is more on the performance of discourse than on the archaeology of discourse. These two implications need to be drawn out in some detail before the argument can proceed: (a) We must understand what it means to treat discourse from the first principle that it is a performance; and (b) we must understand how this first principle affects the way we describe the features of discourse.

TEXTUAL "FRAGMENTS"

With criticism as a master term, we assume that rhetoric is a form or genre of discourse presented for study as are novels, plays, or poems. The question of what constitutes "the text" is unproblematic—the discourse as it is delivered to its audience/readers is considered "finished," whole, clearly and obviously the object (target) of critical analysis. "The text" is Martin Luther King's "I Have a Dream" speech, for example, or Leni Riefenstahl's film *Triumph of the Will*, and close textual analysis will not stray far from the terms and the resources of the target discourse's world.

By contrast, with rhetoric as a master term, we begin by noticing that rhetors *make* discourses from scraps and pieces of evidence. Critical rhetoric does not *begin* with a finished text in need of interpretation; rather, texts are understood to be larger than the apparently finished discourse that presents itself as transparent. The apparently finished discourse is in fact a dense reconstruction of all the bits of other discourses from which it was made. It is fashioned from what we can call "fragments." Further, whether we conceive it in an Aristotelian sense as the art of persuasion, or in a Burkean sense as the social process of identification, rhetoric is *influential* (see Condit, 1987a, 1987b). That is, the rhetor understands that discourse anticipates its utility in the world, inviting its own critique (the interpretation and appropriation of its meaning). So "I Have a Dream" and *Triumph of the Will* are "in between" elided parts that will make them whole. They are simultaneously structures of fragments, finished texts, and fragments themselves to be accounted for in subsequent discourse, either (a) the audience/reader/critic's explanation of their power and meaning, or (b) the audience/reader/critic's rationalization for having taken their cue as an excuse for action. As a finished text, "I Have a Dream" is an arrangement of facts, allusions, and stylized expressions. As a fragment in the critic's text, the speech is only a featured part of an arrangement that includes all facts, events, texts, and stylized expressions deemed useful in explaining its influence and exposing its meaning.

THREE STRUCTURAL RELATIONSHIPS

One can get a more developed picture of a whole "text" by considering three structural relationships, between an apparently finished discourse and its sources, between an apparently finished discourse and culture, and between an apparently finished discourse and its influence.

We are most familiar with the relationship between the apparently finished discourse and its sources. Fledgling orators and writers have for centuries been taught research skills under the heading of "invention." They go to the library, locate other discourses deemed relevant to the topic of their speech or essay, and take note on index cards of "important" or "representative" "essential" passages. Foreign policy expert Henry Kissinger may have chosen 8,000 words to express in *Foreign Affairs* his opinion of U.S. policy in the Middle East. The debater, the public speaker, the journalist, the legislator, or the essayist, however, will represent that discourse in 250 words, reducing and condensing Kissinger's apparently finished text into a fragment that seems more important than the whole from which it came. This fragment is said to be "the point" Kissinger was trying to make, "the bottom line," the argument "in a nutshell." The relationship between the fragment and Kissinger's whole essay is nominalistic or semiotic: The fragment is a sign that consists of a signifier (the whole discourse it represents) and a signified (the meaning we are urged to see in the whole discourse). The relationship between the fragment and its new location—in the rhetor's discourse— is more forensic or approbative: The truncation we call "Kissinger's opinion" is clustered with other similar fragments in relation to a claim we are asked to approve. The clearest abuse of this process is "taking something out of context," allowing the requirements of an approbative structure to determine meaning by ignoring the requirements of the fragment's semiotic structure. In the best of possible arguments, the meaning of a fragment is invariant when structuration changes. That is, the advocate will so fairly represent Kissinger's opinion that the meaning of the fragment will be the same inside a critic's essay as in Kissinger's whole argument.

Though it is frequently featured in rhetorical theories, we are less familiar with the relationship between an apparently finished discourse and *culture*. Aristotle's notion of the *enthymeme* and Cicero's use of the *epicheireme*, as well as the discussion of *doxa* among most of the Greeks, get at what we now call "culture," though in a back-handed way. Human beings, the story goes, exist in a matrix of rules, rituals, and conventions that we "take for granted" by assuming their goodness and truth and accepting the conditions they create as the "natural order of things." This conventional wisdom (*doxa*) is identical to the concept *culture* that is so prominently featured in much contemporary discourse theory. Present-day writers, however, are primarily concerned with problems of *constraint*, investigating why, how, and with what result culture silences people. In contrast, rhetoricians have usually been concerned with *empowerment*, seeking to discover how and with what consequence *doxa* can be used to authorize a redress of human grievances. *Enthymemes* and *epicheiremes* are argument forms that incorporate *doxa* in exhortations to action. Rhetors are advised to ground their arguments in *doxa*, using the taken-for-granted rules of society as the first principle (premise) of a chain of arguments. Further, advocates are urged not to "insult the intelligence" of audiences by directly proving what can safely be taken for granted—*doxa* is silent, and it should be kept silent, unless it becomes itself the source of grievance. When *doxa* is the source of grievance, rhetoricians in both the Platonic and Isocratean schools envision a kind of "social surgery" where new cultural imperatives are substituted for old taken-for-granted conventions. The exhortations of Socrates in Plato's *Apology* and of Isocrates in orations on pan-Hellenism are clear examples, respectively, of inconsequential and influential "surgery" on Greek culture.

Since all apparently finished discourses presuppose taken-for-granted cultural imperatives, all of culture is implicated in every instance of discourse. In principle, even the most basic cultural imperative (that the discourse is in one language as opposed to another—Russian, for example, and not French) is implicated in an apparently finished discourse and is thus part of "the text." In practice, however, only a finite and discrete set of cultural imperatives, discoverable by application of a simple test, need to be treated as implicatives within a specific discourse. The test has to do with the effects of unmasking cultural imperatives, giving voice to the silences of *doxa*: If recognition and statement of a rule, ritual, or convention is necessary to understand any fragment of the discourse, or if such recognition and statement would motivate an audience/reader/critic to resist the claims of the discourse, we can infer that the discourse derives its rhetorical power more from the *silence* of the cultural imperative than from the imperative itself. Whether we supply elided premises of *enthymemes* and *epicheiremes* or keep them silenced should make no difference in interpreting or acting upon apparently finished discourses. If missing premises do make a difference, they must be clearly articulated, thus becoming part of "the text."

Considering the relationship between an apparently finished discourse and its influence calls attention to the fundamental interconnectedness of all discourse. Writing makes no sense unless there are readers. The response of an interlocutor ("feedback") is an essential component of any communicative event. Every bit of discourse, in other words, invites its own critique. It is in this sense, perhaps, that Kenneth Burke keeps reminding us that we are all critics. In the most radical sense of this claim, as "everyday critics," we make a series of "snap judgments" in response to discourse. The first is a judgment of *salience*: The discourse is silenced, dismissed and forgotten, if it seems uninteresting or irrelevant; but if it matters, the discourse will be remembered, structured into our experience. If the discourse is memorable, it will at the very least affect our *attitudes*: Even if we disapprove and disagree with what the discourse seems to be saying, it will influence what we think by altering a motive state (increasing anger, for example, or decreasing anxieties hitch-hiking in descriptions of the world) and providing an example of someone else's foolishness. The discourse may also affect our *beliefs*, in dimensions of intensity and *substance*: With regard to intensity, the discourse could strengthen or weaken our confidence in what we think we know about the world, or our commitment to the truth of facts we have in the past taken on faith. With regard to substance, the discourse could simply add to our store of knowledge, or, with more complicated consequence, it could cause us to discard prior facts as erroneous and to accept new facts as truth. The fourth snap judgment of everyday critics has to do with the translation of our beliefs into *action*: At the very least, we decide to engage in a speech act when we verbalize our motive-ridden beliefs in response to a discourse judged to be salient. At the most, we intervene in the world, physically interposing ourselves upon a problematic condition in an attempt to make the world conform to our will.

Professional critics (whether they be critics of art, society, literature, or any other thing) differ from everyday critics in that *they are always trying to make the world conform to their will*. Their criticism is on its face that sort of action which intervenes in the world. Put another way, professional critics are all rhetorical critics, in either of the two dominant contemporary senses of "rhetoric": In Aristotelian terms, professional criticism functions to persuade readers to make the same judgments of salience, attitude, belief, and action the critic made. In Burkean terms, professional criticism promotes identification with the critic, suggesting that critics give voice to communal judgments of salience, attitude, belief, and action, stating a collective will to which the world should conform. The everyday critic *may* create discourse in response to discourse; but the professional critic *always* creates formal discourse in response to discourse. (The object of criticism is always either discourse or discourse analogue, in the sense that it is treated as meaningful and in need of interpretation.) Professional critics must thus be sensitive to rhetoric in two dimensions: With regard to the object of criticism, they will be perceived as respondents and interpreters responsible for providing in a formal way the missing fragments of the object of criticism, its influence. With regard to their own formal writing, they will function as advocates or adversaries of "the text" who invent, arrange, style, remember, and deliver arguments in favor of particular judgments of salience, attitude, belief, and action (see Brockriede, 1972, 1974).

THE TERMS "TEXT" AND "CONTEXT"

In calling attention to three structural relationships that make an issue out of deciding what a "text" is, I have done no more than change the way we have traditionally described the problematics of rhetorical criticism. In the past we separated "text" from "context" and discussed the sources, presuppositions, and effects of discourse as parts of "context." The result of such conceptual separation, I suggest, has been confusion about the root nature of discourse. Unfortunately, an unkind way of articulating the problem is also the clearest: Separate consideration of text and context makes question-begging too easy and attractive. "Context" can be reduced to any of its parts. If you can't chase down the fragments from which an argument was constructed (if you can't find the prosecution's case in the trial of Socrates, for example), you use the discursive equivalent of the theory of spontaneous generation and treat the argument as *ex nihilo* philosophy and/or literature, words without history, or words with only an "intellectual" or "literary" history. If you can account for the sources of discourse, but have difficulty understanding the cultural milieu in which it was socially and politically significant, you reduce the communicative event to a simple stimulus–response mechanism wherein discourse is said to have discrete and independent effects on history. (This results in such odd critical judgments as Nichols [1972] holding Lincoln to account for failing to stop the Civil War with his "First Inaugural Address.") If you understand the cultural milieu, but discover the difficulty of showing how one bit of discourse contributes to an overdetermined cultural condition, you can ignore the problem of influence altogether by celebrating the artistry (eloquence) of the rhetor who combined sources into an insightful, well-said commentary on his or her life and times. The Chicago School has even given us the conceptual wherewithal to ignore all three parts of context by performing "close textual analysis" on presumptively self-contained discourses.

My way of stating the case (using the concept "fragment" to collapse context" into "text") emphasizes an important truth about discourse: *Discourse ceases to be what it is whenever parts of it are taken "out of context."* Failing to account for "context," or reducing "context" to one or two of its parts, means quite simply that one is no longer dealing with discourse as it appears in the world. The belief that the formation of words we call King's "I Have a Dream" oration can be construed as sufficient unto themselves is sheer fantasy. Put another way, the elements of "context" are so important to the "text" that one cannot discover, or even discuss, the *meaning* of "text" without reference to them. This is not to say that scholarship focused on parts of "the text" (as I describe it) is impossible or nonsensical. Each of the "question-begging" strategies I have discussed (and several others not enumerated here) could be reframed in a sensible and productive way. Even the Chicago School strategy of ignoring "context" altogether can be redeemed by consistently, rigorously acknowledging the "incompleteness" of the analysis. Make it clear that King's speech is a *fragment*. Look for the particular locutions that implicate its sources. Show where cultural conventions are presupposed. Locate the places where "I Have a Dream" is trying to create, or is seeking, its audience. Show where and how the speech anticipates its own "everyday" critique. Frequently the best evidence you have of the missing parts of a text are there in front of you as implications of the fragment you are looking at. Certainly, every fragment is a map of the structures that will make it complete, and in that sense focus on a part can be a speculative, "incomplete" study of the whole.

THE FRAGMENTATION OF CULTURE

I believe that problematizing the concept "text" is generally productive, even in dealing with deeply historical fragments such as *Magna Carta* or Burke's "Speech on Conciliation with the Colonies." If the human condition had not changed so radically in the past seventy years, I could therefore be content to leave this argument with a pluralistic claim, that I have posed one of several plausible ways to account for the relationship between text and context. This announces that I would be pleased to see others follow up the suggestions made here, but that I see no *necessity* in them, nothing that makes choosing my way of thinking better than the traditional disjunction of text and context. Radical change has occurred, however, and our new condition makes it necessary to insist on the concept "fragment" and to suggest that alternatives embrace error. This point can come clear in a line of reasoning that begins by asking what features of discourse inclined critics to treat "text" as self-evident.

In the not-too-distant past, all discourses were what some social theorists call "totalizations" (see, e.g., Mannheim, 1972). That is, all structures of a text were homogeneous. Education was restricted to a scant minority, and as a result the content of an education was so homogeneous that an orator could utter two or three lines in Latin, identified only with the words "as Tully said," in complete confidence that any reader/audience/critic would be able to identify the source of the words–and even recite the next several lines from Cicero's *De oratore*! Except for everyday conversation, all discourse within a particular language community was produced from the same resources. Further, all discourse found its influence on the same small class of people who comprised the political nation. And it was the same small class that received the benefits of a homogenized education. There was little cultural diversity, no question that there was in every state a well-defined dominant race, dominant class, dominant gender, dominant history, and dominant ethnicity. The silent, taken-for-granted creed of all true-blue Americans (Frenchmen, Englishmen, etc.) could have been articulated by any one of them who had been conditioned by the education system and admitted as a member in good standing of the political nation, even those who fancied themselves revolutionaries.

Discourse practices reflected the presumed homogeneity of Western cultures. Rhetors invested a great deal of effort to insure that their discourses appeared to be "harmonious," whole, ending with allusion to their beginning. The same air of formality that dictated proper dress at public occasions and in restaurants also dictated proper discourse practices. Public argument was also formal argument modeled after the courtroom. The dice were loaded in favor of existing circumstances, so that advocates of change were forced to assume a "burden of proof" and to meet the stiff requirements of the prima facie case. Regardless of whom they silenced, what they ignored, or weakness in their argument, advocates tried mightily to write or speak as if they had an "airtight case" that accounted for all possible interpretations of evidence and all conceivable courses of action that appeared to follow from the truths the evidence appeared to support. Ethical public figures, those who refused to "stoop to demagoguery," addressed everyone in their target audiences as if the meanest laborer, the most ignorant rounder among them, had all the skills of reason and wisdom of an appellate judge, a Member of Parliament, or a U.S. senator. Adaptations to ignorance, apathy, and vulgarity were fundamentally linguistic rather than logical, the choice of a smaller vocabulary instead of truncations of what was supposed to be the rational process. This commitment to the rationality of *homo sapiens* led to the cultural imperative that we all should take our time in making deliberate judgments. The wise judgment was precisely the deliberate judgment that carefully weighed evidence and balanced alternatives with the skill of a juggler.

I believe that a persuasive history of the twentieth century could be written with the motif that presumed homogeneity has been replaced by the presumption of cultural heterogeneity. If I were telling the story, I would likely begin with the agitation that led to the passage of the 19th Amendment, the women's suffrage movement. I would point to the "psychologizing" of literally every social–political institution. Clarence Darrow invented the plea of insanity. A parole system evolved based on our presumed capacity to psychologically rehabilitate criminals. Dr. Spock inspired American families to rear children with less emphasis on the formalities and requirements of public life and more emphasis on the psychological contentment of the child. Mainstream religions put less emphasis on Christian doctrine and their role as moral watchdogs than on their community service functions ("good works"), frequently transforming the cleric into a combination social worker and therapist. The Supreme Court legitimized ethnicity in several decisions related to *Brown vs. The Board of Education* which argue, in main part, that America's traditional "melting-pot" rhetoric causes psychological harm to minorities who cannot find themselves in WASP-ish cultural depictions of the ideal society. Politicians, both in campaigns and in executing the duties of office, increasingly consult their audiences as if they were fundamentally irrational, *homo cognito* rather than *homo sapiens*. The "bottom line" of politics these days is the instantaneous public opinion poll which measures popular *reaction* to current conditions rather than the *considered, deliberate judgment* of "We, the People." John Dewey inspired a revolution in education based on our capacity to condition all citizens to the psychology of democracy. People have grown less interested in the *content* than in the *process* of a public education, suggesting that what people know is less important than the process of learning (see Cheney, 1988b). As a result, there is no longer a homogeneous body of knowledge that constitutes the common education of everyone. Students are more likely today to learn English literature by reading science fiction than by reading "the classics," and the ability to remember specific things about a particular essay or novel is no longer valorized.

We stand now in the middle (or at the end, if reactionaries have their way) of a seventy-year movement which has fractured and fragmented American culture. Contemporary discourse practices reflect this fragmentation. Indeed, changes in discourse practices have been so obviously dramatic that several theorists portray new communication technologies as *the cause* of cultural fracturing. Some take the broad view of deep intellectual history, vacillating between near-Luddite polemics that merely implicate technology in a general indictment of capitalism and science (e.g., Burke, 1945, pp. 113–117, 175–176, 214–223, 507–511) and jubilant epideictics that celebrate those fragmenting effects of new media which constitute or presage a recuperation of good things in long-lost "oral cultures" (e.g., McLuhan, 1964, and Ong, 1982). Others take a more political view, oddly enough condemning new discourse practices from both extremes of the relatively narrow spectrum of American politics. From the right, reactionaries worry about "the fate of the book" (Cheney, 1988) and the alleged "closing of the American mind" (Bloom, 1987). From the left comes a voice with French accent, the voice of so-called "post-modernism," worrying about the "colonization" of the psyche (Deleuze and Guattari, 1983) and "the precession of simulacra" (Baudrillard, 1983).

Settling the cause-and-effect issue regarding the relationship between culture and discourse practices is ultimately an ineffable chicken-and-egg problem of scant interest. However we got there, the human *condition* has changed. Put whatever adjectives you want in front of the concept "condition." (I grit my teeth and shudder as I say it, but I think the term *post-modern condition* is likely to prove best.) One clear truth will not change: The public's business is now being done more often via direct mail, television spots, documentaries, mass entertainment, and "quotable quotes" on the evening news than through the more traditional media (broadsides, pamphlets, books, and public speeches). A central requirement of our new circumstance is simply finding a place to start thinking about it. Scholars are all analysts at heart, but nothing in our new environment is complete enough, finished enough, to analyze—and the fragments that present themselves to us do not stand still long enough to analyze. They fly by so quickly that by the time you grasp the problem at stake, you seem to be dealing with yesterday's news, a puzzle that solved itself by disappearing. A few years ago, for example, the Cable News Network broadcast two stories, in tandem, every thirty minutes for forty-eight hours. The first was a Romeo and Juliet tale of a tragic, dramatic teenage suicide. The second reported that a causal connection exists between news of teenage suicide and suicide attempts. By the time the network recognized the contradiction and its potential effect, it was trapped by "the public's right to know" into reporting an epidemic rash of copy-cat suicides. By the time policymakers and academics recognized that public health may require re-examination of traditional attitudes toward "free press" issues, the epidemic was over. The network had other news to confront, policymakers had no immediate cause for study or action, and academics had no opportunity for response other than adding another item to the laundry list of topics that warrant tooth-gnashing polemics against the insensitivity of those who run the culture industry.

I agree with Said (1983a, 1983b) that the fundamental root of frustration in such situations is our inclination to treat scraps of social problems and fragments of texts as if they were whole. In his vocabulary, the solution is to look for *formations of texts* rather than "*the* text" as a place to begin analysis. I like the term "formation," but I want to keep clear that we are dealing with fragments, not texts, and that we mean to treat a "formation" as if it were a singular text—only then can we interpret, analyze, and criticize. I would therefore state the case in two somewhat different ways:

From one angle, provided by the traditional disjunction of text and context, I would want to explore the sense in which "texts" have disappeared altogether, leaving us with nothing but *discursive fragments of context*. By this I would mean that changing cultural conditions have made it virtually impossible to construct a whole and harmonious text such as Edmund Burke's "Speech on Conciliation with the Colonies." If by "text" we mean the sort of finished discourse anticipated in consequence of an essentially homogenous culture, no texts exist today. We have instead fragments of "information" that constitute our *context*. The unity and structural integrity we used to put in our texts as they faithfully represented nature is now presumed to be *in us ourselves*.

From another angle, provided by my proposed collapse of context into text, I would want to explore the sense in which we are constantly harassed by the necessity of understanding an "invisible text" which is never quite finished but constantly in front of us. By this I would mean that changing cultural conditions have forced writers/speakers and readers/audiences to reverse their roles. At one time producers of discourse could circumscribe even the most difficult human problem in a single finished text. (With reference to the enthymeme and epicheireme, one would say that producers of discourse provided more in their texts than they presumed in their audiences.) The communication revolution, however, was accompanied by a knowledge explosion. The result is that today no single finished text could possibly comprehend all perspectives on even a single human problem, let alone the complex of problems we index in the phrase "issues of the day." The only way to "say it all" in our fractured culture is to provide readers/audiences with dense, truncated fragments that cue *them* to produce a finished discourse in their minds. In short, *text construction is now something done more by the consumers than by the producers of discourse.*

In my vocabulary, the problem calls for the skills of a rhetorician. I think we can reconcile traditional modes of analysis with the so-called post-modern condition by understanding that our first job as professional consumers of discourse is *inventing a text suitable for criticism*. I will elaborate on the subject of text construction in a subsequent essay. For now, this first step requires closure: So long as one reads historical documents ("finished" texts produced in consequence of demonstrated cultural homogeneity) it is possible to take a pluralistic attitude toward the concept "fragment." The strategy I propose can be understood as one of many alternatives in the business of managing the theoretical relationship of texts and their context. If you analyze contemporary discourse, however, "fragment" or some concept that can be made equivalent (Said's "formation," for example) is *necessary*. Only something very similar to the strategy I propose has the power to account for discourse produced in consequence of the fragmentation of culture.

References

Apel, K. (1972). "The *A Priori* of Communication and the Foundation of the Humanities." *Man and World* 5: 3–37.

Barthes, R. (1968). *Writing Degree Zero.* Translated byAnnette Lavers and Colin Smith. New York: Hill and Wang.

Baudrillard, J. (1983). *Simulations.* Translated by Paul Foss, Paul Patton, and Philip Beitchman. New York: Semiotext(e).

Black, E. (1978). *Rhetorical Criticism: A Study in Method.* 2d ed. Madison: University of Wisconsin Press.

Bloom, A. (1987). *The Closing of the American Mind.* New York: Simon & Schuster.

Brockriede, W. (1972). "Arguers as Lovers." *Philosophy and Rhetoric* 5: 1–11.

Brockriede, W. (1974). "Rhetorical Criticism as Argument." *Quarterly Journal of Speech* 60: 165–174.

Burke, K. (1945). *A Grammar of Motives.* New York: Prentice-Hall.

Burke, K. (1961). *The Rhetoric of Religion: Studies in Logology.* Boston: Beacon Press.

Cheney, L. V. (1988a). *American Memory: A Report on the Humanities in the Nation's Public Schools.* Washington, DC: National Endowment for the Humanities.

Cheney, L. V. (1988b). *Humanities in America: A Report to the President, Congress, and the American People.* Washington, DC: National Endowment for the Humanities.

Condit, C. M. (1987a). "Crafting Virtue: The Rhetorical Construction of Public Morality." *Quarterly Journal of Speech* 73: 79-97 (reprinted in this volume).

Condit, C. M. (1987b). "Democracy and Civil Rights: The Universalizing Influence of Public Argumentation." *Communication Monographs* 54: 1–18.

Derrida, J. (1981). *Dissemination.* Translated by Barbara Johnson. Chicago: University of Chicago Press.

Frye, N. (1957). *Anatomy of Criticism: Four Essays.* Princeton, NJ: Princeton University Press.

Gronbeck, B. E. (1985). "The Birth, Death, and Rebirth of Public Address." Paper presented at the annual meeting of the Speech Communication Association, Denver, CO.

Habermas, J. (1984). *The Theory of Communicative Action, Vol. 1: Reason and the Rationalization of Society.* Translated by Thomas McCarthy. Boston: Beacon Press.

Hart, R. P. (1985). "Public Address: Should It Be Disinterred?" Paper presented at the annual meeting of the Speech Communication Association, Denver, CO.

Isocrates. (1961). *Antidosis.* In *The Works of Isocrates.* Translated by George Norlin and Larue Van Hook (Cambridge, MA: Harvard University Press), pp. 181–365.

McKerrow, R. E. (1989). "Critical Rhetoric: Theory and *Praxis.*" *Communication Monographs* 56: 91–111 (reprinted in this volume).

McLuhan, M. (1964). *Understanding Media: The Extensions of Man.* New York: McGraw-Hill.

Mannheim, K. (1955). *Ideology and Utopia: An Introduction to the Sociology of Knowledge.* Rev. ed. Translated by L. Wirth and E. Shils. New York: Harvest Books.

Mitchell, W. J. T., ed. (1983). *The Politics of Interpretation.* Chicago: University of Chicago Press.

Nichols, M. H. (1972). "Lincoln's First Inaugural." In R. L. Scott and B. L. Brock, eds., *Methods of Rhetorical Criticism* (New York: Harper and Row), pp. 60–100.

Ong, W. J. (1982). *Orality and Literacy: The Technologizing of the Word.* New York: Methuen.

Ricoeur, P. (1971). "The Model of the Text: Meaningful Action Considered as a Text." *Social Research* 38: 529–562.

Rorty, R. (1979). *Philosophy and the Mirror of Nature.* Princeton, NJ: Princeton University Press.

Said, E. W. (1983a). "Opponents, Audiences, Constituencies, and Community." In W. J. T. Mitchell, ed., *The Politics of Interpretation* (Chicago: University of Chicago Press).

Said, E. W. (1983b). *The World, the Text, and the Critic.* Cambridge, MA: Harvard University Press.

Thonssen, L., and A. C. Baird. (1948). *Speech Criticism: The Development of Standards for Rhetorical Appraisal.* New York: Ronald Press.

Practicing the Arts of Rhetoric

Tradition and Invention

THOMAS FARRELL

Ironically mirroring the fortunes of contemporary politics, two very different senses of practice have begun to merge in our historical understanding. The first, in order of appearance, is the Aristotelian sense of *praxis*, lately articulated by Alasdair MacIntyre and a host of conservative classicists.[1] This original notion suggests a coherent mode of activity with its own internal standards of excellence. Since the cultivation and mastery of recognizable practices usually requires concentration of effort and purpose, this striving for excellence is thought to engender other worthwhile "goods" and virtues of character and civic life.[2] So, as one example, the athlete must be patient, determined, mentally "tough," and so forth. The artist must be aware of her tradition, devoted to her craft, willing to sacrifice, take risks, and so on. This original sense of *practice*, in other words, stresses its unity and coherence as a form of thoughtful action. And in an era that many have indicated as a "dark" time of self-indulgence and incoherent moral discourse,[3] the return to this sense of *practice* has promised an incremental road to recovery.

But to the classical understanding of practice must be added another, more radical understanding: that of critical theory deriving from a Marxist base.[4] This historically determinate rendering regards practice as the concrete embodiment of existent social forces, understood as a mode of production. While this latter understanding preserves the cognitive significance of the practical, it tends to collapse the subjective region of practical choice into the existing conditions of a state of affairs.[5] A revealing recent example is the work of Anthony Giddens on structuration:

> The problem of order in social theory is how *form* occurs in social relations, or (put in another fashion) how social systems "bind" time and space. All social activity is formed in three conjoined moments of difference: temporally, structurally (in the language of semiotics, paradigmatically), and spatially; the conjunction of these express the *situated* character of social practices. The binding of time and space in social systems *always* has to be examined historically, in terms of the bounded knowledgeability of human action.[6]

On the basis of what we read in Giddens' words, there is little to disturb a classical rhetorician, except perhaps the lack of caution: "*All* social activity . . ." "The binding of time and space . . . *always* has to be examined historically." A vision of *praxis* which has banished all nuance and *modality* of indeterminacy may seem formally elegant but ethically troublesome, just as it has proved to be politically troublesome for all those who made the "wrong" choices.[7]

I noted earlier that these two senses of practice seem to have come together in our contemporary understanding. By this, I mean that the traditional understanding of *praxis* has been forced to reconsider and even revise itself in light of the less than amicable climates of modernity. At the same time, even the most sweeping forms of historicism have failed to author a definitive utopian ending for history's discordant, but insistent, voices. If these intuitions make sense, the opening of human practices to both a sense of their history *and* a sense of our human agency would invite a careful reappraisal of the rhetorical tradition. Why?

Primarily, I shall argue, it is because *rhetoric derives its materials from the real conditions of civic life, the appearances of our cultural world. At the same time, this activity makes room for disputation about the meaning, implications, direction, and value of cultural appearances.* This is another way of saying that rhetoric promises to include both of our senses of a practice. However, the discovery of such a preoccupation within rhetoric seems to raise as many issues as it resolves. For instance, it remains to be seen whether our classically grounded understandings of tradition offer a vocabulary of explanation sufficiently rich and responsive to capture the inventional possibilities for practice in contemporary life. I might note in passing that a widespread revival of Aristotelian *ethical* and *political* philosophy has thus far not been accompanied by any great interest in a renewal of the Aristotelian *rhetorical* tradition; and this is despite a much-heralded revival of interest in rhetoric.[8] A closely related issue is whether an informed appraisal of contemporary cultural settings might not disclose an environment so dark and dispirited as to be antagonistic to our classical understandings. This is, of course, our two senses of practice returning to us in more general theoretic terms.

In this essay, I outline a treatment of tradition which should emphasize how rhetorical *practice* allows reflection and invention to occur, given the sometimes diffuse and chaotic materials of civic life. While the impetus to my approach derives from an optimistic reading of Aristotelian rhetorical tradition, I should stress that the term *practice* itself is not without important normative and thus "critical" connotations. One does not have to be an Aristotelian to intuit that virtually any practice admits to a variable quality in performance. One plays the piano well or badly. And if one is "just learning," this terminology also immerses us within a family of concepts in which our aim is to get better: to reach or at least approach our "potential." These normative concerns might be expressed in quite recognizably modern ways as well. For instance, I may ask where you derive your operative notions of "well" or "badly." I may critique those examples of quality chosen as models for emulation. I may bemoan the unequal chances many of us have to perform certain practices in the first place, and so on.

While I cannot address this matter comprehensively here, I find it difficult to avoid the assumption that discourse about *rhetorical* practice would be unintelligible without at least the pretension to rigor afforded by an acquaintance with theory. For it is theory that raises questions about the identity and vitality of rhetorical traditions, the boundaries of genre, the pertinence of conventions and proofs, the "goods" and standards of practice itself, the very *meaning* of "rhetoric" in the first place.[9] This essay, in other words, could not hope to essentialize certain distinctive qualities within the Aristotelian rhetorical tradition without employing the language of theory.

We begin with what will seem to be a paradoxical claim. I want to argue that rhetoric is a higher-order practice; *and*, I want to suggest that rhetorical practice achieves its aims in ways that allow virtually anyone to participate effectively within the practice itself.

REREADING THE RHETORICAL TRADITION

Perhaps the most basic differentiation of activities in all of classical thought is Aristotle's own distinction between the theoretic and the productive sciences. In the productive sciences, of which ethics was one, the point was not so much to *know* virtue for its own sake, but to *become* virtuous through action.[10] Aristotle's distinction provided an important qualifier to the Platonic attempt to subsume all activities, crafts, and sciences under his own monistic philosophic vocabulary. Even within the context of the schema, however, the placement of rhetoric is still problematic. Rhetoric admits to both a theoretic quality, and to a certain form of power. And Aristotle nowhere explicitly says that the aim of rhetoric is to *be* persuasive. As near as we have been able to determine, the aim of rhetoric is to *practice* judgment (to enact *krisis*) where certain sorts of problematic materials are concerned.[11] Perhaps that is what it means to be rhetorical.

But this still leaves unsettled just what sort of practice rhetoric itself is. The modern tendency, I believe, would take rhetoric to be simply a pragmatic exertion of power through discourse, or any manner of partisanship uncovered in discourse. Either concept assumes that rhetoric only is achieving its aims when it is covering over its *true* (that is to say, "false,") intent.[12] But rhetorical practice admits to a broader understanding than this. Some idea of this understanding might be suggested by Alasdair MacIntyre's useful distinction between goods that are *internal* to a practice and goods that are *external* to it. MacIntyre's specific example is that of chess. And he is able to argue, convincingly I think, that there is a recognizable difference between goods that are only casually and contingently related to quality play in chess (such as paying a child to play, or perhaps the publicity accompanying great success, for an adult), and the goods that are fundamental and integral to the mastery of this complex game ("analytic skill, strategic imagination, and competitive intensity," to use MacIntyre's language).[13]

The distinction becomes serviceable for rhetoric if we remember two things: first, that the "goods" internal to an activity are not necessarily the reason one seeks to master the practice. One does not play chess only to acquire and sophisticate these "goods." One plays chess to win. Still, with the acquisition of skill, there comes an appreciation for the well-played match, regardless of results. Second, and despite the singular focus of MacIntyre's repeated examples, the "goods" that are cultivated are not always localized within the autonomous agent alone. There is an unmistakable pedagogical sense in which improved performance by the other improves the quality of play, one's appreciation for the sport, perhaps the resolve of one's opponent. Most important, this means we should not confuse goods that are internal to a practice with virtues that are somehow interior to its practioner alone. It is worth noting that two of MacIntyre's own interior "goods" (strategic imagination and competitive intensity) require another person in order to be practiced and thereby cultivated. They are, in other words, *relational goods*. This does not mean that they are somehow inferior to other goods; no such thing is implied by virtue of being internal to a practice. This is pivotal to rhetoric. I think we are now in a position to claim that the "goods" or qualities *internal* to rhetoric are necessarily relational.[14] Like competitiveness and strategic imagination (which mastery of rhetoric is also capable of providing), they require some *other* in order to be practiced. But beyond this, some very important civic qualities—such as civic friendship, a sense of social justice—are actively cultivated through excellence in rhetorical practice.[15] These qualities, in other words, are not merely distinctions for the autonomous agent to master; they are qualities of the body politic itself. Aristotle's original conception of rhetoric and its operation thus gives us the outline of a most intriguing form of activity, an activity admitting its own distinct goods. Truly, we have been introduced to a *practice*, that is—a coherent, creative activity admitting to certain standards of accomplishment.

But what sort of practice? It remains to be seen, for instance, whether and how this ancient art may engender "goods," "qualities," and "virtues" that are worthy of emulation. My own position, abbreviated here, is that classical rhetoric offers us a practical ideal of the appropriate; *phronesis* or practical wisdom. Rhetoric also provides us with a kind of overarching form of reasoning with *doxa*, the conventions and opinions of the civic-minded "others" around us. This is, of course, the enthymeme. And rhetoric provides a kind of location wherein all of this might occur, by carefully delimiting a certain space of civic engagement, and this we might think of as the rhetorical occasion.

Within the context of classical theory, rhetoric is an art of practice to be developed in real-life settings, where matters are in dispute and there are no fixed or final criteria for judgment.[16] It is significant that the philosopher who invented formal logic and many special disciplines saw some need for rhetoric in the first place. In his oft-cited justification for the art, Aristotle allowed that there is value in encouraging the force of the better argument to prevail, even if the matters discussed are not resolved for all time. Whether or not rhetorical practice always vindicates the force of the better argument is not nearly so important as its continual allowance for critique and improvement.[17] This means that rhetoric, like all other arts, carries with it the *possibility* of refinement.

But most important to our immediate concern, Aristotle considered rhetoric to involve practical questions that took on urgency, immediacy, and pertinence for disputants, because of the institutional time, place, and circumstances of their involvement. In other words, the questions addressed and adjudicated through rhetoric were those that could only be framed, let alone understood, within the context of a particular form of life in a culture. The formal criteria for analytic validity, like the philosophical claims to *a priori* "truth," were here less important than inference-making which invoked the presuppositions of ordinary life, and then applied them to the contingent demands of an occasion.

In earlier projects, I have emphasized the centrality of audience convictions and "habits" of thinking to the kind of practical inference which rhetoric employs to engage, animate, and complete the world of appearances. Once an audience is invoked to think along with an advocate, certain acquired background norms govern the propriety of order, emphasis, direction, subordination, and support for artistic proofs in issues of disputes.[18] By definition, these cannot be universally applicable to all cases equally, of course. Rather, they are guided by the particularity of circumstance, interest, and inclination of those who participate in the very *form* of rhetoric.

We may have happened upon an explanation of why the revival of classical philosophy has generally *not* been accompanied by a revival of Aristotelian rhetoric.

For the most part, the advocates of a recovery of classicism are part of a single-minded program, where community, the *polis*, and solidarity are one and the same thing. The regretable model for this is MacIntyre's chilling image of the "truth-bearers" huddled in the catacombs on the eve of some new dark age.[19] Yet at least as I am interpreting matters here, the whole point of the *Rhetoric* is not its monism, but its circumstantiality and eclecticism. That is what the practical ideal of *phronesis* really is all about.

But the matter that now concerns us is this whole question of *How*. How is it that *phronesis* is evoked by the *Rhetoric*? And how is this rhetorical realm of appearances really engaged by art? In a quite subtle but persistent way, the whole emphasis of the *Rhetoric* is toward the action and agency of others, as an audience in the formation of character, and the rendering of judgments. This is perhaps obvious enough in the most logocentric of Aristotle's devices—the enthymeme.[20] Here, you and I might collaborate on an inference making use of some shared normative consent. Say I observe that it is disgraceful that American-owned companies don't take more responsibility for the damage of acid rain beyond their national borders. If you agree, it is probably because you think, as do I, that their neglect has much to do with the problem, *and* that responsibility does not end at one's national or provincial borders. I don't have to say those things; yet they work as shared background conditions for forming the argument. This is a (somewhat-elliptical) enthymeme.

But I want to suggest as well that this evocation of agency is present all through the *Rhetoric*, in the markers of character, or *ethos*, in the unlikely and often unstable territory of emotion, or *pathos*, as well. Let us begin with Aristotle's ruminations about Honor:

> Honour is the token of a man's being famous for doing good. It is chiefly and most properly paid to those who have already done good; but also to the man who can do good in the future. Doing good refers either to the preservation of life and the means of life, or to wealth, or to some other of the good things which it is hard to get either always or at that particular place or time—for many gain honour for things which seem small, but the place and occasion account for it. The constituents of honour are: sacrifices; commemoration, in verse or prose; privileges; grants of land; front seats at civic celebrations; state burial; statues; public maintenance; among foreigners, obeisances and giving place; and such presents as are among various bodies of men regarded as marks of honour.[21]

For those less than sympathetic to classical rhetoric, this is the sort of passage that could confirm the worst of their stereotypes. It reads as little more than a list. But of what? It is surely an unusual way of approaching the virtue of honor. Here we have "tokens" and "marks" of honor, accounted for by the place and occasion; hence presents, and even seating position, all that persons "regard" as honor. The very mundanity here must be revealing; for this is an overview of the *appearances* of honor presented as materials for rhetoric, how honor might be recognized, presented, framed, and depicted. By whom? Let us remember that rhetoric is practical reasoning in the presence of collaborative others: in this case, those who recognize and enact the visible markers of honor for those they respect and admire. Thus, it is no exaggeration to say that their own public character is invoked and implicated by these conspicuous recognitions. Only when a sense of honor is available can honor itself be accorded. It is interesting that Aristotle moves directly from this overview in Book 1 to an examination of the various public "excellences." When he arrives at "the good," he confounds Platonists and Sophists alike by beginning with "good luck," only to include the "good in itself" as one of over forty differing and often contradictory senses of "goodness."[22] What is going on here? Again, Aristotle is overviewing for us appearances of value construed rhetorically. And far from the monolithic construals of Aristotle's many Platonic commentators, what we find instead is a sense of diversity and eclecticism. In civic life, at least, the "good" must be the outcome of timely, collaborative choice within the particularities of circumstance.

Now let us turn to the unsteady terrain of *pathos*, or emotion. Again, the conventional derogations of Aristotle need to be set aside. Gadamer finds this to be trafficking in the excitation of emotions.[23] Ricoeur views it as the most overburdening sort of pop psychology.[24] I would like to introduce a brief passage from Book 2 of the *Rhetoric*. The passage has not received much notice from rhetoricians, but I think it points in the overall direction of my position. In Chapter 8 of Book 2, Aristotle is in the process of discussing the emotion of pity. He says:

> Again, we feel pity when the danger is near ourselves. Also we pity those who are like us in age, character, disposition, social standing, or birth; for in all these cases it appears more likely that the same misfortune may befall us also. Here too we have to remember the general principle that what we fear for ourselves excites our pity when it happens to others. Further, since it is when the sufferings of others are close to us that they excite our pity (we cannot remember what disasters happened a hundred centuries hereafter, and therefore feel little pity, if any for such things).[25]

Aristotle concludes this remarkable discussion by stating:

> Most piteous of all is it when, in such times of trial, the victims are persons of noble character; whenever they are so, our pity is especially excited, because their innocence, as well as the setting of their misfortunes before our eyes, makes their misfortunes seem close to ourselves.[26]

This is one of the passages that arguably is behind the repeated references to the *Rhetoric* when Aristotle's *Poetics* attempts to explain the nature of tragic pleasure. It is also possible to sense, in the early going, that same partiality to those near and dear (in class, birth, age, character) that has received strenuous criticism from the Kantian universalist position. But who can deny that there is something much more important, even transformational, going on as well? If one lingers over this passage long enough, what emerges is a principle of *translation* among emotions. Fear for ourselves, when the matter in question does not happen to us—but rather others somehow close to us—is not fear at all but pity. While the aforementioned connection of *catharsis* is undeniable, there are also fascinating implications for the cultivation of "civic friendship," belonging, and care that are required for a richly textured community life.[26*] For it is rhetoric that seems to remove us from the immediacy of familiar appearance so that we might formulate conditions for appreciating the needs of others. This same discussion of pity strongly implies that the cultivation of affiliative "goods" might reverse itself as well.[27] To the extent we see others as radically *unlike* ourselves, as distant in appearance, time, and place, our "pity" will recede. So, too, our ability to judge prudently the intersection of their and our interest will narrow accordingly. What may be cultivated may also, in the world of rhetorical practice, be made to disappear. Not quite a virtue, not exactly an individuated passion, pity becomes—through rhetoric—a form of proof.

---

[*]Editor's note: The footnote no. 26 appears twice in the original.

Pivotal to Aristotle's understanding of rhetoric, then, is its peculiar inculcation of cognition, ethos, and emotion in the decisions and acts of collectivities. The norms and conventions for a culture thus find themselves employed as premises of recognition and also inference. The norms of social knowledge that apply to membership groups are the selfsame norms of enthymemes. As these expand or contract, they directly affect the lived reality of culture, including its extensiveness. So perhaps I can sum up this liberal textual reading by suggesting that rhetoric in the classical sense provides an important inventional capacity for the conventions, emotions, and cognitions necessary for us to affiliate in a community of civic life.

We are also on the verge of filling in an understanding of the first claim introduced earlier, that rhetoric, in its classical Aristotelian sense, is a "higher-order" practice. By this, I do not mean that rhetoric is an *elite* or fine art in some hierarchy of practices, but rather that rhetoric, in its most fully elaborated sense, helps to uncover instances of its practice in a great many of our unexamined activities; the discourse surrounding rituals of civic life: art, sports, entertainment; the more mundane practices of collecting and recollecting: diaries, scrapbooks, autobiographies, and memoirs. Each of these activities, while constituted by its own norms and conventions, may be seen to share in qualities that are undeniably rhetorical. This is because, in Allen Gross's felicitous phrase, rhetoric is not so much *something*, as *about* something.[28] And it is in this recognizably Aristotelian sense that we might think of rhetoric as a *higher-order* practice.

The more difficult question, though, is whether this practice admits any real-life practitioners. As has happened many times in the checkered history of this "art," defenders of rhetoric's "nobility" always run the risk of purifying their defendant of any meaningful content. I wish to suggest, however, that a broader picture of rhetoric as a *serial practice* or plurality of activities may help us to avoid this danger. Rhetoric is held in the lowest regard when it is identified solely with the product domain: sham enthymemes, slippery slogans, feel-good sound-bites. It is not until we think of the two-sided argument, the running controversy, the ritual that becomes a crisis: in other words, not until we admit the liminal elements of struggle, difference, and thus reflective judgment that rhetoric itself is redeemed.

REREADING RHETORICAL CULTURE

Rhetorical Practice

This enlarged picture of rhetorical practice should offer a way of developing the second part of my claim: to show that, even in a less than 'eloquent' age, participation within rhetorical practice might cultivate recognizable relational goods. Building from the vocabulary of Aristotle's *Rhetoric*, I now outline a way of looking at contemporary rhetorical occasions, so that we might observe some features of a rhetorical practice at work. As a kind of bedrock assumption for recovering the Aristotelian tradition, we need to concede that not every sense of "culture" is equally compatible with the aims of such a project as this. Prefigured as early as the tension between *Nomos* and *Physis*, there has been a temptation to regard "culture" as *either* an entirely arbitrary assortment of symbols, conventions, and affiliations *or* as a repository of unquestioned truth as real as nature (*Physis*) itself. Each set of assumptions can lead to a kind of paralysis where rhetoric is concerned. The arbitrary assortment view can lead to vicious relativism, a less-than-benign variation on Callicles' dilemma. And the "reality" centered view reinforces either the "pre-Modern" foreclosure of alternatives or the "late Modern" sense that culture is a *second* nature, entirely analogous to the determinism of physical reality.[29]

Without suggesting that any of the above approaches are wrong, I want only to observe that they obscure our appreciation for rhetorical occasions. If all assortments are relative, it would be difficult to imagine any particular configuration which might call for an "appropriate" response. And if our responses are already *over*-determined, then it is difficult to see why anyone would care much about what the nature of any particular response happens to be.

Over and against the above renderings, I want to suggest an understanding of culture as "cultivation," a durable symbolic home with valued traditions and ways of acting. From this standpoint, it becomes possible to appreciate striking differences among cultures, while appreciating that, as Michael Walzer has put it, "where one is is already a place of some value."[30] This more organic vision of culture also seems compatible with modern comprehension of rhetorical practice. For more than simply determining our prevailing patterns of response, contemporary life exposes us to a range of *propriety* where possible rhetorical audiences are concerned, to variable and disputable conceptions of social problems, definitions of the public good, even norms for the attribution of responsibility and judgment. To sense the availability of these radically different means of persuasion is to restore an important dimension of indeterminacy to public "learning."[31] Behavior may be determined, but the agency of human engagement and choice is *occasioned*.

When one is immersed within a cultural "lifeworld," whether it be that of an urban East coast streetperson or that of a Japanese peasant, the rhetorical characteristics of ongoing cultural activities are likely to go unnoticed. This does not mean that they are absent or unimportant, but only that our practices themselves are taken for granted in a way that withholds our sense of their partisanship. What Gibbard has called a community of "isolation" persists to the extent that the activities of other communities have no impact upon us, even though these activities are very different from our own.[32] We are drawn into a more public awareness of rhetoric, when the different activities of others must have an impact upon our needs, priorities, and practices.

Rhetoric, in its venerable sense of an art *form*, emerges when we have recognized features of our activities as directional choices from among an array of options. With each of these cultural prototypes, rhetorical practice does afford a measure of reflection, at least to the extent that the "other" must be acknowledged as a witness to what *we*, as a collective membership group, must do. This means that rhetorical *phronesis* cannot be enacted without at least a partial intuition of what the "appropriate" *is* in each historically specific setting. And so even the most powerful imposition of rhetorical advocacy must have a reciprocal interest in the justification of its own conduct. We might even go so far as to say that public "power" is proportional to this interest.[33] Modern rhetorical *practice* is thus the performance and enactment of our sense of the appropriate with responsive interested *others*. For lack of a better term, let us call these contemporary constituencies of address *audiences*.

Rhetorical Form

Yet the very changes we have addressed in contemporary public cultures require that we employ our rhetorical vocabulary in a more expansive way. For one thing, the notion of rhetorical *form* needs to be broadened to include more than simple emergent "products" of reasoning. Like our comprehension of rhetorical tradition itself, form needs to be extended to include the whole practice of public rhetorical thinking in disputational contexts: what we might think of as *rhetorical cognition*. Our prototype for this process of inference remains the enthymeme: that abbreviated convergence of *doxa* and public conviction with the particularities of circumstance and issue. But our more expansive understanding requires that we reintroduce two characteristics of enthymematic thinking that are vital to modern rhetorical practice. First is the uncertain *referentiality* of enthymematic premises themselves. While most cultures will profess to a conception of what is good or just, honorable or honest, the individuated meanings of any such conception are entirely dependent upon the lifeworld or received traditions of the membership groups themselves. However, this need not be cause for despair. The primary function of enthymematic thinking is to bring a general value horizon together with an individuated audience understanding and a problem or object of contention. Like the practice which gives them form, then, enthymemes express an internal direction (to a membership group) and an external direction (to a larger interested constituency) at the same time. As noted earlier, social knowledge premises creatively affect the lived reality of culture, including its extensiveness. Enthymemes are, in short, *inventional*.

Second, the audience dependence of enthymematic reasoning, even in its traditional construal, gives the form a hybrid, synthetic quality of eclecticism and plurality. Here analysis is refigured by differing senses of the public good, the culturally appropriate, even the venues for proper discussion. As an enactment of *phronesis* for the modern community, then, rhetorical cognition is best seen (in a kind of gloss on Arendt) as a quest for *meaning*, rather than truth.[34] To be more specific, the aim of rhetorical judgment is to particularize meaning by instantiating and refiguring possible categories and criteria through the world of action. It would seem, then, that a sense of rhetorical thinking might inform possible meanings of interested *others*, even as judgment must limit this meaning within a range of actual truths to what real membership groups *do*. From such a deliberately enlarged lens of vision, then, rhetorical cognition is essentially *figurative, informal, and directional reasoning that acquires force through the implied consensus of others*. It is figurative in the same sense that metaphorical and tropical discourses are figurative; in other words, through reliance upon a kind of slippage among literal sense and reference so as to capture—through indirection—some aspect of meaning that eludes exact definition. For instance, former American President Reagan frequently characterized the Contra insurgents in Nicaragua as "freedom-fighters,"[35] and even, "the moral equivalent of the Founding Fathers." Such a turn of phrase forces an inferential choice. Either the Founding Fathers were drug-dealing thugs, or the Contras must have some greater civic virtue than we thought. Rhetorical cognition is informal, for the obvious reason that analytic purity of distribution is here subordinated to the traditional aim of effective collaboration. And it is directional because, as we shall see, there are critical normative implications of rhetorical cognition for accepting authority, engaging issues, and even enriching our domain of responsibility.

The most critical point, however, is that all such convergences of generalizable normative convictions, specific circumstances, and identifiable audiences are likely to be *provisional*. Even in the world of antiquity, there could have been no such thing as an enthymeme that encompassed every aspect of a cultural setting. This is true both by virtue of the *phainomenai* which constitute rhetorical inference *and* by the elliptical quality of enthymematic form. An awareness of this in practice is rhetorical cognition in its revelatory mode, captured by the traction of unfinished rhetorical episodes. This more expansive sense of rhetorical cognition also helps to explain why rhetoric does not need to achieve the rarified horizon of eloquence in order to redeem itself as an art practice. When we achieve that rarity, a monolithic consensus, even the least cynical among us will expect that a healthy portion of "productive ambiguity" has been at work in our discourse. And when we, much more frequently, find ourselves at odds over the causes of strife, the conduct of others, the avenues of *proper* recourse, something every bit as important is occurring. The very episodes we are unfolding are urging an encounter with other partisanships and thus a potential moment of reflection. Viewed this way, it simply misses the point to demean rhetoric as distorted or deformed discourse. For what else is an art practice, but the recognition of how rarely we realize perfection, of how much we must yet master to improve and advance our craft? This is, of course, a rhetorical question.

Rhetorical Community

The practical ideal of *phronesis* or practical wisdom has always involved an uneasy tension among form, content, and context. Ironically enough, those visions of rhetoric which paid least attention to the immediacy of circumstance ("the adjustment of ideas to people and people to ideas")[36] were usually forced to invoke the most utopian contexts to defend their craft. The distance from Socrates' "colloquium" to Aristotle's *polis* to the universal audiences of ideal speech situations may be shorter than we think.

Once more, we can identify two confounding polar approaches to the problem of context. The first option has been to insist upon an idealized "form of life" teleology, or mythic foundation as a precondition for a revitalized practice. The less obvious problem with this option is that we have no way of explaining how such hyper-realities are ever engendered, other than in the rarified horizons of myth and legend. The other option is to suggest that significant literary or rhetorical texts establish their own constitutive conditions for a community in miniature between reader and implied author. But this more optimistic approach shades over the pivotal question of how texts are selected and reflectively engaged in the first place.

Once more, I would like to explore the "excluded middle" by looking to contemporary *places*, where the normative "content" and convictions of membership groups may be identified and expressed. Our century has witnessed the emergence of a broader range of encounter settings where the ensemble of convictions, affiliations, and traditions we know as culture is introduced to a widening circle of acquaintance. These settings may be formal, informal, even conjectural and socially emergent. They are given urgency and impetus by rhetorical occasions; and within such occasions they sometimes constitute and acquire form through the critical controversies of our time. I refer to such places as instances of the local, civic, or global rhetorical *forum*.

As suggested in the work of Toulmin, Rieke, and Janik, a rhetorical "forum" is a more or less formal location, where types of reasoning and argument are practiced.[37] While the beginning made by these authors is most helpful, the very breadth of their conception makes it difficult to identify the institutional constraint of the forum within the operation of real rhetorical practice. Without unduly narrowing the idea of "forum," it may be useful to speculate further about its operation, so as to appreciate better its importance for contemporary *rhetorical* practice.

A rhetorical forum is any encounter setting sufficiently durable to serve as a recurring "gathering place" for discourse. As such, the forum provides a space for multiple expressed positions to encounter one another. And, in its most developed condition, the forum may also provide precedents and modalities for granting a hearing to positions, as well as sorting among their agendas and constituencies. This is a way of saying that a rhetorical forum provides a potential normative horizon, an avenue of mediation among discourses that might otherwise be self-confirming, incommensurable or perhaps not even heard at all.

The clearest historical antecedent for the rhetorical forum is probably found in the sense of public space which emerges in some idealist renderings of the Athenian *polis*. Here, for instance, is that Idealist Aristotelian, Hannah Arendt:

> The polis, properly speaking, is not the city-state in its physical location; it is the organization of the people as it arises out of acting and speaking together, and its true space lies between people living together no matter where they happen to be. "Wherever you go, you will be a polis": these famous words became not merely the watchword of Greek colonization, they expressed the conviction that action and speech can create a space between the participants which can find its proper location almost any time and anywhere. It is the space of appearance in the widest sense of the word, namely the space where I appear to others as others appear to me, where men [*sic*] exist not merely like other living or inanimate things but make their appearance explicitly.[38]

These words from Arendt might provide us with a helpful, albeit somewhat misleading, basis of our own understanding. Along the helpful side, Arendt reminds us that the fact of interpersonal affiliation and individuation is prior to any of its institutional embodiments. This is another way of saying that a sense of forum emerges whenever there is the potential for resistance, the third-party standpoint which might emerge at any time in any ongoing conversation. This sense of potential is critical. It is one reason why, in principle, the idea of a forum may never irreversibly be banished.

A second implication of Arendt's words is the emergence of appearances, in all of their plurality, within the web of interrelationships established through the presencing of others. It is the rhetorical forum which allows the plurality of appearances to be presented, witnessed and regarded, qualified and subverted by the perspectives of others. Yet, for all of this, I think Arendt's treatment tends to mystify and idealize the genuine presence of real live others in her rather primordial conception of classical political life. She thus lends undue weight to her own agenda of "dark times": that long-distance democracy and liberationist social movements are merely the further conformism of mass society in disguise.[39] More important, I think, than the actual physical presence of persons in each other's public space is the *conscious awareness* of each other's presence in the symbolic landscape of prospective thought and decision: the fact that other persons and constituencies make a difference and thus must be "taken into account" in our deliberations.

What is critical to the power and constraint of the forum is that two very different sorts of loci may always intersect there: first, is the cumulative weight of customary practice: convention, commonplace and *communis sensus* associated with the forum's own history; and second, the inevitably uncertain fact of otherness—not only that a sense of constituency has been made available. In principle, this is possible within any real public encounter setting. Much more important than a specific location in geographic space is that a forum have some durability and continuity over time. It needs to be accessible to those who wish to participate, recurrently so. And it needs the capacity for the projection and retrieval of messages. This creates a sense of *reflective* participation: an unavoidable supposition that one's own constituency may be tested by the interests of others who are involved, even if they are unrepresented directly by advocacy. Viewed together, these two intersecting loci provide the tension between strict adaptation and genuine invention. This may be only another way of saying that propriety is always possessed of both an ethical and an aesthetic dimension.

We are now beginning to approach the question of how a forum interacts with rhetorical practice. The answer, which is difficult to generalize, very much depends upon how developed and historically stabilized the forum is, the breadth of its compass or scope of coverage, the genres or types of rhetorical practice involved, and the nature of the rhetorical occasion. The core of a forum may be a kind of disturbance, an issue or contested perspective. It may also be an unfolding event or an emerging public affiliation that demands a name, a language, a form of address. For instance, a live rhetorical controversy among opposition leaders to apartheid will admit to very different frames and thematic constraints upon the rhetorical practice than will—let us say—a state funeral for a fallen leader, or—for that matter—a peace conference among previously hostile groups. But however we conceptualize the meeting point of these intersecting forces, there is within the rhetorical forum a dual sense of constraint and opportunity. In the forum of institutional stability and extended duration, there is usually an accessible, or at least translatable, body of traditions, codified in charters, and made practicable by available rules, roles, and procedures. And in more volatile settings and occasions, a forum may work as a kind of "pocket" of disturbance, an "eye of the storm," or core of tension around which other disparate positions and arguments may hover. In a rough analogy to the "pocket" of modern jazz, in which wide-ranging, virtually random dissonance may and usually does begin to collect and gather itself around a central rhythmic "core," there is in every such forum a *focus* made recognizable by the emergent familiarity of departure and return. Stable or not, the critical function of the forum is to warrant, frame, and constrain the appearance, shape, and direction of rhetorical practice.

This preliminary sketch has been an attempt to show that the rhetorical forum is, like many a "social imaginary,"[40] real in its power and implication. At the point of its greatest impact, it inscribes a set of conditions for rhetoric itself to flourish. Yet, it inevitably raises certain issues itself. How are tensions among forum and practical choice to be addressed and explained? And in occasions of disturbance and controversy, how are we to find, identify, and appraise the intersecting performances of practice and forum? If we are to appreciate fully the importance of the contemporary rhetorical forum for the development of discourse practice, we need to merge our traditional senses of rhetorical *phronesis* and rhetorical cognition within this larger picture. The issues and questions we have raised may then be viewed from perspectives that are internal and external to the occasion at hand.

In what we understand as its "normalized" condition, the rhetorical forum provides loose but recognizable admission criteria as to who may speak, what may be spoken about, and how we might be held accountable for what we say and do. In a very general sense, each of these sets of constraints may be subsumed under the large category of the *appropriate*, perhaps the closest congruence we have between emancipatory reason and *phronesis*. However, a rhetorical sense of the appropriate would identify norms that are more specific than universal validity claims. In the world of *phainomenai* where rhetoric must dwell, norms for speakers, messages, and constituencies are evoked which are provisional and situation-specific. We might think of these in the following ways:

Type	Locus	Value
1. speaker-centered norm	*ethos* or perspective	norm of authority
2. message-centered norm	*stasis* or issue	norm of integrity
3. constituency-centered	*krisis* or judgment	norm of conscience[41]

As stated above, a normalized forum (say, an awards ceremony or a court of law) will admit to fairly specific constraints along all three of these continua. And yet even in these cases, there is a further characteristic worth noting about a rhetorical sense of the appropriate. Instead of presupposing the appropriate as an *a priori* validity claim in advance of speech, *rhetorical practice enacts the norms of propriety collaboratively with interested collective others*. In the rhetorical forum, rhetoric is both the animated and the animator. This is because the very conditions of propriety are continually being reindividuated and renewed with every specific case. And it is also because particularly challenging disputes about what constitutes proper authority, integrity, and responsibility can have the effect of enriching, refraining, and perhaps reinventing the boundaries of rhetorical community itself. As White has suggested of cultural languages generally, this process of change and renewals is not always conspicuous, but it is surely ongoing.[42]

Authority may be considered as a variation of *ethos*, a grounded entitlement to offer a perspective on appearances based upon some claim to a constituency.[43] Even in well-structured forum contexts, the inscription of authority may be opened to propriety dispute. When newly enshrined rhetorical hero Václav Havel visited Kurt Waldheim in Austria, he was quickly denounced for having lent legitimacy to Waldheim's questionable past.[44] Havel's supporters replied by observing that Havel had visited Austria to attend the Salzburg Festival, and not to see Waldheim. His conduct, in other words, could be redeemed by a different understanding of its forum and propriety context. But once the issue is raised, this is not necessarily the end of the matter. Here, for instance, was Havel himself at Salzburg after Waldheim had introduced him:

> A person who is afraid of what is yet to come is generally also reluctant to look in the face of what has been. And a person afraid to look at his own past must fear what is to come . . . Those who falsify history do not protect the freedom of the nation but rather constitute a threat to it. The idea that a person can rewrite his autobiography is one of the traditional self-deceptions of Central Europe. Trying to do that means hurting oneself and one's fellow countrymen. When a truth is not given complete freedom, freedom is not complete.[45]

And perhaps that is why this matter of perspective is unlikely to be so easily resolved, for it is difficult to imagine eloquent and confrontational lines such as these delivered at a purely *aesthetic* occasion.

While some concerns about authority lend themselves to provisional resolution through a more proper positioning within a forum, other cases are not nearly so tidy. When the Reagan administration chose to honor German war dead at Bitburg, for instance, many questioned whether even the President of the United States possessed the breadth of perspective to authorize a redefinition for a twentieth-century marker event.[46] Yet it could be claimed that the debate about this issue was actually a positive development, rekindling an encounter with dark memory as our turbulent century draws to a close.

Integrity, as I am using the term, deals with the way issues and positions fall out and "hold up" over the course of an ongoing episode.[47] In a rhetorical sense, integrity is less an attribute specifically applicable to persons and their characters than it is an emergent, acquired trait of messages that are presented and upheld in public life. The normalized rhetorical forum's persistence in time, its durability, provides a place stable enough for the normative expectation of integrity to emerge. A forum allows the articulation of positions to "hold still" long enough to elicit some sense of *answerability*.[48] It is the openness of a rhetorical forum that brings our positions from a stance of foreclosure to a sense of *exposure*. If one's positions and messages have integrity, they will either withstand public scrutiny, or they will react, respond, and correct themselves in light of opposed positions and messages. Lacking integrity, as a great many political messages do, they will run and hide, grin and spin. There is a sense in which all serious political disputation is about integrity; for this is what allows the very *fact* of dispute to acquire meaning. For this reason, integrity may be seen as the opposite of *hypocrisy*.[49] When Senator Nancy Kassebaum voted against John Tower's confirmation as Secretary of Defense (the only Republican to do so), it was not her motives, but her statement—on the importance of women's issues—that enacted this public sense of integrity;[50] it was an issue that every other Republican Senator in the Senate chose to overlook in the interests of Party loyalty.

While not every personality or type of character easily admits to the possibility of integrity, the *norm* of integrity only becomes available to us through the unfolding of an episodic *process*. When, after nearly ten years, the Sandinistas were not overthrown, but peacefully voted out of office, it proved to be the vindication of something called the Contadora Process, rather than America's covert foreign policy. How that happened is interesting. A number of Central American States—led by President Arias of Costa Rica—began the Contadora process in an attempt to find a peaceful Central American solution to the war in Nicaragua. From the beginning, the United States covertly opposed the process, even attempting to subvert and overturn it[51] at the same time as the United States officially recognized the Sandinista government *and* Congress had expressed itself as in favor of the process.[52] Despite increasingly devious American subterfuge, the process went forward, with Arias himself receiving the Nobel Peace Prize in 1988. Although almost no American newspapers mentioned the matter, I would argue that the integrity of this *public* process accomplished something a twenty-four billion dollar covert war was unable to accomplish: a peaceful transfer of power: It is, in other words, the principle of publicity and exposure that makes integrity a possibility in public life. Once a forum has been acknowledged, it becomes very difficult to ignore.

Responsibility, as conceptualized here, involves the internalization of the voice of others as an encounter with conscience. Here "conscience" may be thought of meta-phorically as the state of acting as an audience and witness for what one is and does.[53] Now the propriety of such an encounter may itself be challenged. The paths and implications of action are continuous, irreversible, and ever completely foreordained. It is a curiosity of the moral claim's generality that almost any decision or act can be charged with ramifications in this area. At the same time, almost everyone would concede that not all choices and concerns are of moral significance. And for those courses of conduct which raise moral issues, there is no easy way to delimit or finalize a proper tribune of judgment.

So this third range of concerns for the practice, forms, and fora of rhetoric is a complex, and even treacherous, territory to chart. It is often the case that our intuitions direct us further than our arguments. Accordingly, I want to borrow liberally from the work of James Boyd White and suggest that the clash of moral stance need not be an end of discussion, but an inventional challenge to continuity of discourse.[54] While it is true that audiences are usually more comfortable judging their adversaries than themselves, this does not mean that reflection and rhetoric are always at odds with one another. At times, as in Lincoln's Second Inaugural, words are found to uncover themes larger than any partisan position. And even in more recent episodes, we may and do agonize over the propriety of our positions, their distance from our deeds, the boundaries for judgment and responsibility in our life and time. Occasionally, as if by a resigned process of elimination, we are reminded that our adversary is ourselves.

To illustrate some of the complexity confronting rhetorical practice as it engages the problem of conscience, we might consider two fascinating modern cases, where the practice of rhetoric occasioned a kind of moral provocation, albeit with very different results. On New Years Day 1990, Czech playwright and dissident Václav Havel spoke as newly-elected President of his nation to a multitude of jubilant citizens.[55] Refusing to evade responsibility for decades of post-war tyranny, Havel confronted his audience directly: "If I speak about a spoiled moral atmosphere I don't refer only to our masters . . . I'm speaking about all of us. For all of us have grown used to the totalitarian system and accepted it as an immutable fact, and thereby actually helped keep it going. None of us are only its victims; we are all also responsible for it."[56] Havel's speech marked and captioned a luminous moment of public recognition; his speech has been widely acclaimed as a touchstone of eloquence.

Now consider a rather striking contrast. About two years prior to Havel's triumph, another European, Phillip Jenninger, the speaker of the West German Parliament, chose to speak publicly about the Nazi extermination policies, on the fiftieth anniversary of Krystallnacht, the date marking the burning of the Reichstag and the intensification of the anti-Jewish pogroms.[57] All evidence indicates that Jenninger's rhetorical aim was a noble one: to remind one and all the depth and gravity of the German historical offense. But the speech apparently so shocked those assembled—diplomats, Greens, Social Democrats, Jewish survivors, Free Democrats—that many walked out.[58] Others tried to shout down passages of the speech. Reaction was so uniformly negative within Germany that Jenninger himself was forced to resign early the next morning. And so we have the spectacle of two distinguished national leaders, each confronting fellow citizens with evidence of willful complicity in past sins. Both are, in other words, well-intentioned attempts to articulate a sense of public responsibility. One speech is acclaimed as a masterpiece of rhetorical eloquence, while the other occasions the disgrace and embarrassment of public exile. Why? An attempt to sketch a less-than-conclusive answer to this question might still shed some light upon the mystery of conscience in the rhetorical forum.

Clearly, one can point to qualitative differences in the craft of the rhetorical agents. Havel's speech beautifully subverts the magisterial style of party encomium by speaking the sad truths hidden by decades of hyperbole.[59] It uses the mechanistic metaphor of determinism to explain the "inevitability" of his predecessor party's collapse. And in its most memorable lines: "How is it possible that so many people immediately understood what to do and that none of them needed any advice or instructions?"[60] it refigures the peaceful revolution itself as a kind of metonymy for the rebirth of the public sphere. Undeniably, then, it is an eloquent speech, if by eloquence we mean rhetoric where *a larger vision is wedded clearly to both the critical judgment and the ordinary convictions of others, all at the same time*. By any such aesthetic standard, the Jenninger speech was a disaster. In the Western press, which printed only small excerpts from the speech, the initial sense was that Jenninger had somehow conveyed the impression that he endorsed the taboo National Socialist sentiments, that he had himself given expression to anti-Semitism.[61] Later interpretations corrected this false impression, but nonetheless concluded that Jenninger had been guilty of a monumental impropriety. As the *New York Times* summed things up, "The consensus among politicians, newspapers and many Germans today was that Mr. Jenninger had seriously erred in the style and timing of his presentation."[62] Even as read in translation, problems in the technical principles of rhetoric abound. Jenninger tried to be contrite and confrontational at the same time, and all within a kind of blurred epic genre. And even as he brought his audience face-to-face with the horrors of the camps and gas chambers, he tried to establish German complicity through the astonishing choice of an ironic tone.[63] There are, in other words, a myriad of purely technical reasons why the speech had to fail.

For all the differences in craft, however, there are also critical contrasts in the way each discourse engages the difficult relationships among responsibility, conscience, and history. Havel presents the evils of the recent past from a stance of great symbolic and historical distance. He repeatedly refers to his nation's "great creative and spiritual potential,"[64] as having been squandered. His people have had "to learn not to believe in anything," as if this cuts against our very nature.[65] By framing post-war tyranny as one monstrous aberration, he is able to remain partially removed from the evil. The revolution can be regarded as a moment of return to a healthier *and a more permanent public condition*. Jenninger, on the other hand, is completely subject to an irreversible fallen condition created and foreordained by the Holocaust. He quotes Nietzsche and Dostoevsky on a world without God, the inevitability and invincibility of evil.[66] In implicating everyone in every respect, he leaves no compensatory room for reflective distance. This is a speech without hope.

Finally, it must be said that weight of events themselves has exacted a different sort of toll on each of these speeches. Havel is, after all, speaking in a moment of recovery. The injuries, while staggering and permanent, may still be placed in a kind of perspective. This is why his treatment of conscience and responsibility may offer an opportunity to recognize our complicity, and thus recover—through our own acknowledgment's redemptive moment—the power to forgive and thus to reinvent ourselves. In Jenninger's case, the speech could not have been adequate to the unfathomable magnitude of the event. Perhaps no speech could. When Jenninger concluded that we are all, even the children, stained by the sins of the forefathers, he had lost the only conceivable redemptive possibility available to him. And so this failed discourse became part of a national trauma of compulsive repetition. It could do little more and nothing less.

But now, a more radical suggestion. Even though Jenninger's speech must be marked as a monumental failure in conventional terms, it also managed to place the very issue of Holocaust war guilt within a larger horizon of late twentieth century constituencies and concerns. It is one of the first in what is likely to be an increasing series of forensic perorations for our millennium. If these speeches are to be honest and truthful, they can not help but be uncomfortable as well. In holding his admittedly confused, out-of-focus mirror up to a clouded taboo subject, Jenninger threw a harsh public light on painful memories. And it is interesting that as the boundaries of his controversial forum of constituency broadened, so did the civic friendship of sympathy appear to deepen. In tens of thousands of letters Jenninger has received from all over the world, he says that all but forty or fifty were supportive of his intent.[67] And so, true to his spirit of atonement, Jenninger now feels that "my sacrifice in resigning from office was very much worthwhile."[68] That, of course, is not the point. It is that this dispute itself may have worked inventionally, to move us beyond pragmatics, and even personal ethics: to prompt us to reconfigure the generational bounds of moral responsibility, to place us in the uncertain horizon of a community of conscience.

Among the many examples I have alluded to throughout this essay, the case of Jenninger is the only one in which the advocate of a contested position abides by judgment in its more traditional form, as if to concede error and conform to an authoritative public verdict. And as we have just seen, even this was not the end of the matter. Even in cases where disputation seems to have been "resolved," what happens is more fittingly encompassed by Burke's "barnyard scramble" metaphor. The arguments of the opposition begin to spread, even as the norms upon which they rest are clarified. Meanwhile the arguments on one's own behalf begin to splinter, falling victim to self-contradiction, and a gradual loss of ethos, and plausibility. In the last echo of this multi-cultural *reductio*, there is usually the shrill remonstrance of faith and good intentions, and then silence. Yet in many more cases than this, and often the most interesting cases, dispute really does not resolve itself. Like the continual reinvention of rhetorical culture, it is ongoing.

ARGUMENTS AND IMPLICATIONS

Earlier in this essay, I raised some issues about rhetorical practice that now should be addressed, along with some implications for more detailed research. Rhetoric has often been dismissed as a form of distorted communication, and one might well draw the conclusion that its most visible function throughout the body of my examples has been to confirm this impression. Beyond this difficulty is the problem of how to ground claims for a rhetoric that would move *beyond* distortion; i.e., express a reflective capacity.

These questions can at least be approached usefully through a broadened contemporary understanding of the rhetorical tradition. We have begun this task by refiguring the notions of *practice*, rhetorical *cognition*, and the concept of the rhetorical *forum*. Part of the mastery of rhetoric as theory consists in gaining an appreciation of the possible range of variation for subject matters of civic and public interest. But if this is all we did, the mission of rhetoric would be virtually indistinguishable from the radically reductive playground of much post-Modernism. And so rhetoric, at least as I understand it, must take another reflective turn: to ask what proofs and possible modes of conviction might best adjudicate conflicts among partisan positions in a world lacking full dialectical closure for practical questions. Put another way, rhetoric does not see the sudden discovery of radical variation (which the tradition has known since the younger Cicero) as proof that "the end is near," but rather as evidence that its own constructive possibilities are far from over.

There is a specific application of this line of thought to the first reservation. Within the enlarged vantage point of rhetorical occasions, the values and norms of any single culture take on a partisan cast. So, of course, does the discourse that must articulate these values. But such a discursive *process* can only be regarded as distorted in a morally deficient manner if it removes itself from any prospect for correcting and broadening the sentiments expressed. By extending our appreciation for the practical activity of rhetoric beyond the singularity of speech acts and univocal claims, it becomes possible to locate a redemptive impetus within the larger unfolding frame of its process. We might thus think of rhetoric as constantly reminding us to make room for error and comedy, for the performance of momentary pleasure: little building blocks of possibility, provisional criteria for the small victories of practical reason.

As in the world of aesthetics generally, we are reminded frequently of the inadequacy of "mere" words to capture the beauty, or perhaps the radical opposite, in a human work. Works such as Alan Resnais' *Night and Fog*, Picasso's *Guernica*, the "No Trespassing" sign from *Citizen Kane* all come to mind. It is not paradoxical, or at least it *should* not be, that these eloquent silences actually have the effect of rejuvenating discourse. Far from devaluing words and works, such willfully failed approximations may enrich and deepen our language of mood, sentiment, and expression. A language of value which is only employed technically will surely reify values. But a language of value which is *never* employed in practical settings will just as surely atrophy. Rhetoric, as I have tried to express it here, is more than the practice; it is the entire process of forming, expressing, and judging public thought in real life.

As a concluding reflection, I would suggest that a broadened vision of rhetorical practice will make little difference if we fail to extend our horizon of appreciation for the rhetorical practitioner as well. In particular, this enhanced understanding needs to include the condition of being a rhetorical audience. This is a condition in which we are called to exert our own critical capacities to a maximum extent.[69] We have to decide—quite literally—what sort of public persons we wish to be. We might be told, for instance, that because of things done in our name, in the past, there is more for us to do now. And we may also be told, and even need to hear, that there are larger affiliative responsibilities that override these past claims on our conviction and commitment. Rhetorical audiences are not known for overarching vision and long memories. Much of the time, they must feel their way through the thicket of contention and conflict. But whatever the durability of our public feelings, they only become possible when rhetoric itself is felt and heard. To make some of the conditions for such a hearing available and perhaps even contagious has been the aim of this study, and, I am tempted to say, the larger aim of rhetorical studies generally.

Notes

1. Alasdair MacIntyre, *After Virtue: A Study in Moral Theory* (South Bend, IN: University of Notre Dame Press, 1981), pp. 175–180. MacIntyre has elaborated upon this notion in his more recent work, *Whose Justice? Which Rationality?* (South Bend, IN: University of Notre Dame Press, 1988), pp. 124–145.

2. D. S. Hutchinson, *The Virtues of Aristotle* (London: Routledge & Kegan Paul, 1986), pp. 35–87.

3. For the "dark times" hypothesis, see MacIntyre, *After Virtue*, pp. 1–23. Also see Hannah Arendt, *The Human Condition* (Chicago:University of Chicago Press, 1958), pp. 248–325; and Max Horkheimer, *Critique of Instrumental Reason* (New York: Seabury Press, 1974). An interesting communicative variation of the critique may be found in Martin Allor, "Relocating the Site of the Audience," *Critical Studies in Mass Communication* 5 (1988): 217–234. For a helpful analysis and criticism of this hypothesis, see Patrick Brantlinger, *Bread and Circuses: Theories of Mass Culture as Social Decay* (Ithaca, NY: Cornell University Press, 1983).

4. A useful introduction to the Marxist notion of *praxis* is offered by Richard Bernstein, in *Praxis and Action: Contemporary Philosophies of Human Activity* (Philadelphia: University of Pennsylvania Press, 1971), pp. 11–83. See also Henri Lefebvre, *The Sociology of Marx*, trans. Norbert Gutterman (New York: Pantheon Books, 1968), pp. 25–58.

5. A most ingenious attempt to grapple with this dilemma may be found in Raymond Williams, *Marxism and Literature* (Oxford: Oxford University Press, 1977), pp. 108–120.

6. Anthony Giddens, *A Contemporary Critique of Historical Materialism: Vol. 1, Power, Property, and the State* (Berkeley and Los Angeles: University of California Press, 1981), p. 30.

7. The examples here, on either end of the political spectrum, are too numerous to mention. But one of the most poignant cases of premature "correctness" and subsequent victimage has to be that of Georg Lukács. Late in life, Lukács was still wrestling with the ethics of an overdetermined *praxis* from nearly fifty years earlier. See Georg Lukács, Hans Heinz Holz, Leo Kofler, and Wolfgang Abendroth, *Conversations with Lukács*, ed. Theo Pinkus (Cambridge, MA: MIT Press, 1975), pp. 106–109.

8. Despite a wealth of classical commentary, recent treatments of rhetorical tradition and its development have given only passing attention to Aristotle's *Rhetoric*. See, for instance, Brian Vickers, *In Defence of Rhetoric* (Oxford: Clarendon Press, 1988), pp. 18–27. Also, see Thomas M. Conley, *Rhetoric in the European Tradition* (New York: Longman, 1990), pp. 13–28. It is not my intention to indict either of these fine works; I simply note the diminished attention paid to the classical tradition's most completely realized *theory* of rhetoric.

9. Thomas Farrell, "Inventing Rhetorical Culture: Some Notes on Theory and Practice," *Rhetoric Society Quarterly* (in press).

10. Aristotle, *Eudemian Ethics, Books I, II, and III*, trans. Michael Woods (Oxford: Clarendon Press, 1982), 1216b.5–25, 6–7.

11. Aristotle, *Rhetoric*, trans. W. Rhys Roberts (New York: Modern Library, 1958), 1.1355b. This is Aristotle's famous defense of *Rhetoric* as essential to that which is distinctive about "man": *logos*. See also Larry Arnhart, *Aristotle on Political Reasoning: A Commentary on the Rhetoric* (DeKalb: Northern Illinois University Press, 1981), pp. 17–51.

12. This critique of rhetoric, a recognizable variation of its Kantian and even Platonic origins, is found in German critical theory. See, for instance, Jürgen Habermas, *The Theory of Communicative Action, Vol. 1: Reason and the Rationalization of Society*, trans. Thomas McCarthy (Boston: Beacon Press, 1984), pp. 286–291. Habermas's own position is a complex one, and there is reason to believe it is shifting, where the normative properties of rhetoric are concerned.

13. MacIntyre, *After Virtue*, pp. 186–189.

14. On this matter, see also Farrell, "The Tradition of Rhetoric and the Philosophy of Communication," *Communication* (1983): 151–180.

15. See Aristotle, *Rhetoric*, 2.1381a; also see Nancy Sherman, "Aristotle on Friendship and the Shared Life," *Philosophy and Phenomenological Research* (1988): 580–613.

16. Aristotle, *Rhetoric*, 1.1354a.

17. Aristotle, *Rhetoric*, 1.1355a.

18. Aristotle, *Rhetoric*, 2.1393a–403b.

19. MacIntyre, *After Virtue*, pp. 238–245.

20. Lloyd F. Bitzer, "Aristotle's Enthymeme Revisited," *Quarterly Journal of Speech* (1959): 399–408.

21. Aristotle, *Rhetoric*, 1.1361a.25–30.

22. Aristotle, *Rhetoric*, 1.136lb–3a.

23. Hans-Georg Gadamer, "Rhetoric, Hermeneutics, and the Critique of Ideology: Metacritical Comments on Truth and Method," in Kurt Mueller-Vollmer, ed., *The Hermeneutics Reader* (New York: Continuum, 1985), p. 278.

24. Paul Ricoeur, *The Rule of Metaphor: Multidisciplinary Studies of the Creation of Meaning in Language*, trans. Robert Czerny (Toronto: University of Toronto Press, 1977), p. 30. To be fair, both Gadamer and Ricoeur attempt to recover substantial elements of the Aristotelian rhetorical tradition for their own respective projects.

25. Aristotle, *Rhetoric*, 2.1386a.15–25.

26. Aristotle, *Rhetoric*, 2.1386a–b.

27. Nancy Sherman, "Aristotle on Friendship," pp. 610–613.

28. Allen Gross, personal correspondence.

29. Eugene Rochberg-Halton, *Meaning and Modernity: Social Theory in the Pragmatic Attitude* (Chicago: University of Chicago Press, 1986), pp. 95–188.

30. Michael Walzer, "Interpretation and Social Criticism," *The Tanner Lectures on Human Values*, 8 (1968) (Salt Lake City: University of Utah Press, 1988), p. 16.

31. While there are, for instance, many variations of the "post-Modernist" position, the most radical postures seem simply to accept the pronouncements of Western technocracy at face value. Cf. Jean Baudrillard, "Consumer Society," in *Selected Writings*, ed. Mark Poster (Stanford, CA: Stanford University Press, 1988), pp. 29–56.

32. Allan Gibbard, *Wise Choices, Apt Feelings: A Theory of Normative Judgment* (Cambridge, MA: Harvard University Press, 1990), p. 236.

33. Maurizio Passerin D'Entreves, "Freedom, Plurality, Solidarity: Hannah Arendt's Theory of Action," *Philosophy and Social Criticism* 15 (1989): 326–327.

34. Hannah Arendt, in Ronald Beiner, ed., *Lectures on Kant's Political Philosophy* (Chicago: University of Chicago Press, 1982), pp. 58–64. The present essay deviates from Arendt's pronouncements by allowing for the prospect that meaning might be made to "appear" in the present through the collaborative practices of reflection. For an illuminating discussion of Arendt's problematic distinction between "meaning" and "truth," see Mark Pollock, *A Reconsideration of the Prospects for Rhetoric in Hannah Arendt's Political Philosophy* (Ph.D. diss., Northwestern University, 1989), pp. 20–37. For a most provocative attempt to synthesize practical reason with some intuitions of critical theory, see Shawn W. Rosenberg, *Reason, Ideology, and Politics* (Princeton, NJ: Princeton University Press, 1998), pp. 85–158.

35. See "Contra Manual: The Sequel," *Harpers Magazine* 272 (1986): 16-18.

36. Donald C. Bryant, "Rhetoric: Its Function and Scope," in Joseph Schwartz and John A. Rycenga, eds., *The Province of Rhetoric* (New York: Ronald Press , 1965), p. 19.

37. Stephen Toulmin, Richard Rieke, and Allan Janik, *An Introduction to Reasoning* (New York: Macmillan, 1979), pp. 14–16.

38. Arendt, *The Human Condition*, pp. 198–199.

39. Hannah Arendt, *Between Past and Future: Eight Exercises in Political Thought* (New York: Viking Press, 1965), pp. 197–227.

40. See Cornelius Castoriadis, *The Imaginary Institution of Society*. (Cambridge, MA: MIT Press, 1987), pp. 340–353, for an elaboration of this fascinating notion.

41. What I have attempted to do with this trichotomy is to take speaker-centered, message-centered, and audience- or constituency-centered approaches to the value assumptions behind contentious practical questions. All three regions, loosely grouped under the terrain of "prudential reason," would be bracketed as validity claims according to the universal pragmatics position; and they would be presupposed as an array of received opinions or *doxa* according to the more conservative Aristotelian position. By treating them as matters of dispute admitting multiple conceptions at cross purposes, we allow for the possibility that there might be disputation about the nature of our assumptions and ends-in-view, while—at the same time—admitting the possibility that practical reason may explore and reinvent applicable criteria for reflective thought and action.

42. See James Boyd White, *When Words Lose Their Meaning: Constitutions and Reconstitutions of Language, Character, and Community* (Chicago: University of Chicago Press, 1984), pp. 290–291.

43. See Thomas Farrell, "Reason and Rhetorical Practice: The Inventional Agenda of Chaim Perelman," in James L. Golden and Joseph J. Pilotta, eds., *Practical Reasoning in Human Affairs: Studies in Honor of Chaim Perelman* (Dordrecht, The Netherlands: D. Reidel, 1987), for an elaboration of this conception of authority.

44. Following an initial editorial criticism of Havel's Salzburg visit (published in the *New York Times*, July 29, 1990), Paul Hartman wrote to the *New York Times* defending Havel (August 1, 1990). For a partial text of Havel's actual remarks, I have relied upon Václav Havel, "The Velvet Hangover," trans. Kaca Polackova Henley, *Harpers* 281 (1990): 18–21.

45. Havel, "Velvet Hangover," p. 20.

46. For a fascinating account of the Bitburg controversy, including many of the primary documents, see Geoffrey Hartman, ed., *Bitburg in Moral and Political Perspective* (Bloomington: Indiana University Press, 1986).

47. While my use of" integrity" will strike some as eccentric, the usage seems loosely consistent with what Habermas has come to call a third level of argumentative presupposition, "the rhetorical level of processes"; see Jürgen Habermas, *Moral Consciousness and Communicative Action*, trans. Christian Lenhardt and Shierry Weber Nicholsen (Cambridge, MA: MIT Press, 1990), p. 87.

48. "The individual must become answerable through and through: all of his constituent moments must not only fit next to each other in the temporal sequence of his life, but must also interpenetrate each other in the unity of guilt and answerability"(Mikhail Bakhtin, *Art and Answerability: Early Philosophical Essays by M. M. Bakhtin*, ed. M. Holquist and V. Liapunov, trans. V. Liapunov [Austin: University of Texas Press, 1990], p. 2). In our own time, we are perhaps more likely to recognize answerability through its widely praised bureaucratic opposite: "deniability."

49. Arendt, *The Human Condition*, pp. 236–246.

50. Sen. Nancy Kassebaum, *Congressional Record-Senate*, Mar. 9, 1989, S2460-2461. See also "Kassebaum Told Bush of Decision," *Washington Post*, March 10, 1989, p. A18.

51. Amazingly, a fairly detailed outline of this long-term subversive campaign surfaced in the mainstream press. See "U.S. Said to Sabotage Peace Talks for Contras," *Chicago Tribune*, May 10, 1987, p. I27. Much more detailed investigative reporting can be found by Alfonso Chardy, in the *Miami Herald*, May 10, 1987, RETLIB, take: OIZ, ver: 1.01. Special appreciation to *Tribune* international editor Judy Peres.

52. The United States Senate voted 97-1 on May 12, 1987 to endorse the Contadora peace process; see *Congressional Record*, Thurs. May 12, 1987, No. 39S3807.

53. On this elusive question of "consciences" which most persons recognize but few can explain, I am particularly indebted to Michael Hyde. See M. Hyde, "The Conscience of Rhetoric: Heidegger's Poetic Mistake" (presentation to Speech Communication Association, November 3, 1990, Chicago).

54. "The paradoxical combination of certainty and uncertainty, of clarity and silence, makes the world at once intelligible and alive with tension, both for us as readers and for the actors within it. No simple print-out of a cultural pattern, this is a world of contention and struggle in which everything can be put into question, a moral and rhetorical universe in which the actors constantly claim meanings for what is said and done and do so in competition with each other. It lives by a politics of persuasion, upon a premise of instability. In this it may be a model of all politics." The world of which James Boyd White speaks is that of Homer's *Iliad* (see White, *When Words Lose Their Meaning*, pp. 55–56).

55. See, for recent background, Thomas Omestad, "Ten-Day Wonder," *New Republic*, December 25, 1989, pp. 19–22. A fine journalistic treatment of the events in Eastern Europe, including the "Prague Fall," is now available in Timothy Garton Ash, *The Magic Lantern: The Revolution of '89 Witnessed in Warsaw, Budapest, Berlin, and Prague* (New York: Random House, 1990), esp. pp. 78–156.

56. Václav Havel, "New Years Day Address," Jan. 1, 1990, *New York Times* translation. The complete text of this speech is available in *Vesnik*, February 1990, pp. 401, 3–5.

57. An initial account of the furor can be found in Serge Schmemann, "Blunt Bonn Speech on the Hitler Years Prompts a Walkout," special to the *New York Times*, November 11, 1988, p. 1.

58. See, for further discussion and response, Judea B. Miller, "Jewish Victims and German Indifference," *Christian Century*, December 14, 1988, pp. 1144–1145. Also see Victoria Barnett, "Jewish Victims and German Sensitivity," *Christian Century*, March 15, 1989, pp. 287–288. For a remarkable misconstrual of the speech and the reasons for its failings, see Jeffrey Herf, "Phillip Jenninger and the Dangers of Speaking Clearly," *Partisan Review* (1989): 225–236.

59. Havel, *New York Times* translation.

60. Ibid.

61. Serge Schmemann, "Bonn Speaker Out after Nazi Speech," *New York Times*, p. 1.

62. Ibid.

63. Phillip Jenninger, "Speech of Commemoration," November 10, 1988. Full German text is available in *Die Zeit*, November 1988, pp. 4-6. Translation by T. Farrell and J. Stoeckler.

64. Havel, "New Years Day Speech."

65. Ibid.

66. Jenninger, "Speech of Commemoration," p. 5.

67. Serge Schmemann, "A Very German Storm: Dust Settles and Unsettles,"*New York Times*, December 14, 1988, p. A4.

68. Phillip Jenninger, quoted in Schmemann, "A Very German Storm."

69. The sense of audience reflection I have in mind is most akin to that discussed by Robert L. Scott in his seminal essay, "The Tacit Dimension and Rhetoric: What It Means to Be Persuading and Persuaded," *Pre-Text* 2(1–2) (1981): 115–124.

The Taming of *Polos/Polis*

Rhetoric as an Achievement Without Woman

JANE SUTTON

Dedication: Theseus who must conquer an image[1]

Invocation
Ornate-throned immortal Aphrodite, wile weaving
daughter of Zeus, I entreat you:
[. . .] do not tame me
Come to me again and deliver me from
oppressive anxieties; fulfil all that my heart
longs to fulfil, and you yourself be my
fellow-fighter.

Sappho, Fragment 1

Woman, in mythic etymology, links with horse.[2] The sex of rhetoric (*rhetorike*), according to gendered grammar, is feminine. As woman is stretched from the *mythos* of animality to the *logos* of speech, rhetoric is patterned within the feminine which embraces the horse. We can see the contours of the archetypal woman/horse/rhetoric marked out in the name of Socrates' adversary in Plato's *Gorgias* (1952). He is *Polis*, the horse. In this dialogue, rhetoric is contemptible, an "untamed filly" giving in to desire (461–481).[3] However, in Plato's *Phaedrus* (1973), Socrates tames rhetoric. As Phaedrus' name would implicate him, he, the domesticated wolf, herds the horse/woman image of rhetoric for Socrates, the rhetorician, to subdue. At last, the most superb wild and black horse, tongue and jaw drenched with blood spilled by the bit of reason, is forced into domestication (255). Broken, rhetoric earns a place in the *polis*. And those who wish to use or study the art can now do so. Thus, before rhetoric could be studied safely, as Michel de Certeau (1988, p. 119) reminds us, its danger as an object of desire had to be eliminated. There had to be no danger in rhetoric, for danger inhibited the possibility of conceptualization. Following the contours of the three archetypes, I have found scraps of the horse/woman pattern to constitute a significant image prefiguring the talk about rhetoric being dangerous. Nothing lies deeper in the fear of rhetoric than this animism.[4]

In this essay I describe how rhetoric came to be written in relation to woman's body—a way that implicates her very being—and what this style of discourse says about the practice and nature of rhetoric itself. There are two distinct phases in my argument. In Part 1, I shall feature the gerund "taming" from my title and construct the subject rhetoric/woman/horse by emplotting tropologically—metaphorically, metonymically, synecdochically, and ironically—rhetoric's history. Then in Part 2 I shall let this constructed subject resist the emplotment because the subject of the narrative has become literalized and, thus, dis-figured. That is to say, there will be "turns"—deviations from customary or literal usage—against the "logic" sanctioned by the narrative, a "logic" that entails the possibility of rhetoric's conceptualization.

According to Harold Bloom, linguistic "turns" are equivalent to a psychological defense mechanism (1975, p. 91). In his *Tropics of Discourse*, Hayden White explains Bloom's statement regarding "turns" in relation to the word *trope*: "[A trope is a] defense against [a turning away from] literal meaning in discourse, in the way that repression, regression, projection, and so forth are defenses against the apprehension of death in the psyche" (1978, p. 2). Following White's lead, my aim is to pursue rhetoric's relation to its past (death), discovered (*inventio*) in the "logic" of its narrativity, and the relation to its future (rebirth), created (*inventio*) by troping or defending against the "logic" of narrativity. In fact, White argues, discourse is "quintessentially a *mediative* enterprise" (1978, p. 4). As such, once found, I will be able to show rhetoric's relation to its past by viewing its aim through representations of theory; and I will be able to show rhetoric's relation to its future by viewing the aim of rhetorical practices as an occasion for rhetoric to be about itself. The occasion—rhetoric being self-rhetorical—gives the art the opportune moment to be a defense from or an oppositional voice to the literal, conventional, or "proper" use of rhetoric, which, theoretically speaking, stipulates that rhetoric should behave itself and be decorous. Deviating from the proper course—troping occasionally—is the "anti"-aim of rhetoric. Nothing is more lively and more feminine than deviation.

With that broad overview, I can be more specific regarding my methodology.[5] In this essay, history unfolds like a collage in which the "data" on horse/woman, embedded in the theoretical discourse, fuses into a configurative pattern about rhetoric itself. The field of history I am constructing starts by marking out descriptions of woman and horse and investing them in rhetoric as archetypes. Following that marking procedure, I notice their place in history by locating discussions and the accounts that concern themselves with rhetoric's "origin." So placed, I pay close attention to the pristine scene, the pre-theoretical context or the occasion of rhetoric, which is itself put into practice. In sum, the "data" or grounds for an "original" understanding of rhetoric are resurrected by considering several kinds of discourse: myth, histories of rhetoric (e.g., Plato, 1952, 1973; Isocrates, 1980a, 1980b, 1980c; Aristotle, 1954; Dionysius of Halicarnassus, 1974; Tacitus, 1942; Macrobis, 1952; Augustine, 1951, 1958; and Todorov, 1977), Renaissance painting, drama, and twentieth-century essays and poetry.

Taking the "data" together, I emplot chronologically the path the archetypal image of rhetoric as horse/woman takes. This path can best be grasped as a narrative sequence that passes through four distinct phases. In turn, each phase unfolds within the purview of a particular trope. As a methodological departure point, I invoke the tropes set forth by White (1973). Thus, the image of rhetoric evolves, from an original [1] metaphorical characterization of the domain of experience, through [2] *metonymic deconstructions* of its elements, to [3] *synecdochic representations* of the relations between its superficial attributes and its presumed essence, to, finally, [4] a representation of whatever *contrasts* or oppositions can legitimately be discerned in the totalities identified in the third phase of discursive representation [irony]. (p. 5; my emphasis)

Moreover, White says that whatever concept—in this case, rhetoric—evolves through this narrative structure must be viewed as an animate subject itself, as a subjective "I" that participates in its own destiny (1978).

I want to preview how this method will be invoked. First, I reconstruct the myth's archetypal plot. I begin by showing how a metaphoric unity between feminine (Amazon woman) and masculine (the traditional Corax and Tisias story) condensed in rhetoric at its origin. From there, I trace a division, in which rhetoric is split along gender lines into a masculine *polis* dweller and a feminine barbaric wanderer. This division may also be read as a metonymic reduction, whereby the domain of rhetoric is restricted to its masculine form. In the complex synecdochical phase, I examine how the undifferentiated feminine/barbaric/wanderer/animal is fractured further into a "good" and "bad" woman. Subsequently, the good woman is readmitted into the rational/masculine/*polis* as keeper of the home (as a microcosm of the *polis*), and this new part of rhetoric (man plus wife) is portrayed as its whole, its essence. In turn, the articulation of feelings and the body are projected onto the bad woman and ostracized as potential disruptions to the newly formed gender alliance between rational man and his supplemental wife. Finally, I show how in its fourth phase this myth reinforces its own misogynistic character by portraying the return of the harlot/untamed woman/rhetoric, only to undercut the portrayal ironically.

But just as figuration itself constantly slips from the grasp of a colonizing logos, in the second part of the essay I show how rhetoric also manages to dance outside of the archetypal plot designed to tame it, and, through particular figurations, to resist the narrative meanings of the myth. To illustrate this slippage, I show how woman, even though she seems caught by the patriarchate in a sociopolitical matrix not of her own making, escapes to an alternative historical moment by making a virtue out of her attributed vice/voice—her body. To show this, I use collage-type procedure—cutting and pasting woman in and out of historical history—which high-lights both woman's oppositional voice to and her affinity with rhetoric. I situate this oppositional stance within the very figures—metaphor, metonymy, synecdoche, and irony—that comprise the archetypal plot itself. Only this time, I concentrate on how woman uses rhetoric/horse attribution to escape from and, in so doing, to undermine the legitimacy of, the myth itself.

It is only through critical awareness of the inadequacies of traditional historiographies that we can begin to understand the ends of rhetoric. In fact, I know that the traditional modes of speaking are complicitous in hiding from view the very understanding I seek. As Nietzsche's *Zarathustra* (1961) would put it, I first "shatter their ears" to teach them "to hear with their eyes."

THE ARCHETYPAL PLOT

Metaphor

I wish to characterize the original domain of the experience of rhetoric in the metaphoric mode. With this trope, I can witness the historical effort to comprehend the art and to make it adequate "to the satisfaction of the felt need of human beings" (White, 1978, p. 5). This need, insofar as comprehension is grounded in the metaphorical pattern, underlies and informs all representations of rhetoric.

We begin at a scene in history when the earth was young and the Amazon ruled. On horseback and armed with bow and arrow, the gorgeous woman allowed no Tyrant [later depicted as *just* man] to direct the affairs of society. There is a legend that the Amazons erected a Temple of Aphrodite "the Warlike" to commemorate her victory over the Tyrant (Sobol, 1972, p. 124). In myth, rhetoric is depicted as a woman in an erotic context. Vase paintings portray rhetoric in an aphrodisiac setting. Buxton (1982) shows persuasion participating with Zeus, Hera, and Eros in the birth of Aphrodite. This event, an image often corroborated in the visual arts, links rhetoric's beginning to Aphrodite's warring female entourage. According to more familiar mythic origins of rhetoric, two (male) sophists, Corax and Tisias, enabled the people to defeat two Tyrants, Gelon and Hieron (cf. 1035, Farenga, 1979). In both the Amazon myth and the story of Corax and Tisias, the hero(ine)s slay the Tyrant(s). Combining the mythic characterizations of rhetoric, we see that the art (*techne*) encompasses a masculine *and* feminine origin.

Metonymy

However, the metaphoric comprehension of the original domain of experience as a masculine/feminine unity that exists within rhetoric—via the story of Corax and Tisias *and* the myth of the Amazons—clashes with the human need to differentiate. Thus, the metaphoric characterization fails and, instead, makes *either* the rhetoric of a true *polis* or the rhetoric of barbarism possible. Insofar as the Amazon is the archetype of the barbarian par excellence (Sobol, 1972, p. 126), her body must be vanquished, since the need is to unite within a *polis* that defines unity vis-à-vis man. The splitting apart of people into *polis* dweller (masculinity) and barbaric wanderer (femininity) is the new reductive social structure projected onto the unity of rhetoric's elements. And in order to have a true rhetoric and a good woman, one that can be situated in the *polis* so that a theory can be put in place "properly," the *logos* must repress woman's destruction of tyranny or, literally, her ability to overcome, even to kill, man. Aphrodite, the feminine face of rhetoric, undergoes metonymic deconstruction. Texts concerned with the origin of rhetoric reveal this loss.

Isocrates extols rhetoric as a victory, a stabilizing force, over woman. Woman is said to have dominated a time of unreason—of passion, emotion, ignorance, superstition, and even, perhaps, an authority over man. Indeed, in the *Panegyricus*, Isocrates (1980c, 65–68) celebrates the defeat of the Amazons. He claims that the total destruction of a race of Woman is a crowning achievement within the overall defeat of the Persians. This conquest affirms the right of the *polis* to expand in the space of the Other and to destroy the feminine within that expansion. On another occasion (*Nicocles or the Cyprians*), Isocrates (1980b) praises speech for making victory over an external force possible. "It is by the power of persuading one another that we have raised ourselves, founded cities, laid down laws and discovered arts" (6–7).[6]

Whether dealing with the destruction of the Amazon—the metaphorical characterization of the feminine—or with rhetoric's power to conquer the life of the wild beast, *external* forces—whether barbarian, Persian, Amazon, or wild animal/horse—loom large. By reading the origin of rhetoric, as Isocrates does, together with the myth of the Amazon, we uncover a tension in the story of rhetoric's origin. The metaphoric unity—the mythic pair of origins balancing the masculine and feminine—is upset. As a result, the story shifts and settles in a reductive version with the triumph of reason over unreason, the triumph of "man" over beast, the triumph of speech (*peitho*) over violence (*bia*), and the triumph of rule (Athens) over being ruled by (the "daughters of Ares" followed by the Persians). The move from a metaphorical apprehension to a metonymical perception of a "strange" or "threatening" reality marks a primary tropological shift in historical description (White, 1978, p. 6). Speeches that recall rhetoric's origin advance the archetypal plot to a new stage of consciousness. So, for example, while Isocrates finds a place for rhetoric in his vision of a future *polis*, his is a repressive picture because it violently disperses the past. Woman in rhetoric vis-à-vis the Amazon is eliminated gloriously. With the Amazon conquered, which destroyed the feminine, rhetoric can no longer be practiced *as* Woman.

To prepare for the scenic change from metonymy to synecdoche, enter Aristotle for an interlude. The art of rhetoric, as well as "man's" life, is praised when it is governed by reason. Reason is an element presumed to be essential to rhetoric and, hence, masculine. There is nothing but a presumption of essence here because the art's elements have already been dispersed metonymically. At any rate, during this scenic change we notice that just as there had to be distinctions in the life of the *polis* between the rational and the irrational (a metonymic division that relies on the metaphoric apprehension of the need for a difference between *polis* dweller [masculine] and barbaric warrior [feminine]), there had to be a theory of rhetoric that embodied that same distinction (Sutton, 1986). For if speech (*Logos*) unites "men," it is a logical and moral imperative for that same speech (*Logos*) to take control over all areas of experience outside the jurisdictions of reason (*logos*). And yet, the feminine (pre*logos*, *mythos*) is always already within the metaphorical domain of man and the art of rhetoric. Mindful of that, the feminine is incarnated in the goddesses of the city—Aphrodite—and of invention—muses of inspiration. This attempt to recover the metaphoric unity of rhetoric, however, disperses woman, indeed as it must, given that dispersion is the aim of rhetoric in its metonymic phase. The body of a goddess or intellect of a muse—the absence of woman, really—is no recovery of the metaphoric unity of the feminine because it forces woman to go outside or around the Real—the political/judicial practices of rhetoric by men. For her to gain access to the Real, the feminine unconscious, also true to metonymic form, disperses. The reductive act divides Woman into symmetrical power contiguities—woman/woman—and projects evil onto *only* part of the series of herself. The projection enables Woman herself to avoid exclusion from the Real; the division of herself enables her to ward off total annihilation. The effect of this division of power, thereby ensuring the possibility of a will to power, is that "Man's" life within the *polis* experiences the return of the repressed and dispersed womanish parts. With this return, rhetoric will direct its attention to a particular type of woman's body. The feminine unconscious is integrated synecdochically, which means that she is assigned to different orders, classes, and places within the *polis*. Synecdochically, her status is characterized as either this kind of woman or, in *sotto voce*, that kind . . .—if you catch my drift.

Synecdoche

This tropological phase traces the continued fragmentation of woman in relation to rhetoric. What we will witness is a scenic division of woman into good wife/homemaker, and bad harlot/ostracized other. Once this split is constructed, the "good" woman can be reintegrated into rhetoric proper as the helpmate of rational man. This partnership then constitutes a new "whole" which can then be set in opposition to the rhetoric of desire, which is projected onto the harlot and oppressed as an ever-present danger to civic rule.

To begin, in "the house of the profligate and abandoned," the harlot is able to secure the wife's position. There is no "home"—no miniaturized *polis*—with this replacement.

> There sits the lawful wife, freeborn and chaste, but with no authority over her domain, while an insensate harlot, bent on destroying her livelihood, claims control of the whole estate, treating the other like dirt and keeping her in a state of terror. (Dionysius of Halicarnassus, 1974, 5 f.)

It should come as no surprise that when Dionysius of Halicarnassus, a Greek rhetorician who lived in Rome during the times of Augustus, wrote this passage *of* women, he is not interested in woman but in something else. The whore, he notes, has a textual analogue: a new rhetoric had sprung up "from some Asiatic death-hole" (the whore) and replaced the "old philosophical rhetoric" (the wife).[7] He is using woman to write a history of classical rhetoric that preserves "true" rhetoric and destroys false rhetoric.[8]

Woman/Woman, Dionysius observes, is the new site upon which rhetoric must struggle since, as his text reveals, the conflict is not yet over. Woman has divided into the "good" (servant of the *polis*) and the "bad" (user of the *polis*) and continues to depotentiate the metaphorical unity in rhetoric's repressed past by activating the metonymical destruction of the feminine. Against this split and the symmetrical projecting power of woman/woman, Dionysius marshals an army of metaphors commonly used in works on religious morality or the moral idealism of the Golden Age. The ease with which he does this signals his own awareness of the Greek and Roman historical consciousness of promoting one ideal, the ideal that woman belongs to man (see note 7 above). Simone de Beauvoir (1952, p. 146) notes that woman/woman, not Woman, "is symmetrical [integrated as wife or whore] only in such societies as [ancient Greece], Fascist Italy, and Nazi Germany, which destines the woman for the State and not for the individual, which regard her exclusively as mother and makes no place for eroticism."

Dionysius' text on the history of rhetoric rehearses the patriarchal setting seen in Isocrates (1980c): It calls for the defeat of an Enemy, who continues to be an Amazonian erotic woman. Further, the killing of the whore is justified as a patriotic sacrifice for the countryman and glosses the issue that her death reenacts the destruction of the Amazon in the origin of rhetoric, a compulsive repetition that makes possible the fatherland. Indeed, the growth of reason and the democrat's *polis* occur soon after the metonymic destruction of the Other woman—Amazon or whore. Thus, the history of rhetoric in a patriarchate will be redirected toward the body of woman, that untamed other of the brothers.[9] It can be said, in sum, that the splitting of woman into polar opposites is her achievement and her failure. One side of her achieves inclusion within certain practices of rhetoric, and, at the same time, excludes her participation from the role of rhetoric as a "real" discipline in history.

As the first historian of rhetoric, Dionysius' perspective on the "two rival Rhetorics" further reflects the historical attitudes toward the Athenian woman. Continuing his figure of thought, Dionysius writes that in every city "the ancient and indigenous Attic Muse [lawful wife], deprived of her possessions, had lost her *civic* rank, while her antagonist [insensate harlot], an upstart . . . claimed the right to rule over Greek cities, expelling her rival from public life" (1974, p. 7; my emphasis). A woman such as the wife of Euphiletus who takes a lover (Lysias, 1976a) or a woman who does not marry (Lysias, 1976b, 21) causes suffering to those held together by the "city's hands." Anticonjugal and nonconjugal use of a woman's body threatens to disunite the *polis*. ("Man" may be dispersed and live disenfranchised from the corporate body of male citizenry—the life of a wild beast [Halperin, 1990, p. 16]). Again, woman is seen as an enemy, for she dissuades the bonds of man. Now her sexuality must be defeated. She must be alienated from herself, but connected to man. That task, we have shown, is accomplished by defining woman's relationship to man as either good or bad.

Moreover, in this relationship, an ambiguously valued sexuality links woman to rhetoric. A woman becomes a harlot when she offers her body for hire to any man who will pay for sex. So too, the rhetorician: "Those who sell it [wisdom] to anyone are called 'sophists,' just like prostitutes" (fr. 79 2a, in Sprague, 1972). By selling her services for sex, woman is separated from the respectable class of women, the wives and brides of the harlot's clients. By selling wisdom, particularly to barbarians, the rhetor is separated from the philosophers, the soldiers, and the citizens who are the guardians and creators of the *polis*. Just as the woman, mythically represented as an Amazon, was a threat to the unity of mankind, the whore is now a threat to the household—that miniaturized *polis*. So identified, the sophist/rhetor poses a threat to those who govern the city state.

Thus far, I have shown that patriachalism recapitulates patriotism to define whore as an opponent of the wife, an image potent enough to be invoked by aspiring politicians and philosophers when conceptualizing the ideal of rhetoric. Now, as the final act, I consider post-Renaissance history. This fourth move takes the representations of contrasts or oppositions from the synecdochical scene (White, 1978, p. 5) and negates them. That is, in the scene of irony, the narrative "I" reflects on the inadequacy of the characterization with respect to the archetypal plot. "I" can resist the emplotment by refusing to satisfy narrative's formal coherencies.

Irony

In the writing of Dionysius of Halicarnassus, and in historians who followed, rhetoric (integrated, synecdochically, as an ideal and not-so-ideal woman) is always already placed together with woman in history, regardless of the particularities of culture or the contingencies of the historical moment. This means that from the representation of the totalities—derived from the synecdochical integrations—begins a series of contrasts, which is the creation of the ironic act; we find binary oppositions maturing in the twentieth century and its feminist enlightenment. Casting history into the ironic mode through contrast or oppositions appears, according to White (1973), to signal the ascent of thought in a given area of inquiry to a level of self-critical conceptualization of its world and the process through which it has become possible (p. 37). For the narrative "I" of rhetoric, the phase of irony means that the art scrutinizes itself and realizes that if eternal vigilance is not maintained over the post-metonymic destruction of the woman into wife/whore (that both terrorizes and preserves the feminine principle in rhetoric), she will rise up to challenge the ultimate justifier, Aristotle, male rule in the household—the miniaturized *polis*—and the state on which it is modeled. Aristotle notes that the usurpation of wife over the husband "is not in virtue of excellence" (1984b, 1161a). As we will see, even in the house of a man like Alexander the Great, who was tutored by Aristotle, there is not only the unremitting conflict of opposites—between reason (the representation of masculinity) and passion (the representation of whore)—but also the possibility of reversing the stakes of man, institution, value, and the idea of excellence, of slipping back into the prerational domain of the Amazon. Viewed ironically, the narrative "I" can negate itself.

By fixing our sight on Alexander the Great's household after the conjunction of myth, poetry, and painting in the Renaissance, we find interesting possibilities for discussion about the ironic negations of rhetoric/woman. In particular, the problematic nature of the synecdochical integrations of the slain Amazon woman, the low hierarchical position of woman in Aristotle, and the Roman moral attitude toward wife and whore in writing the history of rhetoric inspire rhetoric (as the narrative "I") to have second thoughts about itself. For example, engravings, carvings, and the paintings of Rubens and Delacroix that depict Theseus's defense of Athens and the meeting of Alexander the Great and Thalestris, queen of the Amazons, characterize woman as praiseworthy and, at the same time, refuse to praise her insofar as the artists meet the viewer's expectation of woman's savage-like animism (see Dijkstra, 1986; Gardner, 1980; Hall, 1979). In this case, such negation, which, marked by the reflection on the praise of woman, signals that historical discourse, entertains with irony (see White, 1973). I have selected the engraving *Phyllis Rides Aristotle* (Figure 1),[10] combined with the poetry and drama that elaborate upon it, as my focal point of the ironic phase in the archetypal plot because the visual depiction makes clear the ironic shift in the discourse of rhetoric's history.

The theme—beware of woman—is interpreted visually in *Phyllis Rides Aristotle*. There are many versions in art and literature of the so-called apocryphal story of Aristotle's seduction.[11] In general, all the remakings of this tale feature Aristotle being tricked by a woman who is either a wife of a King-like man or his mistress. It is the details that are significant. In the German version (*AinSpil von Maister Aristotiles*, in Hutchinson, 1966, p. 76), the King catches Aristotle being "taken" by woman and confronts him. In his scolding speech, the king uses the imagery of a *horse* "to deride [Aristotle] the learned old man [for allowing] himself to be outwitted by a woman" (Hutchinson, 1966, p. 76, n. 38). The horse signifies the sophisticated dream of the feminine in the historical unconscious of rhetoric. That is, when man represses woman/rhetoric, those repressed contents grow in power in the unconscious and then erupt in the patriarchal speech from which they were once banned.

In the German Renaissance poetry of Henry d'Andely and Ulrich von Eschenbach (cited in Hutchinson, 1966, p. 76, n. 33), the woman is *not a wife*, but a *mistress* who is able *to seduce* Aristotle by singing a song while she picks *flowers*. d'Andely stresses that the woman is *without a veil*. As the dream of the unconscious progresses, the unveiled woman is dangerous because she has lifted her veil, which is to say, she resists being a husband's property under the veil—the symbolic cover signifying protection and submission to the authority of the patriarchy. As do Gerda Lerner (1986) and G. E. M. de Ste. Croix (1970), I read the practice of veiling a woman as not only a way to distinguish types of women but also to discourage men from associating socially with a woman classified as unrespectable. Class formation demands a visible means of distinguishing those belonging to the class of "citizen." A veiled harlot (truly an ambiguity [thus sophistry (Aristotle, 1984d, 165b–166a)]) would be a major offense against the property owners. Since a veiled harlot appears to be something other than what she is, her sexual practices make it possible, albeit indirectly through heirs, to render the distribution of property problematical. In fact, Lerner (1986) notes that a man who does not report a veiled harlot is bridled and whipped. If we push this imagery to the limit in terms of the transformation of rhetoric into a true and false discourse,

FIGURE 1. *Aristotle and Phyllis* engraving by Master M. Z. 1465–1535. Courtesy of the Fogg Art Museum, Harvard University Art Museums, William M. Prichard Fund.

we are back in Plato's (1973) distinction between the good and bad horse and the story of how the wicked horse must be whipped and made to abandon lustful ways. Looking ahead into the political thought of Aristotle, the rule of man over tame animal/woman becomes justified and natural (see Garside, 1971; Gomme, 1967). The style of clothing that institutionalized the body of woman institutionalized the body of rhetoric. What Aristotle veils (protects) and encloses for public discourse is a plain style of rhetoric that has no ornaments of the harlot. This enclosure is the cell out of which rhetoric attempts to protect rhetoric from rhetoric. That is to say, outside the law of the patriarchy, which is the largest veil, woman as unattached outsider or mistress seduces men from their proper course in the homeland with the tropes, those flowers or ornaments of rhetoric.

In this visual depiction, a typical account tells that Aristotle scolds his pupil, Alexander the Great, for neglecting public affairs and spending time with his wife. The woman sets out to defeat this political attitude of public-centeredness by getting Aristotle to agree to be ridden like a horse. She gets on top. He is humiliated, of course. But in the end the woman is bridled and sacrificed.

The ironic tradition of the archetypal plot climaxes with the simple statement that Phyllis rides Aristotle and the opposed meaning of that statement, which suggests this: Alexander and Aristotle were the riders and Phyllis was the ridden. In other words, with real or feigned disbelief, the authors of Phyllis and Aristotle's story characterize woman/rhetoric by negating on the figurative level what is positively affirmed on the literal level. In a poem, Eleanor Wilner (1991) captures the ironic phase in the final conquest of woman and the victory of Aristotelianism as she waxes lyrical on a nineteenth-century "man."

> What a great tradition was born when Alexander whipped his penknife out, cut the knot she carefully had tied, leaped on his mount, a perfect straddle and let the crotch decide who was the horse and who was the rider, who was the muse and who the writer [rhetor]. (p. 94)

This poem informs us about the image of wife and whore which, when taken together with the archetypal plot, enable us to picture rhetoric beyond Athens. "Man" has tamed the horse: the Other: the woman. From then on, "man"/reason/philosopher will ride woman/feelings/rhetoric. Etymologically speaking, "the horse" is the posture of making love (Aristophanes, 1931, p. 276 n. 1). In other words, here in the concept of horse is Amazon/woman as ruler over man and the physical notion of woman literally atop man. To reverse position—to let woman dominate the earth, as in the case of the Amazon, and to let woman be on top of man as in the case of sexual intercourse—haunts the thinking behind the fear of rhetoric, woman, and *pathos*. Disguised in a discussion of argument, this fear is evident in the fable of the horse in Aristotle's *Rhetoric* (1393b 10–24). And through sexual allusion, fear of woman (as tyrant-slayer, Amazon, or whore) is evident in Aristophanes' *Wasps* (1931). Xanthias says:

> Yesterday I went to see a gay girl about noon and suggested she should mount me and ride me; she flew into a rage, pretending I wanted to restore the tyranny of Hippias [*Hippos* means "horse" (Sobol, 1972, p. 162) and Hippias is a rhetorician]. (p. 32)

And finally from *The Thesmophoriazusae*, in the reply to Agathon's suggestion of adopting a woman's habit in order to be placed in character on the stage: "Then you ride the high horse when you are composing a Phaedra" (Aristophanes, 1931, p. 276).

All such *niaiserie* (folly, stupidity, silliness), as Nietzsche (1966) reminds us, belong in comedy (aphorisms 11, 19). Furthermore, Aristotle's "horse" example in illustrating argument is not appropriate to a theory of rhetoric that he claims has risen above the mire of passion, particularly in light of his introduction of the enthymeme (proof by reason, *logos*) to rhetoric.

If we return to the images in the German play and d'Andely's and von Eschenbach's poetry—wife, a woman riding a horse, a mistress without a veil, and the colorful flowers in the story of Aristotle's seduction—we find the ironic impulse carrying woman into a discussion of style. Before we can understand the relation between types of woman and the question of style in the history of rhetoric, we must step back further into Dionysius' history and consider his contrasting images of the wife and the whore. The household that Dionysius talks about indicates a return of the repressed, the metonymic reduction of the feminine elements that makes the fatherland possible. This is so because the world which he portrays reflects the threat of the Amazonian myth in its metaphoric characterization and looks forward to her destruction for the sake of the development of the democratic Greek city-state.

We shall examine the wife and whore and their images in some detail, paying particular attention to differences in women's social practice that have ramifications for style in rhetoric. The control of the wife's house, we recall, has been taken over by a whore. As the whore's reckless extravagance suggests, style is *under* the control of a woman. The whore, being *insensate*, indicates why she is threatening. She has no feeling; that is to say, she is unconscious. The unconscious, being prerational, makes her appear stupid and senseless with respect to the law. By contrast, the wife's place is next to control ("She is chaste"), which is, in effect, to say that she is accustomed to propriety. She is next to rationality ("She is freeborn"), and so has ingested at least enough reason to be given authority for regulating her own, her daughters', and her neighbors' wife's sexual behavior (see Solon's law in Pomeroy, 1975, p. 86). In such a context, Dionysius' interest in the appropriate or proper woman reemerges first as a rhetorical code for the question of style. Then, the question of the harlot in place of the wife sets up the possibility that an author can say one thing and mean another, thereby creating the condition for duplicity in rhetoric.

First, in this code, the feminine is bound to rhetoric through an opposition in style which is manifested in the two kinds of woman. For example, in Tacitus (1942), the clash between styles/women (or, perhaps, one woman and one effeminate male [*Oratory*, 21]) is evident in the description of dress.

> [I] should certainly prefer . . . vehemence . . . or . . . sobriety . . . to . . . curls . . . or . . . jingles . . . : so much better is it for an orator to wear a rough dress than to glitter in many-colored and meretricious attire. (*Oratory* 21, 26)

And, in *On Christian Doctrine* (1958), these visions of woman recur indirectly, through Augustine's justification of the use of the high, eloquent style.

> It is sufficiently apparent, I think, that women are vehemently urged by . . . eloquence not to adulterate their appearance with rouge and to be shameful and fearful. Thus we recognize style is neither subdued nor moderate, but altogether grand. (xxi, 50)

That is, Augustine (1958) affirms Dionysius' rhetorical code of style by justifying the high, harlot style as a strategy on behalf of wifely wisdom. In that sense, and as Richard Lanham (1976) implies, the combined oppositions—between kinds of woman and kinds of style—can be read as a threat. The ornate and high style, represented as the whore "arising out of an Asiatic death-hole" of rhetoric, can overpower the plain and middle style, represented as the wife attached to philosophy.

The distinction I have delineated between the two types of style inscribed on the body of woman has great consequence for the theory and practice of rhetoric. On the ironic stage, the consequences concern truth and the *polis*. After Dionysius' account, this opposition between wife and whore ensures the impossibility of wife and whore being in the same location or place (de Certeau, 1984, p. 117). In this spatial story there is but one place—the household within the institution of marriage, itself within the reason-bound *polis*. Thus, to situate the "right" woman in the "right" place is to situate rhetoric as a *praxis* in theory. Rhetorical theory and methodology exist to tame rhetoric as practice. By reinforcing the connection between *a* theory (place/*polis*/home) and *one* (ideal) practice, the choice of rhetoric/woman is reduced to being either under the control of the state—in the hands of the *polis*, the philosophy/father or husband—or being out of place, which is to say, untamed, a *polos*. (But, of course, woman/rhetoric in "man's" control is even suspect. After all, she has left her home—the fatherland—for the home of a husband and, thus, is a traitor and forever unfaithful). At any rate, her lack of self-control (which is why she needs man's control) will take on the form of frenzy, madness, and passion. Her frenzy is evident in complaints about her ostentatious and showy behavior at funerals, from which she is eventually barred (Pomeroy, 1975, p. 80). And it is equally evident, although less frenzied, in the descriptions of her excesses in eating, drinking, and sexual activity (Powell, 1988, p. 338). Generalizing these abuses to rhetoric, style is either clear, sincere, and faithful, or it is out of hand—excessive, displaying itself to outsiders (Lanham, 1976, pp. 1–9). The classical rhetorician's preferences for the place of woman-as-wife elevates the practice of the plain style. This preference is still with us today in universities where rhetoric is taught as rule-governed courses in English composition.[12]

Indeed, through styles of speaking, classical rhetoric can be seen as the preoccupation of putting and keeping woman in her proper place. Her behavior is systematically scrutinized for what is/is not proper. She must keep her place, which is a place away from the affairs of "man" and the life of the *polis*. Even in the household, her place is still away from her husband. In the home there were separate quarters for man and woman. Woman, Pomeroy (1975) reports, "usually inhabited the more remote rooms, away from the street and from the public areas of the house" (p. 80, n. 9). In taking charge of her everyday existence, the husband regulates the breeding of female slaves and controls his wife's sexuality. The most important function of woman was providing an heir. This was crucial to the survival of a family in an era when the availability of men's "rights"—for example, to speak in an assembly—was increasingly restricted through a dependence on citizenship laws. Given woman's sexual/bestial nature, however, even when continuous care was taken to regulate her actions, woman could slip out of the proper and appropriate. Woman can cause confusion. She could appear in place of the wife, thereby allowing the harlot (and her children) to be mistaken and granted rights of the freeborn and chaste.

This woman who confuses illicit practices of sex with the proper place of sexuality was called the *hetaira* (McKechnie, 1987, p. 153; Pomeroy, 1975, p. 89). She transposed the meaning of freedom with that of noncitizenship and the meaning of wife with that of "sexual companion to man." We meet the same problem when rhetoric also mixed up styles. We have already been warned by Dionysius that the harlot's beauty, artistry, and imagination, in short, stylizing, are excessive practices that slipped into the wife's domain and took over the whole estate. But before turning to this second confusion directly, we need to take a look at what happens, ironically speaking, when woman slips past the patriarchal gaze.

As the practice of woman's everyday life and her place within the life of the *polis* is bound to law, so too is rhetoric bound to the patriarchal rules of reasoned discourse. Policing rhetoric in a structure of the *gynaikonomous*[13] of *letteraturizzazione*[14]–an official structure that keeps both the movement of woman and the functions of rhetoric within the dictates of the *polis*–is explicitly passed along throughout the second period of the history of rhetoric, a period T. Todorov marks as being "from Cicero to Fontanier" (1977, p. 77). That she can easily slip from the plain style (wife) to the high style (whore) is evident in Todorov's successive analysis of the destruction of the link between truth and expression, invention and disposition, or, as the Italian Humanists like to call this dichotomy, *res* and *verba*, and each effect of the reductionistic relations between them. By adapting Todorov's analysis (p. 72), I shall portray, in Figure 2, one victim of the second period in rhetoric's history. Each time there is a division of the woman, there is a victim in the metonymic deconstruction of the metaphoric unity, and the narratives "I" of rhetoric is used to victimize woman/rhetoric further by reducing the art to superficiality and presuming that the new integrative representation is its essence. The diagram is meant to simplify the relation between rhetoric and woman in the archetypal plot so that the resistance to it in Part 2 may be addressed.

In using Todorov's analysis of the link between truth and expression and my analysis of the link between style and woman in complementariness, I aim to show that rhetoric/woman is honored and valued when the expression of the word serves thought or the truth. In other words, rhetoric/woman is respectable when the discovery of ideas (invention) expresses the ideas (disposition) in their "proper" place according to the grammar or rules that constitute language or the *polis*, respectively. And for rhetoric to present itself truthfully, it must not be showy or ostentatious, for that is the sign of the whore. Just as a Greek wife had to wear a *himation*, which was a shawl drawn over the head as a hood in public (Pomeroy, 1975, p. 83), rhetoric must be covered with a

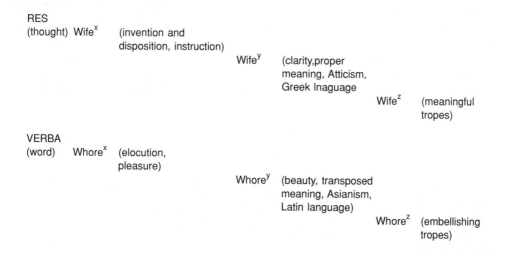

FIGURE 2. The *Gynaikonomous Letteraturizzazione* of Rhetoric.

veil to snsure, Augustine (1951) writes in *Letters* (55), "the [keeping of the] command-ments literally, as they are given, without figurative meaning" (p. 277). The veil here is the sign of the plain style that we have shown to be operative in a neighbor's relationship with another neighbor in the patriarchal place and woman's legitimacy as a woman (read: wife) of the *polis*. In Cicero's *Dream of Scipio* (1952), there is earlier corroboration for this Christian function of the veil. When the woman, not the man, takes off her veil, (Numenius interprets this to mean) she has only the profession of prostitution to practice (Macrobius Ambrosius Theodosius, *Commentary on Scipio's Dream*, 1952, 1.2.19). Lifting the veil from her head indicates that woman has stepped outside the authority of father, husband, or *polis*. Unveiled she can wander the city, available to be chosen by anyone, including the barbarian, and unavailable, according to institutional/political guidelines and the Decalogue, for the citizen to choose her. Both aspects of her political existence can be derived from the politics' root, *pele*, meaning wanderer—even/broad/flatland and settler—policing/high/city (*American Heritage*, App. 1533).

Thus, rhetoric is implicated by this truth of the veil: To be good, style must clearly express that speech plainly (Aristotle, 1954, 1404b5). To do anything else is to lift the veil, expose hair, and risk having rhetoric do something other than what it should properly do. Unveiled rhetoric, for instance, can be used immorally. That rhetoric can be used for immoral purposes is Plato's worry. Rereading Augustine with Aristotle, we must conclude that what is veiled is instrumental or, as Aristotle casts it (1954, 1355a20–25), rhetoric/woman are useful when each faithfully serves an external purpose, whether it is to the truth, to the *polis*, or to her husband. Such usefulness is the necessary condition of virtue and excellence. If the distinctions become ambiguous, as they do for the *hetaira*, the condition becomes useless to the *polis*—barbaric and dangerous.

THE DENOUEMENT TO THE ARCHETYPAL PLOT

But even the unveiled harlot can achieve patriarchal cleansing and forgiveness. In the anticlimactic act of the archetypal plot, woman/rhetoric is ideologically upgraded and represented. Woman and rhetoric, after having fallen completely into embellishing tropes under the sign of the whore (see Figure. 2), is cleaned up and transformed into a bride-to-be. In our own century, Alastair Fowler (1990), writing an apology for rhetoric's ostentations, expurgates the woman in rhetoric without apology or critical examination:

> Lady Rhetoric may be like a beautiful woman of uncertain age, who will want to wear something old and something new for her remarriage with stylish young Poetics (p. 118).

It is now apparent that "that untouch'd bride of quietness" can cause no trouble. The historical outlook in Fowler's passage makes the history of rhetoric truly a reflection of Dark-age life. Patriarchy is the cultural text within which women and rhetoric become something to be given away in marriage to all other arts—first politics, then philosophy, and now (again?) poetics. Side by side, the "mistress of all the arts" (Tacitus, 1942, 32) and her metaphorical extension, woman, will be located by consistent representation of prostitution or virginity or housework. She is a whore, a bride or a wife.

We can now understand the remarriage of rhetoric to Poetics as yet another desire to control the practice of rhetoric by subordinating its place to that of another discipline (and the connotation of that word, as Foucault reminds us, should not be lost).

SUBVERTING THE ARCHETYPAL PLOT

In order to delineate the implications and possibilities that can be drawn from the archetypal plot, I shall move to the second step of my argument, which shows how images of rhetoric/woman/horse resist inclusion within the archetypal plot, thereby calling the narrative "I" into question. The resistance to a coherent subject, plot, and narrative "I" is an illogical movement. By illogical I mean, for example, that the subject (rhetoric/woman), proceeding as the narrative "I," slips the grasp of the narrative logic because it is inadequate for understanding the subject's totality. White (1978, p. 4) describes the dynamism in the movement of the logical/illogical combination. There is movement "'back and forth' (like a shuttle) between alternative ways of encoding reality." I understand this to mean that the history of rhetoric is shaped as a tradition by the archetypal plot and is reshaped by taking account of the alternative possibilities of a subject's (rhetoric/woman) image. Rhetoric is always an occasion to express itself and its history otherwise.

I offer the term *rheotactical* to suggest my conception of this movement. *Rhoe*, derived from the Greek verb meaning *flow* (Coppee, 1860, p. 1), is associated with the element of water through rhetoric's participation in the sea birth of Aphrodite. It is a tactical flow that goes toward its destination, goal, or end point, which is its nature to do so by intention—theoretical (Aristotelian) teleology. And yet, it deviates or swerves from the proper or ideal path. A rheotactic study, then, follows two steps in order to achieve understanding: First, I have arranged rhetoric and ordered its history. Now I notice how the arrangement turns, moves, and maneuvers. With this notion of rheotactic, I will re-present the configural pattern of the wife and whore image and its integration into the archetypal plot so that I can turn to follow how images swerve and maneuver in/out of this pattern. Even though there is a text of rhetoric held together by chronological sequence, an undertow will not let the image of rhetoric stay on the proper track. A rheotactic approach makes evident that rhetoric is a trade-off between conventionalized conceptions, which is its lowest potential (goal) and mythic misconceptions, which is its radical, highest possibility. If we understand this trade-off, we can begin to see that rhetorical theory, particularly Aristotelian, is a product of a need to organize the expression of thought in a particular way, a manner boringly transparent and dead.

Metaphoric Evasion

I return to myth to discover what elements can voice an opposition to the metaphorical characterization of the origin of rhetoric with which the narrative "I" began the archetypal plot. In myth, rhetoric is depicted as a woman in an erotic context. *Eros* is passionate love; it is erotic desire. So cast, rhetoric can fall into a state of madness, which, Prodicus tells us (in Sprague, 1972), can be thought of like two arrows hitting the mark: "Desire doubled is love, and love doubled is madness" (84–87). The problem with doubling passion is that it puts reasoning, the essence of rhetoric from the future synecdochical standpoint, to rest (Aristotle, 1984a, 1202a6–7). The doubling of passion can be blocked and madness avoided only if rhetoric becomes the logic of social life (1954, 1359b9–11), and if Aphrodite's direct link to rhetoric is repressed.

But Aphrodite's repression is impossible for man. Aphrodite is born from the sea after blood from Uranus' (Heaven) castrated genitals renders it fertile. It is out of man's libido, signified by ocean plus the blood of severed genitals, that Aphrodite matures (Eliade, 1982, p. 188). It is through Aphrodite's synthetic (literally man-made) fusion of herself with the mirror and the flower that we find her connection with bodily pleasure called into question (see Dijkstra, 1986).

In erotic settings, Rhetoric holds a mirror, which, being like a pool of water and round like the moon, reflects a mythical connection to seduction. It is also narcissistic and auto-erotic. A woman before a mirror is an image of feminine self-containment and vanity. Her existence is self-contained because she exists in and for what she mirrors; she is vain because she does not mirror the world of man. When she is like the moon, Sappho (1982) says, she is distant, cool, isolated from the *polis* of the stars, those tiny suns symbolizing man (fr. 34). At the mirror, she sets herself apart from the others. But the patriarchal gaze, not the woman, must do the surveying, judging, and regulating of her. Isocrates (1980c), we now recall (from the *Panegyricus*) seeks war against the Persians to secure one Hellenic world, just as had been done previously against the Amazons (see T. Poulakos, 1987, and McKechnie, 1989, pp. 22–28). A woman at a mirror is otherworldly, in another world, and controlled by no one. Thus, she is an oppositional voice with power to destroy the future of her metonymic dispersal.

Elsewhere, Rhetoric holds a flower, mythically signifying an erotic function much like eyes or the breath of perfume (Sappho, 1982, fr. 1.1–4). Woman, the flower-like entity, is a land siren. She can lure even the most wise and most learned man. Further, when a wife adorns her body with perfume, her sexual fidelity is questioned. Thus, in Aristophanes' (1931) *The Ecclesiazusae*, Blepyrus asks about his wife's absence from the home:

> Eh, Praxagora! where do you come from?
> How does that concern you?
> Why greatly! What a silly question!
> You don't think I have come from my lover's?
> No, perhaps not from only one.
> You can make yourself sure of that.
> And how?
> You can see whether my head smells of perfume.
> What? cannot a woman [get screwed] without perfume?
> The gods forfend, as far as I'm concerned.
>   (1931, pp. 354–355)

The "flowers of an eloquent tongue" or the tropes of rhetoric can have a destabilizing effect on the truth, just as Praxogora, in particular, can on the household of her husband, and woman, in general, can on the *polis*. Rhetoric must be placed in the gardener's care if the corporate body of man is to determine who is freeborn and chaste, who is to bloom and when she is to be picked.

If rhetoric follows the course as seen by the Amazon living by the light of the moon or as a harlot living by the light of her mirror, it cannot serve the dictates of man in his home or *polis*. To let her attend to herself is to neglect the possibility of man uniting in a *polis* (as did the Amazon once); and it is at the same time to neglect the reality of public affairs (as did the mistress once in the case of Aristotle's encounter with Phyllis [Figure 1], and as did the wife, as Augustine writes [1951, 1958]). If rhetoric is to become a useful art, then civilized human and political life must cut off the flow of the passion, the body of woman.

And yet rhetoric is already associated with a woman: Aphrodite. This association of rhetoric to the feminine shows that the "data" resist coherence of one image (say the wife) that we try to fashion it into. As the myth establishes Aphrodite as the literal and figurative embodiment of Rhetoric, it does so by showing her origination in man's desire. Man is caught between rejecting "passion" and identifying with it. If he reidentifies with *Polos* (literally, an untamed, bestial, horse [the Amazon]), if he recovers what he has cut off (literally, his genitals), he cannot escape the life of the wild beast and come together to create a *polis*. If he rejects passion, he must do so by castrating himself.

Metonymic Slippage

I turn to Plato's discussion of rhetoric to illustrate his awareness that there are images that resisted inclusion within the metaphoric characterization and now oppose the metonymic destruction of the art's elements. It is rhetoric's rebirth in *Gorgias* that attempts to solve the slippage into the repressed opposition's voice by constructing Aphrodite's birth in terms of its masculinity. Passion is no longer wild, but rather something that is not yet tame. The rebirth of rhetoric in Plato (1973) shifts the art from its Amazonian contrast between wild and tame to an opposition between what has and what has not already been tamed. Moving through a whole field of images associating rhetoric with passion and seduction, Plato reconstructs the wild/tame sensibility as that which must be domesticated before rhetoric can persuade men to act justly in guiding the helm of the state (Plato, 1961, 303e).

The passion of rhetoric, from man's desire; is an object that must be sacrificed. Plato (1973) visualizes a hierarchy of language users, from *polos* or beast at the bottom, through barbarians including the Sophists, to Greeks in general, and then to the summit of the *polis* (248–249). That he entertains the possibility of a "true rhetoric" is clear from the *Phaedrus*, but this rhetoric becomes possible only if the orator, like the charioteer, is able to seize, hoist, gag, and yoke his own bad horse that, like the harlot, dazzles the eyes of the lover (Plato 1973, 254–255). The lustful ways of the bad horse and, as myth has shown us by etymological extension, woman, must be sacrificed for the unity of the *polis*. Ironically, Plato's ideal rhetoric rests upon a second castration— man from his passions.

By shifting from the image of "wild" after the defeat of the Amazons to an image of what has not already been tamed, Plato again sacrifices the horse, and mythically woman is killed again. An unbroken colt is not an ordinary sacrificial victim; a goat is ordinary (Loraux, 1987, p. 36). The horse, and by implication woman, has its place in military sacrifices, a ritual uniting men as hoplites or citizen-soldiers in the democratic city-states and, at the same time, dividing them from what is female (Halperin, 1990, pp. 14–16). The slaying of horses provides a common ground and a collective image of citizens as masculine, competitive, restrained, and aggressive. The image is ideological and politically alien to woman. She is excluded mythically (her association with a horse) and symbolically (her exclusion from military horse).

But Plato's writing resists his intentions. For although the central allegory in the *Phaedrus* is the chariot figure in which the charioteer seeks to tame and control the magnificent black horse, that taming is itself undercut by a more central claim of this dialogue—that divine madness, as a necessary condition for truth, presupposes an

unbridled bodily attraction, as Socrates undoubtedly feels toward the beautiful Phaedrus. Thus we see that the "truth" of bodily desire resides within man himself, is a
prelude to whatever "truth" he seeks, and cannot be willfully controlled or projected
only onto woman. Thus, the feminine truth in language allows Plato to escape the
consequences of his intentions—namely, the second castration should desire be cut off
of/from man.

Synecdochical Resistance

In the synecdochical characterization of rhetoric, I have shown how the art functioned
through the institution of marriage to promote and sustain the polis. I said that
marriage is the political bond that unites men to one another by uniting them to woman
in a particular way. Thus, I suggested that while rhetoric is associated mythically with
the sacrifice of Amazon (woman/horse) in the metaphoric scene and with the taming
(killing?) of the *polos* (woman/Amazon) for the sake of the *polis* in the metonymic scene,
the art in the synecdochical scene enslaves woman (*polos*/horse/Amazon) through a
marriage. So characterized, marriage is a substitute sacrifice or the symbolic killing of
eros (see frs. 82B 8a, 87B 123 in Sprague, 1972). Just as the military has its sacrificial
victim in the horse in the previous scene of the archetypal plot, so, in the next one,
the sacrificial victim "must also by definition be untouched by the yoke" (Loraux, 1987,
p. 36). And the two images overlap in that men of thirty years of age or older, veterans
of the wars, were the husbands of thirteen-year-old girls because they, as untamed fillies,
were to be led away and made passive and docile (Vernant, 1990, pp. 55–77; Pomeroy,
1975, p. 64).

However, there is a counter-example. The *hetaira* opposes rhetoric/woman as it/she
functions only through the politics of marriage. Living as the sexual companion of
man, she is a disruption, a gap in the *polis*. She is the woman of excess. Because she
is unmarried, she is pretending to be a free-born and chaste wife, when, in fact, she is
a prostitute who earns money. The problem with prostitution, insofar as I have revealed
its inextricable link with the art of rhetoric, is that not every rhetoric, which is to say,
not every woman, is a rhetoric (or again, a woman [read: wife]) of the *polis*.

That a rhetoric can negate marriage and a political institution is revealed in the
mythical adventures of Ixion. When a woman is given to him for marriage, Ixion does
not pay the equivalent of a dowry (*charis*), money which is a public seal of the agreement
between two households. The woman is a legitimate wife because she has been given
away according to rules, but she is illegitimate because her husband has not paid for
her. Ixion has made a pretense of marriage. Here is Vernant's (1990) brilliant telling
of the tale:

> Ixion does away with the distinction between the *damar*, or legitimate wife, and the *pallake*
> or concubine. He reduces Dia, whom he has received from her father's hands to be his wife,
> to the level of companion in sexual activity, like a slave captured by force in battle or carried
> off during a pirate raid, or like any woman installed in the house without ceremony to do
> her master's pleasure.

As the story continues, it becomes clear that the violation of marriage also destroys
the unity among men:

> Ixion does not simply deny Dia the status of wife, within the context of marriage. He also
> destroys the alliance with his father-in-law, changing it into its opposite, a relationship of

hostility. When his son-in-law invites him to a feast to celebrate their reconciliation, Hesioneus [father] goes trustingly to attend it and perishes in a trap treacherously set for him. In return for the gift of Hesioneus' daughter Ixion offers only vain and misleading words and then repays the friendly trust of the father with trickery, duplicity, and murder. He negates all forms of exchange and mutual generosity called for by marriage. (p. 158)

When "marriage" operates outside of the patriarchal conceptions of home and state, it functions as an oppositional voice to both. And both official "rhetoric" and "woman" are challenged.

Rhetoric's ability to undercut the official line is recorded by Aristotle as duplicity; he writes that the Sophist's judicial rhetoric has crept into the habit—the wolf into the sheep's clothes—of politics (1954, 1356a 26; see Roberts, 1904; Sutton, 1991). The judicial rhetoric of the sophists, like *Polos*, is dangerous because it addresses the *individual's* need. Thus, rhetoric and politics do have a close connection when they preserve the relationship between citizen and *polis*. And finally, when rhetoric masquerades as politics, the latter is in jeopardy in the same way that marriage is threatened when words replace materiality.

The making of a distinction between judicial and political rhetoric corroborates the close connection among rhetoric, a woman, and marriage. Just as the whore disrupts the center of the home and threatens the lawful wife, so does a sophistical rhetoric challenge the relations of power upon which the *polis* rests. We catch Plato's fear of the sophist as a woman when he describes rhetorical practices as a disguise (1952, p. 23). In other places, he uses figures like "deceitful designer," "masquerader," "smuggler," and "juggler" to depict rhetoric. Nothing, however, illustrates the power of rhetoric as an erotic, seductive woman better than his *Gorgias* (1952). Rhetoric is an illiberal art, a woman in a fallen cosmetic state keeping erotic company. Wearing suggestive dress and excessive make-up and polish, she is far more than a decorative addition providing mere pleasure and gratification. This mistress of the arts projects a pretense of beauty. Her true identity remains hidden, covered-over, perhaps even distorted. As sophistic is to legislation, Plato muses, and as cookery is to medicine, so is rhetoric to justice. Rhetoric is presented as dolled-up woman, the noncitizen lover of man, a relationship that must not influence politics. If a discussion of rhetoric as a harolt has meant mostly a discussion of verbal pleasure, then the art is an unsuitable foundation upon which civilized human social and political life must rest. If we identify with *Polos* (literally the untamed filly), we cannot keep the wild beast out of the household of man.

Ironic Subversion

In the post-Isocratean world, Woman/rhetoric is to serve. She is to wait. She is to come for the sake of—[15] For the sake of Truth, for the sake of the *polis*, for the sake of Beauty? No and Yes. No, she will be there for the truth in arguments that betray her, for the justice of the *polis* that is not equitable, and for beauty that lacks adornment. Yes, she will be there so that she can slip past the grasp of Beauty, Truth, and Justice placed within "logic" and decorum. By slipping the grasp of the logical, decorous placement, she can ask if logic and decorum are adequate to capture the nature of the subject. However, the question, since it is uttered within the ironic phase, is ironical. That is, the deviating rhetoric/woman earns the right to the closure of the archetypal plot. She is getting married to Stylish Poetics in the twentieth century, but she can ask: What is at stake in the control of rhetoric through woman? F. A. Wright offers this:

> The fact is—and it is well to state it plainly—that the Greek world perished from one main cause, a low ideal of womanhood and a degradation of women which found expression in both literature and in social life. The position of women and the position of slaves—for the two classes went together—were the canker spots which, left unhealed, brought about the decay of Athens and then of Greece. (Cf. 58 Pomeroy)

Even though Wright's statement was used to urge the adoption of the Nineteenth Amendment, it recollects the degradation of woman in the literature of the rhetorical tradition. If the Golden Age of Greece is what the rhetor of today has his or her sight set on, that vision, if it is not to succumb to the same decay as happened in Athens, must be liberated. And so to Wright's pronouncement we add that rhetoric has suffered from a low ideal of womanhood. As woman was pushed to the fringes of society, rhetoric was the fringe built around her to keep her out of sight and to limit her influence. This is Nazi Germany's dream. Adolph Hitler dreamed of fighting, wounding, and killing Amazons in space (Dr. Kurt Kreuger, *I Was Hitler's Doctor*, pp. 276–281; cf. Sobol, 1972, p. 155). As long as tyrants are separated from their dreams, rhetoric is separated from man's dream, which is to say, the art separates man from himself and man from woman. To end the theme of separation means to stop speaking like man. It means giving rhetoric a woman's voice. It means the end of political unity *as we know it*.

CONCLUSION AND IMPLICATIONS

In a representative perspective (which is the foundation for a traditional history of rhetoric), the metonymic destruction of metaphoric unity is felt as the need for difference between the masculine (*polis* dweller) and feminine (barbaric wanderer). The masculine image which brings rhetoric into original history signifies its appropriation by ideologically motivated systems of discourse. The most elemental of these takes place at the level of *verba* (the metaphor of *rhetoric as woman*), not at the level of *res*.

The one is prior to the many and to the composite, Aristotle says (1962, 286b.16–17). Without metaphoric unity, which underwent metonymic destruction, rhetoric cannot be one. Dispersed, rhetoric has no essence, which, definitionally, cannot be divided (Aristotle 1960, 32–35). A glance back at *The Gynaikonomous Letteraturizzazione of Rhetoric* (see Figure 2) shows this to mean that rhetoric is brought into philosophy and its history as either a wife or whore. 'Tis a pity she's a whore.

Since a whore is excess and, thus, without essence, rhetoric cannot subsist essentially (1960, 1015b.16–17). Thus, the word *rhetoric* (as used by Plato in his dialogues, et al.) is a misogynist term insofar as woman/rhetoric refuses to incorporate the cultural ideal of patriarchy, particularly the idealization of the *polis* and family, especially the relation between man and woman.[16]

Blind to its repression, rhetoric is fated to the inessential as opposed to the essential. Rhetoric needs to be dominated by man's voice so that she can be defined and so that she knows who she is. She is willingly made a slave. Turned into an object, she is a whore. This is so because even beyond her own desire, awareness, or thoughts, she is forever unfaithful by virtue of the fact that she has been made an object and can be possessed by anyone who chooses her. Locked away in the Peripatetic's Academy (to Aristotelianize her) or pushed outside the walls of Athens (to Platonize her), she still arouses desire. To inspire desire in a stranger is to fail your husband and your society. Through deceit, through sexual promiscuity, she proves she cannot be controlled or possessed. Rhetoric/Woman is doomed to duplicity and to excess because rhetoric/woman has been made an object, a man's possession. This is evident in the fact that at least two kinds of women—wives and whores—are necessary to theorize about how the practice of rhetoric can become a true art.

The wife metaphor is linked with preferred signifiers and this association is read back onto the wife/whore system of representation. Any contradiction to this distinction, as in the case of a *hetaira*, is an *ambiguity*, making it a fallacy by definition according to Aristotle's *Sophistical Refutations* (1984d, 165a.25–166b). If the wife begins to emulate the whore—in other words, to become ambiguous, which is to become a *hetaira*—she can be discounted as a societal evil, which is to say a logical fallacy. In this self-perpetuating system, rhetoric is forever conjoined to reason as the sign of a "true" rhetoric. Moreover, this "true" rhetoric exists in the space where the art and woman struggle to overcome each other. Rhetoric (woman/wife) enters the writing of history employing a discourse system (man/husband) which would exclude it—posing her as wife to satisfy the fetish of respectability.[17] Thus, for rhetoric to count as an authentic person she must erase rhetoric. The problem is self-supporting, circular, and antiwoman to the core. It asks that I write with an eraser.

I go back to the scene of history where a wife/whore metaphor carried woman into rhetoric. While this return now affords me with many possibilities for demonstrating the untenability of the useful/useless, wife/whore, insider/outsider, sophistic/rhetoric opposition, I focus on what is, perhaps, the most powerful source of her oppositional voice, namely, the mythological history of rhetoric as it relates to woman's body, particularly her sexuality. Initially, rhetoric's sexual images arise in myth. Moreover, these mythic images occur within the context of the Athenian *polis*, where they function as a cadre of metaphors which divide woman from man and *polis* and unify the corporal body of man in the fatherland. This location secures an historic basis for woman's subordination to man as well as rhetoric's subordination to philosophy in general and politics in particular. Out of the desire to subordinate rhetoric and woman in these ways, the question of the unity of the *polis* and, by extension, of the household emerges as an ideal that mandates woman's degeneration. This degeneration, in turn, informs the history of rhetoric. Historical consciousness takes advantage of the insignificance of woman in order to exonerate the Tradition, informed by Aristotelian theory, and reproach practices that deviate from it.[18]

They did invent her (de Beauvoir, 1952, p. 174; cf. Nietzsche, *Twilight of the Idols*). Her hope is to give that lie back to the patriarchate. After all, she does exist apart from his inventiveness.[19]

All of this has been a long way to say: All footnotes lead to Plato, except . . .

Notes

1. After Theseus was banished from Athens, he died. "They [the Athenians] built a great tomb for him and decreed that it should be forever a sanctuary for slaves and for all poor and helpless people, in memory of one who through his life had been the protector of the defenseless" (Hamilton, 1940, p. 158). I have dedicated this project to Theseus so that he may return and conquer his image as an Amazonian fighter. This quest I have charged him with will involve the task of carnivalization. Drawing upon William S. Burrough's carnivals in *Nova Express*, Vitanza

(1987, p. 56) writes: "Word begets image and image is virus. 'Image' is what infects us. And what is 'image'? It is the virus power's *reality of an insidious single universe of discourse*, to which we have become addicted and victimized and which is depicted as a figurative viral infection that feeds on 'junk.'" Theseus, then, must conquer the web or maze of meanings left in the wake of the killing of the Amazon.

2. Individual Amazon names inscribed on vases or in myth link woman to horse: Hippolyte, "of the stampeding horse"; Melanippe, "black mare"; and Alcippe, "powerful mare." See Sobol (1972, p. 162) and Lefkowitz (1986, pp. 26–27). For discussion of the invention of etymologies by the Greeks, see Merck (1978, p. 110).

3. My opening image of women's connectedness to an animal is indebted to Simone de Beauvoir (1952). In this essay, citations to classical texts are by line or fragment number, indicated by the omission of the abbreviations *p.* or *pp.*

4. Just a few examples: Lefkowitz, reading Semonides, tells us that "a beautiful woman is like a mare" (1986, p. 115). Octavio Paz (1961, p. 36) describes the Latin American view of woman: "Woman is a domesticated wild animal, lecherous and sinful from birth, who must be subdued with a stick and guided by the reins of religion." The idea of man ruling over woman as one tames a wild animal is discussed by Aristotle (1984c, 1254b–1277b.25). (See Garside, 1971; Lefkowitz and Fant, 1982). Rhetoric is discussed through characters that mean untamed horse. From Thrasymachus, Herodicus told Polos, "You are always coltish" (fr. 6A in Sprague, 1972). The myths and allegories feature horse, such as in *Phaedrus* (Plato, 1973, pp. 246–257). Antiphon uses a metaphor of the horse (fr. B 144 in Sprague, 1972).

5. I have discussed the use of collage as a method suitable to understanding the fragments in rhetoric's history in Sutton (forthcoming). The discussion, in this essay, extends the collage as a method by appropriating White (1987, pp. 1–25; 1973, pp. 45–80); Vernant (1990, pp. 258–259), De Certeau (1988, 1984); Brantlinger (1990, pp. 1–34); and, finally, Cixious and Clement (1975, p. 6).

6. For this translation, see Kane (1986); fn. I.; Isocrates (1980c, 254) makes a similar point in *Antidosis*.

7. Dionysius of Halicarnassus (1974) writes history sensitive to the Greek attitude toward Etruscan women (seventh century b.c.). According to Etruscan Institutions and customs, the wife takes part in the feasts and banquets on a footing of complete equality with her husband. This privileged place of the Etruscan women completely contrasts with the state of inferiority and even of seclusion which was the Greek wife's fate up to Hellenistic times. The Greeks, and the Romans too, considered the Etruscan attitude scandalous and did not spare their attacks on the supposed immorality of the Etruscans. This scorn is reported in the fourth century B.C.; see Bloch (1956) and Warren (1973).

8. Compare Dionysius of Halicarnassus (1974), for example, with Xenophon's (see Sprague, 1972) descriptions three centuries earlier: "But the 'sophists' talk to deceive and write for their own gain and are of no benefit to anyone; for none of them is wise or ever became so, but it is enough for each one of them to be called a 'sophist,' which is an insult, at least to men of sound reasoning. So I exhort you to be aware of the 'sophists,' but not to disregard the considerations of the philosophers" (fr. 79 2a). As told in *Gnomologium Vaticanum* (743 no. 166), it was said even a century earlier: "Gorgias the rhetor said that those neglecting philosophy and devoting themselves to general studies [rhetoric] were like the suitors who, though wanting Penelope, slept with her maids" (fr. 82 B29 in Sprague). The difference between whore or wife or between the maids or Penelope or, finally, between Virtue or Vice is, as Prodicus teaches, the choice of Heracles (fr. 84 B2 in Sprague).

9. I use the future anterior tense for a reason. Rhetoric and Woman are established in language through grammar, the structure of the verb tense of the past definite. My attempt at rewriting the history of rhetoric is similar to what Vitanza (forthcoming) has in mind when he reads Lacan's future anterior as the tense that heals (*Ecrits*, p. 86; cf. deMan, p. 222). My thesis of history is that woman is the representation of, the accumulation of, and the transformation of symbols into an open and available meaning to the question—what is rhetoric/woman?

10. Aristotle ridden by Phyllis, as depicted in a 7-3/16 × 5-1/8″ Renaissance engraving by Master M. Z. (Martin Zazinger). The duplication of the photograph (permission and courtesy of Fogg Art Museum, Harvard University) appears in Horowitz (1976, p. 190).

11. I have relied on Horowitz (1976) and Hutchinson (1966) for a reference to the various sources.

12. For a critical appraisal of writing (the discipline) and rhetoric, see Vitanza (1987).

13. See Wehril (1962). Powell (1988) reports: "The behavior of women was commonly appraised with words from the root *kosm-*, which often implied the orderly separation of things" (p. 338). Other remarks on *gynaikonomous*, having an official to control the movements of women, occur in *Politics* (Aristotle, 1984c). For that discussion, see Garside (1971).

14. This is an Italian term from Vasile Florescu that Kennedy (1980, p. 5) borrows for "shorthand convenience." The term describes "a persistent characteristic of classical rhetoric in almost every phase of its ancient and modern history, to move from primary into secondary forms." See Kennedy's (1980, p. 247) note to his own citation and Sutton (1986) for further discussion.

15. This is based on Semonides's discussion of the different kinds of women whose behaviors are defined in terms of service to their husbands. See Lefkowitz and Fant (1982, p. 14).

16. This misogynistic rendition is particularly evident in the thesis of Schiappa (1990). He writes that Plato coined the term "rhetoric." In fact, he insists, by documenting his claim through his earlier research, that "the evidence concerning the myth that Corax and Tisias 'invented' rhetoric must be reconsidered" (p. 197). I agree—almost—with J. Poulakos's argument (1990) against Schiappa (1990). The difference between him and me is I wish to give the word *rhetoric* to the Schiappa *et als.* of the world. I am not interested in defending a word that is based in Plato's misogyny. For Plato as misogynist and feminist, see Wender (1973).

17. McKechnie (1989, p. 152) writes: "Philosophy was usually regarded as unimpeachably respectable. *Hetaerae*, by contrast, are treated by the ancient authors as having existed in a *demi-monde*."

18. A composte is an alternative to Aristotle. It involves an investigation of decomposition as an image capable not only of organizing information, but of generating a formula for the discovery of the invention process.

19. Cole (1991) claims that rhetoric is a discipline of Aristotle and Plato and a word that both use to describe an alternative version from their predecessors. Also see Sankovitch (1986).

References

Aristophanes. (1931a). *The Ecclesiazusae on Women in Council*. In The Athenian Society, eds., *Aristophanes Comedies* (New York: Rarity Press), vol. 2, pp. 330–392.

Aristophanes. (1931b). *The Thesmophoriazusae or the Women's Festival*. In The Athenian Society, eds., *Aristophanes Comedies* (New York: Rarity Press), vol. 2, pp. 266–326.

Aristophanes. (1931c). *Wasps*. In The Athenian Society, eds., *Aristophanes Comedies* (New York: Rarity Press), vol. 2, pp. 8–80.

Aristotle. (1954). *Rhetoric*. Translated by W. R. Roberts. New York: Modern Library.

Aristotle. (1960). *Metaphysics*. Translated by Richard Hope. Ann Arbor: University of Michigan Press.

Aristotle. (1962). "De caelo." Translated by T. Taylor. In Thomas P. Kiernan, ed., *Aristotle Dictionary* (New York: Philosophical Library), p. 452.

Aristotle. (1984a). *Magna moralia*. Translated by St. G. Stock. In Jonathan Barnes, ed., *The Complete Works of Aristotle* (Princeton, NJ: Princeton University Press), vol. 2, pp. 1868–1921.

Aristotle. (1984b). *Nicomachean Ethics*. Translated by W. D. Ross, revised by J. O. Urmson. In J. Barnes, ed., *The Complete Works of Aristotle* (Princeton, NJ: Princeton University Press), vol. 2, pp. 1729–1867.

Aristotle. (1984c). *Politics*. Translated by B. Jowett. In J. Barnes, ed., *The Complete Works of Aristotle* (Princeton, NJ: Princeton University Press), vol. 2, pp. 1986–2129.

Aristotle. (1984d). *Sophistical Refutations*. Translated by W. A. Pickard-Cambridge. In J. Barnes, ed., *The Complete Works of Aristotle* (Princeton, NJ: Princeton University Press), vol. 1, pp. 278–314.

Arthur, M. (1973). "Early Greece: The Origins of the Western Attitude toward Women." *Arethusa* 6: 7–59.

Augustine. (1951). *Letters*, Vol. 1 [Letters 1–82]. Translated by Sister W. Parsons, S.N.D. Washington, DC: The Catholic University of America Press.

Augustine. (1958). *On Christian Doctrine*. Translated by D. W. Robertson Jr. Indianapolis, IN: Bobbs-Merrill.

Bloch, R. (1956). *The Etruscans*. New York: Praeger.

Bloom, H. (1975). *A Map of Misreading*. New York: Oxford University Press.

Brantlinger, P. (1990). *Crusoe's Footprints*. New York: Routledge.

Buxton, R.G.A. (1982). *Persuasion in Greek Tragedy: A Study in Peitho*. Cambridge: Cambridge University Press.

Cixous, H., and C. Clement. (1975). *The Newly Born Woman*. Translated by Betsy Wing. Minneapolis: University of Minnesota Press.

Cole, T. (1991). *The Origin of Rhetoric in Ancient Greece*. Baltimore: John Hopkins University Press.

Coppee, H. (1860). *Elements of Rhetoric Designed as a Manual of Instruction*. Philadelphia: E. H. Butler.

de Beauvoir, S. (1952). *The Second Sex*. Translated by H. M. Parshley. New York: Knopf.

de Certeau, M. (1984). *The Practice of Everyday Life*. Translated by S. F. Rendall. Berkeley and Los Angeles: University of California Press.

de Certeau, M. (1988). *The Writing of History*. Translated by T. Conley. New York: Columbia University Press.

De Ste. Croix, G.E.M. (1970). "Some Observations of Athenian Woman." *Classical Review* 20: 273–278.

Dijkstra, B. (1986). *Idols of Perversity: Fantasies of Feminine Evil in Fin-De-Siecle Culture*. New York: Oxford University Press.

Dionysius of Halicarnassus. (1974). *On the Ancient Orators*. In *The Critical Essays*, trans. S. Usher (Cambridge, MA: Harvard University Press), vol. 1, pp. 5–15.

Eliade, M. (1982). *A History of Religious Ideas*. Translated by W. R. Trask. Chicago: University of Chicago Press.

Farenga, V. (1979). "Periphrasis on the Origin of Rhetoric." *Modern Language Notes* 94: 1033–1055.

Fowler, A. (1990). "Apology for Rhetoric." *Rhetorica* 8: 103–118.

Gardner, H. (1980). *Art through the Ages*. New York: Harcourt Brace Javanovich.

Garside, C. (1971). "Can a Woman Be Good in the Same Way as a Man?" *Dialogue: Canadian Philosophical Review* 10: 534–544.

Gomme, A. W. (1967). *Essays in Greek History and Literature*. Freeport, NY: Books for Libraries Press.

Hall, J. (1979). *Dictionary of Subjects and Symbols in Art*. New York: Harper and Row.

Halperin, D.M. (1990). "The Democratic Body: Prostitution and Citizenship in Athens." *Differences* 2: 1–15.

Hamilton, E. (1940). *Mythology*. New York: Grosset and Dunlap.

Henle, J. (1973). *Greek Myths: A Vase Painter's Notebook*. Bloomington: Indiana University Press.

Horowitz, M. C. (1976). "Aristotle and Woman." *Journal of the History of Biology* 9: 183–213.

Hutchinson, J. C. (1966). "The Housebook Master and the Folly of the Wise Man." *Art Bulletin* 48: 73–78.

Isocrates. (1980a). *Antidosis*. Translated by G. Norlin. In G. P. Goold, ed., *Isocrates* (Cambridge, MA: Harvard University Press), vol. 2, pp. 184–365.

Isocrates. (1980b). *Nicocles or The Cyprians*. Translated by G. Norlin. In G. P. Goold, ed., *Isocrates* (Cambridge, MA: Harvard University Press), vol. 1, pp. 77–113.

Isocrates. (1980c). *Panegyricus*. Translated by G. Norlin. In G. P. Goold, ed., *Isocrates*, (Cambridge, MA: Harvard University Press), vol. 1, pp. 121–241.

Kane, F.I. (1986). "Peitho and the *Polis*." *Philosophy and Rhetoric* 19: 99–123.

Kennedy, G. A. (1980). *Classical Rhetoric and Its Christian and Secular Tradition from Ancient to Modern Times*. Chapel Hill: University of North Carolina Press.

Lacey, W. K. (1973). "Women in Democratic Athens." In S. G. Bell, ed., *Women: From the Greeks to the French Revolution* (Stanford, CA: Stanford University Press), pp. 21–36.

Lanham, R. A. (1976). *The Motives of Eloquence*. New Haven, CT: Yale University Press.

Lefkowitz, M. R. (1986). *Women in Greek Myth*. Baltimore: Johns Hopkins University Press.

Lefkowitz, M. R., and M. B. Fant. (1982). *Women's Life in Greece and Rome*. Baltimore: Johns Hopkins University Press.

Lerner, G. (1986). *The Creation of Patriarchy*. New York: Oxford University Press.

Loraux, N. (1987). *Tragic Ways of Killing a Human*. Translated by A. Forster. Cambridge, MA: Harvard University Press.

Lysias. (1976a). *Against Eratosthenes*. Translated by W.R.M. Lamb. In G. P. Goold, ed., *Lysias* (Cambridge, MA: Harvard University Press), pp. 221–281.

Lysias. (1976b). *On the Murder of Eratosthenes*. Translated by W.R.M. Lamb. In G. P. Goold, ed., *Lysias* (Cambridge, MA: Harvard University Press), pp. 2–47.

Macrobis. (1952). *Commentary on the Dream of Scipio*. Translated by W. H. Stahl. New York: Columbia University Press.

McKechnie, P. (1989). *Outsiders in the Greek Cities in the Fourth Century B.C.* London: Routledge.

Merck, M. (1978). "The City's Achievements." In S. Lipshitz, ed., *Tearing the Veil* (London: Routledge & Kegan Paul), pp. 95–115.

Morris, W. (1971). *The American Heritage Dictionary*. Boston: Houghton Mifflin.

Nietzsche, F. (1961). *Thus Spoke Zarathustra* . Translated by R. J. Hollingdale. New York: Penguin Books.

Nietzsche, F. (1966). *Beyond Good and Evil*. Translated by W. Kaufmann. New York: Vintage Books.

Paz, O. (1961). *The Labyrinth of Solitude*. New York: Grove Press.

Plato. (1952). *Gorgias*. Translated by W. C. Helmbold. Indianapolis, IN: Bobbs-Merrill.

Plato. (1961). *Statesman*. Translated by J. B. Skemp. In E. Hamilton and H. Cairns, eds., *Plato's Collected Dialogues* (New York: Pantheon Books), pp. 1018–1085.

Plato. (1973). *Phaedrus and Letters VII and VIII*. Translated by W. Hamilton. New York: Penguin Books.

Pomeroy, S. B. (1975). *Goddesses, Whores, Wives, and Slaves*. New York: Schocken Books.

Poulakos, J. (1987). "Isocrate's Use of Narrative in the *Evagoras*: Epideictic Rhetoric and Moral Action." *Quarterly Journal of Speech* 73: 317–328.

Poulakos, J. (1990). "Interpreting Sophistical Rhetoric: A Response to Schiappa." *Philosophy and Rhetoric* 23: 218–228.

Powell, A. (1988). *Athens and Sparta*. London: Routledge.

Roberts, W. R. (1904). "The New Rhetorical Fragment (Oxyrhynchus Papyri, Part 3, pp. 27–30) in Relation to the Sicilian Rhetoric of Corax and Tisias." *Classical Review* 18: 18–21.

Sankovitch, T. (1986). "Inventing Authority of Origin." In Mary Beth Rose, ed., *Women in the Middle Ages and Renaissance* (Syracuse, NY: Syracuse University Press), pp. 227–243.

Sappho. (1982). *Alcaeus*. Translated by D. A. Campbell. In G. P. Goold, ed., *Greek Lyric* (Cambridge, MA: Harvard University Press), pp. 438–473.

Schiappa, E. (1990). "Neo-Sophistic Criticism or the Historical Reconstruction of Sophistic Doctrines?" *Philosophy and Rhetoric* 23: 192–217.

Sobol, D. J. (1972). *The Amazons of Greek Mythology*. London: Thomas Yoseloff.

Sprague, R. K., ed. (1972). *The Older Sophists*. Columbia: University of South Carolina Press.

Sutton, J. (1986). "The Death of Rhetoric and Its Rebirth in Philosophy." *Rhetorica* 4: 203–226.

Sutton, J. (1991). "Rereading Sophistical Arguments: A Political Intervention." *Argumentation* 5: 141–157.

Sutton, J. (Forthcoming). "Structuring the Narrative for the Canon of Rhetoric: The Principles of Traditional Historiography (An Essay) with the Dead's *Differend* (A Collage)." In V. Vitanza, ed., *Writing Histories of Rhetoric*.

Tacitus. (1942). "A Dialogue on Oratory." In M. Hadas, ed., *The Complete Works of Tacitus* (New York: Modern Library), pp. 735–769.

Todorov, T. (1977). *Theories of the Symbol*. Translated by C. Poreter. Ithaca, NY: Cornell University Press.

Vernant, J-P. (1990). *Myth and Society in Ancient Greece*. Translated by J. Lloyd. New York: Zone Books.

Vitanza, V. (1987). "Critical/Subversions of the History of Rhetoric." *Rhetoric Review* 6: 41–66.

Vitanza, V. (Forthcoming). "Taking Account of a (Future-Anterior) History of Rhetoric *as* 'Libidinalized Marxism' (A P.M. Pastiche)." In V. Vitanza, ed., *Writing Histories of Rhetoric*.

Wehrli, C. (1962). "Les gyneconomes." *Museum Helveticum* 19: 33–38.

White, H. (1973). *Metahistory*. Baltimore: Johns Hopkins University Press.

White, H. (1978). *Tropics of Discourse*. Baltimore: Johns Hopkins University Press.

Warren, L. (1973). "The Women of Etruia." *Arethusa* 6: 91–103.

Wender, D. (1973). " Plato: Misogynist, Paedophile, and Feminist." *Arethusa* 6: 75–91.

Wilner, E. (1991, March–April). "Muse." *Ms.*, p. 94.

PART 2

Rhetoric and Epistemology

The suspect status of rhetoric in Western history might well be traced to a continuing belief that rhetorical discourse is deficient in its ability to convey truth. Whether "truth" is defined as the word of God, the result of scientific experiment, or the outcome of philosophical debate, rhetoric has often been seen as self-consciously employing other methods and seeking goals other than the production of truth, such as producing conviction or motivating action.

In the practical world of everyday affairs the philosopher's suspicion represents little more than a minor irritation, for to the extent that it achieves its goals—however framed—rhetorical practices are self-validating. In the academy, however, where the search for "truth" has been valorized as one of the premiere and ultimate goals, rhetorical theorists must constantly defend their object of study. Several routes to that defense are illustrated in the essays below.

The most conservative option is presented by Richard A. Cherwitz and James W. Hikins, who offer "Rhetorical Perspectivism" as a means of putting rhetoric back in harness to the truth. Cherwitz and Hikins believe that truth exists and that it is self-validating, but they restrict rhetoric to the role of a "tool" that enables human beings to approach or uncover the truth. They admit that human beings differ in their relationship(s) to particular dimensions of reality and therefore in their objectively different perspectives on the objects of truth. However, they maintain that such differences of position can be reconciled with a single, multidimensional, object of truth. On their account, when it is operating at its best, rhetoric functions to move audiences beyond their individual and limited perspectives to a mutual understanding of a more complete, unified truth that lies below the surface of discourse.

Thomas Farrell offers a different but nevertheless traditional approach to the problem in "Knowledge, Consensus, and Rhetorical Theory." Employing an Aristotelian framework, Farrell argues that while rhetoric may be irrelevant to some kinds of truth (i.e., technical knowledge), it is the central tool for gaining a particular kind of truth (i.e., social knowledge). Since social knowledge is essential to generating social cooperation, rhetoric is valuable for the kind of truth it produces. Rhetoric is thus not a deficient purveyor of technical knowledge, but rather the only proficient supplier of the knowledge that makes social interaction possible.

A variety of scholars have found these two relatively traditional approaches to the problem of rhetoric and epistemology insufficiently aggressive. In 1967, Robert Scott rekindled the sophistic vision of rhetoric's relationship to truth, arguing that rhetoric is epistemic. In "On Viewing Rhetoric as Epistemic," Scott argues that a more productive conception of the relationship between rhetoric, knowledge, and ethics would emerge from severing ourselves from unnecessarily narrow conceptions of truth. In particular, he maintains that no deliberative argument can produce a conclusion that has the force of certainty, because all such arguments rely on our past experience for their evidence or support. Short of having access to a crystal ball, we can never know if what was true in the past might continue to be true in the future. At best, Scott argues, we can only be certain of a particular claim or belief when we are actually in the presence of the thing that produces it; but of course when we are in the presence of such objects or phenomena, no argument is needed to demonstrate its certainty. Since no argument can produce a certain conclusion, the word "truth" misleads us. Rather than to see rhetoric as a method for conveying truths through argument, therefore, Scott suggests that we ought to see argument as a process of generating time-limited truths. In any given situation, we are always faced with conflicting (and often equally valid) obligations, interests, and values. Participating in argument allows us to choose the best actions for the particular situation, at least so long as we exercise toleration, will, and responsibility in our discussions.

Scott's position was soon widely supported. Barry Brummett, for example, argued that notions of an idealized truth ignored the fact that humans do not have immediate (or unmediated) access to such truth(s), but rather are constrained to operate in a world in which the "meaning" of reality is much more salient. In his highly influential essay "Some Implications of 'Process' or 'Intersubjectivity': Postmodern Rhetoric," Brummett refuted the notion of "objective reality." He pointed out that no one can ever observe nature directly, not even the scientist, for even scientific observation is mediated by observational devices (e.g., microscopes) or recording devices (e.g., rulers, or mass spectrometers). These tools always introduce limiting and biasing perspectives. Hence no objective, unmediated reality is available to humans. As Brummett explains it, "The discovery of reality and the testing of it is never independent of people, but takes place through people." Thus, he emphasizes, the production of knowledge and reality is typically a collective or "intersubjective" process, rather than a simple matter of each of us deciding for ourselves what is true. And it is precisely in this context that he argues that rhetoric provides the best model for producing and understanding the intersubjectivity of knowledge, truth, and reality.

According to the position initially framed by Scott and extended by Brummett, rhetoric is the master practice responsible for the construction of all human truths. This position placed them in opposition to the dictates of modernism, which treated rhetoric as a deficient or deviant form of philosophy, science, or theology, and led to the earliest invocations of a "postmodernist" rhetoric. One consequence of this reorientation was the development of the area of study that is now called the "rhetoric of inquiry." Under this heading rhetorical theorists and critics began to shift their attention away from the traditional texts of rhetorical study (i.e., public discourse that focused primarily on issues of governance) and began to focus attention on the ways in which rhetoric was involved in defining the criteria of truth and knowledge in any discourse community concerned with the problems and possibilities of human inquiry. It is not hard to understand how more humanistic disciplines like literary studies and history are deeply implicated by rhetorical practices, for they are so heavily reliant upon critical and interpretive methodologies that ultimately resist narrowly defined, objective verification. "Science," of course, with its rigid commitments to "neutrality" and "objectivity," is presumably a different matter, and thus provided the "hard case" for determining the ultimate role of rhetoric in human inquiry. If one could prove that "science" was governed by rhetoric, then, it was assumed, rhetoric's role as the master of knowledge would be secured. And it has been precisely the relationship between rhetoric and science that has most fully occupied the interests of those working in the rhetoric of inquiry (e.g., Campbell, 1975; Lessl, 1987; Lyne and Howe, 1986; Nelson, Megill, and McCloskey, 1987; Taylor, 1991).

Dilip Parameshwar Gaonkar's essay, "Rhetoric and Its Double: Reflections on the Rhetorical Turn in the Human Sciences," offers a critique of this development. Gaonkar suggests that an organized academic pursuit of the study of the rhetorical moves of scientific discourse is not needed. Instead, he suggests, scientists are capable of being self-reflective in times of crisis using only the resources of ordinary language. Thus, he concludes, rhetoric may not have an appropriately epistemic function. Instead, Gaonkar maintains that rhetoric is a local practice of persuasion and trope. As the list of additional readings indicates, Gaonkar's essay opens onto many differing perspectives. The ferment thus continues, as rhetorical theorists seek alternate routes by which one might articulate rhetoric to truth.

Additional Readings

Biesecker, Barbara. (1992). "Michel Foucault and the Question of Rhetoric." *Philosophy and Rhetoric* 25: 351–364.

Campbell, John. (1975). "The Polemical Mr. Darwin." *Quarterly Journal of Speech* 61: 375–390.

Leff, Michael C. (1978). "In Search of 'Ariadne's Thread': A Review of the Recent Literature on Rhetorical Theory." *Communication Studies* 29: 73–91.

Lessl, Thomas M. "Heresy, Orthodoxy, and the Politics of Science." (1987). *Quarterly Journal of Speech* 74: 18–34.

Lyne, John, and Henry Howe. (1986). "'Punctuated Equilibria': Rhetorical Dynamics of a Scientific Controversy." *Quarterly Journal of Speech* 72: 132–147.

Nelson, John S., Allan Megill, and Donald N. McCloskey, eds. (1987). *The Rhetoric of the Human Sciences: Language and Argument in Scholarship and Public Affairs*. Madison: University of Wisconsin Press.

Railsback, Celeste Condit. (1983). "Beyond Rhetorical Relativism: A Structural–Material Model of Truth and Objective Reality." *Quarterly Journal of Speech* 69: 351–363.

Scott, Robert. (1976). "On Viewing Rhetoric as Epistemic: Ten Years Later." *Central States Speech Journal* 27: 258–266.

Taylor, Charles A. (1991). "Defining the Scientific Community: A Rhetorical Perspective on Demarcation." *Communication Monographs* 58: 402–420.

Thomas, Douglas. (1994). "Reflections on a Nietzschean Turn in Rhetorical Theory: Rhetoric without Epistemology?" *Quarterly Journal of Speech* 80: 71–76.

On Viewing Rhetoric as Epistemic

ROBERT L. SCOTT

> Every beginning is against nature; the beginning is a leap and
> nature does not make leaps.
>
> *Pierre Thevenaz*[1]

Rhetoric is among the oldest of the arts of Western civilization. As the familiar tradition informs us, it sprung up in the fifth century B.C. during the aftermath of democratic revolts in several Greek *poleis* on the island of Sicily. But professing rhetoric seems always eventually to lead to embarrassment. In Plato's dialogue, Socrates' questions soon silence Gorgias, leaving young Polus to inquire, "Then what do you think rhetoric is?" In one way or another Socrates' answer has had a way of echoing through history.

At best good men grant rhetoric a slight role but grudgingly. A few years ago, Arthur Larson, cast in the role of rhetorician by virtue of his appointment as Director of the United States Information Agency, found himself trying to explain the importance of his mission to a Senate subcommittee. There creeps throughout the testimony the feeling that undertaking to persuade others is not quite right. Recall that Socrates remarks in responding to Polus that Gorgias has not made his profession altogether clear,[2] and consider Senator Fulbright's statement to Larson: "Well, this is a very interesting subject. I would not want to minimize the difficulty, either, by simply saying that you have not made it clear. Certainly all members of Congress have struggled with it. . . . It is a very difficult thing to sit here in peacetime and feel that it is constructive."[3]

Fulbright's remark goes to the heart of the matter. Invoking those well known arguments of Aristotle's from the opening chapter of his *Rhetoric* do no good, for clearly the art of persuasion is granted sufferance only on the grounds that men are not as they ought to be. Were all men able—as some men are—to reason soundly from true premises, then rhetoric would be superfluous.

The assumption that has spanned the centuries from that dialogue in Athens to the one in Washington, DC, is that men can possess truth. If indeed one can, in the sense that "truth" is ordinarily taken, then rhetoric is of limited value. If some men can possess truth, and others understand truth, then what need the former do but present truth to the latter? Only in unusual circumstances, for example, as Fulbright's statement implies, in time of war, or for those incapable of responding to right reason, may rhetoric be sanctioned.

Accepting the notion that truth exists, may be known, and communicated leads logically to the position that there should be only two modes of discourse: a neutral presenting of data among equals and a persuasive leading of inferiors by the capable. The attitude with which this position may be espoused can vary from benevolent to cynical, but it is certainly undemocratic. Still, the contemporary rhetorician is prone to accept the assumption, to say, in effect, "My art is simply one which is useful in making the truth effective in practical affairs," scarcely conscious of the irony inherent in his statement.

It is absurd, of course, to typify in a few paragraphs the attitude that has dominated rhetoric. But inasmuch as my purpose is to set forth a different position as a starting point for rhetoric, a longer consideration would be inappropriate. My undertaking can be described as philosophizing about rhetoric. The result will not be the discovery of a fresh starting point; I merely hope to clarify through a fresh analysis a way which has always been open and sometimes chosen, but seldom in a clear, incisive manner.

Obviously I take as a sufficient meaning for "philosophy" that indicated by Maurice Natanson, who sees it as a study of beginnings, which is to say that every discipline starts with some assumptions and that it is the business of philosophy to discover those assumptions and to study their meanings.[4]

My point of departure will be drawn from the work of Stephen Toulmin. Interestingly, Toulmin's book, *The Uses of Argument*, has had a remarkably potent influence on rhetorical theory and teaching in this decade, but rhetoricians have borrowed from the third chapter of that book, "The Layout of Arguments," tending to ignore the larger concern of which that analysis is a part.

1

Plato's Socrates confronted Gorgias with a choice: "Shall we, then, assume two kinds of persuasion, the one producing belief without certainty, the other knowledge?"[5] The choice seems simple enough, but the grounds involved need examining.

The terms "certainty" and "knowledge" confront one with what has become known as epistemology. It is to a fundamental inquiry about epistemology that Stephen Toulmin directs his analysis in the book mentioned above. He argues that the question "How do I know?" is an ambiguous one. In one sense it seems to ask, "How do my senses work?" and is a physiopsychological question. As such, it requires the compilation of data which can be analyzed in an empirical fashion—*a posteriori*. This is not, however, the fashion in which epistemologists have worked. Their methods have been speculative or at least abstract and *a priori*. The goal has been to obtain some standard or standards to satisfy the question, "How can I be certain of my conclusions?"

Toulmin suggests that we can set aside the psychological aspects of the central question, "How do I know?" This is not to say that these aspects are unimportant; it simply is a maneuver to allow us to concentrate on the philosophical aspects; he sees these as logical.

The quest for certainty presents a question which is often begged simply by entering into epistemological discussion. The question may be posed, "What do you mean by *certain?*" To say, "I am certain that the sun will rise tomorrow," may be to make a common statement which will probably not elicit argument, unless one is engaged in an epistemological discussion. (The fact that this example is often used in logic textbooks is evidence supporting Toulmin's disposition to see epistemology, considered philosophically, as basically an inquiry into logic.) But to say "The sun will not rise tomorrow" does not contradict the grounds on which most people feel certain that the sun will rise. Our conclusion, based on experience, does not follow necessarily from true premises. This is to say that we are *not* certain by the standard required.

The only sort of arguments which will answer the demands of certainty made in epistemological speculation are those arguments which Toulmin calls analytic. It is questionable (although Toulmin does not put the matter in this fashion) whether or not analytic arguments should be called arguments at all since the word "argument" suggests the drawing of conclusions which are somehow fresh, new, unknown, or unaccepted otherwise. Consider Toulmin's model analytic argument:

> Anne is Jack's sister;
> All Jack's sisters have red hair;
> So Anne has red hair.[6]

The conclusion of this argument, Toulmin says quite rightly, might better be introduced with the phrase "in other words" rather than "so" or "therefore." If the argument is to be analytic, the premise, "All Jack's sisters have red hair," can only be asserted in the presence of his sisters, including Anne.

Toulmin contrasts analytic arguments with arguments he calls substantial. He claims that analytic arguments, which have been taken to be the model to which philosophic arguments ought be held, are rare. I am inclined to believe that they are nonexistent, that is, that they can be indicated only with special sorts of notational systems which can never make existential claims. In terms of Toulmin's example, if one is not in the presence of Anne, then the conclusion makes a claim about a present condition on the basis of past experience, i.e., all Jack's sisters *had* red hair when last we saw them. To deny the conclusion is not to contradict the truth of the premises. If one is in Anne's presence, then no argument is necessary.

The famous illustrative syllogism concerning Socrates' mortality is ambiguous. If the major premise, "All men are mortal," is taken as a statement about our past experience, then the argument is not analytic; as a matter of fact, the argument turns out to be quite like that one from which we conclude that the sun will rise tomorrow. On the other hand, if we take the premise to be one defining what we mean in part by "man," then I would have to say that we have no argument; Toulmin would say, at least, that we have no substantial argument. In the case of taking the premise to be a definition, we could define men as being purple, and our argument is as good analytically. The rejoinder, "But men are not purple," appeals to a nonanalytic criterion.

As Toulmin sees them, substantial arguments involve some sort of type shift, that is, the conclusion contains an element not present in the premises, e.g., "cause" or "other minds." The type shift Toulmin concentrates on, and one which in my opinion is crucial, is the shift in time. In substantial arguments a shift in time always occurs. If a shift in time does not occur, then one is simply reporting what is present, not arguing.

That one is able to report, that is, share his perceptions with others, may be called into question if the analytic ideal is taken as the criterion for knowing.[7]

The observations thus far made lead us to believe that analytic arguments must be tenseless; they cannot exist in time.[8] The certainty demanded must arise from what has been true, is true, and shall be true, which is to say that it must be settled once and for all—immutable, changeless. Can there be substantial truths, that is, statements with content, not empty, which can be used in analytic argument? If so, then they must be stated in time and cannot be stated in time. Technically this is the conclusion of a *reductio ad absurdum*. The possibility of such truths can be rejected on formal grounds.

Although the possibility may be rejected formally, one may accept the conclusion labeled as invalid. One may not follow the reasoning or not accept the grounds. These possible responses underscore the use of the word "truth" in the foregoing paragraph. One might argue that "truth" is not coincident with the analytic ideal. It is possible but difficult to use the word without the freight of the analytic ideal. This strong tendency to associate one with the other should make us suspicious of a rhetoric which claims to be based on truth.

By "truth" one may mean some set of generally accepted social norms, experience, or even matters of faith as reference points in working out the contingencies in which men find themselves. In such cases the word might be better avoided, for in it the breath of the fanatic hangs threatening to transmute the term to one of crushing certainty. If truth is somehow both prior and substantial, then problems need not be worked out but only classified and disposed of. Unwittingly, one may commit himself to a rhetoric which tolerates only equals, that is, those who understand his "truths" and consequently the conclusions drawn from them; such a rhetoric approaches those who are not able to take its "truths" at face value as inferiors to be treated as such.

The attractiveness of the analytic ideal, ordinarily only dimly grasped but nonetheless powerfully active in the rhetoric of those who deem truth as prior and enabling, lies in the smuggling of the sense of certainty into human affairs.

2

In order to press further into the possibilities presented by rejecting prior and enabling truth as the epistemological basis for a rhetoric, I shall make several observations about the adaptations of Toulmin's concepts by contemporary rhetorical theorists. The earliest and most thorough use of his concepts has been made by Douglas Ehninger and Wayne Brockriede.[9] They have adapted Toulmin's form for "laying out" argument, holding it to be a more clear and complete pattern than the traditional syllogism, without pushing further into the philosophic issues for which Toulmin's scheme of analysis is preparatory. In this respect, Ehninger and Brockriede do not differ from others who have used Toulmin's "layout" in speech textbooks.

One might argue that these further issues are irrelevant to the interests of rhetorical theorists, although one of the purposes of this paper is to show that such a position is untenable. Furthermore, Ehninger and Brockriede take care to indicate a point of view toward debate which might be well described as a philosophical foundation for their treatment of rhetorical concepts. Although there is no evidence that their treatment owes anything to Toulmin, their description of debate as cooperative critical inquiry[10] is nonetheless congruent with some of the implications of his criticism of analytic argument as he applies it to epistemology.

When Ehninger and Brockriede describe debate as cooperative critical inquiry, they may be interpreted as taking a radical departure from the typical point of view. If debate is critical inquiry, then it is not simply an effort to make a preconceived position effective. It would be absurd for anyone who begins with the attitude that he possesses truth, in the sense in which I began this essay, to embark on any genuine enterprise of cooperative critical inquiry. Of course these statements do not mean that Ehninger and Brockriede reject investigation before speaking or the use by speakers of experience, references to social norms, or even to articles of faith. What these statements do suggest is that truth is not prior and immutable but is contingent. Insofar as we can say that there is truth in human affairs, it is in time; it can be the result of a process of interaction at a given moment. Thus rhetoric may be viewed not as a matter of giving effectiveness to truth but of creating truth.

Ehninger and Brockriede's debate-as-cooperative-critical-inquiry is one vantage point from which to see rhetoric as epistemic. This notion is most coherent when it is taken as *normative* rather than as *descriptive*. When so taken, it calls for a commitment to a standard and several matters become clear: one may be committed and, being human, fall short of the standard; further, one may make use of the attributes associated with the standard without at all being committed to it.

I have already suggested that Ehninger and Brockriede may err in not examining their philosophic position in light of the disclosures toward which Stephen Toulmin leads. I am now arguing that they err in presenting their fundamental position as *descriptive* of debate. A confusion arises from their attempt to describe the process of debate (the title of their second chapter is "The Process of Debate") as the "rationale of debate as an instrument for settling inferential questions critically."[11] As a description this statement is plainly contrary to much of our experience; we commonly use the word "debate" to refer to situations in which anything but cooperative critical inquiry is occurring. The confusion may be cleared away if we recognize that Ehninger and Brockriede's ideal is *one* of the uses of the process of debate to which men may be committed. They do argue that the process tends to assure this use, but that it *tends toward* rather than *determines* such a use is clear. As a matter of fact, the authors modify their statements at times, e.g., "the highest tradition of debate,"[12] and are driven finally to explain that "any control, internal or external, may, of course, be circumvented, or debate may be so ineptly practiced that much of its effectiveness is lost. Such failure, however, is human and is not to be charged against debate as a method."[13] But just as the failure is not to be charged against the method neither should the success, i.e., debate at its "highest tradition," be attributed to the process itself rather than the human commitment and the energy and skill to make that commitment meaningful.

The direction of analysis, from Toulmin through Ehninger and Brockriede, leads to the conclusion that there is no possibility in matters relevant to human interaction to determine truth in any *a priori* way, that truth can arise only from cooperative critical inquiry. Men may have recourse to some universal ideas in which they are willing to affirm their faith, but these must enter into the contingencies of time and place and will not give rise to products which are certain.

3

This analysis has led toward the tragic view of life: man who desires certainty understands that be cannot be certain and, moreover, that he must act in dissonant circumstances. One of the great symbols of man, Faust, sits in his chamber at the point of suicide early in Goethe's drama. He is vastly learned in all four of the great professions, but he is certain only that he cannot be certain.[14]

Later Faust sits translating the Bible. He is working on the beginning of the Gospel according to St. John. The troublesome word is *logos*, which he renders as "word," then "mind," then "power," then "act."[15]

The word *logos* and its derivatives have long had a suggestion of divinity about them. For the ancient Greeks, it was often an expression for "universal mind"; and it retains something of this sense in Plato. Man could know because he was identified with the substance of God, that is, the universal mind. From the universal mind (*logos*), man's mind (*logos*) can reason (*logos*) to bring forth speech (*logos*). The wonderful ambiguity of *logos* retains the identity, that is, truth.

All of this may be quite right, the Greek sophist Protagoras said in effect, but I have no way of knowing that it is.[16] All I have is experiences, and my experiences, being finite, cannot reveal the infinite to me. The argument of the Greek sophist Gorgias for his famous three propositions (nothing is; if anything is, it cannot be known; if anything is and can be known, it cannot be communicated)[17] may be interpreted as an attempt to show that man can be certain of no absolute standard. We may be aware of the attributes of our experiences, but there is no way for us to recognize any attribute which is essential among experiences. (Gorgias' inquiry was into the reality of that primary attribute, *being* itself.) There may be some quality (value, norm, standard) which identifies all experiences with all others, or some with some others, but we cannot make such identifications with absolute certainty.

In human affairs, ours is a world of conflicting claims. Not only may one person contradict another, but a single person may find himself called upon to believe or act when his knowledge gives rise to directives which are dissonant. He may be caught, for example, in a conflict of duty toward his family and his country. As a father, he may reason that he ought to keep a well-paying job to provide for the material necessities of his children and by his presence help guide them during their immaturity. As a citizen, he may reason that he is obligated to lower his income and remove his presence from his home to serve in the armed forces. He may decide that his duty to country must take precedence and even that in following the demands of that duty he will in many ways serve his family, but although he is able to make such a decision, the rightness of the decision does not obviate the responsibilities generated by the rejected claim.

The illustrative example can be easily modified into other quite common sets of circumstances: a draft board considering a particular case, arguments concerning the policy of the draft, or even war as a particular or general policy. All these questions must be settled by specific men in specific circumstances. Even taking uncritically the dictates of some past solution is to take that solution in a particular circumstance.

The sophists facing their experiences found consistently not *logos* (in this context we might read "a simple explanation" or "a solitary moral imperative") but *dissoi logoi*, that is, contradictory claims.[18] From another point of view, Stephen Toulmin gives a similar suggestion: "Practice forces us to recognize that general ethical truths can aspire at best to hold good in the absence of effective counter-claims: conflicts of duty are an inescapable feature of the moral life."[19]

My argument is not that one has the choice to act on prior truth or to act to create truth. One may act assuming that the truth is fixed and that his persuasion, for example, is simply carrying out the dictates of that truth, but he will be deceiving himself. Pierre Thevenaz' statement summarizes this point of view: "The phenomenon of expression cannot be reduced to *logos*: it is both more fundamental and more general. Man acts and speaks *before he knows*. Or, better, it is *by acting* and *in action* that he is enabled *to know*."[20]

4

The attractiveness of the notion that first one must know the truth and that persuasion at its best is simply making the truth effective rests in large part on man's desire to be ethical. "How can I assure myself that my actions are good?" is the question with which he nags himself. The question is a good one. The position I have argued is not one that sets it aside but one that holds that the question cannot be answered in the abstract and that whatever principles one holds are only guides in acting consistently with moral demands.

The point of view that holds that man cannot be certain but must act in the face of uncertainty to create situational truth entails three ethical guidelines: toleration, will, and responsibility. I shall suggest why these principles follow from the point of view set forth.

If one can be certain, then one needs no commands or urgings (either from oneself or from others) to act. Failure to act can only be a sign of a momentary misunderstanding or of a flawed intellect. In either case, there is no good reason to tolerate disagreement. As a matter of fact, if one can be certain, tolerating deviations from the demands of certainty may itself be deemed evil.

On the other hand, uncertainty, taking truth as a toehold to climb into the yet-to-be-created rather than as a program to unfold regardless of the circumstances, demands toleration. It would be inconsistent with one's starting point and one's quest to act otherwise. When one's undertaking involves the belief and action of others, one spoils his own potentiality for *knowing*, by Thevenaz' criterion at least, if one fails to respect the integrity of the expression and action of others.

This demand, the *sine qua non* of a democratic state, is called by Karl Popper one of "the most important principles of humanitarian and equalitarian ethics." His phrasing of the principle is "tolerance towards all who are not intolerant and who do not propagate intolerance."[21]

If one cannot be certain, however, then one must either withdraw from the conflicts of life or find some way to act in the face of these conflicts. He must say with Gorgias, "I know the irreconcilable conflicts, and yet I act."[22] That man can so act, he knows from experience. What is true for that man does not exist prior to but in the working out of its own expression. Although this working out may not always involve attempts to communicate with others, such attempts are commonly involved, and thus we disclose again the potentiality for rhetoric to be epistemic. Inaction, failure to take on the burden of participating in the development of contingent truth, ought be considered ethical failure.

If one can act with certainty of truth, then any effects of that action can be viewed as inevitable, that is, determined by the principles for which the individual is simply the instrument; the individual acting is not responsible for the pain, for example, that his actions may bring to himself or to others. The man who views himself as the instrument of the state, or of history, or of certain truth of any sort puts himself beyond ethical demands, for he says, in effect, "It is not I who am responsible."

On the contrary, one who acts without certainty must embrace the responsibility for making his acts the best possible. He must recognize the conflicts of the circumstances that he is in, maximizing the potential good and accepting responsibility for the inevitable harm. If the person acts in circumstances in which harm is not an ever-present potential, then he is not confronted by ethical questions. Such circumstances are apt to be rare in human interaction. Looking to the future in making ethical decisions, we must be prepared to look to the past. "Certainly nothing can justify or condemn means except results," John Dewey has argued. "But we must include consequences impartially. . . . It is willful folly to fasten upon some single end or consequence [or intention] which is liked and to permit the view of that to blot from perception all other undesired and undesirable consequences."[23] To act with intentions for good consequences, but to accept the responsibilities for all the consequences in so far as they can be known is part of what being ethical must mean. "'That which was' is the name of the stone he cannot move," The Soothsayer tells Zarathustra of man. To redeem the past, man must learn "to recreate all 'it was' into 'thus I willed it.'"[24]

Perhaps a final example is necessary. Consider a story from his youth told by the Italian novelist Ignazio Silone.[25] Briefly, he and other village boys were taken to a puppet show by their parish priest. During the performance a devil-puppet suddenly turned to ask the children where a child-puppet was hiding. Rather than reporting "under the bed," the children lied. The priest was upset, for lying was contrary to the precepts he had taught them. His demands for truth were not met. "But," the children protested, "the truth is that there was the devil on one side and a child on the other. We wanted to help the child."

At best (or least) truth must be seen as dual: the demands of the precepts one adheres to and the demands of the circumstances in which one must act. The children had to act and acted to maximize the good potential in the situation. In chastising the children, as he did, the priest had to act also. He also had to make what he could of the situation as well as of his precepts. One may doubt that insisting repeatedly only that "a lie is always a lie," in the face of the children's question, "Ought we to have told the devil where the child was hiding, yes or no?" as Silone reports, the priest did make maximum the good and minimum the harm potential in the situation.

Man must consider truth not as something fixed and final but as something to be created moment by moment in the circumstances in which he finds himself and with which he must cope. Man may plot his course by fixed stars but he does not possess those stars; he only proceeds, more or less effectively, on his course. Furthermore, man has learned that his stars are fixed only in a relative sense.

In human affairs, then, rhetoric, perceived in the frame herein discussed, is a way of knowing; it is epistemic. The uncertainty of this way may seem too threatening to many. But the other way of looking at the world offers no legitimate role to rhetoric; if one would accept that way, then one may be called upon to act consistently with it.

Notes

1. Pierre Thevenaz, "The Question of the Radical Point of Departure in Descartes and Husserl," in *What Is Phenomenology? and Other Essays*, ed. James M. Edie, and trans. James M. Edie, Charles Courtney, and Paul Brockelman (Chicago, 1962), p. 96.

2. Plato, *Gorgias*, 463.

3. *Hearing before the Subcommittee of the Committee on Appropriations United States Senate, Eighty-fifth Congress, First Session on H. R. 6871, Making Appropriations for the Departments of State and Justice, the Judiciary and Related Agencies for the Fiscal Year Ending June 30, 1958*, p. 530.

4. Maurice Natanson, "Rhetoric and Philosophical Argumentation," *Quarterly Journal of Speech* 48 (1962): 28.

5. *Gorgias*, 454.

6. See Stephen Toulmin, *Uses of Argument* (Cambridge, 1958), pp. 123–130, 222–223.

7. "If a genuine claim to knowledge must be backed by an analytic argument, then there can be no authentic claim to knowledge in such fields as these. The future, the past, other minds, ethics, even material objects: about all of these we ought, strictly speaking, to admit that we *know* nothing" (Toulmin, *Uses of Argument*, p. 231).

8. Ibid., p. 235.

9. Douglas Ehninger and Wayne Brockriede, *Decision by Debate* (New York, 1963). Also see Wayne Brockriede and Douglas Ehninger, "Toulmin on Argument: An Interpretation and Application," *Quarterly Journal of Speech* 46 (1960): 44–53.

10. See Ehninger and Brockriede, *Decision by Debate*, preface and chap. 2. See also Douglas Ehninger, "Decision by Debate: A Re-Examination," *Quarterly Journal of Speech* 45 (1959): 282–287.

11. Ehninger and Brockriede, *Decision by Debate*, p. 15.

12. Ibid., p. viii.

13. Ibid., p. 17.

14. My paraphrase is intended to underscore the argument I have been making. Walter Kaufmann translates:

> Called Master of Arts, and Doctor to boot,
> For ten years almost I confute
> And up and down, wherever it goes,
> I drag my students by the nose—
> And see that for all our science and art
> We can know nothing. It burns my heart.
> (Goethe's *Faust*, 2.360–365 [Garden City, NY, 1962]).

15. *Wort!. . . . Sinn!. . . . Kraft!. . . . Tat!* (2.1225–1237).

16. See Mario Untersteiner, *The Sophists*, trans. Kathleen Freeman (Oxford, 1954), pp. 27–28.

17. Ibid., pp. 146–156.

18. Ibid., passim.

19. Toulmin, *Uses of Argument*, p. 117.

20. Pierre Thevenaz, "What Is Phenomenology?," p. 33.

21. Karl Popper, *The Open Society and Its Enemies, Vol. 1: The Spell of Plato* (New York, 1963), p. 235.

22. Untersteiner, *The Sophist*, pp. 181–182: "If Gorgias speaks of the many virtues and not of absolute virtue, he did not deny 'the formal concept of a supreme ethical law'; rather, Gorgias' ethical concept was intended especially to overcome the rigidity of an absolute concept which historical experience also had shown to be contradictory. To make virtue possible in the active turmoil of life, Gorgias detaches it from the empyrean of an abstraction overruled by the incessant reproduction of the antitheses, and makes it relative. In the face of all idealistic dogmatism he stands for the inner turmoil of a tragic decision which gives so profound a meaning to life."

23. John Dewey, *Human Nature and Conduct* (New York, 1922), pp. 228–229.

24. Friedrich Nietzsche, *Thus Spoke Zarathustra*, Part 2, in *The Portable Nietzsche*, trans. Walter Kaufmann (New York: Viking, 1954), p. 251.

25. See Richard Crossman, ed., *The God that Failed* (New York, 1952), pp. 84–86.

Knowledge, Consensus, and Rhetorical Theory

THOMAS FARRELL

Long ago, Aristotle formulated a functional relationship between a fully developed art of rhetoric and a generally accepted body of knowledge pertaining to matters of public concern. In discussing the value of the rhetorical art, Aristotle urged that the speaker "frame his proofs and arguments with the help of common knowledge and accepted opinions."[1] The reason for such advice is abundantly clear; for rhetoric had application to the common subjects of deliberation, those matters to which this "common knowledge" was pertinent: "Rhetoric is applied to the recognized subjects of deliberation—things for which we have no special art or science."[2] In Aristotle's early expansive vision, then, rhetoric was the art which employed the common knowledge of a particular audience to inform and guide reasoned judgments about matters of public interest.

Aristotle has since been scolded both for the naïve idealism and the unwarranted cynicism of that original vision.[3] But both criticisms ignore the normative foundations of the rhetorical art, a foundation that is in serious need of recovery and reformulation. If such a reformulation is to prove possible, this essay maintains, it is necessary *first*, to clarify what sort of "knowledge" is pertinent to the practical art of rhetoric. A conception of *social knowledge* is defined, and elaborated here.[4] *Second*, it is necessary to explore the functional characteristics of such knowledge in relation to the art of rhetoric. *Third*, it would be valuable to derive some normative implications for the theorist and practitioner of rhetoric from such a revitalized conception of social knowledge. While an admirable beginning to these tasks has been made in recent scholarship,[5] a tentative but more encompassing picture is offered here. This picture, whatever its eventual pattern, will emerge amid some controversy.

I. THE PROBLEM OF DEFINING SOCIAL KNOWLEDGE

The possibility of a kind of knowledge particularly appropriate to the art of rhetoric has varied with our undemonstrated assumptions about how persons come to know and what they are capable of knowing. For Plato, the belief of the populace was but the poorest approximation of truth, a shadow of a shadow. To the extent that rhetoric was forced to depend upon such poor approximations, the poverty of rhetoric itself was sealed. By contrast, Aristotle was able to posit a body of *common knowledge* as a natural corollary to his idealizations of human nature, the potential of human reason, and the norms and procedures of public decision-making.[6] While analytic and dialectic provided foundation and structure for the facts of science and the general truths of philosophy, rhetorical method found its warrant in occasions of particular choice, its form in the enthymeme and example, and its substance in shared contingent knowledge, consisting in signs, probabilities, and examples.[7]

Ever since the prescriptive clarity of Aristotle's vision faded, the derivation and status of this common knowledge has been in question. With Bacon, new modes of scientific discovery began to claim what was previously the product of rhetorical invention. With Campbell and Hume, rhetorical principles themselves began to undergo scientistic reduction; and with Whately, the rhetorical art began its inevitable formalistic reaction.[8] With each alteration in our conception of knowledge, then, the art of rhetoric—which seems to depend upon a kind of collective knowledge—altered its status and function accordingly. If the knowledge relevant to rhetoric is to be given a contemporary redefinition, some attention must be directed toward its current philosophic context.

The early twentieth century witnessed a growth in restrictive and restricting theories of knowledge. Whether knowledge was formally, empirically, or operationally derived, "the aim," according to Jürgen Habermas, "was to exclude practical questions from discourse. They are no longer thought to be susceptible of truth."[9] An explosion of "information" with a corresponding decline in public dialogue seemed the paradoxical implication.

It is neither possible nor practical to exhaustively refute all conceptions of knowledge which once impeded the current inquiry; fortunately, it is also unnecessary. The contradictions of extreme realism, radical empiricism, and logical positivism are now clearly apparent to all but their most steadfast adherents.[10] Contemporary philosophy has now moved away from the detached derivation of criteria for knowledge and toward the more inclusive study of human activity in all its forms—even as this activity informs the process of scientific knowing itself.[11] Minds as diverse as Michael Polanyi and Thomas Kuhn have argued the necessity of a coherent and accessible universe of discourse if the normal scientific processes of reduction, prediction, and law-like explanation are to be possible. Thomas Kuhn terms consensual agreements on a structured universe of discourse "paradigms," and suggests that without such a consensual context, even the developed sciences would lose their rigor and analyticity. In asking, for instance, how scientists are "converted" to a particular paradigm, Kuhn is forced to proceed in the following manner: "What sort of answer to that question may we expect? Just because it is asked about techniques of persuasion, or about argument and counter-argument in a situation in which there can be no proof, our question is a new one, demanding a sort of study that has not previously been undertaken."[12]

Rather than eliminate the collaboration of others as a criterion for knowing, writers such as Kuhn force us to turn our attention to the kinds of cooperation which are necessary and possible in various fields of inquiry. For this much is apparent: No criterion for knowledge can be polemically proclaimed; at the very least, it must require the cooperation of others in some form. John Ziman's study of *Public Knowledge*, for instance, underscores the necessity of consensual agreement—even in the confirmation and explanation of scientific "fact": "What I have tried to show . . . is that the criteria of proof in science are public, and not private; that the allegiance of the scientist is towards the creation of a consensus. The rationale of the 'scientific attitude' is not that there is a set of angelic qualities of mind possessed by individual scientists that guarantees the validity of their every thought . . . but that scientists learn . . . to further the consensible end."[13] The analytic rigor and synthetic precision of any body of knowledge, then, would seem to vary in direct relation to *two* interdependent factors:

1. the degree of actual consensus on methods of investigation, procedures of analysis, and operations of measurement.
2. the knowers' degree of detachment from human interests related to the object of knowledge.

To the extent that either or both of these factors are absent, scientific demonstration (whether realistic, empirical, or positivistic in its root assumptions) becomes rhetorical dispute, presuming a type of knowledge which has yet to be elaborated.

Now if all knowledge must rest upon some sort of human consensus and presume some functional connection with human knowers, then it may logically be asked: What functional characterization of *knowledge* is appropriate to the art of rhetoric? In the argument that follows, I refer to a kind of knowledge which must be assumed if rhetorical discourse is to function effectively. I call this knowledge "social knowledge" and define it as follows:

> Social knowledge comprises conceptions of symbolic relationships among problems, persons, interests, and actions, which imply (when accepted) certain notions of preferable public behavior.

Implicit in this definition are a number of special characteristics of social knowledge which deserve amplification. Social knowledge is a kind of general and symbolic relationship which acquires its rhetorical function when it is assumed to be shared by *knowers* in their unique capacity as audience. Whereas technical or specialized knowledge is actualized through its perceived correspondence to the external world, social knowledge is actualized through the decision and action of an audience. Because of its dependence upon some *subsequent* decision and action, social knowledge is characterized by a state of "potential" or incipience. Yet even in its incipient state, social knowledge is functionally a covert imperative for choice and action; in pragmatic parlance, it is "live" knowledge.[14] Since this analysis is predicated upon special characteristics of social knowledge as an object to be known, as well as its unique relationship to knowers, I begin by considering these.

II. THE FUNCTIONAL CHARACTERISTICS
OF SOCIAL KNOWLEDGE

In Jürgen Habermas' analysis of social systems, *Legitimation Crisis*, two basic environmental contexts for such systems are posited: "outer nature, or the resources of the non-human environment . . . and inner nature, or the organic substratum of the members of society. Social systems set themselves off symbolically from their social environment."[15] The boundaries between systems and environments are, of course, notoriously unstable. Nevertheless, it is possible to infer a general distinction related to the orientation a social system takes to these respective environments, and the kind of knowledge applicable to each orientation. In attempting, for instance, to control, produce, or appropriate resources of the natural and externalized environment, managers and members of a social system must presuppose a technical or specialized knowledge. This knowledge, whether localized in science, craft, or technology, will acquire its character as an object through the general patterns which are found to inhere in the natural environmental process. While reconstruction of these patterns may range from prediction, to empirical generalization, to theories constituted by law-like statements, it is the general and optimally invariant set of relationships among empirical phenomena which must preoccupy the scientist, the specialist, the social engineer. Yet much of our most ordinary and necessary social conduct does not easily reduce to such basic formulations. Whenever members of a social system experience the need for coordinating their conduct, there is a corresponding necessity for assuming a kind of knowledge applicable to this "inner nature." And rhetoric (barring the use of force) is the primary process by which social conduct is coordinated. This process, too, must presuppose a kind of regularity.

When we say, for instance, that, *as a rule*, politicians are not to be trusted, or that, *as a rule*, people do not act against their own perceived interests, or that, *as a rule*, nations do not attack nations which are stronger than they, each utterance points to an important similarity or regularity in the ways human beings understand and act in their social world. The phrase "as a rule"[16] signifies this regularity. Uttered as idle speculation, the phrase is loosely descriptive; but as a ground for advocacy, it is transformed into a generalization of interest, culminating in a prescription for human choice and action. As a minimum condition, then, this rule-like structure of *social* knowledge assumes that persons will regularly respond to problems in similar ways and attach their own human interests to purposes in some recognizable fashion. But if that which is known is a generality inhering—*as a rule*—in matters of human choice and conduct, this same knowledge also involves a rather unique relationship to human knowers.

Conventional theories of knowledge, from Aristotle to Descartes, have made much of the "objective" detachment of knowers from the object of their knowledge. Similarly, traditional scientific method establishes an elaborate series of controls to assure that the knower's own conscious or unconscious commitments and preferences do not intervene to alter the character of what is to be scientifically "known." I have termed this knowledge "technical" or "specialized"; in any case, it is the knowledge of observation. Whenever I participate in a *rhetorical* process, however, I am depending upon much more than information, data, evidence, even the armory of persuasive tactics which still comprise our lexicons. All such conceptions of proof and strategy—*in vacuo*—still view knowledge as externalized proof or observation. And what I call "social knowledge" can be neither discovered nor verified through the detachment which observation demands. Instead, social knowledge depends upon an "acquaintance with" (to use James's phrase) or a *personal relationship* to other actors in the social world. As we decide, advocates and audiences, whether to build a dam, or raise teacher salaries, or to provide for a drug rehabilitation program, we will—of necessity—presume a kind of knowledge which depends upon our direct or indirect experience of collective "others," and which applies an interest to these others which is generalizable. Whenever we are asked to endorse or condemn a person, action, or policy, it is likely that we are also being asked to conduct ourselves as members of a human community. And with each particular decision, a reflexive act is performed—an act which gives increasing form and specificity to our relationship with others as social beings.

Now it may seem as if this conception of social knowledge has the practical effect of making everyone an authority. On some very general matters, this might be the case, but only if one were to depend upon an audience's membership in a cultural "form of life" for the purposes of further argument (as is sometimes the case, for instance, in analytic philosophy). Much more frequently, social knowledge is functionally attributed to a particular audience and applied in quite specific situations. Having considered social knowledge as both an object to be known, and as constituted by a unique kind of relationship to knowers, the nature of this "attribution" will now be explored, as well as several additional rhetorical characteristics of social knowledge: its audience dependence, its generative implications, and its normative force.

Social Knowledge as Consensus

Central to an understanding of social knowledge is the notion of consensus. Originally understood to be a range of agreement on objects of communication, consensus has been broadened by Chafee and McCleod and Thomas J. Scheff to include an awareness or understanding that agreements are held.[17] In the somewhat ideal-typical realm of communication models, consensus is considered to be both a precondition and an outcome of communication. I maintain that social knowledge rests upon a peculiar kind of consensus. That is to say, it rests upon a consensus which is attributed to an audience rather than concretely shared. This means that such knowledge does not rest upon agreement which is both fact and known to be fact. The assumption of agreement may be counterfactual. Some persons may, in fact, disagree with what is attributed. Yet it is this assumed understanding of agreement—as an hypothesis, rather than fact—which makes rhetorical argument possible. In more than an idiomatic sense, then, social knowledge is attributed for the sake of argument. In exploring the foundations of communicative action, Habermas points to the kind of consensus which is presumed in social knowledge: ". . . we cannot explain the validity claim of norms without recourse to rationally motivated agreement or at least to the conviction that consensus on a recommended norm could be brought about with reasons . . . . The appropriate model is rather the communication community of those affected, who as participants in a practical discourse test the validity claims of norms and, to the extent that they accept them with reasons, arrive at the conviction that in the given circumstances the proposed norms are 'right.'"[18] To further illustrate this attributive characteristic of social knowledge, it is appropriate to consider the possible varieties of consensus and the sorts of knowledge which these affirm.

Throughout the decade of the 1960s, demographers and urbanologists alike conducted extensive research on rates of growth and distribution of population in America's urban centers. Among their findings, it was agreed that a growing percentage of the urban wage-earners were leaving the inner city.[19] Now the outcome of this research may be understood as specialized or technical knowledge for the two interdependent reasons discussed above. First, it was the outcome of a mode of inquiry which treats mass behavior as a natural, externalized phenomenon—in Habermas' terms—as a phenomenon of "outer nature"; and second, this knowledge was based upon a real or fully actualized consensus as to appropriate research methods and modes of measurement. This consensus, of course, did not protect such technical knowledge from sources of error; yet even the determination and revision of error in such technical fields owes its orderly efficiency to the underlying methodological consensus held by the experts in the fields in question. By contrast, the consensus of any one segment of the national public on the significance, seriousness, or harm of the "inner-city exodus" must—even today—be attributed to that collectivity in order to employ the urban phenomenon as a reason in an argument for—let us say—governmental assistance to urban centers. Specialized or technical knowledge, then, reflects the outcome of an actual consensus on specialized modes of inquiry or procedures of research. Social knowledge must presume or attribute a consensus concerning the generalizable interests of persons in order that argument may culminate in the advocacy of choice and action.

The distinction is less exact than one might wish, of course. To the extent that our urban researchers become urban reformers (pronouncing the urban environment "desolate" and its future "grim"), they are functioning now as rhetors in that a broader consensus (concerning the limits to human acceptability of urban conditions) is being attributed to a public outside the specialized audience.[20]

Does this mean that all attributed consensus possesses the rhetorical character of social knowledge? Once again, there are complications. When I say, for instance, "Everybody knows that Los Angeles is the most polluted city in the United States," I may or may not be relying on social knowledge for rhetorical purpose. Although the assumption appears to be normative, neither the purpose nor the implications of its explicit statement are yet clear. And when the meteorologist relies upon an actual and increasingly accurate technical consensus to predict an unusually high phosphorous and ozone count in the atmosphere for a particular day, the expert in question has set forth a type of knowledge more specific than our normal understanding of social knowledge, but with clear normative implications. Some cases of attributed consensus may function in a non-rhetorical manner. And some instances of technical or specialized knowledge, when combined with further attributions (as in the case of smog alerts or earthquake predictions) may function rhetorically. What is suggested here is that the attribution of consensus is a necessary, but not a sufficient condition for social knowledge to be rhetorically impactful.

This can be demonstrated logically. If a situation is considered "rhetorical" (in Bitzer's terminology) at least two factors must be present: (1) the outcome of the situation must be indeterminate, i.e., it must always be possible for the audience to refrain from acting in the recommended manner; and (2) the exigence of a situation must be amenable to resolution by an audience's action.[21] Now if audiences and advocates alike were to operate from a fully realized consensus on all norms and "proofs" in a specific rhetorical encounter, then they would *necessarily* act and the situation would cease to be rhetorical. In other words, fully realized consensus would undermine the first constituent of rhetorical situations by rendering them determinate. Yet the above analysis presupposes that the audience was able to act. Suppose, for the sake of argument, that nothing could be done about the problem in question. In such a case, the second constituent of the rhetorical situation is missing (namely, that the exigence be amenable to resolution by the action of an audience). Even if there were a fully realized consensus on the problem of humankind's mortality, this does not undermine the necessity of attributed consensus in social knowledge. Neither the fact of death, nor its terminal character, can be altered through the choice and action of an audience. By definition, then, the knowledge which is distinctly rhetorical in function—that is, social knowledge—must be based upon a consensus which is attributed rather than fully realized.

Social Knowledge as Audience-Dependent

But more than simply being attributed to others, social knowledge is assumed to be shared by other persons in their collective capacity as audience. Even so-called "new" information, if it is to function rhetorically, must depend upon more basic assumptions of audience consensus on certain problems, interests, and actions. And it is this assumption of *audience* consensus which requires explication. As a particular advocate notes, let us say, that inner-city poverty is increasing, this advocate lays claim to a pragmatic faith in the mutuality of social interests. Now, of course, this faith cannot be empirically verified; nor will it always be well-founded. Even an audience consisting entirely of urban dwellers will exhibit, upon occasion, divided loyalties and a disheartening narrow conception of interest. And, no doubt, the number and intensity of potentially opposed interests will expand as the audience becomes broader and more heterogeneous. But if rhetorical argument is to operate with any effectiveness, some region of "beginning" must exist. And if it does not exist in empirical fact, then it must be presupposed. The presupposition is grounded on a formidable possibility, namely, that those who play the collective role of audience—as conscious members of an urban or even a broader social community—may become conscious that the suffering of others is pertinent to their own interests. In microcosm, this is the faith of a democracy. A conscious and civilized audience is therefore representative in more than a statistical sense, for we must assume that its collective nerve endings are alive to the interests of others within the society. The anonymous advocate, in the preceding example of inner-city poverty, does not need to assume of the audience a technical comprehension of Keynesian economics; but (s)he does presume an awareness and appreciation of certain human potentialities and skills within society and the relevance of these to the purposes of a community. In proposing a solution to the problem of inner-city poverty, the advocate presumes, at a bare minimum, some conception of poverty in relation to the social interest; without some such assumption, any real advocacy of action would be premature.

This does not mean that social knowledge is necessarily general and ambiguous. As attributed to particular audiences and referred to concrete exigencies, social knowledge can be quite specific. It may, in some cases, even center upon the character traits of certain public figures, as recent political history has shown. Yet just as this knowledge cannot be validated in each discrete individual, so it cannot be reduced to empirical operationalization. In that sense, social knowledge becomes the emergent property of a collectivity. It is an attribution which is general in scope rather than abstract in epistemic status.

But if this construct is attributed and interest-dependent, what is its epistemic status? H. N. Lee has noted that volitional and emotional factors do not serve to differentiate types of knowledge.[22] Perhaps more provocative is John Ziman's stipulation that, "Normative and moral principles cannot, by definition, be embraced in a consensus; to assert that one ought to do so and so is to admit that some people, at least, will not freely recognize the absolute necessity of not doing otherwise."[23] Ziman evades outward inconsistency by inserting "cannot" instead of "should not" in his stipulation. But this evasion renders the statement counterintuitive in application. On one level, of course, Ziman is acknowledging what has been a central position in this essay, i.e., that social knowledge is, by definition, an attributed or assumed, rather than a fully actualized consensus. Ziman's implicit denial of volitional ingredients in scientific consensus is difficult to reconcile to his own characterization of science (see note 13). But just as problematic, his inclusive use of the term "consensus" is difficult to reconcile with actual experience. Do we not—all of us—assume just such a normative consensus as we exhort our hearers on any number of important practical questions? The matter is not so easily settled. But what might be suggested is that social knowledge, just as the questions for rhetorical disputes, is probable knowledge. It is knowledge in a state of potential or indeterminance. And it is validated through the reasoned judgment and action of an audience. How is one to gain confirmation for an attribution of consensus on the financial decay of the inner city as a community problem? If the audience acts on the problem through available procedures, (s)he will have tentative evidence. Through the reasoned action of an audience, the potential state of social knowledge is actualized. Just as the specialized consensus on modes of investigation and measurement has been validated through repeated operation, so—in a more probable sense— is social knowledge confirmed through recurrent action. The probative force of collective experience has, throughout history, been the test of democratic societies. And if rhetoric is to have application to popular decision-making, it must subject its assumptions to a similar test.

Social Knowledge as Generative

Rather than being fixed, permanent, and static, therefore, social knowledge is transitional and generative. As individual problems are encountered and, through the frustrating incrementalism of human decision-making, managed or resolved, new problems emerge; and with these, new knowledge may be attributed, based reasonably upon the collective judgments which have previously been made. Not only does social knowledge provide a context of relevance for artistic proof in collective inference making; it also establishes social precedents for future attributions of consensus in situations which have yet to be encountered.

This generative characteristic of social knowledge can be illustrated simply in the development of the traditional issues in rhetorical controversy. The four traditional issues of such controversy—conjectural, definitional, qualitative, and procedural or translative—each represent points of "rest" in the development and possible resolution of rhetorical disagreement.[24] Two or more opposing positions may—at various times— reduce their differences to a question of fact, definition, quality, or procedure: that point which, when settled, may determine the direction and eventually the outcome of controversy. Yet if this process of controversy is to operate effectively, we must presume consensus on a prior issue in order to move properly to the next. We may not, for instance, argue over the distinguishing characteristics of the financial crisis in any urban center, or the seriousness of its effects upon relevant human interests, unless we attribute to our audience or opponent a prior consensus on the presence of that crisis. And in considering each subsequent issue, the proof which will be decisive will also rest upon attributed consensus—verified through previous choice and action—for the acceptable standards of proof. Thus the ingredients of social knowledge (whether assertions of fact, definitions of character, rules of quality, or precedents of procedure) should aid each rhetorical exchange in achieving its natural "logic" of completion. When a controversy reaches a point of termination or resolution, a more fully actualized consensus is achieved which functions as a social precedent for future controversy.

Social Knowledge as Normative

The traits of social knowledge which have been considered thus far—its attributive dimension, its audience-dependence, its state of potential, and its generative implications—contribute to an understanding of the most elusive and important characteristic of social knowledge. I refer to its affective or normative impact upon decision-making.

There is an amorphous and indefinite body of knowledge that makes little or no difference to the daily conduct of our lives. We can know, for instance, that the technical ascription for water is H_2O, that Steve Garvey was the 1974 MVP in the National League, that Humphrey Bogart made four films with Lauren Bacall, and unless we happen to be chemists, baseball fans, and film fanatics, each item of knowledge is unlikely to alter our normal decision-making priorities. By contrast, consider the finding of the Citizens Board of Inquiry, in 1968, ". . . that in the wealthiest nation in the history of the world, millions of men, women, and children are slowly starving,"[25] or the rampant starvation in Biafra and, more recently, Bangla Desh. Some knowledge *demands* that a decision be made. It forces our options, insofar as the very apprehension and comprehension of such knowledge requires that some action be taken. Even the attempt to ignore, to detach it from our lives (as a fact of "outer nature") is itself an action of sorts; it is the decision to do nothing. Knowledge which relates problems to persons, interests, and actions often implies, then, a covert imperative for choice and action.

Clearly, this covert imperative will not be a permanent or fixed property peculiar to specifiable items of information. As circumstances and social expectations gradually alter, so too will the specific knowledge which carries this curious normative force. Critics and social observers complained for some time, for instance, that the escalation of violence in America was desensitizing the American public to the mutuality of pain and suffering. Yet David Berg was able to cite one social observer to the effect that televised publicity of wartime suffering may one day render even the just war a practical impossibility.[26] More problematic is the tendency of mass media to publicize, even create social knowledge which forces options without suggesting actional outlets for mass concern. Whether this tendency will lead to mass frustration or ambivalence to public problems is a matter for concerned speculation and research. A matter of related interest is the tendency of radical organizations to attribute consensus far in excess of its actual state. Whether this is a distinguishable trait of radical movements is not clear. What is clear is that such movements, with increasingly refined ideologies, will regard each social discrepancy as evidence of extensive covert imperatives for action. That their attributions of consensus are frequently not actualized should not be surprising.

Having considered several distinguishing rhetorical characteristics of social knowledge, it should now be apparent that rhetoric, whatever its own attributed status, is not a purely formalistic enterprise. There is something which this art is about. That "something" is a kind of knowledge which is attributed, audience-dependent, potential in state, generative, and normative in implication. And yet the functions of this knowledge reach beyond its ability to distinctly characterize the rhetorical process.

Any sophisticated social system will be confronted, throughout its existence, by serious problems which require careful deliberation and concerted action. Imagine a society in which the knowledge required to deal with such problems is absent or confined to narrow quarters. Such a system may be a collectivity of individuals; but it is far from a community of persons. The overarching function of social knowledge is to transform the society into a community. There is no way to overstate the importance of this function; philosophers from Aristotle to the present have dreamed of its possibilities. In our own time, it was John Dewey who simplified and celebrated the social function of rhetorical art:

> Symbols in turn depend upon and promote communication. The results of conjoint experience are considered and transmitted. Events cannot be passed from one to another,

but meanings may be shared by means of signs. Wants and impulses are then attached to common meanings. They are thereby transformed into desires and purposes which, since they implicate a common or mutually understood meaning, present new ties, converting a conjoint activity into a community of interest and endeavor. Thus there is generated what, metaphorically, may be termed a general will and social consciousness.[27]

It is difficult to avoid metaphorical language when speaking of this function. The ability of rhetorical transactions gradually to generate what they can initially only assume appears to possess a rather magical ambience. But lurking in the background is a process which can be understood on more than an aesthetic level. There are at least three interdependent means by which social knowledge fulfills this significant function.

First, social knowledge helps define a "zone of relevance" in matters of human choice. Alfred Schutz defines this zone of relevance as a realm in which data, concepts, and principles pertain to operative human interests.[28] While the actual matters pertinent to our interests multiply, our contact with these matters becomes less and less direct. Schutz writes: "We are less and less determined in our social situation by relationships with individual partners within our immediate or mediate reach, and more and more by highly anonymous types which have no fixed place in the social cosmos. We are less and less able to choose our partners in the social world and to share our social life with them. We are, so to speak, potentially subject to everybody's remote control."[29] Social knowledge cannot, in itself, rectify an increasingly dangerous imbalance between what is and what should be known. But by establishing the outer parameters for feasible attributions of consensus, social knowledge enables both the advocate and the "informed citizen"[30] to determine what should be known and how what is known may be utilized.

Second, social knowledge is a way of imparting significance to the numerous "bits" of information which are disseminated to the mass of public citizens. Not all of this information can even be attended to, let alone successfully assimilated. That which it receives its significance due to what Edelman calls *aesthetic* information, a larger associated body of generalized beliefs, convictions, images, contexts, and norms.[31] These are by no means the same for all. But social knowledge, when employed rhetorically, crystallizes the normative dimension of this aesthetic information, thus enabling isolated "bits" of information to achieve meaning and significance. Rather cryptically put, social knowledge gives *form* to information.

Third, social knowledge allows each social actor to confront a set of generalized assumptions suggesting the relative priority of collective commitments held by others. To say that social knowledge provides a means of reality-testing may be somewhat extreme. What it does do is enable each conscious person to place the content, direction, and intensity of personal knowledge within the context of an attributed distribution of public convictions. While this placement is no sure test of reliability in the traditionally uncertain arena of human decision-making, the ordering of personalized knowledge in a more variegated public context is a necessary prelude to the validation of such knowledge. By providing pertinence, form, and context to the data of our public experiences, then, social knowledge assists in the grand transformation of society into community.

Retracing my procedure, it has been alleged that the rhetorical process implies, indeed *requires* a kind of knowledge appropriate to probable human decision-making. I have argued that it is *social* knowledge which provides foundation and direction to the art of rhetoric. Several rhetorical characteristics of this knowledge have been introduced, as well as its functional contribution to the social community. The moral implications of social knowledge are a difficult matter, complex in scope, and beyond the structure of this essay. But several directions for an analysis of this matter may be suggested here.

III. NORMATIVE IMPLICATIONS FOR RHETORICAL THEORY

Social knowledge, as a characteristic which is actively attributed to persons, must necessarily partake in the active dimension of the rhetorical process itself. As John Searle has suggested, certain types of linguistic utterances become *acts* when set forth in the presence of others.[32] That is, both the fact of linguistic utterance and the *presence* of others are required conditions, if the expression is to take on an active dimension—as in promise-making, or exhortation. Michael Polanyi, in painstakingly exploring the phenomenology of such utterances, finds that many of our most common rhetorical expressions imply commitments which are by no means trivial."[33] The very basic commitment of respect for hearers who are party to our transactions requires, for instance, that the rhetor take seriously that consensus which is attributed to an audience. As Georges Gusdorf has noted in *Speaking*, "To respect one's word is thus to respect others as well as oneself, for it indicates what one thinks of oneself."[34] One should not forget that the rhetor speaks *on behalf of* others. That knowledge which is assumed to be held by other persons thus involves the rhetor with the complicity of *other knowers*, whose interests are now a factor for reasoned consideration.

But the commitment to others implied in the assumption of social knowledge would be purely formalistic were it not for the more concrete interdependence of the self and others. While it is the pragmatic tradition which has most carefully and clearly affirmed this interdependence, it is that most practical of arts—rhetoric—that must test this assumption in social life. Social knowledge is merely the surface tracing of a deeper identity, between the self and its conscious extension—the human community. Charles S. Peirce wrote, in 1903:

> Two things here are all-important to assure oneself of and remember. The first is that a person is not absolutely an individual. His thoughts are what he "is saying to himself," that is saying to that other self that is just coming into life in the flow of time. When one reasons, it is that critical self that one is trying to persuade; and all thought whatsoever is a sign, and is mostly of the nature of language. The next thing to remember is that man's circle of society (however widely or narrowly this phrase may be understood), is a sort of loosely compacted person, in some respects of higher rank than the person of an individual organism.[35]

Social knowledge is thus the assumption of a wider consciousness. And the corollary of such an assumption, commitment, should extend as far as consciousness itself. Both John Dewey and—more recently—his student, Richard McKeon, have defined the great community as a consequence of acting as the members of such a community.[36] Social knowledge is thus an instrument of both this action and its optimal consequence.

It is not suggested here that social knowledge is possessed of an inherent qualitative superiority to personal knowledge. Although the impulse of social knowledge is the perfectibility of personal motive, such knowledge—like the art which assumes and creates it—may be used for noble or diabolical purposes. The moral warrant afforded by the construct I have sketched is thus limited: by the parameters of situations and ultimately by the broader dialectic of history. Rhetoric may be viewed as the counterpart of this dialectic. And it is within this selfcorrecting context that the partiality of a culture's conviction—just as the privacy of an individual's perception will be disclosed.

Notes

1. Aristotle, *The Rhetoric*, trans. Lane Cooper (New York: Appleton-Century-Crofts, 1932), 1355a.

2. Ibid., 1357a.

3. Underlying this sometimes amusing paradox are varying conceptions of "rationalism," "logos," "pathos," and "judgment" as assumptions or features of Aristotle's *Rhetoric*. Among the recent studies which shed light on this paradox are Edwin Black's *Rhetorical Criticism: A Study in Method* (New York: Macmillan, 1965), esp. chaps. 2 and 4; Wayne Brockriede, "Toward a Contemporary Aristotelian Theory of Rhetoric," *QJS* 52 (1966): 33–40; Douglas Ehninger, "On Rhetoric and Rhetors," *Western Speech* 31 (1967): 242–247. J. A. Hendrix, "In Defense of Neo-Aristotelian Criticism," *Western Speech* 32 (1968): 246–251; Stephen Lucas, "Notes on Aristotle's Concept of Logos," *QJS* 57 (1971): 456–458; and Forbes Hill, "The Rhetoric of Aristotle," in James J. Murphy, ed., *A Synoptic History of Classical Rhetoric* (New York: Random House, 1972), pp. 38–48. A significant step toward a resolution of the technical confusion in Aristotle's *Rhetoric* is taken by David P. Gauthier, in *Practical Reasoning* (Oxford: Clarendon POress, 1963), chap. 3. The political dimension of this classical controversy emerges in a recent encounter between Forbes Hill and Karlyn Campbell, in "The Forum," *QJS* 58 (1972): 451–464.

4. The phrase "social knowledge" is used in a somewhat specialized way in this essay. While social knowledge may refer to any beliefs which are generally shared, or even beliefs and knowledge *about* society, the more restricted usage I employ is suggested in Jürgen Habermas, *Legitimation Crisis* (Toronto: Beacon, 1975); therein, social knowledge would seem to be a normative agreement, presumed by communication acts, which generalizes human interests and is applicable to practical questions. This usage is explored at greater length in the body of this essay.

5. The many diverse strands of such scholarship could not be exhausted here. Some recent examples are: Ernest G. Bormann, "Fantasy and Rhetorical Vision: The Rhetorical Criticism of Social Reality," *QJS* 58 (1972): 396–408; Thomas W. Benson and Gerard A. Hauser, "Ideals, Superlatives, and the Decline of Hypocrisy," *QJS* 59 (1973): 99–105; and Henry W. Johnstone Jr., "Rationality and Rhetoric in Philosophy," *QJS* 59 (1973): 381–390; the analysis offered in this essay owes its direction to Lloyd F. Bitzer, "The Rhetorical Situation," *Philosophy and Rhetoric* 1 (1968): 1–14 (reprinted in this volume).

6. The epistemological assumptions of Aristotle's *Rhetoric* have been subjected to careful scrutiny by scholars. While the summary offered here is attenuated, confirmation can be found in Richard McKeon, "Principles and Consequences," *Journal of Philosophy* 56 (1959): 385–401.

7. Richard McKeon, ed., "Introduction," in *The Basic Works of Aristotle* (New York: Random House, 1941), pp. xxix–xxxi.

8. Again, what is stated here is a highly abbreviated paraphrase of a complex philosophical transformation. For a careful analysis of the epistemological assumptions of George Campbell's rhetoric, see Lloyd Bitzer, ed., "Introduction," in *The Philosophy of Rhetoric*, by George Campbell (Carbondale: Southern Illinois University Press, 1963), pp. ix–xxxvii. For an analysis of Whatley's epistemological assumptions, see Douglas Ehninger, ed., "Introduction," in *The Elements of Rhetoric*, by Richard Whately (Carbondale: Southern Illinois University Press, 1963), pp. ix–xxx.

9. Habermas, *Legitimation Crisis*, p. 16.

10. Among the recent works which argue convincingly for the rejection of traditional realism, radical empiricism, and logical positivism are Richard J. Bernstein, *Praxis and Action* (Philadelphia: University of Pennsylvania Press, 1971), part 4; Jürgen Habermas, *Knowledge and Human Interests* (Boston: Beacon Press, 1971), part 2; and Michael Polanyi, *Personal Knowledge* (New York: Harper &

Row, 1962). Daniel J. O'Keefe underscores Frederick Suppe's characterization of logical empiricism as "a view abandoned by most philosophers of science" in O'Keefe, "Logical Empiricism and the Study of Human Communication," *Speech Monographs* 42 (1975): 169–183. O'Keefe provides an excellent summary of the indictments which led to the abandonment of positivism.

11. See, for instance, Bernstein, *Praxis and Action*, pp. 257–269.

12. Thomas S. Kuhn, *The Structure of Scientific Revolutions*, 2d ed, (Chicago: University of Chicago Press, 1970), p. 152.

13. John Ziman, *Public Knowledge* (London: Cambridge University Press, 1968), p. 78.

14. William James first coined the term in "The Will to Believe," in *Pragmatism and Other Essays* (New York: Washington Square Press, 1963), p. 194.

15. Habermas, *Legitimation Crisis*, p. 9.

16. Stephen Toulmin employs the phrase *as a rule* as a naturalistic generalization in "Rules and Their Relevance for Understanding Human Behavior," in Theodore Mischel, ed., *Understanding Other Persons* (Oxford, UK: Blackwell, 1974), p. 190. I am extending Toulmin's initial usage in applying the phrase to human conduct and interests.

17. See Thomas J. Scheff, "Toward a Sociological Model of Consensus," *American Sociological Review* 32 (1967): 32–46, for a survey of alternative conceptions of "consensus."

18. Habermas, *Legitimation Crisis*, p. 105.

19. See esp. Philip Hauser, *Population Perspectives* (New Brunswick, NJ: Rutgers University Press, 1960), and Robert Mowitz and Deil Wright, *Profile of a Metropolis* (Detroit: Wayne State University Press, 1962), for examples of this agreement. For the data base that has governed subsequent projections, see U.S. Bureau of the Census, *Statistical Abstracts of the United State, 1967* (Washington, DC: U.S. Government Printing Office, 1967), pp. 8–10.

20. Among the better examples of "rhetorical" treatments of urban population trends (i.e., treatments which presume social knowledge as a ground of advocacy) are "The Conscience of the City," *Daedalus* 97 (1968); and Jeffrey K. Hadden, Louis H. Masotti, Calvin J. Larson, eds., *Metropolis in Crisis* (Atasca, IL.: F. E. Peacock, 1967).

21. Bitzer, "Rhetorical Situation," pp. 7–8.

22. H. N. Lee, *Percepts, Concepts, and Theoretic Knowledge* (Memphis, TN: Memphis State University Press, 1973), p. 136.

23. Ziman, *Public Knowledge*, p. 15.

24. See, for an illustration of this process, Wayne N. Thompson, "*Stasis* in Aristotle's Rhetoric," *QJS* 58 (1972): 134–141.

25. Citizen's Board of Inquiry, *Hunger USA* (Washington, DC: New Community Press, 1968), p. 7.

26. Robin Day is cited to that effect in David Berg, "Rhetoric, Reality, and Mass Media," *QJS* 58 (1972): 258.

27. John Dewey, *The Public and Its Problems* (1927; rpt., Chicago: Swallow Press, 1954), p. 153.

28. Alfred Schultz, "The Well-informed Citizen: An Essay in the Social Distribution of Knowledge," *Collected Papers 2* (The Hague: M. Nijhoff, 1964), p. 124.

29. Ibid, p. 129.

30. An ideal type which, in Schutz's terminology, refers to the citizen who "stands between the ideal type of the expert and that of the man on the street" (p. 122).

31. Murray Edelman *Politics as Symbolic Action* (Chicago: Markham, 1971), chap. 2.

32. John R. Searle, *Speech Acts* (Cambridge: Cambridge University Press, 1970), p. 23.

33. Polanyi, esp. "Commitment," chap. 10 of *Personal Knowledge*.

34. Georges Gusdorf, *Speaking*, trans. Paul T. Brockelman (Evanston, IL: Northwestern University Press, 1965), p. 122.

35. Charles S. Peirce, "The Essentials of Pragmatism," *Philosophical Writing*, ed. Justus Buchler (New York: Dover, 1940), p. 258.

36. Richard McKeon, "Communication, Truth, and Society," *Ethics* 67 (1957): 89–99, and John Dewey, *The Public and Its Problems*.

Some Implications of "Process" or "Intersubjectivity"

Postmodern Rhetoric

BARRY BRUMMETT

The purpose of this paper is to show some implications for rhetoric of the scientific and philosophical point of view known as "process" or "intersubjectivity." I will argue that process is the most valuable philosophy for the study of rhetoric, and rhetoric is the most valuable study for the intersubjective philosophy. Development of my argument will be in four stages. The first section of this paper will briefly review the traditional, Newtonian, "mechanistic" world view embodied in some philosophies of science and social science. The second section will, in opposition to mechanistic philosophy, explain the world view implied by process or intersubjectivity. The third section will develop an ethic for rhetoric that is appropriate to intersubjectivity. The fourth section will argue for a mode of inquiry into rhetoric that is appropriate to intersubjectivity. More detailed aims and overviews will be found at the start of each section.

PART 1: THE MECHANISTIC POINT OF VIEW

> So here we are together, machines and me.
> I feel about as local as a fish in a tree . . .
>
> *John Sebastian*

The assumptions and methodology of Newtonian mechanics, in science and as extrapolated to social science, are well known and need not receive extensive explication here. My purpose is to show the metaphysical and epistemological bases of mechanism, bases which the process point of view most directly denies.

Apart from the strictly scientific merits of Newtonian mechanics per se, a metaphysics grew up around it designed to make mechanics seem "objective and necessary."[1] I am concerned with this metaphysic of mechanics since it has been borrowed by many branches of the social sciences. Newtonian mechanics was based on two tenets: (1) reality is objective, that is to say, it exists absolutely and apart from mind, the observer's intentions, or tools of observation; and (2) this objective reality is mechanical, causal, and necessary.[2]

I should stress that this world view is one peculiarly appropriate to Newtonian mechanics. Other schools of science such as quantum mechanics do not accept its metaphysics.[3] To a certain extent, mechanics and its social science offsprings have seen to it that assumptions and disciplines implying antagonistic metaphysics were regarded as unacceptable study. This metaphysics restricts itself and epistemology to the study of the physical, which was assumed to be the objective. "In short, all that mattered was matter."[4] Newtonian metaphysics held two assumptions for the role of humanity in this objective reality. First, it was assumed that all of human experience and understanding could be explained by the mechanistic, causal, physical paradigm. What at the moment appeared to be soul, ideas, or will would in time be found to be material. Second, the assumption of reality as causal and determinate placed humanity at the mercy of forces in the environment. A deterministic world view required the belief that humanity could not be an end in itself but merely a cog in the cosmic machine. In psychology, the role of inner motivation was taken over by causal factors in the scene. People became "a passive means to some imposed external end."[5]

The incompatibility between this metaphysic and everyday experience shaped an epistemology appropriate to mechanics. Deterministic reality is objective and orderly; yet every day people see incompatible subjective differences, indeterminacy, uncertainty, chance, and chaos.[6] If the world is not *really* like that, then how can humanity come to know that placid world, and why is it that we don't? This was the challenge for mechanistic epistemology.

Why don't people apprehend objective reality directly in everyday experience? Mechanical epistemology answered this question with a dichotomy between appearance and reality.[7] If the observer doesn't immediately apprehend objective reality, mechanics argued, there must be some gap between the knower and the known, between people and reality.

What is the goal of knowledge? To remove those barriers between knower and known, or in other words, to arrive at the *truth*. Mechanics in the "Modern Age" based its epistemological hopes on the concept of a truth which was as objective, absolute, and empirically verifiable as the reality to which it bore reference.[8]

How to reach the goal of truth? Or, how best to remove those barriers between knower and known, appearance and reality? Mechanical epistemology was based on two assumptions. First, reason and formal logic were considered most appropriate for the apprehension of an essentially mathematical reality.[9] Second, objectivity was required for the observer. Objectivity was appropriate for the apprehension of truth for two reasons: (a) it removed personal bias and shortsightedness which were major alleged causes of the appearance-reality gap; and (b) it removed social or moral bias in the form of value or motive nonmechanistic assumptions.[10] This epistemology stemmed directly from the appearance-reality gap. Since the reality half of that gap remained constant and immutable, it was assumed that appearance, or the human side of the chasm, contained the flaw that created the gap. Thus, human (often read "emotional" or "intuitive") factors in observation were rigidly guarded against.

Let me make two observations at this point. First, mechanics begged the question of values and personal experience. Mechanics *had* to assume that this personal part of life was mechanically structured. But that *was* an assumption and not derived from other "truths." A person arguing *for* the integrity of values, intuitions, or personal experience could not be refuted but only ignored or talked around. Second, mechanics looked forward for the day when metaphysics and epistemology would collapse into one, when the dichotomy between the two would be meaningless. This would happen on the day that humankind came to *know* objective reality. Speculation about human knowledge would then be speculation about reality as well. Mechanics in the modern age saw that as a real if distant inevitability.

The methodology of mechanics was based on the second metaphysical tenet argued above, that of causality and determinacy. A causal reality made two methodological approaches appropriate: *reduction*, and through reduction, *control*.[11]

By reduction I mean the simplification of phenomena and the contexts in which they are observed. The parts of systems are studied rather than whole systems. Reduction's goal was to discover the laws of nature which would explain both human and physical activity.[12] With present research tools our understanding of the whole system, including the whole person, is not amenable to the use of mechanistic methodology. Systems and people don't appear to behave causally and determinately. Selected focus upon certain parts of systems and people will reveal subjects that *do* seem to act causally, and that is why the mechanist reduces.[13] Paradoxically, once the mechanist has reduced, he/she reconstructs. The reconstruction is not a system but an aggregate: many reduced parts are studied together as a category to determine similarities between them which may be laws of nature.[14] Mechanics in psychology, for example, is not concerned with the *whole* person or with any part of *the* person, but rather with an aggregate of parts.[15]

Reduction leads to control in two senses. It leads to experimental control since a concern with only similar parts of systems allows the mechanist to exclude from observation those parts which are deemed irrelevant variables. This allows the mechanist to control that which he/she observes and to concentrate on what are presumably the effects of only the observed. Reduction leads to control in another sense. If reduction is successful in achieving the mechanistic goal of observing objective laws of nature, then by knowing how those laws must operate under certain conditions the scientist can *manipulate* conditions and *control* the motion or experience of the parts that have been isolated.[16] Reduction leads to predictability only if the actions observed are determinate. Mechanics is at heart an extremely pragmatic philosophy and avoids understanding for its own sake; the ability to predict is meaningless in mechanics unless it leads to the ability to control.[17] This urge to manipulate is often extended into the social sciences by mechanists, where an old goal has been the neutral control and manipulation of the body politic.[18]

While many references to mechanistic philosophy have been in the past tense, I must not leave the impression that all this is behind us now. Maslow has complained that mechanics is the mainstream of contemporary psychology, no inconsiderable force in the social sciences.[19] Its major manifestation in psychology is the school of thought known as behaviorism.[20] Of more concern is the growth of the mechanistic viewpoint in speech-communication research, especially in those studies relating to rhetoric. Smith argues that most experimental research in speech that deals with manipulations of variables is deterministic.[21] Smith gives two examples of such prominent researchers in speech: Bowers, making references to prediction,[22] and Miller, praising predictability and manipulation.[23] A greater concern to me is not the flow of mechanism into speech, but the reverse. Social psychology is now doing many things that bear directly upon rhetoric, and is doing them mechanistically. Aronson cites Aristotle as "the world's first published social psychologist," and the footnote is to, maddeningly enough, the *Rhetoric!*[24] Insko and Schopler view persuasion in clearly mechanistic terms, as a one-way process of a source influencing a target audience.[25] It is the growing tendency to view this process of influencing people and establishing cooperation, rhetoric, in mechanistic terms that I see as the challenge to be faced in this paper.

PART 2: "POSTMODERN" REALITY

> She always says, my lord, that facts are like cows. If you look
> them in the face hard enough they generally run away. She is a
> very courageous woman, my lord.
>
> *Dorothy L. Sayers*

In this section I will discuss a view of reality and knowledge in contrast to that of Newtonian mechanics. This perspective will be called, interchangeably, "process" and "intersubjectivity." Authors using the two terms are, I believe, referring to essentially the same thing.

Science and the Direct Observation of Nature

Mechanics relied upon reason and the scientific method to move closer and closer to the perception of objective reality. It also relied upon avoidance of personal or social and moral bias, which were assumed to create the gap between appearance and reality. I will argue in this subsection that these goals were counterproductive or impossible of attainment.

First, I will defend the thesis that reason and the scientific method, or any method whatsoever, will impede the direct observation of any objective reality. Therefore, no science can possibly directly observe absolute nature. This principle is illustrated by two facets of science. The first is the nature of scientific theories. Heisenberg has argued that science does not observe nature directly because it observes nature within the constraints of its theories.[26] The observation of nature is impossible without the influence of a *way* of observing. To the lay public, "facts" about nature such as the laws of nature are supposed to exist apart from methods of observing them. But Toulmin has shown that "laws of nature" are ways of *representing* what is observed and are not nature itself. They are principles for drawing inferences and are constraints upon the observer, not upon reality.[27]

A second facet of science that impedes any direct observation of any direct reality is the nature of reduction itself, which has been assumed to be a necessary step towards such apprehension. If science reduces systems to parts, it must avoid examining just the parts, for that would be much less useful even for its own purposes than the examination of whole particular systems. Examining isolated particulars in the aggregate, which mechanics must do as a consequence of reduction, causes objective physics to deal with ideals and not with realistic exactness concerning individual parts.[28] The major feature of this focus on aggregates is that the aggregates are perceived mathematically, and this is a limitation. Science can then be said to know the mathematical structure of aggregates but not things in themselves.[29] This last consequence of reduction leads to a further barrier between observation and reality. If physics does not examine things in themselves, then it can only know things by examining their *effects*, and even then only their effects taken within the context of the aggregate to avoid misleading random variations.[30] Physics can never know what changes, only the results of the change itself.[31]

Mechanics relied not only upon direct observation but upon the avoidance of personal, social, or moral bias. It sought the detachment from science of the scientist. This goal is impossible for a number of reasons. At a very general level, Bronowski has observed that the practice of science compels the formation of values in the scientist.[32] Observation cannot be value-free. But even if the personal values of the scientist did not exist, detachment of the observer from the observed would be impossible.[33] The very nature of observation, the approach towards the observed by the scientist, is a linking of the two. Real detachment would mean no observation at all. Observation is participation, "a form of interaction or transaction."[34] This relationship is doubly complex, for the unidirectional relationship blurs or reverses at times: the knower and the known reciprocally affect each other, and what the observer observes is the observed affected by the observation, which affects the observer's act of observing, and so on in infinite regression.[35] This relationship is yet triply complex. Objects are not observed entirely in themselves and apart but as part of some background or context. Observation of this background will affect observation of the focal object, and then the complexities of reciprocity in observation apply here, too.[36] The problem for mechanics is this: to *be observed* is to be *different* for the observer.

The conclusion of the preceding argument is that the notion of an objective reality is not a useful concept in science or experience for a number of reasons. Positing objective reality as a concept may be the province of philosophy, but it is not helpful in the pursuit of knowledge. Indeed, it is not *now* helpful in many branches of science. Kuhn writes that "there is, I think, no theory-independent way to reconstruct phrases like 'really there'; the notion of a match between the ontology of a theory and its 'real' counterpart in nature now seems to me illusive in principle."[37] Science gets along very well using concepts whose "real" existence has never been proven such as ether and phlogiston in the past and certain subatomic particles in the present.[38] Relativity in particular does not need or use the idea of an absolute reality. It views the world as events rather than things, and events are things that happen to certain observers, not for all to see in the same way.[39] But perhaps the most important reason against the positing of objective reality in science, if the previous argument against objective observation is accepted, is that such a postulate would never be testable and is thus a poor subject for science. Concerning objective reality, Wheelis argues that "we are free so to imagine; but then must accept that we have composed a fairy tale, not a theory, for it is by definition something that cannot be tested—like saying that turtles, when completely unobserved, become princes."[40]

If objective reality exists people will never know it. Thus, the only reality ever to be encountered is what is observed.[41] The implication of that conclusion is that "reality" will be different with different ways of observing it. For everyday experience, reality will vary with different ways and forms of experiencing it: "This is to say that the world is what we experience—either directly or indirectly."[42] To the extent that a person's ways of observing and experiencing differ from other people's, then he/she can say that reality is different. Kuhn has shown this to be the case in the sciences, since "after a revolution scientists are responding to a different world."[43]

These are the considerations we must accept if we hold a nonmechanistic view of reality. Let me make two observations about this new reality to correspond with the observations in the last section. First, I would argue that intersubjective or process reality begs the question of personal experience quite as much as does mechanism although of course in a different way. While mechanics must assume the physical nature of human emotions, values, morals, and the essentially obfuscating nature of human faculties for the pursuit of knowledge, intersubjectivity begins with the assumption that an objective reality will be outside the realm of that philosophy's concerns. Again, these two points of view cannot argue meaningfully on the question of personal experience. Second, while mechanistic objectivity sought the eventual collapse of metaphysics and epistemology by coming directly to know all of reality, intersubjectivity seeks the same collapse but at this end of the philosophical tunnel. Intersubjectivity begins with the assumption that the study of what and how people know is nothing more or less than the study of the nature of reality. The very existence of a dichotomy between what humanity knows and what there is to know is Newtonian, and intersubjectivity begins with a denial of the dichotomy.

The Nature of an Intersubjective Reality

The central tenet of intersubjectivity, or process, is ambiguity: the idea that there is no objective reality (or considerations of one are excluded). This idea was developed in the physical sciences,[44] and has been taken up by some revisionist scholars in the social sciences and humanities. There is no one standard against which to compare experience, yet people nevertheless do have meaningful experiences and do not generally suffer from any feeling of unreality. Therefore, if reality is not objective, then it must be the case that people make their own reality. This is not to say that I can conjure up whatever reality I like. The sense in which I mean that people make their own reality is that we must *participate* in making reality: "There are no appearances to be photographed, no experiences to be copied, in which we do not take part."[45] To say that people participate in making reality is to say that reality, or what is observed, will be partially determined by the way in which people observe, which is a form of participation. Thus, the world is determined by nature and science jointly.[46]

Let me make it clear that no modern Dr. Johnson need kick a stone to refute me. I am not arguing that I can dream up any reality I like. I am not arguing that reality is subjective. The constraints of sensory data are one bond between human beings and one reason why I cannot imagine a tree and have it appear. But sense data by themselves are not experience. Experience is sensation plus *meaning*. Sensation alone is *meaningless*. To all experiences people give meaning, a process which is inherently and uniquely human. It is in this sense that people make their own reality, for we give to experience its absolutely necessary component of *meaning*. I will argue for the idea that meaning is of first importance in human affairs, and in a real sense *reality is meaning*.

The centrality of meaning should not be difficult to establish. Kuhn argues that in the sciences and elsewhere sensory stimuli may be the same, but the meanings given to the stimuli are quite different and will in effect constitute different realities: "Mere parochialism, I suspect, makes us suppose that the route from stimuli to sensation is the same for the members of all groups."[47] No physical stimulus is inherently meaningful, for meaning must be given to experience; it is not a part of it automatically.[48] Thus, the answer to the old question is that when a tree falls in the woods it does indeed make a sound, but the sound is perfectly meaningless since no person can hear it.

Now, the question is this: If objective reality does not exist, where will people get the reality that we do have? Which is to say, where will we get the meanings that we have? The answer is that people get meanings from other people through communication. This, Barnlund has argued, is the purpose of communication.[49] Meaning is the essential component of the reality of relatively simple aspects of experience like rocks and trees. How much more is meaning an important part of complex political and social situations. Here especially do people get meanings from communication: "Therefore, meaning is not discovered in situations, but *created* by rhetors."[50]

Let me briefly summarize. Reality is what experience *means*. This meaning is taken from personal experience and communication about it with others, the sharing of meaning. Intersubjectivity stems from the principle of no objective reality. From this principle two others are derived. First, if things do not take meaning from an objective reality, then they must take meaning from other components in the systems of which they are a part. Things are not defined objectively but are defined by their *contexts*. Yet, since contexts are made up of other things which are also defined or given meaning by the context, it follows that everything in turn defines or gives meaning to other components of its context. This implies an important element of independence or self-determination for every person: I can define those things that in turn define me. A second principle stems from this first: that if contexts give meaning, then the meaning of a person or thing or idea is constantly changing. This is true for two reasons: (a) any entity is a part of many different contexts, all of which may define it in different ways; and (b) defining contexts are always changing: now I am a teacher, now a husband, now an insurance customer, etc.

This view of reality has often been called "process." Smith quotes Berlo's description of this idea with a focus on the idea of interdefinition of the components of a context: "The ingredients within a process interact; each affects all of the others."[51] This idea of interdefinition is the source of meaning: "The basis for the concept of process is the belief that the structure of physical reality can not be discovered by man; it must be created by man."[52]

To contrast this view of reality with other philosophies is useful. Scott draws a distinction between objectivity, which was examined in the first section, intersubjectivity, which I have just explained, and subjectivity, which is in its pure form solipsism.[53] The difference among the three is essentially one of the source of our meanings: from objective reality, from others, or from ourselves alone. Pemberton has described this trichotomy as the "absolutistic," "transactionist," and "relativistic" perspectives.[54] Stewart's basis for his philosophy of interpersonal communication is the "transactionist," or intersubjective point of view.[55]

Relevance of Process or Intersubjectivity to Rhetoric

Intersubjectivity is the most "realistic" way to view rhetoric. Scott has argued that rhetoric is not one-way, or a matter of a speaker influencing an audience, but involves mutual influence and interdefinitions.[56] This relevance of intersubjectivity to rhetoric I will explore further. But I will also argue that rhetoric is the most "realistic" way to view intersubjectivity. I will show that acceptance of this point of view places rhetoric squarely at the heart of one's world view.

Intersubjectivity holds that the discovery of reality and the testing of it is never independent of people but takes place through people. Yet this reality is found through communication between people if humanity is to escape solipsism. Reality is meaning, yet meaning is something created and discovered in communication. Boulding argues that the "image," which is essentially reality, is built up of messages. This theory has no room for the idea of "facts" without accounting for communicating about those facts.[57] The images that people have which are made by communication are the only ideas of reality people will ever have, for these images can only be compared to other images and never to objective reality.[58] This is what Scott means when he argues that no duality exists between fact and symbol; what is symbolized will be the facts, and the intersubjective way of discovering facts is to symbolize (or communicate) with others.[59] Bormann has essentially agreed in arguing that the most meaningful reality to people will often not be "facts" or objective reality but rather the rhetorical reality created by communication.[60]

Humans are necessarily involved in sharing and manipulating messages to give and gain meanings about experience. But what experience means is not by any means agreed upon. This ambiguity is a feature of the essentially rhetorical nature of reality. Ambiguity generates conflict and disagreement about meaning and a constant striving to resolve these divisions. This striving is rhetoric; while rhetoric may be defined in many ways and on many levels, it is in the deepest and most fundamental sense the *advocacy of realities*.

Let me approach this point from two more beginnings: that reality is shared and that it can be changed. The first point I have made repeatedly: "The world—so far from being a solid matter of fact—is rather a fabric of conventions."[61] Conventions are shared meaning; in Boulding's terms, they are "images," and are the only sort of "facts" ever encountered. The shared nature of this reality is quite important. Participation in shared meanings are requisites for participation in society: madness is by definition an inability to share conventional meanings.[62] Indeed, the reliance upon shared conventions may be so great that it obscures the arbitrary, nonobligatory nature of many meanings. Vatz argues that "consensual symbolism" may so "ritualize" events that their rhetorically induced character may go unrecognized.[63] Indeed, Vatz's indictment of Bitzer is essentially an attempt to call attention to the conventional nature of highly "ritualized" situations.

Now here is the crux of the matter: only if reality is shared, that is to say created by discourse, can it be changed or altered by discourse. This is seen in the link between "social reality" or shared meanings and the "rhetorical vision" or the impulse to change meaning, in Bormann's analysis.[64] Today's social reality is yesterday's rhetorical vision. Scott has expanded the sense of the changeability of reality to include "the most everyday sort of occurrences."[65] The point here is that wherever meanings are shared, they are shared only because discourse has the power to induce people to participate in that shared reality. The same power may be used to change the reality.

Boulding's analysis of how reality changes is interesting and patently rhetorical. Reality is meaning. But the meaning of messages or the reality they advocate are the changes produced in the image (or existing meanings).[66] This focus on *change* means that meaning only occurs to the extent that messages cause change; that which does not change the image is meaningless. Boulding recognizes this as rhetorical, for he argues that persuasion is the art of changing others' images.[67] Boulding has also presented an interesting perspective on political rhetoric. The political process, he argues, is the mutual modification of images.[68] That which ties groups of people together in a society is their shared public image. Although a common image, this shared meaning still grows out of the minds of the individuals within that system.[69] How does this image change? How do individual minds generate a collective change?

Boulding says that a change in the public image comes about through the efforts of a few creative individuals who urge upon others some change in the image.[70] These few creative minds may be taken to be the orators and rhetoricians of a society. They cause the *radical* changes in an ever-changing reality.

PART 3: RHETORIC AND TRUTH

> Certainty is certainty, whether it issues from the Vatican or from the Lawrence Radiation Laboratory.
>
> *Allen Wheelis*

In this section I will attempt to develop some grounds for an ethic of rhetoric that is consistent with an intersubjective or process point of view. I will argue that the most ethical world view is one with rhetoric at its center. I will be most concerned with the term "truth," what it means for mechanistic philosophy, and what it means for process. Scott argues that "truth" traditionally has two meanings.[71] One meaning is that truth is the conformity of a proposition to reality. Thus, the "truth" of "This tree is green" may be established by examining the tree itself to see if it is green. This meaning of truth implies physical verifiability. It essentially deals with physical reality. A second meaning is that truth is some ideal standard that exists apart from humanity. This meaning of truth implies philosophical verifiability and refers to an idealist reality. In this sense some absolute standard of social or symbolic realities exists such as "beauty," or "justice," or "honesty," and to discover that standard is to discover the truth.

Both of the meanings of truth given above are tied to epistemology. They involve finding out about something that people do not know about already: the "truth." They require a dichotomy between the nature of reality and the ways of finding out about reality. They both assume truth to be *correspondence* of ideas to reality. But perhaps this will not do for intersubjectivity, for it collapses metaphysics and epistemology into one mode of inquiry. Objective reality is dispensed with; intersubjectivity is assumed. So if truth in mechanics is the correspondence of ideas to reality, what is truth in process? It is the same thing; but the different definitions of "reality" are the crux of the distinction. Intersubjective truth is still the correspondence of ideas to reality, but remember that the reality is now an intersubjective one. Many writers with this point of view will claim that truth is "relative."[72] By this I believe they mean not that truth is solipsistic but that truth will be determined by the changing contexts in which people move. For each context there will be a different truth. Thus, Boulding argues that truth is "relative," and means by this that any given subculture will generate some standards to serve as "truth" for its members.[73] This process notion of truth attempts to explain how it is that people face contradictory "truths." The problem is not to resolve these contradictions by reference to one objective standard. No such standard exists. Truths are contradictory precisely because they are relative and relative because human-made: "truth lies in man."[74]

This explanation leaves a number of questions unanswered: (1) Some notion of "truth" is still a part of moral experience. People feel justified in claiming ideas as "true" or not. People sometimes feel justified in indicting contexts and social groups as promoting untruths. How can the intersubjectivist still use the term with objective implications? (2) People use the term in the sense of checking on physical experience. I have argued that everything that is meaningful in experience is reality, but people occasionally ask if personal reality is "true" or is an illusion. If I see a pink elephant I will want to know if the reality of that experience is "true." How is the term used here? (3) "Truth" is closely bound up with the question of "ethics." Ethics attempts to discover the truth about the best way to behave. Does a relative truth destroy ethics? How is it possible to make ethical judgments if truth is not absolute?

Intersubjective Truth and the Verification of Experience

Let me consider these first two questions together, since they essentially involve the notion of truth as the confirmation of experience. These questions correspond to Scott's two kinds of truth: idealist and physical. The problem is one of verification of experience.

Truth refers to the correspondence of our physical and cognitive experience with reality. In Newtonian terms, if my experience of X is that it is thus, and it is thus in objective reality, then my experience is true. I *know* the *truth* about X. But no objective standard exists in intersubjectivity. Reality in process is, instead, *shared meanings*. Therefore, truth, for the individual, is *the extent to which the meanings of experience (that is to say, reality) of that individual are shared by significant others*. Truth is agreement. If nobody else shares the meaning that I give to sensory data, then I will usually conclude that those meanings are not *true*, and I will try to grasp the meanings others give to that experience. Once I assign shared meanings to my experience, then that meaning is *true*. The reader will foresee the fulfillment of one of my aims if he/she recalls that this reality of shared meanings was described as a *rhetorical* reality in the last section.

This notion of truth implies *degrees* of truth. Suppose I see something, and the meaning that I give to this sensation is that here is a pink elephant. Since I want to know if that is what I truly see, I will ask someone if they see it, too. If nobody does, then I can be fairly certain that I must remove the meaning "pink elephant" from that experience, and I instead assign the meaning of "hallucination." I then say that it is not *really* (*reality* = shared meanings) a pink elephant. Now suppose that in a group of ten people, two others saw this elephant. I might still think I was hallucinating, but I would be much less sure. I would think that perhaps there "really" was a pink elephant there. And if five of the ten saw it? Then I would be more sure. In these degrees of certainty are degrees of truth. The more my meaning is shared, the more true I assume it to be.

Now for some comments and retractions on my argument so far. I have referred to the sharing of meanings with significant others. By this I mean that people restrict standards of comparison to certain contexts and not to others. People decide who and what in particular situations and issues will be the *validating context* for our meanings. I would not choose as my validating context in the pink elephant issue, for example, the denizens of Joe's Bar. Or if I did, I would want to ask some others, too.

Question number one above asked how it is that we can challenge our social contexts and groups as to the truth of some symbolic or idealist meaning. This question becomes increasingly important if truth is determined by shared meanings. The question is answered by the notion of validating contexts and the element of personal choice and personal influence on the other elements of interdefining contexts to which I referred when defining "process." People can choose to limit validating contexts to only the individual (although I believe that this is rarely done outside of madness). This limiting is possible only if people participate in defining, as well as being defined by, contexts. The individual can challenge the world's shared meanings if he/she believes that he/she is the only person who can validate his/her own meanings.

Question number two above was concerned with the feeling that an absolute standard of truth must exist for verification of sensory experience. I would argue that what are regarded as such standards are actually widely shared or ritualized meanings. They may be meanings that have rarely or never been contradicted. The most fundamental truths are those meanings most universally shared. This leads to one of my conclusions in this section. The intersubjectivist finds truth in agreement with significant others. Yet agreement does not stand still. It is made and unmade by rhetorical discourse. Others are not mirrors that reflect the world back to us. They are active agents that *urge* meanings upon us. When people seek intersubjective truth by comparing their meanings, they are involved in rhetoric; for some meanings will be advocated and some scorned, some chosen and some abandoned. In the last section I argued that only in an intersubjective world created by rhetorical beings could rhetoric be central. But more than that, a world view in which truth is agreement *must* have rhetoric at its heart, for agreement is gained in no other way.

The feeling that contradictory truths exist, or that we can challenge our social groups, is accounted for by this notion of truth. Conflicting truths arise when two or more validating contexts have opposed meanings. For example, people may be torn between the desire to further the common welfare and the desire to protect self-interests. This conflict is possible because the meanings assigned to either pattern are generated by different validating contexts. Motivations for one context or another are in a rhetorical opposition that presents the individual with a choice. That choice raises the question of how it is that people perceive process systems as such and choose between them. Such issues are important but beyond the scope of this paper.

The desire for truth is closely linked to a Newtonian desire for certainty in an indeterminate world. Many seek to find certainty, if not in ethical choices, then in the sciences. Surely certain truths lie here. But this is not the case. The model nature of scientific theory prevents this certainty. Kuhn has shown us the extent to which certainties and truths change with paradigms. What scientists are sure of is not reality but rather the internal mathematical workings of their models which may or may not match experience. Toulmin puts it like this: "Scientists will never be entitled to say to the public . . . that the universe *is* a machine . . . . Models remain models, however far-reaching and fruitful their applications may become."[75]

Certainty is often considered a measure of knowledge. Wheelis writes that "knowledge is the name we give to those of our opinions to which certainty is ascribed."[76] If this is true then it is consistent with the implications of what I have already argued. If I know something with certainty then I share its meanings with a great many people in a great many contexts.

Rhetoric, Ethics, and Truth

I will now attempt to answer the third question that I posed at the start of this section, concerned with the possibility of a "relative" ethic for rhetoric that is based on intersubjectivity. I will argue that in many ways such an ethic is not only possible but much to be preferred over objective ethics.

Let me begin by describing an ethical Scylla and Charybdis to be avoided. Both posit an objective reality, although in extremely different ways. I will first analyze idealist ethics and then semanticist ethics.

Idealist ethics, specifically in rhetoric, made its most important early appearance in Plato. Platonic rhetoric assumes that an absolute truth exists and that the task is to find this truth and employ rhetoric in its service to "treat the soul."[77] The question is, what sort of objective truth is this? For an answer, turn to that friend of traditional rhetoric, Richard Weaver, who is certainly an idealist. Weaver felt that this objective truth was one of ideas, principles, and forms.[78] This focus on the idea is, of course, opposed to the physical orientation of mechanism, but the certainty that Weaver assigns to the Ideal is just as great. The ideal serves as the standard of ultimate good, a fixed standard against which to measure the specific things one would call good.[79] Keep in mind that this ideal order of goods is, according to Weaver, independent of anything else, and that rhetoric, far from creating the good, serves it.[80] This idealist truth is discovered, not by rhetoric, but by the logical process of "dialectic."[81] Rhetoric then serves a subsidiary function: "Rhetoric seeks actualization of a dialectically secured position in the existential world."[82] Weaver's kind of objective truth is to be found in many philosophies that are otherwise opposed to him. Bitzer is probably not a Weaverian idealist, yet Vatz has shown that Bitzer's "situation" implies a similar kind of ethical objectivity.[83]

Let me stress certain aspects of idealist ethics in rhetoric. An objective truth is assumed. The task is to find it, then to "actualize" it. This task implies a dichotomy between the realm of objective truth and the realm of experience. The implication is that finding the truth alone is inadequate for its implementation and that not just everyone can find it. The truth is a special order of ideas that is possible *not* to know. Rhetoric remedies that ignorance. The implication is also clear that rhetoric is a channel for truth, a servant of truth. To the extent that rhetoric is at all *creative*, or adds anything to "reality," then it must be indicted by the idealist, for its task is only to make effective the truth. It cannot create or add to the truth.

Semanticist ethics for rhetoric is also objective. Matson has shown that the semanticist and logical positivist traditions grow out of mechanism. In these philosophies language needs to be made to match a supposed objective reality to reduce confusion and misunderstanding.[84] I will take as illustrative of semanticists S. I. Hayakawa, a gentleman who caused Weaver no small amount of grief. Hayakawa is certainly of mechanist sympathies; he praises science in terms of its abilities to predict and its restriction to physical or "extensional" reality.[85] Hayakawa views language and its use, rhetorical or otherwise, in terms of the relationship between a map and a territory, with the implication that a good map will report a territory and not include mountains and valleys and rivers where there are none in objective reality.[86] This view of language as objectively reporting seems to be widespread. It even creeps into Heisenberg, who argues that while language has "immediate connection with reality," science does not, implying a dichotomy between language and reality over which to have such a connection.[87]

It is plain that while Hayakawa recognizes the existence and uses of rhetoric and describes some strategies in his book, he eyes rhetoric with suspicion. This is only natural given his orientation. "Facts," he believes, if properly reported, can be "affective" (that is to say, rhetorical) without "literary devices" (that is to say, rhetoric) to make them so.[88] While Weaver regarded rhetoric as the servant of truth, Hayakawa's view implies the rejection of rhetoric altogether unless it reports objective reality. Then it would no longer be rhetoric as such but merely the utterance of truth which is sufficient to move people to accept it. Hayakawa does not preclude a dialectic to discover the truth, but it will be a dialectic of mechanical science to discover a truth of fact rather than one of idea. To the extent that rhetoric urges anything that cannot be seen with a microscope, then it is superfluous at best and obfuscating at worst.

I will attempt to avoid the two positions of semanticism and idealism with an ethics of process. I will argue that intersubjectivity is more "realistic" and more responsible by attacking first semantic ethics and then idealism.

The more people recognize and accept grounds for ethical responsibility the more ethical human life will be. Within the scope of this paper I cannot describe or urge specific ethical guidelines, but I am concerned with establishing the grounds for ethical judgments. Whatever ethical standards are taken, the more often people are constrained to compare actions and judgment with those standards, the more will people conform to those standards. Now, the trouble with Hayakawa is that he does not grant language or rhetoric any ethics per se. They are only subject to ethical evaluation to the extent that they report or do not report objective reality. But they are not subject to evaluation in and of themselves. This is all very good within his perspective, but an intersubjective perspective will grant language and rhetoric ethical status.

From an intersubjective point of view, language is indeed subject to ethical considerations. This is because it creates the meanings that are reality, and does so as much as or more than does physical sensation. I. A. Richards has developed a philosophy suited to this view of rhetoric. While process posits the interdefinition of a system, Richards goes further to posit interdefinition or "interdependence of meaning" for language alone.[89] Whereas in process the meaning of a component is determined by its context, in Richards' view the meaning of a word is its "delegated efficacy," by which he means the missing part of its context.[90] While each word means what it means by virtue of its context, so each word is part of the context for some other word and influences other words in turn. This is, of course, process in language. Just as changing or multiple contexts affect the meaning of process components, so do the contexts of language create an ambiguity as to the meaning of words. This ambiguity creates and requires the ability of language to create meanings, that is to say, reality, and thus ambiguity is an important resource of language.[91] Richards argues that his context theory of the meanings of language avoids the semanticist notion that words are restricted to some one meaning that they ought to have.[92] That restriction cannot exist if language is ambiguous. Thus, Richards gives to language itself an element of choice. Because it is ambiguous and because it creates reality, it is the responsibility of the user of language to choose between the reality that his/her language will advocate. This choice is ethical, and it is also rhetorical. It gives to rhetoric itself an ethical ground and is thus preferable to Hayakawa's denial of ethics to rhetoric.

Intersubjective ethics is also preferable to idealist ethics because, again, it offers or demands more ethical accountability. Weaver is very concerned with ethics, and his charge to the rhetor to discover the truth is an admirable and an ethical one. But in Weaver's system, ethical responsibility must inevitably stop at the point that one discovers the truth and actualizes it. It must stop precisely because of the power of the supposed objective truth. Having found the truth, the idealist cannot claim that truth as his/hers and cannot be held accountable for the consequences of the actualization of truth. After all, Truth is being urged by the idealist rhetor, a truth that is the rhetor's responsibility to find, but the rhetor is not responsible for that truth *itself*. The consequences of that truth are charged to the account of Truth, not to the rhetor who is only an agency. This creates for the rhetor a waiver of responsibility at best. At worst, as Scott has shown, it provides the kind of "rationalization" that fanatics feed on.[93]

A better alternative is intersubjectivity. Here, the rhetor still has the responsibility to discover his/her truth in the sense that I have discussed truth so far. But the rhetor also has the responsibility to recognize that this truth is his/her responsibility, and its actualization and consequences are his/her responsibility, for he/she is part of the context that determines in part how others will view reality. Thus, process requires greater ethical responsibility from one end of dialectic to the last consequences of rhetoric.[94] The idea that the truth that is being argued is created as well as discovered puts a greater responsibility on the rhetor. While I am avoiding specific ethical charges, Scott has suggested some good ones for intersubjective truth: toleration, will, and responsibility.[95]

Because the rhetor is responsible for the truth that he/she advocates, he/she is less likely to make the extreme claims for it that irresponsibility encourages. Wheelis put this point very well when he wrote: "Certainty leads us to attack evil; being less sure we would but resist it. The difference between attack and resistance is the difference between violence and argument, the thread on which our lives dangle."[96] Knowledge of the possibility of other truths, that is to say, opposed shared meanings, will reduce certainty of the truth the rhetor advocates. This awareness of other truths must stem from an ethic in which truth itself is rhetorically *made* by agreement, not given or found absolutely. Such a rhetorical ethic is possible only in intersubjectivity.

Process is a point of view good not only for ethics but for rhetoric. Idealist rhetoric assumes that people are deficient in apprehension of the truth, that people would not need rhetoric if humankind could see the truth unaided. Thus, rhetoric's place is as the servant of truth.[97] Because the truth must be discovered rather than created, rhetoric actually becomes parasitic to those studies which can tell what that truth or reality is.[98] Rhetoric for the semanticist is only subsidiary to the science that discovers truth. Neither the idealist nor the semanticist gives to rhetoric the power to create truth. Only in a process philosophy do we find, as Scott has noted, that if no choice exists between discovering and creating truth, we will inevitably do the latter.[99] In a process point of view, indeed in any philosophy that does not discount daily experience, the truths that people can be sure of are bound to be trivial. Rhetoric deals with creating the more important truths that guide choices.[100] Thus, rhetoric in process is doubly ethical: it is the result of a choice on the part of the rhetor as to the reality advocated and the method of doing so, and it *urges* choice rather than complete and necessary acceptance on the part of the audience. Truth which is rhetorically made encourages choice and awareness of alternative realities. Idealist ethics removes that choice and makes acceptance of objective reality an obligation.

PART 4: PROCESS AND RHETORICAL METHODOLOGY

> Is not subjectivity in knowing like pregnancy in a convent,
> whereof the smallest amount is much too much?
>
> *Allen Wheelis*

> ... nor is it shameful for man to sit down when he thinks.
>
> *Otis Walter*

Given the description of intersubjective reality and rhetoric which I have discussed, I will assume in this section that the object of inquiry in rhetorical study will be meaning and the way in which meanings are created, shared, and changed. I hope to describe a proper methodological perspective for that kind of study within the process point of view. I cannot within the scope of this paper discuss an intersubjective perspective for "rhetorical criticism" itself. My concern is with the relationship between the experimental method and methods of rhetorical criticism. The present discussion is restricted to that relationship because some scholars may mistakenly feel that intersubjectivity must imply antagonism between experiment and more holistic forms of criticism. I have shown at the start of this paper that the study of humanity borrowed its philosophy and method from Newton and then rejected mechanics with Heisenberg and others. In accordance with the spirit of this eternal following after, I will borrow a methodological perspective from "post-modern" or process-oriented science.

Intersubjectivity in Science

Let me begin by elaborating a point that has been made before. Natural science is not the objective observation of anything at all. It is instead the personal involvement of the scientist with the observed. As such, science depends on a point of view. Science grows not by mere accumulation of data, as does natural history, but by changes in perspectives.[101] This is a point of Kuhn's book: that science changes by paradigm shifts which do not represent the accumulation of knowledge but rather the reconstruction of data.[102] Thus, science is a way of seeing the world which involves the active participation of the scientist in making that point of view.[103] What is meant when one refers to a "discovery" in science is rarely that something new is observed but rather that something old is observed in quite a different way, and that way is chosen by the scientist.[104] Kuhn's idea of a paradigm as shared by a community of scholars describes the paradigm as an intersubjective reality. It is something created by people, not found in objective reality. Therefore, in the social sciences and humanities where the object of study is intersubjective reality, to the extent that this inquiry proceeds according to various paradigms, it will be the intersubjective study of the intersubjective.

The notion of science and scientific change as reconstructions of data is the first point I would like to make. But how can science reconstruct? What do theories do? Science seeks to discover *unity* in the data that it analyzes.[105] But this unity does not necessarily exist objectively in nature; at any rate, if it does, people will never know it. The unity that science seeks in data is a unity that science gives to data. Laws of nature are created by the scientist rather than discovered.[106] They are created to facilitate the understanding of nature. In this sense, Bronowski has argued, art and science are very much alike. Both seek to re-create and unify experience, rather than simply report it.[107] This means that science, like art, will be a *creative* process.[108] The scientist has no choice but to be creative. Nothing is given to the senses in a whole or organized form. The scientist and the artist, indeed, everybody that perceives anything, must perceive by organizing partial impressions.[109] This perception of unity is absolutely necessary to any inquiry. In science, regularity must be conceived before experimentation can begin.[110] The need for an organizing perspective is as important in the study of rhetoric as it is in the "hard" sciences.

Let me make an observation that will tie this section to the one before. Involved creativity on the part of the scientist is a compulsory choice. The scientist cannot choose not to participate in observation but must decide among alternative ways of observing and objects to be observed. To the extent that methodology in science is a choice, then ethics will lie at the heart of methodology. If the critic can apply these methods of science to rhetoric, rhetorical inquiry is itself a matter of choice and is ethical. Process rhetorical research will be an ethical examination of the ethical and a responsible inquiry into the responsible.

Assumptions of Process Methodology

Smith has specified five "methodological assumptions" for research that are consistent with process or intersubjective reality.[111] They are: (1) objectivity is not assumed, (2) the nature of the observer's perspective is stipulated, (3) different explanations are allowed, (4) different explanations may be held simultaneously, and (5) research is conducted with a holistic point of view. I will not quarrel with these except to modify this last point, but I would like to add to these prescriptions. Smith does not explain the relationship between the use of experimentation in persuasion and the use of more conventional rhetorical criticism. What are the assumptions of mechanical experimentation? Objectivity of the observer and reduction of the observed. Yet process denies objectivity. Does reduction then have a place in intersubjectivity? At first blush it would seem that intersubjectivity would deny the propriety of observing a component as meaningful apart from the context that gives it meaning. I believe that a common assumption among "humanists" is that experimentation alone would not seem to satisfy intersubjective views of reality. Does it have any place in rhetorical research at all?

In the first place, scholars should as a matter of principle be wary of banishing any form of inquiry. To the extent that experimentation has something to offer, it should make that contribution. The sciences themselves recognize that no point of view is adequate to explain all of reality. Toulmin argues that scientific theories are not limited by the "truth" but by the scope of their application which may be limited to special parts of science.[112] Kuhn has shown that different aspects of science may embrace different and incompatible paradigms.[113]

I will argue that the questions I raised at the start of this subsection were questions concerning experimentation performed within the mechanistic point of view. The crucial issue in any methodology is not so much what is done but what is made of the data that are gathered. More important than the experimental focus which produces data is the organizing and guiding perspective which interprets that data. Experiment in mechanism is objectionable not for what it does but for the constructions placed upon data gathered by objectified, simplified, mathematical procedures. Rasmussen has shown this point very well in arguing that no methodology is inherently process or mechanistic but depends on interpretation of data.[114] Rasmussen has criticized Smith's suggestion of certain specific methodological procedures by showing that none of these procedures is inherently process oriented.[115]

I will attempt to develop a productive attitude for joining the experimental and traditional methods of research in rhetoric into a paradigm appropriate to a process reality. This paradigm will be Michael Polanyi's philosophy of focal and subsidiary or tacit knowledge. I will preview a more specific explanation of this philosophy with a brief summary of it. Focal knowledge is knowledge gained by attending to some particular object in and of itself. Subsidiary knowledge is a holistic, intuitive knowledge of the focal object in its background or context. The observer attends *from* subsidiary knowledge *to* focal knowledge; or examines particulars within a sense of their relationship to a context. Both are necessary, but neither is sufficient alone for full knowledge of the object of study.

The experimental method corresponds to focal knowledge and has been explained elsewhere. I will at this point argue for the role of holism and intuition in the pursuit of knowledge. Polanyi has shown that knowledge can never be purely focal or restricted but must include some subsidiary awareness of the context of a thing.[116] Yet a thing has an infinite context. How is the observer to know this infinite context so as to place the object of focal awareness in some sort of perspective? Only through a holistic point of view can the observer comprehend in any way this infinity of context while focusing on some particulars within the context. Knowledge of people (and this would include rhetoric) must include this element of holism. The scholar must study people with a subsidiary awareness of their contexts, and this means not only holism but also a study of the person as an individual rather than merely reducing him/her to his/her parts.[117] This concern for the person as a whole rather than some particular drive or physiological response of the person is necessary because a person's actions can be explained within the motivating context for the whole person rather than for the reduced parts of the person.[118] The infinite ranges of contexts in which people move that define their particular actions in ever-changing ways requires a sort of holistic knowledge that Polanyi calls an infinite range of "anticipations."[119]

A holistic component of methodology is important because intersubjective reality demands the assumption of purpose and self-determination for the person as well as definition by one's context.[120] Yet the purposes that people have can never be examined directly and in isolation. Purpose is largely discoverable by "tacit knowledge" or "subsidiary awareness," in Polanyi's terms. Intuition or tacit knowledge plays an important part in Polanyi's epistemology. People know things, in part, holistically. Yet no rules can be found for determining how people know, how we discover regularities and unities in the observed—we simply know.[121] Polanyi posits an infinite range of peripheral cues that determine holistic perception, but these cues are always internal and out-of-awareness.[122]

So a holistic/intuitive perspective is a necessary part of knowledge, as is a focal/experimental component. The question is, why is Polanyi's system the most appropriate one for the study of a process reality?

I have argued that the experimental method alone is insufficient for process investigations. Even the experimental method taken with what often passes for a process perspective is insufficient. If parts of a system take their meaning from the system, then an experimental focus upon isolated components alone will never have a perspective on the rest of the system that gives those components meaning. To assume that experimental research can meet process requirements by specifying and examining all the relevant parts of a context over time is a mistake. This, for example, is what Brooks and Scheidel have done in a recent monograph.[123] The trouble is, one can never name all the variables in a context and one can never specify all the contexts that may give relevant definitions to the components focused upon. One can never settle on *the* contexts that define the observed. So the experimental method alone can never account for the defining nature of contexts in process. But on the other hand the researcher must close off the system at some point and say that this is what I will study. The experimental method has at least two valuable characteristics which holism does not. It can examine particular things more completely in themselves rather than as part of a context. This focus upon the specific and particular is a perspective upon the object of study which is missed by holism. Also, experimentation more clearly accepts the idea that restriction of human attention at *some* point is necessary for inquiry to begin at all. Observation must eventually come to focus on something. At some time attention must be focal, must be on one component of a system, and must freeze the meaning of a component to study it, although in process reality the meaning may be changing all the time. Some measure of isolation and reduction is as necessary as is an awareness of the larger system that the isolated and reduced component is a part of. Subsidiary knowledge is the necessary component of a methodology that wants to include a process awareness of some system; and focal awareness is necessary to settle upon some object of study since a purely holistic procedure would focus on the entire universe, and the only relevant tool would be the syllable "Aum."

Experimentalism and holism together are necessary for fullest knowledge of an object within the process perspective. I will now try to apply this idea to the study of rhetoric. By way of preliminary assumptions, it seems to be that the spirit behind rhetorical criticism, as opposed to experiment concerned with persuasion, is holistic. Some scholars criticize and some experiment, but rarely do the twain meet in the same publication. The rhetorical critic is certainly concerned with the relevance of his/her study to other knowledge, but he/she is not so concerned with prediction and control. While rhetorical criticism involves focal knowledge, the focus is not quite as sharp as in experimentation. The methodology of most rhetorical criticism seems to be on balance the expression of a holistic understanding of the rhetoric studied.

What is the relationship between holism and experimentation in rhetorical study? I will argue first that holism is necessary in order to gain a perspective from which to draw intersubjective conclusions from experimental data. Part of the advantage of holism in rhetorical study is that it can deal best with many questions that experimentation cannot directly or quickly attack. Walter has argued that "in a world in which half the population is starving and the other half can blow the rest into eternal oblivion, it makes little difference whether, for example, climax order or anticlimax order is sometimes somewhat more or sometimes somewhat less effective."[124] Walter is unfair here. If experimenters were to discover that climax order could in an experiment persuade people, then that would be a useful thing to know. But the trick is to apply that knowledge, gleaned from college sophomores in some laboratory, to the "real world." How will the scholar use that knowledge, what questions can that knowledge address, and how and where does it need to be modified? Matters of morality and choice, of the merits of blowing the world up or not, are not open to experimental investigation.[125] Nor are questions of how to apply restricted experimental findings to the infinity of experience. These applications must involve holistic awareness of the systems in which the focal knowledge is to be applied. Walter has complained that only the easy problems are quantitative.[126] Problems of choice and morality are not. Yet the quantifiable problems are not really the *whole* problems; they can generate answers which serve a holistic perspective on the whole systems. This is what Wheelis means when he argues that the ends of knowledge are determined by faith (or holism) while science gives us the means to reach those ends.[127] The point is not that the easy problems are quantifiable but that the very small components of great problems are quantifiable. Holism is necessary to guide and integrate findings that experimentation gives to us.

Holism in the study of rhetoric gives a perspective to the findings of experimentation. It does this more so than does mechanism for mechanism assumes that experimentation properly done will discover a truth that can stand by itself and is in need of no guiding or orienting perspective. But in an intersubjective reality this is not the case. Isolation of a system's parts, which inevitably occurs in experimentation, results in some problems. Polanyi argues that isolation inevitably leaves out parts of the system, which I have discussed above, it also changes the appearance of the isolated parts.[128] At this point behaviorism stops. Having isolated components of a system, it draws conclusions about the components and system based on the limited data that it has.[129] Intersubjective methodology, however, will recognize that any act of observation must change the appearance of the observed because it has been isolated from a system, because the meaning has been frozen so that the observer can look at it. The trick is to take what experimentation can tell about that isolated segment of a system and apply that data back again to the system which has been evolving all along. This is possible only through a holistic perspective that can take into account the infinite range of changes, meanings, and contexts necessary to apply experimental knowledge to changing intersubjective systems. This perspective involves the integration of both focal and subsidiary awareness; it cannot tell about rhetoric by proceeding in only one way.[130]

Note that the experimental or focal and the holistic methods are opposed to each other. In a certain sense, isolation precludes integration and vice versa. Yet both are *complementary* to each other in arriving at the fullest knowledge possible. Complementarity is an idea well known to the sciences, particularly quantum mechanics, and the study of rhetoric would do well to borrow it. Matson describes the advantages of this point of view:

> The inference ... is not, of course, that the systematic search for natural causes and coefficient correlations must be abandoned forthwith in human affairs, nor that explanation in the qualitative terms of reason and free will is alone sufficient to account for all behavior. The point is rather that the two alternative perspectives or frames of reference are *complementary*: i.e., mutually exclusive if applied simultaneously but mutually "tolerant" if considered as opposite sides of the same coin—differing faces of the same reality.[131]

Polanyi agrees in arguing that focal and subsidiary knowledge are complementary ways of regarding the same reality: "Focal and subsidiary awareness are definitely *not two degrees* of attention but *two kinds* of attention given to the *same* particulars."[132] I have argued that these two kinds of knowing, while opposed, can work together in order to give the observer the specifics of knowledge and the perspective with which to apply that knowledge to systems. Polanyi describes the advantages of both kinds of knowledge working together:

> The concerted advantage of the two processes arises from the fact that normally every dismemberment of a whole adds more to its understanding than is lost through the concurrent weakening of its comprehensive features, and again each new integration of the particulars adds more to our understanding of them than it damages our understanding by somewhat effacing their identity.[133]

Other authors have also argued for similar, complementary ways of knowing about something. Maslow argues a need for both "experiential" and "spectator" knowledge,[134] and says that these methods represent complementary ways of knowing.[135]

SUMMARY

My purpose has been to show that rhetoric is a perspective which is quite important for understanding intersubjectivity and that intersubjectivity is important for understanding the centrality of rhetoric in human affairs. My purpose has been to show some, but by no means all, of the implications of process or intersubjective philosophy for the study of rhetoric. To generalize my conclusions while ignoring many smaller ones, I have advanced arguments in four areas. First, I attempted to describe the mechanistic world view that I believe intersubjectivity addressed most directly. Second, I attempted to describe the process or intersubjective world view. My purpose there was to place rhetoric at the heart of that world and to place process at the heart of rhetoric. Third, I attempted to specify some grounds for ethics in rhetoric as opposed to mechanistic or objective points of view. I particularly contrasted process ethics with the ethics of idealism and semantics. Finally, I attempted to suggest a methodological perspective for the study of rhetoric which would be consistent with process. My concern was to reconcile the vital traditions of experimentation and rhetorical criticism which some scholars may view as opposed or antagonistic. This synthesis was done by reference to Michael Polanyi's system of focal and subsidiary awareness.

Notes

1. Allen Wheelis, *The End of the Modern Age* (New York: Harper and Row, 1971), p. 41.
2. Floyd W. Matson, *The Broken Image* (Garden City, NY: Anchor Books, 1966), p. 3.
3. Werner Heisenberg, *Physics and Philosophy* (New York: Harper and Row, 1962), pp. 144–145.
4. Matson, *Broken Image*, p. 11.
5. Ibid., pp. 52–53.
6. Wheelis, *End of the Modern Age*, p. 29.
7. Matson, *Broken Image*, p. 4.
8. Wheelis, *End of the Modern Age*, pp. 23–24.
9. Ibid., p. 3.
10. Matson, *Broken Image*, p. 69.
11. Ibid., p. 15.
12. Wheelis, *End of the Modern Age*, p. 35.
13. Abraham Maslow, *The Psychology of Science* (Chicago: Henry Regnery, 1969), pp. 3–4.
14. Matson, *Broken Image*, pp. 66–67.
15. Maslow, *Psychology of Science*, p. 8.
16. Matson, *Broken Image*, p. 39.
17. Ibid., p. 56.
18. Ibid., pp. 88–89.
19. Maslow, *Psychology of Science*, p. ix.
20. Matson, *Broken Image*, p. 30.
21. David H. Smith, "Communication Research and the Idea of Process," *Speech Monographs* 39 (1972): 176.
22. Ibid., p. 178.
23. Ibid., pp. 176–177.
24. Elliot Aronson, *The Social Animal* (San Francisco: Freeman, 1972), p. 58.
25. Chester Insko and John Schopler, *Experimental Social Psychology* (New York: Academic Press, 1972), p. 209.
26. Heisenberg, *Physics and Philosophy*, p. 5.
27. Stephen Toulmin, *The Philosophy of Science* (New York: Harper and Row, 1953, paper 1960), pp. 30, 42.
28. Ibid., pp. 71–72.
29. Matson, *Broken Image*, p. 117.
30. Bertrand Russell, *The ABC of Relativity* (New York: Harper and Row, 1953), p. 135.
31. Ibid., p. 143.
32. J. Bronowski, *Science and Human Values* (New York: Harper and Row, 1972), p. xiii.
33. Wheelis, *End of the Modern Age*, pp. 56–57.
34. Matson, *Broken Image*, p. 129.

35. Wheelis, *End of the Modern Age*, p. 78.

36. Michael Polanyi, *Knowing and Being* (Chicago: University of Chicago Press, 1969), p. 111.

37. Thomas Kuhn, *The Structure of Scientific Revolutions* (Chicago: University of Chicago Press, 1970), p. 206.

38. Toulmin, *Philosophy of Science*, p. 137.

39. Russell, *ABC of Relativity*, p. 140.

40. Wheelis, *End of the Modern Age*, pp. 62–63.

41. Heisenberg, *Physics and Philosophy*, p. 58.

42. Robert L. Scott, "On Not Defining 'Rhetoric,'" *Philosophy and Rhetoric* 6 (1973): 87.

43. Kuhn, *Structure*, p. 111.

44. Matson, *Broken Image*, p. 121.

45. Bronowski, *Science and Human Values*, p. 20.

46. Kuhn, *Structure*, pp. 111–112.

47. Ibid., p. 193.

48. Matson, *Broken Image*, p. 84.

49. Dean Barnlund, "Toward a Meaning-Centered Philosophy of Communication," in John Stewart, ed., *Bridges Not Walls* (Reading, MA: Addison-Wesley, 1973), pp. 45–46.

50. Richard E. Vatz, "The Myth of the Rhetorical Situation," *Philosophy and Rhetoric* 6 (1973): 157 (reprinted in this volume).

51. Smith, "Communication Research," p. 175.

52. Ibid., p. 179.

53. Scott, "On Not Defining," pp. 91–92.

54. William Pemberton, "The Transactionist Assumption," in Stewart, ed., *Bridges Not Walls*, p. 30.

55. Stewart, *Bridges Not Walls*, pp. 8–12.

56. Scott, "On Not Defining," pp. 89–90.

57. Kenneth Boulding, *The Image* (Ann Arbor: University of Michigan Press, 1961), p. 173.

58. Ibid., p. 165.

59. Scott, "On Not Defining," p. 85.

60. Ernest G. Bormann, "Fantasy and Rhetorical Vision: The Rhetorical Criticism of Social Reality," *Quarterly Journal of Speech* 58 (1972): 400–401.

61. I. A. Richards, *The Philosophy of Rhetoric* (London: Oxford University Press, 1965), p. 41.

62. Boulding, "Fantasy," pp. 14–15.

63. Vatz, "Myth of the Rhetorical," p. 160.

64. Bormann, "Fantasy," p. 398.

65. Scott, "On Not Defining," pp. 88–89.

66. Boulding, *The Image*, p. 7.

67. Ibid., p. 134.

68. Ibid., pp. 102–103.

69. Ibid., p. 64.

70. Ibid., p. 75.

71. Robert L. Scott, "Some Implications of Existentialism for Rhetoric," *Central States Speech Journal* 15 (1964): 271.

72. Wheelis, *End of the Modern Age*, p. 83.

73. Boulding, *The Image*, p. 167.

74. Scott, "Implications of Existentialism," p. 271.

75. Toulmin, *Philosophy of Science*, p. 167.

76. Wheelis, *End of the Modern Age*, p. 81.

77. Otis M. Walter, "On Views of Rhetoric, Whether Conservative or Progressive," *Quarterly Journal of Speech* 44 (1963): 376.

78. Richard Johannesen, Rennard Strickland, and Ralph Eubanks, in Richard Weaver, *Language Is Sermonic* (Baton Rouge: Louisiana State University Press, 1970), p. 11.

79. Ibid., p. 12.

80. Ibid., p. 17.

81. Weaver, *Language Is Sermonic*, p. 71.

82. Johannesen, Strickland, Eubanks, in Weaver, *Language Is Sermonic*, p. 19.

83. Vatz, "Myth of the Rhetorical," pp. 154–155.

84. Matson, *Broken Image*, p. 93.

85. S.I. Hayakawa, *Language in Thought and Action* (New York: Harcourt, Brace, 1949), p. 282.

86. Ibid., p. 32.

87. Heisenberg, *Physics and Philosophy*, pp. 200–201.

88. Hayakawa, *Language*, p. 127.

89. Richards, *Philosophy of Rhetoric*, p. 10.

90. Ibid., p. 32.

91. Ibid., p. 40.

92. Ibid., p. 61.

93. Scott, "Existentialism," p. 274.

94. Vatz, "Myth of the Rhetorical," p. 158.

95. Robert L. Scott, "On Viewing Rhetoric as Epistemic," *Central States Speech Journal* 18 (1967): 16 (reprinted in this volume).

96. Wheelis, *End of the Modern Age*, p. 114.

97. Scott, "On Viewing Rhetoric," p. 10.

98. Vatz, "Myth of the Rhetorical," pp. 157–158.

99. Scott, "On Viewing Rhetoric," p. 15.

100. Ibid., p. 257.

101. Toulmin, *Philosophy of Science*, p. 53.

102. Kuhn, *Structure*, pp. 84–85.

103. Ibid., p. 103.

104. Toulmin, *Philosophy of Science*, p. 20.

105. Polanyi, *Knowing and Being*, p. 138.

106. Wheelis, *End of the Modern Age*, p. 43.

107. Bronowski, *Science and Human Values*, p. 19.

108. Ibid., pp. 12–13.

109. Ibid., p. 34.

110. Toulmin, *Philosophy of Science*, p. 111.

111. Smith, "Communication Research," p. 179.

112. Toulmin, *Philosophy of Science*, p. 31.

113. Kuhn, *Structure*, p. 50.

114. Karen Rasmussen, "Inconsistency in Campbell's *Rhetoric*: Explanations and Implications," *Quarterly Journal of Speech* 60 (1974): 197.

115. Ibid.

116. Marjorie Greene, "Introduction" to Polanyi's *Knowing and Being*, p. ix.

117. Maslow, *Psychology of Science*, pp. 10–11.

118. Matson, *Broken Image*, p. 236.

119. Polanyi, *Knowing and Being*, p. 141.

120. Maslow, *Psychology of Science*, p. 18.

121. Polanyi, *Knowing and Being*, p. 107.

122. Ibid., p. 122.

123. Robert D. Brooks and Thomas M. Scheidel, "Speech as Process: A Case Study," *Speech Monographs* 35 (1968): 1–7.

124. Walter, "On Views of Rhetoric," p. 376.

125. Wheelis, *End of the Modern Age*, p. 89.

126. Walter, "On Views of Rhetoric," p. 380.

127. Wheelis, *End of the Modern Age*, p. 108.

128. Polanyi, *Knowing and Being*, p. 124.
129. Ibid., p. 152.
130. Ibid., p. 151.
131. Matson, *Broken Image*, p. 136.
132. Polanyi, *Knowing and Being*, p. 128.
133. Ibid., p. 125.
134. Maslow, *Psychology of Science*, p. 49.
135. Ibid., pp. 86–87.

Rhetorical Perspectivism

RICHARD A. CHERWITZ
JAMES W. HIKINS

With characteristic foresight, Douglas Ehninger predicted that the focus of rhetorical studies in the contemporary period would become an epistemological one.[1] Indeed, since Scott's pronouncement that "rhetoric is epistemic," the literature has exhibited numerous attempts to define more precisely the role of communication in the process of coming to know.[2]

As rhetorical epistemology has developed, a number of controversies have arisen. The most notable of these concerns the nature of the "objects of knowledge" and the means by which these objects are apprehended. Some scholars posit that the objects of knowledge are the products of social/linguistic interaction. This position views reality as socially *constructed*.[3] Others contend that the objects of knowledge exist *prior to* social/linguistic interaction and are not *created*, but rather are *discovered* through discourse.[4] The former position—subtleties notwithstanding—has been variously labeled "intersubjectivity," "rhetorical subjectivism," or "rhetorical relativism;" the latter, "rhetorical objectivism," "rhetorical dialectic," or "critical rationalism."[5]

In what follows, a theory of *rhetorical perspectivism* is developed for the purposes of contributing to our understanding of the role played by rhetoric in the acquisition of knowledge, and to account for the disaffection among theorists. The first section develops the fundamental tenets of perspectivism. The second section explores the implications of perspectivism for rhetorical epistemology, identifying a major philosophical problem common to both the intersubjectivist *and* objectivist positions. Finally, it is shown how rhetorical perspectivism better addresses this problem, underscoring important insights for rhetoric as a way of knowing.

THE PHILOSOPHY OF PERSPECTIVE

The term "perspective" has been employed both in technical applications (such as theories of art, physics, psychology, and sociology) as well as in the vernacular. At this stage in its etymological history, the term has become a cliché.[6] Yet the term has found extensive use in philosophical epistemology. Leibniz introduced an epistemological conception of perspective in his theory of *monads*.[7] In addition to a "physical" character, each monad, according to Leibniz, also is endowed with individual consciousness from which arises human consciousness. As a result, each monad mirrors its own *perspective*, perceiving reality from a particular locus or point of view. Whitehead, again within the context of consciousness and perception, contended that one apprehends reality from a particular point in space and time, that is, from a unique perspective.[8] Combining the concepts of space and time, Whitehead advanced a theory of "perspective space" comprised of various "points of view of private space."[9] In similar ways, the theory of perspective has played an important part in the philosophies of Russell, Mead, Biser, and Ushenko.[10] However, the most systematic treatment of perspectives, employing the concept as the cornerstone of a theory of knowledge, was offered by E. B. McGilvary.

McGilvary's chief concern was to develop a defensible formulation of direct realism.[11] Thus, he held the common sense view that, when we perceive, we perceive a world that exists independently of ourselves, "out there," and when we communicate we communicate with other minds that think in large measure as we ourselves think and are located "in other persons."[12] McGilvary did not offer a demonstration for the common sense view. Rather, he followed the accepted practice of advancing direct realism as a *postulate*.

Let us offer a number of postulates as provisionally true. While technical in nature, their formulation is prerequisite to understanding *rhetoric's* inherent epistemological function. The important thing to keep in mind is that the test of any theoretical system is how such a system coheres *qua* system, both in its internal consistency as well as in its ability to account for the world that confronts us in our everyday experience.[13] The most fundamental postulates which bear on an understanding of perspectivism follow.[14]

Postulate 1: The Independence of Reality

In experience there is presented to us, directly, a world of phenomena largely independent of our attitudes, beliefs, and values. This postulate, implying a common sense philosophy somewhat akin to that advocated by Thomas Reid, is put forth solely as a beginning point to be defended in conjunction with other postulates.[15] Yet, it is not an arbitrary notion, for it is sustained by the overwhelming persistence of the belief that reality exists independent of our consciousness of it.[16] Moreover, this conviction sustains us not only as *individuals* who, in our day-to-day affairs act on the presumption that reality is in large measure independent of us, but as *rhetors* and *rhetoricians* as well. For part—indeed a vital part—of our worldview includes such concepts as *audiences*, replete with "other minds" which we inform, persuade, and entertain. What we regard as an independent reality is revealed by our behavior, if not always by our theorizing: not even the most committed subjectivist would support the thesis that reality is *purely* a mental construct by venturing into the path of an oncoming locomotive on the assumption that mind could alter the consequences of the ensuing collision. Most of the events in human experience cannot be wished away. Likewise, McGilvary was fond of pointing out that "even the solipsist continues to have social moments when he tries to convince others of the correctness of his views, and would probably become as mad in behavior as he is in theory if the social denizens of his world were persistently to deny that they and he are what he and they seem to them and to him to be."[17]

Postulate 2: Relationality

The world is comprised of many particulars, each a member of a context of particulars, and each deriving its nature from that context. Each particular exhibits various characters which themselves emerge wholly as a function of the relations in which the particular stands to other members of its context. Simply put, entities in the universe are what they are solely because of the relationships in which they stand to other entities. As we shall see momentarily, this feature of relationality is applicable to "nonempirical" concepts (such as justice, love, and goodness), as well as to "empirical" concepts.

To understand this postulate, consider its contrary: a one-item universe, where nothing stands *in relation to* anything else. It is impossible to imagine such a universe. In experience, for example, we are confronted by tables, chairs, cats, dogs, and a saturnalia of other items. These items of experience exhibit more or less permanent characters because they are apprehended from various points of view. To illustrate, a tree may exhibit the characteristics green or brown, tall or short, rough-barked or smooth-barked, alive, dead, dormant, healthy or diseased, *depending upon the relationships between and among its various parts and the context of particulars in which it, as a whole, stands* (its *relationships* to the things around it). As a result, what makes the green healthy oak tree a green healthy oak and not a dead fir is the presence of some characters and the absence of others, standing in specific *relationships*, that is, the presence of those characters, "arranged" in a certain way. Similarly, Newton's laws of gravitation capture a complex set of *relationships* between "objects" with particular characters, such as mass, distance *from* one another, and velocity. In this way, the "objects" of reality are both understood and comprehended *qua* relationships.

It should be clear that relationality is advanced *not* as a description of the *nature* of the objects of the universe, but as an explanation of how those objects—be they thought of as "material," "spiritual," or whatever—come to possess the natures they have. Moreover, as argued in what follows, it is this feature of relationality which accounts not only for what is, but also for what is *thought*.

Postulate 3: Consciousness

Consciousness is a natural event which occurs when and only when an entity comes to stand in a particular relationship to other entities within a context of particulars. Consciousness is itself a character of a specific kind and is always part of a corresponding asymmetrical relation also of a specific kind. By "natural event" is meant an occurrence independent of individual attitudes, beliefs, and values. For example, while the reader may have *intended* to read these words, and while he or she may choose at any time to stop reading, nonetheless, once a particular set of relations obtains, consciousness will occur independent of what the reader "wishes." For instance, if the individual is within a certain distance of this page, under certain conditions of lighting, and assuming "normal" vision and certain "brain processes," plus the lack of any intervening set of relations (such as closed eyelids "obstructing" the view), consciousness of the words on this page will *necessarily* occur.

Of course, one might argue that a reader who "brings" certain attitudes, beliefs, or values to his or her reading may "read it" or "read *into* it" something quite different from another reader. Moreover, someone reading this paper for the first time may come away with a different "perception" than he or she would after having read it several times. The explanation for this is to be found in the difference between *consciousness of* an object (again, where "object" is to be understood as *object of thought* and not in physicalist terms) and certain notions *additional to* consciousness, such as meaning, reflection, understanding, and comprehension.

By "entity" is meant a discrete collection of characters. It is important to note that the term "entity" should not be thought of as "physical" or "mental," since what have typically been called "physical entities" and "non-physical" or "mental" entities (such as love, justice, and goodness) are not *qualitatively* distinct within the theory of perspectivism herein developed. Thus, people, inanimate objects, and values are all entities. Consciousness, then, is a *purely relational concept*, arising out of the relation in which one particular complex entity of a particular type stands to other entities.

The phrase "context of particulars" denotes all those entities and the various relationships in which they stand to one another which in any way affect or condition some other individual, specifiable entity. Thus, in this postulate, a *complete account* of the conscious state of, say, an astronomer viewing the moons of Jupiter, or a mathematician grappling with a complex equation, or an ethicist struggling to determine a proper course of action, would entail a description of all the entities and relationships among entities which have a significant bearing on the conscious event.

A conscious relation is "asymmetrical" in the sense that when an entity "A" is conscious of some other entity "B," it does not follow that "B" is necessarily conscious of "A," nor that "B" is conscious of "A's" consciousness of "B."

In summary, we have advanced three postulates: (1) there exists a world of entities in some sense independent of our attitudes, beliefs, and values—a world in which we are powerless to either will or wish away most, though certainly not all events; (2) the entities populating the world—be they trees, stones, polar bears, values, thoughts, or human beings—are what they are solely because of the relationships in which they stand to one another; and (3) consciousness is itself an occurrence arising when a particular entity, such as a human being, comes to stand in a certain relationship to another entity or entities. These entities and the conscious subject comprise a complex, interrelated array of constituents, called a "complex of particulars."

PERSPECTIVISM AND RHETORICAL EPISTEMOLOGY

One of perspectivism's most important contributions to an understanding of rhetoric's role in the process of coming to know lies in its ability to account for—and perhaps even mediate—the current debate between the rhetorical subjectivist (intersubjectivist) and rhetorical objectivist positions. As suggested at the outset, the literature in rhetorical theory reflects at least two broad categories of thought regarding the relationship between rhetoric and knowing. Some thinkers claim that reality is socially constructed through discourse; others contend that reality exists independent of and apart from discourse. This section catalogs various positions which are subsumed within these two larger categories, suggesting how the issues they raise may be addressed by perspective theory.

Subjectivism versus Objectivism

A survey of the literature in rhetorical epistemology reveals four varieties of ontological claims. Consider, for example, the claims of the subjectivists. This school, which describes itself as "intersubjectivist," abjures the possibility that there exists an "objective reality" or at minimum contends that *if* there is such a reality, we can never know it.[18] Therefore, so the argument continues, the notion of an objective reality is not a useful concept. We suggest that this school is more properly characterized as subjectivist because of the manner in which they develop the argument against an objective reality. Consider, for example, their reformulation of what reality *is*: "Reality is meaning yet meaning is something created and discovered in communication." Further, "meaning is of first importance in human affairs, and in a real sense, *reality is meaning*."[19] According to this analysis, all of reality *is* a product of meaning, literally. Moreover, the subjectivists wish to claim that this process of *constructing* meaning is an *inter*subjective process—one that is the product of a number of individual, other persons. Yet notice that other *persons*—or, more precisely, what we *know* of other persons—we know in the same sense we know trees, houses, cats, rats, or any other "external" object. This being the case, the *objective* existence of other persons must be regarded with the same ontological suspicion as all other things whose *objective* nature is called into question by the subjectivists. This is because *other persons must be regarded as the product of meaning too*. Now this conclusion may be warmly embraced by the subjectivists and even touted as a rationale for the preeminence of human rhetorical communication. The problem with the view, as we see it, is that it is inherently *solipsistic*. In the absence of any account establishing the *objective* existence of *other subjects*, intersubjectivity collapses altogether. We are left only with the contention that the reality we perceive is created through meaning. And if humans have the capacity to create reality through meaning, who is to say that this activity is not done *purely* subjectively, the notion of "other minds" being an elaborate conceptual illusion, just as the *objective* existence of trees, houses, cats, rats, and everything else is a conceptual illusion according to the subjectivists? Moreover, who is to say there is not just *one* mind, the mind of the thinker, everyone else merely *appearing* to have an intellect? In sum, *inter*subjectivity reduces to solipsism and hence to subjectivity, for, if meaning determines reality, it is just as likely that the world is a product of the *intra*personal communication within *a* mind (subjectivity) as it is of interpersonal communication among *several* minds (intersubjectivity).

A less radical version of rhetorical subjectivism (*mitigated subjectivism*) contends that only some items of reality are the product of discourse. According to this position, the world is divided into two separate realms, a "technical" or "scientific" realm including objects somehow "external" to and "independent" of mind, and a mental or "social" realm, wherein the externality of concepts in such fields as ethics and politics (concepts such as "goodness," "justice," "virtue," and the like) is steadfastly denied.[20] The term "subjectivism" describes this school of thought for much the same reason that the term is applied to the "strict subjectivists." For despite the positing of distinct "technical" and "social" realms, the ontological status of other thinking persons in such a world remains unclear. On the one hand, these writers could be suggesting that such concepts as other persons reside in the social realm because, for example, they are "unobservable," unlike empirical, technical entities. Presumably, it is such persons who generate rhetorical discourse by "creating meaning" in much the same sense as in the case of the strict subjectivists. If this is so, any precise demarcation between what is created by subjects in the social realm and what is observed in the technical realm becomes problematic. Hence, because solipsism is again entailed, the term "subjectivism" applies. On the other hand, the "mitigated subjectivists" could locate other persons in the technical realm—a position which might render the label "subjectivist" inapropos. This, however, seems inconsistent with the spirit in which the technical/social bifurcation was advanced; placing notions like other persons into the technical category casts doubt as to whether *anything* falls into the social realm. Social knowledge, after all, is by implication created by persons and cannot be reduced to "empirical operationalization." It is difficult to see how social knowledge could arise as "probable knowledge . . . knowledge in a state of potential or indeterminance"[21] if it were generated by the kind of automata the "technical" alternative implies.

What are the rationales upon which these two versions of subjectivism are based? The strict subjectivists generally hold that there is no method whereby one can *test* the postulate that there exists an independent reality.[22] In addition, it has been argued that the positing of an independent reality is "not helpful in the pursuit of knowledge," since, for example, "science gets along very well using concepts whose 'real' existence has never been proven such as ether and phlogiston in the past and certain subatomic particles in the present."[23]

Both these arguments seem to hinge on a radical application of a kind of "verifiability criterion" not unlike that developed by the early positivists. Terms such as "test" and "proven" appear to mean "verified" in the sense that one could *measure* or visually *observe* phenomena; for the strict subjectivists, since we cannot escape the fact that our minds are inextricably involved in measuring, observing, and imputing meaning in what is measured and observed, the notion of a reality which exists "out there," independent of mind, is simply not a meaningful and, hence, not a "useful" concept.

The rationale of the mitigated subjectivists is much the same as that of the strict subjectivists. However, there is no radical application of any "verifiability criterion" to what we commonly speak of as empirical matters. These theorists postulate the existence of external objects that can be measured and observed. While denying the validity of positivism in most of their writing outside rhetorical epistemology, they nonetheless adopt what is tantamount to a positivistic approach when treating rhetoric as a way of knowing. That which is "real" and "knowable" in the ultimate sense are such things as the objects of scientific inquiry; that which is the subject of rhetoric are such things as political, moral, and religious questions—matters about which we "create" realities through discourse.[24] The former are independent of our thinking about them; the latter are a product of our mental life interacting (socially) with the mental lives of "others."

The objectivist position, as it appears in the literature in rhetorical epistemology, also evidences at least two emphases. On the one hand are those who suggest that rhetoric's function is to transmit the truths discovered by the other arts and sciences (*strict objectivism*).[25] This view is traditional in the history of rhetoric, and casts for rhetoric a "minimal epistemological role."[26] A second position within the objectivist camp (which has been called *rhetorical dialectic*) argues for the existence of independent realities in both the "empirical" and "social" realms.[27] Terms like "goodness," "justice," and the "rightness" or "wrongness" of an act are as "real" as the subjects treated within the physical sciences. Rhetoric's role is not to *create* realities about such concepts; it is rather to *discover* them and articulate relationships between or among them through the process of argumentative discourse.[28] The rationale for the objectivist position takes a number of forms, including the argument from solipsism just mentioned, and others with which the reader of this essay may be familiar.[29] Rather than assessing the arguments marshaled by both the subjectivists and objectivists, let us take their thesis statements at face value, while suggesting how perspectivism might help close the distance between the two camps.

The Implicit Problem of Dualism in Rhetorical Epistemology

To comprehend, and perhaps mitigate, the differences between the objectivist and subjectivist positions, it is necessary to understand the source of their theoretical disparities. That source is, or is much the same as, the *Cartesian dichotomy between mental entities and physical entities*. Since Descartes penned the *Meditations* in 1641, philosophy in general and epistemology in particular have been plagued by what has become known as the problem of *dualism*.[30] Simply put, if there exist mental occurrences which have their locus in a mind, and these are both quantitatively and qualitatively distinct from physical events, what is to account for the influence of one on the other? The four stances outlined above represent, in effect, four "stands" taken by rhetoricians vis-à-vis this issue.

The *strict subjectivists* circumvent the dualist problem by calling into question the existence of physical realities, emphasizing the priority of mental constructs (such as "meaning") which explain the way the world is and the way it is created or managed via discourse. One consequence of this solution, as we have seen, may be solipsism—the inability to account for or find a theoretical place for other minds, since, if the world is a mental construct, what appear to be other thinking beings may well be a construct of the thinker.

The *mitigated subjectivists*, on the other hand, squarely embrace the dualist position in their separation of mental and physical entities, without commenting on the philosophical problems which such a dualism engenders. Hence, these thinkers leave a major quandary of dualism unanswered, namely, How does one account for the influence of one realm on the other? How is it that two so qualitatively distinct worlds coexist and interact?

The *strict objectivists*, while avoiding the problem of dualism by suggesting that the only knowable objects are "physical" in nature, render impossible the conferring of epistemic status upon those ideas and beliefs which are the subject of day-to-day discourse. And, as those who have taken issue with positivism have indicated, to dismiss all nonempirical matters as meaningless and unknowable, though it may solve the dualist problem, is unacceptably counterintuitive.[31] After all, especially in the world of prudential conduct, such "nonempirical" issues are both meaningful and of crucial importance in managing our lives.

Finally, those who have taken the position of *rhetorical dialectic* have, like the mitigated subjectivists, failed to deal with the problem of reconciling the physical and mental realms which dualism has occasioned. Moreover, these scholars, in maintaining the externality of both social and scientific questions, have left themselves vulnerable to the subjectivists' complaint that questions of a contingent variety (such as moral, religious, and political issues), if they are external to mind in the same way as are empirical ones, should be similarly verifiable.

Perspectivism and Dualism

Perspectivism offers an alternative approach to the dualist enigma. By treating the constituents of the world as collections of characters which cohere *relationally* to form particulars within a context of particulars, and by treating consciousness as a phenomenon which *itself* emerges when an entity of a particular type (e.g., a human being) stands in a particular *relation* to other entities, the perspectivist dispenses with the necessity of bifurcating the world into "physical" and "mental" realms. According to our formulation, the mental/physical distinction—and the dualist problem which has arisen from it—is an unfortunate "category mistake,"[32] that is, an artificial categorization of the objects of experience. All objects of experience, including the objects of scientific inquiry, as well as such characteristics as "good," "bad," "justice," "virtue," and the like are endowed with a similar *ontological* status; they all *exist* and are all *entities* in the world of nature, deriving their separate natures according to the relationships in which they stand, both to their own characters and to the characters and complexes of characters exhibited by other entities.

The foundation of the dualist problem, then, is rooted in the familiar and ubiquitous *subject/object distinction*,[33] one which maintains an *ontological* difference between perceivers and things perceived. The existence of this bifurcation necessarily leads to the kind of epistemological differences so apparent among the four positions taken by rhetoricians. These differences are manifested in the inherent practice of thinking in terms of distinctions such as physical/mental, internal/external, contingent/apodeictic. We have, for centuries, wittingly or unwittingly, labored under the *conceptual* consequences of Cartesian dualism. In the present century, the problem has been exacerbated by the growth of science and the ensuing academic conflicts between science and the arts. In rhetoric, the tendency has been further accentuated by the elevation of Aristotle's contingent/apodeictic distinction to the status of an axiom.

The theory of perspectivism, on the other hand, is premised on the assumption that there is no *ontological* distinction among the entities populating the universe. Because everything which is is what it is by virtue of its relationship to whatever else is, the subject/object distinction is otiose. Such a conclusion is consistent with the first postulate of perspective theory, namely, that reality is independent of human attitudes, beliefs, and values. Such independence does, on the perspectivist view, obtain; however, it obtains in the sense that the *objects* of reality are collections of *relata* standing in an asymmetrical conscious relationship to human subjects that are also collections of *relata*. The ontological cement gluing all entities together, then—be they abstract entities such as justice and goodness, empirical entities such as tables, chairs, and atoms, or conscious entities such as human beings—is *the relation*. For this reason, we may still refer to perceiving entities and perceived entities without becoming ensnared in dualism, so long as we are certain to keep at the forefront of our epistemological system the realization that the perception of entities is made possible *because of relationality*.[34] But as one reader of this essay inquired: "What does it mean to enter into a relationship? Is the relationship objectively real or does *it* depend on a perspective? Do entities have existence outside relationship? Can relationships be socially determined?" These are fair questions, but space permits us only to suggest what direction a response would take.

Technically, it is impossible to enter *anew* into a relationship in the sense of entering *afresh* into the vast relational complex that is the universe. The relational determiners which, for example, prescribed the occurrence of the Beirut Massacre, were as present in the world a thousand years ago as in September, 1982. The only sense, we suggest, in which the notion of entering into a relationship can be understood is the sense in which we *become aware*, as conscious human beings, of the possibility and, in retrospect, the actuality of relationships. Relations *are*, without exaggeration, *more* than objectively real, for they themselves are the determiners of the specific items comprising reality. Hence, rather than being shaped *by* perspectives, relations form the basis *of* human perspectives. Finally, it should be seen to follow that relationships (relations) *themselves* cannot be socially determined. Thus, while a skillful rhetor might convince an audience that the assassination of John Kennedy was the result of a conspiracy, only the existence or nonexistence of individuals other than Lee Harvey Oswald standing, *in fact*, in a conspiracy relationship to the events of November 22, 1963 can make the former President's death the product of a conspiracy. At best, the rhetor can make us aware of a relationship, *possible or actual*, that we were not (or are not) conscious of prior to rhetoric. But the rhetor cannot, strictly speaking, "create" a world of both relations *and* relata in defiance of relations *actually* existing.

The doctrine of relationality underscores how perspectivism may act as a mediating influence among the four positions on rhetorical epistemology. With respect to *strict subjectivism*, relationality accounts for how it is that individuals apprehend the world in distinct and frequently conflicting ways, hence retaining a valuable portion of the strict subjectivist thesis. Because each individual stands in a unique perspective to the multiplicity of events and things in the world, such individuals' accounts of the world are often distinctive. Yet while rhetors can view the world from different perspectives, and while the propagandist may argue for combinations of relations that do not obtain (i.e., are *untrue*), this is a far cry from the strict subjectivist's contention that meaning is wholly a product of individuals or that reality is socially constructed. Thus, perspectivism seems less vulnerable to the charge of solipsism. In a world where everything is intimately *related* in strictly ontological terms, solipsistic estrangement is less likely to occur, for, as all three postulates of perspectivism taken together suggest, the solipsistic implications of strict subjectivism dissolve on the basis of relationality, direct realism, and perspective consciousness.

With regard to *mitigated subjectivism*, perspective theory would echo the belief that not all classes of items comprising reality are the same. The differences among such items stem from the fact that each and every entity within the world stands in a special and unique relationship to all else that is. Unlike the mitigated subjectivists, however, perspectivism avoids the conclusion that classes of items are *ontologically* distinct, which is the source of the dualist enigma. For the perspectivist, there is no division of the world into technical and social phenomena. In terms of the most basic explanation possible for the nature of all phenomena, it is such foundational *relations* as "difference" itself which grounds the objects of knowledge. Differentiations among *classes* of objects of knowledge may be useful for some purposes, but are not, for the perspectivist, to be made on the basis of the role of language (communication) in "creating" some classes or "assessing" others. In sum, while perspectivism recognizes one advantage of the mitigated subjectivist thesis, namely, that the objects of reality exhibit significant differences, it rejects the claim that such differences are a function of, for example, a *qualitative* mind/body-type distinction. Such a distinction is, on the perspectivist view, both artificial and improper, since all objects of reality hold equal ontological status. In this way, the dualist enigma is avoided.

In terms of *strict objectivism*, perspective theory reaffirms the claim that reality, because it is independent of us, cannot be willed into existence nor wished away. The perspectivist, though, rejects the strict objectivist's contention that the only knowable items of reality are those that are "empirical." Like the two schools of subjectivist thought, perspectivism holds that we are capable of knowing, and in fact *do* know, much about the nonempirical world of prudential affairs. As already indicated, perspectivism takes issue with the very attempt to locate qualitative ontological differences among the items comprising reality. For this reason, terms such as "empirical" and "nonempirical" are at best euphemistic, and do *not* refer to a basic ontological distinction. The doctrine of an independent reality is applicable to *all* items in the world. One can, and frequently *does*, stand in a conscious relation to "nonempirical" as well as "empirical" entities. Such a claim is less problematic, according to the perspectivist, if we keep our language and thought free of the empirical connotations which terms such as "test," "proven," and the like (mistakenly) imply. This task becomes more manageable when we remember that all phenomena are what they are because of their relationship to all else.

Finally, perspectivism offers an important extension of the *rhetorical dialectic* thesis. To begin with, the perspectivist would share the contention of the rhetorical dialectic camp that reality is largely independent of the knower's attitudes, beliefs, and values, and is capable of being known. Again, however, the perspectivist posits such a claim without introducing an empirical/nonempirical vocabulary. In this way, the perspectivist both avoids the dualist enigma and helps address the subjectivists' complaint that nonempirical items of reality, if they are independent of us in the same way as empirical items, should be similarly verifiable. For the perspectivist, the problem of verifiability is ensconced within a dualist vocabulary—the tendency to make distinctions between empirical and nonempirical objects, subjects and objects, and contingent and apodeictic knowledge. If one approaches the notion of verifiability—and for that matter the entire process of coming to know—from the standpoint of conscious relations, such distinctions become unnecessary. In short, if we think of the process of coming to know as beginning when a conscious human being becomes aware of a relation, then it is just as easy to imagine how one could have awareness of what euphemistically have been called nonempirical objects as of empirical objects, since that which permits knowledge or understanding is *the relation*.

The relational foundation of awareness can be illustrated by considering some examples of epistemic judgments which arise in day-to-day discourse. Consider:

1. $4 + 5,000,000 = 5,000,004$
2. Jan followed her older, taller sister, Mary, into the room.
3. At a temperature of 459.69 degrees Fahrenheit (absolute zero), there is an absence of molecular movement, i.e., an absence of heat.
4. Richard Nixon was a bad president.

In line with traditional thinking, one might be tempted to label statement one "mathematical," statement two "general descriptive," statement three "scientific" or "empirical," and statement four "contingent." Each statement would be taken as different in kind, perhaps involving a unique type of epistemological judgment. Adopting the point of view of the perspectivist, all four statements purport to describe various constituents of the world as collections of characters which cohere *relationally* and, on this analysis, are *not* qualitatively distinct. Thus, while the perspectivist would certainly hold that the objects comprising the subject matter of each of the four statements are independent of the utterer's attitudes, beliefs, and values, there is no reason to introduce a subject/object vocabulary, contending that the objects in some of the statements are spatially external and, in other cases, spatially internal to mind.

The first statement, "Four added to five million equals five million and four," involves a relationship of equality. It, like other statements within pure mathematics, is a prime example of the notion of relationality, one which should be unproblematic for virtually any reader. For even the most fervent empiricist (including the strict objectivist) experiences much difficulty in explaining the "truth" of such a statement in empirical terms. The reason for this difficulty is clear: the statement treats only nonempirical concepts. It does not deal with quantities of apples or trees or tables or chairs; it deals with the *concepts* "four," "five million," "equality," and "five million and four." Nor do any of us have the slightest trouble operating with the two larger numbers in this equation, though doubtless none of us have ever *experienced* such quantities *of anything*. A consideration of similar and even more complex examples indicates that one often operates in mathematics with relations and concepts which have no instantiation in what has euphemistically (from the perspectivist's point or view) been called the "empirical world," or at least, if they are so instantiated, have never been, and likely will never be, experienced by human beings, *except in a nonempirical* sense. An individual becomes *conscious* of a mathematical equation when he or she stands in a certain relationship to that equation. The equation itself expresses a relationship among its various concepts as well as to the conscious individual, because the concepts it contains all stand in a context of particulars determined by all the interrelationships involved.

An interesting corollary of the perspectivist analysis of mathematics arises in the hypothetical case wherein all conscious entities suddenly perish from the universe (one may define perish as "to come into a state of complete and perpetual relational dissolution, so that consciousness is not possible"). In this event, the mathematical relation expressed by the first example, and all other mathematical examples, would continue to exist, since their ontological status is guaranteed so long as the mathematical relationships they express obtain. Extended to other objects of knowledge, perspectivism affirms the common sense notion that the stars and planets will continue to exist "in space" after all life is extinct on earth and no one is left to "perceive" their existence. This is because all the characters in the relational complex, save those comprising sentient earthlings, will continue to enter into relationships with each other.

In the second example, the statement "Jan followed her older, taller sister, Mary, into the room" was introduced. There are a number of easily identifiable relations which comprise this epistemic judgment, such as "older," "taller," and "followed." Other relations present that are somewhat more covert include "sisterhood." Sisterhood (which we call a "relation" in ordinary discourse) is vacuous unless treated as a relata in a world where at least two entities exist. In addition to these more or less obvious relations, terms such as "Jan" and "Mary" are relational as well, in the sense that they are terms which distinguish particular complexes of particulars from others. When one asks, "Who is Jan?," the response is likely to be, "Jan is the red-haired, short girl who is Mary's sister." Though one rarely thinks of it as such, a certain complex of particulars, Jan, is here being distinguished from among other complexes around her, including "Mary," "Paula," and "Theresa." Similar examples are ultimately analyzable into distinctions of a relational variety.

In "absolute zero," a number of relations are discernible. The numeric interval, 459.69, as well as the scale upon which it is based, namely the Fahrenheit scale, are obvious relational concepts. The requirement that one must think in terms of "external" and "internal" (subject/object) does not appear. An understanding of statement number three (and any other) requires only the recognition that it may be analyzed wholly in relational terms. Most conspicuously absent in this epistemology is the introduction of phrases such as "internal to mind" and "external to mind." Such an account demands only recognition of: (1) independent relata; and (2) their relations. It does not require a positing either of "objects" in the physicalist sense of the term, or reified "social realities" in the subjectivist sense.

Finally, let us consider the question of Richard Nixon's presidency addressed in statement four. Unlike the strict empiricist, the perspectivist analysis of this epistemic judgment begins with the common sense assumption that the statement is as meaningful and as important as any of the others. Thus the term, "bad," like its opposite, "good," is, at minimum, a character which is part of the complex of particular characters together constituting the concept "Richard Nixon's presidency." It is questions like this one which are more traditionally the domain of rhetorical discourse, though as suggested at the beginning of this section, the first three also frequently fall within the scope of rhetoric.[35] The last section of this paper focuses on these traditional rhetorical questions and explains additional implications which the perspectivist approach holds for rhetoric.

PERSPECTIVISM'S IMPLICATIONS FOR RHETORIC

To this stage of the argument it has been suggested that the perspectivist views all objects of experience, broadly conceived, as having an equal ontological status. Morals, ethics, and the questions of politics are as real as trees, houses, planets, and atoms. Yet one might challenge this position on the rationale that most of the objects of the former sort (for example, the objects of astronomical inquiry, such as stars and planets) are readily observable and that the scientific questions which they occasion are not the subject of *disagreement* in the sense that, say, the question of the goodness of Richard Nixon as an American president is the subject of disagreement. After all, the argument might continue, once a scientific question has been identified, a way to *measure* or otherwise *observe* the phenomena in question is found; then, shortly, our disagreement is resolved. Yet in the case of what have been called "contingent questions," debate may continue for centuries without a resolution. How can the perspectivist account for this seeming disparity? Moreover, doesn't this feature of disagreement signal a demarcation between two realms of thought which are, epistemologically, qualitatively distinct, perhaps even serving to confirm the very Cartesian distinction which we have been attempting to dismantle?[36]

The perspectivist account of disagreement begins with the observation that there exists, especially within the more complex and advanced branches of modern science, perhaps an equivalent level of disagreement—disagreement on issues which are as difficult to verify as any question of politics or ethics. Examples range from nuclear physics, where scientists are currently grappling with disagreements that seem almost insoluble, to contemporary astronomy, where the discovery of quasars is prompting a radical reevaluation of previous conceptions of the universe.

But let us examine the fundamental tenets of perspectivism to see if they offer a clue as to both the reason for and the solution to disagreements of a "contingent" nature. Recall that the perspectivist posits a world of relationships, wherein every entity, conscious or inanimate, stands in relationship to one another. It follows that each of us will perceive the world in a different way. Moreover, as each of us confronts very complex collections of relata, the complexity of such collections will have two effects: (1) they will offer the perceiving subject multi-various characters, each one itself a relata of the relational complex; and (2) their "appearance" may alter radically as the perspective changes for each perceiver or with different perceivers.

Let us pursue the question of Richard Nixon's presidency. One could hardly find a contemporary example of a question which would generate more controversy. Was Nixon a good president? Some would answer "yes" and some would say "no." Yet both responses cannot be true, for it is both logically and conceptually impossible to entertain both answers as *knowledge* at the same time and in the same way. How, then, can we account for the existence of actual rhetorical discourse which embraces contradictory answers to the question of whether or not Richard Nixon was a good president?

It is clear that both the strict and mitigated subjectivists would answer that such a question is meaningless, since there is no "truth" or "falsity"—at least in any absolute sense—and, hence, no answer to the question apart from socially constructed attitudes, beliefs, and values. The advocate of rhetorical dialectic, on the other hand, would contend that there is an answer to this question and that it must be true or false, while the strict objectivist would contend that such a question is totally without meaning because of its "nonempirical" character. The perspectivist, however, would take a somewhat different approach. The answer to the disagreement regarding Richard Nixon's presidency lies in an understanding of each arguer's *perspective* and in the fact that they may be conscious at any one time of collections of characters or *aspects*, each of which is a relatum within the collection of particulars comprising the Nixon presidency, but which *appear* to be different because of the differing *perspectives* in which each arguer stands. On this account, the apparently contradictory judgments are really not contradictory at all, since they are *judgments about different aspects of the same object.* One arguer, for example, may frame the answer to the hypothetical question as a result of a close attention to the foreign policy aspects of the Nixon years, with an emphasis on such events as normalizing relations with China or negotiating arms limitation agreements. He or she may conclude "Nixon was a good president." The other arguer may focus on the disastrous effects of Watergate and conclude "Nixon was a bad president." Ultimately, we should be able to reduce the scope of our interest in the relational complex so that we are all "talking about the same thing." Then we should be able to marshal the context of particulars in which arguers stand to an object of disagreement so we are arguing on the "same plane." When this is done we can both agree on what we are disagreeing about and, perhaps, "stand inside the other's perspective." At this point, agreement should be possible.[37]

Of course, one can imagine instances where individuals engage in this argumentative process and, nonetheless, are unable to embrace, understand, or otherwise recognize an other's perspective. An example might be the racist who holds a severe prejudice against blacks. Such an individual might labor under such a prejudice purely out of ignorance, that is, ignorance that no credible studies support the notion that blacks are inherently less intelligent than whites. In an argumentative confrontation, one might enlighten the racist about the actual data. In fact, one might produce a host of research to expose the racist's error. If the evidence were overwhelming, the racist *might* be convinced that his or her former attitude toward black intelligence was, in fact, in error. Yet this person might continue to hold racist views, based on other considerations—that is, based on *other perspectives.* Or, the racist might find himself or herself unable to reconcile a new perspective with the consequences for personal behavior or interpersonal relationships among his or her peer group. In the latter case, the racist might continue to *espouse* racist views, even though the argumentative encounter had undermined the initial rationale upon which those views were grounded.

If the racist eventually abandons his or her prejudice as a result of being made aware of another perspective by the argumentative encounter, then the value of rhetorical perspectivism as a tool of inquiry becomes obvious. On the other hand, if the racist persists in his or her attitude toward blacks, perspective theory may still offer important resources for affecting potential change. First, application of the theory of rhetorical perspectivism allows us to determine whether, in fact, impasse has been reached. Perspectivism may signal, as in the case of the Nixon example, that, because we are not arguing on the same level (that is, because we are not talking about the same aspect of the problem), there are no genuine grounds for disagreement. A perspective account of such discourse, therefore, could reveal imprecision on the part of the interlocutors regarding the object of controversy, thus permitting them to redefine the issue at hand. Perspectivism, then, may make continued discussion and eventual agreement possible through the elimination of what first appeared to be an impasse.

Second, rhetorical perspectivism may allow one to move among *various* perspectives on the *same* issue. Thus, even though a racist might be correct in his or her claim that large numbers of blacks live in ghetto communities, a discussion of how those communities came into existence, covering such topics as economic segregation, the denial of educational opportunities, and the failure of white-dominated city councils to provide essential services, might offer a number of *different perspectives* concerning the *reasons* for ghetto communities. By identifying perspectives the racist may not have considered in the past, his or her attitude toward blacks may be subject to amendment.

Finally, even if additional perspectives are not identified in an argumentative exchange, and even if the isolation of particular issues does not result in continued argumentative progress, still, by identifying precisely where an impasse is occurring, we have an indication of *why* genuine argument has stagnated. Accordingly, a perspective analysis of discourse may tell us something about ourselves *qua* arguers. It may underscore those moments when our emotions, preferences, values, dogmas, and prejudices have interceded to inhibit the most rational and person-building means of inquiry.

This recognition offers us the opportunity to reduce the potential for nondiscursive forms of conflict, in a world where technology renders conflict all the more egregious. By admitting, for example, that *both* we and our potential adversaries—be they Russians, Iranians, wives, or lovers—have reached a point of impasse based on the values and myths which each uniquely holds, we can eschew charges of disingenuousness, deceit, frivolity, and truculence. Thus, while we may be required to terminate our rhetorical efforts because of such an impasse, we can at least leave the negotiating table agreeing, no, *understanding* why negotiations have broken down. By agreeing, if only about the source of disagreement, we may be able to avoid the varieties of inflammatory charges which are the progenitors of nondiscursive conflict.

Perspectivism, then, may remind us that, because we each stand in an unique perspective to all else (thus explaining "intrinsic value differences"), we may, on occasion, be simply unable to find solutions to grave problems. Nevertheless, we may still depart from argumentative confrontations with the knowledge that, having applied perspectivism as a guide to argument, we have done all humanly possible to achieve harmony, hoping that at some future time negotiations can be reconvened and fresh perspectives pursued.[38] It should be clear from what has gone before that perspectivism offers not only the *opportunity* but, in a sense, the *responsibility* for continued efforts to solve disputes on the basis of peaceful, discursive means. This is because the theory assumes the potential for every individual to be brought to a realization of the perspective of any other and to work together to solve differences constructively. For this reason, nondiscursive forms of conflict can, and thus must, be continually set aside, and the invitation to return to the conference table continually held open. While it is doubtless true that many readers will find in such a view more "naïve" idealism than worldly "realism," we suggest there is ample evidence in the history of international diplomacy to warrant continued consideration of this position.

CONCLUSION

Embracing the tenets of perspectivism may allow us to retain useful and meaningful conceptions of "truth" or "knowledge," thus preserving the most important feature of objectivism. Moreover, by relieving rhetorical epistemology of the burden of the dualist enigma, perspectivism permits the introduction of a richly endowed theory of knowledge capable of extending rhetorical knowing across the entire spectrum of what there is to know, from matters previously labeled scientific to those frequently called contingent.

In addition to recasting objectivist statements of how knowledge is possible, perspectivism offers a better understanding of the nature and usefulness of theoretical constructs within subjectivist thought. For example, perspectivism makes clear the contribution of those in rhetoric who have argued for the existence of socially constructed realities. Such realities are, in effect, the perspectives which different societal groups entertain on various social phenomena. However, they do not, for the perspectivist, represent the terminus of inquiry. Rather, such social realities are to be viewed as more or less complete expositions of one perhaps limited perspective. Thus, they may be invaluable in contributing to a fuller understanding of the social phenomena under investigation; yet, for the perspectivist, a thorough understanding of a particular social phenomena can occur only when *all* relevant perspectives have been discovered, evaluated, and juxtaposed to form a more complete view of the object of inquiry. As this study suggests, it is only through an active seeking out of perspectives that such a goal may be approached. The promise of perspectivism, then, inheres in the systematic development and application, by theorist, critic, and arguer alike, of *perspective method*, a goal to which we hope this essay has contributed a modest beginning.

Notes

1. Douglas Ehninger, "Introduction," in Douglas Ehninger,ed., *Contemporary Rhetoric: A Reader's Coursebook* (Glenview, IL: Scott, Foresman, 1972), pp. 1–14. This view may also be seen in his later works. See, e.g., Douglas Ehninger, "Science, Philosophy—And Rhetoric: A Look Toward the Future," in James L. Golden, Goodwin F. Berquist, and William E. Coleman, eds., *The Rhetoric of Western Thought* (Dubuque, IA: Kendall/Hunt, 1978), pp. 323–331.

2. Robert L. Scott, "On Viewing Rhetoric as Epistemic," *Central States Speech Journal* 18 (1967): 17 (reprinted in this volume). A representative list of scholarship in this area includes: Robert L. Scott, "On Viewing Rhetoric as Epistemic: Ten Years Later," *Central States Speech Journal* 27 (1976): 258–266; Lloyd Bitzer, "Rhetoric and Public Knowledge," in Don Burks, ed., *Rhetoric, Philosophy, and Literature* (West Lafayette, IN: Purdue University Press, 1978), pp. 67–98; Thomas Farrell, "Knowledge, Consensus, and Rhetorical Theory," *Quarterly Journal of Speech* 64 (1976): 1–14 (reprinted in this volume); Walter M. Carleton, "What Is Rhetorical Knowledge? A Reply to Farrell—And More," *Quarterly Journal of Speech* 64 (1978): 313–328; and Richard Cherwitz, "Rhetoric as a 'Way of Knowing': An Attenuation of the Epistemological Claims of the 'New Rhetoric,'" *Southern Speech Communication Journal* 42 (1977): 207–219. A good review of research on this topic appears in Michael C. Leff, "In Search of Ariadne's Thread: A Review of the Recent Literature on Rhetorical Theory," *Central States Speech Journal* 29 (1978): 73–91.

3. See, e.g., Barry Brummett, "Some Implications of 'Process' or 'Intersubjectivity': Post-modern Rhetoric," *Philosophy and Rhetoric* 9 (1976): 34 (reprinted in this volume). Although not agreeing with Brummett entirely, this position is also taken by Farrell, Scott, and Carleton. Most of this research seems to be an outgrowth of views expressed by Peter Berger and Thomas Luckmann, in their *The Social Construction of Reality* (Garden City, NY: Doubleday, 1966).

4. In particular, see C. Jack Orr, "How Shall We Say: 'Reality Is Socially Constructed through Communication?'" *Central States Speech Journal* 29 (1978): 263–274. See also Richard A. Cherwitz and James W. Hikins, "John Stuart Mill's *On Liberty*: Implications for the Epistemology of the New Rhetoric," *Quarterly Journal of Speech* 65 (1979): 12–24.

5. The term "intersubjectivity" has become commonplace in the writings of some scholars in rhetorical epistemology, most notably Brummett. Of late, however, several theorists have recognized the subjective or relative implications of intersubjectivity, preferring the terms "rhetorical subjectivism" and/or "rhetorical relativism." See, for example, Earl Croasmun and Richard Cherwitz, "Beyond Rhetorical Relativism," *Quarterly Journal of Speech* 68 (1982): 1–16. Their argument is that intersubjectivity inherently lapses back into subjectivity, despite the contention by the intersubjectivists that subjectivity is avoided. The view of "rhetorical relativism" is embraced by Scott in his 1976 essay. The distinction between "rhetorical objectivism" and "rhetorical dialectic" appears in James W. Hikins, "Plato's Rhetorical Theory: Old Perspectives on the Epistemology of the New Rhetoric," *Central States Speech Journal* 32 (1981): 160–176. "Critical rationalism" is discussed by Orr (cited in full above, note 4).

6. The earliest recorded use of the term "perspective" in English is reported as occurring in 1598. Its various uses are illustrated in, for example, *The Oxford English Dictionary*, q.v. "perspective"; Edmund Burke Feldman, *Varieties of Visual Experience* (Englewood Cliffs, NJ : Prentice-Hall, 1981), pp. 160, 215, 419, 441–444; *The Oxford New English Dictionary on Historical Principles*, q.v. "perspective"; Albert North Whitehead, *Science in the Modern World* (New York: Free Press, 1967), p. 102.

7. See Gottfried Wilhelm Von Leibniz, *The Monadology*, in *Monadology and Other Philosophical Essays*, trans. Paul Schrecker and Anne Martin Schrecker (Indianapolis, IN: Bobbs-Merrill, 1965), p. 157.

8. Whitehead, *Science in the Modern World*, p. 102.

9. Ibid., p. 102.

10. See Bertrand Russell, *The Problems of Philosophy* (London: Oxford University Press, 1959), pp. 15–16, 101ff.; George Herbert Mead, *The Philosophy of the Present*, ed. Arthur E. Murphy (Chicago: Open Court, 1932); Irwin Biser, *General Scheme for Natural Systems* (Philadelphia: Westbrook, 1932); and Andrew Ushenko, "A Theory Of Perception," *Journal of Philosophy* 37 (1940): 141ff.

11. For an excellent discussion of the various formulations of philosophical realism, see Paul Edwards, ed., *The Encyclopedia of Philosophy* (New York: Macmillan/Free Press, 1962), vol, 7, pp. 77–83.

12. Evander Bradley McGilvary, *Toward a Perspective Realism* (La Salle, IL: Open Court, 1956), pp. 11, 12, 15, 16.

13. It is the basic epistemological concern of providing a proper account of how we know what we know about the world confronting us in our everyday experience that has motivated major writings in contemporary phenomenology and existentialism. See, for example, Martin Heidegger, *Being and Time*, trans. John Macquarrie and Edward Robinson (New York: Harper and Row, 1962); Edmund Husserl, *Logical Investigations*, trans. J. N. Findlay (New York: Humanities Press, 1970); and William Richardson, *Heidegger: Through Phenomenology to Thought*, vol. 13 of *Phenomenologica*, 2d ed. (The Hague: Martinus Nijhoff, 1967). The reader will doubtless discover a number of parallels between this essay and the works just cited, especially in terms of the issues that are their most common progenitor. Perhaps the most significant point of departure between this study and those mentioned above involves the resolution of epistemological problems through the employment of a theory which is believed consistent with contemporary science and is treated sympathetically in a number of American and British philosophical systems, including those of Peirce and Russell, to name but two (see notes 9 and 10, above).

14. The postulates developed in this essay are, in large part, based upon the theory of perspectivism advanced by McGilvary. However, in many respects they depart from, and in some cases amplify, McGilvary's thinking.

15. See Thomas Reid, *Essays on the Intellectual Powers of Man*, in Lewis White Beck, ed., *Eighteenth-Century Philosophy* (New York: Free Press, 1966), pp. 134–150.

16. The contention that reality exists independent of consciousness is argued by McGilvary: "While in many respects we find ourselves unable to get on the same plane of meanings on which others take their stand, it is obvious that in other respects and in our unphilosophical moments we are all of us, with some unhappy exceptions, already on the same plane when we speak of 'reality.'" See McGilvary, *Toward a Perspective Realism*, p. 9.

17. Ibid., p 11.

18. In our opinion this is the position of Brummett and Carleton. In many important respects, this thesis is advocated also by Scott, "On Viewing Rhetoric as Epistemic." See also Charles W. Kneupper, "Rhetoric, Argument, and Social Reality: A Social Constructivist View," *Journal of the American Forensic Association* 16 (1980): 173–181.

19. Brummett, "Some Implications of Process," p. 29.

20. One of the more articulate expositions of this thesis appears in Thomas Farrell, "Knowledge, Consensus, and Rhetorical Theory." A reaffirmation of this position is found in Thomas Farrell, "Social Knowledge 2," *Quarterly Journal of Speech* 64 (1978): 329–334.

21. Farrell, "Knowledge, Consensus, and Rhetorical Theory," p. 9.

22. This seems to be the reasoning of Brummett, in his "Some Implications of Process," p. 27. It is interesting to note, however, that to make such a claim and argue for the concept of social realities is itself the advocacy of an independent reality. This was precisely the point made by Orr in his critique of intersubjectivity ("How Shall We Say").

23. Brummett, "Some Implications of Process," p. 27

24. See, e.g., Scott, "On Viewing Rhetoric as Epistemic," and Scott, "Ten Years Later."

25. This thesis is reminiscent of the position adopted by rhetoricians of the modern period who viewed rhetoric's role as one of "making truth effective," a notion found in François Fenelon's *Dialogues on Eloquence*. This position finds sympathetic treatment in the contemporary literature as well. See, e.g., Richard Weaver, *Language Is Sermonic* (Baton Rouge: Louisiana State University Press, 1970), pp. 11, 12, 18, 19, and 71.

26. Vincent M. Bevilacqua, "Philosophical Influences in the Development of English Rhetorical Theory: 1748–1783," *Proceedings of the Leeds Philosophical and Literary Society, Literary and Historical Section* 19(4): 192. See also Scott, "On Viewing Rhetoric as Epistemic," p. 9.

27. See Orr, "How Shall We Say."

28. See Cherwitz and Hikins, "John Stuart Mill's *On Liberty*."

29. A more thorough exploration of these arguments appears in Orr, "How Shall We Say," pp. 263–274. See also Roger Trigg, *Reason and Commitment* (Cambridge: Cambridge University Press, 1973). Their implication for rhetoric is that one cannot possibly embrace the view that all reality is socially generated; to do so would render concepts such as "speaker," "audience," and even "persuasion" meaningless.

30. Rene Descartes, *Meditations on First Philosophy*, trans. Laurence J. Lafleur (Indianapolis, IN: Bobbs-Merrill, 1960). The reader should be careful not to interpret us as suggesting that "the differences between subjectivism and objectivism stem from taking Descartes seriously," as an earlier critic of this essay contended. Obviously, the subjectivist/objectivist debate has its origins in pre-Socratic philosophy. However, Descartes' contribution to the debate has been of signal importance. For one, he was the first to make epistemology the starting point of inquiry and to state the subject/object distinction in a form which caused dualism to "remain at the heart of much contemporary philosophical inquiry, the work of Gilbert Ryle and Ludwig Wittgenstein, for example, being aimed directly against what are still very powerful Cartesian conceptions." Second, Descartes' formulation of the problem of dualism underscores the priority of developing an *epistemology* before contending with questions of *ontology*. Thus, while it is true that an important issue facing rhetorical epistemology is the *meaning* of the objects of knowledge, what is, and how one comes to know what is, are kindred questions. What one may know, how one may come to know, and what are the limits of human knowledge are questions surely conditioned by what, in fact, *is*, i.e., on the way the world is constituted. Hence, the issue of "meaning" is not only merely *part* of what any epistemology (rhetorical or otherwise) must address, but it is a question which must inevitably *be* addressed *in concert with ontological issues*, as soon as the most

fundamental epistemological issues have been decided upon. To *wholly* eschew ontology on the assumption that "meaning" is a prior issue is to beg the question and point immediately toward a particular epistemological world view (subjectivism). See Bernard Williams, "Descartes, René," in Paul Edwards, ed., *The Encyclopedia of Philosophy* (New York: Macmillan, 1967), vol. 2, p. 354.

31. See *The Encyclopedia of Philosophy*, q.v. "Popper, Karl Raimund."

32. The notion of "category mistake" is treated in Gilbert Ryle, in *The Concept of Mind* (London: Hutchinson's University Library, 1949).

33. See note 30, above.

34. This view implies that a fully developed exposition of perspectivism demands discussion of a *theory of perception* and perception's relation to the communicative enterprise. Spatial limitations preclude such a discussion in this essay; however, it should be obvious that a perspective theory of perception would depart significantly from contemporary accounts, especially those advanced in physiology. Here, too, the influence of the Cartesian enigma is evident, as physiologists struggle to make sense of how *physical* phenomena (such as photons and nerve impulses) become transformed into *conscious* acts such as seeing and hearing. See, e.g. Rodney J. Hirst, *Perception and the External World* (New York: Macmillan, 1965).

35. Arguments for this position derive from a number of sources. Most conspicuous among these is the current tendency in our field to view rhetoric as playing a significant role in scientific inquiry. Representative essays in the rhetoric of science are: Mario Finocchiaro, "Logic and Rhetoric in Lavossier's Sealed Note: Toward a Rhetoric of Science," *Philosophy and Rhetoric* 10 (1977): 111–122; Michael A. Overington, "The Scientific Community as Audience: Toward a Rhetorical Analysis of Science," *Philosophy and Rhetoric* 10 (1977): 143–163; and Walter Weimer, "Science as a Rhetorical Transaction: Toward a Nonjustificational Conception of Rhetoric," *Philosophy and Rhetoric* 10 (1977): 1–29.

36. The argument that contingent questions are qualitatively different from apodeictic ones is a distinction that cannot be maintained. The position rests primarily on the observation that contingent questions are somehow opaque to observation or measurement, in contrast to the objects of science, for instance. This does not appear to be a very probative or enlightening remark. After all, the atoms that Lucretius wrote about in his *De rerum natura* were as ephemeral in his day as "values" such as goodness or justice are to us today.

37. At this point it may seem that we have come full circle to admit that agreement is the final arbiter of truth. This is not, however, what the formulation of perspectivism suggests. Unlike the social constructivists, the contention here is not that agreement creates "truth" or "knowledge," but rather that the *independent* (in a relational sense, as *relata*) objects of reality *determine agreement* when viewed by individuals in precisely the same way, from the same "point of view."

38. The reader will undoubtedly notice a similarity between our application of perspectivist theory and the traditional concept of *status* (*stasis*). While there are many similarities, two points must be emphasized. First, the concept of stasis was designed primarily to deal with disputes that took place in courts of law (judicial stasis) and in legislative assemblies (deliberative stasis); in this way, stasis was taken almost exclusively as a method of invention for arriving at decisions. Perspectivism, on the other hand, goes beyond rhetorical discourse in such practical, *advocacy* settings. A perspective theory of rhetoric is concerned not just with arriving at legal and legislative decisions; rather, it is intended to deal with all discourse aimed at seeking truth. Unlike stasis, therefore, perspectivism applies to discovery-oriented discourse. The setting for perspectivism is one of *inquiry*, not advocacy. Second, although perspective theory has direct application to decision making situations, its primary purpose is to provide an *epistemological* foundation for concepts such as stasis. Unlike traditional stasis theory, then, perspectivism accounts on an epistemological level for many of the different approaches to a particular issue. It also explains how and why arguers may not be reaching stasis within particular categories or levels of stasis because of their unique relationships to particular aspects of the object of inquiry.

Rhetoric and Its Double

Reflections of the Rhetorical Turn in the Human Sciences

DILIP PARAMESHWAR GAONKAR

THE FLIGHT FROM "MERE" RHETORIC

Rhetoric cannot escape itself. Rhetoric cannot escape its "mereness," or to use the fashionable vocabulary of our time (here I am alluding to Derridean deconstruction), it cannot escape its status as a "supplement." Yet this simple fact that there is no exit for rhetoric, nor an exit from rhetoric, escapes many friends of rhetoric. Rhetoric cannot efface itself to become its traditional counterpart, dialectic, as Perelman and Valesio would have it.[1] Nor can it recast itself, as Grassi proposes, as the seat of primordial poetic utterance, which apprehends and articulates "the first principles" on which the rational speech of philosophy, in turn, depends.[2] Nor can rhetoric be equated with a hermeneutics of suspicion, as the linguistically inclined followers of Marx, Nietzsche, and Freud would suggest.

To be sure, rhetoric stands in a historically fluctuating relationship with other disciplines, especially those formal disciples which are its neighbors. To a certain measure, its identity and its fortunes are linked to those fluctuating affiliations. For that reason, Roland Barthes tells us that "rhetoric must always be read in the structural interplay with its neighbors (Grammar, Logic, Poetics, Philosophy): it is the play of the system, not each of its parts in itself, which is historically significant."[3] Sometimes its systemic proximity to one of the neighbors is so great and compelling that one is prone to overlook its distinctive character and its essential difference. If such a misreading of rhetoric happened but occasionally, it would be understandable.

However, when scholars repeatedly fail to distinguish rhetoric from its neighbors, and do so even in a period marked by a renewed and self-conscious interest in rhetoric, it is reasonable to suspect that something more than an accident is involved. The tenacity of this error, if error it is, should give us pause and prompt us to review this impulse (this habit of the mind) which urges us to make rhetoric into something other than itself.

What is involved in these misreadings, in my opinion, is simply a "flight from rhetoric," or to be more precise, a flight from "mere" rhetoric—that is, rhetoric conceived as a "supplement." What is so frightening, you may ask, that one should seek to flee from "mere" rhetoric in so deliberate a manner?

Once rhetoric is conceived as a "supplement," it becomes a formal, hence an empty, discipline. It is without substance, without a secure set of referents, or to put it mundanely, it has no subject matter of its own. To be sure, one can take the general and recurrent lines of arguments (topics) and certain structural/functional resources of language (tropes and figures) as the special province or the subject matter of rhetoric. But this does not resolve the difficulty. Such a view, it seems to me, while recognizing rhetoric as a mode of practical reasoning and discourse production does so precisely in terms of its formal character as a language art. Thus deprived of substance, rhetoric stands in a parasitic relationship vis-à-vis substantive disciplines such as ethics and politics. Sometimes this "parasite" becomes so deeply entangled with the affairs of an alien body, especially the "body politic," it forgets its own nature and purpose and pretends to be a substantive entity. Perhaps this is what Aristotle had in mind when he said, "It thus appears that rhetoric is an offshoot of dialectic and also of ethical studies. Ethical studies may fairly be called political: and for this reason rhetoric masquerades as political science, and the professors of it as political experts."[4] For much the same reason, Plato reached a more severe judgment and dismissed rhetoric as a counterfeit art (*Gorgias*, 464–465).

Brian Vickers, a distinguished contemporary champion of rhetoric, notes that rhetoric, having no subject matter of its own, functions a bit like a "service industry," and thereby gets into territorial disputes with other disciplines.[5] The very fact that rhetoric is without a domicile is seen as profoundly threatening to the integrity of substantive disciplines. The territorial disputes between two substantive disciplines, say, law and sociology, are far less acrimonious than when rhetoric enters the picture and attempts to transform and use the materials characteristic of either of those two disciplines. Here I am reminded of Cicero's characterization of Marc Antony as a "homeless" transgressor in the *Fourth Philippic*. According to Cicero, one could negotiate with an enemy on some "settled principle" so long as he has "a republic, a senate house, a treasury, harmonious and united citizens" which he hopes to protect and promote. But Antony, says Cicero, "is attacking your republic, but has none himself; is eager to destroy the Senate, . . . but has no public council himself; he has exhausted your treasury, and has none of his own. For how can a man be supported by the unanimity of the citizens, who has no city at all?"[6] If we substitute rhetoric for Antony, we have an apt image for the kind of danger rhetoric represents to the established disciplines. Rhetoric can spring up any time, from within or without, to pollute and possess what is not its own for the sake of temporary advantage and gratification. Thus, rhetoric is seen as a nomadic discipline that threatens the integrity of the republic of knowledge itself. Why would anyone want to admit such a discipline to the council of learning when it refuses to abide by the academic rules of property and propriety?

Such is the impulse of an empty discipline to become substantive, to become something other than itself. It is as if rhetoric were in search of its other, the substantive other, who, when found, would fill out its formal emptiness. But this other which is to provide rhetoric with a grounding, relieve it from that epistemic anxiety with which it has been burdened since Plato, will always elude us. Perhaps this is the fatal game which animates rhetoric and keeps it going.

The flight from "mere" rhetoric consists of a double movement which, in my view, regulates, shapes, and determines the self-image of rhetoric. This double movement simultaneously propels rhetoric on a vertical axis downward into its past to find itself a suitable history and on a horizontal axis sideways to situate itself within the discursive practices of special "substantive" sciences, especially the human sciences. Rhetoric moves diachronically to discover for itself an alternative historical tradition that will free it from its supplementary status, and it moves synchronically to find itself in the discursive body (textuality) of other disciplines that will confirm its "presence."

These two movements motivated by their distaste for "mere rhetoric" direct us to flee from it, especially if we are serious about this business of rehabilitating rhetoric as "the once and future queen of the human sciences."[7] They play on our disciplinary "lures" and anxieties (which are predictably many), and urge us to make rhetoric into something other than itself.

This double movement in the contemporary self-understanding of rhetoric is not necessarily fully "articulated." Nor is it an entirely "implicit" and subterranean movement which I am somehow magically bringing to light. If this movement is partially "invisible," its invisibility is not due to its obscure presence but to what Alfred Schutz calls its "taken-for-granted" character.[8]

As you may have inferred from my characterization of this double movement as a "lure," I regard it as fundamentally problematic and possibly destructive of rhetoric as a vocation. However, I am not here to reject it but to contest it. In fact, this double movement is not something which can be either accepted or rejected, for it is one of the "essentially contested" features of our discipline.[9]

THE FIRST MOVEMENT: THE SUPPLEMENTARY TRADITION

The idea that rhetoric is no more than a "supplement" makes its initial appearance in the fabled encounter between the Older sophists and the Platonic Socrates, the first site of the so-called quarrel between rhetoric and philosophy. Naturally, there are several strands to this quarrel between rhetoric and philosophy, but both historically and in our own time much of the dispute concerns the epistemic status of rhetoric.[10] The idea that rhetoric is no more than a "supplement" has its origin in the articulation of this question.

The question in its simplest form is this: Does rhetoric, the art of discovering available means of persuasion in a given case (Aristotle), have anything to do with the generation of knowledge? If not, as Socrates, Plato, and Aristotle appear to have assumed, then we may ask, as Heidegger asked of poets: *What are rhetoricians for?*

The Aristotelian compromise on this question, which sets into motion the "supplementary" tradition in rhetoric, is well known. For Aristotle, among other things, rhetoric makes knowledge more readily comprehensible and acceptable in the domain of civic discourse. That is, rhetoric cannot generate knowledge but is useful, possibly indispensable, for the transmission of knowledge discovered by philosophy and the special substantive sciences. Rhetoric, to use a term popularized by Jacques Derrida, is a supplement to knowledge, much as writing is a supplement to Speech.[11]

The placing of Aristotle within the supplementary tradition is somewhat problematic. In the Aristotelian scheme, while demonstrative (apodictic) reasoning belongs to the domain of the necessary, rhetoric and dialectic operate within the domain of the contingent and the probable. Further, neither rhetoric nor dialectic "is a science that deals with the nature of any definite subject, but they are merely faculties of furnishing arguments."[12] Rhetoric, in other words, is a general art consisting not of knowledge about substantive fields but a flexible system of formal and prudential devices—topics, tropes and figures, inferential schemes, probabilities, prudential rules, and so on.[13] At the same time, however, this general art is functionally implicated in managing and transforming common opinion for persuasive ends. This functional link to common opinion, according to Leff, prevents rhetoric from becoming a purely formal discipline, and its practical applications extend to the whole field of human affairs.[14] Moreover, the functional aspect of rhetoric is particularly decisive in the civic arena when citizens have to make judgments on issues without recourse to the special sciences to guide their deliberation.[15] This unresolved tension between the formal and the functional dimensions of rhetoric threatens its identity in two distinct but contradictory ways. On the one hand, rhetoric cannot posit a substantive identity because it has no subject matter of its own; on the other hand, its functional involvement with *doxa* threatens its formal identity by what Ricoeur calls an "overburdening of content."[16] Thus, rhetoric is simultaneously empty of subject matter and overburdened with content.

It is against this background one has to negotiate the question as to whether rhetoric has an epistemic function. The centrality of "invention" in the rhetorical tradition as a whole hints at a generative rather than a purely managerial and transmissive function for rhetoric. Yet a closer examination reveals that the aim of rhetorical inquiry is quite different from that of dialectical inquiry. A distinction introduced by Kenneth Burke is particularly useful in this context. Burke, following Aristotle, recognizes that both dialectic and rhetoric begin their inquiry with a critique of common opinion in the realm of the contingent and the probable. But the two critiques have different ends. Although the dialectical critique occurs in the scenic order of truth with a view toward transcending the conflict intrinsic to opinion, the rhetorical critique occurs in the moral order of action with a view toward managing and transforming conflicting opinions in accordance with the exigencies of a given situation. Hence rhetoric, unlike dialectic, is not constitutive of general truths and propositions but of specific beliefs, attitudes, and actions.[17]

Roland Barthes arrives at a similar conclusion regarding Aristotle's treatment of the passions. What Aristotle offers in his *Rhetoric*, according to Barthes, is a "projected" psychology: a psychology as everyone imagines it—not "what is in the mind" of the public, but what the public believes others "have in mind." In Barthes' view, Aristotle's innovative treatment of the passions (in contrast to the technographers who preceded him) lies precisely in his decision to view them "in their banality" and to classify "the passions not according to what they are, but according to what they are believed to be: he does not describe them scientifically, but seeks out arguments which can be used with respect to the public's ideas about passion."[18] Rhetorical psychology is therefore quite the opposite of a reductive psychology that would try to see what is *behind* what people say and attempt to reduce anger, for instance, to something else, something hidden. For Aristotle, public opinion is the first and last datum; he has no hermeneutic notion (of decipherment): anger is what every one thinks about anger, passion is never anything but what people say it is.[19]

Rhetoric thus puts together a disparate set of materials and insights originating in common opinion and popular understanding by recourse to a flexible system of formal devices on an ad hoc basis. Despite its generality as a formal system, rhetoric is marked by a radical particularity in its practices and products. Thus, unless one is prepared to collapse the distinction between knowledge and belief, understanding and action, it seems unreasonable to invoke the authority of Aristotle to claim that rhetoric has an epistemic function.

At any rate, according to the "supplementary" tradition, the quarrel between sophistic rhetoric and Platonic philosophy, as mediated by Aristotle, was decided in favor of the latter. Rhetoric was pushed into the margins of philosophy and the special sciences, and there it was forced to function as a *supplement to knowledge*. The subsequent history of rhetoric is the history of a supplement, living in the margins of philosophy, periodically attempting to widen that margin, as in the case of Cicero and the Renaissance Humanists, or to deepen the dignity of supplementary function, as in the case of St. Augustine.[20] On the whole, however, it is not a history of violent opposition and rebellion against philosophy, but one of accommodation, adjustment, and redefinition.

This tradition of the *supplement* has led many students of rhetoric into a conceptual impasse, as illustrated by John Quincy Adams, the first holder of the Boylston Professorship of Rhetoric at Harvard. In a lecture given in 1806, he declares that rhetoric "which has exhausted the genius of Aristotle, Cicero, and Quintilian, can neither require nor admit much additional illustration. To select, combine, and apply their precepts, is the only duty left for their followers of all succeeding times, and to obtain a perfect familiarity with their instructions is to arrive at the mastery of the art."[21] The same frame of mind prompted the English scholar J.E.C. Welldon in 1886 to praise Aristotle's *Rhetoric* "as being perhaps a solitary instance of a book which not only begins a science, but completes it."[22] Such is the praise heaped on a text (an incomplete set of lecture notes to be precise) that, whatever its genius, stands profoundly divided against itself. This is the extent to which rhetoric had been emasculated within the rubric of a "supplementary" tradition by the end of the nineteenth century.

Understandably, the revived interest in rhetoric in this century is marked by a desire to break free from such a conceptual impasse. The tale of twentieth-century rhetoric, at least in its theoretical speculations, if not in its critical practice, can be read as a revolt against the "supplementary" tradition.

THE SOPHISTIC TRADITION

This escape from "mere" rhetoric takes many forms and employs many strategies. One way to escape from the conceptual impasse brought about by the "supplementary tradition" is to revive its historical opponent, the sophistic tradition. The rehabilitation of the older sophists that began in the early part of the nineteenth century under the sponsorship of Hegel in Germany and Grote in England has gained considerable momentum in this century. Their name, if not their work, is prominent in the current revival of rhetoric.[23] A return to their skeptical outlook on the "language-ridden" world of human culture is regarded as central to any serious attempt at reviving rhetoric. This revival of the sophistic tradition consists of two related sets of moves, the philosophical and the historical.

The philosophical move in restoring the sophistic tradition to its former glory requires one to decenter the epistemic question. Instead of asking whether rhetoric can generate knowledge, a more fundamental (ontological) question is pushed to the center:

How is rhetoric possible?[24] This Kantian type of question refers to the ultimate grounds of rhetoric. In response to this question, two unavoidable human characteristics are offered as the ultimate grounds of rhetoric. First, to use a phrase of Kenneth Burke, humans are symbol-using (misusing) creatures. Second, to use a phrase of Hannah Arendt, life is given to humans under "the condition of plurality."[25] From these two ultimate grounds, one can derive, in turn (as de Man and Todorov do), two distinct but related concepts of rhetoric.[26] They are rhetoric as persuasion and rhetoric as trope. Although the dimension of plurality, marked by "unity in division" (Burke), imposes on humans the necessity of persuasion, the tropological dimension of language makes them susceptible to persuasion. The basic strategy here is to derive in a global fashion the inevitability of rhetoric from our social relations as they are mediated by language. This strategy clearly favors certain theories of language and social relations over others. For instance, while the theory that views language as a transparent medium for the communication of things and ideas is clearly unacceptable, the thesis that social reality, among other things, is linguistically constructed and legitimated is enthusiastically endorsed.[27] The main difficulty with this strategy, with rare exceptions, is that it operates at an extremely high level of generality and almost equates rhetoric with language use and sociability. As a result, this philosophical strategy is disconnected from the sense of rhetoric as a local phenomenon which is so central to the human experience of rhetoric as a material force.[28]

The historical move is far more intriguing. The return to the sophists requires a reconstitution of the history of rhetoric. One cannot traverse 2,500 years back to the origins of rhetoric without acknowledging the intervening steps. According to this reconstituted history, there are not one but two histories of rhetoric—a manifest history and a hidden history. And they are dominated by two different traditions—the manifest history by the "supplementary" tradition, and the hidden history by the sophistic tradition.

The manifest history begins predictably enough with the older sophists and their celebrated quarrel with the Platonic Socrates; it moves through Aristotle, Isocrates, Cicero, Quintilian, and St. Augustine in the classical world, and then through the Middle Ages and the Renaissance and the eighteenth-century neoclassical rhetoric and the Scottish School. This is the official history of Boethius, Alcuin, George of Trebizond, Agricola, Ramus, Bacon, Fenelon, Lawson, Campbell, and Blair, which finally culminates in Bishop Whatley's *Elements of Rhetoric*. This is the history of rhetoric conceived as a "supplement," a history of obscure places, unfamiliar names, and forgotten texts.

The other history of rhetoric, its hidden history, also begins with the celebrated quarrel between the sophists and the Platonic Socrates, and moves indecisively along-side the manifest history until the end of the classical world; then, suddenly, it disappears, until it is *rediscovered* by Kenneth Burke. The "hidden" history places a somewhat different interpretation on the quarrel between sophistic rhetoric and Platonic philosophy. According to this version, the fabulous quarrel that held the Greek mind captive during the declining years of Periclean Enlightenment involved more than the competing claims of two skirmishing disciplines. Rather, is was a contest between two competing ways of life, the *vita activa* and the *vita contemplativa*. Their competing claims to civic attention is described vividly, but with a decided bias, in the Platonic dialogues, especially in the *Theaetetus* (172c–175e). Such a contest could not be settled in a single generation, even if that generation could produce so rare a phenomenon as Socrates. So it continues to engage our attention to this day in varying degrees of intensity. At any rate, for a variety of reasons, both political and intellectual, this competition for cultural hegemony ended in a defeat for the sophists, and they were promptly driven out of the cultural milieu by their philosophical detractors. Thereafter sophistry, insofar as it is a permanent opening for man, had to live an underground, subterranean existence. Later, when Aristotle made the compensatory move toward rhetoric and granted it the status of a supplement, rhetoric and sophistic became divorced. While rhetoric, in its attenuated form as a "supplement," was allowed to live in the margins of philosophy, sophistic was "repressed." Thus, rhetoric continued to function as a supplement to philosophical knowledge, where it regulated certain discursive practices and products, but it could not function as a supplement to a sophistic *Weltanschauung* marked by ethical relativity and epistemic skepticism. In this managerial placement, style retained a legitimate interest for the art, but rhetoric seems incapable of generating its own grounding as a mode of persuasion. This partly explains why the theory of invention in rhetoric became moribund, but the theory of *lexis* (*eloqutio*) was endlessly refined and elaborated.

But what is "repressed" is not erased. It must resurface in various symptomatic forms. Besides, the natural affinity between rhetoric and sophistic would continually draw the two together. Hence, there follows a series of illicit relations and subterranean connections, which constitute the "hidden" history of rhetoric. In some sense, this is the "return of the repressed." And the most distinguished chronicler of this return is none other than Kenneth Burke.

In Burke's *A Rhetoric of Motives*, this proposed reconstruction of the "hidden" history of rhetoric was brilliantly outlined, if not filled out in detail. His initial project in this book was to extend the range of rhetoric, but that extension, as he quickly realized, required an historical grounding, which forced him to depart from the manifest history. He began "by showing how a rhetorical motive is often present where it is not usually recognized, or thought to belong":

> In part, we would but *rediscover* rhetorical elements that had become obscured when rhetoric as a term fell into disuse, and other specialized disciplines such as esthetics, anthropology, psychoanalysis, and sociology came to the fore (so that esthetics sought to outlaw rhetoric, while the other sciences we have mentioned took over, each in its own terms, the rich rhetorical elements that esthetics would ban).[29]

He continues:

> But besides this job of *reclamation*, we also seek to develop our subject beyond the traditional bounds of rhetoric. There is an intermediate area of expression that is not wholly deliberate, yet not wholly unconscious. It lies midway between aimless utterance and speech deliberately purposive.[30]

In order to analyze this rhetorical area, Burke has to shift from reliance on "persuasion" to "identification" as the key term of rhetoric:

> Particularly when we come upon such aspects of persuasion as are found in "mystification," courtship, and the "magic" of class relationships, the reader will see why the classical notion of clear persuasive intent is not an accurate fit for describing the ways in which the members of a group promote social cohesion by acting rhetorically upon themselves and one another.[31]

At this point, I am not interested in examining Burke's concept of identification, which has already received ample critical attention. What interests me is the implications of this shift from "persuasion" to "identification" for a history of rhetoric. Consider, for instance, the second part of the book, which bears the title: "Traditional Principles of Rhetoric." In the first few pages (49–84), Burke examines some classical texts by Aristotle, Cicero, Quintilian, and St. Augustine where "persuasion" is the key term. Then, on page 90, there occurs a "break," a "rupture," in the text, as Burke begins to move with "identification" as the key concept into what I would call the "hidden" history of rhetoric. Here the task of "reclamation" proper begins: Bentham's theory of fictions, Marx on "Mystification" (*The German Ideology*), Carlyle on "Mystery" (*Sartor Resartus*), Diderot on "Pantomime" (*Neveu de Rameau*), De Gourmont on "Dissociation" (*La Dissociation des Idées*), Pascal on "Directing the Intention," Administrative Rhetoric in Machiavelli, Dante's *De Vulgari Eloquentia*, and so on. After a long underground existence, the sophistic tradition in rhetoric has been rediscovered, reclaimed, and reconstituted.

Here Burke, the "reclaimer," is in his "true form." While tracking down the implications of "persuasion" in classical texts, Burke is impatient, restrained, like a tiger in a cage, summarizing the formal/topological principles laboriously catalogued by Cicero in a mere page or two, and then quickly moving on to something else, say, Longinus' *On the Sublime*. But once we come to Bentham's *Book of Fallacies*, a dazzling intellectual journey begins, a veritable *tour de force* through the corridors of the history of ideas, interweaving text upon text, in the same breath speaking of Pascal and Joyce. It is a consummate performance.

It is almost impossible not to be seduced by this other "hidden" history of rhetoric, as "reconstituted" by Burke, especially when he invites "other analysts" to join him in "the task of tracking down the ways in which the realm of sheerly worldly powers become endowed with attributes of 'secular divinity.'"[32]

Who can refuse such an invitation, especially someone about to embark on rhetoric as a vocation. If accepted, this invitation calls at one level for extending the range of rhetoric, which I find perfectly legitimate. But that extension, in turn, requires a "reinterpretation" of the history of rhetoric that is problematic, if not ill-conceived.

Such is the seductive tale of the two histories of rhetoric. There are, to be sure, many other tales about the birth, the rise, the decline, the fall, and even the "death" of rhetoric. These tales have been constructed frequently by those who are not themselves, as I am not, full-fledged historians of rhetoric. They are clearly political tales, meant to account for the troubled relationship between rhetoric and other disciplines and culture in general. They are designed so as to legitimate its claim to renewed intellectual and cultural attention. Each putative revivalist of rhetoric has to tell a tale of its glorious origins, its civilizing effects, its unjustified suppression, and its eventual demise and dispersion. So the tale I have told above on behalf of Kenneth Burke (unauthorized, to be sure) is only one among many tales circulating among the current revivalists of rhetoric. As a revivalist tale it is only partly true. And this tale, like so many of the recent tales about the history of rhetoric, is espistemologically driven. It speaks as though the quarrel between Plato and the older sophists over the epistemic status of rhetoric continually and exclusively shaped its complex history. It fails to acknowledge that from late antiquity to the High Middle Ages, Latin rhetorical instruction was largely dominated by two manuals of what George Kennedy calls "technical rhetoric": *De Inventione* and *Rhetorica ad Herrennium*.[33] It completely overlooks the third tradition in rhetoric, the tradition of civic humanism that stretches from Protagoras through Isocrates and Cicero to the Renaissance humanists, and continues to manifest itself in the activities of great orators like Edmund Burke. But these errors, repeatedly corrected by the orthodox historians like Kennedy and Vickers, continue to remain occluded from a disciplinary consciousness obsessed with abstract epistemological questions.

My reservations are quite simple. The "lure" of the hidden history has led to a denigration of the manifest history of rhetoric. One simple fact attests to this. Despite all the talk about the "Revival of Rhetoric" and the coming of the "New Rhetoric" in this century, we have yet to produce a definitive history of rhetoric. As an intellectual enterprise, rhetoric cannot continue to be viable without an adequate understanding of its own history, even if that history is an uninspiring one, which I don't think it is. If there is one thing we can learn from Jacques Derrida, it is that the history of a supplement may be more interesting than the history of that which is in need of a supplement.

THE SECOND MOVEMENT: THE RHETORIC OF INQUIRY

The second horizontal movement that propels rhetoric to constantly reconfirm its "presence" in the discourse of other disciplines is fashionably characterized these days as the "rhetorical turn" in the human sciences, or as the Iowa School prefers to call it the "rhetoric of inquiry."

In this paper I am not primarily concerned, as the Iowa School avowedly is, with the discovery of rhetoric by the practitioners of human sciences and the consequences of that discovery for the discursive practices of their disciplines. What interests me at this moment is the impact of that discovery on the self-understanding of rhetoric itself. To be sure, I recognize that rhetoric and the human sciences interpenetrate one another in innumerable ways, and the evolving dialectic between the two has a long history. What I seek to problematize here is but a single aspect of that dialectic.

The "rhetorical turn" refers to the growing recognition of rhetoric in contemporary thought, especially among the special substantive sciences. It means that the special sciences are becoming increasingly rhetorically self-conscious. They are beginning to recognize that their discursive practices, both internal and external, contain an unavoidable rhetorical component. *Internal* here refers to those discursive practices that are internal to a specific scientific language community; external refers to the discursive practices of that scientific language community in respect to its dealings with other scientific (or nonscientific) language communities and the society in general. While the external dimension is sometimes noted, the work of the Iowa School clearly emphasizes the internal dimension.

The existing body of literature pertaining to the internal dimension of the rhetorical turn in contemporary thought can be further divided into two groups: the explicit rhetorical turn and the implicit rhetorical turn. By explicit rhetorical turn, I refer to those works that explicitly recognize the relevance of rhetoric for contemporary thought and where rhetoric is used as a critical and interpretive method. The works of the following scholars, including those generally identified as the new rhetoricians (Chaim Perelman, Kenneth Burke, Richard McKeon, I. A. Richards, and Richard Weaver), may be placed in this category: Wayne Booth, Paul de Man, Walter J. Ong, Ernesto Grassi, Paolo Valesio, Northrop Frye, Tzvetan Todorov, Harold Bloom, Hugh Dalziel Duncan.

Clearly, however, those authors are not equally enthusiastic about rhetoric. While some of them have written several books on rhetoric, others confine their observations on rhetoric to a mere essay or two. While some of them view rhetoric as a general theory of discourse (hence a metadiscipline), others simply admit the importance of rhetoric for the human sciences and employ it as a critical instrument in their analyses of literary and social texts; and there are those who simply scatter the word *rhetoric* carelessly through their texts. For instance, there is a renewed interest in rhetoric among the literary critics. But the nature and intensity of interest varies significantly. Thus, while Wayne Booth, operating from a distinctly humanistic perspective, concentrates on the argumentative dimension of literature, especially novels, Paul de Man, operating from a deconstructionist perspective, stresses the figural dimensions of literary language.[34] Other critics, like Frye, Todorov, Mailloux, and Bloom, have paid varying degrees of attention to rhetoric, but as opposed to Booth and de Man, we could not properly entitle them "rhetorical critics."

Finally, and perhaps most important, there are also texts that evince signs of an implicit rhetorical turn. These are texts whose authors, while relatively unaware of the rhetorical lexicon, seem to be groping for a vocabulary that could adequately characterize the tropological and suasory aspects of the discursive practices that remain occluded from disciplinary consciousness.

The list of authors and their texts that evince signs of such an implicit rhetorical turn is truly formidable: Thomas Kuhn's *The Structure of Scientific Revolutions*, Paul Feyerabend's *Against Method*, Steven Toulmin's *The Uses of Argument*, Lacan's *Ecrits*, Gadamer's *Truth and Method*, Foucault's *Archeology of Knowledge*, and Habermas's *Legitimation Crisis*, to name a few. These are the master texts of our time, and they are, we are told, bristling with rhetorical insights, even though they often are not consciously recognized.

Furthermore, on some accounts, whole "schools of thought" reveal a decisively rhetorical orientation. Here one might list the sociology of knowledge tradition (from Scheler to Berger and Luckmann), the symbolic interactionists, the dramatistic movement in anthropology and sociology (Geertz, Turner, and Goffman), and various philosophical positions that stress the role of language and language action (e.g., the "later" Wittgenstein and the "early" Heidegger, Austin, Searle, and other speech-act theorists). The contemporary intellectual landscape is, thus, replete with signs of an implicit rhetorical turn. With a bit of diligence and, of course, with requisite faith, anyone could read those signs and celebrate what they portend.

The *locus classicus* of this implicit rhetorical turn in contemporary thought is Kuhn's *The Structure of Scientific Revolutions*.[35] The reasons for the choice of this text are quite obvious. *First*, it examines the discursive practices of the hard sciences, such as physics and chemistry. Second, it brings to light the rhetorical aspect of discursive practices internal to the scientific language community. Third, Kuhn makes these profound observations without the slightest awareness of the rhetorical lexicon. Fourth, though unconscious of rhetoric, he makes a fairly radical claim for the primacy of rhetoric when he asserts that "paradigm shifts" in any scientific community are more like religious conversions than carefully considered and well-reasoned shifts in scientific practices. Fifth, he calls for a reexamination of the history of science from a sociological perspective. He rejects the textbook version of the history of science as an idealization which assumes that the growth of knowledge is a purely logical-rational enterprise. These aspects of Kuhn's work have made him into the very embodiment of the rhetorical turn. If the discourse of the physicists cannot detach itself from rhetoric, how can the chatter of lesser mortals, such as historians and sociologists, hope to emancipate itself from rhetoric?

In short, it appears that there is more to the "rhetorical turn" than the mundane explicit turn. Just as there are two histories of rhetoric, the manifest and the hidden, there are two rhetorical turns, the explicit and the implicit. The lure of the implicit rhetorical turn is infinitely greater than the reality of the explicit rhetorical turn. Although the explicit rhetorical turn is a result of practical necessity—a literary critic like Booth, for example, is unable to make sense of novelistic prose without recourse to a rhetorical vocabulary and rhetorical sensibilities—the implicit rhetorical turn is a largely theoretical and epistemological enterprise. If the explicit rhetorical turn is only a decade or two old, the implicit rhetorical turn is of more ancient vintage. Its roots can be traced all the way back to that celebrated quarrel between Platonic Socrates and the older sophists. If Kenneth Burke is the chronicler of the hidden history of rhetoric, Professors Nelson and Megill have undertaken to chronicle the story of the implicit rhetorical turn. Nelson and Megill, along with Donald McCloskey, are the leading figures in the Iowa School, which has done much to place claims of the rhetorical turn before the scholarly community.

THE NELSON AND MEGILL MYTH

In a recent essay, Nelson and Megill set out to furnish the "rhetoric of inquiry" with what they call an "animating myth."[36] They write:

> Rather, we sketch the development of the field so far, focusing on how early contributors have regarded rhetoric and inquiry. This is not the history of rhetoric, science, or philosophy widely familiar to scholars of communication. It is instead an animating myth of the new field.[37]

They are, however, certain that "what begins as myth ends as history." A myth of this sort requires a set of precursors who were but dimly aware of what they were doing, that is, preparing the way for the progressive dismantling of a logic of inquiry which is to be replaced by a rhetoric of inquiry.

Nelson and Megill do, indeed, give us a myth, a good one at that. It is reminiscent of Protagoras's reply in Plato's dialogue of that name when Socrates asks him to identify what he does. Protagoras admits to being "a sophist and an educator" (317b). But he claims to practice an ancient art and not something new and fashionable as people assume. According to Protagoras, since sophistry seems to arouse, however unjustifiably, suspicion among people, those who practiced it before did not admit to being sophists. They adopted suitable disguises and worked under the cover of some other profession. Homer, Hesiod, and Simonides claimed to be poets, Orpheus and Musaeus claimed to be musicians, and Herodicus of Selymbria claimed to be a physician. In fact, however, they were all sophists (316d–e). But that strategy of concealment did not work. They were discovered for what they were, and their attempt to disguise their art excited even greater mistrust. So Protagoras freely admits to being a sophist and welcomes any opportunity to explain and defend his art, for only through constant public exposure can sophistry hope to overcome the undeserved fear and suspicion with which it is presently regarded.

However, the myth which Nelson and Megill want to weave for us cannot be a simple Protagorean tale of exposing one's timorous and somewhat inept precursors.

For them, rhetoric, and by implication the rhetoric of inquiry, is a ubiquitous and unavoidable component in human belief and behavior. Since rhetoric always already exists, it cannot be simply discovered and enunciated. It has to be rediscovered and reconstituted. For that reason, it must be first repressed and made to disappear. If someone is going to be credited with recovering and recuperating rhetoric, then someone must be charged with its prior repression and dispersion.

The story of the progressive repression of the rhetoric of inquiry begins, predictably enough, in the seventeenth century with the birth of modern philosophy—with Descartes' quest for "clear and distinct ideas." In the quest for certainty, the "empiricist" Locke and the "idealist" Kant follow the "rationalist" Descartes. They embrace mathematics as the ideal model of conviction and "dream of dispelling disagreement through demonstration." Thus, rhetoric comes to be repressed. The repression is carried out through a series of dichotomies: truth vs. opinion, object vs. subject, conviction vs. persuasion, all of which valorize the logic of inquiry over rhetoric. This repression also had political implications. According to Nelson and Megill,

> Plato denigrated opinion and rhetoric so as to celebrate truth and order at a time of Greek conflict and Athenian decline. Similarly, Aristotle subordinated rhythms to logos and rhetoric to dialectic. In an era when radical disagreements racked the peace of Europe, Descartes wrote off rhetoric in favor of mathematical reason and Hobbes enslaved language to the sovereign. Later, Kant sought perpetual peace through pure and practical reason.[38]

The sole voice of dissent on behalf of rhetoric in the late seventeenth and early eighteenth century was Vico, who opposed Cartesianism with the same sort of vigor with which Isocrates had once opposed Platonisim. According to Nelson and Megill, effective opposition to the hegemonic rule of modern philosophy over scholarly inquiry did not occur until the late nineteenth century, and it is Nietzsche who emerges as the leading *persona*: "One implicitly rhetorical challenge to the sovereignty that modern philosophy claims over scholarship actually begins with Nietzsche's assault on the subject/object dichotomy."[39] As the opposition gathered speed and momentum in the twentieth century, the privileged set of dichomoties was challenged, undermined, and dissolved. The quest for certainty was questioned. The fear of disagreement abated. The mathematic model of conviction began to yield to the discursive model of persuasion. Modern epistemology came to be seen as a source of, rather than a shield against, the philosophical anxiety about "skepticism, solipsism, and nihilism." This challenge to "the Cartesian foundations and Kantian principles of modern philosophy" followed from a series of internal discursive crises and tensions in philosophy and science. Nelson and Megill identify three such crises (but do not discuss them): the philosophical attack on foundationalism, the philosophical reconstruction of science, and, the rhetorical conception of epistemology. And they enumerate a list of twentieth-century thinkers (a now familiar litany from Dewey and Heidegger through MacIntyre and Rorty) who recognize and grapple with these crises and thus, unwittingly, open the way to a rhetoric of inquiry.

All this intellectual ferment, Nelson and Megill conclude, leads to Iowa City in the 1980s, where the logic of inquiry is officially transformed into a rhetoric. This transformation yields a good many benefits: We will escape from the clutches of "Western rationalism and its paradox of authoritarian liberation." As we begin to pay more attention to the actual reasoning that goes on in scholarly inquiry, we will learn to "recognize that rhetoric is reasonable and reason is rhetorical." As we begin to notice that scholarship is also a mode of communication addressed to an audience, we will learn to "insist that rhetoric is contextual and context is rhetorical."

Such, then, is the history of the implicit rhetorical turn. (Note that, of the writers cited in this history, only Perelman, Burke, Booth, and White make systematic use of a rhetorical lexicon in their studies.) Nelson and Megill are, indeed, worthy successors to Kenneth Burke. They do for the implicit rhetorical turn what Burke has done for the hidden history of rhetoric.

THE LURE OF THE IMPLICIT RHETORICAL TURN

Once again, in my opinion, the lure of the implicit rhetorical turn will gradually overwhelm, if it has not done so already, the promise of the explicit rhetorical turn. The implicit rhetorical turn will have the same sort of psychological hold over our disciplinary imagination as the hidden history of rhetoric has had since the publication of Burke's *A Rhetoric of Motives*.

The reason for this is quite simple. The study of the explicit rhetorical turn is, in the long run, a tedious affair, which is only occasionally redeemed by critical excellence and achievement, while the pursuit of the implicit rhetorical turn is a boldly constitutive, well-nigh archeological, venture, which "lures" us to discover "traces" of rhetoric virtually everywhere. The explicit rhetorical turn suffers from sheer obviousness. Once it is recognized, as it ought to be, that the discourse of the human sciences contains an unavoidable rhetorical component, the task of analysis consists in making explicit the functioning of that component in the production and the reception of discourses. There are some brilliant instances of such critical analysis. In an excellent essay, Hexter unpacks the rhetoric of history in terms of the historian's habitual and distinctive use of quotations, footnotes, and statistics in writing history, and he shows how the rhetoric of history differs from the rhetoric of natural sciences.[40] The type of rhetorical analysis of historiography that Hexter offers is unlikely to unsettle the self-understanding of rhetoric. For Hexter has merely shown how the discourse of history cannot productively emulate the rhetoric of natural sciences; and his explication of rhetorical elements in historiography is analogous to the explication of "manifest" rhetoric in any discursive practice. The model for unpacking the argumentative strategies and the play of stylistic devices is much the same in history as in oratory.

In contrast, the implicit rhetorical turn is engaged in a far more grandiose project. It is, in essence, a philosophical enterprise, or to be more precise, it is a critique of Western metaphysics that begins with Nietzsche and continues in the work of Heidegger and his deconstructive followers. It is preoccupied with the theme of the end of philosophy (modernism, or the end of modernism), and sees in rhetoric an alternative to the foundationalist epistemology. The implicit rhetorical turn is thus largely a product of an internal crisis in philosophy. Here rhetoric becomes entangled in the schemes of those who are attempting to articulate a counter-tradition in philosophy. And the story of rhetoric's initial suppression and the subsequent recuperation is read, in the Nelson and Megill version, in terms of an objectivist/subjectivist dichotomy that has fractured Western consciousness since the beginning of philosophical reflection. Nelson and Megill are quite correct in asserting that an objectivist epistemology is generally damaging to the fortunes of rhetoric, while a subjectivist/relativist epistemology is more encouraging to its growth. But this observation is so broad as to be banal

and not easily translatable into concepts for use. Moreover, such an enlarged epistemological perspective makes the idea of rhetoric so thoroughly elastic as to incorporate
anyone averse to objectivism and foundationalism. In short, while the explicit rhetorical
turn is local in its application, the implicit rhetorical turn is global in its aspirations.

Thus, it is hardly surprising that Nelson and Megill's prospectus for the "rhetoric
of inquiry" should end, not with a whimper, but with a bang:

> Our world is a creature and a texture of rhetorics: of founding stories and sales talks,
> anecdotes and statistics, images and rhythms; of tales told in nursery, pledges of allegiance
> or revenge, symbols of success and failure, archetypes of action and character. Ours is a
> world of persuasive definitions, expressive explanations, and institutional narratives. It is
> replete with figures of truth, models of reality, tropes of argument, and metaphors of
> experience. In our world, scholarship is rhetorical.[41]

This is, alas, the fate of rhetoric. Like Blanche DuBois in Tennessee Williams's *A
Streetcar Named Desire*, we, the rhetoricians, have always relied on "the kindness of
strangers," but too much kindness could kill us. We are either dismissed out of hand,
excommunicated, cast out from the realm of light and truth, or we are given the whole
world all to ourselves and asked to preside over "the conversation of mankind."[42]

Such is Nelson and Megill's myth for the new field. But the myth calls for some
finer interpretation. How important is this story of repression and the subsequent
regeneration of rhetoric of inquiry in the development of modern philosophy from
Descartes to Derrida? Even Nelson and Megill will not venture to place it on the center
stage. There are, to be sure, some negative comments about rhetoric in Descartes,
Locke, and Kant. On the whole, however, they and their philosophical followers simply
ignored rhetoric. If their work had the effect of repressing a rhetoric of inquiry, which
I admit that it did, it was a latent outcome rather than a manifest intent. It would be
preposterous to imagine that Kant set out to write the three critiques in order to repress
rhetoric or to obviate a rhetoric of inquiry. The motivation for his labor came from
different sources. Similarly, the dismantling of the modernist dogma in this century by
Heidegger, Dewey, Wittgenstein, and others was not motivated by a manifest desire to
make space for a rhetoric of inquiry. (I am not trying to suggest here that the suffocation
of the rhetoric of inquiry under the modernist dogma was not genuine and severe
simply because it was latent. Perhaps, it was more insidious because of its latency.)

Nelson and Megill will probably disagree with me on this point. For them the
repression and the subsequent regeneration of the rhetoric of inquiry in modern
philosophy is a critical thread. For me, it is a sideshow. The fact that it is a sideshow
does not make me apologetic about the place of rhetoric in the life of the mind. The
fact that it is a sideshow is in keeping with the nature and function of rhetoric.[43]

In the long and enduring quarrel between rhetoric and philosophy, the latter has
not always set out to undermine the former.[44] Rhetoric has often been trampled on
accidentally in philosophy's quest for certainty or whatever else it is bent on pursuing
at any given time. Historically, philosophers have not evinced a profound concern with
rhetoric. There is a sort of narcissistic streak in philosophy, an overdetermination of
its own self-sufficiency and autonomy, which keeps it from seriously entertaining the
competing claims of rhetoric.

There was only one philosopher, in my opinion, who set out earnestly to repress
rhetoric; and when he couldn't, he sought to and pretty much succeeded in emasculating it. That was Plato. There was only one orator/rhetorician who seriously attempted

to reconcile the competing claims of rhetoric and philosophy and pretty much succeeded in uniting the competing claims of eloquence and wisdom in his own person. That was Cicero. We might add other names to either column in this list, but, even by a liberal standard, the list would not be long.

This brings me to the main point. Academically rhetoric has never been able to determine its own fortune. It lies embedded in the cultural practices of the time. It is always already there as a supplement, as an insert. Extract it from that to which it is a supplement or from that within which it is embedded, and it evaporates. It is present, to borrow a phrase from Lacan, only in "the discourse of the other." Ironically, the art of eloquence has no voice of its own within the academy. Pure persuasion is possible, as Kenneth Burke tells us, only in the furthest regions of religion and poetry where one hesitates, as in *Finnegans Wake*, between sound and sense.

The fortunes of rhetoric, more than any other discipline, turn on the roll of cultural dice. Rhetoric has good days and bad days, mostly bad days. This is one of the good days. If there is a myth about rhetoric, it is that of an outsider whose day of reckoning is deferred, time and again.

This is my countermyth for an old discipline which constantly seeks to escape itself. If you had to choose between the two myths, I suspect Nelson and Megill would carry the day, despite my carping . . . At least, that is what my myth requires me to believe. After all, this is one of the good days for rhetoric.

CONCLUSION

Finally, what is the significance of the rhetorical turn in the self-understanding of rhetoric? At the sociological level, the rhetorical turn implies a renewed disciplinary legitimacy for rhetoric as an intellectual enterprise. If rhetoric is an unavoidable component in discourses as diverse as theoretical physics, economics, literary criticism, and psychoanalysis, then the story of rhetoric is a tale well worth telling. However, this would also suggest that the "legitimacy" of a formal discipline, such as rhetoric, is relative to its measurable "presence" in the substantive disciplines. This could be problematic, because, if rhetoric requires a constant "reconfirmation" of its "presence" in the discourse of other disciplines, it would suggest that rhetoric is a supplement to those discourses rather than constitutive of them. To put it differently, one could argue that rhetoric is parasitic vis-à-vis the special discourses rather than productive of them in the way that a "rule" is productive of a series of rule-governed actions, or that the "deep structure" of a natural language is said to be productive of its "surface structure." I believe (and this is a provisional statement) that an adequate understanding of the rhetoric of the human sciences is possible only when we have an adequate grasp of the logic of supplementarily within which rhetoric is habitually caught.

At another level, the rhetorical turn sets up an expectation that there would be a renaissance in rhetoric in the near future—that rhetoric would regain its lost glory as "the queen of the human sciences" in our time, and that it would preside over other disciplines as the metascience of culture in the Isocratean sense. The anticipation of a rhetorical turn could, thus, revive and set in motion the dormant foundational aspirations characteristic of formal, hence empty, disciplines like rhetoric, dialectic, and hermeneutics. That is, one has to travel but a short psychological distance to make that fatal move from anticipating a rhetorical turn in contemporary thought to proclaiming rhetoric as the foundational discipline (obviously, in its capacity as the general theory of discourse) for the human sciences.

Before we become intoxicated with such visions of grandeur, we have to ascertain exactly what role, if any, rhetoric as an academic discipline has played in bringing about this rhetorical turn, other than recognizing and celebrating its alleged arrival. As I indicated earlier, Kuhn's *The Structure of Scientific Revolutions*, which is treated as the *locus classicus* of the rhetorical turn, is entirely innocent of rhetoric as a discipline. This innocence or ignorance of rhetoric is not uncommon among the writers and the texts cited earlier as participating in the implicit rhetorical turn.

Even among those who write self-consciously about rhetoric and its presence, and whose texts were cited earlier as constituting the explicit rhetorical turn, few are conscious of rhetoric as an academic discipline. As for the majority, if they acknowledge their debt to rhetoric, it is usually to some classical texts, especially to Aristotle's *Rhetoric*; among the moderns, it is invariably Kenneth Burke and occasionally Perelman, and rarely I. A. Richards. For these writers, contemporary rhetoric simply means the idiosyncratic works of Kenneth Burke. This is best exemplified in the work of sociologist Hugh Dalziel Duncan, who has systematically, albeit mechanically, sought to reinterpret social theory from a decidedly rhetorical perspective, but the rhetorical perspective here simply means a Burkian perspective.[45] For other American writers like Geertz, Goffman, and Hayden White, who are clearly conscious of rhetoric, Burke provides the only link between classical rhetoric and its contemporary possibilities. The continental writers like Lacan, Derrida, Ricoeur, Genette, and Gadamer, whose texts bristle with rhetorical concepts and terms, are either entirely unaware of Burke's work or only marginally aware of it.

But on the whole, it is clear that rhetoricians have played but a limited role in bringing about this rhetorical turn. What concerns me here is not the sociological embarrassment resulting from the fact that we who celebrate this "rhetorical turn" in contemporary thought have contributed so little to its making. What does concern me is the fact that people like Kuhn and Toulmin were driven to make certain observations, which we characterize as marking a rhetorical turn in their respective thinking, by the internal logic (both synchronic and diachronic) of their own special discourses. They became, as it were, infected with a "rhetorical consciousness" by immersing themselves in their own special discourses and by tracing the discursive implications of their own distinctive theory and practice. It was not as if they were struggling for a vocabulary, absent in the ordinary language, that could articulate their "break" from the traditional discourse. The "break," or the "rupture," in the traditional discursive practices with which their names are associated neither occurred nor came to be articulated as a result of their sudden acquaintance with the rhetorical lexicon. Kuhn was not awakened from his dogmatic slumber after reading Aristotle or Burke, as Kant allegedly was after reading Hume.

To be sure, one could argue that it would have been easier for Kuhn to articulate his rhetorical insights had he been acquainted with the rhetorical tradition. This could serve as an argument for a greater dissemination of rhetorical lore in our culture, especially in the academy. But one could just as easily argue that in some situations a familiarity with the rhetorical lexicon could be a hindrance. Perhaps people like Kuhn do not really need a stylized rhetorical lexicon to recognize rhetoric; and their rhetorical insights are possibly richer, less labored, and more firmly grounded precisely because they are the insights of someone driven by the compulsions of a special discourse in search of a special knowledge, the knowledge of the world, so to speak. The ordinary language which, as Cicero reminds us, is the language of rhetoric, is sufficiently versatile to meet the needs of a Kuhn or a Toulmin. If we follow this logic, then, it would appear that an institutionalized presence of rhetoric is neither necessary nor sufficient for the rhetorical turn.

Furthermore, it may be interesting to note that these fabled rhetorical turns occur in times of crisis. Clearly, Kuhn's theory about paradigm shifts, Habermas's thesis regarding the legitimation crisis in the modern welfare state, and Derrida's method of reading as a textual "deconstruction" refer to and have their origin in specific crisis situations, be they in scientific theory, social theory, or literary theory. Perhaps it is during the discursive crises that a scientific language community becomes "rhetorically conscious." Further, we could argue that every special discourse and every scientific language community periodically goes through "rhetorical stages." And sometimes the general culture itself, passing through a general crisis, becomes rhetorically self-conscious. But with the passing of that crisis, the rhetorical consciousness once again erodes. That is, the emergence of a rhetorical consciousness is directly related to a crisis within a special discourse. That relation can be formulated as follows: A crisis, discursive or otherwise, makes rhetoric visible; that is, a crisis brings to the fore the incipient rhetorical consciousness. The sheer possibility of a rhetorical consciousness, the possibility that rhetoric is a permanent though unrealized opening for man, does not by itself induce a crisis, but it is something always waiting to be exploited when the crisis comes. In short, rhetoric is the medium and not the ground of discursive and cultural crises.

Notes

1. Chaim Perelman and L. Olbrechts-Tyteca, *The New Rhetoric: A Treatise on Argumentation*, trans. John Wilkinson and Purcell Weaver (South Bend, IN: University of Notre Dame Press, 1969); Paolo Valesio, *Novantiqua: Rhetoric as Contemporary Theory* (Bloomington: Indiana University Press, 1980). For a tendency to subordinate rhetoric to dialectic, see Maurice Natanson, "The Limits of Rhetoric," *Quarterly Journal of Speech 41* (1955): 133–139; and Richard Weaver, "The Phaedrus and the Nature of Rhetoric," in his *The Ethics of Rhetoric* (Chicago: Henry Regnery, 1953), pp. 3–26.

2. Ernesto Grassi, *Rhetoric as Philosophy: The Humanistic Tradition* (University Park: Pennsylvania University Press, 1980).

3. Roland Barthes, "The Old Rhetoric: An Aìde-Memoire," in his *The Semiotic Challenge*, trans. Richard Howard (New York: Hill and Wang, 1988), p. 46.

4. Aristotle, *The Art of Rhetoric*, ed. and trans. Lane Cooper (New York: Appleton-Century-Croft, 1932), p. 9.

5. Brian Vickers, "Territorial Disputes: Philosophy versus Rhetoric," in Brian Vickers, ed., *Rhetoric Revalued* (Binghamton, NY: Medieval and Renaissance Texts and Studies, 1982), p. 248.

6. Cicero, "Fourth Philippic," in Lewis Copeland and Lawrence W. Lamm, eds., *The World's Great Speeches*, 3rd ed. (New York: Dover, 1973), p. 48.

7. This phrase *alte und neue Konigin der Wissenschaften* comes from Walter Jens, Von Deutscher Rede (Munich: Piper, 1969), and is cited by Chaim Perelman, in *The Realm of Rhetoric*, trans. William Kluback (South Bend, IN: University of Notre Dame Press, 1982), p. 162.

8. Alfred Schutz, *The Phenomenology of the Social World*, trans. George Walsh and Frederick Lehnert (Evanston, IL: Northwestern University Press, 1967). Also see his *Collected Papers, Vol. 1: The Problems of Social Reality*, ed. Maurice Natanson (The Hague: Martinus Nijhoff, 1971).

9. For a discussion of "essentially contested concepts," see W. B. Gallie, *Philosophy and the Historical Understanding* (New York: Schocken, 1964), pp. 157–191.

10. For an excellent critical survey of the literature on this question in the speech communication journals, see Michael Leff, "In Search of Ariadne's Thread: A Review of the Recent Literature on Rhetorical Theory," *Central State Speech Journal 29* (1978): 65–91.

11. Jacques Derrida, *Of Grammatology*, trans. Gayatri Chakravorty Spivak (Baltimore: Johns Hopkins University Press, 1976). Also see "Plato's Pharmacy," in Derrida, *Dissemination*, trans. Barbara Johnson (Chicago: University of Chicago Press, 1981), pp. 61–171.

12. Aristotle, *The "Art" of Rhetoric*, trans. John Henry Freese, Loeb Classical Library (Cambridge, MA: Harvard University Press, 1926), 1856a, p. 19

13. Lloyd Bitzer, "Political Rhetoric," in Dan Nimmo and Keith Sanders, eds., *Handbook of Political Communication* (Beverly Hills, CA: Sage, 1981), pp. 225–248.

14. Michael Leff, "The Habitation of Rhetoric," in Joseph Wenzel et al., eds., *Argument and Critical Practices: Proceedings of the Fifth SCA/AFA Conference on Argumentation* (Annandale, VA: SCA, 1987), p. 5 (reprinted in this volume).

15. Bitzer, "Political Rhetoric," p. 231.

16. Paul Ricoeur, *The Rule of Metaphor: Multidisciplinary Studies in the Creation of Meaning in Language*, trans. Robert Czerny with Kathleen McLaughlin and John Costello (Toronto: University of Toronto Press, 1976), p. 30.

17. Kenneth Burke, *A Rhetoric of Motives* (Berkeley and Los Angeles: University of California Press, 1969, 1950), pp. 54–55.

18. Barthes, "The Old Rhetoric," p. 73.

19. Ibid., p. 75.

20. Cicero, *De oratore*, 2 vols., trans. E. W. Sutton, Loeb Classical Library (Cambridge, MA: Harvard University Press, 1942); Saint Augustine, *On Christian Doctrine*, trans. D. W. Robertson Jr. (New York: Bobbs-Merrill, 1958). In Cicero's *De oratore*, there are a number of references to rhetoric (the art or theory of oratory) as a supplement to inborn talent and correct practice based on imitation of suitable models. Cicero, while exalting the powers of the orator in a variety of ways, repeatedly observes that the art of oratory cannot produce the orator by itself without assistance from nature, which supplies talent, and practice, which deepens and perfects talent. The art itself, according to Cicero, plays but a minor role, and what is there to understand of the art can be obtained easily and quickly. Augustine is more explicit about the status of rhetoric as a supplement. In the fourth book of *De doctrina christiana*, rhetoric is clearly drawn into the orbit of hermeneutics as a supplement to elucidate what interpretation has uncovered of the sacred texts.

21. Cited in George A. Kennedy, *Classical Rhetoric and Its Christian and Secular Tradition from Ancient to Modern Times* (Chapel Hill: University of North Carolina Press, 1980), p. 240.

22. Cited by Lane Cooper, trans. and ed., in *The Rhetoric of Aristotle* (New York: Appleton-Century-Croft, 1932), p. xii.

23. For a general overview on the sophists in the light of the current revival of scholarly interest in them, see W.K.C. Guthrie, *The Sophists* (New York: Cambridge University Press, 1971), and G. B. Kerferd, The Sophistic Movement (New York: Cambridge University Press, 1981).

24. For an early attempt to articulate the ontological basis of rhetoric, see Karlyn K. Campbell, "The Ontological Foundation of Rhetorical Theory," *Philosophy and Rhetoric 3* (1970): 97–108.

25. Hannah Arendt, *The Human Condition* (New York: Anchor, 1958), p. 10.

26. Paul de Man, *Allegories of Reading* (New Haven, CT.: Yale University Press, 1979), pp. 103-131; Tzvetan Todorov, *Theories of the Symbol*, trans. Catherine Porter (Ithaca, NY: Cornell University Press, 1982), pp. 60–110.

27. For the most influential account of the "reality construction" thesis, see Peter L. Berger and Thomas Luckmann, *The Social Construction of Reality: A Treatise in the Sociology of Knowledge* (New York: Anchor Books, 1967).

28. For an account of rhetoric as a "material force," see Michael Calvin McGee, "A

Materialist's Conception of Rhetoric," in R. E. McKerrow, ed., *Explorations in Rhetoric: Studies in Honor of Douglas Ehninger* (Glenville, IL: Scott, Foresman, 1982), pp. 23–49.

29. Burke, *A Rhetoric of Motives,* p. xiii.

30. Ibid.

31. Ibid., p. xiv.

32. Kenneth Burke, *A Grammar of Motives and A Rhetoric of Motives* (New York: Meridian Books, 1962), p. 523.

33. Kennedy, *Classical Rhetoric,* pp. 86–107.

34. Wayne C. Booth, *The Rhetoric of Fiction* (Chicago: University of Chicago Press, 1983); Paul de Man, *The Rhetoric of Romanticism* (New York: Columbia University Press, 1984).

35. Thomas S. Kuhn, *The Structure of Scientific Revolutions* (Chicago: University of Chicago Press, 1970).

36. John S. Nelson and Allan Megill, "Rhetoric of Inquiry: Projects and Prospects," *Quarterly Journal of Speech* 72 (1986): 20–37. McCloskey appears to share the views of Nelson and Megill on the prospects of a rhetoric of inquiry. This same essay, with minor modifications, appears as the introductory essay in the volume of papers from the Iowa conference held on March 28–31, 1984. See John S. Nelson, Allan Megill, and Donald N. McCloskey, eds., *The Rhetoric of the Human Sciences: Language and Argument in Scholarship and Public Affairs* (Madison: University of Wisconsin Press, 1987), pp. 3–18.

37. Nelson and Megill, "Rhetoric of Inquiry," p. 20.

38. Ibid., pp. 22–23.

39. Ibid., p. 24.

40. J. H. Hexter, "The Rhetoric of History," *History and Theory* 6 (1967): 1–14. For an expanded version of the same essay, see the chapter by the same title in his *Doing History* (Bloomington: Indiana University Press, 1971), pp. 15–76.

41. Nelson and Megill, "Rhetoric of Inquiry," p. 36.

42. This popular phrase among the proponents of the rhetorical turn was originally coined by Michael Oakeshott in "Poetry as a Voice in the Conversation of Mankind," in his *Experience and Its Modes* (1933), and reprinted in his *Rationalism in Politics* (New York: Methuen, 1962), pp. 197–247.

43. On the "marginality" of rhetoric in the disciplinary contest for "status," see Robert Hariman, "Status, Marginality, and Rhetorical Theory," *Quarterly Journal of Speech* 72 (1986): 38–52 (reprinted in this volume).

44. The literature on the quarrel between philosophy and rhetoric is quite extensive. For both an historically and conceptually informed general view of the quarrel, see Brian Vickers, *In Defense of Rhetoric* (Oxford: Clarendon Press, 1988), especially chaps. 2 and 3, pp. 83–213.

45. Hugh Dalziel Duncan, *Communication and Social Order* (New York: Oxford University Press, 1968).

PART 3

The Character of the Rhetorical Situation

Rhetorical discourse is frequently distinguished from philosophical, scientific, and artistic discourses because it is judged according to criteria of particularity, contingency, and propriety. Where philosophical and scientific discourses typically seek universal, transcendent knowledge or truth, rhetorical discourse seeks timely and fitting action. Where great art is judged for its "timeless" quality, great rhetoric is seen as that which aptly responds to a particular moment in historical time. Put simply, while other forms of discourse have generally been treated as if they aspired to a universalized context, or indeed to pure and contextless meaning, rhetoric has generally been understood in terms of its linkages to local moments and the exigencies of political pragmatism. In contrast to philosophy, science, and art, then, rhetoric is a discourse that addresses pressing needs in particular situations.

Although rhetoric has long been defined by its pragmatic purpose and context, this is not to say that the nature of the rhetorical situation is either self-evident or obvious. Rhetorical theory in the late twentieth century has occupied itself in substantial measure with filling out the theoretical implications and dimensions of the historical bindings of rhetorical discourse. Lloyd F. Bitzer initiated a significant phase of this analysis in 1968 in the inaugural issue of the then new journal *Philosophy and Rhetoric*. In this essay, entitled "The Rhetorical Situation," Bitzer outlined the working assumptions that had guided the practice of rhetorical critics in the first half of the twentieth century. According to Bitzer, human relations operated in the context of rhetorical situations governed by *exigencies*, that is, social, political, economic, and ethical urgencies that invited discursive responses. Rhetoric occured when a speaker responded to the perception of exigency by addressing an audience that could be persuaded to make changes that would modify the urgency.

Bitzer's analysis of the rhetorical situation derived from his philosophical and epistemological commitments to realism. From this perspective, an exigency is an objective occurrence that demands particular forms of response. The rhetor who neglects to address the factors demanded by an exigent situation thus fails (at least potentially) to produce an adequate rhetorical response. So, for example, on the occasion of a eulogy for a prominent politician, Bitzer would argue that the rhetorical situation dictates that the speaker praise the important virtues and accomplishments of the deceased. If the speaker delivering the eulogy chose to ignore such conventional expectations and to focus explicitly upon the deceased's moral shortcomings and failures, Bitzer would judge that he or she had failed to respond appropriately to the exigency that called forth the speech.

Almost immediately, Richard E. Vatz and others (Consigny, 1974; Patton, 1979) challenged Bitzer's realism and its implications for how we understand the importance of a rhetorical situastion. In an essay titled "The Myth of the Rhetorical Situation," Vatz maintained that exigences are not the product of objective events, but rather are a matter of perception and interpretation. Hence, to say that exigencies call forth rhetoric is to put the cart before the horse; rather, Vatz argued, we would be better served if we understood the sense in which rhetoric creates the perception of exigency. Bitzer had used as a prime example the way in which the assassination of President John Kennedy constituted a rhetorical situation that demanded the speaking of a eulogy as a fitting response. Vatz called this example into question, arguing that the particular situation it described—at least as Bitzer characterized it—might be too ritualistic and conventional to serve as a paradigm case for fully understanding the complexities of the relationship between "rhetoric" and "situation." Less conventionalized examples, he suggested, might lead to a richer understanding of how situations themselves are rhetorically constructed.

Whereas Vatz challenged Bitzer's notion that the exigency dictated the appropriate response, and thus maintained a controlling force over the speaker, Barbara A. Biesecker argued that we need to reconsider the very nature of the two concepts "situation" and "speaker." Biesecker suggested that Vatz's formulation was correct as far as it went, but in the end it simply reversed the relationship that Bitzer had described. Instead of viewing context as the controling factor in a rhetorical situation, it granted some sense of overarching control to the speaker. According to Biesecker, this merely replaced a realist conception of "context" as objective with a realist conception of the "rhetor" or "speaker" as an autonomous, self-directed agent who consciously constructs exigencies according to a carefully planned set of interests. From this perspective, she argued, the members of the audience were similar to rhetors in their autonomy and willfullness, albeit more passive. In "Rethinking the Rhetorical Situation from within the Thematic of *Différance*," Biesecker offered a new tool for disrupting such overly simple understandings of rhetors and their audiences. This tool is called "deconstruction," and it derives from the French theorist Jacques Derrida. Deconstruction urges us to see that the identities of audiences and speakers are themselves constructed in the process of the rhetorical transaction. Rhetoric is not, therefore, a simple linear process by which one individual attempts to influence others, but rather a complex interactive process whereby persons and collectivities articulate their shifting identities to each other within changing historical circumstances.

The notion of the rhetorical situation has thus become more fluid in contemporary rhetorical theory than it was in earlier periods. This increased fluidity necessitates our reconsideration of the concepts of history and pragmatics as well. Simultaneously, the notion that philosophy, art, or even science can be "timeless" has been under attack. If these human pursuits also prove to be transient and contextual, is all human discourse ultimately rhetorical? The stage is thus set for continuing the reconsideration of the character of rhetoric as situated discourse.

Additional Readings

Bitzer, Lloyd F. (1980). "Functional Communication: A Situational Perspective." In E. White, ed., *Rhetoric in Transition: Studies in the Nature and Uses of Rhetoric.* (State College: Pennsylvania State University Press), pp. 21–38.

Consigny, Scott. (1974). "Rhetoric and Its Situations." *Philosophy and Rhetoric* 7: 172–182.

Garret, Mary, and Xiaosui Xiao. (1993). "The Rhetorical Situation Revisited." *Rhetoric Society Quarterly* 23: 30–40.

McGee, Michael C. (1977). "The Fall of Wellington: A Case Study of the Relationship Between Theory, Practice, and Rhetoric in History." *Quarterly Journal of Speech* 63: 28–42.

Miller, Caroyln R. (1984). "Genre as Social Action." *Quarterly Journal of Speech* 70: 151–167.

Patton, John. (1979). "Causation and Creativity in Rhetorical Situations: Distinctions and Implications." *Quarterly Journal of Speech* 65: 36–55.

Smith, Craig R., and Scott Lybarger. (1996). "Bitzer's Model Reconstructed." *Communication Quarterly* 44: 197–213.

Tompkins, Phillip K., John H. Patton, and Lloyd Bitzer [Discussants]. (1980). "The Forum." *Quarterly Journal of Speech* 66: 85–95.

The Rhetorical Situation

LLOYD F. BITZER

If someone says, That is a dangerous situation, his words suggest the presence of events, persons, or objects which threaten him, someone else, or something of value. If someone remarks, I find myself in an embarrassing situation, again the statement implies certain situational characteristics. If someone remarks that he found himself in an ethical situation, we understand that he probably either contemplated or made some choice of action from a sense of duty or obligation or with a view to the Good. In other words, there are circumstances of this or that kind of structure which are recognized as ethical, dangerous, or embarrassing. What characteristics, then, are implied when one refers to "the rhetorical situation"—the context in which speakers or writers create discourse? Perhaps this question is puzzling because "situation" is not a standard term in the vocabulary of rhetorical theory. "Audience" is standard; so also are "speaker," "subject," "occasion," and "speech." If I were to ask, "What is a rhetorical audience?" or "What is a rhetorical subject?," the reader would catch the meaning of my question.

When I ask, What is a rhetorical situation?, I want to know the nature of those contexts in which speakers or writers create rhetorical discourse: How should they be described? What are their characteristics? Why and how do they result in the creation of rhetoric? By analogy, a theorist of science might well ask, What are the characteristics of situations which inspire scientific thought? A philosopher might ask, What is the nature of the situation in which a philosopher "does philosophy"? And a theorist of poetry might ask, How shall we describe the context in which poetry comes into existence?

The presence of rhetorical discourse obviously indicates the presence of a rhetorical situation. The Declaration of Independence, Lincoln's Gettysburg Address, Churchill's Address on Dunkirk, John F. Kennedy's Inaugural Address—each is a clear instance of rhetoric and each indicates the presence of a situation. While the existence of a rhetorical address is a reliable sign of the existence of a situation, it does not follow that a situation exists only when the discourse exists. Each reader probably can recall a specific time and place when there was opportunity to speak on some urgent matter, and after the opportunity was gone he created in private thought the speech he should

have uttered earlier in the situation. It is clear that situations are not always accompanied by discourse. Nor should we assume that a rhetorical address gives existence to
the situation; on the contrary, it is the situation which calls the discourse into existence.
Clement Attlee once said that Winston Churchill went around looking for "finest
hours." The point to observe is that Churchill found them—the crisis situations—and
spoke in response to them.

No major theorist has treated rhetorical situation thoroughly as a distinct subject
in rhetorical theory; many ignore it. Those rhetoricians who discuss situation do so
indirectly—as does Aristotle, for example, who is led to consider situation when be treats
types of discourse. None, to my knowledge, has asked the nature of rhetorical situation.
Instead, rhetoricians have asked: What is the process by which the orator creates and
presents discourse? What is the nature of rhetorical discourse? What sorts of interaction
occur between speaker, audience, subject, and occasion? Typically the questions which
trigger theories of rhetoric focus upon the orator's method or upon the discourse itself,
rather than upon the situation which invites the orator's application of his method and
the creation of discourse. Thus rhetoricians distinguish among and characterize the
types of speeches (forensic, deliberative, epideictic); they treat issues, types of proof,
lines of argument, strategies of ethical and emotional persuasion, the parts of a
discourse and the functions of these parts, qualities of styles, figures of speech. They
cover approximately the same materials, the formal aspects of rhetorical method and
discourse, whether focusing upon method, product, or process; while conceptions of
situation are implicit in some theories of rhetoric, none explicitly treat the formal
aspects of situation.

I hope that enough has been said to show that the question What is a rhetorical
situation? is not an idle one. I propose in what follows to set forth part of a theory of
situation. This essay, therefore, should be understood as an attempt to revive the
notion of rhetorical situation, to provide at least the outline of an adequate conception of it, and to establish it as a controlling and fundamental concern of rhetorical
theory.

I

It seems clear that rhetoric is situational. In saying this, I do not mean merely that
understanding a speech hinges upon understanding the context of meaning in which
the speech is located. Virtually no utterance is fully intelligible unless meaning-context
and utterance are understood; this is true of rhetorical and non-rhetorical discourse.
Meaning-context is a general condition of human communication and is not synonymous with rhetorical situation. Nor do I mean merely that rhetoric occurs in a setting
which involves interaction of speaker, audience, subject, and communicative purpose.
This is too general, since many types of utterances—philosophical, scientific, poetic, and
rhetorical—occur in such settings. Nor would I equate rhetorical situation with persuasive situation, which exists whenever an audience can be changed in belief or action
by means of speech. Every audience at any moment is capable of being changed in
some way by speech; persuasive situation is altogether general.

Finally, I do not mean that a rhetorical discourse must be embedded in historic
context in the sense that a living tree must be rooted in soil. A tree does not obtain
its character-as-tree from the soil, but rhetorical discourse, I shall argue, does obtain
its character-as-rhetorical from the situation which generates it. Rhetorical works belong

to the class of things which obtain their character from the circumstances of the historic context in which they occur. A rhetorical work is analogous to a moral action rather than to a tree. An act is moral because it is an act performed in a situation of a certain kind; similarly, a work is rhetorical because it is a response to a situation of a certain kind.

In order to clarify rhetoric-as-essentially-related-to-situation, we should acknowledge a viewpoint that is commonplace but fundamental: a work of rhetoric is pragmatic; it comes into existence for the sake of something beyond itself; it functions ultimately to produce action or change in the world; it performs some task. In short, rhetoric is a mode of altering reality, not by the direct application of energy to objects, but by the creation of discourse which changes reality through the mediation of thought and action. The rhetor alters reality by bringing into existence a discourse of such a character that the audience, in thought and action, is so engaged that it becomes mediator of change. In this sense rhetoric is always persuasive.

To say that rhetorical discourse comes into being in order to effect change is altogether general. We need to understand that a particular discourse comes into existence because of some specific condition or situation which invites utterance. Bronislaw Malinowski refers to just this sort of situation in his discussion of primitive language, which he finds to be essentially pragmatic and "embedded in situation." He describes a party of fishermen in the Trobriand Islands whose functional speech occurs in a "context of situation."

> The canoes glide slowly and noiselessly, punted by men especially good at this task and always used for it. Other experts who know the bottom of the lagoon . . . are on the look-out for fish. . . . Customary signs, or sounds or words are uttered. Sometimes a sentence full of technical references to the channels or patches on the lagoon has to be spoken; sometimes . . . a conventional cry is uttered. . . . Again, a word of command is passed here and there, a technical expression or explanation which serves to harmonize their behavior towards other men. . . . An animated scene, full of movement, follows, and now that the fish are in their power the fishermen speak loudly, and give vent to their feelings. Short, telling exclamations fly about, which might be rendered by such words as: "Pull in," "Let go," "Shift further," "Lift the net."

In this whole scene, "each utterance is essentially bound up with the context of situation and with the aim of the pursuit. . . . The structure of all this linguistic material is inextricably mixed up with, and dependent upon, the course of the activity in which the utterances are embedded." Later the observer remarks: "In its primitive uses, language functions as a link in concerted human activity, as a piece of human behaviour. It is a mode of action and not an instrument of reflection."[1]

These statements about primitive language and the "context of situation" provide for us a preliminary model of rhetorical situation. Let us regard rhetorical situation as a natural context of persons, events, objects, relations, and an exigence which strongly invites utterance; this invited utterance participates naturally in the situation, is in many instances necessary to the completion of situational activity, and by means of its participation with situation obtains its meaning and its rhetorical character. In Malinowski's example, the situation is the fishing expedition consisting of objects, persons, events, and relations—and the ruling exigence, the success of the hunt. The situation dictates the sorts of observations to be made; it dictates the significant physical and verbal responses; and, we must admit, it constrains the words which are uttered in the same sense that it constrains the physical acts of paddling the canoes and throwing the nets. The verbal responses to the demands imposed by this situation are clearly as functional and necessary as the physical responses.

Traditional theories of rhetoric have dealt, of course, not with the sorts of primitive utterances described by Malinowski—"stop here," "throw the nets," "move closer"—but with larger units of speech which come more readily under the guidance of artistic principle and method. The difference between oratory and primitive utterance, however, is not a difference in function; the clear instances of rhetorical discourse and the fishermen's utterances are similarly functional and similarly situational. Observing both the traditions of the expedition and the facts before him, the leader of the fishermen finds himself obliged to speak at a given moment—to command, to supply information, to praise or blame—to respond appropriately to the situation. Clear instances of artistic rhetoric exhibit the same character: Cicero's speeches against Cataline were called forth by a specific union of persons, events, objects, and relations, and by an exigence which amounted to an imperative stimulus; the speeches in the Senate rotunda three days after the assassination of the President of the United States were actually required by the situation. So controlling is situation that we should consider it the very ground of rhetorical activity, whether that activity is primitive and productive of a simple utterance or artistic and productive of the Gettysburg Address.

Hence, to say that rhetoric is situational means: (1) rhetorical discourse comes into existence as a response to situation, in the same sense that an answer comes into existence in response to a question, or a solution in response to a problem; (2) a speech is given *rhetorical* significance by the situation, just as a unit of discourse is given significance *as* answer or *as* solution by the question or problem; (3) a rhetorical situation must exist as a necessary condition of rhetorical discourse, just as a question must exist as a necessary condition of an answer; (4) many questions go unanswered and many problems remain unsolved—similarly, many rhetorical situations mature and decay without giving birth to rhetorical utterance; (5) a situation is rhetorical insofar as it needs and invites discourse capable of participating with situation and thereby altering its reality; (6) discourse is rhetorical insofar as it functions (or seeks to function) as a fitting response to a situation which needs and invites it. (7) Finally, the situation controls the rhetorical response in the same sense that the question controls the answer and the problem controls the solution. Not the rhetor and not persuasive intent, but the situation is the source and ground of rhetorical activity—and, I should add, of rhetorical criticism.

II

Let us now amplify the nature of situation by providing a formal definition and examining constituents. Rhetorical situation may be defined as a complex of persons, events, objects, and relations presenting an actual or potential exigence which can be completely or partially removed if discourse, introduced into the situation, can so constrain human decision or action as to bring about the significant modification of the exigence. Prior to the creation and presentation of discourse, there are three constituents of any rhetorical situation: the first is the *exigence*; the second and third are elements of the complex, namely, the *audience* to be constrained in decision and action, and the *constraints* which influence the rhetor and can be brought to bear upon the audience.

Any *exigence* is an imperfection marked by urgency; it is a defect, an obstacle, something waiting to be done, a thing which is other than it should be. In almost any sort of context, there will be numerous exigencies, but not all are elements of a rhetorical situation—not all are rhetorical exigencies. An exigence which cannot be modified is not rhetorical; thus, whatever comes about of necessity and cannot be changed—death, winter, and some natural disasters, for instance—are exigencies to be sure, but they are not rhetorical. Further, an exigence which can be modified only by means other than discourse is not rhetorical; thus, an exigence is not rhetorical when its modification requires merely one's own action or the application of a tool, but neither requires nor invites the assistance of discourse. An exigence is rhetorical when it is capable of positive modification and when positive modification requires discourse or can be assisted by discourse. For example, suppose that a man's acts are injurious to others and that the quality of his acts can be changed only if discourse is addressed to him; the exigence—his injurious acts—is then unmistakably rhetorical. The pollution of our air is also a rhetorical exigence because its positive modification—reduction of pollution—strongly invites the assistance of discourse producing public awareness, indignation, and action of the right kind. Frequently rhetors encounter exigencies which defy easy classification because of the absence of information enabling precise analysis and certain judgment they may or may not be rhetorical. An attorney whose client has been convicted may strongly believe that a higher court would reject his appeal to have the verdict overturned, but because the matter is uncertain—because the exigence *might* be rhetorical—he elects to appeal. In this and similar instances of indeterminate exigencies the rhetor's decision to speak is based mainly upon the urgency of the exigence and the probability that the exigence is rhetorical.

In any rhetorical situation there will be at least one controlling exigence which functions as the organizing principle: it specifies the audience to be addressed and the change to be effected. The exigence may or may not be perceived clearly by the rhetor or other persons in the situation; it may be strong or weak depending upon the clarity of their perception and the degree of their interest in it; it may be real or unreal depending on the facts of the case; it may be important or trivial; it may be such that discourse can completely remove it, or it may persist in spite of repeated modifications; it may be completely familiar—one of a type of exigencies occurring frequently in our experience—or it may be totally new, unique. When it is perceived and when it is strong and important, then it constrains the thought and action of the perceiver who may respond rhetorically if he is an a position to do so.

The second constituent is the *audience*. Since rhetorical discourse produces change by influencing the decision and action of persons who function as mediators of change, it follows that rhetoric always requires an audience—even in those cases when a person engages himself or ideal mind as audience. It is clear also that a rhetorical audience must be distinguished from a body of mere hearers or readers: properly speaking, a rhetorical audience consists only of those persons who are capable of being influenced by discourse and of being mediators of change.

Neither scientific nor poetic discourse requires an audience in the same sense. Indeed, neither requires an audience in order to produce its end; the scientist can produce a discourse expressive or generative of knowledge without engaging another mind, and the poet's creative purpose is accomplished when the work is composed. It is true, of course, that scientists and poets present their works to audiences, but their audiences are not necessarily rhetorical. The scientific audience consists of persons capable of receiving knowledge, and the poetic audience, of persons capable of participating in aesthetic experiences induced by the poetry. But the rhetorical audience must be capable of serving as mediator of the change which the discourse functions to produce.

Besides exigence and audience, every rhetorical situation contains a set of *constraints* made up of persons, events, objects, and relations which are parts of the situation because they have the power to constrain decision and action needed to modify the exigence. Standard sources of constraint include beliefs, attitudes, documents, facts, traditions, images, interests, motives, and the like; and when the orator enters the situation, his discourse not only harnesses constraints given by situation but provides additional important constraints—for example, his personal character, his logical proofs, and his style. There are two main classes of constraints: (1) those originated or managed by the rhetor and his method (Aristotle called these "artistic proofs"), and (2) those other constraints, in the situation, which may be operative (Aristotle's "inartistic proofs"). Both classes must be divided so as to separate those constraints that are proper from those that are improper.

These three constituents—exigence, audience, constraints—comprise everything relevant in a rhetorical situation. When the orator, invited by situation, enters it and creates and presents discourse, then both he and his speech are additional constituents.

III

I have broadly sketched a conception of rhetorical situation and discussed constituents. The following are general characteristics or features.

1. Rhetorical discourse is called into existence by situation; the situation which the rhetor perceives amounts to an invitation to create and present discourse. The clearest instances of rhetorical speaking and writing are strongly invited—often required. The situation generated by the assassination of President Kennedy was so highly structured and compelling that one could predict with near certainty the types and themes of forthcoming discourse. With the first reports of the assassination, there immediately developed a most urgent need for information; in response, reporters created hundreds of messages. Later as the situation altered, other exigencies arose: the fantastic events in Dallas had to be explained; it was necessary to eulogize the dead President; the public needed to be assured that the transfer of government to new hands would be orderly. These messages were not idle performances. The historic situation was so compelling and clear that the responses were created almost out of necessity. The responses—news reports, explanations, eulogies—participated with the situation and positively modified the several exigencies. Surely the power of situation is evident when one can predict that such discourse will be uttered. How else explain the phenomenon? One cannot say that the situation is the function of the speaker's intention, for in this case the speakers' intentions were determined by the situation. One cannot say that the rhetorical transaction is simply a response of the speaker to the demands or expectations of an audience, for the expectations of the audience were themselves keyed to a tragic historic fact. Also, we must recognize that there came into existence countless eulogies to John F. Kennedy that never reached a public; they were filed, entered in diaries, or created in thought.

In contrast, imagine a person spending his time writing eulogies of men and women who never existed: his speeches meet no rhetorical situations; they are summoned into existence not by real events, but by his own imagination. They may exhibit formal features which we consider rhetorical—such as ethical and emotional appeals, and stylistic patterns; conceivably one of these fictive eulogies is even persuasive to someone; yet all remain unrhetorical unless, through the oddest of circumstances, one of them by chance should fit a situation. Neither the presence of formal features in the discourse nor persuasive effect in a reader or hearer can be regarded as reliable marks of rhetorical discourse: A speech will be rhetorical when it is a response to the kind of situation which is rhetorical.

2. Although rhetorical situation invites response, it obviously does not invite just any response. Thus the second characteristic of rhetorical situation is that it invites a fitting response, a response that fits the situation. Lincoln's Gettysburg Address was a most *fitting* response to the relevant features of the historic context which invited its existence and gave it rhetorical significance. Imagine for a moment the Gettysburg Address entirely separated from its situation and existing for us independent of any rhetorical context: as a discourse that does not "fit" any rhetorical situation, it becomes either poetry or declamation, without rhetorical significance. In reality, however, the address continues to have profound rhetorical value precisely because some features of the Gettysburg situation persist; and the Gettysburg Address continues to participate with situation and to alter it.

Consider another instance. During one week of the 1964 presidential campaign, three events of national and international significance all but obscured the campaign: Khrushchev was suddenly deposed, China exploded an atomic bomb, and in England the Conservative Party was defeated by Labour. Any student of rhetoric could have given odds that President Johnson, in a major address, would speak to the significance of these events, and he did; his response to the situation generated by the events was fitting. Suppose that the President had treated not these events and their significance but the national budget, or imagine that be had reminisced about his childhood on a Texas farm. The critic of rhetoric would have said rightly, "He missed the mark; his speech did not fit; he did not speak to the pressing issues—the rhetorical situation shaped by the three crucial events of the week demanded a response, and he failed to provide the proper one."

3. If it makes sense to say that situation invites a "fitting" response, then situation must somehow prescribe the response which fits. To say that a rhetorical response fits a situation is to say that it meets the requirements established by the situation. A situation which is strong and clear dictates the purpose, theme, matter, and style of the response. Normally, the inauguration of a President of the United States demands an address which speaks to the nation's purposes, the central national and international problems, the unity of contesting parties; it demands speech style marked by dignity. What is evidenced on this occasion is the power of situation to constrain a fitting response. One might say metaphorically that every situation prescribes its fitting response; the rhetor may or may not read the prescription accurately.

4. The exigence and the complex of persons, objects, events, and relations which generate rhetorical discourse are located in reality, are objective and publicly observable historic facts in the world we experience, are therefore available for scrutiny by an observer or critic who attends to them. To say the situation is objective, publicly observable, and historic means that it is real or genuine—that our critical examination will certify its existence. Real situations are to be distinguished from sophistic ones in which, for example, a contrived exigence is asserted to be real; from spurious situations in which the existence or alleged existence of constituents is the result of error or ignorance; and from fantasy in which exigence, audience, and constraints may all be the imaginary objects of a mind at play.

The rhetorical situation as real is to be distinguished also from a fictive rhetorical situation. The speech of a character in a novel or play may be clearly required by a fictive rhetorical situation, a situation established by the story itself; but the speech is not genuinely rhetorical, even though, considered in itself, it looks exactly like a courtroom address or a senate speech. It is realistic, made so by fictive context. But the situation is not real, not grounded in history; neither the fictive situation nor the discourse generated by it is rhetorical. We should note, however, that the fictive rhetorical discourse within a play or novel may become genuinely rhetorical outside fictive context—if there is a real situation for which the discourse is a rhetorical response. Also, of course, the play or novel itself may be understood as a rhetorical response having poetic form.

5. Rhetorical situations exhibit structures which are simple or complex, and more or less organized. A situation's structure is simple when there are relatively few elements which must be made to interact; the fishing expedition is a case in point—there is a clear and easy relationship among utterances, the audiences, constraints, and exigence. Franklin D. Roosevelt's brief Declaration of War speech is another example: the message exists as a response to one clear exigence easily perceived by one major audience, and the one overpowering constraint is the necessity of war. On the other hand, the structure of a situation is complex when many elements must be made to interact: practically any presidential political campaign provides numerous complex rhetorical situations.

A situation, whether simple or complex, will be highly structured or loosely structured. It is highly structured when all of its elements are located and readied for the task to be performed. Malinowski's example, the fishing expedition, is a situation which is relatively simple and highly structured; everything is ordered to the task to be performed. The usual courtroom case is a good example of a situation which is complex and highly structured. The jury is not a random and scattered audience but a selected and concentrated one; it knows its relation to judge, law, defendant, counsels; it is instructed in what to observe and what to disregard. The judge is located and prepared; he knows exactly his relation to jury, law, counsels, defendant. The counsels know the ultimate object of their case; they know what they must prove; they know the audience and can easily reach it. This situation will be even more highly structured if the issue of the case is sharp, the evidence decisive, and the law clear. On the other hand, consider a complex but loosely structured situation: William Lloyd Garrison preaching abolition from town to town. He is actually looking for an audience and for constraints; even when be finds an audience, he does not know that it is a genuinely rhetorical audience—one able to be a mediator of change. Or consider the plight of many contemporary civil rights advocates who, failing to locate compelling constraints and rhetorical audiences, abandon rhetorical discourse in favor of physical action.

Situations may become weakened in structure due to complexity or disconnectedness. A list of causes includes these: (a) a single situation may involve numerous exigencies; (b) exigencies in the same situation may be incompatible; (c) two or more simultaneous rhetorical situations may compete for our attention, as in some parliamentary debates; (d) at a given moment, persons comprising the audience of situation A may also be the audience of situations B, C, and D; (e) the rhetorical audience may be scattered, uneducated regarding its duties and powers, or it may dissipate; (f) constraints may be limited in number and force, and they may be incompatible. This is enough to suggest the sorts of things which weaken the structure of situations.

6. Finally, rhetorical situations come into existence, then either mature or decay or mature and persist—conceivably some persist indefinitely. In any case, situations grow

and come to maturity; they evolve to just the time when a rhetorical discourse would be most fitting. In Malinowski's example, there comes a time in the situation when the leader of the fisherman should say, "Throw the nets." In the situation generated by the assassination of the President, there was a time for giving descriptive accounts of the scene in Dallas, later a time for giving eulogies. In a political campaign, there is a time for generating an issue and a time for answering a charge. Every rhetorical situation in principle evolves to a propitious moment for the fitting rhetorical response. After this moment, most situations decay; we all have the experience of creating a rhetorical response when it is too late to make it public.

Some situations, on the other hand, persist; this is why it is possible to have a body of truly *rhetorical* literature. The Gettysburg Address, Burke's Speech to the Electors of Bristol, Socrates' Apology—these are more than historical documents, more than specimens for stylistic or logical analysis. They exist as rhetorical responses *for us* precisely because they speak to situations which persist—which are in some measure universal.

Due to either the nature of things or convention, or both, some situations recur. The courtroom is the locus for several kinds of situations generating the speech of accusation, the speech of defense, the charge to the jury. From day to day, year to year, comparable situations occur, prompting comparable responses; hence rhetorical forms are born and a special vocabulary, grammar, and style are established. This is true also of the situation which invites the inaugural address of a President. The situation recurs and, because we experience situations and the rhetorical responses to them, a form of discourse is not only established but comes to have a power of its own—the tradition itself tends to function as a constraint upon any new response in the form.

IV

In the best of all possible worlds, there would be communication perhaps, but no rhetoric—since exigencies would not arise. In our real world, however, rhetorical exigencies abound; the world really invites change—change conceived and effected by human agents who quite properly address a mediating audience. The practical justification of rhetoric is analogous to that of scientific inquiry: the world presents objects to be known, puzzles to be resolved, complexities to be understood—hence the practical need for scientific inquiry and discourse; similarly, the world presents imperfections to be modified by means of discourse—hence the practical need for rhetorical investigation and discourse. As a discipline, scientific method is justified philosophically insofar as it provides principles, concepts, and procedures by which we come to know reality; similarly, rhetoric as a discipline is justified philosophically insofar as it provides principles, concepts, and procedures by which we effect valuable changes in reality. Thus rhetoric is distinguished from the mere craft of persuasion which, although it is a legitimate object of scientific investigation, lacks philosophical warrant as a practical discipline.

Note

1. "The Problem of Meaning in Primitive Languages," sections 3 and 4. This essay appears as a supplement in Ogden and Richards' *The Meaning of Meaning*.

The Myth
of the Rhetorical Situation

RICHARD E. VATZ

In the opening lines of "The Rhetorical Situation," Lloyd Bitzer states, "if someone says, That is a dangerous situation, his words suggest the presence of events, persons or objects which threaten him, someone else or something of value. If someone remarks, I find myself in an embarrassing situation, again the statement implies certain situational characteristics."[1]

These statements do not imply "situational characteristics" at all. The statements may ostensibly describe situations, but they actually only inform us as to the phenomenological perspective of the speaker. There can be little argument that the speakers *believe* they feel fear or embarrassment. Their statements do, however, tell us about qualities within the situation. Kenneth Burke once wrote of literary critics who attributed to others the characteristic of seeking escape: "While apparently defining a trait of the person referred to, the term hardly did more than convey the attitude of the person making the reference."[2] The same goes for the attribution of traits to a situation. It is a fitting of a scene into a category or categories found in the head of the observer. No situation can have a nature independent of the perception of its interpreter or independent of the rhetoric with which he chooses to characterize it.

In his article Bitzer states, "Rhetorical discourse is called into existence by situation"[3] and "It seems clear that rhetoric is situational."[4] This perspective on rhetoric and "situation" requires a "realist" philosophy of meaning. This philosophy has important and, I believe, unfortunate implications for rhetoric. In this article I plan to discuss Bitzer's view and its implications and suggest a different perspective with a different philosophy of meaning from which to view the relationship between "situations" and rhetoric.

MEANING IN BITZER'S "RHETORICAL SITUATION"

Bitzer's perspective emanates from his view of the nature of meaning. Simply stated, Bitzer takes the position that meaning resides in events. As sociologist Herbert Blumer describes this point of view,

> [it is] to regard meaning as intrinsic to the thing that has it, as being a natural part of the objective makeup of the thing. Thus, a chair is clearly a chair in itself, a cow a cow, a rebellion a rebellion, and so forth. Being inherent in the thing that has it, meaning needs merely to be disengaged by observing the objective thing that has the meaning. The meaning emanates, so to speak, from the thing, and as such there is no process involved in its formation; all that is necessary is to recognize the meaning that is there in the thing.[5]

This is Bitzer's point of view: there is an intrinsic nature in events from which rhetoric inexorably follows, or should follow. Bitzer states, "When I ask, What is a rhetorical situation, I want to know the nature of those contexts in which speakers or writers create rhetorical discourse . . . what are their characteristics and why and how do they result in the creation of rhetoric."[6] He later adds, "The situation *dictates* the sorts of observations to be made; it *dictates* the significant physical and verbal responses."[7] This view is reiterated in various forms throughout the article. Situations are discrete and discernible. They have a life of their own independent in meaning of those upon whom they impinge. They may or may not "require" responses. If they do the situation "invites" a response, indeed a "fitting response" almost as a glaring sun requires a shading of the eyes, a clear S-R response.

Bitzer's views are all quite consistent given his Platonist *Weltanschauung*. He sees a world in which "the exigence and the complex of persons, objects, events and relations which generate rhetorical discourse are located in reality, are objective and publicly observable historic facts in the world we experience, are therefore available for scrutiny by an observer or critic who attends to them. To say the situation is objective, publicly observable, and historic means that it is real or genuine—that our critical examination will certify its existence."[8] If the situation is as Bitzer states elsewhere "a natural *context* of persons, events, objects, and *relations*,"[9] it is hard to see how its "existence" can be certified.

Bitzer claims there are three constituents of the rhetorical situation prior to discourse: exigence, audience, and constraints. It is the "exigence" component which interests us most. In describing "exigence" Bitzer most clearly indicates his view of the source of meaning. He states, "Any exigence is an imperfection marked by urgency; it is a defect, an obstacle, something waiting to be done, a thing that is other than it should be."[10] Not only is a "waiting to be done" now existing in the event, but we also learn that it contains an ethical imperative supposedly independent of its interpreters. Bitzer adds that the situation is rhetorical only if something *can* be done, but apparently it is only rhetorical also if something *should* be done. Bitzer seems to imply that the "positive modification" needed for an exigence is clear. He seems to reflect what Richard Weaver called a "melioristic bias." We learn, for example, that the obvious positive modification of pollution of our air is "reduction of pollution." One wonders what the obvious "positive modification" of the military–industrial complex is.

THE MYTH OF THE RHETORICAL SITUATION

Fortunately or unfortunately, meaning is not intrinsic in events, facts, people, or "situations," nor are facts "publicly observable." Except for those situations which directly confront our own empirical reality, we learn of facts and events through someone's communicating them to us. This involves a two-part process. First, there is a choice of events to communicate. The world is not a plot of discrete events. The world is a scene of inexhaustible events which all compete to impinge on what Kenneth Burke calls our "sliver of reality."

Bitzer argues that the nature of the context determines the rhetoric. But one never runs out of context. One never runs out of facts to describe a situation. What was the "situation" during the Vietnam conflict? What was the situation of the 1972 elections? What is any historical situation? The facts or events communicated to us are *choices*, by our sources of information. As Murray Edelman points out in *Politics as Symbolic Action*, "People can use only an infinitesimal fraction of the information reaching them. The critical question, therefore, is what accounts for the choice by political spectators and participants of what to organize into a meaningful structure and what to ignore."[11] Any rhetor is involved in this sifting and choosing, whether it be the newspaper editor choosing front-page stories versus comic-page stories or the speaker highlighting facts about a person in a eulogy.

The very choice of what facts or events are relevant is a matter of pure arbitration. Once the choice is communicated, the event is imbued with *salience*, or what Chaim Perelman calls "presence," when describing this phenomenon from the framework of argumentation. Perelman says: "By the very fact of selecting certain elements and presenting them to the audience, their importance and pertinency to the discussion are implied. Indeed such a choice endows these elements with a *presence*. . . . It is not enough indeed that a thing should exist for a person to feel its presence."[12]

The second step in communicating "situations" is the translation of the chosen information into meaning. This is an act of creativity. It is an interpretative act. It is a rhetorical act of transcendence. As Perelman states, "Interpretation can be not merely a simple choice but also a creation, an invention of significance."[13]

To the audience, events become meaningful only through their linguistic depiction. As Edelman points out, "Political events can become infused with strong affect stemming from psychic tension, from perceptions of economic, military, or other threats or opportunities, and from interactions between social and psychological responses. These political 'events,' however, are largely creations of the language used to describe them."[14] Therefore, meaning is not discovered in situations, but *created* by rhetors.

As soon as one communicates an event or situation he is using evocative language. As Richard Weaver and others have pointed out language is always value-laden. Clearly the adjectives into which a "situation" are communicated cannot be the "real situation"; they must be a translation. Surely we learn from Bentham that rhetors can arbitrarily choose eulogistic or dyslogistic coverings for the same situation: We have "leaders" or "bosses," "organizations" or "machines," and "education" or "propaganda," not according to the situation's reality, but according to the rhetor's arbitrary choice of characterization. No theory of the relationship between situations and rhetoric can neglect to take account of the initial linguistic depiction of the situation.

IMPLICATIONS FOR RHETORIC

There are critical academic and moral consequences for rhetorical study according to one's view of meaning. If you view meaning as intrinsic to situations, rhetorical study becomes parasitic to philosophy, political science, and whatever other discipline can inform us as to what the "real" situation is. If, on the other hand, you view meaning as a consequence of rhetorical creation, your paramount concern will be how and by whom symbols create the reality to which people react. In a world of inexhaustible and ambiguous events, facts, images, and symbols, the rhetorician can best account for choices of situations, the evocative symbols, and the forms and media which transmit these translations of meaning. Thus, if anything, a rhetorical basis of meaning requires a disciplinary hierarchy with rhetoric at the top.

The ethical implications for this rhetorical perspective of meaning are crucial. If one accepts Bitzer's position that "the presence of rhetorical discourse obviously indicates the presence of a rhetorical situation,"[15] then we ascribe little responsibility to the rhetor with respect to what he has chosen to give salience. On the other hand, if we view the communication of an event as a choice, interpretation, and translation, the rhetor's responsibility is of supreme concern. Thus, when there are few speeches on hunger, and when the individual crime and not the corporate crime is the dominant topic of speakers and newspaper and magazine writers, we will not assume it is due to the relative, intrinsic importance of the two or even to a reading or misreading of the "exigencies." Instead, the choices will be seen as purposeful acts for discernible reasons. They are *decisions* to make salient or not to make salient these situations.

To view rhetoric as a creation of reality or salience rather than a reflector of reality clearly increases the rhetor's moral responsibility. We do not just have the academic exercise of determining whether the rhetor understood the "situation" correctly. Instead, he must assume responsibility for the salience he has *created*. The potential culpability of John F. Kennedy in the "missile crisis" is thus much greater. The journalists who choose not to investigate corruption in government or the health needs of the elderly are also potentially more culpable. In short, the rhetor is responsible for what he chooses to make salient.

ESSENCE: RHETORIC AND SITUATIONS

The essential question to be addressed is: What is the relationship between rhetoric and situations? It will not be surprising that I take the converse position of each of Bitzer's major statements regarding this relationship. For example: I would not say "rhetoric is situational,"[16] but situations are rhetorical; not "exigence strongly invites utterance,"[17] but utterance strongly invites exigence; not "the situation controls the rhetorical response,"[18] but the rhetoric controls the situational response; not "rhetorical discourse . . . does obtain its character-as-rhetorical from the situation which generates it,"[19] but situations obtain their character from the rhetoric which surrounds them or creates them.

When George Aiken suggested several years ago that the United States should declare that she had won the war in Vietnam and get out, it was a declaration of rhetorical determination of meaning. No one understands or understood the "situation" in Vietnam, because there never was a discrete situation. The meaning of the war (war?, civil war?) came from the rhetoric surrounding it. To give salience to a situation in an area roughly the size of one of our middle-size states and to translate its exigencies into patriotism-provoking language and symbolism was a rhetorical choice. There was no "reality" of the situation's being in or not being in our national interest. At least George Aiken saw that the situation was primarily rhetorical, not military or political. And since it was produced rhetorically it could be exterminated rhetorically! As Edelman states ". . . political beliefs, perceptions and expectations are overwhelmingly not based upon observation or empirical evidence available to participants, but rather upon cuings among groups of people who jointly *create* the meanings they will read into current and anticipated events. . . . The particular meanings that are consensually accepted *need not therefore be cued by the objective situation*; they are rather established by a process of mutual agreement upon significant symbols."[20]

Political crises, contrary to Bitzer's analysis of Churchill, are rarely "found," they are usually created.[21] There was a "Cuban Missile Crisis" in 1962, not because of an event or group of events, but mainly because acts of rhetorical creation took place which created a political crisis as well.[22] A President dramatically announced on nationwide television and radio that there was a grave crisis threatening the country. This was accompanied by symbolic crisis activity including troop and missile deployment, executive formation of *ad hoc* crisis committees, unavailability of high government officials, summoning of Congressional leaders, etc. Once the situation was made salient and depicted as a crisis, the situation took new form. In 1970, however, in a similar situation the prospects of a Russian nuclear submarine base off Cienfuegos was *not* a "crisis" because President Nixon chose not to employ rhetoric to create one.[23]

Bitzer refers to the controlling situation of President Kennedy's assassination. The creation of salience for certain types of events such as Presidential assassinations may be so ritualized that it is uninteresting to analyze it rhetorically. This does not mean, however, that the situation "controlled" the response. It means that the communication of the event was of such consensual symbolism that expectations were easily predictable and stable. Even Bitzer describes the reaction to the assassination as resulting from "reports" of the assassination. Again, one cannot maintain that reports of anything are indistinguishable from the thing itself. Surely Bitzer cannot believe that there was an intrinsic urgency which compelled the rotunda speeches following the killing of President Kennedy (note, that the killing of important people is communicated with the evocative term "assassination"). In fact, the killing of a President of this country at this time is not a real threat to the people in any measurable way. How smooth in fact is the transference of power. How similar the country is before and after the event. (How similar are the President and Vice-President?) *But* since rhetoric *created* fears and threat perception, the rotunda speeches were needed to communicate reassurances.

CONCLUSION

As Edelman states, "Language does not mirror an objective 'reality' but rather creates it by organizing meaningful perceptions abstracted from a complex, bewildering world."[24] Thus rhetoric is a *cause* not an *effect* of meaning. It is antecedent, not subsequent, to a situation's impact.

Rhetors choose or do not choose to make salient situations, facts, events, etc. This may be the *sine qua non* of rhetoric: the art of linguistically or symbolically creating salience. After salience is created, the situation must be translated into meaning. When political commentators talk about issues, they are talking about situations made salient, not something that became important because of its intrinsic predominance. Thus in 1960 Kennedy and Nixon discussed Quemoy and Matsu. A prominent or high-ethos rhetor may create his own salient situations by virtue of speaking out on them. To say the President is speaking out on a pressing issue is redundant.

It is only when the meaning is seen as the result of a creative act and not a discovery, that rhetoric will be perceived as the supreme discipline it deserves to be.

Notes

1. Lloyd Bitzer, "The Rhetorical Situation," *Philosophy and Rhetoric* 1 (1968): 1 (reprinted in this volume).

2. Kenneth Burke, *Permanence and Change* (New York: New Republic, 1936), p. 16.

3. Bitzer, "Rhetorical Situation," p. 9.

4. Ibid., p. 3.

5. Herbert Blumer, *Symbolic Interactionism: Perspective and Method* (Englewood Cliffs, NJ: Prentice-Hall, 1969), pp. 3–4.

6. Bitzer, "Rhetorical Situation," p. 1.

7. Ibid., p. 5; my emphasis.

8. Ibid., p. 11.

9. Ibid., p. 5; my emphasis.

10. Ibid., p. 6.

11. Murray Edelman, *Politics as Symbolic Action* (Chicago: Markham, 1971), p. 33.

12. C. Perelman and L. Olbrechts-Tyteca, *The New Rhetoric*, trans. John Wilkinson and Purcell Weaver (London: University of Notre Dame Press, 1969), pp. 116–117.

13. Ibid., p.121.

14. Edelman, *Politics*, p. 65.

15. Bitzer, "Rhetorical Situation," p. 2.

16. Ibid., p. 3.

17. Ibid., p. 5.

18. Ibid., p. 6.

19. Ibid., p. 3.

20. Edelman, *Politics*, pp. 32–33.

21. For a similar view regarding presidential rhetorical "crisis creation," see Theodore Otto Windt Jr., "Genres of Presidential Public Address: Repeating the Rhetorical Past" (paper delivered at the annual meeting of the Speech Communication Association of America, December 1972).

22. Quiet diplomacy was ruled out, as were Adlai Stevenson's recommendations of a "trade" of our obsolete missiles in Turkey for Russia's in Cuba. Many of our allies who had lived in the shadow of Russia's nuclear capability could not understand why the United States would find such a situation so intolerable. Moreover, Secretary of Defense McNamara did not feel that the missiles in Cuba would present an unendurable military situation for the United States. See Elie Abel, *The Missile Crisis* (New York: J. B. Lippincott, 1966), and Theodore Sorensen, *Kennedy* (New York: Harper & Row, 1965), pp. 667–718.

23. Benjamin Welles, "Soviet's Removal of Vessel in Cuba Is Awaited by U.S.," *New York Times*, November 15, 1970, p. 1, col. 8.

24. Edelman, *Politics*, p. 66.

Rethinking the Rhetorical Situation from within the Thematic of *Différance*

BARBARA A. BIESECKER

Critics bring to the analysis of rhetorical events various assumptions about the nature of symbolic action. Yet almost invariably they share common presuppositions about the constituent elements of the rhetorical situation and the logic that informs the relations between them. Whether theorists and critics adhere to an "old" or a "new" rhetoric, they continue to operate under the assumption that a logic of influence structures the relations between the constituent elements in any particular rhetorical situation. Symbolic action (what has historically been a linguistic text) is almost always understood as an expression that, wittingly or unwittingly, shapes or is shaped by the constituent elements of the situation out of which and for which it is produced. This long-held conception of the rhetorical situation as an exchange of influence defines the text as an object that mediates between subjects (speaker and audience) whose identity is constituted in a terrain different from and external to the particular rhetorical situation. Hence, the rhetorical situation is thought to modify attitudes or induce action on the part of consummate individuals.

I believe a rethinking of the rhetorical situation is called for on two interrelated grounds. One, the understanding of the rhetorical text as a discourse whose meaning is constituted by its relation to either an exigence operative at a particular historical moment or a consciousness anterior to the rhetorical event commits us to a naïve notion of influence and blinds us to the discourse's radically historical character. Two, the construal of the rhetorical situation as an event made possible by way of an exchange between consummate individuals severely limits what we can say about discourse which seeks to persuade: if any symbolic act is no more than an event that links distinct and already constituted subjects, then rhetorical discourse bumps up against the impenetrable and unalterable space of the subject, "a threshold which none of the strategic [responses] manages to cross."[1] That is to say, if we posit the audience of any rhetorical event as no more than a conglomeration of subjects whose identity is fixed prior to the rhetorical event itself, then we must also admit that those subjects have an essence that cannot be affected by the discourse. Thus, the power of rhetoric is circumscribed: it has the potency to influence an audience, to realign their allegiances, but not to form new identities. Clearly, the traditional concept of the rhetorical situation forces theorists and critics to appeal to a logic that transcends the rhetorical situation itself in order to explain the prior constitution of the subjects participating or implicated in the event. If the identities of the audience are not constituted in and by the rhetorical event, then some retreat to an essentialist theory of the subject is inevitable.[2] Ultimately, this commits us to a limited conception of the subject and, in turn, to a reductive understanding of the rhetorical situation. In this essay I want to suggest that a reexamination of symbolic action (the text) and the subject (audience) that proceeds from within Jacques Derrida's thematic of *différance* enables us to rethink the rhetorical situation as articulation. Indeed, deconstructive practice enables us to read symbolic action in general and rhetorical discourse in particular as radical possibility.[3]

Obviously this is not the first attempt to mark a productive relation between the rhetorical analysis of texts and deconstruction. A plethora of theorists and critics, both within and outside the discipline of Rhetoric, have availed themselves to deconstructive practice under the shared conviction that, more than any other theoretical or critical perspective, deconstruction takes the rhetoricity of all texts seriously.[4] Deconstructive critics decipher all events as strategic impositions: as willed and therefore provisional limitations of a potentially unlimited and indeterminate textuality. Typically, Jacques Derrida and his disciples work toward the disclosure of the tropological structure of modes of thinking which, while purporting to be mere "means of expression," affect or infect the meaning produced. Beyond its demystifying function, however, deconstruction has yet to be appropriated in a productive way by critics working in the field of Rhetoric. What still remains to be done—and what this essay seeks to offer—is a reading of the rhetorical situation from within the frame of deconstructive practice in order to specify what can be produced that is useful for the analysis of rhetorical events. This essay will proceed in the following manner: In the first section, I will take up the text as a constituent element of the rhetorical situation. Here I will delineate what I take to be the productive relation between the rhetorical analysis of discrete symbolic actions and deconstruction. By way of a close reading of Jacques Derrida's thematic of *différance* as it is performed in a number of his essays, and particularly as it is staged in *Glas*,[5] I will suggest that deconstruction is a way of reading that seeks to come to terms with the way in which the language of any given text signifies the complicated attempt to form a unity out of a division, thereby turning an originary condition of impossibility into a condition of possibility in order to posit its ostensive argument. I will argue that from within the thematic of *différance* the "rhetorical dimension" of the text signifies not only the play of the tropological figures operating on its surface level, but also the (non)originary finessing of a division that produces the meaning of the text as such. That is to say, the "rhetorical dimension" names *both* the means by which an idea or argument is expressed and the initial formative intervention that, in centering a differential situation, makes possible the production of meaning.[6] In the second section of the essay, I will fix my glance on the audience as a constituent element of the rhetorical situation. Here I will show how a deconstruction of the subject gives rhetorical critics and theorists access to the radical possibilities entailed in rhetorical events: if, as I will argue with Derrida, we conceive audience as the effect of *différance* and not the realization of identities, then our conception of rhetorical events must allow the potential for the displacement and condensation of those provisional identities. I will recommend that we rethink the rhetorical situation as governed by a logic of articulation rather than influence. Once we take the identity of audience as an effect-structure, we become obliged to read every "fixed" identity as the provisional and practical outcome of a symbolic engagement between speaker and audience.

SITUATION AND SPEAKER

Twenty years ago Lloyd Bitzer simultaneously opened his seminal essay "The Rhetorical Situation" and inaugurated the journal *Philosophy and Rhetoric* with a series of questions, all of which boil down to one: How are we to define the rhetorical text? Bitzer's answer is widely known and based upon an onto-phenomenological differentiation between instrumental and expressive utterance:

> a work of rhetoric is pragmatic; it comes into existence for the sake of something beyond itself; it functions ultimately to produce action or change in the world; it performs some task. In short, rhetoric is a mode of altering reality, not by the direct application of energy to objects, but by the creation of discourse which changes reality through the mediation of thought and action.[7]

"Rhetoric," here, is the name given to those utterances that serve as instruments for adjusting the environment in accordance to the interests of its inhabitants. Of course, absolutely central to Bitzer's definition of rhetoric is the suggestion that rhetorical discourse is a response to and is called into existence by "some specific condition or situation which invites utterance."[8] In his view rhetorical discourse is an effect structure; its presence is determined by and takes its character from the situation that engenders it. As he puts it, "Rhetorical discourse comes into existence in response to a question, a solution in response to a problem." According to Bitzer, the situation is the "necessary condition of rhetorical discourse," and as such it "controls the rhetorical response in the same sense that the question controls the answer and the problem controls the solution": "Not the rhetor and not persuasive intent, but the situation is the source and ground of rhetorical activity—and, I should add, of rhetorical criticism."[9]

In 1973 Richard E. Vatz published "The Myth of the Rhetorical Situation," a gesture which challenged the validity of Bitzer's definition of rhetoric. Vatz indicts, quite correctly, Bitzer's definition of the rhetorical text as an operation that "disengage[s] the meaning [that] resides in events," and argues, to the contrary, that "statements do not imply 'situational characteristics at all': the statements may ostensibly describe situations, but they actually only inform us as to the phenomenological perspective of the speaker."[10] Vatz brought into the discussion what Bitzer had excluded—the intervention of an intending and interpreting speaker-subject. Citing Chaim Perelman and Murray Edelman, Vatz notes both how "the very choice of what facts or events are relevant is a matter of pure arbitration [on the part of the speaker]" and how the communication of "'situations' is the translation of the chosen information into meaning."[11] Hence, for Vatz rhetorical discourse is "an act of creativity ... an interpretative act," and not something discovered in situations.

As an alternative to conceiving rhetorical discourse as the determined outcome of a situation, Vatz calls for a reversal of the cause–effect relation between situation and discourse proposed by Bitzer. Since, as Edelman states, "Language does not mirror an objective 'reality' but rather creates it by organizing meaningful perceptions abstracted from a complex, bewildering world," rhetoric "is a cause not an effect of meaning. It is antecedent, not subsequent, to a situation's impact."[12] For Vatz, as for Edelman, rhetorical discourse is to be analyzed as an expression of a speaker's intentions and interpretations which bring rhetorical situations into being.

Several essays have since been published that take up the question of the relation between the rhetorical text and the rhetorical situation. Continuing the debate between Bitzer and Vatz, critics have defended, rejected, or modified Bitzer's and Vatz's views of rhetoric and the rhetorical situation. In all cases, however, critics still take as their founding presumption a causal relation between the constituent elements comprising the event as a whole. Either speaker or situation is posited as logically and temporally prior, one or the other is taken as origin.[13] The present discussion will not try to review this body of arguments; rather, it will attempt to turn what appears to be an impasse (does situation or speaker occupy the position of origin?) into a productive contradiction, one that makes it possible for us to rethink rhetoric in a new way. Such a task may begin with Vatz's essay which, more than any other, makes visible the contradiction that rules both sides of the debate. As already noted, Vatz's ostensive purpose is to propose an alternative to Bitzer's definition of rhetoric and the rhetorical situation. Whether or not we agree with Vatz's own proposition, we may at least see his essay as a successful counterstatement. Nevertheless, and this is the mark of the double-gesture that inhabits his own writing, even as it questions the validity of Bitzer's central proposition, Vatz's essay simultaneously confirms it. After all, Vatz's statement is a response to Bitzer's essay; Vatz reads "The Rhetorical Situation" as itself a situation with an exigence that invites a response. And yet, is not Vatz's own article an effect of arbitration on the part of a choosing individual? So, then, is Bitzer right or is Vatz right? Is situation or speaker the origin of rhetorical discourse?

It is at this juncture that a deconstructive intervention might prove productive and has, in fact, already been set into operation by Vatz. As I have shown, Vatz inverts the hierarchy between situation and speaker posited by Bitzer. What if, rather than simply choosing sides, we were to suggest with Derrida that by upsetting the hierarchy and producing an exchange of properties between situation and speaker, Vatz unwittingly uncovers and undoes the operation responsible for the hierarchization, and thus displaces both the foundational logic of his own and Bitzer's argument? If both situation and speaker can stand in for cause, "if either cause or effect can occupy the position of origin, then origin is no longer originary; it loses its metaphysical privilege."[14] How, then, are we to account for the production of rhetorical texts? What are we to read rhetoric as the sign of? To answer these questions, I turn to a discussion of *différance* and try to flesh out its implications for the theorization of the rhetorical situation.

Rethinking Speaker and Situation from within the Thematic of *Différance*

Any serious consideration of the productive interface between rhetorical analysis and Derridean deconstruction must begin by charting the ontotheoretical precepts that inform deconstructive practice. Within the parameters of the present essay, this means thinking through the concept-metaphor *différance* that plays a formidable role both morphologically and historically in the works of Derrida. Derrida's notion of *différance* is rooted in Saussure's *Cours de linguistique generale*. In one of his earliest essays Derrida remarks how, in conceiving language as a system of signs whose identity is the effect of difference and not of essence, Saussure is put in the peculiar position of having to conclude that, contrary to common sense,

> in language, there are only differences *without positive terms*. Whether we take the signified or the signifier, language has neither ideas nor sounds that existed before the linguistic system, but only conceptual and phonic differences that have issued from the system. The idea or phonic substance that a sign contains is of less importance than the other signs that surround it.[15]

For Derrida, Saussure's text proposes a notion of difference that unwittingly points to a division within as well as between distinct elements in the linguistic system: the play of difference which Saussure saw operating *between* elements and thus constituting the value of any discrete element in the linguistic system is for Derrida always already at work *within* each element. This internal difference, this interval which separates every element from that which it is not, while "by the same token, divid[ing] the present [element] in itself," is, for Derrida, what lends every element its value.[16] *Différance*, as Derrida names it, marks an originary internal division, a "fundamental" nonidentity which, he tells us in *Positions*,

> forbid[s] at any moment, or in any sense, that a simple element be *present* in and of itself, referring only to itself. Whether in the order of spoken or written discourse, no element can function as a sign without referring to another element which itself is not simply present. This interweaving results in each "element"–phoneme or grapheme–being constituted on the basis of the trace within it of the other elements of the chain or system. This interweaving, this textile, is the *text* produced only in the transformation of another text. Nothing, neither among the elements nor within the system, is anywhere ever simply present or absent. There are only, everywhere, differences and traces of traces.[17]

The sign as "trace-structure," the sign as "constituted" out of a structural principle of original nonidentity or radical alterity, is precisely that which Derrida elsewhere names the "graphematic structure."[18]

In a way that will soon become evident, Derrida's *différance* effects a link between deconstruction and the analysis of rhetorical texts by supplying rhetorical critics with a mechanism that enables them to specify more adequately the rhetoricity of a text. For now, it is important to note that the thematic of *différance* is operative throughout Derrida's early as well as late essays. In fact, we could even decide to decipher most of his essays as variations on this theme. For example, we might read Derrida's essay entitled "Différance" in *Speech and Phenomena and Other Essays on Husserl's Theory of Signs* as something like the logic of *différance* or the questioning of the arche; we might decipher his earlier essay on Rousseau in *Of Grammatology* as the attempt to rename *différance* as "the graphic of the supplement"; we might describe "Signature Event Context" and "Limited Inc." in terms of a reinscription of *différance* as iteration or radical citationality. We might even go so far as to suggest that in every case Derrida's essays re-mark the trace of "the systematic play of differences, of the traces of differences, of the *spacing* by means of which elements are related to each other" in any given text.[19] In short, we could take the entire lot of Derrida's essays as an assemblage seeking to play and sometimes even perform the *différance* that structures all texts but which is always covered over in the writing.[20]

But what about this *différance*? Why should rhetorical critics struggle with this complicated internal division that is said to inhabit all writing, structure all speech, and scandalize all texts? What is so critical about this seemingly critical difference? In his essay "Différance" Derrida provides a possible answer: "*Différance* is what makes the movement of signification possible."[21] The play of *différance*, as Derrida puts it, is "the possibility of conceptuality, of the conceptual system and process in general":

> What we note as *différance* will thus be the movement of play that "produces" (and not by something that is simply an activity) these differences, these effects of difference. This does not mean that the *différance* which produces differences is before them in a simple and in itself unmodified and indifferent present. *Différance* is the nonfull, nonsimple "origin"; it is the structured and differing origin of differences.[22]

To repeat, *différance* makes signification possible. Only to the extent that we are able to differ, as in spatial distinction or relation to an other, and to defer, as in temporalizing or delay, are we able to produce anything. "*Différance*" is, as Derrida puts it, "the formation of form."[23] Here we do well to look a bit closer at an essay in which Derrida provides an extensive structural description of *différance* and then proceeds to discuss at even greater length its enabling power. In "Linguistics and Grammatology" he says,

> [*Différance*] does not depend on any sensible plentitude, audible or visible, phonic or graphic. It is, on the contrary, the *condition of such a plentitude*. Although it does not exist, although it is never a being-present outside of all plentitude, its possibility is by rights anterior to all that one calls sign . . . concept or operation, motor or sensory. This *différance* is therefore not more sensible than intelligible and it *permits the articulation of signs* among themselves within the same abstract order . . . or between two orders of expression. *It permits the articulation of speech and writing*—in the colloquial sense—as it founds the metaphysical opposition between the sensible and the intelligible, then between signifier and signified, expression and content, etc.[24]

Derrida's *différance* is, as Gayatri Chakravorty Spivak points out, the name for "the lack at the origin that is the condition of thought and experience"; all writing in the narrow sense, like all speech, marks the play of this productive nonidentity.[25] *Différance*, Derrida writes, is the structural condition which makes it possible for us to perform any act.

For a concrete example of the enabling power of *différance* we can turn briefly to Derrida's *Glas*. In this work Derrida binds Hegel to Genet, Genet to Hegel. In so doing, he constructs two columns of discourse which make reading or decipherment a problem. How are we to read this two-pronged, two-pegged text? As I have already suggested, we can decide to decipher this text as the dramatization of *différance*. Indeed, it seems to me that no other work by Derrida more proficiently stages the play of *différance* than *Glas*. The very typographic form of the text ("if one decides to concentrate on one column the eye is drawn by the other"[26]) as well as the writing on both sides ("how the seeming exposition in the Hegel section seems upheld yet undone by the unruly Genet column"[27]) dramatizes the structural power of *différance* by performing it graphically. Briefly said, in *Glas* Derrida transposes the logic of *différance* into the graphic of *différance*: it is the white, what we usually take to be empty, space between the Hegel column and the Genet column that gives rise to the text. The space between the (in)dependent columns marks a differencing zone that, as Derrida puts it in "The Double Session," "through the re-marking of its semantic void, it in fact begins to signify. Its semantic void *signifies*, but it signifies spacing and articulation; it has as its meaning the possibility of syntax; it orders the play of meaning."[28]

Glas performs the vantage point from which it becomes possible to see in a very vivid and concrete way how the value of a symbolic act, like the value of any element in a system, is a function of its place in an economy of *différance*. It is in the middle or the suspense of the two previously unjoined texts that meaning can be said to have been made. In fact we might go so far as to suggest that the blithe proposition in *Glas* is: everything deliberately and unavoidably happens in its crease, in its fold. It is in the structural space between the Hegel column and the Genet column that Derrida's text would play out its "meanings." Again, the space between the two (in)dependent texts deliberately and unavoidably stages the incision, the cut, the introduction of a differencing zone, a structure of *différance* that in being divided makes meaning possible. *Différance* is deliberately performed as the fold, where the border between inside (Hegel or Genet) and outside (Genet or Hegel) becomes undecidable as the text slips erratically from one column to the other. In short, the enabling power of *différance* is expressed or demonstrated in *Glas* as the asymmetrical (non)engagement of Hegel and Genet: "each page is folded dissymmetrically down the middle, for Hegel and Genet can never be identical. The equation is never balanced, reading and writing never coincide, and the page is never quite folded *up*."[29]

In shuttling us between the Hegel and Genet columns, Derrida's *Glas* involves us in the "active" movement of *différance*. Typographically dramatizing the economy of *différance*, he engages us in the work of a decipherment which produces the suggestion that all activity is made possible only by finessing a divided origin, a *différance*.

Such finessing, Derrida points out, in what might be taken as a metacritical comment in *Glas*, is hardly without interest:

> Before attempting an active interpretation, verily a critical displacement (supposing that is rigorously possible), we must yet patiently decipher this difficult and obscure text. However preliminary, such a deciphering cannot be neutral, neuter, or passive. It violently intervenes, at least in a minimal form.[30]

The reader as well as the writer, and in the case of *Glas*, the philosopher as well as the poet, generates a discourse whose "meaning" is already, and thoroughly, constituted by a tissue of differences.[31] That meaning emerges as nothing more than a tissue of differences, however, should not be taken as a disabling discovery. In fact, Derrida points out that it is in deciphering difference as *différance* that we begin to read, and it is in transforming this condition of impossibility into a condition of possibility that we are enabled to speak and write—intervene.

Returning to the central question raised in this section of the essay, we can ask once again: How can Derrida's decision to read all texts as the trace of an inaugurating *différance* help rhetorical theorists and critics account for the production of rhetorical texts? As I mentioned at the start, deconstruction allows us to take seriously the *rhetoricity* of discursive practices. What does this mean in terms of the discussion on *différance* and what implications can it have for the practice of contemporary rhetorical criticism that takes the text as one of the constituent elements of the rhetorical situation?

Derridean deconstruction begins by considering the way in which all texts are inhabited by an internally divided nonoriginary "origin" called *différance*. The divisiveness of that "originating" moment is, so to speak, covered over or, as I put it earlier, finessed into a unity by the writing and the speaking. In fact, the finessing of the nonidentical into an identity is, as was noted above, precisely the activity that makes signification happen.

At this point, it might be emphasized that the provisional imposition of something like a unified origin is both a necessary and an interested gesture. It is necessary since the articulation of anything requires the temporary displacement of plurality, the provisional limitation of a potentially unlimited and indeterminate textuality (i.e., historical, discursive field). It is interested since, as I have shown, *différance* underwrites all discursive practices and thus exposes all beginning points, all primordial axioms, and all founding principles as constructions—impositions, traces of a will to knowledge.[32] In "Linguistics and Grammatology" Derrida describes the necessary and interested gesture this way:

> If words and concepts receive meaning only in sequences of differences, one can justify one's language, and one's choice of terms, only within a topic [an orientation in space] and an historical strategy. The justification can therefore never be absolute and definitive. It corresponds to a condition of forces and translates an historical calculation.[33]

All symbolic action marks an intervention and an imposition—a deferral of and differencing between the historically produced discursive field—whose own authority is historically produced and, thus, provisional. As Derrida put it elsewhere, "If the word 'history' did not carry with it the theme of a final repression of *différance*, we could say that differences alone could be 'historical' through and through and from the start."[34]

The transitory character of one's choice of foundational terms is precisely that which any text cannot admit if it is going to make anything like "truth" appear; however, the text's own provisionality is also that which the language of the text repeatedly performs, despite all efforts to conceal it. We are continually reminded that although our own desire for unity and order compels us to "balance the equation that is the text's system," the textuality of the text itself "exposes the grammatological structure of the text," and reveals "that its 'origin' and its 'end' are given over to language in general."[35] Because the text is always and already given over to language in general, there is invariably a moment in the text "which harbors the unbalancing of the equation, the sleight of hand at the limit of a text which cannot be dismissed simply as a contradiction."[36] This textual knot or inadvertent "sleight of hand" marks the rhetoricity of the text and, in so doing, enables us to locate the unwitting and interested gesture that finessed *différance* in such a way that the writing could proceed. In every case the rhetoric of the text marks the intervention of *différance* onto the scene of writing. Moreover, the rhetoricity of the text also sustains the trace of the unwitting and interested gesture that, in rewriting the "originary" division as an identity, effected the text. Thus rhetoric can neither be taken as mere ornamentation for nor accessory to the "essential" argument or proposition of a text. While *différance* constitutes the structural "condition" for signification, rhetoric is the name for both the finessing of *différance* that inaugurates a text *and* the figurality of the text that puts us on its track.

The deconstructive displacement of questions of origin into questions of process frees rhetorical theorists and critics from reading rhetorical discourses and their "founding principles" as either the determined outcome of an objectively identifiable and discrete situation or an interpreting and intending subject. In fact, it implicates them in a much more complicated and unwieldy project: it obliges them to read rhetorical discourses as "the interweaving of different texts (literally 'web'-s) in an act of criticism that refuses to think of 'influence' or 'interrelationship' as *simple* historical phenomena."[37] That is to say, neither the text's immediate rhetorical situation nor its author can be taken as simple origin or generative agent since both are underwritten by a series of historically produced displacements. The implications this has for rhetorical theory and criticism will be made evident after we examine the rhetorical situation from the side of reception rather than production. Thus, the next section will suggest how we might begin to rewrite the rhetorical situation from within the thematic of *différance* by taking up the relation between the text and the audience.

TEXT AND AUDIENCE

So far I have tried to show that Derrida's *différance* provides us with a critical edge for rethinking the relation between a rhetorical text and its speaker or situation. A deconstruction of those relations obliges us to question both the speaker's and the situation's presumed authority over the production of discourse. But where does that leave us? I would like to suggest that if we supplement our deconstructive reading of rhetorical discourse by a reading of audience that proceeds from within the thematic of *différance*, it becomes possible for us to rethink the logic of the rhetorical situation as articulation.

I begin the discussion on text and audience with the observation that whenever rhetorical theorists and critics contemplate the rhetorical situation, they do so with some notion of audience in mind. Indeed, at least in the twentieth century a preoccupation with audience has often served as *the* distinguishing characteristic of critical practice in our discipline. Yet, even in essays explicitly seeking to develop a theory of the rhetorical situation (with audience invariably identified as one of its constituent elements), the concept of audience itself receives little critical attention: in most cases, audience is simply named, identified as the target of discursive practice, and then dropped. For the most part, theorists do not approach audience as a problematic category. Lloyd Bitzer exemplifies this general complacency best when he remarks,

> What characteristics, then, are implied when one refers to "the rhetorical situation"—the context in which speakers or writers create rhetorical discourse? Perhaps this question is puzzling because "situation" is not a standard term in the vocabulary of rhetorical theory. "Audience" is standard; so also are "speaker," "subject," "occasion," and "speech." If I were to ask, "What is a rhetorical audience?" or "What is a rhetorical subject?"—the reader would catch the meaning of my question.[38]

Indeed, one is expected to catch the meaning of Bitzer's question "What is a rhetorical audience?" because one is trained, at least in terms of the theoretical/critical lexicon, to think of audience as a self-evident, if not altogether banal, category. Based on what has been said about it, theorists and critics seem to agree on the nature and function of audience. Surveying the history of the concept as it has been used in the theorization and analysis of rhetorical events, Thomas Benson remarks: the term "audience" signifies for theorists and critics the presence of a body "*influencing* the design of and being *influenced* by a symbolic action."[39] In other words, as a collective animated by an identifiable and shared predisposition, audience implicitly figures into discussions about the rhetorical situation as a constraint upon rhetorical discourse. As a recipient of rhetorical messages, audience also figures forth as a confederate body susceptible to persuasion and, ultimately, "capable of serving as mediators of the change which the discourse functions to produce."[40]

There can be no doubt that the dominant concept of audience as a collectivity that both influences and is influenced by discourse is based on the traditional humanistic conception of the subject. As Michael C. McGee puts it, rhetorical theorists and critics "presuppose a 'people' or an 'audience'" that is "either (a) an objective, literal extension of 'person,' or (b) a 'mob' of individuals whose significance is their gullibility and failure to respond to 'logical' argument."[41] In both cases they hold firmly to a conception of the human being that presumes an essence at the core of the individual that is coherent, stable, and which makes the human being what it *is*. Across the board, the subject, and by extension the audience, is conceived as a consciousness, an "I" which thinks, perceives, and feels, an "I" whose self-presence or consciousness to itself is the source of meaning. For example, even though they disagree with each other on the generative ground of rhetorical discourse, both Bitzer and Vatz presume the presence of an audience that finds, in any rhetorical situation, its ontological and epistemological foundation in the notion of a sovereign, rational subject. In Bitzer's words, an audience signifies "only ... those persons who are capable of being influenced by discourse and of being mediators of change."[42] Implied in this statement is the suggestion that rational persons respond appropriately to reasonable propositions—a suggestion Vatz's argument presupposes. What must be noted here is that theorists as diverse as Bitzer and Vatz predicate their views of audience on the common presumption that fixed essences encounter variable circumstances. Given this conceptualization of the audience, Benson is justified to define the rhetorical situation as a complex governed by the logic of influence. In the next section of the essay, I intend to problematize the feasibility of the notion of audience modeled after the sovereign subject and, by way of conclusion, offer a theorization of the rhetorical situation that provides us with an alternative to the logic of influence.

Rethinking Text and Audience from within the Thematic of *Différance*

In several of his works, Derrida challenges the presumed integrity of the phenomenological subject, the subject of the humanistic tradition that, as I have shown, plays a formidable role in our understanding of the rhetorical situation. He launches a deconstruction of the centered subject by attempting to think presence, including the subject as a consciousness present to itself, as "starting from/in relation to time as difference, differing, and deferral."[43] In short, Derrida takes seriously the possibility that the subject, like writing and speech, is constituted by *différance*.

Before fleshing out the various implications the deconstruction of the humanistic subject has for traditional notions of audience and situation, we must examine more closely Derrida's elaborate argument, one that enables him to forge the polemic suggestion that the centered subject is an effect-structure and not an ontological *a priori*. Derrida's deconstruction of the humanistic subject turns in great part on the effacement of the subject/structure binary that allows humanists like Husserl and Freud[44] to posit a self-present I, "a fixed origin" that itself "escape[s] structurality" in such a way as to limit "the play of structure."[45] Perry Anderson puts it this way:

> What Derrida had seen, acutely, was that the supposition of any stable structure had always depended on the silent postulation of a center that was not entirely "subject" to it: in other words, of a *subject* distinct *from* it. His decisive move was to liquidate the last vestige of such autonomy.[46]

As Anderson intimates, Derrida deconstructs the subject by showing us how the identity of any subject, what I earlier called the core of the human being, like the value of any element in any system is structured by *différance*. This forces us to think of subjectivity not as an essence but as an effect of the subject's place in an economy of differences. For example, in his essay "Semiology and Grammatology" Derrida writes that,

> Nothing—no present and in-*different* being—thus precedes *différance* and spacing. There is no subject who is agent, author, and master of *différance*, who eventually and empirically would be overtaken by *différance*. Subjectivity—like objectivity—is an effect of *différance*, an effect inscribed in a system of *différance*.[47]

In this essay, Derrida recommends that we think the subject not as a stable presence constituted and operating outside the play of *différance*, but instead as a production or effect-structure of *différance*.

If the identity of the subject is to be taken as the effect of *différance* and not of essence, then it is marked, like any sign or any object, by an internal difference that prevents it from being present in and of itself. As Derrida puts it,

> This is why the *a* of *différance* also recalls that spacing is temporization, the detour and postponement by means of which intuition, perception, consummation—in a word, the relationship to the present, the reference to a present reality, to a *being*—are always *deferred*. Deferred by virtue of the very principle of difference which holds that an element functions and signifies, takes on or conveys meaning, only by referring to another past or future element in an economy of traces.[48]

By way of the operation of *différance*, Derrida underscores the radically historical character of the subject. Against an irreducible humanist essence of subjectivity, Derrida advances a subjectivity which, structured by *différance* and thus always differing from itself, is forever in process, indefinite, controvertible. In fact,

> "absolute subjectivity" would . . . have to be crossed out as soon as we conceive the present on the basis of *différance*, and not the reverse. The concept of *subjectivity* belongs *a priori and in general* to the order of the *constituted*. . . . There is no constituting subjectivity. The very concept of constitution must be deconstructed.[49]

Like any other object, the subject is a historical construct precisely because its "unique" and always provisional identity depends upon its operations within a system of differences and the larger movement of *différance*: the subject is neither present nor "above all present to itself before *différance*." Like speech and writing, "the subject is constituted only in being divided from itself, in becoming space, in temporizing, in deferral."[50] Rather than marking a place of identity, the subject designates a noncoincidence, "a complex and differential product"[51] continuously open to change.

Rewriting the Logic of the Rhetorical Situation as Articulation

What implications might the deconstruction of the subject have for our definition of the audience and, thus, for the rhetorical situation? Simply put, the deconstruction of the subject opens up possibilities for the field of Rhetoric by enabling us to read the rhetorical situation as an event structured not by a logic of influence but by a logic of articulation. If the subject is shifting and unstable (constituted in and by the play of *différance*), then the rhetorical event may be seen as an incident that produces and reproduces the identities of subjects and constructs and reconstructs linkages between them. From the vantage of the de-centered subject, the rhetorical event can not signify the consolidation of already constituted identities whose operations and relations are determined *a priori* by a logic that operates quite apart from real historical circumstances. Rather it marks the articulation of provisional identities and the construction of contingent relations that obtain between them. From within the thematic of *différance* we would see the rhetorical situation neither as an event that merely induces audiences to act one way or another nor as an incident that, in representing the interests of a particular collectivity, merely wrestles the probable within the realm of the actualizable. Rather, we would see the rhetorical situation as an event that makes possible the production of identities and social relations. That is to say, if rhetorical events are analyzed from within the thematic of *différance*, it becomes possible to read discursive practices neither as rhetorics directed to preconstituted and known audiences nor as rhetorics "in search of" objectively identifiable but yet undiscovered audiences. *Différance* obliges us to read rhetorical discourses as processes entailing the discursive production of audiences, and enables us to decipher rhetorical events as sites that make visible the historically articulated emergence of the category "audience."

Such perspective, of course, implicates us in a larger, radically historical project that works against essentializing and universalizing claims. If rhetorical discourses (which are themselves played by *différance*) are deciphered as practices that perform the situated displacement and condensation of identities and audiences, then our tendency to gloss over differences and find refuge in a common existential or ontological condition will be checked. I believe, however, that the gift of deconstruction is that it obliges us to resist universalizing gestures, enabling us to open up a space wherein it becomes possible for us to discern the considerable heterogeneity of the social sphere and the formidable role that rhetoric plays in articulating this heterogeneity. Significantly enough, a reading of the rhetorical situation that presumes a text whose meaning is the effect of *différance* and a subject whose identity is produced and reproduced in discursive practices, resituates the rhetorical situation on a trajectory of becoming rather than Being. Finally, then, the deconstruction of the rhetorical situation and its constituent elements has taken us to a point where we are able to rethink rhetoric as radical possibility.

This essay has attempted to provide an answer to the following question: How, if at all, can the insights of deconstruction assist in the explanation and understanding of rhetorical events? Speaking generally now, the appropriation of deconstruction by rhetorical theorists and critics can bring intelligibility to the rhetorical event by enabling them to read rhetoric as a divided sign: as the name for both the unwitting and interested gesture that structures any symbolic action *and* the figurality that puts us on its track. Derridean deconstruction does not merely help rhetorical critics analyze texts; in addition, it promotes a rigorous reevaluation and rebuilding of the concept-metaphor "rhetorical situation" that drives and delimits much contemporary critical practice in this field.

This call for the appropriation of deconstructive insights deserves a final word. My attempt to use deconstructive insights as a means through which the rhetorical situation can be rethought was not meant to suggest that traditional rhetorical theories and critical practices are indefensible or that they should be replaced by Derridean deconstruction. I take deconstructive practice as one possible way to reinvigorate the field, not as the first step towards a renunciation of it. In short, I believe it is possible to open up the field of Rhetoric by using deconstruction not as a transcendental signifier that will lead the way to truth, but as a *bricoleur's* or tinker's tool—a "positive lever"[52]—that produces rather than protects the exorbitant possibilities of rhetoric.

Notes

1. Ernesto Laclau and Chantal Mouffe, *Hegemony and Socialist Strategy: Towards a Radical Democratic Politics*, trans. Winston Moore and Paul Cammack (Great Britain: Thetford, 1985), p. 76.

2. This is precisely the kind of move that traditional theorists and critics have had to make in analyses of the rhetorical situation. For example, see: Lloyd Bitzer, "The Rhetorical Situation," *Philosophy and Rhetoric* 1 (1968): 1–14 (reprinted in this volume); Richard Larson, "Lloyd Bitzer's 'Rhetorical Situation' and the Classification of Discourse," *Philosophy and Rhetoric* 3 (1970): 165–168; K. E. Wilkerson, "On Evaluating Theories of Rhetoric," *Philosophy and Rhetoric* 3 (1970): 82–96; Ralph Pomeroy, "Fitness of Response in Bitzer's Concept of Rhetorical Discourse," *Georgia Speech Communication Journal* 4 (1972): 42–71; Richard Vatz, "The Myth of the Rhetorical Situation," *Philosophy and Rhetoric* 6 (1973): 154–161 (reprinted in this volume); Scott Consigny, "Rhetoric and Its Situations," *Philosophy and Rhetoric* 7 (1974): 175–186; and Alan Brinton, "Situation in the Theory of Rhetoric," *Philosophy and Rhetoric* 14 (1981): 234–248.

3. Political theorists have already begun to appropriate deconstruction for the purposes of social critique. For instance, in their most recent book, *Hegemony and Socialist Strategy: Towards a Radical Democratic Politics*, Ernesto Laclau and Chantal Mouffe consciously struggle to open up a powerful Marxist tradition which they believe no longer helps us to think social struggles in their historical specificity. They point out how from a strict Marxist perspective "diverse subject positions are reduced to manifestations of a single position; the plurality of differences is either reduced or rejected as contingent; the sense of present is revealed through its location in an *a priori* succession of stages" (p. 21). Dissatisfied with the reductionism they see as inherent in orthodox Marxism, Laclau and Mouffe recommend a post-Marxist perspective which takes as its point of departure the indeterminacy of the identity of social agents. Such a view, of course, refuses the suggestion that economically based class relations determine political relations: there "is no necessary or logical relation between social agents and productive relations." While my own discussion is informed by the work of Laclau and Mouffe, it should be noted that they do not deal explicitly with the role of rhetoric in the constitution of hegemonic groups or formations.

4. While it is not possible here to offer a comprehensive list of essays and books addressing the interface between rhetoric and deconstruction, the texts cited below (in addition to the articles cited above) are particularly useful: Jonathan Arac et al., *The Yale Critics: Deconstruction in America* (Minneapolis: University of Minnesota Press, 1984)—this volume includes essays emphasizing the early work of de Man, Hartman, Miller, and Bloom; Bloom et al., *Deconstruction and Criticism* (New York: Seabury Press, 1979)—contributors to this volume include Harold Bloom ("The Breaking of Form"), Paul de Man ("Shelley Disfigured"), Jacques Derrida ("Living On: Border Lines"), Geoffrey H. Hartman ("Words, Wish, Worth: Wordsworth"), and J. Hillis Miller ("The Critic as Host"); Jonathan Culler, *On Deconstruction: Theory and Criticism after Structuralism* (Ithaca, NY: Cornell University Press, 1982); Paul de Man, *Allegories of Reading: Figural Language in Rousseau, Nietzsche, Rilke, and Proust* (New Haven, CT: Yale University Press, 1979), and "The Epistemology of Metaphor," *Critical Inquiry* 5 (1978): 13–30; Denis Donoghue, *Ferocious Alphabets* (Boston: Little, Brown, 1981); Rodolphe Gasche, "Deconstruction as Criticism," *Glyph* 6 (1979): 177–216; Barbara Johnson, *The Critical Difference: Essays in the Contemporary Rhetoric of Reading* (Baltimore: Johns Hopkins University Press, 1980); J. Hillis Miller, "Narrative and History," *ELH* 41 (1974): 455–473; and Richard Rorty, *Philosophy and the Mirror of Nature* (Princeton, NJ: Princeton University Press, 1980).

5. Jacques Derrida, *Glas*, trans. John P. Leavey Jr. and Richard Rand (Lincoln: University of Nebraska Press, 1986).

6. Here I would like to set my own argument in counterdistinction to the approach taken by recent theorists advocating a "rhetoric as epistemic" position who, quite correctly, mark the way in which any discursive gesture is contaminated by the patterns of the perceiving subject. However, I wish to move the argument forward one more step by suggesting that the structure of the binary oppositions that engender "subjectivism" itself can be questioned by grammatological reading. As one deconstructivist put it, "The solution is not merely to say 'I shall not objectify.' It is rather to recognize at once that there is no other language but that of 'objectification' and that any distinction between 'subjectification' and 'objectification' is as provisional as the use of any set of hierarchized oppositions" (Gayatri Chakravorty Spivak, "Translator's Preface," in *Of Grammatology* [Baltimore: Johns Hopkins University Press, 1974], p. lix). As will become evident over the course of this essay, it is imperative that we refuse to take the subject as a "given," as something that interprets. To the contrary, the subject must be thought as process, as becoming.

7. Bitzer, "Rhetorical Situation," pp. 3–4.

8. Ibid., p. 4.

9. Ibid., pp. 5–6.

10. Vatz, "Myth of the Rhetorical," p. 154.

11. Ibid., p. 157.

12. Cited in Vatz, "Myth of the Rhetorical," p. 160.

13. See essays on the rhetorical situation cited in note 2, above.

14. Jonathan Culler, *On Deconstruction*, p. 88.

15. Ferdinand de Saussure, *Course in General Linguistics*, trans. Wade Baskin (New York: Philosophical Library, 1959), p. 120.

16. Jacques Derrida, "Différance," in *Speech and Phenomena and Other Essays on Husserl's Theory of Signs*, trans. David B. Allison (Evanston, IL: Northwestern University Press, 1973), p. 143.

17. Jacques Derrida, "Semiology and Grammatology," in *Positions*, trans. Alan Bass (Chicago: University of Chicago Press, 1981), p. 26.

18. See Jacques Derrida, "Of Grammatology as a Positive Science," in *Of Grammatology*, pp. 74–93.

19. Derrida, "Semiology and Grammatology," p. 27.

20. On pages 131–132 of his essay "Différance," Derrida describes his own texts as an "assemblage." He says, "I insist on the word 'assemblage' here for two reasons: on the one hand, it is not a matter of describing a history, of recounting the steps, text by text, context by context, each time showing which scheme has been able to impose this graphic disorder, although this could have been done as well; rather, we are concerned with *the general system of all these schemata*. On the other hand, the word 'assemblage' seems more apt for suggesting that the kind of bringing-together proposed here has the structure of an interlacing, a weaving, or a web, which would allow the different threads and different lines of sense or force to separate again, as well as being ready to bind others together." In the attempt to mark the same sort of subtle operations, I reiterate Derrida's word choice.

21. Derrida, "Différance," p. 142.

22. Ibid., p. 141.

23. Derrida, "Linguistics and Grammatology," in *Of Grammatology*, p. 63.

24. Ibid., pp. 62–63; emphasis added.

25. Spivak, "Translator's Preface," p. xvii.

26. Gayatri Chakravorty Spivak, "Glas-Piece: A Compte Rendu," *Diacritics* (1977): 26.

27. Ibid., p. 26.

28. Jacques Derrida, "The Double Session," in *Dissemination*, trans. Barbara Johnson (Chicago: University of Chicago Press, 1981), p. 222.

29. Spivak, "Glas-Piece," p. 26.

30. Derrida, *Glas*, p. 5a.

31. Derrida, "Semiology and Grammatology," p. 33.

32. We should, of course, be reminded here that even though *différance* is more "primordial" than the substance or presence of each element in a structure, it can never be present. It also

participates in the radical alterity that makes anything like "identity" possible. See Derrida, "Différance," esp. pp. 140–143.

33. Derrida, "Linguistics and Grammatology," p. 70.

34. Derrida, "Différance," p. 141.

35. Spivak, "Translator's Preface," p. xlix.

36. Ibid., p. xlix.

37. Ibid., p. lxxxiv.

38. Bitzer, "Rhetorical Situation," p. 1.

39. Thomas Benson, "The Senses of Rhetoric: A Topical System for Critics," *Central States Speech Journal* 29 (1978): 249.

40. Bitzer, "Rhetorical Situation," p. 8.

41. Michael Calvin McGee, "In Search of 'the People': A Rhetorical Alternative," *Quarterly Journal of Speech* 61 (1975): 238 (reprinted in this volume).

42. Bitzer, "Rhetorical Situation," p. 6.

43. Cited in Culler, *On Deconstruction*, p. 95.

44. See Jacques Derrida, "Freud and the Scene of Writing," in *Writing and Difference*, trans. Alan Bass (Chicago: University of Chicago Press, 1978), pp. 196–231.

45. Jacques Derrida, "Structure, Sign, and Play in the Discourse of the Human Sciences," in *Writing and Difference*, pp. 278-279.

46. Perry Anderson, *In the Tracks of Historical Materialism* (Chicago: University of Chicago Press, 1983), p. 54.

47. Derrida, "Semiology and Grammatology," p. 28.

48. Ibid., p. 28–29.

49. Jacques Derrida, "The Voice that Keeps Silent," in *Speech and Phenomena*, pp. 84–85n.

50. Derrida, "Semiology and Grammatology," p. 29.

51. Culler, *On Deconstruction*, p. 162.

52. As Spivak puts it in her "Preface" to *The Grammatology*, "The *bricoleur* makes do with things that were meant perhaps for other ends" (p. xix).

PART 4

Rhetoric, Reason, and Public Morality

Rhetoric's primary domain has generally been the field of the "contingent" and the "probable"—those social and civic places where reasoned judgments and policies are desirable, but where there is no necessary or certain knowledge from which to draw in making such decisions. Generally we think of the law courts and legislative assemblies as two of the primary sites of the rhetorical, for in each instance those who make decisions (Is the accused guilty or innocent? Is the proposed policy or legislation expedient or inexpedient?) must do so on the basis of inferences and probabilities rather than on rock-solid knowledge of an immutable truth. After all, how can one truly "know" that a crime was committed if one was not there to witness it oneself? Or how can one truly "know" if going to war in a particular situation represents the "public good"? Yet such judgments must be made, and in many instances they must be made in ways that draw upon and implicate the moral bearings and considerations of the public or community being enacted and/or addressed. Should we legalize abortion? Does affirmative action best facilitate our commitment of "equality for all"? Ought we to close down a local "adult" video store in the interests of prevailing community standards concerning pornography? Or should be keep it open in the interest of freedom of speech and expression? And so on. Instead of being presented as a rigid logic or form of scientific demonstration, then, rhetoric has typically been cast as an art of practical reason that functions to negotiate the course of communal belief and action where disagreement and chaos would otherwise reign.

The role of rhetoric as practical reason in public decision making, or what is currently being called "deliberative democracy," has long been complicated by a number of factors, including most prominently the nature of its particular form and its force in effecting public morality. Some argue, as does G. Thomas Goodnight in "The Personal, Technical, and Public Sphere of Argumentation: A Speculative Inquiry into the Art of Public Deliberation," that the quality of public deliberation has atrophied as arguments drawn from the private and technical spheres, which operate through very different forms of invention and subject matter selection, have invaded, and perhaps even appropriated, the public sphere. The effect has been to undermine and impoverish the quality of deliberation as a means of determining social knowledge and the public good. In the conclusion to his essay Goodnight offers an impassioned appeal to refashion our sense of deliberative argument by examining the forums and modes of argument in public controversies.

Perhaps one of the most elaborate responses to the role of rhetoric in public moral decision making in recent times has been the attempt to rethink the very form of public argument as narrative. In "Narrative as a Human Communication Paradigm" Walter R. Fisher urges us to reconceptualize human communication, and by extension public moral argument, as the function of a "narrative paradigm." According to Fisher, humans are storytelling animals, and therefore the "reason" of public moral deliberation or argumentation is better understood (and perhaps more fulsomely enacted) in and through the narratives one tells, rather than through the more-or-less rigid logics prescribed by the "rational world paradigm" of the eighteenth-century Enlightenment.

Thomas S. Frentz extends Fisher's argument in "Rhetorical Conversation, Time, and Moral Action" by suggesting that the significance of such narratives is that they provide coherence and moral unity for human life. According to Frentz, however, the problem that rhetoric faces in addressing contemporary moral conundrums is that our narratives lack coherence and moral unity, a result of twentieth-century emotivism (a version of radical relativism) and the (im)perfection of liberal individualism, which together have undermined any true sense of moral community. Without such moral community there can be no solid foundations upon which to argue toward or make impersonal moral decisions. Frentz thus urges us to think of public moral argument as a "rhetorical conversation" in which interlocutors connect their moral present with their collective past and potential future as a means of recovering and animating a more spiritual or universalizing *telos*.

An alternate approach to the problem of public moral decision making is contained in Celeste Michelle Condit's "Crafting Virtue: The Rhetorical Construction of Public Morality." According to Condit, models of public moral action that reduce public decision making to "narratives" and "conversations" reify the rhetorical process in terms of private discourse forms that ignore and undermine the ways in which collectivities actually constitute a sense of public morality. So, for example, she argues that in conversations (a privileged form of private interaction) all is lost if one of the interlocutors fails to understand the meaning of the other; in the public forum, however, advocates don't have to understand or even persuade one another so much as they have to achieve a consensus of opinion and judgment among a larger public audience. Rhetoric, she maintains, is best understood as a "craft" that draws upon and manages prevailing public vocabularies—which include ideographs, common *topoi*, cultural myths and metaphors, narratives, and the like—as they embody and enable the collective sense of public moral good. That embodiment, which bears the mark of the community's history and experience, establishes a kind of localized objectivity that produces what others have called a "rhetorical culture." And it is in that rhetorical culture, according to Condit, that one finds the capacity to "live the moment, through the legacies of the past, with just an eye to the fact that we are crafting the future as well."

The essays here represent only some of the most recent and provocative efforts to understand the relationship(s) between rhetoric, reason, and public morality. However one evaluates the particular choices made by these scholars, it should be clear that the problem of constituting an effective deliberative democracy for the twenty-first century, particularly in an increasingly multicultural society, will require sustained attention to the range of ways in which rhetoric constitutes and is implicated in the process of public decision making.

Additional Readings

Burgess, Parke. (1970). "The Rhetoric of Moral Conflict: Two Critical Dimensions." *Quarterly Journal of Speech* 56: 120–130.

Ehninger, Douglas. (1970). "Argument as Method: Its Nature, Its Limitations, and Its Uses." *Communication Monographs* 37: 101–110.

Farrell, Thomas B., and G. Thomas Goodnight. (1981). "Accidental Rhetoric: The Root Metaphors of Three Mile Island." *Communication Monographs* 48: 271–300.

Goodnight, Thomas G., and Kathryn Olsen. (1994). "Entanglements of Consumption, Cruelty, Privacy, and Fashon: The Social Controversy over Fur." *Quarterly Journal of Speech* 80: 249–276.

Jonsen, Albert R., and Stephen Toulmin. (1988). *The Abuse of Casuistry: A History of Moral Reasoning*. Berkeley and Los Angeles: University of California Press.

Klumpp, James F., and Thomas A. Hollihan. (1989). "Rhetorical Criticism as Moral Action." *Quarterly Journal of Speech* 1: 84–96.

McGee, Michael Calvin. (1984). "Secular Humanism: A Radical Reading of 'Culture Industry' Production." *Critical Studies in Mass Communication* 1: 1–33.

Sloop, John M. & James P. McDaniel, eds. *Judgement Calls: Rhetoric, Politic and Indeterminacy*. Boulder, CO: Westview Press, 1998.

Wander, Phillip. (1983). "The Ideological Turn in Modern Criticism." *Central States Speech Journal* 34: 1–18.

The Personal, Technical, and Public Spheres of Argument

A Speculative Inquiry into the Art of Public Deliberation

G. THOMAS GOODNIGHT

Deliberative arguments in the public sphere necessarily pertain to the domain of probable knowledge—that kind of knowledge which, although uncertain, is more reliable than untested opinion or guesswork.[1] Public deliberation is inevitably probable because the future is invariably more and less than expected. The full worth of a policy is always yet to be seen. Argumentation offers a momentary pause in the flow of events, an opportunity to look down the present road as well as paths untaken. As deliberation raises expectations that are feared or hoped for, public argument is a way to share in the construction of the future.

To debate the public good or public policy presupposes that arguers and audiences have a sense of before and after, of that which leads to debate and that which may extend beyond it. To encounter controversy over the course of future events is always to raise the question, where will our deliberations lead? If public argument can yield no more than a probable answer to questions of preferable conduct, it can offer no less than an alternative to decisions based on authority or blind chance.

My purpose here is to consider the status of deliberative rhetoric. My guiding assumptions are that rhetoric is an art, a human enterprise engaging individual choice and common activity, and that deliberative rhetoric is a form of argumentation through which citizens test and create social knowledge in order to uncover, assess, and resolve shared problems.[2] As any art may fall into periods of disuse and decline, so it is possible for the deliberative arts to atrophy. Barring anarchic conditions, though, when one way of fashioning a future is foregone, another takes its place. Distinguishing deliberative argument from the social practices which have replaced it is difficult. Many forms of social persuasion are festooned with the trappings of deliberation, even while they are designed to succeed by means inimical to knowledgeable choice and active participation. The increasing variety of forums, formats, styles, and institutional practices—each claiming to embody the public will or to represent the public voice—demands careful attention. If such practices continue to evolve uncritiqued, deliberative argument may become a lost art.

I hope to elaborate this claim by proving three propositions. First, argumentative endeavors characteristically involve, *inter alia*, the creative resolution and the resolute creation of uncertainty. Second, particular arguments emerge in concert with or in opposition to ongoing activity in the personal, technical, and public spheres. Third, argument practices arising from the personal and technical spheres presently substitute the semblance of deliberative discourse for actual deliberation, thereby diminishing public life. Each claim involves a progressively greater degree of speculation. Hopefully, by attending to the creative enterprises of argument, and by examining the inherent tensions among the variety of alternative groundings, the present status of deliberative rhetoric can be uncovered and critiqued.

UNCERTAINTY AND THE GROUNDING OF DISAGREEMENT

Whatever else characterizes an argument, to be recognizable as such, a statement, a work of art, even an inchoate feeling must partake in the creative resolution and the resolute creation of uncertainty. Some say the argumentative impulse, the quest to advance or dispense with the "incomprehensible, illogical and uncertain," arises from the human capacity for symbolization. Language itself imparts an ought which is forever broken and formed anew.[3] Others maintain that this impulse arises from a primitive feeling of dread, an unquenchable desire for completeness.[4] Of the ultimate source of uncertainty, I am not sure; but, my sentiments are in line with de Gourmont: "All activity has uncertainty for its principle."[5]

To say that all argument arises in uncertainty is not to say that all arguments are immediately controversial. O'Keefe performed a valuable service in directing attention toward ordinary encounters in life where words are exchanged instead of blows, and in pointing out that while these disputes are different from "products" produced in less personal contexts, they are nonetheless significant varieties of argument.[6] But I contend that even self-evident reasoning, the highest form of argument by some standards, while not immediately inviting clash, is argumentative as well. To the medieval world, for example, the stars were luminescenses, intelligences placed in the heavens by God. That they represented the eternal in the world was made self-evident by the fact that they neither disappeared nor varied from their orbits. When a super nova appeared in 1572, as Lewis reports, what had been self-evident became the focus of controversy which ultimately contributed to the collapse of a world view.[7] Not all disconfirmations of the "obviously true" are so dramatic. Nor do all occur in this way. But since arguments involve more than simple sensory perception, being made with some ingenuity, even those propositions which seem to be well instantiated within a cultural perspective persist only against a background of uncertainty.

The recognition that some human endeavors are commonly joined by uncertainty does not lead to any particular theory of argumentation. Indeed, such a recognition is a bit subversive of the traditional task of theorists who, since the breakdown of the Medieval Synthesis, have labored mightily to construct methods, procedures, explanations, and even whole philosophies of argument. Scholars, seeking to establish that argument itself is grounded in particular theories of logic, psychology, sociology, or linguistics (or some combination), have sought to discover some underlying capacity of human existence which governs and gives meaning to the process of argument making. The work continues apace. Uncertainty persists. Until such a time when all the creative enterprises are reduced to a single underlying certainty, it may be useful to add to the repertoire of study the investigation of the manifold ways in which individuals and communities attempt to create and reduce the unknown. The study of why uncertainties appear, what they mean, how they are banished only to be reformed, and what practices shape the course of future events is important, for knowledge of argument's varieties may illuminate the values, character, and blindspots of an era, society, or person.

Members of "societies" and "historical cultures" participate in vast, and not altogether coherent, superstructures which invite them to channel doubts through prevailing discourse practices. In the democratic tradition, we can categorize these channels as the personal, the technical, and the public spheres. "Sphere" denotes branches of activity—the grounds upon which arguments are built and the authorities to which arguers appeal. Differences among the three spheres are plausibly illustrated if we consider the differences between the standards for arguments among friends versus those for judgments of academic arguments versus those for judging political disputes. Permitting a breadth between personal, professional, and public life is characteristically American. The independence of the spheres is protected by a variety of laws protecting privacy and discouraging government intervention in private affairs.

The standards for deciding which events fit into which spheres are sometimes ambiguous and shifting. Burke's notion of identification, however, lends precision to our thinking about this.[8] One form is invoked when a person tries to show "consubstantiality" with another. Another form is invoked through partisan appeals—partisanship being a characteristic of the public. The third form is invoked through a person's identification with his work in a special occupation—the essential ingredient of technical argument. These alternative modes of identification make the personal, technical, and public groundings of arguments possible.

The term "sphere" is not altogether a felicitous one because of its eighteenth- and nineteenth-century connotations of discrete, unchanging arenas where the virtuous play out life according to prevailing custom. One use of spheres as a grounding for rhetorical argument was to justify discrimination against females. Some anti-suffrage speakers justified discrimination on the basis that God had suited women to rule the home and men the professions. Their arguments were grounded in what appeared to be a natural order.[9] Yet from the changing activities of personal and public life, it should be evident that the spheres of argument are not entirely constant over time, and are subject to revision by argument.

Though it may seem historically inevitable that all groundings of argument change as lifestyles are reconfigured, as methods for discovering knowledge become modified, and as the institutions of governance change. But to reduce the spheres of argument themselves to ephemeral contexts or mere points of view is mistaken because all arguers face a similar problem in dealing with uncertainty.[10] An arguer can accept the sanctioned, widely used bundle of rules, claims, procedures, and evidence to wage a dispute. Or the arguer can inveigh against any or all of these "customs" in order to bring forth a new variety of understanding. In the first case, the common grounds for arguing are accepted, and argument is used to establish knowledge about a previously undetermined phenomenon. In the second, argument is employed as a way of reshaping its own grounds. In classical logic this choice was expressed in the contrast between inductive and deductive logic. In the variety of argument endeavors, this tension is expressed by attempts to expand one sphere of argument at the expense of another.

DISTINCTIONS AMONG THE SPHERES OF ARGUMENT, AND AN EXPLANATIONOF HOW THE GROUNDINGS OF ARGUMENT CHANGE

Scholars seek a single explanation of the varieties of argumentative endeavors. Earlier in this century, an attempt was made to ground argument in restricted notions of reasons; variations on the basic forms were imperfections awaiting correction.[11] Contemporary theorists, recognizing that not all arguing is comprised of rigorous adherence to stipulated forms, have turned to psychology and sociology to provide explanatory principles in describing the variety of processes. Cognitive psychologists maintain, roughly speaking, that individuals must make sense of the world through whatever apparatus they can employ; thus, since all argument must be conceived and perceived by individuals, the study of mental processes is preeminent.[12] In contrast, other theorists maintain that humans develop through language into an universe of symbols which shapes and is shaped by intersubjective forms of understanding; hence, since individuals can only be known through social expressions, the study of language is preeminent.[13] Others split the difference by developing theories of interaction among individuals and society.[14] These arguments about arguments are useful in extending our concepts about what any particular disagreement may *mean*. But, if the study of argument *per se* is unhinged from particular epistemological commitments, then the creative tension among alternative groundings of disagreement can be uncovered. From a critic's perspective, argument may be approached as a way of coming to understand the transformations of human activity through the variety of practices employed in making argument.

Studying the current practices of the personal, technical, and public spheres is a useful way to uncover prevailing expressions of the human conditions (the views of the world implicit in particular practices of making argument), and perhaps to discover avenues for criticism. A relatively complete investigation of these practices is the subject of a much longer treatise. However, I would like to present an illustration to demonstrate some of the divergent aspects of practice.

Begin with an example made classic by Willard, strangers arguing in a bar at the airport.[15] This is a relatively private affair. Unless an ethnomethodologist is present, it probably will not be preserved. The statements of the arguers are ephemeral. Since no preparation is required, the subject matter and range of claims are decided by the disputants. Evidence is discovered within memory or adduced by pointing to whatever is at hand. The rules emerge from the strangers' general experience at discussion, fair judgment, strategic guile, and so forth. The time limits imposed on the dispute probably have no intrinsic significance to the disagreement. The plane will take off. An interlocutor will leave. Others may join in and continue the discussion. Those formerly involved in the dispute may replay the disagreement, embroidering it in the retelling. But the chance encounter is at an end.

Suppose that the conversation is preserved, however, and that the arguments are abstracted from their original grounding to serve as examples in supporting claims about a theory of argument. Consider Professor Willard's own arguments about the argument. In his transformation of assertions, grimaces, glances, and self-reports from the original dispute into examples which illustrate observations about the nature of argument, the concrete particularity of the original dispute is lost. But what is to be gained is the advance of a special kind of understanding among members of a professional community of which Willard is a part, the community of argumentation scholars. In creating his statement, Willard narrows the range of subject matter to that of the interests of the requisite community. He brings together a considerable degree of expertise with the formal expectations of scholarly argument (footnotes, titles, organization, documentation, and so forth). The technical arguments are judged by referees as worthy of preservation. Once the research is published, the community addressed may join into the dispute. Of course, Willard and his critics may engage in *ad hominem* attacks, vestigial products of the private sphere, but what engages the community—and continues to do so long after the disputants turn to other battles— is the advance of a special kind of knowledge.

Now if the illustration can be extended just one more step, suppose that the disagreement within the technical field grows so vehement that there arises two groups in unalterable opposition: Willard followers and Willard opponents. Then neither informal disagreement nor theoretical contention is sufficient to contain the arguments involved. The dispute becomes a matter of public debate. Both groups may take to the public forums governing the technical community's business, each contesting for leadership and control of scarce resources. If one side or the other is dissatisfied with the verdict, then the boundaries of the special community are in jeopardy, as disgruntled advocates appeal to a more general public. Willard may be taken to court and tried by his peers, or he may attempt to have legislation passed that would outlaw what he and his followers believe to be harmful teachings. Once the public sphere is entered, the private and technical dimensions of the disagreement become relevant only insofar as they are made congruent with the practices of public forums.

If a public forum is appropriately designed as a sphere of argument to handle disagreements transcending private and technical disputes, then the demands for proof and the forms of reasoning will not be as informal or fluid as those expressed in a personal disagreement. Yet, since the public must encompass its sub-sets, the forms of reason would be more common than the specialized demands of a particular professional community. Moreover, whereas the public forum inevitably limits participation to representative spokespersons (unlike a chance discussion), an appropriately designed public forum would provide a tradition of argument such that its speakers would employ common language, values, and reasoning so that the disagreement could be settled to the satisfaction of all concerned. Most characteristically, though, the interests of the public realm—whether represented in an appropriate way or not—extend the stakes of argument beyond private needs and the needs of special communities to the interests of the entire community.

The illustration need not be pursued further. The major point to be made is that the ways of making arguments are various. The notions of private, technical, and public spheres are useful in describing the manners in which disagreements can be created and extended in making argument. Some disagreements are created in such a way as to require only the most informal demands for evidence, proof sequences, claim establishment, and language use. These may typify arguments in the personal sphere where the subject matter and consequences of the dispute are up to the participants involved. Other disagreements are created in such a way as to narrow the range of permissible subject matter while requiring more specialized forms of reasoning. These typify the technical sphere where more limited rules of evidence, presentation, and judgment are stipulated in order to identify arguers of the field and facilitate the pursuit of their interests. Transcending the personal and technical spheres is the public, a domain which, while not reducible to the argument practice of any group of social customs or professional communities, nevertheless may be influenced by them. But the public realm is discrete insofar as it provides forums with customs, traditions, and requirements for arguers in the recognition that the consequences of dispute extend beyond the personal and technical spheres.

The preceding illustration is intended to be a starting point in examining the differences among argumentative practices. It is not intended to be the foundation of a taxonomical scheme which approaches the study of argumentation by the classification of statements, situations, and customs within established contexts. In the world of arguers, any particular argumentative artifact *can be taken* to be grounded in any one of the spheres or a combinatory relationship. But the question confronting those who would create ways of raising uncertainty or settling it (and this includes argumentation theorists and critics as well) is the direction in which the dispute is to be developed.

Some critics of argument attempt to provide the links between one sphere and another. Thus, neo-Aristotelian scholars attempted to explain the relation between the private life of orators and their public successes.[16] Others, perhaps musing over the creative possibilities of providing a "perspective by incongruity," rip arguments from generally accepted grounding by idiosyncratically extending the argument by analogy. Hauser and his colleagues, for example, attempted to construe Nixon's Cambodia address as comparable to a potlatch ceremony, a ritual practiced among certain tribes of North American Indians.[17] These informed criticisms *reflect* the ongoing attempts of arguers themselves to reform the grounding of disagreement.

To demonstrate how grounds of argument may be altered, I would like to draw upon several historical examples. In each case, what had been accorded as an appropriate way of arguing for a given sphere was shifted to a new grounding; different kinds of disagreement were created. The first example shows how matters of private dispute can take on a public character. The second demonstrates how matters of public judgment can become subjected to the technical domain. The final illustration involves the cooptation of the technical by the public.

In nineteenth-century America, the poor were generally considered to be poor because of personal character flaws. As explained by adherents of the Gospel of Wealth, poverty was a sign of God's disfavor. The poor were poor because they were lazy, spendthrift, or simply engaged in pursuits that did not deserve reward. Arguments made to the poor and about the poor were grounded in the private sphere; poverty was essentially an issue between a man and his Maker.[18] Thus harder work, more saving, and greater self-reliance were encouraged so that all could share in a prosperous abundance provided by God. Help was cajoled from the rich only as a gesture of Christian charity. With the advent of the Progressive movement, however, the grounding of arguments about poverty gradually shifted from the private to the public sphere. Converting the doctrines of Darwin and his social proponents to a recognition that the environment shaped people and the environment could be altered, Progressives gradually transformed the issue of poverty to a public concern, one that was a shared rather than an individual responsibility.[19] Even though attempts to return the issue of poverty to the private sphere sometimes arose, the Progressives were successful in placing the issue on the public docket.

The public question of the treatment of the "environment" offers another example of the transformation of argument grounding. Extending from the early part of the twentieth century were various public movements to protect the heritage of all Americans from the pursuit of private interests by preserving part of pristine America. The vanishing wilderness was the common concern of artists, preachers, naturalists, indeed any citizens who wished to see nature's works preserved.[20] While these movements were successful in restricting some exploitative practices and protecting some of the wilderness, it was not until the public environmentalist movement of the 1970s that the grounds of appeal became more restricted. Rachel Carson's *Silent Spring*, a work combining lyric style and limited scientific fact, projected a future world where the growing poisonous by-products of industry permeated the cellular structure of all living individuals.[21] So strong was the public concern that a relatively new technical community blossomed, ecologists. Yet, with the competing demands for energy, a private interest made public in terms of job loss, the ecologists could not take the environmental protection principle to its ultimate extent. Rather, state-of-the art practice becomes a tentative balancing between projections of competing demands of energy and ecology. These complicated equations are the only answer to a public movement that finds itself making opposing demands.[22]

The realm of public argument can give rise to the ascendancy of technological fields, but public interest may also circumscribe the practice of technical argument. Certainly one of the most outrageous "perspectives by incongruity" of all times was the forlorn attempt by Nazi partisans to create by act of national will a purely German science. Less obviously, national governments influence the conduct of argument communities by providing resources for equipment, training, and information transmittal. These inducements made in the "public" interest may influence the selection of subjects, techniques, and results that are made by theoretically apolitical communities of inquirers. The degree to which present defense efforts induce scientists away from other possible avenues of research is well-known. What the configuration of technical argument communities might be if they were not so subordinated to the limits placed by the public interest is an open question.

In each example, the transformation of grounding is evident. Poverty could be the matter of private disagreement so long as the issue was not grounded in questions of public interest and responsibility. The environment was a public issue; but as the implications of public interest demanded trade-offs that could be made only by technical judgments, ecology was given over largely to the technical sphere. Finally, whereas scientists at least in theory should be able to create communities of inquirers without regard to the demands of the public, public leaders nevertheless provide parameters for scientific argument. Although these examples illustrate how some disputes become transformed, it can be demonstrated that some theories of argument attempt to create an organizing perspective where a single sphere grounds all argument practice.

One example of an attempt to harness the varieties of reason under the aegis of a single sphere is that of Toulmin in *Human Understanding*.[23] In this work, it may be recalled, Toulmin seeks to explain the evolutionary development of fields. In the grand synthesis, the most highly developed forms of reason are mirrored in, but not perfectly reproduced by, developing other disciplines. At the crown sits physics. The court is made up of "compact disciplines"; the hinterlands are ruled by the "diffuse disciplines"; the colonies, by "would-be disciplines"; and political and ethical argument are found only in the wilds of the "undisciplinable." The advance of reason is equated with single-mindedness of purpose. Society supports these communities of reasoners, presumably because it benefits from the technological applications of discoveries. Such a hierarchical explanation of the uses of reason, I submit, is a technical view *par excellence*.[24] The rules and procedures of the forums guarantee critique; individual allegiances and commitments make little difference in the long run, and the relationship of the disciplines to the public is guaranteed to be felicitous.

If Toulmin's notion of fields is to be accepted as the governing method by which arguments are to be recognized, constructed, and evaluated, then what becomes of the personal and public spheres of argument? One of the contributions of Willard's critique of Toulmin is that he points out the personal dimensions to any argument which cannot be accounted for within a strict technical view.[25] It may be added that it is uncertain whether the personal inclinations, stubbornness, and curiosity of men and women attracted to scientific endeavors influence the ways in which problems come to be known and accepted as resolved as much as the independent methods to which they ascribe. The relation between Toulmin's view of argument and the public sphere is also open to question. Is it the case that a scientist's work is without intrinsic political significance? Opponents of eugenics and proponents of creationism would certainly not agree with the claim that scientific communities are propelled only by a curiosity more intense than lay folk. Is it the case that public reasoning itself can be improved by specialization and compactness? This question will receive more detailed analysis in the latter portion of the essay. For now, though, it is important to note that a theory of argument that would ground reason giving in the technical sphere is in opposition to requirements of personal and public life.

THE STATUS OF DELIBERATIVE ARGUMENT

What sphere of argument seems to be prevalent at this time? This is an important question because changes in the grounds of reason cannot be viewed as unequivocal advances. Susanne Langer reminds us that "each new advance is bought with the life of an older certainty."[26] My belief is that the public sphere is being steadily eroded by the elevation of the personal and technical groundings of argument. The decline is not entirely a new phenomenon because it is rooted in the dilemmas of twentieth-century American life.

Writing in the late 1920s, Charles Beard, a great Progressive historian, saw that America had changed. Whereas his country in the eighteenth century was characterized by "congeries of provincial societies," modern technology introduced greater specialization, interdependence, and complexity. These changing conditions challenged the loose-knit governmental structure of an earlier era. Psychology did offer new opportunities to serve the common good, especially through public health programs, but it also carried with it new problems. He observed, "Technology brings new perils in its train: falling aircraft, the pollution of streams, and dangerous explosives. It makes possible new forms of law violation: safe blowing, machine-gun banditry, wiretapping, and submarine smuggling."[27] Beyond the capacity of government to deal with new social responsibilities, the historian noted an even more fundamental issue.

Beard believed that the nature of government was being inexorably transformed to "an economic and technical business on a large scale." As "the operations of public administration become increasingly technical in nature," the governors turn increasingly to specialized knowledge provided by "chemistry, physics, and higher mathematics."[28] What startled Beard were the implications of this transformation for democratic self- government. If it is the case that specialization is necessary to make knowledgeable decisions, then what value is the participation of common citizens? Entertaining the notion that the United States might best be ruled by a technically trained elite, he concluded that even though such a group might be better acquainted with a range of facts, "it would be more likely to fall to pieces from violent differences than to attain permanent unity through a reciprocal exchange of decisions." His reason: "[T]ranscending the peculiar questions of each specialty are the interrelations of all the specialties; and the kind of knowledge or intelligence necessary to deal with these interrelations is not guaranteed by proficiency in any one sphere."[29]

Since Beard's time, the bill of particulars has changed. Presently, concerns that trouble the administration of government include unanticipated missile launchings, ozone depletion, and atomic power incidents. New technology makes possible plutonium theft, computer crime, and airplane hijacking. But the essential issue persists. Certainly technical knowledge has burgeoned over the past fifty years, but it is not certain that the general knowledge which Beard thought necessary to govern a Republic has become any more refined.

The reasons for this doubt are many. Even as politicians have come to rely upon pollsters and mass-communication strategists to formulate sophisticated rhetorics, audiences seem to disappear into socially fragmented groups. Denial of the public sphere is accompanied by celebration of personal lifestyle, producing what one critic has called the "me generation,"[30] and another, "the culture of narcissism."[31] As arguments grounded in personal experience (disclosed by averaging opinion) seem to have greatest currency, political speakers present not options but personalities, perpetuating government policy by substituting debate for an aura of false intimacy. Thus is privatism celebrated and the discourse continued.

Meanwhile, issues of significant public consequence, what should present live possibilities for argumentation and public choice, disappear into the government technocracy or private hands. As forms of decisionmaking proliferate, questions of public significance themselves become increasingly difficult to recognize, much less address, because of the intricate rules, procedures, and terminologies of the specialized forums. These complications of argument hardly invite the public to share actively the knowledge necessary for wise and timely decisions. Given the increasing tendency of political rhetoricians to produce strings of "ideographs," untrammeled by warrants or inferences, and given the tendency of government to proceed by relying upon the dictates of instrumental reason, the realm of public knowledge, identified by Dewey and later addressed by Bitzer, may be disappearing.[32]

Of course, what once constituted public argument is not entirely gone. Some of its semblance remains.[33] The mass media continue to present the drama of politics, but some vital elements of a deliberative rhetoric are carefully excised. At this juncture, I would like to reconstruct a series of "news reports," aired on some major networks during the spring and summer of 1981. Actually, the stories were not "news" at all, but projected happenings should the Reagan forces find success in making budget reductions. Each "spot" was presented on a day when the Reagan adherents had made some headway in passing their version of reform.

Typically, a female reporter comes on camera saying that she is in some small town in the hinterlands of the United States. An issue is identified, usually the reduction of funds for domestic policy or the termination of a federal program. Residents are interviewed. Some are led to say that, yes, there is no fraud or corruption, and the money has been well spent by hard-working souls. When asked what could be done if the funds were to be terminated, to a person, the interviewees responded with a rueful grin, "I just don't know. There is nowhere else to go." Since my political sentiments are somewhat in line with the implied argument of the narrative, I first mistook the reports for a reinvigorated form of public critique. But, on one evening just after the Reagan administration had won a particularly key vote in the Congressional budget battles, an especially gripping narrative was broadcast.

The media found a woman's prison in Florida, where, in what appeared to be something like a summer cottage, female prisoners were incarcerated but allowed to stay with their newly born offspring. As the camera zooms in, the reporter says that a movement is afoot in the Florida legislature to shut down the program which would permit mother and child to remain together. The scene abruptly shifts to two wizened legislators, speaking in deep southern accents. One says in effect, "We need to save the taxpayer every dime we can." The other rejoins: "These women deserve to be punished." Back to the cottage. The female reporter asks the mother/inmate with babe in arms: "What will you do if they pass the cut?" The woman becomes terrified, and clutching the child, tearfully cries: "I don't know. He is all I have. Don't let them take my baby away."

The story was so startling that I began to wonder what could be done for this person, but upon reflection I found that there was not enough information to even begin acting. Later, as I came to think about the entire series of stories as arguments, I discovered that while the reports superficially appeared to be a form of political propaganda—which although one-sided, invites public participation at least through influencing attitudes—actually, they were a different species altogether. The reports always presented the individual as a victim of social forces. Decision-making bodies, apparently bereft of human emotion and lacking common sense, were to make decisions based upon inscrutable principles. Like viewing the winds of a rising hurricane, the signs of power politics were to be seen as a kind of natural disaster, sweeping up the deserving and undeserving alike. The reports were crafted in such a way that no intelligent assessment could be made concerning the issues involved. One had no idea of the reasons for the cuts, the credibility of the sources, the representativeness of the examples, etc. But even beyond these characteristic inadequacies, the stories simply did not invite action. These were reports of human tragedies in the making, and, like witnessing other calamities of fate, the participation invited was that of watching the drama play out.

The paradox of expanding communication technology and the decline of the public sphere is not unique to our own time. Dewey puzzled over the simultaneous appearance of new devices (the telephone, motion picture, and radio) and the disappearance of the public.[34] Another communication revolution is taking place, with the advance of improvements in broadcasting techniques, satellite transmission, and computer processing. Instead of expanding public forums, these devices seem to be geared to producing either refined information or compelling fantasy. That the media could be employed to extend knowledgeable public argument but do not suggests the decline of deliberative practice. Mass communications by and large seem to be committed to technical modes of invention. These artfully capture the drama of public debate even while systematically stripping public argument of consequences beyond the captured attention given to the media itself. And the media's own patterns of argument create a view of life where the trivial and mundane eternally interchange with the tragic and spectacular by the hour. What could be a way of sharing in the creation of a future is supplanted by a perpetual swirl of exciting stimuli. Thus is deliberation replaced by consumption.

While Beard did not project a comfortable solution to the problems of meshing technical and public argument, he did formulate a significant challenge:

> [G]overnment carries into our technological age a cultural heritage from the ancient agricultural order and yet finds its environment and functions revolutionized by science and machinery. It must now command expertness in all fields of technology and at the same time its work calls for a super-competence able to deal with the interrelations of the various departments. It must also reflect the hopes and energies, the dreams and consummation, of the human intelligence in its most enormous movements. Constantly it faces large questions of choice which cannot be solved by the scientific method alone—questions involving intuitive insight, ethical judgment, and valuation as of old. Science and machinery do not displace cultural considerations. They complicate these aspects of life; they set new conditions for social evolution but they do not make an absolute break in history as destiny and opportunity. The problem before us, therefore, is that of combining the noblest philosophy with the most efficient use of all instrumentalities of the modern age—a challenge to human powers on a higher level of creative purpose. Its long contemplation lights up great ranges of sympathies and ideas, giving many deeds that appear commonplace a strange and significant evaluation.[35]

Beard's summary of the dilemmas of *The Republic in the Machine Age* points to a critical enterprise for argumentation theorists. If the public sphere is to be revitalized, then those practices which replace deliberative rhetoric by substituting alternative modes of invention and restricting subject matter need to be uncovered and critiqued. In pointing out alternatives to present practice, the theorist of argument could contribute significantly to the perfection of public forms and forums of argument. If this task is undertaken, then deliberative argument may no longer be a lost art.

Notes

1. For a discussion of the relation between knowledge, rhetoric, and the public, see Lloyd F. Bitzer, "Rhetoric and Public Knowledge," in Don M. Burks, ed., *Rhetoric and Philosophy and Literature: An Exploration* (West Lafayette, IN: 1978), pp. 57–58. My own assumptions are that the public argument is a viable mode of arguing to the extent that (1) the future is not seen as completely determined; (2) discourse is viewed as capable of presenting and evaluating alternatives for acting or restraining action; (3) individual judgment and action are relevant to the options at hand; (4) the process adheres to freedom of inquiry and expression, with the longer term goal of establishing a true consensus; and (5) a community of common interests can be discovered and articulated through discourse. See G. Thomas Goodnight, "The Liberal and the Conservative Presumptions: On Political Philosophy and the Foundations of Public Argument," in Jack Rhodes and Sara Newell, eds., *Proceedings of the [First] Summer Conference on Argumentation* (Annandale, VA: Speech Communication Association, 1980), p. 308.

2. Thomas Farrell, "Knowledge, Consensus, and Rhetorical Theory," *Quarterly Journal of Speech* 62 (1976): 1–14 (reprinted in this volume). This essay maintains Farrell's distinctions between social and technical knowledge. Although Carleton's observation that the lines between social and technical knowledge are sometimes ambiguous is correct, the reply is nonresponsive to a basic problematic uncovered by Farrell. The arguer must rely either upon an actual consensus such as that which characterizes a technical field with exact specifications for argument or the arguer must project consensus from his or her own personal experience or estimation of the social milieu. See Carlton, "What Is Rhetorical Knowledge? A Response to Farrell—and More," *Quarterly Journal of Speech* 64 (1968): 313–328. That some aspects of social knowledge become

subjected to technical transformation and that the implications of some fields must be resolved by social knowledge indicates merely that arguers are able to reshape the grounds upon which arguments occur.

3. Charles W. Kneupper, "Paradigms and Problems: Alternative Constructivist/Interactionist Implications for Argumentation Theory," *Journal of the American Forensic Association* 15 (1979): 223.

4. Charles A. Willard, "On the Utility of Descriptive Diagrams for the Analysis and Criticism of Arguments," *Communication Monographs* 43 (1976): 316; Charles A. Willard, "A Reformulation of the Concept of Argument: The Constructivist/Interactionist Foundations of a Sociology of Argument," *Journal of the American Forensic Association* 14 (1978): 126.

5. Remy de Gourmont, *Remy de Gourmont: Selections from All His Works*, ed. Richard Aldington (New York: Covici-Friede, 1929), p. 472.

6. Daniel J. O'Keefe, "Two Concepts of Argument," *Journal of the American Forensic Association* 11 (1978): 121–128.

7. C. S. Lewis, *The Discarded Image: An Introduction to Medieval and Renaissance Literature* (Cambridge: Cambridge University Press, 1974), pp. 92–198.

8. Kenneth Burke, *The Rhetoric of Motives* (New York: Prentice-Hall, 1952), pp. 20–29. Burke establishes three major modes of identification: consubstantiality, "in being identified with B, A is 'substantially one' with a person other than himself"; partisanship, "the ways in which individuals are at odds with one another, or become identified with groups more or less at odds with one another"; and "autonomous" identification [quotation marks Burke's], "the autonomous activity's place in this wider context [a larger unit of action in which a specialized activity takes place], a place where the agent may be unconcerned." Although these modes of identification aid us to understand the groundings of each argument sphere, arguers typically import one kind of argument to serve another's function. Thus, the politician can appeal to consubstantiality in order to masque partisan interests. A partisan movement can grow by having its participants uncover consubstantial interests, as the consciousness raising techniques of the woman's liberation movement were used to increase awareness of a shared identity. Moreover, disputes over what kinds of activities are autonomous occur as responsibility and authority are contested.

9. Joseph Emerson Brown, "Against the Woman's Suffrage Amendment," in Ernest J. Wrage and Barnet Baskerville, eds., *American Forum: Speeches on Historic Issues, 1788–1900* (Seattle: University of Washington Press, 1960), pp. 333–342.

10. It may be tempting to replace the concept of argument spheres with a more popular term like "social context." Most arguments are social productions. Those that are preserved and seem recurrent enough to be labeled as providing a custom or role may be subjected to sociological mapping. See, e.g., Bruce E. Gronbeck, "Sociocultural Notions of Argument Fields: A Primer," in George Ziegelmueller and Jack Rhodes, eds., *Dimensions of Argument: Proceedings of the Second Summer Conference on Argumentation* (Annandale, VA: Speech Communication Association, 1981), pp. 1–21. Such mappings may be useful to arguers, who sometimes must project social expectations in order to frame a useful statement. But to view social characterizations as determinative is but to reify the perspectives of a sociologist who may see argument as independent of any particular arguer. So long as one can speak ironically, cross-up and recross expectations, and transvalue social norms, social context—no matter how delicately construed or thoroughly proscribed—cannot be said to be determinative.

11. William Kneale and Martha Kneale, *The Development of Logic* (Oxford: Oxford University Press, 1962), pp. 628–651.

12. See, e.g., Dale Hample, "A Cognitive View of Argument," *Journal of the American Forensic Association* 16 (1980): 151–159.

13. Ray E. McKerrow, "Argumentation Communities: A Quest for Distinctions," in *Proceedings of the [First] Summer Conference on Argumentation*, pp. 214–228; Brant R. Burleson, "On the Analysis and Criticism of Arguments: Some Theoretical and Methodological Considerations," *Journal of the American Forensic Association* 15 (1979): 137–148.

14. For an attempt to bridge the gap, see Earl Croasmun and Richard A. Cherwitz, "Beyond

Rhetorical Relativism," *Quarterly Journal of Speech* 68 (1982): 1–16. In the view of these authors, "reality" somehow "impinges" on individuals thereby supplying the prerequisite veridicality to guide the arguer's judgment. While the extramental universe need not be denied as a phenomena which sometimes thwarts the best-laid theories of arguers, it is difficult to rid arguers of dialectical maneuvers which not only alter the grounds upon which world views are constructed but also present problems that cannot be resolved in a purely positivistic manner.

15. Charles Arthur Willard, "Some Speculations About Evidence," in *Proceedings of the [First] Summer Conference on Argumentation*, pp. 267–268.

16. The changing trends of rhetorical criticism mark the different ways in which the relation between or among spheres of argument can be viewed. Neo-Aristotelian critics often attempted to explain public success by exploring the private training, talents, and inclinations of the orator. Symbolic interactionist criticism often focuses on the public significance of private symbol systems, as movement studies demonstrate how the public sphere is reformed through opposition. Fantasy theme analysis charts the personal responses to public statement through its attempt to uncover social dramas.

17. Richard B. Gregg and Gerard A. Hauser, "Richard Nixon's April 30, 1970, Address on Cambodia: The 'Ceremony' of Confrontation," *Communication Monographs* 40 (1973): 167–181. By taking Nixon's address away from its most obvious grounding, namely, the tradition of presidential war rhetoric, the rhetorical critics performed the critical function through poetic extension. In this manner, the grounds of argument are extended to the point that the speech itself is made to seem arbitrary. But why compare Nixon's address to a potlatch ceremony? Why not a potato harvest, a pair of cufflinks, or any other random item? Any critic, through analogical extension, can ignore the processes through which the argument is made by a person or institution and supplant his or her private identification. Unless something is made known about the relation between argument and practical grounds, or at least live alternatives, a criticism of an argument may tell us more about the critic than the argument.

18. See, e.g., Moses Rischin, ed., *The American Gospel of Success* (Chicago: Quadrangle Books, 1968), pp. 3–91.

19. Richard Hofstadter, *The Age of Reform: From Bryan to F.D.R.* (New York: Vintage Books, 1955), pp. 174–214.

20. Roderick Nash, *Wilderness and the American Mind* (New Haven, CT: Yale University Press, 1967), pp. 141–160.

21. Rachel Carson, *Silent Spring* (Boston: Houghton Mifflin, 1962).

22. Thomas B. Farrell and G. Thomas Goodnight, "Accidental Rhetoric: The Root Metaphors of Three Mile Island," *Communication Monographs* 48 (1981): 271–300.

23. Stephen Toulmin, *Human Understanding: The Collective Use and Evolution of Concepts* (Princeton, NJ: Princeton University Press, 1972), pp. 364–411. There is a variety of views extending and supplementing Toulmin's. See Ray E. McKerrow, "On Fields and Rational Enterprises: A Reply to Willard," in *Proceedings of the [First] Summer Conference on Argumentation*, pp. 401–413; Charles Arthur Willard, "Argument Fields and Theories of Logical Types," *Journal of the American Forensic Association* 17 (1981): 129–145; see also essays in this issue. Whether fields are differentiated by subject matter, logical type, language use, sociological character, or purpose is a matter of some disagreement. Perhaps one of the major characteristics of a field is the effort to define the boundaries of a specialized community of argument users. Given the tendency of those involved in rational enterprises to see the world through their specialty (Burke's notion of "occupation psychosis"), it would be surprising if a single notion of field could be acceptable.

24. The rubric of argument fields, in my estimation, is not a satisfactory umbrella for covering the grounding of all arguments. If it is claimed that anytime an arguer takes a perspective there is a field, then one term has been merely substituted for another. Alternatively, to claim that all arguments are grounded in fields, enterprises characterized by some degree of specialization and compactness, contravenes an essential distinction among groundings. Personal argument is created in a durational time dimension, as Willard and Farrell have pointed out. Points at issue can be dropped, appear again years later, be returned to, or entirely forgotten.

From an external perspective, the private dispute may seem to be serendipitous, even while the interlocutors pursue the matter in its own time. The establishment of a field more or less objectifies time insofar as common procedures, schedules, measurements, and argument/decision/action sequences are set up by common agreement. Herein the personal dimension may seem to be not strictly relevant or even counterproductive, except in special cases. A time of public debate may lead to the enactment of a future which increases or decreases individual and/or field autonomy as an outcome of what are figured to be pressing exigencies. Within a democracy at least, public time is not reducible to the rhythms of any individual (unlike a pure dictatorship) or the objectifications of technicians (unlike a purely positivistic state).

25. Charles A. Willard, "On the Utility of Descriptive Diagrams," pp. 308–312.

26. Susanne Langer, *Philosophy in a New Key: A Study in the Symbolism of Reason, Rite, and Art* (Cambridge, MA: Harvard University Press, 1978), p. 294.

27. Charles A. Beard and William Beard, *The American Leviathan: The Republic in the Machine Age* (New York: Macmillan, 1930), p. 7.

28. Ibid., pp. 3–19.

29. Ibid. pp. 10–16.

30. Richard Sennett, *The Fall of Public Man: On the Social Psychology of Capitalism* (New York: Knopf, 1978), pp. 313–338.

31. Christopher Lasch, *The Culture of Narcissism: American Life in an Age of Diminishing Expectations* (New York: Norton, 1978), pp. 31–70.

32. John Dewey, *The Public and Its Problems* (Chicago: Swallow Press, 1927).

33. Although all rhetoric uses language, and although all language may be viewed as "incipient action" as it excites attitudes, distinctions should be made between those forms of discourse designed to keep us watching, while the symbols continue to dance, and those forms which invite the knowledgeable conjoining of motion and action to construct a future. If distinctions are not drawn between the aesthetic and deliberative uses of argument, then the public sphere may be coopted by default, given over to those who control the means of producing elaborate symbolic events. How can untimely, irrelevant and even fatuous "public communication" be critiqued, if all rhetoric is fantasy?

34. Dewey, *The Public and Its Problems*.

35. Beard and Beard, *American Leviathan*.

Narration as a Human Communication Paradigm

The Case of Public Moral Argument

WALTER R. FISHER

> The corrective of the scientific rationalization would seem necessarily to be a *rationale of art*—not, however, a performer's art, not a specialist's art for some to produce and many to observe, but an art in its widest aspects, an *art of living*.
>
> *Kenneth Burke*

When I wrote "Toward a Logic of Good Reasons" (Fisher, 1978), I was unaware that I was moving toward an alternative paradigm for human communication. Indications of it are to be found in the assumption that "*Humans as rhetorical beings are as much valuing as they are reasoning animals*" (p. 376) and in the conception of good reasons as "*those elements that provide warrants for accepting or adhering to the advice fostered by any form of communication that can be considered rhetorical*" (p. 378). While the assumption does not seriously disturb the view of rhetoric as practical reasoning, the conception implies a stance that goes beyond this theory. The logic of good reasons maintains that reasoning need not be bound to argumentative prose or be expressed in clear-cut inferential or implicative structures: Reasoning may be discovered in all sorts of symbolic action—nondiscursive as well as discursive.

That this is the case was demonstrated in an exploration of argument in *Death of a Salesman* and *The Great Gatsby* (Fisher and Filloy, 1982). The authors concluded that these works provide good reasons to distrust the materialist myth of the American Dream (Fisher, 1973, p. 161), for what it requires to live by it and for what it does not necessarily deliver even if one lives by it "successfully." This finding confirms Gerald

Graff's thesis that a theory or practice of literature that denies reference to the world, that denies that literature has cognitive as well as aesthetic significance, is a *Literature Against Itself* (Graff, 1979). In other words, "some dramatic and literary works do, in fact, argue" (Fisher and Filloy, 1982, p. 343).

The paradigm I was moving toward did not become entirely clear until I examined the current nuclear controversy, where the traditional view of rationality did not serve well, and I read Alasdair MacIntyre's *After Virtue: A Study in Moral Theory* (1981). What impressed me most about the book was the observation that "man is in his actions and practice, as well as in his fictions, essentially a story-telling animal" (p. 201). Given this view, "enacted dramatic narrative" (p. 200) is the "basic and essential genre for the characterization of human actions" (p. 194). These ideas are the foundation of the paradigm I am proposing—the narrative paradigm. Thus, when I use the term "narration," I do not mean a fictive composition whose propositions may be true or false and have no necessary relationship to the message of that composition. By "narration," I refer to a theory of symbolic actions—words and/or deeds—that have sequence and meaning for those who live, create, or interpret them. The narrative perspective, therefore, has relevance to real as well as fictive worlds, to stories of living and to stories of the imagination.

The narrative paradigm, then, can be considered a dialectical synthesis of two traditional strands in the history of rhetoric: the argumentative, persuasive theme and the literary, aesthetic theme. As will be seen, the narrative paradigm insists that human communication should be viewed as historical as well as situational, as stories competing with other stories constituted by good reasons, as being rational when they satisfy the demands of narrative probability and narrative fidelity, and as inevitably moral inducements. The narrative paradigm challenges the notions that human communication—if it is to be considered rhetorical—must be an argumentative form, that reason is to be attributed only to discourse marked by clearly identifiable modes of inference and/or implication, and that the norms for evaluation of rhetorical communication must be rational standards taken essentially from informal or formal logic. The narrative paradigm does not deny reason and rationality; it reconstitutes them, making them amenable to all forms of human communication.

Before going further, I should clarify the sense in which I use the term "paradigm." By paradigm, I refer to a representation designed to formalize the structure of a component of experience and to direct understanding and inquiry into the nature and functions of that experience—in this instance, the experience of human communication. Masterman designates this form of paradigm "metaphysical" or as a "meta-paradigm"(1970, p. 65; see also Kuhn, 1974). Since the narrative paradigm does not entail a particular method of investigation, I have not used a designation that might be suggested: "narratism." The narrative perspective, however, does have a critical connection with "dramatism," which will be discussed later.

Consistent with Wayne Brockriede's concept of perspectivism (1982), I shall not maintain that the narrative paradigm is the only legitimate, useful way to appreciate human communication or that it will necessarily supplant the traditional rational paradigm of human decision-making and action. As already indicated, I will propose the narrative paradigm as an alternative view. I do not even claim that it is entirely "new." W. Lance Bennett has published a book with Martha S. Feldman, *Reconstructing Reality in the Courtroom* (1981), and two essays that directly bear on the present enterprise, one concerning political communication (Bennett, 1975) and one on legal communication (Bennett, 1978; see also Farrell, 1983; Gallie, 1964; Hawes, 1978; Mink, 1978; Schrag, 1984; Scott, 1978; and Simons, 1978). Except for these studies, I know of no other attempt to suggest narration as a paradigm. There is, of course, a tradition in rhetorical theory and pedagogy that focuses on narration as an element in discourse and as a genre in and of itself (e.g., Ochs and Burritt, 1973). In addition, there is an increasing number of investigations involving storytelling (e.g., Kirkwood, 1983). Here again, narration is conceived as a mode, not a paradigm, of communication.

The context for what is to follow would not be complete without recognition of the work done by theologians and those interested in religious discourse. The most recent works in this tradition include Goldberg (1982) and Hauerwas (1981). It is worth pausing with these studies, as they foreshadow several of the themes to be developed later. Goldberg claims that:

> a theologian, regardless of the propositional statements he or she may have to make about a community's convictions, must consciously strive to keep those statements in intimate contact with the narratives which give rise to those convictions, within which they gain their sense and meaning, and *from which they have been abstracted.* (p. 35)

The same can be said for those who would understand ordinary experience. The ground for determining meaning, validity, reason, rationality, and truth must be a narrative context: history, culture, biography, and character. Goldberg also argues:

> Neither "the facts" nor our "experience" come to us in discrete and disconnected packets which simply await the appropriate moral principle to be applied. Rather, they stand in need of some narrative which can bind the facts of our experience together into a coherent pattern and it is thus in virtue of that narrative that our abstracted rules, principles, and notions gain their full intelligibility. (p. 242)

Again, the statement is relevant to more than the moral life; it is germane to social and political life as well. He observes, as I would, that "what counts as meeting the various conditions of justification will vary from story to story" (p. 246). I will suggest a foundation for such justifications in the discussion of narrative rationality.

With some modifications, I would endorse two of Hauerwas' (1981) ten theses. First, he claims that "the social significance of the Gospel requires recognition of the narrative structure of Christian convictions for the life of the church" (p. 9). I would say: The meaning and significance of life in all of its social dimensions require the recognition of its narrative structure. Second, Hauerwas asserts that "every social ethic involves a narrative, whether it is conceived with the formulation of basic principles of social organization and/or concrete alternatives" (p. 9; see also Alter, 1981; and Scult, 1983). The only change that I would make here is to delete the word "social." Any ethic, whether social, political, legal or otherwise, involves narrative.

Finally, mention should be made of the work on narration by such scholars as Derrida (1980), Kermode (1980), and Ricocur (1980). Especially relevant to this project are essays by White (1980; see also White, 1978), Turner (1980), and Danto (1982; see also Nelson, 1980; Todorov, 1977).

PURPOSE

If I can establish that narration deserves to be accepted as a paradigm, it will vie with the reigning paradigm, which I will refer to as the rational world paradigm. In truth, however, the narrative paradigm, like other paradigms in the human sciences, does not so much deny what has gone before as it subsumes it.

The rational world paradigm will be seen as one way to tell the story of how persons reason together in certain settings. For now, it is enough that the narrative paradigm be contemplated as worthy of coexisting with the rational world paradigm.

I shall begin by characterizing and contrasting the two paradigms. I shall then examine the controversy over nuclear warfare, a public moral argument, noting particular problems with the rational world paradigm and indicating how the narrative paradigm provides a way of possibly resolving them. Following this discussion, I shall reconsider the narrative paradigm and conclude with several implications for further inquiry. Needless to say, this essay does not constitute a finished statement. It offers a conceptual frame which, I am fully aware, requires much greater development for it to be considered compelling. At this point, as I have suggested, it is sufficient that it receive serious attention. From such attention, a fuller, more persuasive statement should emerge.

THE RATIONAL WORLD PARADIGM

This paradigm is very familiar, having been in existence since Aristotle's *Organon* became foundational to Western thought. Regardless of its historic forms, the rational world paradigm presupposes that: (1) humans are essentially rational beings; (2) the paradigmatic mode of human decision-making and communication is argument— clear-cut inferential (implicative) structures; (3) the conduct of argument is ruled by the dictates of situations—legal, scientific, legislative, public, and so on; (4) rationality is determined by subject matter knowledge, argumentative ability, and skill in employing the rules of advocacy in given fields; and (5) the world is a set of logical puzzles which can be resolved through appropriate analysis and application of reason conceived as an argumentative construct. In short, argument as product and process is *the* means of being human, the agency of all that humans can know and realize in achieving their *telos*. The philosophical ground of the rational world paradigm is epistemology. Its linguistic materials are self-evident propositions, demonstrations, and proofs, the verbal expressions of certain and probable knowing.

The actualization of the rational world paradigm, it should be noted, depends on a form of society that permits, if not requires, participation of qualified persons in public decision-making. It further demands a citizenry that shares a common language, general adherence to the values of the state, information relevant to the questions that confront the community to be arbitrated by argument, and an understanding of argumentative issues and the various forms of reasoning and their appropriate assessment. In other words, there must exist something that can be called public or social knowledge and there must be a "public" for argument to be the kind of force envisioned for it (Bitzer, 1978; Farrell, 1976). Because the rational world paradigm has these requirements and because *being rational* (being competent in argument) *must be learned*, an historic mission of education in the West has been to generate a consciousness of national community and to instruct citizens in at least the rudiments of logic and rhetoric (Hollis, 1977, pp. 165–166; Toulmin, 1970, p. 4).

Needless to say, the rational world paradigm, which is by and large a heritage of the classical period, has not been untouched by "modernism." The impact of modernism has been recounted and reacted to by many writers (Barrett, 1979; Booth, 1974;

Gadamer, 1981, 1982; Lonergan, 1958; MacIntyre, 1981; Rorty, 1979; Schrag, 1980; Sennett, 1978; Toulmin, 1972, 1982; Voegelin, 1952, 1975). The line of thought that has done most to subvert the rational world paradigm is, along with existentialism, naturalism. One of its schools starts with physics and mathematics and makes the logical structure of scientific knowledge fundamental; the other school, involving biology, psychology, and the social sciences, adapts this structure and conception of knowledge to the human sciences. According to John Herman Randall Jr.:

> The major practical issue still left between the two types of naturalism concerns the treatment of values. The philosophies starting from physics tend to exclude questions of value from the field of science and the scope of scientific method. They either leave them to traditional non-scientific treatment, handing them over, with Russell, to the poet and mystic; or else with the logical empiricists they dismiss the whole matter as "meaningless," maintaining with Ayer, that any judgment of value is an expression of mere personal feeling. The philosophies of human experience—all the heirs of Hegel, from dialectical materialism to Dewey—subject them to the same scientific methods of criticism and testing as other beliefs; and thus offer the hope of using all we have learned of scientific procedure to erect at last a science of values comparable to the science that was the glory of Greek thought. (1976, p. 651)

It is clear: With the first type of naturalism, there can be neither public or social knowledge nor rational public or social argument, for both are permeated by values. As Habermas notes, "The relationship of theory to practice can now only assert itself as the purposive rational application of techniques assured by empirical science" (1967, p. 254; Heiddegger, 1972, pp. 58–59).

With the second type of naturalism, one can hope with Randall that it produces the work he sees possible in it. But the fact is that no science of values has appeared or seems likely to do so; further, Dewey (1927) himself noted the eclipse of the "public" and doubted its reemergence. His hope was the development of "communities." Interestingly, fifty-five years later, MacIntyre concludes *After Virtue* with the observation: "What matters at this state is the construction of local forms of community within which civility and the intellectual and moral life can be sustained" (1981, p. 245).

The effects of naturalism have been to restrict the rational world paradigm to specialized studies and to relegate everyday argument to an irrational exercise. The reaction to this state of affairs has been an historic effort to recover the rational world paradigm for human decision-making and communication by: (1) reconstituting the conception of knowledge (e.g., Bitzer, 1978; Farrell, 1976; Habermas, 1973; Lyric, 1982; McGee and Martin, 1983; Polanyi, 1958; Ziman, 1968); (2) reconceptualizing the public—in terms of rational enterprises, fields, and/or communities (e.g., McKerrow, 1980a, 1980b; Toulmin, 1958, 1972; Toulmin, Rieke, and Janik, 1979; Willard, 1982; see also the first nineteen essays in Ziegelmueller and Rhodes, 1981); (3) formulating a logic appropriate for practical reasoning (e.g., Fisher, 1978; Perelman and Olbrechts-Tyteca, 1969; Toulmin, 1958; Wenzel, 1977); and (4) reconceiving the conceptions of validity, reason, and rationality (e.g., Apel, 1979; Ehninger, 1968; Farrell, 1977; Fisher, 1980; Gottlieb, 1968; Johnstone, 1978; McKerrow, 1977, 1982). Many of the studies cited here intimate, if not specifically state, proposals for reconstructing the concept of argument itself. Writers explicitly working on this task include Brockriede (1975, 1977), Burleson (1981), Jacobs and Jackson (1981), McKerrow (1981), O'Keefe (1977, 1982), Wenzel (1980), and Willard (1978).

The motive underlying these various studies, and the movement of which they are an energizing force, is, as I have suggested, to repair the rational world paradigm so that it once again will serve everyday argument. One may well applaud the motive and the movement and yet ask two questions: (1) Has the reformation been successful? (2) Is there a more beneficial way to conceive and to articulate the structures of everyday argument? It is too early to answer the first question with finality but one cannot deny that much useful work has been done, especially in establishing at least the semblance of rationality for fields of argument. I shall maintain, however, that similar progress has not been made in the arena where argument is most general and is most obviously concerned with values, public moral argument, as the examination of the nuclear controversy will show later.

This failure suggests to me that the problem in restoring rationality to everyday argument may be the assumption that the reaffirmation of the rational world paradigm is the only solution. The position I am taking that another paradigm, the narrative paradigm, may offer a better solution, one that will provide substance not only for public moral argument, but also all other forms of argument, for human communication in general. My answer to the second question, then, is: "Yes, I think so." Adoption of the narrative paradigm, I hasten to repeat, does not mean rejection of all the good work that has been done; it means a rethinking of it and investigating new moves that can be made to enrich our understanding of communicative interaction. Representative of the good work that has already been done on public argument are essays by Cox (1981), Goodnight (1980), Hynes, Jr. (1980), Lucaites (1981), Pryor (1981), Sillars and Ganer (1982), and Zarefsky (1981).

THE NARRATIVE PARADIGM

Many different root metaphors have been put forth to represent the essential nature of human beings: *homo faber, homo economous, homo politicos, homo sociologicus,* "psychological man," "ecclesiastical man," *homo sapiens,* and, of course, "rational man." I now propose *homo narrans* to be added to the list.

Preliminary to an attempt to delineate the presuppositions that structure the narrative paradigm, I should indicate how the *homo narrans* metaphor relates to those that have preceded it. First, each of the root metaphors may be held to be the master metaphor, thereby standing as the ground, while the others are manifest as figures. In the terminology of the narrative perspective, the master metaphor sets the plot of human experience and the others the subplots. When any of the other metaphors are asserted as the master metaphor, narration is as it is considered now: a type of human interaction-activity, an art, a genre, or mode of expression.

Second, when narration is taken as the master metaphor, it subsumes the others. The other metaphors are then considered conceptions that inform various ways of *recounting or accounting for* human choice and action. Recounting takes the forms of history, biography, or autobiography. Accounting for takes the forms of theoretical explanation or argument. Recounting and accounting for can be also expressed in poetic forms: drama, poetry, novel, and so on. Recounting and accounting for are, in addition, the bases for all advisory discourse. Regardless of the form they may assume, recounting and accounting for are stories we tell ourselves and each other to establish a meaningful life-world. The character of narrator(s), the conflicts, the resolutions, and the style will vary, but each mode of recounting and accounting for is but a way of relating a "truth" about the human condition.

Third, the *homo narrans* metaphor is an incorporation and extension of Burke's definition of "man" as the "symbol-using (symbol-making, symbol-misusing) animal" (Burke, 1968, p. 16; Cassirer, 1944, p. 26; see also Langer, 1953, pp. 264ff.). The idea of human beings as storytellers indicates the general form of all symbol composition; it holds that symbols are created and communicated ultimately as stories meant to give order to human experience and to induce others to dwell in them to establish ways of living in common, in communities in which there is sanction for the story that constitutes one's life. And one's life is, as suggested by Burke, a story that participates in the stories of those who have lived, who live now, and who will live in the future. He asks: "Where does the drama get its materials?" I would modify the question to read: "Where do our narratives get their materials?" And I would accept his answer:

> From the "unending conversation" that is going on in history when we are born. Imagine that you enter a parlor. You come late. When you arrive, others have long preceded you, and they are engaged in a heated discussion, a discussion too heated for them to pause and tell you exactly what it is about. In fact, the discussion had already begun long before any of them got there, so that no one present is qualified to retrace for you all the steps that had gone before. You listen for awhile, until you decide that you have caught the tenor of the argument; then you put in your oar. Someone answers; you answer him; another comes to your defense; another aligns himself against you, to either the embarrassment or gratification of your opponent, depending upon the quality of your ally's assistance. However, the discussion is interminable. The hour grows late, you must depart. And you do depart, with the discussion still vigorously in process. (Burke, 1957, pp. 94–97; for a discussion of the nature of conversation as narration, see MacIntyre, 1981; Campbell and Stewart, 1981)

As Heidegger observes, "We are a conversation . . . conversation and its unity support our existence" (Heidegger, 1949, p. 278; Gadamer, 1982, pp. 330ff.; Rorty, 1979, pp. 315ff.).

To clarify further the narrative paradigm, I should specify how it is related to Bormann's (1972) concepts of "fantasy themes" and "rhetorical visions," and to the Frentz and Farrell (1976) language action paradigm. Fantasy, Bormann holds, is a technical term, meaning "the creative and imaginative interpretation of events that fulfills a psychological or rhetorical need" (1983, p. 434). Fantasy themes arise "in group interaction out of a recollection of something that happened to the group in the past or a dream of what a group might do in the *future*" (1972, p. 397). When woven together, they become composite dramas, which Bormann calls "rhetorical visions" (1972, p. 398). From the narrative view, each of these concepts translates into dramatic stories constituting the fabric of social reality for those who compose them. They are, thus, "rhetorical fictions," constructions of fact and faith having persuasive force, rather than fantasies (Fisher, 1980b). Nevertheless, without getting into the problem of how group-generated stories become public stories, I would note that Bormann (1973) and others have demonstrated that "rhetorical visions" do exist (e.g., Bantz, 1975; Kidd, 1975; Rarick, Duncan, Lee, and Porter, 1977.) I take this demonstration as partial evidence for the validity of the narrative paradigm. (For further empirical evidence, see Bennett, 1978; Campbell, 1984.)

With minor adaptation, I find no incompatibility between the narrative paradigm and the language action paradigm. Indeed, language action is meaningful only in terms of narrative form (Ricoeur, 1976). What Frentz and Farrell (1976) designate as "form of life" and "encounters"—implicit matters of knowledge, aesthetic expectations, institutional constraints, and propriety rules—can be considered the forces that determine the structure of narratives in given interpersonal environments. What they call an "episode," a "rule-conforming sequence of symbolic acts generated by two or more actors who are collectively oriented toward emergent goals," can be thought of as the process by which one or more authors generate a short story or chapter—deciding on plot, the nature of characters, resolutions, and their meaning and import for them and others (p. 336).

I do not want to leave the impression that the narrative paradigm merely accommodates the constructs of Bormann, Frentz and Farrell. Their work enriches the narrative paradigm. I shall rely specifically on the language action paradigm in what follows.

The presuppositions that structure the narrative paradigm are: (1) humans are essentially storytellers; (2) the paradigmatic mode of human decision-making and communication is "good reasons" which vary in form among communication situations, genres, and media; (3) the production and practice of good reasons is ruled by matters of history, biography, culture, and character along with the kinds of forces identified in the Frentz and Farrell language act; (4) rationality is determined by the nature of persons as narrative beings—their inherent awareness of *narrative probability*, what constitutes a coherent story, and their constant habit of testing *narrative fidelity*, whether the stories they experience ring true with the stories they know to be true in their lives (narrative probability and narrative fidelity, it will be noted, are analogous to the concepts of dramatic probability and verisimilitude; as MacIntyre (1981, p. 200) observes, "The difference between imaginary characters and real ones is not in the narrative form of what they do; it is in the degree of their authorship of that form and of their own deeds"); and (5) the world is a set of stories which must be chosen among to live the good life in a process of continual recreation. In short, good reasons are the stuff of stories, the means by which humans realize their nature as reasoning-valuing animals. The philosophical ground of the narrative paradigm is ontology. The materials of the narrative paradigm are symbols, signs of consubstantiation, and good reasons, the communicative expressions of social reality.

The actualization of the narrative paradigm does not require a given form of society. Where the rational world paradigm is an ever-present part of our consciousness because we have been educated into it, the narrative impulse is part of our very being because we acquire narrativity in the natural process of socialization (Goody and Watt, 1962–1963; Krashen, 1982). That narrative, whether written or oral, is a feature of human nature and that it crosses time and culture is attested by historian White: "Far from being one code among many that a culture may utilize for endowing experience with meaning, narrative is a metacode, a human universal on the basis of which trans-cultural messages about the shared reality can be transmitted . . . the absence of narrative capacity or a refusal of narrative indicates an absence or refusal of meaning itself" (1980, p. 6); by anthropologist Turner: "If we regard narrative ethically, as the supreme instrument for building 'values' and 'goals,' in Dilthey's sense of these terms, which motivate human conduct into situational structures of 'meaning,' then we must concede it to be a universal cultural activity, embedded in the very center of the social drama, itself another cross-cultural and transtemporal unit in social process" (1980, p. 167); and by linguist-folklorist Dell Hymes: "The narrative use of language is not a property of subordinate cultures, whether folk, or working class, or the like, but a universal function" (1980, p. 132; see also Barthes, 1977; Ong, 1982).

Gregory Bateson goes so far as to claim that "if I am at all fundamentally right in what I am saving, then *thinking in terms of stories* must be shared by all mind or minds, whether ours or those of redwood forests and sea anemones" (1979, p. 14). And Burke observes that "We assume a time when our primal ancestors became able to go from SENSATIONS to WORDS. (When they could duplicate the experience of tasting an orange by saying 'the taste of an orange,' that was WHEN STORY CAME INTO THE WORLD)" (1983, p. 1).

In theme, if not in every detail, narrative, then, is meaningful for persons in particular and in general, across communities as well as cultures, across time and place. Narratives enable us to understand the actions of others "because we all live out narratives in our lives and because we understand our own lives in terms of narratives" (MacIntyre, 1981, p. 197).

Rationality from this perspective involves, as I have proposed, the principles of narrative probability and narrative fidelity. These principles contrast with but do not contradict the constituents of rationality I have outlined earlier (Fisher, 1978, 1980). They are, in fact, subsumed by the narrative paradigm. The earlier notion was attuned to the rational world paradigm and essentially held that rationality was a matter of argumentative competence: knowledge of issues, modes of reasoning, appropriate tests, and rules of advocacy in given fields. As such, rationality was something to be learned, depended on deliberation, and required a high degree of self-consciousness. Narrative rationality does not make these demands. It is a capacity we all share. It depends on our minds being as Booth (1974, pp. 114–137) represents them in *Modem Dogma and the Rhetoric of Assent*, a key point of which is: "Not only do human beings successfully infer other beings' states of mind from symbolic clues; we know that they characteristically, in all societies, build each other's minds. This is obvious knowledge—all the more genuine for being obvious" (p. 114). The operative principle of narrative rationality is identification rather than deliberation (Burke, 1955, pp. 20–46).

Narrative rationality differs from traditional rationality in another significant way. Narrative rationality is not an account of the "laws of thought" and it is not normative in the sense that one must reason according to prescribed rules of calculation or inference making. Traditional rationality posits the way people think when they reason truly or with certainty. MacIntyre notes, "To call an argument fallacious is always at once to describe and to evaluate it" (1978, p. 258). It is, therefore, a normative construct. Narrative rationality is, on the other hand, descriptive, as it offers an account, an understanding, of any instance of human choice and action, including science (Gadamer, 1982; Heidegger, 1972; Holton, 1973; Ramsey, 1969). At the same time, it is a basis for critique, because it implies a *praxis*, an ideal democratic society (McGee, Scult, and Kientz, 1983). Traditional rationality implies some sort of hierarchial system, a community in which some persons are qualified to judge and to lead and some other persons are to follow.

For the sake of clarity, I should note that, while the narrative paradigm provides a radical democratic ground for social-political critique, it does not deny the legitimacy (the inevitability) of hierarchy. History records no community, uncivilized or civilized, without key story-makers/story-tellers, whether sanctioned by God, a "gift," heritage, power, intelligence, or election. It insists, however, that the "people" do judge the stories that are told for and about them and that they have a rational capacity to make such judgments. It holds, along with Aristotle (1954, bk. 1, ch. 1, 1355ª 20) that the "people" have a natural tendency to prefer the true and the just. Neither does the narrative paradigm deny that the "people" can be wrong. But, then, so can elites, especially when a decision is social or political. And neither does the theory deny the existence and desirability of genius in individuals or the "people" to formulate and to adopt new stories that better account for their lives or the mystery of life itself. The sort of hierarchy condemned by the narrative *praxis* is the sort that is marked by the will to power, the kind of system in which elites struggle to dominate and to use the people for their own ends or that makes the people blind subjects of technology.

Narrative rationality, then, is inimical to elitist politics, whether fascist, communist, or even democratic—if traditional rationality is the prevailing societal view. And this seems to be the case with American democracy, as subsequent examination of the nuclear controversy will show. The prevalent position is that voters are rational if they know enough about public issues; are cognizant of argumentative procedures, forms, and functions; and weigh carefully all the arguments they hear and read in a systematic, deliberative process. Contrary to this notion is that of V. O. Key Jr. In a classic study of presidential voting between 1936 and 1960, he concluded that "voters are not fools," which is what they must be considered if measured by traditional rationality. His data led him to conclude that the American electorate is not "straitjacketed by social determinants or moved by subconscious urges triggered by devilishly skillful propagandists." They are moved by their perceptions and appraisals of "central and relevant questions of public policy, of governmental performance, and of executive personality" (1966, pp. 7–8). These perceptions and appraisals of political discourse and action become stories, narratives that must stand the tests of probability and fidelity. And these stories are no less valuable than the stories constructed by persons who are rational in the traditional way. There is no evidence to support the claim that "experts" know better than anyone else who should be elected president.

Obviously, as I will note later, some stories are better than others, more coherent, more "true" to the way people and the world are—in fact and in value. In other words, some stores are better in satisfying the criteria of the logic of good reasons, which is attentive to reason and values. Persons may even choose not to participate in the making of public narrative if they feel that they are meaningless spectators rather than co-authors. But, all persons have the capacity to be rational in the narrative paradigm. And, by and large, persons are that—at least in the fashioning of their daily lives. Persons do not have the capacity to be equally rational in the rational world paradigm. Because persons have the capacity of narrative rationality, it is reasonable to have juries of lay persons and popular elections, as Bennett (1978; Bennett and Feldman, 1981) has well demonstrated. I want to stress, however, that narrative rationality does not negate traditional rationality. It holds that traditional rationality is only relevant in specialized fields and even in those arenas narrative rationality is meaningful and useful.

Certain other features of the narrative paradigm should be noted before moving to the case of public moral argument. First, the paradigm is a ground for resolving the dualisms of modernism: fact-value, intellect-imagination, reason-emotion, and so on. Stories are the enactment of the whole mind in concert with itself. Second, narratives are moral constructs. As White asserts: "Where, in any account of reality, narrativity is present, we can be sure that morality or a moral impulse is present too" (1980, p. 26; Benjamin, 1969). Third, the narrative paradigm is consonant with the notion of reason proposed by Schrag: "Reason, as the performance of vision and insight, commemoration and foresight, occasions the recognition of a process of meaning-formation that gathers within it the logic of technical reason and the *logos* of myth" (1980, p. 126). The appropriateness and validity of this view of reason for the narrative paradigm is supported by Angel Medina (1979). In a statement that reiterates several of the points I have made, he writes:

It is necessary to define our reason primarily as biographical, that is, above all narrative and then symbolic. Human reason is narrative because it extends from its inception and in every one of its acts toward the foreshadowing of its total course. It is symbolic in that the major aim in the formation of this totality is its own self-presentation within the dialogue of consciousness. The meaning of my whole life is communicative; it emerges, as such, for the benefit of another consciousness when I attempt to present myself totally to it. Reciprocally, the meaning of another life becomes a totality only when received fully within my life. (p. 30)

And, fourth, as I will attempt to show, the narrative paradigm offers ways of resolving the problems of public moral argument.

THE CASE: PUBLIC MORAL ARGUMENT

It should be apparent by now that I think that MacIntyre's (1981) *After Virtue* is a remarkable work. Equally remarkable, in its own way, is Jonathan Schell's (1982) *The Fate of the Earth*. Schell's book is exemplary of contemporary moral argument intended to persuade a general audience, the "public." His concluding argument is:

Either we will sink into the final coma and end it all or, as I trust and believe, we will awaken to the truth of our peril, a truth as great as life itself, and, like a person who has swallowed a lethal poison but shakes off his stupor at the last moment and vomits the poison up, we will break through the layers of denials, put aside our faint-hearted excuses, and rise up to cleanse the earth of nuclear weapons. (p. 231)

The validity of Schell's argument is not the question here. Our concern is its reception, which reveals the limits, perhaps the impossibility, of persuasive moral argument in our time, given the rational world paradigm.

Critical response to *The Fate of the Earth* is of two sorts. The first is celebratory. Reviewers in this group are obviously in sympathy with the book's moral thrust, its depiction of the results of nuclear war, and its call for action—for life instead of death—but not with every detail of its argument. Although reviewers in this group include distinguished figures from a variety of professions—journalists Walter Cronkite, James Reston, and James Kilpatrick; historians Harrison Salisbury, John Hersey, and Henry Steele Commager; and politicians Barry Commener, W. Averell Harriman, and Walter Mondale—none is a current member of the federal administration or the defense establishment. Each of them bears witness to an attitude—opposition to nuclear annihilation—but none testifies to the technical merits of Schell's representation of "deterrence theory," his inferences about its meaning in regard to strategy and tactics, or his conclusions about national sovereignty. They, like Schell, are not "experts" in the field in which the argument is made. They, like Schell, are active in the realm of rhetorical knowledge, in the sphere of social-political policy and behavior (Bitzer, 1978; Farrell, 1976).

Reviewers in the second group, on the other hand, are purveyors of ideological, bureaucratic, or technical arguments. Such arguments may overlap, be used by the same arguer, but each is distinguished by a particular privileged position: political "truth," administrative sanction, or subject matter expertise. The thrust of the ideological argument is that one violates ultimate "facts," is fundamentally wrong-headed; the bureaucratic argument stresses feasibility in regard to administrative approval; and the technical argument alleges ignorance of the "facts," that opponents are "unrealistic," meaning they do not have a firm grasp on reality. These are, of course, the lines of refutation or subversion. Their opposites would be constructive arguments of affirmation or reaffirmation.

The subversive pattern of ideological, bureaucratic, and technical arguments is evident in the following attacks on Schell's reasoning. McCracken (1982) labels Schell an "alarmist" and concludes: "The danger is that Mr. Schell's followers may triumph and bring about a freeze that by making present inequities permanent will prove destabilizing in the short run and in the long run productive of both redness and deadness" (p. 905). Focusing on the lynch-pin arguments of *The Fate of the Earth* (Schell's interpretation of deterrence theory and his suggested solution of abolishing national sovereignty), Hausknecht (1982) first cites Alexander Haig and then observes that "it is not hard to imagine Ronald Reagan saying, 'Okay, so it may be the end of the species, but we can't let the bastards get away with it.'" In regard to Schell's solution, he concludes that "successful political action demands significant but realizable goals" (p. 284). The same charge is leveled by Pierre (1982), who approves the moral force of Schell's position but then charges that "Schell provides no realistic alternative to our nuclear policy based on the concept of deterrence. His argument—that knowledge that nuclear weapons can extinguish mankind must be the new deterrent in a disarmed world—is very weak" (p. 1188).

The strategy of these reviews is clear: reaffirmation of the moral concern, subversion of the reasoning. The tactics are also obvious: juxtapose Schell's reasoning with what is right-headed, what is approved by the administration, or what is "realistic." Insofar as there is merit in these "arguments," it lies not in the way they foreclose dialogue but in their narrative probability and narrative fidelity. Yet this is not their intended appeal or effect. The effects are to discredit Schell as an arguer and to dismiss his argument as unfounded. Public moral argument is thus overwhelmed by privileged argument. Put another way, it is submerged by ideological and bureaucratic arguments that insist on rival moralities and technical argument which denudes it of morality altogether, making the dispute one for "experts" alone to consider (see Farrell and Goodnight, 1981).

The question that arises at this point is: What happens when "experts" argue about moral issues in public? Before considering this question, however, it is essential to sketch the general characteristics of "public moral argument."

Public moral argument is to be distinguished from reasoned discourse in interpersonal interactions and arguments occurring in specialized communities, such as theological disputes, academic debates, and arguments before the Supreme Court. The features differentiating *public* moral argument from such encounters are: (1) it is publicized, made available for consumption and persuasion of the polity at large; and (2) it is aimed at what Aristotle called "untrained thinkers," or, to be effective, it should be (1954, bk. 1, ch. 2, 1357[a] 10). Most important *public* moral argument is a form of controversy that inherently crosses fields. It is not contained in the way that legal, scientific, or theological arguments are, by subject matter, particular conceptions of argumentative competence, and well recognized rules of advocacy. Because this is so and because its realm is public-social knowledge, *public* moral argument naturally invites participation by field experts and is dominated by the rational superiority of their arguments. *Public* moral argument, which is oriented toward what ought to be, is undermined by the "truth" that prevails at the moment. The presence of "experts" in *public* moral arguments makes it difficult, if not impossible, for the public of "untrained thinkers" to win an argument or even judge them well—given, again, the rational world paradigm.

Public *moral* argument is moral in the sense that it is founded on ultimate questions—of life and death, of how persons should be defined and treated, of preferred patterns of living. Gusfield (1976) designates such questions "status issues." Their resolution, he writes, indicates "the group, culture, or style of life to which the government and society are publicly committed" (p. 173). In addition to nuclear warfare, desegregation would be included in the category as well as abortion and school prayer.

Public moral *argument* refers to clear cut inferential structures, in the rational world paradigm, and to "good reasons," in the narrative paradigm. Public moral *argument* may also refer to public controversies—disputes and debates—about moral issues. The nuclear warfare controversy is an obvious case in point, but so are the others mentioned above. One could add disputes over pornography, the ERA, and crime and punishment. This characterization of public moral *argument* is attentive to argument as product and as process (Wenzel, 1980).

The problem posed by the presence of experts in public moral argument is illustrated by the dispute between Hans Bethe and Edward Teller over the 1982 nuclear freeze proposition in California. Their positions were published in the *Los Angeles Times* (1982, October 17, Part 4, pp. 1–2), so they were public. They obviously concerned a moral issue and they were reasoned statements. Both persons are credible. Which one is to be believed and followed? Who in the general public could contend with them? Teller answers the second question in unequivocal terms: "The American public is ignorant, even of the general ideas on which they [nuclear weapons] are based" (p. 2). Here is revealed the fate of non-experts who would argue about nuclear warfare. Only experts can argue with experts and their arguments—while public—cannot be rationally questioned. As Perelman (1979) notes, rationality in and of itself forecloses discussion and debate. In the audience of experts, the public is left with no compelling reason, from the perspective of the rational world paradigm, to believe one over the other. One is not a judge but a spectator who must choose between actors. From the narrative paradigm view, the experts are storytellers and the audience is not a group of observers but are active participants in the meaning-formation of the stories.

It may be asked at this point: How is it that freeze referendums were approved in eight out of nine states and in twenty-eight cities and counties in 1982? One answer is "fear," the "most intelligent feeling of our time" (Wieseltier, 1983, p. 7). Another answer is "distrust," distrust of those responsible for the development, deployment, and use of nuclear weapons. This answer is, I believe, more accurate. It does not deny the existence of fear. It insists on the "rationality" of those who voted for and against the referendum. Those who opposed the referendum did so because of a basic distrust of Soviet leaders and a fundamental trust of our own. What I am saying is that there are good reasons for trust and distrust, that the response of voters was rational, given the narrative paradigm. The good reasons that are expressed in public moral argument relate to issues not accounted for in the rational world paradigm. These issues include the motivations and values of the characters involved in the ongoing narrative of nuclear warfare, the way in which they conceive and behave in respect to the conflict, and the narrative probability and narrative fidelity of the particular stories they tell, which may well take the form of "reasoned argument." Experts and lay persons meet on common ground, given the narrative paradigm. As Toulmin observes, "A scientist off duty is as much an 'ordinary' man as a tinker or a bus-conductor off duty" (1982, p. 81).

From the narrative perspective, the proper role of the expert in public moral argument is that of a counselor, which is, as Benjamin (1969) notes, the true function of the storyteller. His or her contribution to public dialogue is to impart knowledge, like a teacher, or wisdom, like a sage. It is not to pronounce a story that ends all storytelling. The expert assumes the role of public counselor whenever she or he crosses the boundary of technical knowledge into the territory of life as it ought to be lived. Once this invasion is made, the public, which then includes the expert, has its own criteria for determining whose story is most coherent and reliable as a guide to belief and action. The expert, in other words, then becomes subject to the demands of narrative rationality. Technical communities have their own conceptions and criteria for judging the rationality of communication. But, as Holton (1973) has demonstrated, the work even of scientists is inspired by stories; hence, their discourse can be interpreted usefully from the narrative perspective. Holton writes tellingly of the "nascent moment" in science, the impulse to do science in a particular or in a new way, and how science is informed by "themes"—thematic concepts, methods, and hypotheses inherited from Parmenides, Heraclitus, Pythagoras, Thales, and others (pp. 28–29; see also Ong, 1982, p. 140).

Viewed from the perspective of the rational world paradigm, Schell's case, his argument and its reception, evokes despair. If one looks to MacIntyre's *After Virtue* for relief, one will be disappointed and disheartened further, for he provides the historical and philosophical reasons for the fate of *The Fate of the Earth* and similar arguments. His own argument is that "we still, in spite of the efforts of three centuries of moral philosophy and one of sociology, lack any coherent, rationally defensible statement of a liberal individualist point of view" (1981, p. 241). He offers some hope with the idea that "the Aristotelian tradition can be restated in a way that restores intelligibility and rationality to our moral and social attitudes and commitments." He observes, however, "the new dark ages" are "already upon us." The "barbarians are not waiting beyond the frontiers; they have already been governing us for quite some time. And it is our lack of consciousness of this that constitutes part of our predicament. We are waiting not for Godot, but for another—doubtless very different—St. Benedict" (p. 245).

The reasons for this state of affairs are: (1) the rejection of a teleological view of human nature and the classical conception of reason as embodied in Aristotelian logic and rhetoric; (2) the separation of morality from theological, legal, and aesthetic concerns; and (3) the evolution of the individualistic sense of self and the rise of emotivism. The consequence of these movements is a situation in which ethical arguments in public are rendered ineffectual because of "conceptual incommensurability."

A case in point is protest—where advocates of reform argue from a position of "rights" and those who oppose them reason from the stance of "utility." MacIntyre observes:

> The facts of incommensurability ensure that protestors can never win an *argument*; the indignant self-righteousness of protestors arises because the facts of incommensurability ensure equally that the protestors can never lose an argument either. Hence, the *utterance* of protest is characteristically addressed to those who already *share* the protestors' premises. . . . This is not to say that protest cannot be effective; it is to say that protest cannot be *rationally* effective. (p. 69)

Thus, when arguers appealing to justice and equality contend with adversaries who base their case on success, survival, and liberty, they talk past each other.

From the perspective of the narrative paradigm, the dynamic of this situation is that rival stories are being told. Any story, any form of rhetorical communication, not only says something about the world, it also implies an audience, persons who conceive of themselves in very specific ways. If a story denies a person's self-conception, it does not matter what it says about the world. In the instance of protest, the rival factions' stories deny each other in respect to self-conceptions and the world. The only way to bridge this gap, if it can be bridged through discourse, is by telling stories that do not negate the self-conceptions people hold of themselves.

It may be germane to note at this point that narrative as a *mode of discourse* is more universal and probably more efficacious than argument for nontechnical forms of communication (Fisher, 1982, p. 304). There are several reasons why this should be true. First, narration comes closer to capturing the experience of the world, simultaneously appealing to the various senses, to reason and emotion, to intellect and imagination, and to fact and value. It does not presume intellectual contact only. Second, one does not have to be taught narrative probability and narrative fidelity; one culturally acquires them through a universal faculty and experience. Obviously, one can, through education, become sophisticated in one's understanding and application of these principles. But, as Gadamer observes, "I am convinced of the fact that there are no people who do not 'think' sometime and somewhere. That means there is no one who does not form general views about life and death, about freedom and living together, about the good and about happiness" (1981, p. 58; see also Ogden, 1977, p. 114; Lonergan, 1958, xiv–xv, xxii–xxx). In other words, people are reflective and from such reflection they make the stories of their lives and have the basis for judging narratives for and about them. On the other hand, appreciation of argument requires not only reflection, but also specialized knowledge of issues, reasoning, rules of rationality, and so on. Third, narration works by suggestion and identification; argument operates by inferential moves and deliberation. Both forms, however, are modes of expressing good reasons—given the narrative paradigm—so the differences between them are structural rather than substantive.

SUMMARY AND CONCLUSIONS

This essay began as a study of public moral argument—the nuclear controversy. It was undertaken with the rational world paradigm well in mind. The results of my analysis were disturbing not only in what I found to be the inevitable subversion of *The Fate of the Earth* and similar such arguments, but also in that the rational world paradigm was at least partly responsible for that fate. Then came MacIntyre's (1981) *After Virtue*. Reflection set in and the narrative paradigm came out of it. I was concerned with the concept of technical reason and the way it rendered the public unreasonable; with the idea of rationality being a matter of argumentative competence in specialized fields, leaving the public and its discourse irrational; with the apparent impossibility of bridging the gaps between experts and the public and between segments of the public; and with the necessity to learn what was supposed to be of the essence of persons—rationality—so that one class of citizens can always be superior to another.

Although I do not mean to maintain that the narrative paradigm resolves these problems out of existence, I do think that it provides a basis for reconsideration of them. Before that, I am aware, the narrative paradigm itself needs further scrutiny. I know that I do not need to tell critics how to do their work—the examination of my representation of the rational world paradigm, the presuppositions of the narrative paradigm and its relationship to other constructs, my concept of public moral argument, and the analysis of the specific case. I welcome the "stories" the critics will tell.

In closing, I should like to make two additional comments. First, I think that the concepts of public and social knowledge should be reconceived in light of the narrative paradigm. The effect would be to give shape to these ideas as identifiable entities in the discourse of the citizenry, to give public knowledge a form of being. To consider that public-social knowledge is to be found in the stories that we tell one another would enable us to observe not only our differences, but also our commonalities, and in such observation we might be able to reform the notion of the "public."

Second, and closely related to the discovery of our communal identity, is the matter of what makes one story better than another. Two features come to mind: formal and substantive. Formal features are attributes of narrative probability: the consistency of characters and actions, the accommodation of auditors, and so on. In epistemological terms, the question would be whether a narrative satisfied the demands of a coherence theory of truth. The most compelling, persuasive stories are mythic in form (Campbell, 1973; Cassirer, 1944, 1979, p. 246; Eliade, 1963). Substantive features relate to narrative fidelity. Bormann has proposed two concepts pertinent to the problem of narrative fidelity: "corroboration" (1978) and "social convergence" (1983, p. 436). These concepts concern how people come to adhere to particular stories. They do not solve the problem of narrative fidelity because both suggest that narratives are valid by virtue of consensus and provide no criteria by which one can establish that one narrative is more sound than another. While there is work to be done on the problem, I think the logic of good reasons is the most viable scheme presently available by which narratives can be tested. Its application requires an examination of reasoning and "inspection of facts, values, self, and society" (Fisher, 1978, p. 382). In epistemological terms, narrative fidelity is a matter of truth according to the doctrine of correspondence. Though the most engaging stories are mythic, the most helpful and uplifting stories are moral. As John Gardner wrote, "Moral action is action that affirms life" (1978, p. 23).

One may get the impression that the conception of rationality I have presented leads to a denial of logic. It does, but only as logic is conceived so that persons are considered irrational beings. With Heidegger (1973, p. 170), I would assert that "to think counter to logic does not mean to stick up for the illogical, but only means to think the *logos*, and its essence as it appeared in the early days of thought; i.e. to make an effort first of all to prepare such an act of reflecting (*Nachdenka*)." In an earlier essay, I attempted to make such an effort by showing the relationship of the logic of good reasons to Aristotle's concept of "practical wisdom" (Fisher, 1980, pp. 127–128).

Application of narrative rationality to specific stories may further clarify its nature and value. From the perspective of narrative rationality, Hitler's *Mein Kampf* must be judged a bad story. Although it has formal coherence in its structure, as McGuire (1977) demonstrated, it denies the identity of significant persons and demeans others. It also lacks fidelity to the truths humanity shares in regard to reason, justice, veracity, and peaceful ways to resolve social-political differences. On the other hand, one may cite the cosmological myths of Lao-tse, Buddha, Zoroaster, Christ, and Mohammed which satisfy both narrative probability and narrative fidelity for those cultures for whom they were intended—and many others across time and place. Far from denying the humanity of persons, they elevate it to the profoundest moral and metaphysical level the world has known. One could also cite such works as *The Iliad* and *The Odyssey*; the tragedies of Aeschylus, Sophocles, Euripides; Virgils' *Aeneid*; Dante's *Commedia*; the plays of

Shakespeare; and the novels of Tolstoy, Melville, Thomas Mann, and James Joyce. One could point to the lives of Jesus, Socrates, Lincoln, and Gandhi. Regarding political discourse, one could mention many of the speeches and writings of Adlai Stevenson and Winston Churchill. While these classic manifestations of religious, social, cultural, and political life have been celebrated by persons committed to traditional rationality, it has been because they have not restricted themselves to "logic" but have recognized and responded to the values fostered by them, by their reaffirmation of the human spirit as the transcendent ground of existence.

For a more detailed illustration of how narrative probability and fidelity can be usefully applied, I offer this brief analysis of *The Epic of Gilgamesh*, "the finest surviving epic poem from any period until the appearance of Homer's *Iliad*: and it is immeasurably older" (Sandars, 1982, p. 7). It is, in fact, 1,500 years older.

The story, in sum, is as follows: Gilgamesh, the King of Urak, two-thirds god and one-third man, is possessed of a perfect body, unbounded courage, and extraordinary strength. He is a hero, a tragic hero, the "first tragic hero of whom anything is known" (Sandars, 1982, p. 7). His youth is spent in pursuit of fame as the means of immortality.

He is restless, with no one to match his appetites and physical feats. His people ask the gods to create a companion for him, which they do in Enkidu. Enkidu is Gilgamesh's counterpart in strength, energy, and exuberance for life. After a wrestling match, they become inseparable, brothers in every way but birth. Gilgamesh learns what it means to love.

Because Enkidu begins to lose his physical prowess—he had been an inhabitant of the wilds and ran with animals—Gilgamesh proposes that they pursue and slay Huwawa, a terrible monster. At first, Enkidu is reluctant but is chided into joining the quest. The monster is met, subdued, and, because of an insult, is slain by Enkidu.

When they return to Urak, the goddess Ishtar proposes to Gilgamesh. He not only refuses her, but he and Enkidu heap scorn upon her. She goes to her father, Anu, and asks him to have the bull of heaven kill Gilgamesh. But Gilgamesh and Enkidu kill the bull instead. It appears at this point that the "brothers" cannot be defeated by man, monsters, or the gods.

It turns out, however, that in killing Huwawa, Gilgamesh and Enkidu incurred the wrath of Enlil, guardian of the forest in which the monster lived. Enlil demands the death of Gilgamesh, but the sun god intervenes and Enkidu is doomed and dies.

With Enkidu's death, the world of Gilgamesh is shattered. He has not only lost his loving companion, he must now directly confront the fact of death. Up to this point, he has lived as a willful child, acting as though the meaning of life is a matter of dominating it.

At first, Gilgamesh refuses to accept Enkidu's death as real. He becomes obsessed with death and starts a quest to learn the secret of immortality. His journey is tortured and long. He finally arrives, after incredible hardships, at the island of Utanapishtim and asks him how one gains eternal life. Utanapishtim suggests that he try not to sleep for six days and seven nights. But he soon falls asleep, for seven days, a form of living death. He is awakened and realizes there is no escape from death. He resigns himself to his fate, the fate of all humankind, and returns home. On his return he learns to value the wall he has built around the city: immortality is, he apparently concludes, to be found in the monuments that one leaves behind.

The story provides good reasons to accept not only this truth, but others as well: Life is fullest when one loves and is loved; death is real; and maturity is achieved by accepting the reality of death. We learn these truths by dwelling in the characters in the story, by observing the outcomes of the several conflicts that arise throughout it, by seeing the unity of characters and their actions, and by comparing the truths to the truths we know to be true from our own lives. In other words, the story exhibits narrative probability and fidelity across time and culture (Jacobsen, 1976).

Finally, I do not mean to maintain that "knowledge of agents" is superior to "knowledge of objects." With Toulmin, I would hold that "A decent respect for each kind of knowledge is surely compatible with conceding the legitimate claims of the other" (1982, p. 244). With knowledge of agents, we can hope to find that which is *reliable or trustworthy*; with knowledge of objects, we can hope to discover that which has the quality of *veracity*. The world requires both kinds of knowledge.

Karl Wallace was right: "One could do worse than characterize rhetoric as the art of finding and effectively presenting good reasons" (1963, p. 248). MacIntyre is also right:

> The unity of human life is the unity of a narrative quest. Quests sometimes fail, are frustrated, abandoned or dissipated into distractions; and human lives may in all these ways also fail. But the criteria for success or failure in a human life as a whole are the criteria of success or failure in a narrated or to-be-narrated quest. (1981, p. 203)

And that quest is "for the good life" for all persons.

References

Alter, R. (1981). *The Art of Biblical Narrative*. New York: Basic Books.

Apel, K.O. (1979). "Types of Rationality Today: The Continuum of Reason between Science and Ethics." In T. F. Geraets, ed., *Rationality Today* (Ottawa: University of Ottawa Press), pp. 309–339.

Aristotle (1954). *Rhetoric*. Translated by W. R. Roberts. New York: Modern Library.

Baier, A. (1983). "Secular Faith." In S. Hauerwas and A. MacIntyre, eds., *Revisions: Changing Perspectives on Moral Philosophy* (South Bend, IN: University of Notre Dame Press), pp. 203–221.

Bantz, C. R. (1975). "Television News: Reality and Research." *Western Journal of Speech Communication* 39: 123–130.

Barrett, W. (1979). *The Illusion of Technique: A Search for Meaning in a Technological Civilization*. Garden City, NY: Anchor Press/Doubleday.

Barthes, R. (1977). "Introduction to the Structural Analysis of Narratives." In S. Heath, ed., *Image-Music-Text* (New York: Hill and Wang), pp. 79–124.

Bateson, G. (1979). *Mind and Nature: A Necessary Unity*. Toronto: Bantam Books.

Benjamin, W. (1969). "The Storyteller." In H. Arendt, ed., *Illuminations* (New York: Schocken Books), pp. 83–109.

Bennett, L. W. (1975). " Political Scenarios and the Nature of Politics." *Philosophy and Rhetoric* 8: 23–42.

Bennett, L. W. (1978). "Storytelling and Criminal Trials: A Model of Social Judgment." *Quarterly Journal of Speech* 64: 1–22.

Bennett, L. W., and M. S. Feldman. (1981). *Reconstructing Reality in the Courtroom: Justice and Judgment in American Culture*. New Brunswick, NJ: Rutgers University Press.

Bitzer, L. F. (1978). "Rhetoric and Public Knowledge." In D. Burks, ed., *Rhetoric, Philosophy and Literature: An Exploration* (West Lafayette, IN: Purdue University Press), pp. 67–93.

Booth, W. C. (1974). *Modern Dogma and the Rhetoric of Assent*. South Bend, IN: University of Notre Dame Press.

Bormann, E. G. (1972). " Fantasy and Rhetorical Vision: The Rhetorical Criticism of Social Reality." *Quarterly Journal of Speech* 59: 143–159.

Bormann, E. G. (1973). "The Eagleton Affair: A Fantasy Theme Analysis." *Quarterly Journal of Speech* 59: 143–159.

Bormann, E. G. (1979). "The Tentative and the Certain in Rhetoric: The Role of Corroboration on the Rigidity or Flexibility of Rhetorical Visions." Paper presented at the annual meeting of the Central States Speech Association, Minneapolis.

Bormann, E. G. (1983). "Fantasy Theme Analysis." In J. L. Golden, G. F. Berquist, and W. E. Coleman, eds., *The Rhetoric of Western Thought*, 3rd ed. (Dubuque, IA: Kendall/Hunt), pp. 430–449.

Brockriede, W. (1975). "Where Is Argument?" *Journal of the American Forensics Association* 11: 179.

Brockriede, W. (1977). "Characteristics of Arguments and Arguing." *Journal of the American Forensics Association* 13: 129–132.

Brockriede, W. (1982). "Arguing about Human Understanding." *Communication Monographs* 49: 137–147.

Burke, K. (1955). *A Rhetoric of Motives*. New York: George Braziller.

Burke, K. (1957). *The Philosophy of Literary Form*. Rev. ed. New York: Vintage Books.

Burke, K. (1968). "Definition of Man." In *Language and Symbolic Action: Essays on Life, Literature, and Method* (Berkeley and Los Angeles: University of California Press), pp. 3–24.

Burke, K. (1983). "Lecture Outlines. Logology: An Overall View." Personal correspondence.

Burleson, B. R. (1981). "Characteristics of Argument." In G. Ziegelmueller and J. Rhodes, eds., *Dimensions of Argument: Proceedings of the Second Conference an Argumentation* (Annandale, VA: Speech Communication Association), pp. 955–979.

Campbell, J. (1973). *Myths to Live By*. New York: Bantam Books.

Campbell, J. A. (1984). "On the Rhetoric of History: Epochal Discourse and Discovery of the Universal Audience." Unpublished paper, Department of Speech Communication, University of Washington.

Campbell, J. A., and J. R. Stewart. (1981). "Rhetoric, Philosophy, and Conversation." Paper presented at the annual meeting of the Western Speech Communication Association, San Jose, CA.

Cassirer, E. (1944). *An Essay on Man: An Introduction to a Philosophy of Human Culture*. New Haven, CT. Yale University Press.

Cassirer, E. (1979). "The Technique of Our Modern Political Myths." In D. P. Verent, ed., *Symbol, Myth, and Culture: Essays and Lectures of Ernst Cassirer* (New Haven, CT: Yale University Press), pp. 242–267.

Cox, J. R. (1981). "Investigating Policy Argument as a Field." In G. Ziegelmueller and J. Rhodes, eds., *Dimensions of Argument: Proceedings of the Second Conference on Argumentation* (Annendale, VA. Speech Communication Association), pp. 126–142.

Danto, A. C. (1982). "Narration and Knowledge." *Philosophy and Literature* 6: 17-32.

Derrida, J. (1980). "The Law of Genre." *Critical Inquiry* 7: 55–81.

Dewey, J. (1927). *The Public and Its Problems*. Chicago: Swallow Press.

Dijk, T. A. (1976). "Philosophy of Action and Theory of Narrative." *Poetics* 5: 287–388.

Ehninger, D. (1968). "Validity as Moral Obligation." *Southern Speech Journal* 33: 215–222.

Eliade, M. (1963). *Myth and Reality*. New York: Harper Colophon Books.

Farrell, T. B. (1976). "Knowledge, Consensus, and Rhetorical Theory." *Quarterly Journal of Speech* 62: 1–14 (reprinted in this volume).

Farrell, T. B. (1977). "Validity and Rationality: The Rhetorical Constituents of Argumentative Form." *Journal of American Forensics Association* 13: 142–149.

Farrell, T. B. (1983). "The Tradition of Rhetoric and the Philosophy of Communication." *Communication* 7: 151–180.

Farrell, T. B., and G. T. Goodnight. (1981). "Accidental Rhetoric: The Root Metaphor of Three Mile Island." *Communication Monographs* 48: 271–300.

Fisher, W. R. (1973). "Reaffirmation and Subversion of the American Dream." *Quarterly Journal of Speech* 9: 160–169.

Fisher, W. R. (1978). "Toward a Logic of Good Reasons." *Quarterly Journal of Speech* 64: 376–384.

Fisher, W. R. (1980). "Rationality and the Logic of Good Reasons." *Philosophy and Rhetoric* 13: 121–130.

Fisher, W. R. (1982). "Romantic Democracy, Ronald Reagan, and Presidential Heroes." *Western Journal of Speech Communication* 46: 299–310.

Fisher, W. R., and R. D. Burns. (1964). *Armament and Disarmament: The Continuing Dispute.* Belmont, CA: Wadsworth.

Fisher, W. R., and R. A. Filloy. (1982). "Argument in Drama and Literature: An Exploration." In J. R. Cox and C. A. Wilard, eds., *Advances in Argumentation Theory and Research* (Carbondale: Southern Illinois University Press), pp. 343–362.

Frentz, T. S., and T. B. Farrell. (1976). "Language-Action: A Paradigm for Communication." *Quarterly Journal of Speech* 62: 333–349.

Gadamer, H. G. (1980). *Dialogue and Dialectic: Eight Hermeneutical Essays on Plato.* Translated by P. Christofer Smith. New Haven, CT: Yale University Press.

Gadamer, H. G. (1981). *Reason in the Age of Science.* Cambridge, MA: MIT Press.

Gadamr, H. G. (1982). *Truth and Method.* New York: Crossword.

Gallie, W. B. (1964). *Philosophy and Historical Understanding.* New York: Schocken Books.

Gardner, J. (1978). *On Moral Fiction.* New York: Basic Books.

Goldberg, M. (1982). *Theology and Narrative.* Nashville, TN: Parthenon Press.

Goodnight, G. T. (1980). "The Liberal and the Conservative Presumptions: On Political Philosophy and the Foundation of Public Argument." In J. Rhodes and S. Newell, eds., *Proceedings of the Summer Conference on Argumentation* (Falls Church, VA: Speech Communication Association), pp. 304–337.

Goody, J., and I. Watt. (1962-1963). "The Consequences of Literacy." *Comparative Studies in Society and History* 5: 304–326, 332–345.

Gottlieb, G. (1968). *The Logic of Choice: An Investigation of the Concepts of Rule and Rationality.* New York: Macmillan.

Graff, G. (1979). *Literature Against Itself: Literacy Ideas in Society.* Chicago: University of Chicago Press.

Gusfield, J. R. (1976). *Symbolic Crusade: Status Politics and the American Temperance Movement.* Urbana: University of Illinois Press.

Habermas, J. (1967). *Theory and Practice: The History of a Concept.* South Bend, IN: University of Notre Dame Press.

Habermas, J. (1973). *Knowledge and Social Interests.* Boston: Beacon Press.

Hauerwas, S. (1981). *A Community of Character: Towards a Constructive Christian Ethic.* South Bend, IN: University of Notre Dame Press.

Hausknecht, M. (1982). "Waiting for the End? Prospects for Nuclear Destruction." *Dissent* 29: 282–284.

Hawes, L. C. (1978). "The Reflexivity of Communication Research." *Western Journal of Speech Communication* 42: 12–20.

Heidegger, M. (1949). *Existence and Being.* Chicago: Henry Regnery.

Heidegger, M. (1972). *On Time and Being.* Translated by J. Stanbaugh. New York: Harper and Row.

Heidegger, M. (1973). "Letter on Humanism." In R. Zaner and D. lhde, eds., *Phenomenology and Existentialism* (New York: Capricorn Books/G. P. Putnam's Sons), pp. 147–181.

Hollis, M. (1977). *Models of Man: Philosophical Thoughts and Social Action.* Cambridge: Cambridge University Press.

Holton, G. (1973). *Thematic Origins of Modern Science.* Cambridge, MA: Harvard University Press.

Hymes, D. (1980). "A Narrative View of the World." In D. Hymes, *Language in Education: Ethnolinguistic Essays* (Washington, DC: Center for Applied Linguistics), pp. 129–138.

Hynes, T. J., Jr. (1980). "Liberal and Conservative Presumptions in Public Argument: A Critique." In J. Rhodes and S. Newell, eds., *Proceedings of the Summer Conference on Argumentation* (Falls Church, VA: Speech Communication Association), pp. 338–347.

Jacobs, S., and S. Jackson. (1981). "Argument as a Natural Category: The Routine Grounds for Arguing in Conversation." *Western Journal of Speech Communication* 45: 118–132.

Jacobsen, T. (1976). *The Treasurer of Darkness: A History of Mesopotamian Religion*. New Haven, CT. Yale University Press.

Johnstone, H. W., Jr. (1978). *Validity and Rhetoric in Philosophical Argument*. University Park, PA: Dialogue Press of Man and World.

Kernmode, F. (1980). "Secrets and Narrative Sequence." *Critical Inquiry* 7: 83–101.

Key, V. O. (1966). *The Responsible Electorate: Rationality in Presidential Voting, 1936–1960*. New York: Vintage Books.

Kidd, V. (1975). "Happily Ever After and Other Relationship Styles: Advice on Interpersonal Relations in Popular Magazines, 1951–1973." *Quarterly Journal of Speech* 61: 31–39.

Kirkwood, W. G. (1983). "Storytelling and Self-Confrontation: Parables as Communication Strategies." *Quarterly Journal of Speech* 69: 58–74.

Krashen, S. D. (1982). *Principles and Practice in Second Language Acquisition*. Oxford, UK: Pergamon Press.

Kuhn, T. S. (1974). "Second Thoughts on Paradigms." In F. Suppe, ed., *The Structure of Scientific Theories* (Urbana: University of Illinois Press), pp. 459–482.

Langer, S. K. (1953). *Feeling and Form: A Theory of Art*. New York: Charles Scribner's Sons.

Lonergan, B.J. F., SJ. (1958). *Insight: A Study of Human Understanding*. New York: Harper and Row.

Lucaites, J. L. (1981). "Rhetoric and the Problem of Legitimacy." In G. Ziegelmueller and J. Rhodes, eds., *Dimensions of Argument: Proceedings of the Second Conference on Argumentation* (Annandale, VA: Speech Communication Association).

Lyne, J. (1982). "Discourse, Knowledge, and Social Process: Some Changing Equations." *Quarterly Journal of Speech* 68: 201–214.

MacIntyre, A. (1978). "Rationality and the Explanation of Action." In A. MacIntyre, *Against the Self-Image of the Art: Essays on Ideology and Philosophy* (South Bend, IN: University of Notre Dame Press), pp. 244–259.

MacIntyre, A. (1981). *After Virtue: A Study in Moral Theory*. South Bend, IN: University of Notre Dame Press.

Masterman, M. (1970). "The Nature of a Paradigm." In I. Lakatos and A. Musgrave, eds., *Criticism and the Growth of Knowledge* (London: Cambridge University Press), pp. 59–89.

McCracken, S. (1982, July 23). "The Peace of the Grave." *National Review*, pp. 904–905.

McGee, M. C., and M. A. Martin. (1983). "Public Knowledge and Ideological Argumentation." *Communication Monographs* 50: 47–65.

McGee, M. C., A. Scult, K. Kuntz. (1983). "Genesis 1–3 as Sacred Text: An Inquiry into the Relationship of Rhetoric and Power." Unpublished paper, Department of Communication, University of Iowa.

McGuire, M. (1977). "Mythic Rhetoric in *Mein Kampf*: A Structural Critique." *Quarterly Journal of Speech* 68: 1–13.

McKerrow, R. E. (1977). "Rhetorical Validity: An Analysis of Three Perspectives on the Justification of Rhetorical Argument." *Journal of the American Forensics Association* 13: 133–141.

McKerrow, R. E. (1980a). "Argument Communities: A Quest for Distinctions." In J. Rhodes and S. Newell, eds., *Proceedings of the Summer Conference on Argumentation* (Falls Church, VA: Speech Communication Association), pp. 214–227.

McKerrow, R. E. (1980b). "On Fields and Rational Enterprises: A Reply to Willard." In J. Rhodes and S. Newell, eds., *Proceedings of the Summer Conference on Argumentation* (Falls Church, VA: Speech Communication Association), pp. 401–411.

McKerrow, R. E. (1981). "Senses of Argument: Uses and Limitations of the Concept." In G. Ziegelmueller and J. Rhodes, eds., *Dimensions of Argument: Proceedings of the Second Conference on Argumentation* (Annandale, VA: Speech Communication Association), pp. 990–986.

McKerrow, R. E. (1982). "Rationality and Reasonableness in a Theory of Argument." In J. R. Cox
    and C. A. Willard, eds., *Advances in Argumentation Theory and Research* (Carbondale:
    Southern Illinois University Press), pp. 105–122.
Medina, A. (1979). *Reflection, Time, and the Novel: Toward a*
Communicative Theory of Literature. London: Routledge & Kegan Paul.
Mink, L. O. (1978). "Narrative Form as a Cognitive Instrument." In R.H. Canary, ed., *The Writing
    of History* (Madison: University of Wisconsin Press), pp. 129–149.
Nelson, J. S. (1980). "Tropal History and the Social Sciences: Reflections on Struever's Remarks."
    History and Theory 19: 80–101.
Ochs, D. J., and R. J. Burritt. (1973). "Perceptual Theory: Narrative Suasion of Lysias." In C. J.
    Stewart, D. J. Ochs, and G. P. Mahrmann, eds., *Explorations in Rhetorical Criticism* (University
    Park: Pennsylvania State University Press), pp. 51–74.
Ogden, S. M. (1977). "Myth and Truth." In S. M. Ogden, *The Reality of God* (San Francisco: Harper
    and Row), pp. 99–129.
O'Keefe, D. J. (1977). "Two Concepts of Argument." *Journal of the American Forensic Association*
    13: 121–128.
O'Keefe, D. J. (1982). "The Concepts of Argument and Arguing." In J. R. Cox and C. A. Willard,
    eds., *Advances in Argumentation Theory and Research* (Carbondale: Southern Illinois University
    Press), pp. 3–23.
Ong, W. (1982). *Orality and Literacy: The Technologizing of the Word*. London: Methuen.
Perelman, C. (1979). "The Rational and the Reasonable." In *The New Rhetoric and the Humanities:
    Essays on Rhetoric and Its Applications* (Boston: D. Reidel), pp. 117–123.
Perelman, C., and L. Olbrechts-Tyteca. (1969). *The New Rhetoric: A Treatise on Argument*.
    Translated by J. Wilkinson and P. Weaver. South Bend, IN: University of Notre Dame Press.
Pierre, A. J. (1982). [Review of *The Fate of the Earth*, by Jonathan Schell]. *Foreign Affairs* 60: 1188.
Polanyi, M. (1958). *Personal Knowledge: Towards a Postcritical Philosophy*. Chicago: University of
    Chicago Press.
Pryor, B. (1981). "Saving the Public through Rational Discourse." In G. Ziegelmueller and J.
    Rhodes, eds., *Dimensions of Argument: Proceedings of the Second Conference on Argumentation*
    (Annandale, VA.: Speech Communication Association), pp. 848–864.
Ramsey, I. T. (1969). "Religion and Science: A Philosopher's Approach." In D. M. High, ed., *New
    Essays on Religious Language* (New York: Oxford University Press), pp. 36–53.
Randall, J. H., Jr. (1976). *The Making of the Modern Mind*. New York: Columbia University Press.
Rarick, D. L., M. B. Duncan, and L. W. Porter. (1977). "The Carter Persona: An Empirical
    Analysis of the Rhetorical Visions of Campaign '76." *Quarterly Journal of Speech* 63: 258–273.
Ricoeur, P. (1976). *Interpretation Theory: Discourse and the Surplus of Meaning*. Fort Worth: Texas
    Christian University Press.
Ricoeur, P. (1980). "Narrative Time." *Critical Inquiry* 7: 169–190.
Rorty, R. (1979). *Philosophy and the Mirror of Nature*. Princeton, NJ: Princeton University Press.
Sandars, N. K. (1982). *The Epic of Gilgamesh*. New York: Penguin Books.
Schell, J. (1982). *The Fate of the Earth*. New York: Avon Books.
Schrag, C. O. (1980). *Radical Reflection and the Origins of the Human Sciences*. West Lafayette, IN:
    Purdue University Press.
Schrag, C. O. (1984). "Rhetoric, Hermeneutics, and Communication." Unpublished manuscript,
    Department of Philosophy, Purdue University.
Scott, R. L. (1978). "Evidence in Communication: We Are Such Stuff." *Western Journal of Speech
    Communication* 42: 29-36.
Scutt, A. (1983). "The Rhetorical Character of the Old Testament and Its Interpretation." Paper
    presented at the annual meeting of the International Society for the History of Rhetoric,
    Florence, Italy.
Sennett, R. (1978). *The Fall of Public Man: On the Social Psychology of Capitalism*. New York: Vintage
    Books.
Sillars, M. O., and P. Ganer. (1982). "Values and Beliefs: A Systematic Basis for Argumentation."

In J. R. Cox and C. A. Willard, eds., *Advances in Argumentation Theory and Research* (Carbondale: Southern Illinois University Press), pp. 184–201.

Simons, H. D. (1978). "In Praise of Muddleheaded Ancedotalism." *Western Journal of Speech Communication* 42: 21–28.

Todorov, T. (1977). *The Poetics of Prose*. Translated by R. Howard. Ithaca, NY: Cornell University Press.

Toulmin, S. E. (1958). *The Uses of Argument*. Cambridge: Cambridge University Press.

Toulmin, S. E. (1970). "Reasons and Causes." In R. Borger and F. Cioffi, eds., *Explanation in the Behavioral Sciences* (Cambridge: Cambridge University Press), pp. 1–41.

Toulmin, S. E. (1972). *Human Understanding*. Princeton, NJ: Princeton University Press.

Toulmin, S. E. (1982). *The Return to Cosmology: Postmodern Science and the Theology of Nature*. Berkeley and Los Angeles: University of California Press.

Toulmin, S. E., R. Rieke, and A. Janik. (1979). *Introduction to Reasoning*. New York: Macmillan.

Turner, V. (1980). "Social Dramas and Stories about Them." *Critical Inquiry* 7: 141–168.

Voegelin, E. (1952). *The New Science of Poetics*. Chicago: University of Chicago Press.

Voegelin, E. (1975). *From Enlightenment to Revolution*. Durham, NC: Duke University Press.

Wallace, K. (1963). "The Substance of Rhetoric: Good Reasons." *Quarterly Journal of Speech* 49: 239–249.

Wenzel, J. W. (1977). "Toward a Rationale for Value-Centered Argument." *Journal of the American Forensics Association* 13: 150–158.

Wenzel, J. W. (1980). "Perspectives on Argument." In J. Rhodes and S. Newell, eds., *Proceedings of the Summer Conference on Argumentation* (Falls Church, VA: Speech Communication Association), pp. 112–133.

White, H. (1978). *Metahistory: Tropics of History*. Baltimore: Johns Hopkins University Press.

White, H. (1980). "The Value of Narrativity in the Representation of Reality." *Critical Inquiry* 7: 5–27.

Wieseltier, L. (1983, January 10 and 17). "The Great Nuclear Debate." *New Republic*, pp. 7–38.

Willard, C. A. (1978). "A Reformulation of the Concept of Argument: The Constructivist/Interactionist Foundations of a Sociology of Argument." *Journal of the American Forensics Association* 14: 121–140.

Willard, C. A. (1982). "Argument Fields." In J. R. Cox and C. A. Willard, eds., *Advances in Argumentation Theory and Research* (Carbondale: Southern Illinois University Press), pp. 24–77.

Zarefsky, D. (1981). "Reasonableness in Public Policy Argument: Fields as Institutions." In G. Ziegelmueller and J. Rhodes, eds., *Dimensions of Argument: Proceedings of the Second Conference on Argumentation* (Annandale, VA: Speech Communication Association), pp. 99–100.

Ziegelmueller, G., and J. Rhodes. (1981). *Dimensions of Argument: Proceedings of the Second Conference on Argumentation*. Annandale, VA: Speech Communication Association.

Ziman, J. (1968). *Public Knowledge*. London: Cambridge University Press.

Rhetorical Conversation, Time, and Moral Action

THOMAS S. FRENTZ

> Quality, then, seems to have practically two meanings, and one of
> these is the more proper. The primary quality is the differentia
> of the essence, and of this quality in numbers is a part; for it is a
> differentia of essences, but either not of things that move or not
> of them *qua* moving. Secondly, there are the modifications of
> things that move, *qua* moving and the differentia of movements.
> Virtue and vice fall among these modifications; for they indicate
> differentia of the movement or activity, according to which things
> in motion act or are acted on well or badly; for that which can he
> moved or act in some way is good, and that which can do so in
> another—the contrary—way is vicious. Good and evil indicate quality
> especially in those which have purpose.
>
> *Aristotle*, Metaphysics

In ancient Greece, rhetoric was "a practical art . . . for cultivating and enacting practical reason in audiences with the potential for moral action."[1] Over the centuries, especially since the rise of science and the advent of positivism, rhetoric and morality became disjoined, leaving both adrift, depreciated, and vulnerable to redefinition in terms of the presuppositions of contemporary philosophies.[2] In the twentieth century, however, rhetoric and morality have enjoyed a renaissance of sorts. Writers as diverse as Thomas Kuhn, Chaim Perelman, Jürgen Habermas, Hans-Georg Gadamer, Kenneth Burke, and Robert Pirsig—not to mention historians, linguists, classicists, philosophers, and speech communication scholars—have revived the ancient disciplines in a variety of ways. And yet, for many rhetorical scholars, one of the most intriguing works for reconstituting and re-uniting rhetoric and moral action, ironically, says nothing about rhetoric:

Alasdair MacIntyre's *After Virtue*.[3] When tied to a classical conception of rhetoric and an actional conception of time, his work provides a ground for conceiving a paradigmatic form of human communication, what I will call *rhetorical conversation*.

To begin, we must first establish MacIntyre's position. He begins by noting a disturbing feature of contemporary moral arguments. Although public arguments appear in the guise of rationality, at base they derive from premises containing concepts (e.g., human rights and utility) divorced from the moral traditions which originally gave them meaning. Consequently, MacIntyre observes, there is no rational way to decide between competing moral positions and moral arguments become shrill and interminable.[4] The cause of this situation is that when moral philosophers rejected Aristotelian teleology, moral arguments could no longer be generated from impersonal premises concerning the optimal good for humankind, and their authoritative force could no longer be validated rationally.[5] For without a teleological conception of morality, all rational attempts to justify moral action culminate in some variant of "emotivism." Emotivism, MacIntyre tells us, grounds premises for moral action in the desires, preferences, and needs of the individual, values the ahistorical "autonomous moral agent" who is free to choose his or her moral actions, and views people as means to be manipulated as opposed to ends to be valued. The philosophical terminus of this liberal individualistic morality is Nietzsche's *Übermensch*, "the great man."[6]

To understand fully MacIntyre's alternative to emotivism, we must first recount Aristotle's moral position, because it is Aristotle to whom MacIntyre is most indebted. For Aristotle, morality entails a three-fold scheme in which practical reason and experience with political contingencies lead people from a present condition of moral happenstance to a future condition of moral excellence as persons approach their *telos* of happiness (*eudaimonia*). Practical reason and experience, the moral constituents of ethics, are guided by the virtues—e.g., courage, justice, truthfulness, friendship, and so on. Some virtues define a person's character and are acquired through habit (*hexis*), while others are intellectual and must be learned through instruction. As MacIntyre notes, "The immediate outcome of the exercise of a virtue is a choice which issues in right action."[7]

MacIntyre's account of moral action fuses Aristotle's teleological perspective with concepts whose root origins trace back to the Homeric epics and the mythology of pre-Socratic Greece.[8] The centerpiece of MacIntyre's moral perspective is a *practice* which is:

> any coherent and complex form of socially established cooperative human activity through which goods internal to that form of activity are realized in the course of trying to achieve those standards of excellence which are appropriate to, and partially definitive of, that form of activity, with the result that human powers to achieve excellence, and human conceptions of the ends and goods involved, are systematically extended.[9]

If we unpack this highly compressed definition, several features stand out. First, a practice is a cooperative human activity engaged in by persons who conjointly value the goods intrinsic to the practice. Thus, to use MacIntyre's own example, throwing a football (an individual act) would not be a practice, while the game of football (a collective activity) would be.[10] Further, practices have internal goods which can only be achieved by participating in that practice. Internal goods, like the satisfaction derived by scoring in football, are sharply contrasted with external goods, like receiving money and prestige from playing the game.[11] Finally, practices are constituted and regulated by standards of excellence which participants in the practice must honor. It is through allegiance to and the possible extension of the standards of practices that the goods internal to those practices are themselves extended and improved.

Practices must be understood in relation to two additional concepts. The moral unity of an individual life MacIntyre identifies as a *narrative,* and it is while presenting the moral import of personal narratives that MacIntyre relies upon rhetoric's not-too-distant cousin in communication, the conversation: "For conversation . . . is the form of human transactions in general. . . . I am presenting both conversations in particular and human actions in general as enacted narratives."[12] Conceptualizing an individual's life as a narrative allows an interpretation of a particular act as an instance of a story which gives moral continuity to the actor's life. If an individual's life is best understood as a narrative, a story in the process of being told, then the *telos* for humanity reflects the dramatic form of the Homeric epic—the quest.[13] The optimal end for humanity is neither the deification of human reason nor the stipulation of a transcendent God who commands moral obedience. Rather, MacIntyre's concept of *telos* is fluid and indeterminate; it is a *telos* of potential (*dynamis*), a nascent power to extend.[14]

Collectively constituted practices and personal narratives do not occur in a moral vacuum. Practices and narratives unfold in *moral traditions* which provide the cultural contexts for understanding moral action historically. Virtues such as courage, honesty, justice, and constancy bond practices, personal narratives, and moral traditions into a unified moral perspective. "The virtues find their point and purpose not only in sustaining those relationships necessary if the variety of goods internal to practices are to be achieved and not only in sustaining the [narrative] form of an individual life in which that individual may seek out his or her good as the good of his or her whole life, but also in sustaining those traditions which provide both practices and individual lives with their necessary historical context."[15]

This rather lengthy summary of MacIntyre's position has been undertaken because any assessment or extension of his framework must consider the complete perspective and not just constituents of it. What, then, are we to make of this work? Clearly, it is a most important treatise in moral philosophy. But, because MacIntyre's central concept of a practice is separated from an understanding of rhetoric, it is difficult to see how practices, as he conceives of them, could promote moral action.[16] Further, the concept of a narrative is oddly restricted to explaining the unity of an individual life.

If MacIntyre's moral posture is extended in a way which conjoins an Aristotelian sense of rhetoric with a temporal conception of narrative, we can derive a more adequate explanation of how rhetoric can affect moral action in contemporary society. In this essay, I will (1) argue that certain kinds of conversations are practices whose internal goods lead participants to recover their own potential as moral agents, (2) use the language-action paradigm to explain the distinctive narrative form of these conversations in relation to temporality, and finally (3) offer an extended exemplar of such a conversation—namely, the film *My Dinner with Andre.*

RHETORICAL CONVERSATIONS AS PRACTICES

By grounding practices in action (*praxis*), MacIntyre preserves the important Aristotelian notion that morality is less a form of knowing than of doing.[17] Practices include "arts, sciences, games, politics in the Aristotelian sense, the making and sustaining of family life."[18]

Although gaining the goods internal to a practice requires engaging in it in accordance with the virtues, not all goods internal to practices are directly relevant to moral action. For example, the goods MacIntyre finds internal to the practice of chess are "a particular kind of analytic skill, [and] strategic imagination and competitive intensity."[19] In like manner, one internal good of portrait painting in Western Europe from the late middle ages to the eighteenth century was the realization of how such portraits reveal the souls of their subjects.[20] Even in a period in which some teleological morality is embraced, it is difficult to see how "analytic skills" and "revealed souls" could directly influence moral action. And in modern society, which, as MacIntyre demonstrates so clearly, is sedimented in liberal individualism, most of the practices mentioned in *After Virtue* and their attendant internal goods seem woefully incapable of dislodging the sedimentation. Certain practices, then, seem more capable than others of facilitating moral tasks. Although MacIntyre does not identify those for us, Aristotle does.

In the context of the Greek *polis*, the possibility of an autonomous moral agent who exercised choice on the basis of personal preferences and desire would have been a moral aberration of the first order. For the Athenian statesperson, moral action occurred within a teleologically based moral tradition in which each act contributed to the cumulative narrative history of an individual's character as well as to the tradition in which the act was embedded. Against this backdrop, the central practice for honing practical reason and personal character to a moral sharpness was rhetoric.

Yet rhetoric, as Aristotle envisioned it, is often inadequate for confronting the moral dilemmas of modern societies. Where once agents could be presumed to share a common social knowledge from which moral action might emanate, that presumption has become all but untenable in an age of increased specialization and the concomitant proliferation of technical knowledge.[21] Moreover, the progressive separation of rhetorical audiences from advocates has largely eliminated the audience as the efficient cause of rhetoric—those who judge.[22] In its place, we often find a pre-packaged spectacle, which, when ingested by an apathetic public, creates the illusion of moral involvement in public decision-making.[23] But perhaps the most damaging blow to the classical rhetorical tradition is described by MacIntyre himself. For, as a practice which led to morally defensible action, Aristotelian rhetoric presupposed moral agents who possessed a sense of their own individual moral histories as well as an awareness of how particular choices extended the impersonal teleology of the Greek moral tradition. This presupposition is precisely what MacIntyre denies is possible in liberal individualistic conceptions of morality. Put somewhat differently, any contemporary approach to rhetoric which attempts to preserve the Aristotelian roots of the art must do so with the full realization that modern rhetorical advocates and audiences have lost their sense of individual moral coherence and a teleologically grounded moral tradition.

But the prospect for such a classical approach to rhetoric in modern times is not quite as bleak as the preceding account might suggest. To give some credence to this optimism, however, we will need to entertain the possibility that the form of such a rhetoric might differ significantly from its Aristotelian prototype and, further, that its functions might have to be more rudimentary than was the case for rhetoric in the classical tradition. I want to argue that in contemporary society the closest analogue to Aristotelian rhetoric is a special kind of conversation, which I will call "rhetorical."[24] A rhetorical conversation is a narrative episode in which a conflict over opposing moral viewpoints re-unites the agents with their own moral histories, with the moral traditions of which they are a part, and—perhaps most important—with an awareness of the virtues.[25] As a practice, the goods internal to rhetorical conversations are an awareness of the moral unity of individual life and a sense of the quest for the ultimate good for self and humanity. Unlike MacIntyre's concept of practices, the goods internal to rhetorical conversations are themselves morally essential concepts which can be achieved only by acting in accordance with the virtues.

Before considering how rhetorical conversations promote moral action, it seems necessary to demonstrate that certain conversations—or parts of them—may assume a traditional rhetorical character. Recent inquiries into the relationship between rhetoric and conversation have revealed some basic similarities. For one, Thomas Farrell observes that both may derive from the same common origin—the poetic narrative of the Homeric epic.[26] For another, both conversation and rhetoric value relationships among interacting agents. For Aristotle, friendship was essential to ensure that agents expressing opposing positions would not forget that the best political decisions demanded a cooperative spirit of fraternity in the face of controversy. On a very different level, conversational theorists also underscore how conversations affect the interpersonal relationships between or among participants.[27] To these commonalities, Farrell adds three conditions by which ordinary conversations assume rhetorical characteristics:

1. Cases where the content or expected direction of the conversation has been prepared in advance by at least one of the conversants.
2. Cases where the emergent status of the conversation, as a potentially complete unit of discourse, comes to rest upon the reflective and collaborative practical choices of the conversants themselves.
3. Cases where conversational discourse becomes disputational.[28]

I would add a fourth condition: cases where the conversational narrative structures time so that conversants experience past and future moral traditions—individual and impersonal—as an eternal present. I turn now to an elaboration of this fourth condition in relation to the language-action paradigm.[29]

NARRATIVE EXTENSION AND THE TEMPORAL PRESENT

Echoing the Homeric tradition, MacIntyre claims that individual acts become intelligible by placing them in personal narrative settings in which they are seen as interdependent parts of wholes. "We identify a particular action," he writes, "only by invoking two kinds of context, implicitly if not explicitly. We place the agent's intentions . . . in causal and temporal order with reference to their role in his or her history; and we also place them with reference to their role in the history of the setting or settings to which they belong."[30] Narratives are dramatic stories with beginnings, middles, and ends which give individual actions meaning, provide unity and self-definition to individual lives, and facilitate improvement of the impersonal good for humankind by showing the future as potential extensions of the present. Some important rhetorical applications of narrative are provided in a recent essay by Walter R. Fisher.[31] He uses MacIntyre's notion of narrative as the basis for a paradigm for all human discourse that inevitably leads to moral action. Like MacIntyre, Fisher is distressed over the degenerate state of contemporary public moral argument. MacIntyre argues that there are no rational grounds for deciding between competing moral arguments, and when this is the case, Fisher observes, those "purveyors of ideological, bureaucratic, or technical arguments" often carry the day because of the privileged status of their roles in a hierarchical society and the presumed superiority of their attendant knowledge.[32]

It is clear that for MacIntyre and Fisher, narration is a pivotal construct in any modern teleological moral system. But it is also clear that very little has been said about how narrative structures—whether conversations, histories, or even full-blown paradigms—facilitate moral action. If narration is to fulfill its promise as a form of discourse which promotes moral action, the question of *how* must be addressed.

Some preliminary answers have been suggested by on-going work with the language-action paradigm.[33] Originally, the actional paradigm was a heuristic perspective on conversation designed to explain the structure and meaning of varied instances of interpersonal communication. The paradigm consists of three hierarchical layers of context. *Form of life contexts* are ranges of shared experience among agents—sometimes cultural, sometimes institutional, and sometimes interpersonal.[34] *Encounter contexts* are physical locations where social actors are mutually aware of each other's presence.[35] Finally, *episodic contexts*—those regions defined by conversations themselves—are rule-conforming sequences of symbolic acts generated by two or more actors collectively oriented toward emergent goals.[36]

To explain how rhetorical conversation may lead toward moral action, we need to understand how such interactions affect conversant's experience of *time*. The central categories of the language-action paradigm were originally justified as contexts essential for understanding the meaning of symbolic acts. Yet these same constituents also function as more than analytic categories; they mark the ways in which time may be asserted, understood, even undermined, in the intentions and choices of actors. For example, we can easily recall conversations so involving that we thought they lasted a few minutes—only to discover that we had been engaged for hours. And the obverse is equally common; what we were sure was the drudgery of several eternal hours turned out to be only ten minutes by our watch. In both instances, we are faced with the complex interplay of communication and temporality.

As soon as we view our actional contexts as temporal modalities, however, we confront head-on the philosophical jungles involved in any reflective analysis of time. In part, this is because, as experienced directly, *time is pure change*. And because of that, temporality has become the Darth Vader for philosophical traditions whose ideological commitments lean toward permanency and universality. For when time becomes timeless, it ceases to be the phenomenon we set out to explain. For example, Cassirer notes that when Newton postulated "absolute time" as the foundation of his physics, he had created, in Kant's words, an "existing non-entity."[37] Of both realistic ontology and psychological empiricism, Cassirer concludes:

> neither things in themselves nor sensations in themselves explain the fundamental relation that confronts us in temporal consciousness. The succession of ideas is by no means synonymous with the representation of succession—nor is there any way of seeing how the latter might simply result from the former. For as long as the flow of representations is taken purely as an actual change, an objectively real process, it contains no consciousness of change as such—of that mode in which time is posited as sequence and yet as unremitting present.[38]

If we are to understand how social actors experience time-as-change in rhetorical conversation, we shall have to seek assistance from those who preserve the transitory nature of the concept. Many of those thinkers turn out to be Christian theologians. As an exemplar of this tradition, Augustine observes that we always experience time in the present, but that the present is only knowable as a narrative which encapsulates both the past as memory and the future as expectation.[39] Centuries later, Paul Tillich makes the same point.

> The mystery is that we *have* a present; and even more, that we have *our* future also because we anticipate it in the present; and that we have *our* past also, because we remember it in the present. In the present, our future and our past are *ours*. . . . This is possible because every moment of time reaches into the eternal . . . . It is the eternal "now" which provides for us a temporal "now."[40]

For Augustine and Tillich, temporal consciousness means to experience the past, which was but is no more, and the future, which is not yet but will be, in the present, which is now. And the form of this temporal consciousness, as MacIntyre clearly recognizes, is narration. But not all narratives affect how we experience time in the same way, and if we are to understand how narration functions vis-à-vis rhetorical conversation, we will have to distinguish conversations which structure time as an emergent historical unity from conversations in which time is experienced as a linear sequence of temporal units. The distinction becomes clear in the different ways we experience time-in-conversation on the encounter and form of life levels of the language-action paradigm.

When we experience time on the encounter level, it is the quantitative cumulation of temporal units—seconds, minutes, hours, days. Ontically real, encounter time is the stuff that ages us, makes cars rust, and codifies nicely into the maxim, "The longer you live the older you get." Conversations in which agents experience time as encounter time are transitory and easily forgotten because the present is not extended into the past and future, is not an "eternal now," to use Tillich's phrase, but is rather a mere additive sequencing of chronological units. And when time in conversations is disconnected from past and future, a surrogate continuity can only be supplied by conventions and habitual choices. In the words of a particularly skilled phrasemaker, "When conversations are enacted simply to pass time, they become the time they are passing."[41] When we experience time on the encounter level, our temporal connection to past and future is limited to the spatio-temporal boundaries of the encounter context in which the episode occurs. But occasionally something unusual happens temporally, and it is to those instances that I now turn.

When conversations transcend encounter time, the participants experience time on the form of life level. As its name implies, form of life is an historical concept—fusing past and future in the present. When agents experience the temporal holism of a form of life all at once, in the consciousness of the present in an on-going conversation, they place themselves in a narrative context—in which past and potential conversations are experienced as an historical unity emerging in the present—a unity whose evolving direction can be determined in part through cooperative action. By experiencing time in this way, agents are compelled to rediscover two preconditions to moral action: the unity of their individual lives as actors in a dramatic story, and the moral tradition within which the present narrative is being acted out.

Rhetorical conversations, then, manifest these features: The topic or content is morality. Conversants experience the tension of *agon*—a contest between opposing moral systems. And most important, such conversations are narrative structures in which participants experience time-present as an extended form of life.[42] What we must now ask is whether rhetorical conversations actually occur in a moral universe which seems so alien to them. To answer affirmatively, we are led to an unusual place.

MY DINNER WITH ANDRE

Conversations—rhetorical ones included—are difficult to pin down. No sooner are they enacted than they evaporate, leaving barely a trace of their existence. And so our task becomes doubly difficult—to find a permanent record of a particular type of conversation when permanent records of conversations in general demand planning and extreme care if the constituents of conversations (e.g., rules, strategies, etc.) are to function normally. Fortunately, a memorable rhetorical conversation has not only been preserved, but it also comes to us in the highly accessible form of a film entitled *My Dinner with Andre*.[43] In a cinematic era of Jedi Knights, Valley girls, and Richard Gere, many people found *Andre* a rather tedious anachronism. After all, the action high-point of the film occurs when the head waiter brings Wally and Andre their main course. But like other superb films that did not exactly become box office smashes, *Andre* has already found a cult following of sorts, including diverse scholars in communication.[44] My purpose here, however, is to examine *Andre* as a paradigm example of a rhetorical conversation.

Andre is an unusual instance of a rhetorical conversation. Andre Gregory and Wallace Shawn did not simply have dinner at a New York restaurant in which their spontaneous remarks were filmed. Although the film creates the illusion that an emergent conversation has occurred, it is only an illusion. In reflecting on the incidents which led to the film, Shawn notes, "What if, instead of a play, we just did a very simple film, with lots of closeups, in which I would be talking with Andre? . . . And instead of just writing it myself out of my imagination, Andre and I would really talk for a while, and then my script would be based on our real conversations. . . . It wouldn't just be me! And the piece would say what he wanted it to say, as well as what I wanted it to say" (pp. 13–14). Andre seems even more aware of the potential impact of this theatrical conversation on film than Shawn: "It immediately struck me that the most necessary and appropriate piece that one *could* possibly do at this particular moment in history would be a piece about two friends sitting and talking to each other" (pp. 10–11).

On the surface, the film is an interesting hybrid. As a cinematic event, *Andre* exhibits a contemporary poetic form. In being premeditated and scripted in accordance with the dictates and intentions of both Shawn and Gregory, the work has a pronounced rhetorical flavor. And yet, the exclusively conversational form of the plot harkens back, at least in structure, to matters more properly termed dialectical. I am not concerned with a "correct" labeling of the film—elements of each classical genre are readily apparent in the finished product. It is more important that the plot of *Andre* makes it rhetoric in conversational form, and that the two main characters play themselves.

As in the case with any richly textured discourse, *Andre* is far more than a blueprint of its observable action—of which there is very little. Still, some general overview seems warranted as a departure point. Andre and Wally work in the New York theater—Shawn as a playwright and part-time actor and Gregory as an award-winning director. Both are concerned with the theater's incapacity to present audiences with "reality" in a way that might change their lives. Both are also distressed with the quality of their own lives—although to different degrees and, as we discover, for different reasons. But each approaches their impending dinner with quite different expectations. For Andre, the dinner will afford an opportunity to share a series of "happenings" over the past several years with someone who was once a very close friend, but who—Andre correctly senses—has been avoiding him. For Wally, the dinner promises to be a nightmare with a possible madman, who, allegedly, hallucinates regularly and has taken to chatting with plants; Wally's task is to survive. Their conversation, of course, transcends both sets of expectations. Plotted in encounter time, Andre shares his experiences, both agree on the degenerate quality of contemporary life, they disagree as to the role of the theater vis-à-vis the quality of life, and finally they confront one another's moral traditions and in the process learn something morally important.

As a prelude to our analysis, we note that Wally and Andre bring to their conversation incomplete moral selves. In his five years of travels, of living purely by his impulses, Andre has rediscovered a vital moral truth—that genuine living demands that we experience every moment to its fullest and that such living generates an interconnectedness with all people and all things. After recounting his experiences in Poland, Andre muses: "What I think I experienced was for the first time in my life to know what it means to be truly alive. . . . Now, that's very frightening, because with that comes an immediate awareness of death . . . because they go hand in hand . . . you know, that feeling of being connected with everything, means to also be connected with death" (p. 38). But in gaining some moral acuity through his experiences, Andre has lost other qualities. Principally, he has lost a sense of teleology, of purpose, of the moral life as a continual narrative quest in which the individual moves from a present moral condition toward something better.

Wally is an ideal moral counterpoint to Andre. Where Andre's international adventures in impulse have left him individually alive and vibrant, Wally's own existence has left him—as Andre himself might have put it—a lobotomized performer with no sense of the person behind the mask. Wally is not unreflective, however. On his way to meet Andre, he laments: "When I was ten years old I was rich, I was an aristocrat, riding around in taxis, surrounded by comfort, and all I thought about was art and music. Now I'm thirty-six, and all I think about is money" (p. 17). At this point, it is clear that while Andre has lost the teleological sense of moral tradition, Wally instinctually retains it. Well into their conversation, Wally tells Andre:

> You know . . . I think I do know what really disturbs me about the work that you've described, . . . if I've understood what you've been saying, it somehow seems that the whole point of the work that you did in those workshops . . . was to enable the people in the workshops, including yourself, to somehow sort of strip away every scrap of purposefulness from selected moments. And the point of it was so that you would then be able to experience somehow just pure being. . . . And I think I just simply object to that. (pp. 103–104)

Despite his objection, Wally's sense of moral purpose has been perverted into making lists of errands to do and taking empty pleasure in doing them.

And so as they approach their evening together, Wally and Andre are oddly incomplete moral agents. Wally has some sense of tradition, but a crippled sense of self, while Andre is literally brimming over with "selfness," but has no idea what to do with it. But both are quite clear that *something* is wrong with their lives and that the theater—their vocation—seems ill-suited to address the malady—whatever it may be. With this preview, we turn now to the conversation itself.

It begins as a typical dialogue unfolding in encounter time. We do not experience that portion of the interaction directly. Rather we are told about it by Wally: "So we talked for a while about my writing and my acting and about my girlfriend, Debby, and we talked about his wife, Chiquita, and his two children, Nicolas and Marina. Finally, I got around to asking him what he'd been up to in the last few years. He seemed a little reluctant to go into it, but that made me all the more anxious to know the story. I was sure I would feel very relaxed with him if only he'd tell his story. So I just kept asking, and finally he started to answer" (pp. 21–22). And when Andre begins to answer by telling his story, the conversation transcends encounter time and becomes a narrative grounded in form of life.

As a rhetorical conversation, the interaction has three phases, each conveniently correlated with a portion of the meal. The first phase begins with hors d'oeuvres and ends with the serving of the main course and is "Andre's story." The second begins with the entre and concludes with the ordering of the after dinner drinks and involves "identification and conflict." The final phase starts with the after dinner drinks and ends with Andre paying the check. This phase, more subtle and complex than the preceding two, entails "moral closure."

"Andre's Story" is really a composite of five stories spanning several years of his life: (1) a theater workshop in Poland conducted with his friend and mentor, Jerzy Grotowski; (2) a trip to Tibet and an aborted plan to direct *The Little Prince* with a buddhist monk, Kozan, playing the lead role; (3) a brief trip to India; (4) a stay in the experimental Scottish community of Findhorn; and (5) a death and rebirth ritual conducted on Halloween at a friend's estate on Montauk, Long Island. Andre has shared these stories before—with other friends and acquaintances. This telling is different from previous versions because it is rhetorical. As such, Andre experiences two morally relevant insights, insights we may presume he did not encounter previously, or the dinner with Wally would not exhibit the ultimate moral import it had. Andre seems aware that these five adventures are not merely chronological sequences in encounter time, but rather a personal narrative which gives the past five years of his life moral continuity. It is significant that the Poland episode ends with his group christening Andre and re-naming him "Yendrush," and that the Montauk event symbolically kills Andre so that he may be born again—rather transparent evidence of the narrative force of the stories for Andre. But there is a more disquieting revelation as well. Andre seems increasingly aware of the incompleteness and even the potential for evil if his story were extended. In retrospectively examining the Polish workshop and his fascination with the *Little Prince*, Andre uses Nazi references as a means both of self-criticism and as a ploy to coax the detached Wally to offer his own critical appraisal of Andre's story. When Wally does not respond, Andre intensifies the references and in so doing induces the reluctant Wally to enter the form of life narrative. After the entre is served, both silently reflect on Andre's experiences when Andre says:

> Yes, you know, frankly, I'm sort of repelled by the whole story, if you really want to know .... I mean, who did I think I was? You know? I mean that's the story of some kind of spoiled princess. I mean, you know, who did I think I was, the Shah of Iran? I mean, you know, I wonder if people such as myself are not really Albert Speer, Wally. You know, Hitler's architect, Albert Speer. . . . Well, I've been thinking a lot about him recently. Because I think I am Speer. . . . Well, he was a very cultivated man, . . . so he thought the ordinary rules of life didn't apply to him. I mean, I would really like to be stripped and unmasked. I feel I deserve it. Because I really feel that everything I've done is horrific. Just horrific. (pp. 57–58)

Once Andre rediscovers the unity of his life as a personal narrative, he also discovers that he will somehow be judged, held accountable, for the moral integrity of his life when he leaves it. And his fear is that he will not measure up in a narrative composed of "impulse living" (p. 58).

The second phase of the conversation begins as Wally leaves the detached context of encounter time by coming to his friend's defense. They share an intense interlude where both acknowledge that people in contemporary society have become mechanical automatons, persons who have lost the capacity to feel and who focus all their energy on accomplishing occupational goals. (We might note in passing that this precise view of humanity was offered by MacIntyre as the societal consequence of living in an age where morality is defined by liberal individualism.)[45] Ironically, Wally is diffidently unaware that he is one of the zombies himself. Andre's story may have left Andre raw and morally incomplete, but at least he knows it! Wally, on the other hand, has forgotten his story and in its place we find a craving for comfort, a distrust and fear of genuine emotion, and a life filled with the empty security of routine.

The confrontation begins innocently enough. Wally has just mentioned that sleeping under an electric blanket has subtly changed how he sleeps and even how he dreams (pp. 75–76). But Andre sees the blanket for what it is—a technological device designed to intensify comfort and anesthetize feeling:

> Well, I wouldn't put an electric blanket on for anything, . . . turn on that electric blanket, and its like taking a tranquilizer, or it's like being lobotomized by watching television. I think you enter the dream world again. I mean, what does it do to us, Wally, to live in an environment where something as massive as the seasons and the cold and the winter don't in any way affect us? (pp. 76–77)

Wally's response, a defense actually, involves his occupation as a playwright. He admits that he succumbs to the dream world by valuing creature comforts in his personal life, but in his plays, he attempts to jar audiences to acknowledge the harsh reality around them (p. 83). But Andre is relentless:

> But, Wally, don't you see the dilemma? You're not taking into account the period we live in! I mean, of *course* that's what the theater *should* do. . . . But, Wally, the question is whether the theater *now* can do for an audience what Brecht tried to do or what Craig or Duse tried to do. . . . Because . . . I think people are so deeply asleep today that unless you're putting on those sort of superficial plays that help your audience sleep more comfortably, I think it's very hard to know what to do in the theater. (pp. 84–85)

It is important to understand what Andre has done here. He has torn Wally loose from his moorings, and in so doing, has prepared both of them for a partial rediscovery of their roles in a moral tradition. Wally has conceded that his personal life is defined by creature comforts and habit. And now his vocation—often a surrogate tradition in a society governed by emotivism—has been challenged by someone who has intimate knowledge of it.

When backed against this wall, Wally strikes back and Andre is forced to admit some things too. After questioning Andre intensely over whether dropping out of society is necessary, Wally chides: "So I mean, is that our problem? Is that what you're saying? Are we just bored, spoiled children who've been lying in the bathtub all day, playing with their plastic duck, and now they're thinking. What can I do?" (p. 91). Andre's response places him squarely in the liberal individualist moral tradition, a tradition, MacIntyre tells us, which in one variant expresses a paranoid distrust of institutions which would suppress the freedom of the autonomous moral agent.[46] Andre says:

> Okay. Yes. We're bored now. We're all bored. But has it ever occurred to you, Wally, that the process which creates this boredom that we see in the world now may very well be a self-perpetuating unconscious form of brainwashing created by a world totalitarian government based on money? And that all of this is much more dangerous, really, than one thinks? And that it's not a question of individual survival, Wally, but that somebody who's bored is asleep? And somebody who's asleep will not say no. (pp. 91–92)

And what is Andre's solution? How does the liberal individual confront this moral apocalypse? His solution seems even more detached and ethereal then his account of the problem.

> I keep thinking that we need a new language, a language of the heart, a language, as in the Polish forest, where language wasn't needed—some kind of language between people that is a new kind of poetry, that is the poetry of the dancing bee, that tells us where the honey is. (p. 95)

Andre is wrong, of course, and both he and Wally know it. Moral action cannot be reinvented through a language of the heart. The heart itself must somehow be stirred from its moral slumbering and moved to a better place. And to do that, Wally must recover his own moral legacy and impart its significance to Andre.

It is unfortunate that as the final phase of the conversation begins, the audience may feel the emotional fatigue from what has transpired and, like Andre and Wally, be ready to sit back, relax, and enjoy some espresso and an amaretto. But it is in this final phase that the disparate moral pieces of two lives become reassembled, and if we are not prepared for it, the moral closure is apt to slip by us quietly along with dessert.

Wally begins by sharing with Andre what he, Wally, "really thinks" of Andre's experiences and proclamations. Wally's thoughts are too long and complex to reproduce here in their entirety, but they contain two important clues to his own moral tradition (pp. 97–100). The first is Wally's genuine joy over the everyday continuities of life, those very same continuities which Andre's sees as unthinking habits that lead to ultimate passivity: "I mean . . . isn't it pleasant just to get up in the morning, and there's Chiquita, there are the children, the *Times* is delivered . . . why not lean back and just enjoy these details?" (p. 98). The second is his commitment to science. Wally's allegiance here is not to the naïve belief that science will solve the world's problems. On the contrary, Andre and Wally believe that science is causing more problems than it is solving (p. 103). But science is an undeniable force in an *evolving moral universe*. To deny that force, as Andre tries to do by becoming a slave to his impulses, is to deny a teleological morality and to float adrift in the uncharted seas of the encounter moment.

What is the moral heritage beneath Wally's impassioned comments? While no characterization would be uncontestable, the signs point toward Aristotelianism. The grounding of action in the practical world, the importance of familial ties and kinship to self-identity, the exercise of practical reason and experience as the arbiters of action—all point to the classical tradition. Subtly, Andre learns his Aristotelian lesson. "And I mean, as long as you're really alive inside, then of course there's no problem. I mean, you know, if you're living with someone in one little room, and there's a life going on between you and the person you're living with, well then, you know a whole adventure can be going on right in that room" (p. 106). Again, less hypothetically: "And when I allowed myself to consider the possibility of not spending the rest of my life with Chiquita, I realized that what I wanted most in life was to always be with her" (p. 108). And finally, as their conversation ends, Andre acknowledges the continual mystery of life even within the unending narrative in which each individual plays but a small part: "A baby holds your hands, and then suddenly there's this huge man lifting you off the ground, and then he's gone. Where's that son?" (pp. 112–113).

And what is learned? Wally rediscovers the wonderment of being alive as an individual and connected with all that surrounds him. "I rode home through the city streets. There wasn't a street—there wasn't a building—that wasn't connected to some memory in my mind" (p. 113). Andre realizes that self-awareness devoid of moral tradition has no purpose and that surrendering life to disconnected moments of "pure being" can lead to the fascistic horrors of Nazism which forever haunt his mind. Andre and Wally are re-united through a rhetorical conversation. They have rediscovered the constituents of a moral perspective each needed the other to supply. Andre imparted a sense of selfhood to Wally, while Wally gave Andre a renewed appreciation for a teleological tradition. The continuity of an individual life and a moral tradition are the goods internal to rhetorical conversations as practices and achieveable only through enacting such conversations in accordance with the virtues of justice (the desserts each owe the other), courage (to risk one's self for the other), and honesty (to be truthful beyond all else).

IMPLICATIONS

The continuing work with the language-action paradigm reveals increasing similarities between rhetoric and conversation. Aristotle began the *Rhetoric* with the claim that rhetoric was the counterpart of dialectic; both were general methods for dealing with probabilities in the political realm of *praxis*.[47] To those initial similarities, Farrell has added others.[48] We may now add one, perhaps two, more. If the argument and extended example presented here specify the function of rhetorical conversations, then moral action—in its most general sense—would seem to be the *telos* of both public rhetoric and its conversational analogues. But, if MacIntyre is correct that moral premises in modern times take root in individual desires, then no common moral grounds (except desires—which are indefinitely variable) bond reasons together and no collectively deliberated moral decisions can be expected as a matter of course. Thus, I suggested with guarded optimism that the best we might hope from rhetorical conversations is that agents might become united with the necessary *preconditions* to moral action in the Aristotelian tradition

Rhetoric and conversation may also be linked to temporal experience. I argued that rhetorical conversations are narratives in that conversants experience time-present as a narrative extension into the past and future forms of life in which they enact multiple stories simultaneously—their own, others' stories, and those of their respective moral traditions. It is this protracted temporal experience which reunites agents with the moral goods internal to rhetorical conversations. We might now ask whether the temporal experience of time-present as extended forms of life is found in more traditional rhetorical artifacts. For if it is, it might provide additional clues to the suasory impact others find in public moral argument reconceptualized as narrative.

Our account of rhetorical conversations and moral action would not be complete without commenting retrospectively on the work that most centrally stimulated this effort. I refer, of course, to *After Virtue*. MacIntyre is quite clear that if the *telos* of humanity is not impersonal in nature, the resultant moral system will ultimately be reducible to some variant of emotivism when scrutinized rationally. But can MacIntyre's own impersonal ultimate good for humanity withstand the very test he devises? MacIntyre's *telos* is clearly set forth: "We have then arrived at a provisional conclusion about the good life for man: the good life for man is the life spent in seeking for the good life for man, and the virtues necessary for the seeking are those which will enable us to understand what more and what else the good life for man is."[49] But in defining the ultimate good for humanity as an indeterminant future condition which we constantly expand even as we search for it, MacIntyre commits himself to a humanism which contains the seeds of a collective emotivism. For if the ultimate good for humanity can only be created by cooperative human action, then this impersonal *telos* is also, in the final analysis, grounded in the collective wills, needs, and desires of human agents. If practices are cooperative human activities, then their internal goods must be rooted in human action. And if the virtues are set forth by human agents— whether Aristotle, Jane Austin, or MacIntyre himself—then they too are determined by humanity. And if the question were asked, which moral ends, which practices, or which virtues are best, the ultimate grounds for responding, I fear, would be the very grounds MacIntyre strives so diligently to avoid—the collective wills of the group or community in which moral action takes place. As long as the ultimate good *for humanity* is something which can be exclusively defined, changed, and acted upon *by humanity*, the moral philosophy which results will turn out to be another form of an emotivist moral system.

I believe MacIntyre has fallen prey to the same trap he argues has ensnared other modern moral philosophers. Throughout his work, MacIntyre claims that most contemporary moral philosophers try to construct coherent moral systems from concepts which represent ahistorical fragments of antithetical moral traditions.[50] If MacIntyre's own position suffers the same fate as those he so successfully indicts, perhaps he too is working with concepts from competing moral traditions. In fact, this turns out to be the case.

At the outset, I suggested that MacIntyre's moral philosophy contains concepts from two quite different moral traditions. The concepts of "the virtues," "practices," and "practical reason" are clearly Aristotelian. But the concepts of "narration," "quest," and "historical unity," while surely discussed in the Aristotelian corpus, are more centrally remnants of an older moral tradition we might call pre-Socratic, or more simply, Homeric. When concepts from one tradition are dislodged from their heritage and placed in another tradition, there is always the danger that the original meanings of the displaced concepts will have been lost. Two such concepts are "quest" and "teleology" and we must ask how their respective meanings changed as they assumed new roles within MacIntyre's moral system.

The answer is a complex one. For Aristotle, the ultimate *telos* for humankind is happiness, and the pursuit of happiness is "an activity of the soul and consists in actions performed in conjunction with the rational element."[51] MacIntyre rejects this view because "Aristotle's teleology presupposed his metaphysical biology," which has been shown to be untenable.[52] While rejecting Aristotle's animism, MacIntyre preserves a teleology by recasting it in Homeric terms, as a narrative quest. What MacIntyre fails to see is that a narrative quest in the Homeric tradition is inextricably linked to a supernatural *telos*—the desires and actions of the gods, as memorialized in poetry. As narrative quests, Homeric poetry presents the stories of the gods (*nomoi* or "custom laws") as normative models of the stories humans should live if their lives are to be characterized by *aretē*—overall excellence.[53] By divorcing the narrative quest from the gods, MacIntyre has changed its meaning and, in so doing, created a moral fiction of his own. When he then grafts that fiction onto a teleological tree, itself having been pruned of its theological impulse in the form of Aristotelian animism, the resultant bush does not exactly burn with moral authority. For when the *telos* for humanity is a quest plus humanly derived moral concepts, all that can follow is a humanly grounded morality, and those are at base emotivist, no matter how persistent the protests to the contrary.

Is there any way to construct a teleological morality that transcends emotivism and still preserves the classical system? Any satisfactory answer would be well beyond the scope of this work. We can, however, sketch one direction an answer might take. Suppose the concept of the narrative quest were re-united with "the gods." Such a move is not as radical as it might appear. In fact, if history is conceptualized as a narrative quest, then some sense of spirit is necessary if that quest is to be meaningful. As Ken Wilber notes, "If we assume that history has some sort of *meaning*, then we must also assume that it points to something *other* than itself, which is to say, something other than individual men and women. . . . Nothing can stay long removed from God, nor long divorced from that Ground of Being outside of which nothing exists, and history . . . is the story of men and women's love affair with the Divine."[54] This sense of human history evolving in concert with the gods epitomizes the teleology of the Homeric tradition. In such a system, practices and their attendant virtues would be vehicles for gaining access to the moral truths of the gods. The narrative unity of an individual's life and the historical unity of moral traditions would be narrative quests in the fullest Homeric sense, quests for universal moral truths.

This Homeric teleology would enrich our understanding of the classical rhetorical tradition by reaffirming aspects of the tradition which have long been neglected. For example, if moral truths are transcendent, they must comprise *archai* or first moral principles. Moral *archai* capture relationships between the universal and the particular, between the gods and humankind. According to Giambattista Vico, one central function of rhetoric is to set forth these *archai*: "This requires that rhetoric be understood as a science of narration which can comprehend the particulars of the human world in terms of necessity. Narration must tell us the story of the human world as the necessary sequence of the ideal eternal history. Narration and necessity are joined."[55] What is good in any given case is based upon moral principles which link the stories of the gods to the emergent narrative of human history.

But how are moral *archai* discovered? Writing of *archai* in the theoretical sciences, Aristotle concludes: "There will be no scientific knowledge of the primary premisses, and since except intuition nothing can be truer than scientific knowledge, it will be intuition that apprehends the primary premisses."[56] Moral *archai*, like their theoretical counterparts, are discoverable only through intuition, and intuition, Vico tells us, is grounded in the inventional facet of memory called *ingegno* or ingenuity.[57] *Ingegno* is the capacity to see immediately and directly a relationship between a moral problem in the human world and a solution in the spiritual world—what Vico refers to as "ideal eternal history."[58]

Although moral *archai* are discovered through *ingegno*, they are most clearly expressed through metaphor. As the grounds of moral argument, *archai* exhibit an imaginative quality neither reducible to nor derivable from rational argument. Extending the Homeric tradition through Vico, Ernesto Grassi captures well the expressive quality of this metaphorical discourse: "The *true rhetorical speech* . . . springs from the *archai* [and is] nondeducible, moving, and indicative, due to its original images. The original speech is that of the wise man, of the *sophos*, who is not only *epistetai*, but who with insight leads, guides, and attracts."[59] And so the initial vision of rhetoric which emerges from the Homeric tradition is quite un-Aristotelian with its emphasis upon moral *archai*, ingenious invention, and metaphorical expression.

But there is great danger if we stop here. For if moral action entails the unreflective acceptance of the advocacy of a rhetor who claims to have been to the mountaintop and received "the Truth," we are surely faced with a rhetoric having little to do with morality and the virtues. For every Moses, history sadly records a hundred Hitlers and the tragic consequences of uncritically following false prophets. Perhaps Aristotle's greatest legacy to the classical tradition was his insistence that practical reason, *phronesis*, should be the final arbiter of moral action. Whereas the Homeric tradition allows us to recover the imagistic nature of moral insight, it is the classical heritage which reminds us that the muse must be broken, interrupted, and reflectively examined if the ensuing action is to be rationally justified.[60] But who initiates the interruption? We may take a clue from Farrell's careful reading of Aristotle's *Rhetoric*. Farrell notes that for Aristotle, the end of rhetoric is not the production of persuasive discourse, but rather the enactment of moral choice "through the adjudication of a reasoning and competent audience."[61] The rhetorical audience is entrusted with the responsibility of critically assessing the genuineness of the original vision, and is—as such—the ultimate guardian of moral action.

We have perhaps extended this fragment further than its speculative nature would warrant. My point is to suggest that if we reunite the Homeric concepts of narration, quest, and the universal moral truth of the gods with the Aristotelian concepts of the classical rhetorical tradition, we may well gain a deeper understanding of the tradition and share MacIntyre's enthusiasm—however guarded—for the potential of that tradition for dealing with contemporary moral problems.

Notes

1. Thomas B. Farrell, "The Tradition of Rhetoric and the Philosophy of Communication," *Communication* 7 (1983): 152.

2. Ibid., p. 151.

3. Alasdair MacIntyre, *After Virtue* (South Bend, IN: University of Notre Dame Press, 1981).

4. Ibid., pp. 6–11

5. Ibid., pp. 49–53.

6. Ibid., pp. 239–240.

7. Ibid., p. 140.

8. In commenting on the narrative structure of individual lives which makes their actions intelligible, MacIntyre writes: "Hence, there is no way to give us an understanding of any society, including our own, except through the stock of stories which constitute its initial dramatic resources. Mythology, in this original sense, is at the heart of things" (*After Virtue*, p. 201).

9. Ibid. p. 175.

10. Ibid., p. 175.

11. Ibid., pp. 175–176.

12. Ibid., p. 197.

13. Ibid., p. 204.

14. Farrell makes much the same point in arguing that Aristotle saw virtue in the *Rhetoric* as "a powerful capacity awaiting propitious enactment" ("Tradition of Rhetoric," p. 165).

15. MacIntyre, *After Virtue*, p. 207.

16. I could discover only minimal uses of "rhetoric" in *After Virtue* and all support the claim made here. For example, on p. 69, MacIntyre qualifies his indictment of emotivist morality by noting that "the major protagonists of the distinctively modern moral causes of the modern world ... offer a rhetoric which serves to conceal behind the masks of morality what are in fact the preferences of arbitrary will and desire is not of course an original claim." Again, on p. 235, in a rare tip-of-the-hat to Marx, MacIntyre credits Marx with recognizing that fragmented social concepts "are used at one and the same time to express rival and incompatible social ideals and policies *and* to furnish us with a pluralist political rhetoric whose function is to conceal the depth of our conflict." These usages, as well as the others, reveal the negativism common to naïve contemporary nontechnical uses of rhetoric.

17. Aristotle, *Eudemian Ethics*, trans. J. Solomon, in *The Works of Aristotle*, ed. W. E. Ross (London: Oxford University Press, 1915), I, 5, 1216^b.

18. MacIntyre, *After Virtue*, p. 175.

19. Ibid., pp. 175–176.

20. Ibid., p. 176.

21. For an account of the changes in the type of knowledge which underlies rhetoric, see Thomas Farrell, "Knowledge, Consensus, and Rhetorical Theory," *Quarterly Journal of Speech* 62 (1976): 1–15 (reprinted in this volume); and Thomas B. Farrell and G. Thomas Goodnight, "Accidental Rhetoric: Root Metaphors of Three Mile Island," *Communication Monographs* 48 (1981): 271–300.

22. Farrell, "Tradition of Rhetoric," p. 161.

23. There are numerous elaborations of this claim, each with slightly different colorations. The two most germane to this essay are Daniel J. Boorstin, *The Image* (New York: Atheneum, 1962), esp. pp. 9–12; and Thomas B. Farrell, "The Forms of Social Knowledge: *Praxis* and Spectacle" (paper presented at the Speech Communication Association Convention, San Francisco, California, December 1976).

24. Two caveats are necessary. First, "persuasion" is not a necessary condition for conversations to be rhetorical, because persuasion occurs in all conversations to some extent. Second, rhetorical conversations occur very rarely—as we should expect in a society dominated by emotivism.

25. Rhetorical conversations share some features with what others have called "dialogic communication." See, for example, Richard J. Bernstein, *Beyond Objectivism and Relativism: Science, Hermeneutics, and Praxis* (Philadelphia: University of Pennsylvania Press, 1983); Richard L. Johannesen, "The Emerging Concept of Communication as Dialogue," *Quarterly Journal of Speech* 57 (1971): 373-382; and John Stewart, "Foundations of Dialogic Communication," *Quarterly Journal of Speech* 64 (1978): 183–201.

26. Thomas B. Farrell, "Aspects of Coherence in Conversation and Rhetoric," in Robert Craig and Karen Tracey, eds., *Conversational Coherence: Studies in Form and Strategy* (Berkeley, CA: Sage, 1983), pp. 259–285.

27. The "content-relationship" distinction permeates most modern treatments of interpersonal communication. One of the earliest statements of the distinction is Paul J. Watzlawick, J. H. Bevin, and Don D. Jackson, *Pragmatics of Human Communication* (New York: W. W. Norton, 1967).

28. Farrell, "Aspects," p. 271.

29. See, e.g., Thomas S. Frentz and Thomas B. Farrell, "Language-Action: A Paradigm for Communication," *Quarterly Journal of Speech* 62 (1976): 333–349; Thomas B. Farrell and Thomas S. Frentz, "Communication and Meaning: A Language-Action Synthesis," *Philosophy and Rhetoric* 12 (1979): 215-55; and Thomas S. Frentz and Thomas B. Farrell, "Discourse, Coherence, and Episodic Duration" (paper presented at the Western Speech Communication Convention, Denver, Colorado, February 1981).

30. MacIntyre, *After Virtue*, p. 194. It is interesting to note that MacIntyre's entire discussion of the intelligibility of human action in terms of contexts parallels quite closely the language-action approach to meaning in communication. See, e.g., Frentz and Farrell, "Language-Action"; Farrell and Frentz, "Communication and Meaning"; and Frentz and Farrell, "Discourse."

31. Walter R. Fisher, "Narration as a Human Communication Paradigm: The Case of Public Moral Argument," *Communication Monographs* 51 (1984): 1–22 (reprinted in this volume).

32. Ibid., p. 11.

33. Frentz and Farrell, "Discourse."

34. Frentz and Farrell, "Language-Action," pp. 334–335

35. Ibid., pp. 335–336.

36. Ibid., p. 336.

37. Ernst Cassirer, *The Philosophy of Symbolic Forms* (New Haven, CT: Yale University Press, 1957), vol. 3, p. 163.

38. Ibid., p. 173.

39. Saint Augustine, *Confessions*, trans. Rex Warner (New York: Mentor-Omega Books, 1963), p. 273.

40. Paul Tillich, *The Eternal Now* (New York: Charles Scribner's Sons, 1963), pp. 130–131.

41. My compliments to Thomas Farrell for this aphorism in a personal letter long gone but not forgotten.

42. I am not implying that only rhetorical conversations restructure the experience of time on the form of life level. Clearly, many conversations I would not identify as "rhetorical" perform this temporal function. Intense discussions about important relationships, philosophical issues, or even the Green Bay Packers can result in the participants experiencing time as an extended narrative through discourse. I am claiming that experiencing time as an extended present is a necessary, but not sufficient, condition for a conversation being rhetorical.

43. Subsequent references to the film will cite pages from the screenplay by Wallace Shawn and Andre Gregory, *My Dinner with Andre* (New York: Grove Press, 1981).

44. The Mass Communication Interest Group co-sponsored a program with the Language Behavior Interest Group to explore different approaches to *Andre* at the Western Speech Communication Association's regional convention in Seattle, Washington, February 18–21, 1984.

45. MacIntyre, *After Virtue*, pp. 22–34.

46. Ibid., p. 33.

47. Aristotle, *Rhetoric*, trans. W. Rhys Roberts, I, 1, 1354[a].

48. Farrell, "Aspects."

49. MacIntyre, *After Virtue*, p. 204.

50. Ibid., pp. 1–5.

51. Aristotle, *Nicomachean Ethics*, trans. Martin Ostwald, I, 7, 1098[a].

52. MacIntyre, *After Virtue*, p. 152.

53. See Eric A. Havlock, *Preface to Plato* (New York: Grosset and Dunlap, 1967), pp. 61–86.

54. Ken Wilber, *Up From Eden: A Transpersonal View of Human Evolution* (Boulder, CO: Shambhala Publications, 1981), p. 1.

55. Donald Phillip Verene, *Vico's Science of Imagination* (Ithaca, NY: Cornell University Press, 1981), p. 165.

56. Aristotle, *Posterior Analytics*, trans. G.R.G. Mure, in *The Basic Works of Aristotle*, ed. Richard McKeon (New York: Random House, 1941), II, 19, 100[b]. It is true that for Aristotle dialectic can critically assess first principles to ascertain their casual efficacy and thereby their degree of belief (*pistis*), but the initial discovery of *archai* is a matter for intuition and not dialectic.

57. Verene, *Vico's Science*, p. 105.

58. Ibid., pp. 65–95.

59. Ernesto Grassi, *Rhetoric as Philosophy* (University Park: Pennsylvania State University Press, 1980), p. 32.

60. Havelock, *Preface to Plato*, pp. 208–209.

61. Farrell, "Tradition of Rhetoric," p. 165.

Crafting Virtue

The Rhetorical Construction
of Public Morality

CELESTE MICHELLE CONDIT

Throughout its history, rhetorical theory has bristled with disputes about the relationship between morality and rhetoric. In the founding years, Plato, Aristotle, Isocrates, and others focused some of their most determined attention on the moral status of rhetoric in the community.[1] In our own century, several refounding studies in the renaissance of rhetoric concentrated on the ethical choices faced by individual rhetors.[2] More recently, as interest in the social functions of rhetoric has become recentralized, the issue of rhetoric's impact on public morality has gained the spotlight.[3]

Recent theorists, however, have tended to derogate public moral discourse and have resorted to privatized models of morality. In a social community where no one may "impose their religious views on others," and where religion is taken as the sole or primary source of morality, privatization of morality may provide an appealing retreat. Nonetheless, I will suggest that it is possible and preferable to maintain a theory that recognizes collective discourse as the source of an active public morality. This essay will trace the errant root metaphors that nourish the "privatization" of morality, defend a theory of public morality, and provide an empirical study of race relations in America to illustrate and support that theory.

THE PRIVATIZATION OF MORALITY

The case for the "privatization of morality" has been constructed through recent works by Walter Fisher, Thomas Farrell, and Thomas Frentz, all of whom draw heavily on Alasdair MacIntyre.[4] Frentz's statement of the position is the most explicit, but the perspective rests on three shared assumptions: a pessimistic view of public morality, a "conversational" model of moral discourse, and the promotion of individual moral growth rather than collective moral argument.

The pessimistic strand in these works is most striking. In Fisher's view, for example, contemporary public moral argument is in such a desperate state that there is perhaps an "impossibility, of persuasive moral argument in our time, given the rational world paradigm."[5] Fisher is so concerned as to demand an entirely new metaparadigm of thought. His despair is echoed by Farrell, who, in an insightful defense of the rhetorical tradition, nonetheless labels the human position as "tragic," refers to "the barbarism of our times," and laments that "rhetoric no longer mimes an ordered world."[6] Frentz completes the triadic chorus, bemoaning the contemporary preoccupation with vocation and lack of appreciation for Aristotelian virtues such as "family."[7] He argues that "modern rhetorical advocates have lost their sense of individual moral coherence and a teleologically grounded moral tradition" and that "rhetoric, as Aristotle envisioned it, is often inadequate for confronting the moral dilemmas of modern societies."[8] Pessimism about public morality thus provides a central motivation for the move to privatized morality.

The reliance upon a "conversational" model of discourse is also a common element among the privatized moral theories, as it is in a wide range of academic fields today.[9] In MacIntyre and Fisher, the conversational metaphor is not consciously recognized, but it is explicitly used.[10] Fisher, for example, suggests the conversational metaphor is incomplete, but claims to incorporate it.[11] More importantly, although he begins by locating the "problem" of morality in the public realm, Fisher eventually falls back on the two-party "conversation" between Plato's "Callicles" and "Socrates" for illustration. In this private conversation, the moral issue shifts to a consideration of how individuals ought to live their lives, rather than how a collectivity comes to "act morally." Fisher's conclusions about the Platonic dialogue feature, for example, the suggestion that "persons have found these [Calliclean] values *relevant* to their material lives, *consequential* in determining their survival and well-being."[12] Thus, although Fisher, like MacIntyre, begins with a concern about collective action, he is diverted by a model that returns the focus to the private realm.

It is Frentz, however, who pushes the conversational model most directly. He labels his perspective "rhetorical conversation" and focuses his critique on a movie about a dinner conversation. Frentz presents as paradigmatic *My Dinner with Andre*, the filmic account of a conversation between two effete male intellectuals who, while feasting at an expensive French restaurant, stumble by the admission that they are "bored, spoiled children who've been lying in the bathtub all day, playing with their plastic duck."[13] Frentz lauds, as an example of moral development, the journey of self-discovery that these two well-fed and self-indulgent American males go through. No doubt, for these two individuals, the social interaction provided by an enlightened conversation produces improved individual virtue. Their discovery, however, lacks breadth and depth. For example, according to Frentz's portrayal, Wally learns that he should be content to live with his family and his newspaper and his comfortable way of life. This is far from a significant answer to the moral quandaries with which Fisher, MacIntyre, and (by bequeathal) Frentz begin—collective international problems such as nuclear war, resource allocation, and abortion.

The source of the deficiencies in this conversational model can be unearthed by returning to the original presentation of the perspective by Alasdair MacIntyre. In *After Virtue*, MacIntyre describes the positions held by competing groups on issues such as nuclear weapons, abortion, and resource distribution. Essentially he sets up a "conversation" between advocates of critical social issues, portraying the goal of this encounter as that of an academic conversation—the two parties ought to convince each other. He finds, however, that the differences between the views of the parties are so great that persuasion seems impossible. The hope of moral resolution is therefore suspended. MacIntyre's response is to insist that everyone return to a uniform set of individual moral precepts—evolving from the Aristotelian virtues—even if that means a retreat from the public realm to "local" communities of like-minded individuals.

Frentz follows MacIntyre's path closely. He sees "rhetorical conversation" as functioning in the same manner—the two parties are supposed to learn from or persuade each other. Given the impossibility of this in a world where shared ideals (or a hegemonic moral order) have broken down, Frentz also seeks an escapist solution: he turns to ambiguous "gods" and "ingenious" leaders to prod individuals toward morally enlightening conversations.[14]

Both MacIntyre's and Frentz's escape from the collective are necessitated by the conversational model around which their arguments are molded. In a conversation the outcomes of concern are the beliefs and actions of the conversational partners—the advocates themselves. If the speakers cannot be made to understand one another or learn from each other, all is lost. Fortunately, however, this is not generally the manner in which public discourse functions. Public advocates rarely convince each other, but given a rhetorical model, they do not have to do so. Competing rhetors persuade third parties—audiences—and create a "public consensus" that does not require the approval of every individual on every point—although it requires a general minimal satisfaction.[15] This course of affairs is evident, for example, in the "public consensus" on the abortion issue which, as reflected both in the Supreme Court decision and in public opinion polls, is neither that of the Pro-choice nor Pro-life view.[16] Rather, values, facts, and interests of both groups have been combined.

The abortion controversy is no historical exception. The same ongoing process of resolutions occurred for the battle over slavery, on which Americans held views which were as hostile and polar as in modern controversies. In the concluding section of this essay, I will argue that the discursive process is also evident in the controversy over Civil Rights.

Therefore, because it leads us to expect the wrong kind of results in the wrong places, a conversational model feeds pessimism, despair over the public realm, and the wrenching alternative of private morality in an immoral social world. If it can be constructed, a model that explains how public advocacy crafts a viable collective morality will lead us rather to understand the possibility of slow, painful, moral resolutions in the public realm.

THE OPERATION OF RHETORIC IN MORALITY

Pragmatically, the assertion that public morality is constructed, implemented, and improved through public argument requires the establishment of three subordinate claims. First, it requires that we believe that morality can be *humanly* generated. Second, the claim demands that such a morality be *both* situational *and* objective; otherwise no standards for "improvement" are available or there is no solidity to that morality. Finally, the claim presumes the denial of pessimism about humanity—suggesting that in particular conditions, we are capable of, though not necessarily destined to, "doing good."

Humanity

The suggestion that morality is humanly grounded has long generated strong resistance. Frentz's attack is fresh, but representative. He claims that any humanly created morality is both capricious and limited, and hence is "relativist."[17] Frentz requires, therefore, that morality be based in some other agency that is in some way external to humanity. He seems to label this agency ambiguously as "the gods."[18] Frentz arrives at this conclusion by means of the assumption that a "collective will," as a composite entity, is no more than a group of divided individual wills (which he deprecates as mere "individual desires").[19] Specifically, Frentz opposes a moral theory that rests on "collective wills of the group or community in which moral action takes place," because, he suggests, "as long as the ultimate good *for humanity* is something which can be exclusively defined, changed, and acted upon *by humanity* the moral philosophy which results will turn out to be another form of an emotivist moral system."[20]

Frentz's position rests upon a fallacy of composition and division. Frentz and others before him falsely assume that a "collective will," because its components are individual desires, can be *no more than* a bundle of individual desires, and similarly that a collective will cannot transcend the interests of the collectivity. Neither is the case. It is precisely the practice of public rhetoric that converts individual desires into something more—something carrying *moral* import, which can anchor the will of the community.

This transformation of desires is possible because *public* rhetoric requires that an individual speak a public language that includes linguistic *commitments* shared by all who are constituents of a community. This language, as Michael McGee has described it, includes the unique linguistic elements, "ideographs," which constitute social narratives for public action.[21] Collective language also includes shared social "myths" and "characterizations."[22] Such sociopolitical language units are different in quality from the same terms in private usage. The "liberty" sought by a sailor on shore leave is morally empty, whereas the "liberty" of a class of people in South Africa is a morally dense concept. Similar differences exist between isolated personal "narratives" and broad social myths.

Social discourse units carry moral import beyond individual interest, in part, then, because they indicate *shared* commitments and prescribe what each person as a member of a collectivity is *obligated* to do within the collectivity. More fundamentally, these terms are moral because the public arena, by its very nature, requires the use of terms that match the essential requirements of morality—the sacrifice of self interests for larger goods. Public argument centers on those greater goods because the contest between competing interest groups leads each group to attempt to identify their interests with larger goods. Unlike the participants of private conversations, the "public" does not endorse enactment of social policies for apparently selfish interests. Only when a policy can be presented as bearing greater goods will it be endorsed. Moreover the "goods" themselves are created and defined within these contests, because agonistic attempts to apply general concepts of "goodness" to particular issues require the definition, challenge, and transformation of "general goods" themselves. There is, thus, a "duality of communication"; moral terms in communication are "both medium and outcome."[23] All this is true even where "special interests" govern a vote; the public rationale for an action must always be expressible in the form of general goods.[24] Thus, even where discourse is ideologically distorted, the moral element (although limited or overridden) is necessarily engendered by the process of public argument.

Through particular applications, public discourse thus creates and requires the general or universal element that constitutes the core of morality. Consequently, general principles do not preexist particular moral quandaries but are produced from them. Because the general "goods" have a history of many competing particular applications, they transcend the particular situation. These generalized moral terms will even transcend the interests of the community itself, as will be indicated shortly. First, however, we must consider the reasons why Frentz and others tend to deny "objective" status to anything that is not "external" to humanity.

The problem resides in the mis-evaluation of "human desires." Frentz, for example, appears to be agreeing with MacIntyre in claiming that *because* "moral premises in modern times take root in individual desires, then no common moral grounds (except desires—which are indefinitely variable) bond reasons together and no collectively deliberated moral decisions can be expected as a matter of course."[25] The statement assumes that individual desires are somehow immoral or amoral and definitely unworthy. Their "infinite variability" feeds their unworthiness because of the presumption that only unitary and permanent things may hold "real" value.

It is possible, however, to view individual desires—for food, peace, security, and love—in a radically different light. While desires take varied forms, their basic sources are finite in their variability and widely shared. Moreover, these basic forms provide the substrate of morality. Such desires alone are not "moral"—they must be transformed by public discourse to craft a moral code—but they are nonetheless the *substance* of morality.

The strongest proof of the centrality of basic needs and desires to morality is the fact that the needs and desires of others are the foundation of the morality expressed in the general moral concept of the categorical imperative, the pervasive Christian version of which is "Do unto others as you would have them do unto you." Other moral precepts—"Thou shalt not kill" or even "Be kind"—are based similarly on the nature of human needs and desires and the human ability, radicalized and reinforced by public rhetoric, to generalize those needs to other humans and potentially to other beings. The ability to take the perspective of the other is a basic requisite of morality, and the contents of perspective-taking are human needs, desires, values, and ideas. Consequently, the presence of individual desire and even emotion do not disqualify a code from moral status, but rather indicate the possibility of moral valuation.

Why then do Frentz, MacIntyre, and others exert so much effort to disparage individual desire? The answer, it seems, is that the many grave and evident wrongs committed on the basis of human desire lead us naturally to seek some outside, limiting force. However, it is specifically *individual desires*, or the desires of *particular* interest groups marshalled against the desires of others, that are problematic. We should not confuse these particularized interests with the underlying human capacity for desire nor with the moral force collectively forged from those basic human desires. The moral outrage of a Nazi Reich was the product of the limited desires of a narrow interest group, enforced by the brutish power of the SS. Hitler's oratory was never awe-inspiring to the Jews. In that case and similar cases it was not the basic commodity of human desire, but the limitation of the universality of the *audience* for the public moral rhetoric (a limiting of the collectivization of desire) that was at fault.

Here, a rhetorical morality must meet the challenge of ideology. To the extent that dominant elites control the means of communication and the public vocabulary, they can represent *singular* partisan interests as universal or moral ones. They can thereby evade the modifications, compromises, and larger goods wrought through agonistic competition between values and interests. Dominant elites thus hijack the moral potential for partisan ends.

Although it is probably true that the pattern of public discourse in history is more "distorted" or ideological than it is moral, two responses can be offered here. First, a history of distortion does not deny the potential for future emancipation. Second, I would also crawl out on an unpopular limb to suggest that the history of Western Civilization can be read as a patchy struggle to decrease the control of public communication by elites, and a consequent increase in collective moral breadth and depth in some areas at some times.[26] The rise of a sociopolitical philosophy advocating equality in communication as a base for morality (most notably described by Jürgen Habermas) may be a good sign of the coming-to-maturity of this particular moral code.[27] Although Habermas's criteria indisputably remain as ideals, they nonetheless point out and describe the ongoing process of a battle for greater inclusiveness, and they force us to consider a definitional set that would declare ideological discourse to be that which is relatively more partial, exclusionary, and partisan, as opposed to moral discourse, which in the public realm can be identified in part as more inclusive and open. A fuller story of the relationship between ideology and public morality will need to be told elsewhere, but I suspect it will unify our understanding of *partisan* desire and *general* good.

Objectivity

Public rhetoric can therefore be viewed as a process in which basic human desires are transformed into shared moral codes. However, to make this theory palatable for those of us who believe that morality is not simply a matter of human whim (and hence is not *solely* equivalent to ideology), we can defend the potential for "objectivity" or "solidity" in such a moral code. To do so requires that we understand "objectivity" in a somewhat different manner than may be customary. Specifically, the "objectivity" borne by a moral code is an inductive and locally derived objectivity rather than a "principled" morality imposed by the dictates of external, universal commands invariantly applied. Such an "objectivity" exerts the compelling force sought by Frentz (and many of us), because it is not fully under the control of personal or even cultural "taste." Instead, the source of the compelling, restraining, or demanding power it exercises rests in complex sets of factors in particular situations.

In order to clarify the inductive character of morality, it is useful to distinguish among arenas or types of "moral discourse." I suggest that corresponding to a hypothetical idealist realm, to the collective arena, and to individual reflection there are, respectively, "principles," "rights," and "oughts."

Moral "principles" have their greatest substantiality in the discourse arenas of religion, theology, and philosophy. As inductive ideals, however, they provide crucial reference points for all arenas. Such principles are general statements of those moral actions and beliefs that are felt to be required of every human person. Ultimately, even the professional theologians, ministers, and philosophers do not agree on any such principles, precisely. Nonetheless, the *attempt* to locate such principles is grounded in an important facet of morality—the boundary conditions of human morality.

Although relativists, structuralists, and semiologists of many stripes have argued forcefully against simple theories of objectivism that postulate one-to-one correspondences between an "objective reality" and "truth," their cases do not impugn the postulation of objective boundary conditions that impinge upon human morality. Once we accept some kind of "reality" as a probable and useful concept, we can locate universal conditions such as the existence of language, sexuality, and mortality, which have moral consequences. The fact that cultures generally have some form of proscriptions against things such as killing humans, lying in cooperative communication situations, and random sexual liaisons provides an indication of these universal boundary conditions. That is, although there is no universal proscription of *particular* types of killing, lying, and promiscuity, there are signs of these boundary conditions in the fact that these behaviors present *moral problematics* for all societies. Each culture creates careful (if differing) rules and sanctions surrounding such activities. Moreover, the general trend of these proscriptions, though not universally consistent, is similar in direction. Therefore, the widespread existence of some form of proscriptions surrounding certain behaviors does not indicate (as philosophers, theologians, and religious figures seeking unity or hegemony have maintained) a "universal" moral code, but it does signal the existence of very broad universal boundary conditions that constrain human coexistence and communication and thereby constrain, without fully determining, the construction of moral codes.

As an example, we may consider the fact that, as Ricoeur puts it, "man is not radically alien to man, because he offers signs of his own existence."[28] As a consequence, there is a forceful potential for people to feel an empathy that compels recognition of killing as horrible. On a grander scale, the costs of war always exert a restraint on the possibilities of declaring war. These restraints may be overridden by a variety of factors, but their existence and force is always indicated by cultural devices for carefully controlling and compensating for them. Moral principles, therefore, are simply attempts to sum up the underlying force implied by the existence of crucial boundary conditions on human life. In practice, such attempts always fail, because there is no direct translation from the multiplicitous set of objective boundary conditions to their "moral meaning." Cultures and languages must *substantialize* morality and so few societies believe in or practice the absolute "Thou shalt not kill." It is at the level of rights that moral discourse becomes concrete.

"Rights" are the moral prescriptions of sociopolitical units. In small homogeneous communities they take on the character of customs or rituals, and thus "rights-customs" form a continuum, but the social character of morality at this level is the same at both poles. Rights (and the negative form, restrictions) are general social formulations of moral boundaries. Rights and restrictions may be influenced by "principles" that are carried as salient components of the public vocabulary, but they are influenced by other elements as well. Thus, rather than the principle "Thou shalt not kill," in our society we have "first degree murder" and "involuntary manslaughter," along with "justified homicide," "just wars," and other socially sanctioned categories of human life taking. These rights and restrictions are induced from a complex set of shared experiences, a collective history that includes moral codes, incidents of killing, values, other rights, and a variety of other objective factors that constrain killing. Although it is the social code that creates meaning and therefore formulates concrete "rights," the social definition process is influenced by objective conditions derived both from the general boundary conditions noted above and from specific material factors in a particular society's situation. (Urbanization, for example, may have caused formalization of moral prescriptions against drinking because close quarters made previous drinking practices more problematic.[29])

It is a special strength of this inductive theory that it ties morality to objective forces, while leaving room for contingency—thereby allowing both variety and error. Sometimes a society may have moral prescriptions requiring its members to "do what they ought not do." Especially where participation in the public dialogue is limited, the gravitational pull of moral imperatives serving the general interest may be overridden by power conditions and particular clusters of competing objective conditions (for example, South African apartheid or the Indian custom of burning wives on their husband's funeral pyres, while grounded in sound local economics, present such cases). Nonetheless, there are also many areas in which vastly varying social customs are perfectly defensible (as with other characteristics of most burial customs or puberty rites, for example). The recognition that there are both defensible and condemnable cultural variations is an important advance in moral theory and is necessary to avoid the twin perils of "utter relativism" and "imperialist objectivism." The adjudication between tolerance and reprobation for particular cultural practices is always an ongoing matter for public advocacy, within and without the culture.[30]

Situationalism does not, therefore, represent the application of "modifications" to universal principles so that those principles are "relativized," turning us all loose to make exceptions for ourselves at will. Rather, any principle is merely a shorthand summary for the complex and objectively compelling moral imperatives that arise from the specific conditions of moral situations, including the broad, shared boundaries of the human condition. To say therefore, that a culture's moral code arises inductively and includes its own history is not to say that it is capricious and relative. No culture freely chooses its history, but rather it faces many restraints. The cultural realm of moral "rights" is therefore objective, constrained, and yet not determined, in all cases, to "be right."

The realm of the individual "ought" is created, in part, by this gap. Because governments can be wrong, individuals and the religious institutions within which they gather in our time have a separate moral obligation that may require them to act against the social prescriptions. Moreover, because cultures can be wrong, they may choose not to prescribe all behaviors (even if they could). Individuals thus have the option to choose to violate cultural prescriptions (accepting social penalties) or, they may feel they have a moral obligation (that they "ought") to do more than is required by the society. Thus, a woman who believes she has a moral right to abortion may choose not to have one because she believes it is morally *better* not to do so.

The general, societal, and individual realms are therefore quite interdependent. Individuals will attempt to enact what they think everyone "ought" to do as cultural rights and restrictions. Battles between the individual and social realm will be augmented by arguments about what is really a "universal principle" and what merely a social or individual preference. It is the interactive dynamic of these three realms that provides us a wealth of moral protections (even if also creating a great deal of confusion about morality).

With this multiplicity of layers we can now see how the construction of human morality extends, not only beyond the interests of an individual, but also beyond the interests of specific human collectivities, or even humanity as a whole.

There are moral situations in which a collectivity recognizes that "its interests" compete with other interests and are in some moral sense outweighed by larger interests surrounding it. This may result from the boundary conditions discussed above or from the substantiality and logic of the moral code itself. Once universal terms, narratives, and characterizations are created and supported, they carry a force separate from the wishes of the collectivity. Great labor is required to restrain or reshape such commitments. Additionally, a code does not simply and univocally reflect the wishes of its creators, even at the instant of its creation—the rhetorical process and moral codes adhere to their own logic. For example, it is doubtful that when the American Catholic Bishops promoted the "sanctity of human life" as a moral warrant for banning abortion, they intended to reverse their stand on the death penalty, but that is what the public commitment to "life" pressured them to do. In this way, a "collective will," through public discourse, creates something outside its own will. Although the collectivity always retains power to modify the code, it cannot exert unlimited control. As long as the discourse process is relatively open, the nature of the code itself, as well as the broad biological, psychological, and social limitations upon human beings, exerts an important external moral force.

Consequently, in response to Frentz and other opponents of grounding morality in humanity itself, I offer the rhetorical production of moral codes. Such codes are generated by human collectives, yet they also formulate objective restraints on humanity. This model allows us to take one last bold step to suggest that there can be improvement of the public moral code.

Against Pessimism

Optimism about human morality has been, in most places and times, hard to come by. Saturated with the petty lies of politicians and the grand larcenies of corporate plunderers, we find it difficult to defend moral optimism as anything other than a charming naïveté. I have already indicated the importance of this pessimism for the "privatization of public morality" and have suggested some grounds, in the form of examples of collective American actions, for resisting such blanket despair. The demise of direct human slavery, a decreased tolerance of starvation in "developed" countries, as well as the declining acceptance of infanticide provide other examples of moral improvements made by human collectives. Further, a similar argument can be made with regard to the character of public arguments themselves. If we look, for example, at the arguments in the Civil Rights controversy, it seems difficult to maintain that "modern rhetorical advocates have lost their sense of individual moral coherence and a teleologically grounded moral tradition."[31] If we compare the Civil Rights activists' religiously and traditionally grounded plea for "life" or "freedom" with the claims of an Athenian orator urging war for booty, a feeling of moral progress might even seem to be warranted (and even our current public "warrants for war" may be marginally better than in the past).[32]

While individual human beings may or may not differ radically in their moral qualities from times past, it is possible to concede that, in two thousand years, human societies have made at least a few laudable advances in a few particular areas. All of this is not to say that we have *universally* improved ourselves, or that we have, overall, "progressed." It would be easy enough to cite a list of our continued and new moral transgressions. Nor do the patchy improvements in moral conditions authorize us to expect that moral improvement is a necessary and inevitable process of "progress" that will continue.

Our stance, therefore, cannot be joyously optimistic; we can only deny the necessity of pessimism. There is no structural, biological, or social necessity for moral impoverishment, nor for moral improvement. It is neither true that "everything will turn out all right in the end," nor that "everything" will necessarily end soon in a nuclear explosion. Instead, we simply can say that some portions of the moral code and collective behavior can be improved by particular human actions. Human morality is contingent; optimists and pessimists alike lack firm grounds, because human beings must daily and locally, as well as by the century and continent, actively craft human morality.

A quick survey of the public discourse relating Black and White Americans can illustrate this process of open crafting. I present the example of race relations in direct contrast to the foundational example offered by Frentz. Frentz examined an aesthetic object, a movie, the agents of which were two self-indulgent Americans seeking satisfaction in self-understanding. If our understanding of morality is bound by such models, I think our rhetorical theory will be impoverished by the lack of long-term perspective, of public participation, and of action. To add these dimensions, I offer a view of Americans, locked in bitter contest, speaking in public across decades, to enact a better way of life.

"JUSTICE" FOR AFRO-AMERICANS

The historical relationships between Black Americans and White Americans confronts us with two conflicting moral "intuitions." On one side, there is the sense of contemporary White academics that equality between Anglo-Americans and Afro-Americans is and always has been "just." The concept or relation seems worthy of universality. On the other side, there is the disturbing and compelling fact that millions of morally sane and responsible individuals did not believe this for many years.

The typical response to this quandary has been to deny the morality of supporters of slavery and discrimination. We have tended to suggest that, by using psychological defense mechanisms such as "rationalization," otherwise good individuals were able to delude themselves or be deluded into ignoring an ever-present truth. Or, we have occasionally suggested that they knew all along that this moral truth was "self-evident" but they let their human greed interfere with their moral impulses.[33] As a result, we have tended to portray the movement towards equal rights as "inevitable," a historical necessity motivated by the American Conscience."[34] Good people had to triumph over evil.

None of these moves is sufficient. The best evidence we have indicates that there were caring and moral individuals who sincerely believed that slavery, and later, discrimination, were morally defensible institutions.[35] Moreover, to suggest the "inevitability" of the change may be comforting, but it glosses deceptively the uncertainty and struggle that was necessary to enact the moral code. We need, then, a different account.

Looking at the rhetoric produced in the situation gives us a means to understand this moral problem in historical perspective. Simply put, when racial slavery was instituted, Anglo-Americans had not yet crafted a public moral code that included Afro-Americans in the demands of "equal justice." It is taking hundreds of years to modify that original relationship.

Two elements have been central to the development and evolution of justice for Afro-Americans. As I have suggested, one component of morality is the human need for resources—food, clothing, and material for "the pursuit of happiness." By recognizing these needs, human beings recognize that there is something about which to be just. In addition, however, in order for perspective-taking to occur, we must feel that the "other" is in some fundamental ways the "same" as us—experiencing similar needs and wants. The story of "civil rights" in America is the tale of a gradual amelioration of resource shortages and increasing identification of Whites with Blacks. These elements together, through the operation of public discourse, produced an improved (because more universalized) moral code. The resource situation, especially the resource of labor, is testified to by various historians.[36] The rhetorical process of "identification" can be sketched by a brief glance at the chief contents of the public rhetoric between 1840 and 1960.[37]

The need for rhetorical effort to build "identification" was generated by the nature of the early contact period, when Whites tensely characterized Blacks as both "similar" and radically "different." Early descriptions of Africans by Europeans indirectly recognized a basic similarity by identifying Blacks as persons (or, in the locution of the time, "men"). However, the sixteenth- and seventeenth-century travelers, traders, and chroniclers emphasized the exoticness of the people and places, downplaying the similarities There were indeed many dramatic differences of dress, religion, eating habits, and kinship relations.[38]

These differences in the practices of daily life were morally problematic because the Western world had not yet elaborated a moral code capable of universality that transcended them. The first impediment to such a code was the lack of familiarity with the concept of "human racial difference." There was not even any clear scientific concept of "species" or "family," and the ambivalence between "human *race*" and ethnically differentiated "race" was symptomatic of the confusion.[39]

This ambiguity allowed "race" to be rapidly shaped by existing dominant social principles. The social code of the day was rife with hierarchy and "order." Monarchies survive on inequity and inferiority, and these principles were only gradually giving way to a concept of justice that included political "equality" and religious tolerance. Without a clear description of humanity in the code, and with a strong practice of coding hierarchy, the differences between Africans and Europeans were apt to be interpreted as "inferiorities," and in the most extreme cases Africans were classed as "bestial."[40]

The dominant moral codes of the day solidified and exacerbated this differentiation. The Christian Bible was the indisputable moral authority and it explicitly allowed one to enslave "strangers," but not those who were of "one's own." It said in part that "you may buy male and female slaves from among the nations that are round about you. You may also buy from among the strangers who sojourn with you . . . but over your brethren the people of Israel you shall not rule."[41]

Finally, the initial sense of difference and the acceptance of economic, political, and social inequality were amplified and reified by the economic need for labor and the subsequent patterns of slavery, which haphazardly developed. Such an economic relationship not only gave further motive to the intensification of "difference," it also led to a physical and cultural separation that prevented recognition of "similarity."

Upon these conditions—economic need, an underdeveloped code of "equality," and an ambivalent linguistic code that allowed Afro-Americans to be classed as "different" and hence outside the normal laws and bounds of "justice"—racial slavery was formed and flourished. The institution was increasingly challenged as (1) Blacks and Whites came into prolonged contact in social situations that decreased Black cultural differences such as dress, dating habits, and language, and (2) the control of "justice" was placed in the hands of those who endorsed "equality" and had direct contact with the increasingly "similar" Blacks (that is, in the North, after the American Revolution). Gradually, the operative weight of the new American code of justice began to exert force towards including Blacks.

The abolitionists' arguments were clearly based on this increasing awareness of similarity. One of the most repeated and vivid strands of abolitionist discourse was the insistence on the fundamental humanity of Blacks.[42] William Lloyd Garrison testified that his own conversion to abolitionism was based on his effort at imagining himself as a Black man, and he provides one of the most forceful statements of similarity. Responding to Henry Clay's assertion of general White supremacy, Garrison declared, "I deny the postulate that God has made, by any irreversible decree, or any inherent qualities, one portion of the human race superior to another."[43] Once Blacks were included in this manner with Whites, the dictates of the newly crafted American "justice," proclaiming all men equal, mandated that Africans could not be enslaved by other human beings.[44]

The centrality of the issue of "identification" is equally clear in the opposing proslavery rhetoric, which focused a large portion of its effort on "difference," in the form of the rhetoric of "White supremacy."[45] Albert Taylor Bledsoe was employing normal usage when he referred to the Africans as the "inferior race," and insisted that

> Slavery is not the mother, but the daughter, of ignorance, and degradation. It is, indeed, the legitimate offspring of that intellectual and moral debasement which, for so many thousand years has been accumulating and growing upon the African race.[46]

The second major strand of proslavery rhetoric similarly emphasized "difference," but this time as a general principle. Bledsoe and others denied "equality" as a viable moral obligation.[47] James A. Sloan, for example, insisted that "a system of complete equality does not seem to be in accordance with the providence of God, or with the Bible."[48]

Neither of these arguments from difference were ultimately successful in the national arena. From the pre-Revolutionary War period until just before the Civil War, the "antislavery impulse" spread in breadth and intensity (albeit unevenly). Gradually, the "South" was driven to *cut off public discussion* in the Congress and in the public presses. As Frederick Douglass predicted, "Slavery cannot bear discussion."[49] Latent material conditions could not be made explicit without challenging the vocabulary of public values or the conditions themselves.

Eventually, however, change was produced through rhetorical effort, adequate time to disseminate the new code, and bullets to force the acquiescence of those who would not allow persuasion. By 1865 a revolutionary moral code excluding the "rightness" of racial slavery had been publicly enacted. As a result of economic shifts, but also as a result of and through the medium of public discourse, a broader, more universal moral code had come to be accepted. "Justice" no longer could include human racial slavery, and the claims of other forms of "equality" among human beings had been expanded and strengthened.

The moral code nonetheless faced further evolution. The end of slavery came with a formal, militarily enforced recognition of the humanity of Blacks. Even many abolitionists who recognized this humanity, however, had never fully erased from their minds a sense of "difference" that implied inferiority of some sort. The merely formal sense of equality during the postwar era was translated into a very limited political equality, which was increasingly circumscribed by social and economic "difference" and "separation" in a mutually augmenting spiral. This state of affairs was legally codified in 1896 by the Supreme Court in *Plessy v. Ferguson*.[50] The Court's ruling that the races could remain "separate but equal" was a basically unstable compromise, however. "Separate" at the time clearly meant "unequal," and the continuance of separation meant a continuance of "difference." The lack of a sense of "identity" clashed with the basis of a justice premised on equality.

As a consequence of these conditions, the "post-Reconstruction rhetoric" of both

Blacks and Whites consisted primarily of efforts to identify the Negroes more closely with Whites. Not a merely formal membership in the human race, but "essential similarity" was projected. Both extremes of Black rhetors worked toward the same ends. Booker T. Washington, the ultramoderate, sought to teach Blacks the "important lessons of cleanliness, promptness, system, honesty, and progressiveness" in order that each Black could contribute "his share" and smooth "the pathway for this and succeeding generations."[51] More radical men such as Marcus Garvey and W. E. B. DuBois were to develop "Black pride" in their humanity, emphasizing the worthiness of the best members of their race.[52]

Between 1940 and 1960 the White press amplified this refrain, gradually recharacterizing all Blacks as similar to Whites even in the realm of the day to day. The redefinition began during World War II with descriptions of Black workers and soldiers as "loyal," "heroic," "brave," "pleasant," "accustomed to hard work," as well as "spic and span" and "friendly."[53] After the war, the more liberal elements of the press incorporated Blacks into narratives that testified to their essentially positive nature—allowing White audiences to come to know and like Black characters, and to perceive them as *like* themselves.

Gradually, the narratives went further, suggesting that it was unjust to treat these "people like us" in nonsimilar ways. Tales of worthy "Negroes" being disallowed reward solely because of their Blackness began to arouse the emotional sympathy we call a "sense of injustice." The concept of "race" gradually was reduced to the less potent identifier, "skin color"—an item devoid of the general baggage of "race" and linguistically less capable of carrying it.

This rhetorical effort primarily reached the liberal, northern, elite, but this group was crucial. They controlled much of the public discourse and legal processes, a factor evident in the Supreme Court ruling in *Brown v. Board of Education*, which held that "separate" could not be "equal" because it inherently bred a sense of inferiority (a clear form of "difference").[54]

This rhetoric of identification also encouraged Blacks to demand "justice." Ultimately, Martin Luther King Jr. could draw on the strengthened sense of identification and, on a national platform, call forth the ultimate dream of identity that "little black boys and black girls will be able to join hands with little white boys and white girls as sisters and brothers."[55] By the late sixties, even in the South, an adequate *public* presumption had been built to identify Blacks and Whites and include Blacks in the code of justice.[56] "Massive Resistance" never materialized in large part because the similarity of Blacks and the justice of their inclusion was nominally accepted by an adequate number of active social agents. Although even today that expanded code is not universally shared within the United States, North or South, nor outside of our states (especially in private), it has strong and wide support among the politically active, and it meets public resistance only when it tends to encroach on other senses of "justice" (as in "affirmative action programs" felt to be unjust to others.)[57]

Across two hundred years or more, therefore, new rhetorical structures of great importance have been created. Blacks and Whites are now publicly identified, not only as human, but also as essentially similar. Moreover, a strong moral code that demands human equality has gained currency. The original Anglo-American moral code of "justice" has thus evolved into a broader "American" code that belongs to and includes persons of all descents and skin colors.

Viewing the Civil Rights controversy as a situational process of the crafting of morality through rhetoric thus allows us to understand the change in the moral code

through American history. White slave owners were not necessarily deceiving themselves or allowing crass self-interests to overrule their moral impulses. Rather, because
Afro-Americans had been coded as "different," and because the dominant moral code
of the day featured hierarchy, there was no moral code that included Blacks in White
"justice." A sense of compassion and a morality of "care" may have often dictated
humane treatment, but that was different from treatment as "brothers." The inclusion
of Blacks in White conceptions of justice (or better, the construction of shared
White/Black justice) was a *new* moral code that had to be crafted through time and
rhetorical effort. We "understand" now that the Black person and the White person
objectively deserve equal treatment, but we had to craft the moral code and the
conditions that allowed this moral understanding to be widely available to a working
plurality of citizens. Moreover, individual rhetors, both Whites like Garrison and Lydia
Maria Child and Blacks like Douglass, Washington, and DuBois had to empathize, to
sacrifice, to speak and write, in order to work out and spread that code.

The temptation remains to say that, nonetheless, the moral relationship or
principle was there all along—simply "unrealized." With the new code, we simply
"recognized" a transcendent "truth." More softly, we might say that once even a few
radicals discovered the "truth" of Black/White identity, it took "a century long lag of
public morals" for the rest of the population to catch up.[58]

Either of these moves obscures the fundamental nature and complexity of morality
as a public process. Generally, Blacks and Whites now publicly perceive each other as
fundamentally similar and agree that we should treat each other similarly. However,
until the two sets of peoples came into extensive contact with each other, no moral
relationship could exist. The process of constructing a moral definition of the relationship necessarily took time and discourse, and although the process might be characterized as one of "recognizing" potent objective boundary conditions, it was nonetheless
an active, historically concrete process of constructing a new code. Therefore, although
it may be psychologically comforting to argue that we should *always* have had that
recognition, to do so is not only futile, it deprives humanity of further moral growth.

We must view morality as an open process of crafting in order to continue the
process of crafting. Our broader history shows this crafting. The statement penned by
Thomas Jefferson that "all men are created equal [but Negroes aren't fully men?]" as
an *official document* was a radical assertion of new material from the English public
moral code. The post-Civil War rewriting of that code to state that "all men are created
equal" was a further rewriting and expansion of the morality. Similarly, our current
efforts to once again rewrite the code to state that "all persons are created equal" may
result in another step.

Our moral capacity as a people can grow, and increasing "universality" has been
one aspect of that growth. If, however, we reify the current best principles, we put
ourselves exactly in the position of the Southern slaveholders in 1850—we preserve an
old moral order at the cost of a newer, broader one. If, for example, we maintain that
the use of the Bible as an authority worked for Black rhetors in the past so we should
not challenge its use for the future, or if we hold that "all persons are created equal"
is a universal principle, always existent, but simply misunderstood or misapplied at
times, then we stunt our ability to craft an even grander moral code as we turn the
corner. The current code may be used, as such codes historically have been used, to
prevent the development of a better code. To say that America has always relied on the
Judeo-Christian tradition is not only to distort history by reifying that tradition, it is
also not to say that she should or must be so limited in the future. To hazard a guess

at an example, we can note that our current public moral code justifies the "cycle of poverty" in terms of a rhetoric of "equal opportunity," where equal opportunity counts only technical numbers of resources, not the kinds of resources necessary to make individuals capable of equality of opportunity. Blind and rigid defense of that code forestalls the development of a moral code that may someday express clearly our now vague sentiment that "because all persons are not born equal in their social and natural situation, we must shape our society to insure that they are able to develop all of their natural potential."

THE "CRAFT" OF MORALITY

I have tried to suggest that "morality" is constructed by collectivities through their public discourse in a process of reflexive reproduction that utilizes the capacity of discourse simultaneously to create, extend, and apply moral concepts. I have gone further, to suggest that this process is bounded by an inductive, historical objectivity. I have also tried to illustrate what this might mean for our understanding of the collective moral controversies in our past and present. I do not expect this account to be universally persuasive, but I hope I have increased the plausibility of such a perspective. There remains the issue, however, of why such an account ought to be chosen over, for example, a conversational theory, a religious explanation, or a pessimistic dismissal of all morality. The usual tests of the "explanatory power" of a theory will eventually apply here, but given the nature of the subject, another kind of test is relevant as well.

Baldly stated, for moral reasons, the best metaphor for the rhetorical construction of morality is neither MacIntyre's individual intellectual quest nor Frentz's private conversation, but the simple, collective "craft."

MacIntyre's "quest" metaphor contains two major faults. First, the requirement that all members of communities share all the same individual values and virtues is unlikely given the multiplicity of levels and dimensions of moral practices. Moreover, it is probably undesirable as well. Uniformity in morality has too often been bought at the price of oppression. MacIntyre's alternative—to ignore the public realm and form small "survival" groups for moral practice—is a retreat from responsibility that, I have suggested, is unjustified by contemporary conditions, if those conditions are compared to human history rather than to some imaginary ideal or golden age.

Second, MacIntyre concludes that the virtues and the good "are those which will enable us to understand what more and what else the good life for man is."[59] To promote, in this way, the intellectuals' pet standard of "understanding" as the central *activity* of moral practice misguidedly urges all human beings to spend their lives doing what academics do only as a matter of profession—thinking about morality rather than actively crafting it in the world. That seems to threaten moral impoverishment, rather than offering collective growth.

Frentz's "rhetorical conversation" is more constructive for the building of private virtue through local social interactions, but it too does not help us to act morally in the public realm, nor to understand collective morality. Understanding the "craft" of morality-building as including all forms of rhetoric—conversation, debate, discussion, and harangue—would seem to allow us to go farther. Like all crafts, the rhetorical construction of morality partakes of the workshop. Individual workers may produce individual creations, but the large practice of the collectivity is mostly anonymous. The rare individual may nonetheless radically revise the social practice through particular action, insight, or merit; even in routine, each social practice is dependent on individuals. Thus, the collective and the individual interact to produce morality. The "duality of communication" dictates that it is through the arguments of individuals about enactment of particular moral rulings that the collective moral code is built. Additionally, the rhetor constructing morality, like any craftsperson, is limited by objectives, situations, and the available materials.

Lastly, as with all crafts, the rhetorical construction of morality fulfills the human urge for goodness, creativity, and perfection.[60] We have too often viewed morality as we might a great art, where a painfully transcendent beauty outside normal day-to-day experience is the high ideal. With such a model, only "the gods" can offer us morality, for indeed the bounds of the human condition are too great. But morality is not an art. It is not free to take beauty and run unbound with it. Morality must partake of beauty, and truth, and power in the conditions of the world.

In spite of these limits, a craft can, nonetheless, fulfill the human urge for unity, continuity, and teleology—an urge for good and perfection. It cannot give us "transcendence" in stepping outside of daily meaning, but it can give us a perfecting of action through meaning. Carefully monitored water systems, well-designed transportation, and accessible communication media are as important to human life as the statue of *David*, the Taj Mahal, and the *Enterprise*. When we fail to recognize the value of human craft, we sadly deplete the quality of human life. And so it is with the craft of morality. Art gives us greater beauty. Philosophy gives us grander truths. Science gives us greater power. But without rhetoric to produce and maintain morality, human life would be more seriously diminished.

Ultimately, then, to recognize morality as a collective craft is also to call ourselves to account for our participation in the ebb and flow of human morality. As Thomas Farrell would seem to indicate, the rhetorical practices of the collective are "tenuous"[61]; rhetoric indeed may be used more frequently for evil and partisan gain than for the general good. It is, however, that very contingency that makes our individual participation in the collective so crucial, infusing each of our moves with broad meaning.

Together, then, people have built the good, not with an architectural blueprint, but with a traditional knowledge of the way the tribe has built in the past and through daily assessment of the probabilities involved in a local outcome. Proceeding day by day, we do not live the moments of the present as though they sucked in the past and future at once in some dizzying, transcendent manner. Rather, the moral craft requires us to live the moment, through the legacies of the past, with just an eye to the fact that we are crafting the future as well.

Notes

1. For example, Plato in the *Phaedrus*, *Republic*, and *Laws*; Aristotle in the *Rhetoric*, *Politics*, and *Ethics*; Isocrates in *Nicocles or the Cyprians*; Cicero in *De officii*, *De oratore*, and *De finibus*; Quintilian in the *Institutes*.

2. As in B. J. Diggs, "Persuasion and Ethics," *Quarterly Journal of Speech* 50 (1964): 359–373; Franklyn Haiman, "A Re-examination of the Ethics of Persuasion," *Central States Speech Journal* 3 (1952): 4–9; Edward Rogge, "Evaluating the Ethics of a Speaker in Democracy," *Quarterly Journal of Speech* 45 (1959): 419–425; Thomas R. Nilsen, *Ethics of Speech Communication* (Indianapolis, IN: Bobbs-Merrill, 1966); Richard Weaver, *The Ethics of Rhetoric* (South Bend, IN: Gateway Editions, 1953).

3. Walter R. Fisher, "Narration as a Human Communication Paradigm: The Case of Public Moral Argument," *Communication Monographs* 51 (1984:) 1–22 (reprinted in this volume); Thomas S. Frentz, "Rhetorical Conversation, Time, and Moral Action," *Quarterly Journal of Speech* 71 (1985): 1–18 (reprinted in this volume); Michael Calvin McGee, "Secular Humanism: A Radical Reading of 'Culture Industry' Production," *Critical Studies in Mass Communication* 1 (1984): 1–33; Philip Wander, "The Ideological Turn in Modern Criticism," *Central States Speech Journal* 34 (1983): 1–18; Martha Solomon, "Robert Schuller: The American Dream in a Crystal Cathedral," *Central States Speech Journal* 34 (1983): 172–186; Steven Goldwig and George Cheney, "The U.S. Catholic Bishops on Nuclear Arms: Corporate Advocacy, Role Redefinition, and Rhetorical Adaptation," *Central States Speech Journal* 35 (1984): 8–23.

4. Fisher, "Narration"; Frentz, "Rhetorical Conversation"; Walter R. Fisher, "The Narrative Paradigm: An Elaboration," *Communication Monographs* 52 (1985): 347–367; Thomas B. Farrell, "Rhetorical Resemblance: Paradoxes of a Practical Art," *Quarterly Journal of Speech* 72 (1986): 1–19; Alasdair MacIntyre, *After Virtue: A Study In Moral Theory* (South Bend, IN: University of Notre Dame Press, 1981).

5. Fisher, "Narration," p. 1.

6. Farrell, "Rhetorical Resemblance," pp. 16, 2, 15.

7. Frentz, "Rhetorical Conversation," pp. 11, 13.

8. Ibid., p. 4.

9. E.g., Richard Rorty, *Philosophy and the Mirror of Nature* (Princeton, NJ: Princeton University Press, 1979); and Richard J. Bernstein, *Beyond Objectivism and Relativism: Science, Hermeneutics, and Praxis* (Philadelphia: University of Pennsylvania Press, 1983).

10. Farrell ("Rhetorical Resemblance") does not employ the conversational metaphor. Instead, ironically I think, he resorts to the metaphor of "form," as he attacks the aestheticians.

11. Fisher, "An Elaboration," p. 353.

12. Ibid., p. 363.

13. Frentz quotes the movie; "Rhetorical Conversation," p. 12.

14. Ibid., pp. 15–16.

15. The limits are reached at the level where legitimacy of the governing unit is itself challenged. See John Louis Lucaites, "Rhetoric and the Problem of Legitimacy," *Dimensions of Argument: Proceedings of the Second Summer Conference on Argumentation* (Annandale, VA.: Speech Communication Association. 1981), pp. 799–811.

16. Celeste Condit Railsback, "The Contemporary American Abortion Controversy: Stages in the Argument," *Quarterly Journal of Speech* 70 (1984): 410–423.

17. Frentz, "Rhetorical Conversation," pp. 1–3, 5, 14.

18. Ibid., p. 16.

19. Ibid., p. 14.

20. Ibid., p. 14.

21. Michael Calvin McGee. "The 'Ideograph': A Link Between Rhetoric and Ideology," *Quarterly Journal of Speech* 66 (1980): 1–16.

22. The role of "characterizations" and "public myths" is very similar to that of ideographs, although each of these works at different levels. For explanations and illustrations, see Celeste Michelle Condit, "Democracy and Civil Rights: The Universalizing Influence of Public Argumentation," *Communication Monographs*, forthcoming.

23. Anthony Giddens, *Central Problems in Social Theory: Action, Structure and Contradiction in Social Analysis* (Berkeley and Los Angeles: University of California Press, 1979), p. 5.

24. Michael Calvin McGee, "The Rhetorical Process in Eighteenth Century England," in Walter R. Fisher, ed., *Rhetoric: A Tradition in Transition* (East Lansing: Michigan State University Press, 1974), pp. 99–121.

25. Frentz, "Rhetorical Conversation," p. 13.

26. An example is presented below, but another might be read, against the author's intentions, perhaps, in Raymond Williams, *The Long Revolution* (Westport, CT: Greenwood Press, 1975), or in Stuart Hall, "The State in Question," in G. McLennan, D. Held, and S. Hall, eds., *The Idea of the Modern State* (Milton Keynes, UK: Open University Press, 1984), pp. 1–28.

27. See Jürgen Habermas, *Communication and the Evolution of Society*, trans. Thomas McCarthy (1976; rpt., Boston: Beacon Press, 1979).

28. Paul Ricocur, *Hermeneutics and the Human Sciences*, ed. and trans. John B. Thompson (Cambridge: Cambridge University Press, 1981), p. 49.

29. For an elucidation of situational objectivism in morality, see Renford Bambrough, *Moral Skepticism and Moral Knowledge* (Atlantic Highlands, NJ: Humanities Press, 1979). For a further elaboration of the epistemological foundations of such localistic thought, see Ludwig Wittgenstein, *Philosophical Investigations*, trans. G.E.M. Anscombe (Oxford, UK: Basil Blackwell, 1963), and Jean-François Lyotard, *The Postmodern Condition: A Report on Knowledge*, trans. Geoff Bennington and Brian Massumi (Minneapolis: University of Minnesota Press; 1984).

30. This is where I part company with Stephen Toulmin's *An Examination of the Place of Reason in Ethics* (Cambridge: Cambridge University Press, 1950). He would limit such discussion to the members of a culture only.

31. Frentz, "Rhetorical Conversation," p. 4.

32. For example, see Demosthenes, "The First Phillipic," in W. Robert Connor, ed., *Greek Orations* (Ann Arbor: University of Michigan Press, 1966), or the speeches of Cleon and Diodotus to the Athenian *Ecclesia*, in Thucydides, *The Peloponnesian War*, trans. E. Crawley (New York: Random House, 1951), 3.37–48. Although these two may be juxtaposed as examples of ideal and material justifications, both offer pecuniary interests as the underlying goal.

33. William Lloyd Garrison launched this attack in a forceful, early version in "William Lloyd Garrison Abandons Colonization (1830)" in John L. Thomas, ed., *Slavery Attacked: The Abolitionist Crusade* (Englewood Cliffs, NJ: Prentice- Hall, 1965), reprinted from "Henry Clay's Colonization Address," *Genius of Universal Emancipation*, February 12, 1830. Later, materialist versions tend to describe how the belief or argument that Blacks were inferior developed only after the economic interests of the slaveholders were threatened. They covertly insert the vocabulary that implies the beliefs were nongenuine. George Frederickson, for example, says the arguments began their "career as a rationale" and were a "defensive ideological consciousness." He says the southerners were "putting out propaganda" and "seeking to put to rest their own nagging fears." See "Slavery and Race: The Southern Dilemma," in Allen Weinstein and Frank Otto Gatell, eds., *American Negro Slavery*, 2d ed. (New York: Oxford University Press, 1973), esp. pp. 227–233. Similarly, Stanley M. Elkins, *Slavery: A Problem in American Institutional and Intellectual Life*, 2d ed. (1959, 1968; rpt., Chicago: University of Chicago Press, 1971), e.g., pp. 208–212.

34. Probably the most influential of such works is that by Gunnar Myrdal, with Richard Sterner and Arnold Rose, *An American Dilemma: The Negro Problem and Modern Democracy* (1944; rpt., New York: Harper and Row, 1962), pp. 24, 215.

35. Albert Taylor Bledsoe, for example, specifically objects to the abolitionists' assumption that they have moral right on their side and says that "the institution of slavery, as it exists among us in the South, is founded in political justice, is in accordance with the will of God and the designs of his providence, and is conducive to the highest, purest, best interests of mankind" (Bledsoe, *An Essay on Liberty and Slavery* [Philadelphia: J. B. Lippincott, 1856], p. 8). See also John Bell Robinson, *Pictures of Slavery and Anti-Slavery* (Philadelphia, 1863), "Introduction"; and John Henry Hopkins, *A Scriptural, Ecclesiastical, and Historical View of Slavery, from the Days of the Patriarch Abraham, to the Nineteenth Century* (New York: W. I. Pooley and Co., n.d.).

36. For instance, George M. Fredrickson, *White Supremacy: A Comparative Study in American and South African History* (New York: Oxford University Press, 1982), p. 55, or Winthrop D. Jordan, *White over Black: American Attitudes toward the Negro, 1550–1812* (Chapel Hill: University of North Carolina Press, 1968), esp. pp. 91, 320–331, 47–48.

37. These conclusions are based on the study of three separate sets of discourse. For the abolitionist period it includes an incomplete sampling of pro-slavery and abolitionist pamphlets from 1820–1860, especially during the period 1850–1860, supplemented by secondary histories of the period, of which the most helpful is William Sumner Jenkins, *Pro Slavery Thought in the Old South* (Gloucester, MA: Peter Smith, 1960). The Black rhetoric was surveyed through readings of the speeches and writings of major figures, especially Frederick Douglass, Booker T. Washing-

ton, William E. B. Dubois, Marcus Garvey, Malcolm X, and Martin Luther King Jr. The most intensive research segment was the focus on the White magazine press 1940–1960. A 10 percent structured random sample of all articles concerning "Negroes" listed in the *Reader's Guide to Periodical Literature* forms the basis of the conclusions given here.

38. Jordan, *White over Black*, pp. 3–98.

39. Ibid., pp. 216–239.

40. Ibid., pp. 29–32.

41. Lev. 25: 39–47, *The New Oxford Annotated Bible*, rev. standard ed. (New York: Oxford University Press). There was great dispute about the meanings of various biblical texts on slavery during the abolitionist period, but it seems clear that, whether or not the Bible sanctioned racial slavery in America, it explicitly sanctioned some form of slavery in the past. (Especially, but not solely, in the Old Testament)

42. The other major strands of argument included a restatement and insistence on the principle of the Declaration of Independence that "All men are created equal" (the biblical version of which was "do unto others as you would have them do unto you") and a recounting of the horrors of slavery. See, e.g., Rev. William H. Boole, *Antidote to Rev. H. J. Van Dyke's Pro-Slavery Discourse* (New York: Edmund Jones and Co., 1861); Frederick Douglass, assorted speeches collected in *The Life and Writings of Frederick Douglass*, 2 vols., ed. Philip S. Foner (New York: International Publishers, 1950), and works of Theodore Weld and others collected in various anthologies including John L. Thomas, ed., *Slavery Attacked: The Abolitionist Crusade* (Englewood Cliffs, NJ: Prentice-Hall, 1965), and Louis Ruchames, ed., *The Abolitionists: A Collection of Their Writings* (New York: G. P. Putnam's Sons, 1963).

43. William Lloyd Garrison, "Henry Clay's Colonization Address," in Thomas, ed., *Slavery Attacked*, p. 7.

44. Some emancipationists were colonizationists, and they generally presumed both that the Negro was inferior and that slavery was bad, but this argument, held even by Abraham Lincoln, was not the rationale eventually incorporated into the public documents and consensus. The material humanity (in numbers and form) of the Blacks prevented that rhetoric's success.

45. See, e.g., Bledsoe, *An Essay on Liberty*; Robinson, *Pictures of Slavery*, pp. 51, 67, 139, 241; Hopkins, *A Scriptural . . .View of Slavery*, p. 11; and Henry Field James, *Abolitionism Unveiled* (Cincinnati, OH: E. Morgan and Sons, 1856), pp. 17, 114, 123–125, 131.

46. Bledsoe, *An Essay on Liberty*, pp. 288, 54.

47. James, *Abolitionism Unveiled*, pp. 201–204; Robinson, *Pictures of Slavery*, pp. 227–228; Hopkins, *A Scriptural . . . View of Slavery*, pp. 18–21, 27.

48. James A. Sloan, *The Great Question Answered; or, Is Slavery a Sin in Itself* (Memphis: Hutton, Galloway and Co., 1857), p. 48.

49. Douglass, in Foner, ed., *Life and Writings*, vol 2, p. 252.

50. See *Plessy v. Ferguson*, 163 U.S. 537, 16 S.Ct. 1128, 41 L. Ed. 256 (1896).

51. Booker T. Washington, "First Annual Address as President: National Negro Business League, August 14, 1900," in *Selected Speeches of Booker T. Washington*, ed. Ernest Davidson Washington (Garden City, NY: Doubleday, Doran and Co., 1932), p. 90, and other speeches.

52. Marcus Garvey, "Speech Delivered on Emancipation Day at Liberty Hall, New York City, January 1, 1922," in *Philosophy and Opinions of Marcus Garvey*, ed. Amy Jacques-Garvey (New York: Arno Press/New York Times, 1968), pp. 79–81. W.E.B. DuBois, "On Segregation," in *A W.E.B. DuBois Reader*, ed. Andrew G. Paschal (New York: Collier Books, 1971), p. 143.

53. The description of the discourse in the White press is drawn from Condit, "Democracy and Civil Rights."

54. See *Brown v. Board of Education* 73 S.Ct. 2; 74 S.Ct. 347; 75 S.Ct. 753, 346 U.S. 483, and 349 U.S. 294 (1954, 1955). The importance of the gradual spread of a rhetoric and its relative dominance among elite power groups is particularly evident here. Harlan's dissent in *Plessy v. Ferguson* was very much similar to the decision in *Brown v. Board of Education*, but the majority in *Plessy* referred continually to the existing "customs," North and South, which legitimized "separation."

55. Martin Luther King Jr., "I Have a Dream," in Wil A. Linkugel, R. R. Allen, and Richard L. Johannesen, eds., *Contemporary American Speeches*, 5th ed. (Dubuque, IA: Kendall Hunt, 1982), p. 369.

56. This controversial claim requires two distinctions and evidence. The first distinction is that of "public" vs. "private." That which remained acceptable in local and private contexts became unacceptable in national and public contexts. Second, a numerical majority is not necessary for such changes to take effect. All that is required is a working coalition of powerful social actors and complacency by the majority. Third, the evidence is available in polls of the period. For example, one of the closest measures of acceptability and identity is the willingness to live near members of another race. The opinion polls indicate that the desirability of Black neighbors to Whites was first and more radically altered in the South in the 1950s and 1960s, and later in the North. See George H. Gallup, *The Gallup Poll: Public Opinion, 1935–1971* (New York: Random House, 1972), pp. 1572–1573, 1824, 1941.

57. This theme, that "affirmative action" is limited to those cases where it does not result in "reverse discrimination" against the rights of other individuals, is clearly articulated in *Regents of University of California v. Bakke* 438 U.S. 265 (1978).

58. Myrdal, *An American Dilemma*, p. 24.

59. MacIntrye, *Against Virtue*, p. 204.

60. Kenneth Burke, "Definition of Man," in *Language as Symbolic Action: Essays on Life, Literature, and Method* (Berkeley and Los Angeles: University of California Press, 1966), pp. 3–24.

61. Farrell, "Rhetorical Resemblance," p. 17.

PART 5

The Nature of the Audience

Rhetorical discourse is *addressed* to particular audiences. To speak rhetorically is neither to articulate abstract truths in a universal void nor to practice a purely aestheticized self-expression through language. To address an audience is rather to create a message that accounts for the character of a specific group of people who are imagined as the receivers of that message. To unravel what it means to address an audience, however, is a more difficult task than it might at first seem.

The paradigm case for rhetoric in the early part of the twentieth century was the political oration, a speech presented by a speaker to an audience understood as "the public." From this perspective, the public was an extension of the Enlightenment conception of the "individual" as a rational actor, the difference being that when cast as a decision-making body, the public represented an aggregation or community of rational individuals who operated on the basis of what some thinkers have called "public knowledge." In this context, public knowledge refers to a stable and relatively homogeneous body of facts, values, and opinions that constitute the community's "objective" knowledge (e.g., Bitzer, 1978).

Michael Calvin McGee challenges this notion in his essay "In Search of 'the People': A Rhetorical Alternative." According to McGee, audiences are neither stable nor homogeneous; nor, for that matter, do they inherently preexist a given rhetorical encounter as one might imagine an objectifiable "public" waiting to be addressed. Rather, he argues that at least in the Anglo-American experience, the premiere audience has always been "the people," a gross fictionalization of a national, collective identity that achieves reality only in the context of being called into existence by a specific rhetoric. Moreover, such rhetoric is not rooted in an objectively verifiable "public knowledge," but in ideology. In calling "the people" a rhetorical fiction McGee does not mean to suggest a lack of power or collective agency; much to the contrary, he suggests that "the people" have an enormous capacity to shape their world, but that their power is transitory and constituted solely through rhetoric. Whereas a "public" exists over time by virtue of the knowledge that it shares, a "people" exists only so long as groups of individuals see themselves in an active public discourse that successfully constitutes a collective identity for them.

A related approach to exploring the rhetorical dimensions of the audience is provided by the concept of "persona." In an essay entitled "The Second Persona," Edwin Black posits that each instance of rhetoric constructs an implied auditor. So, for example, a speech reveals not only what the rhetor wants his or her audience to know or believe as a consequence of the particular topic of the speech, but it also implies who the ideal auditor for the message would be. According to Black, the character of this implied auditor is made evident in recurring stylistic tokens, such as the repetition of key metaphors. Identifying and analyzing the implications of these recurring elements allows the critic to isolate the moral character of the implied audience, and thus obligates him or her to offer a moral judgment of the rhetor's vision.

Philip Wander extends Black's insight in an essay entitled "The Third Persona: An Ideological Turn in Rhetorical Theory." In this essay Wander calls attention to the fact that just as a rhetorical discourse implies an ideal auditor, so too it excludes potential audience members from inclusion within its boundaries. According to Wander, those who are silenced by being "written out" of the public discourse represent a rhetoric's "third persona." If a primary function of public discourse is to constitute the identity of "the people" and their interests, then Wander's argument suggests the importance of analyzing and evaluating the ways in which certain groups or interests are excluded from consideration by virtue of the stylistic construction of the audience. Only by understanding who gets to be included in "the people" and whose identity and interests are excluded can we fully and fairly evaluate the potential effects and moral import of any public discourse.

Put simply, the rhetorical study of the audience is much more than a matter of public opinion polling. It entails examining the complex of relationships between speakers, texts, and the society as a whole.

Additional Readings

Bitzer, Lloyd. (1978). "Rhetoric and Public Knowledge." In Don M. Burks, ed., *Rhetoric, Philosohy, and Literature: An Exploration* (West Lafayette, IN: Purdue University Press), pp. 67–94.
Brummett, Barry, and Margaret Carlisle Duncan. (1990). "Theorizing without

Totalizing: Specularity and Televised Sports." *Quarterly Journal of Speech* 76: 227–246.

Campbell, Karlyn Kohrs. (1973). "The Rhetoric of Women's Liberation: An Oxymoron." *Quarterly Journal of Speech* 59: 74–86.

Charland, Maurice. (1987). "Constitutive Rhetoric: The Case of the Peuple Québécois." *Quarterly Journal of Speech* 73: 133–150.

Cohen, Jodi R. (1991). "The 'Relevance' of Cultural Identity in Audiences' Interpretations of Mass Media." *Critical Studies in Mass Communication* 8: 442–454.

Hauser, Gerard. (1998) "Vernacular Dialogue and the Rheotricality of Public Opinion." *Communication Monographs* 65; 83–107.

Lucaites, John Louis. (1997). "Visualizing 'The People': Individualism and Collectivism in *Let Us Now Praise Famous Men*." *Quarterly Journal of Speech* 83: 269–288.

McGee, Michael Calvin, and Martha Martin. (1983). "Public Knowledge and Ideological Argument." *Communication Monographs* 50: 47–65.

The Second Persona

EDWIN BLACK

The moral evaluation of rhetorical discourse is a subject that receives and merits attention. It is not necessary to dwell on why rhetorical critics tend to evade moral judgments in their criticism, or on why the whole subject has the forbiddingly suspicious quality of a half-hidden scandal. Suffice it to note that the motives for doubting the enterprise are not frivolous ones. Most of us understand that the moral judgment of a text is a portentous act in the process of criticism, and that the terminal character of such a judgment works to close critical discussion rather than open or encourage it.

Moral judgments, however balanced, however elaborately qualified, are nonetheless categorical. Once rendered, they shape decisively one's relationship to the object judged. They compel, as forcefully as the mind can be compelled, a manner of apprehending an object. Moral judgments coerce one's perceptions of things. It is perhaps for these reasons that critics are on the whole diffident about pronouncing moral appraisals of the discourses they criticize. They prefer keeping their options open; they prefer allowing free play to their own perceptual instruments; they prefer investigating to issuing dicta. These are preferences that strongly commend themselves, for they are no less than the scruples of liberal scholarship.

Nevertheless, there is something acutely unsatisfying about criticism that stops short of appraisal. It is not so much that we crave magistracy as that we require order, and the judicial phase of criticism is a way of bringing order to our history.

History is a long, long time. Its raw material is an awesome garbage heap of facts, and even the man who aspires to be nothing more than a simple chronicler still must make decisions about perspective. It is through moral judgments that we sort out our past, that we coax the networks and the continuities out of what has come before, that we disclose the precursive patterns that may in turn present themselves to us as potentialities, and thus extend our very freedom. Even so limited a quest as conceiving a history of public address requires the sort of ordering and apportioning that must inevitably be infected with moral values. The hand that would shape a "usable past" can grasp only fragments of the world, and the principles by which it makes its selections are bound to have moral significance.

The technical difficulty of making moral judgments of rhetorical discourses is that we are accustomed to thinking of discourses as objects, and we are not equipped to render moral judgments of objects. Ever since Prometheus taught us hubris, we in the West have regarded objects as our own instruments, latent or actual, and we have insisted that an instrument is a perfectly neutral thing, that it is solely the use to which the instrument is put that can enlist our moral interest. And it was, of course, the ubiquitous Aristotle who firmly placed rhetoric into the instrumental category.[1] Thanks in part to that influence, we are to this day disposed to regard discourses as objects, and to evaluate them, if at all, according to what is done with them. If the demagogue inflames his audience to rancor, or the prophet exalts their consciousness, in either case we allow ourselves a judgment, but the judgment is of consequences, real or supposed. We do not appraise the discourse in itself except in a technical or prudential way. Our moral judgments are reserved for men and their deeds, and appropriately the literature of moral philosophy is bent toward those subjects. My purpose here is by no means to challenge this arrangement. Instead, I propose exploring the hypothesis that if students of communication could more proficiently explicate the saliently human dimensions of a discourse—if we could, in a sense, discover for a complex linguistic formulation a corresponding form of character—we should then be able to subsume that discourse under a moral order and thus satisfy our obligation to history.

This aspiration may seem excessively grand until we remember that we have been at least playing about its fringes for a long time in criticism. The persistent and recurrently fashionable interest among rhetorical and literary critics in the relationship between a text and its author is a specific expression of the sort of general interest embodied in the hypothesis. Despite our disputes over whether the Intentional Fallacy is really a fallacy, despite our perplexities over the uses of psychoanalysis in criticism and the evidentiary problems they present, despite even the difficulties posed the critic by the phenomenon of ghost writing, where the very identity of the author may be elusive, we still are inclined to recognize, as our predecessors have for many centuries, that language has a symptomatic function. Discourses contain tokens of their authors. Discourses are, directly or in a transmuted form, the external signs of internal states. In short, we accept it as true that a discourse implies an author, and we mean by that more than the tautology that an act entails an agent. We mean, more specifically, that certain features of a linguistic act entail certain characteristics of the language user.

The classic formulation of this position is, of course, in the *Rhetoric* and the *Poetics*. There we find the claim developed that a speech or set of speeches, constituting either the literal discourse of a public man or the lines associated with a role in a play, reveal two dimensions of character: the moral and the intellectual. It is common knowledge that the discussion of moral character—*ethos*—in the *Rhetoric* is for many reasons an intriguing account, that the discussion of intellectual character—*dianoia*—which appears mainly in the *Poetics* is cryptic and evidently incomplete in the form in which we have it, and that there are ample textual hints that we are to take ethos and dianoia as distinguishable but complementary constituents of the same thing. They are aspects of the psyche. In a play their tokens suggest to the audience the psyche of a character. In a speech they suggest the speaker.

It is also common knowledge that today we are not inclined to talk about the discursive symptoms of character in quite the way men did in Aristotle's time. We are more skeptical about the veracity of the representation; we are more conscious that there may be a disparity between the man and his image; we have, in a sense, less trust. Wayne Booth, among others, has illuminated the distinction between the real author of a work and the author implied by the work, noting that there may be few similarities between the two, and this distinction better comports than does the classical account with our modern sense of how discourses work.[2] We have learned to keep continuously before us the possibility, and in some cases the probability, that the author implied by the discourse is an artificial creation: a persona, but not necessarily a person. A fine illustration of this kind of sensibility appears in a report on the 1968 Republican convention by Gore Vidal:

> Ronald Reagan is a well-preserved not young man. Close-to, the painted face is webbed with delicate lines while the dyed hair, eyebrows, and the eyelashes contrast oddly with the sagging muscle beneath the as yet unlifted chin, soft earnest of wattle soon-to-be. The effect, in repose, suggests the work of a skillful embalmer. Animated, the face is quite attractive and at a distance youthful, particularly engaging is the crooked smile full of large porcelain-capped teeth. The eyes are the only interesting feature: small, narrow, apparently dark, they glitter in the hot light.[3]

Note that last twist of the knife: the eyes are "*apparently* dark." Not even the windows of the soul can quite be trusted, thanks to optometry.

The Vidal description is more nearly a kind of journalism than a kind of criticism, but its thrust is clearly illustrative of the distinction we have become accustomed to making—the distinction between the man and the image, between reality and illusion. And we have to acknowledge that in an age when 70 percent of the population of this country lives in a preprocessed environment, when our main connection with a larger world consists of shadows on a pane of glass, when our politics seems at times a public nightmare privately dreamed, we have, to say the least, some adjustments to make in the ancient doctrine of ethical proof. But however revised, we know that the concept amounts to something, that the implied author of a discourse is a persona that figures importantly in rhetorical transactions.

What equally well solicits our attention is that there is a second persona also implied by a discourse, and that persona is its implied auditor. This notion is not a novel one, but its uses to criticism deserve more attention.

In the classical theories of rhetoric the implied auditor—this second persona— is but cursorily treated. We are told that he is sometimes sitting in judgment of the past, sometimes of the present, and sometimes of the future, depending on whether the discourse is forensic, epideictic, or deliberative.[4] We are informed too that a discourse may imply an elderly auditor or a youthful one.[5] More recently we have learned that the second persona may be favorably or unfavorably disposed toward the thesis of the discourse, or he may have a neutral attitude toward it.[6]

These typologies have been presented as a way of classifying real audiences. They are what has been yielded when theorists focused on the relationship between a discourse and some specific group responding to it. And we, of course, convert these typologies to another use when we think of them as applying to implied auditors. That application does not focus on a relationship between a discourse and an actual auditor. It focuses instead on the discourse alone, and extracts from it the audience it implies. The commonest manifestation of this orientation is that we adopt when we examine a discourse and say of it, for example, "This is designed for a hostile audience." We would be claiming nothing about those who attended the discourse. Indeed, perhaps our statement concerns a closet speech, known to no one except ourselves as critics and its author. But we are able nonetheless to observe the sort of audience that would be appropriate to it. We would have derived from the discourse a hypothetical construct that is the implied auditor.

One more observation must be made about these traditional audience typologies before we leave them. It is that one must be struck by their poverty. No doubt they are leads into sometimes useful observations, but even after one has noted of a discourse that it implies an auditor who is old, uncommitted, and sitting in judgment of the past, one has left to say—well, everything.

Especially must we note what is important in characterizing personae. It is not age or temperament or even discrete attitude. It is ideology—ideology in the sense that Marx used the term: the network of interconnected convictions that functions in a man epistemically and that shapes his identity by determining how he views the world.

Quite clearly we have had raging in the West at least since the Reformation a febrile combat of ideologies, each tending to generate its own idiom of discourse, each tending to have decisive effects on the psychological character of its adherents. While in ages past men living in the tribal warmth of the *polis* had the essential nature of the world determined for them in their communal heritage of mythopoesis, and they were able then to assess the probity of utterance by reference to its mimetic relationship to the stable reality that undergirded their consciousness, there is now but the rending of change and the clamor of competing fictions. The elegant trope of Heraclitus has become the delirium of politics. Thus is philosophy democratized.

It is this perspective on ideology that may inform our attention to the auditor implied by the discourse. It seems a useful methodological assumption to hold that rhetorical discourses, either singly or cumulatively in a persuasive movement, will imply an auditor, and that in most cases the implication will be sufficiently suggestive as to enable the critic to link this implied auditor to an ideology. The best evidence in the discourse for this implication will be the substantive claims that are made, but the most likely evidence available will be in the form of stylistic tokens. For example, if the thesis of a discourse is that the communists have infiltrated the Supreme Court and the universities, its ideological bent would be obvious. However even if a discourse made neutral and innocuous claims, but contained the term "bleeding hearts" to refer to proponents of welfare legislation, one would be justified in suspecting that a general attitude—more, a whole set of general attitudes—were being summoned, for the term is only used tendentiously and it can no more blend with a noncommittal context than a spirochete can be domesticated.

The expectation that a verbal token of ideology can be taken as implying an auditor who shares that ideology is something more than a hypothesis about a relationship. It rather should be viewed as expressing a vector of influence. These sometimes modest tokens indeed tend to fulfill themselves in that way. Actual auditors look to the discourse they are attending for cues that tell them how they are to view the world, even beyond the expressed concerns, the overt propositional sense, of the discourse. Let the rhetor, for example, who is talking about school integration use a pejorative term to refer to black people, and the auditor is confronted with more than a decision about school integration. He is confronted with a plexus of attitudes that may not at all be discussed in the discourse or even implied in any way other than the use of the single term. The discourse will exert on him the pull of an ideology. It will move, unless he rejects it, to structure his experience on many subjects besides school integration. And more, if the auditor himself begins using the pejorative term, it will be a fallible sign that he has adopted not just a position on school integration, but an ideology.

Each one of us, after all, defines himself by what he believes and does. Few of us are born to grow into an identity that was incipiently structured before our births. That was, centuries ago, the way with men, but it certainly is not with us. The quest for identity is the modern pilgrimage. And we look to one another for hints as to whom we should become. Perhaps these reflections do not apply to everyone, but they do apply to the persuasible, and that makes them germane to rhetoric.

The critic can see in the auditor implied by a discourse a model of what the rhetor would have his real auditor become. What the critic can find projected by the discourse is the image of a man, and though that man may never find actual embodiment, it is still a man that the image is of. This condition makes moral judgment possible, and it is at this point in the process of criticism that it can illuminatingly be rendered. We know how to make appraisals of men. We know how to evaluate potentialities of character. We are compelled to do so for ourselves constantly. And this sort of judgment, when fully ramified, constitutes a definitive act of judicial criticism.

A PARADIGM

Since a scruple of rationality mandates that claims be warranted, and since the most convincing sanction of a critical position is its efficacy, we turn now to a test. That test will be an essay in the original sense of the word: a trial, an attempt, an exploration. The subject of the essay is a small but recurrent characteristic of discourses associated with the Radical Right in contemporary American politics. That characteristic is the metaphor, "the cancer of communism."

The phrase, "the cancer of communism," is a familiar one. Indeed, it may be so familiar as to approach the condition of a dead metaphor, a cliché. What is less familiar is that this metaphor seems to have become the exclusive property of spokesmen for the Radical Right. Although speakers and writers who clearly are unsympathetic to the Right do sometimes use "cancer" as the vehicle of metaphors, the whole communism-as-cancer metaphor simply is not present in "liberal" or Leftist discourses.[7] Yet it seems to crop up constantly among Rightists—Rightists who sometimes have little else in common besides a political position and the metaphor itself. Perhaps the best source of illustration of the metaphor is the Holy Writ of the John Birch Society, *The Blue Book* by Robert Welch. More than most of his compatriots, Welch really relishes the metaphor. He does not simply sprinkle his pages with it, as for example does Billy James Hargis. Welch amplifies the figure; he expands it; he returns to it again and again. For example: "Every thinking and informed man senses that, even as cunning, as ruthless, and as determined as are the activists whom we call Communists with a capital 'C,' the conspiracy could never have reached its present extensiveness, and the gangsters at the head of it could never have reached their present power, unless there were tremendous weaknesses to make the advance of such a disease so rapid and its ravages so disastrous."[8] And again: "An individual human being may die of any number of causes. But if he escapes the fortuitous diseases, does not meet with any fatal accident, does not starve to death, does not have his heart give out, but lives in normal health to his three score years and ten and then keeps on living—if he escapes or survives everything else and keeps on doing so, he will eventually succumb to the degenerative disease of cancer. For death must come, and cancer is merely death coming by stages, instead of all at once. And exactly the same thing seems to be true of those organic aggregations of human beings, which we called cultures or civilizations."[9] And again: "Collectivism destroys the value to the organism of the individual cells—that is, the individual human beings—without replacing them with new ones with new strength. The Roman Empire of the West, for instance, started dying from the cancer of collectivism from the time Diocletian imposed on it his New Deal."[10] And again: "Until now, there is a tremendous question whether, even if we did not have the Communist conspirators deliberately helping to spread the virus for their own purposes, we could recover from just the natural demagogue-fed spread of that virus when it is already so far advanced."[11] And again: "We have got to stop the Communists, for many reasons. One reason is to keep them from agitating our cancerous tissues, reimplanting the virus, and working to spread it, so that we never have a chance of recovery."[12] And finally: "Push the Communists back, get out of the bed of a Europe that is dying with this cancer of collectivism, and breathe our own healthy air of opportunity, enterprise, and freedom; then the cancer we already have, even though it is of considerable growth, can be cut out."[13]

There are other examples to be taken from Welch's book, but we have a sample sufficient for our biopsy. Welch, of course, is an extreme case even for the Radical Right. He cultivates the metaphor with the fixity of a true connoisseur. But though the metaphor is not present in the discourses of all Rightists, it seems almost never to appear in the discourses of non-Rightists. It is the idiomatic token of an ideology, the fallible sign of a frame of reference, and it is what we essay to explore.

This metaphor is not the only idiomatic token of American right-wing ideology. There is, to name another, the inventory of perished civilizations that crops up in discourses that are right of center. It is a *topos* that goes a long way back into our history, and that has evidently been associated with a Rightist orientation for more than a century. Perry Miller, writing of the political conservatism of nineteenth-century revivalism, notes of a sermon delivered in 1841 that it "called the roll . . . of the great kingdoms which had perished—Chaldea, Egypt, Greece, Rome—but gave America the chance, unique in history, of escaping the treadmill to oblivion if it would only adhere to the conserving Christianity. In the same year, George Cheever, yielding himself to what had in literature and painting become . . . a strangely popular theme in the midst of American progress, told how he had stood beneath the walls of the Colosseum, of the Parthenon, of Karnak, and 'read the proofs of God's veracity in the vestiges at once of such stupendous glory and such a stupendous overthrow.'"[14] Miller goes on to observe, "William Williams delivered in 1843 a discourse entitled 'The Conservative Principle,' and Charles White one in 1852 more specifically named 'The Conservative Element in Christianity.' These are merely examples of hundreds in the same vein all calling attention to how previous empires had perished because they had relied entirely upon the intellect, upon 'Political Economy,' and upon 'false liberalism.'"[15]

That *topos* is with us yet, and it is almost as much a recurrent feature of Rightist discourse as the communism-as-cancer figure. Both the *topos* and the metaphor are examples of an idiomatic token of ideology.

Regarding the communism-as-cancer metaphor, it could make considerable difference to critical analysis whether a preoccupation with or morbid fear of cancer had any psychopathological significance, whether such a fear had been identified by psychiatrists as a symptom of sufficient frequency as to have been systematically investigated and associated with any particular psychological condition. If that were the case—if psychiatry had a "line" of any kind on this symptom—such clinical information could be applicable in some way to those people who are affected by the communism-as-cancer metaphor. Moreover, if an obsessive fear of cancer were the symptom of an acknowledged and recognizable psychological condition, the tendency of Rightist discourse to cultivate this fear may work to induce in its auditors some form of that psychological condition. Such would be the enticing prospects of a marriage between science and criticism, but unfortunately both psychiatry and clinical psychology are frigid inamoratas, for the literature of neither recognizes such a symptom. It remains, then, for the critic alone to make what sense he can of the metaphor:

1. Cancer is a kind of horrible pregnancy. It is not an invasion of the body by alien organisms, which is itself a metaphor of war, and therefore suitable to the purposes of the Radical Right. Nor is it the malfunction of one of the body's organs—a mechanical metaphor. The actual affliction may, of course, be related to either or both of these; that is, some kinds of cancer may in fact be produced by a virus (invasion), or they may be the result of the body's failure to produce cancer-rejecting chemicals (malfunction), but these are only the hypotheses of some medical researchers, and not associated with the popular conception of cancer. Cancer is conceived as a growth of some group of the body's own cells. The cancer is a part of oneself, a sinister and homicidal extension of one's own body. And one's attitude toward one's body is bound up with one's attitude toward cancer; more so than in the case of invasions or malfunctions, for neither of these is an extension of oneself. It is a living and unconscious malignancy that the body itself has created, in indifference to, even defiance of, the conscious will. And because one's attitude toward one's body is bound up with one's attitude toward cancer, we may suspect that a metaphor that employed cancer as its vehicle would have a particular resonance for an auditor who was ambivalent about his own body. We may suspect, in fact, that the metaphor would strike a special fire with a congeries of more generally puritanical attitudes.

2. In the popular imagination, cancer is thought to be incurable. Now this is a curious aspect of the metaphor. If the metaphor serves to convey the gravity, agony, and malignancy of communism, why would it not convey also its inexorability, and thus promote in the auditor a terror that robs him of the will to resist? That consequence would seem to be contrary to the Rightist's objectives. Why, then, is the metaphor not excessive? Some auditors possibly are affected by the metaphor or understand it in this way—that is, as a metaphor conveying not just the horror of communism but also the inevitability of its triumph. Hence, Rightists seem less inhibited by the fear of nuclear war than others. Perhaps there is associated with this metaphor not a different estimate of the probable effects of nuclear war, but rather a conviction that the body-politic is already doomed, so that its preservation—the preservation of an organism already ravaged and fast expiring—is not really important.

We must understand the *Weltansicht* with which the metaphor is associated. The world is not a place where one lives in an enclave of political well-being with a relatively remote enemy approaching. No, the enemy is here and his conquests surround one. To the Rightist, communism is not just in Russia or China or North Vietnam. It is also in the local newspaper; it is in the magazines on the newsstand; it is in television and the movies; it has permeated the government at all levels; it may even be in the house next door. We understand well enough that when the Rightist speaks of communism he refers to virtually all social welfare and civil rights legislation. What we understand less well is that when he refers to America, he refers to a polity already in the advanced stages of an inexorable disease whose suppurating sores are everywhere manifest and whose voice is a death rattle.

And what organs of this afflicted body need be spared amputation? The country is deathly ill. Its policies are cowardly; its spokesmen are treasonous; its cities are anarchical; its discipline is flaccid; its poor are arrogant; its rich are greedy; its courts are unjust; its universities are mendacious. True, there is a chance of salvation—of cure, but the chance is a slight one, and every moment diminishes it. The patient is *in extremis*. It is in this light that risks must be calculated, and in this light the prospect of nuclear war becomes thinkable. Why not chance it, after all? What alternative is there? The patient is dying; is it not time for the ultimate surgery? What is there to lose? In such a context, an unalarmed attitude toward the use of atomic weapons is not just reasonable; it is obvious.

3. The metaphor seems related to an organismic view of the state. The polity is a living creature, susceptible to disease; a creature with a will, with a consciousness of itself, with a metabolism and a personality, with a life. The polity is a great beast: a beast that first must be cured, and then must be tamed. The question arises, What is the nature of other organisms if the state itself is one? What is the individual if he is a cell in the body-politic? Contrary to what one might expect, we know that the Rightist places great emphasis on individualism, at least verbally. Recall, for example, Goldwater's often-used phrase, "the whole man," from the 1964 campaign.[16] It is true, the Rightist is suspicious of beards, of unconventional dress, of colorful styles of living. He has antipathy for deviance from a fairly narrow norm of art, politics, sex, or religion, so that his endorsement of individualism has about it the aura of a self-indulgent hypocrisy. Nonetheless, there is something of great value to him that he calls individualism, and if we would understand him, we must understand what he means by individualism. He probably acts consistent with his own use of the term.

It appears that when the Rightist refers to individualism, he is referring to the acquisition and possession of property. Individualism is the right to get and to spend without interference, and this is an important right because a man asserts himself in his possessions. What he owns is what he has to say. So conceived, individualism is perfectly compatible with an organismic conception of the polity. And moreover, the polity's own hideous possession—its tumor—is an expression of its corruption.

4. At first glance the metaphor seems to place communism in the category of natural phenomena. If one does not create a cancer, then one cannot be responsible for it, and if communism is a kind of cancer, then it would seem that one cannot develop a moral attitude toward its agents. This would constitute a difficulty with the metaphor only if people behaved rationally. Fortunately for the metaphor—and unfortunately for us—there is a demonstrable pervasive and utterly irrational attitude toward cancer that saves the metaphor from difficulty. Morton Bard, a psychologist who investigated the psychological reactions of a hundred patients at Memorial Sloan-Kettering Cancer Center, found that forty-eight of them spontaneously expressed beliefs about the cause of their illness that assigned culpability either to themselves or to others or to some supernatural agent.[17] His study suggests, in other words, that an extraordinarily high proportion of people who have cancer—or for our purposes it may be better to say *who become convinced* that they have cancer—are disposed to blame the cancer on a morally responsible agent. Surely it is no great leap from this study to the suspicion that an auditor who is responsive to the metaphor would likely be just the sort of person who would seek culpability. The link between responsiveness to the metaphor and the disposition to seek culpability lies, perhaps, in religious fundamentalism. Various studies indicate that the members of Radical Right organizations tend also to be affiliated with fundamentalist religious sects.[18] Surely it is possible that a lifetime of reverent attention to sermons that seek a purpose behind the universe can end by developing a telic cast of mind, can end by inducing some people to seek purpose and plan behind everything,

so that they must explain political misfortunes and illnesses alike by hypothesizing conspiracies.

5. Cancer is probably the most terrifying affliction that is popularly known. So terrible is it, in fact, that medical authorities have reported difficulty in inducing people to submit to physical examinations designed to detect cancer. For many, it seems, cancer has become unthinkable—so horrifying to contemplate that one cannot even admit the possibility of having it. The concept of cancer is intimately connected with the concept of death itself. Thus, to equate communism with cancer is to take an ultimately implacable position. One would not quit the struggle against death except in two circumstances: either one acknowledged its futility and surrendered in despair, or one transmuted the death-concept into a life-concept through an act of religious faith.

Given the equation, communism = cancer = death, we may expect that those enamored of the metaphor would, in the face of really proximate "communism," tend either to despairing acts of suicide or to the fervent embrace of communism as an avenue to grace. The former, suicidal tendency is already discernible in some Rightist political programs, for example, the casual attitude toward nuclear warfare that has already been remarked in another connection. If it were possible for a communist agency to increase its pressure on the United States, we could expect to see the latter tendency increasing, with some of our most impassioned Rightists moving with equal passion to the Left. John Burnham, Elizabeth Bentley, Whitaker Chambers, and others famous from the decade of the fifties for having abandoned the Communist Party have already traveled that road in the opposite direction. The path clearly is there to be trod.

6. Finally, we may note the impressive measure of guilt that seems to be associated with the metaphor. The organism of which one is a cell is afflicted with a culpable illness. Can the whole be infected and the part entirely well?

As the Archbishop in the second part of *Henry IV* says in the midst of political upheaval:

> . . . we are all diseas'd;
> And with our surfeiting and wanton hours
> Have brought ourselves into a burning fever
> And we must bleed for it . . .

The guilt is there. Coherence demands it, and the discourse confirms it. It finds expression in all the classic patterns: the zealous righteousness, the suspiciousness, the morbidity, the feverish expiations. The condition suits the metaphor; the metaphor, the condition.[19]

What moral judgment may we make of this metaphor and of discourse that importantly contains it? The judgment seems superfluous, not because it is elusive, but because it is so clearly implied. The form of consciousness to which the metaphor is attached is not one that commends itself. It is not one that a reasonable man would freely choose, and he would not choose it because it does not compensate him with either prudential efficacy or spiritual solace for the anguished exactions it demands.

In discourse of the Radical Right, as in all rhetorical discourse, we can find enticements not simply to believe something, but to *be* something. We are solicited by the discourse to fulfill its brandishments with our very selves. And it is this dimension of rhetorical discourse that leads us finally to moral judgment, and in this specific case, to adverse judgment.

If our exploration has revealed anything, it is how exceedingly well the metaphor of communism-as-cancer fits the Rightist ideology. The two are not merely compatible; they are complementary at every curve and angle. They serve one another at a variety of levels; they meet in a seamless jointure. This relationship, if it holds for all or even many such stylistic tokens, suggests that the association between an idiom and an ideology is much more than a matter of arbitrary convention or inexplicable accident. It suggests that there are strong and multifarious links between a style and an outlook, and that the critic may, with legitimate confidence, move from the manifest evidence of style to the human personality that this evidence projects as a beckoning archetype.

Notes

1. Aristotle, *Rhetoric,* 1355a–b.
2. Wayne C. Booth, *The Rhetoric of Fiction* (Chicago, 1961), esp. Part 2, "The Author's Voice in Fiction."
3. "The Late Show," *New York Review of Books,* September 12, 1968, p. 5.
4. Aristotle, *Rhetoric*, 1.3.
5. Aristotle, *Rhetoric* 2.12–13.
6. See, e.g., Irving L. Janis et al., *Personality and Persuasibility* (New Haven, 1959), esp. pp. 29–54.
7. Norman Mailer, for example, has lately been making "cancer" and "malignancy" the vehicles of frequent metaphors, but the tenor of these metaphors, usually implied, seems to be something like "the dehumanization that results from technological society." It clearly is not "communism," although Soviet society is not exempt from Mailer's condemnations. One can also find occasional references to the "cancer of racism" among left-of-center spokesmen, but these references seem to be no more than occasional. Where, as in Mailer, cancer is a frequently recurring metaphorical vehicle, the analysis that follows may, with appropriate substitution of tenors, be applied. In Mailer's case, at least, it works.
8. Robert Welch, *The Blue Book of the John Birch Society* (Belmont, MA, 1961), p. 41.
9. Ibid., p. 45.
10. Ibid., p. 46.
11. Ibid., pp. 53–54.
12. Ibid., p. 55.
13. Ibid.
14. Perry Miller, *The Life of the Mind in America* (New York, 1965), pp. 70–71.
15. Ibid., p. 71.
16. For example, roughly the last third of Goldwater's speech accepting the Republican nomination in 1964 was a panegyric to individuality and nonconformity.
17. Morton Bard, "The Price of Survival for Cancer Victims," *Transaction* 3 (March–April 1966): 11.
18. See, e.g., Daniel Bell, ed., *The Radical Right* (Garden City, NY, 1964), esp. Seymour Martin Lipset, "Three Decades of the Radical Right: Coughlinites, McCarthyites, and Birchers (1962)," pp. 373–446.
19. Some illuminating comments on the component of guilt in Rightist style and ideology can be found in Richard Hofstadter, "The Paranoid Style in American Politics," in *The Paranoid Style in American Politics and Other Essays* (New York, 1967), esp. pp. 30–32.

In Search of "the People"

A Rhetorical Alternative

MICHAEL CALVIN McGEE

Though concerned almost exclusively with public, social life, students of rhetoric have not been much involved with the topics of social theory. I do not mean, of course, that we are ignorant and sloppy in our scholarship; there has been, especially in so-called movement theory, a good deal of borrowing from the rubrics of empirical sociology and social psychology.[1] But as a rule, we tend not to recognize the significance of our own concepts in describing man's social condition. We bind ourselves to Greek and Roman understandings of rhetoric, and thus tend to underplay our intellectual associations with such social philosophers as Voltaire, Hegel, Guizot, Burckhardt, Lamprecht, Marx, Dilthey, and Huizinga.[2] So, for example, rhetorical scholars were for a time intent on categorizing Kenneth Burke as an "Aristotelian" when in fact his writing is part of a much newer intellectual tradition, that of Hegel, Marx, and Freud.[3]

One manifestation of our continued orientation to conventional rhetorical topics is our general failure fully to exploit the organic conception of human existence presupposed in nearly all rhetorical documents. Whether one's reference is to Marxist "communism" or to Hegelian *Volksgeist*, most all of social theory has been warranted by understanding "humanity" to be a collective entity, "the people."[4] And central to all of rhetorical theory has been a similar organic concept, the advocate's "audience." The consistent appearance in rhetorical literature of appeals to "the people," however, has been considered usual argumentative gymnastics. Especially in analyzing *messages*, critics have taken "people" and "audience" to be no more than plural abstractions of "person" or "individual." In consequence, any appeal to a "people" is almost by definition an argumentative fallacy, and hence an "irrational" form of persuasion. It even has a Latin name, *argumentum ad populam*. The attitude one adopts toward such "fallacies" seems to have determined that one of two general lines of research will be pursued.

First, there are those who rarely encounter a problem of ethics in rhetoric. Such writers, typically critics in an Aristotelian tradition or technicians engaging in attitude research, note the *fact* of appeals to the "people" and attempt to isolate as well as they can a list of "effects" which those appeals are supposed to have. Critics study election results, votes in deliberative assemblies, and reports of witnesses to guess at the impact of great speeches. Experimenters attempt scientifically to describe the changes in attitude and belief which are attributable to persuasion in controlled circumstances. In both cases, "people" or "audience" are terms used in a different, more specific sense than when, for example, our Founding Fathers wrote about the "will" of "We the People." In the current sense, "people" is no more than the plural of "person," a grammatic convention which encourages the notion that the people of a nation are objective, literal extensions of the individual.[5] To determine the "effects" of an argument, or to describe "the will of the people," a poll or survey is taken, and terms like *majority* or *plurality* are used to define the collective life. So in any age studied, individuals are distinguished, divided, and weighed by age, sex, occupation, religion, education, income, *ad nauseum*. It is supposed that an arithmetic of sorts can capture the spirit of a "people."[6]

Another group of writers (typically rhetoricians trying to improve the academic reputation of their art or philosophers seeking to "rehabilitate" a renegade discipline convicted by Plato[7]) apparently believes that pointing up a fallacy in argument is enough in itself to warrant either dismissing an advocate entirely, apologizing for him, or composing a polemic against him. The significance of "the people" in argument, in other words, seems to be that appeals to them instead of to reasoning and evidence short-circuit the reasoning processes. A position of this sort presupposes that the human condition ought to be a rational one; as Marcuse argued, the impulse is to make reality over into a thing with only one, fashionably reasonable, dimension—to create a "one-dimensioned man." Marcuse further argues that this impulse is in a straight-line tradition of Western logic, from Socrates and Plato to date.[8] And as E. L. Hunt observed, the oldest traditions of rhetoric are grossly misrepresented and falsely served by imposing on them the rationalistic ideals of Platonism.[9]

The impulse to continue humanity's reduction to one dimension, partly by deploring such "sophistries" as arguments *ad populam*, is exhibited even by the group of philosophers whose recent rediscovery of rhetoric has led them to resist Plato's blanket moral condemnation of rhetoric. Perelman, for example, will not take rhetoric as he finds it in nature, replete with sophistries, propaganda, myths, and visions. Such things seem specifically "irrational," and his mission is to create a "new rhetoric" which is conceived as a species of reason, the contrary both of experiment and logical deduction on the one hand, and of "irrational forces, instincts, suggestion, and violence" on the other.[10] "People" are more important to Perelman than they were to Plato, for he understands that "audience" is a central, defining concept in any idea of rhetoric. But he will not take audiences as he finds *them* in nature, dominated by individuals moved, as Aristotle observed, more by maxims and self-interest than by reason and evidence.[11] Such audiences are anathema for a rhetoric conceived as a stopgap for formal logic. A redefinition is thus attempted, and Perelman creates (or borrows from literary theory) a "universal audience" which is not universal at all, but rather a series of intellectual elites which do no more than "stand at the vanguard of humanity."[12] So as Plato ignored the *real* "people" in attempting to remake rhetoric for *Phaedrus*, Perelman ignores *real* "people" in writing a *New Rhetoric* which is not more than *A Treatise on Argumentation* for the elite.

One might conclude that, with few exceptions, most rhetorical scholarship presupposes a "people" or an "audience" which is either (a) an objective, literal extension of "person," or (b) a "mob" of individuals whose significance is their gullibility and failure to respond to "logical" argument.[13] The purpose of this essay is to describe an alternative means of defining "the people" based on organic conceptions of human society, depending neither on the observed behavior of individuals nor on Platonic prejudices about the role of reason in human affairs. The essay incidentally explores one part of the reciprocal relationship between rhetoric and social theory—implicitly, it is suggested that a central concept in rhetoric ("audience/people") is better understood within the meanings and intentions of social philosophy than those of logic or the philosophy of science; further, it is argued that attention to the use of the concept "people" in rhetorical documents can illuminate serious problems which have plagued the development of social theories.

I

Describing an alternative conception of "the people" in rhetoric demands first an understanding of A. F. Pollard's observation that "the 'people' is so indeterminate an expression that its use, let alone its abuse, obscures almost all political discussions."[14] Typically, "the people" justify political philosophies; their only concrete significance is their existence, for not even their *identity* is agreed upon by those who appeal to them. About the only point of agreement is that, in politics, "the people" are omnipotent; they are an idea of collective force which transcends both individuality and reason. John Locke's "people," for example, are perceptive in ways no philosopher could be, powerful in a way no army could match, patient in a way any behavioral scientist would envy.[15] Hitler writes of "historical avalanches" which are "movements of the people," "volcanic eruptions of human passions and spiritual sensations" which do not involve individuals.[16] In China, Chairman Mao plots strategy which matches nuclear bombs against nothing more than masses of "the people."[17] Thus, in each of the three major ideological systems of the twentieth century (Whig, Fascist, and Communist), "the people" warrant a whole political system: but their identity varies from system to system, no political philosopher surely describes them, no political leader for long can be assured that he has captured the spirit even of his own people.[18]

Stated simply, the problem is this: How can one conceive the idea "people" in a way which accounts for the rhetorical function of "the people" in arguments designed to warrant social action, even society itself? A possibility most recently was suggested by Bormann's reassertion of arguments advanced some time ago by Sorel, Lippmann, Burke, Mannheim, Ortega, and Weaver.[19] Bormann believes that such concepts as "The People" may be strictly *linguistic* phenomena introduced into public argument as a means of "legitimizing" a collective fantasy. The advocate, he suggests, dangles a dramatic vision of the people before his audience. The audience, essentially a group of individuals, reacts with a desire to participate in that dramatic vision, to *become* "the people" described by the advocate. "The people," therefore, are not objectively real in the sense that they exist as a collective entity in nature; rather, they are a fiction dreamed by an advocate and infused with an artificial, rhetorical reality by the agreement of an audience to participate in a collective fantasy. As Bormann observes:

> When there is a discrepancy between the word and the thing the most important cultural artifact for understanding the events may not be the things of "reality" but the words or the symbols. Indeed, in many vital instances the words, that is, the rhetoric, are the social reality

and to try to distinguish one symbolic reality from another is a fallacy widespread in historical and sociological scholarship which the rhetorical critic can do much to dispel.[20]

An alternative to collecting the votes of "persons," therefore, may be to conceive "people" as an essential rhetorical fiction with both a "social" and an "objective" reality.

This notion of dual realities is specifically "nonrational" in traditional terms. Contrary to the law of identity, the assertion is explicit that "the people" are both real and a fiction simultaneously. I would like to consider this possibility in some detail by using as a context Hitler's description of the rhetorical process in which a leader transforms individuals into a "people":

> By "people" I mean all those hundreds of thousands who fundamentally long for the same thing without finding the words in detail to describe the outward appearance of what is before the inner eye. For with all great reforms the remarkable thing is that at first they have as their champion only a single individual, but as their supporters many millions. For centuries their goal is often the inner ardent wish of hundreds of thousands, till one man stands up as the proclaimer of such a general will and as the flag-bearer of an old longing he helps it to victory in the form of a new idea.[21]

Hitler's suggestion is that individuals have a predisposition toward a particular expression of the popular will, but that they are unaware of it. Their identity as a "people" is contained in general propositions—maxims, commonplaces, national ideological commitments—that remain attitudes, "inner ardent wishes." While they are in a condition of quiescence, therefore, *there is no such thing as a people*. In terms of objective reality, there are only individuals who perhaps "long for the same thing," but who have no collective identity because they cannot describe "what is before the inner eye," the urge to achieve collective unity and collective goals.

The vision of Hitler's "champion" (advocate) extends not just to a particular audience at a particular time, but to an entire nation over a period of centuries. The duty of a champion is to find "an old longing" and "help it to victory." This duty necessarily involves a search of the nation's history with a constant sensitivity toward the character of the "people" who executed it. When "one man stands up as the proclaimer of a general will," what he says, *at the time he originally says it*, is a fiction, for it is his personal interpretation of his "people's" history.[22] Though he warrants his argument with abundant examples, he creates, not a description of *reality*, but rather a political *myth*. Often such myths are confused with descriptions of reality by historians writing in a later day; the result is entertaining and meaningless polemic. So, for example, Namier draws himself up to the height of self-righteousness in recognizing one of Edmund Burke's political myths to be nothing but a product of the writer's "fertile, disordered and malignant imagination."[23] In two short pages, Brooke calls the same myth every name he can think of to discredit it, a "legend," a "bogy," a "myth," a "fantasy," a "hotch-potch," and a "fiction." Burke's *Thoughts on the Causes of the Present Discontents* is all of this and more: it is a vision of the "people" of England in 1770, drawn from their history, and offered to a general audience as an expression of what Burke believed to be "the inner ardent wish of hundreds of thousands."[25]

Hitler asserts that the curious chemistry mixing the single advocate, his vision of "the people," and the social commitments of a million or more persons is characteristic of "all great reforms," and is the *process* which he finds "remarkable." The advocate is a "flag-bearer" for old longings, and by transforming such longings into a new idea, he actualizes his audience's predisposition to act, thus creating a united "people" whose collective power will warrant any "reform" against any other power on earth. Once the process is complete, "the people" have an objective existence defined by their collective behavior.[26] But that reality is still "mythical" in two important respects.

First, in the purely rhetorical encounter Hitler describes (as distinguished from leaderless group encounters), "the people" focus on the Leader to establish a group identity.[27] The advocate is recognized as Leader only when he transcends his own individuality in the estimation of his audience. That is, an advocate brings to the confrontation with his audience a battery of entirely personal convictions and opinions; he then adapts them to his vision of what a "people," when created, will want to hear.[28] If he is successful in dragging "the people" into objective reality, he (the focal point for collective identity) is transformed by their faith in him and his ideas into a *Leader*, an image or mirror of collective forces. And as Frazer argued, the new Leader is himself a kind of fiction, for he wears the magic mask of Kingship, an anonymous face which conceals the powers of a demigod.[29]

Second, "the people," even though made "real" by their own belief and behavior, are still *essentially* a mass illusion. In purely objective terms, the only human reality is that of the individual; groups, whether as small as a Sunday-school class or as big as a whole society, are infused with an artificial identity. So, from a rhetorical perspective, the entire socialization process is nothing but intensive and continual exercises in persuasion: individuals must be seduced into abandoning their individuality, convinced of their sociality, not only when their mothers attempt to housebreak them, but also later in life when governors ask them to obey a law or to die in war for God and country. When in Hitler's vision a champion offers individuals group identity as a "people," therefore, the invitation is to assume an anonymous mask, the kind of face that a timid storekeeper might don to lynch an alleged criminal, to kill an enemy in war, or simply to confront a dominant personality in group discussion.[30]

II

Hitler's rhetoric has not been used here as an object of criticism, but rather as an example of the sense in which "people" exist in objective reality and as social fantasies at the same time. The more important point, however, is that "the people" are more *process* than *phenomenon*. That is, they are conjured into objective reality, remain so long as the rhetoric which defined them has force, and in the end wilt away, becoming once again merely a collection of individuals. As Namier observes of eighteenth-century England, "Even the principles of the Glorious Revolution, after victory had been irrevocably won and they had changed into an accepted profession of faith, came to sound somewhat hollow."[31] An active "people," tired of "tyranny" and jealous of "liberty," existed in 1688. But when Whiggism came to dominate the politics of the 1750s, individuals were no longer inclined to do battle for it. As a result, Namier argues, politics in England were "personal," Whiggish references to "the people" were formulary, and the whole population was generally content to pursue selfish interests.[32] If Namier's observations (and Hitler's) are correct, one cannot speak of "the people" of Anglo-America without reference to stages of development.

I would argue that a kind of rhetoric defines "the people" at each stage in a "collectivization process" of coming-to-be, being, and ceasing-to-be an objectively real entity. "The people" may be defined rhetorically, therefore, from four distinct perspectives. The seeds of collectivization stay dormant in the popular reasonings (aphorisms, maxims, and commonplaces) which Mannheim identifies as the "total ideology" of a particular culture.[33] Such dormant arguments do not define "the people" at a specific moment, but they do represent the parameters of what "the people" of that culture could possibly become.[34] From time to time, advocates organize dissociated ideological commitments into incipient political myths, visions of the collective life dangled before individuals in hope of creating a real "people." Regardless of its actual effects, such a myth contains "the people" of a particular time more surely than general ideological commitments, for it focuses on specific problems in specific situations. A third kind of rhetoric emerges when masses of persons begin to *respond* to a myth, not only by exhibiting collective behavior, but also by publicly ratifying the transaction wherein they give up control over their individual destinies for sake of a dream. At this state, a "people" actually exists in a specific, objective way. As rhetoric defines each of the first three stages of collectivization, so there is a rhetoric of decay as society becomes quiescent and ideological commitments are once again dissociated. Such rhetoric is marked by its hostility toward collectivism ("the people are a monster"[35]); the collective life exists only in legend, and, as Edmund Burke writes of his own time, the tendency is to treat collective existence as an abstraction:

> I have constantly observed, that the generality of people are fifty years, at least, behind-hand in their politicks. . . . Men are wise with but little reflection, and good with little self-denial, in the business of all times except their own. . . . To be a Whig on the business of a hundred years ago is very consistent with every advantage of present servility. This retrospective wisdom, and historical patriotism, are things of wonderful convenience.[36]

The heart of the collectivization process is a political myth, a vision of mass man dangled before persons in the second stage of their metamorphosis into a "people." In a sense, the myth contains all other stages of the process: it gives specific meaning to a society's ideological commitments; it is the inventional source for arguments of ratification among those seduced by it; and it is the central target for those who will not participate in the collective life either because they are hostile to the myth itself or because they have tired of the myth and are not inclined to defend it. Edmund Burke's *Present Discontents*, for example, is almost a textbook summation of the Whig ideology made to justify the use of seventeenth-century value judgments in 1770. The pamphlet was a prime influence on politicians attempting to develop a system of parliamentary democracy and among historians who attempted to rationalize the emergence of parliamentary democracy.[37] It was also a prime target for opponents of the eighteenth-century version of Whig liberalism, and in the twentieth century, it became a symbol of "political dogma" which "clouds thought" by recommending collective fervor and passion (rather than reason and evidence) in the defense of "liberty."[38] This one document, in other words, can be said to contain the entire collectivization process from coming-to-be to ceasing-to-be a "people."

Though many have attempted to define such myths as the *Present Discontents* in terms of collective behavior or historical criticism, they are purely *rhetorical* phenomena, mass fantasies in which grown men justify their intention to act by "playing like" the world is a more comfortable place than it appears to be. Sorel writes: "Myths are not descriptions of things, but expressions of a determination to act. . . . A myth . . . is, at bottom, identical with the convictions of a group, being the expression of those convictions in the language of movement; and it is, in consequence, unanalysable into parts which could be placed on the plane of historical description."[39]

So-called "objective reality" is made more comfortable by making an alternate "reality," what Marx called "false consciousness."[40] The fantastic world of political myths make possible an almost absolute control over the environment—as anyone who has ever attended a traditional Christian funeral can testify, even the most final reality can be controlled by faith in an "afterlife." Though myths defy empirical or historical treatment, therefore, it is easy to recognize them rhetorically as ontological arguments relying not so much on evidence as on artistic proofs intended to answer the question, What is "real"? So political myths were made, for example, when Winston Churchill redefined the reality of Dunkirk, when Franklin Roosevelt redefined the reality of the Great Depression, and when John Kennedy made apparently insoluble social and political problems seem like a "New Frontier."

Political myths technically may represent nothing but a "false consciousness," but they are nonetheless *functionally* "real" and important, as Peter Schrag noted in describing "the failure of political language" in the Presidential campaign of 1972:

> In the past, there was always some assurance about certain fundamentals. Political language began with . . . a set of unquestioned givens . . . Such assurance . . . survived for nearly two centuries as the true-blue, one-for-all, now-and-forever, American creed. With some exceptions, we shared a common set of political axioms . . . and so we . . . could feel relatively certain about what bothered people . . . and about what they expected. What is new and striking about the 1972 campaign is that even that fundamental assurance is missing. . . . It is as if a dozen candidates . . . are running for the Presidency of an undiscovered country, looking for connections, for a nerve to touch, seeking a language.[42]

Each political myth presupposes a "people" who can legislate reality with their collective belief. So long as "the people" believe basic myths, there is unity and collective identity. When there is no fundamental belief, one senses a crisis which can only be met with a new rhetoric, a new mythology.

From the moment of its first utterance, the political myth is in a dual competition with at least two other ontological constructs. Because it is an attempt to redefine material conditions, the myth most obviously conflicts with "objective reality." Because it is a response, not only to discomfort in the environment, but also to the failure of previous myths to cope with such discomfort, a new political myth also conflicts with all previous myths. Each new vision of the collective life, in other words, represents a movement of ideas (and of "the people") from one "world" of attitudes and conditions to another. The result is the sort of silent revolution Walter Bagehot observed in describing "the people's" accommodation to a new set of governing maxims, a new "constitution": "A new constitution does not produce its full effect as long as all its subjects were reared under an old Constitution. . . . Generally one generation in politics succeeds another almost silently; at every moment men of all ages between thirty and seventy have considerable influence; each year removes many old men, makes all others older, brings in many new. The transition is so gradual that we hardly perceive it."[43]

As Bagehot translates it, the objective conflict involves disagreements in attitude among overlapping "generations" whose perceptions both of reality and of valuative myths differ noticeably.

Recognition of an argumentative competition in history (usually characterized as "dialectical") is commonplace in social theory. If one is an idealist, he sees rational "laws" of history, perhaps an eternal struggle between "good" and "evil." If one is a materialist, he sees a competition between "bourgeois" and "proletariat," or in the West, between the "haves" and the "have-nots." And a pragmatist might see competition between "establishment" and "antiestablishment," or "ins" and "outs" with reference to power. Bagehot's contribution was his association of such competition with attitudes developed by "generations" who shared a roughly comparable socialization process. The political "generation" is a biological phenomenon, but it is defined by its "Constitution." A rhetorical analyst might suggest further that, regardless of their biological age, all who accept the same system of myths constitute a "generation" of "the people." As myths change, "generations" change, and with the new "generation" comes a new "people," defined not by circumstances or behavior, but by their collective faith in a rhetorical vision.

Analyzing the collective beliefs presupposed in one myth, however, does not give the rhetorician a satisfactory description of "the people," for, as Bagehot observed, there are several myths and several political generations at any one time, each with a modicum of influence in the society. How many myths, and how many peoples, for example, were envisioned by other advocates at the time Hitler dangled National Socialism before the German public? Can one automatically assume that all Germans were Nazi, or at least enough of them to constitute a "people"? If that judgment can be made, can one decide at which point the myth of super-race came to dominate the German public mind? Such questions indicate that "the people" exist, not in a single myth, but in the *competitive relationships* which develop between a myth and antithetical visions of the collective life.

If we believe Ortega, the competitive relationship between myths is not a haphazard political or economic tension; it is rather a tension within each individual between contrary impulses, one to credit the lessons of the past forced upon us in the socialization process, the other to credit our own "root feeling in the presence of life" regardless of social dicta.[44] Because life conditions are always changing, there is a constant choice between a "stable" impulse to see objective reality as tending to confirm traditional judgments of life (old myths) and a contrary "vital" impulse to perceive objective reality as tending to refute traditional judgments (a condition calling for new myths). Because such impulses are a product of the learning condition itself, Ortega argues, the tension between stable and vital impulses is a drama which must be replayed with each biological generation.[45] Over a period of time, several generations making different judgments about the life condition establish a cultural "rhythm" within which all myths are born, grow useless, and are superseded by new myths better fit to new life conditions. So, for example, Roosevelt's "people" judged their condition by predominately vital criteria and therefore abandoned an economic tradition in favor of a "New Deal," a new myth. In time, the "New Deal" stabilized, became a part of the stable tradition of subsequent generations, an "old deal." In the 1960s, children of affluence reacted with vitality against the security-conscious morality of the 1930s, creating what Means calls a "crisis in American values."[46]

Because myths can be classified within a culture's vital and stable rhythm, "the people" of that culture can be described rhetorically. One begins with the understanding that political myths are purely rhetorical phenomena, ontological appeals constructed from artistic proofs and intended to redefine an uncomfortable and oppressive reality. Such myths are endemic in the human condition and, though technically they represent nothing but a "false consciousness," they nonetheless function as a means of providing social unity and collective identity. Indeed, "the people" *are* the social and political myths they accept. But because a new myth competes for public faith both against objective reality and against other myths, it is difficult to get a clear view of a "people" by analyzing a single myth. Myths dominant during the socialization process are generally accepted, and thus come to represent "generations" of "the people." But these myths, and the generations they represent, conflict with new and old myths, new and old generations, all existing in some degree of influence at a single moment in history. The tension existing between competing myths is a product of the contradiction between an individual's impulse to accept "stable" representations of reality derived from the collective experience of the past, and a contrary impulse to yield to "vital" impressions of reality derived from personal experience with the life condition. Political myths and generations may therefore be classed as predominately "stable" or "vital." So the rhetorical analyst might argue that a description of the argumentative tensions between stable and vital political myths would constitute a portrait of "the people" at a particular time. One might investigate the possibility, for example, that "the people" of Germany in 1934 were somewhere in a competitive tension between National Socialist myths of *Übermensch* (a predominately stable, nationalistic reaffirmation and extension of the rhetoric used to unify the "Fatherland") and a contrary Marxist myth of the classless society (a predominately vital, immediate rebellion against such economic conditions as those described in the didactic drama of Brecht).[47]

III

The analysis of political myths can reveal but one face of "the people," for though the myth is central to the collectivization process, it is evidence of but one stage in the metamorphosis of "persons" into "people." It is nonetheless a productive and important line of inquiry because it illustrates the significance of pursuing the rhetorical alternative in search of "the people." The arguments developed here could be used to explain in theory a new approach to rhetorical criticism; but it has not been my purpose to contribute still another monistic set of categories to aid in the appreciation of oratory. Rather, it has been my intention to follow Kenneth Burke's lead by arguing that studies of rhetoric should contribute positively to understanding the social process and the human condition.[48] So the analysis of rhetorical documents should not turn inward, to an appreciation of persuasive, manipulative techniques, but outward to *functions* of rhetoric.[49] Studies of the collectivization process through rhetorical analysis of political myths orients the researcher to problems of social/rhetorical theory rather than to myopic questions of causation so common in contemporary historical methods.[50]

Consider the rhetorician's advantage in dealing with the collectivization process: When a writer such as Ortega or Marx must describe "the people," he is hampered by lack of evidence. It is admitted in social theory that "the diagnosis of . . . a people or an age must begin by establishing the repertory of its convictions," since social man is a creature of beliefs and not of truths.[51] To discover those convictions, however, social theorists typically ignore rhetorical documents, arguing that a people's repertory of convictions is apparent in the material life conditions of the age.[52] While it may be true that life conditions dictate structures of belief, it does not follow that a history of *events* is equal to a history of *convictions*. As Lichtheim observes, "History is always the history of *this* particular event and *those* particular actors, whose appearance at *this* particular moment must be understood in all its concreteness."[53] The suggestion is that, contrary to conventional wisdom, historical "facts" do no speak for themselves in defining the "people" of a nation. In the Marxist litany, for example, I would suggest that it was not working conditions which made a class struggle in England inevitable, but rather *human responses to working conditions*.[54] These human responses (rhetoric) constitute a filter for "facts" which translates them into *beliefs*. If such filters are ignored (as they have been by all orthodox Marxist writers), the result is what Butterfield called the "Whig fallacy," imposing on the past one's own conviction and perception of what human responses to conditions ought to have been.[55]

My argument here has been that through the analysis of rhetorical documents (particularly political myths), it should be possible to speak meaningfully, not of one's own, but of *the people's* repertory of convictions, not as they ought to be, but as they *are* (or have been). When a writer works with rhetorical documents, he sees material forces, events, and themes in history *only as they have already been mediated or filtered by the Leader whose words he studies*. What he sees, in other words, is not a dialectical materialism, but rather a "rhetorical idealism." It may be that Peter Rodino, for example, was wrong when he suggested that the impeachment of Richard Nixon was linked to Magna Carta, to Locke's *Civil Government*, to the wishes of our "Founding Fathers," and to Burke's impeachment of Warren Hastings.[56] It is true that no thought of democracy or rule of law as we understand it was involved in the extraction of the Magna Carta. It is true that Rodino argued a lie, therefore, that he imposed a meaning on the past in precisely the same way Marx did. The difference rests in the fact that Rodino was a politician arguing a *real* case, before *real* people, and before the *actualization* of the "repertory of convictions" held in his society. If "the people" of Anglo-America *believe* that there is a Whig theme or motion in history, then for that moment there *is* such a "movement" *in fact*. The rhetorical theorist working with the sort of speech Rodino gave should be able to *document* the existence of themes, movements, or rhythms in a way that historicists such as Marx and Ortega could not.[57]

Such possibilities, I would conclude, develop when we begin to realize the significance of our own concepts. Pursuing a rhetorical alternative in defining "the people" leads one to the importance of recognizing the collective life as a condition of being the "audience" of those who pretend to lead the society. Rather than turn the concept "audience" upon itself by inquiring into the effects of rhetoric or by exhorting fledgling advocates to avoid *argumentum ad populam*, I suggest that we use it to explore the reciprocal relationship between rhetoric and social theory and to participate in the serious Hegelian and Marxist dialogues of the previous two centuries which have so greatly affected life in our own time.

Notes

1. Empirical sociologists, social psychologists, and most contemporary rhetoricians seem to be studying "movement" only by a stretch of the imagination. As Black has indicated, Griffin's pioneer work with social and historical "movements" was little more than an attempt to extend the range of traditional Aristotelian rhetorical criticism. Griffin began with *philosophical* descriptions of determinism, with the attempt to understand the connection between rhetoric and the movement of ideas in history. But he conceived rhetoric to operate within historical matrices (rather than seeing history executed within a range of rhetorical possibilities), and thus he was led to think of "movement" as a *physical* motion toward the repeal of a law or condition. Griffin thus confused an event—"agitation"—with a situation—"movement." Though Aristotelian categories have largely been abandoned, contemporary writers still give little evidence of conceiving "movement" in its traditional sense (the *historical* movement of ideas), concentrating instead on

the restrictive definitions of empirical sociology (a *social* movement of "*forces*"). Bowers and Ochs, for example, concentrate only *on messages* generated in the context of what someone else defines as the "movement," in effect giving up the right of definition and interpretation to empirical sociology, politics, and history. The result is the same as Griffin's—we study not "movement," but rhetorical documents existing in "movement" contexts. Such persistence seems strange, especially when it should be possible for rhetoricians *directly* to study "movement" as *linguistic* process contained in and defined by the rhetorical *situation*, not the rhetorical *event*. See Edwin Black, *Rhetorical Criticism: A Study in Method* (New York: Macmillan, 1965), pp. 19–21; Leland Griffin, "The Anti-Masonic Persuasion: A Study of Public Address in the American Anti-Masonic Movement" (Ph.D. diss., Cornell University, 1949), pp. i–iv; John W. Bowers and Donovan J. Ochs, *The Rhetoric of Agitation and Control* (Reading, MA.: Addison-Wesley, 1971), pp. 1, 15; and Michael C. McGee, "Edmund Burke's Beautiful Lie: An Exploration of the Relationship Between Rhetoric and Social Theory" (Ph.D. diss., University of Iowa, 1974), pp. 11–66.

2. At least in part, this was the point of the Wingspread Committee on the Nature of Rhetorical Invention in asserting that, because of significantly changed realities, the "conventional view" of the process of invention, having to do "with the making of arguments by a speaker for an audience for the purpose of gaining assent to a predetermined proposition," should be altered. As the Wingspread Committee points out, the study of "rhetorical invention" in effect is a study of "the core social process." In its broader contemporary sense, then, rhetoricians have a stake in, and can make significant contributions to the sort of conceptual, cultural dialogues envisioned in the Hegelian social/philosophical tradition. The relevance of social theory to the study of rhetoric is apparent even from a cursory look at the writings of the "philosophers of culture." See Lloyd F. Bitzer and Edwin Black, eds., *The Prospect of Rhetoric* (Englewood Cliffs, NJ: Prentice-Hall, 1971), pp. 228–233; and Karl J. Weintraub, *Visions of Culture* (Chicago: University of Chicago Press, 1966).

3. See, e.g., L. Virginia Holland, *Counterpoint: Kenneth Burke and Aristotle's Theories of Rhetoric* (New York: Philosophical Library, 1959), esp. pp. 39–85, and compare with the easier, more obvious Hegelian/Marxist associations noted by Don Abbott, in "Marxist Influences on the Rhetorical Theory of Kenneth Burke," *Philosophy and Rhetoric* 7 (1974): 217–233.

4. See Irving L. Horowitz, *Radicalism and the Revolt against Reason* (New York: Humanities Press, 1961), and Irving M. Zeitlin, *Ideology and the Development of Sociological Theory* (Englewood Cliffs, NJ: Prentice-Hall, 1968).

5. Aristotle placed more trust in the judgments of the many than of the few, noting in one place that the many are more incorruptible than the few (*Politics*, III.11–12, 1281a39–1283a20), and in another that judgments were less likely to be perverted by emotional arguments among the many than with one judge (*Rhetoric*, I.1.1354b22–1355a3). His attitude toward the many, however, is contradictory. By urging advocates to adapt to individual characteristics displayed by members of an audience, he seems to be adhering to the grammatical conception of "the people" (*Rhetoric*, II.12–17). But by treating the audience as an irrational "mob" responding almost unpredictably to emotional appeals and assurances of what they knew already, he seems to join Plato in conceiving the "people" to be, at best, childlike (*Rhetoric*, II.21.1395b1–10; 22.1395b27–1396a4). In any case, the only examples of nongrammatical organic conceptions of "the people" in either the Platonic or the Aristotelian traditions with which I am familiar follow the theme that "Demos" is a monster. See Karl R. Popper, *The Open Society and Its Enemies: The Spell of Plato*, 4th ed. (Princeton, NJ: Princeton University Press, 1962).

6. This attitude is endemic in the social sciences. It is also at the center of a dispute between proponents of a romantic style in history (so-called Whig history) and proponents of the "Namierite" style ("revisionism" in this country). See McGee, "Burke's Beautiful Lie," pp. 106–188, 264–346. A critique of the cause–effect syndrome in rhetorical criticism is provided by Black's *Rhetorical Criticism*.

7. See Franklyn S. Haiman, "Democratic Ethics and the Hidden Persuaders," *QJS* 44 (1958): 385–392. Even in criticizing "antirhetoric" and exploring the possibilities of a "new rhetoric," for example, Florescu seems to be saying that the function of rhetoric is to fill "gaps" in classical

logical theory. See Vasile Florescu, "Rhetoric and Its Rehabilitation in Contemporary Philosophy," *Philosophy and Rhetoric* 3 (1970): 207.

8. See Herbert Marcuse, *One-Dimensional Man: Studies in the Ideology of Advanced Industrial Society* (Boston: Beacon Press, 1964), pp. 123–169, esp. pp. 123–127.

9. See Everett Lee Hunt, "Plato and Aristotle on Rhetoric and Rhetoricians," in R. F. Howes, ed., *Historical Studies of Rhetoric and Rhetoricians* (Ithaca, NY: Cornell University Press, 1961), pp. 29–54.

10. Chaim Perelman and L. Olbrechts-Tyteca, *The New Rhetoric: A Treatise on Argumentation*, trans. John Wilkinson and Purcell Weaver (South Bend, IN: University of Notre Dame Press, 1969), pp. 1–3.

11. See Aristotle, *Rhetoric*, II.21.1395b1–10.

12. See Richard Burke, "Rhetoric, Dialectic, and Force," *Philosophy & Rhetoric* 7 (1974): 154–155, and Perelman, *New Rhetoric*, pp. 30–45. In an Aristotelian sense, Perelman has come closer to a "new dialectic" than to a "new rhetoric." Though he draws extensively from treatises in the rhetorical tradition, his development of "universal audience," his stated motives for undertaking the treatise, and the character of his conclusions are more reminiscent of Aristotle's *Topics* than of the *Rhetoric*, I.1.1354a–1355b25, especially where Aristotle appears to hold that, in function, rhetoric is a species of force, a kind of violence which Perelman specifically wishes to avoid in his new rhetoric.

13. Though in the last few years (since 1960) there have been rumblings of a change in attitude, the most conspicuous exception remains Kenneth Burke, who has always seen a symbolic rather than an objective reality, and who has consistently modified his rationalism with the idea of "orientation." See Kenneth Burke, *Attitudes Toward History* (1939; rpt., Boston: Beacon Press, 1961).

14. A. F. Pollard, *The Evolution of Parliament* (London: Longmans, Green, 1934), p. 343.

15. In Locke's vision of civil government, "the people" are God's earthly embodiment. It is they who punish "tyrannical" governments by appealing to heaven in a trial by combat called revolution. The notion is carried so far that a willingness to engage the collective life in a holy struggle for Liberty is *a condition of humanity* in Locke's philosophy. See John Locke, *An Essay Concerning the True and Original Extent of Civil Government*, in *Great Books of the Western World*, 54 vols., ed. J. Hutchins (Chicago: Wm. Benton for Encyclopedia Brittanica, 1952), vol. 35, p. 63. Classic works at hand in this collection hereafter cited as *GBWW*.

16. Adolph Hitler, *Mein Kampf*, trans. Alvin Johnson (New York: Houghton Mifflin/Reynal & Hitchcock, 1939), pp. 491–492, 496.

17. Mao Tse-Tung, *Quotations from Chairman Mao Tse-Tung* (Peking: Foreign Languages Press, 1966), p. 89: "The richest source of power to wage war lies in the masses of the people. It is mainly because of the unorganized state of the Chinese masses that Japan dares to bully us. When this defect is remedied, then the Japanese aggressor, like a mad bull crashing into a ring of flames, will be surrounded by hundreds of millions of our people standing upright, the mere sound of their voices will strike terror into him, and he will be burned to death."

18. Boas uncovers this ambiguity as it has emerged through history by examining the old proverb "*vox populi, vox Deus.*" Whether in reference to popular taste as an aesthetic standard or to "the people" as a warrant for a certain type of government, appeals to "the people" in modern times have assumed the same proportion and character as appeals to "the will of God" in former times. The difference is that, among Christians, there is a tolerably consistent guideline for "the will of God" in the Holy Bible: "the people" are not contained in a scripture, nor are there many priests to aid us in interpreting their "will." See George Boas, *Vox Populi: Essays in the History of an Idea* (Baltimore: Johns Hopkins Press, 1969), esp. pp. 39–71, 248–277.

19. See Ernest G. Bormann, "Fantasy and Rhetorical Vision: The Rhetorical Criticism of Social Reality," *QJS*, 58 (1972): 396–407. Bormann's piece links commonplace arguments in twentieth-century rhetorical and social theory with recent findings in communicology. Though such writings are, as I have suggested previously, rarely referred to in contemporary rhetorical theory, there is a long tradition behind ideas of social realities that are essentially fictional (or

"dramatistic"). As part of the antirationalist movement in nineteenth-century philosophy, Sorel used the idea of "group fantasy" to argue for his invention of the concept "political myth." Lippmann picked up on Le Bon's notion of a "popular mind" made up of dreamlike commitments to policies and values in his description of "the reality of the mind," the "public mind" which rules in a democracy. Kenneth Burke's "dramatism" was originally grounded in the observation that masses of people make decisions in the context of rituals executed within poetic categories. Though he believed it possible to reduce such fantasies to the system of an empirical science, Karl Mannheim began his invention of the "sociology of knowledge" by comparing objective reality with "ideological" reality (false consciousness). In Ortega's last major work, he began directly to speak of "the people" and of "public opinion" as linguistic phenomena. Richard Weaver's polemic assertion that *Ideas Have Consequences* was predicated upon a defense of linguistic "realities" against the universally fashionable exclusion of all dimensions of humanity except an empirically defined "objective" reality. See, resp., Georges Sorel, *Reflections on Violence*, trans. T. E. Hulme (1916; rpt., New York: Peter Smith, 1941); Gustave Le Bon, *The Crowd* (1895; rpt., New York: Viking Press, 1960); Walter Lippmann, *Public Opinion* (New York: Harcourt-Brace, 1922); P. H. Odegard, *The American Public Mind* (New York: Harcourt-Brace, 1930); Kenneth Burke, *Attitudes toward History*; Karl Mannheim, *Ideology and Utopia*, trans. Louis Wirth and Edward Shils (1929; rpt., New York: Harvest Books, 1952), esp. pp. 55–108; José Ortega y Gassett, *Man and People*, trans. Willard R. Trask (New York: W. W. Norton, 1957), esp. pp. 192–272; and Richard M. Weaver, *Ideas Have Consequences* (Chicago: University of Chicago Press, 1948), esp. pp. 92–112.

20. Bormann, "Fantasy," pp. 400–401.

21. Hitler, *Mein Kampf*, pp. 456–457. With a friendly stretch of the imagination, a reader might see in this section of *Mein Kampf* a sketchy philosophy of history. I am reluctant, however, to accuse Hitler of committing philosophy; what he argues is more properly a macrorhetoric, an explanation of the *uses* of *Volksgeist* by "reformers" who seek to define and preserve national identity and purpose.

22. As Muller indicates, even the historian who sets his goal at re-creating the past through simple description faces problems of his own subjectivity. The writer who aims even higher, at the discovery of a "popular will" running as a theme within history, is more properly an "ideologue" than an "historian," for he must argue constantly, not in concrete episodes, but in metaphors. See Herbert J. Muller, *The Uses of the Past* (New York: Oxford University Press, 1952), pp. 31–32; Robert A. Nisbet, *Social Change and History* (New York: Oxford University Press, 1969), esp. pp. 104–125, 240–304; and Thomas Molnar, *Sartre: Ideologue of Our Time* (New York: Funk & Wagnalls, 1968).

23. Sir Lewis Namier, "Monarchy and the Party System," *Personalities and Powers: Selected Essays by Sir Lewis Namier* (1955; New York: Harper Torchbook, 1965), p. 21.

24. John Brooke, *The Chatham Administration, 1766–1768* (London: Macmillan, 1956), pp. 231–232.

25. See McGee, "Burke's Beautiful Lie," pp. 67–105.

26. As LaPiere indicated some time ago, most "mass movements" are conceived as fantasies by those caught up in them. In the first textbook on the subject, he suggested that it was all but impossible to analyze the mythical content of a movement; so he abandoned the intentions of Sorel and claimed that the only "real" part of a social movement was observable, collective behavior. See Richard T. LaPiere, *Collective Behavior* (New York: McGraw-Hill, 1934), esp. the definition of "mass movement" in highly poetic terms, p. 504.

27. I am referring to "leader" in a historical sense. I am not willing to argue that one conception is better than another, but it is necessary to distinguish between that "leadership" which makes a shavetail fit to be an officer and a gentleman, and that other kind of "leadership" which defines for a moment in history the identity of a whole people. In the former view, leadership is a quality defined by the behavior of a person highly esteemed by his peers; the notion is abstracted to theory with a lengthy checklist of behaviors which, if followed like a recipe, will produce an extraordinary man. In the latter view, leadership is defined by the topics of

epideictic rhetoric, the process of comparing the words and deeds of one man who led a whole people with the words and deeds of other recognized leaders. In the former view, any man is "leader" if he exhibits certain preconceived behavior; in the latter view, a man is not "Leader" until his people are inclined to compare him with Pericles, Cicero, Savonarola, Cromwell, Danton, Chatham, Jefferson, Lincoln, Hitler, and Churchill.

28. Though an advocate is seeking to get his audience to exhibit belief or action they might not otherwise have contemplated, still he is but a mirror of the commonplace judgments of his society; he must argue from socially defined "good reasons." See Karl R. Wallace, "The Substance of Rhetoric: Good Reasons," *QJS* 49 (1963): 239–249. It was because rhetoric functioned more as a mirror of mass opinion than as an arbiter of truth that Plato called it a knack and not an art. In this vein he argued that "rhetoricians and tyrants have the least possible power in states . . . for they do literally nothing which they will, but only what they think best" (Plato, *Gorgias*, 466).

29. See Sir James G. Frazer, *The Golden Bough: A Study in Magic and Religion*, 2d ed. (London: Macmillan, 1900), and *Lectures on the Early History of Kingship* (London: Macmillan, 1905).

30. This seems to have been what Isocrates had in mind when he scoffed at conceptions of rhetoric that were tied to particular occasions (deliberative, forensic, ceremonial). The sort of rhetoric he professed was a kind of social surgery, the study and practice of manufacturing a Greek "people" from the "old longings" recorded in the history of individual city-states. For him, the transubstantiation of persons into a *people* was the highest function of rhetoric, as unlike argument in a courtroom or at a marriage ceremony as Pheidias' statue of Athena was unlike the mannikin fashioned by a doll-maker. See *Isocrates*, trans. George Norlin, Loeb Classical Library (Cambridge, MA: Harvard University Press, 1961), vol. 2, pp. 185, 187.

31. Sir Lewis Namier, "Human Nature in Politics," in *Personalities and Powers*, pp. 4–5.

32. Namier, *The Structure of Politics at the Accession of George III* (London: Macmillan, 1929).

33. Mannheim, *Ideology and Utopia*, pp. 59–94.

34. An inquiry of the sort I am attempting to describe was recently completed at the University of Florida. See Woodrow Wilson Leake Jr., "Ideological Rhetoric: Systemic Arguments on War and Peace in High School American History Textbooks" (Ph.D. diss., University of Florida, 1973).

35. An excellent example of the kind of rhetoric which might be analyzed from this perspective is Eric Hoffer's polemic reaction to Hitler's National Socialism. A more systematic development of arguments designed to justify a retreat from the collective life is Popper's lengthy polemic, *The Open Society and Its Enemies* (Princeton, NJ: Princeton University Press, 1950). See Eric Hoffer, *The True Believer* (New York: Harper & Row, 1951).

36. Edmund Burke, *Thoughts on the Causes of the Present Discontents*, in *The Works of the Right Honorable Edmund Burke*, 4th ed. (Boston: Little, Brown, 1871), vol. 1, p. 442.

37. In commenting on Burke's influence in the transition from "balanced government" to parliamentary democracy, Lecky observes that "No other politician or writer has . . . impressed his principles so deeply on both of the great parties in the State, and has left behind him a richer treasure of political wisdom applicable to all countries and to all times" (W.E.H. Lecky, *A History of England in the Eighteenth Century*, 4th ed. [London: Longmans, Green, 1890], vol. 3, pp. 181–182). The *Present Discontents* was received as a satisfactory, though exaggerated, account of the early years of George III's reign by such writers as Robert Huish, Lord John Russell, William Nathaniel Massey, Erskine May, Lecky, and William Hunt. See Herbert Butterfield, *George III and the Historians* (London: Collins, 1957), pp. 75, 104, 146–147, 152–153, 163, and 179, resp.

38. For an account of the none-too-friendly reception of the pamphlet by those who distrusted "incendiary" justification of "mob" behavior, see Donald C. Bryant, "Burke's *Present Discontents*: The Rhetorical Genesis of a Party Testament," *QJS* 42 (1956): 115–126. I have already referred to the passionate attacks on the pamphlet created by those whose mission is to discredit what Namier called "beautiful and very rational legends"; see Sir Lewis Namier, *England in the Age of the American Revolution*, 2d ed. (London: Macmillan, 1961), pp. 128–131.

39. Sorel, *Reflections on Violence*, pp. 32, 33.

40. See Karl Marx, *The Poverty of Philosophy*, trans. with intro. by Frederick Engels (New York: International Publishers, 1963), pp. 103–125; and Mannheim, *Ideology and Utopia*, pp. 70–75.

41. See Kenneth Burke, *Attitudes Toward History*, pp. 317–319. The physical world *exists*, but it has no *meaning* until it has been defined by individuals coping with it. Such individuals bring "perspective" or "orientation" to the physical world, mythically and ritualistically redefining it, causing themselves to be "reborn" in a new world of their own making. So if it happens in my life that I become economically insecure, I do not need to respond to my situation with a direct action such as getting a job, standing in a welfare line, or robbing a bank. I can avoid my problem, and perhaps solve it, by redefining my environment. I may argue that the rich are robbing me and ought to be made to shoulder my economic burden; or I may argue that poverty is only apparent, that I should count my blessings and stop worrying about economic security. With each argument I create a new world, and I feel more comfortable because I am "reborn" in a world where my problem does not exist.

42. Peter Schrag, "The Failure of Political Language," *Saturday Review*, March 25, 1972, pp. 30–31.

43. Walter Bagehot, *The English Constitution* (New York: Appleton, 1877), pp. 3–4.

44. See José Ortega y Gassett, *The Modern Theme*, trans. James Cleugh (New York: Harper Torchbook, 1961), pp. 1–13; *History as a System*, trans. H. Weyl (New York: Norton Library, 1962); and *Man and Crisis*, trans. Mildred Adams (New York: Norton Library, 1962).

45. Ortega is careful to qualify his argument with the obvious notation that no generation is *purely* vital or stable. Rather, the general tension between vital and stable judgments makes each generation more-vital-than-stable or more-stable-than-vital. I am uncertain as to whether the tension might be characterized as *balance, equation,* or *stasis*. There is something of Festinger's dissonance theory in the observation that vital judgments inconsistent with stable teachings make individuals receptive to new political myths. This makes the term "balance" or "congruity" attractive. There is something akin to a Marxist dialectic of social class in Ortega's assertion of the inevitability of conflict between stable and vital impulses. This makes the term "equation" or "conflict" seem attractive. And there is also something like the relationship between affirmative and negative arguments in a courtroom in Ortega's description of the practical relationship between vital and stable. This makes me want to refer the whole concept to the stasis doctrine of classical rhetoric. I will settle here for the more neutral term "tension" to avoid tangents and to leave open possible associations with communicology, Marxist philosophy, and the classical rhetorical tradition.

46. See Richard L. Means, *The Ethical Imperative* (Garden City, NY: Doubleday, 1969). Toffler has made much of the difficulty of communicating lessons learned in the Great Depression to a generation incapable of experiencing extreme economic deprivation. See Alvin Toffler, *Future Shock* (New York: Random House, 1970), pp. 7–48, 124–182.

47. See Milton Mayer, *They Thought They Were Free: The Germans, 1933–1945* (Chicago: University of Chicago Press, 1955), pp. 95–98; George W. F. Hallgarten, "Adolf Hitler and German Heavy Industry, 1931–1933," *Journal of Economic History* 12 (1952): 223–246; Gerard Braunthal, "The German Free Trade Unions during the Rise of Nazism," *Journal of Central European Affairs* 15 (1956): 339–353; and Gerhard Ritter, "The Fault of Mass Democracy," in Maurice Baumont, ed., *The Third Reich* (New York: Praeger, 1955), pp. 389–412.

48. Even in his first book, before his language-oriented arguments led him to consider *The Rhetoric of Motives*, Burke used literary and rhetorical documents, not as objects of esthetic or formal criticism, but as evidence of social and human processes. See *Attitudes Toward History*, pp. 3–33.

49. Though ultimately he retreated to a method which, as Black suggests, did little more than "illuminate the history of rhetorical practice," this was Griffin's argument in observing that "we have now sat long enough upon the ground and told sunny stories of the kings and counsellors of the platform." It is also a position Black seems inclined to in his discussions of

"the functions of argumentation" and "clusters of opinion," though the end of Black's "Alternative Frame of Reference" for rhetorical criticism seems to lie more in the rhetorical event itself than in the social and human significance of the event. See Leland M. Griffin, "The Rhetoric of Historical Movements," *QJS* 38 (1952): 185, and Black, "Alternative Frames," pp. 21, 132–137, 161–164, 168–176.

50. My fear is that the use of faddish historical methods might obscure more productive rhetorical methods resulting in the kind of myopia now endemic among writers of histories. See Isaiah Berlin, "History and Theory: The Concept of Scientific History," in Alexander V. Riasanovsky and Barnes Riznik, eds., *Generalizations in Historical Writing* (Philadelphia: University of Pennsylvania Press, 1963), pp. 60–113. "Revisionism" and "Namierism" in history have produced too many comments like this from Barzun and Graff: "An historian would say, for example, that under the conditions prevailing in this country today it is not probable that a public official, e.g., the governor of a state, could be entirely misrepresented to posterity as regards his appearance, actions, and character. Too many devices of publicity are continually playing on public figures." It is evident even to the neophyte in rhetorical method that "devices of publicity" distort rather than clarify public character. Historians are mistaken greatly if they believe that even a cinematographic footnote will be taken seriously. No twentieth-century reporting, for example, will render Neville Chamberlain in his complete character. He will be, for purposes of argument and action, a weak and despicable villain so long as the possibility of "appeasement" exists in conflict situations. The "devices of publicity" which have "played" on him have rendered, not a portrait, but a caricature. See Jaques Barzun and Henry Graff, *The Modern Researcher* (New York: Harcourt-Brace, 1957), p. 138.

51. Ortega, *History as System*, p. 166.

52. Ibid., p. 168.

53. George Lichtheim, *The Concept of Ideology and Other Essays* (New York: Random House Vintage, 1967), p. 296.

54. This is one point I believe Sorel successfully illuminates in another historical context than that chosen by Marx. See Georges Sorel, *The Illusions of Progress*, trans. John Stanley and Charlotte Stanley (Berkeley and Los Angeles: University of California Press, 1969).

55. For a detailed discussion of the Whig fallacy as it exists in the writing of history, see Herbert Butterfield, *The Whig Interpretation of History* (New York: W. W. Norton, 1965). For a discussion of the fallacy as it appears in philosophies of history, see Robert A. Nisbet, *Social Change and History* (New York: Oxford University Press, 1969). And for a discussion of the fallacy as it has existed in the study of rhetoric, see Michael C. McGee, "The Rhetorical Process in Eighteenth-Century England," in Walter R. Fisher, *Rhetoric: A Tradition in Transition* (Lansing: Michigan State University Press, 1974), pp. 99–121.

56. Peter Rodino, "Opening Remarks at the Public Inquiry of the Committee on the Judiciary of the U.S. House of Representatives Relative to the Impeachment of Richard M. Nixon," July 24, 1974; videotape in possession of this author, reel 1: 252.

57. Speculative philosophical themes have an objective reality only when, by accident, social theorists arguing for Utopian systems happen also to be practicing advocates engaged in the persuasion of a mass society. Marx, for example, had no contact with the reality of any people's repertory of beliefs; rather, Lenin, a rhetorician, is responsible for making Marxist beliefs real, not as a result of the *truth* of his argument, but because of the *persuasiveness* of his appeal. This is an old point central to the rhetorical method, made by Aristotle: "Whatever men wish to be, rather than seem, is the greater good, *since it is nearer reality*" (Aristotle, *Rhetoric*, I.7.1365b10–14; my italics).

The Third Persona

An Ideological Turn
in Rhetorical Theory

PHILIP WANDER

> In the Word is involved the unity of humanity, the wholeness
> of the human problem, which permits nobody, and today less
> than ever to separate the intellectual and artistic from the
> political and social, and to isolate himself within the ivory
> tower of the "cultural" alone.
>
> *Thomas Mann (1937)*[1]

This was what Mann wrote the Dean of the Philosophical Faculty at Bonn University on learning that his name had been struck off the list of Honorary Doctors. He had fled Germany four years earlier as the fascists came to power. The great German universities failed to provide a bulwark against the dictatorship; when they did not quietly comply, they actively endorsed the fall of the Weimar Republic and the repression of the Jews. Mann, in his response, warns against the isolating potential of the ivory tower. It is in this tension between the privileged space of the university and the public space of political activity that I should like to consider the problem of understanding the nature of criticism and to respond to objections regarding an earlier effort to get at such matters, "The Ideological Turn in Modern Criticism."[2]

American scholarship is ill-equipped to understand criticism in the way that Mann would have us look at it. This becomes evident in our efforts to appropriate European thought as a source of authority, inspiration, or new methods for our own work. We are, I think, just beginning to appreciate the extent to which European intellectual activity is shaped by and centers on Marxist themes and an assumption that one has, under certain conditions, an obligation not only to oppose the state, but also to undermine the existing order.

Those themes and that assumption grow out of an historical context radically different from ours. Over the past forty years both Germany and France have had rulers who were fascists, a power elite, in other words, who controlled the state and who secured if not full then sufficient cooperation from every other institution in society— the civil service, army, courts, churches (with significant exceptions), the great universities—for among other things the slaughter of millions of innocent men, women, and children. The upper classes and the professionals in France and Germany did not renounce their privileges during this period. We read and remember those who went into exile or those who became leaders in the resistance, but the vast majority simply adapted either through silence or through actual participation in the ceremonies marking a change in government.

The only analogue in American experience which might suggest that resistance to the state could be a patriotic duty and a moral obligation lies in Vietnam. Yet even here, the comparison falters. Those who, during the Vietnam War, poured blood on induction files had to be willing to "pay the price." No records exist of debates among French, Yugoslavian, Danish, or Italian partisans over whether they should allow themselves to be arrested for climbing over fences, demonstrating without a permit, or throwing rocks and bottles at the minions of law and order. I point this out not to suggest that more violent protest was either justified or would have been theoretically defensible during the course of Vietnam, but to suggest how pale and limited the analogue is between European and American notions of intellectual activity and political resistance.

While academic scholars and literary intellectuals in Europe, after the Second World War, assumed a critical stance in relation to the state and dominant culture, and took political commitment and activity ("*praxis*") as a matter of course, American scholars, even now, worry over the implications of an arrest for trespassing at a nuclear power plant or a research laboratory designing genocidal weapons. Our teachers before us, during what we now call the "McCarthy period," blanched at the thought of having been photographed at a cocktail party with someone who might have had an affair with a fellow traveler.

It may be that on his return to Germany after the war, Theodore Adorno was accused of being "un-German," or that Sartre at some point was accused of being "un-French," or that E. P. Thompson has been charged with being "un-English." I suspect that we would find it amusing, if we did unearth some such accusation. But when in this country during the 1950s scholars and scientists such as W. E. B. Dubois, Owen Lattimore, Robert Oppenheimer, and M. I. Finley were accused of being "un-American," it was not amusing. The extent of such activities during this period is truly remarkable. In 1955 Paul Lazarsfeld reported the results of a survey involving over two thousand interviews on 165 college campuses. More than half the respondents indicated that one colleague or another had been accused, by other faculty, citizens committees, or student informers, of having subversive sympathies.[3] The files compiled during the 1960s and 1970s by the Central Intelligence Agency, Army Intelligence, and the Federal Bureau of Investigation became, with the Freedom of Information Act, a matter of public record. It would, I believe, be naïve to think that this kind of intelligence gathering no longer occurs.

THE "IDEOLOGICAL TURN": CRITICISM AND RESPONSE

Echoes of the McCarthy period, amplified during the Reagan administration, may be heard in reactions to the "Ideological Turn." They are not so much reflections of belligerent Americanism as they are of apoliticism and prudential neutralism—fears about being mistaken for a "partisan" or a fanatic, of being confused by political controversy or failing to achieve a balanced view. My respondents recoil from "dogmatic materialism," "avante-garde revolutionism," and the "intense connotations" associated with "Marxian polemics." Professor McGee, with his ear to the ground, solemnly declares that he is not now nor ever has been a "Comsymp."[4] His phrasing mocks the loyalty oaths and charges made by members of the House UnAmerican Activities Committee during the 1950s.

It is true that ideological criticism may lead one into a dangerous, foreboding, and deathlike environment—in Professor Rosenfield's term, a "miasma."[5] This is because such criticism leaves the asylum offered by a world of ideas to confront the world of affairs, the sensual, material "is" of everyday life. Because it seeks to understand and enter into political struggle, ideological criticism recalls the "is" shattered over Vietnam, and similar policies in the Middle East as well as Central and South America, where CIA employees and their hired mercenaries "defend freedom" and once again presume to counter, with the exception of China, a monolithic "Communist Menace." Ideological criticism, because it insists on a historical perspective in relation to cultural artifacts and political issues, need not ignore the vast slaughter of humanity in Indonesia, Chile, and Vietnam attending American policies in those areas. Because it takes humanity and not some arbitrary segment as its focus, ideological criticism is also prepared to hear the cries of victims in Poland, Afghanistan, and the Gulag. Because it is not confined by academic barriers, ideological criticism is able to address the unprecedented buildup of genocidal weapons in the United States and the Soviet Union. Because it is not a "method" of research, but rather indicates the ground on which research, scholarship, and criticism *can* be conducted, if one chooses to do so and if conditions allow for it, ideological criticism joined with rhetorical theory is prepared to critique rhetoric legitimizing actions, policies, and silences relevant to the great issues of our time.

Clearly, Rosenfield is correct: Ideological criticism can lead one into the miasma, but it is not a miasma created by the critic. Rosenfield would have the critic transcend such realities to enjoy the fullness, the ripeness, of being. Yet, it is one thing to celebrate the manifold splendors of Being; it is quite another to treat this experience as a precondition for doing criticism, to renounce deliberation, debate, and rationality, to confine criticism to the epideictic and then only to the bright side (i.e., praise). The problem here is similar to that Ernst Cassirer noted in Heidegger's work in the late 1920s. Like Heidegger, Rosenfield penetrates beyond the sphere of life into that of personal existence, which he makes exhaustive use of in a religious way. Yet he remains confined to it.[6] Rosenfield's critic may be prepared to hear the survivor's scream but not, I am afraid, the cry of the victim. Cries for help call for much more than appreciation.

Does that mean that Rosenfield is wrong, that his work is unworthy? Not at all. He is right to remind us that, in the midst of political controversy, love, gentleness, and even joy may be unwittingly sacrificed. Is one who would confront political issues automatically fixed in an attitude of outrage? Is reason in such matters barred from the poetic consciousness? Is the blinding insight of the individual to be lost on the pyre of collective struggle? These are not idle questions, nor are they irrelevant to political struggle. In light of the grim conclusion of so many seemingly noble efforts, I believe that they strike at the center of some profound theoretical issues. In the "Ideological Turn," however, I questioned the assumption that the poetic, that Being in the way Rosenfield speaks of It, has to be or should be separated from the world of affairs.[7] I approached this, in light of the challenge laid down by the appreciative critic, at two levels: stylistically, in relation to a politicized Heidegger, and dialectically, in relation to the Manichean universe attributed to those who confront disturbing moral, political, or historical issues. I will return to these questions in my response to Professor Megill.

From Rosenfield's "appreciative" or Transcendental Critic, I now turn to Professor Hill's "rhetorical" or Professional Critic. Like Rosenfield's, Hill's critic also draws back from political controversy. But unlike Rosenfield, who promises bursts of insight and rapture, Hill has trouble explaining why his critic should not address the social, political, and moral issues taken up in rhetorical discourse he, unlike Rosenfield, agrees the critic ought to be examining. In his essay on Nixon's Vietnam speech of 1969, Hill denounced those who challenged Nixon's motives, facts, or the consequences of his policies on the grounds that Aristotle's treatise on rhetoric did not allow for such license. I suggested that only in the sequestered world of the academy would invoking Aristotle to ignore preventable human suffering be found anything other than bizarre. In his response, Hill leaves off Aristotle in favor of maxims about scholarship. The critic who would engage in controversy, he tells us, must wait until he or she "discover[s] the truth, the whole truth, and nothing but the truth."[8]

At first glance, because of its honored place in courts of law, I was inclined to let it slide, but on closer inspection and recalling the oath administered to witnesses to "tell the truth, the whole truth, and nothing but the truth," it became clear that the oath had been amended. To *tell* the whole truth as one knows it is quite different from being required to remain silent until one has *discovered* the whole truth. A critic with a philosophical bent or a respect for what the Greeks called *hubris* might be loathe to claim that he or she ever could discover or know the "whole truth" about anything. Hill does not indicate how one discovers or how one knows that he or she has discovered so vast a thing. What he does tell us is that, in its absence, critics were wrong to question Nixon's speech in 1969 about its policy implications, and that it remains wrong over a decade later because Professor Kissinger still claims that it was the Vietnamese who made us kill Vietnamese.

Even if we decided that Hill's standards were not too high or that his sensitivity to controversy did not approach the condition of a nervous disorder, we should pause at the prospect of having our freedom to contest official rhetoric depend on our access to official documents. However much concerned about the fate of humanity or convinced that great moral, social, and political issues are at stake, Hill's critic must wait for those in power to throw open the archives, for until the critic knows all the secrets, motivations, and information available to those in a position to make policy, he or she must stifle such concerns or relinquish the role "rhetorical critic."[9]

There are truths about the human consequences of government policy which may be and can be known before government documents are made available and while there is still time to change bad policy. It is not at all clear why Hill's critic should ignore them. But beyond this, in the real world of politics, even a subliminal acquaintance with the nature and extent of government classification in this country along with the misinformation on which government officials, during the war in Vietnam, were willing to rely and the disinformation they were willing to provide, should make one skeptical about discovering even the half-truths underlying official rhetoric.[10]

What is it that leads Hill to confine rhetorical critics, to so restrict their ability to critique official rhetoric? It would appear to be fear: fear, on the one hand, of the "partisan" who threatens the ideals of scholarship—the association is of course with the "fanatics" he refers to in his article on Nixon and not to the partisans venerated in European history; fear, on the other hand, of the decline of rhetorical studies in the hands of "rhetorical partisans" who, shifting their gaze away from the canon and traditional methods of research, may be blinded by the glare of politics and deafened to the demands of truth. So great is his concern over these matters that he is unwilling to risk a distinction between engaged scholarship and uninformed and poorly reasoned harangues. He would rather, like the ancient Athenians, banish those who utter impieties or who otherwise prove troublesome. In doing so, though, he contracts criticism into little more than a technical exercise and reveals, quite inadvertently, why rhetorical criticism has, over the years, rarely been troubled by the demands of either an academic or a popular audience of people genuinely concerned about the meaning and significance of public address.

I believe in the power and utility of rhetorical theory, including Hill's contribution. This should have been obvious in the "Ideological Turn"; it should become even more apparent later in this essay. I believe that rhetorical theory offers a perspective on historical struggle that would be employed even if the "field" as we know it, responding to current calls for relevant courses, is transformed into an apprenticeship program for the corporate state. My differences with Hill pivot not on his theoretical advance but on his use of it to mark off the boundaries of criticism.

The problems with ideological criticism spelled out by Rosenfeld and Hill appear to gain support from Professor Megill's response to the "Ideological Turn."[11] Megill focused his attack on the discussion of Heidegger. He notes errors, but even if there were no errors, he believes that the approach taken precludes any real understanding of Heidegger. Critics committed to a "materialist" interpretation cannot grasp the symbolic domain. They cannot "listen" to rhetorical, literary, and philosophical texts addressing attitudes and consciousness. Except for a few political speeches, Heidegger's is an "ideal world." The personal dimension in Heidegger's work, and in much modernist and postmodernist literature, makes such texts "unpromising territory" for ideological criticism.

When the issue concerns dates, bibliographic sources, or a particular reading, Megill's comments are useful. It is another matter when he attempts theory and criticism. Theory, for Megill, does not have to do with understanding the world but with prescribing interpretive strategies and texts. There are, he believes, two approaches to interpretation: Materialism, which assumes that ideas are distorted reflections of an underlying material-economic base, and Symbolism, which stresses the transcendent and the potential of the mind. There are two kinds of texts, sociopolitical texts and highly personal texts focusing on attitudes, consciousness, and ideal worlds. Materialism and Symbolism are not mutually exclusive (Megill denounces dogmatic Materialists), yet it appears that sociopolitical and highly personal texts are mutually exclusive. What is clear, however, is Megill's insistence that Materialists (i.e., ideology critics) not be allowed to interpret certain texts.

Given Megill's view of Materialism and the fact that sociopolitical texts also may focus on attitudes, consciousness, and an ideal world, there is no basis for Materialist criticism—it does not and, in Megill's view, cannot produce understanding. The case for doing away with Materialist interpretations of all symbolist and some "sociopolitical" texts, however, stands ultimately not on the properties of the texts or the intent of the author (neither of which will withstand scrutiny), but on his narrow definition of Materialism. What Megill calls Materialism he locates in the Marxist canon. The materialism Megill thinks is representative, however, was a doctrine propounded by Stalin and promoted by party ideologues during the 1930s called "mechanical Materialism." At the heart of this doctrine is the belief that ideas are not only distorted reflections of but also in some way determined by an underlying economic base. This doctrine has been the subject of a vigorous debate among Marxist scholars for several decades. Out of this debate have emerged other conceptions of both Materialism (i.e., "historical" and "dialectical" as well as "mechanical" materialism) and ideology.[12]

Following this debate, one discovers that Marx, contrary to Megill's claim, does not use the term ideology, only in the "pejorative sense" as distorted ideas. While the pejorative sense is appropriate in certain contexts and reflects the approach taken in *The German Ideology*, Marx, in the *Contribution to the Critique of Political Philosophy* (1859), writes:

> The distinction should always be made between the material transformation of the economic conditions of production and the legal, political, religious, aesthetic or philosophic—in short, ideological—forms in which men become conscious of this conflict and fight it out.[13]

One also discovers, contrary to Megill, that not all Marxists hold that ideas find their "real" meaning in the productive relations underlying the social order. The Frankfurt School of critical theorists explores the "partiality" of ideas in relation not only to party interests but also to an ideal world or Totality. Herbert Marcuse warns against thinking ignoring this second dimension, for without it it would be impossible to identify the limitations of what is.

A prominent Marxist historian, Leszek Kolakowski, summed up the debate over materialism. Historical materialism is, he argues, a valuable heuristic principle; it enjoins the "student of conflicts and movements of all kinds—political, social, intellectual, religious, and artistic—to relate his observations to material interests including those derived from the class struggle." This kind of rule, he goes on,

> does not mean that everything is "ultimately" a matter of class interest; it does not deny the independent role of tradition, ideas, or the struggle for power, the importance of geographical conditions or the framework of human existence.[14]

This understanding avoids the "sterile" debate over economic determinism. At the same time, it takes seriously Marx's principle that our spiritual and intellectual life is not self-contained and wholly independent but *also* an expression of material interests. Though grounded in Marx, this view of Materialism, notes Kolakowski, is certainly not unique to Marxism.

If Megill, with his narrow definition, sensed a relationship between Symbolism and Materialism, one might assume that the relationship would blossom with a Materialism acknowledging the force of ideas and realities beyond the workings of a socioeconomic base. But Megill fails to specify the relationship, and when it comes to concrete examples of Materialist criticism, it would seem that none exists. The criticisms he comments on do not merely contain errors; they prove "abortive." They are "failures." He points to Bronner's critique of Heidegger and is dismayed ("alas") that Sheehan's "highly damaging" rejoinder was not cited. There is an affinity here. Sheehan's refutation, like Megill's, pivots on *ad hominem* attacks and dualistic thinking:

> To judge by this article, Bronner is either an incompetent or a fraud. He is the latter if he was actually aware of the many errors he makes, the former if in fact he was not aware of them.[15]

Either-or logic (either a success or a failure, either Symbolist or Materialist, either a real or an ideal world, either political-social or personal texts), an inclination to take up sides (upholding one, damaging the other), the arguments advanced by Megill and Sheehan play off unresolvable dualities. Whatever burden an encounter with "Being" or dialectical reasoning might place on a Manichean view of the world, it is a burden Megill and Sheehan have managed to overcome.

What Megill has done with the "Ideological Turn" is to arrest a few themes and interrogate them over their Materialist tendencies. He draws back from the debate over the place of politics in criticism, refuses to talk about the need to address real issues, remains indifferent to the poetry, the song, the dialectical movement between different historical contexts, the "dance of creation," in sum, the obvious and unrelenting symbolism in the critique. Professor Francesconi is puzzled by Megill's response:

> The drastic materialist interpretation Megill attributes to Wander draws attention away from the symbolic interpretation of the translation of philosophy to the world of everyday life.[16]

I am also puzzled, especially so since the question of ideology and Materialism was addressed early on in the "Ideological Turn":

> A more catholic and, I think, surer grip on ideological analysis understands that it does not force a doctrinaire rejection of Idealism in favor of Materialism or the dismissal of Aristotle in favor of Marx or Habermas. (p. 4)

It is tempting to suggest that symbolist critics do not read, cannot "listen," etc., but it would, I think, be fairer to conclude that Megill, with his notion of Materialism and ignorance of rhetorical theory, was unable to grasp the argument either substantively or stylistically. Not only does the "Ideological Turn" fail to reflect the exclusivity attributed to it (against Symbolism or Idealism, for example), but it pursues the possibilities of inclusiveness ("coalition building" to use Gouldner's phrase) aesthetically, professionally, academically, theologically (a "catholic" grip), politically, and theoretically. The issues facing us, the real issues, are much too demanding to go it alone.

If we can agree that the critic is not and should not be prevented from talking about the implications of or the silences in the most lyrical, self-indulgent flights of spiritualism (i.e., in Heidegger, or in modernist and post-modernist literature), then the great barrier between Symbolist and Materialist falls or, more accurately, is subsumed in a larger conception of criticism. Perhaps, as ideal types, the Materialist is obliged to make errors and the Symbolist is obliged to ignore history, but we do not have to look upon criticism as a struggle between ideal types. In the everyday world of doing criticism, there is not contest.

But, while there are no sides, there are different moments. In textual analysis, for example, one selects a text; one listens to what it says; and one comments on it. It is like a conversation. What the critic says will vary. Sometimes the critic will summarize what he or she has heard and the result will be largely expository. Sometimes the critic will argue with what was said or what was left unsaid, and the result will be largely polemical. Whether expository or polemical, the choice is up to the critic, the critic as a real person who listens, speaks, studies the speaking situation; who meditates on purpose, considers the audiences, examines the issues; who does his or her best to say something worthwhile about matters of importance; and who recognizes that there are times when words are not enough.

Transcendental, Professional, and Symbolist criticism—each in turn has been examined and found wanting. Are we not in a position to say that these approaches should be discarded? Have they not been outmoded? Should we not now pursue ideological criticism? If the answer is yes, we are now in a position to consider the question of method. What methods of research does ideological criticism have to offer? This line of reasoning is precisely what Professor McGee, in his response, predicts will occur. But the legitimacy of ideological criticism as a method of research must not become the issue. This is the way of "repressive tolerance." One of the questions raised through an ideological perspective concerns method—the assumption that "method" contains within it a sense of purpose or the promise of understanding. McGee rightly argues that method is better understood as a way of organizing materials than as an instrument of discovery. When a "method" acquires epistemic status, argues McGee, criticism succumbs to the lure of methodological pluralism and its promise that somewhere, sometime, some method or combination of methods will achieve certainty (i.e., will produce knowledge and, presumably, generate understanding or wisdom).

What do we have to show for our faith in method? In rhetorical studies, in communication research, and in various other fields, the result has been work which speaks only to the professional concerns of technically trained scholars. *Techne* has become an end in itself. It is no longer related to a product. McGee's argument here, and it is an important one, is not that we have been cursed with bad criticism, or that rhetorical studies has become too specialized, or that the field has not yet matured, or that we need a more "holistic" approach. It is that what is now called "criticism" is the result of an established order willing to tolerate work which is morally, socially, and politically meaningless so long as it reproduces forms associated with technical reason. It is the product of a system which asks not why is this subject important, what does it add to human knowledge, or what is its emancipatory potential, but committed to technocratic solutions, what is the "text" or object of research, what have other researchers said about it, and, above all, what method or methods are going to be employed?

McGee is quite right—ideological criticism is not a method or a professional stance. But, I would argue contrary to McGee that it is much more than a perspective. It entertains possibilities for action, and the actions it considers may go beyond actions sanctioned in the academy, namely the production of texts. This becomes apparent when we take up issues meaningful in our everyday lives—the impact, for example, of the established order, through various institutional arrangements, on how we think and talk about the victims of official violence.

But such analysis, as I conceive of it, requires a reformulation of rhetorical theory. It is, therefore, time to leave off "he said this, but I wrote this, and she failed to grasp this" format which threatens to become little more than a contest, a Heart of America Tournament for postdoctorates. My own reflections prior to the publication of the "Ideological Turn," and most certainly my encounter with a body of challenging and insightful criticism related to it—and I should here express how much I appreciate the efforts of my respondents to come to grips with the partial truths of that work—have led me to explore issues lying somewhere between theory and criticism. The remainder of my response, therefore, will consist of two meditations: (1) Ideology and dogmatism; and (2) Idealism and Materialism.

IDEOLOGY AND DOGMATISM

> We should let ourselves be guided by what is common to all. Yet,
> although the Logos is common to all, most men live as if each of
> them had a private intelligence of his own.
>
> *Heraclitus*[17]

Partisanship, orthodox Marxism, dogmatism—these terms, in the context of American scholarship, point to concerns about narrowed sensibilities or party discipline in contrast to freethinking and well-rounded academic humanism. The fear is that intense commitment will result not only in a loss of intellectual independence, but will also render one intolerant, unable to give other than perverse readings of those with whom one does not agree. The underlying ideal is disinterested scholarship and balanced views. In my concern with "partial" or party interests in a particular world view or "ideology," there is implicitly affirmed a whole, a total world view, or Totality ever present but never fully realized. It is here that we can, I think, get beyond the clash. The Totality does not require a revelation or even a gloss of Hegelianism. It may be posited in the face of the reality of change; in the limits of language where, even if one knew the truth whole, it could not be contained in words, and if contained could never be heard but only interpreted in light of the limits of the other; in myriad perspectives seducing one away from solipsistic isolation to engage in dialogue where question invites answer invites question into an infinite progress; or in the sheer impossibility of announcing the Totality without inventing a mode of expression beyond the ordinary—in a word, "poetry."

In an era of scientism and calculations of cost-efficiency, the Totality lies under a shroud of positivism, unbelief, and the absence of financial support. To speak of It is grounds for arrest on charges of mysticism or, worse, mystification. But while I do not presume to bring news of the cosmos, I believe that, as a theoretical construct, the Totality plays an important, even practical, role in ideological criticism. It enables such criticism to move beyond even the most persuasive bit of dogma, truth, fact, philosophy, common sense, or party line. The same principle obtains in the ancient argument between rhetoric and philosophy. The Totality or, as Perelman would have it, the "Universal Audience" moderates all claims: "The discourse of the philosopher and his [or her] conception of the universal audience is not the discourse of a god—of a universal, and eternal truth—but that of a man [or woman], inevitably conditioned by the understandings, the aspirations, and the problems of his [or her] milieu, hence the inevitable pluralism in philosophy, where incontestable truth does not exist."[18]

The Totality is that which laughs at efforts to trick up existence to look like eternity. Perelman, along with the Frankfurt School (he specifically refers to Habermas), links the Totality to democratic political theory and the assumption that no one, no party, no institution holds the truth whole. McGee alludes to this when discussing Gouldner's realm of critical discourse. In a recent essay, he explores the problem of citing God as an authority in argument.[19] God's word does not invite rebuttal; it terminates debate—a conclusion as obvious to the unbeliever as to a believer. With regard to Marxism, an important element in Critical Theory, it is the Totality which stands above and beyond attempts to use "Marxism" to legitimize party or government policy. Similarly with regard to capitalism, there is a reminder that claims made on behalf of the "Free World" also have their limits. In heaven we can set aside the need to work for worthwhile change. Change occurs in the world of affairs. The question is, To what extent can we work to make change progressive? To be progressive, change must progress toward something. That something, oriented around traditional humanist notions of human potential, is grounded in the emancipation of human potential.[20] Human potential may be blunted by the existing order; it may be effaced in a one-dimensional society where "ought" collapses into "is" and potential is equated with trend or trajectory. It also may be lost in a society lacking the means for its realization. When this is the case, humanism—whether Marxist, neo-Marxist, liberal, conservative, or academic—is obliged to consider the social, political, and economic conditions necessary for human emancipation.[21] But if history is seen as a mechanism automatically heading in some direction, an aggregate of accidental moments and meaningless events, or a past wholly detached from the present and the future, then action becomes irrelevant. History, however, as Vico understood it—a succession of presents with people whose lived present includes the possibility of constructing a future—gives meaning to concepts such as "progress," "action ... potential," and the effort to "make history."

Bringing what is into the light of could be and ought to be, ideological criticism makes sense in an historical context—the struggle to create the future—only if a space exists where people can deliberate and act to bring about change. In democratic political theory, this is called the "public space." Without a public space, criticism lapses into eulogy or falls silent. Criticism rooted in democratic political theory, therefore, works to create and sustain a space wherein people or "publics" can reason through the possibilities for collective action. Within each party or faction, there must be room for debate; between various parties, room to negotiate; between individuals and between parties, room for deliberation. There is a pragmatic reason for this: only through coalition building can a public space become an agency for progress.[22] A critic, working within this tradition, therefore, keeps his or her own party's world view open not merely out of respect for free thinking, but also out of a practical need to join together party interests and partial truths into larger ideological configurations or, in Gouldner's term, an ideological "umbrella" under which a coalition might find a way to articulate what common interest makes possible.

Politics of this sort disappears in historical accounts interested not in the meaning but in the significance of actions and events. The meaning of an action, event, or text lies in what it means for those who participate in it. The significance lies in what it holds for an observer. To be sure, an event does not become an "event" unless someone takes an interest in it. The action making up an event and indicated through the text becomes a unit of analysis because someone after the fact finds it important. This is the meaning of "significance." Finding an event important, however, does not create it. This remains true even though calling it an "event" provides a form through which to assemble what interests us now. If the critic denies that an action, event, or text meant something to those who produced it, or that it cannot be understood or appreciated now, then all action, including the critical act, threatens to become meaningless.

There are two problems here: one is how people know what they are doing is meaningful; the other is how someone, after the fact, can determine what the meaning was for the actors. The first problem faces the critic as forcefully as it faces the historical subject. The second problem may be resolved by claiming that the critic possesses either unique sensibilities or powerful methods of investigation enabling him or her to penetrate the mask, identify the symptom, or get at a deeper structure eluding the actors. This claim does not necessarily deny that what the critic is studying was meaningful to the participants, and, however grandiose the claim to knowledge, neither sensibility nor method can, by itself, decide from among a number of acts, events, or texts which one merits observation. Whatever it meant to the participants and however compelling the critic's insights, the question of significance takes the critic beyond self-pride and pride of method to engage in the same kind of reflection as other historical actors.

The critic may escape the labyrinth of the meaning of significance and the significance of meaning by becoming a systematic observer whose only task is to report accurately his or her findings. But this flight into technical reason, and the fascinating things it does to critical choice, flutters back to the ground when actions, events, and texts are not treated as givens, mere things divorced from human purpose, but as things lying on a state where efforts to create the future enacted in the here-and-now of real people may be likened to the critic's effort, through research, meditation, and writing, to create something in the here-and-now.

But what have we done to the critic, by introducing this person into the world of contingency facing other historical actors—an everyday world of shadows and fra-grances, unspoken fears and the delights of the human voice? What are we now to make of this once familiar figure, the "critic"? The "critic," on the surface, is only a fiction—a noun, a role, a convention of academic and literary writing. The term "critic" encourages the writer to rise above the whims of subjectivity. The "critic" is less personal than "I," more formal than "we," and, aligned with "one," clearly an invitation to universalize. Like the "scholar," "researcher," "scientist," "philosopher," or "intellec-tual," the "critic" is another name for Ideal Observer.

But what of the Totality in the face of the more interesting Critic and the more personable Ideal Observer? What are the limits of the Critic or Ideal Observer in light of the Totality? Ideally speaking, none, for the Critic and the Ideal Observer are but other names for the Totality. Practically speaking, however, the Ideal Observer does not act, while in the world of affairs the act of "observation," especially systematic observation, is highly rewarded. And the Critic, when brought to earth in professional publications, takes on the guise of Omniscient Professional.[23] In the world of affairs, the Critic personifies the ideology of a particular profession at a certain time and place; hence the myriad qualifiers preceding the Critic such as "social," "literary," "rhetorical," "media," "film," etc.

I should like to explore the tension between Critic and "critic" in rhetorical studies, taking the humbling concept of the Totality into the *inner sanctum* of the field, rhetorical theory. In order to do this, I shall return to an issue raised during the course of the debate over the "Ideological Turn," the rules by which texts and events not mentioned in the text may be linked.

IDEALISM AND MATERIALISM

> Rhetorical speech. . .is a "dialogue," that is, that which breaks out with vehemence in the urgency of the particular human situation and "here" and "now" begins to form a specifically human order in the confrontation with other human beings. And because the material belonging to language consists in the interpretation of the meaning of sensory appearances—for the main thing is to order and form these—it is laden with figurative expressions, colors, sounds, smells, tangibles.
>
> *Ernesto Grassi*[24]

Where is the link between "Being" and the Great War, or between Heidegger on art and the rise of Fascism? How can we move between the "text" and historical events to which the text does not refer? What sanction does this movement have outside partisan interest or personal whim? The question becomes more manageable if we ask: Where does the critic get permission to link events in the material world with the ideas in a speech when the speaker does not refer to or may even deny the relevance of such things in the speech?

In everyday life, the link between materialism and idealism is fairly obvious. Those who do not appreciate the practical are said to be "too idealistic," and those who can see only the almighty dollar are called "too materialistic." If we take this everyday observation into history and philosophy, we can explore one possibility for making a link between word and object, text and thing, speech and events—the audience and the part it can play in the absence of reference or inference through implication and connotation. Survey research in communication studies begins with a simple proposition, and I believe it applies here: The "meaning" of a speech will vary with the audience. It is useful, therefore, in debates over meaning to distinguish between the audience or audiences for whom the speech had meaning at the moment of utterance, and the audience or audiences for whom it holds significance later on. This distinction may shed some light on what for Megill is a preemptory objection regarding an interpretation of Heidegger. "Alas," he writes,

> one gets no sense that Wander has bothered to ask himself why *Being and Time* is a philosophically significant work. Instead, in lurid language, he reminds us of the "shrieking iron and flame" of the First World War, the "blood red poppies of Flanders' fields," the "vast wasteland littered with rotting corpses."[25]

If the relevant audience for the lectures that became *Being and Time* is an audience of contemporary professional philosophers, those for whom "philosophically significant" takes on special meaning, then the "meaning" of *Being and Time* will be confined to disputes over interpretation, the precise point at which the celebrated "turn" occurred, and other questions presupposing that the whole of the Heideggerian canon is before us to be explicated. Megill is quite right. For this audience the context in which Being was or is talked about will not include dreaded events or lurid details.

But let us begin with the assumption that the audience for whom Heidegger's Being—the "Being" he articulated—took on meaning in Germany when the lectures were being presented was an audience well aware of the awesome disaster Megill serializes as the "First World War"; that this audience had experienced, was experiencing, and knew people who were experiencing, as Jung wrote at the time, the threat of insanity brought on by the collapse of what is and the fragile hope and sense of purpose anchored in existing institutional arrangements; and that this audience would, on the whole, not have found the details of the Great War "lurid," but instead common knowledge, the sort of shared experience a speaker may call upon to flesh out an argument or breathe life into a figure of speech.

For this audience, for people confronting hopelessness, the meaning of "Being" can hardly be confined—and would not have been confined for so popular a lecturer— to the responses of professional philosophers. Those who were or who might have been seeking positions in philosophy in the universities at the time—students like Marcuse, Sartre, Arendt, and Grassi—have proven less likely, over the course of their careers, to limit the context and associations to what Megill in both his response and his essay on Heidegger indicates is appropriate.

The link between Heidegger and art, specifically between his Frankfort Lectures in 1936 and recollections of starvation and the triumph of the National Socialists in Germany at that time, is of particular interest. This link calls for an augmentation of the concept of audience in rhetorical theory to include audiences not present, audiences rejected or negated through the speech and/or the speaking situation. This audience I shall call the Third Persona. In order to approach this concept, however, we need to locate it in relation to actual audiences and in relation to a First and Second Persona.

Communication researchers using descriptive methods identify real or actual audiences—people who in fact heard, or read, or saw the speech (program, advertisement, play, etc.). Hill's contribution has been to identify the audience or audiences aimed at through the speech. There is the audience in fact reached, including both those the speaker-sender wished to reach (the "primary" audience) and those who are reached inadvertently ("secondary" audiences). The actual audience, however, does not reveal the audience or persona commended through the speech. It is one thing to say the speaker reached X and Y; it is another to say what the speaker was, on the basis of what was said, suggesting what X or Y become.

In a conscious break with Aristotelian tradition, Professor Black notes the absence of any treatment of the audience the message or "discourse," by virtue of the language employed, would create.[26] Black sets aside the question of the impact on real audiences as well as the intent of the speaker to dwell on the implications for the auditor confronted with the language of his or her community. Language, in this view, becomes a refuge for being, a medium in which it exists as a possibility for being in the world. The persona frozen in language and commended through discourse, because it gives human shape to things and because it may entail significant behavior, becomes the proper subject, in Black's view, for moral judgment. In this way Black resurrects the individual as actor and, even as the ethos of the speaker is set aside, preserves the notion of moral evaluation even in a world in which the center does not hold.

The Second Persona—being commended through discourse—is meaningful in a society made up of competing groups and rival ideologies. It enables one to look into the heart of various bodies of belief or world views and describe the being in the world it commends. Beyond rejection and ridicule, the Second Persona exists as a fact and an invitation. It may be an invitation turned down; it may even be an offensive invitation; but it is an invitation which can be heard and responded to here and now. It becomes morally important, when one realizes that it is, beyond being, an invitation to act.

In the text conceived as speech or "discourse" involving exchange (in contrast to "sending" and "receiving" or "speaking" and "listening"), there is implied a speaker and a speaker's intent. This is the "I," or the First Persona. There is also implied, through certain features of the discourse entailing specific characteristics, roles, actions, or ways of seeing things for one who can use the language, a "you" or a Second Persona.

But, just as the discourse may be understood to affirm certain characteristics, it may also be understood to imply other characteristics, roles, actions, or ways of seeing things to be avoided. What is negated through the Second Persona forms the silhouette of a Third Persona—the "it" that is not present, that is objectified in a way that "you" and "I" are not. This being not present may, depending on how it is fashioned, become quite alien, a being equated with disease, a "cancer" called upon to disfigure an individual or a group; or an animal subordinated through furtive glance or beady eye; or an organism, as a people might be transformed, through a biological metaphor, into "parasites." The potentiality of language to commend being carries with it the potential to spell out being unacceptable, undesirable, insignificant.

The Third Persona, therefore, refers to being negated. But "being negated" includes not only being alienated through language—the "it" that is the summation of all that you and I are told to avoid becoming—but also being negated in history, a being whose presence, though relevant to what is said, is negated through silence. The moral significance of being negated through what is and is not said reveals itself in all its anguish and confusion in context, in the world of affairs wherein certain individuals and groups are, through law, tradition, or prejudice, denied rights accorded to being commended or, measured against an ideal, to human beings. The objectification of certain individuals and groups discloses itself through what is and is not said about them and through actual conditions affecting their ability to speak for themselves. Operating through existing social, political, and economic arrangements, negation extends beyond the "text" to include the ability to produce texts, to engage in discourse, to be heard in the public space.

Establishing links between what is said and audiences denied access to public space brings rhetorical theory back to earth. Was what Heidegger said in his lectures on art in Frankfurt on November 17, 24, and December 4, 1936, irrelevant to those suffering under Fascism? Might they not and should they not have interpreted what was said in ways quite different from what professional philosophers, intellectual historians, or rhetorical critics propose half a century after the moment of utterance?

Regarding the lectures, it can be argued that Heidegger did not intend to address the politically oppressed. Certainly this cannot be shown to be his primary audience. No mention of Jews, Communists, or labor organizers, for example, appears in the text. There is no evidence in the Heideggerian canon of such concern. I shall return to the limits of textual analysis and the political "intent" of these lectures, but for now the question is, Was what Heidegger said about art in his lectures relevant to this group?

If we accept that audiences at the time can provide links between, for example, a reference to food and the experience of starvation, then we have begun to establish a connection between Heidegger's imagining a woman trudging through a field and allusions to bread, childbirth, death, and events not mentioned in the text. The peasant woman's shoes, "pervaded by uncomplaining worry as to the certainty of bread, the wordless joy of having once more withstood want, the trembling before the impending childbed and shivering at the surrounding menace of death,"[27] would, less than a generation after the Great War, have touched on lived experience as well as stories heard while growing up.

The link is even clearer with an audience unable to assemble to hear the lectures, an audience composed of those persecuted by an all-powerful fascist state. For this audience, the uncertainty of bread, joy of withstanding want, trembling before the impending childbed, and the surrounding menace of death would have resonated not only with the past, but also with a problematic present.

Less than three years before the Frankfurt lectures, all non-Aryans and anyone else who opposed the dictatorship had been removed from government jobs and from teaching. The "People's Court" had been in operation for over two years trying cases of treason (broadly defined) in secret, with appeal only to the Fuhrer. A national boycott against Jewish businesses and professions had been in effect for over three years; the

Nuremberg Laws, denying citizenship to Jews and forbidding intermarriage, had been in effect for a year. Labor unions had been crushed, their political parties outlawed.

For this audience, reflections on peasant life (a major theme in Nazi propaganda), paintings, a failure to address pressing issues, and a stoic or "quietistic" response would have, in a political context, and, given this context, should have taken on meaning quite different from what Heidegger intended and from the response of his primary or actual audience.

In Megill's view this is all beside the point. He does not envision a link. He worries about "overmaterializing" Heidegger's text and points to the Frankfurt lectures—he wants to call them an "essay"—as a prime example of where ideological criticism fails:

> It is odd that Wander should choose to make these connections when he completely ignores the explicit topic of the essay, namely the ontological significance of the work of art. Perhaps Wander believes that Heidegger's discussion of that topic is beneath consideration.

There is, he states, "nothing in the essay that points to the war and its aftermath."[28]

Now while I agree with Megill that the world Heidegger wants to embrace is not the extant world as "Wander understands it," the extant world Heidegger urges his audience to transcend points to war and its aftermath in a variety of ways. One textual link concerns the "things" Heidegger likens to works of art:

> works of art are familiar to everyone.... If we consider the works in their untouched actuality and do not deceive ourselves, the result is that the works are as naturally present as things. The picture hangs on the wall like a rifle or a hat. A painting, e.g., the one by Van Gogh that represents a pair of peasant shoes, travels from one exhibition to another. Works of art are shipped like coal from the Ruhr and logs from the Black Forest. During the First World War Holderlin's hymns were packed in the soldier's knapsack together with cleaning gear. Beethoven's quartets lie in storerooms of the publishing house like potatoes in a cellar.[29]

Note that there is a reference to the Great War in the text, though Megill's caution about the lectures being altered for publication years later is also supported by the fact that the reference is to a war occurring before a "second" World War.

But even if there were no reference, the "things" picked out were familiar, had common associations for the audience listening to the lectures. As things naturally present—coal, logs, and potatoes—they merely exist; but they also may be thought of as symbols of security. For the primary and, in all probability, for the actual audience, such things could be transcended, and the insecurities associated with an earlier period including not only the Great War, when such things were scarce, but also the Great Depression, when they were often not affordable, could be set aside. Why? Because of the prosperity enjoyed under the National Socialists. Coal was once more coming from the Ruhr; winter did not have to be so cold. Logs were once again coming from the Black Forest; homes could be built and heated. Potatoes once more could be laid up in the cellar; no need to fear an empty stomach. When such things no longer present a problem, they become "naturally present."

From the point of view of the audience which could not assemble and could not protest, and which was being negated in and through every channel of communication, however, the suggestion that rifles be treated as commonplace and the military be associated with hymns and cleaning gear might have and, given the situation in 1936, should have struck a different note. With the imposition of police power, the abolition of free speech and assembly, a rapid buildup of the armed forces, and the omnipresent voice of the Fuhrer over newly installed radios, this audience might have found the things indicated by Heidegger more disturbing than natural. "Airplanes and radio sets," he went on, only, seven months after the reintroduction of conscription in Germany, "are nowadays among the things closest to us, but when we have in mind the last things we think of something altogether different." For the fearful and the oppressed, these "last things" might have been marked with dread, anger, or resignation: "Death and judgment—these are the last things."[30]

But consider Heidegger's method for approaching the "naturally present"—taking the familiar and making it unfamiliar by reattaching it to work and, through work with what is (i.e., equipment), to a problematic future. The peasant shoes in Van Gogh's painting become, through the critical narrative, equipment for work. They are productive of something. What kind of life are they associated with? What sort of future does this life bring into being? What is the value in and quality of this effort? What are the fears attending or underlying the use of this equipment? These are questions addressed to what is beneath the surface of the thing—the work of art—revealed through the object imbedded in the process of living.

Francesconi puts the question in this way: "Wouldn't a complete 'releasement toward things' acknowledge our social being, our nature as beings of purpose in social involvement? Wouldn't such an analysis realize that a technological tool has an impact upon the social organization in which it operates?" (p. 52). What occurs if this type of analysis is applied to other things specified by Heidegger, and if we make comparisons between equipment and the future instead of focusing on the differences between art and non-art? Coal, logs, potatoes, radios, and airplanes, if only through government propaganda, blend symbols of security and symbols of progress and power into an overarching sense of national prosperity, pride, and potential under National Socialism. In this way "prosperity" also may become a thing whose essence must be penetrated if one is to rise above what is "naturally present." Prosperity is the product not only of work but also, in the case of "national" prosperity, of decisions made by government.

As a thing, then, "national prosperity" is associated not only with a particular government, with decisions made by those in power over the collection of taxes, distribution of funds, future projects and policies, etc. The problem with a term like "prosperity" is that it gathers in too much and, at the same time, not enough. "National Prosperity" depends, in the modern world, on abstractions such as employment statistics and productivity indexes (during 1933–1937 unemployment in Germany dropped from 6.4 to 1.8 million and productivity almost doubled). Such abstractions, however, barely touch on what is experienced in everyday life or the future being fashioned out of economic decisions made by governments summed up under terms like "economic security," "productivity," or "national prosperity."

A similar problem occurs with things treated as "objects," except that when things become objects-of-perception they may reclaim some small portion of a world of fragrances and shadows. In both cases, the entities—abstractions and objects—are detached from the lives of those who experience them over time and in light of their importance in a world of purpose and action. With objects such as coal, logs, potatoes, radios, and airplanes, and with abstractions such as national prosperity, they too, like a work of art, may become things unnoticed, part of our second nature. Disturbing their "natural presence" invites inquiry into their origin, their function in a human world, and the future they are intended to or are likely to provide.

Alongside a pair of shoes, Heidegger places other things which also hint at scenes of desolation. Grasping this requires us to penetrate our knowledge of concentration camps and World War II to reach a point from which to survey a future which, while not holding these specific events, held such grave possibilities that it had become dangerous to talk about them. It also requires us to grasp the ideological nature of our historical explanations for what occurred in Germany, specifically our understanding the causes of the economic boom following the takeover in 1933.

Traditional explanations for this boom center on Keynesianism and demand management. Recent research, however, according to V. R. Berghan, emphasizes the relationship between national prosperity and arms expenditure. The Four Year Plan, begun in 1936, writes Berghan,

> fixed both the ultimate object of all this hectic rearmament activity, namely a war in four years' time, and pointed to the inexorability of national bankruptcy unless the military expenditure of the 1930s was recouped in such a war. It was clear that the debts which the government had incurred when ordering weapons and increasing the size of the armed forces would one day have to be paid.[31]

The wars such expenditures pointed to were not "world wars"—this is where thinking may become blocked by subsequent events. The National Socialists were not advocating a "Second World War." There was a need for a strong defense, for a well-armed Germany, for protecting a sphere of influence, for warding off one menace or another, for protecting Germans in other countries.

But however enormous increases in defense spending were officially explained, there were people in Germany in late 1936 who recognized the potential for war and knew its horrors. For this audience, the things associated with economic security, national prosperity, military power—coal, logs, potatoes, radios, airplanes, a desolate landscape, the "shivering menace of death," and the last things, "death and judgment"— would have seemed less arbitrary or merely illustrative. This audience would not have been reluctant to look beneath the surface of the lecture because of the reputation of the speaker. Here again our thinking may be blocked. For us Heidegger's membership in the Party and his speeches favoring the Fuhrer in 1933 predominate; for an audience attending the lectures in 1936, the speaker was a famous philosopher who had left the Party, resigned his administrative post, was being attacked by party ideologues, and, strangely enough, had taken up the topic of "art" on a public platform.

I say "strangely enough" because for us talk about art is harmless, the sort of thing found in museum brochures or journals of aesthetics. It was not innocuous in the context in which Heidegger spoke. The difference between what "art" referred to then and what it refers to now, along with the conditions under which talk about "art" is monitored and the penalties that can be inflicted, is so great that the meaning of Heidegger's lectures is all but lost to us.

Politically sensitive is one way of characterizing the topic, the "origin of art." The government extended its control over art as far as it could. The Reich Chamber of Culture covered literature, music, films, radio, theater, fine arts, and the press. Membership in the Chamber was compulsory in every artistic profession. Denial of membership meant that one could not, in a public sense, be an "artist." The financing of art fell under government jurisdiction. Unauthorized art could be destroyed. All forms of expression were subject to censorship.

Politically dangerous is another way of characterizing efforts to talk about art under such conditions. On November 27, 1936, one week before Heidegger's third lecture, Dr. Goebbels, head of the Ministry of Propaganda and Enlightenment, announced:

> Because this year had not brought an improvement in art criticism, I forbid once and for all the continuance of art criticism in its present form, effective as of today. From now on, the reporting of art will take the place of art criticism which has set itself up as a judge of art—a complete perversion of the concept "criticism" which dates from the time of the Jewish domination of art. The critic is to be superseded by the art editor. The reporting of art should not be concerned with values, but should confine itself to description.[32]

Whether or not there was an intentional link between Goebbels' announcement and Heidegger's lectures—whether Goebbels "meant" to silence Heidegger or his approach to interpretation—this much is evident: There was, under the National Socialists, a well-defined political context for anyone who would talk about "art."

Given the constraints on what could and could not be said and the clarity of the official position in these matters, one would expect to find a number of themes, like racial explanations for art, expounded. One would expect to find these themes, that is, if the speaker were one with the government and the Party. If the speaker were not in agreement, one would expect to find the topic treated in ways as far removed from sociopolitical realities as possible. Ontology, like irony and allegory, offers refuge for a speaker who is vulnerable to political attack. How far ontology may be conceived of as a rhetorical strategy in this instance I have no idea. So much depends on "intent," and so little is known about Heidegger's thinking on the underlying issues.

Clearly, ideological criticism must be able to step outside the barriers of intent when assessing the meaning of a body of discourse or a "text." This is true not only when the discourse is being treated as a symptom of some social or political problem, but also when the discourse, perhaps unintentionally, grapples with problems which can be shown to exist in context. Professor Corcoran's objection to a concept of ideology which fails to provide for the unintentional production of ideologically significant formations and his insistence on including structuralist and deconstructionist contributions to the concept are pertinent here. Ideology, he observes, is all the more effective for not being recognized as such.[33] I would only add that ideology, even when intentional, is sometimes possible only when those in power do not or cannot identify it as such.

With regard to Heidegger, while there is little room to argue that he was aware of the implications of his lectures for those whose existence lay outside the university, there is evidence to suggest that he was concerned about the impact of Nazi policies on those who worked within the university.[34] But whatever Heidegger's intent in these matters, when the political constraints about public address and the topic of art in particular are taken into account, certain contextual ambiguities appear which help to explain why Heidegger, during the middle 1930s, came increasingly under attack. Ambiguity attends both form and content at the close of his third lecture. After declaring that a people's historical existence is found in art, he asks: "Are we in our existence historically at the origin?" For Party leaders and government officials, this was no longer open to question. National Socialism was the answer—it was a New Order, the beginning of a Thousand Year Reich. "Do we know, which means do we give heed," he goes on, "the essence of the origin? Or do we still," he asks amidst an official revival of classical realism, "merely make appeal to a cultivated acquaintance with the past?"

How did Heidegger answer these questions? He did not answer them directly; instead, he offered a standard for arriving at answers. It was not a standard endorsed by the Party, dictated by the government, or articulated by the Leader. Nothing was said about the racial origins of the "standard," though it did come from one of the heroes in the nationalist canon. It was a standard provided by a poet, and Heidegger raised it up before the established order as a standard to which it too could be held accountable:

> Holderlin the poet—whose work still confronts the Germans as a test to be stood—named it in saying:
>
>> Reluctantly
>> that which dwells near its origin departs.[35]

There are ambiguities in Heidegger's lectures on art which grow out of treating them rhetorically and situating them in the here and now of historical struggle. They rest on certain facts about the speaker—the fact that Heidegger left the Party and his administrative post in 1934, no longer praised the government or the Leader, in his seminars denounced official attempts to ground art in racial theories, and did not employ such theories in his lectures on art. They rest on references in the text—references to "coal," "logs," "potatoes," a "rifle," "soldiers," "radios," and "airplanes"—which, in the false security of a war economy and an official call for protecting Germany's sphere of influence, makes such things problematic, the same things which, when likened to works of art, should not be taken for granted as "things."[36] They rest also on the fact that the language of the text and the nature of the argument were shaped to some extent by a government which had assumed control over production, content, communication, and interpretation of the arts and of language itself.[37]

Finally, they rest on the existence of different audiences: a primary audience concerned about or interested in the "origin of art" in a society where such questions were given official answers; a secondary audience composed of Party ideologues and government censors whom Heidegger had to take into account and who already were denouncing him; and a tertiary audience, an audience which may or may not have been part of the speaker's awareness, existing in the silences of the text, the reality of oppression, and the unutterable experience of human suffering, an audience for whom what was said was relevant in ways that traditional approaches to interpretation may overlook.

I am not promoting a "new" interpretation of Heidegger or contributing another gloss on his lectures. Such things are rightly left up to those who study the "texts," know the languages, spend time in the archives. I stand in their debt in trying to puzzle out the issues. As for the interpretation offered, I take some solace from the poet:

> What is spoken is never,
> and in no language,
> What is said.[38]

What interests me is the theoretical issue centered on the ways in which theory in general, rhetorical theory in particular, is shaped by the context in which it is propounded. To what extent does rhetorical theory oblige us to ignore audiences not addressed, unable to attend, and unable to respond to the "text?" To what extent do our academic assumptions or commitments prompt us to reflect on the meaning and significance of what is said in ways that ignore or, with Heidegger's lectures on art, actually conceal important silences?

Whatever the limitations of my critique, I believe that the Third Persona merits serious consideration as a contribution to rhetorical theory. It focuses on audiences negated through the "text"—the language, the speaking situation, the established order shaping both. It provides a space in rhetorical theory for those unable not only to find shelter in, but also to take part in the discourse. Through the Third Persona we may examine the rules for producing discourse (criticism) about discourse (rhetoric). The tendency for such rules to reflect, sanction, or obscure rules for the production of discourse in the public space when it comes to the negation of human beings (i.e., transforming some group, or class, or sex, or race into an "it") suggests a link between theory and the institutional framework underwriting the production of theory. This is, I think, a point where Critical Theory, Sartrean existentialism, and deconstructionism intersect. And it is the ground on which hermeneutics, in its flight from the heavens of purpose and potential, can alight on discovering that texts are produced by real people and that the process of production, interpretation, and communication may veil what is in various ways.

SUMMARY

It takes two to maintain a silence: the one who remains silent, and the other who either doesn't ask questions or who is satisfied with unsatisfactory answers.

Michael Schneider[39]

Something fruitful, I hope, has emerged out of the exchange over the "Ideological Turn." It has forced me to reflect on and make explicit certain theoretical assumptions regarding a Third Persona. It is important to understand, however, that this concept refers not merely to groups of people with whom "you" and "I" are not to identify, who are to remain silent in public, who are not to become part of "our" audience or even be allowed to respond to what "we" say. Beyond its verbal formulation, the Third Persona draws in historical reality, so stark in the twentieth century, of peoples categorized according to race, religion, age, gender, sexual preference, and nationality, and acted upon in ways consistent with their status as non-subjects. The Third Persona directs our attention to beings beyond the claims of morality and the bonds of compassion. It does so not only in the past, but also, in an age of genocidal weapons, in a future of generations yet unborn whose claims on the present grow increasingly faint. There is, to be sure, a technical ring about the "Third Persona." Properly understood, however, it bursts the limits of technical reason to join the intellectual and the artistic with the political and social. Properly understood, it involves the unity of humanity and the wholeness of the human problem.

Notes

1. Thomas Mann, "Letter to the Dean of the Philosophical Faculty of the University of Bonn, 1936," in *The Thomas Mann Reader*, ed. J. W. Angell (New York: Grosset and Dunlap, 1950), p. 518.

2. Philip Wander, "The Ideological Turn in Modern Criticism," *Central States Speech Journal* 34 (1983): 1–18.

3. Paul F. Lazarsfeld and Wagner Thielens Jr., *The Academic Mind* (Glencoe, IL: Free Press, 1958), p. 50. For an excellent overview of this era, see David Caute, *The Great Fear: The Anti-Communist Purge Under Truman and Eisenhower* (New York: Simon and Schuster, 1978), esp. "Purge of the 'Reducators,'" pp. 403–431.

4. Michael Calvin McGee, "Another Philippic: Notes on the Ideological Turn in Criticism," *Central States Speech Journal* 35 (1984): 43–50.

5. Lawrence W. Rosenfield, "Ideological Miasma," *Central States Speech Journal* 34 (1983): 119–121.

6. Ernst Cassirer, "'Mind' and 'Life': Heidegger," trans. John Michael Krois, *Philosophy and Rhetoric* 16 (1983): 162.

7. This question was also explored in my "The Aesthetic Dimension: A Note on Ideology, Criticism, and Reality," in David Zarefsky, Malcolm A. Sillars, and Jack Rhodes, eds., *Argument in Transition: Proceedings of the Third Summer Conference on Argumentation* (Annandale, VA: Speech Communication Association, 1983), pp. 159–169; and "The Aesthetics of Fascism," *Journal of Communication* 33 (1983): 70–78.

8. Forbes Hill, "A Turn Against Ideology: Reply to Professor Wander," *Central States Speech Journal* 34 (1983): 122.

9. The exchange between Professors Campbell and Hill illustrates the kind of debates which occur over the question of who can or cannot lay claim to academic legitimacy. Campbell presses Hill over the arbitrary definitions of the "field" he advances, his inability to tolerate different approaches, and the arbitrary manner in which he defends his views on Vietnam. (See Karlyn Kohrs Campbell, "Response to Forbes Hill," *Central States Speech Journal* 34 [1983]: 126–127.)

10. See Paul Joseph, "The Politics of 'Good' and 'Bad' Information: The National Security Bureaucracy and the Vietnam War," *Politics and Society* 7 (1977): 105–126.

11. Allan Megill, "Heidegger, Wander, and Ideology," *Central States Speech Journal* 34 (1983): 114–119. Megill's positions on Heidegger are laid out in more complete form in his *Prophets of Extremity: Nietzsche, Heidegger, Foucault, Derrida* (Berkeley and Los Angeles: University of California Press, 1985).

12. On "mechanical," "historical," and "dialectical" materialism, see Raymond Williams, *Keywords: A Vocabulary of Culture and Society* (New York: Oxford University Press, 1976), pp. 163–167.

13. Quoted in Williams, *Keywords*, p. 128.

14. Leszek Kolakowski, *Main Currents of Marxism*, trans. P. S. Falla (New York: Oxford University Press, 1978), vol. 1, p. 371. For the context surrounding the debate over materialism, see "Marxism as the Ideology of the Soviet State," in *Main Currents*, vol. 3, pp. 77–116.

15. Thomas Sheehan, "Philosophy and Propaganda: Response to Professor Bronner," *Salmagundi* 43 (1979): 174. Bronner, in his response, captures the tone. Sheehan, he writes, "employs pedantry and bellicose verbosity in order to smother contradictions, suppress controversies, and divert the reader from real issues" (Stephen Eric Bronner, "The Poverty of Scholasticism/A Pedant's Delight: A Response to Thomas Sheehan," *Salmagundi*, p. 185).

16. Robert Francesconi, "Heidegger and Ideology: Reflections of an Innocent Bystander," *Central States Speech Journal* 35 (1984): 51–53.

17. Heraclitus, "Fragments," in Philip Wheelwright, ed., *The Presocratics* (New York: Oddyssey Press, 1966), p. 69.

18. Chaim Perelman, "The New Rhetoric and the Rhetoricians: Remembrances and Comments," *Quarterly Journal of Speech* 70 (1984): 193–194. On the historical struggle between philosophy and rhetoric, see Nancy S. Struever's incisive statement in *The Language of History in the Renaissance: Rhetoric and Historical Consciousness in Florentine Humanism* (Princeton, NJ: Princeton University Press, 1970), pp. 5–39.

19. See Michael Calvin McGee, "Secular Humanism: A Radical Reading of 'Culture Industry' Productions," *Critical Studies in Mass Communication* 1 (1984): 1–33.

20. Mihailo Markovic, *From Affluence to Praxis: Philosophy and Social Criticism* (Ann Arbor: University of Michigan Press, 1974). This book has a "Forward" by Eric Fromm, whose entire body of work may be seen as a critique of the established order in light of human potential.

21. See my "Introduction" to the new edition of Henri Lefebvre, *Everyday Life in the Modern World* (New York: Transaction Press, 1984).

22. See Alvin Gouldner, *The Dialectic of Ideology and Technology* (New York: Seabury Press, 1976).

23. "At the heart of the debate between the 'old' and 'new' left in France in the late 1960s and early 1970s was a re-evaluation of the role of the critic or 'intellectual.' Sartre identified the May 1968 'events' as pivotal. In the contrast between his 'A Plea for Intellectuals,' lectures delivered at Tokyo and Kyoto in September–October 1965, and 'A Friend of the People,' an interview given in October 1970, may be seen this change" (Jean-Paul Sartre, *Between Existentialism and Marxism* [New York: William Morrow and Company, 1976], pp. 228–298). Michel Foucault attacked the notion of the intellectual as spokesperson for the "universal," contrasting it with the realization that the intellectual, even while critiquing the established order, is part of it. Even while serving the function of "representing" others not able to speak, the intellectual perpetuates "silences" (see "Intellectuals and Power," a conversation with Gilles Deleuze recorded March 4, 1972, in *Michel Foucault: Language, Counter-Memory, Practice*, ed. D. F. Bouchard, trans. D. F. Bouchard and S. Simon [Ithaca, NY: Cornell University Press, 1977], pp. 205–217). For a brilliant attempt to integrate philosophy, criticism, and history, see Arthur Hirsh, *The French New Left: An Intellectual History from Sartre to Gorz* (Boston: South End Press, 1981).

24. Ernesto Grassi, *Rhetoric as Philosophy: Humanist Tradition* (University Park: Pennsylvania State University Press, 1980), p. 113.

25. Megill, "Heidegger, Wander, and Ideology," p. 115.

26. Edwin Black, "The Second Persona," *Quarterly Journal of Speech* 56 (1970): 109–119 (reprinted in this volume).

27. Martin Heidegger, *Poetry, Language, Thought*, trans. Albert Hofstadter (New York: Harper & Row, 1975), p. 34.

28. Megill, "Heidegger, Wander, and Ideology," p. 115.

29. Heidegger, *Poetry, Language, Thought*, pp. 18–19.

30. Ibid., p. 21.

31. V. R. Berghahn, *Modern Germany: Society, Economy, and Politics in the Twentieth Century* (New York: Cambridge University Press, 1982), p. 148.

32. George L. Mosse, ed., *Nazi Culture: Intellectual, Cultural, and Social Life in the Third Reich* (New York: Grosset and Dunlap, 1966), p. 162.

33. "The Widening Gyre: Another Look at Ideology in Wander and His Critics," *Central States Speech Journal* 35 (1984): 54–56. The partiality of a speech, message, formation, or world view may be explained through the "bad faith" of the speaker, the vested interests shaping the process of communication, or simply stand revealed in the structure or silences in the product. The *technique* for conducting an ideological critique must not overshadow its purpose, but Corcoran is quite right about the problems, especially in relation to mass media, of ignoring methods which rise above intent. See his "Television as Ideological Apparatus: The Power and the Pleasure," *Critical Studies in Mass Communication* 1 (1984): 131–145. For another approach to the same problem, see my "Cultural Criticism," in Dan D. Nimmo and Keith R. Sanders, eds., *Handbook of Political Communication* (Beverly Hills, CA: Sage, 1981), pp. 497–528.

34. In his recollection of the events of 1933–1934, when he served as Rector, Heidegger stresses his disillusionment over political pressures placed on the university as well as the political divisions within the university. When he turns to his Rectoral Speech of May 1933, Heidegger reveals his sensitivity to ideological concerns. Minister Wacker, after the rectoral dinner on the same day as the speech, he recalls, commented on the "private" National Socialism it contained, disagreed with the refusal of the idea of a "political science" promoted by the Party, and "above everything else" objected that the whole was not based upon the concept of race. Heidegger reflects on the political consequences of this speech at some length (Martin Heidegger, *The*

Rectorate 1933/4: Facts and Thoughts [unpub. manuscript., n.d.], trans. R. P. Nicholls and Krin Zickler, University of Waterloo, August 1983).

35. Heidegger, *Poetry, Language, Thought*, p. 78. The ambiguity introduced by a sociopolitical context continues in the "Addendum" to these lectures added twenty years later in 1956. Because "Being . . . is a call to man" there is a human relation with regard to art. "The setting-into-work of truth" does not make it clear "who does the setting or in what way it occurs." This, writes Heidegger, referring to *"the relation between Being and human being"* (underlining in the original), has presented a "distressing difficulty" since *Being and Time* (*Poetry, Language, Thought*, pp. 86–87). When the state assumes control of the production, communication, and interpretation of art, and is willing to destroy both the creators of and audiences for certain kinds of art, the connection between Being and human being becomes doubly problematic.

36. Even the peasant in the "desolate" field becomes ideologically significant in context, in the contrast, for example, between Heidegger's figure and both the Party's view of the peasant and its depiction in popular culture. By 1937, according to George Mosse, some 50–75 percent of book sales were for "approved" National Socialist literature, and peasant novels were among the biggest sellers. Josef Berens-Totenohl was a popular novelist of the period. Her novel, *Der Femhof*, published in 1935 and characterized as "typical" of the peasant novel by Mosse, reveals a strong, virtuous, somewhat troubled peasant hero bent on purifying his life, protecting his manor, and lamenting a youthful affair with a dark-eyed, dark-haired, "gypsy" woman he wishes he had killed. Against a background of the official and the popular view of the peasant, Heidegger's stoical woman laboring in bleak surroundings was, more than atypical, antithetical (see Mosse, *Nazi Culture*, pp. 133–140, 168–176). Thus while a "textual" critic may note Heidegger's "quietistic" philosophy and call on the peasant in the "Origin of Art" to support the claim, the scene of desolation and the stoical peasant in the lectures constitute a rejoinder to perhaps even a prediction about the consequences of an optimistic, activist, militarist state.

37. On the attempt, through censorship, official dictionaries, and the like, by the National Socialists to control language itself, see Claus Mueller, *The Politics of Communication: A Study in the Political Sociology of Language, Socialization, and Legitimation* (New York: Oxford University Press, 1973), pp. 25–34.

38. Martin Heidegger, "The Thinker as Poet," in *Poetry, Language, Thought*, p. 11.

39. Michael Schneider, "Fathers and Sons Retrospectively: The Damaged Relationship between Two Generations," *New German Critique* 31 (1984): 5.

PART 6

The Role of Discourse
in Social Change

Rhetoric is central to all efforts to bring about social change, as it is to the maintenance of social stability. It is appropriate, therefore, that the issue of rhetoric's role in social change processes has been a dominant concern of contemporary rhetorical theory. There are, however, many different situations in which social change processes occur, and therefore many different theoretical approaches to the relationship between rhetoric and social change.

The oldest investigations of social change in rhetorical studies focused on the electoral realm. Bruce Gronbeck's essay, "The Functions of Presidential Campaigning," reviews many of the findings of this enduring strand of research. Gronbeck emphasizes that the hostile and negative critiques of presidential campaigns prominent in journalistic commentaries and many academic treatises fail to account for the broader and important ritualistic and collectivizing effects of campaigns. Political campaign rhetoric is important not merely because it helps citizens to choose between candidates, but also because it holds the polity together in a variety of crucial ways. Political campaigns promote participation in the political system, they legitimize the system, they provide grounds for social interaction and aesthetic experiences, and they also serve other functions. Gronbeck's essay thus emphasizes that the effects of rhetoric are not always narrow and immediate, confined to the explicit issues and arguments raised in the discourse, but rather should be understood as broad and sometimes diffuse.

In the late 1960s the civil rights movement, the women's movement, and antiwar protests generated intense scrutiny of a different type of social change process. The label "social movement studies" was applied to investigations of the quasi-organized collectivities that spoke and operated outside of the established political apparatus, pursuing changes in the policies, actions, and structures of the government and society. Herbert W. Simons's essay, "Requirements, Problems, and Strategies: A Theory of Persuasion for Social Movements," was one of the early contributors to this line of research. Simons argued that movement leaders did not simply face the classic set of rhetorical goals—to persuade the public. Instead, the movement leader faced conflicting demands from two different audiences with vastly different expectations: the public and the movement's members. The rhetoric of movement leaders thus manifested a distinctive tension in accounting for the competing demands of different audiences, both of whom were integral to achieving the leader's goals.

The tendency to focus on prominent leaders was only one of the many precepts of classical rhetorical studies that was challenged by Karlyn Kohrs Campbell's essay, "The Rhetoric of Women's Liberation: An Oxymoron." Campbell's analysis of the rhetoric of the women's liberation movement in the 1960s argued that the efforts of women to speak violated such fundamental assumptions of Anglo-American public discourse that their rhetoric radically challenged both the traditional discourse and the classical modes of rhetoric. Campbell pointed out how the consciousness-raising group served as a model for women's liberation rhetoric. Such rhetoric occurred in fundamentally leaderless small groups that focused on raising one's consciousness and thus altering one's identity, rather than on promoting particular policies in the more traditional model of public deliberation. Such rhetoric, and its study, also seriously challenged the classical definition of rhetoric as *public* discourse. In her analysis Campbell highlighted the fact that personal and public discourse are so highly interdependent that it becomes virtually impossible to understand rhetoric as operating solely in the public sphere. Campbell's essay thus stimulated multiple challenges to the classical assumptions of rhetorical studies of social change.

The work of Maurice Charland argues for a continued extension of rhetorical studies in these directions so as to put the disciplines of rhetoric and social theory in closer proximity to one another. In "Rehabilitating Rhetoric: Confronting Blindspots in Discourse and Social Theory" Charland outlines the changes he deems necessary for rhetorical theory to encompass a broader and more productive understanding of the relationship between discourse and social processes in what we might refer to as "postmodern times." So, for example, he urges an understanding of rhetoric and social theory that begins with an expansive notion of culture and society in a mass-mediated world, rather than one that narrowly restricts its scope to the examination of electoral and legislative politics. Although Charland praises rhetorical studies for its contribution in revealing the "structure of reasons in discourse motivating political power and collective action," he argues that rhetorical study needs to be more reflective about the social and institutional forces that give rise to particular political situations and identities in the first place. He suggests that a profitable combination might occur if the rhetorical study of *discourse in action* could be combined with theories that attend to the *social production of discourse*, such as those offered by cultural studies.

Another important essay that urges a more complex undertanding of the relationship between rhetoric and social theory by looking beyond the campaign event or the organized social movement is Michael Calvin McGee's "The 'Ideograph': A Link Between Rhetoric and Ideology." According to McGee, public discourse is not simply a conveyer belt that brings "ideas" to the public; rather, it is a material entity in its own right. To characterize rhetoric or discourse as material is to recognize the substantive effect that it has on an audience at the moment of its impact. And according to McGee, that impact is a direct result of the unique and complex configurations of language—not merely the ideas supposedly "carried" by such language—employed by rhetors at particular moments in time. To this end, McGee encourages the study of the meaning and uses of "ideographs," the key terms that define the ideological contours of a community or collectivity, terms such as "liberty," "property," and "public service." According to McGee, such terms appear in public discourse primarily as a means of warranting or justifying otherwise troubling or problematic acts of collective power. On McGee's account, the key thing to know about an ideograph is that it is not an abstract, timeless ideal to which cultures universally aspire. Rather, the meaning (and effect) of an ideographic term, such as "liberty," is created by the actual discourse in a particular society. Thus, the term "liberty" does not refer to an ideal that means the same thing to all people in all cultures, however distorted its universal meaning might be by different local vocabularies. Rather, as an ideograph, the meaning of "liberty" is specific to a particular rhetorical culture; as the culture changes across time, so too will the range of legitimate meanings accorded to its understanding of "liberty."

Because such ideographs circumscribe the possible identities of the members of the culture and specify what actions the collectivity can take, ideographs constitute the substance of any social group. McGee's theory envisions the shifting contents of the public vocabulary across the centuries as the product of both the tensions and contrasts among many voices and the structural interplay among different vocabularies. He thus understands our contemporary social structures as the product of a history of different and competing usages of different key terms and the resulting social and political relationships that those terms constitute.

Raymie E. McKerrow's widely cited essay, "Critical Rhetoric: Theory and *Praxis*," offers yet a further exploration of the implications and suppositions of extending the study of sociopolitical rhetoric beyond the boundaries of a narrowly drawn situational framework. McKerrow articulates a critical theoretical program that is substantially different from earlier examinations of the rhetorical processes of social change. Whereas the study of political campaigns, social movements, and even ideographic forces have typically been heavily descriptive and explanatory, often narrowly restricting its offices to the consideration of the instrumental and strategic dimensions of rhetoric, McKerrow recalibrates the central goal for rhetorical studies in terms of a critical rhetoric concerned to "unmask and demystify the discourse of power" at the same time that it offers a reconstructive vision of what the society can become, if only for the moment. His essay synthesizes a range of important insights drawn from contemporary rhetorical and social theories to encourage rhetoricians to question more directly the basic terms of the societies in which they live.

Many other avenues have been opened up in social change studies in recent decades. The following list of additional readings provides a starting point for exploring some of these.

Additional Readings

Blair, Carole. (1992). "Contested Histories of Rhetoric: The Politics of Preservation, Progress, and Change." *Quarterly Journal of Speech* 78: 403–428.

Burgess, Parke G. (1968). "The Rhetoric of Black Power: A Moral Demand?" *Quarterly Journal of Speech* 44: 122–133.

Carlson, A. Cheree. (1986). "Gandhi and the Comic Frame: 'Ad Bellum Purificandum.'" *Quarterly Journal of Speech* 72: 446–455.

Hasian, Marouf, Jr., Celeste Michelle Condit, and John Louis Lucaites. (1996). "The Rhetorical Boundaries of 'The Law': A Consideration of the Rhetorical Culture of Legal Practice and the Case of the 'Separate but Equal' Doctrine." *Quarterly Journal of Speech* 82: 323–342.

Lucas, Stephen E. (1988). "The Renaissance of American Public Address: Text and Context in Rhetorical Criticism." *Quarterly Journal of Speech* 74: 241–260.

McGee, Michael Calvin. (1980). "The Origins of 'Liberty': A Feminization of Power." *Communication Monographs* 47: 23–45.

Newman, Robert P. (1975). "Lethal Rhetoric: The Selling of the China Myths." *Quarterly Journal of Speech* 61: 113–128.

Ono, Kent A., and John Sloop. (1992). "Commitment to *Telos*: A Sustained Critical Rhetoric." *Communication Monographs* 59: 48–60.

See also special issues on social movements in the *Central States Speech Journal*, Winter 1980, Spring 1983, and Spring 1991.

Requirements, Problems, and Strategies

A Theory of Persuasion for Social Movements

HERBERT W. SIMONS

Given the usual problems of estimating the effects of a single speech, of assessing the factors that may have produced those effects, and of evaluating the speech in light of the speaker's intent,[1] it is not surprising that few rhetoricians have undertaken the much more difficult task of analyzing the role of persuasion in social movements.[2] When one advances to the movement as a unit of study, these problems are magnified and others are introduced. As any number of currently unemployed college presidents can attest, it is frequently impossible to separate detractors from supporters of a social movement, let alone to discern rhetorical intentions,[3] to distinguish between rhetorical acts and coercive acts,[4] or to estimate the effects of messages on the many audiences to which they must inevitably be addressed. Actions that may succeed with one audience (e.g., solidification of the membership) may alienate others (e.g., provocation of a backlash).[5] For similar reasons, actions that may seem productive over the short run may fail over the long run (the reverse is also true).[6]

Add to these problems of analysis the sheer magnitude of the unit of study: a time span that may extend through several stages[7] for a decade or longer; a host of varied and often unconventional symbols and media;[8] not one leader and one following but several of each (themselves frequently divided into competing factions).[9] Designed for microscopic analysis of particular speeches, the standard tools of rhetorical criticism are ill-suited for unravelling the complexity of discourse in social movements or for capturing its grand flow. Hence it is with good cause that the major contributor to the development of an appropriate methodology has himself cautioned the uninitiated against study of any but the most minute social movements, and then only in the light cast by historical perspective.[10]

Professor Griffin has prescribed a relativistic and essentially clinical process for identifying and evaluating "the pattern of public discussion, the configuration of discourse, the physiognomy of persuasion, peculiar to a movement."[11] Yet the analyst could probably fulfill and even go beyond Griffin's definition of his task if only he could draw more heavily on theory.[12] No theory of persuasion in social movements can as yet be applied predictively to particular cases or tested rigorously through an analysis of such cases. But theory can nevertheless be illuminative. In addition to suggesting categories for descriptive analysis (a skeletal typology of stages, leaders, media, audiences, etc. has already been provided by Griffin),[13] it can indicate—admittedly in general terms—the requirements that rhetoric must fulfill in social movements, the means available to accomplish these requirements, and the kinds of problems that impede accomplishment. By enumerating rhetorical requirements, theory identifies the ends in light of which rhetorical strategies and tactics may be evaluated. By suggesting parameters and directions to the rhetorical critic, theory places him in a better position to bring his own sensitivity and imagination to bear on analyses of particular movements.

This paper is aimed, in preliminary fashion, at providing a leader-centered conception of persuasion in social movements.[14] Rooted in sociological theory, it assumes that the rhetoric of a movement must *follow*, in a general way, from the very nature of social movements. Any movement, it is argued, must fulfill the same functional requirements as more formal collectivities. These imperatives constitute *rhetorical requirements* for the leadership of a movement. Conflicts among requirements create *rhetorical problems*, which in turn affect decisions on *rhetorical strategy*. *The primary rhetorical test of the leader–and, indirectly, of the strategies he employs–is his capacity to fulfill the requirements of his movement by resolving or reducing rhetorical problems.*

A social movement may be defined, combining concepts offered by Smelser and by Turner and Killian, as an uninstitutionalized collectivity that mobilizes for action to implement a program for the reconstitution of social norms or values.[15] Movements should be distinguished, as such, from panics, crazes, booms, fads, and hostile outbursts, as well as from the actions of recognized labor unions, government agencies, business organizations, and other institutionalized decision-making bodies.

The focus of this paper is on reformist and revolutionary movements. Blumer distinguished these "specific" social movements from "general" social movements (amorphous social trends) and from "expressive" social movements, of which religious cults are a prototype.[16] Although geared to specific social movements (and especially to contemporary cases), the theory is applicable with somewhat less consistency to general and expressive movements, perhaps neglected by Blumer's classification scheme, as secessionist movements and movements aimed at the restoration or protection of laws, rules, and/or agencies.[17]

In the pages that follow, examination is made of the necessary functions of reformist and revolutionary rhetoric and of the types of problems that arise from inherently conflicting demands. Presentation of the theory next proceeds to a consideration of alternative strategies of adaptation: the tactics and styles appropriate to each and their respective advantages and disadvantages.

RHETORICAL REQUIREMENTS

Sociological theorists have inferred the functional imperatives of formal organizations from an analysis of their structural characteristics.[18] A social movement is not a formal social structure, but it nevertheless is obligated to fulfill parallel functions.[19] Like the heads of private corporations or government agencies, the leaders of social movements must meet a number of rhetorical requirements, arranged below under three broad headings:

1. *They must attract, maintain, and mold workers (i.e., followers) into an efficiently organized unit.* The survival and effectiveness of any movement are dependent on adherence—to its program, loyalty to its leadership, a collective willingness and capacity to work, energy mobilization, and member satisfaction. A hierarchy of authority and division of labor must be established in which members are persuaded to take orders, to perform menial tasks, and to forego social pleasures. Funds must be raised, literature printed and distributed, local chapters organized, etc.[20]

2. *They must secure adoption of their product by the larger structure* (i.e., the external system, the established order). The product of any movement is its ideology, particularly its program for change.[21] Reformist and revolutionary rhetorics both seize on conditions of real deprivation or on sharp discrepancies between conditions and expectations—the reformist urging change or repair of particular laws, customs, or practices, the revolutionary insisting that a new order and a vast regeneration of values are necessary to smite the agents of the old and to provide happiness, harmony, and stability.[22]

3. *They must react to resistance generated by the larger structure.* The established order may be "too kind" to the movement or it may be too restrictive. It may steal the movement's thunder by anticipating its demands and acting on some of them, by appointing a commission to "study the problem," or by bribing or coopting personnel. On the other hand, it may threaten, harass, or socially ostracize the membership, refuse to recognize or negotiate with the movement, or deny it access to the mass media.[23] The leadership of a social movement must constantly adjust to backlash reactions and pseudosupportive reactions as well as to overreactions by officials on which it may capitalize.

Social movements are severely restricted from fulfilling these requirements by dint of their informal compositions and their positions in relation to the larger society. By comparison to the heads of most formal organizations, the leaders of social movements can expect minimal internal control and maximal external resistance. Whereas business corporations may induce productivity through tangible rewards and punishments, social movements, as voluntary collectivities, must rely on ideological and social commitments from their members. At best, the movement's leadership controls an organized core of the movement (frequently mistaken for the movement itself) but exerts relatively little influence over a relatively larger number of sympathizers on its periphery.[24] Existing outside the larger society's conceptions of justice and reality, moreover, movements threaten and are threatened by the society's sanctions and taboos: its laws, its maxims, its customs governing manners, decorum, and taste, its insignia of authority, etc.

Although organizational efficiency and adaptation to pressures from the external system are clearly prerequisite to promotion of a movement's ideology, in other respects the various internal and external requirements of a movement are incompatible. *Shorn of the controls that characterize formal organizations, yet required to perform the same internal functions, harassed from without, yet obligated to adapt to the external system, the leader of a social movement must constantly balance inherently conflicting demands on his position and on the movement he represents.*

RHETORICAL PROBLEMS

Unless it is understood that the leader is subjected to incompatible demands, a great many of his rhetorical acts must seem counterproductive. An agitator exhorts his following to revolutionary fervor and then propounds conservative solutions to the evils he has depicted.[25] Another leader deliberately disavows the very program he seeks to achieve.[26] A third leader encourages his supporters to carry Viet Cong flags or to "raze the Pentagon" or to heckle another spokesman for the movement, despite advance knowledge that these acts will fragment the movement and invite bitter reactions from outsiders.[27]

On the other hand, the disintegration of a movement may be traced to its failure to meet one or more of the demands incumbent upon it. To deal with pressures from the external system, a movement may lose sight of its ideological values and become preoccupied with power for its own sake.[28] Careful, by contrast, to remain consistent with its values, the movement may forsake those strategies and tactics that are necessary to implement its program.[29] To attract membership support from persons with dissimilar views, the movement may dilute its ideology, become bogged down with peripheral issues, or abandon all substantive concerns and exist solely to provide membership satisfactions.[30]

Short of causing disintegration, the existence of cross-pressures enormously complicates the role of the leader, frequently posing difficult choices between ethical and expediential considerations. The following are illustrative of these dilemmas and of other rhetorical problems created by conflicting demands.

1. When George Wallace vowed, after losing a local election, that he would never again be "out-niggered," he was referring to a phenomenon that has its counterpart on the left as well. Turner and Killian have suggested that strong identification by members with the goals of a movement—however necessary to achieve *esprit de corps*—may foster the conviction that any means are justified and breed impatience with time-consuming tactics. The use of violence and other questionable means may be prompted further by restrictions on legitimate avenues of expression, imposed by the larger structure. Countering these pressures may require that the leader mask the movement's objectives, deny the use of tactics that are socially taboo, promise what he cannot deliver, exaggerate the strength of the movement, etc. A vicious cycle develops in which militant tactics invite further suppression, which spurs the movement on to more extreme methods. Lest the moderate leader object to extremist tactics, he may become a leader without a following.[31]

2. The leader may also need to distort, conceal, exaggerate, etc., in addressing his own supporters. To gain intellectual respectability within and/or outside the movement, ideological statements should be built on a logical framework and appear consistent with verifiable evidence.[32] Yet mass support is more apt to be secured when ideological statements are presented as "generalized beliefs," oversimplified conceptions of social problems, and magical, "if-only" beliefs about solutions.[33] Statements of ideology must provide definition of that which is ambiguous in the social situation, give structure to anxiety and a tangible target for hostility, foster in-group feelings, and articulate wish-fulfillment beliefs about the movement's power to succeed.[34] Hence the use of "god words" and "devil words"[35] as well as "stereotypes, smooth and graphic phrases and folk arguments."[36]

Among isolated individuals, those anxiety, hostility, and wish-fulfillment beliefs that are socially taboo are likely to be repressed or inhibited. They are expressed unconsciously, or if consciously, only to one's self, or if expressed to others, said more to expunge feelings than to share them.[37] What is largely expressive for the isolated individual is rhetorical for the movement's leadership. Particularly in militant movements, the leader wins and maintains adherents by saying to them what they cannot say to others or even to themselves. A major rhetorical process, then, consists of legitimizing privately-held feelings by providing social support and rationalizations for those feelings.

Apart from placing a strain on the ideological values of the movement and its leaders, the deliberate use of myths, deceptions, etc. creates practical problems. When outsiders discover that the size of the membership has been exaggerated or when followers learn that they are far from united, the leader must invent rationalizations for his deceptions through a new rhetoric of justification or apology. Worst of all, the leadership may come to believe its own falsehoods. As Kenneth Keniston has noted, "Movement groups . . . tend to develop strong barriers on their outside boundaries, which impede communication and movement outside the group; they frequently exhibit an 'anti-empirical' inability to use facts in order to counter emotion-based distortions and impressions; interaction within the group often has a quality of 'surreality.'"[38]

3. Pressures for organizational efficiency are incompatible with membership needs. An energized membership is the strength of any movement and its *esprit de corps* is essential to goal implementation. Yet morale cannot be secured through abdications of leadership. Members may feel the need to participate in decision-making, to undertake pet projects on their own initiatives, to "put down" leaders or other followers, to obstruct meetings by socializing, or to disobey directives. The leadership cannot ignore these needs; yet it cannot accede to all of them either. The problem is especially acute in movements that distrust authority and value participatory democracy. During the hectic days of Vietnam Summer, according to Keniston, the secretarial staff of the central office demanded and received equal status and responsibilities with a seasoned political staff. As a result, experienced organizers were forced to perform menial chores while the former clerical workers advised local projects.[39]

4. The leaders of social movements face discrepancies between role expectations and role definitions. The leader must appear to be what he cannot be. Expected to be consistent, for example, he must nevertheless be prepared to renounce previously championed positions. Expected to be sincere and spontaneous, he must handle dilemmas with consummate manipulative skill. When, in one year, Malcolm X broke with Elijah Muhammad, shifted positions on integration and participation in civil rights demonstrations, and confessed his uncertainties on other issues, he inevitably alienated some followers and invited charges of weakness and inconsistency from his enemies.[40] When Allard Lowenstein politicked with student groups in behalf of Senator Eugene McCarthy, he had to seem as unlike a "pol" as possible.[41]

5. The leader must adapt to several audiences simultaneously. In an age of mass media, rhetorical utterances addressed to one audience are likely to reach others. Outsiders include those who are sympathetic, indifferent, and opposed. As shall later be argued, another key variable is the extent to which those in the larger structure are susceptible to threats of force. Within the movement interfactional conflicts invariably develop over questions of value, strategy, tactics, or implementation. Purists and pragmatists clash over the merits of compromise. Academics and activists debate the necessity of long-range planning. Others enter the movement with personal grievances or vested interests. Preexisting groups, known to have divergent ideological positions,

are nevertheless invited to join or affiliate with the movement because of the power they can wield.[42]

6. Movements require a diversity of leadership types with whom any one leader must both compete and cooperate.[43] Theoreticians, agitators, and propagandists must launch the movement; political and bureaucratic types must carry it forward. Ideological differences among the leadership must also be expected insofar as the leadership reflects internal divisions among the following. Finally, there may well be cleavages among those vested with positions of legitimate authority, those charismatic figures who have personal followings, those who have special competencies, and those who have private sources of funds or influence outside the movement. Much of the leader's persuasive skill is exhibited in private interactions with other leaders.

RHETORICAL STRATEGIES

From the foregoing discussion it should be quite clear that the leader of a social movement must thread his way through an intricate web of conflicting demands. How he adapts strategies to demands constitutes a primary basis for evaluating his rhetorical output. Along a continuum from the sweet and reasonable to the violently revolutionary, one may identify *moderate, intermediate,* and *militant* types of strategies, each with its own appropriate tactics and styles.

Little needs to be said about the strategy of the moderate. His is the pattern of peaceful persuasion rhetoricians know best and characteristically prescribe, the embodiment of reason, civility, and decorum in human interaction. Dressed in the garb of respectability and exhibiting Ivy League earnestness and midwestern charm, the moderate gets angry but does not shout, issues pamphlets but never manifestos, inveighs against social mores but always in the value language of the social order. His "devil" is a condition or a set of behaviors or an outcast group, never the persons he is seeking to influence. They, rather, are part of his "we" group, united if only by lip-service adherence to his symbols. In textbook terms, the moderate adapts to the listener's needs, wants, and values; speaks his language; adjusts to his frame of reference; reduces the psychological distance between his movement and the larger structure. Roy Wilkins exemplified the approach when he argued that the "prime, continuing racial policy looking toward eradication of inequities must be one of winning friends and influencing people among the white majority."[44]

If moderates assume or pretend to assume an ultimate identity of interests between the movement and the larger structure, militants act on the assumption of a fundamental clash of interests. If moderates employ rhetoric as an alternative to force, militants use rhetoric as an expression, an instrument, and an act of force. So contradictory are the rhetorical conceptions of moderate and militant strategists that it strains the imagination to believe that both may work. Yet the decisive changes wrought by militant rhetorics in recent years gives credence to the view that the traditionally prescribed pattern is not the only viable alternative.

The core characteristic of militant strategists is that they seek to change the actions of their primary targets as a precondition for changes in attitudes.[45] By means of direct-action techniques and verbal polemics, militants threaten, harass, cajole, disrupt, provoke, intimidate, coerce. Hostility is also expressed in dress, manners, dialect, gestures, in-group slogans, and ceremonies.[46] Although the aim of pressure tactics may be to punish directly (e.g., strikes, boycotts), more frequently they are forms of "body rhetoric," designed to dramatize issues, enlist additional sympathizers, and delegitimatize the established order.[47] The targets of sit-ins, sleep-ins, and other confrontational activities are invited to participate in a drama of self-exposure. Should they reject militant demands, they may be forced to unmask themselves through punitive countermeasures, thus helping to complete the rhetorical act.[48] Confrontation, according to Scott and Smith, "dissolves the line between marches, sit-ins, demonstrations, acts of physical violence, and aggressive discourse. In this way it informs us of the essential nature of discourse itself as human action."[49]

Militant and moderate strategies are antithetical, yet each has highly desirable characteristics. Decisions to employ "intermediate" strategies may be viewed as efforts to obtain the following advantages of each while still avoiding their respective disadvantages. Once again, the following dilemmas derive from conflicting rhetorical requirements.

1. Militant tactics confer visibility on a movement; moderate tactics gain entry into decision centers. Because of their ethos of respectability, moderates are invited to participate in public deliberations (hearings, conferences, negotiating sessions, etc.), even after militants have occasioned those deliberations by prolonged and self-debilitating acts of protest. On the other hand, the militant has readier access to the masses. Robert C. Weaver has lamented that "today, a publicized spokesman may be the individual who can devise the most militant cry and the leader one who can articulate the most far-out position."[50]

2. For different reasons, militants and moderates must both be ambivalent about "successes" and "failures." Militants thrive on injustice and ineptitude by the larger structure. Should the enemy fail to implement the movement's demands, the militant is vindicated ideologically, yet frustrated programmatically. Should some of the demands be met, he is in the paradoxical position of having to condemn them as palliatives. The moderate, by contrast, requires tangible evidence that the larger structure is tractable in order to hold followers in line; yet "too much" success belies the movement's reason for being.

3. Militant supporters are easily energized; moderate supporters are more easily controlled. Having aroused their following, the leaders of a militant movement frequently become victims of their own creation, Robespierres and Dantons who can no longer contain energies within prescribed limits or guarantee their own tenure.[51] On the other hand, moderate leaders frequently claim that their supporters are apathetic. As Turner and Killian have pointed out: "To the degree to which a movement incorporates only major sacred values its power will be diffused by a large body of conspicuous lip-service adherents who cannot be depended upon for the work of the movement."[52]

4. Militants are effective with "power-vulnerables"; moderates are effective with "power-invulnerables"; neither is effective with both.

As the writer has argued in an earlier article, a distinction needs to be made between two objects of influence.[53] Persons most vulnerable to pressure tactics are the leaders of public and quasi-public institutions: elected and appointed government officials who may be removed from office or given an unfavorable press; church and university leaders who are obliged to apply "high-minded" standards in dealing with protests; executives of large corporations whose businesses are susceptible to loss of income and who are publicly committed to an ethic of social responsibility.

"Power-invulnerables" are those who have little or nothing to lose by publicly voicing their prejudices and acting on their self-concerns. With respect to the movement for black equality:

> They are the mass of white Americans who are largely unaffected by rent strikes and boycotts and who have so far defended their neighborhood sanctuaries or have physically and psychologically withdrawn to the suburbs. The average American may fear riots but he can escape from them. He may or may not approve of boycotts and demonstrations but in either case he is largely unaffected by them. He is subject to legislation but in most cases until now he has been able to circumvent it. Only through communications aimed at a change in his attitudes or through carefully formulated and tightly enforced government policies can his actions be appreciably modified.[54]

By reducing the psychological distance between the movement and the external structure, the moderate is likely to win sympathizers, even among "power-vulnerables." But as those in positions of power allocate priorities (they, too, are subjected to conflicting demands), they are unlikely to translate sympathy into action unless pressured to do so. Should the leader of a movement strike militant postures, he is likely to actuate "power-vulnerables" but at the same time prompt backlash groups to apply their own pressure tactics.

Where the movement and the larger structure are already polarized, the dilemma is magnified. However much he may wish to plead reasonably, wresting changes from those in public positions requires that the leader build a sizable power base. And to secure massive internal support, the leader must at least *seem* militant.

So the leader of a social movement may attempt to avoid or resolve the aforementioned dilemmas by employing "intermediate" strategies, admittedly a catchall term for those efforts that combine militant and moderate patterns of influence. The leader may alternate between carrot and stick or speak softly in private and stridently at mass gatherings. He may form broadly based coalitions that submerge ideological differences or utilize spokesmen with similar values but contrasting styles. Truly the exemplar of oxymoronic postures, he may stand as a "conservative radical" or a "radical conservative," espousing militant demands in the value language of the established order or militant slogans in behalf of moderate proposals. In defense of militancy, he may portray himself as a brakeman, a finger in the dike holding back an angry tide. In defense of more moderate tactics, he may hold back an angry tide without loss of reputation, as Jerry Rubin and Abbie Hoffman did in urging nonviolence on their "Yippie" following during the Democratic Convention in Chicago: "We are a revolutionary new community and we must protect our community. . . . We, not they, will decide when the battle begins. . . . We are not going into their jails and we aren't going to shed our blood. We're too important for that. We've got too much work to do."[55]

Intermediacy can be a dangerous game. Calculated to energize supporters, win over neutrals, pressure power-vulnerables, and mollify the opposition, it may end up antagonizing everyone. The well-turned phrase may easily appear as a devilish trick, the rationale as a rationalization, the tactful comment as an artless dodge. To the extent that strategies of intermediacy require studied ambiguity, insincerity, and even distortion, perhaps the leader's greatest danger is that others may find out what he really thinks.

Still, some strategists manage to reconcile differences between militant and moderate approaches and not simply to maneuver around them. They seem able to convince the established order that bad-tasting medicine is good for it and seem capable, too, of mobilizing a diverse collectivity within the movement.

The key, it would appear, is the leader's capacity to embody a higher wisdom, a more profound sense of justice; to stand above inconsistencies by articulating over-arching principles. Few will contest the claim that Martin Luther King Jr. epitomized the approach. Attracting both militants and moderates to his movement, King could win respect, even from his enemies, by reconciling the seemingly irreconcilable. The heart of the case for intermediacy was succinctly stated by King himself in a speech which Professor Robert Scott has analyzed: "What is needed is a realization that power without love is reckless and abusive and love without power is sentimental and anemic. Power at its best is love implementing the demands of justice, and justice at its best is power correcting everything that stands against love."[56]

Viewed broadly, the great contemporary movements all seem to require combinations of militant and moderate strategies. Tom Hayden can be counted upon to dramatize the Vietnam issue; Arthur Schlesinger, to plead forcefully within inner circles. Threats of confrontation may prompt school boards to finance the building of new facilities in ghetto areas, but it may take reasonableness and civility to get experienced teachers to volunteer for work in those facilities. Demands by revolutionary student groups for total transformations of university structures may impel administrators to heed quasi-militant demands for a redistribution of university power. Support for the cause by moderate groups may confer respectability on the movement. Thus, however much they may war amongst themselves, militants and moderates each perform essential functions.

SUMMARY

This paper has attempted to provide a broad framework within which persuasion in social movements, particularly reformist and revolutionary movements, may be analyzed. Derived in large measure from sociological theory and from an examination of contemporary cases, it has examined rhetorical processes from the perspective of the leader of a movement: the requirements he must fulfill, the problems he faces, the strategies he may adopt to meet those requirements.

What emerges most sharply from the foregoing discussion are the extraordinary rhetorical dilemmas confronting those who would lead social movements. Movements are as susceptible to fragmentation from within as they are to suppression from without. Impelled to fulfill the same internal and external requirements as the heads of most formal organizations, their leaders can expect greater resistance to their efforts from both insiders and outsiders. The needs of individual members are frequently incompatible with organizational imperatives; appeals addressed to the intelligentsia of a movement incompatible with appeals addressed to the masses; the values for which the movement stands incompatible with tactical necessities. In the face of these and other problems, the leader may adopt the traditionally prescribed tactics and style of the moderate or those of his more militant counterpart. Yet the choice between moderate and militant strategies introduces still other dilemmas. The great leaders (and the great movements) seem capable of combining these seemingly antithetical strategies without inconsistency by justifying their use with appeals to higher principles.

Notes

1. See, e.g., Lester Thonssen and A. Craig Baird, *Speech Criticism* (New York, 1948), chap. 17.

2. For the decade prior to the writing of his text, Professor Edwin Black found only three such studies reported in *QJS* or *Speech Monographs*; see his *Rhetorical Criticism: A Study in Method* (New York, 1965), pp. 22–23.

3. For a discussion of the problem of discerning intent, see Rudolf Heberle, *Social Movements* (New York, 1951), pp. 94–95. According to Lang and Lang, "The ideology presented to the mass of followers is a 'mask' for the real beliefs of the inner core. Its 'real' ideology is hidden from all but the initiated"; see Kurt Lang and Gladys Engel Lang, *Collective Dynamics* (New York, 1961), p. 539.

4. To understand the rhetoric of a militant movement requires an analysis of force as the backdrop against which communication frequently takes place and similarly requires an analysis of communication, not as an alternative to force, but as an instrument of force. Four recent articles in *QJS* have dealt with the problem and the questions of ethics raised by it. See Parke G. Burgess, "The Rhetoric of Black Power: A Moral Demand?," *QJS* 44 (1968): 122–133; Franklyn S. Haiman, "The Rhetoric of the Streets: Some Legal and Ethical Considerations," *QJS* 53 (1967): 99–114; James R. Andrews, "Confrontation at Columbia: A Case Study in Coercive Rhetoric," *QJS* 55 (1969): 9–16; and Robert L. Scott and Donald K. Smith, "The Rhetoric of Confrontation," *QJS* 55 (1969): 1–8.

5. One variant of the problem is discussed by Wayne E. Brockriede and Robert L. Scott, in "Stokely Carmichael: Two Speeches on Black Power," *Central States Speech Journal* 19 (1968): 3–13.

6. The problems of estimating long-range effects are nicely illustrated in Howard H. Martin's appraisal of the effects of the antiwar "teach-ins"; see "Rhetoric of Academic Protest," *Central States Speech Journal* 17 (1966): 244–250.

7. For a classic typology of stages, see Carl A. Dawson and Warner E. Gettys, *An Introduction to Sociology*, rev. ed. (New York, 1935), chap. 19.

8. For an intriguing analysis of nonobvious symbols, see Hugh D. Duncan, *Communication and Social Order* (New York, 1962).

9. For example, during its heyday, the civil rights movement encompassed SNCC, CORE, and the NAACP, each of which was torn by internal fragmentation.

10. Leland M. Griffin, "The Rhetoric of Historical Movements," *QJS* 38 (1952): 184–188.

11. Ibid., p. 185.

12. Griffin has suggested that the development of theory must await further research. Yet there is reason to believe, here as elsewhere, that theory and research must develop apace of each other. As Black has argued (*Rhetorical Criticism*, p. 22), the researcher can do little without a framework for analysis.

13. Griffin, "Rhetoric of Historical Movements," pp. 185–187.

14. Consistent with Scott and Smith's view of rhetoric as *managed* public discourse ("Rhetoric of Confrontation," p. 8), the paper focuses on the intentional symbolic acts of those who lead social movements. Emphasis on more spontaneous acts of communication (rumor, milling, social contagion, etc. by nonleaders) has been provided by those who have stressed the primitive features of social movements. The "classic" study is Gustave Le Bon's *The Crowd: A Study of the Popular Mind* (London, 1897).

15. Neil J. Smelser, *Theory of Collective Behavior* (New York, 1962), pp. 110 and 129–130, and Ralph H. Turner and Lewis M. Killian, *Collective Behavior* (Englewood Cliffs, NJ, 1957), p. 308.

16. Herbert Blumer, "Social Movements," in A. M. Lee, ed., *New Outline of the Principles of Sociology* (New York, 1946), pp. 200, 202, and 214.

17. Any classification of social movements must have arbitrary features. For other categorizations, see Lang and Lang, *Collective Dynamics*, pp. 497–505.

18. See, for example, Chester I. Barnard, *The Functions of the Executive* (Cambridge, MA, 1938) and Robert K. Merton, *Social Theory and Social Structure* (Glencoe, IL, 1949).

19. According to Lang and Lang (*Collective Dynamics*, p. 493), it is the quasi-structural character of social movements that distinguishes them from formal organizations on the one hand and spontaneous mass behavior on the other. Although claiming to stress the nonstructural aspects of social movements, Lang and Lang have provided the most adequate account of their structural imperatives; see pp. 495–496 and 531–537. See also C. Wendell King, *Social Movements in the United States* (New York, 1956).

20. See H. H. Gerth and C. Wright Mills, eds., *From Max Weber: Essays in Sociology* (New York, 1946); Barnard, *Functions of the Executive* ; Peter M. Blau, *The Dynamics of Bureaucracy* (Chicago, 1955); and Philip Selznick, *TVA and the Grass Roots* (Berkeley and Los Angeles, 1949).

21. Blumer, "Social Movements," pp. 210–211.

22. See Smelser, *Theory of Collective Behavior*, pp. 109–110 and 121–122.

23. Ibid., pp. 282–286.

24. Lang and Lang, *Collective Dynamics*, p. 495.

25. See Christopher Lasch on Stokely Carmichael, in "The Trouble with Black Power," *New York Review of Books*, February 29, 1968, pp. 4–14.

26. According to Turner and Killian (*Collective Behavior*, p. 337), this is the usual case for revolutionary movements. They are forced to retain several identities. The same should also be true of retrogressive movements. See, for example, Henry Kraus, *The Many and the Few* (Los Angeles, 1947).

27. See Norman Mailer, "The Steps of the Pentagon," *Harper's Magazine*, March 1968, pp. 47–142. Mailer described the disruptive effects of Yippie leaders on "straights."

28. The "iron law of oligarchy" may be overstated, but it is not without merit. See Turner and Killian, *Collective Behavior*, p. 372.

29. Norman Mailer and others have ascribed just this failure to Eugene McCarthy. See "Miami Beach and the Siege of Chicago," *Harper's Magazine*, November 1968, pp. 41–130. Cf. pp. 77 and 93.

30. See, e.g., Sheldon L. Messinger, "Organizational Transformation: A Case Study of a Declining Social Movement," *American Sociological Review* 20 (1955): 3–10.

31. Turner and Killian, *Collective Behavior*, p. 373.

32. Blumer, "Social Movements," p. 210.

33. Smelser, *Theory of Collective Behavior*, p. 82.

34. The writer has inferred these rhetorical functions from Smelser's thorough analysis of the belief components common to all forms of collective behavior and to social movements in particular (*Theory of Collective Behavior*, pp. 79–130, 292–296, and 348–352). For comparable statements of these leadership requirements, see Eric Hoffer, *The True Believer* (New York, 1951).

35. See Leland M. Griffin's use of the terms in his "The Rhetorical Structure of the 'New Left' Movement: Part 1," *QJS* 50 (1964): 113–135. According to Eric Hoffer (*True Believer*, p. 89), "Mass movements can rise and spread without belief in a God, but never without belief in a devil."

36. Blumer, "Social Movements," p. 210.

37. For a discussion of such nonrhetorical speech functions, see, e.g., Jon Eisenson, J. Jeffery Auer, and John V. Irwin, *The Psychology of Communication*, rev. ed. (New York, 1963), pp. 20–29.

38. Kenneth Keniston, *Young Radicals: Notes on Committed Youth* (New York, 1968), p. 159.

39. Ibid., pp. 160–161.

40. See Malcolm X, as told to Alex Haley, *The Autobiography of Malcolm X* (New York, 1965).

41. See David Halberstam, "The Man Who Ran Against Lyndon Johnson," *Harper's Magazine*, December 1968, pp. 47–66.

42. For a discussion of other intramovement divisions, see Smelser, *Theory of Collective Behavior*, pp. 302–306 and 361–364.

43. Like Margaret Sanger or Martin Luther King Jr., the same leader may encompass all or almost all of the necessary roles. This is rare, however. See Turner and Killian, *Collective Behavior*, pp. 472–476.

44. "What Now?—One Negro Leader's Answer," *New York Times Magazine*, August 16, 1964, p. 11.

45. Considerable experimental evidence suggests that where actions and attitudes are discrepant, the latter are more likely to change. See Ralph L. Rosnow and Edward J. Robinson, *Experiments in Persuasion* (New York, 1967), pp. 297–308.

46. In the "black power" movement, for example, what may actually be most frightening to whites are its nonprogrammatic symbols: faded levis, "hang loose" manners, clenched-fist salutes, the "honkie" epithet, "soul" and "brother" identifications, the ritual handshake, etc. For an excellent analysis of nonverbal symbolism among black militants, see Ulf Hannerz, "The Rhetoric of Soul: Identification in Negro Society," *Race* 9 (1968): 453–465.

47. See, e.g., John R. Searle, "A Foolproof Scenario for Student Revolts," *New York Times Magazine*, December 29, 1968, pp. 4–5 and 12–15; Daniel Walker, *Rights in Conflict* (New York, 1968), chaps. 2 and 3; and Herbert W. Simons, "Confrontation as a Pattern of Persuasion in University Settings," *Central States Speech Journal* 20 (1969): 163–169.

48. See Scott and Smith, "Rhetoric of Confrontation," p. 8.

49. Ibid., p. 7.

50. *Philadelphia Bulletin*, March 2, 1966, p. 3. See also Paul L. Fisher and Ralph L. Lowenstein, *Race and the News Media* (New York, 1967).

51. Walker, *Rights in Conflict*, pp. 49–51.

52. Turner and Killian, *Collective Behavior*, p. 337.

53. Herbert W. Simons, "Patterns of Persuasion in the Civil Rights Struggle," *Today's Speech* 15 (1967): 25–27.

54. Ibid., p. 26.

55. Quoted in Walker, *Rights in Conflict*, pp. 136–137.

56. Quoted in Robert L. Scott, "Black Power Bends Martin Luther King," *Speaker and Gavel* 5 (1968): 84.

The Rhetoric of Women's Liberation

An Oxymoron

KARLYN KOHRS CAMPBELL

Whatever the phrase "women's liberation" means, it cannot, as yet, be used to refer to a cohesive historical–political movement. No clearly defined program or set of policies unifies the small, frequently transitory groups that compose it, nor is there much evidence of organizational unity and cooperation.[1] At this point in time, it has produced only minor changes in American society,[2] although it has made the issues with which it is associated major topics of concern and controversy. As some liberation advocates admit, it is a "state of mind" rather than a movement. Its major manifestation has been rhetorical, and as such, it merits rhetorical analysis.

Because any attempt to define a rhetorical movement or genre is beset by difficulties, and because of the unusual status of women's liberation I have briefly described, I wish to state explicitly two presuppositions informing what follows. First, I reject historical and sociopsychological definitions of movements as the basis for rhetorical criticism on the grounds that they do not, in fact, isolate a genre of *rhetoric* or a distinctive body of *rhetorical acts*.[3] The criteria defining a rhetorical movement must be rhetorical; in Aristotelian terminology, such criteria might arise from the relatively distinctive use or interpretation of the canons and modes of proof. However, rather than employing any codified critical scheme, I propose to treat two general categories— substance and style. In my judgment, the rhetoric of women's liberation (or any other body of discourses) merits *separate* critical treatment if, and only if, the symbolic acts of which it is composed can be show to be distinctive on both substantive and stylistic grounds. Second, I presume that the style and substance of a genre of rhetoric are interdependent.[4] Stylistic choices are deeply influenced by subject matter and context,[5] and issues are formulated and shaped by stylistic strategies.[6] The central argument of this essay is that the rhetoric of women's liberation is a distinctive genre because it evinces unique *rhetorical* qualities that are a fusion of substantive and stylistic features.

DISTINCTIVE SUBSTANTIVE FEATURES

At first glance, demands for legal, economic, and social equality for women would seem to be a reiteration, in a slightly modified form, of arguments already familiar from the protest rhetoric of students and blacks. However, on closer examination, the fact that equality is being demanded *for women* alters the rhetorical picture drastically. Feminist advocacy unearths tensions woven deep into the fabric of our society and provokes an unusually intense and profound "rhetoric of moral conflict."[7] The sex role requirements for women contradict the dominant values of American culture—self-reliance, achievement, and independence.[8] Unlike most other groups, the social status of women is defined primarily by birth, and their social position is at odds with fundamental democratic values.[9] In fact, insofar as the role of rhetor entails qualities of self-reliance, self-confidence, and independence, *its very assumption is a violation of the female role.* Consequently, feminist rhetoric is substantively unique by definition, because no matter how traditional its argumentation, how justificatory its form, how discursive its method, or how scholarly its style, it attacks the entire psychosocial reality, the most fundamental values, of the cultural context in which it occurs. As illustration, consider the apparently moderate, reformist demands by feminists for legal, economic, and social equality—demands ostensibly based on the shared value of equality. (As presented here, each of these demands is a condensed version of arguments from highly traditional discourses by contemporary liberationists.)

The demand for legal equality rises out of a conflict in values. Women are not equal to men in the sight of the law. In 1874 the Supreme Court ruled that "some citizens could be denied rights which others had," specifically, that "the 'equal protection' clause of the Fourteenth Amendment did not give women equal rights with men," and reaffirmed this decision in 1961, stating that "the Fourteenth Amendment prohibits any arbitrary class legislation, except that based on sex."[10] The legal inferiority of women is most apparent in marriage laws. The core of these laws is that spouses have reciprocal—not equal—rights and duties. The husband must maintain the wife and children, but the amount of support beyond subsistence is at his discretion. In return, the wife is legally required to do the domestic chores, provide marital companionship, and sexual consortium but has no claim for direct compensation for any of the services rendered. Fundamentally, marriage is a property relationship. In the nine community property states, the husband is considered the head of the "community," and so long as he is capable of managing it, the wife, acting alone, cannot contract debts chargeable to it. In Texas and Nevada, the husband can even dispose of the property without his wife's consent, property that includes the income of a working wife. The forty-one common law states do not recognize the economic contribution of a wife who works only in the home. She has no right to an allowance, wages, or income of any sort, nor can she claim joint ownership upon divorce. In addition, every married woman's surname is legally that of her husband, and no court will uphold her right to go by another name.[11]

It seems to me that any audience of such argumentation confronts a moral dilemma. The listener must either admit that this is not a society based on the value of equality or make the overt assertion that women are special or inferior beings who merit discriminatory treatment.[12]

The argument for economic equality follows a similar pattern. Based on median income, it is a greater economic disadvantage to be female than to be black or poorly educated (of course, any combination of these spells economic disaster). Although half of the states have equal pay laws, dual pay scales are the rule. These cannot be justified economically because, married or single, the majority of women who work do so out of economic necessity, and some 40 percent of families with incomes below the poverty level are headed by women. Occupationally, women are proportionately more disadvantaged today than they were in 1940, and the gap between male and female income steadily increases.[13] It might seem that these data merely indicate a discrepancy between law and practice—at least the value is embodied in some laws—although separating values and behavior is somewhat problematic. However, both law and practice have made women economically unequal. For example, so long as the law, as well as common practice, gives the husband a right to the domestic services of his wife, a woman must perform the equivalent of two jobs in order to hold one outside the home.[14] Once again, the audience of such argumentation confronts a moral dilemma.

The most overt challenge to cultural values appears in the demand for social or sexual equality, that we dispense forever with the notion that "men are male *humans* whereas women are human *females*,"[15] a notion enshrined in the familiar phrase, "I now pronounce you *man* and wife." An obvious reason for abolishing such distinctions is that they lead to cultural values for men as men and women as wives. Success for men is defined as instrumental, productive labor in the outside world whereas "wives" are confined to "woman's place"—child care and domestic labor in the home.[16] As long as these concepts determine "masculinity" and "femininity," the woman who strives for the kind of success defined as the exclusive domain of the male is inhibited by norms prescribing her "role" and must pay a heavy price for her deviance. Those who have done research on achievement motivation in women conclude that: "Even when legal and educational barriers to achievement are removed, the motive to avoid success will continue to inhibit women from doing 'too well'—thereby risking the possibility of being socially rejected as 'unfeminine' or 'castrating.'"[17] And "the girl who maintains qualities of independence and active striving (achievement-orientation) necessary for intellectual mastery defies the conventions of sex appropriate behavior and must pay a price, *a price in anxiety*."[18] As long as education and socialization cause women to be "unsexed" by success whereas men are "unsexed" by failure, women cannot compete on equal terms or develop their individual potentials. No values, however, are more deeply engrained than those defining "masculinity" and "femininity." The fundamental conflict in values is evident.

Once their consequences and implications are understood, these apparently moderate, reformist demands are rightly seen as revolutionary and radical in the extreme. They threaten the institutions of marriage and the family and norms governing childrearing and male-female roles. To meet them would require major, even revolutionary, social change.[19] It should be emphasized, however, that these arguments are drawn from discourses that could not be termed confrontative, alienating, or radical in any ordinary sense. In form, style, structure, and supporting materials, they would meet the demands of the strictest Aristotelian critic. Yet they are substantively unique, inevitably radical, because they attack the fundamental values underlying this culture. The option to be moderate and reformist is simply not available to women's liberation advocates.

DISTINCTIVE STYLISTIC FEATURES

As a rhetoric of intense moral conflict, it would be surprising indeed if distinctive stylistic features did not appear as strategic adaptations to a difficult rhetorical situation.[20] I propose to treat "stylistic features" rather broadly, electing to view women's liberation as a persuasive campaign. In addition to the linguistic features usually considered, the stylistic features of a persuasive campaign include, in my view, characteristic modes of rhetorical interaction, typical ways of structuring the relationships among participants in a rhetorical transaction, and emphasis on particular forms of argument, proof, and evidence. The rhetoric of women's liberation is distinctive stylistically in rejecting certain traditional concepts of the rhetorical process—as persuasion of the many by an expert or leader, as adjustment or adaptation to audience norms, and as directed toward inducing acceptance of a specific program or a commitment to group action. This rather "antirhetorical" style is chosen on substantive grounds because rhetorical transactions with these features encourage submissiveness and passivity in the audience[21]—qualities at odds with a fundamental goal of feminist advocacy: self-determination. The paradigm that highlights the distinctive stylistic features of women's liberation is "consciousness raising," a mode of interaction or a type of rhetorical transaction uniquely adapted to the rhetorical problem of feminist advocacy.

The rhetorical problem may be summarized as follows: women are divided from one another by almost all the usual sources of identification—age, education, income, ethnic origin, even geography. In addition, counter-persuasive forces are pervasive and potent—nearly all spend their lives in close proximity to and under the control of males—fathers, husbands, employers, and so on. Women also have very negative self-concepts, so negative, in fact, that it is difficult to view them as an audience, i.e., persons who see themselves as potential agents of change. When asked to select adjectives to describe themselves, they select such terms as "uncertain, anxious, nervous, hasty, careless, fearful, dull, childish, helpless, sorry, timid, clumsy, stupid, silly, and domestic . . . understanding, tender, sympathetic, pure, generous, affectionate, loving, moral, kind, grateful, and patient."[22] If a persuasive campaign directed to this audience is to be effective, it must transcend alienation to create "sisterhood," modify self-concepts to create a sense of autonomy, and speak to women in terms of private, concrete, individual experience, because women have little, if any, publicly shared experience. The substantive problem of the absence of shared values remains: when women become part of an audience for liberation rhetoric, they violate the norms governing sex appropriate behavior.

In its paradigmatic form, "consciousness raising" involves meetings of small, leaderless groups in which each person is encouraged to express her personal feelings and experience. There is no leader, rhetor, or expert. All participate and lead; all are considered expert. The goal is to make the personal political: to create awareness (through shared experiences) that what were thought to be personal deficiencies and individual problems are common and shared, a result of their position as women. The participants seek to understand and interpret their lives as women, but there is no "message," no "party line." Individuals are encouraged to dissent, to find their own truths. If action is suggested, no group commitment is made; each must decide whether, and if so which, action is suitable for her.[23] The stylistic features heightened in this kind of transaction are characteristic of the rhetoric as a whole: affirmation of the affective, of the validity of personal experience, of the necessity for self-exposure and self-criticism, of the value of dialogue, and of the goal of autonomous, individual decision making. These stylistic features are very similar to those Maurice Natanson has described as characteristic of genuine argumentation:

What is at issue, really, in the risking of the self in genuine argument is the immediacy of the self's world of feeling, attitude, and the total subtle range of its affective and conative sensibility. . . . I open myself to the viable possibility that the consequence of an argument may be to make me *see* something of the structure of my immediate world . . . the personal and immediate domain of individual experience. . . .

. . . feeling is a way of meaning as much as thinking is a way of formulating. Privacy is a means of establishing a world, and what genuine argument to persuade does is to publicize that privacy. The metaphor leads us to suggest that risking the self in argument is inviting a stranger to the interior familiarity of our home.[24]

Even a cursory reading of the numerous anthologies of women's liberation rhetoric will serve to confirm that the stylistic features I have indicated are characteristic. Particularly salient examples include Elizabeth Janeway's *Man's World; Woman's Place*, "The Demise of the Dancing Dog,"[25] "The Politics of Housework,"[26] *A Room of One's Own*,[27] and "Cutting Loose."[28] The conclusion of the last essay cited will serve as a model:

The true dramatic conclusion of this narrative should be the dissolution of my marriage; there is a part of me which believes that you cannot fight a sexist system while acknowledging your need for the love of a man. . . . But in the end my husband and I did not divorce. . . . Instead I raged against him for many months and joined the Woman's Liberation Movement, and thought a great deal about myself, and about whether my problems were truly all women's problems, and decided that some of them were and that some of them were not. My sexual rage was the most powerful single emotion of my life, and the feminist analysis has become for me, as I think it will for most women of my generation, as significant an intellectual tool as Marxism was for generations of radicals. But it does not answer every question. . . . I would be lying if I said that my anger had taught me how to live. But my life has changed because of it. I think I am becoming in many small ways a woman who takes no shit. I am no longer submissive, no longer seductive. . . .

My husband and I have to some degree worked out our differences. . . . But my hatred lies within me and between us, not wholly a personal hatred, but not entirely political either. And I wonder always whether it is possible to define myself as a feminist revolutionary and still remain in any sense a wife. There are moments when I still worry that he will leave me, that he will come to need a woman less preoccupied with her own rights, and when I worry about that I also fear that no man will ever love me again, that no man could ever love a woman who is angry. And that fear is a great source of trouble to me, for it means that in certain fundamental ways I have not changed at all.

I would like to be cold and clear and selfish, to demand satisfaction for my needs, to compel respect rather than affection. And yet there are moments, and perhaps there always will be, when I fall back upon the old cop-outs. . . . Why should I work when my husband can support me, why should I be a human being when I can get away with being a child?

Women's liberation is finally only personal. It is hard to fight an enemy who has outposts in your head.[29]

This essay, the other works I have cited here, and the bulk of women's liberation rhetoric stand at the farthest remove from traditional models of rhetorical discourse, judged by the stylistic features I have discussed. This author, Sally Kempton, invites us into the interiority of her self, disclosing the inner dynamics of her feelings and the specific form that the problem of liberation takes in her life. In a rhetorically atypical fashion, she honors her feelings of fear, anger, hatred, and need for love and admits both her own ambivalence and the limits of her own experience as a norm for others.

She is self-conscious and self-critical, cognizant of the inconsistencies in her life and of the temptation to "cop out," aware of both the psychic security and the psychic destruction inherent in the female role. She is tentatively describing and affirming the beginnings of a new identity and, in so doing, sets up a dialogue with other women in a similar position that permits the essay to perform the ego functions that Richard Gregg has described.[30] The essay asks for the participation of the reader, not only in sharing the author's life as an example of the problems of growing up female in this society, but in a general process of self-scrutiny in which each person looks at the dynamics of the problems of liberation in her own life. The goal of the work is a process, not a particular belief or policy; she explicitly states that her problems are not those of all women and that a feminist analysis is not a blueprint for living. Most importantly, however, the essay exemplifies "risking the self" in its most poignant sense. The Sally Kempton we meet in the essay has been masochistic, manipulative, an exploiter of the female role and of men, weak, murderous, vengeful and castrating, lazy and selfish. The risk involved in such brutal honesty is that she will be rejected as neurotic, bitchy, crazy, in short, as not being a "good" woman, and more importantly, as *not like us.* The risk may lead to alienation or to sisterhood. By example, she asks other women to confront themselves, recognize their own ambivalence, and face their own participation and collaboration in the roles and processes that have such devastating effects on both men and women. Although an essay, this work has all the distinctive stylistic features of the "consciousness raising" paradigm.

Although the distinctive stylistic features of women's liberation are most apparent in the small group processes of consciousness raising, they are not confined to small group interactions. The features I have listed are equally present in essays, speeches, and other discourses completely divorced from the small group setting. In addition, I would argue that although these stylistic features show certain affinities for qualities associated with psychotherapeutic interaction, they are rhetorical rather than expressive and public and political rather than private and personal. The presumption of most psychotherapy is that the origins of and solutions to one's problems are personal;[31] the feminist analysis presumes that it is the social structure and the definition of the female role that generate the problems that individual women experience in their personal lives. As a consequence, solutions must be structural, not merely personal, and analysis must move from personal experience and feeling to illuminate a common condition that all women experience and share.

Finally, women's liberation rhetoric is characterized by the use of confrontative, nonadjustive strategies designed to "violate the reality structure."[32] These strategies not only attack the psychosocial reality of the culture, but violate the norms of decorum, morality, and "femininity" of the women addressed. Essays on frigidity and orgasm,[33] essays by prostitutes and lesbians,[34] personal accounts of promiscuity and masochism,[35] and essays attacking romantic love and urging man-hating as a necessary stage in liberation[36] "violate the reality structure" by close analysis of tabooed subjects, by treating "social outcasts" as "sisters" and credible sources, and by attacking areas of belief with great mythic power. Two specific linguistic techniques, "attack metaphors" and symbolic reversals, also seem to be characteristic. "Attack metaphors" mix matrices in order to reveal the "nonconscious ideology"[37] of sexism in language and belief, or they attempt to shock through a kind of "perspective by incongruity."[38] Some examples are: "Was Lurleen Wallace *Governess* of Alabama?" A drawing of Rodin's *Thinker* as a female. "Trust in God; She will provide."[39] "Prostitutes are the only honest women because they charge for their services, rather than submitting to a marriage contract which forces them to work for life without pay."[40] "If you think you are emancipated, you might consider the idea of tasting your menstrual blood—if it makes you sick, you've got a long way to go, baby."[41] Or this analogy:

> Suppose that a white male college student decided to room or set up a bachelor apartment with a black male friend. Surely the typical white student would not blithely assume that his black roommate was to handle all the domestic chores. Nor would his conscience allow him to do so even in the unlikely event that his roommate would say, "No, that's okay. I like doing housework. I'd be happy to do it. . . ." But change this hypothetical black roommate to a female marriage partner, and somehow the student's conscience goes to sleep.[42]

Symbolic reversals transform devil terms society has applied to women into god terms and always exploit the power and fear lurking in these terms as potential sources of strength. "The Bitch Manifesto" argues that liberated women are bitches—aggressive, confident, strong.[43] W.I.T.C.H., the Women's International Terrorist Conspiracy from Hell, says, in effect, "You think we're dangerous creatures of the devil, witches? You're right! And we're going to hex you!"[44] Some feminists have argued that the lesbian is the paradigm of the liberated female;[45] others have described an androgynous role.[46] This type of reversal has, of course, appeared in other protest rhetorics, particularly in the affirmation that "black is beautiful!" But systematic reversals of traditional female roles, given the mystique associated with concepts of wife, mother, and loving sex partner, make these reversals especially disturbing and poignant. Quite evidently, they are attempts at the radical affirmation of new identities for women.[47]

The distinctive stylistic features of women's liberation rhetoric are a result of strategic adaptation to an acute rhetorical problem. Women's liberation is characterized by rhetorical interactions that emphasize affective proofs and personal testimony, participation and dialogue, self-revelation and self-criticism, the goal of autonomous decision making through self-persuasion, and the strategic use of techniques for "violating the reality structure." I conclude that, on stylistic grounds, women's liberation is a separate genre of rhetoric.

THE INTERDEPENDENCE
OF SUBSTANTIVE AND STYLISTIC FEATURES

The rhetorical acts I have treated in the preceding section, particularly as illustrated by the excerpt from an essay by Sally Kempton, may seem to be a far cry from the works cited earlier demanding legal, economic, and social equality. However, I believe that all of these rhetorical acts are integral parts of a single genre, a conclusion I shall defend by examining the interdependent character of the substantive and stylistic features of the various discourses already discussed.

Essays such as that of Sally Kempton are the necessary counterparts of works articulating demands for equality. In fact, such discourses spell out the meaning and consequences of present conditions of inequity and the implications of equality in concrete, personal, affective terms. They complete the genre and are essential to its success as a persuasive campaign. In the first section, I argued that demands for equality for women "attack the entire psychosocial reality." That phrase may conceal the fact that such an attack is an attack on the *self* and on the roles and relationships in which women, and men too, have found their identities traditionally. The effect of such an argument is described by Natanson: "When an argument hurts me, cuts me, or cleanses and liberates me it is not because a particular stratum or segment of my world view is shaken up or jarred free but because *I* am wounded or enlivened—*I* in my particularity, and that means in my existential immediacy: feelings, pride, love, and sullenness, the world of my actuality as I live it."[48] The only effective response to the sensation of being threatened existentially is a rhetorical act that treats the personal, emotional, and concrete directly and explicitly, that is dialogic and participatory, that speaks from personal experience to personal experience. Consequently, the rhetoric of women's liberation includes numerous essays discussing the personal experiences of women in many differing circumstances: black women, welfare mothers, older women, factory workers, high school girls, journalists, unwed mothers, lawyers, secretaries, and so forth. Each attempts to describe concretely the personal experience of inequality in a particular situation and/or what liberation might mean in a particular case. Rhetorically, these essays function to translate public demands into personal experience and to treat threats and fears in concrete, affective terms.

Conversely, more traditional discourses arguing for equality are an essential counterpart to these more personal statements. As a process, consciousness raising requires that the personal be transcended by moving toward the structural, that the individual be transcended by moving toward the political. The works treating legal, economic, and social inequality provide the structural analyses and empirical data that permit women to generalize from their individual experiences to the conditions of women in this society. Unless such transcendence occurs, there is no persuasive campaign, no rhetoric in any public sense, only the very limited realm of therapeutic, small group interaction.

The interrelationship between the personal and the political is central to a conception of women's liberation as a genre of rhetoric. All of the issues of women's liberation are simultaneously personal and political. Ultimately, this interrelationship rests on the caste status of women, the basis of the moral conflict this rhetoric generates and intensifies. Feminists believe that sharing personal experience is liberating, i.e., raises consciousness, because all women, whatever their differences in age, education, income, etc., share a common condition, a radical form of "consubstantiality" that is the genesis of the peculiar kind of identification they call "sisterhood." Some unusual rhetorical transactions seem to confirm this analysis. "Speak-outs" on rape, abortion, and orgasm are mass meetings in which women share extremely personal and very negatively valued experiences. These events are difficult to explain without postulating a radical form of identification that permits such painful self-revelation. Similarly, "self-help clinics" in which women learn how to examine their cervixes and look at the cervixes of other women for purposes of comparison seem to require extreme identification and trust. Feminists would argue that "sisterhood is powerful" because it grows out of the recognition of pervasive, common experience of special caste status, the most radical and profound basis for cooperation and identification.

This feminist analysis also serves to explain the persuasive intent in "violating the reality structure." From this point of view, women in American society are always in a vortex of contradiction and paradox. On the one hand, they have been, for the most part, effectively socialized into traditional roles and values, as research into their achievement motivation and self-images confirms. On the other hand, "femininity" is in direct conflict with the most fundamental values of this society—a fact which makes women extremely vulnerable to attacks on the "reality structure." Hence, they argue, violations of norms may shock initially, but ultimately they will be recognized as articulating the contradictions inherent in "the female role." The violation of these norms is obvious in discourses such as that of Sally Kempton; it is merely less obvious in seemingly traditional and moderate works.

CONCLUSION

I conclude, then, that women's liberation is a unified, separate genre of rhetoric with distinctive substantive-stylistic features. Perhaps it is the only genuinely *radical* rhetoric on the contemporary American scene. Only the oxymoron, the figure of paradox and contradiction, can be its metaphor. Never is the paradoxical character of women's liberation more apparent than when it is compared to conventional or familiar definitions of rhetoric, analyses of rhetorical situations, and descriptions of rhetorical movements.

Traditional or familiar definitions of persuasion do not satisfactorily account for the rhetoric of women's liberation. In relation to such definitions, feminist advocacy wavers between the rhetorical and the nonrhetorical, the persuasive and the nonpersuasive. Rhetoric is usually defined as dealing with public issues, structural analyses, and social action, yet women's liberation emphasizes acts concerned with personal exigences and private, concrete experience and its goal is frequently limited to particular, autonomous action by individuals. The view that persuasion is an enthymematic adaptation to audience norms and values is confounded by rhetoric which seeks to persuade by "violating the reality structure" of those toward whom it is directed.

Nor are available analyses of rhetorical situations satisfactory when applied to the rhetoric of women's liberation. Parke Burgess' valuable and provocative discussion of certain rhetorical situations as consisting of two or more sets of conflicting moral demands[49] and Thomas Olbricht's insightful distinction between rhetorical acts occurring in the context of a shared value and those occurring in its absence[50] do not adequately explicate the situation in which feminists find themselves. And the reason is simply that the rhetoric of women's liberation appeals to *what are said to be* shared moral values, but forces recognition that those values are *not* shared, thereby creating the most intense of moral conflicts. Lloyd Bitzer's more specific analysis of the rhetorical situation as consisting of "one controlling exigence which functions as the organizing principle" (an exigence being "an imperfection marked by urgency" that "is capable of positive modification"), an audience made up "only of those persons who are capable of being influenced by discourse and of being mediators of change," and of constraints that can limit "decision and action needed to modify the exigence"[51]—this more specific analysis is also unsatisfactory. In women's liberation there are dual and conflicting exigences not solely of the public sort, and thus women's liberation rhetoric is a dialectic between discourses that deal with public, structural problems and the particularly significant statements of personal experience and feeling which extend beyond the traditional boundaries of rhetorical acts. A public exigence is, of course, present, but what is unavoidable and characteristic of this rhetoric is the accompanying and conflicting personal exigence. The concept of the audience does not account for a situation in which the audience must be *created under the special conditions* surrounding women's liberation. Lastly, the notion of constraints seems inadequate to a genre in which to act as a mediator of change, either as rhetor or audience member, is itself the most significant constraint inhibiting decision or action—a constraint that requires the violation of cultural norms and risks alienation no matter how traditional or reformist the rhetorical appeal may be.

And, similarly, nearly all descriptions of rhetorical movements prove unsatisfactory. Leland Griffin's early essay on the rhetoric of historical movements creates three important problems: he defines movements as occurring "at some time in the past"; he says members of movements "make efforts to alter their environment"; and he advises the student of rhetoric to focus on "the pattern of public discussion."[52] The first problem is that the critic is prevented from examining a contemporary movement and is forced to make sharp chronological distinctions between earlier efforts for liberation and contemporary feminist advocacy; the second problem is that once again the critic's attention is diverted from efforts to change the self, highly significant in the liberation movement, and shifted toward efforts to change the environment; and the third is a related deflection of critical concern from personal, consciousness raising processes to public discussion. Herbert Simons' view of "a leader-centered conception of persuasion in social movements" defines a movement "as an uninstitutionalized collectivity that mobilizes for action to implement a program for the reconstitution of social norms or values."[53] As I have pointed out, leader-centered theories cannot be applied profitably to the feminist movement. Further, women's liberation is not characterized by a *program* that mobilizes feminist advocates to reconstitute social norms and values. Dan Hahn and Ruth Gonchar's idea of a movement as "socially shared activities and beliefs directed toward the demand for change in some aspect of the social order"[54] is unsuitable because it overlooks the extremely important elements of the personal exigence that require change in the self. There are, however, two recent statements describing rhetorical movements that are appropriate for women's liberation. Griffin's later essay describing a dramatistic framework for the development of movements has been applied insightfully to the inception period of contemporary women's liberation.[55] What makes this description applicable is that it recognizes a variety of symbolic acts, the role of drama and conflict, and the essentially moral or value-related character of rhetorical movements.[56] Also, Robert Cathcart's formulation, again a dramatistic one, is appropriate because it emphasizes "*dialectical enjoinment in the moral arena*" and the "*dialectical tension growing out of moral conflict.*"[57]

And so I choose the oxymoron as a label, a metaphor, for the rhetoric of women's liberation. It is a genre without a rhetor, a rhetoric in search of an audience, that transforms traditional argumentation into confrontation, that "persuades" by "violating the reality structure" but that presumes a consubstantiality so radical that it permits the most intimate of identifications. It is a "movement" that eschews leadership, organizational cohesion, and the transactions typical of mass persuasion. Finally, of course, women's liberation is baffling because there is no clear answer to the recurring question, "What do women want?" On one level, the answer is simple; they want what every person wants—dignity, respect, the right to self-determination, to develop their potentials as individuals. But on another level, there is no answer—not even in feminist rhetoric. While there are legal and legislative changes on which most feminists agree (although the hierarchy of priorities differs), whatever liberation is, it will be something different for each woman as liberty is something different for each person. What each woman shares, however, is the paradox of having "to fight an enemy who has outposts in your head."

Notes

1. A partial list of the numerous groups involved in women's liberation and an analysis of them is available in Julie Ellis, *Revolt of the Second Sex* (New York: Lancer Books, 1970), pp. 21–81.

A similar list and an analysis emphasizing disunity, leadership problems, and policy conflicts is found in Edythe Cudlipp, *Understanding Women's Liberation* (New York: Paperback Library, 1971), pp. 129–170, 214–220. As she indicates, more radical groups have expelled members for the tendency to attract personal media attention, used "counters" to prevent domination of meetings by more articulate members, and rejected programs, specific policies, and coherent group action (pp. 146–147, 166, 214–215). The most optimistic estimate of the size of the movement is made by Charlotte Bunch-Weeks, who says that there are "perhaps 100,000 women in over 400 cities" (see her "A Broom of One's Own: Notes on the Women's Liberation Program," in Joanne Cooke, Charlotte Bunch-Weeks and Robin Morgan, eds., *The New Women* [1970; rpt., Greenwich, CT: Fawcett, 1971], p. 186). Even if true, this compares unfavorably with the conservative League of Women Voters with 160,000 members (Cudlipp, *Understanding Women's Liberation*, p. 42) and the National Council of Women representing organizations with some 23 million members whose leadership has taken an extremely antiliberationist stance (see Lacey Fesburgh, "Traditional Groups Prefer to Ignore Women's Lib," *New York Times*, August 26, 1970, p. 44.)

2. Ti-Grace Atkinson said: "There is no movement. Movement means going some place, and the movement is not going anywhere. It hasn't accomplished anything." Gloria Steinem concurred: "In terms of real power—economic and political—we are still just beginning. But the consciousness, the awareness—that will never be the same." ("Women's Liberation Revisited," *Time*, March 20, 1972, pp. 30, 31.) Polls do not seem to indicate marked attitude changes among American women. (See, e.g., *Good Housekeeping*, March 1971, pp. 34–38, and Carol Tavris, "Woman and Man," *Psychology Today*, March 1972, pp. 57–64, 82–85.)

3. An excellent critique of both historical and sociopsychological definition of movements as the basis for rhetorical criticism has been made by Robert S. Cathcart in "New Approaches to the Study of Movements: Defining Movements Rhetorically," *Western Speech* 36 (Spring 1972): 82–88.

4. A particularly apt illustration of this point of view is Richard Hofstadter's "The Paranoid Style in American Politics," in *The Paranoid Style in American Politics and Other Essays* (New York: Knopf, 1965), pp. 3–40. Similarly, the exhortative and argumentative genres developed by Edwin Black are defined in both substantive and stylistic grounds in *Rhetorical Criticism: A Study in Method* (New York: Macmillan, 1965), pp. 132–177.

5. The interrelationship of moral demands and strategic choices is argued by Parke G. Burgess in "The Rhetoric of Moral Conflict: Two Critical Dimensions," *QJS* 56 (1970): 120–130.

6. The notion that style is a token of ideology is the central concept in Edwin Black's "The Second *Persona*," *QJS* 56 (1970): 109–119 (reprined in this volume).

7. See Burgess, "Rhetoric of Moral Conflict," and "The Rhetoric of Black Power: A Moral Demand?" *QJS* 54 (1968): 122–133.

8. See Matina S. Horner, "Femininity and Successful Achievement: A Basic Inconsistency," in Michele Hoffnung Garskof, ed., *Roles Women Play: Readings toward Women's Liberation* (Belmont, CA.: Brooks/Cole, 1971), pp. 105–108.

9. "Women's role, looked at from this point of view is archaic. This is not necessarily a bad thing, but it does make woman's position rather peculiar: it is a survival. In the old world, where one was born into a class and a region and often into an occupation, the fact that one was also sex-typed simply added one more attribute to those which every child learned he or she possessed. Now to be told, in Erik Erikson's words, that one is 'never not-a-woman' comes as rather more of a shock. This is especially true for American women because of the way in which the American ethos has honored the ideas of liberty and individual choice . . . woman's traditional role in *itself* is opposed to a significant aspect of our culture. It is more than restricting, because it involves women in the kind of conflict with their surroundings that no decision and no action open to them can be trusted to resolve" (Elizabeth Janeway, *Man's World; Woman's Place: A Study in Social Mythology* [New York: William Morrow, 1971], p. 99).

10. Jo Freeman, "The Building of the Gilded Cage," *The Second Wave* 1 (1971): 33.

11. Ibid., pp. 8–9.

12. Judicial opinions upholding discriminatory legislation make this quite evident. "That woman's physical structure and the performance of maternal functions place her at a disadvan-

tage in the struggle for subsistence is obvious. . . . The physical well-being of woman becomes an object of public interest and care in order to preserve the strength and vigor of the race. . . . Looking at it from the viewpoint of the effort to maintain an independent position in life, she is not upon an equality. . . . She is properly placed in a class by herself. . . . The reason . . . rests in the inherent difference between the two sexes and in the different functions in life which they perform" (*Muller v. Oregon*, 208 U.S. 412 [1908] at 421-23). This and similar judicial opinions are cited by Diane B. Shulder, in "Does the Law Oppress Women?," in Robin Morgan, ed., *Sisterhood Is Powerful* (New York: Vintage Books, 1970), pp. 139–157.

13. Ellis, *Revolt*, pp. 103–111. See also Caroline Bird, with Sara Welles Briller, *Born Female: The High Cost of Keeping Women Down* (1968; rpt., New York: Pocket Books, 1971), esp. pp. 61–83.

14. "The Chase Manhattan Bank estimated a U.S. woman's hours spent at housework at 99.6 per week" (Juliet Mitchell, "Women: The Longest Revolution [Excerpt]," in Deborah Babcox and Madeline Belkin, eds., *Liberation Now!* [New York: Dell, 1971], p. 250). See also Ann Crittenden Scott, "The Value of Housework," *Ms.*, July 1972, pp. 56–59.

15. Aileen S. Kraditor, *Up from the Pedestal: Selected Writings in the History of American Feminism* (Chicago: Quadrangle Books, 1968), p. 24.

16. The concepts underlying "woman's place" serve to explain the position that women hold outside the home in the economic sphere: "Are there any principles that explain the meanderings of the sex boundaries? One is the idea that women should work inside and men outside. Another earmarks service work for women and profit-making for men. Other rules reserve work with machinery, work carrying prestige, and the top job to men. Most sex boundaries can be explained on the basis of one or the other of these three rules" (Bird and Briller, *Born Female*, p. 72).

17. Horner, "Femininity and Successful Achievement," p. 121.

18. From E. E. Maccoby, "Woman's Intellect," in S. M. Farber and R.H.L. Wilson, eds., *The Potential of Woman* (New York: McGraw-Hill, 1963), pp. 24–39; cited in Horner, "Femininity and Successful Achievement," p. 106.

19. In the economic sphere alone, such changes would be far reaching. "Equal access to jobs outside the home, while one of the pre-conditions for women's liberation, will not in itself be sufficient to give equality for women. . . . Society must begin to take responsibility for children; the economic dependence of women and children on the husband-father must be ended. The other work that goes on in the home must also be changed—communal eating places and laundries for example. When such work is moved into the public sector, then the material basis for discrimination against women will be gone" (Margaret Bentson, "The Political Economy of Women's Liberation," in Garskof, ed., *Roles Women Play*, pp. 200–201).

20. The individual elements described here did not originate with women's liberation. Consciousness raising has its roots in the "witnessing" of American revivalism and was an important persuasive strategy in the revolution on mainland China. Both the ancient Cynics and the modern Yippies have used violations of the reality structure as persuasive techniques (see Theodore Otto Windt Jr., "The Diatribe: Last Resort for Protest," *QJS* 58 [1972]: 1–14), and this notion is central to the purposes of agit-prop theater, demonstrations, and acts of civil disobedience. Concepts of leaderless persuasion appear in Yippie documents and in the unstructured character of sensitivity groups. Finally, the idea that contradiction and alienation lead to altered consciousness and revolution has its origins in Marxian theory. It is the combination of these elements in women's liberation that is distinctive stylistically. As in a metaphor, the separate elements may be familiar; it is the fusion that is original.

21. The most explicit statement of the notion that audiences are "feminine" and rhetors or orators are "masculine" appears in the rhetorical theory of Adolf Hitler and the National Socialist Party in Germany. See Kenneth Burke, "The Rhetoric of Hitler's 'Battle,'" in *The Philosophy of Literary Form* (1941; rpt., New York: Vintage Books, 1957), p. 167.

22. Jo Freeman, "The Social Construction of the Second Sex," in Garskof, ed., *Roles Women Play*, p. 124.

23. The nature of consciousness raising is described in Susan Brownmiller, "Sisterhood Is

Powerful," and in June Arnold, "Consciousness Raising," in Stookie Stambler, ed., *Women's Liberation: Blueprint for the Future* (New York: Ace Books, 1970), pp. 141-161; Charlotte Bunch-Weeks, "A Broom of One's Own," pp. 185-197; Carole Hanisch, "The Personal Is Political," Kathie Sarachild, "A Program for Feminist 'Consciousness Raising,'" Irene Peslikis, "Resistances to Consciousness," Jennifer Gardner, "False Consciousness," and Pamela Kearon, "Man-Hating," all in Shulamith Firestone and Anne Koedt, eds., *Notes from the Second Year: Women's Liberation, Major Writings of the Radical Feminists* (New York: By the Editors, 1970), pp. 76-86.

24. Maurice Natanson, "The Claims of Immediacy," in Maurice Natanson and Henry W. Johnstone Jr., eds., *Philosophy, Rhetoric, and Argumentation* (University Park: Pennsylvania State University Press, 1965), pp. 15, 16.

25. Cynthia Ozick, "The Demise of the Dancing Dog," in Cooke, Bunch-Weeks, and Morgan, eds., *The New Women*, pp. 23-42.

26. Redstockings, "The Politics of Housework," *Liberation Now?*, pp. 110-115. Note that in this, as in other cases, authorship is assigned to a group rather than an individual.

27. Virginia Woolf, *A Room of One's Own* (New York: Harbinger, 1929).

28. Sally Kempton, "Cutting Loose," *Liberation Now!*, pp. 39-55. This essay was originally published in *Esquire*, July 1970, pp. 53-57.

29. Ibid., pp. 54-55.

30. Richard B. Gregg, "The Ego-Function of the Rhetoric of Protest," *Philosophy & Rhetoric* 4 (1971): 71-91. The essay is discussed specifically on pp. 80-81.

31. Granted, there are humanistic or existential psychological theorists who argue that social or outer reality must be changed fully as often as psychic or inner reality. See, for example, Thomas S. Szasz, *The Myth of Mental Illness* (1961; rpt., New York: Dell, 1961); R. D. Laing and A. Esterson, *Sanity, Madness, and the Family* (1964; rpt., New York: Basic Books, 1971); and William H. Grier and Price M. Cobbs, *Black Rage* (New York: Basic Books, 1968). However, the vast majority of psychological approaches assumes that the social order is, at least relatively, unalterable, and that it is the personal realm that must be changed. See, for example, Sigmund Freud, *A General Introduction to Psychoanalysis*, trans. Joan Riviere (1924; rpt., New York: Washington Square Press, 1960); Wilhelm Stekel, *Technique of Analytical Psychotherapy*, trans. Eden Paul and Cedar Paul (London: William Brown, 1950); Carl A. Whitaker and Thomas P. Malone, *The Roots of Psychotherapy* (New York: Blakiston, 1953); and Carl R. Rogers, *Client-Centered Therapy* (Boston: Houghton Mifflin, 1951).

32. This phrase originates with the loose coalition of radical groups called the Female Liberation Movement (Ellis, *Revolt*, p. 55). See also Pamela Kearon, "Power as a Function of the Group," in Firestone and Koedt, eds., *Notes from the Second Year*, pp. 108-110.

33. See, e.g., Anne Koedt, "The Myth of the Vaginal Orgasm," in *Liberation Now!*, pp. 311-320; Susan Lydon, "The Politics of Orgasm," and Mary Jane Sherfey, M.D., "A Theory on Female Sexuality," in Morgan, ed., *Sisterhood Is Powerful*, pp. 197-205, 220-230.

34. See, e.g., Radicalesbians, "The Woman-Identified Woman," in *Liberation Now!*, pp. 287-293; Ellen Strong, "The Hooker;" Gene Damon, "The Least of These: The Minority Whose Screams Haven't Yet Been Heard," and Martha Shelley, "Notes of a Radical Lesbian," in Morgan, ed., *Sisterhood Is Powerful*, pp. 289-311; and Del Martin and Phyllis Lyon, "The Realities of Lesbianism," in Cooke, Bunch-Weeks, and Morgan, eds., *The New Woman*, pp. 99-109.

35. Sally Kempton's essay is perhaps the most vivid example of this type. See also Judith Ann, "The Secretarial Proletariat," and Zoe Moss, "It Hurts to Be Alive and Obsolete: The Ageing Woman," in Morgan, ed., *Sisterhood Is Powerful*, pp. 86-100, 170-175.

36. See Shulamith Firestone, "Love," and Pamela Kearon, "Man-Hating," in Firestone and Koedt, eds., *Notes from the Second Year*, pp. 16-27, 83-86.

37. This term originates with Sandra L. Bem and Daryl J. Bem, "Training the Woman to Know Her Place: The Power of a Nonconscious Ideology," in Garskof, ed., *Roles Women Play*, pp. 84-96.

38. This phrase originates with Kenneth Burke and is the title of Part 2 of *Permanence and Change*, 2d rev. ed. (Indianapolis, IN: Bobbs-Merrill, 1965).

39. Emmeline G. Pankhurst, cited by Ellis, in *Revolt*, p. 19.

40. Ti-Grace Atkinson, cited by Charles Winick and Paul M. Kinsie, in "Prostitutes," *Psychology Today*, February 1972, p. 57.

41. Germaine Greer, *The Female Eunuch* (New York: McGraw-Hill, 1970), p. 42.

42. Bem and Bem, "Training the Woman," pp. 94–95.

43. Joreen, "The Bitch Manifesto," in Firestone and Koedt, eds., *Notes from the Second Year*, pp. 5–9.

44. "WITCH Documents," in Morgan, ed., *Sisterhood Is Powerful*, pp. 538–553.

45. See, for example, Martha Shelley, "Notes of a Radical Lesbian," in Morgan, ed., *Sisterhood Is Powerful*, pp. 306–311. Paralleling this are the negative views of some radical groups toward heterosexual love and marriage. See "The Feminists: A Political Organization to Annihilate Sex Roles," in Firestone and Koedt, eds., *Notes from the Second Year*, pp. 114–118.

46. See, for example, Carolina Bird, "On Being Born Female," *Vital Speeches of the Day*, November 15, 1968, pp. 88–91. This argument is also made negatively by denying that, as yet, there is any satisfactory basis for determining what differences, if any, there are between males and females. See, e.g., Naomi Weisstein, "Psychology Constructs the Female, or the Fantasy Life of the Male Psychologist," in Garskof, ed., *Roles Women Play*, pp. 68–83.

47. Elizabeth Janeway makes a very telling critique of many of these attempts. She argues that the roles of shrew, witch, and bitch are simply reversals of the positively valued and socially accepted roles of women. The shrew is the negative counterpart of the public role of the wife whose function is to charm and to evince honor and respect for her husband before others; the witch is the negative role of the good mother—capricious, unresponsive, and threatening; the bitch is the reversal of the private role of wife—instead of being comforting, loving, and serious, she is selfish, teasing, emasculating. The point she is making is that these are not new, creative roles, merely reversals of existing, socially defined roles (*Man's World; Woman's Place*, pp. 119–123, 126–127, 199–201).

48. Natanson, "Claims of Immediacy," pp. 15–16.

49. Parke G. Burgess, "Rhetoric of Moral Conflict."

50. Thomas H. Olbricht, "The Self as a Philosophical Ground of Rhetoric," *Pennsylvania Speech Annual* 21 (1964): 28–36.

51. Lloyd F. Bitzer, "The Rhetorical Situation," *Philosophy & Rhetoric* 1 (1968): 6–8 (reprinted in this volume).

52. Leland M. Griffin, "The Rhetoric of Historical Movements," *QJS* 38 (1952): 184–185.

53. Herbert W. Simons, "Requirements, Problems, and Strategies: A Theory of Persuasion for Social Movements," *QJS* 56 (1970): 3 (reprinted in this volume).

54. Dan F. Hahn and Ruth M. Gonchar, "Studying Social Movements: A Rhetorical Methodology," *Speech Teacher* 20 (1971): 44, cited from Joseph R. Gusfield, ed., *Protest, Reform, and Revolt: A Reader in Social Movements* (New York: Wiley, 1970), p. 2.

55. Brenda Robinson Hancock, "Affirmation by Negation in the Women's Liberation Movement," *QJS* 58 (1972): 264–271.

56. Leland M. Griffin, "A Dramatistic Theory of the Rhetoric of Movements," in William H. Rueckert, ed., *Critical Responses to Kenneth Burke* (Minneapolis: University of Minnesota Press, 1969), p. 456.

57. Robert S. Cathcart, "New Approaches to the Study of Movements," p. 87.

The Functions
of Presidential Campaigning

BRUCE E. GRONBECK

We all, of course would like to think that the millions of dollars spent, untotaled hours put in by volunteers, and thousands of miles tallied in visiting far-reaching communities, engineered every four years in the name of presidential elections, amounts to something useful. We all would like to think that presidential campaigning is worth the candle—and the floodlight. In view of gnawing doubts, however, many often buy into the post-election analyses of cynics: journalists are fond of laughing at or crying over the time-consuming, energy-draining spectacle of too many dollars chasing too few votes. The presidential election of 1972 cost some $40 million, and produced Richard Nixon.

Before we dismiss the electoral process, and especially that surrounding the selection of a President, as cultural waste second only to the squandering of fossil fuels, we should attempt to specify as clearly as possible the range of functions served by campaigning. In this essay, I contend that the instrumental benefits of presidential campaigning extend beyond the flick of a few levers on a machine, and that, perhaps even more important, the consummatory benefits accrued during "electing time" probably could not be replaced by any other combination of cultural rituals.[1] Presidential elections serve a wide variety of practical, social, and idiosyncratic functions, ultimately affecting the culture's routines, distribution of resources, and even conceptions of itself. If these propositions have more than face validity, then the ways we go about examining campaign communication need to be rethought.

In elaboration of the propositions, I will offer a list of functions previous research has investigated or at least suggested. To account for ways those functions are performed in communicative interactions, I will discuss briefly the nature of the political objects and acts to which this culture attributes "symbolic meaning." In thus offering functional "whats" and symbolic-rhetorical "hows," I hope to lay the groundwork for a comprehensive theory of presidential campaign communication.

THE INSTRUMENTAL FUNCTIONS OF CAMPAIGNING

The political ritual of actively seeking the office of President of the United States has existed something over a century, going back at least to Horace Greeley's stumping on his own behalf in the 1872 election and even farther in some of its manifestations. One can speculate, furthermore, that the practice of pre-election public communication was not simply the invention of fringe-area politicians such as Greeley, desperately seeking popular support in the face of flagging party zeal. The practice, rather, developed into its present-day polished performance for a number of important reasons rooted in the *realpolitik* of modern democracies.

Behavioral Activation

Most important is the simple notion that elections depend upon voters; and, as a corollary, that persons become "voters" only by voting. Campaigning, one suspects, came into being in this country in response to the need of a popular democracy—especially one with a growing sense of "the people," with no legal requirements for voting, and with the disintegration of cultural consensus following the Civil War, westward expansion, and immigration—to "get out the vote." Getting out the vote, as Lazarsfeld, Berelson, and Gaudet so simply put it, involves:

> *Reinforcement*—appealing to the predispositions and prejudices of party sympathizers;
> *Activation*—creating "new" voters from the pool of nonvoters, and moving current voters into more active forms of support (monetarily, behaviorally); and,
> *Conversion*—attracting undecided, nonaligned, and other-party voters to one's party and candidate.[2]

No matter what the demographic or communicative variables involved, a primary function of campaigning is that of stirring previous voters, crossover voters, and nonvoters on the Tuesday of an election.

Cognitive Adjustments

Similarly, campaigns can serve the important function of fostering multifaceted dialogues—of providing a mutual exchange on "issues" among candidates, press representatives, and voters. Pre-election campaigning allows a constituency to "tell" politicians what is important, a candidate and/or the media to tell each other what positions are foolhardy, unrealistic, or vacuous. Such advisory activities involve essentially a series of cognitive adjustments, i.e., the supplying of new or restructured political information, the overlaying of valuative and motivational schemata on that information, and the mapping of social-political-economic priorities. Thus, campaigning can involve:

> *Reflection*—encouraging candidates to come to grips with "issues" on people's minds (usually mediated through the press and polls), to rank-order problems and solutions in ways palatable to a constituency and consistent with its perceptions of reality;
> *Refraction*—modifying or even abandoning analyses of problems and/or their

solutions in the face of attacks from other candidates and press interpretations or commentary; and,

Reconstitution—setting, for the voters, economic-social-political agenda according to the judgments (or strategic assessments) of candidates, their parties, and the press.[3]

Hence, 1960 was considered a year dominated by "communism" and the "New Frontier"; 1964, by the "Great Society" and Indochina; 1968, by law and order; 1972, by peace negotiations and the limits of domestic progressivism; and 1976, by "trust." Many additional issues, of course, were addressed each of these years, but they held lower priorities and were accorded less or only temporary headline coverage through the campaigns. Political terrain, in an important sense, became reduced to cognitive maps with distinctive intellectual-emotional hills and valleys because of reflection, refraction, and reconstitution. Now, questions of agenda-setting, of information flow, of issue saliency—and of the cognitive processes by which such agenda, data polls, and judgments of saliency change—still in most respects represent moot questions, as the research on these topics is relatively new. Nevertheless, its power and importance cannot be overestimated.

The Assignation of Legitimacy

A final cluster of instrumental functions centers on the notion of "legitimation," the idea that the campaigning process, at least as much as the act of voting per se, provides Presidents with assigned or delegated power. Louis Koenig emphasizes this idea when he remarks that campaigns yield or "reflect a social and political consensus that will sustain constructive programs for major public programs."[4] Particularly, two important features of the political system are thus instrumentally sustained:

Leadership—winnowing through all of the presidential aspirants, via a series of tests or trials (in caucuses, primaries, conventions, and the press) to find some*one* to lead the country; and,

Programmatic Endorsement—encouraging a leader to pursue "campaign promises" into law, into bureaucratic expansion or contraction, into the realm of moral statement or edict.

Thus, President after President refers back to campaign speeches, to commitments made, and to approval "expressed" by a voting public, as he issues orders (Kennedy's desegregation of the University of Alabama), proposes legislation (Johnson's Civil Rights Act of 1964), and signs or vetoes bills (Carter's positive reaction to legislation reorganizing the executive branch in 1977). The number of campaign promises actually kept, of course, is small. But the legitimacy of acting in *the name of* those promises, on the basis of the hard-won "mandate," is unquestionable.

Activating the electorate, reassembling and reviewing the nation's problems and their proposed solutions, and actually filling the Executive Office with a person armed with consensual powers—these functions alone are enough to justify "autumnal madness," I suppose. Yet, I believe that campaigning achieves even more far-flung goals, the goals we can smile at, parody, take personal satisfaction in, and deify on the Fourth of July. Such goals are reached through the "consummatory" functions of campaign communication, functions performed as much if not more by the act than by the substance of communication.

THE CONSUMMATORY FUNCTIONS OF CAMPAIGNING

If "instrumental functions" are thought of as ways in which additional behaviors (voting, legislating, thinking) are generated by pieces of communication, then "consummatory functions" are embodied in those communication processes which produce end-states or "products" that go beyond (or stop short of) voting and electing per se. That is, campaigning creates second-level or meta-political images, personae, myths, associations, and social-psychological reactions which may even be detached or at least distinct from particular candidates, issues, and offices. Simply put, one may (and most probably do) "use" a presidential campaign for some things other than selecting Presidents and ordering priorities.

To get at these uses, one must deal with two aspects of a vigorous presidential campaign. The first is its ubiquity. Door-to-door volunteers, mass mailings, rallies, wire service photos, commercials, bumper stickers, buttons, billboards, airplane streamers, the six o'clock news reports, and a steady diet of election speeches over radio and television conspire to make a campaign unavoidable in this culture. We are forced by mini- and mass media to "get involved," and such involvement cannot but affect us, perhaps even in profound ways. We may consciously choose not to vote, we may toss leaflets into the nearest trash can, and we may switch channels sanctimoniously when a political commercial is punched up, but even these are acts of involvement, paradoxically. We must actively choose not to be active; hence we are participating symbolically even if not actually.

Furthermore, that involvement is not "meaningless" because presidential campaigning has become a traditional, rule-governed ritual in this society. Both as individuals and as a society we possess a series of expectations concerning how candidates ought to communicate, when and where they ought to say what. Generally, for example, we are aware that the ritual is composed of a sequence of happenings (pre-primary events, primaries and caucuses, conventions, post-convention events, and election day). We generally are able to identify a series of genres of campaign discourse—announcement speeches, press conferences, concession speeches, discourses interpreting primary or poll results, keynote addresses, nomination and acceptance speeches, apologia (to compensate for *faux pas* or unseemly behaviors), election-eve appeals, etc. We even know our ritual well enough to be able to process non-explicit messages (the "meaning" generated by someone campaigning in shirtsleeves instead of three-piece suits) and paradoxical ones (how it is that a candidate can claim "victory" in a primary where he finished second or third). The communicative expectations we possess, individually and culturally, in the phrase of Paul Weaver, make us "captives of melodrama."[5] Because we know the "rules"— legal and traditional—we are drawn into at least intellectual if not physical participation.

The ubiquity of campaigning, therefore, guarantees some level of participation by the vast majority of Americans, and its ritualistic features allow us to specify certain of the consummatory by-products likely to be generated.

Involvement

"Political involvement" is a many-headed hydra, especially as recent research on "the uses and gratifications" of mass communication is demonstrating.[6] That involvement accounts for at least five classes of consummatory effects:

> *Participation*—reminding traditional or habitual activists that it is once again time
>   to start raising money, preparing placards, licking envelopes, or in other words

banding together in social-political minisocieties of like-minded citizens for the duration of the campaign;[7]

Self-Reflection—permitting individuals to examine their political preferences, social-economic priorities and needs, and the like, in terms of their own plights and perceptions and in terms of group judgments (as in unions);

Social Interaction—giving people a tremendous variety of "topics" (role perform-ances, "issues," "styles," etc.) for informal discussion around water coolers, over luncheons and cocktails;

Parasocial Interaction—providing persons with "messages" and "sources"—via radio, television, newspapers, brochures—with which to "interact," as when people "argue" with their television sets' projected personae;[8] and,

Aesthetic Experiences—fostering new and even vital forms of "drama" on television, especially through the construction of essentially poetic universes wherein heroes and villains, would-be saviors and chastised subverters, do battle in the comedic, melodramatic, and tragic "scripts" individuals can build out of a campaign and its coverage.[9]

In other words, presidential campaigning invades myriad personal-social "occasions" in people's lives, generating many types and degrees of involvement. It can range from thirty hours a week manning phones in the county party headquarters to the detached amusement some feel once every four years watching party delegates make fools of themselves in convention cities. One can be involved for positive (goal-directed) or for negative (ego-enhancing) reasons. One can regard campaigning as vital or ludicrous. One can celebrate groupness or belongingness, cerebrate over the meaning of life, critique expected role-performances, communicate with crooks and commercials, or construct sociodramas. The uses to which individuals can put a campaign seem limited only by their experience and creativity.

Legitimation of the Process

Finally, campaigning, to the consternation of its detractors and the joy of its celebrants, ultimately legitimates itself as much as it does its instrumental output. As people engage in campaign activities, they symbolically reinforce the values for which the activities stand. Each time one waits in a long line to vote, one is committed even more deeply to the value of voting—"participatory democracy."[10] Each time one hands out campaign literature on a street corner, the literature itself acquires more significance because we value "political information" as a systemic "right." Each time a debate is held, America's commitment to "open inquiry" and "freedom of examination" deepens. Each time a baby is kissed, another citizen discovers that "the people count." And each time another candidate says "I was a poor boy myself," the American Dream is born anew. Thus, each time the country spends its tens of millions on an election, it commits itself to as much if not more the next time; that is not only a matter of inflation but of moral dedication as well. Hence, presidential campaigning is an almost insidiously self-rein-forcing or self-justifying activity. It functions to perpetuate primal American myths:

Acquiescence—providing a paradigmatic, "fail-safe" rationale for choosing leaders and fostering programs with particularly "American" bents, making it difficult for anyone to object to the process (for if you do, the system's ideological web reaches out, telling you to seek the desired change by participating—running for office, pressuring the parties, voicing your opinions in public forums); and,

Quiescence—reasserting the values associated with campaigning and its outcomes (free-and-open decision making, public accountability, habitual and even mandatory modes of campaigning, the two-party system), in order to remind a citizenry that it is "happy" and "content" with its electoral system; emphasizing the mores and ceremonial rituals associated with elections which make the country "devil-proof," invincible to attacks from within or without.[11]

The only major change in presidential campaign politics made in recent years—the alteration of campaign financing—has only further ingrained myths concerning "people's" participation. Otherwise, the process continues to mandate traditional behaviors. Overall, we may carp about it, about spending levels, about the undesirability of judging a candidate's strength from results of the New Hampshire primary or from a ten-second TV spot, and on and on, yet we do little to change any of these features. We probably would evoke considerable psychic and ideological discomfort by destroying the accepted, tested way of picking a Commander-in-Chief and overseer of the State of the Union. We have been educated in the myths and rituals, and now they protect us.[12]

Overall, then, presidential campaigns function as both means and ends, as evidenced in several of the works mentioned in this essay's footnotes. More could be said about both instrumental and consummatory functions, but we should move to the question more pertinent to communications scholars: How are these functions manifested in the routines and rituals which comprise campaigning?

THE COMMUNICATIVE MANIFESTATIONS
OF CAMPAIGNS' FUNCTIONS

Presidential campaigns perform the functions we have identified, of course, primarily via communicative symbols and acts. This is not to assert that power relationships, situational exigencies, money, etc., do not affect electoral outcomes, but rather is to say that even these aspects of systemic input and structures become salient and determinative in the public decision-making process principally through the mediating capabilities of communications. Thus, the power of a party boss is made salient verbally in his commands or symbolically in his behavior, as when he shows up at and blesses a fundraising benefit for a candidate; a particular situation, such as the Gulf of Tonkin incident in 1964, must be configured and interpreted symbolically by candidates before features of that exigency are adjudged politically relevant;[13] and even money must be put to some communicative use—buying TV time, paying for stationery, updating computerized lists of voters—before it affects an electorate. Hence, communicative symbols and acts are the mediating entities necessary to the bridging of candidates' aspirations and constituencies' behaviors.

How, then, can we talk usefully about communicative symbols and acts? While other typologies are available,[14] in this essay I will define "symbols" and "acts" and then subdivide each, producing a four-fold breakdown of communicative artifacts—nonverbal objects (emblems), verbal objects (slogans and habituated vocabulary), verbal acts (discourse), and nonverbal acts (politicized behaviors). Such fractioning will allow us generally to relate each sort of communicative artifact to its central campaign functions and to draw some global—and, potentially, some theoretically interesting—conclusions concerning the campaign process. We will, in other words, gain a vocabulary and a point of view.

Campaignings' Communicative Symbols

By "communicative symbol," first of all, I simply mean a thing or verbal construct to which political meaning is attributed. "Donkeys" and "elephants" as well as more abstract words such as "trust" have everyday denotations; but, through habitual usage in political environments, they come to acquire political meanings and to express political preferences. Two kinds of political-communicative symbols are easily identified.

Nonverbal Objects

Most readily observable are the innumerable political objects which inundate a campaign—buttons, pictures, placards, red/white/blue bunting, bumper stickers with words or icons, the kinds of typeface in which slogans are cast, the Democrats' donkey and the Republicans' elephant, and even more personal symbols with which particular candidates are identified, such as Roosevelt's cigarette holder, Carter's peanut, and George Wallace's bulletproof glass enclosure. Such symbols can be considered communicative in that they perform political functions: (1) they are expressive of people's identifications and commitment, denoting voter activation or conversion (as in the case of 1972's "Democrats for Nixon" buttons); (2) they can be used instrumentally to engage party or ideological loyalties and to stir patriotic impulses, as when a political parade sweeps through a downtown district with the full regalia of flags, confetti, bunting, car-top signs, and limousines; and (3) they of course can have some degree of consummatory value, in that they can be discussed, enjoyed, laughed at, collected, prized, or even revered.[15]

Indeed, as the reference to a parade suggests, we may go even farther and suggest that "settings" can be considered nonverbal political symbols. Murray Edelman has written at some length on this subject. He notes that they are "the emotional context of the acts they enfold," and indicates that "a pragmatic definition of political setting, then, must recognize it as whatever is background and remains over a period of time, limiting perception and response. It is more than land, buildings, and physical props. It includes any assumptions about basic causation and motivation that are generally accepted."[16] Thus, for example, the place a candidate chooses to declare presidential aspirations allows us in part to characterize his or her "leadership style" (see below). The Washington Press Club luncheon is associated with traditional campaign expectations, a war to be waged with the blessing of the party and press establishment, while a circus tent in one's backyard in Shirkieville, Indiana, signals more populist urges (at least Birch Bayh assumed it did when he chose that strategy, as Trent argues in another essay in this volume). A convention hall plastered with mammoth posters of the party's war horses provides a setting with more "loyalist" associations than does one without them. We read into such choices-among-settings, as Edelman says, assumptions about "basic causation or motivation"; settings are significant campaign objects.

Verbal Objects

Many of the nonverbal objects or symbols just mentioned, of course, have verbal dimensions; and some objects are purely verbal, such as slogans and habituated catchwords of certain campaigns. It may seem odd to term a slogan an "object." I do so because it functions in much the same way any other symbolic object does—as an emblem. It becomes a "thing" or concept to which special political meanings are attached; verbal "objects" distill philosophies, ideologies, preferences, and belief-structures. They become what have been termed "condensation symbols,"[17] encapsulating a veritable flood of belief statements, attitudinal preferences, and valuative orientations. "I Like Ike" in 1952 and 1956; "The New Frontier" in 1960; "All the Way with LBJ" in 1964; "Nixon's the One," "Dump the Hump," and "Clean Gene [McCarthy]" in 1968; "Nixon Now" (shortened to "Nixon No" by his ingenuous detractors) in 1972—these slogans and cants were short-hand terms which condensed party platforms and political rationales. They provide the same expressive, instrumental, and consummatory outlets that technical or physical symbols do. In addition, they can be forged into litanies, as witness the almost hypnotic chants used to express political loyalties in 1968 ("Hey, hey, LBJ, how many kids have you killed toady?") and 1972 ("Four more years!" ringing a full ten minutes from the upper balconies of the Republican National Convention).

Verbal and nonverbal objects, therefore, are symbols—perceivable in a single sweep—which through traditional use or an innovative process of meaning attribution convey even complex political messages. In a time when candidates are committed to "grassroots" campaigns, when electronic media (radio, television, photo transmitters, computerized news letters) can wire the nation for the lightning diffusion of political information, and when the pace of political life has accelerated to a point of psychic shock, the explosion of these symbols across the culture is hardly news. They allow for expressive, instrumental, and consummatory messages to be transmitted, sanctioned by tradition, and magnified by a press establishment paid directly and indirectly to repeat them.

Campaignings' Communicative Acts

Sustained discourse and other complex behaviors likewise communicate political meanings. Indeed, for most communication scholars, the heart and soul of campaigning-as-process are found in verbal and physical acts.

Verbal Acts

Historically, verbal acts have occupied most of the attention of communication analysts, which comes as no surprise to those who know that "rhetoric" and "communication" traditionally have been defined in terms of "words" and that "political communication" has been dominated by researchers nurtured in speech communication departments in universities. "Talk" has been the stuff of which campaigning for centuries has been constituted; Aristotle gave us lists of message strategies, and the twentieth-century social sciences taught us how to take them apart systematically. Whether oral or written, face-to-face or electronically mediated, verbal acts pervade campaigns and provide the largest pile of grist for scholarly mills. The ubiquity (and academic attractiveness) of verbiage needs little explanation. Its theoretical importance, however, probably does.

On the assumption that governments are constituted by collectivities to provide protection and service, one must note that "problems" necessarily justify a government's reason for being. Hence, campaigning, as we have noted, is (at least in theory) devoted to cognitive mapping, making salient and concrete problems as well as solutions to them. Of course, it takes many words to describe politically advantageous perspectives and to indicate the proper—collectively sanctioned—solutions. Such political rationalizations often become complicated, especially as candidates find themselves buffeted by special interests and the press to the point where they must explain, re-explain, and even alter positions. Verbal acts are needed to elaborate the "issues" which comprise the political information of a campaign.

In a campaign, however, such issues are not simply "stands" on welfare and warfare. Rather, the issues of a presidential campaign, especially, converge on the "leadership styles" of competing candidates.[18] Election campaigns, after all, are in a very real sense "dry runs"—hypothetical experiments in governance. They are expensive versions of the childhood game "What If?" If America is to avoid basing its presidency in either heritability (traditional power) or mere charisma, it must rely upon a symbolic version of trial-by-combat, a struggle for Weber's legitimate rule.[19] Hence, in a presidential campaign, an electorate witnesses candidates' "styles"—their habitual modes of thought and action. The way a candidate goes about answering a question—"What about Quemoy and Matsu?" (1960), "When does political commitment become a matter of 'extremism'?" (1964), "What can be done to restore law and order in America?" (1968), "What can we do to keep the 'Great Society' from stagnating?" (1972), "Will Americans ever trust government again?" (1976)—is of the utmost importance. Candidates' patterns of response to such questions provide voters with grounds for answers to questions of style: What beliefs does a candidate bring to bear upon a problem? What attitudes are exhibited toward the problem and the people it affects? What evaluative orientations appear over and over in the answers? How are these beliefs, attitudes, and values forged into habituated responses to problems? How candidates "handle" themselves verbally may even determine electoral outcomes. "Handling themselves," indeed, is of concern in all arenas of political talk. An answer to an "important" question, such as Goldwater's reaction to nuclear weapons or his analysis of the Social Security system in 1964, and to an "unimportant" question, such as Carter's use of the phrase "ethnic purity" or Ford's reference to the independence of Iron Curtain countries in 1976, will be *equally* relevant to the judgment of how candidates handle themselves.

One's leadership style, therefore, is in good measure plumbed by judgments of the web of words spun through speeches, news conferences, interviews, ads, brochures, and so on.[20] If Eugene McCarthy can talk only of "peace," where will we find the leadership for solving our domestic problems? If George McGovern one day is "1000 percent" behind a vice-presidential candidate but a week later under pressure accepts his resignation from the ticket, what will he do when he must assemble a cabinet, appoint ambassadors, and lean on a bureaucracy? If Ronald Reagan celebrates conservative ideals in one breath, only to select a liberal Republican as a running mate in the next, will he be able to live up to his own promise once he is President? Answers to questions concerning *competency* and *trustworthiness* from context to context, problem to problem, hinge upon the electorate's perceptions of such "style" issues. Hence, while the cynics among us disdain the "pat answers" and "set speeches" produced by pre-programmed candidates, they miss the point of it all; paradoxically, perhaps, the pat-ness and set-ness epitomize campaign discourse because of the particular kinds of cognitive maps the electorate needs traced and retraced. Furthermore, in terms of campaigning's consummatory functions, those selfsame characteristics of discourse allow for judgments about role performance; the "same old campaign rhetoric" provides grounds for social interaction, parasocial interaction, and aesthetic inquiries into the way a candidate's campaign is being "orchestrated."

Nonverbal Acts

If competency and trustworthiness can be thought to be revealed through verbal acts, two other dimensions of credibility—dynamism and personal attractiveness—are, I would argue, principally established by nonverbal political acts. By "physical" or "nonverbal" acts I mean nothing more complicated than behaviors to which we attribute political significance. These acts include political clichés such as kissing babies, wearing Indian headdresses on the reservation, going to church, shaking hands at airports, and waving a "V for Victory" at crowds from the motorcade. They also encompass acts given political meaning in more recent times—walking among the electorate instead of riding through it, campaigning in workshirt and blue-jean suit, holding "citizens' news conferences" from which the press is barred (started by Reagan in 1976), shooting the rapids of the Colorado River (Robert Kennedy), sleeping at the home of an "ordinary" voter while on the campaign trail (as did Jimmy Carter in his resurrection of Andrew Jackson). Both traditional and nontraditional acts are assigned symbolic import by an electorate because generally they are thought to be less "manipulative" than words (as "actions speak louder than words" in American folklore), they can convey messages concerning "personality" often less well carried through words (the "real-man-and-not-the-image" myth), and they ultimately communicate a fundamental American fiction. That fiction is the consuming dream that electing time is an occasion for Would-Be-Leader to reach down to Follower for strength, support, and ratification. In the ritualized acts of campaigners, thus, we find reasons for voting and we see played out most of the legitimizing functions of a campaign.

Verbal and nonverbal objects, verbal and nonverbal acts—these constitute campaign communication. These symbols and acts are the embodiments of the political process, allowing the functions which campaigning ought to serve to work themselves out publicly.

PARTING THOUGHTS

Neither space nor the current state of political knowledge permits the presentation of an elaborated theory—one predictive of specific outcomes and explanative of all significant behaviors. What we have in this essay, rather, is the start of a point of view. From the list of functions and the isolation of their communicative manifestations flow two conclusions about the state of political communication (especially campaign) theory.

First, because "political meaningfulness" can be attached to such an array of things, words, slogans, hymnodic rhapsodies, discourses, and behaviors, and because the "uses" to which any datum can be put are so varied, any comprehensive theory of campaign communication must be predicated on the notion of multidimensionality. Take, for example, Carter's celebrated interview with *Playboy* in 1976. That incident could be used by voters to (1) assess his moral character, (2) measure his political savvy (what kind of candidate would grant such a high-risk interview?), (3) check on his abilities to rationalize his public behavior, (4) judge the competencies of the staff that allows such an interview, (5) estimate the degree to which as President he will let personal ethics interfere with public decision-making, (6) interpret his sensitivities to party traditions (because of his commentary on Lyndon Johnson), and (7) see what array of public opinion leaders—from the party, the religious establishment, and the black community—

come to his defense. Conceivably, any voter could employ that event to make judgments of morality, attractiveness, competency, trustworthiness, sensitivity to expectations, and future behavior. Such judgments in turn affect voting (instrumentally) and people's interactions, degree of political optimism/cynicism, vision of the drama, etc. (consummatorily). Any simple "limited effects" model which does not allow for the construct of multidimensional contexts for judgments seems doomed.[21]

Second, a review of the footnotes reveals several "theoretical" positions which are being integrated here—agenda-setting research, demographic analyses, uses and gratifications, dramaturgical discussions, and even more pure forms of rhetorical analyses, much of which is summarized in Trent's catalogue of campaign studies.[22] The knowledges to which I have alluded are varied because we have had no solid holistic theory set out convincingly in our literature. Scholars in "rhetorical" traditions have assimilated an Aristotelian view of the political world, one which ontologically is committed to the idea of "rhetorical choice" and hence which concentrates upon rhetorical intentions and message strategies. Concomitantly, scholars in a "communication" tradition have been guided by positivistic assumptions and hence have attempted to systematize message characteristics (via content analysis) or parse audience variables (seeking principally demographic antecedents for behavioral consequents). For the most part, therefore, rhetorical scholars have labored to make sense out of and to judge the propriety of "inputs," and communication scholars, the same for "outputs." Both groups at least implicitly, have worked within a kind of systems model. Perhaps they have been forced to do so because the wide-ranging holistic models—dramaturgical, interactionist, ethnographic, and other rule-governed viewpoints—have not lived up to their promise, via case studies of specific campaigns.[23] This volume, as well as a special issue of *Quarterly Journal of Speech* (October 1977) and other collections, is a start toward a grand, high-order theory which potentially bridges C. P. Snow's "two cultures."

Tradition has it that the sign spanning Shakespeare's Globe Theatre read *Totus Mundus Agit Histrionem*. To take seriously the assertion that "all the world's a stage," especially when one is scrutinizing mass social behavior, is to enter a perhaps bizarre intellectual world. It can be studied sequentially, as Trent does later in this volume when she looks at "the first act" of campaigning. It can be examined generically, as does Gold when she ferrets out some "rules" for campaign apologia. Or, it can be discussed ritualistically, as does Farrell when he attempts to underscore the functional orchestration of communicative stimuli in the 1976 Republican and Democratic conventions. These studies in this issue as well as those in the Sage volume on "uses and gratifications" are indications of some of the directions holistic theories—most of which are tied to dramaturgical assumptions of performance, performance rules, and contextual judgment—will take us. That world may seem bizarre to us now, but only because it confronts some of the narrower parameters of campaign theory. Once we open ourselves to consider the range of communicative functions and communicative artifacts as they are achieved and constructed in campaigns, that world may well become as comfortable as that which Shakespeare built for drama.

Notes

1. "Electing time" is a phrase I borrow from Edwin Black, "Electing Time," *Quarterly Journal of Speech* 59 (1973): 125–129, to connote the set of event-related expectations participants bring

to any presidential campaign; the distinction between "instrumental" and "consummatory" effects is similar to the one drawn by Wallace C. Fotheringham, in *Perspectives on Persuasion* (Boston: Allyn and Bacon, 1966), p. 22. I realize that most of the "benefits" I list have not been validated by empirical research. This, though, may be because the attempt has not yet been made or has not yet been made in sufficiently sophisticated a way. Such research could be useful not only for testing the existence of these functions, but also for discovering the degree of interdependence among them.

2. See Paul F. Lazarsfeld, Bernard Berelson, and Hazel Gaudet, *The People's Choice* (New York: Columbia University Press, 1948).

3. For a discussion of what I have termed "refraction," see Robert O. Anderson, "The Characterization Model for Rhetorical Criticism of Political Image Campaigns," *Western Speech* 37 (1973): 75–96. For overviews of the whole question of political thought patterns, see Lee B. Becker, Maxwell E. McCombs, and Jack M. McLeod, "The Development of Political Cognitions," in Steven H. Chaffee, ed., *Political Communication: Issues and Strategies for Research* (Beverly Hills, CA: Sage, 1975), pp. 21–64: and David L. Swanson, "Political Information, Influence, and Judgment in the 1972 presidential Campaign," *Quarterly Journal of Speech* 59 (1973): 130–142.

4. Louis W. Koenig, *The Chief Executive*, 3d ed. (San Francisco: Harcourt Brace Jovanovich, 1975), p. 35.

5. Paul H. Weaver, "Captives of Melodrama," *New York Times Magazine*, August 29, 1976, pp. 6, 48–50, 54–56. This is one of the finest analyses of television's role in campaign impression management available.

6. See, for example, Jay G. Blumler and Elihu Katz, eds., *The Uses of Mass Communication* (Beverly Hills, CA: Sage, 1974).

7. For further discussion, see esp. Nelson W. Polsby and Aaron Wildavsky, *Presidential Elections*, 4th ed. (New York: Charles Scribner's Sons, 1976), p. 158.

8. All of these "uses" are reviewed in Blumler and Katz, *Uses of Mass Communication*.

9. The role of the mass media in fostering "aesthetic experiences" is underscored by Weaver, in "Captives of Melodrama."

10. Here and throughout the rest of this essay, I shall be assuming that "behaviors" and "actions"—as much as "words" and other "symbols"—can reflect the valuative priorities, and even reinforce the legitimacy, of the culture's political system and process. In other words, "political reality" is nothing other than a special, institutional case of "social reality"—the perceptual filters endemic to social organizations. I do not have room to elaborate these theses here, but they are developed at considerable length in Peter L. Berger and Thomas Luckmann, *The Social Construction of Reality: A Treatise in the Sociology of Knowledge* (Garden City, NY: Doubleday, 1966), esp. pp. 47–128. I expand them somewhat in "The Rhetoric of Political Corruption: Sociolinguistic, Dialectical, and Ceremonial Processes," *Quarterly Journal of Speech* 64 (1978): 155–172.

11. The theme of politics as the means by which a culture engineers acquiescence and quiescence is the burden of Murray Edelman, *The Symbolic Uses of Politics* (Urbana: University of Illinois Press, 1964), esp. "Introduction" and "Symbols and Political Quiescence," pp. 1–43.

12. See the discussion of socialization and legitimation, esp. in "marginal situations," in Berger and Luckmann, *Social Construction of Reality*, passim.

13. The notion that "situations" have social effect only through their rhetorical elaborations is developed in Lloyd Bitzer, "The Rhetorical Situation," *Philosophy & Rhetoric* 1 (1968): 1–14 (reprinted in this volume).

14. Edelman (*Symbolic Uses*) approaches "communication" through analyses of "administrative system," "leadership," "settings," "language," "forms" of language, and "goals." Nimmo prefers to break down campaign communications by medium (Dan Nimmo, *The Political Persuaders* [Englewood Cliffs, NJ: Prentice-Hall, 1970]). Simons invokes a developmental model stressing the sequence of communicative acts: Planning, Mobilization, Legitimation, Promotion, and Activation (Herbert W. Simons, *Persuasion: Understanding, Practice, and Analysis* [Reading, MA: Addison- Wesley, 1976], esp. pp. 227–243). Furthermore, numerous articles in speech communication journals especially will present variations on Edelman's segmental stress, Nimmo's

mediational concerns, and Simons' systemic orientation. I here hold to simple conceptual distinctions so that they may be employed by any analyst in any more theoretical scheme (modular, mediational, or systemic).

15. For another approach to nonverbal political symbols, see Haig A. Bosmajian, "The Persuasiveness of Nazi Marching and *Der Kampf um die Strasse*," in Haig A. Bosmajian, ed., *The Rhetoric of Nonverbal Communication: Readings* (Glenview, IL: Scott, Foresman, 1971), pp. 157–165. Specific symbols—flags, armbands, etc.—are treated in other essays in the book.

16. Edelman, *Symbolic Uses*, pp. 99, 102–103.

17. This term goes back to Edward Sapir's essay on "symbolism" for the *Encyclopedia of the Social Sciences* (1934). Our current understanding of it is developed in Edelman, *Symbolic Uses*, esp. pp. 6–12, and in Doris A. Graber, *Verbal Behavior and Politics* (Urbana: University of Illinois Press, 1976), chap. 10.

18. Floating through a body of political literature is a distinction between two major sorts of issues: "position issues" ("stands" on problem areas) and "style issues" (what I will here be calling "leadership" questions particularly). It seems to go back to Lewis A. Froman, *People and Politics* (Englewood Cliffs, NJ: Prentice-Hall, 1962), pp. 24–25, and has been used effectively in Richard M. Merelman, "The Dramaturgy of Politics," in James E. Combs and Michael W. Mansfield, eds., *Drama in Life: The Uses of Communication in Society* (New York: Hastings House, 1976), pp. 285–301. Actually, I think it is almost impossible to separate the two sorts of issues or questions, because I believe one judges "style" from the habitual modes by which candidates deal with "positions."

19. See Hans H. Gerth and C. Wright Mills, eds., *From Max Weber: Essays in Sociology* (New York: Oxford University Press, 1958), pp. 246ff.

20. Relevant to this notion of "style issues" is the research concentrating upon political "image." More specific operationalizations of "image" than the one offered here can be found in: Dan Nimmo and Robert L. Savage, *Candidates and Their Images* (Pacific Palisades, CA: Goodyear, 1976); Robert S. Sigel, "Image of the American Presideny," *Midwest Journal of Political Science* 10 (1966): 123–137; Jay G. Blumler and Denis McQuail, *Television in Politics* (Chicago: University of Chicago Press, 1969); Joseph Trenaman and Denis McQuail, *Television and the Political Image* (London: Nithuen, 1961); Bill O. Kjeldahl et al., "Factors in a Presidential Candidate's Image," *Speech Monographs* 38 (1971): 129–131; Lynda Lee Kaid and Robert O. Hirsh, "Selective Exposure and Candidate Image Over Time," *Central States Speech Journal* 24 (1973): 48–51; Barbara A. Hinkley et al., "Information and the Vote: A Comparative Election Study," *American Politics Quarterly* 2 (1974): 131–158; and Leonard V. Gordon, "The Image of Political Candidates: Values and Voter Preference," *Journal of Applied Psychology* 56 (1972): 382–387. I am indebted to Prof. Patrick Devlin for help in assembling this list; he also has several convention papers relating to political image.

21. The "mosaic" model of communication is presented in Samuel L. Becker, "Rhetorical Studies for the Contemporary World," in Lloyd F. Bitzer and Edwin Black, eds., *The Prospect of Rhetoric: Report of the National Developmental Project* (Englewood Cliffs, NJ: Prentice-Hall, 1971), p. 43–91. The "limited effects" model is critiqued harshly but effectively by theorists unhappy with "hypodermic" persuasion studies following the Yale school of campaign research. Researchers in this model tended to search out only cognitive or attitudinal change points as ways of measuring political effect. See several critiques in Chaffee, ed., *Political Communication*: Becker, McCombs, and McLeod, "Development of Political Cognitions," pp. 21–64; Garrett J. O'Keefe, "Political Campaigns and Mass Communication Research," pp. 129–164; and Jay G. Blumler and Michael Gurevitch, "Towards a Comparative Framework for Political Communication Research," pp. 165–194.

22. Judith S. Trent, "A Synthesis of Methodologies Used in Studying Political Communication," *Central States Speech Journal* 26 (1975): 287–297.

23. As samples, see essays in volume 63 of *Quarterly Journal of Speech*: W. Lance Bennett, "The Ritualistic and Pragmatic Bases of Political Campaign Discourse" (pp. 219–238); David L. Swanson, "And That's the Way It Was? Television Covers the 1976 Presidential Campaign" (pp.

239–248); John H. Patton, "A Government as Good as Its People: Jimmy Carter and the Restoration of Transcendence to Politics" (pp. 249–257); David L. Rarick, "The Carter Persona: An Empirical Analysis of the Rhetorical Visions of Campaign '76" (pp. 258–273); and John F. Cragan, "Foreign Policy Communication Dramas: How Mediated Rhetoric Played in Peoria in Campaign '76" (pp. 274–289). One even can go well beyond "drama" and fully into "dream" or "fantasy" understood psychoanalytically. See, e.g., Lloyd DeMause, "Jimmy Carter and American Fantasy," *Journal of Psychohistory* (1977): 151–174; and John J. Hartman, "Carter and the Utopian Group-Fantasy," *Journal of Psychohistory* 5 (1977): 239–258; the first proposes a four-stage psychic cycle in American politics generally, while the second concentrates upon the 1976 Democratic convention.

The "Ideograph"

A Link Between Rhetoric and Ideology

MICHAEL CALVIN McGEE

In 1950, Kenneth Burke, apparently following Dewey, Mead, and Lippmann, announced his preference for the notion "philosophy of myth" to explain the phenomenon of "public" or "mass consciousness" rather than the then-prevalent concept "ideology."[1] As contemporary writers have pushed on toward developing this "symbolic" or "dramatistic" alternative, the concept "ideology" has atrophied. Many use the term innocently, almost as a synonym for "doctrine" or "dogma" in political organizations;[2] and others use the word in a hypostatized sense that obscures or flatly denies the fundamental connection between the concept and descriptions of mass consciousness.[3] The concept seems to have gone the way of the dodo and of the neo-Aristotelian critic: As Bormann has suggested, the very word is widely perceived as being encrusted with the "intellectual baggage" of orthodox Marxism.[4]

Objecting to the use or abuse of any technical term would, ordinarily, be a sign of excessive crabbiness. But in this instance conceptualizations of "philosophy of myth," "fantasy visions," and "political scenarios," coupled with continued eccentric and/or narrow usages of "ideology," cosmetically camouflage significant and unresolved problems. We are presented with a brute, undeniable phenomenon: Human beings in collectivity behave and think differently than human beings in isolation. The collectivity is said to "have a mind of its own" distinct from the individual qua individual. Writers in the tradition of Marx and Mannheim explain this difference by observing that the only possibility of "mind" lies in the individual qua individual, in the human organism itself. When one appears to "think" and "behave" collectively, therefore, one has been tricked, self-deluded, or manipulated into accepting the brute existence of such fantasies as "public mind" or "public opinion" or "public philosophy." Symbolists generally want to say that this trick is a "transcendence," a voluntary agreement to believe in and to participate in a "myth." Materialists maintain that the trick is an insidious reified form of "lie," a self-perpetuating system of beliefs and interpretations foisted on all members of the community by the ruling class. Burke, with his emphasis on the individuals who are tricked, concerns himself more with the structure of "motive" than with the objective conditions that impinge on and restrict the individual's freedom to develop a political consciousness. Neo-Marxians, with their focus on tricksters and the machinery of trickery, say that the essential question posed by the fact of society is one of locating precise descriptions of the dialectical tension between a "true" and a "false" consciousness, between reality and ideology.[5]

Though some on both sides of the controversy would have it otherwise, there is no *error* in either position. Both "myth" and "ideology" presuppose fundamental falsity in the common metaphor which alleges the existence of a "social organism." "Ideology," however, assumes that the exposure of falsity is a moral act: Though we have never experienced a "true consciousness," it is nonetheless theoretically accessible to us, and, because of such accessibility, we are morally remiss if we do not discard the false and approach the true. The falsity presupposed by "myth," on the other hand, is amoral because it is a purely poetic phenomenon, legitimized by rule of the poet's license, a "suspension of disbelief." A symbolist who speaks of "myth" is typically at great pains to argue for a value-free approach to the object of study, an approach in which one denies that "myth" is a synonym for "lie" and treats it as a falsehood of a peculiarly redemptive nature. Materialists, on the other hand, seem to use the concept "ideology" expressly to warrant normative claims regarding the exploitation of the "proletarian class" by self-serving plunderers. No error is involved in the apparently contradictory conceptions because, fundamentally, materialists and symbolists pursue two different studies: The Marxian asks how the "givens" of a human environment impinge on the development of political consciousness; the symbolist asks how the human symbol-using, reality-creating potential impinges on material reality, ordering it normatively, "mythically."

Errors arise when one conceives "myth" and "ideology" to be contraries, alternative and incompatible theoretical descriptions of the same phenomenon. The materialists' neglect of language studies and the consequent inability of Marxian theory to explain socially constructed realities is well publicized.[6] Less well described is the symbolists' neglect of the nonsymbolic environment and the consequent inability of symbolist theory to account for the impact of material phenomena on the construction of social reality.[7] I do not mean to denigrate in any way the research of scholars attempting to develop Burke's philosophy of myth; indeed, I have on occasion joined that endeavor. I do believe, however, that each of us has erred to the extent that we have conceived the rubrics of symbolism as an *alternative* rather than *supplemental* description of political consciousness. The assertion that "philosophy of myth" is an alternative to "ideology" begs the question Marx intended to pose. Marx was concerned with "power," with the capacity of an elite class to control the state's political, economic, and military establishment, to dominate the state's information systems and determine even the consciousness of large masses of people. He was politically committed to the cause of the proletariat: If a norm was preached by the upper classes, it was by virtue of that fact a baneful seduction; and if a member of the proletarian class was persuaded by such an argument, that person was possessed of an "ideology," victimized and exploited. Not surprisingly, symbolists criticize Marx for his politics, suggesting that his is a wonderfully convenient formula which mistakes commitment for "historically scientific truth." By conceiving poetic falsity, we rid ourselves of the delusion that interpretation is scientific, but we also bury the probability that the myths we study as an alternative are thrust upon us by the brute force of "power." While Marx overestimated "power" as a variable in describing political consciousness, Burke, Cassirer, Polanyi, and others do not want to discuss the capacity even of a "free" state to determine political consciousness.[8]

If we are to describe the trick-of-the-mind which deludes us into believing that we "think" with/through/for a "society" to which we "belong," we need a theoretical model which accounts for both "ideology" and "myth," a model which neither denies human capacity to control "power" through the manipulation of symbols nor begs Marx's essential questions regarding the influence of "power" on creating and maintaining political consciousness. I will argue here that such a model must begin with the concept "ideology" and proceed to link that notion directly with the interests of symbolism.

I will elaborate the following commitments and hypotheses: If a mass consciousness exists at all, it must be empirically "present," itself a thing obvious to those who participate in it, or, at least, empirically manifested in the language which communicates it. I agree with Marx that the problem of consciousness is fundamentally practical and normative, that it is concerned essentially with describing and evaluating the legitimacy of public motives. Such consciousness, I believe, is always false, not because we are programmed automatons and not because we have a propensity to structure political perceptions in poetically false "dramas" or "scenarios," but because "truth" in politics, no matter how firmly we believe, is always an illusion. The falsity of an ideology is specifically rhetorical, for the illusion of truth and falsity with regard to normative commitments is the product of persuasion.[9] Since the clearest access to persuasion (and hence to ideology) is through the discourse used to produce it, I will suggest that ideology in practice is a political language, preserved in rhetorical documents, with the capacity to dictate decision and control public belief and behavior. Further, the political language which manifests ideology seems characterized by slogans, a vocabulary of "ideographs" easily mistaken for the technical terminology of political philosophy. An analysis of ideographic usages in political rhetoric, I believe, reveals interpenetrating systems or "structures" of public motives. Such structures appear to be "diachronic" and "synchronic" patterns of political consciousness which have the capacity both to control "power" and to influence (if not determine) the shape and texture of each individual's "reality."

HYPOTHETICAL CHARACTERISTICS OF IDEOGRAPHS

Marx's thesis suggests that an ideology determines mass belief and thus restricts the free emergence of political opinion. By this logic, the "freest" members of a community are those who belong to the "power" elite; yet the image of hooded puppeteers twisting and turning the masses at will is unconvincing, if only because the elite seems itself imprisoned by the same false consciousness communicated to the polity at large. When we consider the impact of ideology on freedom, and of power on consciousness, we must be clear that ideology is transcendent, as much an influence on the belief and behavior of the ruler as on the ruled. Nothing *necessarily* restricts persons who wield the might of the state. Roosevelts and Carters are as free to indulge personal vanity with capricious uses of power as was Idi Amin, regardless of formal "checks and balances." The polity can punish tyrants and maniacs after the fact of their lunacy or tyranny (if the polity survives it), but, in practical terms, the only way to shape or soften power at the moment of its exercise is prior persuasion. Similarly, no matter what punishment we might imagine "power" visiting upon an ordinary citizen, nothing *necessarily* determines individual behavior and belief. A citizen may be punished for eccentricity or disobedience after the fact of a crime, but, at the moment when defiance is contemplated, the only way to combat the impulse to criminal behavior is prior persuasion. I am suggesting, in other words, that social control in its essence is control over consciousness, the *a priori* influence that learned predispositions hold over human agents who play the roles of "power" and "people" in a given transaction.[10]

Because there is a lack of necessity in social control, it seems inappropriate to characterize agencies of control as "socializing" or "conditioning" media. No individual (least of all the elite who control the power of the state) is *forced* to submit in the same way that a conditioned dog is obliged to salivate or socialized children are required to speak English. Human beings are "conditioned," not directly to belief and behavior, but to a vocabulary of concepts that function as guides, warrants, reasons, or excuses for behavior and belief. When a claim is warranted by such terms as "law," "liberty," "tyranny," or "trial by jury," in other words, it is presumed that human beings will react predictably and autonomically. So it was that a majority of Americans were surprised, not when allegedly sane young men agreed to go halfway around the world to kill for God, country, apple pie, and no other particularly good reason, but, rather, when other young men displayed good common sense by moving to Montreal instead, thereby refusing to be conspicuous in a civil war which was none of their business. The end product of the state's insistence on some degree of conformity in behavior and belief, I suggest, is a *rhetoric* of control, a system of persuasion presumed to be effective on the whole community. We make a rhetoric of war to persuade us of war's necessity, but then forget that it is a rhetoric—and regard negative popular judgments of it as unpatriotic cowardice.

It is not remarkable to conceive social control as fundamentally rhetorical. In the past, however, rhetorical scholarship has regarded the rhetoric of control as a species of argumentation and thereby assumed that the fundamental unit of analysis in such rhetoric is an integrated set-series of propositions. This is, I believe, a mistake, an unwarranted abstraction: To argue is to test an affirmation or denial of claims; argument is the means of proving the truth of grammatical units, declarative sentences, that purport to be reliable signal representations of reality. Within the vocabulary of argumentation, the term "rule of law" makes no sense until it is made the subject or predicable of a proposition. If I say "The rule of law is a primary cultural value in the United States" or "Charles I was a cruel and capricious tyrant," I have asserted a testable claim that may be criticized with logically coordinated observations. When I say simply "the rule of law," however, my utterance cannot qualify logically as a claim. Yet I am conditioned to believe that "liberty" and "property" have an obvious meaning, a behaviorally directive self-evidence. Because I am taught to set such terms apart from my usual vocabulary, words used as agencies of social control may have an intrinsic force—and, if so, I may very well distort the key terms of social conflict, commitment, and control if I think of them as parts of a proposition rather than as basic units of analysis.

Though words only (and not claims), such terms as "property," "religion," "right of privacy," "freedom of speech," "rule of law," and "liberty" are more pregnant than propositions ever could be. They are the basic structural elements, the building blocks, of ideology. Thus they may be thought of as "ideographs," for, like Chinese symbols, they signify and "contain" a unique ideological commitment; further, they presumptuously suggest that each member of a community will see as a gestalt every complex nuance in them. What "rule of law" means is the series of propositions, all of them, that could be manufactured to justify a Whig/Liberal order. Ideographs are one-term sums of an orientation, the species of "God" or "Ultimate" term that will be used to symbolize the line of argument the meanest sort of individual *would* pursue, if that individual had the dialectical skills of philosophers, as a defense of a personal stake in and commitment to the society. Nor is one permitted to question the fundamental logic of ideographs: Everyone is conditioned to think of "the rule of law" as a *logical* commitment just as one is taught to think that "186,000 miles per second" is an accurate empirical description of the speed of light even though few can work the experiments or do the mathematics to prove it.[11]

The important fact about ideographs is that they exist in real discourse, functioning clearly and evidently as agents of political consciousness. They are not invented by observers; they come to be as a part of the real lives of the people whose motives they articulate. So, for example, "rule of law" is a more precise, objective motive then such observer-invented terms as "neurotic" or "paranoid style" or "*petit bourgeois.*"

Ideographs pose a methodological problem *because* of their very specificity: How do we generalize from a "rule of law" to a description of consciousness that comprehends not only "rule of law" but all other like motives as well? What do we describe with the concept "ideograph," and how do we actually go about doing the specific cultural analysis promised by conceptually linking rhetoric and ideology?

Though both come to virtually the same conclusion, the essential argument seems more careful and useful in Ortega's notion of "the etymological man" than in Burke's poetically hidden concept of "the symbol-using animal" and "logology":

> Man, when he sets himself to speak, does so *because* he believes that he will be able to say what he thinks. Now, this is an illusion. Language is not up to that. It says, more or less, a part of what we think, and raises an impenetrable obstacle to the transmission of the rest. It serves quite well for mathematical statements and proofs.... But in proportion as conversation treats of more important, more human, more "real" subjects than these, its vagueness, clumsiness, and confusion steadily increase. Obedient to the inveterate prejudice that "talking leads to understanding," we speak and listen in such good faith that we end by misunderstanding one another far more than we would if we remained mute and set ourselves to divine each other. Nay, more: since our thought is in large measure dependent upon our language . . . it follows that thinking is talking with oneself and hence misunderstanding oneself at the imminent risk of getting oneself into a complete quandary.[12]

All this "talk" generates a series of "usages" which unite us, since we speak the same language, but, more significantly, such "talk" *separates* us from other human beings who do not accept our meanings, our intentions.[13] So, Ortega claims, the essential demarcation of whole nations is language usage: "This gigantic architecture of usages is, precisely, society."[14] And it is through usages that a particular citizen's sociality exists:

> A language, *speech*, is "what people say," it is the vast system of verbal usages established in a collectivity. The individual, the person, is from his birth submitted to the linguistic coercion that these usages represent. Hence the mother tongue is perhaps the most typical and clearest social phenomenon. With it "people" enter us, set up residence in us, making each an example of "people." Our mother tongue socializes our inmost being, and because of this fact every individual belongs, in the strongest sense of the word, to a society. He can flee from the society in which he was born and brought up, but in his flight the society inexorably accompanies him because he carries it within him. This is the true meaning that the statement "man is a social animal" can have.[15]

Ortega's reference, of course, is to language generally and not to a particular vocabulary within language. So he worked with the vocabulary of greeting to demonstrate the definitive quality of linguistic usages when conceiving "society."[16] His reasoning, however, invites specification, attention to the components of the "architecture" supposedly created by usages.

Insofar as usages both unite and separate human beings, it seems reasonable to suggest that the functions of uniting and separating would be represented by specific vocabularies, actual words or terms. With regard to political union and separation, such vocabularies would consist of ideographs. Such usages as "liberty" define a collectivity, i.e., the outer parameters of a society, because such terms either do not exist in other societies or do not have precisely similar meanings. So, in the United States, we claim a common belief in "equality," as do citizens of the Union of Soviet Socialist Republics; but "equality" is not the same word in its meaning or its usage. One can therefore precisely define the difference between the two communities, in part, by comparing the usage of definitive ideographs. We are, of course, still able to interact with the Soviets despite barriers of language and usage. The interaction is possible because of higher-order ideographs—"world peace," "detente," "spheres of influence," etc.—that permit temporary union.[17] And, in the other direction, it is also true that there are special interests within the United States separated one from the other precisely by disagreements regarding the identity, legitimacy, or definition of ideographs. So we are divided by usages into subgroups: Business and labor, Democrats and Republicans, Yankees and Southerners are *united* by the ideographs that represent the political entity "United States" and *separated* by a disagreement as to the practical meaning of such ideographs.

The concept "ideograph" is meant to be purely descriptive of an essentially social human condition. Unlike more general conceptions of "Ultimate" or "God" terms, attention is called to the social, rather than rational or ethical, functions of a particular vocabulary. This vocabulary is precisely a group of *words* and not a series of symbols representing ideas. Ortega clearly, methodically, distinguishes a usage (what we might call "social" or "material" thought) from an *idea* (what Ortega would call "pure thought"). He suggests, properly, that *language gets in the way of thinking*, separates us from "ideas" we may have which cannot be surely expressed, even to ourselves, in the usages which imprison us. So my "pure thought" about liberty, religion, and property is clouded, hindered, made irrelevant by the existence in history of the ideographs "Liberty, Religion, and Property."[18] Because these terms are definitive of the society we have inherited, they are *conditions* of the society into which each of us is born, material ideas which we must accept to "belong." They penalize us, in a sense, as much as they protect us, for they prohibit our appreciation of an alternative pattern of meaning in, for example, the Soviet Union or Brazil.

In effect, ideographs—language imperatives which hinder and perhaps make impossible "pure thought"—are bound within the culture which they define. We can *characterize* an ideograph, say what it has meant and does mean as a usage, and some of us may be able to achieve an imaginary state of withdrawal from community long enough to speculate as to what ideographs *ought* to mean in the best of possible worlds; but the very nature of language forces us to keep the two operations separate: So, for example, the "idea" of "liberty" may be the subject of philosophical speculation, but philosophers can never be *certain* that they themselves or their readers understand a "pure" meaning unpolluted by historical, ideographic usages.[19] Should we look strictly at material notions of "liberty," on the other hand, we distort our thinking by believing that a rationalization of a particular historical meaning is "pure," the truth of the matter.[20] Ideographs can *not* be used to establish or test truth, and vice versa; the truth, in ideal metaphysical senses, is a consideration irrelevant to accurate characterizations of such ideographs as "liberty." Indeed, if examples from recent history are a guide, the attempts to infuse usages with metaphysical meanings, or to confuse ideographs with the "pure" thought of philosophy, have resulted in the "nightmares" which Polanyi, for one, deplores.[21] The significance of ideographs is in their concrete history as usages, not in their alleged idea-content.

THE ANALYSIS OF IDEOGRAPHS

No one has ever seen an "equality" strutting up the driveway, so, if "equality" exists at all, it has meaning through its specific applications. In other words, we establish a meaning for "equality" by using the word as a description of a certain phenomenon; it has meaning only insofar as our description is acceptable, believable. If asked to make a case for "equality," that is, to define the term, we are forced to make reference to its history by detailing the situations for which the word has been an appropriate description. Then, by comparisons over time, we establish an analog for the proposed present usage of the term. Earlier usages become precedents, touchstones for judging the propriety of the ideograph in a current circumstance. The meaning of "equality" does not rigidify because situations seeming to require its usage are never perfectly similar: As the situations vary, so the meaning of "equality" expands and contracts. The variations in meaning of "equality" are much less important, however, than the fundamental, categorical meaning, the "common denominator" of all situations for which "equality" has been the best and most descriptive term. The dynamism of "equality" is thus paramorphic, for even when the term changes its signification in particular circumstances, it retains a formal, categorical meaning, a constant reference to its history as an ideograph.

These earlier usages are vertically structured, related each to the other in a formal way, every time the society is called upon to judge whether a particular circumstance should be defined ideographically. So, for example, to protect ourselves from abuses of power, we have built into our political system an ideograph that is said to justify "impeaching" an errant leader: If the president has engaged in behaviors which can be described as "high crimes and misdemeanors," even that highest officer must be removed.

But what is meant by "high crimes and misdemeanors"? If Peter Rodino wishes to justify impeachment procedures against Richard Nixon in the Committee on the Judiciary of the House of Representatives, he must mine history for touchstones, precedents which give substance and an aura of precision to the ideograph "high crimes and misdemeanors." His search of the past concentrates on situations analogous to that which he is facing, situations involving actual or proposed "impeachment." The "rule of law" emerged as a contrary ideograph, and Rodino developed from the tension between "law" and "high crimes" an argument indicting Nixon. His proofs were historical, ranging from Magna Carta to Edmund Burke's impeachment of Warren Hastings. He was able to make the argument, therefore, only because he could organize a series of events, situationally similar, with an ideograph as the structuring principle. The structuring is "vertical" because of the element of *time*; that is, the deep meanings of "law" and "high crime" derive from knowledge of the way in which meanings have evolved over a period of time—awareness of the way an ideograph can be meaningful *now* is controlled in large part by what it meant *then*.[22]

All communities take pains to record and preserve the vertical structure of their ideographs. Formally, the body of nonstatutory "law" is little more than literature recording ideographic usages in the "common law" and "case law."[23] So, too, historical dictionaries, such as the *Oxford English Dictionary*, detail etymologies for most of the Anglo-American ideographs. And any so-called professional history provides a record in detail of the events surrounding earlier usages of ideographs—indeed, the historian's eye is most usually attracted precisely to those situations involving ideographic appli-cations.[24] The more significant record of vertical structures, however, lies in what might be called "popular" history. Such history consists in part of novels, films, plays, even songs; but the truly influential manifestation is grammar school history, the very first contact most have with their existence and experience as a part of a community.

To learn the meanings of the ideographs "freedom" and "patriotism," for example, most of us swallowed the tale of Patrick Henry's defiant speech to the Virginia House of Burgesses: "I know not what course others may take, but as for me, give me liberty or give me death!" These specific words, of course, were concocted by the historian William Wirt and not by Governor Henry. Wirt's intention was to provide a model for "the young men of Virginia," asking them to copy Henry's virtues and avoid his vices.[25] Fabricated events and words meant little, not because Wirt was uninterested in the truth of what really happened to Henry, but rather because what he wrote about was the definition of essential ideographs. His was a task of socialization, an exercise in epideictic rhetoric, providing the youth of his age (and of our own) with general knowledge of ideographic touchstones so that they might be able to make, or comprehend, judgments of public motives and of their own civic duty.

Though such labor tires the mind simply in imagining it, there is no trick in gleaning from public documents the entire vocabulary of ideographs that define a particular collectivity. The terms do not hide in discourse, nor is their "meaning" or function within an argument obscure: we might disagree metaphysically about "equal-ity," and we might use the term differently in practical discourse, but I believe we can nearly always discover the functional meaning of the term by measure of its grammatic and pragmatic context.[26] Yet even a complete description of vertical ideographic structures leaves little but an exhaustive lexicon understood etymologically and diachronically—and no ideally precise explanation of how ideographs function *presently*.

If we find forty rhetorical situations in which "rule of law" has been an organizing term, we are left with little but the simple chronology of the situations as a device to structure the lot: Case 1 is distinct from Case 40, and the meaning of the ideograph thus has contracted or expanded in the intervening time. But time is an irrelevant matter *in practice*. Chronological sequences are provided by analysts, and they properly reflect the concerns of theorists who try to describe what "rule of law" *may* mean, potentially, by laying out the history of what the term *has* meant. Such advocates as Rodino are not so scrupulous in research; they choose eight or nine of those forty cases to use as evidence in argument, ignore the rest, and impose a pattern of organization on the cases recom-mended (or forced) by the demands of a current situation. As Ortega argues with reference to language generally, key usages considered historically and diachronically are purely formal; yet in real discourse, and in public consciousness, they are *forces*:

> [A]ll that diachronism accomplishes is to reconstruct other comparative "presents" of the
> language as they existed in the past. All that it shows us, then, is changes; it enables us to

witness one present being replaced by another, the succession of the static figures of the language, as the "film," with its motionless images, engenders the visual fiction of a movement. At best, it offers us a cinematic view of language, but not a *dynamic* understanding of how the changes were, and came to be, *made*. The changes are merely results of the making and unmaking process, they are the externality of language and there is need for an internal conception of it in which we discover not resultant *forms* but the operating *forces* themselves.[27]

In Burke's terminology, describing a vertical ideographic structure yields a culture-specific and relatively precise "grammar" of one public motive. That motive is not captured, however, without attention to its "rhetoric."

Considered rhetorically, as *forces*, ideographs seem structured horizontally, for when people actually make use of them presently, such terms as "rule of law" clash with other ideographs ("principle of confidentiality" or "national security," for example), and in the conflict come to mean with reference to synchronic confrontations. So, for example, one would not ordinarily think of an inconsistency between "rule of law" and "principle of confidentiality." Vertical analysis of the two ideographs would probably reveal a consonant relationship based on genus and species: "Confidentiality" of certain conversations is a control on the behavior of government, a control that functions to maintain a "rule of law" and prevents "tyranny" by preserving a realm of privacy for the individual.

The "Watergate" conflict between Nixon and Congress, however, illustrates how that consonant relationship can be restructured, perhaps broken, in the context of a particular controversy: Congress asked, formally and legally, for certain of Nixon's documents. He refused, thereby creating the appearance of frustrating the imperative value "rule of law." He attempted to excuse himself by matching a second ideograph, "principle of confidentiality," against normal and usual meanings of "rule of law." Before a mass television audience, Nixon argued that a President's conversations with advisers were entitled to the same privilege constitutionally accorded exchanges between priest and penitent, husband and wife, lawyer and client. No direct vertical precedent was available to support Nixon's usage. The argument asked public (and later jurisprudential) permission to expand the meaning of "confidentiality" and thereby to alter its relationship with the "rule of law," making what appeared to be an illegal act acceptable. Nixon's claims were epideictic and not deliberative or forensic; he magnified "confidentiality" by praising the ideograph as if it were a person, attempting to alter its "standing" among other ideographs, even as an individual's "standing" in the community changes through praise and blame.[28]

Synchronic structural changes in the relative standing of an ideograph are "horizontal" because of the presumed consonance of an ideology; that is, ideographs such as "rule of law" are meant to be taken together, as a working unit, with "public trust," "freedom of speech," "trial by jury," and any other slogan characteristic of the collective life. If all the ideographs used to justify a Whig/Liberal government were placed on a chart, they would form groups or clusters of words radiating from the slogans originally used to rationalize "popular sovereignty"—"religion," "liberty," and "property." Each term would be a connector, modifier, specifier, or contrary for those fundamental historical commitments, giving them a meaning and a unity easily mistaken for logic. Some terms would be enshrined in the Constitution, some in law, some merely in conventional usage; but all would be constitutive of "the people." Though new usages can enter the equation, the ideographs remain essentially unchanged. But when we engage ideological argument, when we cause ideographs to *do work* in explaining, justifying, or guiding policy in specific situations, the relationship of ideographs changes. A "rule of law," for example, is taken for granted, a simple connector between "property" and "liberty," until a constitutional crisis inclines us to make it "come first." In Burke's vocabulary, it becomes the "title" or "god-term" of all ideographs, the center-sun about which every ideograph orbits. Sometimes circumstance forces us to sense that the structure is not consonant, as when awareness of racism exposes contradiction between "property" and "right to life" in the context of "open-housing" legislation. Sometimes officers of state, in the process of justifying particular uses of power, manufacture seeming inconsistency, as when Nixon pitted "confidentiality" against "rule of law." And sometimes an alien force frontally assaults the structure, as when Hitler campaigned against "decadent democracies." Such instances have the potential to change the structure of ideographs and hence the "present" ideology—in this sense, an ideology is dynamic and a *force*, always resilient, always keeping itself in some consonance and unity, but not always the *same* consonance and unity.[29]

In appearance, of course, characterizing ideological conflicts as synchronic *structural* dislocations is an unwarranted abstraction: An ideological argument could result simply from multiple usages of an ideograph. Superficially, for example, one might be inclined to describe the "busing" controversy as a disagreement over the "best" meaning for "equality," one side opting for "equality" defined with reference to "access" to education and the other with reference to the goal, "being educated." An ideograph, however, is always understood in its relation to another; it is defined tautologically by using other terms in its cluster. If we accept that there are three or four or however many possible meanings for "equality," each with a currency and legitimacy, we distort the nature of the ideological dispute by ignoring the fact that "equality" is made meaningful, not within the clash of multiple usages, but rather in its relationship with "freedom." That is, "equality" defined by "access" alters the nature of "liberty" from the relationship of "equality" and "liberty" thought to exist when "equality" is defined as "being educated." One would not want to rule out the possibility that ideological disagreements, however rarely, could be simply semantic; but we are more likely to err if we assume the dispute to be semantic than if we look for the deeper structural dislocation which likely produced multiple usages as a disease produces symptoms. When an ideograph is at the center of a semantic dispute, I would suggest, the multiple usages will be either metaphysical or diachronic, purely speculative or historical, and in either event devoid of the force and currency of a synchronic ideological conflict.[30]

In the terms of this argument, two recognizable "ideologies" exist in any specific culture at one "moment." One "ideology" is a "grammar," a historically-defined diachronic structure of ideograph meanings expanding and contracting from the birth of the society to its "present." Another "ideology" is a "rhetoric," a situationally-defined synchronic structure of ideograph clusters constantly reorganizing itself to accommodate specific circumstances while maintaining its fundamental consonance and unity. A division of this sort, of course, is but an analytic convenience for talking about two *dimensions* (vertical and horizontal) of a single phenomenon: No present ideology can be divorced from past commitments, if only because the very words used to express present dislocations have a history that establishes the category of their meaning. And no diachronic ideology can be divorced from the "here-and-now" if only because its entire *raison d'être* consists in justifying the form and direction of collective behavior. Both of these structures must be understood and described before one can claim to have constructed a theoretically precise explanation of a society's ideology, of its repertoire of public motives.

CONCLUSION

One of the casualties of the current "pluralist" fad in social and political theory has been the old Marxian thesis that governing elites control the masses by creating, maintaining, and manipulating a mass consciousness suited to perpetuation of the existing order.[31] Though I agree that Marx probably overestimated the influence of an elite, it is difficult *not* to see a "dominant ideology" which seems to exercise decisive influence in political life. The question, of course, turns on finding a way accurately to define and to describe a dominant ideology. Theorists writing in the tradition of Dewey, Burke, and Cassirer have, in my judgment, come close to the mark; but because they are bothered by poetic metaphors, these symbolists never conceive their work as description of a mass consciousness. Even these writers, therefore, beg Marx's inescapable question regarding the impact of "power" on the way we think. I have argued here that the concepts "rhetoric" and "ideology" may be linked without poetic metaphors, and that the linkage should produce a description and an explanation of dominant ideology, of the relationship between the "power" of a state and the consciousness of its people.

The importance of symbolist constructs is their focus on *media* of consciousness, on the discourse that articulates and propagates common beliefs. "Rhetoric," "sociodrama," "myth," "fantasy vision," and "political scenario" are not important because of their *fiction*, their connection to poetic, but because of their *truth*, their links with the trick-of-the-mind that deludes individuals into believing that they "think" with/for/through a social organism. The truth of symbolist constructs, I have suggested, appears to lie in our claim to see a legitimate social reality in a vocabulary of complex, high-order abstractions that refer to and invoke a sense of "the people." By learning the meaning of ideographs, I have argued, everyone in society, even the "freest" of us, those who control the state, seem predisposed to structured mass responses. Such terms as "liberty," in other words, constitute by our very use of them in political discourse an ideology that governs or "dominates" our consciousness. In practice, therefore, ideology is a political language composed of sloganlike terms signifying collective commitment.

Such terms I have called "ideographs." A formal definition of "ideograph," derived from arguments made throughout this essay, would list the following characteristics: An ideograph is an ordinary-language term found in political discourse. It is a high-order abstraction representing collective commitment to a particular but equivocal and ill-defined normative goal. It warrants the use of power, excuses behavior and belief which might otherwise be perceived as eccentric or antisocial, and guides behavior and belief into channels easily recognized by a community as acceptable and laudable. Ideographs such as "slavery" and "tyranny," however, may guide behavior and belief negatively by branding unacceptable behavior. And many ideographs ("liberty," for example) have a nonideographic usage, as in the sentence, "Since I resigned my position, I am at liberty to accept your offer." Ideographs are culture-bound, though some terms are used in different signification across cultures. Each member of the community is socialized, conditioned, to the vocabulary of ideographs as a prerequisite for "belonging" to the society. A degree of tolerance is usual, but people are expected to understand ideographs within a range of usage thought to be acceptable: The society will inflict penalties on those who use ideographs in heretical ways and on those who refuse to respond appropriately to claims on their behavior warranted through the agency of ideographs.

Though ideographs such as "liberty," "religion," and "property" often appear as technical terms in social philosophy, I have argued here that the ideology of a community is established by the usage of such terms in specifically rhetorical discourse, for such usages constitute excuses for specific beliefs and behaviors made by those who executed the history of which they were a part. The ideographs used in rhetorical discourse seem structured in two ways: In isolation, each ideograph has a history, an etymology, such that current meanings of the term are linked to past usages of it diachronically. The diachronic structure of an ideograph establishes the parameters, the category, of its meaning. All ideographs taken together, I suggest, are thought at any specific "moment" to be consonant, related one to another in such a way as to produce unity of commitment in a particular historical context. Each ideograph is thus connected to all others as brain cells are linked by synapses, synchronically in one context at one specific moment.

A complete description of an ideology, I have suggested, will consist of (1) the isolation of a society's ideographs, (2) the exposure and analysis of the diachronic structure of every ideograph, and (3) characterization of synchronic relationships among all the ideographs in a particular context. Such a description, I believe, would yield a theoretical framework with which to describe interpenetrating material and symbolic environments: Insofar as we can explain the diachronic and synchronic tensions among ideographs, I suggest, we can also explain the tension between *any* "given" human environment ("objective reality") and any "projected" environments ("symbolic" or "social reality") latent in rhetorical discourse.

Notes

1. Kenneth Burke, *A Rhetoric of Motives* (New York: Prentice-Hall, 1950), pp. 197–203; John Dewey, *The Public and Its Problems* (New York: Henry Holt, 1927); George H. Mead, *Mind, Self, and Society* (Chicago: University of Chicago Press, 1934); and Walter Lippmann, *Public Opinion* (1922; rpt., New York: Free Press, 1965). Duncan groups the American symbolists by observing that European social theorists using "ideology" were concerned with "consciousness" (questions about the *apprehension* of society), while symbolists using poetic metaphors were concerned with a "philosophy of action" (questions about the way we do or ought to *behave* in society). In rejecting the concept and theory of "ideology," Burke refused to consider the relationship between consciousness and action except as that relationship can be characterized with the agency of an *a priori* poetic metaphor, "dramatism." His thought and writing, like that of a poet, is therefore freed from truth criteria: Supposing his *form*, no "motive" outside the dramatistic terminology need be recognized or accounted for *in its particularity*. Though Burkeans are more guilty than Burke, I think even he tends to redefine motives rather than account for them, to cast self-confessions in "scenarios" rather than deal with them in specific. One might say of "dramatism" what Bacon alleged regarding the Aristotelian syllogism, that it is but a form which chases its tail, presuming in its metaphoric conception the truth of its descriptions. See Hugh Dalziel Duncan, *Symbols in Society* (New York: Oxford University Press, 1968), pp. 12–14; Richard Dewey, "The Theatrical Analogy Reconsidered," *American Sociologist* 4 (1969): 307–311; and R. S. Perinbanayagam, "The Definition of the Situation: An Analysis of the Ethnomethodological and Dramaturgical View," *Sociological Quarterly* 15 (1974): 521–541.

2. See, e.g., Arthur M. Schlesinger Jr., "Ideology and Foreign Policy: The American Experience," in George Schwab, ed., *Ideology and Foreign Policy* (New York: Cyrco, 1978), pp. 124–132; and Randall L. Bytwerk, "Rhetorical Aspects of the Nazi Meeting: 1926–1933," *Quarterly Journal of Speech* 61 (1975): 307–318.

3. See, e.g., William R. Brown, "Ideology as Communication Process," *Quarterly Journal of Speech* 64 (1978): 123–140; and Jürgen Habermas, "Technology and Science as 'Ideology,'" in *Toward a Rational Society*, trans. Jeremy J. Shapiro (1968; Boston: Beacon Press, 1970), pp. 81–122.

4. Bormann's distrust of "ideology" was expressed in the context of an evaluation of his "fantasy theme" technique at the 1978 convention of the Speech Communication Association (S.C.A.). See "Fantasy Theme Analysis: An Exploration and Assessment," S.C.A. 1978 Seminar Series, audiotape cassettes. For authoritative accounts of the various "encrustations," see George Lichtheim, "The Concept of Ideology," *History and Theory* 4 (1964–1965): 164–195; and Hans Barth, *Truth and Ideology*, 2d ed., trans. Frederic Lilge (Berkeley and Los Angeles: University of California Press, 1976).

5. See Kenneth Burke, *Permanence and Change*, 2d ed., rev. (1954; rpt., Indianapolis, IN: Bobbs-Merrill, 1965), pp. 19–36, 216–236; Karl Marx and Frederick Engels, *The German Ideology* (1847), trans. and ed. Clemens Dutt, W. Lough, and C. P. Magill, in *The Collected Works of Karl Marx and Frederick Engels*, 9 vols. (Moscow: Progress Publishers, 1975–1977), vol. 5, pp. 3–5, 23–93; Karl Mannheim, *Ideology and Utopia*, trans. Louis Wirth and Edward Shils (1929; rpt., New York: Harvest Books, 1952); and Martin Seliger, *The Marxist Conception of Ideology: A Critical Essay* (Cambridge: Cambridge University Press, 1977). My purpose here is to expose the issue between symbolists (generally) and materialists (particularly Marxians). This of course results in some oversimplification: With regard to the brute problem of describing "consciousness," at least two schools of thought are not here accounted for, Freudian psychiatry and American empirical psychology. Freudians are generally connected with the symbolist position I describe here, while most of the operational conceptions of American empirical psychology (especially social psychology) may fairly be associated with Marxian or neo-Marxian description. Moreover, I treat the terms "ideology" and "myth" as less ambiguous than their history as concepts would suggest. My usage of the terms, and the technical usefulness I portray, reflects my own conviction more than the sure and noncontroversial meaning of either "myth" or "ideology."

6. See, e. g., Willard A. Mullins, "Truth and Ideology: Reflections on Mannheim's Paradox," *History and Theory* 18 (1979): 142–154; William H. Shaw, "'The Handmill Gives You the Feudal Lord': Marx's Technological Determinism," *History and Theory* 18 (1979): 155–176; Jean-Paul Sartre, *Critique of Dialectical Reason*, trans. Alan Sheridan-Smith (London: NLB, 1976), pp. 95–121; and Jean-Paul Sartre, *Search for a Method*, trans. Hazel E. Barnes (New York: Vintage, 1968), pp. 35–84.

7. See W. G. Runciman, "Describing," *Mind* 81 (1972): 372–388; Perinbanayagam, "Definition of the Situation"; and Herbert W. Simons, Elizabeth Mechling, and Howard N. Schreier, "Mobilizing for Collective Action From the Bottom Up: The Rhetoric of Social Movements" (unpublished manuscript, Temple University), pp. 48–59, forthcoming in Carroll C. Arnold and John Waite Bowers, eds., *Handbook of Rhetorical and Communication Theory*.

8. Adolph Hitler, this century's archetype of absolute power—as well as absolute immorality—rose to dominance and maintained himself by putting into practice symbolist theories of social process. Hitler's mere existence forces one to question symbolist theories, asking whether "sociodramas" and "rhetorics" and "myths" are things to be studied scientifically or wild imaginings conjured up from the ether, devil-tools playing upon human weakness and superstition, and therefore things to be politically eradicated. In the face of Hitler, most symbolists adopted a high moral stance of righteous wrath, concentrating on the evil of the man while underplaying the tools he used to gain and keep power. But subtly they modified their logics: Burke is most sensitive to the problem, but in the end he does little more than demonstrate the moral polemical power of dramatistic methods of criticism, becoming the "critic" of his early and later years rather than the "historian" and "theorist" of his middle years. Cassirer's reaction is more extreme, backing away from the logical implications of the symbolist epistemology he

argued for before Hitler, begging the problem of power by characterizing the state itself as nothing but a "myth" to be transcended. Hitler was an inspiration to Polanyi, causing him to take up epistemology as a vehicle to discredit social philosophy generally. In the process Polanyi became an unabashed ideological chauvinist of his adopted culture. See, resp., Kenneth Burke, "The Rhetoric of Hitler's 'Battle,'" in *The Philosophy of Literary Form*, 3d ed. (Berkeley and Los Angeles: University of California Press, 1973), pp. 191–220, and cf. Kenneth Burke, *Attitudes Toward History* (Boston: Beacon Press, 1961), pp. 92–107; Ernst Cassirer, *The Philosophy of Symbolic Forms*, trans. Ralph Manheim (New Haven, CT: Yale University Press, 1953), vol. 1, pp. 105–114; Ernst Cassirer, *The Myth of the State* (New Haven, CT: Yale University Press, 1946); Michael Polanyi, *The Logic of Liberty* (Chicago: University of Chicago Press, 1951), pp. 93–110, 138–153; and Michael Polanyi, *Personal Knowledge: Towards a Post-Critical Philosophy* (Chicago: University of Chicago Press, 1962), pp. 69–131, 203–248, 299–324.

9. I am suggesting that the topic of "falsity" is necessary whenever one's conception of consciousness transcends the mind of a single individual. This is so because the transcendent consciousness, by its very conception, is a legitimizing agency, a means to warrant moral judgments (as in Perelman) or a means to create the fiction of verification when verification is logically impossible (as in Ziman and Brown). To fail to acknowledge the undeniable falsity of *any* description of mass or group consciousness is to create the illusion that one or another series of normative claims have an independent "facticity" about them. In my view, Brown and Ziman are reckless with hypostatized "descriptions" of the consciousness of an intellectual elite, a "scientific community," which itself is in fact a creature of convention, in the specific terms of "description" a fiction of Ziman's and Brown's mind and a rhetorical vision for their readers. See Brown, "Ideology as a Communication Process"; P. Perelman and L. Olbrechts-Tyteca, *The New Rhetoric: A Treatise on Argumentation*, trans. John Wilkinson and Purcell Weaver (South Bend, IN: University of Notre Dame Press, 1969), pp. 31–35, 61–74; J. M. Ziman, *Public Knowledge: An Essay Concerning the Social Dimension of Science* (Cambridge: Cambridge University Press, 1968), pp. 102–142; and contrast George Edward Moore, *Principia Ethica* (Cambridge: Cambridge University Press, 1965), esp. pp. 142–180; and Bruce E. Gronbeck, "From 'Is' to 'Ought': Alternative Strategies," *Central States Speech Journal* 19 (1968): 31–39.

10. See Kenneth Burke, "A Dramatistic View of the Origins of Language and Postscripts on the Negative," in *Language as Symbolic Action* (Berkeley and Los Angeles: University of California Press, 1966), pp. 418–479, esp. pp. 453–463; Hannah Arendt, "What Is Authority?," in *Between Past and Future* (New York: Viking, 1968), pp. 91–141; Hannah Arendt, "Lying in Politics: Reflections on the Pentagon Papers," in *Crises of the Republic* (New York: Harcourt Brace Jovanovich, 1972), pp. 1–47; Jürgen Habermas, "Hannah Arendt's Communications Concept of Power," *Social Research* 44 (1977): 3–24; J.G.A. Pocock, *Politics, Language, and Time* (New York: Atheneum, 1973), pp. 17–25, 202–232; and Robert E. Goodwin, "Laying Linguistic Traps," *Political Theory* 5 (1977): 491–504.

11. See Kenneth Burke, *A Grammar of Motives* (New York: Prentice-Hall, 1945), pp. 43–46, 415–418; Burke, *Rhetoric*, pp. 275–276, 298–301; Ernst Cassirer, *Language and Myth*, trans. Susanne K. Langer (New York: Dover, 1953), pp. 62–83; Richard M. Weaver, *The Ethics of Rhetoric* (Chicago: Gateway, 1970), pp. 211–232; and Rosalind Coward and John Ellis, *Language and Materialism* (London: Routledge & Kegan Paul, 1977), pp. 61–152.

12. José Ortega y Gasset, *Man and People*, trans. Willard R. Trask (New York: Norton 1957), p. 245.

13. Ibid., pp. 192–221, 258–272.

14. Ibid., p. 221.

15. Ibid., p. 251.

16. Ibid., pp. 176–191.

17. See Murray Edelman, *Political Language* (New York: Academic Press, 1977), pp. 43–49, 141–155; Schwab, *Ideology and Foreign Policy*, pp. 143–157; and Thomas M. Franck and Edward Weisband, *Word Politics: Verbal Strategy Among the Superpowers* (New York: Oxford University Press, 1972), pp. 3–10, 96–113, 137–169.

18. Ortega, *Man and People*, pp. 243–252. Further, contrast Ortega and Marx on the nature

of "idea"; see José Ortega y Gasset, *The Modern Theme*, trans. James Cleugh (New York: Harper, 1961), pp. 11–27; and Marx and Engels, *German Ideology*, pp. 27–37. See also Coward and Ellis, *Language and Materialism*, pp. 84–92, 122–135.

19. Ortega, *Man and People*, pp. 57–71, 94–111, 139–191. Husserl's recognition of *praxis* and contradiction in his doctrine of "self-evidence" confirms Ortega's critique; see Edmund Husserl, *Ideas: General Introduction to Pure Phenomenology*, trans. W. R. Boyce Gibson (London: Collier Macmillan, 1962), pp. 353–367. See also Alfred Schutz and Thomas Luckmann's elaboration of the bases of Carneadean skepticism, in their *The Structures of the Life-World*, trans. Richard M. Zaner and H. Tristram Engelhardt Jr. (Evanston, IL: Northwestern University Press, 1973), pp. 182–229.

20. Michel Foucault, *The Archaeology of Knowledge*, trans. A. M. Sheridan Smith (New York: Pantheon, 1972), pp. 178–195; H. T. Wilson, *The American Ideology: Science, Technology, and Organization as Modes of Rationality in Advanced Industrial Societies* (London: Routledge & Kegan Paul, 1977), pp. 231–253; and Roger Poole, *Towards Deep Subjectivity* (New York: Harper & Row, 1972), pp. 78–112.

21. Michael Polanyi and Harry Prosch, *Meaning* (Chicago: University of Chicago Press, 1975), pp. 9, 22: "We have all learned to trace the collapse of freedom in the twentieth century to the writings of certain philosophers, particularly Marx, Nietzsche, and their common ancestors, Fichte and Hegel. But the story has yet to be told how we came to welcome as liberators the philosophies that were to destroy liberty.... We in the Anglo-American sphere have so far escaped the totalitarian nightmares of the right and left. But we are far from home safe. For we have done little, in our free intellectual endeavors to uphold thought as an independent, self governing force." Contrast this "personal knowledge" explanation with Max Horkheimer and Theodor W. Adorno, *Dialectic of Enlightenment*, trans. John Cumming (New York: Herder and Herder, 1972), pp. 255–256; and Jacques Ellul, *Propaganda: The Formation of Men's Attitudes*, trans. Konrad Kellen and Jean Lerner (New York: Vintage, 1973), pp. 52–61, 232–257.

22. See Peter Rodino's opening remarks in "Debate on Articles of Impeachment," U.S. Congress, House of Representatives, Committee on the Judiciary, 93rd Cong., 2nd sess., 24 July 1974, pp. 1–4. The "vertical/horizontal" metaphor used here to describe the evident structure of ideographs should not be confused with Ellul's idea (*Propaganda*, pp. 79–84) of the structural effects of "propaganda." Lasky's analysis of "the English ideology" represents the "vertical" description I have in mind; see Melvin J. Lasky, *Utopia and Revolution* (Chicago: University of Chicago Press, 1976), pp. 496–575.

23. See Edward H. Levi, *An Introduction to Legal Reasoning* (Chicago: University of Chicago Press, 1948), esp. pp. 6–19, 41–74; Perelman and Tyteca, *The New Rhetoric*, pp. 70–74, 101–102, 350–357; and Duncan, *Symbols in Society*, pp. 110–23, 130–140.

24. Collingwood suggests that the content or ultimate subject matter of history should consist of explaining such recurrent usages ("ideographs") as "freedom" and "progress"; see R. G. Collingwood, *The Idea of History* (London: Oxford University Press, 1972), pp. 302–334. See also Herbert J. Muller, *The Uses of the Past* (New York: Oxford University Press, 1952), pp. 37–38.

25. See William Wirt, *Sketches of the Life and Character of Patrick Henry*, 9th ed. (Philadelphia: Thomas Cowperthwait, 1839), Dedication and pp. 417–443; Judy Hample, "The Textual and Cultural Authenticity of Patrick Henry's 'Liberty or Death' Speech," *Quarterly Journal of Speech* 63 (1977): 298–310; and Robert D. Meade, *Patrick Henry: Portrait in the Making* (New York: Lippincott, 1957), pp. 49–58.

26. At least two strategies (i.e., two theoretical mechanisms) have the capacity to yield fairly precise descriptions of functional "meaning" within situational and textual contexts: see Hans-Georg Gadamer, *Philosophical Hermeneutics*, trans. David E. Linge (Berkeley and Los Angeles: University of California Press, 1976), pp. 59–94; and Umberto Eco, *A Theory of Semiotics* (Bloomington: Indiana University Press, 1976), pp. 48–150, 276–313.

27. Ortega, *Man and People*, p. 247. Cf. Ferdinand de Saussure, *Course in General Linguistics*, trans. Wade Baskin, ed. Charles Bally and Albert Sechehaye in collaboration with Albert Riedlinger (New York: McGraw-Hill, 1966), pp. 140–190, 218–221.

28. See Richard M. Nixon, "Address to the Nation on the Watergate Investigation," in *Public*

Papers of the Presidents of the United States (Washington, DC: U.S. Government Printing Office, 1975), Richard Nixon, 1973, pp. 691–698, 710–725. Lucas's analysis of "rhetoric and revolution" (though it is more "idea" than "terministically" conscious) represents the "horizontal" description I have in mind; see Stephen E. Lucas, *Portents of Rebellion: Rhetoric and Revolution in Philadelphia, 1765–76* (Philadelphia: Temple University Press, 1976).

29. See Jürgen Habermas, *Communication and the Evolution of Society*, trans. Thomas McCarthy (Boston: Beacon Press, 1979), pp. 1–68, 130–205.

30. See Foucault, *Archaeology of Knowledge*, pp. 149–165.

31. See Nicholas Abercrombie and Bryan S. Turner, "The Dominant Ideology Thesis," *British Journal of Sociology* 29 (1978): 149–170.

Critical Rhetoric
Theory and *Praxis*

RAYMIE E. McKERROW

Since the time of Plato's attack marginalizing rhetoric by placing it at the service of truth, theorists have assumed a burden of explaining why rhetoric is "*not* an inferior art" (Hariman, 1986, p. 47). Attempts to rescue rhetoric from its subservient role have often been dependent on universal standards of reason as a means of responding to Plato's critique. While rehabilitating rhetoric in some degree, the efforts nonetheless continue to place it on the periphery, at the service of other, more fundamental standards. Habermas's (1984, 1987) "ideal speech situation," Perelman's (1969) "universal audience," and Toulmin's (1972) "impartial standpoint of rationality" all privilege reason above all else as the avenue to emancipation. In so doing, they preserve for rhetoric a subordinate role in the service of reason. If we are to escape from the trivializing influence of universalist approaches, the task is not to rehabilitate rhetoric, but to announce it in terms of a critical practice.

In response to this challenge, this essay articulates the concept of a *critical rhetoric*—a perspective on rhetoric that explores, in theoretical and practical terms, the implications of a theory that is divorced from the constraints of a Platonic conception. As theory, a critical rhetoric examines the dimensions of domination and freedom as these are exercised in a relativized world. Thus, the first part of this essay focuses on what I am terming a "critique of domination" and a "critique of freedom." The critique of domination has an emancipatory purpose—a *telos* toward which it aims in the process of demystifying the conditions of domination. The critique of freedom, premised on Michel Foucault's treatment of power relations, has as its *telos* the prospect of permanent criticism—a self-reflexive critique that turns back on itself even as it promotes a realignment in the forces of power that construct social relations. In practice, a critical rhetoric seeks to unmask or demystify the discourse of power. The aim is to understand the integration of power/knowledge in society—what possibilities for change the integration invites or inhibits and what intervention strategies might be considered appropriate to effect social change. The second part of the essay delineates the *principles* underlying a critical practice. While the principles are not an exhaustive account, they constitute the core ideas of an *orientation* to critique. As will be argued, the principles also recast the nature of rhetoric from one grounded on Platonic, universalist conceptions of reason to one that recaptures the sense of rhetoric as contingent, of knowledge as doxastic, and of critique as a performance. In so doing, a critical rhetoric reclaims the status (Hariman, 1986) of centrality in the analysis of a discourse of power.

Before considering the twin critiques of domination and freedom, the generic features of a "critical rhetoric" need to be set forth. These features name the enterprise and determine its overall *telos*. First, a critical rhetoric shares the same "critical spirit" that is held in common among the divergent perspectives of Horkheimer, Adorno, Habermas, and Foucault. Second, what Slack and Allor (1983) identify as the "effectivity of communication in the exercise of social power" (p. 215) refers to the manner in which discourse insinuates itself in the fabric of social power, and thereby "effects" the status of knowledge among the members of the social group. As Mosco (1983) suggests, "Critical research makes explicit the dense web connecting seemingly unrelated forces in society" (p. 239). By doing so, a critical rhetoric serves a demystifying function (West, 1988, p. 18) by demonstrating the silent and often nondeliberate ways in which rhetoric conceals as much as it reveals through its relationship with power/knowledge. As Marx (1843) put it, a critique serves as "the self-clarification of the struggles and wishes of the age" (cited in Fraser, 1985, p. 97). Third, "a critical social theory frames its research program and its conceptual framework with an eye to the aims and activities of those oppositional social movements with which it has a partisan though not uncritical identification" (Fraser, 1985, p. 97). Critique is not detached and impersonal; it has as its object something which it is "against."[1] Finally, a critical practice must have consequences. In Misgeld's (1985) view, "The ultimate test for the validity of a critical theory of society consists in the possibility of the incorporation of its insights into practically consequential interpretations of social situations" (p. 55). Whether the critique establishes a social judgment about "what to do" as a result of the analysis, it must nonetheless serve to identify the possibilities of future action available to the participants.

A THEORETICAL RATIONALE
FOR A CRITICAL RHETORIC

A critical rhetoric encompasses at least two complementary perspectives. The critiques of domination and freedom may not embrace all of those possible, but they allow us to establish the general thrust of critical rhetoric's analysis of discourse. A specific critique may focus on one or the other, or may select elements of both in exploring rhetoric's central role in the creation of social practices. Following the "theoretical rationale," the essay considers the principles that govern analysis within or across these perspectives.

The Critique of Domination: The Discourse of Power

The focus of a critique of domination is on the discourse of power which creates and sustains the social practices which control the dominated. It is, more particularly, a critique of ideologies, perceived as rhetorical creations. The interrelationships between these key concepts deserves closer examination.

Domination, Power, and Ideology

A traditional critique of ideology has been in terms of the domination thesis. Giddens (1979) provides a theoretical rationale for viewing power in terms of the dominant or ruling class. He distinguishes between "ideology *as referring to discourse* on the one hand, and ideology *as referring to the involvement of beliefs within 'modes of lived existence'*" (p. 183), and goes on to insist *"that the chief usefulness of the concept of ideology concerns the critique of domination"* (p. 188). This does not mean that the emphasis on discourse itself has been reduced or rejected. Instead, the emphasis has shifted from the question "is this discourse true or false?" to "how the discourse is mobilized to legitimate the sectional interests of hegemonic groups[?]" (p. 187). The critique is directed to an analysis of discourse as it contributes to the interests of the ruling class, and as it empowers the ruled to present their interests in a forceful and compelling manner.

Domination occurs through "the construction and maintenance of a particular order of discourse ... [and] the deployment of non-discursive affirmations and sanctions" (Therborn, 1980, p. 82). The ruling class is affirmed by recourse to *rituals* wherein its power is expressed; its role as ruler is sanctioned, in a negative sense, by the ultimate act of *excommunicating* those who fail to participate in or accede to the rituals. The social structures of discourse, taking their cue from Michel Foucault's "orders of discourse," begin with *"restrictions* on who may speak, how much may be said, what may be talked about, and on what occasion" (Therborn, 1980, p. 83). These restrictions are more than socially derived regulators of discourse; they are institutionalized rules accepted and used by the dominant class to control the discursive actions of the dominated. The ruling class does not need to resort to overt censorship of opposing ideas, as these rules effectively contain inflammatory rhetoric within socially approved bounds—bounds accepted by the people who form the community. As Hall (1988) notes:

> Ruling or dominant conceptions of the world do not directly prescribe the mental content of the illusions that supposedly fill the heads of the dominated classes. But the circle of dominant ideas *does* accumulate the symbolic power to map or classify the world for others; its classifications do acquire not only the constraining power of dominance over other modes of thought but also the inertial authority of habit and instinct. It becomes the horizon of the taken-for-granted: what the world is and how it works, for all practical purposes. (p. 44)

Within the world of the "taken-for-granted," discourse is further *shielded* by accepting only certain individuals as the authorities who can speak. The Moral Majority, for example, would typify this order of discourse by limiting the "word" to the Bible and its author, God. Their discourse is further shielded by allowing repetition by God's servants on earth, only so long as their pronouncements conform to the valid meaning of the original text. Governmental "gag orders" perform the same function, only in this case the intent is to protect interests by limiting the privilege of speech to those whose words can be counted on to be supportive of the establishment. Finally, the structuring of the discursive order involves the *delimited appropriation of discourse,* whereby its reception is restrictively situated. This is not a new category, as research on genre has already established the nature and form of "delimited" address in particular contexts (see Simons and Aghazarian, 1986).

Those who are dominated also participate in the social structure and are affected by—and affect—the orders of discourse by which their actions are moderated. Bisseret (1979) suggests that "the more the speaker is subjected to power, the more he situates himself conceptually in reference to the very place where power is concretely exercised" (p. 64). A person cannot escape from the influence of dominant actors, even though the discourse of the latter involves no overt attempt to censor or to entrap the dominated. One can participate in the "dialectic of control" (Giddens, 1979, p. 149) and thereby affect the discourse of power by which individual choice is governed. Nevertheless, the impetus to so function, and the possibility of change, is muted by the fact that the subject already is interpellated with the dominant ideology. Actions oriented toward change will tend to be conducive to power maintenance rather than to its removal.

The locus of the "dialectic of control" can be found in discourse which articulates between class and people. The dominant and the dominated both have recourse to a rhetoric which addresses the people in terms of the classes to which they belong. Domination requires a subject—and the manner of articulation will determine the mode of discourse required to address either "class" or "people." There is no necessary connection between a given ideology and a given class, either ruling or subordinate, at any moment in history (Therborn, 1980, p. 54). As Hall (1988) notes, "Ideologies may not be affixed, as organic entities, to their appropriate classes, but this does not mean that the production and transformation of ideology in society could proceed free of or outside the structuring lines of force of power and class" (p. 45). An emphasis on class does not mean that the "people" either cease to exist or fail to be of major theoretical import in the analysis of power relationships. Laclau (1977) differentiates class struggles (dominated by the relations of production) and struggles between a people and the ruling elite (when antagonism cannot be traced clearly to relations of production alone). In the latter sense,

> The "people" or "popular sectors" are not, as some conceptions suppose, rhetorical abstractions or a liberal or idealist conception smuggled into Marxist discourse. The "people" form an objective determination of the system which is different from class determination; the people are one of the poles or the dominant contradiction in a social formation, that is, a contradiction whose intelligibility depends on the ensemble of political and ideological relations of domination and not just the relations of production. If class contradiction is the dominant contradiction at the abstract level of the mode of production, the people-power bloc contradiction is dominant at the level of the social formation. (pp. 107–108)

The *people*, as is clear from the above, have no clear class content. As subjects, they are very much involved in the struggle for hegemony: "The very articulation of the subject's diverse positions is the result of a struggle for hegemony. . . . Hegemony is the very process of constructing politically the masses' subjectivity and *not* the practice of a pre-constituted subject" (Laclau, 1983, p. 118). What is important here is the interaction between class and people in the articulation of a "position" as subject: To win adherence to a class position, the themes are expressed in terms of the rhetoric of the "people." To maintain power, the ruling class also must address themes in terms of a "people." Where, in Therborn's formulation, the nexus of struggle is between differentiated ideological themes or terms, here the nexus is between the ruling elite's and the class's demarcation of the people. The ideological discourse that expresses the will of the people at the same time it constitutes the people as a rhetorical force (Charland, 1987) will reflect a broader interpretation of the "interests" of both dominant and dominated. The creation of a sense of ideological unity derives from the constitution of a discourse of the people; the discourse of the people overrides that of the class in establishing an overall ideological structure. In Laclau's formulation, *"Classes cannot assert their hegemony without articulating the people in their discourse"* (1977, p. 196). Additionally, the ruling class cannot maintain its hegemony without clearly articulating its motives for support in terms of the "people."

The "people" are both real and fictive. They exist as an "objective determination" (Laclau, 1977, p. 165); one can define their presence in economic and social terms. An agent can construct a definition of "people" to whom discourse is addressed. They are fictive because they exist only inside the symbolic world in which they are called into being (McGee, 1975). They are constituted in the "field of the symbolic" (Laclau and Mouffe, 1985, p. 97) and have no meaning outside of this context. As Charland (1987) notes in his case study of the constitutive nature of rhetoric, the *peuple québécois* "do not exist in nature, but only within a discursively constituted history" (p. 137). They are called into being by discourse (McGee, 1980), and from that moment forward, are "real" to those whose lives their discourse affects—the boundaries of their membership can have "real" economic indexes and sociopolitical connections.

Critical Practice

A critique of domination can proceed from Therborn's (1980) classification of ideology types, keeping in mind that these are "class-specific *core themes* of discourses that vary enormously in concrete form and degree of elaboration" (p. 79). Therborn isolates "ego" ideologies as those core themes identifying "who we are"; these exist in conjunction with "alter" ideologies that define what we are not. In the 1950s "patriot" was a key term of the ego ideology, while "communist" was a key term of the corresponding "opposing" ideology. Within contemporary feminism, a core egocentric theme might be "cooperation," with "competition" serving as the "alter" term. In the case of class formations, the conflict between ego and alter ideologies serves as the battleground. Both are inscribed in the social practices of the society and both serve as the impetus for maintenance and change: "From the standpoint of the constitution of class-struggle subjects, the crucial aspect of the alter-ideology is, in the case of exploiting classes, the rationale for their domination of other classes; in the case of exploited classes, it is the basis for their resistance to the exploiters" (Therborn, 1980, p. 61). In pre-Civil War days, to property owners, the perception of slaves as "property" served as a reason to keep them under control. To the slaves, the same perception served as the impetus for revolt. In this sense, it is not so much how I see myself as how I see the Other—my appropriation of an alter ideology for the Other defines the locus of our struggle. The "ego–alter" distinction, as with others Therborn delineates, serves as potential *topoi* for the unraveling of universes of discourse, as well as for locating the nexus of struggle.

A second key element in the unraveling of the discourse of power within this context is to recognize that the issue is not one of simple oppositions. If it were, societal members would be in a relatively "fixed" state, they would "relate to a given regime in a conscious, homogeneous . . . and consistent manner" (Therborn, 1980, p. 102). If this were the case, one would assume the following:

> *Either* a regime has legitimacy *or* it does not; people obey *either* because of normative consent *or* because of physical coercion; *either* the dominated class or classes have a conception of revolutionary change *or* they accept the status quo or are content with piecemeal reforms; people *act* either on the basis of true knowledge *or* on the basis of false ideas. (Therborn, 1980, p. 102)

The world of the social is not this simple. There are a variety of positions which the dominated and dominant alike can take at any given moment. Hegemony, as Laclau and Mouffe (1985) note, is "not a determinable location within the topography of the social" (p. 139). The analysis of the discourse of power thus must begin with the assumption that any articulatory practice may emerge as relevant or consequential— nothing can be "taken-for-granted" with respect to the impact of any particular discursive practice.

Finally, a critical practice must recognize that the critique of domination alone is not an exhaustive account of the potential discourses of power which govern social practices. This is not to deny the importance of a focus on domination, as there is a compelling sense in which power is negative or repressive in delimiting the potential of the human subject. It is easy to accept the force of the dominant thesis—if you were a Black American in the 1840s, or even in the 1940s, if you are a contemporary feminist, the power of the ruling group may indeed be (if not only appear to be) repressive. The discourse which flows from or expresses power functions to keep people "in their place" as that status is defined and determined by the interest of the dominant class in maintaining its social role. Nevertheless, a focus on the hierarchy of dominant/domi-nated may deflect attention from the existence of multiple classes, groups, or even individuals with varying degrees of power over others. For this reason, there is a need to examine the critique of power relations across a broader social spectrum.

The Critique of Freedom and the Discourse of Power

Michel Foucault, whose works concern the pervasive effects of power in daily life, articulates a broader conception of power by challenging the power–repression formula endemic to the domination thesis. In the process, he articulates a specialized form of critique that is amenable to the needs of a critical rhetoric. In his terms, "The work of profound transformation can only be done in an atmosphere which is free and always agitated by permanent criticism" (Foucault, 1982, p. 34). The search is not towards a freedom *for* something predetermined. As noted at the outset of this essay, the *telos* that marks the project is one of never-ending skepticism, hence permanent criticism. Results are never satisfying as the new social relations which emerge from a reaction to a critique are themselves simply new forms of power and hence subject to renewed skepticism. His is not the skepticism of Descartes or Hume. Attempts at transformation do not end in futility. As Rajchman (1985) observes, "Sextus Empiricus is Foucault's precursor. Foucault's philosophy does not aim for sure truths, but for the freedom of withholding judgment on philosophical dogmas" (p. 2). Skepticism is a healthy response to a society which takes universalist dogma and the "truths" it yields for granted: "To question the self-evidence of a form of experience, knowledge, or power, is to free it for our purposes, to open new possibilities for thought and action" (Rajchman, 1985, p. 4).

This approach to questions of social relations yields, for Foucault, a nontraditional historical analysis. Reacting against the "totalizing" emphasis of traditional intellectual history, Foucault is decidedly "anti-Whig" (Kent, 1986). By seeking differences rather than similarities, Foucault's analysis of history focuses on discontinuities in an attempt to discover why certain social relations occurred and not others. History teaches us that there are no certainties, there are no universalizing truths against which we can measure our progress toward some ultimate destiny (Clark and McKerrow, 1987). In conse-quence, the most we can do is to ever guard against "taken for granteds" that endanger our freedom—our chance to consider new possibilities for action.

Concomitantly, Foucault is not seeking a particular normative structure—critique is not about the business of moving us toward perfection (it is not transcendental in the Neo-Kantian, Habermasian sense), nor is it avowedly anarchistic (Fields [1988, p. 143] overstates the case). Rather, it is simply nonprivileging with respect to the options its analysis raises for consideration. On demonstrating the manner in which our social relations constrain us, often in ways that are virtually invisible, which occur at such a deep and remote level in our past as to be anonymous, the possibility of revolt is opened. Anarchism is freedom without a point, and once realized is content to defend its privileged position. Foucault's project privileges nothing, hence contains no such contentment.[2]

The Pervasiveness of Power

As noted earlier, the analysis of power relations need not focus solely on the question of the legitimacy of the state. As Foucault (1980a) notes, "One impoverishes power if one poses it solely in terms of legislation and constitution, in terms solely of the state and the state apparatus" (p. 158). Foucault's analysis of power, in terms of relations that are existent throughout the "social body" (1980a, p. 119), is a radical critique that eschews both analyses of state and economic power, and politically-oriented analyses that have as their motive the "demystification of ideologically distorted belief systems" (Fraser, 1981, p. 272).[3] Instead, the focus is on power as it is manifest across a variety of social practices. His contrast between two historically grounded conceptions of power offers a beginning point for our examination: "The contract–oppression schema, which is the juridical one, and the domination–repression or war–repression schema for which the pertinent opposition is not between the legitimate and illegitimate, as in the first schema, but between struggle and submission" (1980a, p. 92). Within these two versions, it is clear that the discourse of power will be qualitatively different. That is, discourse which upholds a juridical theme of power will speak in terms of rights, obligations, and of the possibility of exchanging power through the legal mediation of conflicting interests. In essence, it is a Western, democratic conception of power that is rational and orderly, and whose discursive themes are deeply imbedded in the historical consciousness of the participants. Contemporary criticism of political rhetoric "buys in" to this perception of power as a model which grounds evaluative claims.

The discourse emanating from what Foucault terms "Nietzsche's hypothesis," on the other hand, will draw on the themes of the opposition of forces in conflict, struggle, and ultimately war. The theme of oppression in the juridical perspective will occur when rights are overextended, contracts are broken, or obligations are left unfulfilled. In the case of power as "the hostile engagement of forces," the discursive theme of repression will occur both as a justification for a resort to force and as an account of the "political consequences of war" (1980a, p. 91). One could argue that critical assessments of Western "war rhetoric" are implicitly trapped by the established vision of the dominant group. They are not, as Wander (1983) would argue, essays which take an "ideological turn," as this "reflects the existence of crisis, acknowledges the influence of established interests and the reality of alternative world-views, and commends rhetorical analyses not only of the actions implied but also of the interests represented" (p. 18).

Over against these orientations toward power, Foucault presents a third perspective in his attempt to relate the "mechanisms [of power] to two points of reference, two limits; on the one hand, to the rules of right that provide a formal delimitation of power; on the other, to the effects of truth that this power produces and transmits, and which in their turn reproduce this power. Hence, we have a triangle: power, right, truth"

(1980a, pp. 92–93). Of importance for our purpose is the role of discourse in this interactive network: "There are manifold relations of power which permeate, characterize and constitute the social body, and these relations of power cannot themselves be established, consolidated nor implemented without the production, accumulation, circulation and functioning of a discourse" (1980a, p. 93). The discourse identified herein brings power into existence in social relations and gives expression to the ideology that the exercise of power in that relation represents. The sense of "power" brought into being through discourse is not conceived as a stable, continuous force:

> Discourses are not once and for all subservient to power or raised up against it, any more than silences are. We must make allowance for the concept's complex and unstable process whereby discourse can be both an instrument and an effect of power, but also a hindrance, a stumbling block, a point of resistance and a starting point for an opposing strategy. Discourse transmits and produces power; it reinforces it, but also undermines and exposes it, renders it fragile and makes it possible to thwart it. (1980b, pp. 100–101)

Discourse is the tactical dimension of the operation of power in its manifold relations at all levels of society, within and between its institutions, groups, and individuals. The task of a critical rhetoric is to undermine and expose the discourse of power in order to thwart its effects in a social relation (the task is not so dissimilar from Burke's [1961] own attempt in *Attitudes Toward History*).

In this context, an examination of the power of the state would take on a special cast: "The power of the state would be an *effet d'ensemble,* the result of an attempt to immobilize, to encode, to make permanent, and to serialize or realign or homogenize innumerable local (and necessarily unstable) confrontations. The state gives an immobilizing intelligibility to the scattered, wildly productive effects of these power generating confrontations" (Bersani, 1977, p. 3). Outside the state, the localization of power lies within an unstable and shifting environment of social relations: "There is no single underlying principle fixing—and hence constituting—the whole field of differences" between and among the social practices that could be energized by a discourse of power (Laclau and Mouffe, 1985, p. 110). Foucault's object in analyzing this dimension of power, in his *History of Sexuality,* for example, is "to define the regime of power-knowledge-pleasure that sustains the discourse on human sexuality in our part of the world" (1980b, p. 11). In this context, the analysis of power in terms of a juridical model, or in terms of a "war" model, would be too far from the mark to be helpful. As Fraser (1981) notes, "If power is instantiated in mundane social practices and relations, then efforts to dismantle or transform the regime must address those practices and relations" (p. 280). The critic must attend to the "microphysics of power" in order to understand what *sustains* social practices. Power, thus conceived, is not repressive, but productive—it is an active potentially positive force which creates social relations and sustains them through the appropriation of a discourse that "models" the relations through its expression.

Underlying Foucault's approach is the belief that power, exercised in terms of law and sovereign right, transforms, or in Therborn's terms, "naturalizes" the social relation: it becomes the norm, and discourse related to its maintenance is "normal." Challenges are therefore abnormal and irrational by definition. This stigma attached to the agents of change is present even though they might work within the confines of the "order of power." Consider, for example, Edelman's (1988) observation that "the language of the helping professions functions as a form of political action" (p. 107) within the established social structure. Challenges to the social relations normalized within the "helping professions" would be met, by those still adhering to the established order, with arguments that assert naïveté or irrationality on the part of the "naysayers." Power, in this context, is *not a possession or a content*—it is instead an integral part of social relations. The discourse of power creates and perpetuates the relations, and gives form to the ideology which it projects. Ideology, regardless of its expression, begins with these social relations as integral to its creation, continuance, and change. A thoroughgoing Foucauldian critique, however, would go beyond Edelman's (1988) analysis, conducted primarily at the level of "agents of change." Power is expressed anonymously, in nondeliberate ways, at a "deep structure" level, and may have its origins in the remoteness of our past (carried forward through a particularizing discursive formation).

To be an agent for change requires, from a Foucauldian perspective, an understanding of the reasons for the current social relations of power—and those reasons do not necessarily have to presuppose an earlier production via a named agent. The "denial" of an agent as productive of contingently derived social practices does not rule out the present role of persons as active participants in "revolt" against the present dangers. Otherwise, there is no point to positing the possibilities of freedom—and a Sartrean angst is preordained as the condition of passive acceptance of one's fate.

Power and Truth in the Critique of Freedom

Foucault's analysis of the relationship between power and truth raises the question of the role of discourse as an agent of truth. The rejection of transcendental or universalist standards against which rhetoric is evaluated, as suggested in the beginning of this essay, raises a question: "Have we abandoned the Platonic quest and embraced sophism?" The answer is "yes." The orientation is shifted from an expression of "truth" as the opposite of "false consciousness" (and away from the naïve notion that laying bare the latter would inevitably move people toward revolution on the basis of a revealed truth). Engels stated the case for a view of ideology predicated on "false consciousness": "Ideology is a process accomplished by the so-called thinker consciously, it is true, but with a false consciousness. The real forces impelling him remain unknown to him" (1893, p. 459, cited in Therborn, 1980, p. 4). This assumes, however, that (1) all ideology is necessarily false and (2) that "only scientific knowledge is 'true' or 'real' knowledge" (Therborn, 1980, p. 8). In contemporary accounts of culture, this perception has been discredited (Hall, 1988; but see Markovic, 1983). There is an advantage to dispensing with a perception of truth that is hidden behind a "cloud of unknowing" (Hall, 1988, p. 44): If ideology is not equated with false consciousness, it "is no longer treated as untextual, homogeneous, cultural mush—as a synonym for ideas in general, distorted ideas in general, *Weltanschauung*, ethos, spirit of the times, and so forth" (Mullins, 1979, p. 153). To consider ideology in terms of truth and falsity is to focus attention on its character and to typify it as product rather than as process.

Nevertheless, a consideration of "truth" is an appropriate focus of a critical rhetoric. In Foucault's (1980a) words, "The problem does not consist in drawing the line between that in a discourse which falls under the category of scientificity or truth, and that which comes under some other category, but in seeing historically how effects of truth are produced within discourses which in themselves are neither true nor false" (p. 118). By focusing on the "effects of truth," as expressed in a social relation typified by power, one approximates an Isocratean sense of "community knowledge":

The important thing here, I believe, is that truth isn't outside power, or lacking in power: Contrary to a myth whose history and functions repay further study, truth isn't the reward of free spirits, the child of protracted solitude, nor the privilege of those who have succeeded in liberating themselves. Truth is a thing of this world: It is produced by virtue of multiple forms of constraint. And it induces regular effects of power. Each society has its regime of truth, its "general politics" of truth: that is, the types of discourse which it accepts and makes function as true; the mechanisms and instances which enable one to distinguish true and false statements, the means by which each is sanctioned; the techniques and procedures accorded value in the acquisition of truth; the status of those who are charged with saying what counts as true. (Foucault, 1980a, p. 131)

The analysis of the discourse of power focuses on the "normalization" of language intended to maintain the status quo. By producing a description of "what is," unfettered by predetermined notions of what "should be," the critic is in a position to posit the possibilities of freedom. Recharacterization of the images changes the power relations and re-creates a new "normal" order. In this interaction, "truth" is that which is supplanted by a newly articulated version that is accepted as a basis for the revised social relation. Once instantiated anew in social relations, the critique continues.

THE PRINCIPLES OF *PRAXIS*

> Discourse lives, as it were, beyond itself, in a living impulse . . .
> toward the object; if we detach ourselves completely from this
> impulse all we have left is the naked corpse of the word, from
> which we can learn nothing at all about the social situation or
> the fate of a given word in life.
>
> *Bakhtin*, The Dialogic Imagination, *p. 292*

Bakhtin's observation about the relation between selves and words is an appropriate grounding for the discussion of the "principles of *praxis*." This section of the essay does not seek to establish the *methodology* (in the narrow sense of formula or prescription) appropriate to a critical rhetoric. Rather, it seeks to outline the "orientation" (invoked in Burke's sense) that a critic takes toward the object of study. The "object" of a critical rhetoric, however, requires reconsideration prior to a discussion of the principles of a critical practice.

Critical Practice as Invention

Public address, as traditionally conceived, is *agent-centered.* Even the study of social movements has been dominated by this perspective. Given public address's "quasi-theological" (to borrow Cawelti's [1985] term) nature, there is the danger that the inclusion of a "critical rhetoric" perspective would merely perpetuate the traditional model of criticism. The acceptance of a critical rhetoric is premised on the reversal of the phrase "public address"—we need to reconceptualize the endeavor to focus attention on *that symbolism which addresses publics.* The term "address" conjures up the image of a preconceived message, with a beginning, a middle, and an end—a ratiocinative discourse which can be located in space and time as an isolated event, or can be placed in a "rhetorical situation" out of which it grew and to which it responds. More often than not, the products of discourse are mediated—are no longer the simple property of a speaker–audience relation. In the context of such mediated communication, Becker (1971) noted the *fragmented* nature of most of the messages impinging on any one consumer. More recently, McGee (1987) has exhorted critics to attend to "formations of texts" in their original fragmented form. What he calls for is the role of a critic as "inventor"—interpreting for the consumer the meaning of fragments collected as *text* or *address*. To approach mediated communication as rhetorical is to see it in its fragmented, unconnected, even contradictory or momentarily oppositional mode of presentation. The task is to construct addresses out of the fabric of mediated experience prior to passing judgment on what those addresses might tell us about our social world. The process one employs is thus geared to uncovering the "dense web" (Mosco, 1983, p. 239), not by means of a simple speaker–audience interaction, but also by means of a "pulling together" of disparate scraps of discourse which, when constructed as an argument, serve to illuminate otherwise hidden or taken for granted social practices.

The reversal of "public address" to "discourse which addresses publics" places the critic in the role of "inventor." As such, s/he is more than an observer of the social scene. And s/he will have as the *text* more than traditional "speaker–audience" scenarios in engaging in a critique. The movement toward communication as "mediated," including the analysis of popular culture, is one way to recover what Turner (1986) refers to as "missed opportunities" in the practice of criticism. If the reversal is not in place, there is the danger that a "public address" vision of popular culture would be constrained to think in terms of "agent" rather than symbol as the focus of attention. There also is the danger that such extension of traditional forms of analysis would simply perpetuate modernist clichés in constructing, through the myopic lenses of a predefined vision of the media as a "cultural wasteland," elitist standards of excellence. *Facts of Life* may never aspire to inclusion in the "canons of oratorical excellence," but it may have more influence on a teenager's conception of social reality than all the great speeches by long-dead great speakers. To ignore "symbols which address publics" in all their manifest forms has, as its ultimate consequence, the perpetuation of sterile forms of criticism.

Principles of a Critical Practice

In the discussion which follows, the principles of a critical *praxis*, and the alterations in rhetoric's nature they imply, encompass both the critique of domination and of freedom. Neither critique, although it may be carried out alone, is ultimately "complete" without attention to the other. It *is* the case that state power exists, is repressive, and is accessible to critique. It is *equally* the case that power is not only repressive but potentially productive, that its effects are pervasive throughout the social world, and that these effects are accessible to analysis. While a critical practice need not focus on both, the overall analysis of the impact of the discourse of power requires, at a minimum, attention to each dimension. A thoroughgoing critical rhetoric, therefore, is one whose principles provide an orientation common to both perspectives on *ideologiekritik*. More precisely, then, an *ideologiekritik* is "the production of knowledge to the ends of power and, maybe, of social change" (Lentricchia, 1983, p. 11). Whether cast as a critique of domination or of freedom, the initial task of a critical rhetoric is one of re-creation—constructing an argument that identifies the integration of power and knowledge and delineates the role of power/knowledge in structuring social practices. Reconceptualizing address as textual fragments, and assuming the orientation of a critical rhetoric, brings a critic to the discourse of power with a blank slate if there are no additional principles underwriting the perspective. While not pretending to catalog an exhaustive list, the following "principles" serve to describe, without limiting, the orientation suggested by a critical rhetoric.

Principle #1: "Ideologiekritik Is in Fact Not a Method, But a Practice" (McGee, 1984, p. 49).

McGee (1984, 1987) is correct in chastising critics for paying too much attention to methodological concerns. If reading Burke prompts any lesson, it is that creative insights are constrained by the systematicity of method. This lesson was lost on legions of academics who, by imposing a system on an unmethodological critic, created their own fiction and termed it a method.[4] Considered as practice, understanding and evaluation are one: "Understanding is impossible without evaluation. Understanding cannot be separated from evaluation: they are simultaneous and constitute a unified integral act. . . . In the act of understanding [unless one is a dogmatist and therefore impervious to change] a struggle occurs that results in mutual change and enrichment" (Bakhtin, 1986, p. 142). In this context, "description" implies evaluation by the very fact of choice with respect to what is described, as well as what is not. Burke's (1966, p. 45) dictum that a selection of reality is also a deflection and a rejection applies to the act of criticism as well as to other symbolic acts that are taken as the object of a critical perspective. This does not mean a critic functions as an anarchist. Rather, it means one operates from a "perspective" (McGee, 1984, p. 47) or an "orientation": embracing a set of principles does not commit one to prescriptivism any more than it renders the critical act directionless. An orientation is the least restrictive stage from which the critical act might be launched; it maximizes the possibilities of what will "count" as evidence for critical judgment, and allows for creativity in the assessment of the "effects of truth" upon social practices.

Principle #2: The Discourse of Power Is Material.

An ideology exists, in a material sense, in and through the language that constitutes it (McGee, 1982). As Therborn (1980) notes, "Ideology operates as discourse. . . . [It] is the medium through which men make their history as conscious actors" (pp. 15, 3). Participants are not passive bystanders, simply absorbing the ideology and having no power to alter its force or its character. Ideology is a property of the social world, but agents have the capacity to interact in that world to modify the discourse (see Mumby, 1987). They do not come to the particular ideology as a tabula rasa: They come to a system of discourse with an ideological grid already in place and participate in terms of that grid's determinative nature. This is the implication of Burke's (1966) "terministic screens" as mechanisms which control how alternate discourses are heard. As Althusser (1971) has noted, "Ideology has always-already interpellated individuals as subjects" (p. 164). This focuses our attention on the social dimension or consciousness of the collectivity that utilizes or adheres to a particular discourse. As Charland (1987) has illustrated, a traditional speaker–audience model presumes that an audience is already constituted as subject, and employs discourse in a manner to sustain present relations of domination. He succeeds in carrying the "constitution of a subject" a step backward to its initiation in a discourse—as the audience is called into being as a *peuple québécois* (p. 134). In either case, the rhetor is capable of participating in a "dialectic of control" to shape the ongoing nature of the social relation being sustained or entered into. In fact, to the extent that a person fails to enter into a dialectical relation with the ideology, that individual ceases to function as an *agent* in the social system (see Giddens, 1979, p. 149).

The materiality of discourse focuses attention on the sense of *"praxis"* utilized in a critical rhetoric. Aristotle's vision of *praxis* identified it with the goals of *phronesis* or practical wisdom (the "doing of fine and noble deeds" [Benhabib, 1986, p. 157] in the service of virtue). A critical rhetoric no longer looks at *praxis* in its ethical dimension, tying it to an ideal lifestyle. Rather, a critical rhetoric links *praxis*, both as object of study and as style, to "a mode of *transformative activity*" (Benhabib, 1986, p. 67) in which the social relations in which people participate are perceived as "real" to them even though they exist only as fictions in a rhetorically constituted universe of discourse. What is differentiated for the purposes of critical practice is not a rejection of ethical values, but a reordering of the perspective to one in which *transformation* (or at minimum, the delineation of the possibilities for transformation) is seen as the ultimate aim. Even theorizing, in this sense, is critical practice, as it lays out the preconditions for transformation within a set of social relations. The product of a critique may be seen in the Aristotelian sense of a "noble deed," but that is not its *raison d'être*.

What is constituted as "real" is not only so structured through discursive practices. What is perceived as real to the populace, in economic, social, and political terms also is created in nondiscursive ways. Following Laclau and Mouffe (1985), the practice of a critical rhetoric

> rejects the distinction between discursive and non-discursive practices. It affirms: (a) that every object is constituted as an object of discourse insofar as no object is given outside every discursive condition of emergence; and (b) that any distinction between what are usually called linguistic and behaviourial aspects of a social practice is either an incorrect distinction or ought to find its place as a differentiation within the social production of meaning which is structured under the form of discursive totalities. (p. 107)

This is not to diminish the importance of nondiscursive practices, but rather to acknowledge that the discussion of such practices takes place in terms of discursive practices. The analysis of social *praxis* must, if it is to accomplish its transformative goal, deal in concrete terms with those relations which are "real"—that do in fact constrain discourse, and do so in ways that are seldom seen without such analysis.

Principle #3: Rhetoric Constitutes Doxastic Rather Than Epistemic Knowledge.

A critical rhetoric must be grounded on a reconstitution of the concept of *doxa* (Hariman, 1986). Plato's impact on the status of rhetoric needs little elaboration—the attempts to rehabilitate rhetoric, to save it from its own "shame" are many and varied (Hariman, 1986; Nelson and Megill, 1986). In essence, that is what the "epistemic"[5] movement attempts, regardless of its claim to establish rhetoric's role in the constitution of subjects. By subsuming the constitution of subjects under the rubric of *episteme,* theorists do no more than attempt to rescue rhetoric from the oblivion to which Plato consigned it. Considerations of rhetoric as epistemic are inextricably linked to a neo-Kantian definition of what constitutes knowledge, as that will always be seen in terms of independent, universal standards of judgment (whether invoked by Perelman, Toulmin, or Habermas). In the process, the rehabilitation remains subservient to a

Platonic, neo-Kantian perception of rhetoric's "true" role in society. A more positive approach is to reassert the value of rhetoric's province—*doxa*—and thereby resituate theory and practice in a context far more amenable to its continuance.

Nelson and Megill (1986), writing on the nature of the "rhetoric of inquiry," observe the history of "certitude" under which rhetoric has served:

> Plato denigrated opinion and rhetoric so as to celebrate truth and order at a time of Greek conflict and Athenian decline. Similarly, Aristotle subordinated mythos to logos and rhetoric to dialectic. In an era when radical disagreements racked the peace of Europe, Descartes wrote off rhetoric in favor of mathematical reason and Hobbes enslaved language to the sovereign. Later, Kant sought perpetual peace through pure and practical reason. Craving certainty as a path to peace and order in our own troubled times, many of us may be tempted by similar visions. But after more than three centuries of such abstract utopias, not to mention the programs for their enforcement, we have every reason to resist their temptation and revise their anti-rhetorical premises. (p. 23)

As they demonstrate, there is a wealth of philosophical support for the rejection of such antirhetorics. Their own limitation, notwithstanding brief references to the social and political facets of inquiry, is that the rhetoric of inquiry ends in description.[6] In this sense, the rhetoric of inquiry, as is the case with the Habermasian project, remains locked into a mode of reason (even when viewed as rhetorical [Brown, 1987]) that aims for universalizing the standards of judgment—in this case, across the academy. A critical rhetoric ends in transformation of the conditions of domination or in the possibility of revolt as the consequence of a critique of freedom. Thus, even though the rhetoric of inquiry is premised on a positive reassertion of rhetoric's role in society, its rationale (wedded to rhetoric as epistemic) does not go far enough to embrace the practice of a critical rhetoric.

Hariman (1986) offers a reconceptualization of *doxa* that removes it from an opposition to *episteme*. *Doxa*, as he notes, includes not only the traditional characteristic of "opinion" but also "reputation" or "regard" and functions as much by concealment as by revelation: "*Doxa* is created by acts of concealment, and so a complete conceptualization of *doxa* must include the idea that regard is in part achieved by the concealment of rank. This interpretation repositions *doxa*: it is no longer contrasted with *episteme*, but rather with *alethia*, truth (literally 'unhiddenness'). . . . This dynamic of concealment and unconcealment [truth]—of authorizing and marginalizing—is the means by which we determine what we believe, what we know, and what we believe to be true" (pp. 49–50). Doxastic knowledge functions as the grounding of a critical rhetoric.[7] Rather than focusing on questions of "truth" or "falsity," a view of rhetoric as doxastic allows the focus to shift to how the symbols come to possess power—what they "do" in society as contrasted to what they "are."

The sense of *doxa* as concealment is implied in Bourdieu's (1977, 1979) notion of *doxa* as the realm of the "undiscussed." Bourdieu (1977, 1979, 1980) employs metaphors of capitalism in his examination of the relationships between authority to speak and the appropriation of symbols—those in authority simply have more "capital" at their disposal, as well as enjoy control of the means of distribution of symbols. They have, as a result, the interest of conserving or preserving the "state of *doxa* in which the established structure is not questioned" (Thompson, 1984, p. 49). Bringing the "undiscussed" or concealed to the forefront is an act of heterodoxical rhetoric, met, naturally enough, by an orthodox rhetoric of defense of the status quo. Central to this discussion of *doxa*, as in the case of Hariman's analysis, is the recognition of its contingent nature, as well as its implicit sense of having an inscribed status (estimate of worth) by having been appropriated as the symbolic capital of the dominant group. Those with less capital are accordingly "marginalized" until or unless their heterodoxical rhetoric can successfully supplant that of the ruling elite.

Principle #4: Naming Is the Central Symbolic Act of a Nominalist Rhetoric.

The power of language to constitute subjects implicit in "naming as an interpretive act" (in Burke's [1941, pp. 5–71] sense; see Blankenship, 1976, p. 236) suggests that it is a justifiable principle to incorporate in a critical perspective. The principle encompasses all that has been said in criticism under the rubric of "rhetorical visions," "ideographs," and "condensation symbols." As a specific example, though it is not discussed in any of these terms, consider Hall's (1985) own treatment of his personal experience as a "coloured" person in Jamaica and then as a person from Jamaica. As the contexts shift, so too do the meanings inherent in social practices legitimated by reactions to a label. The subject is "fractured" into a multiplicity of selves as the perception/label shifts. Bakhtin's (1986) observation that "nothing is absolutely dead: every meaning will have its homecoming festival" (p. 170) applies: A return to Jamaica brings with it all of the old associations that one has grown away from in another cultural milieu. In the recent Iran-Contra hearings, McFarlane legitimated a foreign country's contribution to the Contras, at a time when solicitation was expressly forbidden by Congress, as "not a solicitation per se." One can't put too fine an edge on the power or process of naming, when potentially illegal actions are justified by linguistic sleights of hand.

What is left out of the above analysis is perhaps the most crucial aspect of the process of naming. Consonant with recapturing a sense of rhetoric as doxastic rather than epistemic, a reinterpretation of rhetoric as nominalist fits well with the contingent nature of the social reality in which humans are both subject and subjected (Therborn, 1980). Rajchman (1985) observes of Foucault that "his histories are *themselves* nominalist histories. They are not histories of things, but of the terms, categories, and techniques through which certain things become at certain times the focus of a whole configuration of discussion and procedure" (p. 51). For a critical rhetoric, the significance is the parallel sense in which rhetoric itself adopts a nominalist stance. Foucault's nominalist history is directed against the totalizing and deterministic effects of an intellectual (Whiggish) history which sacrifices difference in the search for similarity. In similar fashion, a nominalist rhetoric is directed against the universalizing tendencies of a Habermasian communicative ethics or a Perelmanesque philosophical rhetoric (see Benhabib, 1986; McKerrow, 1986).

The implications of a nominalist rhetoric are evidenced in a comparison of different forms of hermeneutic analysis:

> Hermeneutic realism, for example, assumes a stability of meaning before any rhetorical acts take place. Meaning is determinate, objective, and eternally fixed because of constraints in the text itself that are independent of historically situated critical debate. In a strangely similar way, hermeneutic idealism also assumes a stability of meaning outside situated practices. Meaning is determinate, intersubjective, and temporarily fixed because of constraints provided by the communal convention in readers' and critics' minds. (Mailloux, 1985, p. 630)

Rhetorical hermeneutics, on the other hand, tries to correct the error of "presupposing the possibility of meaning outside specific historical contexts of rhetorical practices" (Mailloux, 1985, p. 630). A nominalist rhetoric shares, with Mailloux's formulation of a rhetorical hermeneutics, a sense that terms are contingently based—the reasons for their emergence are not premised on fixed, determinative models of inquiry.

Principle #5: Influence Is Not Causality.

This simple claim has profound implications for understanding the assumptive framework underlying the analysis of the discourse of power. As Condit (1987) argues, "To say that something 'influences' a process, or has 'force,' eschews the determinism latent in the term 'cause.' An influence or force may be overridden or supplemented by other forces. It may even require the active participation of other forces (e.g., 'human choice') to become actualized" (p. 2). Thus, given the contingency with which rhetoric historically concerns itself, to say that a symbol has influence is to claim that it impacts on others (one might term this a soft cause if one wished to retain the term).

Presence of a symbol is not actuality, but at least is potentiality. The potential for images of crime to influence the social reality of the elderly is present through the depiction of such symbolic acts on nightly crime drama. As empirical studies have shown, such acts do in fact influence the elderly's perception of the amount of actual crime in their own social community.

The claim separates a critical rhetoric from the structural causality inherent in an Althusserian critique of culture, as well as from other "pure" Marxist reductionisms of the determinist stripe. Seen in this context, the notion of "influence" rejects the twin claims that nothing is connected to anything else (culturalism) and that everything is determined by something (structuralism) (see Hall, 1985). Hall's own cultural perspective is far more amenable to this principle, as it allows for contingency in the convergence of events that would determine social practices, or social change. Noting that there is no "necessary correspondence" between an ideological expression and one's social class does not invalidate the possibility of social change. From a rhetorical perspective, what it implies is that the impetus for change has not yet been articulated— the necessary symbolic act bridging the ideology and the social position has not yet been created. This doesn't imply that it won't or can't be formulated. The following statement from Hall (1985) identifies the role of rhetoric, without so naming it: "The aim of a theoretically-informed political practice must surely be to bring about or construct the articulation between social and economic forces and those forms of politics and ideology which might lead them in practice to intervene in history in a progressive way—an articulation which has to be *constructed* through practice precisely because it is not guaranteed by how those forces are constituted in the first place" (p. 95).

If there is a lack of correspondence between an ideology and a class position, symbols must be invented in such a way as to accommodate the "difference" that exists. In the various analyses of Hart's debacle, there is ample suggestion of the variance between cultural mores and the position of the candidate. Hart's "affair," or more recently, the travails of Jimmy Swaggart, are not morality plays. They are, much more fundamentally, failures to bridge the gap between a lived practice and a noncorresponding ideology. As Abravanel (1983) points out, the contradiction is between a moral sense of "what should be done" and "what is being done" (p 280). The contradiction is mediated, both in the life of the individual and within the public realm, by recourse to suitable myths that gloss the incompatibilities, and thereby provide a rationalization for action. The task of a critical rhetoric is to call attention to the myth, and the manner in which it mediates between contradictory impulses to action.

Principle #6: Absence Is as Important as Presence in Understanding and Evaluating Symbolic Action.

Hall's experience is again helpful; as he writes, "Positively marked terms 'signify' because of their position in relation to what is absent, unmarked, the unspoken, the unsayable. Meaning is relational within an ideological system of presences and absences" (1985, p. 109). Terms are not "unconnected"; in the formation of a text, out of fragments of what is said, the resulting "picture" needs to be checked against "what is absent" as well as what is present. Wander's analysis of media also supports the influence of the "not said," particularly as it reinforces that which is said (1981). To the extent that the following is an accurate statement about what appears on television, the negation also may be considered an accurate reflection of reality:

> Most characters on prime time conform to conventional standards of beauty—they tend to be white or near white, fine-featured, young, well proportioned, and of average height.
> NEGATION: Few characters appear on prime time who are fat. Not many have scars, limps, or protruding lips. Few adult characters are under five feet or over six feet, four inches tall. Not many characters appear to be over 65. When physically "deviant" characters do appear, they tend not to be cast as intelligent, strong, or virtuous. (pp. 518–519)

As the culture changes, and the "said" shifts in identifiable patterns, the negation can be revised.

The Iran-Contra hearings provide a very different exemplar: over and over, the concern was with what was left out, the "unsaid" in a situation. McFarlane may have said that such and such knowledge is "not known concretely" but did not say that such knowledge is known in some degree. Answers to specific questions may only be partial statements, accurate insofar as they are expressed, but certainly not the answers that would be given if other questions were asked. Inferences based on such answers more often than not play directly into the hands of those in control of both knowledge and the power that it provides.

Principle #7: Fragments Contain the Potential for Polysemic Rather Than Monosemic Interpretation.

This probably shouldn't need saying. Nevertheless, given the dominance of a modernist critique which, as a particularizing example, sees mediated communication as a corruptive influence, as promoting the declining standards of the culture, such a claim deserves renewed attention. First, to use Cawelti's (1985) term, the early "quasi-theological" cast of much media criticism is on the wane. As Grossberg (1984) and Becker (1986) suggest in their respective surveys of media criticism, there is a much stronger influence from ideological, social/cultural perspectives currently in vogue. Even so, as Fiske (1986) notes, ideological criticism has been myopic in its vision of television as a monosemic text, underwriting the dominant cultural forces at work in society. An underlying weakness of a critique which sees the viewer as ultimately passive and unable to participate in social change limits ideological criticism to that "of increasing the viewer's ability to resist the imposition of cultural meanings that may not fit one's own social identity, and in so doing to resist the homogenization of culture" (p. 399). While this has value, it is, in the main, a negative one. A polysemic critique is one which uncovers a subordinate or secondary reading which contains the seeds of subversion or rejection of authority, at the same time that the primary reading appears to confirm the power of the dominant cultural norms. As Fiske (1986) says, "Different socially located viewers will activate" the meaning of a text differently. Those who come to the experience from the domain of power may see only legitimization, while those subjected to power can "take the signifying practices and products of the dominant" and "use them for different social purposes" (p. 406).

Principle #8: Criticism Is a Performance.

This is the thrust of McGee's (1987) analysis of the critique of culture. In the sense of a critical rhetoric, it places the focus on the activity as a statement; the critic as inventor becomes arguer or advocate for an interpretation of the collected fragments. Is this to say anything more than Brockriede (1974), who long ago acknowledged that criticism is an argumentative activity? If I understand McGee's point, the emphasis goes beyond the simple assertion that any interpretation must give reasons. In McGee's (1987) words, "Rhetoricians are performers" (p. 8). The act of performing, within the context of our expertise as critics/readers of the social condition, moves the focus from criticism as method to critique as practice.

This principle also encompasses the recent advocacy of an "ideological turn" in criticism. Wander (1983) argues that "criticism takes an ideological turn when it recognizes the existence of powerful vested interests benefiting from and consistently urging politics and technology that threatens life on this planet" (p. 18). As written, however, the frame of reference for the insertion of ideological intent is unnecessarily confined to a narrow range of human experience. The function of an *ideologiekritik* is to counter the excesses of a society's own enabling actions, its "repressive tolerance" in Marcuse's terms, that underwrites the continuation of social practices that ultimately are harmful to the community (see McGee, 1984). Thus, the sense of that which is harmful may be much broader than Wander implies.

To escape the implication that what Wander desires is for academics to take to the streets as practicing revolutionaries (and that may, in fact, be what he desires) there is an important caveat. The practice of a critical rhetoric can take refuge in Foucault's (1980a) defense of his own writing as that of a *specific intellectual* (p. 126). To borrow Lentricchia's (1983) statement of the practice, a specific intellectual is "one whose radical work of transformation, whose fight against repression is carried on at the specific institutional site where he [she] finds himself [herself] and on the terms of his [her] own expertise, on the terms inherent to his [her] own functioning as an intellectual" (pp. 6–7). This also gives meaning to theorizing as a critical practice—as a performance of a rhetor advocating a critique as a sensible reading of the discourse of power.

SUMMARY: THEORY, *PRAXIS,* AND THE FUTURE

I have, in this essay, taken Jensen's (1987) observation, "communication media engage audiences in the construction of cultural forms" (p. 24) as a given. My purpose has been to suggest a theoretical rationale and a set of principles for the critique of domination and of freedom. As such, this essay serves as a "synthetic statement" of both forms of critique. There are many other forms of criticism, and of critiques; the conception of a critical rhetoric need not displace all other rhetorics. What it must do, however, is provide an avenue—an orientation—toward a postmodern conception of the relationship between discourse and power. In so doing, it announces a critical practice that stands on its own, without reliance on universal standards of reason. Instead, a critical rhetoric celebrates its reliance on contingency, on *doxa* as the basis for knowledge, on nominalism as the ground of language meaning as doxastic, and critique viewed as a performance. Rhetoric, in the context of these principles, emerges with *status* (Hariman, 1986) in the analysis of a discourse of power.

What then of the "future" of a critical rhetoric? If I have been marginally successful in setting forth the "image" of a critical rhetoric as theory and *praxis*, I rest my case on Blankenship and Muir's (1987) observation that such an image contains "both the vision of the future and the [instrument] for realizing it" (p. 6).

Notes

1. As may be obvious, this is a more violent wrenching of traditional modes of rhetorical criticism than some may tolerate (e.g., Campbell, 1983; Hill, 1983).

2. It is in this sense that his project is antihumanist (see Blair and Cooper, 1987, and Fisher, 1985, to the contrary). By privileging no one subject or topic, Foucault is not antihuman, but antihumanist in the sense that he does not place humans at the center or core of our philosophical tradition. He places nothing, and especially not transcendental reason, at the center, so to claim an "antihumanism" stance is simply to affirm that "human choice and freedom" (Blair and Cooper, 1987, p. 167) will not be constrained by an *a priori* privilege.

3. In the process, Foucault suspends traditional rationalistic orientations toward truth and falsity (a tradition Marxist analysis of false consciousness embraces, though for different effects), and "brackets" questions of epistemic and normative justifications of social practices (Fraser, 1981, pp. 273-275). The suspension of criteria of justification is consonant with the absence of privilege alluded to earlier.

4. There is a similar danger in perceiving Foucault's "perspective" as a "method" (Blair and Cooper, 1987, p. 161). As Shiner (1982) argues, "If one persists in seeing Foucault as a methodologist, the phrase 'genealogy of power' which from 1972 replaces 'archaeology of knowledge' will be even more grossly misinterpreted. . . . His method is an anti-method in the sense that it seeks to free us from the illusion that an apolitical method is possible" (p. 386). There is not an apparent contradiction between a political project (any analysis of the relations of knowledge and power is inherently political) and the absence of privilege, even of a method of analysis. To privilege any one method, including genealogy or its precursor, archaeology, is to preordain the conclusion and hence restrict freedom. What Blair and Cooper (1987) see as a method is in actuality a parody—what a method might be if one were to consciously adopt it—that Foucault has no intention of following slavishly (Clark and McKerrow, 1987).

5. For representative essays, see Scott (1967, 1976), Farrell (1976, 1978), Leff (1978), and Cherwitz and Hikins (1986).

6. For representative essays, see Simons (1985), McGee (1980, 1987), Lyne (1985), Nelson and Megill (1986), Nelson, Megill, and McCloskey (1987), and Hariman (1986).

7. The orientation to knowledge grounds the critique of domination's focus on what is concealed as well as revealed in the discourse of power (thereby conferring status on the elite and marginalizing the dominated). Foucault's concern with understanding how certain "mentali-

ties" came into being at a particular time also resonates well with this reconceptualized sense of *doxa*—certain discursive formations are granted status within social relations while others are marginalized. The aim of a Foucauldian critique is, in these terms, to set forth the conditions by which the nature of what is taken to be doxastic knowledge at any given time can be recast.

References

Abravanel, H. (1983). "Mediatory Myths in the Service of Organizational Ideology." In L. R. Pony, P. J. Frost, G. Morgan, and T. C. Dandridge, eds., *Organizational Symbolism* (Greenwich, CT: JAI Press), pp. 273–293.

Althusser, L. (1971). *Lenin and Philosophy, and Other Essays.* Translated by B. Brewster. London: NLB.

Bakhtin, M. M. (1981). *The Dialogic Imagination.* Edited by M. Holquist. Translated by C. Emerson and M. Holquist. Austin: University of Texas Press.

Bakhtin, M. M. (1986). *Speech Genres and Other Late Essays.* Edited by C. Emerson and M. Holquist. Translated by V. McGee. Austin: University of Texas Press.

Becker, S. (1971). "Rhetorical Studies for the Contemporary World." In E. Black and L. Bitzer, eds., *The Prospect of Rhetoric* (Englewood Park, NJ: Prentice-Hall), pp. 21–43.

Becker, S. (1986, November). "Rhetoric, Media, and Culture, or the Rhetorical Turn in Media Studies." Paper presented at the annual meeting of the Speech Communication Association, Chicago.

Benhabib, S. (1986). *Critique, Norm, and Utopia: A Study of the Foundations of Critical Theory.* New York: Columbia University Press.

Bersani, L. (1977). "The Subject of Power." *Diacritics* 7: 3.

Bisseret, N. (1979). *Education, Class Language, and Ideology.* London: Routledge & Kegan Paul.

Blair, C., and M. Cooper. (1987). "The Humanist Turn in Foucault's Rhetoric of Inquiry." *Quarterly Journal of Speech* 73: 151–171.

Blankenship, J. (1976). "The Search for the 1972 Democratic Nomination: A Metaphorical Perspective." In J. Blankenship and H. G. Stelzner, eds., *Rhetoric and Communication: Studies in the University of Illinois Tradition* (Urbana: University of Illinois Press), pp. 236–260.

Blankenship, J., and J. K. Muir. (1987). "On Imaging the Future: The Secular Search for 'Piety.'" *Communication Quarterly* 35: 1–12.

Bourdieu, P. (1977). *Outline of a Theory of Practice.* Translated by R. Nice. Cambridge: Cambridge University Press.

Bourdieu, P. (1979). "Symbolic Power." Translated by R. Nice. *Critique of Anthropology* 4: 77–85.

Bourdieu, P. (1980). "The Production of Belief: Contribution to an Economy of Symbolic Goods." Translated by R. Nice. *Media, Culture, & Society* 2: 261–293.

Brockriede, W. (1974). "Rhetorical Criticism as Argument." *Quarterly Journal of Speech* 60: 165–174.

Brown, R. H. (1987). *Society as Text: Essays on Rhetoric, Reason, and Reality.* Chicago: University of Chicago Press.

Burke, K. (1941). *The Philosophy of Literary Form.* Baton Rouge: Louisiana State University Press.

Burke, K. (1961). *Attitudes Toward History.* Boston: Beacon Press.

Burke, K. (1966). *Language as Symbolic Action.* Berkeley and Los Angeles: University of California Press.

Campbell, K. K. (1983). "Response to Forbes Hill." *Central States Speech Journal* 34: 126–127.

Cawelti, J. G. (1985). "With the Benefit of Hindsight: Popular Cultural Criticism." *Critical Studies in Mass Communication* 2: 363–379.

Charland, M. (1987). "Constitutive Rhetoric: The Case of the *Peuple Québécois.*" *Quarterly Journal of Speech* 73: 133–150.

Cherwitz, R. A., and J. Hikins. (1986). *Communication and Knowledge: An Investigation in Rhetorical Knowledge.* Columbia: University of South Carolina Press.

Clark, E. C., and R. E. McKerrow. (1987). "The Historiographical Dilemma in Myrdal's American Creed: Rhetoric's Role in Rescuing a Historical Moment." *Quarterly Journal of Speech* 73: 303–316.

Condit, C. (1987). "Democracy and Civil Rights: The Universalizing Influence of Public Argumentation." *Communication Monographs* 54: 1–18.

Edelman, M. (1988). *Constructing the Political Spectacle.* Chicago: University of Chicago Press.

Engels, F. (1942). "Engels to Mehring, July 14, 1893." In *K. Marx and F. Engels: Selected Correspondence, 1846–1895*, trans. D. Torr (New York: International Publishers), vol. 29, pp. 511–512.

Farrell, T. B. (1976). "Knowledge, Consensus, and Rhetorical Theory." *Quarterly Journal of Speech* 62: 258–266 (reprinted in this volume).

Farrell, T. B. (1978). "Social Knowledge, Part 2." *Quarterly Journal of Speech* 64: 329–334.

Fields, A. B. (1988). "In Defense of Political Economy and Systemic Analysis: A Critique of Prevailing Theoretical Approaches to the New Social Movements." In C. Nelson and L. Grossberg, eds., *Marxism and the Interpretation of Culture* (Urbana: University of Illinois Press), pp. 141–156.

Fisher, W. (1985). "The Narrative Paradigm: An Elaboration." *Communication Monographs* 52: 347–367.

Fiske, J. (1986). "Television: Polysemy and Popularity." *Critical Studies in Mass Communication* 3: 391–408.

Foucault, M. (1980a). *Power/Knowledge.* Edited by C. Gordon. Translated by C. Gordon, L. Marshall, J. Mephau, and K. Soper. New York: Pantheon Books.

Foucault, M. (1980b). *The History of Sexuality*, Vol. 1. Translated by R. Hurley. New York: Vintage Books.

Foucault, M. (1982). "Is It Really Important to Think? An Interview." Translated by T. Keenan. *Philosophical and Social Criticism* 9: 29–40.

Fraser, N. (1981). "Foucault on Modern Power: Empirical Insights and Normative Confusions." *Praxis International* 1: 272–287.

Fraser, N. (1985). "What's Critical about Critical Theory? The Case of Habermas and Gender." *New German Critique* 35: 97–131.

Giddens, A. (1979). *Central Problems in Social Theory.* Berkeley and Los Angeles: University of California Press.

Giddens, A. (1984). *The Constitution of Society: Outline of a Theory of Structuration.* Cambridge, UK: Polity Press.

Grossberg, L. (1984). "Strategies of Marxist Cultural Interpretation." *Critical Studies in Mass Communication* 1: 391–421.

Habermas, J. (1984). *The Theory of Communicative Action, Vol. 1: Reason and Rationalization of Society.* Translated by T. McCarthy. Boston: Beacon Press.

Habermas, J. (1987). *The Philosophical Discourses of Modernity.* Translated by F. Lawrence. Cambridge, MA: MIT Press.

Hall, S. (1985). "Signification, Representation, Ideology: Althusser and the Post-Structuralist Debates." *Critical Studies in Mass Communication* 2: 91–114.

Hall, S. (1988). "The Toad in the Garden: Thatcherism among the Theorists." In C. Nelson and L. Grossberg, eds., *Marxism and the Interpretation of Culture* (Urbana: University of Illinois Press), pp. 35–57.

Hariman, R. (1986). "Status, Marginality, and Rhetorical Theory." *Quarterly Journal of Speech* 72: 38–54 (reprinted in this volume).

Hiley, D. (1984). "Foucault and the Analysis of Power." *Praxis International* 4: 192–207.

Hill, F. (1983). "A Turn against Ideology: Reply to Professor Wander." *Central States Speech Journal* 34: 121–126.

Jensen, K. B. (1987). "Qualitative Audience Research: Toward an Integrative Approach to Reception." *Critical Studies in Mass Communication* 4: 21–36.

Kent, C. A. (1986). "Michel Foucault: Doing History or Undoing It?" *Canadian Journal of History* 21: 371–396.

Laclau, E. (1977). *Politics and Ideology in Marxist Theory.* London: NLB.

Laclau, E. (1980). "Populist Rupture and Discourse." Translated by J. Grealy. *Screen Education* 34: 87–93.

Laclau, E. (1983)."'Socialism,' the 'People,' 'Democracy': The Transformation of Hegemonic Logic." *Social Text* 7: 115–119.

Laclau, E., and C. Mouffe (1985). *Hegemony and Socialist Strategy: Towards a Radical Democratic Politics.* Translated by W. Moore and P. Cammack. London: Verso.

Leff, M. (1978). "In Search of Ariadne's Thread: A Review of the Recent Literature on Rhetorical Theory." *Central States Speech Journal* 29: 73–91.

Lentricchia, F. (1983). *Criticism and Social Change.* Chicago: University of Chicago Press.

Lyne, J. (1985). "Rhetorics of Inquiry." *Quarterly Journal of Speech* 71: 65–73.

Mailloux, S. (1985). "Rhetorical Hermeneutics." *Critical Inquiry* 11: 620–641.

Markovic, M. (1983). "The Idea of Critique in Social Theory." *Praxis International* 3: 108–120.

McGee, M. C. (1975). "In Search of 'the People': A Rhetorical Alternative." *Quarterly Journal of Speech* 61: 235–249 (reprinted in this volume).

McGee, M. C. (1980). "The 'Ideograph:' A Link Between Rhetoric and Ideology." *Quarterly Journal of Speech* 66: 1–16 (reprinted in this volume).

McGee, M. C. (1982). "A Materialist's Conception of Rhetoric." In R. E. McKerrow, ed., *Explorations in Rhetoric* (Glenview, IL: Scott, Foresman), pp. 23–48.

McGee, M. C. (1984). "Another Philippic: Notes on the Ideological Turn in Criticism." *Central States Speech Journal* 35: 43–50.

McGee, M. C. (1987, April). "Public Address and Culture Studies." Paper presented at the annual meeting of the Central States Speech Association, St. Louis.

McKerrow, R. E. (1986). "Pragmatic Justification and Perelman's Philosophical Rhetoric." In J. Golden and J. J. Pilotta, eds., *Practical Reasoning in Human Affairs: Studies in Honor of Chaim Perelman* (Dordrecht, The Netherlands: D. Reidel), pp. 207–225.

Misgeld, D. (1985). "Critical Hermeneutics versus Neoparsonianism?" *New German Critique* 35: 55–82.

Mosco, V. (1983). "Critical Research and the Role of Labor." *Journal of Communication* 33: 237–248.

Mullins, W. A. (1979). "Truth and Ideology: Reflections on Mannheim's Paradox." *History and Theory* 18: 141–154.

Mumby, D. K. (1987). "The Political Function of Narrative in Organizations." *Communication Monographs* 54: 113–127.

Nelson, J. S., and A. Megill. (1986). "Rhetoric of Inquiry: Prospects and Projects." *Quarterly Journal of Speech* 72: 20–37.

Nelson, J. S., A. Megill, and D. N. McCloskey, eds. (1987). *The Rhetoric of the Human Sciences.* Madison: University of Wisconsin Press.

Perelman, C., and L. Olbrechts-Tyteca. (1969). *The New Rhetoric: A Treatise on Argumentation* Translated by J. Wilkinson and P. Weaver. South Bend, IN: University of Notre Dame Press.

Rajchman, J. (1985). *Michel Foucault: The Freedom of Philosophy.* New York: Columbia University Press.

Ross, S. D. (1985). "Foucault's Radical Politics." *Praxis International* 5: 131–144.

Scott, R. L. (1967). "On Viewing Rhetoric as Epistemic." *Central States Speech Journal* 18: 9–17 (reprinted in this volume).

Scott, R. L. (1976). "On Viewing Rhetoric as Epistemic: Ten Years Later." *Central States Speech Journal* 27: 258–266.

Shiner, L. (1982). "Reading Foucault: Anti-Method and the Genealogy of Power/Knowledge." *History and Theory* 21: 382–398.

Simons, H. (1985)."Chronicle and Critique of a Conference." *Quarterly Journal of Speech* 71: 52–64.

Simons, H., and A. A. Aghazarian, eds. (1986). *Form, Genre, and the Study of Political Discourse.* Columbia: University of South Carolina Press.

Slack, J. D., and M. Allor. (1983). "The Political and Epistemological Constituents of Critical Communication Research." *Journal of Communication* 33: 208–218.

Therborn, G. (1980). *The Ideology of Power and the Power of Ideology.* London: NLB.

Thompson, J. B. (1984). *Studies in the Theory of Ideology.* Berkeley and Los Angeles: University of California Press.

Toulmin, S. (1972). *Human Understanding.* Princeton, NJ: Princeton University Press.

Turner, K. (1986, April). "Rhetoric of, by, and for the Media: Public Address Studies in an Age of Mass Communication." Paper presented at the annual meeting of the Central States Speech Association, Cincinnati.

Wander, P. (1981). "Cultural Criticism." In D. Nimmo and K. Sanders, eds., *Handbook of Political Communication* (Beverly Hills, CA: Sage), pp. 497–528.

Wander, P. (1983). "The Ideological Turn in Modern Criticism." *Central States Speech Journal* 34: 1–18.

West, C. (1988). "Marxist Theory and the Specificity of Afro-American Oppression." In C. Nelson and L. Grossberg, eds., *Marxism and the Interpretation of Culture* (Urbana: University of Illinois Press), pp. 17–29.

Rehabilitating Rhetoric

Confronting Blindspots in Discourse and Social Theory

MAURICE CHARLAND

Rhetorical theory is the oldest (if not most venerable) theory of discourse in the Western tradition. Furthermore, as Terry Eagleton (1981: 101) points out, rhetorical theory was at its root practical and political. We should not be surprised, therefore, that Eagleton, a Marxist literary theorist, has rediscovered rhetoric. Rhetorical theory and its practice provide Eagleton with the means to reassert a link between discourse and *praxis*, and thus evade the compartmentalization of the "literary" within the realm of psychological effects and personalized or romantic conceptions of aesthetics. While Eagleton writes seemingly unaware of the American discipline of rhetorical studies within communication studies, he does realize the significance of rhetoric's conceptual framework to the critical study of discursive practices within the social order.

Paradoxically, Eagleton's discovery of a rhetorical criticism not merely based in Derridean deconstruction coincides with the emergence of a critical tendency within communication studies that has cast a blind eye to rhetoric. Those critics and theorists of cinema, of mass communication, and ultimately of culture who ride the poststructuralist wave have encountered the Nietzschean uncertainties of the sign, have seen the power of discourse, and have written on practice. Yet they have not engaged the harlot of the arts. Thus, within communication studies, we find one community of scholars known as rhetoricians, and another loosely termed "cultural theorists." Furthermore, while these two groups share a concern with the structuration of power through discourse, and will often employ similar concepts, they form distinct speech communities. While there are certainly historical and sociological reasons for this *écart*, the exigencies of theory and *praxis* call for the forging of a broader and more inclusive discursive field. I assert this, not in the name of a facile pluralism, but in the hope for a theoretical engagement and alliance informed by an appreciation for and a confrontation with theoretical difference.

While I am unsure of how Eagleton might assess American rhetorical studies, particularly from within the *optique* of Marxism, I am sure that the theoretical and practical foundation of both classical and American versions of rhetorical studies does provide a basis for a fundamental analysis of the relationships of discourse, communication, power, and culture. This is not, however, to assert that rhetoric has developed a complete and sufficient theory of the relationship of discourse to power. Furthermore, I concede from the outset that the contemporary practice of American rhetorical studies suffers from a number of political and theoretical blindspots. Nevertheless, I insist on the value of its primary insight and call therefore for its rehabilitation. In my view, rhetorical study needs to be rehabilitated in a double sense: its proper place within the human sciences and contemporary cultural theory should be recognized; also, however, those working within the rhetorical tradition need to shed their insularity, enter into the grand debates within the human sciences, and critically reexamine the assumptions of their own practice. Rhetoric's contribution to cultural theory will only be realized if those within the rhetorical tradition understand and situate the significance of their own work.

RHETORIC AS SITUATED DISCOURSE

In focusing on the effects of language upon knowledge, upon understanding, and indeed upon being, rhetorical theory anticipated by over a millennium the recent "linguistic turn" of the human sciences. However, and this must be emphasized, rhetoric's aim is modest. It seeks only to explore the status of language-in-action. Thus, while rhetorical theory can contribute to epistemology and ontology, its main object is *praxis*. Rhetorical studies share much with those human sciences that affirm the fundamental linguisticality of humans. However, and this unlike the most formal of structuralisms, such as Lévi-Strauss's anthropology, rhetorical studies insist that humans *act*. This insistence on human agency affirms that humans live in a meaningful universe, and that discourse (language-in-use) mediates meaning. Furthermore, and this is key, the artful deployment of language, through topics, arguments, tropes, and figures, has real effects upon language itself, upon meaning, and finally, upon what humans do.

In the American tradition of rhetorical studies, this has led to an emphasis on the study of communicative acts that produce "exigency" within what Lloyd Bitzer (1968) has termed the "rhetorical situation." In other words, the study of rhetoric begins with a concern for the potential real effects of a discourse. It considers discourse to provide, or at least articulate, the "good reasons" (Wallace, 1963) that motivate social action. Thus, rhetorical analysis begins by situating discourse within the social formation. Rhetoric is a form of discourse that is always *addressed* (Burke, 1950: 37–39) to some audience and speaks to a particular historical conjuncture. Of course, it then follows that rhetorical scholars pay considerable attention to the speeches of Presidents, of parliamentarians, and of leaders of "movements." Rhetorical studies consider the terms of the policies, practices, values, and ideologies such speeches or writings articulate, the forms in which these prescriptions are thereby cast, and the manner in which these articulate *with* existent discourses and the at least attributed logics and understandings of their audience.

The audience-oriented hermeneutic of rhetorical theory can be clearly seen, for example, in David Zarefsky's (1986) discussion of the "Lincoln–Douglas" debates. Zarefsky dismisses those criticisms of the debates that focus on their lack of innovation or philosophical depth. Such debates must be understood, Zarefsky makes clear, as performed by candidates before an audience in the view of developing voter support. The debaters were constrained by the situation in which they found themselves as they tried to articulate their positions, and their *ethos*, before a portion of the electorate with its own prejudices. Similarly, the notion of audience is fundamental to Michael McGee's (1980b) study of Queen Elizabeth's rhetoric before Parliament. Elizabeth, as a woman, needed to overcome the resistance of a Parliament of men if she were to be an effective sovereign. Elizabeth deployed language in a particular way that we can understand once we become aware of what opposition she faced. Furthermore, through Elizabeth's and Parliament's rhetorical transactions, the meaning and power of the monarchy in England were transformed. Indeed, it is in the relationship of speaker to audience that the structuration of power occurs. Finally, the importance of audience in rhetorical analysis is illustrated by Randall A. Lake's (1983) analysis of the American Indian Movement's tactics. There, it is argued that critics who consider such tactics as the occupation of the offices of the Bureau of Indian Affairs to be counter-productive have erred because they consider AIM's audience to be whites, rather than native people. Particular audiences will be moved by different symbolic acts, depending upon their (symbolically mediated) interests.

Rhetorical analysis proceeds with "audience" as its ground. It is important to note, however, that its audience is not the concrete individual human beings who listen to or read and interpret a discourse. Rather, following Aristotle, rhetorical theory considers the audience as a *class*. In Aristotle, this meant analyzing audiences on the basis of what today we would term "basic demographics." Among contemporary theorists, this means considering the audience as existing within a rhetorical culture, which is to say a culture in which "good reasons" for interests and motives exist in discourse. Thus, Zarefsky's Lincoln and Douglas are not only performing to each other, but are speaking to the (discursively constituted) prejudices (in Gadamer's sense) of the culture they address. This culture, for rhetorical theory, consists not in the multiplicity of practices and differences within any particular social formation, but in what Farrell (1976) terms its "social knowledge," an ethical rather than empirical form of knowledge, attributed to that formation by the rhetor on the basis of a received consent. The creativity and productivity of rhetoric lies in its reshaping of that knowledge by articulating the tensions and contradictions within the formation experienced by individual social subjects. Thus, rhetoric produces new social knowledge as it offers public interpretations of social experience and proceeds to make normative claims. In this, then, rhetoric forms prescriptives and fosters ethical judgment, not in terms of what is, but in terms of what should be. Furthermore, rhetoric can only succeed to the degree its audience recognizes or discovers a "truth" in these articulations. Rhetoric's audience then, which lives through and enacts judgments, is a mediating ground that halts a random or capricious overlaying of one discourse upon another. Rhetorical theory's audience does not consist of transcendental subjectivities, nor even necessarily of reflexively conscious agents. It does consist of historically and discursively situated subjectivities whose experience is the condition of possibility for rhetorical creativity as well as a site of resistance to semiotic free play. To the degree that social existence produces *malaise*, or that a gap is felt between attributed social knowledge and personal experience, or indeed that particular conjunctures render social knowledge itself evidently contradictory or problematic, a potential audience for rhetoric emerges. That audience, more than an assemblage of individuals, is rhetorically constituted as a collective ethical subject through an articulation of experience.

As I hope the above has made evident, rhetorical theory recommends a particular form of interpretive and political practice and so takes its place among the human or cultural sciences. Rhetorical theory directs the cultural critic to the study of the publicly articulated motivations and reasons for actions, institutionalized practices, and relations of power. Furthermore, rhetorical theory provides the critic with the analytic machinery to deconstruct the sense of these articulations and so provides the possibility to chart their possible reconstruction. But there is a bias in all of this that is fundamental to the rhetorical project: It is that even "irrational" cultures and orders of power have their reasons. Rhetorical theory has no illusion that the discourses of the social evince the philosopher's rationality. Indeed, since Socrates philosophers have been suspicious of rhetorical reasoning. Nevertheless, modes of practical reasoning within culture do exist and rhetorical theory insists upon the possibility of an audience-grounded cultural hermeneutic that is more than an encounter with schizophrenia.

With a postulate of intelligibility, rhetorical theory mandates a particular mode of criticism. The rhetorical critic seeks to identify how discourse configures the world as meaningful and consequently mandates "reasonable" courses of action. Not surprisingly, then, much rhetorical criticism begins with argument. On the basis of an attributed "What Is," and of postulated warrants that assert relations between objects, arguments produce new understandings, knowledge, or commitments. Rhetorical criticism permits an analysis and deconstruction of this productivity. The analysis of arguments reveals the taken-for-granted "common sense" that Stuart Hall (1982, pp.76–77) identifies as fundamentally ideological, for as Aristotle noted, rhetorical argumentation deals with the "probable," with what seems likely, and not with the necessary. Rhetorical theory examines and lays bare for critique the expectations or prejudices of a discursively constituted audience. Argument analysis also identifies the semiotic operations that produce knowledge or commitment through a calculus of appeals. Arguments do more than demonstrate the probable: they configure the probable by positing or interpreting, rather than merely representing, a state of affairs. Arguments thus organize understanding and motives by creating relations in discourse between objects and by invoking and reconstructing the prejudices and interests of the claimed audience.

For the rhetorical critic, then, "good reasons" are not immanent to the "facts," but are produced. Furthermore, while rhetorical theory places stress upon argument, it is under no illusion that argument represents pure cognition about objective realities. Rather, rhetorical theory fully recognizes that the force of argument is partly based in interest and emotion; that *ethos*, the rhetorically effected trust or respect for the rhetor, and *pathos*, an effect of empathy and sympathy, can serve as proper proofs of a claim; and that the very words used to signify value have unstable meaning even as they invoke commitment. Thus, while rhetorical theory and criticism are very concerned with argument, they go beyond it and concern themselves in general with the production of meaning and reason through public discourse. Argument is simply one of the more explicit and overt forms of discourse that is concerned with social relations and makes claims upon commitment and action. Consequently, rhetorical theory and criticism evince a highly ambiguous logocentrism. Certainly, rhetoric is concerned with reasons and motives as configured or configurable in propositions. However, rhetoric is not concerned with mere pure cognition. Rhetorical force is not simply the logical force of statement entailment inherent to pure logic's propositional calculus. Rhetorical force arises in the deployment of signs in concrete historical situations, where signs rework and configure both affect and interest. As such, much rhetorical force is pre- or extra-argumentive. Arguments work within and upon other discursive configurations of the reasonable. Thus, in rhetorical theory: the metaphor is fundamental to the creation of new meaning and the determination of topics of demonstration and lines of enquiry (Richards, 1936: 89–138); the narrative configures a universe in terms of ethical value and moral action, all the while including its audience through a process of identification (Charland, 1987; Condit and Lucaites, 1985; Fisher, 1984); language acts as a "terministic screen" that orients actions (Burke, 1966: 44–62); and tradition prescribes the usage of ideological key terms, "ideographs," in seeking to secure legitimacy and marshal consent (McGee, 1980a). Rhetorical critics trace the power of words as *logos* in the pre-Socratic sense of "constitutive utterance" through a semiotic and political play of signs. Consequently, rhetoric's logocentrism is not based on theoretical categories of reason, but in the manifest configuration of reasons and motives within language. Rhetorical criticism and theory study the practical reason manifest in the concrete public performance of discourse, of historically and situationally activated texts. To paraphrase a colleague, "Reason is as reason does."

In insisting that discourse-in-action *makes* reasons, rhetorical theory shares much with theories of discourse and culture influenced by poststructuralism. Both eschew a representational function for language in favor of one that is configurational; both see meaning as an effect of the surface of the text; and both recognize the deep intermingling of discourse and power. Rhetorical theory refuses, however, the pure structuralist project of eliminating positivity in favor of only relations of difference. Rather, rhetoric makes meaning through an *act* of signification. In this, rhetorical theory shares a terrain with certain strands of Marxist poststructuralism, particularly those influenced by the work of Stuart Hall and British Cultural Studies, which have found it necessary to rediscover signifying practice in the wake of structuralist reifications. While rhetoric is quite modest in its scope in comparison with what in communication is increasingly being known as "cultural studies," the latter will end up reproducing rhetorical theory if it wishes to enquire into the meaning structures of "ideological" discourse, of publicly articulated representations, legitimations, assertions, or arguments that make an implicit or explicit claim upon consent, commitment or action.

Rhetorical theory's particular contribution, as one of the human sciences, is to reveal the structure of reasons in discourse motivating political power and collective action. Consequently, interpretive analyses of the discourse of public power and real politics will tread along rhetoric's path. Such is the case, for example in Hartley's analysis of the news. His typology (1982: 118–119) of "framing," "focusing," "realizing," and "closing" reproduce classical rhetoric's parts of a speech: "exordium," "narratio," "proof," and "peroration." Indeed, it is hardly surprising that Bill Nichols (1981: 174–182), in his treatment of film, acknowledges rhetoric as the theory of expository discourse and makes use of its categories in discussing documentary film. To ignore these categories is to condemn oneself to reinvent them. Admittedly, not all visual presentations are amenable to rhetorical analysis. Rhetorical theory's concern is reason-giving in language acts. However, to the degree that audio-visual presentations are reducible to expositions, propositions, or rhetorical (expository and prescriptive) narratives, they become accessible to rhetorical categories, and such reductions necessarily occur in the operation of ideology and are necessary to practical politics. While discursive configurations of representations, of subject positions, of desire, and of pleasure have political and ideological implications, those implications are only realized within the social hierarchy through the articulation of empirical and normative claims.

In other words, the implications are manifest as demands are made, relationships are justified, and difference is suppressed.

In asserting the place of rhetorical theory and criticism within the human sciences, I do not intend to dismiss the significant work of cultural or critical theorists operating out of postmarxism, poststructuralism, or postmodernism. While my claim is that a theory of discourse concerned with practical politics cannot ignore rhetoric, I see in the "posts-" both points of complementarity with and significant challenges to the rhetorical tradition. In other words, I see the existence of sufficient common ground to permit the interrogation of one intellectual practice by the other. This common ground is apparent if one considers, for example, the affinities of Roland Barthes' criticism to rhetorical analysis, of Burke's "dramatism" to poststructuralist deconstruction, or of McGee's (1975; 1980a) treatment of ideographs and collectivization with Stuart Hall's (1985) discussion of ideology and the subject. Indeed, the rhetorical tradition even has a certain compatibility with Baudrillard's work, for as Lyotard (1985: 5) observes, the rhetorician is the "maker of simulacra." These affinities provide, I would submit, the ground for a more *praxical* theorization of the relationship of discourse and power.

In calling for a renewed critical and interpretive discourse within communication studies that would include both rhetorical theory and the "posts-," I have no illusion of the obstacles that such a project would encounter. Rhetorical studies and critical or cultural studies form two relatively distinct "speech communities" or "discursive formations," as the choice of terms in this sentence illustrates. These two communities are divided by interpretive orientations, politics, and style. The former community is, frankly, rather staid. Even though, since Plato, rhetoric has been *the* marginalized discourse in the face of philosophy, being treated as mere "knack" or as "harlot," it nevertheless moves within the "mainstream," both within and outside the university. The community of "posts-," on the other hand, valorizes difference and *différance*, and is energized by its status as Other. Indeed, its preoccupation is precisely with that which slips through or refuses the "mainstream's" normalization. In calling for a productive—and public—dialectic (in the sense of Socratic dialogue) between these two communities, I am not favouring the development of a new unitary "affective apparatus," to borrow from another context one of Grossberg's (1984) terms, that would replace the two now existent. I am calling for a partial unhinging of theory and practice from personal style and affect. This would permit an encounter of one with the other, where each could serve as a corrective to the other's blindspots.

Rhetoric proceeds within the "mainstream." This is an unavoidable consequence of its practical roots. Since antiquity, it has been concerned with the management of affairs before the court and the state. Rhetorical theory places no value upon the marginal or the avant-garde, except in their attempts to move or transform institutionalized formations of power, or, in Gramscian terms, to effectively challenge and reconstruct hegemony. In this, rhetorical theory rejects the Foucaultian preoccupation with the other, with the marginalized and the silenced, particularly when their practices reinforce and valorize their marginality. Rhetoric is not as such politically insensitive or inherently allied to the powerful and the "right." Rather, rhetoric is pragmatically impatient before what it considers ineffective political and intellectual practice. Rhetoric understands that power will not be restructured by the intellectual's fascinated gaze upon the oppressed; power will be changed through both their mobilization and through discursive and non-discursive acts that win concessions from the powerful. Furthermore, from the rhetorical perspective, prescriptives and political programs derived from philosophy and abstract theorizations (such as Marxism) are doomed to ineffectiveness. As Burke argued to the American Writers Congress in 1935 (Lentricchia, 1983: 21–25), there must be a consonance between the language of practice and theory. Burke recognized that political practice is a rhetorical enterprise that must always begin within a discourse, and must rework that discourse from the inside. Thus, for Burke, in the United States at least, a strong tradition of discourse mandates the "people" as warrant for the exercise of political power. A successful American politics of the left would of necessity proceed by arguing for the "people, " and not for some other totalization such as the "workers" or the "proletariat." The AWC effectively expelled Burke for this heresy. In spite of the Gramscian (and hence rhetorical) turn of the New Left, the rhetorical tradition remains absent, if not indeed silenced, within the new left of communication scholarship. Ironically, because it doubts the efficacy of marginal practices that operate only from outside of hegemony and the discourses of power, the rhetorical tradition itself is unspoken and unacknowledged by those whom I am convinced should be its theoretical and practical allies.

Much of what is termed critical or cultural studies proceeds from outside of the mainstream of political practice. It is at times driven by philosophy, or by Marxist theory, or by an interest in or fascination with popular (and not so popular) cultural forms. While such theorizations clearly espouse an emancipatory interest, their political focus is often displaced by the theorizing of pleasure or the pleasure of theorizing. This is the case with much film or television criticism that begins with a preoccupation with mediated texts. This is also the case with much Marxist political theory that expends its energies in rigorous theoretical constructions that finally only serve as cultural capital within the world of left intellectuals. All too often, practical politics is elided in a conflation of theoretical practices, aesthetic practices, and style. Of course, I hasten to add that I am not claiming that all work in cultural studies is politically and theoretically inconsequential, nor am I claiming that all critical or cultural study within communication studies ignores practical politics. Furthermore, much critical or cultural theory that does not lead to practical politics succeeds where rhetoric does not in identifying networks and sedimentations of power within social and cultural formations. Thus, my argument is not against the theorization of the "posts" per se. It is against their reluctance to admit the presence of the rhetorical tradition and to entertain rhetorical theory's challenge to think about politics and power pragmatically, from within a social formation's institutions and discourses, and from within the realm of the possible. In other words, this silence, I would suggest, is symptomatic of a reluctance to deal with practical politics in realistic terms.

Of course, there are exceptions to this tendency that I indict. The work of Stuart Hall, for example, evinces a keen sensitivity to the importance of public discourse, to the institution of power in the state, and to the basically rhetorical character of gaining consent through ideology. In his discussion of Thatcherism, Hall (1988) warns of the dangers of theoreticism, insists on the necessity of grounded and concrete political analyses, and emphasizes the indeterminate outcome of history and the role of ideologues in forming consent. Thus, even though he proceeds from Gramsci and does not speak from within the rhetorical tradition nor use its terms, Hall's position is consonant with that of rhetorical scholars. Of course, there remain differences between Hall's project and that of rhetorical theory. First, Hall begins with a Marxist analysis of the social formation and is committed to Marxism's prescriptions. Rhetorical theory's commitment is to a culture where prescriptions *emerge* in speech. Rhetorical theory differs from Hall's Marxism in that it not only recognizes that the future is contingent upon today's practice, but also asserts that a determination of what is right and proper, of what is ethical and not merely effective, can only be made contingently; ethical judgment arises through the rhetorical situation. Second, while Hall stresses the gaining of consent through the configuration of "common sense" in ideological discursive practices, he is not particularly concerned with the precise rhetoric of ideology. He does not focus on the way tropes, figures, narratives, and arguments rework meaning and motive. Rather he lays stress on something rhetorical critics should keep in mind but usually do not: the non-discursive forces that structure and constrain what can and will be spoken.

Rhetorical theory has a blindspot. Its apparent "conservatism," or at least absence of radicalism, is not merely the product of a theoretically derived political realism. It results as well from its own history as an institutionalized discourse and from an ideological commitment that tends to inhibit a reflection upon its own presuppositions. In its American incarnation, rhetorical theory is fundamentally founded in a belief in the existence of democratic life. The project of rhetorical theory and criticism is a democratic political culture. Contemporary rhetorical theory is naïve when it presumes that the culture of good reasons can be attained simply through the study and practice of public speaking. In rhetorical theory we rarely find an adequate account of social and political forces and determinations. Rhetorical theory usually does not render problematic the categories of the rhetorical situation. It tells us neither why certain occasions, speakers, and topics are privileged, nor what unspoken interests are served, nor what audiences are excluded. Indeed, rhetorical criticism has far too often focused on "official" discourses in the less-than-open public sphere, and thus has failed to bring to light the rhetoric of those hegemony would silence (Wander, 1983: 1–6). Also, as Philip Wander (1984) has observed, rhetorical studies have ignored "the third persona," those who neither speak nor are spoken to in public address.

Of course, the roots to the study of rhetoric in the United States are in literature, not political theory. Its aim initially was to contribute to the quality of public discourse, which was ignored by traditional literary studies. The progressive moment in this should not be ignored: rhetorical studies re-politicized the study of language. Nevertheless, because it lacked a materialist foundation, and attributed too much to the power of words, and because it developed in an intellectual tradition where idealism and then positivism dominated, the study of rhetoric has not been characterized by the development of a fundamental political or cultural critique. On the other hand, rhetorical criticism has contributed a wealth of concrete and very specific analyses of the workings of the discourses of "good reasons" that have marshalled or undermined consent at particular historical moments. This well illustrates the boundary of the discipline of rhetorical studies. Its concern is with discourse-in-action, its creation, its deployment, and its effects. For a theory of the conditions of production of such discourse, and of the social forces that constitute such conditions, one must look elsewhere.

Both the emancipatory interest of rhetorical theory and the theoretical interest of rhetorical scholars would be well served by an opening to the new critical discourses within communication studies. Such a rehabilitation of rhetorical studies will require an increased attention to political and cultural theory by rhetorical theorists, for McGee's (1975: 235–238) arguments regarding the tradition's reluctance to engage the major currents in social theory are still far too true. In order that rhetorical studies successfully undertake an increasingly called-for critical turn and thus realize their radical potential, rhetorical scholars will need to theorize properly the position of their project within the human sciences as well as within the social formation. Such an understanding would lead to a recognition of its limitations as well as its theoretical and analytic power.

The corrective that critical and cultural theory, including "cultural studies," can bring to rhetorical studies is an adequate theorization of the place of discourse, the forces that put it in place, the ideological and affective grounds from which it proceeds, and the silences that are imposed. Furthermore, critical and cultural theory can identify the sites in which rhetorical action is needed, the audiences that await being addressed, and the interests that such rhetorics must confront. Rhetorical theory, conversely, should remind cultural or critical theory that practical politics requires ideological work in the form of arguments and narratives that create good and compelling reasons or motives to act. Furthermore, such reasons can only proceed from the existent discursive ground. Rhetorical theory rejects pessimism in considering the realistic politics of possibility. Rhetorical theory also remains committed to the development of prescriptives not grounded in descriptive statements. In other words, and finally, the rhetorical tradition refuses to abandon ethics and the faculty of judgment in favor of sheer political commitment, descriptive theoretical analysis, or a politics grounded solely in affect or aesthetics. Rhetoric, at least in the sophistic and Aristotlean tradition, remains committed to the contingent judgment and to *phronesis*, or practical wisdom.

In taking its place among the human sciences of the Western intellectual tradition, rhetorical theory will face many challenges. There will be, of course, the modern Platonists who will attempt to reduce it to a mere pure *tekhnè* at best, or untrue obfuscation at worse. There are others who will dismiss it on aesthetic grounds, seeking more elegant theorizations. But the real challenge to rhetoric will come not from theory but from the real. Rhetorical theory is pertinent only if what Farrell has termed a "rhetorical culture" is possible. Should public spaces, always threatened, finally disappear, or should a culture reach the point where consistency or reason-giving are no longer valued or recognized, rhetoric would be irrelevant. Such a world is to be resisted however, for the absence of reasons and judgment are the mark of a reign of terror.

References

Bitzer, Lloyd F. (1968). "The Rhetorical Situation." *Philosophy of Rhetoric* 1: 1–14 (reprinted in this volume).

Burke, Kenneth. (1950). *A Rhetoric of Motives*. Berkeley and Los Angeles: University of California Press.

Burke, Kenneth. (1966). *Language as Symbolic Action*. Berkeley and Los Angeles: University of California Press.

Charland, Maurice. (1987). "Constitutive Rhetoric: The Case of the *Peuple Québécois*." *Quarterly Journal of Speech* 73: 133–150.

Eagleton, Terry. (1981). *Walter Benjamin or Towards a Revolutionary Criticism*. London: New Left Books.

Farrell, Thomas B. (1976). "Knowledge, Consensus, and Rhetorical Theory." *Quarterly Journal of Speech* 62: 1–14 (reprinted in this volume).

Fisher, Walter R. (1984). "Narration as Human Communication Paradigm: The Case of Public Moral Argument." *Communication Monographs* 51: 1–22 (reprinted in this volume).

Grossberg, Lawrence. (1984). "Another Boring Day in Paradise: Rock and Roll and the Empowerment of Everyday Life." *Popular Music* 4: 225–258.

Hall, Stuart (1982). "The Rediscovery of Ideology: Return of the Repressed in Media Studies."

In Michael Gurevitch et al., eds., *Culture, Society, and the Media* (New York: Methuen), pp. 56–89.

Hall, Stuart. (1985). "Signification, Representation, Ideology: Althusser and the Post-Structuralist Debates." *Critical Studies in Mass Communication* 2: 91–114.

Hall, Stuart. (1988). "The Toad in the Garden: Thatcherism among the Theorists." In Cary Nelson and Lawrence Grossberg, eds., *Marxism and the Interpretation of Culture* (Urbana: University of Illinois Press), pp. 35–57.

Hartley, John. (1982). *Understanding News*. London: Methuen.

Lake, Randall A. (1983). "Enacting Red Power: The Consummatory Function in Native American Protest Rhetoric." *Quarterly Journal of Speech* 69: 127–142.

Lentricchia, Frank (1983). *Criticism and Social Change*. Chicago: University of Chicago Press.

Lucaites, John Louis and Celeste Michelle Condit. (1985). "Reconstructing Narrative Theory: A Functional Perspective." *Journal of Communication* 35: 90–108.

Lyotard, Jean-François, and Jean-Loup Thébaud. (1985). *Just Gaming*. Translated by Wlad Godzich. Minneapolis: University of Minnesota Press.

McGee, Michael C. (1975). "In Search of 'the 'People': A Rhetorical Alternative." *Quarterly Journal of Speech* 61: 235–249 (reprinted in this volume).

McGee, Michael C. (1980a). "The Ideograph: A Link Between Rhetoric and Ideology." *Quarterly Journal of Speech* 66: 1–16 (reprinted in this volume).

McGee, Michael C. (1980b). "The Origins of 'Liberty': A Feminization of Power." *Communication Monographs* 47: 23–45.

Nichols, Bill (1981). *Ideology and the Image: Social Representation in the Cinema and Other Media*. Bloomington: Indiana University Press.

Richards, I. A. (1936). *The Philosophy of Rhetoric*. London: Oxford University Press.

Wallace, Karl. (1963). "The Substance of Rhetoric: Good Reasons." *Central States Speech Journal* 35: 197–216.

Wander, Philip (1983). "The Ideological Turn in Modern Criticism." *Central States Speech Journal* 34: 1–18.

Wander, Philip. (1984). "The Third Persona: The Ideological Turn in Rhetorical Theory." *Central States Speech Journal* 35: 197–216 (reprinted in this volume).

Zarefsky, David. (1986). "The Lincoln–Douglas Debates Revisited: The Evolution of Public Argument." *Quarterly Journal of Speech* 72: 162–184.

PART 7

Rhetoric in the Mass Media

Classical rhetorical theory was formulated to account for the relationship between discourse and power in ancient Greece and Rome. Contemporary rhetorical theory has endeavored to modify the formulations of classical rhetoric to account for the changing circumstances and practices of rhetoric in our own time. The most obvious difference between the classical era and our own time is the dominance of the mass media, particularly television and film, as well as the increasing importance of computer-mediated communication.

The rhetorical study of television and film requires a fairly substantial shift in some of the underlying assumptions concerning the relationship between public discourse and social and political power. The most substantial shift concerns the fact that film and television are predominantly commercial media. The primary goal of most television programming and film releases is to attract a paying audience, not to gain political support for a particular policy, party, or person. Nonetheless, wittingly or not, the content of television programs and movies almost always incorporates significant political messages. Sometimes these messages relate to specific policies currently being deliberated in the public sphere. For example, a program portraying the horrible results of an illegal abortion conveys a message about the desirability of legalizing abortion. More often, perhaps, a film or program conveys messages about more diffuse social practices or hidden threats. Thus, a program on abortion probably also conveys images of appropriate gender roles, while a film such as *Blade Runner* may convey more subtle messages about the threat that advanced technology poses to individual identity.

Because the political messages in film and television are often not explicitly connected with particular policies being publically debated, the study of the rhetorical practices embedded in such mass media involves a shift of focus. Rhetoric is thus not solely a study of governance, but is also, and significantly, a study of culture and identity. For rhetoricians, of course, culture is not an apolitical phenomenon. Nevertheless, to interpret the political through the lenses of culture and entertainment rather than through the lens of deliberative governance is to change the way in which one understands the functions and scope of rhetoric. Most significantly, such a perspective diffuses the nature of the rhetorical situation. The exigences that create the conditions for the production and dissemination of the movie *Jaws*, or even for more politically charged movies like *Amistad*, are not specifically locatable incidents, such as the assassination of a president or a military attack. Rather, they create and respond to trends that span much larger periods of time, such as rapid technological change, the closing of the frontier, and changing perceptions of the roles that gender and race play in U.S. history.

There is an enormous range of approaches to the modes of rhetoric represented in the mass media. Barry Brummett's examination of "Burke's Representative Anecdote as a Method for Media Criticism," for example, views the contents of mass media as though they were directed at helping individuals to cope with situations in their personal lives. As such, Brummett argues that in periods when technological change has been perceived as particularly intimidating, movies have helped audiences to cope with the apparent threats to their individuality and livelihood.

In contrast, Janice Hocker Rushing and Thomas S. Frentz's essay, "Reintegrating Ideology and Archetype in Rhetorical Criticism," describes the ways in which broadly universal human archetypes interact with particular ideological imperatives. Rushing and Frentz draw on Jung's psychoanalytic theory, which indicates that there are fundamental and recurring human images, relationships, or forms. They suggest that mass media programs such as *Jaws* or *E.T.* adapt those enduring archetypes to particular modern conditions. Thus, basic human needs are modified through time to fit changing human consciousness.

Yet a third approach to understanding the rhetoric of the mass media is offered by Celeste Michelle Condit in her essay, "The Rhetorical Limits of Polysemy." This essay examines the ways in which two audience members—a pro-life activist and a pro-choice activist—respond to an episode of the television show *Cagney and Lacey* that dealt with abortion. Condit argues that the differences in interpretations offered by these readers and their respective enjoyment of the program are constrained by a variety of factors, including the content of the episode itself, the availability of other media images of abortion, the amount of labor each viewer has to perform to produce a profitable interpretation of the episode, and the exposure of each viewer to other interpretations of abortion. Her conclusion is that a rhetorical reading of the mass media needs to be situated in sociopolitical contexts with regard both to ongoing political initiatives and the range of coverage of a topic within the mass media and alternative media as a whole.

Attention to the ways in which the media of film and television change rhetoric and demand its retheorization are well under way. At the same time, the analysis of the rhetorical implications of the computer and the Internet as primary communication media are barely beginning. No rhetorical theories treating of these dimensions of contemporary communication are included here, though preliminary works listed in the additional readings by Aune, Chesebro and Bertelson, Gurak, and Lanham suggest the richness and significance of the theoretical implications of these new ways of doing rhetoric.

Additional Readings

Aune, James Arnt. (1997). "The Work of Rhetoric in the Age of Digital Dissemination." *Quarterly Journal of Speech* 83: 230–242.

Chesebro, James W., and Dale A. Bertelsen. (1996). *Analyzing Media: Communication Technologies as Symbolic and Cognitive Systems*. New York: The Guilford Press.

Cuklanz, Lisa M. (1996). *Rape on Trial: How the Mass Media Construct Legal Reform and Social Change*. Philadelphia: University of Pennsylvania Press.

Dow, Bonnie J. (1996). *Prime-Time Feminism: Television, Media Culture, and the Women's Movement since 1970*. Philadelphia: University of Pennsylvania Press.

Fiske, John. (1986). "Television: Polysemy and Popularity." *Critical Studies in Mass Communication* 3: 391–408.

Frentz, Thomas S., and Janice Hocker Rushing. (1993). "Integrating Ideology and Archetype in Rhetorical Criticism, Part 2: A Case Study of *Jaws*." *Quarterly Journal of Speech* 79: 61–81.

Gurak, Laura J. (1997). *Persuasion and Privacy in Cyberspace: The Online Protests over Lotus Marketplace and the Clipper Chip*. New Haven, CT: Yale University Press.

Haynes, W. Lance. (1988). "Of That Which We Cannot Write: Some Notes on the Phenomenology of Media." *Quarterly Journal of Speech* 74: 71–101.

Lanham, Richard. (1993). *The Electronic Word: Democracy, Technology, and the Arts* Chicago: University of Chicago Press.

Lucaites, John Louis and Maurice Charland. (1989). "The Legacy of [LIBERTY]: Rhetoric, Ideology, and Aesthetics in the Postmodern Condition." *Canadian Journal of Political and Social Theory* 13: 31–48.

Burke's Representative Anecdote as a Method in Media Criticism

BARRY BRUMMETT

INVASION OF THE BODY SNATCHERS

One of Kenneth Burke's central concepts is the idea that literature is "equipment for living" (1941/1967, pp. 293–304; 1935/1965). By that he means that through types, components, or structures of literature people confront their lived situations, celebrate their triumphs and encompass their tragedies. For instance, some literary *forms* seem to be used reliably to help people adjust to agriculture lifestyles, while other forms seem better adapted to urban and industrial situations (Burke, 1935/1965, pp. 37–49, 237–246; 1937). Elsewhere Burke argues that people communicate using clusters of key terms which anchor symbolic structures of association and dissociation necessary for social life (1945/1962a). He describes the ways in which classical plot forms of tragedy and comedy are used by people to assuage guilt and repair social rifts (1937, vol. 1, pp. 41–118; 1941/1967, pp. 191–220; 1945/1962a). Writing in the Depression, Burke recommended new forms of public discourse to provide more effective symbolic equipment for a changing economy, and to replace the existing modes of discourse which had resulted in "trained incapacities" (1935/1965, pp. 7–9, 48–49). Throughout his writings runs the idea that types, components, or structures of literature *recur* as appropriate responses to recurring types of situations; that there are ways of *speaking about* war, victory, civil unrest, marital problems, etc., which will reliably equip us to live through those situations.

Thus, it becomes the task of the Burkean critic to identify the modes of discourse enjoying currency in a society and to link discourse to the real situations for which it is symbolic equipment. In this way, by examining what people are *saying*, the critic may discover what cultures are celebrating or mourning—and the critic may recommend

479

other ways of speaking which may serve as better equipment for living. For Burke, criticism is epistemic rather than merely evaluative; it generates knowledge of the human condition.

Burke focused more on fiction and poetry than on any other form of discourse; but he draws upon a wide variety of discourses in different media, including news reports, sermons, popular songs, etc. There is nothing in his theories which disqualify them for application today to all forms of mass media, including the electronic media. In fact, the major purpose of this article is to suggest one method of Burkean criticism which is a fruitful tool for analyzing mass media content. I shall also argue that the dramatic characteristics of the media make Burke's dramatistic method relevant for media criticism. To reflect this wider application, I shall substitute the term *discourse* for Burke's *literature*, and include in that term mass media content. That content is, of course, the equipment for living relied upon by millions today. That raises for the critic these epistemological and methodological questions: What aspect of media content should one look at, and how, if one wishes to discover ways in which that discourse equips people for living? What critical methods will allow the critic to take the pulse of a society, to link the discourse it uses with the situations it encounters?

THE METHOD

The generic term for Burke's methodology is *dramatism* (1945/1962a). The Burkean studies all symbolic action as if it were a play, even if the discourse under study displays no explicit narrative or fictional characteristics. All of Burke's more specific methods flow from, and are informed by, this root metaphor of the drama.

Burke picks drama as the central metaphor for his method because of his insistence that any method should represent rather than reduce its subject matter. To *represent* something is to sum up its essence; and the *dramatic* aspects of what people do and say are the *essence* of human action (Burke, 1950/1962b, pp. 13–15). One aspect of the drama is the *plot* or *story line* that it follows. Burke argues that to treat discourse as if it were the enactment of a plot represents (and thus, *reveals*) the essence of that discourse well (1941/1967, p. 103; 1937, p. 208). And therefore, one key Burkean method stemming from his dramatistic metaphor is his insight that the content or "terminology" of whole discourses or groups of discourses will imply, or will seem to be based upon, a *representative anecdote* (Burke, 1945/1962a, pp. 59–60, 323–325, 503–507). He means for us to take "anecdote" explicitly in the dramatic sense of a story, a tale. For instance, he argues that the discourse of the psychologists of his time was based upon anecdotes containing the central claims that "humans are chemicals" or "humans are white rats" (Burke, 1945/1962a, p. 59). Burke identifies the "making of the Constitution" explicitly as an anecdote underlying his *Grammar of Motives* (1945/1962a, pp. 323–401), and he analyzes his own discourse to show why that anecdote was better than others based upon war or train terminals. He explicitly bases the first part of his *Rhetoric of Motives* (1950/1962b, p. 17) on the anecdote of Samson among the Philistines. The anecdote is a macroscopic tool in the array of Burkean methods, in contrast to the pentadic, cluster agon, or other more word-specific approaches. And we shall see that this is a method that represents well what happens in the media because the *media* are anecdotal.

What *is* a representative anecdote; what does one look for? An anecdote is a dramatic form which underlies the content, or the specific vocabulary, of discourse.

Burke says (1945/1962a, p. 49) that "dramatism suggests a procedure to be followed in the development of a given calculus, or terminology. It involves the search for a 'representative anecdote,' to be used as a form in conformity with which the vocabulary is constructed." To identify an anecdote, one should ask, "If this discourse were based upon a story, an anecdote, what would the form, outline, or bare bones of that story be"?

The anecdote need not have been explicitly uttered in the discourse under analysis. Instead, the anecdote is a method used by the *critic*. The anecdote is a lens, filter, or template through which the critic studies and reconstructs the discourse. The critic *represents* the essence of discourse by viewing it as if it follows a dramatic plot. The psychologists Burke indicts for using the white rat anecdote did not explicitly say that people were white rats; but Burke reveals the essence of their claims by showing that their discourse implies that anecdote. The critic in search of an anecdote must therefore exercise his or her powers of abstraction to detect a form or pattern which is a plot, a story line, immanent within the content of the discourse and able to represent the discourse. To take an explicitly dramatic example so as to illustrate the point easily, the critic might boil down the play *Pygmalion* or the musical and film *My Fair Lady* to the essential anecdote underlying it: "A person of high economic and social status patronizes a younger person of lower status for motives that seem not entirely altruistic. The younger person is radically altered and encounters difficulties adjusting to his or her new status. A break between the two people occurs, and it is healed through the alteration of the older person as well," etc.

Because one is looking for an abstract dramatic form, one is looking for the same *story structure* to be told in different guises. The representative anecdote underlying *Pygmalion* and *My Fair Lady* underlies other discourse in other media: the play and television special *The Corn Is Green*, the television series *Diff'rent Strokes*, nonfictional documentaries on paternalism in our society, news coverage of an elder statesperson who took a younger politician into tutelage, etc. One does not look for *Pygmalion* per se, one looks for the anecdote upon which it is based. Thus, the representative anecdote is useful for studying widely used symbolic strategies in many different media, because it sifts out those discourses which offer the same formal symbolic equipment to an audience.

Sometimes the initial examination of explicitly dramatic discourse suggests the anecdote most clearly, but the critic need not start from fictional or dramatic discourse at all. Using the anecdote as a form, the critic then *displays* the discourse under examination according to the pattern of the form. Now, when a critic analyzes a thing or a discourse, the critic does not present the whole discourse but rather chooses certain aspects of it that can stand for the whole; and in doing so, one must be careful not to choose *un*representative aspects which will reduce the discourse. Burke argues that psychologists who approached humans as white rats reduced rather than represented humanity. But Burke must be careful, in finding that anecdote within the psychologists' discourse, not to become reductive in turn. This is the pitfall to be guarded against with the representative anecdote. A choice of anecdotes is representative rather than reductive if much of the discourse under analysis can be shown to embody it. If a critic is aware of the representative anecdote underlying *Pygmalion*, etc., then he or she can search across many media for messages of different sorts that can be arrayed according to the dramatic form of the anecdote.

Of course, many different representative anecdotes underlie discourses. For instance, one such anecdote is, "There is something that serves as a safe but confining haven for people. It is moving towards a goal in time or space. It is surrounded by hostile forces which attempt to invade or destroy it. The people in the haven must rely entirely on their inner resources within the haven or what comes to them by chance for survival." That anecdote underlies a number of recent discourses, including the television show *Battlestar Galactica*, the venerable *Robinson Crusoe* and *Swiss Family Robinson*, newscasts of bathysphere explorations and of spacecraft flight, documentaries about Asian and Haitian "boat people," westerns about covered wagon trains moving through Indian territory.

To identify a representative anecdote as immanent within a number of media discourses is to sum up the essence of a culture's values, concerns, and interests in regard to some real-life issues or problems. The anecdote is one component of discourse that equips for living because its dramatic form (1) allows people to express their hopes and fears in familiar (and thus manageable) patterns (Duncan, 1968, pp. 61, 64; Burke, 1941/1967, p. 109). If one fears that he or she will lose a job, seeing a television show about unemployment better equips one to live through that experience. Running throughout Burke's writings is the theme that *articulation* of a situation in discourse "vicariously" helps the audience to understand and act through their own similar situations, and that such articulation suggests helpful motives for the audience to embrace in confronting their trials (1935/1965, parts 1 and 2; 1945/1962a). The dramatic form of the anecdote also, (2) naturally "invites participation" in its rhythms (Burke, 1950/1962b, p. 58), thus enabling "the mind to follow processes amenable to it" (Burke, 1931/1968, p. 143). Burke defines form as "the creation of an appetite in the mind of the auditor, and the adequate satisfying of that appetite" (1931/1968, p. 31). By posing the problem of unemployment to the unemployed, for instance, discourse activates or addresses their "appetites" or concerns. When discourse satisfactorily shows a "solution" to unemployment, following one of several narrative forms accepted in a culture, the formal *completion* of the discourse is satisfying to the audience and thus provides them with the motives, hope, and symbolic resources to face their real situations. *Stories* do not merely pose problems, they suggest ways and means to resolve the problems insofar as they follow discursively a pattern that people might follow in reality.

The critic's task is then to *link* discourse embodying the formal anecdote to an audience's problems, to show how the anecdotal form equips a culture for living in that situation. The critic follows Burke's idea that recurrent *types* of anecdotes are "good for" types of situations. Sometimes that linkage can be done by showing *who* attends to discourses enacting a particular anecdote. If it were discovered that the young and poor tend to follow discourses embodying the *Pygmalion* anecdote, for instance, then the critic might speculate that such an anecdote, whenever it is reindividuated in discourse, is used as a symbolic remedy for poverty and social immobility. At other times, it may be discovered that discourse embodying an anecdote appears more often during some periods or in response to some exigencies than others. An examination of those periods, with special attention to complaints or celebrations common to both periods, may show how the anecdote is available for use by audiences facing such trials or triumphs. This essay provides an example of that second sort of analysis.

The representative anecdote is a critical tool especially well-suited to analysis of the media, first, because of their "anecdotal" nature. Television, newspapers, film, popular magazines, etc., mediate reality to people by recasting the chaotic, disjointed world into "story exposition forms" (National Institute of Mental Health, 1982, p. 23), presenting the world to audiences in the brief, one-half-hour to two-hour dramas of newscasts, articles, sitcoms, limited series, etc. "The parallels between television and story-telling are quite obvious" (Granzberg, 1982, p. 48), so that it is more real than metaphorical to refer to "media dramas" (Duncan, 1968, pp. 33–34; Nimmo and Combs, 1983). Because the audience *expects* the world to be mediated to them dramatically, and because the media do so by calling up standard, recurrent, culturally ingrained *types* of dramas, the anecdotal form of the media fits well with Burke's notion of form as the arousing and satisfying of expectations. We expect newscasts of Presidential election results to be cast into a "horse-race" plot, for instance. Because the media are anecdotal, because audiences expect dramatic structure in media content, critical analysis of the media ought to be sensitive to form and drama. That kind of sensitivity is precisely what is engendered by the method of the representative anecdote, which is trained awareness of types of dramatic form. Because the anecdote detects the same dramatic form within different discourses across several media, it alerts critics to the essential similarity in diverse media content. The anecdote can help us to see what is *anecdotal about* the media, and what ties together some diversity in media exposure.

A second reason why the representative anecdote is particularly appropriate for media analysis is that audiences use the dramatic or anecdotal nature of the media as equipment for living. Burke's argument, noted above, that people receive from discourse the symbolic resources to cope with life is thus similar to Gerbner's "cultivation effect" thesis (Gerbner, Gross, Morgan, & Signorielli, 1980). Basing their work on Gerbner's theory, Buerkel-Rothfuss and Mayes (1981, p. 108) found that "heavy systematic exposure to any systematically distorted view of the world will result in similarly distorted viewer perceptions." In their study of daytime television serials, or soap operas, the authors found that people who watch the serials tend to have problems similar to those of soap characters. They disclaim assertion of a causal relationship (p. 114); however, Burke's concept of discourse as equipment for living suggests that viewing the dramatic and formal expression and resolution of one's real problems is psychologically satisfying, even necessary, so that perhaps people with problems are drawn to the anecdotal treatment of them. Through the dramatic form embodied in a representative anecdote, as Herzog noted for soap opera audiences, "listeners are helped to accept their fate" (Herzog, 1965, p. 55). "Help" seems to be a function of media in general. For instance, the National Institute of Mental Health reports that "films and videotape have been used successfully to help people learn to cope with fears and phobias" (1982, p. 5), that "television leads its viewers to have television-influenced attitudes" (p. 7), and that "television does contribute to viewers' conceptions of social reality" (p. 62). The representative anecdote is a particularly *representative* tool for media analysis, then, because it resonates with the anecdotal, representative, dramatic form of the media, and because the content carried by that form is used by millions as equipment for living, a function to which the method of the anecdote is especially well attuned. The representative anecdote is therefore a method that taps what a culture *most* deeply fears and hopes, and how that culture confronts those concerns symbolically. The remainder of this essay illustrates the utility of Burke's anecdotal method in media criticism. First, I shall identify some economic and political concerns shared by the Fifties and late Seventies. Then, I shall identify a representative anecdote that has been embodied in different types of discourse and media, an anecdote that I shall call *xeroxing*. Since the anecdote emerged during periods that shared similar fears and concerns, the Fifties and late Seventies, I shall argue that discourse embodying the xeroxing anecdote served as equipment for living.

THE SITUATION

Let me begin by showing the kind of situation in which discourse embodying the xeroxing anecdote helps people to live. A complex of concerns occurred nationally in both the Fifties and in the late Seventies. To make historical judgments about a period as near to us as the late Seventies is perilous unless it can be anchored in the analogous, and better-understood Fifties. So let us briefly examine some historians' conclusions about the Fifties and its exigencies, and let us consider how such exigencies mirror those of the late Seventies.

The Fifties were a time of change and transition "more swift and sweeping than any previous generation of Americans had known" (Goldman, 1965, p. 119). The post-war world was "a strange and unruly world" (Goldman, 1965, p. 249). Changes and fears arose in many areas: "The pressures and crises of the cold war continued undiminished. Inflation and recession posed threats to prosperity. Racial, religious, and ideological tensions added their disruptions to the normal problems of a mobile society" (Link and Catton, 1974, p. 160). The same might be said for the Seventies; let us examine technological, economic, and political instability.

Both the Fifties and late Seventies saw vast technological changes, including automation in the Fifties and, in the late Seventies, the new wave of genetic engineering and computer technology. These changes in each case presaged a new era of technology that would be unfamiliar to the average worker (Degler, 1968, p. 173). The worker in the Fifties was threatened by an "expanding revolution in technology" (Link and Catton, 1974, p. 19), as was the worker of the late Seventies. The Fifties saw the introduction of "an increasingly automated and sophisticated economic system" (Link and Catton, 1974, p. 54), as did the late Seventies at the start of the ongoing genetic and silicon chip revolution (Link and Catton, 1974, pp. 20, 54). Technological change found many workers in both periods unprepared, for "it took a heavy toll of unskilled laborers, farmhands and inexperienced young manual workers" (Leuchtenberg, 1973, p. 719). Personal inadequacy took the form of fear that one would be *replaced* by technology: "The word 'automation' struck fear in the heart of the American working man. 'The worker's greatest worry,' explained a writer, 'is that he will be cast upon the slag heap by a robot'" (Leuchtenberg, 1973, p. 719). Such fears are likely to arise in eras when technological change forces dislocation in the economy, as did the flood of inexpensive computers in the late Seventies. The Fifties and late Seventies also saw a collective anxiety about the quality of American technology in relation to the rest of the world. While the Fifties experienced the embarrassment of Sputnik (Goldman, 1965, pp. 308–310), the late Seventies experienced the embarrassment of Japanese and European advances in technology such as automotive engineering, and a fear that despite rapid change, our industry would become obsolete. Therefore, fear of foreign superiority joined with suspicion of technology. Whittaker Chambers, for instance, proclaimed "the scientific method" as the very source of Communism (Wittner, 1974, p. 123).

Economically, the Fifties was a time of instability (Goldman, 1965, p. 265), as were the late Seventies. The Fifties saw relatively high inflation (Goldman, 1965, p. 200), as did the late Seventies. The economic influence upon the social structure changed in both periods, for new respect for business shifted personal allegiance to one's corporate affiliations (Goldman, 1965, p. 264). In both the Fifties and the Seventies, one consequence of the "incorporation" of America was the growth in power and prestige of a "business elite" allied with government (Wittner, 1974, p. 114), "a distant corporate bureaucracy" (p. 132) manipulating business beyond the control or knowledge of the average worker. Herbert Lehman wrote of the Fifties, and could have said of the late Seventies, that "the big business firms not only dominate our economy to an increasing extent; they are, in fact, beginning seriously to affect our culture, our education, and the intellectual climate of our times" (Lehman, 1969, p. 74).

The growth of big business in both eras led to a fear that the nation was becoming too careful and too conformist. The bland, careerist and consumerist orientation felt on so many campuses in the late Seventies mirrored the "near-unanimity" of concern in the Fifties that society was breeding a generation of "careful young men" (Leuchtenberg, 1973, p. 747). Henry Steele Commager declared "the new loyalty" in the Fifties to be, "above all, conformity" (Wittner, 1974, p. 122). "The typical American, social analysts complained, had become both conformist and bland" (Leuchtenberg, 1973, p. 744). "Whether the individual survives as a self-reliant, self-providing person or becomes a regimented automaton of the state" (Shanks, 1969, p. 28) was a Fifties concern echoed in such late Seventies discourse as Ronald Reagan's campaign rhetoric; we find repeatedly a fear that the individual would become "a calculating automaton cut off from the social context" (Hecksher, 1969, p. 35).

The political atmosphere of both the Fifties and late Seventies presented similar problems. Both periods followed controversial wars with Communist opponents. The Fifties saw the intensification of the cold war while the late Seventies saw the collapse of detente. The Fifties saw (and the late Seventies presaged) the election of conservative Republican Presidents, and a perceived swing of the political mood to the right (Goldman, 1965, pp. 212–213). Underlying these events was a deep sense that the nation was losing control over events at home and abroad: "America found that it could not control the world it had won fair and square. Things would've been different if it hadn't been for the Communists" (Lester, 1969, p. 20). In the Fifties, "irritation rasped through American life" (Goldman, 1965, p. 201) and "gloom was pervasive" (Link and Catton, 1974, p. 56). This sense of frustration and irritation released "a chronic American tendency to suspect that their way of life is being subverted by an internal conspiracy of evildoers" (Link and Catton, 1974, pp. 19, 56). The enemy was an alleged international Communist conspiracy that "was so powerful and so pervasive that its agents might strike anywhere, from within the country as well as from without" (Degler, 1968, p. 36). This "popular fear ... that the nation, and particularly the federal government, swarmed with communist espionage agents" (Wittner, 1974, p. 87) amounted to a "political stampede" (p. 97). At times concern for lurking conspiracies reached the level of "hysteria" (Christie and Dinnerstein, 1976, p. 5). One never knew in the Fifties when one's neighbor may have fallen victim to that conspiracy, for "it was enough for a man to be considered a Communist because he would not say he wasn't" (Lester, 1969, p. 21). Although the Fifties were more explicitly paranoid than the late Seventies in terms of the Communist threat, the latter era nonetheless had its share of conspiracy fears, with the belief that monolithic Communism was on the march again, orchestrating terrorism at home and abroad, violating the SALT treaty, contributing to the downfall of Iran.

I have reviewed a number of fears and hopes that concerned the nation in the Fifties and late Seventies. I shall now show that some of the media content of these two periods also shows similarities. Specifically, the discourses I shall examine follow the same dramatic *form* insofar as they all seem to be following the same representative anecdote, which I shall call *xeroxing*. And these discourses engage, literally and metaphorically, those shared concerns of the Fifties and late Seventies. The discourses express the concerns and develop them dramatically through the representative anecdote. Therefore, the media contained equipment for living through technological, economic, and political change. I am not arguing that those real-life concerns never occurred at any other period, nor am I claiming that media content never followed the xeroxing anecdote in, let us say, the Sixties. Rather, I am arguing that these problems and this form of discourse occurred together, in those two eras, rather more often and more intensely than in other periods, and that therefore the discourse was available as a symbolic remedy for the problems had a troubled audience chosen to attend to it.

THE ANECDOTE

The representative anecdote analyzed in this essay could be summed up like this: Xeroxing is the duplication and replacement of humans with evil, inhuman copies that are difficult to detect. The act of duplication occurs in a scene of rapid change and decay. This act of duplication is carried out through technological conspiracies. The replacements themselves are marked by a poverty and uniformity of purpose, the sign of a loss of humanity.[1]

A number of discourses in different media which appeared in the Fifties and again in the late Seventies followed the form of xeroxing. Two films and a book serve as paradigm cases of that anecdote. Jack Finney's (1955/1978) book, *Invasion of the Body Snatchers*, was produced as a film in 1956 (Wanger, 1956) and remade in 1978 (Solo, 1978). A shower of spores from outer space falls on the earth (landing near a small town in Finney's book and in the 1956 film, or near San Francisco in the 1978 film). These spores produce flowering pods which, when placed near sleeping people, take on the form of those people; in the process of reproducing them, the pods destroy the original. The pods are distributed by a conspiracy of technocratic pod people in a scene of social and physical change and decay. A small group resists this threat (Doctor Miles Benell in Finney and in the 1956 film, Health Inspector Matthew Benell in the 1978 film; Becky Driscoll in Finney and in the 1956 film, Elizabeth in the 1978 film; and the Belicecs, Jack and Theodora, in all versions). Pods are produced *en masse*, and although the replacements look like the individual, differentiated originals, they have absolutely uniform emotions, drives, and motives.

Although the *Body Snatchers* films and book embody the xeroxing anecdote clearly, the anecdote informs much discourse about *automation* that appeared in the Fifties especially, but also in the late Seventies in response to computer technology. The anecdote underlies much late Seventies discourse about *cloning*. Cloning mass-produces uniform duplicates of living things, and some fear that it might duplicate humans. Cloning is but a part of the genetic engineering revolution that developed in the late Seventies. The structure of my analysis will follow the structure of the xeroxing anecdote as given at the start of this section. In reviewing each component of the dramatic form, I shall show how it corresponds to the situational concerns given in the previous section.

A Changing, Decaying Scene

As noted in the previous section, the social and political context of the Fifties and late Seventies was one of change and instability. Contexts put into anecdotal form become scenes, stage-settings. We find this fear of a strange world changing beyond one's control articulated in discourse grounded in the xeroxing anecdote. In xeroxing, as in the reality of both eras, change and strangeness seem universal and growing. In Finney, Earth's moon and Mars for instance, were thriving planets that were zapped by pod invasions (1955/1978, pp. 184–185). In the 1956 film, Miles and Becky witness the distribution of pods to representatives from surrounding communities. Miles pounds on the passing cars in an attempt to warn them of the danger and shouts, "It's here already. You're next." In the 1978 film, the pod threat has become global. Matthew sees pods being loaded onto oceangoing freighters, bound for distant ports.

The late Seventies and the Fifties fear of rapid change is also reflected in xeroxing. The 1956 film covers three days and three nights, and in that time the entire town goes under. The 1978 film shows just as rapid a change. "It was like the whole city had changed overnight," says Elizabeth on the morning of the second day. In nonfiction discourse about automation, one finds uncontrolled technological change articulated as a fear: "As a button-pusher on an automated machine, a man now stands outside his work and whatever control existed is finally shattered" (Karsh, 1957, p. 209). The bewildering scene of automation was "a society of such complexity that an individual with the best of motives may be powerless either to grasp or to deal with the many facets of a specific situation" (Carr, 1956, p. 667). Toffler (1970, p. 197) describes the scene of clone xeroxing as one of rapid change: "Advances in genetics have come tripping over one another at a rapid pace," so that soon "man will be able to make biological carbon copies of himself."

With a fear of change comes a sense that change means decay. Finney's city (1955/1978, p. 88) abounds with broken glass and "For Rent" signs, and prior to the pod invasion Miles remarks that "the town's dying" (p. 123). In the 1956 film, creeping decay accompanies the pod invasion; Miles notices that farmer Grimaldi's vegetable stand is littered and closed, and we discover that Grimaldi has become a pod. Scenic decay reaches its peak in the 1978 film. Matthew Benell plies his trade among the garbage cans of the city and delights in the discovery of "rat turds" masquerading as capers in restaurants. Elizabeth notes after some research in the 1978 film that the tiny pod-flowers seem to "thrive on devastated ground."

The average worker of the Fifties and Seventies, faced with overwhelming change, felt unskilled and weak in the face of newness. And so we find xeroxing discourse articulating that fear. Nonfiction discourse of the Fifties stressed the superiority of robots over the ordinary "American worker [who] is pitifully *undereducated* and *under-skilled*" (Gerbracht and Scholfield, 1957, p. 113). Automation especially threatened a "decline in unskilled jobs" (Wolfert, 1955, p. 45; Bronowski, 1958, p. 250). Writing on the issue of automation and robots, Rorvik refers to Arthur Clarke's belief that "man will ultimately be superseded by humanlike computer entities. . . . The computer being will go on to construct even greater intelligences" (1970, p. 155).[2] Human weakness and unpreparedness can pave the way for undesirable change; that concern is reflected in the *Body Snatchers* as the need to stay awake, for one becomes a pod when one sleeps. "He's got to go to sleep some time" say the pod people as they hunt for Matthew in the 1978 film. In the 1956 film, Jack Belicec warns, after he has turned into a pod, "Sooner or later you'll have to go to sleep." Miles recognizes the danger: "We can't close our eyes all night." But Becky is weak and cannot resist sleeping as she and Miles try to escape. This weakness is fatal: "A moment's sleep and the girl I loved was an inhuman enemy bent on my destruction. That moment of sleep was death to Becky's soul." Because audiences are accustomed to seeing the world mediated to them, these literal and literary media depictions of a *strange* world would conform to their private anxieties.

The Enemies

The troubled Fifties and Seventies attributed their strange world, as we have seen, to the conspiratorial machination of Communists, big business elites, and government bureaucrats. Xeroxing expresses that fear of The Enemy. And because story-telling depends upon antagonists and protagonists, because the media do well at unidimensional caricature instead of complex characterization, we find The Enemy given as monsters embodying both eras' concerns. The word "strange" or "strangers" is often used to describe these conspirators. In the 1956 film, Miles Benell perceived that "there must be strangers in town" on the morning that pods were trucked in for secret distribution. In the 1978 film, "strange people" is a recurring remark made by the protagonists: "Geoffrey was meeting all sorts of strange people." Agents who perpetrate automation and cloning are also perceived as alien. A 1954 story, "The Father Thing," by Philip K. Dick, depicts an automated robot "bug" that duplicates a little boy's father, and the father now seeks to xerox the child. This creature's eyes contain "something alien and cold" (Dick, 1959, p. 246).

Much of the strangeness of the villainous enemies stems from their overwhelming power. Miles Benell in the 1956 film notes that the pods are "fantastically powerful, beyond any comprehension." The title of Aute Carr's article (1956, p. 667) asks, "Automation–Substitute for God?" and foresees "the danger that this new, wonder-working technology will become the 20th century substitute for God." More recently, cloning "smacks of scientists playing God" (Randall, 1978, p. 12). The cloned replacements might even become deathless: "A person's own awareness of the world might somehow survive the death of the body—in the locus of cloned consciousness" (Rorvik, 1978, p. 21).

A fear of powerful strangers spreading change in the world is expressed dramatically as the presence of conspiracies. Xeroxing thus gives shape to the Fifties and late Seventies fear of secretive, organized forces at work. Elizabeth says in the 1978 film, "I keep seeing these people recognize each other. Something is passing between them. It's a conspiracy, I know it." Matthew's inability to persuade the police of the pod danger does not surprise Jack, who says, "Of course, it's a conspiracy." In the 1956 film, Dr. Benell suspects that "somebody or someone wants this duplication to take place." As Miles and Becky try to escape through the haunted streets of Mill Valley, Miles "wondered if phones were being lifted in the houses we passed and if the air wasn't filled with messages about us" (Finney, 1955/1978, p. 41).

Xeroxing expresses the paranoid fear that conspiracies are both pervasive *and* invisible. In the 1956 film, when Miles returns to Mill Valley, "at first glance, everything looked the same. But it wasn't. Something evil had taken possession of the town." In Finney, "Something impossibly terrible, yet utterly real was menacing us in a way beyond our comprehension or abilities" (Finney, 1955/1978, pp. 112–113). Xeroxing in other kinds of discourse also contains conspiracies that insinuate themselves quietly into the scene. Rorvik (1970, p. 83) speculates that "when the [robot] 'takeover' comes it is likely to be a bloodless one; possibly it won't even register as a takeover in the consciousness of man. It could be argued, even, that the takeover has already taken place."

The technocrats of the Fifties and late Seventies become characters in the xeroxing anecdote. In Finney (1955/1978, p. 74) Miles's friend Mannie Kaufman, having become a pod, tries to explain strange occurrences by appealing to Benell's scientific training: "Hell, you're a doctor, Miles; you know something about how this sort of thing works."

In the 1956 film, the conspirator Kaufman appeals to Miles as a technologist: "Miles, you and I are scientific men, you can understand the wonder of what's happened." In the 1978 film, the conspirators corner the protagonists in Benell's office, amid a vast array of scientific apparati. Articles by technocrats in the Fifties reflected a sinister optimism in automation as "dynamic and forward looking" (Sotzin, 1956, p. 151). Workers could not possibly have been cheered by the technocrats' hope that automation's "promise of future usefulness is vast" (Wolfert, 1955, p. 43).

Conspirators in xeroxing are so powerful that they control government and business, reflecting the Fifties and late Seventies concern with those two sectors. In the 1978 film, Matthew Benell's attempt to notify the federal authorities is hopeless. As Jack Belicec says, "The FBI? The CIA? They're pods already"! In recent xeroxing an MIT professor said, "It wouldn't surprise me at all if the government had some crazy cloning scheme going on" (Johnson, 1978, p. 100). Observers of automation feared that it would lead to "a totalitarian form of government" (Bronowski, 1958, p. 250; Shull, 1959, pp. 339–340). In a 1954 story, "The Tunnel Under the World," by Frederik Pohl (1975), businessmen control an entire town that was destroyed and then copied in miniature for the purpose of advertising research. These conspirators control every experience the "townspeople" robots have. In Finney, pod people control that symbol of corporate power, the telephone company. Jack Belicec cries in despair, "They've got the phones" when an operator feigns inability to connect him with the FBI (Finney, 1955/1978, p. 111). In the 1978 film, the operator knows Matthew Benell's name even though he has not given it to her, prompting strong suspicion that the pods have hold of AT&T. Thus, xeroxing confirms and sanctions the workers' fears that their employers are evil strangers up to no good.

Dehumanization and Uniformity

The key action of xeroxing is duplication of people. That element of the anecdote articulates the real-life fear of "replacement of human beings by machines" (Harrington, 1955, p. 177): "These new brains are going to replace workers—a lot of workers" (Bendiner, 1955, p. 15). A worker might arrive on the job to find a clanking, steaming, whirring copy of him or herself performing a job with more efficiency. In Robert Heinlein's "Waldo" (1959), for instance, the inventor Waldo's hands have been copied: "Everywhere were pairs of Waldoes, large, small, and life-sized" (p. 188).

Duplication is repugnant. In Niven's *A World Out of Time* (1976), an omniscient computer-robot offers to clone the hero to extend his life: "We can clone men. We can clone you." But the protagonist replies, "You're talking about grinding me up into chemically leeched hamburger" (p. 49). Why should it be so terrible to be replaced?

The danger of duplication articulates the real-life fear of uniformity, blandness, corporate amalgamation, and sterility, fears that haunted the Fifties and late Seventies. Those fears are expressed in xeroxing where uniformity of *appearance* signals uniformity of substance. For instance, although most experts agree that physically identical clones would be emotionally different ("The Road to Cloning," 1978, p. 26; Johnson, 1970, p. 102), laymen often assume that physical sameness indicates emotional and intellectual uniformity as well (Bylinsky, 1978, p. 108).

In the *Body Snatchers*, when the pods mature, their emotions and purposes are uniform. Sameness of feeling was forecast by physical sameness in the pods' early development. Details make people individuals, and the fetal pods have none. In the 1978 film, Jack Belicec finds that the new pod meant for him has "no detail, no character, it's unformed." In the 1956 film, Dr. Benell noted that, physically, Jack's pod "has all the features but no character, no details, no lines." Finney (1955/1978, p. 37) echoes the same theme: "No lines, no *details*, no character."

The physical sameness of xeroxing is evident in automation if one remembers that robots or machines, being mass-produced, look very much alike. Rod Serling's "Mighty Casey" features a robot of the same name with "a face that looked as if it had been painted on. Even the voice. Dead. Spiritless" (1960, p. 7). His story "The Lonely" features an isolated criminal who is given a robot companion "made in his image" (Serling, 1960, p. 167). But the robot gives no physical sign of purpose and life: "There was no expression in the eyes. There was a deadness, a lack of vitality" (pp. 155–156).[3]

Once a person becomes a pod, all individuating purpose, all emotional difference and character is gone. This development is the articulation of what people feared would happen to them in factories and offices. In the 1956 *Body Snatchers* film, Wilma Lenz fears that her Uncle Ira, who has become a pod, has lost all feeling: "There's no emotion." Dan Kaufman, having turned into a pod, says that "There's no need for love," and Miles Benell responds, "No emotion. Then you have no feelings." Finney (1955/1978, p. 184) also shows no individuating purpose in the pod agents: "There's no real joy, fear, hope or excitement in you, not any more. You live in the same kind of grayness as the filthy stuff that formed you."

Xeroxed replacements in other discourses also have no individuating emotions and thus share an internal sameness of purpose. Technocrats seek a uniform "mechanization without purpose" (Kelley, 1957, p. 558). The only value allowed replacements is "dynamic conformity" with no originality or independence (Kelley, 1957, p. 560). Dick's "The Father-Thing" (1959, p. 252) depicts a father who has been duplicated by a robot alien. He/it is "humorless and utterly without emotion." Neurosurgeon Robert White, discussing cybernetic amalgamations of humans and robots, foresees "the stage where you can turn men into robots, obedient sheep," without purposes of their own (Toffler, 1970, p. 214). Loss of individual purpose proves the replacements, in xeroxing as in the fears of the Fifties and late Seventies, are not human. Kael (1978, p. 48) sees a major theme of the *Body Snatchers* as "trying to hang on to your human individuality while those around you are contentedly turning into vegetables." Becoming uniform means losing one's humanity. "We may wake up changed to something evil and inhuman," says Becky in the 1956 film. In the 1978 film, Elizabeth's friend Geoffrey "has become less human" as a result of turning into a pod. Some commentators in the Fifties complained that "the human being and his efforts are almost entirely by-passed" by those who "rush to embrace every new non-human force" (Memoli, 1955, p. 23; Karsh, 1959, p. 383). The new, inhuman technocrat of the Fifties was described as "the Martian prototype, the new race, all brain" (Mannes, 1957, p. 39). Being xeroxed through cloning also leads to a loss of humanity. Rorvik (1970, pp. 55–56) hypothesizes that "a cloned individual might suffer a serious identity crisis, finding it difficult to distinguish himself from his donor." This enforced sameness threatens the humanity of the clone: "When you start manipulating genes at the level of cloning, you are changing our whole concept of what it is to be human" (Dobbie, 1978, p. 69). Jeremy Rifkin argues "that human cloning is an antisocial, inhuman, criminal technology. It's the assembly-line production of carbon copies of humans, and our whole value system about the uniqueness of life is based on the essential difference between individuals" (Johnson, 1978, p. 98).

We have seen xeroxing discourses *articulate* the fears and hopes of the Fifties and late Seventies, and we saw that articulation in and of itself equips people for living.

The formal rhythm which completes the cycle of xeroxing is important, too, for it provides audiences with closure of one sort or another. The book and 1956 film versions of the *Body Snatchers* end happily: The FBI is called in, with promise of salvation. Dick (1959) also ends happily, with escape from "the father thing." Such is not the case for the 1978 *Body Snatchers* film, which gives strong indications that the pod invasion is irresistible. And the townspeople in Pohl's 1954 "The Tunnel Under the World" (1975) are doomed to never-ending slavery under their industrialist captors. In each case, although the stories end differently, an answer is given to the question of "What will happen to me at the factory, office, etc.?" Thus symbolically prepared, audiences are armed to accept, reject, or attempt to change the real course of events depicted in the media.

CONCLUSION

A time of rapid and uncontrolled change, fear of conspirators at home and abroad, new technological developments and their corresponding social and economic changes: these are the exigencies which formed the context for some distinctive discourses in several media in the Fifties and late Seventies. Xeroxing reveals the essence of that media content as symbolic medicine which equips people for living when they face those difficulties. The anecdote is individualized in fiction and nonfiction, in print and electronic media, and in both serious and entertaining discourse. Knowing this, critics may be on the lookout for discourses in the future which embody xeroxing. The anecdote that some discourse embodies may explain why the discourse appears and how or whether it appeals to its audiences.

The task remains for critics to catalogue other representative anecdotes and to link them with the situations that they equip people to confront. Xeroxing only illustrates the central goal of this essay: to show how Burke's anecdotal method allows the critic to study mass media content as equipment for living. Other fears and hopes confront society, and people turn to mass media for the symbolic means to encompass those situations. The media are equipment for living because they recast this world, its hopes and fears, into anecdotal form, and thus an anecdotal method can help reveal that form. Burke would remind us that media content tells a story, and that critical methods which look for stories are thus appropriate tools for media analysis. To reveal the formal stories being told, and the real or symbolic ills they cure, gives media criticism the ability to move from social commentary to social knowledge.

Notes

1. Although this anecdote bears some resemblance to the "Frankenstein" or "Doppelganger" myths, its uniqueness as a whole lies in the combination of its elements, especially the *mass* production of copies, the element of *conspiracy*, and the loss of *purpose* in copies.

2. Although Rorvik (1970) was originally printed before the late Seventies, the popularity of Rorvik (1978) caused the earlier work to be marketed again at the end of the decade. The same was true of Toffler (1970).

3. Serling's book is, of course, based on original *television* shows, broadcast during the Fifties.

References

Bendiner, R. (1955, April 7). The age of the thinking robot, and what it will mean to us." *Reporter*, pp. 12–18.

Bronowski, J. (1958, March 22). Planning for the year 2,000. *Nation*, pp. 248–251.

Buerkel-Rothfuss, N. L., & S. Mayes. (1981). Soap opera viewing: The cultivation effect. *Journal of Communication 31*: 108–115.

Burke, K. (1937). *Attitudes toward history*. New York: New Republic.

Burke, K. (1962a). *A grammar of motives*. Berkeley and Los Angeles: University of California Press. (Original work published 1945)

Burke, K. (1962b). *A rhetoric of motives*. Berkeley and Los Angeles: University of California Press. (Original work published 1950)

Burke, K. (1965). *Permanence and change*. Rev. ed. Berkeley and Los Angeles: University of California Press. (Original work published 1935)

Burke, K. (1966). *Language as symbolic action*. Berkeley and Los Angeles: University of California Press.

Burke, K. (1967). *Philosophy of literary form*. Rev. ed. Berkeley and Los Angeles: University of California Press. (Original work published 1941)

Burke, K. (1968). *Counter-statement*. Rev. ed. Berkeley and Los Angeles: University of California Press. (Original work published 1931)

Bylinsky, G. (1978, June 19). "The cloning era is almost here" *Fortune*, pp. 100–104, 108–110.

Carr, A. L. (1956, May 30). Automation substitute for God? *Christian Century*, pp. 666–667.

Christie, L., & L. Dinnerstein (Eds.) (1976). *America since World War II*. New York: Praeger.

Degler, C. N. (1968). *Affluence and anxiety*. Glenview, IL: Scott, Foresman.

Dick, P. K. (1959). The father thing. In A. Boucher (Ed.), *A treasury of great science fiction* (vol. 1, pp. 245–254). Garden City, NY: Doubleday.

Dobbie, J. (1978, April 3). Cloning: Has man's reach exceeded his grasp? *Maclean's*, pp. 68–69.

Duncan, H. D. (1968). *Symbols in society*. New York: Oxford University Press.

Finney, J. (1978). *Invasion of the body snatchers*. New York: Dell. (Original work published 1955)

Gerbner, G., L. Gross, M. Morgan, & N. Signorielli. (1980). The "mainstreaming" of america: violence profile no. 11. *Journal of Communication 30*: 10–29.

Gerbracht, C., & F. Scholfield (1957, April). . . . And the problems of life related to these changes. . . *Industrial Arts and Vocational Education*, pp. 113–114.

Goldman, E. F. (1965). *The crucial decade–and after*. New York: Knopf.

Granzberg, G. (1982). Television as a storyteller: The Algonkian Indians of Central Canada. *Journal of Communication 32*: 43–52.

Harrington, M. (1955, May 20). The advance of automation. *Commonweal*, pp. 175–178.

Hecksher, A. (1969). Liberalism, conservatism, and freedom. In D. G. Baker & C. H. Sheldon (Eds.), *Postwar America: The search for identity* (pp. 34–35). Beverly Hills, CA: Glencoe Press.

Heinlein, R. (1959). Waldo. In A. Boucher (Ed.), *A treasury of great science fiction* (vol. 1, pp. 170–244). Garden City, NY: Doubleday.

Herzog, H. (1965). Motivations and gratifications of daily serial listeners. In W. Schramm (Ed.), *The process and effects of mass communication* (pp. 50–55). Urbana: University of Illinois.

Johnson, J. (1970). *As man becomes machine*. New York: Pocket Books.

Kael, P. (1978, December 25). The current cinema: Pods. *New Yorker*, pp. 48–51.

Karsh, B. (1957, October 5). Automation's brave new world. *Nation*, pp. 208–210.

Karsh, B. (1959). Work and automation. In H. Jacobson & J. Roucek (Eds.), *Automation and society*. New York: Philosophical Library.

Kelley, J. B. (1957, February 16). Man and automation. *America*, pp. 558–560.

Lehman, H. H. (1969). Big business and the plight of the individual. In D. G. Baker & C. H. Sheldon (Eds.), *Postwar America: The search for identity* (pp. 73–74). Beverly Hills, CA: Glencoe Press.

Lester, J. (1969). *Search for the new land*. New York: Dial Press.

Leuchtenberg, W. E. (1973). *The unfinished century*. Boston: Little, Brown & Co.

Link, A. S., & W. B. Catton (1974). *American epoch*. 4th ed. New York: Knopf.

Mannes, M. (1957, July 11). Channels: Lonely men and busy machines. *Reporter*, pp. 39–41.

Memoli, F. (1955, February 12). Ignorant of values. *Saturday Review*, p. 23.

National Institute of Mental Health. (1982). *Television and behavior: Ten years of scientific progress and implications for the eighties*, Vol. 1. Rockville, MD: U.S. Department of Health.

Nimmo, D., & J. E. Combs. (1983). *Mediated political realities*. New York: Longman.

Niven, L. (1976). *A world out of time*. New York: Ballantine.

Pohl, F. (1975). *The best of Frederik Pohl*. Garden City, NY: Doubleday.

Randall, J. (1978, May). The cloning controversy. *Progressive*, pp. 11–12.

Randall, J. (1978, October). The road to cloning. *Chemistry*, pp. 25–27.

Rorvik, D. (1970). *As man becomes machine*. New York: Pocket Books.

Rorvik, D. (1978). *In his image: The cloning of a man*. New York: Pocket Books.

Serling, R. (1960). *From the Twilight Zone*. Garden City, NY: Doubleday.

Shanks, C. M. (1969). Common man in an uncommon decade. In D. G. Baker & C. H. Sheldon (Eds.), *Postwar America: The search for identity* (pp. 28–29). Beverly Hills, CA: Glencoe Press.

Shull, C. W. (1959). Political aspects of automation. In H. Jacobson & J. Roucek (Eds.), *Automation and society*. New York: Philosophical Library.

Solo, R. [Producer]. (1978). *Invasion of the body snatchers*. [Film]. Culver, CA: United Artists.

Sotzin, H. A. (1956, May). Automation—A blessing or a menace? *Industrial Arts and Vocational Education*, pp. 149–151.

Toffler, A. (1970). *Future shock*. New York: Random House.

Wanger, W. [Producer]. (1956). *Invasion of the body snatchers*. [Film]. New York: Allied Artists.

Wittner, L. S. (1974). *Cold war America: From Hiroshima to Watergate*. New York: Praeger.

Wolfert, I. (1955, May). What's behind this word "automation"? *Reader's Digest*, pp. 43–48.

The Rhetorical Limits
of Polysemy

CELESTE MICHELLE CONDIT

The recent, energetic critical program focused on the receivers of mass communication emphasizes the autonomy and power of audiences to exert substantial control of the mass communication process, and hence to exercise social influence. The polysemic character of texts, these studies argue, allows receivers to construct a wide variety of decodings and thereby prevents simple domination of people by the messages they receive (Fiske, 1986; Hall, 1980; Morley, 1980; Radway, 1986).

These theoretical claims are supported by substantial evidence demonstrating the active character of audience viewing. The theoretical conclusions, however, overstate the evidence because they oversimplify the pleasures experienced by audience members. As many of the preeminent scholars in critical audience studies themselves admit, audiences are not free to make meanings at will from mass-mediated texts (Fiske, 1987c, pp. 16, 20, 44). Consequently, the pleasures audiences experience in receiving texts are necessarily complicated. In this essay I employ a multidimensional rhetorical critique of a single television text to suggest that the ability of audiences to shape their own readings, and hence their social life, is constrained by a variety of factors in any given rhetorical situation. These factors include audience members' access to oppositional codes, the ratio between the work required and pleasure produced in decoding a text, the repertoire of available texts, and the historical occasion, especially with regard to the texts' positioning of the pleasures of dominant and marginal audiences. I conclude that mass media research should replace totalized theories of polysemy and audience power with interactive theories that assess audience reactions as part of the full communication process occurring in particular rhetorical configurations.

CRITICAL STUDIES OF THE AUDIENCE

Audience-centered critical research argues that viewers and readers construct their own meanings from texts. Audiences do not simply receive messages; they decode texts.

Members of mass audiences are therefore not mere "cultural dupes" of message producers. As John Fiske (1987c, p. 65) describes the process, viewers have the "ability to make their own socially pertinent meanings out of the semiotic resources provided by television." As a consequence, "viewers have considerable control, not only over its meanings, but over the role that it plays in their lives" (p. 74). Janice Radway (1984, p. 17) makes a similar argument about mass-produced fiction: "Because reading is an active process that is at least partially controlled by the readers themselves, opportunities exist within the mass-communication process for individuals to resist, alter, and reappropriate the materials designed elsewhere for their purchase."

Critical audience analysts position their work as a radical break with the history of critical media studies, which they depict as having emphasized the power of the media to impose a dominant ideology or to control beliefs and behaviors (Fiske, 1986; Morley, 1980; Radway, 1986). The new studies indicate that disparate audiences do not decode messages in uniform ways (Katz and Liebes, 1984; Morley, 1980; Palmer, 1986), in the precise directions critics have suggested they might (Radway, 1984), or even as the messages' authors seemed to have intended (Hobson, 1982; Steiner, 1988).[1] These studies conclude that texts which link producers' intended messages and actual audiences are not univocal. Reworking structuralist insights, they emphasize that all texts are polysemic (Fiske, 1986; Newcomb, 1984), that is, capable of bearing multiple meanings because of the varying intertextual relationships they carry (esp. Bennett and Woollacott, 1987) and because of the varying constructions (or interests) of receivers.

The study of the polysemic character of texts has thus included two research schools, often not clearly distinguished. Works in the American school (Kellner, 1982; Newcomb, 1984) emphasize the variety of ideological positions contained within the mass media. In contrast, the British approach highlights the variety of decodings possible from a single text or message (e.g., Burke, Wilson, and Agardy, 1983; Morley, 1980).

Whether based in the variety of available texts or in the flexibility of decoding processes, polysemy has been taken to be a widespread or even dominant phenomenon, bearing significance for theories of social change. Rather than portraying the mass media as the channel of oppression generated through the top-down imposition of meanings, such a perspective allows for the suggestion that the pleasures of the popular media might in fact be liberating. Radway (1984, p. 184), for instance, claims that because of the pleasure women derive from romance reading, "they at least partially reclaim the patriarchal form of the romance for their own use." Fiske (1987c, p. 239) finds similar pleasures and effects are operative in television: "The pleasure and the power of making meanings, of participating in the mode of representation, of playing with the semiotic process—these are some of the most significant and empowering pleasures that television has to offer." Fiske argues that, even without the active step of circulating one's own representations, these pleasures may offer a real resistance to the dominant ideology. Escape, he indicates (p. 318) may itself be liberating, because to escape from dominant meanings is to construct one's own subjectivity, one that is an important step in more collective moves toward social change. Fiske (p. 230) concludes:

> While there is clearly a pleasure in exerting social power, the popular pleasures of the subordinate are necessarily found in resisting, evading, or offending this power. Popular pleasures are those that empower the subordinate, and they thus offer political resistance, even if only momentarily and even if only in a limited terrain.

Recent critical audience studies thus repudiate prior portrayals of television as a sinister social force in favor of a celebration of the ability of audiences, enabled by the broad referential potentiality of texts, to reconstruct television messages. Television, because it is popular, therefore becomes a force for popular resistance to dominant interests.

These audience studies and the theories they are generating offer a useful counter-balance to the flat assertion that messages produced by elites necessarily dominate social meaning-making processes. Nonetheless, the scope and character of audience power have not yet been delimited, and I believe they are as yet over-stated.[2] It is clear that there are substantial limits to the polysemic potential of texts and of decodings. If television offered a true "semiotic democracy" (Fiske, 1987c, p. 236) we would have to assume either that television—with all the distortions described by the last fifty years of quantitative and critical analysts—is in fact an accurate producer of the popular interest or that it will soon reform itself to be such. This seems either too dark a description or too optimistic a forecast. The underlying agonistic theory common to British cultural studies, postmodern theory, and American rhetorical studies seems to offer a more appropriate line of approach. We need to begin to describe the precise range of textual polysemy and the power held by the audience in its struggle with texts and message producers.

These limits ought to be found both in production and reception conditions (Meehan, 1986) and in texts. As a rhetorical critic, I will focus my attention on the latter, exploring, in a variety of ways, the communication event occasioned by the broadcast on November 11, 1985, of an episode of *Cagney and Lacey* concerning the topic of abortion. Because rhetorical criticism focuses on language usage as a means of distributing power among a particular group of agents who are uniquely situated in a communication process (e.g., McGee, 1982), this critique examines two particular audience members for the program, then the specific political codes made present in the message, and, finally, the historical occasion of the broadcast. While this case study leads to a focus on television, the implications extend to other national mass media as well.

THE POLYSEMOUS *CAGNEY AND LACEY*

My own viewing of the abortion episode leads me to describe the central plot as follows: Police detectives Cagney and Lacey help a pregnant woman (Mrs. Herrera) to enter an abortion clinic where pickets (led by Arlene Crenshaw) are blocking access. Lacey, married and pregnant, eagerly helps Mrs. Herrera, while Cagney, feeling conflicted, resists any assistance beyond that necessitated by her job. When the abortion clinic is bombed and a vagrant dies as a result, the detectives investigate and locate the bomber who, in a climatic scene, threatens to blow up herself and the detectives. She gives up when confronted with the inconsistency of killing Lacey's "pre-born" child for a Pro-life cause.[3]

Two viewers, selected from a larger project I am conducting, offer particularly interesting responses to the episode. The two were college students recruited through local-scale organizations active in the abortion controversy. They were asked to view the program and to respond, during commercial breaks and after the program ended, to my open-ended and nonjudgmental questions. These two college students and their responses are not presented because of their "typicality." I do not claim their responses are representative, but rather that they are suggestive of new questions that must be asked in order to gain an accurate picture of the relative power of encoding and decoding as social processes. The first respondent, whom I'll call "Jack," was the leader of a student Pro-life group. A twenty-one-year old male, first exposed to the abortion issue through a required essay in a Catholic all-boys high school, Jack described himself as not being a particularly successful student and as having a life goal of becoming a major league baseball umpire. "Jill," a first-year student, was the daughter of a feminist mother. Active in the student Pro-choice organization, her goal was to complete a doctorate. Neither of these two leaders of politically active groups had seen the episode previously, but both reported having heard about it and having talked about it in their organizations when the episode was broadcast. While Jill displayed more familiarity with the series, Jack showed more knowledge about the political preferences and activities of the actresses and producers and reported having read about the episode in newspapers and magazines.

At one important level, the eighteen single-spaced pages of responses provided by these two opposed activists confirm the polysemy thesis. Their replies to my questions agreed less than 10 percent of the time. For example, when asked about the fairness of the presentation, Jill replied "Yeah, I think it is fair," whereas Jack said "I think it's really grossly unfair." Jill responded to Arlene Crenshaw by saying "I don't like her. I don't respect her," whereas Jack listed her as his favorite character, noting that she was the "lone good-guy type of figure in the show." Similarly, Jill claimed that the value of "family" was "definitely portrayed as positive," whereas Jack concluded "I don't think they take a very pro-family type response." Throughout their interviews, Jill and Jack provided virtually diametrically opposed opinions of the episode.

There were, nonetheless, important elements in their responses which lead me to suggest that the term "polyvalence" characterizes these differences better than does the term "polysemy." Polyvalence occurs when audience members share understandings of the denotations of a text but disagree about the valuation of those denotations to such a degree that they produce notably different interpretations. In this case, it is not a multiplicity or instability of textual meanings but rather a difference in audience evaluations of shared denotations that best accounts for the two viewers' discrepant interpretations. Careful listening and examination of the transcripts make it clear that neither Jill or Jack misunderstood the program, and they did not decode the images and words as holding different denotations. Their plot summaries, although extremely rough, were not inconsistent. More importantly, perhaps, each advocate was able to predict what the other's response to the program would be. If we accept the premise that understanding is effectively assessed by the ability to predict another's interpretation, this is an important test that both pass. After claiming that the episode "presents both sides of the story," for example, Jill admitted that "I'm sure that a lot of Pro-life people would hate it because it ends up that they are criminals at the end." Jack shared the ability to reflect on how the text might be read by others with different values: "A lot of people . . . would say, 'Oh, it's great, it's a fair portrayal, it presents our side very well and does a good job of the other one too,' whereas the Pro-lifers would say 'It's a terrible portrayal, it's absolutely biased against our side.'" On another occasion, in talking about his preference for Arlene Crenshaw as a character, he noted "You know, obviously, coming from my point of view, I can see if I was pro-abortion, she'd be like the 'bad-guy.'"

On a number of specific counts it further becomes clear that both viewers shared a basic construction of the denotations of the text. Both described Cagney as the character "in the middle." Both cited the transformation of the lieutenant's attitudes.

Both noted the poverty and minority status of Mrs. Herrera. Ultimately, there was nothing in their responses to suggest that they did not share a basic understanding of what the program was trying to convey.

This finding is consistent with other major audience studies. In Morley's (1980) published transcripts of interviews surrounding the program *Nationwide*, I detect little fundamental inconsistency in the denotations processed by the viewers; instead, it is the valuation of those denotations and the attached connotations that they draw upon which become important (see also Eco, 1979, pp. 54–56). Similarly, in Radway's (1984) contrast of the professional critics with the Smithton readers, it is not that these two sets of readings are inconsistent, but simply that the critics disvalue any patriarchal codings, whereas the Smithton women accept some of those codings as consistent with their values. The only instance in which true shifts in denotations are recorded, to my knowledge, is Katz and Liebe's (1984) study of Arab readers of *Dallas*, and in this case it requires massive cross-cultural differences and language shifts to produce such discrepant interpretations.

The emphasis on the polysemous quality of texts thus may be overdrawn. The claim perhaps needs to be scaled back to indicate that responses and interpretations are generally polyvalent, and texts themselves are occasionally or partially polysemic. It is not that texts routinely feature unstable denotation, but that instability of connotation requires viewers to judge texts from their own value systems. Different respondents similarly understand the messages that a text seeks to convey. They may, however, see the text as rhetorical—as urging positions upon them—and make their own selections among and evaluations of those persuasive messages. As I note in the conclusion, this will have profound implications for the practice of critical reading. For clarity, then, we might reserve the term "inter-textual polysemy" to refer to the existence of variety in messages on mass communication channels, the terms "internally polysemous" or "open texts" for those discourses which truly offer unstable or internally contradictory meanings, and the term "polyvalence" to describe the fact that audiences routinely evaluate texts differently, assigning different value to different portions of a text and to the text itself. Such revisions imply the need to generate a more careful account of the actual social force of popular or mass communication. Such an endeavor begins with a more detailed exploration of audience interpretations.

AUDIENCES: GROUPS OF INDIVIDUALS

The claim that audiences have the ability to create their own empowering responses to mass-mediated texts loses little of its force when it is acknowledged that the polysemic freeplay of discourse has been overestimated. Whether deriving from decoding processes related to denotation or connotation, critical audience studies have indicated fairly clearly that viewers can construct a variety of responses to any given mass-mediated text. The central issue remains, however, to what extent do these responses constitute liberating pleasure and social empowerment? The situation of audiences as members of groups in a social process constructs some fundamental limits to these pleasures and powers which can now be explored.

The proposition that decoding a message always requires work is a fundamental postulate supporting the claim that audiences have control of the mass communication process. As Morley (1980, p. 10) puts it, "The production of a meaningful message in the TV discourse is always problematic 'work.'" The work receivers must do inserts them into a position of influence in relationship to the text. Such accounts, however, fail to note that decoding requires *differential* amounts of work for different audiences. Jack's responses to *Cagney and Lacey* consumed more than twice the space and time of Jill's replies. Jill was positioned to give a reading of the text that was dominant or only slightly negotiated (e.g., she objected to the tokenization of minorities in the program and the lack of women in the more powerful job hierarchies). Jack was required to provide a largely oppositional reading.

Not only did Jack's interpretation require more space, and visibly more effort (his nonverbal behavior was frequently tense and strained), it showed itself to be more incomplete and problematic in other ways. Frequently, Jack's responses departed from the program altogether to provide the background of a fairly extended Pro-life argument. In reacting to the abortion clinic's male physician, Jack cited the doctor's story about a twelve-year-old girl who came in to get an abortion, arguing

> . . . little does he tell them now, however, that it is easier for the younger, anywhere from a twelve- to eighteen-year-old, statistically and medically, to bear children than it is for women who are over twenty-five or thirty, only because it's like, their bodies are ripe and just developing, as opposed to either at the peak or really past that. See, they don't want to get into that; he just talks about how terrible it allegedly or supposedly is for the young women to have children. So it's the best thing to do, get them in there, you know, do the abortion, and get them out, no worries. Do they ever talk about post-abortion counseling that that doctor might do? . . . Are they willing to go so far as to say that he just does the abortion and have [*sic*] nothing more to do with her?

Jack thus worked very hard to oppose his own ideology to the program. At times this entailed distortions of the truth which were probably unintentional. For example, Jack's statistics are skewed. More importantly for Jack, at times he was simply unsuccessful at producing a consistent response. At several key points he was reduced to a position of virtual incoherence, and he indicated his frustration in nonverbal ways. For example, at one point he became trapped between his denial that normal Pro-life people are violent and his attempt to project how the network should portray abortion clinic bombers. He concluded:

> If I was [*sic*] nuts enough to bomb, I'd go about it real calmly, talk to them, and wait until they dig up some more information before I went, got overly nervous. I think they did a good job of portraying her as, well, see, she was involved in the sixties and seventies and all these demonstrations, the typical type. Why couldn't they portray, if they are going to, a bomber who is just an average everyday American? They did a good job of portraying her as an extreme fanatic. That is to say that, see, they're all like this. They're the type who did that and they'll do this again. It's rather illogical.

Jack was unable to come up with a consistent characterization of clinic bombers. He described them as "nuts" and asked that they be portrayed as "an average everyday American," displaying his difficulty in putting together a response to the text that was persuasive (either to himself or to me). Jill did not show such strain in her interpretations.

Finally, Jill and Jack differed with regard to the chief tests they put to the text. For Jill, the recurrent test was "Is this realistic?" Accusing the text of committing errors, she argued that the portrayal of the Pro-life leaders and the bomber as women was inaccurate, but that Pro-lifers in fact generated violence, and so on. For Jack, the reality criterion emphasized motives rather than facts. His most frequent strategy was to talk about what the text omitted: the character of the fetus, the "ripeness" of young women, the poor quality of counseling the women received. For Jill, therefore, the negotiation process was simply one of relatively minor factual corrections. For Jack, the process was a matter of filling in major motivational absences in the text (see Scholle, 1988; Wander, 1984).

For Jack, in short, the work of interpreting the text and resisting its persuasive message was much more difficult than the accommodative response was for Jill. Although these differences may have been caused by factors other than their political positions (e.g., differential academic ability or familiarity with the series), they provide grounds for considering the important possibility that oppositional and negotiated readings require more work of viewers than do dominant readings. This possibility is reinforced as well by work with public speakers (Lucaites and Condit, 1986). Three factors give impact to the difference in audience work load: its silencing effects, its reduction of pleasure, and its code dependence.

The first consequence of the greater work load imposed on oppositionally situated audience groups is the tendency of such burdens to silence viewers. In its most stark form, this leads to turning off the television, a widespread phenomenon, especially among minority groups (Fiske, 1987c, p. 312; Morley, 1980, p. 135). If the particular range of television's textual polysemy excludes marginal group messages, and if oppositional reading requires comparatively oppressive quantities of work, then minority groups are indeed silenced, even as audiences, and therefore discriminated against in important ways.

Another consequence of this work load is disproportional pleasure for oppositional and dominant readers. As Fiske (1987c, p. 239) points out, it is clearly the case that viewers can take great pleasure in constructing oppositional readings simply because of the human joy in constructing representations. Nonetheless, this does not mean that the pleasures of the text are fairly distributed. Jill indicated that she enjoyed the episode of *Cagney and Lacey* very much, she found it "powerful," and her nonverbal response indicated a restful, enjoyable experience. Jack, on the other hand, clearly took some pleasure in his ability to argue against the text, but he also displayed clear signs of pain and struggle in that decoding. Jack's relative displeasure may be widely shared, given that even a popular program enlists only twenty million viewers out of a population of over two hundred and forty million, and that most of those viewers are simultaneously engaged in other activities (Meyrowitz, 1985, p. 348). The disparity is made pernicious given that the most highly sought audiences have the characteristics of more elite groups (Feur, 1984a, p. 26; Kerr, 1984, p. 68). Programs are tailored for the greater pleasure of a relative elite.

A similar disparity of pleasures in the mass publishing industry is suggested by Radway (1984, pp. 104, 165–167) when she reveals that the repressed pornography that producers of romance believe to be attractive to women may not actually be women's primary interest and that an extremely different genre of stories might bring greater pleasures to these audiences. As Fiske (1987c, p. 66) notes, to be popular enough to gain economic rewards, mass media must attract a fairly large audience. That popularity, however, is only relative to other programming the producers are willing to construct. Hence, the trade-off among what majority audience groups want, and what the producers are willing to give them as a compromise may still retain a great deal of control for producers and dominant groups.

Mass-mediated texts might be viewed, therefore, not as giving the populace what they want, but as compromises that give the relatively well-to-do more of what they want, bringing along as many economically marginal viewers as they comfortably can, within the limitations of the production teams' visions and values. If so, the differential availability of textual pleasures and the costs in pain become as important as any absolute statements about viewer abilities. It is not enough to argue that audiences can do the work to decode oppressive texts with some pleasure. We need to investigate how much more this costs them, and how much more silencing of oppositional groups this engenders. In addition, we need to understand better the various conditions that best enable oppositional decoding.

A third consequence of the differential work load required of viewing groups provides further clues to the variability of audience experiences. Among oppositional readers of the *Cagney and Lacey* text, Jack was in a particularly empowered position. As a leader of a Pro-life group, he was experienced in producing Pro-life representations and had access to a large network of oppositional codes. This experience and access were evident throughout his interview (as in the instance here he used Pro-life rhetoric to point out "gaps" in the doctor's story). The utility of such experience and skill in helping viewers produce self-satisfying decodings is echoed throughout the audience literature. Morley (1980, p. 141) especially notes the enhanced ability of shop stewards to produce oppositional codings more successfully than do rank and file union members. Importantly, most of the content-based audience research thus far taps into audiences where group leadership exists and where audience members have access to counter-rhetorics. Radway's study (1984) relies on a group centered on Dorothy Evans, who encodes negotiated readings, giving access to a resistive code to her group members. Linda Steiner's study (1988) relies similarly on a site, *Ms.* magazine, where oppositional rhetorics are provided.

In sum, the strongest evidence about the actualization of audiences' abilities to decode messages to their own advantage comes from studies that select audiences or conditions in which we would expect the receivers to be relatively advantaged as opponents to the message producers. Moreover, in cases with the weakest access to group organization, it also seems that the oppositional interpretations are weaker. In his study of adolescent female responses to Madonna, for example, Fiske (1987a, p. 273; 1987c, p. 215) suggests that the young girls are only "struggling" to find counter-rhetorics. They experience only distinctly limited success at resistance.

The commonalities in these studies suggest two conclusions. First, there is a need for research to assess the typicality of oppositional readings. The tendency to notice successful oppositional decodings may have led scholars to overplay the degree to which this denotes typical behavior. Correctives could come from comparing audiences with different access to oppositional codes on a particular topic and from studies of the relative degrees of oppositionality in typical decodings. Only if a strong and pervasive response to dominant messages can be demonstrated can we assert that the limited repertoire of mass-mediated messages really co-exists with a semiotic democracy.

Second, these commonalities also re-establish the importance of leadership and organized group interaction. Leadership always has been largely a matter of the ability to produce rhetorics that work for the group. While being human may mean having the ability to encode and decode texts (Burke, 1966), it is not the case that all human beings are equally skilled in responding to persuasive messages with countermessages. The masses may not be cultural dupes, but they are not necessarily skilled rhetors. Here, another fragment from the abortion communication event is instructive.

In interviews of abortion activists in California, Kristin Luker (1984, p. 111) noticed an interesting phenomenon. The women who became abortion activists reported one factor that led to replacing their guilt and negative feelings about abortions with active campaigning for a right to choose. It was not the experience of abortion per se; many of them had had abortions long before the change in their attitude. It was, they said, the ability of a few articulate rhetors that had been instrumental in helping them to resist the prior, dominant views. The presentation of different codings had helped them to resist the dominant rhetorics. If popular media are only oppositional to the extent that countermedia exist to help audiences decode dominant messages, the mass media's role in social change processes may be extremely limited. In this case, Fiske (1987c, p. 326) is not wrong when he concludes that "resistive reading practices that assert the power of the subordinate in the process of representation and its subsequent pleasure pose a direct challenge to the power of capitalism to produce its subjects-in-ideology." It is simply that we do not yet know how widespread such resistive interpretative practices are, given the more substantial obstacles outlined here. In contrast, we should weigh the power that these texts give to dominant audiences.

CODES AND THE PUBLIC

The disproportional viewing pleasures experienced by elite groups might present only a minor social problem if turning off the television set sufficiently closed down the influence of its texts. However, even in such relative silence, the television texts continue to go about constructing hegemony in important ways. This becomes evident if we shift our perspective so that the important audience for television is no longer individual viewers (even grouped by social interest) but "the public."

The term "public" is highly contested (Bitzer, 1987; Goodnight, 1987; Hauser, 1987; McGee, 1987). By it I mean those members of a nation-state who have had their interests articulated to a large enough mass of people to allow their preferred vocabulary legitimacy as a component in the formation of law and behavior. I suggest that television's political functions are not confined to its address to the pleasures of individuals. In addition, television "makes present" particular codings in the public space (Perelman and Olbrechts-Tyteca, 1971). Once such codings gain legitimacy they can be employed in forming public law, policy, and behavior. Even if they are not universally accepted, their presence gives them presumption (the right to participate in formulations, and even the need for others to take account of them in their policy formulations). Crucially, the upscale audience courted by television advertisers is also the group most likely to constitute the politically active public (e.g., "Young Blacks Have," 1987). Hence, television, or any mass medium, can do oppressive work solely by addressing the dominant audience that also constitutes the public.

It is because television "makes present in public" a vocabulary that prefers the dominant audience's interests that the dominant audience gets the most pleasure from television and that television actively promotes its interests. The fact that other groups can counter-read this discourse, and enjoying doing so, does not disrupt the direct functions of governance that television serves for dominant groups. A return to the case of the broadcast of abortion practices will explain this point more thoroughly.

Prime-time television addressed the practice of abortion in clearly patterned ways. The very few, highly controversial programs concerning abortion in the sixties and early seventies occasioned sponsor withdrawal, boycotts of sponsors who did not withdraw, and extended editorial treatment by opponents of legalized abortion (Condit, 1987).

Probably as a consequence of this extra-popular control mechanism, a second round of abortion programs did not really appear until the mid-eighties, more than a decade after abortion had been legalized through the actions of state legislators and the Supreme Court. For many years, television producers were dissuaded from making present the practice of abortion. When abortion re-appeared, it did so with a dominant-preferring code firmly, if cleverly, in place.

The evolution of prime-time television's treatment of abortion between the years 1984 and 1988 was such that it began to include increasingly more problematic cases of abortion, and it featured distinctive types. Nonetheless, the main clump of programs between 1984 and 1986 constructed a limited repertoire of meanings.

Different viewers, with different viewing habits, may have found themselves introduced to abortion in the mass culture in one of three ways. For viewers with traditional affiliations, those who enjoyed "family" programs, *Call to Glory*, *Webster*, *Family*, *Dallas*, or *Magruder and Loud* would have provided them with episodes in which prominent female characters found themselves unintentionally pregnant, decided against having an abortion, and then were relieved of the consequences of that decision through miscarriage or the discovery that they were not pregnant after all. Fans of MTM productions, and their liberal values (Feuer, 1984b), would have been introduced to abortion in a different manner. On *Cagney and Lacey*, *Hill Street Blues*, and *St. Elsewhere*, professionals supported the choices of transitory female characters to have abortions, and confronted the violence of the Pro-life movement. Finally, viewers might have first encountered televised abortion in a more sharply conflicted manner through *Spenser for Hire*, *L.A. Law*, or a second episode of *St. Elsewhere*. In these programs, central women characters made highly contested choices to undergo abortions.

Prime-time television thus introduced the public to the practice of abortion with a polysemic voice. The mass-mediated *message* itself appeared to bring different textual resources to different audiences. As has been previously argued, however, this textual polysemy had very clear limits (Condit, 1987). Regardless of whether the program was primarily "pro" or "anti," abortion was portrayed as a morally problematic act that was nonetheless the woman's choice. Although female characters decided in favor of and against abortions in a wide variety of problem situations, the abortions presented in prime time were never those of women in optimal reproductive situations. Women in caring, financially secure marriages did not abort healthy fetuses. Moreover, the practicalities of abortion were absent. There was no direct mention of the problem of payment, the pain of the operation, or the real but difficult alternatives of adoption or contraception.

As a consequence, dominant group vocabularies and practices were normalized (Condit, in press). Career women could get abortions and feel more comfortable with the practice, even though their role or obligation as mothers was not erased. This was both an attractive enactment of career women's own reproductive practices and a discursive instantiation of their "choices" in the public vocabulary. The power distributed through such reinforcement is immense; it is virtually the entire social glue that allows dominant groups to coordinate their efforts in a democracy, and thereby maintain power. Moreover, the reinforcement shields dominant groups from understanding the ways in which different conditions might make different practices necessary or right for others. In the face of such a public culture, it was relatively easy for the Reagan administration, in its second term, to withdraw virtually all indirect financial support of abortion *and* of family planning both in the national and international arenas.

In contrast, prime-time television neither informed the poor how to finance abortions nor told the young how to avoid needing them and why they might want to avoid such need. No constructive efforts on their behalf provided useful information or created pleasurable self-validation for these other groups of women. Hence, even if other groups were active interpreters of these programs, in order to seek legitimacy or cultural sympathy for their own practices they would have had to do double work—deconstructing the dominant code and reconstructing their own. In addition, to effect favorable policies, marginal groups also would have had to make a public argument in some other, *less pleasurable* arena, counterposing their interests and vocabulary to this now-dominant vocabulary. Finally, even if they were able to present an equally attractive argument, they would still, at best, be able to win a compromise with this already-legitimated dominant code (a position they would not have faced, absent its broadcast).

In sum, television disseminates and legitimates, in a pleasurable fashion, a political vocabulary that favors certain interests and groups over others, even if by no other means than consolidating the dominant audience by giving presence to their codes. Given the interest of advertisers in dominant economic groups, the ability of marginal groups to break this grip seems particularly unlikely. Fiske's conclusion (1987c, p. 319) that homogenization will lead to the inclusion of these other groups presumes much about the demographics of television audiences that is yet to be established. It also rests on imprecise definitions of "the popular" which do not seem to distinguish who the dominant elites are (the rich or the middle and well-to-do working class [e.g., automotive unions]?) and who the "resisting populace" might be (secretaries or the unemployed?). Further examination of that relationship will require more careful studies of the economic side of this question. If, however, maximal economic return can be purchased through appeal to dominant audiences, then the fact that programs also attract oppositional readers around the globe may be only of minimal importance. In short, the jury is still out on the "popularity" of the mass media.

A second political consequence of television's coding of abortion practices has to do with the dissemination of new information to individuals. It can be explored through a turn to the third component of rhetorical events.

OCCASION: HISTORICAL AGENTS

Historical agents are embedded in particular occasions with specific power relationships, communicated through ideologies. Recent interpretations of ideology have begun to explore its character as information (Foucault, 1972; Lyotard, 1984; Scholle, 1988). In place of the old "ideology vs science" equation, some analyses suggest that one of the primary ways that ideology functions is by making present or dominant certain pieces of information to certain audiences. On this account, one important function of the broadcast of the *Cagney and Lacey* abortion episode was the extent to which it gave access to new and useful information about the practice of abortion.

To make such an evaluation of the *Cagney and Lacey* episode requires an accounting of the historical situation and self-consciousness about criteria. In the mid-1980s, it was clear that the legality of abortion was a widely shared knowledge. Less widely shared was information of many kinds: about the types of women who have abortions and their reasons, about the experience of the operation, about women's control over their sexuality and fertility, and perhaps about the character of the fetus. *Cagney and Lacey* distribute information about some of these issues (especially about the wide variety of "good" women who have abortions), but not about others (the character of the operation and of the fetus).

The social impact of the program was in part a matter of the particular information it disseminated to different groups, even to groups able to decode the program through their own value structures. Jack, for example, was forced by the program's presence to confront the fact of abortion's "so-called social acceptability by too many people." Television programs distribute varying sorts of information about abortion, even to viewers who wish to change that practice and who actively and negatively decode the program.

Evaluating the impact of *Cagney and Lacey* on this learning dimension might seem to imply survey research, but that approach is unlikely to be cost-effective. Research in the "direct effects" tradition of rhetorical studies indicated the virtual impossibility of quantitatively tracking learning and persuasion impacts on large audiences (e.g., Baran & Davis, 1975). Most important, in historical studies scholars can never go back and get the kind of data that would meet the tests of quantitative-style knowledge claims. Further, academics are rarely prescient enough to know what programming is important with enough lead time to prepare for such surveys. Knowledge claims thus must be critically based.

Historically based evaluations need to take into account a more sensitive gauge than has been applied previously (and this might well be the most important moral of Radway's work on romance novels). Rather than describing a text and its readings simply as good or bad, critics need to develop judgments of better and worse. From this perspective, *Cagney and Lacey* should be evaluated on several comparative grounds. First, it should be placed as the earliest of the second wave of televisualization of abortion. Second, it should be compared to other programs and entertainment media. On this scale, the episode was far more conservative in the amount of information it provided than *St. Elsewhere*, with its far greater detail about the experience and emotions of having an abortion and inclusion of the issue of contraception. However, it is far more informative than episodes such as *Webster* or *Call to Glory*, neither of which ever directly even name abortion as "the option" nor deal with the consequences.

Such an evaluation process will lead not to a condemnation or simple praise of a program but to a calibrated understanding of the particular role it played in introducing certain limited pieces of information to different ranges of audiences at different times. Critical analysis should therefore, at least at times, be rhetorical; it should be tied to the particularity of occasions: specific audiences, with specific codes or knowledges, addressed by specific programs and episodes (McGee, 1982; Wichelns, 1972). Such an approach does not deny the wisdom of also exploring the intertextuality of programs, the stripped character of the viewing experience (Newcomb, 1984, p. 44), and the disengaged character of much viewing. It merely adds one additional vector to our understanding.

EVALUATION

After considering the historical moment, the public code constructed, and the range of audience readings, we might be in a position to provide an evaluation of *Cagney and Lacey*. I wish to turn that evaluation to the key criterion on which I see Fiske, Hall, Morley, Radway, and others (but probably not Newcomb) converging, that is, the judgment of a mass communication event based on its "resistance" to the dominant ideology. This judgmental criterion rests on the assumption that academics have a duty to the society that pays their salaries to try to produce a better world. This is a duty widely accepted for the ever more technically oriented scientists, although with admittedly different procedures. In the humanities and social sciences, however, the execution of that criterion is eternally and politically controversial, and that deters us from encouraging scholars in communication studies to undertake endeavors of a sort we virtually demand from scholars in natural studies. I nonetheless support such efforts.

For many years, critics interested in bringing about positive social changes assumed that the deconstruction of the dominant ideologies contained in popular and political texts was the best contribution toward human progress. This kind of criticism gradually became too predictable to suit the tastes of an academic machine that voraciously devours "new ideas" in preference to the good execution of old ones. Furthermore, at its worst, and too frequently, such criticism merely imposed the ideology/methodology of a particular political preference upon dominant texts, threatening to produce nothing but a blanket condemnation of the status quo, rather than insight into how to improve society.

Today, with the rise of attention to audiences, such a textual approach has come under further attack. Fiske (1987c, p. 64; see also 1987b) writes, for example, that

> Textual studies of television now have to stop treating it as a closed text, that is, as one where the dominant ideology exerts considerable, if not total, influence over its ideological structure and therefore over its reader. Analysis has to pay less attention to the textual strategies of preference or closure and more to the gaps and spaces that open up to meanings not preferred by the textual structure.

In placing enormous faith in the capacity of audiences to resist, however, a similar blindness may be on its way to being produced on the other side. We can endlessly generate studies that demonstrate that clever readers can take pleasure in reconstructing texts, but this does not certify that mass communication in general functions as a force for positive social change.

The assumption that pleasure liberates is too simplistic on a myriad of counts. To begin with, note that Fiske's argument (1987c, p. 19) is based on the premise that "Pleasure results from a particular relationship between meanings and power. Pleasure for the subordinate is produced by the assertion of one's social identity in resistance to, in independence of, or in negotiation with, the structure of domination." This is a flat assertion with no support. It is based on the claim that "escape" is always escape from the dominant ideologies' subjective positioning of the marginal person (p. 317). While Fiske documents that this kind of escape can and does sometimes occur, he does not demonstrate that it is the only kind or primary kind of pleasure to be gained from a text by a subordinate. There are a wide variety of pleasures, some of them are merely temporary escape from truly painful thoughts and activities, and these do not challenge the subjective identity television programs present. The most important of these is what Kenneth Burke (1969, p. 19) has called "identification." One can fully identify with the rich patrons of *Dynasty*, enjoying the vicarious experience of opulence, without building any oppositional identity. I have reveled in such play, the pleasure coming from a temporary "giving in" rather than from resistance. My female career-oriented students generally admit relishing the Cinderella myth offered by *An Officer and a Gentleman*. Such pleasurable identification does not require that we are naïvely confusing reality and our own position (a different thesis which Fiske [1987c, pp. 44–47, 63–72] argues against forcefully and accurately). We know that we are not as rich as Krystal and will never be. Nonetheless, we can enjoy playing that we are. This kind of pleasure offers only temporary escape.

I would not willingly deny any of us such pleasures. Human life is hard, under capitalism or any other system human beings have yet devised. Radway's Smithton readers need a pleasurable escape from their oppressive husbands and demanding children. However, we should be very cautious about our portrayal of such escape as liberating. Attention to the discrepancies between critical readings of television's embedding of subjects in patriarchy and those subjects' own readings (the opening of Radway's book) should not obscure the realization that both personal pleasure and collective domination can go on at the same time (the conclusion of Radway's book). We need to make a clear distinction between the personal or "private" experience of pleasure which temporarily liberates us from the painful conditions of our lives and the collectivized pleasures which, in the right historical conditions, may move us toward changing those conditions. Because of the character of the mass media, both are social pleasures, but *collectivized* (grouped, internally organized through communication production) action and pleasure are essential to social change. Alterations in subjectivity may indeed provide a first step in that later process, but it is an extremely limited step and it is not the case that all pleasurable readings produce such resisting subjectivities (Scholle, 1988, p. 33). Moreover, if the cost of mildly altered subjectivities is complacence, the potential for change may be offset. Television does not, therefore, simply offer "a set of forces for social change" (Fiske, 1987c, p. 326); television is engaged in a set of social forces within which actors may or may not promote social change.

To assess the social consequences of a mass communication event requires, consequently, that we dispense with the totalized concept of "resistance." It is not enough to describe a program or an interpretation of a program as oppositional. It is essential to describe what particular things are resisted and how that resistance occurs. In part, this requires taking more seriously the melding of liberal interest group theory and Marxism evident in Fiske's work (1987c, p. 16). Fiske's explicit political theory dismantles views of politics that portray it either as an evenhanded barter between various interest groups (the classic liberal account) or as the dominance of a unified, all-powerful elite. Instead, he argues (1987c, p. 16) as do I (in press), that politics is a battle and barter among a wide range of groups, each of which is differently and unevenly empowered. Unfortunately, like most other audience theorists, Fiske does not carry this theory through into his analysis. Instead, he reduces the multiplicity of differently empowered groups to "the dominant" and "the resistant." Such a totalized concept of resistance from a system is at odds with a theory that posits a wide range of groups with a wide range of investments in the system they share. Given that perspective, for my interpretation of *Cagney and Lacey*, I would offer the following evaluations.

From the perspective of women like Jill, the decisions by the production team headed by Barney Rosenzweig, which resulted in this particular treatment of abortion on prime-time television, were mildly progressive. Jill's interpretation needs to be supplemented by that of other women, but for her, the program portrayed powerful characterizations of "good" women having abortions and reaffirmed the evaluation that abortion was not a repudiation of familial love. Most importantly, it affirmed that even though abortion is the morally problematic termination of the potential of a growing creature's life, it is always the woman who must weigh the principles and factors involved to make the decision. This is perhaps surprisingly mild progressive ideological work for a production team that dealt in outstanding detail with the experience of rape and that treated the fallout of the AIDS crisis on single adults with gingerly directness. The program, however, was the leader of the second wave of telecasts and took a great deal of public criticism even for these steps. For Jill's group, it accomplished some important ideological work.

For women in poverty and women of color the program is more mixed. It explicitly affirmed the choices of a particular minority woman, but it did not deal with the ways in which poor women might fund abortion or contraception. It did not deal with the options provided by extended families, or with the importance of motherhood in different cultures. It offered a sugary and unrealistic moral, "Have an abortion so you can go to school and get off welfare," that may have appealed to latent racism in white audiences more than assisting poor women with real options. In the face of such silences, the Republican administration could continue its largely hidden work at pro-natalism by dismantling funding for family planning. From the perspective of these groups of viewers, this represents a serious short-coming of this episode.

The situation is much grimmer from Jack's perspective as a clearly marginal viewer of this text, and in many ways a person whom I sensed to be involved in popular culture (especially sports), but disempowered by the dominant political economy. I find it difficult to argue that Jack found his reading of this text, resistant and skilled as it was, to be either a predominantly pleasurable or liberating experience. Jack expressed the following general response to the program's significance: "I think it's a [*sic*] pretty much a devastating blow, not that it's totally going to stop the movement, but it set us back." For Jack, as for other relatively unempowered males, especially of Pro-life positions, *Cagney and Lacey* did not promote the social changes they preferred. Even their resistant readings left them with the feeling of oppression by the media.

The *Cagney and Lacey* broadcast about abortion broke new ideological ground, inserting new political codes into the public culture. It was thus a progressive but not radical text that tended to oppose the interests of marginally positioned traditional males. It favored the interests of career women, but only marginally supported other groups of women.

I have, of course, stacked the deck here by probing readings that scramble the left's general presumption that marginal readers of texts are the potential source of liberation, the groups with whom we, as academics, ought to identify and praise. I have done so to heighten my point that "resistance" and the metaphor of a "dominant system" is a bad way to phrase what it is those interested in social change should praise. History creates "hegemonies," but hegemonies are not equivalent to dominant ideologies. A hegemony is a negotiation among elite and nonelite groups and therefore always contains interests of nonelite groups, though to a lesser degree. To resist the power of dominant groups may be safe, but to resist the hegemony that is constructed in negotiation with those groups is always also to resist what is partially of one's own interests. The totalizing concept of resistance should give way to historically particular acts in order to bring about specific social changes. This shift will require academics to affirm particular goals, rather than to simply critique that which is.

CONCLUSIONS

Recent reemphasis on the audience as an important component of what happens in the process of mass communicating is a useful redress of an old imbalance. We should avoid, however, totalizing the audience's abilities. The receiver's political power in mass mediated societies is dependent upon a complex balance of historically particular forces which include the relative abilities of popular groups and their access to oppositional codes, the work/pleasure ratio of the available range of the media's intertextual polysemy, the modifications programs make in the dominant code, and the degree of empowerment provided to dominant audiences.

To scholars, this balance of forces presents a series of challenges. There is a need to explore more precisely the relative decoding abilities of audiences and their access to counter-rhetorics. There is also a need to continue to explore what texts "make present," even without regard to their "seams," through careful historically grounded studies of the particular issue contents of television programming. There is, finally, a need to explore the "occasion" of a discourse in terms other than the family viewing context (contexts emphasized in Fiske [1987c, p. 239] and Morley [1986, p. 14]). Different families and different members of families are always embedded in larger political occasions that create collective experiences across family walls. Unless we ask about the particular contents of particular sets of programs, the relationship of those contents to the stasis of the issue for viewers and for the larger society at the time of broadcast, we will not be able to assess fully television's roles in the process of social change for its various constituencies.

There are additional implications for scholars as teachers. One of the primary ways through which we can bring about positive social change is through our teaching of undergraduates for whom our arcane battles about research protocols are rightfully boring and meaningless. For our students, decoding alternatives, through painful effort, can become pleasurable resources they can use throughout life. A perspective that emphasizes the receiver's placement within a complexly balanced process suggests the need to continue to use classrooms to teach students a range of decodings for possible texts, a project that may include increasing their ideological range (the ability to see *An Officer and a Gentleman* as Cinderella, Sonny Crocket as a 1980's John Wayne, *Dallas* as the costs inherent to capitalism). It might also include familiarizing students with the history of the various issue contents of the mass media. Studies of the participation of news and entertainment programming in particular social movements and issues might be added to genre studies and analyses of private audiences (e.g., Hallin, 1986; Rushing, 1986a, 1986b).

As a whole, the effort to gain a more variegated picture of audiences is an important one. However, the tendency to isolate the audience from the communication process and then pronounce the social effects of mass communication based on the ability of some receivers to experience pleasure in producing oppositional decoding is undesirable. It simply repeats the error of message-dominated research which attempted to describe the mass media's influence solely by investigating texts (or, in the other research strands, presumed intents of sources). Audience members are neither simply resistive nor dupes. They neither find television simply pleasurable, simply an escape, nor simply obnoxious and oppressive. The audience's variability is a consequence of the fact that humans, in their inherent character as audiences, are inevitably situated in a communication *system*, of which they are a part, and hence have some influence within, but by which they are also influenced. To study the role of that communication system in the processes that change our humanity and the system itself therefore requires a multiplicity of approaches to the critical analysis of the massive media.

Notes

1. I am aware that to locate intent in television programs is a difficult matter because of the multiplicity of inputs into such productions. However, this multiplicity does not negate the

fact that messages have sources and therefore some collection of intended meanings. To abrogate the use of the term simply because intent is complex would be to ignore an important component of the communication process.

2. Radway (1984, 1986) begins such a delimitation with regard to her case study of romance readers.

3. I choose the terms "Pro-life" and "Pro-choice" because they are the names employed by the members of the respective movements to define themselves.

References

Baran, S. J., and D. K. Davis. (1975). "The Audience of Public Television: Did Watergate Make a Difference?" *Central States Speech Journal* 26: 93–98.

Bennett, T., and J. Woollacott. (1987). *Bond and Beyond: The Political Career of a Popular Hero*. New York: Methuen.

Bitzer, L. F. (1987). "Rhetorical Public Communication." *Critical Studies in Mass Communication* 4(4): 425–428.

Burke, J., H. Wilson, and S. Agardy. (1983). A Country Practice *and the Child Audience: A Case Study*. Melbourne: Australian Broadcasting Tribunal.

Burke, K. (1966). "Definition of Man." In *Language as Symbolic Action*. Berkeley and Los Angeles: University of California Press.

Burke, K. (1969). "Identification." In *A Rhetoric of Motives*. Berkeley and Los Angeles: University of California Press.

Condit, C. (1987). "Abortion on Television: The 'System' and Ideological Production." *Journal of Communication Inquiry* 11: 47–60.

Condit, C. (in press). *Decoding Abortion Rhetoric: Communicating Social Change*. Urbana: University of Illinois Press.

Eco, U. (1979). "Denotation and Connotation." In *A Theory of Semiotics*, 54–56. Bloomington: Indiana University Press.

Feuer, J. (1984a). "MTM Enterprises: An Overview." In Jane Feuer, Paul Kerr, and Tise Vahimagi, eds., *MTM: "Quality Television"* (London: British Film Institute), pp. 1–31.

Feuer, J. (1984b). "The MTM Style." In Jane Feuer, Paul Kerr, and Tise Vahimagi, eds., *MTM: "Quality Television"* (London: British Film Institute), pp. 32–60.

Fiske, J. (1986). "Television: Polysemy and Popularity." *Critical Studies in Mass Communication* 3(4): 391–408.

Fiske, J. (1987a). "British Cultural Studies and Television." In R. C. Allen, ed., *Channels of Discourse* (Chapel Hill: University of North Carolina Press).

Fiske, J. (1987b). "*Cagney and Lacey*: Reading Character Structurally and Politically." *Communication* 9: 399–426.

Fiske, J. (1987c). *Television Culture*. New York: Methuen.

Foucault, M. (1972). *The Archaeology of Knowledge*. New York: Pantheon Books.

Goodnight, G. T. (1987). "Public Discourse." *Critical Studies in Mass Communication* 4(4): 428–432.

Hall, S. (1980). "Encoding/Decoding." In S. Hall, D. Hobson, A. Lowe, and P. Willis, eds., *Culture, Media, Language* (London: Hutchinson), pp. 128–138.

Hallin, D. C. (1986). *The "Uncensored War": The Media and Vietnam*. New York: Oxford University Press.

Hauser, G. A. (1987). "Features of the Public Sphere." *Critical Studies in Mass Communication* 4(4): 437–441.

Hobson, D. (1982). *Crossroads: The Drama of a Soap Opera*. London: Methuen.

Katz, E, and T. Liebes. (1984). "Once Upon a Time in *Dallas*." *Intermedia* 12(3): 28–32.

Kellner, D. (1982). "TV, Ideology, and Emancipatory Popular Culture." In H. Newcomb, ed., *Television: The Critical View*, 3rd ed. (New York: Oxford University Press), pp. 386–421.

Kerr, P. (1984). "The Making of (the) MTM (Show)." In Jane Feuer, Paul Kerr, and Tise Vahimagi, eds., *MTM: "Quality Television"* (London: British Film Institute), pp. 61–98.

Lucaites, J., and C. Condit. (1986). "Equality in the Martyrd Black Vision." Paper presented at the annual meeting of the Speech Communication Association, Chicago.

Luker, K. (1984). *Abortion and the Politics of Motherhood*. Berkeley and Los Angeles: University of California Press.

Lyotard. J. F. (1984). *The Postmodern Condition: A Report on Knowledge*. Minneapolis: University of Minnesota Press.

McGee, M. (1982). "A Materialist's Conception of Rhetoric." In R. E. McKerrow, ed., *Explorations in Rhetoric* (Glenco, IL: Scott, Foresman, and Co.), pp. 23–48.

McGee, M. C. (1987). "Power to 'The People.'" *Critical Studies in Mass Communication* 4(4): 432–437.

Meehan, E. R. (1986). "Conceptualizing Culture as Commodity: The Problem of Television." *Critical Studies in Mass Communication* 3(4): 448–457.

Meyrowitz, J. (1985). *No Sense of Place*. New York: Oxford University Press.

Morley, D. (1980). *The "Nationwide" Audience: Structure and Decoding*. London: British Film Institute.

Morley, D. (1986). *Family Television: Cultural Power and Domestic Leisure*. London: Comedia.

Newcomb, H. (1984). "On the Dialogic Aspects of Mass Communication." *Critical Studies in Mass Communication* 1: 34–50.

Palmer, P. (1986). *The Lively Audience: A Study of Children around the TV Set*. Sydney: Allen and Unwin.

Perelman, P., and L. Olbrechts-Tyteca. (1971). *The New Rhetoric: A Treatise on Argumentation*. South Bend, IN: University of Notre Dame Press.

Radway, J. (1984). *Reading the Romance: Woman, Patriarchy, and Popular Literature*. Chapel Hill: University of North Carolina Press.

Radway, J. (1986). "Identifying Ideological Seams: Mass Culture, Analytical Method, and Political Practice." *Communication* 9: 93–123.

Rushing, J. (1986a). "Mythic Evolution of 'The New Frontier' in Mass-Mediated Rhetoric." *Critical Studies in Mass Communication* 3(3): 265–296.

Rushing, J. (1986b). "Ronald Reagan's 'Star Wars' Address: Mythic Containment of Technical Reasoning." *Quarterly Journal of Speech* 72(4): 415–433.

Scholle, D. J. (1988). "Critical Studies: From the Theory of Ideology to Power/Knowledge." *Critical Studies in Mass Communication* 5(1): 16–41.

Steiner, L. (1988). "Oppositional Decoding as an Act of Resistance." *Critical Studies in Mass Communication* 5(1): 1–15.

Wander, P. (1984). "The Third Persona: An Ideological Turn in Rhetorical Theory." *Central States Speech Journal* 35(4): 197–216.

Wichelns, H. (1972). "The Literary Criticism of Oratory." In Robert L. Scott and Bernard L. Brock, eds., *Methods of Rhetorical Criticism: A Twentieth-Century Perspective* (New York: Harper and Row), pp. 27–60.

Young Blacks Have Higher Voting Rate than 18–24 Whites. (1987, October 7). *Champaign-Urbana News-Gazette*, p. A13.

Integrating Ideology and Archetype in Rhetorical Criticism

JANICE HOCKER RUSHING
THOMAS S. FRENTZ

Ideological approaches to textual criticism have not always had the prominence they enjoy today. Little over a decade ago, for example, James Carey commented that European "cultural studies" had been generally misunderstood and ignored in the United States, with the result that ideology was virtually absent in American media studies.[1] A year later, Michael McGee lamented that the ideological interpretation of rhetorical texts "seems to have gone the way of the dodo and of the neo-Aristotelian critic."[2] And as late as seven years ago, Farrell Corcoran noted that television had been particularly slow to submit to ideological criticism.[3] But with the increased endorsement of European Marxist-oriented thought, ideological approaches have been more and more frequently employed in rhetorical/communication criticism.[4] While a few short years ago, Marxism was a series of fragmented "oppositional texts" struggling for legitimacy in the face of the dominant modernist trends in academic criticism, it is now the standard against which those once-privileged alternatives must justify their own existence.

Clearly, the acceptance of ideological studies within communication has introduced important changes into rhetorical criticism. Perhaps the most profound contribution has been the acknowledgement that discourses often function covertly to legitimate the power of elite social classes. Typically, this function is enacted by posturing the political necessities of a ruling class as "natural," universal, and immune to history, thereby insulating the social order against change. Identifying this rhetorical operation implies a moral commitment, for if texts primarily reaffirm the ruling ideology in a class society, they also perpetuate the social oppression of the subordinate classes. To practice criticism from an ideological viewpoint, then, is to perform the morally significant act of fighting oppression by unmasking the rhetorical strategies that maintain it.[5] For ideological critics, the overarching telos that warrants ethical judgments is, explicitly or implicitly, some utopian vision of a classless society in which hierarchy and thereby oppression are eliminated.

But like all interpretive schemes, ideological criticism has its limitations. For example, by grounding textual meaning in the historical contingencies of material conditions, ideological analysis either marginalizes or misunderstands symbols that index the inner workings of the human psyche—both individual and cultural. In many cases, psychological processes are dismissed as the insignificant preoccupations of an historical period obsessed with the individual.[6] Even when the psyche is valued as an important constituent of ideological study, it is often constructed by "historicizing" the work of Sigmund Freud.[7] Thus, the unconscious aspects of the psyche are viewed as the site where intolerable political oppressions are repressed (forgotten) so that everyday life can masquerade as "normal."

Two problems arise when the psyche is so conceived. First, if the unconscious contains nothing but repressions caused by the socio-economic order, then it must follow that there are no real universals in the psyche, and the positing of such is itself an ideological disguise of historically determined factors. But if some textual symbols do originate from ahistorical dimensions of the unconscious, they will be impervious to ideological analysis. Second, ideological criticism restricts its moral telos to an idealized social condition with no psychological corollary other than (in some cases) the lifting of repressions. In this view, consequently, moral action cannot emanate from psychological sources; it can only occur in social *praxis*. But if the psyche possesses moral potentials not always originating in material conditions, these potentials, like possible "universal" psychic processes, will be either missed or misunderstood.

In this work, we develop an integrated approach to rhetorical criticism which assumes that the external world of historical conditions and the internal world of psychological processes are separate, but interrelated, domains of human experience. Some texts reflect both material conditions and psychic states, and if those two realms are neither coterminous nor derivable one from the other, then any adequate reading of such texts presupposes an integrated perspective. Our intent is not to replace ideological analyses with psychological ones, nor to pick and choose randomly from select ideological and psychological approaches to criticism; rather, we try to preserve the existing insights of ideological criticism while redressing the limitations of viewing the psyche as a corrupt interiorization of material circumstances. As we hope to show, once the human psyche is reconceptualized *on its own terms*, we must rethink the rhetorical and moral functions of discourses in general and reposition the critic as an agent of moral change.

We proceed by placing one major spokesperson for the ideological framework and one for the psychological alternative in dialectical tension. By using each to critique the other, we derive a synthetic perspective not solely dependent on either. Clearly, such a procedure is limited to the extent that other ideological and psychological theorists differ from the ones we choose to examine. However, given the restrictions of this forum, a focused, specific analysis seems preferable to a more global, but necessarily cursory approach. Our ideological source is the work of Marxist literary critic, Fredric Jameson, most centrally his important book, *The Political Unconscious*. Not only is Jameson widely respected in critical circles, but many consider him the best and most influential Marxist critic writing in America today.[8] Moreover, unlike many ideological critics, the centerpiece of Jameson's critical framework is a psychological concept—namely, "the political unconscious." Thus, his work attempts to account not only for social conditions as they impinge upon textuality, but also for the interaction of history with the psyche. Finally, in deriving a model of the psyche from an historicized reinterpretation of Freud, Jameson offers a particularly revealing view of the problems that arise when psychological operations are derived exclusively from material causes.

As a counterpoint to Jameson, we juxtapose the work of depth psychologist C. G. Jung. Unlike Freud and the neo-Freudian tradition in postmodern criticism, Jung treats the unconscious as a cognitively significant domain of human experience which is related, but not primarily a reaction to, the societal conditions of conscious life. Moreover, he grounds his model in ahistorical processes called "archetypes." And while these may evaporate into ideological fictions in the materialist worldview, they have a legitimate status in relation to moral action in Jung's framework. Jung also posits "individuation" as the optimal moral state for the human psyche, and in so doing, he offers an interior analogue to the ideologist's own utopian wish for a classless society.

Although we construct our own position from the disjunctions between Jameson and Jung, our voice is intentionally oppositional. That is, we contend that ideological approaches like Jameson's represent the valorized perspective in much rhetorical/cultural criticism today, while archetypal perspectives like Jung's are typically marginalized and dismissed as "religious," "ideological," "outdated," or "ethicist." Our attempt, then, is to redress this imbalance by raising the subordinate archetypal position while at the same time decentering the privileged ideological alternative. To accomplish this, we do not always give equal critical attention to both Jameson and Jung. Whereas Jung wrote in relative ignorance of the ideological perspective, part of Jameson's (and other ideologists') rise to prominence has been achieved through a derogation (and often misinterpretation) of the archetypal perspective. Thus, in order to challenge the hegemonic order that has emerged between the two perspectives, we sometimes need to interrogate the ideological stance at greater length.

We develop our perspective by examining Jameson's and Jung's divergent views on the cultural psyche, narrative texts, and the critic as moral agent. In each case, we invoke three general standards in constructing our framework. First, we grant both Jameson's ideological perspective and Jung's archetypal position their own integrity— that is, we do not reconstruct either as a derivative of the other. Second, we posit a moral telos for criticism that is based in *both* material conditions and psychological processes. Finally, we attempt to preserve a moral role for the critic that allows him or her to function as an agent of cultural change.

THE CULTURAL PSYCHE

For Jameson, an understanding of unconscious processes is essential to textual criticism, for the very act of interpretation "always presupposes, if not a conception of the unconscious itself, then at least some mechanism of mystification or repression in terms of which it would make sense to seek a latent meaning behind a manifest one, or to rewrite the surface categories of a text in the stronger language of a more fundamental interpretive code."[9] For his own conception, Jameson begins with Freud's notion of the unconscious, which he adopts because of its pervasive impact upon interpretation and because he considers it "the only really new and original hermeneutic developed since the great patristic and medieval system of the four senses of scripture" (61).

For Freud, as is well known, the unconscious is the seat of sexual and aggressive energy (libido) within all individuals that is prevented from manifesting itself in adult waking society, and thus is repressed and hidden from conscious awareness. Whereas unconscious libido operates in accord with the "Pleasure Principle"—that is, it relentlessly pursues its own gratification, the ego learns to operate in accord with the "Reality Principle"—that is, to postpone or sublimate gratification in order to meet the demands of society. Thus, the individual is locked into a fatefully antagonistic relationship with society (Necessity) which thwarts desire (Freedom), substituting for the fullness of pleasure the punier purpose of avoiding pain.[10]

Jameson retains Freud's basic outline of the dynamics between consciousness and the unconscious.[11] For Jameson and Freud, the unconscious is the repository of repressions caused by the imposition of society upon desire; thus, consciousness in a real sense *creates* the unconscious, which has no *raison d'être* except as a reaction to restraint. Jameson also adopts Freud's essentially negative stance on the relationship between society and desire. "History is what hurts," Jameson remarks; "it is what refuses desire and sets inexorable limits to individual as well as collective praxis. . ."[12]

As a Marxist critic rather than a psychoanalyst, however, Jameson's subject is the maladies of History rather than of the individual patient. In order to amend Freud's version of the unconscious for his own purposes, he must strip it of its universalist pretensions and contextualize it within History. He accomplishes this by arguing that Freud necessarily wrote within the limits of his own historical era, one in which capitalism had succeeded in destroying the fullness of collective life, replacing it with the fragmented, privatized individual who is irrevocably alienated from the group. As the individual is isolated, sexual desire and activity are also banished from collective practice, and relegated to the private sphere of repression and fantasy. "[A]s long as sexuality remains as integrated into social life in general as, say, eating," Jameson explains, "its possibilities of symbolic extension are to that degree limited, and the sexual retains its status as a banal inner-worldly event and bodily function" (64). But with its exile from the collective, it becomes charged with a semiotic significance far in excess of its functions for reproduction and pleasure; that is, sex comes to function as a "vocabulary" in which the workings of a more primal desire may be expressed.[13] That more primal desire, Jameson claims, is for the alienated individual to return to the communal totality from which it was torn with the onset of modes of production following primitive communism.[14]

When Jameson translates Freud's universal version of the *individual* unconscious into his own historicized version of the *political* unconscious, he switches the emphasis from sexual to political repression—to how society forgets and hides from sight the ugly results of hierarchical domination. Referring to the eternal struggle between the oppressed and the oppressor, Jameson thus defines the political unconscious: "It is in detecting the traces of that uninterrupted narrative, in restoring to the surface of a text the repressed and buried reality of this fundamental history, that the doctrine of a political unconscious finds its function and necessity" (20). Since it is History, in its inevitable march toward Necessity, that has produced the individual as a fragmented chip off the old block of collectivity, it is still History that hurts. But whereas Jameson, with Freud, sees the individual and society as radically opposed, society *in its primitive, collective aspect* becomes associated now with pleasure, and individualization with pain. The moral telos underlying Jameson's criticism, then, is a collective, "Utopian" society, presumably one in which oppression and hence also the political unconscious have been eliminated (292).

Jameson's historicizing of Freud is a useful contextualization, for certainly the unconscious is affected by history and is composed of more than sexual repressions. It is what Jameson retains unaltered from Freud, however, that produces the limitations in his understanding of the psyche. In what follows, we argue that Jung's amendments to Freud's model of the psyche are improvements because they grant the unconscious an existence and a moral potential not totally derived from material circumstances.

From their few scattered references to Jung, it is clear that Jameson and his interpreters regard Jungian-based criticism as one of the worst offenders of the "psychologizing" or "ethical" kind. By "ethical," Jameson does not mean the moralizing or didactic criticism typical of the Victorian age, but that in which "notions of personal identity, myths of the reunification of the psyche, and the mirage of some Jungian 'self' or 'ego' stand in for the older themes of moral sensibility and ethical awareness . . ." (60). These various "liberal ideologies . . . all find their functional utility in the repression of the social and the historical, and in the perpetuation of some timeless and ahistorical view of human life and social relations."[15] "In its narrowest sense," Jameson claims, "ethical thought projects as permanent features of human 'experience,' and thus as a kind of 'wisdom' about personal life and interpersonal relations, what are in reality the historical and institutional specifics of a determinate type of group solidarity or class cohesion."[16] To challenge such interpretive systems, therefore, is "a political act of some productiveness."[17]

The name generally given to differentiate Jung's system from that of Freud is "depth psychology," an apt description, for Jung's conceptualization of the psyche is based upon layers of increasing depth or degrees of unconsciousness.[18] Jameson's objection to Jungian analyses (shared by Marxists in general) centers upon the bottom layer, what Jung has variously called the "collective unconscious," the "transpersonal unconscious," or the "objective psyche"—that dimension of the unconscious which is of a given, generally human character, rather than merely the result of personal or cultural repressions, and which he claims accounts for the phenomenon that certain symbolic motifs from dreams, myths, and legends repeat themselves all over the world.[19] The objective psyche should not be defined in terms of static *contents*, according to Jung, but in terms of *processes* known as "archetypes" or "primordial images"; these are not, as has often been interpreted, "inherited ideas," but innate *pathways*—that is, tendencies toward expression that are ingrained in the psyche. Although the *images* or symbols that give them form vary from culture to culture, the patterns underlying symbol formation in the psyche are everywhere the same.[20]

One typical ideological response to this argument counters that so-called universal symbols are created in response to common human experience. Everyone, so the argument goes, has a mother and a father, encounters the nurturing and destructive sides of nature, and lives through some form of seasonal change. From these and other common apprehensions, we generate the "archetypes" of the Mother, Rebirth, Spirit, and so on. Universal symbols, therefore, can be explained without recourse to ahistorical psychic processes, but simply as symbolic responses to shared human experience.[21] If, however, any common human experience is in large part determined by the particular historical conditions in which it occurs, then this ideological explanation will only hold for persons who live in the same material circumstances. For if we take historicity seriously, then the experience of the seasons, say, from within the social formation of feudalism will differ from that same experience within late capitalism. If these perceptual differences are not acknowledged, then the impact of history upon experience would be annulled. By contrast, the recurrence of some symbols at different periods of history, in societies manifesting different modes of production, and in locales so geographically removed from one another that social contact is extremely improbable, seems to justify the hypothesis that the symbols in question are transcultural.

Mythologists have gathered much evidence, of course, that supports this hypothesis in detail.[22] For example, humans have a tendency to express the potential wholeness of the self and its relationship to the world and the cosmos in a circular pattern enclosing a geometric shape, or *mandala*. But whereas this archetype may manifest itself in a crude drawing of a primitive tribe, it may materialize in a highly advanced technological culture as a flying saucer; in the tribe, the symbol points to the undifferentiated wholeness of the group, while in the technological culture, it represents the intuited *need* for unity that the fragmentation of the age has introduced.[23] Moreover, Joseph Campbell notes the striking, detailed similarity between the 4000-year-old meditational practice of *kundalini* yoga, experienced and represented pictorially as the uncoiling of a serpent along seven spinal centers known as *chakras*, and the Navajo ritual journey of the Pollen Path, a ceremony in which an initiate physically traverses the serpentine map of a sand drawing. Both rituals guide the initiate in a journey toward transcendent awareness, healing, or spiritual strength.[24] The appearance and persistence of these underlying archetypes in widely dispersed cultures with radically different modes of production illustrate both the essential connectedness among the cultures and their historically influenced difference. Archetypes cannot be expressed abstractly, but only in particular symbols. "When an archetypal motif is activated by experience in the social world, it is filled in with the contents present in the society," Ira Progoff explains. "The form that the [symbol] takes in any given culture, then, is the bridge between the universal and the historical; it is the point at which the archetype becomes particularized into its social manifestations."[25]

What Jung does, in effect, is to conceptualize the collective unconscious as a semi-autonomous mechanism pre-existing the development of consciousness.[26] This is no more "ideological" than are the equally universal claims that all physically unimpaired people will learn to walk and talk, that the human brain is predisposed to learn language at a particular period of maturation,[27] that complex psycho-motor processes unfold in a genetically programmed way, or that narrative is an *a priori* form of perception (a claim advanced by Jameson himself).[28] It is obviously the case that universals *may* erroneously be posited where there are none, and that this positing may be employed to justify hegemonic exploitation. But this does not mean that *all* stipulations of archetypal presence are likewise.

Jung's model of the psyche consists of more than the collective unconscious, of course. He also speaks of a "personal" or "subjective" unconscious, which is what Freud usually refers to when he speaks of the unconscious; it contains psychic contents that have been repressed from awareness, and also those drives and desires arising from the collective unconscious that have not yet reached consciousness. The personal unconscious is in a compensatory relationship with consciousness, in that it balances it and becomes particularly active when the person focuses too exclusively on the affairs of the ego.

Jung does not give it an explicit name, but it is possible to infer that a "cultural unconscious" exists at a parallel level with the personal unconscious, for he says that every culture has a certain "conscious outlook," and that this activates a compensatory movement at an unconscious level for the entire culture.[29] He argues, for example, that cultures develop certain psychological temperaments, or types, at the expense of repressing other potentialities. Modern Western cultures have developed *extraversion*—an

orientation to action and the outer object—to the great detriment of *introversion*—
an orientation to contemplation and the inner self. "It is characteristic of our present
extraverted sense of values," Jung notes, "that the word 'subjective' usually sounds like
a reproof; at all events the epithet 'merely subjective' is brandished like a weapon over
the head of anyone who is not boundlessly convinced of the absolute superiority of the
object."[30] Jung's comments about the impact of culture on the unconscious indicate,
contrary to Jameson's charge, that his view of human life and social relations is not
entirely "timeless and ahistorical."

Although Jung extends his notion of the personal unconscious to cultural life, he
has little to say about the psychic consequences of the repressions of class structure. It
is here, then, that Jameson's political unconscious repairs a deficiency in Jung. For if
the desires for revolution against inequitable economic conditions are repressed in
order to hide them from view, then surely this process must be accommodated within
any adequate conception of the cultural unconscious.

Our own view of the cultural unconscious includes, but transcends, the positions
of Jameson and Jung. Since it is composed not only of repressed societal contents, but
also of images that have risen from the collective unconscious,[31] it is the site of a
collision of psychic energies from two separate origins—the archetypes from the
collective unconscious and the repressed contradictions from oppressive social formations. It is often the expression of these clashing energies from the cultural unconscious
that impart symbolic power to rhetorically significant texts. The cultural unconscious
also includes repressed material that does not originate from *economic* relations. Jung
refers to one aspect of this, as we noted above, when he observes that the general
psychic orientation of Western culture is toward extraversion. Moreover, while it is still
a contested issue, many feminists argue that gender is a source of repression that
transcends particular socio-economic conditions and is endemic to a patriarchal world
view. The personal/cultural unconscious, then, is a large and varied construct consisting of emanations from the collective unconscious and repressions from many facets
of conscious life, and is often the psychic source of textual energies.

On the surface of the psyche, in Jung's conception, is the thinnest and most fragile
layer, that of "ego-consciousness," or the "ego-complex." The ego is consciousness of
personal identity that extends through time and space, and is capable of reflecting
about itself; it is the seeming originator of personal choices and the will which translates
decisions into goal-directed actions.[32] As the human agent clashes with the constraints
of a particular social order, the individual ego is formed by differentiating itself out of
the collective unconscious. Thus, like the personal/cultural unconscious, it is at least
partially constructed from social, historical forces. As Jung explains, "Our consciousness
does not create itself—it wells up from unknown depths. In childhood it awakens
gradually, and all through life it wakes each morning out of the depths of sleep from
an unconscious condition. It is like a child that is born daily out of the primordial
womb of the unconscious."[33] Consciousness does not, then, create the unconscious for
Jung; rather, it grows out of the collective unconscious, which is older and larger than
consciousness, which is compensatory to it, and which goes on functioning with or
without it.[34]

Although neither Jameson nor Jung is content to leave matters in the hands of
ego-consciousness, they differ radically concerning what to do about the problem of
the ego. As we have seen, Jameson, in his historicizing of Freud, regards the emergence
of the individual (or the "fully constituted subject") as an unfortunate residue of the
splintering of the group brought on by modes of production occurring after primitive

communism. Since the individual self is constituted by the ego as a correlative of societal repressions, and since such repressions would by definition disappear with the occurrence of a truly political revolution that abolished class society, then presumably the individual ego would also disappear as a distinct structure; that is, the individual would be reabsorbed back into the collective. This assumption leads Jameson to speculate on what a future "Utopian society" would be like: "For Marxism, indeed, only the emergence of a post-individualistic social world, only the reinvention of the collective and the associative, can concretely achieve the 'decentering' of the individual subject . . . ; only a new and original form of collective social life can overcome the isolation and monadic autonomy of the older bourgeois subjects in such a way that individual consciousness can be lived—and not merely theorized—as an 'effect of structure.' . . . ."[35]

If we juxtapose two phrases from this quotation, however, "new and original form of collective social life" and "reinvention of the collective and the associative," we can pinpoint a contradiction that underlies Jameson's program for social reform. For that which is *re*invented cannot be truly new and original. Furthermore, it is worth asking whether, once the individual ego has emerged, it can or should be reassimilated back into the collective, as if it never existed. The "individual" comes into being not only through modes of production, but also through *awareness of separation,* and once that knowledge has been attained, it is difficult to imagine how it could be lost. It is analogous to the expectation that an adult might climb back into the womb of protection and ignorance, or that our advanced technological society could "forget" its knowledge of how to build the bomb. In sum, the moral standard at the foundation of Jameson's view of criticism is transparently revisionist.

Jung's view of what to do about the individual seems more realistic. He acknowledges that the emergence of the ego, though necessary, is also a problem, because the ego has a tendency to overdevelop, to protect its own sovereignty through defenses that result in repression, and to devalue the life of the unconscious.[36] But the ego is not the end point of psychic maturation for Jung. Rather, Jung's "reintegrated self" depends upon an additional phase of psychic development, "individuation," which is really more a goal than an absolutely achievable destination.[37] This word carries the double meaning of "becoming an individual" and "becoming undivided." Whereas these two meanings would be incommensurable for Jameson, they are not for Jung. For becoming an individual implies developing *beyond* the ego stage, which is merely a way station on the path to full maturity. Individuation is an urge and a latent potential within every person, although it is by no means a predetermined end, and must be consciously sought in order to be effected. It entails a conscious recognition of the archetypes—a return to the primordial for the purpose of revitalization by the collective in order to achieve something truly new. Moreover, as Jung notes, individuation facilitates the development of a non-repressive collectivity. "As the individual is not just a single, separate being, but by his very existence presupposes a collective relationship, it follows that the process of individuation must lead to more intense and broader collective relationships and not isolation" (448).

The most important archetype in the individuation process is the Self, which is experienced as "a postulated encompassing personality characterized by individual wholeness and expressing a central guidance system directed toward conscious experience and fulfillment, a center which is not in consciousness and therefore is not identical with the center of consciousness."[38] The Self is not, like the ego, confined to time and space; it expresses itself in the form of nascent wholeness—both general, human wholeness and the unity of an individual life. It is represented in dreams and myths as an ideal personality, as God, or in images of oneness, wholeness, eternalness, and centeredness (216, 219, 236). Whereas the ego strives to preserve the *status quo* of the personality, the Self often wants change, and may threaten the established ego. Thus, psychological maturity demands a confrontation between the Self and the ego, in which the ego is not destroyed, but eventually decentered to make way for the Self as the ultimate guide to moral action (220). What is sought in individuation is a conscious Self-sense in which the ego is recognized as one part of a larger psychic totality. Jameson's equating of self and ego ("some Jungian 'self' or 'ego'"), as well as his implication that the reunification of the psyche means a consolidation of the ego, are serious misrepresentations of Jung's position.

By themselves, Jameson and Jung each offer only a partial ethical solution to the moral problem of the ego. For while Jung localizes the moral impetus in the archetypes, primarily the Self, Jameson positions his own utopian vision in the idealized social relationships arising from non-oppressive material conditions. But if one central ethical function of any adequate moral system is to liberate oppression, and if oppressions occur within the psyche as well as within the society, then any moral standard for criticism must address both domains. Moreover, as we have argued throughout this section, it will not do either to ignore the relevance of psychological processes to social action, or to argue that psychological liberation will occur as a result of material reform, because the former cannot be adequately understood as a corrupt form of the latter.

We offer the construct of *cultural individuation* as a provisional moral ideal which captures the central ethical commitments of both Jameson and Jung. It is beyond the scope of this paper to construct a detailed description of cultural individuation; indeed, at this point in history, it is difficult to offer much more than broad speculation. Within those constraints, however, we would posit that a culture moving toward individuation would struggle against oppression based upon economic class structure and other forms of hierarchic domination, and hence would progressively assimilate more and more of the cultural unconscious into awareness. Further, we suggest that the ego-consciousness of individuals would expand outward to encompass a social collectivity which includes others as part of the Self; individuals would retain, but re-contextualize, their separate senses of self within this greater whole. Finally, while still maintaining their uniqueness, separate cultures would expand their identities outward into a more global, even universal, consciousness.[39] In the sections which follow, we adopt "cultural individuation" as a moral ideal to guide the critic in making ethical judgments of rhetorical texts.

NARRATIVE TEXTS

Given an integrated view of the cultural psyche, we turn our attention to rhetorical texts. As in the previous section, we generate our position from the clash between Jameson and Jung. In this context, however, that tension manifests itself through the two theorists' different approaches to texts as narrative.

Narrative is a crucial construct for Jameson, not only because people make up stories about the world in order to understand it, but because the world comes to people in the shape of stories. Narrative is not a literary form for Jameson, but an epistemological category like the Kantian concepts of space and time, "a contentless form that our perception imposes on the raw flux of reality, giving it, even as we perceive, the comprehensible order we call experience."[40] History, or "the Real," is not itself a narrative, but an "absent cause" which is inaccessible to the critic except in textual form—that is, its narrativization in the political unconscious.[41] Jameson looks at narrative texts similarly to the way that Freud looks at dreams and other manifestations of the unconscious, and to the way that Claude Lévi-Strauss looks at myths and cultural rituals. The analogy at work is: cultural narratives are to the political unconscious what dreams are to the personal unconscious. Jung relies on a similar analogy, considering mythology to be "the dream of the race,"[42] which expresses activity of the collective and personal/cultural unconscious.

Libidinal energy is expressed in dreams as unconscious wish fulfillment, according to Freud. Such libidinal wishes are unacceptable to the dreamer's ego because the ego has assimilated society's Reality Principle in contradistinction to the infantile Pleasure Principle. Therefore, dreams both express the wish and censor it simultaneously; in *dream-work*, the wish is distorted so as not to disturb sleep. "The dream as remembered is not the real thing at all," Freud writes, "but a *distorted substitute* which, by calling up other substitute-ideas, provides us with a means of approaching the thought proper, of bringing into consciousness the unconscious thoughts underlying the dream."[43] In order to interpret a dream correctly, the individual must search for the *latent content* behind the confusing, distorted symbolism of the *manifest content*. Similarly, when Lévi-Strauss interprets a myth or ritual, he looks for the *deep structure* beneath the *surface structure*; the myth always expresses and simultaneously resolves some contradiction, such as the "fact" of hierarchy in a society of equals, which is unconscious to the culture, and which the myth helps to keep in the unconscious.[44]

Narrative always demands interpretation, according to Jameson, because it has something like the distinction between manifest and latent meaning written into it. Narrative is "normal"—it belongs to everyday life as lived on the social surface—but is at the same time "abnormal"—it represses an intolerable reality underneath it; it both reveals and hides, and thus has the same doubleness that dreams have for Freud. What narrative reveals is the social and political equivalent of the repressed instinctuality of Freud's unconscious, or the impulse to revolution that would destroy the class structure and replace it with a collective unity. But since such wishes are intolerable both to the bourgeoisie and to the oppressed, they must also be kept hidden. Jameson argues, then, that "the effectively ideological [narrative] is also, at the same time, necessarily Utopian."[45] The text simultaneously represents and distorts the desire for the collective.[46]

Narrative employs what Jameson terms a "strategy of containment," a way of achieving coherence by shutting out the truth about History.[47] It is a symbolic, imaginary solution to an objective, historical problem—the desire for revolution, coupled with the fact that it has not occurred (118). Jameson explains how such a strategy may work as "a process of compensatory exchange" in mass media and culture: the viewer is offered specific gratifications—visions of collective life, of preternatural sexual gratification—in return for his or her consent to passivity. Otherwise dangerous and protopolitical impulses are first awakened, and then managed, defused, and offered spurious satisfactions through "a complex strategy of rhetorical persuasion in which substantial incentives are offered for ideological adherence" (287). Although narratives do express the upward movement of libido, they are ultimately repressive because libidinal wishes are not fulfilled, but compensated, displaced, and dissipated.

Jameson's strategy of containment articulates an important and pervasive rhetorical function of narrative texts. Though the concept is a significant contribution, however, it is not without problems. For example, there seems to be no reason why the functions of unrepression, projection, and re-repression must operate in the invariant pattern Jameson formalizes in his overall strategy. Could a narrative not lift a repression without projecting it? Similarly, it seems unlikely that re-repression is the final function of all narratives. As a case in point, films like *The China Syndrome* (1979) and *Silkwood* (1983) raised cultural repressions concerning the dangers of nuclear energy, but did not resolve those lifted repressions symbolically within their narrative structures; rather, films like these and other related narrative artifacts functioned rhetorically to precipitate genuine political action.[48] Finally, the threefold narrative functions that comprise Jameson's strategy of containment do not exhaust the rhetorical possibilities of narrative texts. If the limitations in Jameson's view of narrative derive from restrictions in Freud's understanding of dreams, then perhaps we can uncover other functions of narrative from Jung's alternative position on dreams.

Although Jung shares with Freud the assumption that a dream relates a message which is unknown to the dreamer, his notions of how that message is communicated are radically different. A dream does not censor or distort; rather, it is "the expression of an involuntary psychic process not controlled by the conscious outlook. It presents the subjective state as it really is."[49] Emanating from either or both levels of the unconscious, dreams are complex admixtures of archetypal and cultural elements. But they do not hide, lie, or exclusively express wishes; they reveal the situation of the dreamer at a given point in his or her life. The reason that dreams may seem to distort is that they communicate in the prerational imagery of the unconscious, which is not readily comprehended by the linguistically-attuned ego-complex. Dreams invite interpretation so that the dreamer might better understand him- or herself, but they do not demand *unmasking*.

Jung's extended model of the psyche, as well as his more positive interpretation of dreams, alerts him to a function of narrative that Jameson's Freudian-based system disallows. Arguing against Freud's claim that art can be explained as the neurotic symptoms of the artist, Jung counters that some art is based on a vision which "is not something derived or secondary, and it is not a symptom of something else. It is true symbolic expression—that is, the expression of something existent in its own right, but imperfectly known. [It] may not be conjured away" (161–162). Such "visionary art" *reveals* nonrepressed material from the collective unconscious, and is compensatory to consciousness (152–172). Narratives of this sort, we would agree, reveal archetypal images that the culture needs in order to produce new solutions to existing problems, and in order to advance past its present stage of ego-consciousness. When one tries to dismiss the truly visionary, one is guilty of the opposite charge that Marxists make against "ethicists" such as Jung; that is, one politicizes the universal, thereby refusing, as Jung's associate Carl Kerenyi puts it, to "be bold enough to take the things of the spirit spiritually"; one reduces the psychological to the merely material.[50]

Thus far we have isolated two rhetorical operations of narrative: Jameson sets forth the complex ways narrative texts work ideologically to preserve the political *status quo*, and Jung demonstrates how other narrative structures reveal to consciousness knowledge from the collective unconscious that is vital to societal growth. While containment and revelation are significant aspects of narration, they still do not completely encompass the rhetorical dimensions of narrative. And while a project of the present scope cannot dispose of all the possibilities, in what follows, we articulate several additional functions, and conclude by discussing the moral imperative entailed in the view of narration that grows out of our model of the cultural psyche.

Jameson's strategy of containment describes the operation whereby narrative texts repress knowledge that was previously repressed, but temporarily elevated to consciousness within the text. But clearly, a narrative could serve to erase a memory of something which has not been repressed. For example, Harry Haines demonstrates how administrative powers "instructed" the American people to forget the Vietnam War. For most people, except the combat veterans, this administrative rhetoric succeeded. Here is a clear case where narrative functions to *repress* previously unrepressed materials.[51]

Narratives can also *inhibit* the revelation of archetypes. Since material from the collective unconscious is compensatory to an overemphasis on consciousness, the cultural ego often has a large stake in keeping it from emerging, for that which is powerful rarely wants to relinquish control; and, as we have argued above, the conscious recognition of archetypes implies cultural change. For example, the feminine archetype often imagined as the Great Goddess has been inhibited for centuries by the dominance of male archetypes in Western cultures, and has only recently begun to reemerge.[52]

Jameson obviously adopts "displacement" (metonymy), one of Freud's rules of transformation by which latent thoughts become manifest symbols, when he describes the projection of real historical problems onto the narrative symbols of the text. But it seems that narratives could also employ Freud's "condensation" (metaphor), for they may also *condense* two or more symbols into a single image.[53] Thus, two symbols from different levels of the unconscious sometimes merge into a hybridized image that fuses and intensifies the meanings of both. In the 1962 film *The Manchurian Candidate*, for instance, we argued that our largely repressed fears of technological manipulation (depicted as Communist brainwashing) from the personal/cultural unconscious and even more deeply repressed fears of the Terrible Mother archetype from the collective unconscious are both projected from their respective levels in the unconscious and condensed into the same narrative vehicle—namely, the personage of Eleanor Iselin—the mother of the film's tragic hero/victim.[54] Without knowledge of this condensation function, the unusual power and density of many narrative symbols cannot be explained.

Finally, reasoning from the position we have developed thus far, cultural narratives perform *moral*, as well as rhetorical, functions. Jameson would certainly not disagree, for he evaluates narrative texts in relation to his own moral Utopia—the return to the pre-differentiated societal collectivity. However, because the historical problem is resolved only within the boundaries of the symbolic text, this "praxis" substitutes for action in the world of the Real, and thus ultimately reaffirms the inequalities of class society. For Jameson, all narratives are tainted by the sin of political pacification; they cannot be *morally* good, it seems, but only *rhetorically* effective—and this latter to the extent that they perform the strategy of containment with subtlety and/or dexterity.

In our view, by contrast, narratives may implicitly advocate any number of courses of moral action in relation to the end point of cultural individuation. Those that imply a movement toward individuation would be judged as morally superior to those that imply a movement away from it.[55] Such advocacy, of course, is often subtle, ambiguous, or contradictory. And one moral function might be simply to reveal accurately the relationship between the current state of the psyche and its potential, and in so doing, to provide the culture with a self-diagnosis, which the society can then decide whether and how to act upon. Although our framework does not dictate that the meaning of any text is univocal, or that the application of this perspective exhausts its meaning, it does allow for a rich diversity of moral judgment.

THE CRITIC AS MORAL AGENT

Our final task is to suggest how the critic can function as a moral agent given a synthetic view of the psyche and narrative texts. As we have noted throughout, both Jameson and Jung see their work as morally significant. Thus, when Jameson casts his own criticism as a political act insofar as it reveals how texts repress the reality of social oppression, he implies that his work is moral. And for Jung, facilitating individuation through dream or myth analysis entails a moral outlook because it helps persons to withdraw projections, become conscious of the activity of the archetypes in one's life, and allow ego-consciousness to give way to the Self archetype as a guide for ethical action.[56] The moral dimensions in the work of Jameson and Jung are embedded within the metaphor of "health," so that health/morality is contrasted with illness/immorality of the patient/culture.[57] In this section we build a case for the critic as moral agent from the different ways that Jameson and Jung understand the health metaphor of critic as therapist to the body politic. We begin by examining the critical horizons or contexts within which the critic may analyze the culture through the texts it produces, and then consider the capacity of the critic to advocate cultural change through the analysis of texts. We end by commenting on the experiential relationship between the critic and the text.

In Jameson's view, narratives are to be subjected to what William Dowling calls "symptomatic analysis," which is "a mode of interpretation that reveals (1) the specific ways in which they deny or repress History, and (2) what, once brought up out of the nether darkness into the light of rational scrutiny, the History thus denied or repressed looks like."[58] This sort of symptomatic analysis unfolds against three "concentric frameworks" or "semantic horizons," which "mark a widening out of the sense of the social ground of a text."[59] Considering narrative as a *symbolic act*, Jameson places it within its immediate political context, regarding the text as itself a rewriting of a prior historical or ideological subtext. The text, "as though for the first time, brings into being that very situation to which it is also, at one and the same time, a reaction" (82). The text cannot directly address the real social contradiction, the "absent cause," which can only be resolved through social *praxis*; rather, it generates a subtext which takes the form of an *aporia* or *antinomy*—the "logical scandal or double bind" that presents itself to the "purely contemplative mind" as unsolvable, and thus is resolved within the narrative itself (82–83).

In the second horizon, Jameson looks at the *ideologeme* as the minimal conceptual unit, or "narrative paradigm," within which the tension and struggle between social classes takes place; here, he focuses on the text as *parole* to the *langue* of class discourse. Following Mikhail Bakhtin, Jameson argues that class discourse should be interpreted dialogically—as a clash in which the dominant class suppresses oppositional voices. It is the critic's job to reconstruct these voices from dispersed fragments, which typically exist in "popular cultures" such as folk songs, fairy tales, local festivals, and occult systems of belief, and to point out the ways in which the dominant ideology co-opts or universalizes such oppositional forces. The critic will also note that social conflicts between classes are generally carried on within shared communicative codes, such as kinship, religion, or politics (84–88).

In the third and final horizon, the *ideology of form*, Jameson views the text against "history now conceived in its vastest sense of the sequence of modes of production and the succession and destiny of the various human social formations, from prehistoric life to whatever far future history has in store for us" (75). History is viewed diachronically as a series of modes of production, but also synchronically as the conflict between modes which overlap and compete with each other in the same chronological era. Thus, on this level, Jameson considers "cultural revolutions," not as so-called "transitional" periods during which one social formation is replaced by another, but as perpetual struggles between social formations, which sometimes come to the fore in moments of transition. In Jameson's own critical analyses, he notes how the contradictions of history intensify with each successive mode of production, and how, consequently, narratives become ever more adept at resolving them on the imaginary, symbolic level.

As we have argued throughout, both Jameson's strengths and his limitations as a critic stem from his psychological constructs which he derives exclusively from an outward focus upon History. His three horizons for the analysis of a narrative text, for example, place the discourse within its *social* ground, but not within its *psychological* ground of interior reality; consequently, Jameson has much to say about the repressions of society, but little to say about symbols originating in the psyche. In contrast, whereas Jameson turns outward to find his critical contexts, Jung characteristically turns inward. Jung is as interested in the way myths reveal the unconscious as he is in dreams; thus, he often acts as a *de facto* narrative critic. However, since he is primarily a psychologist and not a literary critic, his own critical method is less explicit than Jameson's and must be reconstructed from his scattered comments on method, as well as from his practice—the analysis of myths and dreams.

Although he does not specify formal semantic horizons, Jung's three layers of the psyche (collective unconscious, personal/cultural unconscious, ego-consciousness) are in some ways internal analogues to Jameson's, for they too serve as "contextual" categories of analysis. And where Jameson views narrative within one of three historical horizons, Jung sees the symbols of a dream or myth within the internal ground of one or more of these levels. Moreover, just as Jameson finds it necessary to reconstruct the oppositional voices of the class struggle (the ideologeme) from dispersed fragments, Jung also deems it important to study dreams in a series in order to recover the narrative history of a person's life; in fact, Jung warns that a single dream taken in isolation may be highly misleading.[60] As the Jungian analyst Edward Whitmont explains, "The myth of one's life does not ordinarily appear in a single installment. There is a 'to-be-continued' element and no single dream or situation is *the* myth. Each dream sees the myth from a new angle. As we go on the story unfolds and may even change direction. The myth for each individual is to be intuited from the total tableau as it reveals itself in time and space."[61]

According to the argument developed thus far, a set of contexts for criticism must accommodate both psychological and material phenomena; thus, we must move beyond the singular frameworks of both Jameson and Jung. We propose three critical horizons that combine Jung's insights concerning psychological reality with Jameson's ideas on the historical struggle. On the level of the *text*, the critic interprets symbols in narrative discourses that function to repress, reveal, inhibit, and/or condense, etc., unconscious and/or societal contents. Given that texts function rhetorically in complex combinations, it is important to differentiate the functions at this level so as to avoid either politicizing the universal (e.g., interpreting *all* symbolic functions as repressive) or universalizing the political (e.g., interpreting *all* symbolic functions as archetypally revealing).

When a story is part of a greater narrative of mythic proportions, the apparent rhetorical strategy of a single text often gives way to a more basic strategy which can only be apprehended by embedding the text within a second frame of reference, which we call the *cultural myth*.[62] A cultural myth is a narrative whole which the critic reconstructs from singular texts often separated in time and genre but tied together by a single, unifying theme. The idea of a cultural myth is indebted to Jameson's notion that an ideologeme is critically reconstructed by piecing together fragments in order to determine an oppositional voice (although we do not limit our construct to oppositional texts), and to Jung's dictum that dreams should not be interpreted in isolation from one another. For example, as a singular film, *Rocky IV* appears to be little more than a banal example of Jameson's strategy of containment insofar as contradictions of American capitalism are raised, projected onto the Russian prize-fighter, Ivan Drago, and then symbolically resolved (re-repressed) when Rocky (American) defeats Drago (Russia) in a battle of single-combat warriors. But when seen as an early installment of a cultural myth that raises our collective fears of technology (*Blade Runner* and *The Terminator* being later enactments), this same film may be read as revealing, albeit in an unsophisticated form, these repressed fears.[63]

To determine the moral dimension of texts, either in isolation or as part of a cultural myth, the critic needs an ethical standard, which, in turn, suggests a third horizon we call the *master myth*. The master myth is the narrative of human evolution, including both material modes of production and psychological modes of consciousness. The end point of the master myth is cultural individuation—the ideal we posited earlier—in which economic domination would cease, the culture would become more aware of its unconscious, and the separate ego-consciousness of individuals and cultures would expand to encompass a sense of community.[64] The positing of a Utopian end for human development, however hypothetical and provisional, is necessary if the critic is to render moral judgment as an integral part of critical practice, for such a judgment requires some comparison between what is and what should be. The above-mentioned cultural myth that expresses our fears of technology, for example, evokes a positive moral judgment when seen in relation to the master myth of cultural individuation, for it reveals (without re-repressing) an unconscious compensation for the dominant cultural outlook of "progress" that extols only the beneficial, and not the oppressive, effects of technology on human beings.

Given these critical horizons, we derive our position on the critic as agent of moral change from the contrasts between Jameson's and Jung's understanding of the therapeutic metaphor. As we have seen, Jameson sees all class society as ill (immoral) and texts as placebos that perpetuate the maladies by offering the illusions of a cure. Thus, for Jameson, the task of the morally responsible critic is limited to diagnosing the seemingly infinite array of strategies with which the cultural patient tries, unsuccessfully, to ward off the illness or pretend it is not sick. Jameson himself denies the critic a role in any possible "cure":

> Even the Freudian model of the unconscious, which has been exemplary in our own proposal of a properly political unconscious here, is everywhere subverted by the neo-Freudian nostalgia for some ultimate moment of *cure*, in which the dynamics of the unconscious proper rise to the light of day and of consciousness and are somehow "integrated" in an active lucidity about ourselves and the determinations of our desires and our behavior. But the cure in that sense is a myth, as is the equivalent mirage within a Marxian ideological analysis: namely, the vision of a moment in which the individual subject would be somehow fully conscious of his or her determination by class and would be able to square the circle of ideological conditioning by sheer lucidity and the taking of thought.[65]

Consciousness cannot effect a cure, according to Jameson, because it is one more imaginary substitute for the reconstruction of an *actual* collective unity.

There are at least two ironies underlying the fact that Jameson positions himself as a sort of moral psychoanalyst, and yet refuses a curative role for the critic. The most obvious is that his entire project relies upon a model of consciousness—in fact, is concerned with penetrating the darkness of our political unconscious—and yet he denies that there is any efficacy in becoming more conscious. But what is the point of shedding light on our lack of consciousness if the achievement of such lucidity is itself a ruse, an *illusion* of cure? Not even Freud, from whom Jameson draws so heavily, denies the importance of becoming conscious of repressed processes; to do so would have undercut the practical utility of psychoanalysis. A second irony arises when Jameson, as a Marxist, debunks consciousness as a cure because it is another remnant of his frequent target, that of "psychologizing" or "ethical" criticism. Psychologizing is impotent, Jameson claims, because it substitutes an illusive "integration of the psyche" for *action* in the world of the Real. Presumably, action occurs only within the collective (which he values) and psychologizing only within the individual (which he vilifies). And yet, Jameson so constricts himself, as the critic/therapist, that his criticism can only *act* to show us the impossibility of *action*.[66] His position implies a radical split between knowing and doing, which, along with the privileging of the latter, seems to reaffirm the aforementioned Western, and particularly American, penchant for external action over internal contemplation.

Unlike Jameson, Jung does not conceive of psychological analysis as restricted to the sick or neurotic client; rather, it is a conversational method designed to increase conscious awareness in order to instigate personal transformation in *any* individual—whether mentally unhealthy or "normal."[67] Although he does consider contemporary Western cultures to be suffering from a sort of illness brought on by dissociation of the ego from the unconscious,[68] myths do not only *symptomize* the modern malaise, but often compensate or complete it by *symbolizing* the depths of the unconscious. They may also parallel the conscious attitude, or even anticipate the future in a prospective or oracular form.[69] Whereas Jameson's form of criticism is "symptomatic," therefore, Jung's is best termed "symbolic," for the symbols of myth and dream, whether they represent personal or cultural neurosis or the desire for individuation, contain the resources for renewal and transformation.

In our view, Jung's symbolic approach to criticism is preferable to Jameson's symptomatic alternative because it does not assume beforehand that all narrative texts indicate and sustain cultural infirmity. A narrative *may* symptomize illness and/or function to maintain it, but because it may contain material from the depths of the psyche, it may also be palliative. Jung avoids the disjunction between "practice" and "cure" that threatens to render Jameson's criticism impotent; consciousness is not a *substitute* for action, but a *precursor*. Permeating Jung's entire system is the conviction that effective moral action depends upon consciousness—indeed, that action without consciousness is often the root of evil. In sum, whereas Jameson endorses action in the world of the Real and denies the efficacy of consciousness, Jung endorses the efficacy of consciousness in guiding action in the world of the Real.

We have been working toward articulating the moral implications of viewing the critic as therapist to the body politic. In so doing, we have claimed that the critic has a responsibility not only to diagnose, but also to assist the culture in understanding its options. We are not claiming, of course, that any critic can single-handedly effect a "cure" of cultural disorders as serious as those brought about by the domination of the egoic mode of consciousness and the capitalistic mode of production. We do believe, however, that our perspective preserves a role for *praxis* as well as diagnosis, both for cultural narratives and for the critics who interpret them.

In the therapeutic practices of both Freud and Jung, the relationship between analyst and analysant is a crucial element affecting any practical change that is to occur. To extend the therapeutic metaphor, we now consider the relationship between critic and text, which is also implicitly a relationship between critic and culture (or readers), since the text is symptomatic or symbolic of the culture that produces it. Reasoning from the therapeutic system that informs the work of Jameson and Jung on the psyche and narrative, we may ask how the critic personally experiences the text.[70]

The Freudian psychoanalyst attempts to produce a kind of talking shock treatment when dealing with a patient. This is necessary because the patient inevitably resists the conscious recognition of repressions and counters the analyst's suggestions in that regard with denials and evasions. The analyst uses this recalcitrance on the part of the patient as further evidence of the patient's illness. The general psychoanalytic goal is to break through the patient's defenses, thereby convincing him or her both of the presence of the illness and of the changes that would bring about a cure.[71] Adopting this general approach (as modified by his Marxist commitments and his denial that any cure is possible), Jameson tends to see the culture as sick and its narrative texts as attempts to hide that sickness. Thus he assumes an agonistic, power relationship with the texts he critiques, practicing what Paul Ricoeur calls "the hermeneutics of suspicion."[72] Dowling explains Jameson's complex posture as "style as enactment: a way of writing that *shows* as well as *tells* what it is trying to get across." In Jameson's view, Dowling explains, "The plain style is the limpid style of bourgeois ideology where there is no need for obscurity because all truths are known in advance"; a genuinely Marxist style, then, produces a sense of "'dialectical shock,' that is, the price of its intelligibility again and again forces the reader out of customary and comfortable positions and into painful confrontations with unsuspected truths."[73] Jameson's adversarial encounter with the text thus extends to his relationship with the reader.

The Jungian practice has less to do with shock treatment than with listening and conversing.[74] As Whitmont explains, the analyst strives for an "I–Thou" connection with the client: "The therapeutic relationship becomes an existential encounter, and indeed Jung felt that if any change is to occur at all it must touch and affect both participants" (296). Jung's reason for doing away with Freud's psychoanalytic couch was that it made the analytic relationship too objective and detached. "He considered a direct, personal encounter to be absolutely unavoidable and essential. The absence of the couch is one expression of an unpremediated and unprejudiced affirmation of the unfolding reality of the other, in whatever fashion he happened to present himself" (297). Jung also advised the beginning therapist to "'learn the best, know the best—and then forget everything when you face the patient'"—that is, to keep an open mind, throw out concepts from the Jungian corpus that do not fit, and adopt any from other systems that do (296–297).

Jung's style of psychotherapy suggests a far different relationship between critic and text than is implied by Freud and adopted by Jameson, and we think his general approach is more productive of critical insight. If the text is not automatically assumed to mask some cultural illness, then it does not necessarily require a critical inquisition to force it to disclose its secrets. Rather, it invites an attitude of *caring* for the text as one would care for a valued other.[75] Progoff provides a clue as to what such an attitude would entail:

[T]he intellect can contribute only a small part of the knowledge necessary for understanding the material which Jung studies. It must be experienced more comprehensively by the personality as a whole, at least partially lived through and validated existentially, before it can be thoroughly grasped on a conscious level.[76]

It is a question of a quality of feeling for the nature of human beings, the depth and magnitude of the person. . . . And one proceeds from there whether it be in the interpretation of the dream life of individuals or the quasi-conscious life of societies. . . . Intellectual preparation by itself is by no means sufficient (255).

A personal relationship of respect, of course, does not demand compliant subservience. To the extent that a conversational partner is duplicitous, a person is rightly suspicious, and Jameson's lessons are valuable when a text hides or distorts its hidden truths. But we would suggest that such suspicions be subordinated to a more receptive pose in which the critic *listens* to what texts have to say. Such a stance requires experiencing narratives "by the personality as a whole," living with them on an unconscious as well as a conscious level, and then attempting to communicate something of the "quality of feeling for the nature of human beings" contained in them to one's audience.

CONCLUSION

By offering a framework for rhetorical criticism that integrates a concern for external, economic relations with internal, psychological realities, we have attempted to redress an imbalance that currently favors the former over the latter. In constructing this perspective, we have argued that moral values may emanate from inner, as well as outer, ideals. Obviously, an interest in values is not new to rhetorical criticism. Since Edwin Black's seminal 1965 critique of neo-Aristotelianism as monolithic and amoral,[77] rhetorical critics have considered the relevance of moral judgment to their work. Although they are not the only ones to take up the call to moral responsibility,[78] ideologically-oriented critics have produced the most substantive and coherent body of value-laden criticism to date, perhaps owing partially to Philip Wander and Steven Jenkins' influential essay on criticism and values in 1972, as well as to a series of responses in later years.[79] These contributions are a vital sign that the field has broken irrevocably from the sterile restrictions of "academic objectivity." As we have attempted to demonstrate here, however, the ideological perspective cannot by itself generate a *complete* set of moral standards for the critical act. Indeed, if the ideological approach is allowed, through the default of alternative voices, to coopt the moral territory as exclusively its own, rhetorical criticism will be impoverished by what it ignores—namely, the role of the interior world of the psyche in the visualization of a cultural ideal. The liberation of the material person becomes the oppression of the soul.

Notes

1. James Carey, "Mass Communication Research and Cultural Studies: An American View," in J. Curran, M. Gurevitch, and J. Woollacott, eds., *Mass Communication and Society* (Beverly Hills, CA: Sage, 1979), 410.

2. Michael Calvin McGee, "The Ideograph: A Link Between Rhetoric and Ideology," *Quarterly Journal of Speech* 66 (1980): 1–2 (reprinted in this volume).

3. Farrell Corcoran, "Television as Ideological Apparatus: The Power and the Pleasure," *Critical Studies in Mass Communication* 1 (1984): 131–145.

4. See, for example, Philip Wander and Steven Jenkins, "Rhetoric, Society, and the Critical Response," *Quarterly Journal of Speech* 58 (1972): 441–450; Michael C. McGee, "In Search of 'the People': A Rhetorical Alternative," *Quarterly Journal of Speech* 61 (1975): 235–249; Lawrence Grossberg, "Marxist Dialectics and Rhetorical Criticism," *Quarterly Journal of Speech* 65 (1979): 235–249; McGee, "The Ideograph"; Philip Wander, "Cultural Criticism," in Dan Nimmo and K. Sanders, eds., *Handbook of Political Communication* (Beverly Hills, CA: Sage, 1981), 497–528; Philip Wander, "The Ideological Turn in Modern Criticism," *Central States Speech Journal* 34 (1983): 1–18; Samuel L. Becker, "Marxist Approaches to Media Studies: The British Experience," *Critical Studies in Mass Communication* 1 (1984): 66–80; Lawrence Grossberg, "Strategies of Marxist Cultural Interpretation," *Critical Studies in Mass Communication* 1 (1984): 392–421; Cary Nelson and Lawrence Grossberg, eds., *Marxism and the Interpretation of Culture* (Urbana: University of Illinois Press, 1988); and Raymie E. McKerrow, "Critical Rhetoric: Theory and *Praxis*," *Communication Monographs* 56 (1989): 91–111 (reprinted in this volume).

5. James F. Klumpp and Thomas A. Hollihan, "Rhetorical Criticism as Moral Action," *Quarterly Journal of Speech* 75 (1989): 84–97.

6. Fredric Jameson, *The Political Unconscious: Narrative as a Socially Symbolic Act* (Ithaca, NY: Cornell University Press, 1981), 62–68.

7. Louis Althusser, "Ideology and Ideological State Apparatuses," in *Lenin and Philosophy and Other Essays*, trans. B. Brewster (New York: Monthly Review Press,1971), 127–186. Major spokespersons who rely on Freud to reveal the ideological struggles within language include Julia Kristeva, *Powers of Horror: An Essay on Abjection*, trans. Leon S. Roudiez (New York: Columbia University Press, 1982), *Revolution in Poetic Language*, trans. Margaret Waller (New York: Columbia University Press, 1984), and *About Chinese Women*, trans. Anita Barrows (New York: Marion Boyars, 1986); and Jacques Lacan, *Ecrits: A Selection*, trans. Alan Sheridan (New York: W. W. Norton, 1977), and *The Four Fundamental Concepts of Psycho-Analysis*, trans. Alan Sheridan (New York: W. W. Norton, 1981).

8. We focus primarily on *The Political Unconscious* because this work is Jameson's major theoretical statement to date on the political unconscious and narrative. Other major works by Jameson include *Marxism and Form* (Princeton, NJ: Princeton University Press, 1971), *The Prison-House of Language* (Princeton, NJ: Princeton University Press, 1972), and *Fables of Aggression: Wyndham Lewis, The Modernist as Fascist* (Berkeley and Los Angeles: University of California Press, 1979). Collected essays appear in Fredric Jameson, *The Ideologies of Theory: Essays 1971–1986, Vol. 1: Situations of Theory* (Minneapolis: University of Minnesota Press, 1988), and *The Ideologies of Theory: Essays 1971–1986, Vol. 2: Syntax of History* (Minneapolis: University of Minnesota Press, 1988). For comments on Jameson's importance, see William C. Dowling, *Jameson, Althusser, Marx: An Introduction to* The Political Unconscious (Ithaca, NY: Cornell University Press, 1984), 9; Hayden White and Jonathan Culler, cited on back cover of Jameson, *The Political Unconscious*; Peter Fitting, "Futurecop: The Neutralization of Revolt in *Blade Runner*," *Science-Fiction Studies* 14 (1987): 340–354.

9. Jameson, *The Political Unconscious*, 60.

10. Sigmund Freud, *A General Introduction to Psycho-Analysis*, trans. Joan Riviere (New York: Pocket Books, 1952), 348–366.

11. In addition to the ego and the id, of course, Freud also identified the "super-ego" as an objectified agency which functions as the ego's conscience. The super-ego is only partly conscious, but is allied with the Reality Principle, since it judges libidinal drives. Thus, Freud's model of the psyche is essentially bipartite. See Sigmund Freud, *New Introductory Lectures on Psychoanalysis*, trans. James Strachey (New York: W. W. Norton, 1964), 59–60, 73–79. Freud also entertained the idea of a collective unconscious or archaic mental heritage, which he employed, for example, in his study of totemism and of fixed symbols; see Sigmund Freud, *Totem and Taboo*,

trans. James Strachey (New York: W. W. Norton, 1950), 157; and J. A. C. Brown, *Freud and the Post-Freudians* (New York: Penguin, 1961), 112–113. However, his concept of a collective unconscious was not developed into a full-fledged theory of archetypes, as in Jung, and played little or no part in his practice of psychotherapy; see Brown, *Freud*, 46, and Peter Gay, *Freud: A Life for Our Time* (New York: W. W. Norton, 1988), 238.

12. Jameson, *The Political Unconscious*, 102.

13. Dowling, *Jameson, Althusser, Marx*, 32–33.

14. Jameson, *The Political Unconscious*, 64–65.

15. Fredric Jameson, "Interview with F. Jameson," *Diacritics* 12 (1982): 73; see also *The Ideologies of Theory*, 126–128.

16. Jameson, *The Political Unconscious*, 59.

17. Jameson, "Interview," 73.

18. This discussion of layers of the psyche is drawn from Progoff, *Jung's Psychology*, 55–57; see also C. G. Jung, *Two Essays on Analytical Psychology*, 2d. ed., Bollingen Foundation Series, trans. R. F. C. Hull (New York: Pantheon Books, 1966), 64–79, 127–138.

19. Edward C. Whitmont, *The Symbolic Quest: Basic Concepts of Analytical Psychology* (Princeton, NJ: Princeton University Press, 1978), 41–42. Whitmont explains that Jung used the term "objective psyche" in his later writings in order to avoid the seeming advocacy of a mass psyche.

20. Progoff, *Jung's Psychology*, 59.

21. Although she is not writing from an explicitly ideological framework, Estella Lauter clarifies this point of view in *Women as Mythmakers: Poetry and Visual Art by Twentieth-Century Women* (Bloomington: Indiana University Press, 1984), 208.

22. A classic work is James George Frazer, *The Golden Bough*, 12 vols. (New York: Macmillan, 1922). A more recent source is Joseph Campbell's four-volume work, *The Masks of God: Primitive Mythology*, *The Masks of God: Oriental Mythology*, *The Masks of God: Occidental Mythology*, and *The Masks of God: Creative Mythology* (New York: Penguin Books, 1976).

23. C. G. Jung, *Flying Saucers: A Modern Myth of Things Seen in the Skies*, trans. R. F. C. Hull (Princeton, NJ: Princeton University Press, 1978).

24. Joseph Campbell, *The Inner Reaches of Outer Space: Metaphor as Myth and as Religion* (New York: Alfred Van Der Marck Editions, 1986), 63–100. He also notes many other examples of similar archetypal phenomena in different cultural settings.

25. Progoff, *Jung's Psychology*, 71.

26. For an attempt to show how Jung's archetypes can command support from various movements in ethology and neurobiology, see Anthony Stevens, *Archetypes: A Natural History of the Self* (New York: William Morrow, 1982).

27. See, e.g., Emmon Bach and Robert T. Harms, eds., *Universals in Linguistic Theory* (New York: Holt, Rinehart and Winston, Inc., 1968).

28. Dowling, *Jameson, Althusser, Marx*, 95.

29. C. G. Jung, *The Spirit in Man, Art, and Literature*, trans. R. F. C. Hull (Princeton, NJ: Princeton University Press, 1966), 98.

30. C. G. Jung, *Psychological Types*, a revision by R. F. C. Hull of the trans. by H. G. Baynes, Bollingen Series XX (Princeton, NJ: Princeton University Press, 1976), 375.

31. Progoff, *Jung's Psychology*, 56.

32. Jung, *Psychological Types*, 425; Whitmont, *Symbolic Quest*, 232.

33. C. G. Jung, *Psychology and Religion: West and East*, 2d. ed., trans. R. F. C. Hull, Bollingen Series XX (Princeton, NJ: Princeton University Press, 1969), 569–570.

34. Whitmont, *Symbolic Quest*, 50.

35. Jameson, *The Political Unconscious*, 125.

36. Whitmont, *Symbolic Quest*, 250–264.

37. Jung, *Psychological Types*, 448–450.

38. Whitmont, *Symbolic Quest*, 219. Jung typically indicated the difference between "ego" and the "Self" archetype as "self" vs. "Self."

39. Fritjof Capra, *The Turning Point: Science, Society, and the Rising Culture* (New York:

Bantam Books, 1983); Ken Wilber, *Up from Eden: A Transpersonal View of Human Evolution* (Boulder, CO: Shambhala, 1983); and David Ray Griffin and Huston Smith, *Primordial Truth and Postmodern Theology* (Albany: State University of New York Press, 1989).

40. Dowling, *Jameson, Althusser, Marx*, 95. For a nonideological conception of narration as a perceptual filter on experience, see Walter R. Fisher, *Human Communication as Narration: Toward a Philosophy of Reason, Value, and Action* (Columbia: University of South Carolina Press, 1987).

41. Jameson, *The Political Unconscious*, 35.

42. Progoff, *Jung's Psychology*, 64.

43. Freud, *Introduction*, 121; see also 19–131, 143–155.

44. Claude Lévi-Strauss, *Structural Anthropology*, trans. C. Jacobsen and B. G. Schoeff (New York: Basic Books, 1963).

45. Jameson, *The Political Unconscious*, 286.

46. Dowling, *Jameson, Althussher, Freud*, 98, 115–118.

47. Jameson, *The Political Unconscious*, 53–54.

48. Thomas B. Farrell and G. Thomas Goodnight, "Accidental Rhetoric: The Root Metaphors of Three Mile Island," *Communication Monographs* 48 (1981): 271–300.

49. C. G. Jung, *Modern Man in Search of His Soul*, trans. W. S. Dell and Cary F. Baynes (New York: Harcourt Brace Jovanovich, 1933), 5.

50. C. G. Jung and Carl Kerenyi, *Essays on a Science of Mythology*, trans. R. F. C. Hull, Bollingen Series XXII (New York: Pantheon Books, 1949), 146.

51. As Haines notes, however, the veterans could not forget, and to handle this problem, the administration coopted the meaning of the Vietnam Veterans Memorial, thereby lifting repressed memories of Vietnam only to manage them by casting the Memorial as a sacred site for therapeutic healing. Although the narrative functions surrounding the Memorial exemplify Jameson's strategy of containment, those preceding the Memorial do not. See Harry W. Haines, "What Kind of War? An Analysis of the Vietnam Veterans Memorial," *Critical Studies in Mass Communication* 3 (1986): 1–20.

52. Merlin Stone, *When God Was a Woman* (New York: Harcourt Brace Jovanovich, 1976); Marija Gimbutas, *The Goddess and Gods of Old Europe, 7000–35000 B.C.* (Berkeley and Los Angeles: University of California Press, 1982); Raine Eisler, *The Chalice and the Blade: Our History, Our Future* (New York: Harper & Row, 1988).

53. Freud, *Introduction*, 179–180.

54. Thomas S. Frentz and Janice Hocker Rushing, "The Technological Shadow in *The Manchurian Candidate*," in Martin J. Medhurst, Alberto Gonzalez, and Tarla Rai Peterson, eds., *Communication and the Culture of Technology* (Pullman: Washington State University Press, 1990), 239–256.

55. Thomas S. Frentz, *Mass Media as Rhetorical Narration*, The Van Zelst Lecture in Communication (Evanston, IL: Northwestern University School of Speech, Northwestern University, 1984), 3–15.

56. For a critique of Jung's work as the foundation of an ethical system, see Don S. Browning, *Religious Thought and the Modern Psychologies: A Critical Conversation in the Theology of Culture* (Philadelphia: Fortress Press, 1987), 161–203.

57. For a related perspective which uses a therapeutic metaphor as an approach to rhetoric, see David Payne, "*The Wizard of Oz*: Therapeutic Rhetoric in a Contemporary Media Ritual," *Quarterly Journal of Speech* 75 (1989): 25–39; and *Coping with Failure: The Therapeutic Uses of Rhetoric* (Columbia: University of South Carolina Press, 1989).

58. Dowling, *Jameson, Althusser, Marx*, 78.

59. Jameson, *The Political Unconscious*, 75.

60. Progoff, *Jung's Psychology*, 118–120.

61. Whitmont, *Symbolic Quest*, 92.

62. For an extended justification of this procedure, see Frentz, "Rhetorical Narration."

63. Janice Hocker Rushing and Thomas S. Frentz, "The Frankenstein Myth in Contemporary Cinema," *Critical Studies in Mass Communication* 6 (1989): 61–80.

64. There have been many attempts to tell the complete story of human development, but because of the complexity of the tale, no single text can be completely adequate. Nevertheless, for an intriguing version that combines the psychological and the economic considerations of this project see Wilber, *Up from Eden*. For a defense and critique of Wilber's position, see Griffin and Smith, *Primordial Truth*. For a comparison of Wilber's system to that of Jung, see Michael Washburn, *The Ego and the Dynamic Ground* (Albany: State University of New York Press, 1988).

65. Jameson, *The Political Unconscious*, 283.

66. Jameson, in "Interview," defends himself against the question put by L. Green of whether his exclusively literary analyses will "help shake the foundations of capitalism?" (72). He answers that systemic change in this country is not possible without the achievement of a social democratic movement, and that this depends partly upon the creation of a Marxist intelligentsia, of which his own efforts are a part (73). We agree that efforts such as Jameson's are not irrelevant to social change; however, Jameson's very defense also undermines his charge against the efficacy of lucidity.

67. Whitmont, *Symbolic Quest*, 295.

68. Jung, *Modern Man*, 196–220.

69. Edward C. Whitmont and Sylvia Brinton Perera, *Dreams: A Portal to the Source* (London: Routledge, 1989), 56–66.

70. See Lawrence Rosenfield, "The Experience of Criticism," *Quarterly Journal of Speech* 60 (1974): 489–496.

71. Freud, *Introduction*, 297–311.

72. Paul Ricoeur, "Narrative Time," in W. J. T. Mitchell, ed., *On Narration* (Chicago and London: University of Chicago Press, 1981), 173–174.

73. Dowling, *Jameson, Althusser, Marx*, 11.

74. Whitmont, *Symbolic Quest*, 291–310.

75. Rosenfield: Robert M. Pirsig, *Zen and the Art of Motorcycle Maintenance: An Inquiry into Values* (New York: Bantam Books, 1975).

76. Progoff, *Jung's Psychology*, xxii.

77. Edwin Black, *Rhetorical Criticism: A Study in Method*, 2d ed. (Madison: University of Wisconsin Press, 1978).

78. See, for example, Richard L. Johannesen, "Richard Weaver's View of Rhetoric and Criticism," *Southern Speech Communication Journal* 32 (1966): 133–145; Anthony Hilbruner, "The Moral Imperative of Criticism," *Southern Speech Communication Journal* 40 (1975): 228–247; Richard L. Johannesen, "Richard M. Weaver on Standards for Ethical Rhetoric," *Central States Speech Journal* 29 (1978), 127–137; Thomas B. Farrell, "The Tradition of Rhetoric and the Philosophy of Communication," *Communication* 7 (1983): 151–180; Thomas S. Frentz, "Rhetorical Conversation, Time and Moral Action," *Quarterly Journal of Speech* 71 (1985): 1–18; Fisher.

79. Wander and Jenkins, "Rhetoric, Society, and the Critical Response"; Wander, "The Ideological Turn"; Allan Megill, "Heidegger, Wander, and Ideology," *Central States Speech Journal* 34 (1983): 114–119; and in the same issue Lawrence W. Rosenfield, "Ideological Miasma," 119–121, and Forbes Hill, "A Turn Against Ideology: Reply to Professor Wander," 121–126. Michael Calvin McGee, "Another Philipic: Notes on the Ideological Turn in Criticism," *Central States Speech Journal* 35 (1984): 43–51; and in the same issue Robert Francesconi, "Heidegger and Ideology: Reflections of an Innocent Bystander," 51–54, and Farrel Corcoran, "The Widening Gyre: Another Look at Ideology in Wander and His Critics," 54–56. In addition, see Celeste Condit, "Crafting Virtue: The Rhetorical Construction of Public Morality," *Quarterly Journal of Speech* 73 (1987): 79–97 (reprinted in this volume).

PART 8

Challenging the Tradition of Rhetorical Theory from the Margins

Historically marginalized groups—women, various ethnic minorities, people of color, gays and lesbians, the disabled, and so on—have long struggled in Western societies to achieve the enlightened values of universal human rights and equality. Occasionally—and in contemporary times more frequently—these struggles have been formalized and the otherwise silenced voices of these marginalized groups have been mobilized and given an empowering public presence through a wide range of social and political movements. Since the early 1970s the discipline of rhetorical studies has given increased attention to such groups, focusing both on the ways in which rhetoric has been used to effect such efforts and on the implications such efforts have had for who and what we are as a "people." Additionally, attention has recently begun to focus on the implications of such rhetoric for how we think of the discipline of rhetorical studies itself.

The incorporation of marginalized voices into the contemporary study of rhetoric has significantly challenged the historical biases represented in the canon of great works privileged by the rhetorical tradition, including both technical and philosophical treatises, as well as those texts identified as exemplars of rhetoric-in-action. The addition of such voices has also challenged the methods employed in the study and enactment of rhetoric. The majority of groups marginalized in Western society fall into one or more categories of class, gender, race (broadly construed to include the interests and concerns of both ethnic minorities and postcolonial groups), and sexual preference.

The essays in this section offer the theoretical work of representatives from each of these groups. However, it is important to note
that the primary route by which marginalized voices have been incorporated within the discipline of rhetorical studies has not been the
avenue of philosophically oriented, theoretical work, but rather has
traveled the various byways of critical and historically grounded theory.
Such work typically has either incorporated the rhetorical practices of
marginalized groups as instances of rhetoric worthy of criticism, or it
has employed the rhetorical and ideological insights of marginalized
groups as a site from which to critique mainstream rhetorical practices.
The more philosophical (re)theorizing of contemporary rhetorical studies from the perspective of the margins, a relatively recent event, has
emerged in the wake of such historical and critical theoretial engage-
ments. The novelty and provocative thrust of this work is reflected in
the essays that we have chosen to reproduce. With regard to the issue
of sexual preference, it is reflected in the worst possible way as a
continuing absence, for we have no published piece to offer. This
absence indicates a major gap in the development of contemporary
rhetorical theory, and we are hopeful that it is an absence that will soon
be rectified. For now, we offer theoretically motivated essays that
examine the problems and possibilities of rhetoric from three marginalized positions: class, gender, and race.

James Arnt Aune's "Cultures of Discourse: Marxism and Rhetorical
Theory" examines the dual repression of "rhetoric" within Marxist
theory and of "Marxist" terminologies within the history and theory of
public argument and debate. His argument is a provocative one that
urges a revitalized conception of "traditional rhetorical theory" through
a Marxist vocabulary organized around the metaphor of "modes of
production" as a means of engaging the "social dislocations and class
tensions" so prominent in contemporary social and political discourse.
Although only speculative at this stage, Aune suggests that it might well
be time to effect a critical and theoretical articulation of Marxism and
rhetoric with the goal of producing "a more humane practice of public
argument."

Carole Blair, Julie R. Brown, and Leslie A. Baxter's "Disciplining the
Feminine" speaks directly to the ways in which the discipline of rhetorical studies may well be animated by an oppressive patriarchalism. As
the case for their study they examine a set of comments written by
anonymous journal reviewers who rejected the publication of an earlier
study by Blair, Brown, and Baxter that was critical of the methodological
and theoretical assumptions undergirding the evaluation of female
scholars in rhetorical and communication studies. The essay speaks to
the problems and concerns of rhetorical theory at a number of important levels, but none more so than in the ways in which it appropriates
Michel Foucault's theory of discipline and punishment to demonstrate

and evaluate the dominance of a masculinist ideology within the "discipline" of speech communication. The essay has been highly controversial, both for its suggestion that speech communication imposes a masculinist discipline on all its scholars, and for its critique of the larger, academic practice of "blind review" of journal articles, that is, the practice of allowing the reviewers of journal articles to maintain anonymity.

The dominant rhetorical tradition in departments of communication has typically been written from within a Westernized and Caucasian perspective. As global communication and transportation systems have increased interaction among world cultures, it has become increasingly evident that such rhetorical theory does not embrace sufficiently the full range of human rhetorical possibilities. Accordingly, it should be obvious that there is a major need to identify and evaluate rhetorical theories that have been developed in non-Western contexts and with attention to the implications of racial and ethnic difference. As a consequence of this recognition, there has been increasing attention to a variety of non-Western perspectives on rhetoric from Asian, Aboriginal, and Middle and Near Eastern cultural contexts. Raka Shome's "Postcolonial Interventions in the Rhetorical Canon: An 'Other' View" and Molefi Kete Asante's "An Afrocentric Theory of Communication" represent some of the work pushing in such directions.

Both Shome and Asante operate from the assumption that Western theories of rhetoric are hampered in their ability to speak to the problems of communication because they are grounded in a narrow and limited "Eurocentrism," that is, the modernist assumption that Western European beliefs and values, particularly those that emphasize the autonomous rational individual, have universal applicability. The alternative Shome presents is "postcolonialism," a theoretical perspective that questions the role that modernist, neocolonial patterns of intellectual domination play in reproducing the hegemony of "first world" nations, and thus examines more closely the ways in which dominant, Western rhetorical theories and practices serve to facilitate such reproduction. Additionally, it emphasizes the "hybrid location of cultural values" and thus offers the basis for reconceptualizing the inventional practices of rhetoric as a form of "border-crossing." Asante's alternative is "Afrocentrism," a philosophy that "views the communication person as at the center of all systems, receiving information from all equally, and stimulating all with the power of his or her personality." According to Asante, when we treat the rhetoric (in his vocabualry, the "pragmatics of communication") from within an Afrocentric perspective, we develop a more complete view of the position and role of communication in the world-at-large; as such, Afrocentrism locates the study of rhetoric and communication precisely "in the middle of theoretical and philosophical debates about the nature of society."

Additional Readings

Asante, Molefi Kete. (1987). *The Afrocentric Idea*. Philadelphia, PA: Temple University Press.

Aune, James Arnt. (1994). *Rhetoric and Marxism*. Bolder, CO: Westview Press.

Biesecker, Barbara. (1992). "Coming to Terms with Recent Attempts to Write Women in the History of Rhetoric." *Philosophy and Rhetoric* 25: 140–161.

Campbell, Karlyn Kohrs. (1989). *Man Cannot Speak for Her: A Critical Study of Early Feminist Rhetoric*. 2 vols. New York: Greenwood Press.

Dow, Bonnie J. (1995). "Feminism, Difference(s), and Rhetorical Studies." *Communication Studies* 46: 106–117.

Foss, Sonja K., and Cindy L. Griffin. (1995). "Beyond Persuasion: A Proposal for an Invitational Rhetoric." *Communication Monographs* 62: 2–18.

Garrett, Mary M. (1993). "Pathos Reconsidered from the Perspective of Classical Chinese Rhetorics." *Quarterly Journal of Speech* 79: 19–39.

Gearhart, Sally Miller. (1979). "The Womanization of Rhetoric." *Women's Studies International Quarterly* 2: 195–201.

Kennedy, George A. (1998). *Comparative Rhetoric: An Historical and Cross-Cultural Introduction*. New York: Oxford University Press.

McPhail, Mark Lawrence. (1998). "From Complicity to Coherence: Rereading the Rhetoric of Afrocentricity." *Western Journal of Communication* 62: 114–140.

Nakayama, Thomas K., and Robert L. Krizek. (1995). "Whiteness: A Strategic Rhetoric." *Quarterly Journal of Speech* 81: 291–309.

Ratcliffe, Krista. *Anglo-American Feminist Challenges to the Rhetorical Traditions: Virginia Woolf, Mary Daly, Adrienne Rich*. Carbondale: Southern Illinois University Press.

Cultures of Discourse
Marxism and Rhetorical Theory

JAMES ARNT AUNE

On November 10, 1837, soon after becoming a student at the University of Berlin, Karl Marx wrote a letter to his father. The letter described the development of Marx's two great loves: for Hegel's philosophy and for his future wife, Jenny von Westphalen. There are at least two items of interest in the letter for the student of rhetoric. First, in the introduction Marx deprecated the love poems he recently sent to Jenny: "All the poems of the first three volumes I sent to Jenny are marked by attacks on our times, diffuse and inchoate expressions of feeling, nothing natural, everything built out of moonshine, complete opposition between what is and ought to be, rhetorical reflections instead of poetic thoughts." Second, he described the writing of a twenty-four-page dialogue, "Cleanthus, or the Starting Point and Necessary Continuation of Philosophy," where in attempting to unite art and science, he was led to the acceptance of the Hegelian system. His philosophical endeavors left him in an agitated state. He sought relief by joining his landlord on a hunting expedition and, on his return, by immersing himself in what he called "positive studies." These "positive studies" included the reading of works on the law of property, criminal law, canon law, and a work on the artistic instincts of animals. He then translated parts of Aristotle's *Rhetoric* (Marx and Engels, 1975, pp. 10–21).

It is unclear from the letter or from other writings of Marx what parts of the *Rhetoric* he translated or what effect they had on his work. Nonetheless, I choose this letter for an introduction to a discussion of Marxism and public argument because it serves as a kind of representative anecdote for the reception of rhetoric in the Marxist tradition: if mentioned at all, rhetoric is consigned to the margins of serious discourse, is rigidly separated from both art and philosophy, and is considered, at best, to be a branch of "positive studies." As Kenneth Burke writes, "The Marxist persuasion is usually advanced in the name of no-rhetoric" (Burke, 1969, p. 102), a lesson which Burke no doubt first learned when his venture into Marxist rhetorical theory, *Revolu-*

tionary Symbolism in America, "was roundly condemned at the Communist Writer's Congress in 1935" (Burke, 1935).

The possibility that Marx knew something about the rhetorical tradition is at first sight an intriguing one, but the inevitable conclusion to be drawn from his writings is that the tradition had a negligible influence. To be sure, the historical writings, especially *The Eighteenth Brumaire of Louis Bonaparte* (Marx, 1963), display a nearly Ciceronian style, full of antitheses and copia, but the absence of classical notions of invention or audience is rather obvious. In contrast, we know that the father of capitalist political economy, Adam Smith, wrote a series of lectures on rhetoric and that two of the most important nineteenth-century rhetorical theorists, Thomas De Quincey and Richard Whately, wrote books defending free trade.[1] One wonders what a Marxist rhetoric would look like, then and now.[2]

On the other hand, if Marxism has been silent about the rhetorical tradition, the rhetorical tradition has been almost equally silent about Marxism, both as a historical phenomenon and as a theoretical perspective on discourse. Despite Philip Wander's (1983) immensely important work on ideological criticism and Michael Calvin McGee's (1982) ongoing project for a materialist rhetoric, serious discussion of Marxism (as opposed to a sort of eclectic American radicalism) remains limited to a few partisans of political economy or cultural studies, two research traditions notable for their inattention to rhetoric. The term "ideology" has attained quasi-canonical status in rhetorical criticism, but Marx's central focus on class struggle has been thoroughly ignored by rhetorical scholars. Students of social movements in our field virtually have ignored labor, perhaps because many of them came to political consciousness at a time when the working class was no longer in fashion among liberal academics. Perhaps the most impressive work of Marxist rhetorical theory yet produced, Lawrence Grossberg's (1979) "Marxist Dialectics and Rhetorical Criticism," uses the concept of "class" only once, and there it is in the context of a discussion of Stalinism.

At first sight, the substitution of "ideology" for "class" in left academic discourse seems to solve some problems. It eliminates the putative economic determinism of classical Marxism and opens up the possibility of explaining larger patterns of argument in a culture instead of just focusing on a single speech and its effects. The work of Celeste Condit is perhaps the best example of a productive use of the concept of ideology in the study of public argument. One could also point out that substituting "ideology" for "class" also opens up left academic discourse for the analysis of oppression based on race and gender divisions (Condit, 1987). It seems curious, however, to claim that an analysis of public discourse based on certain observations about the capitalist mode of production is incomplete or maybe even "patriarchal," when no one has examined seriously how capitalism has affected the theory and practice of rhetoric. Further, substituting "ideology" for "class struggle" as a key term runs the risk of making oppression largely a linguistic or cultural matter. The ambiguous position of academics within the class structure of advanced capitalism makes ideological criticism appealing but scarcely more useful politically than when the Frankfurt School invented it in the 1930s.

The focus of this essay, then, is on the repression of rhetoric in Marxist theory and on the reading of the history of theories of public argument in Marxist terms. A critical "articulation" of Marxism and the rhetorical tradition is perhaps premature.[3] It may well be the case that a commitment to Marxist categories by its nature eliminates a rhetorical understanding of public argument. It may also be the case that a commitment to the rhetorical tradition necessitates that one be either a reformist or a conservative. This essay is intended to be an invitation to dialogue, not the raising of a dogmatic flag. I will proceed by: (1) outlining the communicative dilemma created by certain key silences in the classical texts of Marx and Engels, (2) creating a typology of later Marxist responses to this communicative dilemma, and (3) proposing a rereading of the history of rhetorical theory in Marxist terms.

THE TWO MARXISMS AND MARX'S RHETORICAL PROBLEM

Sometimes it appears that the term "Marxist" is so ambiguous as to be useless, unless one is using it solely for propaganda purposes, as in "The Marxist regime in Nicaragua. . . ." Inasmuch as mainstream historians and social scientists accept many of Marx's once controversial doctrines, why keep using the term? Or, given the tremendous political (and moral) distance between, say, Antonio Gramsci and Joseph Stalin, is it reasonable to argue that both were "Marxists"? These objections aside, I do believe that it is possible to describe the outlines of a Marxist "paradigm," at least as an analytic method. It seems less possible to argue that there exists a specific Marxist *politics*, mainly because Marxism after Marx has realized that Marx lacked a politics (among other things). On the other hand, to suggest that Marxism is simply a method, deserving of a sort of affirmative action treatment in the contemporary university, ignores Marx's own intention, which was, quite simply, "to change the world" (Marx, 1972, p. 145).

At a rather high level of abstraction, the following assumptions are common to the many "Marxisms" (see Heilbroner, 1985): (1) "Labor" is a central, if not the central, characteristic of human beings. (2) The mode of production in a given social totality—the level of development of productive forces in addition to the type of work relations that accompany those forces—is a determining factor in establishing that totality's social "being." (3) All hitherto existing societies have been characterized by a class struggle over the control or allocation of the surplus from production. (4) The level of development of the productive forces determines, in the sense of setting boundary conditions for, the sort of class structure and class struggle in a given social system. (5) Because the productive forces tend to develop over time, "history" is generally predictable in terms of the succession of modes of production. (6) That class which controls the mode of production in a given society tends to repress, either through the threat of violence or through promoting a particular set of beliefs in the legitimacy of the existing order, radical alterations in control of the productive forces. (7) Capitalism has outlived its usefulness as a mode of production; that is, it helped develop the productive forces to their currently high level, but its chronic crises, and its wastefulness of natural resources and human talent, mean that it will pass away eventually. (8) The precise mode of capitalism's passing away will vary, depending on the political assumptions of the various schools of Marxism.

Despite the great number of Marxisms, Alvin Gouldner's (1980) division of all hitherto existing Marxisms into "Two Marxisms" is a useful category system. The first is scientific Marxism, and the second is critical Marxism. Followers of the first school would include Lenin, Althusser, and "evolutionary" social democrats such as Eduard Bernstein. These writers view Marxism as science, not critique, and their "canon within the canon" of Marx's writings is the "mature" political economy of *Capital* and not the "ideologized" anthropology of the *1844 Manuscripts*. They stress a deterministic view of ideology, devalue individual experience and action, and emphasize the law-like character of historical change. In contrast, critical Marxists "conceive of Marxism as critique rather than science, they stress the continuity of Marx with Hegel, the importance of the young Marx, the ongoing significance of the young Marx's emphasis on 'alienation,' and are more historicist" (Gouldner, 1980, p. 39). Representative critical Marxists are Gramsci, Sartre, and the Frankfurt School.

Critical Marxism sought to respond to an apparent contradiction in Marx's texts. Gouldner (1980) writes, "The problem is that if capitalism is indeed governed by lawful regularities that doom it to be supplanted by a new socialist society (when the requisite infrastructures have matured), why then stress that 'the point is to change it'? Why go to great pains to arrange capitalism's funeral if its demise is guaranteed by science? Why must persons be mobilized and exhorted to discipline themselves to behave in conformity with necessary laws by which, it would seem, they would in any event be bound?" (p. 32). In other words, Marxism has a rhetorical problem: either the classless society is inevitable and scientifically grounded with individual choice being irrelevant, *or* the classless society comes about through the persuasion of individuals and thus ceases to be grounded in scientific laws of history—laws that, as Kenneth Burke ([1950] 1969b) has pointed out, are a major source of Marxism's rhetorical power in the first place (p. 101). The source of the dilemma is Marx's own failure to create a political theory that would explain how the working class struggles and gains power in or over the state. More precisely, Marx did not explain the psychological and rhetorical prerequisites for revolution.

The Marxist tradition has tended to fill in the gap between what we might call *structure* and *struggle* in roughly four ways:

The first is *Leninism*, which is given its quintessential philosophical expression in the work of Lukács. As Lenin (1961) writes in *What Is to Be Done?*, the working class, left to its own devices, will develop at best trade union consciousness, but never revolutionary consciousness (pp. 31–32). Hence the need for a revolutionary vanguard party that anticipates a fully realized class consciousness (Lukács 1971, pp. 41–42, 51). This party can prepare for revolution and guide the masses at the time of collapse of the capitalist system. In order for the party to be ready for revolution, it must be tightly disciplined, periodically purge itself, and possess a rigidly correct theory of Marxism— concepts that can be summarized by Lenin's wonderfully Orwellian phrase, "democratic centralism." A Leninist party, of course, runs the risk of losing touch with the workers, privileging the role of intellectuals, and eventually becoming totalitarian. The Leninist model of organization also has been notably unsuccessful in advanced industrial societies.

A second alternative, which can be traced back to Rosa Luxemburg, and perhaps even further back to Bakunin, does not privilege the role of the party in fomenting revolution, but rather depends on the spontaneous revolution in the masses themselves, who at the time of capitalist crisis will form naturally the councils to deal with political and economic issues (see Albert and Hahnel, 1978). This view is represented also by the early new left, which called for participatory democracy. It also has been influential in the abandonment of what C. Wright Mills (1969) called Marxism's "labor metaphysic" (p. 28). In Herbert Marcuse's (1964) view, for example, the agent of revolution will not necessarily be the industrial working class, but those people marginalized by the status quo—blacks, students, women, homosexuals, for example (pp. 256–257). The danger in this version of Marxism is its tendency toward leftist adventurism or toward what Lukács, in a moment of self-criticism, called "revolutionary messianism." Perhaps a more important limitation is that "new class" theorists from Marcuse to Gouldner were unable to predict the reversion of capitalism to more brutal ideological forms (Reaganism, Thatcherism) after the economic crisis of the 1970s (see Gouldner, 1979, p. 92).

Two other variants of Marxism specifically address problems of communication. The first, the Frankfurt School, views all mass communication in advanced industrial society as inherently manipulative. Perhaps the most popular expression of this view is Christopher Lasch's (1977) *The Culture of Narcissism*, although Horkheimer and Adorno's (1972) *Dialectic of Enlightenment* and Marcuse's (1964) pre-New Left *One-Dimensional Man* remain the most important. The Frankfurt School's position can be distilled into three main propositions: (1) The working class has been bought off by the "safety net" introduced by Keynesian welfare capitalism. (2) The media (or "consciousness industry") have replaced the family as the main agent of socialization, leading to a repressive desublimation of aggressive and erotic instincts. (3) The only legitimate forms of communication are philosophy and high art. Philosophic discourse is critique, "negative thinking," which must be obscure in order to avoid capitulating to the established universe of discourse. High art preserves memories of freedom and happiness or else explicitly condemns the existing world. For Marcuse (1978), Samuel Beckett emerges as the greatest artist of the contemporary period, for he brings a clear message to his audience: put an end to things as they are.

Although Frankfurt Marxism remains the most coherent and intellectually satisfying of all varieties of critical Marxism to date, it too easily lapses into political quietism and elitist rejection of all forms of popular culture. Even Jürgen Habermas, of the Frankfurt School's second generation, shares with Adorno, Horkheimer, and Marcuse a tendency to reject strategic discourse (what we would call "rhetoric") as inherently manipulative (Habermas, 1979, p. 41).

A fourth and final variant of Marxism has not been articulated fully as yet, but derives from Antonio Gramsci's (1971) *Prison Notebooks*. Gramsci has had tremendous influence on British cultural studies and on American media critics such as Todd Gitlin (1982) and Douglas Kellner (1982). The first steps toward the appropriation of Gramsci for rhetorical theory have been made by Michael McGee and Martha Martin (1983), and by Frank Lentricchia (1983) in his book on Kenneth Burke. In contrast to Marx, Gramsci believed that capitalism obtained consent (at least in Western societies) through persuasion, its ability to make the status quo seem reasonable and necessary. Lentricchia points out the similarity between Gramsci's idea of "hegemony" (the persuasive domination of the masses by the ruling class) and Kenneth Burke's analysis in *Attitudes Toward History*:

> [T]he various "priests" of the pulpit, schools, press, radio, and popular arts, (and we add television), educate the socially dispossessed person to feel "that he 'has a stake in' the authoritative structure that dispossesses him; for the influence exerted upon the policies of education by the authoritative structure encourages the dispossessed to feel that his only hope of repossession lies in his allegiance to the structure that dispossessed him." (Lentricchia, 1983, pp. 76–77)

Gramsci's idea of hegemony, especially as interpreted by Gitlin and Kellner, leads to a more optimistic view of mass communication. The task of the intellectual class at the present time is to help construct a counter-hegemony. A counter-hegemony would be based on the following assumptions: (1) Mass communication addresses real human needs for happiness, diversion, and self-assertion but is flawed because those needs are shown to be met only through the purchase of commodities (Gitlin, 1982, p. 452; Kellner, 1982, p. 403). (2) Hegemony is "leaky" in contemporary mass communication because of the contradictory character of liberal capitalism itself (Kellner, 1982, pp. 386–387). One could interpret the television series *M*A*S*H*, for example, as reinforcing traditional American values on one hand, while de-legitimating war on the other. (3) The Left should learn how to use mass communication more effectively. As Douglas Kellner (1982) writes, "The left should learn how to produce, or how to participate in, the production of popular television, as well as documentaries, news commentaries, and programs, and political discussion suitable for broadcast media. . . . There must be a cultural/media politics to ensure public access and open new channels of communication" (p. 421).

The neo-Gramscians clearly possess an attitude toward communication that is more congenial to the traditional concerns of rhetorical studies. Most, however, have not addressed the problem of rhetoric and rational argument. They lack a theory of the production of discourse and of audience effects. They also lack a response to the charge of more traditional critics such as Wayne Booth (1974) that concepts such as "ideology" and "hegemony" undercut the possibility of rational argument because of their "motivism" (pp. 2–40). A similar charge is made by the Norwegian philosopher Jon Elster (1979), when he attacks the "functionalism" of the Marxist view of ideology in *Ulysses and the Sirens* (pp. 28–35).[4]

Terry Eagleton has begun a project for the reconstruction of traditional rhetorical theory along Marxist lines, although it largely is formulated as a critique of the field of English literature. In Eagleton's (1983) *Literary Theory: An Introduction* he argues that "literature" as a privileged concept in the academy is of recent invention. In his view, the rise of departments of English in the nineteenth century was tied to an ideological quest to legitimate the existing class society. The study of literature was seen as a "humanizing" force, one that could replace religion as a prop for the existing order (pp. 17–53). In contrast, he says that the earlier study of rhetoric in British and American universities made clear the political thrust of humanistic knowledge. In what is perhaps the most useful definition of rhetoric I have read, Eagleton (1981) writes that rhetoric "is the process of analyzing the material effects of particular uses of language in particular social conjunctures" and that traditional rhetoric was "the textual training of the ruling class in the techniques of political hegemony" (p. 101). He goes on to describe a brief program for the development of a Marxist rhetoric:

> As far as rhetoric is concerned, then, a Marxist must be in a certain sense a Platonist. Rhetorical effects are calculated in the light of a theory of the *polis* as a whole. . . . Since all art is rhetorical, the tasks of the revolutionary cultural worker are essentially threefold: First, to participate in the production of works and events which, within transformed "cultural" media, so fictionalize the "real" as to intend those effects conducive to the victory of socialism. Second, as "critic" to expose the rhetorical structures by which non-socialist works produce political undesirable effects, as a way of combatting what is now unfashionable to call false consciousness. Third, to interpret such works where possible against the grain, so as to appropriate whatever is valuable for socialism. (Eagleton, 1981, p. 113)

It should be clear that I am in basic sympathy with Eagleton's ideas, although they need to be extended and made more relevant to the American experience. One major problem with Eagleton's formulation is that, like most leftist intellectuals, he privileges critique over the teaching of advocacy skills. He also still privileges art and literature over the more humble modes of communication such as public speaking and debate. It is not enough to do Marxist analyses of Richardson and Emily Brontë. Nor is it enough to say, for instance, that Ronald Reagan abuses the ideograph of "family" in order to reinforce existing patterns of economic and sexual oppression. One would need to go on to understand the lived experience of American audiences that predisposes them, often in ways that have nothing at all to do with "false consciousness," to accept family-based arguments. One would also need to show students and politicians how to "steal the symbol" of the family and use it for liberatory purposes (Burke, 1984, p. 328).

If it is the case that Marxism has effaced the role of communication in mediating between social structure and human action and that students of communication have ignored capitalism as a determining force in society, how might we combine both fields' virtues while eliminating some of their vices? It may be that the *aporia* which Gouldner and others find in classical Marxism may be the result more of confusion over levels of abstraction in social analysis than a failure of Marxism itself. Erik Olin Wright (1985) suggests, in his recent book *Classes*, that Marxist social analysis operates at three levels of abstraction: mode of production, social formation, and conjuncture (p. 9). Further, within each of these three levels, Marx himself moved back and forth between describing an abstract structural map of class relations (as in the first part of *Capital*, where he develops a "pure" model of capitalism) and describing concrete conjunctural maps of classes-as-actors (as in the chapter of *Capital* where he describes the battles over the length of the working day or as in the historical writings such as the *Eighteenth Brumaire*). Marx's conjunctural maps are much less "reductive" than his other writings, and it is important to note that neither the critical nor scientific Marxists have given as much weight to them as to the *1844 Manuscripts* or to the first part of *Capital*.

In fitting together Marxism and argumentation, it is necessary to clarify the levels of abstraction at which one is working. In focusing on the mode of production, one wants to isolate the way in which dominant forms of argument relate to forces and relations of production *in the most abstract way*. One can avoid both Booth's critique of Marxian motivism and Elster's refutation of Marxian functionalism if the focus is on argumentative forms. This sort of periodization is no different from that which intellectual historians of rhetoric have already done, except that it provides for greater parsimony of explanation. In focusing on social formation, one traces patterns of argument as they relate to a specific nation or region (as revealed, for instance, in Eugene Debs's appropriation of the images of the American Revolution in his arguments for socialism). In focusing on conjuncture, one evaluates the relationship between text and audience in a concrete rhetorical situation, much as traditional neo-Aristotelian criticism did.

Capitalism, in my view, is ultimately determining only in the sense of establishing general patterns and rules for argument. Not all discourse in a given social formation is conducted in class terms, although it certainly is important to study the ways in which public languages of class are created or inhibited. The rhetorical construction and/or repression of class consciousness in American culture, the rhetorical representation of work relations in the mass media, not to mention the very real needs of American workers to develop rhetorical means to combat the deindustrialization of America and the deskilling of work—all these are potentially rich topics for the critic of American public argument to pursue.

To recast Marxist communication studies in terms of the study of labor and of the often heroic resistance of American workers against capitalist domination seems to me much more productive than the narrow focus on the prison-house of ideology, which many of us inherited from the Frankfurt School. To proclaim as Marcuse did or as more recent poststructuralist Marxists do that we are all imprisoned in a one-dimensional society of spectacle ignores the reality of resistance to capitalism that we have seen in the British miners, American farmers, and Local P-9 in Austin, Minnesota. By maintaining Marx's original dialectical tension between structure and struggle we may be able to avoid the passivity that both scientific Marxism and critical Marxism seem to encourage at their worst moments.

CULTURES OF DISCOURSE: RHETORIC, CRITICISM, AND POSTSTRUCTURALISM

If the map of the research program implied by classical Marxism makes sense, how can we use it to direct research in the study of communication? The rest of this essay attempts to describe what an analysis of the history of rhetorical theory would look like in mode-of-production terms.

The recent resurgence of rhetorical studies, inside and outside of departments of communication, is simultaneously encouraging and depressing. Arguably, rhetoric shares with Marxism the distinction of being the only research tradition capable of uniting the various disciplines in the university and of combatting the specialization that prevents academic discourse from affecting the public world. (Positivism once served such a function, but at last count even social scientists were hastening to arrange its funeral rites.) Rhetoric, however, in its privileging of symbol-use over labor as the constitutive activity of human beings, risks being coopted by larger forces of domination in our culture. Please note that I am neither impugning the motives of many contemporary rhetoricians (as if they were all covertly in the employ of the National Association of Manufacturers), nor am I arguing that the revival of rhetoric is somehow *functional* in the reproduction of late capitalist economic relations. I am suggesting, rather, that particular stages in the development of a mode of production—in this case capitalism—will create certain social dislocations or class tensions with which given discourses will attempt to cope.

The resurgence of rhetorical studies, whether in its wholesome American form or in its rather sleazy French version, is tied to a common conviction among intellectual elites that the transcendental signifiers of God, Truth, and the Classless Society have failed us. What remains is rhetoric itself, the free play of signifiers, which the belatedly canonized Kenneth Burke (1965) tells us to contemplate with dismay and delight as we "huddle, nervously loquacious, at the edge of the abyss" (p. 272). The heroic impulse at the heart of rhetorical studies, however, is too easily subverted into the glorification of power. If, following Gramsci, we can conclude that capitalist hegemony is a persuasive process, it may be possible to read dominant theories of rhetoric as attempts to describe, explain, and occasionally criticize hegemonic techniques. Even when not explicitly or self-consciously "rhetorical," intellectuals and other wielders of power in society always develop cultures of discourse or argumentative grammars. These cultures of discourse exist in an occasionally uneven relationship with economic forces and relations of production, but reciprocally influence and are influenced by them. Cultures of discourse, then, are conventions for the production of discourse and are as historically material as a factory or a Hitler speech.

I will argue that three cultures of discourse are currently competing for the allegiance of rhetorical scholars. The first, which can simply be called "rhetoric," is largely dead in its classical and humanistic forms, especially as it existed in American colleges prior to 1850. The second, the culture of critical discourse (Alvin Gouldner's CCD), has been dominant for many years but is now collapsing under the weight of its own internal contradictions. The third, which lacks an appropriate name, although "the new rhetoric" or even "poststructuralism" may do, while it lacks the political and social influence of the other two cultures of discourse, reflects a society of "spectacle," in which nothing is experienced directly except as a sign.

Traditional rhetoricians can be characterized above all by their nostalgia. S. M. Halloran's important article, "Rhetoric in the American College Curriculum," draws an inspiring picture of American education before the decline of rhetoric. He concludes his essay by contrasting the miserable character of the public debate over AWACS with the intense involvement of the American public in Webster's debates with Hayne and Calhoun (Halloran, 1982, pp. 244–262). Halloran is right, of course, that the decline of rhetoric in American universities did parallel the decline of public involvement in politics (although the 1930s certainly come to mind as a counterexample). Nonetheless, he obscures the class character of the decline of traditional rhetoric. Rhetoric declined because it ceased to be an efficient means of education once the university shifted to a larger, more egalitarian constituency. Rhetoric was a useful tool for a propertied elite, but seemingly less necessary when public discourse became controlled by technical experts.

The culture of discourse or argumentative grammar associated with traditional rhetoric seems to have been based on the following communicative rules. (I rewrite here Gadamer's great synthesis of the rhetorical tradition in the first part of *Truth and Method* [1975, pp. 10–39].) First, speak in such a way that one embodies the values of one's culture in one's own character. Second, always adapt one's discourse to the common sense of one's listeners. Third, study past rhetorical situations in order to develop a sense of judgment, the virtue of prudence that will generalize to future rhetorical situations. Finally, study great speeches and history and literature in order to develop a sense of timing and taste.

This culture of discourse at its best sacrificed individual ambition to the needs of the community and at its worst, as Eagleton says, was simply a form of training the ruling class in the techniques of textual domination. And yet, rhetoric in its traditional form had to die. It had to be replaced by a new standard of discourse, one more tied to print and to the initially egalitarian drive of capitalism to find new markets. The culture of critical discourse arose to meet technological and economic needs—and it also served as a site of class struggle, since Marxism itself arose within the culture of critical discourse.

Gouldner (1979), in his account of the culture of critical discourse, ties it to the potential rise to power of the new class of humanistic intellectuals and technical intelligentsia (p. 28). I believe that his prediction that this new class will come to power eventually in both the East and the West is invalidated largely by the return of capitalism to earlier and more primitive forms of domination because of the world recession. I also believe that the culture of critical discourse is more a set of formal assumptions about the conduct of public communication than a set of propositions about the public world (despite the notorious difficulties, familiar to every rhetorician, of separating form and content). My point here, however, is less to criticize Gouldner's theory than to use it to characterize the type of speech about speech that replaced rhetoric in intellectual circles.

The rules of the culture of critical discourse as an argumentative grammar can be summarized as follows: (1) Make one's own speech problematic and try to account for its origins. Be reflexive and self-monitoring. (2) Justify claims without reference to the speaker's societal position or authority; in other words, eliminate the classical function of *ethos*. (3) Stand apart from the common sense of the culture in which the speech is occurring, since the common sense of a culture is ultimately a rationalization for that culture's power relations. (4) Thus, privilege theoretical discourse, speech that is relatively context-free (Gouldner, 1979, p. 29). This culture of discourse, which perhaps has its finest expression in Habermas's notion of the ideal speech situation, has been dominant in universities for a long time. The culture of critical discourse is inherently hostile to traditional rhetoric (as the tortured career of rhetorical studies in America's elite universities in the last fifty years or so indicates), even though the culture of critical discourse has become the main standard of speech among theorists of argumentation. The culture of critical discourse helped break down traditional class and race prejudices, the patriarchal family, and religion, but rather than being tied to the needs of Gouldner's new class, it was simply the rhetorical justification for that process which Marx and Engels (1972) so cogently described in *The Communist Manifesto*:

> Constant revolutionizing of production, uninterrupted disturbance of all social conditions, everlasting uncertainty and agitation distinguish the bourgeois epoch from all earlier ones. All fixed, fast-frozen relations, with their train of ancient and venerable prejudices and opinions are swept away, all new-formed ones become antiquated before they can ossify. All that is solid melts into air, all that is holy is profaned, and man is at last compelled to face with sober senses, his real conditions of life, and his relations with his kind. (p. 338)

The culture of critical discourse was and is the argumentative grammar that justifies technological revolution, the expansion of markets by giving workers a larger share of profits, and also managerial control over the workplace and over society in general—but not, I must add, at the level of propositional argument, but at the level of form. By translating questions of political practice and class struggle into questions of technical expertise, the culture of critical discourse consolidated the transition of capitalism from anarchic competition to corporate liberalism.

The culture of critical discourse, however, and corporate liberalism itself cannot survive the worldwide crisis of capitalism. It has been replaced in the political realm by the politics of pure image as represented by Ronald Reagan. It has been replaced—or is being slowly replaced—by a new ideology of communication that denies the existence of objective reality, proclaims that everything is constructed rhetorically and that there is nothing outside the text. Ironically enough, it is the lapsed Marxist Kenneth Burke and the avowed Marxist Jacques Derrida who seem to provide the best ideological justification for the new rhetorical world of late capitalism.

A grossly enlarged conception of rhetoric plays directly into the hands of corporate capitalism, which would just as soon have us believe that mass persuasion is the solution to our collective problems. To assume that all social problems are problems of communication glosses over the presence of real problems that might, at some point, require direct action, even violence. When our most radical rhetoric-as-epistemicists (what we might call left-Burkeians) tell us that even trees are created rhetorically we are offered what Fredric Jameson (1972) described in another context as "the spectacle of a world from which nature as such has been eliminated, a world saturated with messages and information, whose intricate commodity network may be seen as the very prototype of a system of signs" (pp. viii–ix). The new orthodoxy that there is nothing outside the text, nothing outside of rhetoric itself, is the perfect ideological representation of life under late capitalism, in which nothing, it seems, is experienced outside of its media images.

It seems silly, however, to claim that poststructuralism is somehow "functional" in preserving capitalist domination. It makes more sense to indict poststructuralism's current influence in the academy as a distraction from more productive uses of rhetorical theory. It is silly, too, to claim that late capitalism has created a seamless web of ideological images—Marx himself wrote books and participated in the labor movement in order to dispell the myth that capitalism is an eternal and natural type of social order. My contention in this essay has been that a revitalized conception of traditional rhetoric, one informed by Marxist theory and practice, may be of some use in advancing, if not the Revolution, at least a more humane practice of public argument. I want to conclude by summarizing the main themes of my overall argument in the context of some theses toward a Marxist rhetorical theory:

1. The Marxist representative anecdote of human beings as producers rather than simply as symbol-users may help correct the "trained incapacity" or "occupational psychosis" of rhetorical theory. By foregrounding the role of labor in constructing our human world, a Marxist approach to communication may help revitalize the criticism of public discourse.
2. By foregrounding class struggle rather than public consensus, a Marxist rhetorical theory may be better able to explain broad historical shifts in rhetorical practice and pedagogy than do existing theoretical alternatives.
3. Traditional rhetoric, in privileging common sense as a starting point for the construction of enthymemes, may provide a needed corrective to Marxism's tendency to view the common sense of a culture merely as a rationalization of that culture's relations of domination.
4. Uniting Marxism's traditional concern for economic democracy with rhetoric's traditional (if at times ambiguous) concern for political democracy may provide a narrative structure for a new politics, one that views revolution as a struggle against racial, sexual, and economic oppression and against the specialized languages of expertise, which have characterized "liberal" reform in this century. Marxism needs to correct rhetoric's avoidance of the category of labor in the construction of the social world, while rhetoric needs to correct Marxism's one-sided focus on labor at the expense of other forms of domination.

The preceding four points are perhaps too facile a sketch of a theory that needs further justification, revision, and empirical validation. I have tried to make a case, at a rather high level of abstraction, for the connection of developments in rhetorical theory with developments in modes of production. The next step is to develop longitudinal analyses of public discourse within a given social formation, using Marxist categories. As I suggested earlier, even traditional public address study has largely ignored the rhetoric of the American labor movement. Given what might be called "American exceptionalism," it still remains to be proved empirically that Marxist categories can illuminate the development of languages of labor and class in the United States. But the attempt must be made.

What Marxism has taught us, in admittedly flawed ways, is that human beings have the potential to build a heroic society. What students of rhetoric and communication can give Marxism is a more humane way of bridging the critique of ideology with political action. The ultimate point is that audiences, when presented with the contradictions inherent in their social systems, have a choice about the ideological narratives to which they will subscribe or which they will create. That these narratives may not be limited to the banal yet frightening ones of the White House or the Kremlin depends on our ability to extend our imaginative range. As Marx (1975) himself wrote, "Every emancipation is a restoration of the human world and of human relationships to man himself" (p. 240).

Notes

I am grateful to Joli Jensen, John Rodden, M. S. Piccirillo, and the members of my seminar on Marxism and Communication Studies at the University of Virginia (Spring 1986) and the University of Iowa (Summer 1986) for conversations that helped me clarify the ideas presented in this chapter.

1. Marx, of course, cites Smith's economic and ethical writings in *Kapital*; he also cites De Quincey's *The Logic of Political Economy*; Whately was professor of political economy at Oxford from 1829 to 1831. One sign of the remarkably insular character of much scholarship in the history of rhetorical theory is that rhetoricians write about Smith, De Quincey, and Whately as if rhetoric were the only interest of these theorists.

2. By "rhetoric" here I mean a comprehensive rhetorical theory; for a more limited, practical rhetoric, see the work of Angelica Balabanoff and Willkie (1974).

3. See Ryan (1982) for a useful explication of the metaphor of "articulation," a term from metallurgy referring to the joining of two distinct metals. The nightmare side of my current project is that rhetoric and Marxism may be related more like two magnets opposing one another.

4. I first started reading Elster at the beginning of the final revision of this essay; were I to redraft the project from the bottom up I would make Elster's work central, including also his *Making Sense of Marx* (1985). Elster opens up the prospect of a Marxism without functionalist explanation, a prospect, alas, that most Marxist students of communication, whether in political economy or cultural studies, have yet to consider.

References

Albert, M., and R. Hahnel. 1978. *Unorthodox Marxism*. Boston: South End Press.

Booth, Wayne. 1974. *Modern Dogma and the Rhetoric of Assent*. South Bend, IN: University of Notre Dame Press; paperback edition, Chicago: University of Chicago Press.

Burke, Kenneth. 1935. "Revolutionary Symbolism in America." In Henry Hart, ed., *American Writer's Congress* (New York: International Publishers), pp. 87–93.

Burke, Kenneth. [1950] 1969. *A Rhetoric of Motives*. Englewood Cliffs, NJ: Prentice-Hall; rpt., Berkeley and Los Angeles: University of California Press.

Burke, Kenneth. 1965. *Permanence and Change*. 2d ed. Indianapolis: Library of the Liberal Arts.

Burke, Kenneth. 1984. *Attitudes Toward History*. Berkeley and Los Angeles: University of California Press.

Condit, Celeste M. 1987. "Democracy and Civil Rights: The Universalizing Influence of Public Argumentation." *Communication Monographs* 54: 1–18.

Elster, Jon. 1979. *Ulysses and the Sirens*. Cambridge: Cambridge University Press.

Elster, Jon. 1985. *Making Sense of Marx*. Cambridge: Cambridge University Press.

Gadamer, H. 1975. *Truth and Method*. Translated by Garrett Barden and John Cumming. New York: Seabury Press.

Gitlin, Todd. 1982. "Prime Time Ideology: The Hegemonic Process in Television Entertainment." In Horace Newcomb, ed., *Television: The Critical View*, 3rd ed. (New York: Oxford University Press), pp. 507–532.

Gouldner, Alvin. 1979. *The Future of Intellectuals and the Rise of the New Class*. New York: Seabury Press.

Gouldner, Alvin. 1980. *The Two Marxisms*. New York: Oxford University Press.

Gramsci, Antonio. 1971. *The Prison Notebooks: Selections*. Translated by Quintin Hoard and Geoffrey Nowell Smith. New York: International Publishers.

Grossberg, Lawrence. 1979. "Marxist Dialectics and Rhetorical Criticism." *Quarterly Journal of Speech* 65: 235–249.

Habermas, Jürgen. 1979. *Communication and the Evolution of Society*. Translated by Thomas McCarthy. Boston: Beacon Press.

Halloran, S. M. 1982. "Rhetoric in the American College Curriculum." *PRE/TEXT* 3: 244–269.

Heilbroner, R. 1985. *Marxism For and Against*. New York: Norton.

Horkheimer, M., and T. W. Adorno. 1972. *The Dialectic of Enlightenment*. Translated by John Cumming. New York: Herder and Herder.

Jameson, Fredric. 1972. *The Prison-House of Language: A Critical Account of Structuralism and Russian Formalism*. Princeton, NJ: Princeton University Press.

Kellner, Douglas. 1982. "TV, Ideology, and Emancipatory Popular Culture." In Horace Newcomb, ed., *Television: The Critical View*, 3rd ed. (New York: Oxford University Press), pp. 386–421.

Lasch, Christopher. 1977. *The Culture of Narcissism*. New York: Norton.

Lenin, V.I. 1961. *What Is to Be Done?* Translated by Joe Fineberg and George Hanna. New York: International Publishers.

Lentricchia, Frank. 1983. *Criticism and Social Change*. Chicago and London: University of Chicago Press.

Lukács, Georg. 1971. *History and Class Consciousness*. Translated by Rodney Livingstone. Cambridge, MA: M.I.T. Press.

Marcuse, Herbert. 1964. *One-Dimensional Man: Studies in the Ideology of Advanced Industrial Society*. Boston: Beacon Press.

Marcuse, Herbert. 1978. *The Aesthetic Dimension: Toward a Critique of Marxist Aesthetics*. Boston: Beacon Press.

Marx, Karl. 1963. *The Eighteenth Brumaire of Louis Bonaparte*. New York: International Publishers.

Marx, Karl. 1972. "Theses on Feuerbach." In Robert C. Tucker, ed., *The Marx-Engels Reader* (New York: Norton).

Marx, Karl. 1975. "On the Jewish Question." In *Early Writings*, trans Rodney Livingston and Gregor Benton (New York: Vintage Books).

Marx, Karl, and Frederick Engels. 1972. *The Communist Manifesto*. In Robert C. Tucker, ed., *The Marx-Engels Reader* (New York: Norton).

McGee, Michael Calvin. 1982. "A Materialist's Conception of Rhetoric." In Raymie E. McKerrow, ed., *Explorations in Rhetoric: Studies in Honor of Douglas Ehninger* (Glenview, IL: Scott, Foresman).

McGee, Michael Calvin, and Martha A. Martin. 1983. "Public Knowledge and Ideological Argumentation." *Communication Monographs* 50: 47–65.

Mead, George Herbert. [1934] 1962. *Works of George Herbert Mead, Vol. 1: Mind, Self, and Society from the Standpoint of a Social Behaviorist*. Edited by C. W. Morris. Chicago: University of Chicago Press.

Mills, C. Wright. 1969. "The Politics of Responsibility." In Carl Oglesby, ed., *The New Left Reader* (New York: Grove Press).

Ryan, M. 1982. *Marxism and Deconstruction: A Critical Articulation*. Baltimore: Johns Hopkins University Press.

Wander, Philip. 1983. "The Ideological Turn in Modern Criticism." *Central States Speech Journal* 34: 1–18.

Willkie, R. W. 1974. "The Marxian Rhetoric of Angelica Balabanoff." *Quarterly Journal of Speech* 60: 450–458.

Wright, Michael. 1985, March 3. "National Security's New Insiders." *New York Times Magazine*.

An Afrocentric Communication Theory

MOLEFI ASANTE

I am concerned with nothing less than human maturity. It is my intention to address in a systematic way the pragmatics of communication, particularly with respect to the way we are affected by our environment. Such a task undertakes a reorientation of the enterprise of social science, a reformulation of assumptions, and a more thorough response to the diversity of human experiences in communication. Some writers have begun to see a crisis in the field of social sciences. I see no such crisis, because those who profess belief in the system are inclined to continue their faith. Perhaps what we see is a need for a new world voice. Those who do not believe in the system are the ones expressing difficulty; we are concerned and disturbed.

The historical epoch of Eurocentric social science has its own bases, its own prophets, and its own holy places. We cannot question the integrity of what the system does merely by charging a crisis; we must demonstrate a more righteous way to explore human issues. It is, therefore, the purpose of this present enterprise to present a clarifying portrayal of human beings, in the generic sense, as they exist in contemporary society.

What I propose is a comprehensive plan for analysis rather than the legitimization of any political, economic, or social system. This is in line with the Afrocentric philosophy which views the communication person as at the center of all systems, receiving information from all equally, and stimulating all with the power of his or her personality. Based upon the assumption that the material and spiritual are really parts of the same system, the communication person thrusts himself or herself into the world of the unknown, knowing at all times that messages, symbols, and signs are the influences penetrating his or her every action. Thus, there is no quest here to establish any orientation toward social science based upon a materialistic view or a spiritualistic view.

It is hard to escape the fact that the ideal of social science is rooted in the grounds of materialism. In the works of Europeans, from Plato and Aristotle, from John Locke and B. F. Skinner, we have the full flowering of a material consciousness which led to the compartmentalization of social sciences into sociology, psychology, economics, political science, *ad nauseum*; the process is not yet finished, although social science seems near its end. Even though we find these antecedents in history, the idea of social science as an autonomous field is relatively recent. In fact, in many other parts of the world, outside of Europe and America, it was unheard of until the advent of academic imperialism. Its lateness as a historical phenomenon, however, has not prevented it from exercising a strong influence in the development of human studies. What concerns me is the position which has led us to accept this limited view of reality, and the disastrous effects our acceptance has had on the events of the world. The discovery of "society" as a concept did not really occur in Europe until the eighteenth century, although societies, organized groups of people, had existed thousands of years before. Thus, the special characterization of living arrangements as societies meant that it became possible for people to be studied in numerous ways. The philosophical roots of the works of the Europeans were the same; Europeans all attested to the emergence of societal man on their continent. Hence, Hegel wants the world to know that there is no society unless all are free, meaning, essentially, all whites. The special character of this view as it related to freedom, even in a European sense, had been possible to a greater degree even in classical Africa. At the same time that we see the rise of society as a concept in Europe, and at the same time that European scholars insisted on the "freeness" of those within the society, most European societies held either indentured servants or slaves. A different world would have been created if "family sciences" had become the core of analytic studies.

There have been studies of economic, sociological, and political science dimensions of society for a number of years now. They have inquired into the nature of origins, determinants, norms, potentialities, spheres of influence, and categories of production. But what the European authors have failed to reckon with is the vagueness of their use of the term society. If they have wanted to speak of New Guineans, Africans, or certain groups in South America, they have forced themselves to use the term without meaning what they mean when they use it in a Eurocentric sense. This ambiguity is the cause of much analytical difficulty. But it grows naturally out of a myopic perspective on the world. The balkanization of academic studies as was done with the development of the social disciplines is anathema to the African world voice, except where that view is following or adopting a European view. Some Europeans themselves, however, have pointed out the inherent problems in the conceptualization. One may point to the work of Heinrich von Treitschke, whose work really centers on the importance of the state. Left to von Treitschke, we may be discussing a form of "state sciences," inasmuch as he believed that no society could exist apart from the state. Yet the argument he makes is one that we could easily make for communication of "family sciences" in the African sense. Social science cannot be separated from political science, but neither can it be separated from communication, either as art or science. Indeed, the very gluon of society is communication. While politics may regulate how and where people will live, communication provides the substance of their living together within certain territorial boundaries.

Understanding the context of this rise of society is important to our view of the communication person, a person at once free, collective, global, and aspiring; a person no longer bound by state sentiments, no longer encapsulated by political structures, and no longer one-dimensional; a person becoming, potentializing, and establishing himself or herself. This is not to deny that the social attitude was at one time unprecedented, dynamic, powerful, and controlling. It has not always been so, and will not always be so. We so easily fall into the trap of believing that what is will always be; that is a serious analytical fallacy.

We live in an era, or rather an epoch, and already the new epoch is approaching, bringing with it new concepts, terms, and challenges. Growing from the field of human liberation sentiment, the concept of society was a responsible concept, perhaps in its initial formulation even a positive one. This contextual discussion demonstrates the response of scholarship to the changes within the environment. Our present situation calls for a new formulation which will place communication squarely in the middle of any theoretical and philosophical discussion on the nature of society.

COMMUNICATION CHARACTERISTICS

The characteristics of communication which related to this new humanized epoch are based upon these postulates: (1) A systematic understanding of human interaction across cultures is basic to an effective critique of societies; (2) the potential of human communication resides in the creative development of personality; (3) communication is itself the new social environment; (4) a social situation that distorts human development is illegitimate; and (5) the communication person is holistic.

There are a few scholars, but only a few, who have even fully understood these premises. Some have seen only the viability of communication as analogue; others have misunderstood the creative development of culture and personality as a part of human communication. It is left, however, to more Afrocentric scholarship to capture the true essence of the communication person.

Michael Appiah sees in the Okyeame an integrative function of communication, because it is this person who holds the Akan society together even though the Okyeame serves the state in an official capacity.[1] The Okyeame is not the state; neither is he the people. The Okyeame is the integrator, bringing both the state—in this instance, the king—and the people together. In just this manner, communication serves as the gluon of society, binding all its parts. Nhiwatiwa subscribes to the same view as Appiah, arguing that communication is the source and end of interaction; it is a creation, a collective production.[2] She notes that until we expand the horizon of communication thinkers beyond European models, we will not be able to grasp the holistic nature of the communication person. Support for these positions will continue to gain ground because we are fed up with fragmentation and particularization. Ancient Africans believed in the unity of the universe and demonstrated in their daily work the continuity of the sacred and secular, the spiritual and material; it is this holistic view, characterized by a strong sense of personalism, which establishes the communication person.

I think it is clear that the social science model we have been living with is not able to produce viable patterns of holistic science, nor is it able to transcend the immanent normative characteristics of Western models. This lack has been evident whether the user of the model has been European or not. The problem is not in the person but in the model, inherently so. Thus, the more well-trained, and without intervening training, an individual is in the European model, the more likely he is to interpret the world through inadequate eyes. So we get strange social science from African-American and Chinese-American social scientists, because they have been encapsulated by the European social science model. Stranger still is the fact that they cannot see the problem because they are so closely tied to it, adopting the same justifying phrases, upholding the same positions, and arguing on the same pathological grounds, without knowing the origin or the cause of the model; they embarrass themselves. Fortunately, such intellectual deviance has been seen more in sociology, psychology, anthropology, and economics than in Africology.

Under the present social science model, the potentialities of the academic devoted to a full explication of contemporary society will only be partially realized, because society does not allow the academic to place communication at the center of the analysis. Unable to fulfill the intellectual needs of the scholars who seek a holistic approach to the world, the compartmentalized model forces everyone into frozen blocks. It does not take much imagination to see what happens to the society because of this unnatural arrangement. Sociologists argue in terms of psychologists taking over their territory; anthropologists do not want to be confused by communicationists who insist that they who are not political scientists are not economists, and so on. On the practical side, jobs, orientations, prophets, and textbooks are particularized; they allow one to know one side of the knowledge but not others. Indeed, you may not know all about the particular discipline you choose to know about. The complexity of the field may prevent you from knowing anything but your specialty. Unfortunately, this means that you probably know very little about the nature of humankind. The communication person repudiates cryptic views of humanity. The Afrocentric attempt is to find a just place for integrative knowledge and to enthrone the communication person, trained to have substantive reasons and to provide good choices. The elevation of communication to its proper position in the micro- and macroanalysis of society will eliminate the feuds between disciplinary areas; communication serves as the arbiter of all social science disciplines through messages, information, and persuasion.

NATURE OF HUMAN BEINGS

Until the present epoch, communication theory has been unaware of the age's assumptions about the nature of man and the universe. Almost no Western communicationist has postulated a concept of humanity. Indeed, I do not believe that any theorist in the past thought that he or she should formulate a clear view of humanity and the universe; so many things were given that the communicationist merely followed the formula already established by the Europeans who articulated the concept of social science, later defined more precisely by the Americans. Nevertheless, not even the American communicationists refined the place of humanity in the universe for those interested in studying about the processes which impinge upon people acting and people behaving. It is as if we were playing out the music already set down by some Ellingtonian master without finding our own way. There is, however, nothing wrong with following what others have done, so long as it can be determined that what they have done is consistent with what one must do to make an adequate analysis of the place of humanity in the universe. All our predictions in communication rest upon certain foundations which, if they did not exist, would render the whole process questionable. We cannot take any theoretical formulations for granted; they must be questioned in the light of our conceptualizations of humanity.

To suggest that people communicating was a universal phenomenon but that how they communicate was a specific historical manifestation would have caused the early communicationists considerable difficulty. They were seemingly unable to raise their sights any higher than the European frame of reference which had nurtured, stroked, and comforted them. Thus, it is only in this epoch of communication history that the total enterprise of a philosophical foundation for the study of communication can be properly placed. A theory cannot forever remain innocent of its assumptions about human nature, because it runs the risk of being pocketed by the interests of a given system and of failing to be a true instrument of optimizing the human condition. It is not surprising that rhetoricians like Bryant and Brigance saw communication as a servant of democracy. For them, the adjustment of ideas to people and of people to ideas was the full adventure of human beings communicating. Such a view made any theory of persuasion and information a captive of vested interests. To maximize human recourse, a theory of communication needs to break away from the boundary of specific social or political systems and reach for universal assumptions which can then be tested by those interested in applying them to particular situations.

Communication theory, as developed by contemporary Eurocentric scholars, tends to become like psychology, whereas in the past what communicationists did was often modeled, methodologically, along the lines of a historical approach. This is itself a moment in the history of social science. Since the 1950s, communicationists have been turning more and more toward the empiricism of psychology in an effort to raise the stature of the discipline and to combat all of those who criticize communication for not being able to make predictions. This fact alone has pushed communicationists to consider psychology valuable. Therefore, the postulates that are presented here are indeed a new chapter in the philosophical underpinning of communication. As social science grew out of a certain European climate, social and political, the development of the various models of communication, that is, in terms of method, coincided with certain historical pressures. But even such coincidence was not enough to drive the early communicationists to formulate a view of humanity. An increase in awareness—even more, a revolution in consciousness—occurred in the classrooms and in the streets, but it was largely ignored by theorists who were trying to perfect their newly discovered psychological formulas for application to communication. They were hell bent to walk in the ruts already created for them without ever once giving thought to what contribution they could make to the understanding of society. Thus, as history lost its ability to hold the communicationists in a methodological vise, psychology was tightening its own vise around the necks of a whole generation who never raised their eyes from the statistical chart.

In the present epoch, the dominant methodological motif of communication research derives from psychology. We have no complete formulation of communication as a social science, although we have numerous treatises on how certain aspects of psychology relate to communication. Models of humanity are needed to shed some light on the nature of our whole communication enterprise. It may be of some value to explore the models which have been offered by others, to see where communicationists can make worthwhile contributions. Models of humanity have been given by many scholars in the social sciences. The psychological types seem to predominate, even when the discipline is organization theory. Thus, we have the organization person, the adjusted person, the upwardly mobile person, the encapsulated person, the indifferent person, the manipulator, and the one-dimensional person. There is also the psychological person, the technological person, the historical person, the global person, the parenthetical person, the protean person, the temporary person, the post-Christian person, the irrational person, the multivalent person, the fallible person, the transparent person, the deliberate person, the unitary person, the hopeful person, the transcendent person, the phenomenological person, and the Mozartian person. All these models attempt to address the major problems of human existence. The authors of these models are concerned with diagnosis, description, and prescription for human illness; they all assume that something is seriously wrong with the way we approach the question of human beings in the universe, and each seeks to provide a solution by giving us a method of analyzing ourselves. Frustration, particularly as it figures in keeping people from doing their best work, is the key psychological problem confronting all of these models.

The formulation of a framework for a sound conceptualization of the communication person is the most urgent task of this discussion. I am indebted to both social scientists in a general sense and to Afrocentric scholars in a particular sense for their background contributions to this quirk in my mind. As I have said previously, the idea of the communication person involves an integrated system; the human being stands at the center of the communication environment, acting as organizer of messages. The communication person is a sensory being, responsive to images, sights, and sounds, addicted to urban settings with their inexhaustible supply of visual and auditory stimuli, comfortable with electronic media, at one with computer technology and yet in harmony with the manifestations of humanism, and untrapped by any one political doctrine but open to all human possibilities. Unlike other profiles of humanity, that of the communication person reveals the human being as singularly master of all he or she surveys without becoming a dictator over others; although the communication person possesses the power of information, he or she is checked by a creative belief in the human personality. Communication people are in charge of their own wills because they coordinate from their own centers the information they receive, and at the same time produce and send messages. You may say that communication people are right in the middle of the action, making it logical to themselves and to those who are around them. They sit in board meetings, serve as public relations consultants, study architecture, collect your taxes, and for all practical purposes you may even be one of them. This view of humanity is in opposition to those views that hold the standards of normality to be the norms of any one social system. Most of the models which have been developed have assumed certain individual norms from the society of the model's author and therefore have been compromised in their true value as analytical tools. Thus, the "normal" person is one who conforms to the norms of whatever social or political system the author is highlighting. In such a situation it would be hard for the Chinese scholar to hold the same standards of normality as the person from England. Furthermore, in terms of psychology it may be that to the African the European's quiet expression when he greets a long-missed friend is abnormal. This would be a system-based normality. We must reject system-based normalities for those which cut across or rise above specific systems. Communication man by his very nature is a creature apart from the narrow confines of a limiting view of the world. Our researchers have been blind to inherent fallacies in a system which bases its criteria of normality on those which are immanent in existing social arrangements.

David Berlo's *The Process of Communication* and Hugh Duncan's *Symbols in Society* constitute two of the best examples of efforts by white communicationists (in the case of Duncan, a sociologist-turned-communicationist) to tackle the problem of the nature of humanity.[3] In both cases, however, we get the system-trapped normality which I have been criticizing. Berlo, to be fair to him, never really gives a view of humanity in any clear sense; he implies and infers certain things about the nature of human beings. His linear approach to communication sets him up as a defender of a point of view, a perspective, and some immanent criteria which are indefensible. Berlo is a victim of the social science methodological school which sets criteria for all systems and places by appealing to Eurocentric models. His linear approach to communication, the sender-message-receiver-feedback paradigm, is one-dimensional.[4] It is a historical development not unlike that which brought in the social science paradigm in the first place.

Hence, what David Berlo really articulates is a view of communication similar to the prevailing views of humanity in disciplines such as psychology, sociology, anthropology, economics, and political science. Inasmuch as these disciplines in their present form originated in the Western world, it is not so farfetched to conceive of Berlo's entrapment as natural; to do otherwise would be to ask Western scholars to transcend their own cultural and social situations in ways that few people have ever done in history. We could think of a Martin Luther King, Jr., a Gandhi, and, perhaps, a John Brown. None of these people were in any strict sense scholars, though all possessed that unique ability of great people to analyze situations and to cast their eyes in a visionary way toward the general good of humankind. Berlo's perspective, although closest to that of a communicationist, is still far away from a developed perspective on the nature of humanity.

Duncan, on the contrary, approaches communication from the standpoint of society, and, as a sociologist gathering strength from the critique of Durkheim and Weber, shows that symbols function to create order and disorder in societies. By establishing the link between sociology and communication through society and symbols, Duncan becomes the essential bridge between the fields. His view of human nature, however, is also difficult to discern, unless, of course, one wants to suggest that Duncan is interested in the dramatic person. Following Kenneth Burke even more closely than he follows the sociologists, Duncan sets up his own dramatic stage for analysis of symbols in society.[5] What we must ask is whether or not he has any view other than that of Burke. The answer seems obvious from a reading of both of his major works. Duncan was a prisoner of Burke. He could not get out of the Second European World War. It defined for him the whole nature of humanity; this was his most telling flaw. Berlo, on the other hand, was content to allow his views to emerge from his treatment of the processor of communication; Duncan based his views of humanity on a dramatic metaphor. This metaphor was itself faulty inasmuch as it was only a slice of life. Having seen the disorder created by the displacement of symbols and signs during the war, he could hardly see what was beyond the boundaries of Europe. What Duncan did must be accepted and applauded, on the one hand, because no one had done for sociology what he did for it by showing the connectedness between drama and life. Although George Herbert Mead must be credited with touching on the area as a fruitful intellectual enterprise, it was Duncan who explained how the symbol worked to destabilize and to stabilize societies. His view of human beings was obviously that they are manipulatable creatures, capable of being molded by the drama being played out on the stage of life. On the other hand, Duncan's unawareness of the richness and vastness of the varieties of communication in the African world left his theories pallid and limp when faced with the world communication society. There is a school of communicationists, mainly represented by the likes of Frank E. X. Dance, Samuel Becker, and Gerald Miller, that seems to indicate that the person is less of a factor in communication than, say, the message. Others have contended that a person-centered perspective is most rewarding for the study of communication. They argue from the notion of person-centeredness. But in neither the case of the first group nor that of the second have we had any consistent speculations about the nature of man from a communicationist's point of view. It was as if no systematic formulation could be derived from the field of communication. This was, of course, not the case; it was only an appearance created because, until recently, communicationists have acted like second-class citizens in the world of social science. Those who were able to escape that appearance have often sailed in different waters. Thus, Schramm, McLuhan, Rogers, and Klapper are said to have mixed loyalties. However, it is not so much that their loyalties are mixed as that what they study keeps them away from the personal dyads of the communication situation.

Communication is one of today's most powerful fields. Its expansion as an art and science has not been equaled in the history of American academics. Almost everything in our contemporary society is influenced by communication; it is truly the "becoming" environment. Nothing is extraneous to it as a field of inquiry. The growth of media industries has had an expanding impact on the discipline. Students in universities want to learn about media influences, media development, presentation of messages, development of audiences, and interpersonal communication.

The rising degree of international trade and commerce has opened new possibilities for intercultural communication and diplomatic communication. New arrangements in organizations have called into question our understanding of communication in organizations. These are only a few of the areas to which communication as a field of inquiry is now committed. However, communication cannot succeed as an area of inquiry if it makes systematic commitment, that is, political or social commitment, to any established social order. The reason for this is that certain communication analyses may end up demonstrating in communication terms the non-viability of a given organization or international communication setup. All systems must remain available for communication analysis.

NEW PERSPECTIVE

The methodological posture which the communication field must take is that all sectors of a society and all societies can be explored, analyzed, and questioned on the basis of their contribution to the human personality. Any society that distorts, hinders, or damages the human personality must be called into question. No value-free attitude toward communication situations is possible; indeed, it is an existential impossibility. Unfortunately, too many Eurocentric communicationists have tried to make the discipline respond to the framework of existing social systems; the results have been dismal examples of poor and irrelevant research. They have made the field of communication nothing more than a mimic of the prevailing ideology and, as such, they have been unable to effect any real changes in the condition of the human race.

Communication must transcend what is defined as its purview. Only in this transcendence can it really become the field that it should be for the scholars of this and the next century. Doyin A. Abiola, in her brilliant study of the Nigerian press under military governments, has demonstrated how freedom of the press was a culturally determined term and, in fact, proved that the Nigerian press was, perhaps, "freer" under military rule than it had been under civilian rule.[6] She showed that the press still had the ability to criticize the government and its policies to a degree equal to or greater than that existing prior to military rule. Furthermore, she contended that the press of the Western nations was hopelessly controlled by commercial interests. Here it is necessary to suggest that no press is absolutely free of external constraints, although some may be economically constrained and not politically constrained. Doyin A. Abiola could not have done this study without looking beyond the narrow confines of traditional perspectives, which would not have allowed her to argue that freedom of the press was not objective, but relative. In this sense, she becomes one of the most clarifying critics of the overextended concept of freedom of the press, as well as of the idea that the press is some special preserve for objective advocacy for the people. What she does for the field is to question some of the holy cows, and when she is done, we are directed to the fact that those cows are merely chewing different grass or grazing in different meadows. With her critique of the idea of press advocacy, she states profoundly the cultural connectedness of all institutions within societies. Thus, in Nigeria, where the press is a creation—rather, a development which came with the Europeans—one must look to the traditional cultural relationships in order to determine precisely how the people, the readers, and the audiences view the work of the press. Perhaps, she argues, in the cultural pattern of the society we will be able to find the answer to the press's role in contemporary Nigeria. Since the traditional court announcer or news carrier or drummer was attached to the palace, we have some idea of what the people expect. It is not too much to understand that the audience may very well not comprehend the role of a press that attacks government when the traditional cultural patterns emphasize harmony and dictate that the propagation of news speaks for the royal court. Surely, the leaders of a government in a society where this had been the traditional pattern would be disturbed by a press taking an antagonistic stance. Doyin A. Abiola does not propose that we act one way or the other; she simply lays out the cultural peculiarities of different societies and tells us that we had better look at the patterns within a society before we start to make prescriptions. Her views are controversial and they are certain to receive some criticism from those who believe that communication is the defender of particular worldviews. In the final analysis, such people will continue to hide behind their self-perpetuating, defensive mechanisms. If the human personality is not being elevated, exalted, and healed, then our role as communicationists and communication people is not being fully realized.

All communication begins with the self. The basis of any general view of communication in society, regardless of the particular emphasis—mass, interpersonal, rhetorical, intercultural, or organizational—is the degree to which the individual has minimized his or her message contradictions. One definition of neurosis is a discrepancy between one's potential and one's actual achievement. Sometimes the neurosis may be due to external factors; indeed, this may be the general and common state of neurotic people. They have not been able to achieve their potential because of their environments. Nevertheless, the person who seeks to minimize communication contradictions must do so willingly and with the idea that all communication begins with the self. The ability to find in oneself the source of one's own communication problems is only part of the truth. It is only when an individual remains ineffective as a communicator, in spite of favorable environmental conditions and good natural gifts, that we have to question that individual's functional ability.

What people can communicate to others effectively, they should communicate if it will contribute to the development of their human personalities. A true view of the communication field must rest on what human beings can be as communicators. The field must come alive, make a difference in our lives, as the messages with which we are bombarded influence each of us. In one sense the field of inquiry has yet to live up to the vast dimension of communication in contemporary society.

Edward Hall gives popular voice to the concerns of the masses who are affected by the growth of communication in every sphere by demonstrating how anthropologists can make some sense out of the cultural messages each of us receives.[7] He deliberately addresses the same subjects that we would expect a communicationist to address. He does not defend the indefensible. Some scholars believe that a certain type of communication worldview must emerge and be supported as the only possible outcome. Hall is content to show that different societies have different ways of expressing themselves and that this has nothing to do with inferiority. We have not had any popular works by communicationists to compete with Hall's viewpoint, either in a supportive or a questioning manner. This is not because we do not have ideas or do not know the facts, but rather because we are intoxicated by psychological and physical science methods and have almost abandoned good common sense in our research. Thus, it is not an accident that communicationists are forever questioning themselves, and others are forever questioning them, because what they do is often not derived from systematic concern with human development. Hall, at least, gives the impression that his research is concerned with making life better for human beings, whether they are capitalist businessmen or Marxist proletarians; he feels that he has something to offer the person who wants to improve her or his communication. He is one of the few European-American scholars to come close to the intellectual thrust of the Afrocentric scholars.

Put simply, the communication person, as reflected in the best thinking of the age, is now closer to the African than at any other time in history. This is because of the congruence of African society with the demands of a person's inner-self for harmony. A total environment of symbols, where the communication of needs, wants, and desires operates to maintain the equilibrium of the village, is very much upon us. Quite frankly, there exist numerous villages rather than one single global village. We, as individuals within the various villages, are instruments of the natural harmony. Despite runaway media technology and our insertion into the post-modern communication system, we have emerged and will emerge more concretely as keepers of the society. Our theoretical view must not emphasize the Western conflict view, but the more humanistic voice which is based on harmony. It is not the tradition of African societies to see conflict as a method of progress; in fact, societies are made livable and kept that way by removing and keeping out conflict as much as possible.

Communication is the key ingredient in such a world voice because it is only through symbols that harmony can be restored once it is lost. If it is not regained during one communication event, it is continued at another, perhaps with different players, until it is worked out. In the event of a disagreement between persons, the problem is discussed, and if no solution is forthcoming, the talk is joined by others who may play the major role in devising a solution. In most modern states, such a system would probably prove practical where all kinds of disputes arise over social and behavioral problems. Consider the fact that in a dispute between labor and management the aim is usually to achieve a different synthesis, whereas according to the model suggested by harmony, the aim would be to achieve a justness based upon the relationship between the persons involved in the dispute. Relationship is the operative value in the communication person's view of the world. How do we become mature in a world where relationships are spurious, nonpermanent, and shaky? The communication person is a relationship person, in the sense that relationships are meaningful, because they bind society and are also the source of harmony. When we can learn from the engineer, the computer programmer, the mail carrier, the chemist, the entertainer, or the lawyer with whom we happen to have a relationship, we are secure in a harmonious situation. Individuals who lack relationships are anathema to the new maturity of the communication age; it is too fleeting, too changeable to be caught without relationships. Permanence resides in the maturity of the relationships we possess.

Notes

1. M. K. Appiah, "Okyeame: An Integrative Model of Communication" (Ph.D. diss., State University of New York at Buffalo, 1979).

2. N. Nhiwatiwa, "International Communication Between the African and European World-views" (Ph.D. diss., State University of New York at Buffalo, 1979).

3. David Berlo, *The Process of Communication* (New York: Holt Rinehart &Winston, 1968).

4. Ibid.

5. Hugh Duncan, *Symbols in Society* (New York: Oxford University Press, 1968).

6. Doyin A. Abiola, "The Nigerian Press under Military Rule" (Ph.D. diss., State University of New York at Buffalo, 1979).

7. Edward Hall, *Beyond Culture* (Garden City, NY: Doubleday, 1976), *The Hidden Dimension* (Garden City, NY: Doubleday, 1966), and *The Silent Language* (Garden City, NY: Doubleday, 1959).

Disciplining the Feminine

CAROLE BLAIR
JULIE R. BROWN
LESLIE A. BAXTER

I am reminded of a male colleague, a communication scholar, who has been trying to convince me that I and other feminists lack an internal grace or beauty of character that, once adopted, would allow us to move graciously through the world without anger and confrontation. I have responded that the admonition to "be nice" is precisely what is used to keep us in our places. We will be called crazy. We may be thought churlish and petty. We may be thought unscholarly and unintellectual. If so, we will be joining a long line of honorable women.

Rakow, 211

The ministers of knowledge have always assumed that the whole universe was threatened by the very changes that affected their ideologies and their positions. They transmute the misfortune of their theories into theories of misfortune.

de Certeau, 95–96

Academic writing of the kind published in this or any other professional journal is regulated by clear norms, usually among them the demand for a refined, ahistorical, smoothly finished univocality. That is, works published in most of our academic journals display as little as possible the circumstances and activities of their production. Notably missing, or at least reduced to virtual silence, is the passion that obviously drives our choices to write about particular topics in particular ways. Our writings suppress our convictions, our enthusiasm, our anger, in the interest of achieving an impersonal, "expert" distance and tone. Similarly, journal articles rarely reveal their own histories.

The formative history of an essay is reduced to a notation of an "earlier version," or its history is constituted as a "disciplinary past" by situating the essay in the context of a literature review. Masked also are the mistakes we inevitably make in the process of research and writing. These cannot remain, for we seek a coherent, authoritative, cleanly argued, singular, and defensible position, devoid of "extraneous" or "tangential" details. And gone are any overt signs, except perhaps in a note crediting them, of the "extra" voices of those who provided suggestions or sanctions for revision, in particular the voices of journal editors and referees. These voices are accommodated in such a way as to subsume them, to make them inaudible, to render them part and parcel of the unitary, uncomplicated speech of the author. Finally, the scholarly essay that addresses the working conditions or institutional apparatuses situating the professional scholar is rare indeed. "Scholarship," we would prefer to think, is vouchsafed by academic freedom and intellectual ethics. As a result, issues of institutional or professional power are deemed superfluous to the substance and character of our scholarly efforts.[1] These are but a few of the norms that govern our academic writing, but they surely are recognizable as vital rules to most of us who write in the professional academic milieu of speech communication.

Our approach in this essay is to misunderstand purposefully these norms in the interest of our goal: to point to and critique a constellation of practices in our discipline that some of us would prefer to believe were the relics of a time long past. We refer to the particular themes and enabling mechanisms of a masculinist disciplinary ideology, whose professionalized and seemingly liberal thematic motifs serve as a benign cover for a selectively hostile and exclusionary disciplinary practice.

Our belief that we must break the sacrosanct rules of scholarly writing in order to display these practices is worth examining. In fact, such a move would not be wholly necessary if we were to limit our objective to the one with which we began this project; our goal had been to urge our disciplinary colleagues to eschew any professional/institutional/authoritative use of the findings or rationale of Hickson, Stacks, and Amsbary's 1992 report, "Active Prolific Female Scholars in Communication." However, our project took on added dimension as we attempted to pursue that goal along the ordinary paths toward publication. We wrote an essay responding to the Hickson et al. report and submitted our essay to another prominent speech communication journal for editorial consideration. The anonymous reviews we received (attached to a rejection letter) themselves seemed sufficiently important as ideological fragments that we decided to "up the critical ante," to do more than comment on the Hickson et al. report. Those reviews constitute a rare find, tangible and unusually explicit fragments of what is almost certainly a larger, intolerant disciplinary text that typically remains implicit, unreadable, and deniable.[2] Thus, *in addition to* arguing against use of the Hickson et al. report, which we attempted to do before, we will suggest also that their report is a thematic marker of a masculinist ideology and that the anonymous reviews of our original essay are unusually explicit manifestations of the apparatuses that sustain and enable those ideological themes. We will begin in the next section with a description of our critical stance and with a narrative that chronicles the construction of this manuscript. The sections following are critical readings, in turn, of the Hickson et al. report and of the anonymous referees' reviews of our original response essay. We will conclude by discussing the implications for feminist scholarship of the ideological themes and mechanisms represented by Hickson et al. and by the reviews of our original essay.

FOLLOWING *AND* BREAKING RULES:
PROFESSIONAL PRECEDENTS
AND UNPROFESSIONAL WRITING

If the professional disciplinary rules that we have specified were to find absolute adherence, this essay would have been derailed by now, for it already has revealed something of the history of its production, hinted of a motivation grounded in anger, and staked for itself an explicitly politicized position. Worse, perhaps, we have claimed that it is our *own* disciplinary apparatus that is under indictment. That claim entails two unpleasant possibilities, first, that we *all* have helped to perpetuate the undesirable practices of our discipline by reinforcing and accommodating ourselves to its rules, and second, that the rules themselves are in need of scrutiny and possibly of change. We suspect that a great many journal article submissions have been rejected for far less serious breaches of disciplinary etiquette than these.[3] However, there are precedents for breaking the rules, and this essay takes its particular stance at a nexus among several of them: a specific iteration of the rhetoric of inquiry project, as well as the general positions of the ideological turn, critical rhetoric, feminist theory, and the recent revelatory narrative project on sexual harassment in the *Journal of Applied Communication Research*.

The rhetoric of inquiry project is committed to understand the specific rhetorical constructions of various academic disciplines.[4] While most self-described adherents of POROI attend to the rhetorics of other fields, the aim of the project can and should be reflexive. That is, it can be turned back to examine its own professional instantiation.[5] As Hariman argues, "If rhetorical studies are read into a disciplinary scheme they are read poorly; if they are read sympathetically they subvert the disciplinary reading" (212). He suggests that "the rhetoric of inquiry can itself be aggressively rhetorical—which means more than recognizing that one's own text is as fabricated as any other. The full-blown rhetorical perspective replaces disinterestedness with advocacy, balances specialization with generality, and confronts expertise with an assertion of voice" (213). Hariman's point stands as a precedent, for it suggests that we confront rhetorically the professionalization of university culture, which "has become more a repressive power than a productive power" (212), and it implies that we consider our own field of inquiry in light of that power.

Such an extension of POROI toward a reflection on the professional codes and practices of speech communication is consistent with another set of precedents found in the literature of the "ideological turn," advocated first by Wander and Jenkins, elaborated by Wander ("Ideological Turn"; "Third Persona") and Crowley, and supplemented by discussions of a "critical rhetoric" (McGee, "Text"; McKerrow; Ono and Sloop). The "ideological" project clearly names our discipline's assumptions and apparatuses as targets of critical analysis. What the ideological turn and critical rhetoric literatures highlight and share with Hariman's construction of POROI is the element of the political. All three are explicitly attuned to issues of power as they are inscribed and exercised in all varieties of rhetorical practice, including academic work. They also are committed to understanding the repressive nature of power as it is constructed and acted in discourse. Wander suggests that we attend to the "third persona," a rhetorical excision of the "unacceptable, undesirable, insignificant" elements ("Third Persona," 209), the "audience/s ignored or denounced through the speech, the discourse, the text" ("Politics," 288). And McKerrow specifies a "critique of domination" as a component part of critical rhetoric. Both the ideological turn and critical rhetoric, also like Hariman's position, are animated by poststructuralist thinking, which frequently demands a grounding in practice (rather than in grand theory) and which counts the most "local," everyday life events as legitimate objects of critique (de Certeau; Foucault). The critical writings within the poststructuralist stance often assume extraordinary forms, because the orthodox and prescribed modes of academic writing are unfit or unable to accommodate their positions. Thus, this group of writings also serves as a precedent; it understands the professional as political and academic norms as, in part, repressive. Moreover, it points us to the "local"; it is our position that our own disciplinary practices can and should be counted among the localities we engage critically. Finally, this literature is willing to count as possibly legitimate those writings that would be delegitimized and/or silenced when held to the traditional strictures of professional academic work.

The same is frequently true of feminist theory. Writing is often differentially inscribed and valued in feminist theory; it legitimizes experiential and narrative "evidence," redirection and misappropriation of language, and celebration of *pathos*.[6] In addition, like ideological critique of the type advocated by Wander, feminist theory works at the focal point of power relations, but it understands them principally (sometimes exclusively) as sexually em-bodied or gender-normed. Virtually every iteration of feminist theory, from its most moderate to its most radical construction, claims a transformative or interventionist political stance. That entails changes in academic politics no less than it does alterations in the politics of the public sphere.[7] We see feminist theory as a precedent, for some of the same reasons that we have named the others, but feminist theory specifies our project further; it situates us within a resistant political stance, but one that recognizes the particularity of repressive academic politics with regard to gender-normed practices.

That gender politics are played out in material ways with material effects is starkly clear in the recent special issue of *JACR*, " 'Telling our Stories': Sexual Harassment in the Communication Discipline." The vivid and poignant narratives about personal experiences of sexual harassment in the discipline must lead, as Taylor and Conrad suggest, away from the comforting but inaccurate characterization of gender politics as "someone else's problem" (402, note). They also point out that the university structure is "conditioned by popular images of its pastoral innocence, and of its highly cognitive and theoretical workers—seemingly 'disinterested' intellectuals" (405). Strine recognizes essentially the same image, and she links the disembodied, cognitive realm to material practices in her suggestion that those who engage "their academic work as dispassionate, tough minded 'objectivity' and methodological rigor" may fear "feminine sensibilities and supposedly softer, more experimental and participatory approaches to knowledge" as "contaminants to the rationalistic male-centered academic workplace" (399).

The narrative accounts of sexual harassment ("Our Stories") and the attendant critical analyses by Strine and Taylor and Conrad thus serve notice in two ways that our position takes as precedent. First, they confront our discipline's unique twist on the NIMBY (Not In My Back Yard) syndrome. While acknowledging that increasing numbers of women have populated the discipline, they display the manner in which some of them have been mistreated, not somewhere else, but here—in our midst. Second, they display the effects of gender politics concretely; they set the supposedly disembodied neutrality of academic professionals off against the em-bodied materiality of their persons.

Certainly the story we have to tell is *far* less frightening and grotesque than those told by the survivors of these sexual harassment events. However, in a sense, our story is of a piece with those events. "How things work," the "norms governing the rational operation of the academic sphere," constitute the ideological background (Strine, 391). This ideology enables both the episodic sexual harassment described in the narratives as well as the incidents of erasure and devaluation of women represented by the Hickson et al. report and enforced by the journal referees' reviews of our initial response essay.

The Hickson et al. report rank orders women in the field according to the number of articles they have published in journals indexed by Matlon and Ortiz. According to Hickson and his colleagues, the purpose of this ranking project is to "determine a yardstick for active, female researchers in communication" (351). They suggest that such a guideline is important for three reasons: (1) its use in tenure and promotion decisions; (2) its value in the sociology of knowledge, to determine where influence has been located in the discipline; and (3) its value to persons in other disciplines who want to know the comparative status of one individual's scholarly record (351). The report is one of several studies undertaken in recent years by Hickson and his colleagues to assess scholarly productivity in the discipline.[8] The research program by Hickson et al. represents but a portion of what Erickson, Fleuriet, and Hosman have recently described as the discipline's growing "cottage industry of counting articles authored by prolific researchers" (329).[9] However, the Hickson et al. study of active, prolific female researchers is unique in its exclusive focus on a specific demographic/cultural group.

Soon after the report was published, we found ourselves locked in conversations about it. Although the three of us are in most respects professionally dissimilar (in rank, in research and teaching interests, in intellectual assumptions, etc.), we found each other to be equally dismayed by the *idea* of the report and in agreement that we should write an essay responding to it. Our dismay was grounded in both general and particular concerns. At a general level, the Hickson et al. report represented evidence of our discipline's continuing fascination with identifying the most prolific scholars in our midst, a fascination we find misguided. However, because others have recently argued that this fascination is problematic, we will not elaborate here on these general concerns.[10] At a more particular level, we were fearful that Hickson et al.'s analysis of prolific female scholars would be embraced as a positive statement about women and for women in the discipline and that the masculinist ideology that ironically undergirds the analysis might be disregarded. This ideology is pervasive in the academy, including speech communication, and thus may not be immediately apparent to most readers in the absence of explicit discussion. The Hickson et al. report thus constitutes a fruitful "local" target for critique; it is, on one level, a seemingly benign if not positive statement about and for women but which, upon closer scrutiny, functions in precisely the opposite manner. By examining ways in which the masculinist ideology is apparent in the Hickson et al. report, we hoped to enter into the ongoing conversation about speech communication scholarship as gendered.[11]

Our response essay was, from our point of view, rather modest. In fact, we worried that it might be too moderate, an irony in light of what our referees' reviews would suggest about it and about us. Nonetheless, we submitted the essay and, within a few weeks, received those reviews. After the initial shock of reading the reviews wore off, we realized that what we had received was a gift of sorts—two institutionally sanctioned documents that displayed the enabling mechanisms that support the kinds of ideological themes Hickson et al. advance.

In the next section, we have reproduced almost the entirety of our original essay that responded to Hickson et al. We have eliminated one set of arguments and incidental markers thereof from the original version. This set of arguments addressed the factual accuracy, stylistic competence, and logical coherence of the Hickson et al. report.[12] Our decision to excise that component of the manuscript here is based on our realization that it probably served as a diversion from the principal point of our essay. We had attempted to link this set of arguments to our general ideological point by suggesting the possibility that such concerns as accuracy, style, and coherence simply might have been too easily disregarded in the case of an essay "merely" about women. However, ultimately the issues of accuracy and logical coherence seemed the only explicit substantive concerns of the initial referees; we had essentially provided them with an alibi for their refusal to address the primary arguments of our response. In the interest of providing the reader with an accurate rendering of our ideologically-based objections to the Hickson et al. report, we have refrained from revising our original argument, despite the fact that any number of minor changes have occurred to us with the passage of time. However, none of these changes would alter the substance of our reaction to the report. The next section, thus, contains the remainder of our original essay.

SUBJECT OF OR SUBJECT TO RESEARCH?: A RESPONSE TO HICKSON, STACKS, AND AMSBARY'S "ACTIVE PROLIFIC FEMALE SCHOLARS IN COMMUNICATION"

A number of scholars have described the "chilly climate" that confronts female faculty members in higher education.[13] We believe that the temperature has dropped even further for females in the speech communication discipline with the publication of Hickson, Stacks, and Amsbary's report of "research productivity" among "active prolific" female scholars. The Hickson et al. article constitutes an overt, if unintended, display of insensitivity toward and aggression against women in the discipline. In writing this response, we hope to persuade our female and male colleagues in the field to resist any use of its results.

Our desire to resist the Hickson et al. report is based in one simple observation: Although it is a report about women, it neglects or implicitly denies the fact that it is about women in virtually all of its constituent features—rationale, assumptions, method, and language. That is, Hickson et al. have named "female" as a category and then failed to consider the gendered specificity of the category. Their omission of any hint of the female gender among their "Key Concepts" list is a telling marker of a discourse that *effaces* women even as it specifies them as a group for observation. We submit that a discourse about women must not forget or erase women. But that is, paradoxically, what the Hickson et al. report accomplishes. And it does so by means much more significant and consequential than neglecting to name as a key concept the gendered group it purports to study.

Before exploring our specific concerns with the Hickson et al. article, however, let us be clear about our own stance. First, we do not wish to detract from the many scholarly accomplishments of the particular women listed in Table I ("Most Prolific Active Female Scholars in Communication, 1915–1990") of the Hickson et al. report. These women and many more not listed in Table I merit our respect for their scholarly contributions. Second, we do not believe or assume that the three *individuals* named

Hickson, Stacks, and Amsbary are themselves aggressors against women. Neither do we believe or assume that the "aggressor" label is appropriate to describe the *persons* who reviewed or approved publication of this article. But it is not necessary to assume or make such individual attributions in order to conclude that the Hickson et al. *discourse* functions as an act of aggression against women in the field. We adhere to the general positions taken by a number of contemporary thinkers that entire groups, institutions, or other power networks are speaking when individuals speak.[14] To put it most simply, a discourse of right, power, and privilege is approved within our (or any) discipline, and that discourse is spoken by individual members of the discipline. In this case, it is being spoken by Hickson, Stacks, and Amsbary. "Their" discourse indicts us all to the degree that we allow it to stand without resistance, because it is also *our* disciplinary discourse. So, when we refer to "Hickson et al.," "the authors," "they," "them," etc., we do not point to the individuals Hickson, Stacks, and Amsbary alone, but also to the entire institutional/discursive structure that legitimates their report.

Disciplinary discourses enable and ratify certain lines of argument and certain actions. In this case, "our" disciplinary discourse has authorized a ranking project grounded in an agenetic perspective of impersonal abstraction, disciplinary territoriality, individuation, and hierarchy. A number of scholars have identified this perspective with the "male paradigm" that dominates higher education.[15] These scholars, of course, are highlighting the themes of agency and communion that have been associated with males and females, respectively, in much social scientific research.[16] The fact that female scholars were subjects of, and arguably subject *to*, the Hickson et al. agenetic project is particularly distressing to us, because it is precisely this paradigm, and all that it represents, which constitutes the central obstacle to female achievement in academia. . . . A consideration of what/whose interests are likely to be served by their report [intensifies our distress]. We turn . . .[now] to the assumptions and ideological difficulties we find most disturbing in the Hickson et al. report. . . .

The Imposition of the "Male Paradigm"

The "male paradigm" is characterized, first, by *impersonal abstraction*. Initially, we wish to challenge the legitimacy of a project whose purpose is to develop context-free, universalistic "yardsticks" that can be applied in particular cases, in this instance, to female researchers in the field. Such a project, according to many scholars, is anchored by a male-centered system of logic and morality, in contrast to the personalized and contextualized ways of knowing that are more typical of female socialization.[17] The male-centered model of agency fundamentally is predicated on the separation of the person from contextual particulars. Thus, from the perspective of the "male paradigm," judgment should be based on universal principles and abstract laws that are characterized by "objectivity." The imposition of this male-centered model on females is offensive on its face, because it essentially forgets that they are female. Moreover, the resulting "yardsticks" ignore important contextual factors that distinguish female and male career patterns of research performance.

One of the most important of these contextual factors is the differing temporal rhythms that characterize the scholarly performances of female and male academics. Graphic representations of scholarly activity over the entire life of a career tend to be saddle-shaped for men and to be of a linear progression pattern for women. That is, male research activity tends to be high for the first five to ten years after the doctorate, then levels off at the associate level before picking up again at a later point in the career.[18] By contrast, female research activity tends to be less than male research activity prior to tenure, but greater than male activity after the point of tenure (Task Force on Women in Higher Education). We recognize that the possibility of different temporal rhythms in the research activities of female and male scholars in speech communication has not been systematically researched, but we note with interest that the descriptions of gender-linked patterns "ring true" for the three of us, based on our own career paths to date. Hickson et al. display insensitivity to the possibility of gender-linked trajectories of scholarly activity in electing to measure productivity "outputs" at a single point in time. Further, in emphasizing the importance of females publishing early in their careers (355), Hickson et al. promulgate the male career trajectory as the universal standard against which female scholars should be assessed. Obviously, females whose careers are better characterized by the linear progression pattern as opposed to the saddle-shaped pattern are ill-served early in their professional careers by evaluation grounded in the male career model. The issue of who is served (or not) by the Hickson et al. "yardsticks" is one we return to later in this response.

Also obscured in the Hickson et al. abstraction is the *character* of the publications they enumerate. While Hickson et al. claim that their report is "valuable in the sociology of knowledge to determine where influence has been in the discipline" (351), nowhere do they make even cursory mention of what is said in any of the articles they list. Their failure to do so suggests a cynically reductionistic view of scholarship and its purpose: *That* writing occurs is somehow more significant or influential than *what* is written or *how* that writing is read. This unidimensional portrait of scholarly activity insults both writers and readers by rendering their labors invisible and irrelevant.

Moreover, the authors' preoccupation with tabulating individual output evidences a naïve conception of "influence," a narrow conception of "knowledge," and a rather thorough misunderstanding of the sociology of knowledge project. Based on their operational definitions, Hickson et al. appear to believe that influence is strictly a function of output rate and that "output" can be unproblematically equated with "knowledge." Accepting these beliefs seems to require that we ignore an entire range of *institutional* routines that enable production, that set the priorities used to assess the significance of that production, and that condition the acceptance or rejection of something *as* "knowledge." In other words, Hickson et al. assume that "influence" and "knowledge" inhere in the fact of production. They fail to consider how these latter characteristics are indeed *interpretations* made possible by the social, historical, and ideological context surrounding scholarly production/consumption. What, for instance, leads the authors to focus on journal publications as an index of influence? Why choose the narrow range of publications indexed by Matlon and Ortiz? These questions cannot be answered at the level of product/output alone. The answers reside in the context surrounding product/output, that is, in the history and politics of this discipline and the disciplinary system generally. And it is these systemic, contextual factors—the ones that lead us to "produce" in certain ways and to define the relative influence of that production—that Hickson et al. leave unexamined.

In light of the authors' silence concerning the institutional dimensions of scholarly production and the assessment thereof, we find it difficult to accept their report as "valuable in the sociology of knowledge" (351). Simply put, their report lacks a clear *sociological* dimension. Rather, their report displays and attempts to aggregate *individual* profiles. This approach displaces the social by construing it as essentially epiphenomenal (i.e., as the by-product of aggregated individual activity). In so doing, Hickson et al. place themselves at conceptual odds with much existing work in the sociology of knowledge. From the vantage point of Berger and Luckmann, Bourdieu, Toulmin, and others, social systems prefigure individual actors and provide the logics in and against which individuals may justify and give meaning to activity. Individual activity, while not necessarily determined by extant social systems, occurs in continual *relationship* to these systems. This view of the individual–social relationship is fundamentally dissimilar to the one suggested by Hickson et al. Insofar as the authors attempt to justify their project by aligning it with a literature obviously not amenable to the perspective they advance, we find their justification considerably less than compelling.

The "male paradigm" is characterized, second, by *disciplinary territoriality*. Concern with strict disciplinary boundaries certainly varies among scholars in the field.[19] Our point is that concern with clearly demarcated disciplinary boundaries displays a kind of territoriality that is likely to be gender-linked. Female scholars in the humanities and social sciences, in fact, tend to be more interdisciplinary than their male counterparts (Ward and Grant). A number of scholars have argued that female academics may be attracted more than their male colleagues to scholarly projects that bridge several disciplines because of differing gender socialization experiences.[20] Females are social-ized to construct social reality by connecting the multiple perspectives that constitute their relationship-oriented worlds.[21] An interdisciplinary perspective, in turn, could result in high rates of publication in interdisciplinary outlets or in the journals of other disciplines. In developing statistical "yardsticks" cast narrowly along disciplinary lines, Hickson and his colleagues render a portrait of scholarship by females in speech communication that may be seriously distorted in both quantity and profile. Although the three of us hardly constitute an adequate sample of female scholars in speech communication, we nonetheless note with interest that our own career experiences are captured much better by an interdisciplinary model of knowledge as opposed to a male-centered model of narrow disciplinarity; of our total of 66 scholarly publications, only 36 percent are included in the journals indexed by Matlon and Ortiz. Hickson et al. attempt to pre-empt this concern about interdisciplinary work by acknowledging that people, including those females listed as the "most active and prolific," may publish elsewhere (354–355). What Hickson et al. ignore is that females in the discipline may display disproportionately less disciplinary territoriality than males in their publication habits; if that is the case, Hickson et al.'s use of the Matlon and Ortiz index is inappropriate for establishing anything like a "yardstick" to measure scholarly activity among females in the field. Yet Hickson et al. *assert* that, "Certainly the journals in this study constitute where the vast majority of professors in the field of communication consider that they strive [*sic*] to publish" (355). This claim is open to serious question, and the confidence with which it is advanced itself reveals a territorial presumption.

Also revealing of the presumptiveness of disciplinary territoriality in the Hickson et al. report is their question: "Why are such yardsticks important to the discipline?" (351). If women are less territorial with respect to disciplines than their male colleagues, then Hickson et al. fail in their attempt to warrant the legitimacy of their project by answering this question. More pertinently, their question betrays the very territoriality that they presume to be characteristic of female scholars. The question manifests concern for a bloodless, abstract construct—"the discipline"—and not the material individuals and groups that constitute it. In fact, the three authors seem interested in "the discipline" at the *expense* of individuals and groups. They understand the results of previous studies of research activity as an "indictment" of individuals' publication records (351). Thus, this report and others like it are taken to be important on the grounds that they enable "the discipline" (or those who speak for it) to survey the "territory" of disciplinary publication records and render judgments on them. If publication records within the disciplinary territory are deemed inadequate, then indictment of individuals seems the only conclusion; on this logic, the possibility that individuals simply have crossed the disciplinary borders apparently is unthinkable.

Individuation is the third characteristic of the "male paradigm." By "individuation," we refer to a set of beliefs that revolve around the presumed autonomy or independence of the individual agent, in contrast to a communal view of the individual as embedded in a web of connections with others.[22] One of the beliefs implicated in the male model of individuation is a monadic conception of "influence." Hickson and his colleagues claim that their purpose is to "determine where influence has been in the discipline" (351). However, their understanding of "influence" is a male-centered, individualistic one in contrast to a more relationally-centered conception. Certainly, a person is positioned to be influential by publishing in scholarly outlets, but we would argue that "influence" is inherently a relational phenomenon; that is, whether or not an individual is "influential" can be determined only by what happens *between* people. If Hickson et al. were interested in the "influence" of published authors, perhaps their project would have been better advanced by studying citation patterns, that is, determination of the frequency with which a given author's work has been cited by others in the ongoing scholarly dialogue. Such an alternative approach would have the added benefit of broadening the domain of potentially influential publications to include articles published in other disciplines' journals, as well as books and articles published in interdisciplinary journals. And if citation patterns were studied across several disciplines, we might gain insight into the "influence" of given authors as their ideas and research gain currency outside the parameter of the journals indexed in Matlon and Ortiz.

A second belief implicated in the male model of individuation is the presumption of individual volition. Hickson et al. treat issues of female employment, publication, etc., as if they were entirely volitional. The authors remind readers of the importance of publishing early in one's career and of the correlation between research productivity and working in a doctoral-granting institution. But such advice presupposes that individual female academics are in sole control of their own scholarly activity, making choices without constraint concerning where to work and when to publish. Unfortunately, such advice, however well intended, ignores the structural constraints that still face female academics with respect to problems of sponsorship and mentorship, access to scholarly informal networks, burdens of institutional committee service, and so forth, all of which affect female research activity in ways unrelated to matters of individual volition.[23]

Last and perhaps most important, the "male paradigm" is characterized by *hierarchy*. By "hierarchy," we refer to the acceptance of asymmetrical relations between people, with some groups or individuals gaining dominance or empowerment through the subordination and disempowerment of others. "Hierarchy" is a simple and relatively straightforward concept in the abstract but one which surfaces in a myriad of insidious ways in the Hickson et al. report. It is in its hierarchical assumptions that we believe the Hickson et al. report most clearly moves from "mere" insensitivity and inappropriateness to aggression. The ranking offered by Hickson et al. discursively positions women against one another. The women ranked among the most "prolific" are transformed into evidence for a negative commentary about those not ranked. The hierarchical nature of the list also discursively casts the women on the list against one another; being ranked as #1, according to the obvious hierarchical logic of ranking, is "better than" being ranked as #2. In addition, "active" female scholars are discursively privileged over "inactive" female scholars. Thus, women are cast not merely in the role of objectified, scrutinized subjects; they are cast also in a hierarchically competitive position vis-à-vis one another. Such individually-based competition seems particularly inappropriate when applied to women who are socialized to work more relationally and collaboratively than are men.[24] And to play female scholars off against one another, when they have been playing against a stacked deck in any case, is nothing short of offensive.

Equally offensive is Hickson et al.'s description of their report as an attempt to establish a "yardstick for active, female researchers in communication" (351). Hickson et al.'s report-as-yardstick hearkens to the vulgar (and frequently brutal) political arrangements characterizing dominant/non-dominant group relations in times we have come to believe were "less enlightened." The yardstick (along with its metonymic associates, such as "the ruler" and "the rod") often functioned as the instrument used to "articulate" and reinforce the punitive politics of domination and oppression. The teacher took the ruler to the unruly or obstreperous child; the paternalistic master took the rod to the wayward or disobedient slave; the male authors of this report take the yardstick to females scholars—such is the associational chain summoned in their choice of language. In each case the yardstick (or its equivalent) is used by one individual to *discipline* another. In so doing, *discipline* and those traditionally charged with its preservation are maintained.

Yet, Hickson et al. explicitly link the yardstick with its most literal use—measurement. On its face, measurement seems to be a neutral enough activity. When we consider the myriad choices and assumptions made in even the most routine acts of measurement, however, even this seeming "neutrality" quickly disappears. Measurement necessitates division, categorization, and (more or less explicitly) comparison. Given that persons can be divided, categorized, and compared according to a variety of logics, and that choosing one logic over another changes the shape, orientation, or sense of value associated with the persons measured, acts of measurement, like language choices, are never free of tendency.

Equally significant is the fact that measurements are performed *on* (as opposed to, say, *with*) persons. In this sense, then, measurements function *to order*, *to contain*, and in these senses, *to discipline*. These functions certainly argue for the sociopolitical dimensions of measurement. Consequently, the "yardstick-that-measures" functions similarly to the "yardstick-that-punishes." While not as obviously brutal, the "yardstick-that-measures" functions as a show of strength by the institutionally powerful to those whose "unchecked" activities threaten order and discipline.

The fact that Hickson et al. have used the term "yardstick" in other studies ("Active Prolific Scholars") not segregated by gender fails to serve as an alibi for its use in a study about women. They are *communication* scholars, as are those who approved their manuscript for publication. It is no secret to any of us in this discipline that language comes laced with connotative history and unavoidable tendentiousness. These connotations and tendencies change with the context of utterance. The "yardstick" metaphor, when used by male authors to describe their examination of women, has a more sinister ring than it does when used inside a less lopsided set of power relations. Language choices are rarely innocent, even if motives are.

Hierarchy seems to be implicated as well in the authors' apparent lack of rationale for this research undertaking. It is important to note that they make no explicit case for the value of ranking *female* scholarly activity. They do include a paragraph that, we presume, is supposed to count as a rationale; in it, they note the number of women who have acted as president of the Speech Communication Association or as editors of three SCA journals.[25] That observation is the *only* initial remark Hickson et al. make about *women's* roles in the discipline. However, it is problematic on two counts. First, it implies that contributions to the field are or should be measured according to people's occupancy of positions at the "top" of organizational hierarchies. Second, it provides utterly no justification for the measurement of active scholarship. The suggestion that women have been journal editors and SCA presidents and that, *therefore*, an enumeration and ranking of women's publication records is legitimate, is a non sequitur.

Hickson and his colleagues also claim that, given prior research, "it is now possible" (351) to conduct their research project. Possibilities aside, the question of the *desirability* of this project still remains. It evidently *is* possible, but we are left with the issue of what licenses three men to single out women as a group for scrutiny. There is no obvious reason that presents itself in the literature for segregating research production by gender; no corresponding ranking of active *male* prolific scholars, for example, has presented itself. Rather, one must assume for purposes of warranting the Hickson et al. study that active female researchers have published systematically less than their active male colleagues in the field, in order to see any need at all for this research.[26] It may even be true that women have published less than men, but that is an unsupported hypothesis, not a documented claim. So, how can this unsupported hypothesis serve as an assumptive premise of this report? How, in fact, can it be assumptive when it is, itself a testable hypothesis? Its status as an assumption marks the ease with which women can be seen as inherently less accomplished than their male counterparts. The very taken-for-grantedness of the premise is itself the problem. To be less accomplished is one thing; to always be assumed to be less accomplished is another. Unfortunately, the assumption may well contribute to the condition. Whether or not it does, the assumption itself, and the apparent ease with which it is accepted, are offensive and inherently damaging to women.

The fact that Hickson et al. articulate no clear rationale for this study is disturbing not only because of what it forces the reader to accept as a premise; the lack of persuasive rationale is also troubling, given what the study *does*. Without any clear warrant, three men have conducted surveillance on women's research records (the bodies of their research?) and proceeded to rank order the most prolific among them (those whose bodies of research have the best measurements?). Our parenthetical questions suggest that we take this to be the academic equivalent of a beauty pageant. Indeed, it does seem an appropriate analog. It has all of the necessary trappings: line up the women, gaze on the parts you believe most pertinent, total up the points, and rank order them. That *this* pageant should be conducted strictly by men even does "real" beauty contests one better; the latter frequently have female judges or administrators. Of course, the analog breaks down on another profoundly telling point as well—women in beauty contests presumably choose to participate in such displays.[27]

The authors' consistent use of the term "prolific" to describe the women they display reinforces this sense of woman-as-object-of-male-surveillance. The reader comes away from the report knowing little more than which female bodies produced more than which other female bodies. This, coupled with the "prolific" language, summons an age-old way of construing female identity: Women are what their bodies can produce. And men monitor and regulate female production/reproduction as a means of asserting control over both the products and the power such products might afford the women who produce them.

It is neither fair nor convincing to assume that a woman's choice to publish in scholarly journals entitles three men, in essence, to reduce her activities to the fact of her physiology, to display her as a "better breeder" than other women, or to pit her "academic measurements" against other women's. These uses of women's labor are unfair, regardless of the interests such exhibitions may purport to serve and regardless of the voyeuristic pleasures such exhibitions offer. Just what purposes, and whose, might be served are issues to which we turn in the next section.

What/Whose Interests Are Served?

Hickson et al. conclude their "rationale" with the assertion that their report ought to provide colleagues in other disciplines with information useful in evaluating an individual female from the field "in a comparative sense" (351). But if the intended use of the "yardsticks" developed in the Hickson et al. piece is for tenure and promotion decisions, to whom would it be useful in the process of rendering such decisions? The majority of women named in Table I are full professors. The overwhelming majority are tenured. We have no wish or right to speak for these female colleagues or to comment on the personnel procedures at their respective institutions, but we suspect that the "yardsticks" would be of marginal utility, at least in terms of tenure and promotion issues, for most of those listed. What of the women in the discipline *not* named to the list? Does this ranking have value for them? That seems even more doubtful. We find it exceptionally difficult to believe that anyone would volunteer to a personnel committee that she was not ranked among the most active female scholars of her field. So, if the ranking is of use to someone in personnel decisions, it seems unlikely that someone is the female candidate for promotion or tenure. Instead, the ranking seems more likely to be useful as an *impediment* to a woman's advancement. It requires little imagination to summon a scenario in which a female scholar is taken to task by her colleagues for not having accomplished "enough" or in the "right places" to be considered among the field's most active female scholars. Thus, this ranking serves the interests of those who would obstruct a woman's progress, for it makes acts of professional aggression against women even less difficult than they otherwise might be.

The Hickson et al. report threatens to work against the interests of women at a more "intimate" level as well. That is, what sorts of responses does the report most likely provoke in female readers? What do these likely responses "do" in terms of constructing, reinforcing, or modifying a sense of personal or professional identity? What do these likely responses suggest about how a given female reader sees herself in relation to both male and female colleagues?

As we see it, three types of response seem most likely given how the report was compiled and presented. First, someone who does not appear on the list is likely to feel anxious about her own rate of scholarly activity and thus about her professional future. This response also leads to nervousness about being shown up by "one's own." Second, what if one does appear on the list? Shouldn't this provide some measure of security and gratification? Perhaps. Yet, given the hierarchical nature of the list and the competitiveness that hierarchy almost inevitably promotes, we can imagine that women ranked lower than first might feel less than gratified. Even the number one spot could be an awkward one to occupy. Such a position may create the alienation that comes from being raised—presumably without being offered a choice—above one's peers.

A third response is to be disheartened, as we are, by the fact that such a list exists at all. We are disheartened to see women set against each other in this fashion. We are disheartened to see some of our male colleagues' apparent obliviousness to how this may harm and discourage us. We are disheartened by the fact that "our" discipline would, however tacitly, condone and encourage this sort of activity. We are disheartened when we consider what this says about the state of our collective consciousness regarding gender issues. And we are disheartened when we consider the kind of precedent this report threatens to set. Are "we" entitling the already secure to wield the "yardstick" against a host of marginalized groups? Does the publication of this report give the green light to future rankings of "prolific" African-American scholars? Hispanic scholars? Gay or Lesbian scholars? Are "we" authorizing the institutionally powerful to continue speaking *about* the less powerful, rather than encouraging the powerful to speak *with* us, or, more importantly, to let us speak?

Each of these reactions potentially invoked by the Hickson et al. report is painful in its own right. These reactions taken as a group are even more so. We find it difficult to imagine how any woman could be encouraged, gratified, or take any pleasure when she considers herself in relation to the report. Certainly it would be difficult to do so without simultaneously experiencing some sense of alienation from what could be a sustaining community—other women.

Finally, Hickson et al.'s report functions to reinscribe a disempowering form of subjectivity "offered" to women all too frequently in this culture. As John Berger describes it:

> To be born a woman has been to be born, within an allotted and confined space, into the keeping of men. The social presence of women has developed as a result of their ingenuity in living under such tutelage within such a limited space. But this has been at the cost of a woman's self being split in two. A woman must continually watch herself. . . . From earliest childhood she has been taught and persuaded to survey herself continually.
>
> And so she comes to consider the *surveyor* and the *surveyed* within her as the two constituent yet always distinct elements of her identity as a woman. (46)

The Hickson et al. report, then, serves to demarcate the space of female productivity and to remind us that we are under surveillance by male "colleagues."

More insidiously, however, reports such as this encourage us, quite literally, to split ourselves from ourselves. They do so at two levels. Most obviously, such reports isolate individual women from each other. And such reports isolate us from an integrated sense of self by handing us "the yardstick" so that we might survey and (often negatively) evaluate ourselves. We are hard pressed to think of a way that any community could more effectively control any group of members. We are equally hard pressed to imagine how reinforcing such an isolated and self-limiting form of identity could possibly be in the best interests of those to whom it is offered. Finally, we are hard pressed to see how splitting scholars from themselves and from each other serves "the discipline" in any meaningful way. How could encouraging isolation and self-alienation possibly lead to greater intellectual growth and creativity? How can any community flourish when more and more of its members are limited, made fearful, absorbed in self-surveillance, and, quite literally, broken? This is in no one's best interest, not even those with the most invested in maintaining traditional disciplinary boundaries and relations of power.

APPROVED IDENTITIES, READINGS, AND POLITICS: THE ANONYMOUS REVIEWS AND THE DENOUEMENT

Within a few weeks of submitting "Subject Of or Subject To Research?" we received a rejection letter, accompanied by two reviews that recommended against publication of our essay. In general we found the reviews to be overt displays of ideological mechanisms that not only approve the themes of the masculinist paradigm, but which seek to ensure that the masculinist paradigm represents the exclusive thematic directive for professional work in the discipline. The two reviews do more than reproduce the themes of the masculinist paradigm; they buttress its privilege by advancing what can count as approved (and disapproved) identities, readings, and politics within the discipline. In using these two reviews as explicit objects of analysis, we bring them into the public conversation of scholarly discourse. As Myers observes, a scholarly community's review of a text can be viewed as "a negotiation of the status that the ... community will assign to the text's knowledge claim" (328).[28]

Before we turn to a discussion of the approved (and disapproved) identities, readings, and politics that are embedded in these two reviews, we think it is important to emphasize that the mechanisms of the masculinist paradigm, like those of any ideology, perform enabling functions for a scholarly community. The masculinist paradigm, like other paradigms, provides a scholarly community with what Foucault calls "apparatuses of knowledge" (*Power/Knowledge*, 106); these apparatuses enable the production of research by invoking shared motivations, vocabularies, assumptions, and methods. At the same time, however, these knowledge apparatuses constitute systems of control that exclude alternative intellectual practices.[29]

The focal work of both these reviews is the designation of approved and disapproved identities; that is, articulation of the range of what one is able to say and how, as well as who one can be as an acceptable member of a group, in this case the discipline. The related issues of approved readings and approved politics emerge in connection with the identity prescriptions. By approved readings, we mean prescriptions for "correct" ways of reading. By implication, "incorrect" ways of reading can be identified, rendered unacceptable, and, preferably, silenced. As Crowley observes, "[S]ince there are correct readings, misreading must occur through some fault in the reader who produces it. If two readers disagree, one of them has failed somehow" (459).[30] An approved politics refers to the roles particular individuals and groups are allowed to play vis-à-vis one another or the moves they are allowed to make—especially in cases of conflict or competition for scarce resources. In the case of an academic discipline, these supposedly "scarce resources" might be prestige, designations of "expertise," or even career survival.[31]

The overarching identity approved in the reviews of our essay is that of the professional intellectual or scholar.[32] Referee #1 questions our status as scholars by rejecting our manuscript's status as a "scholarly article," indicating, in part, that "there are too many feline, petty attacks in this manuscript and too much ball-bashing to be a scholarly article." Referee #2 marks us immediately as "unprofessional" and "anti-intellectual," indicating that he or she is "embarrassed" for the academic field for producing persons who have written "the single worst piece of 'scholarship'" that he or she has ever reviewed. Both reviews further specify the stances and attitudes that "professionals," "intellectuals," or "scholars" must demonstrate in order for these roles to be designated as approved identities within the discipline. Appropriately "professional" scholars should be: (1) politically neutral, (2) respectful toward science, (3) mainstream, and (4) politely deferential.[33]

Disciplinary professionals, first, must be *politically neutral*. Referee #2 opines that our manuscript was not a "critique of the published article" but a "political harangue against so-called 'male paradigm,' which is nothing more than the typical male-bashing brought forth by Marxist writers." This reviewer differentiates sharply between "critique" and "political harangue" but does not specify the boundary between them, apparently believing that it should be apparent to anyone wearing an approved identity. Certainly not all "political" discourse is "harangue," nor would most of us wish to be seen as engaging in the latter. But critique is always political and that seems to be the real problem for referee #2. That becomes clearer in an examination of the next identity characteristic and its attendant prescriptions for approved modes of reading.

The second identity characteristic, *respectfulness toward science*, is invoked in the second referee's claim that our manuscript was "laced with extreme anti-science orientations with the mask of the 'male' paradigm doing the front work." We understand the reproach of "anti-science" to define negatively a range of approved behaviors by which professionals either subscribe to the supposed value-neutrality of scientific work or at least agree not to expose the tendentious and valued character of so-called objective work.

The approved respect for the value-neutrality of science links naturally with a related directive for producing an approved reading. According to this view, published texts are transparent, easily and "correctly" readable; to read for or infer assumptions is unnecessary and apparently even unacceptable. This stance promulgates the naïve understanding of scholarly languages (prose, tabulations, calculations, and the like) as neutrally privileged and magically exempt from tendency. Both reviewers find our reading of the Hickson et al. report to be "wrong" because we challenged its value-neutrality. Referee #1 "find[s] it insulting," in her capacity as one of the original reviewers of the Hickson et al. report, that we were "incapable of seeing" that its goal was straightforwardly "to identify and recognize women in the field who have sustained records of scholarship." The second referee also concludes that our analysis of the Hickson et al. report was in error because we failed to read the piece as a celebratory documentation of the discipline's "advancement" of women in the field.

Ironically, however, these referees appear to speculate freely about the objectives of the Hickson et al. report. According to the referees' approved mode of reading, some readers (e.g., these referees) apparently may draw inferences about a text, provided that their inferences are consistent with other attributes of an approved reading. So, delegitimized readers "erroneously" "read into the piece" false inferences; they are deemed "criminal," "Marxist," and so forth. How can the referees' inferences be approved while our own cannot? The answer, of course, has to do in part with their institutional roles as referees and ours as mere authors of a manuscript. But that explanation, by itself, is too simple.

The answer is linked as well to a third element of approved identity—*occupancy of the mainstream*. Referee #2 suggests that our manuscript "represents the extremist fringe of the so-called feminist movement" and that it "does not represent the views of mainstream females in the field, or even that of most of us who see ourselves as feminists." As we will suggest further on, anyone who could characterize our response essay as "extremist" feminism cannot be very familiar with much contemporary feminist scholarship in this field or others. For now, it is enough to observe that referee #2 appears to define the "mainstream" of feminism as the ground occupied by most individual females in the field, not a ground of substantive views or reasoned stances. Feminism, thus, seems to be defined epiphenomenally.

Characterization of the mainstream as a population center provides an excellent opportunity for dismissing those who disagree. This practice makes it possible for an approved reader to draw inferences and to dismiss the inferences of disapproved readers, for example. Because the second referee reads our work as out of step with that of most other women or feminists, only one small move remains to reach the inevitable—dismissal or silencing. Precisely this move appeared in this referee's concluding remarks to us. S/he suggested the formation of "a whole new field that was off limits to males and heterosexual females. That field would appear to be more to the liking of these authors." By casting us as lesbians, a minority supposedly outside the mainstream female population center, this reviewer invokes the approved politics of exclusion and silencing accomplished via segregation. To be different, especially to be vocal about one's differences, is simply unacceptable, and action must be taken to silence those who would express their differences so openly. This stance is consistent with the remaining identity characteristic, which points also to the approved politics of exclusion/silencing.

Polite deference is the fourth and final characteristic, and its most important role seems to be to vouchsafe hierarchy. Referee #1 demonstrates the linkage in her claim that the Hickson et al. rank order list serves "to identify and recognize women in the field who have sustained records of scholarship and point them out as role models for others to follow." The notions of role models and their followers, of course, reference a hierarchy. And everyone, apparently, should be arranged according to it. Referee #1 concludes that our response was "puffy and arrogant" and infers that we "didn't make the list (or weren't as high as [we'd] like to be)." This reviewer immediately proceeds to discuss her own ranking, noting that the Hickson et al. list "reflected a little over half of my journal articles (and, of course, none of my books)" and even claims that "this was the case for most of the women on the list." It apparently is difficult for this referee to believe that anyone would not *want* to be ranked, that anyone actually on the list could *object* to it, or that there could be any *discomfort* with the ranking except not being as high as one would like. This referee then concludes her comments with the hint that we should have "counted to ten" before sending off our response essay in order to avoid looking like "an immature ass." Clearly, this referee invokes a politics of exclusion in this comment. She equates anti-hierarchical positions with "immaturity," and this label functions to legitimate the silencing of unauthorized stances.

Referee #2 is no less clear about reinvesting hierarchy. S/he claims that "In the past 20 years this field has made giant strides toward empowering females to rise to the highest levels of our profession, both scholarly and otherwise. I read the Hickson et al. article as a celebration of that advancement." Again, the approved identity is to rise, to occupy the "highest levels." And the appropriate reaction for others is to honor those who have risen. What Referee #2 also honors is the hierarchical arrangement itself and particularly that which Hickson, Stacks, and Amsbary themselves have since referred to as the "numbers game" ("Active Prolific Scholars," 231). Referee #2 argues that it is "this field" that has "made giant strides toward empowering women." Apparently women have not been responsible for their own successes or in charge of their own careers; the field has been. As with the other prescriptions, if we are unable or unwilling to recognize the sanctity of hierarchical arrangements, the approved, exclusionary politics is put into play. Referee #2 goes so far as to advise that "since these authors publish two-thirds of their work outside the field, might I suggest that they raise that percentage to 100%?"

Rarely are the mechanisms of approval and enforcement so explicitly espoused as in these reviews, but then most referees probably do not expect that their reviews will appear in print. This kind of discourse is allowed to function to control and censor what is said in this discipline; it is absolutely privileged discourse, typically exempt from public scrutiny and always protected by anonymity. Certainly we believe, in fact we know, that all referees do not subscribe to the ideological prescriptions of these two referees. That attempts of this sort to censor and silence occur at all, however, should give us cause for consternation.[34]

CONCLUSIONS/CONTINUATIONS

No conclusions offer themselves easily, for it is not up to the three of us alone to resolve the issues raised here. "Conclusions" will come only from the collective actions of the group we call our "discipline," a term which itself warns us against the seductive powers and dangers of our shared intellectual orthodoxies. We do wish to make three final points, however, that are more about continuing than with concluding.[35]

First, the Hickson et al. report must not be invoked or used in any of our workplaces. It misrepresents the accomplishments of women in the field, refuses to understand their experiences in context, and subordinates their interests to the abstraction called "the discipline." Women *not* included in the Hickson et al. ranking will be those most profoundly affected by it if we sanction its use. The effect will be institutional punishment. That is not to suggest that those women who *are* ranked have been or will be unaffected. This report domesticates them and their work, disciplining them with the "yardstick," ignoring *what* they have had to say, and refusing to acknowledge that their work (as well as that of other female scholars) often has been accomplished against great odds and at serious personal cost. Certainly they *and other women* of academic stripe should be recognized, even lauded, for their work. Ensnaring them within a hierarchical ranking, however, cannot be construed as a "celebration"; this hierarchy exploits women and their work, pressing them into service as unconsenting tokens and thereby perpetuating the ideology that diminishes women. Female tokenism is in play when "the power withheld from the vast majority of women is offered to a few, so that it may appear that any truly qualified woman can gain access to leadership, recognition, and reward" (Adrienne Rich, quoted by Biesecker, 43).

The men and women who identify themselves as members of this discipline must not comply with such an arrangement. All of us—women and men alike—have been "trained" to speak in the assumptive argot of the masculinist paradigm. The issues are whether we are able or willing to retrain ourselves to think and speak outside of its impersonal abstractions, disciplinary territoriality, individuation, and hierarchy. One way to begin could be to acknowledge that everyone in the field—men as well as women—might be better served by different arrangements. We believe that competitive, hierarchical rankings projects of individuals' publication rates peculiarly damage women in the ways we discuss above. But we are not convinced that they serve the men in this discipline either. Perhaps we need to locate and sanction new ways of judging our scholarly efforts and effects besides simply counting them up and arranging them by rank. No one denies that judgment is a component of our working lives, but we *all* might benefit if the discipline's sanctioned grounds for judgment were reconfigured.

Second, the ideological apparatuses that approve a very narrow range of identities and readings and that force a politics of exclusion must not be allowed to silence other voices. The ideological mechanisms of professionalism as they are expressed in the initial referees' reviews would silence virtually any feminist voice.

Feminist stances of any ilk simply *are* political. As Campbell argues, "Feminist scholarship is distinguished by the systematic inclusion of women, by an absence of language and/or perspective that degrades women or minorities, by rigorous testing of assumptions that hark back to stereotypes and social mythology, and by a concern to rectify the omissions, the degradation, and the errors of the past" ("What Really Distinguishes," 4). To suggest that feminist critique must not be political is to suggest that it should not exist at all.[36]

Moreover, feminist stances cannot necessarily respect traditional science. As Gregg acknowledges, "Feminists have been concerned with the equation of the findings of science with truth and knowledge, the designation of scientists as experts, the distance between scientific concepts and research and everyday life: in short, the power of science to predict, control, define, and restrict reality by virtue of its privileged position among other social activities" (8). Such concerns are not "anti-scientific." They are sites of critique. Feminist critique of intellectual practice is neither unusual enough to be "radical," nor limited to challenging the tenets of traditional science. Within our own field, feminists have targeted intellectual practices of rhetorical theory, ethnography, histories of rhetoric, and postmodernism, as well as those of conservative science.[37] Feminist positions must not be silenced on the grounds of their "opposition" to science. Such an accusation is inaccurate, and it misses the transformative point of feminist critique, which is to change any academic stance that devalues, excludes, or effaces women's experience.

Feminism, similarly, does not respect "mainstream" or unitary stances. If the ideology of academic professionalism is allowed to accomplish such a reduction, feminism's virtues will be essentially obliterated. As Schwichtenberg suggests, "Feminism itself is a highly diverse terrain, which challenges monolithic assumptions deriving from a single feminist approach or style" (291). To silence any feminism, whether Marxist, African, Hispanic, Lacanian, or lesbian, is to diminish the extraordinary power of its diversity. Moreover, if arguments for the "mainstream" are allowed to prevail, it is very likely that we will return to the era (if, in fact, we ever left it) that witnessed feminist study of *any* kind declared to be outside the mainstream. Johnson describes it rather pointedly: "It is also not uncommon to hear one's colleagues describe a woman who does such research [gender studies] as 'a one-issue person,' 'narrowly focused,' 'politically motivated,' and 'not in touch with the mainstream of the field.' These comments are seldom heard about individuals who devote themselves to the study of, say, family communication, war rhetoric, communication theory, or small group communication; such individuals are, of course, 'specialists'" (320). If the "mainstream" is to serve as the arbiter, feminism will not pass muster.

Nor can feminist stances be held to the strictures of polite deference and survive. The demand for deference forces women's submission or surrender to masculinist conceptions. Deference simply reinforces a masculine hierarchy as if it characterized *human* ways of thinking, being, and acting. Women have no deference option except to submit and be counted against the measures created to characterize men. The result, as Tavris argues, is to be "mismeasured," to always be found inadequate.

Every ideological apparatus wielded by the initial referees would silence virtually any feminist statement. The silences would not be limited to those the referees would consider extremist, Marxist, lesbian, and so forth—those they clearly do wish to squelch. All of feminism would be quarantined at the disciplinary border and ultimately deported. Such an ideology cannot be allowed to govern an academic field that so proudly espouses pluralism, diversity, and communication. Disagreement is to be valued and kept in play in the dialogue of such a field, not silenced or kept cloistered behind the secretive curtain of blind reviewing.

Third, the writing practices that mark what counts as scholarly discourses in this field must not be maintained without scrutiny. It surely is incumbent upon the adherents of any academic field to scrutinize and evaluate their own rules of engagement and practice. It is the more so for scholars of rhetoric and communication; our written work reveals the assumptions and rules to which we hold vis-à-vis communicative practice and expression. If we have identified correctly the rules for writing the field's scholarship at the beginning of this essay, then we are obliged to acknowledge that these rules demand personae of singular, neutral, authoritative, observers who are detached from or ambivalent about their own histories and contexts. We are also bound to observe the coherence of these rules with the apparatuses that police the professional academic's approved identity and modes of reading by means of an exclusionary politics.

We began this essay by identifying several potent, yet rarely discussed, assumptions and practices characteristic of scholarly activity in the speech communication discipline. Our purpose in doing so goes well beyond the desire to vindicate our original manuscript or to settle scores with referees. We see this essay as the beginning of a process as well as the end of another, and as an invitation to invest in one conversation as well as an argument against investing in another.

We could include an additional entry on the list of troubling norms governing academic writing: the production and consumption of individual journal articles as if they were (or should be) free standing and finalized utterances on the topic at hand. Our talk about \"scholarly dialogue" and "scholarly communities" notwithstanding, we tend to construe our work in monologic terms. We think in terms of single articles; rarely do articles past enter future discussions except as citations. In our estimation, this tendency to focus on single, isolated "scholarly turns" rather than on extended, interactive "scholarly conversations" reduces the chances for the kind of reflexive examination we suggest in this essay. The examination of ourselves as a community requires that we look at patterns in our writing and speaking and at the ideological positions such patterns depend on, reproduce, or refuse. Moreover, insofar as such examination focuses on ourselves as a community, it needs to be done as a community.

We hope, then, that our essay will evoke additional discussion of the issues we have raised. We hope that this discussion will be honest and passionate. We also hope that it will help to reinvest our scholarly activities with a sense of what is (or could be) at stake in them.

Notes

1. For further comment on these and other such academic writing practices, see Bazerman; Brodkey; Wander and Jenkins; Wander, "Politics"; and Nothstine, Blair, and Copeland. Disciplinary practices—among them writing practices—seem to be at least a subtext of most of the essays

in the Spring 1993 special issue of the *Western Journal of Communication* on "Ideology and Communication." See especially Wander's editorial introduction, as well as the essays by Rodden, Owen and Ehrenhaus, Condit, Rigsby, West, Lee, and Wood and Cox.

2. We are using the terms "text" and "fragment" in a fashion almost, but perhaps not entirely, consonant with their uses by McGee, in "Text," and Barthes. One understanding of "text" in their works is that of a combinatory fabric of multiple textual fragments constructed by a critic. Our use of the term here suggests that it may be constructed from material discursive fragments *and* the silences that surround those fragments. These silences might be the unarticulated "rules" of cultural or discursive codes or the silences of strategically unarticulated positions. In that sense, our use of the term links it to notions like Althusser's ideological apparatus, Foucault's discursive practice (*Archaeology*), or Lyotard's phrase regimen (*régime de phrase*) that link phrases or discursive fragments to one another (*The Differend*). In any case, Barthes' injunctions are ones we accept, that "the Text is a process of demonstration," and that it is "experienced only in an activity of production" (157).

3. For example, as Condit describes, the referees for Wander's "The Politics of Despair" expressed "a general rejection-reaction" to the essay ("Introduction," 249). It probably is no coincidence that Wander committed a number of disciplinary "violations" in that essay, one of which was a description of some of the negative consequences of academic writing norms. For example, he suggested that "as the system works to quash surprise, improvisation, and controversy, criticism begins to echo an established order" (278).

4. See Nelson, Megill, and McCloskey, eds.; and Simons, ed.

5. This seems to be consistent with Conquergood's point, when he argues that "it is ironic that the discipline of communication has been relatively unreflective about the rhetorical construction of its disciplinary authority. It would be illuminating to critique the rhetorical expectations and constraints on articles published in the *Quarterly Journal of Speech*, or *Communication Monographs*. What kinds of knowledge, and their attendant discursive styles, get privileged, legitimated, or displaced? How does knowledge about communication get constructed? What counts as an interesting question about human communication? What are the tacitly observed boundaries—the range of appropriateness—regarding the substance, methods, and discursive styles of communication scholarship? And, most importantly for critical theorists, what configuration of socio-political interests does communication scholarship serve?" (195). We find Conquergood's questions to be vital to the discipline at large, necessary for those who are concerned with the rhetoric of inquiry, and formative for our own critique in this essay.

6. For an elaboration, see Johnson's review of books on women's language, particularly her discussion of Mary Daly's book, *Pure Lust*.

7. This is the case, almost regardless of the particular feminist stance assumed or of the particular disciplinary specialty of the advocate. See, for example, Balsamo; Biesecker; Campbell, "Sound"; Cirksena; Dervin; Fine; Foss and Foss; Foss and Griffin; Gallagher; Gregg; Jarratt, "Performing"; Jarratt, "Speaking"; Kauffman; Muto; Press; Rakow; Rushing; Schwichtenberg; Self; Spitzack and Carter, "Women"; Steeves; Wood, "Feminist Scholarship"; and Wood and Phillips.

8. Other studies in the Hickson et al. research program include: Hickson ("Profiling the Chairs"); Hickson, Stacks, and Amsbary ("An Analysis of Prolific Scholarship"); Hickson, Stacks, and Amsbary ("Administrator-Scholars"); Hickson, Stacks, and Amsbary ("Active Prolific Scholars"); Hickson, Scott, Stacks, and Amsbary ("Scholarship in Mass Communication"). For convenience, we will refer to the report "Active Prolific Female Scholars" simply as the Hickson et al. report without further designation. Other articles by these three authors will be differentiated from this one—the object of our response—by parenthetical designation of title.

9. Other research in the bibliometric tradition of Hickson et al. includes Barker, Roach, and Underberg ("An Investigation of Articles . . . 1970 through 1978"); Barker, Roach, and Underberg ("An Investigation of Articles . . . Journal-by-Journal"); Burroughs, Christophel, Ady, and McGreal; Watson, Barker, Rav, and Hall.

10. See Erickson et al. for a discussion of general concern about studies that rank prolific scholars.

11. In the interest of fair reporting, we should note that none of our names appears on the Hickson, Stacks, and Amsbary list. As noted later in this essay, one of our initial referees accused us of list envy. The accusation is, of course, quite insulting. However, there are two very narrow senses in which it is quasi-accurate. First, one of our number would have been on the Hickson, Stacks, and Amsbary list but for an error in the Matlon and Ortiz index. Second, we were relatively concerned that our colleagues might raise the question about our nonpresence on the list in the context of merit or promotion meetings. Our concerns were not ill-founded. One of our colleagues "casually" observed in a conversation that he had noticed that we were not included on the Hickson list. In those senses, and those only, we had self-interested reactions to our own non-inclusion. Principally, we were disgusted by the ideology of the report and worried about its likely uses.

12. We should note that the journal that published the Hickson, Stacks, and Amsbary report did later print corrections to the mistakes in the report, errors that had resulted in some women being mistakenly excluded from the ranking and in others being misranked. However, the tone of the correction should also be noted. Unlike the other item on the erratum page, which was listed as a "correction" and carried with it an apology, the Hickson et al. item was listed as an "update" and bore no traces of apologetic language. That women's careers had been placed potentially at risk apparently was not sufficient cause for regret.

13. For a review, see Sandler.

14. See, for example, Deetz and Mumby; Foucault, *Power/ Knowledge*; Taylor; and Volosinov.

15. See, for example, Ward and Grant. Throughout our response to the Hickson et al. article, we refer to the "male paradigm." Elsewhere in this essay, we use the term "masculinist paradigm." We regard these terms as synonymous; neither is essentialist in nature.

16. For a general review of the agency-communion distinction, see McAdams.

17. See, for example, Belenky, Clinchy, Goldberger, and Tarule; Gilligan; and Lyons.

18. See, for example, Baldwin and Blackburn.

19. See, for example, the related essays by Charles R. Berger and by Redding.

20. See, for example, Renharz.

21. See Belenky et al.; Gilligan; and Lyons.

22. See Gilligan; and Lyons.

23. See, for example, Clark and Corcoran; Menges and Exum; Sandler; and the Task Force on Women in Higher Education.

24. See Belenky et al.; and Ward and Grant.

25. Why they would not acknowledge female editors of other SCA journals is unclear. They name only *QJS*, *CM*, and *CE*. What of *CSMC*? One of its most recent editors is Sari Thomas. And what of the current editor of *TPQ*, Kristin M. Langellier?

26. We suppose one could also justify the segregation on the assumption that women publish systematically more than men, but that seems inconsistent with the general tenor of the essay.

27. In respect to the issue of choice, the better analogs might be livestock shows or slave auctions.

28. We are not the first to conduct an analysis of the reviewing process as a lens through which to analyze the functioning of a scholarly community. See, for example, Cohen: Myers; Peters and Ceci. For an example within the speech communication discipline, see Medhurst.

29. The dual capacity of any social convention or practice to both enable and constrain is a theme addressed by a number of scholars, including Giddens and Foucault, among others.

30. For a further discussion of the implications of approved or correct readings, see Crowley's critique of Wander's respondents in the ideological turn discussion (Campbell, "Response"; Corcoran; Francesconi; Hill; McGee, "Another Philippic"; Megill; and Rosenfield). Crowley's discussion particularly turns on the responses of Megill, Hill, and Rosenfield. She argues that their responses to Wander turn on two warrants: (1) "that correct readings are possible," and (2) "that some critics cannot give correct readings of some texts" (456). These warrants, she argues, are conditioned by an ideology that appears under various names: "Kantian idealism, Enlightenment epistemology, liberal humanism, modernism" (457). Crowley's discussion points to the consequences of subscrip-

tion to these warrants, in her argument that traditional critics "must perforce denigrate the work of critics whose readings . . . do not fall within the range of approved readings. More seriously, they must denigrate the work of critics who for some reason cannot become the readers they need to be in order to read the texts 'properly'" (459). Here Crowley notes not only the issue of approved readings but approved identities as well. Moreover, the notion of "denigration" points us to the political, for in the hands of sanctioned judges like journal manuscript reviewers, denigration is all too easily transformed into silencing and exclusion.

31. For a discussion of these issues, see Lyotard, *The Postmodern Condition*; Wilshire; and Nothstine, Blair, and Copeland. Also see Spitzack and Carter, "Feminist Communication," who argue that "The third lie concerns the cultural portrayal of power as a scarce resource. Attempting to get power is charged by the belief that power exists in limited quantities. There is only enough for a few, and those who struggle to get power must override the competition. This lie endorses a hierarchy in which few are winners and many are losers. In order to 'win,' the competitors must show themselves to be superior to others. . . . When feminists compete with each other, striving to 'win' . . . we run the risk of perpetuating the very hierarchy we criticize. The three lies about power serve to fragment communities of women and assure that none of us will generate fundamental changes either for ourselves or for women in general" (34).

32. In quoting from the two manuscript reviews in what follows, we will come close to exhausting their content. That is, they contain very little besides what is represented below. Both *do* also address issues of accuracy in the Hickson et al. report, as we have noted earlier. Beyond that, they are almost completely contained in our quotations. As a means of insuring that our quotations represent the reviews fairly, we have provided the editor of this journal with copies of the reviews. We should note also that we refer to the first referee as a woman and the second in gender-neutral ways. Referee #1 identifies herself as female in her review; referee #2 does not so specify.

33. At least *female* professionals must fit this profile. That the three of us identified ourselves as female in our response essay complicates the ideological profile to some degree, particularly in these referees' prescriptions of disapproved identities. Disapproved identity characteristics cited in the two reviews include being "vehement," "egotistical," "feline," "petty," "ball-bashing," "extremist," "puffy," "arrogant," "political," and "male-bashing." It hardly seems worth asking if it is acceptable for male professionals to be vehement or egotistical or political. But we are compelled to ask if the more stereotypical female descriptors here might have been transformed to read "assertive," "argumentative," "emphatic," "forthright," "direct," or "confident," if we had cloaked our gender under third-person references. In fact, we wonder if either of the referees would have been as likely to recite for us their professionalism lessons at all had we written in an androgynous tongue. Regardless, the uncertainty about whether male professionals would be required to assume the identities, read in these ways, and be subject to the politics that are all specified here, remains.

34. It is *not* sufficient, in our judgment, to dismiss these reviews as merely aberrant and thus insignificant. We cannot prove that there have been other cases just like these, but it is unnecessary to do so. For one thing, they represent privileged discourse, both because of the shielding provided by referee anonymity and because they were the sanctioned discourse of a journal in this field. In addition, we agree with the point made so clearly by Foucault, that statements actually uttered are those legitimized by the rules of a discursive practice. Such statements, even if rare, are indicators of the forces of power within a discursive field. See *Archaeology* 28, 120.

35. We are interested in continuations more than conclusions, because, despite Referee #2's invitation to us to leave the field, we have decided to stay.

36. Of course, it is equally absurd to suggest that any academic discourse be politically neutral, from our point of view. Feminist scholarship, though, is particularly vulnerable to this kind of demand, for it cannot effectively disguise itself as apolitical as many forms of academic discourse can.

37. See, for example, Balsamo; Biesecker; Foss; and Griffin and Kauffmann.

References

Althusser, Louis. (1971). "Ideology and Ideological State Apparatuses (Notes Towards an Investigation)." In *Lenin and Philosophy and Other Essays*, trans. Ben Brewster (London: New Left Books), 121–173.

Baldwin, Roger G., and Robert T. Blackburn. (1981). "The Academic Career as a Developmental Process." *Journal of Higher Education* 52: 598–614.

Balsamo, Anne. (1987). "Un-Wrapping the Postmodern: A Feminist Glance." *Journal of Communication Inquiry* 11: 64–72.

Barker, Larry, Robert Hall, Deborah Roach, and Larry Underberg. (1979). "An Investigation of Quantity of Articles Produced in the Communication Discipline by Institutions: 1970 through 1978, Part 1." *Association for Communication Administration Bulletin* 30: 18–22.

Barker, Larry, Robert Hall, Deborah Roach, and Larry Underberg. (1980). "An Investigation of Articles Produced in the Communication Discipline by Institution: A Journal by Journal, Year by Year Analysis, Part 2." *Association for Communication Administration Bulletin* 34: 37–48.

Barthes, Roland. (1977). "From Work to Text." In *Image, Music, Text*, trans. Stephen Heath (New York: Hill and Wang), 155–164.

Bazerman, Charles. (1988). *Shaping Written Knowledge: The Genre and Activity of the Experimental Article in Science*. Madison: University of Wisconsin Press.

Belenky, Mary Field, Blythe McVicker Clinchy, Nancy Rule Goldberger, and Jill Mattuck Tarule. (1986). *Women's Ways of Knowing: The Development of Self, Voice, and Mind*. New York: Basic Books.

Berger, Charles R. (1991). "Communication Theories and Other Curios." *Communication Monographs* 58: 101–113.

Berger, John. (1977). *Ways of Seeing*. New York: Penguin Books.

Berger, Peter L., and Thomas Luckmann. (1967). *The Social Construction of Reality: A Treatise in the Sociology of Knowledge*. New York: Doubleday.

Biesecker, Barbara. (1992). "Coming to Terms with Recent Attempts to Write Women into the History of Rhetoric." *Philosophy and Rhetoric* 25: 140–161.

Bourdieu, Pierre. (1988). *Homo Academicus*. Translated by Peter Collier. Cambridge, UK: Polity Press.

Brodkey, Linda. (1987). *Academic Writing as Social Practice*. Philadelphia: Temple University Press.

Burroughs, Nancy F., Diane Christophel, J. Cole Ady, and Elizabeth A. McGreal. (1989). "Top Published Authors in Communication Studies." *Association for Communication Administration Bulletin* 67: 37–45.

Campbell, Karlyn Kohrs. (1983). "Response to Forbes Hill." *Central States Speech Journal* 34: 126–127.

Campbell, Karlyn Kohrs. (1986). "What Really Distinguishes and/or Ought to Distinguish Feminist Scholarship in Communication Studies?" *Women's Studies in Communication* 11: 4–5.

Campbell, Karlyn Kohrs. (1989) "The Sound of Women's Voices" [Review essay]. *Quarterly Journal of Speech* 75: 212–220.

Cirksena, Kathryn. (1987). "Politics and Difference: Radical Feminist Epistemological Premises for Communication Studies." *Journal of Communication Inquiry* 11: 19–28.

Clark, Shirley M., and Mary Corcoran. (1986). "Perspectives on the Professional Socialization of Women Faculty." *Journal of Higher Education* 57: 20–43.

Cohen, Ed. (1993). "Are We (Not) What We Are Becoming?: "Gay Identity," "Gay Studies," and the Disciplining of Knowledge." In Ellen Messer-Davidow, David R. Shumway, and David J. Sylvan, eds., *Knowledges: Historical and Critical Studies in Disciplinarity* (Charlottesville: University Press of Virginia), 397–421.

Condit, Celeste Michelle. (1993). "The Critic as Empath: Moving Away from Totalizing Theory." *Western Journal of Communication* 57: 178–190.

Conquergood, Dwight. (1991). "Rethinking Ethnography: Towards a Critical Cultural Politics." *Communication Monographs* 58: 179–194.

Corcoran, Farrel. (1984)."The Widening Gyre: Another Look at Ideology in Wander and His Critics." *Central States Speech Journal* 35: 54–56.

Crowley, Sharon. (1992). "Reflections on an Argument That Won't Go Away; or, A Turn of the Ideological Screw." *Quarterly Journal of Speech* 78: 450–465.

Daly, Mary. (1984). *Pure Lust*. Boston: Beacon Press.

de Certeau, Michel. (1984). *The Practice of Everyday Life*. Translated by Steven Rendall. Berkeley and Los Angeles: University of California Press.

Deetz, Stanley, and Dennis K. Mumby. (1990). "Power, Discourse, and the Workplace: Reclaiming the Critical Tradition." In James A. Anderson, ed., *Communication Yearbook 13* (Newbury Park, CA: Sage), 18–47.

Dervin, Brenda. (1987). "The Potential Contribution of Feminist Scholarship to the Field of Communication." *Journal of Communication* 37: 107–120.

Dervin, Brenda, Lawrence Grossberg, Barbara J. O'Keefe, and Ellen Wartella, eds. (1989). *Rethinking Communication, Vol. 2: Paradigm Exemplars*. Newbury Park, CA: Sage.

Erickson, Keith V., Cathy A. Fleuriet, and Lawrence A. Elosman. (1993). "Prolific Publishing: Professional and Administrative Concerns." *Southern Communication Journal* 58: 328–338.

Fine, Marlene G. (1986). "What Makes It Feminist?" *Women's Studies in Communication* 11: 18–19.

Foss, Sonja K., and Karen A. Foss. (1986). "What Distinguishes Feminist Scholarship in Communication Studies?" *Women's Studies in Communication* 11: 9–11.

Foss, Sonja K., and Cindy L. Griffin. (1992). "A Feminist Perspective on Rhetorical Theory: Toward a Clarification of Boundaries." *Western Journal of Communication* 56: 330–349.

Foucault, Michel. (1972). *The Archaeology of Knowledge and The Discourse on Language*. Translated by A. M. Sheridan Smith. New York: Pantheon Books.

Foucault, Michel. (1980). *Power/Knowledge: Selected Interviews and Other Writings, 1972–1977*. Edited by Colin Gordon. Translated by Colin Gordon, Leo Marshall, John Mepham, and Kate Soper. New York: Pantheon Books.

Francesconi, Robert. (1984). "Heidegger and Ideology: Reflections of an Innocent Bystander." *Central States Speech Journal* 35: 51–53.

Gallagher, Margaret. (1989). "A Feminist Perspective for Communication Research." In Brenda Dervin, Lawrence Grossberg, Barbara J. O'Keefe, and Ellen Wartella, eds., *Rethinking Communication, Vol. 2: Paradigm Exemplars* (Newbury Park, CA: Sage), 75–87.

Giddens, Anthony. (1984). *The Constitution of Society: Outline of the Theory of Structuration*. Berkeley and Los Angeles: University of California Press.

Gilligan, Carol. (1982). *In a Different Voice: Psychological Theory and Women's Development*. Cambridge, MA: Harvard University Press.

Gregg, Nina. (1987). "Reflections on the Feminist Critique of Objectivity." *Journal of Communication Inquiry* 11: 8–18.

Hariman, Robert. (1989). "The Rhetoric of Inquiry and the Professional Scholar." In Herbert W. Simons, ed., *Rhetoric in the Human Sciences* (Newbury Park, CA: Sage), 211–232.

Hickson, Mark, III. (1990). "Profiling the Chairs of Prolific Speech Communication Departments." *Association for Communication Administration Bulletin* 73: 4–14.

Hickson, Mark, III, Randall K. Scott, Don W. Stacks, and Jonathan H. Amsbary. (1992). "Scholarship in Mass Communication, 1915–1990: An Analysis of Active Researchers' Productivity." *Association for Communication Administration Bulletin* 82: 13–17.

Hickson, Mark, III, Don W. Stacks, and Jonathan H. Amsbary. (1989). "An Analysis of Prolific Scholarship in Speech Communication, 1915–1985: Toward a Yardstick for Measuring Research Productivity." *Communication Education* 38: 230-236.

Hickson, Mark, III, Don W. Stacks, and Jonathan H. Amsbary. (1992a). "Active Prolific Female Scholars in Communication: An Analysis of Research Productivity, II." *Communication Quarterly* 40: 350–356.

Hickson, Mark, III, Don W. Stacks, and Jonathan H. Amsbary. (1992b). "Administrator-Scholars in Speech Communication: An Analysis of Research Productivity, II." *Association for Communication Administration Bulletin* 79: 66–74.

Hickson, Mark, III, Don W. Stacks, and Jonathan H. Amsbary. (1993). "Active Prolific Scholars in Communication Studies: An Analysis of Research Productivity, II." *Communication Education* 42: 224–233.

Hill, Forbes. (1983). "A Turn against Ideology: Reply to Professor Wander." *Central States Speech Journal* 34: 121–126.

Jarratt, Susan C. (1990). "Speaking to the Past: Feminist Historiography in Rhetoric." *Pre/Text* 11: 189–209.

Jarratt, Susan C. (1992). "Performing Feminisms, Histories, Rhetorics." *Rhetoric Society Quarterly* 22: 1–5.

Johnson, Fern L. (1986). "Coming to Terms with Women's Language" [Review essay]. *Quarterly Journal of Speech* 72: 318–330.

Kauffman, Bette J. (1992). "Feminist Facts: Interview Strategies and Political Subjects in Ethnography." *Communication Theory* 2: 187–206.

Lee, Wen-Shu. (1993). "Social Scientists as Ideological Critics." *Western Journal of Communication* 57: 221–232.

Lyons, Nona P. (1983). "Two Perspectives on Self, Relationships, and Morality." *Harvard Educational Review* 53: 125–145.

Lyotard, Jean-François. (1984). *The Postmodern Condition: A Report on Knowledge.* Translated by Geoff Bennington and Brian Massumi. Minneapolis: University of Minnesota Press.

Lyotard, Jean-François. (1988). *The Differend: Phrases in Dispute.* Translated by Georges van den Abbeele. Minneapolis: University of Minnesota Press.

Matlon, Ronald J., and Sylvia P. Ortiz. (1992). *Index to Journals in Communication Studies through 1990.* Annandale, VA: Speech Communication Association.

McAdams, Dan P. (1988). "Personal Needs and Personal Relationships." In Steve Duck, ed., *Handbook of Personal Relationships: Theory, Research and Interventions.* New York: John Wiley and Sons, 7–22.

McGee, Michael Calvin. (1984). "Another Philippic: Notes on the Ideological Turn in Criticism." *Central States Speech Journal* 35: 43–50.

McGee, Michael Calvin. (1990). "Text, Context, and the Fragmentation of Contemporary Culture." *Western Journal of Speech Communication* 54: 274–289.

McKerrow, Raymie E. (1989). "Critical Rhetoric: Theory and Praxis." *Communication Monographs* 56: 91–111 (reprinted in this volume).

Medhurst, Martin J. (1989). "Public Address and Significant Scholarship: Four Challenges to the Rhetorical Renaissance." In Michael C. Leff and Fred J. Kauffeld, eds., *Texts in Context: Critical Dialogues on Significant Episodes in American Political Rhetoric* (Davis, CA: Hermagoras Press), 29–42.

Megill, Allan. (1983). "Heidegger, Wander, and Ideology." *Central States Speech Journal* 34: 114–119.

Menges, Robert J., and William H. Exum. (1983). "Barriers to the Progress of Women and Minority Faculty." *Journal of Higher Education* 54: 123–144.

Messer-Davidow, Ellen, David R. Shumway, and David J. Sylvan, eds. (1993). *Knowledges: Historical and Critical Studies in Disciplinarity.* Charlottesville: University Press of Virginia.

Muto, Jan. (1986). "If I'm Reading This, I Must Not Be by the Pool." *Women's Studies in Communication* 11: 20–21.

Myers, Greg. (1993). "The Social Construction of Two Biologists' Articles." In Ellen Messer-Davidow, David R. Shumway, and David J. Sylvan, eds., *Knowledges: Historical and Critical Studies in Disciplinarity* (Charlottesville: University Press of Virginia), 327–367.

Nelson, John S., Allan Megill, and Donald N. McCloskey, eds. (1987). *The Rhetoric of the Human Sciences: Language and Argument in Scholarship and Public Affairs.* Madison: University of Wisconsin Press, 1987.

Nothstine, William L., Carole Blair, and Gary A. Copeland. (1994). "Professionalization and the Eclipse of Critical Invention." In William L. Nothstine, Carole Blair, and Gary A. Copeland, eds., *Critical Questions: Invention, Creativity, and the Criticism of Discourse and Media*. (New York: St. Martin's Press), pp.15–70.

Ono, Kent A., and John M. Sloop. (1992). "Commitment to *Telos*—A Sustained Critical Rhetoric." *Communication Monographs* 59: 48–60.

"'Our Stories': Communication Professionals' Narratives of Sexual Harassment." (1992). *Journal of Applied Communication Research* 20: 363–390.

Owen, Susan A., and Peter C. Ehrenhaus. (1993). "Critical Rhetoric." *Western Journal of Communication* 57: 169–177.

Peters, Douglas P., and Stephen J. Ceci. (1982). "Peer Review Practices of Psychological Journals: The Fate of Published Articles, Submitted Again." *Behavioral and Brain Sciences* 5: 187–255.

Press, Andrea. (1989). "The Ongoing Feminist Revolution." *Critical Studies in Mass Communication* 6: 196–202.

Rakow, Lana F. (1989). "Feminist Studies: The Next Stage." *Critical Studies in Mass Communication* 6: 209–215.

Redding, W. Charles. (1992). "Response to Professor Berger's Essay: Its Meaning for Organizational Communication." *Communication Monographs* 59: 87–93.

Reinharz, Shulamit. (1992). *Feminist Methods in Social Research*. New York: Oxford University Press.

Rigsby, Enrique D. (1993). "African American Rhetoric and the 'Profession.'" *Western Journal of Communication* 57: 191–199.

Rodden, John. (1993). "Field of Dreams." *Western Journal of Communication* 57: 111–138.

Rosenfield, Lawrence W. (1983). "Ideological Miasma." *Central States Speech Journal* 34: 119–121.

Rushing, Janice Hocker. (1992). "Introduction to 'Feminist Criticism.'" *Southern Communication Journal* 57: 83–85.

Sandler, Bernice R. (1986). *The Campus Climate Revisited: Chilly for Women Faculty, Administrators, and Graduate Students*. Washington, DC: Project on the Status and Education of Women, Association of American Colleges.

Schwichtenberg, Cathy. (1989). "The 'Mother Lode' of Feminist Research: Congruent Paradigms in the Analysis of Beauty Culture." In Brenda Dervin, Lawrence Grossberg, Barbara J. O'Keefe, and Ellen Wartella, eds., *Rethinking Communication, Vol. 2: Paradigm Exemplars* (Newbury Park, CA: Sage), 291–306.

Self, Lois S. (1986). "What Distinguishes/Ought to Distinguish Feminist Scholarship in Communication Studies?: Progress Toward Engendering a Feminist Academic Practice." *Women's Studies in Communication* 11: 1–3.

Simons, Herbert W., ed. (1989). *Rhetoric in the Human Sciences*. Newbury Park, CA: Sage.

Spitzack, Carole, and Kathryn Carter. (1986). "Feminist Communication: Rethinking the Politics of Exclusion." *Women's Studies in Communication* 11: 32–36.

Spitzack, Carole, and Kathryn Carter. (1987). "Women in Communication Studies: A Typology for Revision." *Quarterly Journal of Speech* 73: 401–423.

Steeves, Leslie. (1986). "What Distinguishes Feminist Scholarship in Communication Studies?" *Women's Studies in Communication* 11: 12–17.

Strine, Mary S. (1992). "Understanding 'How Things Work': Sexual Harassment and Academic Culture." *Journal of Applied Communication Research* 20: 391–400.

Task Force on Women in Higher Education. (1988). *Women in Academe: Progress and Prospects*. New York: Russell Sage Foundation.

Tavris, Carol. (1992). *The Mismeasure of Woman*. New York: Simon & Schuster.

Taylor, Bryan C. (1992). "The Politics of the Nuclear Text: Reading Robert Oppenheimer's Letters and Recollections." *Quarterly Journal of Speech* 78: 429–449.

Taylor, Bryan, and Charles Conrad. (1992). "Narratives of Sexual Harassment: Organizational Dimensions." *Journal of Applied Communication Research* 20: 401–418.

Toulmin, Stephen. (1972). *Human Understanding: The Collective Use and Evolution of Concepts*. Princeton, NJ: Princeton University Press.

Volosinov, V.N. (1973). *Marxism and the Philosophy of Language*. Translated by Ladislav Mateejka and I. R. Titunik. Cambridge, MA: Harvard University Press.

Wander, Philip. (1983). "The Ideological Turn in Modern Criticism." *Central States Speech Journal* 34: 1–18.

Wander, Philip. (1984). "The Third Persona: An Ideological Turn in Rhetorical Theory." *Central States Speech Journal* 35: 197–216.

Wander, Philip. (1990). "The Politics of Despair." *Communication* 11: 277–290.

Wander, Philip. (1993). "Introduction: Special Issue on Ideology." *Western Journal of Communication* 57: 105–110.

Wander, Philip, and Steven Jenkins. (1972). "Rhetoric, Society, and the Critical Response." *Quarterly Journal of Speech* 58: 441–450.

Ward, Kathryn B., and Linda Grant. (1991). "Coauthorship, Gender, and Publication among Sociologists." In Mary Margaret Fonow and Judith A. Cook, eds., *Beyond Methodology: Feminist Scholarship as Lived Research* (Bloomington: Indiana University Press), 248–264.

Watson, Kittie W., Larry L. Barker, Vernon O. Ray, and Robert N. Hall. (1988). "A Study of Quantity of Articles Produced in the Communication Discipline by Institution, 1980 through 1985, I." *Association for Communication Administration Bulletin* 63: 85–90.

West, James T. (1993). "Ethnography and Ideology: The Politics of Cultural Representation." *Western Journal of Communication* 57: 209–220.

Wilshire, Bruce. (1990). *The Moral Collapse of the University: Professionalism, Purity, and Alienation*. Albany: State University of New York Press.

Wood, Julia T. (1986). "Feminist Scholarship in Communication: Consensus, Diversity, and Conversation among Researchers." *Women's Studies in Communication* 11: 22–27.

Wood, Julia T., and Robert J. Cox. (1993). "Rethinking Critical Voice: Materiality and Situated Knowledges." *Western Journal of Communication* 57: 278–287.

Wood, Julia T., and Gerald M. Phillips. (1984). "Report on the 1984 Conference on Gender and Communication Research." *Communication Quarterly* 32: 175–177.

Postcolonial Interventions in the Rhetorical Canon

An "Other" View

RAKA SHOME

> There are times in life when the question of knowing if one can think differently than one thinks, and perceive differently than one sees, is absolutely necessary if one is to go on looking and reflecting at all.
>
> *Michel Foucault*, The Use of Pleasure

In recent times, the discipline of rhetorical studies—a discipline that for years has celebrated the public voices of white men in power, and has derived most of its theories from such foci—is being challenged in various ways. Perhaps two of the most significant challenges that rhetorical studies has had to deal with in recent years are those posed by critical rhetoricians (McGee, 1990; McKerrow, 1989, 1991; Ono and Sloop, 1992; Pollock and Cox, 1991) and feminist rhetorical scholars (Biesecker, 1992, 1994; Condit, 1988, 1993; Campbell, 1973, 1988, 1989; Dobris, 1989; Foss, 1989; Foss and Foss, 1988, 1989; Spitzack and Carter, 1987, 1988). Arguing that the aim of contemporary rhetorical studies should be to "escape from the trivializing influence of universalist approaches" (McKerrow, 1989, p. 91) and that the canons of rhetorical studies "[are] overwhelmingly biased towards men, especially towards white men of the Western tradition" (Condit, 1993, p. 214), these incursions into the field have begun to question and problematize some of the criteria, assumptions, and methods (such as a transcendental subject, universal audience, critical objectivity, the "right" standards of eloquence) on which rhetorical scholarship has rested. In so doing, critical and feminist scholarship have begun to push the discipline's traditional paradigms of criticism and theory in significant ways.

In this essay, my aim is to continue this task of pushing the paradigms of rhetorical scholarship even further by underscoring the necessity of a postcolonial perspective for rhetorical studies. I believe that while postmodern and feminist perspectives are challenging the paradigms of rhetoric in useful and much needed ways, there is still more to be done if rhetorical studies is to truly open itself up to alternative and marginalized voices and dialogues. That "still more" that I have in mind are issues of racism and neocolonialism about which both traditional and nontraditional scholarship in the discipline have expressed little concern.[1]

In the paper, I thus argue for the importance of a postcolonial perspective for rhetorical studies. Postcolonialism, which is a critical perspective that primarily seeks to expose the eurocentrism and imperialism of western discourses (both academic and public),[2] has significantly influenced a wide range of fields across the humanities such as sociology, anthropology, education, literature, cultural studies, and even some areas in communication such as mass communication and development communication. However, the field of rhetorical studies has not adequately recognized the critical importance of a postcolonial perspective. By working from a postcolonial perspective, I argue that as we engage in rhetorical understandings of texts, or produce rhetorical theories, it is important to place the texts that we critique or the theories that we produce against a larger backdrop of neocolonialism and racism, and interrogate to what extent these discourses and our own perspectives on them reflect the contemporary global politics of (neo)imperialism. I believe that in today's world, when people are constantly discriminated against by virtue of their skin color, or by virtue of their belonging to "other worlds," to avoid the issues of racism and neocolonialism in our critical politics is to "avoid questions concerning ways in which we see the world; it is to remain imprisoned . . . by conditioned ways of seeing . . . without the self-consciousness that must be the point of departure for all critical understanding" (Dirlik, 1990, p. 395).

In order to highlight the importance of a postcolonial critical perspective for rhetorical studies, I provide in the first section of this essay a theoretical overview of postcolonialism and discuss how it calls for a self-reflexive perspective on academic work. In the second section, I delineate the implications of postcolonial theory and criticism for rhetorical studies and discuss how they point to a need for a reorientation of our field to the present historical and social exigencies of racism and neocolonialism.

POSTCOLONIALISM: AN OVERVIEW

> The interpretation of our reality through patterns not our own serves only to make us ever more unknown, ever less free, ever more solitary.
>
> *Gabriel García Márquez, "The Solitude of Latin America"*

My aim here is not to provide an exhaustive survey of postcolonialism (for which I do not have space) but rather to introduce those themes/issues of postcolonialism that I perceive as having important implications for rhetorical studies. Specifically, I discuss three broad perspectives of postcolonialism, and the theoretical and critical issues they raise for the critical scholar: discursive imperialism, hybrid and diasporic cultural identities, and postcolonial academic self-reflexivity.

Discursive Imperialism

Articulated mainly within the intersectional critical space of cultural studies, postcolonialism primarily challenges the colonizing and imperialistic tendencies manifest in discursive practices of "first world" countries in their constructions and representations of the subjects of "third world" countries and/or racially oppressed peoples of the world. Although most postcolonial critics writing today are from nations that were or are (in the case of Ireland or Hong Kong) historically under european imperial powers such as England and France, their critical focus is not restricted to the discursive practices of these nations during the time they were empires. Rather, many postcolonial critics now also focus on the neocolonialism of nations such as the United States and the United Kingdom, in their representations of subjects of developing countries and racially oppressed groups (whether in popular media or in academia), as an "other"— racially inferior and hence open to subjection by (white) western discursive practices. As Edward Said (1976) suggests, a postcolonial critic investigates those "system[s] of discourse by which the 'world' is divided, administered, plundered, by which humanity is thrust into pigeonholes, by which 'we' are 'human' and 'they' are not" (p. 41).

Among others, two questions that are central to the postcolonial project are: how do western discursive practices, in their representations of the world and of themselves, legitimize the contemporary global power structures? To what extent do cultural texts of nations such as the United States and England reinforce the neoimperial political practices of these nations? These are very important questions to investigate, for they illustrate how, in the present times, discourses have become one of the primary means of imperialism. Whereas in the past, imperialism was about controlling the "native" by colonizing her/him territorially, now imperialism is more about subjugating the "native" by colonizing her or him discursively.

There are a number of reasons, some of course very obvious, why the focus on western discursive imperialism—especially that of the United States and England—has been a relatively major preoccupation of postcolonial criticism. Here I will mention two. The first has to do with the historical relation of colonialism between the East and the west. While discursive imperialism is and was surely in operation in countries such as Japan and the former U.S.S.R, countries that have wielded considerable influence in world politics, these countries do not have the same history of centuries of global colonialism and expansion behind them as England and France, for example. The historically colonized lands of the East such as India, Africa, parts of Southeast Asia, and Latin America, do not have the same relation of subjection and subordination with them as they do with western empires.

The second reason, which today is even more important, has to do with the tremendous global media presence of western nations, and it is here that the United States's role as a neoimperial power gets established. U.S. communication products (both print and tele/visual, popular and academic) penetrate most parts of the world. As Said (1993) notes, "Rarely before in human history has there been so massive an intervention of force and ideas from one culture to another as there is today from America to the rest of the world" (p. 319). The issue is not merely one of technological or cultural power, but also one of linguistic power. The universality of English makes communication products produced in the United States and England accessible to most parts of the world. In the case of the United States, such accessibility is even more significant because it is backed by financial and technological resources which are able to transport its culture to almost every part of the world. It is this tremendous global

American presence that invites examination of U.S. discourses as neocolonial texts; for texts, after all, are sites of power that reflect the politics of their surroundings.

The construction of the people of non-western cultures as an insignificant "other"—an object of "study" and "interest" in "first world" discourses—is defined by Said (1978) as "Orientalism." Although in using the term *Orientalism,* Said had in mind specifically the construction of Eastern subjects by western discourses, this phenomenon that stereotypes and dehumanizes subjects of "underdeveloped" countries is also applicable to those countries and racial groups that are not regarded as "Oriental," but yet subject to the same processes of misrepresentation and colonization in eurocentric western discourses. Countries of Latin America and Africa, and racial groups in the U.S. such as Hispanics and African-Americans, to name a few, can surely fall in this category.

For Said (1978), "Orientalism" is a function of "intellectual power" (p. 41) that frames and studies the racial "other" in classrooms, in illustrated manuals, in the media, in scholarship, for scrutiny, judgement, discipline, and governing. To do so is to have "knowledge" of such subjects—who in the process become objects—and such "knowledge" then provides the intellectual power "to dominate it, to have authority over it," and in the process "deny autonomy to 'it'" (p. 32). Thus the study of the Orient and marginalized groups becomes "a learned field" (p. 63)—and because it is a learned "field," the subjects who are "learned about" are confined to a narrow and discursive space created by the west.

Such discursive confinement is not merely a scholarly confinement, but is ultimately a reflection of the ideological and political practices of "developed" nations; for it is only when two-thirds of the world can be so confined into such a manageable discursive field, which erases and neutralizes their differences and individualities, that it becomes possible for "first world" subjects to devise and adopt a generalized attitude toward natives of "third world" countries or "third world" origins. Abdul JanMohamed (1985) refers to this strategy of generalization as the "commodifi[cation]" of the native, "so that he is now perceived as a generic being that can be exchanged for any other native (they all look alike, act alike, and so on)" (p. 64). Said (1978) further observes that such generalizing strategies also depend on a "flexible *positional* superiority, which puts the westerner in a whole series of possible relationships with the Orient without ever losing him the relative upper hand" (p. 7).

Such a strategy of generalization that effaces cultural differences between peoples of various nonwhite cultures has, for instance, been a significant feature of much of western feminist discourse on the "third world." In such discourse, cultural differences between women of various "third world" cultures are often effaced in order to construct a monolithic image of a "third world" woman as passive, powerless, backwards, uneducated, victimized, and more (Mohanty, 1991)—categories that are easily interchangeable for the "other" must always be a generic "other" if the task of discursive colonization is to be made manageable.

Cultural Hybridity and Diasporic Identity

Although critique of western discursive imperialism is one of the central aims of postcolonial criticism, the postcolonial project is more than that. Postcolonialism is about borderlands and hybridity. It is about cultural indeterminacy and spaces in between. Resisting attempts at any totalizing forms of cultural understanding (whether imperialistic or nationalistic), the postcolonial perspective argues for a recognition of the "hybrid location of cultural value[s]" (Bhabha, 1992, p. 439). Just as postcolonial critics challenge the hegemonic operations of western discourses, many of them also rightly recognize that the answer to western hegemony does not reside in closing off boundaries and resorting to high nationalism (as has often been the case in some third world nations such as Iran). As Arif Dirlik (1990) points out, taking refuge in a pre-western past and indigenous traditions as a source for articulating identities is a "native chauvinism" (p. 401) that reproduces a kind of "internal orientalism" (Breckenridge and Van der Veer, 1993, p. 11) and rearticulates the binary of "us" versus "them" on which much of modernist understandings of identities rest. Instead of holding on to some notion of an indigenous cultural or national identity as a means to reject and resist western hegemony, the point is to recognize that today, with increasing globalization of the world, it is not possible to conceive of cultures and nations monolithically (Appadurai, 1990; Dirlik, 1990; Giddens, 1990; Hall, 1994; Said, 1993). As Said (1993) points out, everyone is at cultural intersections today. We cannot think of culture as an enclosed system of practices.

> [N]ew alignments made across borders, types, nations, and essences are rapidly coming into view, and it is those new alignments that now provoke and challenge the fundamentally static notion of *identity* that has been the core of cultural thought during the era of imperialism. (Said, 1993, pp. xxiv–xxv)

These perceptions of the postcolonial critic typically emerge from the experiential ambivalence that marks the position of the critic. Living between two (or more) cultures or between two nations, and yet not being of either one, the postcolonial "subject" is forced into a nomadic, diasporic position that is marked by what Gloria Anzaldua (1987) calls a "mestiza" consciousness—a consciousness of the borderlands. This mestiza consciousness shuttles between two or more cultures but is unable to situate itself in either one.

> But every place she went
> they pushed her to the other side
> and that other side pushed her to the other side
> of the other side of the other side. . . .
> Pushed to the edge of the world
> there she made her home on the edge. . . .
> Always pushed toward the other side
> In all lands alien, nowhere citizen. (Anzaldua, 1994, p. 3)

The postcolonial individual is thus cultureless (as we normally perceive culture), and yet cultured because she or he exists in a culture of borderlands (Anzaldua, 1987). It is this that bestows on the postcolonial subject's position an unique ambivalence. I emphasize this ambivalence not to delineate it as a weakness. Rather, this ambivalence is what makes the postcolonial perspective so significant in deconstructing grand cultural master narratives. Being a part of two or more cultures, and yet not belonging to either one, the postcolonial subject is equipped to see that national and cultural identities cannot be essentialized, that they are protean, that they cross borders, and that they are transnational.

Postcolonialism and Academic Self-Reflexivity

The importance of a postcolonial position to any scholarly practice is that it urges us to analyze our academic discourses and connect them to the larger political practices of our nations. This means that in examining our academic discourses, the postcolonial question to ask is: To what extent do our scholarly practices—whether they be the kind of issues we explore in our research, the themes around which we organize our teaching syllabi, or the way that we structure our conferences and decide who speaks (and does not speak), about what, in the name of intellectual practices—legitimize the hegemony of western power structures?

In posing this question, the postcolonial perspective does not suggest that, as scholars writing in the west, all that we do is legitimize the imperial political practices of western nations. Rather, the argument is that we need to examine our academic discourses against a larger backdrop of western hegemony, neocolonial, and racial politics. We need to engage in "contrapuntal lines of a global analysis" where we see "texts and worldly institutions . . . working together" (Said, 1993, p. 318). In the pursuit of our scholarly goals, we often do not stop to think or ask questions about why research agenda A seems more important to us than research agenda B? What is the ideology that operates in us that makes research agenda A seem more significant than research agenda B? How are we always already "interpellated" into examining A but not B? What does that interpellation say about our role in reproducing and participating in the hegemonic global domination of the Rest by the west? What does it mean, for instance, when I am told that there is a market for research agenda A but none for research agenda B? Or that if I did pursue research agenda B, I would have to do it in a way that would make it marketable? And what way would that be? Whose way would that be? Who decides what is marketable? What does that decision have to do with the political practices of our nations? How does this market serve the capitalistic and racist hegemony of western nations? And what is my position, as an intellectual, in reproducing this hegemony?

The point in asking such questions is to recognize the latent ideological structures that inform our scholarship and practices. As Van Dijk (1993) puts it, often "under the surface of sometimes sophisticated scholarly analysis and description of other races, peoples, or groups . . . we find a powerful ideological layer of self-interest, in-group favoritism, and ethnocentrism" (p. 160).

In fact, even when we do sometimes try to break out of the eurocentric canons informing contemporary academic scholarship by including alternate cultural and racial perspectives in our syllabi, we often do not realize that instead of really breaking free of the canon, all that we do is stretch it. Add things to it. But the canon remains the same and unchallenged. Our subject positions in relation to the canon remain the same and unchallenged.[3] Instead of examining how the canon itself is rooted in a larger discourse of colonialism and western hegemony, we frequently use the canon to appropriate "other" voices.[4]

The question then arises, "So what is to be done?" Perhaps the first step here is to do what Gayatri Spivak (1990) suggests: to unlearn our privilege (p. 9). And the first step towards that unlearning requires self-reflexivity, it requires seeing ourselves not sequestered in an academic institution, but connecting things that we think or not think, say or not say, teach or not teach, to the larger political and ideological practices of our nations in their interactions with the rest of the world.

A second aspect of postcolonial self-reflexivity is the problem of essentialism that a postcolonial critic is often faced with when she or he challenges the discursive constructions of nonwhite cultures and racially oppressed peoples of the world in hegemonic western discourses. The problem of essentialism that this critical task brings about is that of having to challenge the misrepresentations of racial "others" in western discourses, while at the same time avoiding the suggestion that there *is* an authentic racial identity that the critic knows is being misrepresented. So for instance, when a postcolonial critic argues that a particular western feminist discourse on a third world culture, say India, is a misrepresentation of the lives of the women of that culture, the critic implicitly falls prey to a problem of essentializing because one has to know what it means to be an "Indian woman" to argue that a subaltern Indian woman is being misrepresented. This, then, raises the ensuing question about essentialism: "Is there anything such as an 'Indian woman'?" And if, to engage in her or his critical practice, the critic has to assert that there is, then does that not lead to a kind of colonization all over again, where the critic becomes the voice of authority that determines what constitutes or does not constitute a particular cultural or racial identity ? The question then is: How can the critic engage in such postcolonial criticism without being once again the totalizing voice of authority that determines an "authentic" racial or cultural identity?

A way out of this critical dilemma is provided by Gayatri Spivak's (1988, 1990) notion of strategic essentialism. Spivak suggests that while it is true that to engage in a postcolonial criticism that challenges the misrepresentations of racial "others" in hegemonic discourses, one does to a certain extent end up essentializing, nonetheless that essentializing is only a necessary "strategic" essentializing—a risk that the critic *must* take "in a scrupulously visible political interest" (1988, p. 205): "In deconstructive critical practice, you have to be aware that you are going to essentialize anyway. So then strategically you can look at essentialisms, not as descriptions of the way things are, but as something one must adopt to *produce a critique of anything*" (1990, p. 51; italics added). Strategic essentialism, then, is only a political tool that the postcolonial critic often has to adopt to resist any kind of hegemony. The important point about strategic essentialism is that the critic always remains *aware* that she or he is essentializing only in order to realize certain political goals.

In suggesting that the essentialism that a postcolonial critic engages in has to be a *strategic* political essentialism, Spivak thus warns us against the temptation of really essentializing and carving a fixed and "authentic" identity for a particular racial group that we, as critics, claim is being misrepresented. Such a temptation is problematic because it has the potential to reproduce the colonizing power relations that postcolonialism is out to challenge in the first place. If, in strategically essentializing, the critic lapses into really essentializing and believing in the cultural essence that she/he creates (say of an Indian woman), then the critic ends up being the hegemonic voice that has already predetermined an indigenous cultural/racial identity.

The self-reflexivity that the term *strategic essentialism* then asks us to engage in has to do with constantly examining our subject positions as postcolonial critics when we challenge the misrepresentations of racial "others" in western texts. In Foucauldian terms, this means that instead of engaging only in a juridical/hierarchical examination of power in western discourses, the postcolonial critic also needs to conduct an "ascending analysis of power" (Foucault, 1980, p. 99) by seeing how she or he might be inscribed in the power relations that she or he is attempting to resist. That is, instead of merely uncovering hegemony in western discourses, the critic also needs to examine the power relations that structure her or his own discourses. This is especially important, because having been primarily schooled in western academic mode (even those of us who write from the "margins" or who write from metropolis institutions of non-western countries), the postcolonial critic's intellectual perspectives cannot wholly be free of the power relations that she or he is out to displace.

For me, as a person from the third world writing in western academia, such a postcolonial self-reflexive examination entails asking questions such as: What does it mean when I, as a postcolonial/"third world" critic, am able to be heard in the west? How much of a compromise do I make to be recognized and established as a postcolonial critic? What does the particular "postcolonial position" that I articulate in the western academy have to do with the institutional operations of power in western educational institutions? And if that power contributes to the capitalist hegemony of western nations, then what is my participation in that power that I am out to critique in the first place? These are important questions to ask because it is by asking such questions and engaging in such constant autocritiques that postcolonial critics will be able to recognize and resist the possible operation of the very same colonial power in their critical endeavor that they are out to challenge in the first place.

RETHINKING OUR PARADIGMS: IMPLICATIONS OF POSTCOLONIAL THEORY AND CRITICISM FOR RHETORICAL STUDIES

As superpowers realign and markets diversify, many of the conventional boundaries of earlier eras have been dismantled. Yet our critical languages and our methodologies continue to refer to these older constructs.

Caren Kaplan, "The Politics of Location as Transnational Feminist Critical Practice"

So far, I have presented a theoretical overview of postcolonialism and discussed the kind of theoretical issues that it raises for the critic and critical practice. Now I want to draw out some of the implications of postcolonial theory and criticism for rhetorical studies. First, one of the most significant implications of postcolonial theory and criticism for rhetorical studies is the notion of a postcolonial self-reflexivity. As I have already suggested, a postcolonial self-reflexivity entails that as scholars practicing in the west, we be aware of how our scholarly practices are often engaged in reproducing neocolonial patterns of intellectual domination (Breckenridge and Van der Veer, 1993). This has important implications for rhetoric. Rhetoric as a discipline that is largely based on humanist theories and speeches of white men in power has not been adequately self-reflexive about its scholarship in relation to issues of race and neocolonialism. In fact, as Dwight Conquergood (1991) recently and quite directly suggested, the limitation of rhetorical and communication scholarship is that it has ironically been "unreflexive about the rhetorical construction of its own disciplinary authority" (p. 193). Although calls for other kinds of self-reflexivity (feminist, postmodern, ideological) have been made, albeit all too briefly, the discipline on the whole has been disturbingly silent about its own disciplinary position in relation to issues of race and neocolonialism. The silence that I am talking of is not about the lack of studies on nonwhite people. (In fact there have been some rhetorical studies, although few, on nonwhite issues and cultures. Condit and Lucaites' [1993] valuable work on "equality" which, among other things, examines African American public rhetoric is a recent example.) The silence that I have in mind has to do with not rereading (and problematizing) our dominant rhetorical paradigms, our theories, our critical tools, and our research agendas, against a larger backdrop of racial and neocolonial politics. It has to do with not interrogating the extent to which our white universalistic rhetorical paradigms (whether of Aristotle, Plato or of Burke, Perelman, Toulmin, Bitzer) that we keep drawing on, as well as passing down to students without problematizing their eurocentric limits, inhibits alternative racial and cultural perspectives on rhetoric from emerging, and continues a pattern of eurocentric intellectual domination.[5]

Even the recent postmodern incursions in the field seem to be somewhat problematic in this regard. Scholars (McGee, 1990, 1975; McKerrow, 1989) operating from such a perspective have problematized the modernist subject on which the rhetorical tradition is largely based; however, they have not extended this problematizing to also identify this modernist subject (as well as the modernist canon) as being the subject of colonialism. For as Homi Bhabha (1990) reminds us, the advent of modernism in the west was also the moment of colonialism.[6]

The solution, however, is not merely to do more rhetorical studies on nonwhite people (e.g., Campbell's [1986] study on African American women speakers), for that only becomes a matter of extending, instead of displacing or challenging, the canon by adding "others." Rather, the solution is to critically examine and challenge the very value system on which the rhetorical canon and our scholarship is based. For instance, Rhetoric as a discipline has been traditionally built on public address. But historically public address has been a realm where imperial voices were primarily heard and imperial policies were articulated. The colonized did not always have access to a public realm, or if they did, their speeches were not always recorded in mainstream documents, since the means of production rested with the imperial subject. All this perhaps means that we have built a lot of our understanding of rhetoric, and the canon of rhetoric, by focusing on (and often celebrating) imperial voices. This calls for a reexamination of our paradigms. The move here is parallel to that made by feminists in their challenges of the masculinist biases of the discipline.

If rhetorical scholars are to reexamine the discipline in relation to issues such as imperialism, neocolonialism, and race, then they need to perhaps do what Spivak suggests, "unlearn" a lot of the rhetorical tradition and evaluate critically what kinds of knowledge have been (and continue to be) "privileged, legitimated, [and] displaced" in our texts and theories (Conquergood, 1991, p. 193). And "what configuration of socio-political [and racial] interests" this privileging, displacing, and legitimizing has served (and continues to serve) (p. 193). For one thing, this means engaging in some serious "soul searching" to uncover why scholarship in our discipline has been and continues to be so white (Rakow, 1989, p. 212).[7] It is through such postcolonial self-reflexivity of our discipline, as well as our individual scholarship, that we will be able to continue the task of pushing the traditional paradigms of rhetoric further in order to create spaces for racially and culturally marginalized voices and perspectives on rhetoric to emerge—voices and perspectives that would be comprised of sensitive postcolonial responses to the neocolonial and racist circumstances of our present time.

Second, the postcolonial critique of western discursive imperialism that constructs racial "others" and that legitimizes the contemporary global power structures has important implications for rhetorical criticism, in that it beckons us to recognize postcolonialism as a timely and important critical and political perspective. As Williams and Chrisman (1994) emphasize with great urgency in their introduction to *Colonial Discourse and Post-Colonial Theory*, it is alarming "how many of the attitudes, the strategies, and even how much of the room for manoeuvre of the colonial period [still] remain in place" (p. 3) in contemporary social, cultural, and I would add, academic practices. Given this, it is unfortunate that in our literature we hardly find articles, especially in our mainstream journals, that examine neocolonial representations of racial "others" or that analyze, for instance, the discursive processes through which the (white) "west" gets constantly legitimized in political, cultural, and social discourses.

For instance, it is significant that while other kinds of analyses were done on George Bush's Gulf War rhetoric,[8] there were hardly any analyses of how the U.S. rhetoric on the Gulf War constructed the Middle Eastern people (and different Muslim cultures) as uncivilized and immoral, and always already inclined towards barbaric terrorist activities. (The recent depictions of Muslims and Middle Eastern people in the media during the World Trade Center bombing is also an example of this kind of rhetoric). Nor has there been any rhetorical study, that I am aware of, that examines how the U.S. political and media discourse always constructs the countries with whom U.S. foreign relations reach an impasse, as devilish "others" bent on destroying the world order envisioned by U.S. imperialism. (The media coverage of North Korea as "The headless *beast*" [my emphasis], a caption that *Newsweek* ran on its cover after the death of Kim Il Sung, North Korea's former Head of State, is a recent example).[9] My point here is not necessarily to condone the activities of any of these groups or countries but rather to suggest that when the rhetoric of cultural "othering" is manifest in almost every aspect of public discourse, it is unfortunate that rhetorical scholars have not done much to expose and decry the neocolonial strategies through which such discourse operates. At a time when every form of bigotry (racial, cultural, and sexual) prevails, our discipline, by not adequately focusing on issues of neocolonialism and racism, seems to be imprisoning itself in an ivory tower from which it seems more and more unable to hear the many oppressed who are struggling to be heard.

The implications of all this for our discipline are simple. We simply *need* to engage in postcolonial analyses of texts. We *need* to develop critical perspectives that now seek to examine and expose to what extent neocolonial forces, whether they be representations of "others" or representations of Self, underwrite cultural, political, and academic discursive practices, for as I have already suggested, if texts are sites of power that are reproduced by their social conditions, then neocolonial and racial forces are, to some extent, always already written into our texts. It is when we embrace postcolonialism as a significant critical perspective that rhetorical studies will be able to adequately engage in the present historical and social conditions.

A promising collusion between rhetoric and postcolonialism is also possible given that neocolonialism operates more discursively, in contrast to colonialism, which was more territorial and that neocolonialism operates subtly. On the point of subtlety, Spivak (1991) states that "neocolonialism is like radiation—you feel it less like you don't feel it" (p. 221). Both of these aspects of neocolonialism, its discursivity and its subtlety, suggest that rhetorics constitute neocolonial discourses in their attempts to obscure power and their interpellating capacity.[10] Given this, it seems to me that rhetorical scholars could make significant contributions to the present historical moment if they took upon themselves the task of revealing and examining the various subtle rhetorical strategies through which neocolonialism establishes its hegemony. As I already mentioned earlier, one such strategy is the strategy of generalization whereby "others" are generically constructed, which makes the task of affirmation of the (white) western self that much easier. We need similar and more detailed insights into the various other rhetorical tropes through which discursive imperialism operates. While scholars (Spurr, 1993; Suleri, 1992) in other fields such as literature have done some work in this area, I believe that this is a critical terrain that rhetorical scholars, given their orientation, are best suited to engage in as well as contribute to.

Third, the postcolonial argument about diasporic cultural identities has important implications for the way identity has traditionally been conceptualized in rhetorical studies. Our mainstream rhetorical theories have generally presumed the "reality of the speaker and listener as transcendental subjects engaged in a mutual process of coming together" (Grossberg, 1979, p. 249). Although this position has been problematized by scholars in various ways (Biesecker, 1989; Grossberg, 1979; McKerrow, 1989, 1991), I believe that the postcolonial notion of diaspora and hybridity still has much to offer in this dialogue. As I have already discussed, the postcolonial notion of diasporic identity suggests that with increased globalization of the world, whereby people, technology, ideas, cultures and ethnic groups constantly cross borders (although not often physically) everyone is at cultural intersections. With the softening of national boundaries and the growth of a global economy, we are all in some way cultural hybrids (although some of us more than others) influenced by various transglobal movements of media, of ideas, of peoples, of cultures. In fact, as Tololyan (1991) points out, "diasporas *are* the exemplary communities of the transnational moment" (p. 5; emphasis added). Given this, it is no longer possible to conceive of cultures and cultural identities homogeneously, for each of us in some way occupies borderland territories.

This is slightly different from, or rather an extension of, the position articulated by postmodernism. In postmodernism, what is in question is the individual subject; in postcolonialism what is in question, among other things, is a homogeneous conception of culture. While this position overlaps with postmodernism, much of postmodern theory often itself (albeit implicitly) tends to view cultures homogeneously, since it works from a homogeneous notion of the western world as having reached the last stage of capitalism, which tends to efface cultural differences between countries.

The postcolonial notion of diasporic cultural identity calls for rhetorical theories that are able to address the rhetorical situations and experiences of disjunctured diasporic cultural identities. We now need insights into how rhetoric functions in hybrid borderlands and cultural spaces, as well as how rhetoric aids in the creation of diasporic disjunctured identities. For instance, a pertinent question here would be: How do cultural diasporas use rhetoric to negotiate through their different culturally disjunctured or pastiched states to enable some kind of shared meaning with people in their daily existence? In this connection, the concept of *shared* meaning and understanding, which has traditionally been regarded as one of the goals of rhetoric, also perhaps needs to be reexamined. How much meaning is shared when fractured and pastiched cultural states engage in rhetorical interactions? Furthermore, in dealing with issues of cultural diasporas, we also need to rethink many of our tools and methods of rhetorical criticism, most of which are laden with universalist implications, and examine to what extent, if any, they allow us to deal with and understand identity formation in a postcolonial world.

Fourth, the postcolonial notion of discursive imperialism, and its attendant rhetoric of generalization that tends to appropriate and efface differences between cultural groups, has important implications for feminist scholarship in rhetorical studies. Much of feminist scholarship in rhetorical studies has been carried out from a relatively liberal and generalized perspective. As feminist rhetorical scholars have begun arguing for the need to include and recognize womens' rhetorical and communicative perspectives, they have not adequately addressed the important point (although it sometimes gets mentioned in passing, usually at conferences, and then forgotten) that a white woman's rhetorical and communicative perspectives, practices, and experiences are not the same as nonwhite womens', and cannot be universalized therein. Much of feminist rhetorical scholarship, by ignoring issues of race, implicitly tends towards a discursive colonization, whereby the discourses, more often than not, express and speak to the perspectives and voices of white women. Adrienne Rich has called such a phenomenon "white solipsism" which is a tendency "to think . . . and speak as if whiteness described the world" (cited in Spelman, 1988, p. 116).

Especially problematic in this regard is the generalized notion of a "woman's/feminist rhetorical or communication perspective" that often gets articulated by feminists in the discipline.[11] I believe that this notion needs to be problematized. As Stanback (1988) suggests, the rhetorical goals and experiences of women of different races are different. For instance, a white woman might use rhetoric to negotiate with a patriarchal structure, but a nonwhite woman may use rhetoric to negotiate simultaneously with a patriarchal and a racial structure, and perhaps more with the latter than the former. In other words, the experience, functions, and goals of rhetoric differ in the different cultural spaces of women, and hence the generic concept "feminist or woman's rhetorical/communication perspective" tends to erase the element of race (and other kinds of differences that are beyond the category of sexual difference). Such a perspective also falls prey to a concept of rhetoric that McKerrow (1991) terms (and critiques) as "unidimensional" instead of "multidimensional" (p. 76)—a perspective that once again secures, instead of displaces, the traditional rhetorical canon that feminist scholarship is out to challenge in the first place. Thus, feminist rhetorical scholarship, even though it is pushing the paradigms of the discipline in a laudable manner, still needs culturally localized perspectives, critical or theoretical, that address how race and gender work together to influence and often inhibit womens' communicative experiences. Much of what I am saying here might seem obvious to some, but despite its obviousness, I believe that the point still begs to be made again. It is perhaps by recognizing and embracing postcolonialism as a significant critical practice that feminist scholarship in our discipline will be able to move into its next stage—where, in devising feminist interventions into the traditional rhetorical paradigm, it is also simultaneously able to examine, how and in what ways, it might be using gender as a signifier that covers up issues of race and neocolonialism (Spivak, 1990).

Having said this, I recognize that as feminist rhetorical scholars are engaged in the task of pushing the (white) male oriented paradigms of the discipline, it may not always be possible to fracture the term *woman* or splinter the politics around it. It may sometimes be necessary to engage in feminist interventions in a somewhat monolithic way. And it is perhaps here that the postcolonial notion of strategic essentialism provides us with a helpful political strategy for intervening in the discipline, whereby in strategically essentializing the term "woman," or mobilizing as a group, we are also simultaneously engaged in a vigilant self-reflexivity where we remain *aware* of the politics and power of race and neocolonialism that might be operating through us. It is hopefully through such postcolonial self-reflexivity that our feminist scholarship will become characterized by what Spivak (1994) defines as "an impossible risk" of a lasting essence (p. 3).

A postcolonial rhetorical intervention, as I have laid it out, has much in common with the theory of critical rhetoric developed by McKerrow (1989). McKerrow's call for "a critique of domination" (p. 92), critical self-reflexivity, a move towards heterogeneity, and a focus on the "absences" (p. 107) in texts also underlies a postcolonial rhetorical perspective. The important difference, however, is that McKerrow's postmodern rhetorical perspective does not extend the notion of critical rhetoric to issues of imperialism and neocolonialism. Although such a perspective might be implicit in Mckerrow's postmodern perspective, I believe that the postcolonial move still needs to be explicitly made; for as Appiah (1991) rightly suggests, the "post-" in postmodernism is not necessarily the "post-" in postcolonialism. That is, engaging in a postmodern critical practice does not necessarily mean that one is also engaging in a critique of neocolonialism or imperialism. In fact, a postmodern perspective itself may be eurocentric and hegemonizing (Fredric Jameson's [1986] article "Third-World Literature in the Era of Multinational Capitalism" is a case in point).[12] Mishra and Hodge (1994) provide us with an important distinction here. They state: "If for postmodernism the object of analysis is the subject as defined by humanism, with its essentialism and mistaken historical verities, its unities and its transcendental presence, then for post-colonialism the object is the imperialist subject,. . .[and] the processes of imperialism" (p. 281). There are thus significant intersections between the two, but they are not the same.

Given this, I think that a postcolonial rhetorical perspective needs to be recognized as a challenge that productively adds to that posed by critical rhetoric (as well as feminist rhetoric, since it also has points of intersections with the latter). It is perhaps when all these critical forces come together, as well as draw resources from each other, that Rhetoric as a discipline will undergo its next paradigmatic shift where it is able to sensitively listen to all those diverse groups of people who, because of the stark historical reality of the late twentieth century, have been relegated to places "out there." For as Janice Radway (1992) reminds us:

> [T]here are people "out there" who have voices. They speak in languages and practices that we don't ordinarily try to hear. The problem is our ability to hear different speech. The issue is that they're already speaking—with actions, with fury, with anger, and we don't know how to hear them yet. (p. 668)

Notes

1. I am referring here to the rhetoric of racism/neocolonialism of the dominant culture, as opposed to examinations of the rhetoric of marginalized racial groups. Examining the rhetorical aspects of marginalized and nonwhite cultures, although important, is not the same as examining the rhetoric of racism and neocolonialism. While there surely have been studies (although few) in our discipline that have examined the rhetoric of nonwhite groups or rhetors, there are only very few studies that have examined racist rhetoric/discourse. Some examples of the latter are Celeste Condit and John Lucaites (1991), Cal. M. Logue (1976, 1981), James Klumpp and Thomas Hollihan (1979), and Gordon Nakagawa (1990). A recent study that can also be included here (although it does not explicitly address racist rhetoric) is Nakayama and Krizek's (1995) exploration of the discursive space of whiteness.

I should also mention here that when I refer to the dearth of studies in our discipline/literature on the issues of racism and neocolonialism, I do not include the journal *Critical Studies in Mass Communication* (CSMC) as a part of this literature. Although CSMC is sponsored by the Speech Communication Association (SCA) and some rhetorical scholars have published in this journal, it is not oriented towards rhetorical studies in ways that *Quarterly Journal of Speech*, *Communication Monographs*, or some of the regional journals of SCA are. CSMC is primarily oriented towards mass communication theory and criticism, cultural studies and popular culture, and political economy—areas that have historically (and even now to a large extent) not been a focus of rhetorical scholarship.

2. Critique of eurocentric discourse and western imperialism is one of the primary thrusts of postcolonial criticism. However, it is not the only thrust. For instance, various critiques of indigenous nationalisms engaged in by scholars from many postcolonial and "third world" countries, who demonstrate the often hegemonizing and the elitist, colonialist, and eurocentric

inflections of these nationalist discourses are also a part of the expanding literature on postcolonial criticism. See, for example, the subaltern project of South Asian scholars, specifically the different volumes of Guha's (1982) *Subaltern Studies: Writings on South Asian History and Society*; various essays in Sangari and Vaid's (1990) *Recasting Women: Essays in Indian Colonial History*, especially Chatterjee's chapter, "The Nationalist Resolution of the Women's Question"; Radhakrishnan's (1992) "Nationalism, Gender, and the Narrative of Identity"; Natarajan's (1994) "Woman, Nation, and Narration in *Midnights Children*"; and Spivak's (1994) "Woman in Difference" in her *Outside in the Teaching Machine*.

Some other works in postcolonial literature have examined the hegemonic cultural productions of postcolonial female subjects in many contemporary cultural discourses of some postcolonial countries. See, for example, Rajan's (1993) insightful book, *Real and Imagined Women: Gender, Culture, and Postcolonialism*.

Given the objective of my paper (and my own subject position in the United States), I will, however, limit my discussion of postcolonialism to what I perceive to be its most dominant impulse—the critique of eurocentrism, and (neo)colonialism and imperialism. This understanding should guide the reader's reading of my essay.

3. The argument here is similar to JanMohamed and Lloyds's (1990) caution that we must be wary of a particular kind of liberal "pluralism" in multiculturalism which "along with assimilation, continues to be the Great White Hope of conservatives and liberals alike" (p. 8). The authors note that "Such pluralism tolerates the existence of salsa, it even enjoys Mexican restaurants, but it bans Spanish as a medium of instruction in American schools" (p. 8).

4. See also, in this connection, essays by Giroux (1992), McCarthy (1993), McLaren (1994), and Mohanty (1989–1990).

5. Although I recognize that there are a few scholars such as Asante (1987) who have pointed out the eurocentric limits of some of our rhetorical conceptions, it is still a fact that such works are very few. It is also a fact that such reflexibility has not permeated most sections of our discipline. A dominant silence still prevails about the eurocentric limits of much of our scholarship.

6. Bhabha's (1990) argument here is worth quoting:

> I think we need to draw attention to the fact that the advent of Western modernity, located as it generally is in the 18th and 19th centuries, was the moment when certain master narratives of the state, the citizen, cultural value, art, science, the novel, when these major cultural discourses and identities came to define the "Enlightenment" of Western society and the critical rationality of Western personhood. The time at which these things were happening was the same time at which the west was producing another history of itself through its colonial possessions and relations. That ideological tension, visible in the history of the West as a despotic power, at the very moment of the birth of democracy and modernity, has not been adequately written in a contradictory and contrapuntal discourse of tradition. (p. 8)

7. Although Lana Rakow (1989) makes this point specifically in relation to feminist scholarship in Communication, I find it valid to extend it to the discipline of Rhetoric as well.

8. See, for example, Stuckey's (1992) "Remembering the Future: Rhetorical Echoes of World War II and Vietnam in George Bush's Public Speech on the Gulf War."

9. This particular issue of *Newsweek* is dated July 18, 1994.

10. For an excellent analysis of the tropes of imperialism, see Spurr's (1993) *The Rhetoric of Empire: Colonial Discourse in Journalism, Travel Writing, and Imperial Administration*.

11. For instance, Foss and Foss (1989) in their essay "Incorporating the Feminist Perspective in Communication Scholarship: A Research Commentary" discuss in a significantly generalized manner some of the "essential features" (p. 65, n. 1) of "the feminist perspective." Although the authors briefly mention in a footnote that such a perspective may include many approaches, yet their elaboration of "the essential features" of "the feminist perspective," without adequately factoring in issues of difference, especially racial difference, remains problematic. (Race is only

cursorily addressed in a later section of the essay when the authors survey the "use of the feminist perspective in communication research" [p. 74]).

See also Dobris (1989), which provides a "rhetorical theory accounting for gender." Once again, race is not adequately addressed in the author's discussion of "a gender perspective on rhetorical theory and criticism" (p. 148) (and the author herself seems to acknowledge this when she indicates in her conclusion the need for research that addresses race, class, and culture).

See also Campbell's (1973) essay "The Rhetoric of Women's Liberation: An Oxymoron" (reprinted in this volume). In this essay, Campbell's discussion of what she perceives to be some of the "distinctive" rhetorical features of women's liberation such as leaderlessness—"There is no leader, rhetor, or expert" (p. 79)—and participatory dialogue, tends to, I believe, express an egalitarian and privileged view of the feminist movement that elides the other issues of power, privilege, and silencing, which underwrite feminist rhetoric.

While these are only some examples, much of what passes in our discipline under notions such as "feminist rhetoric" or "women's communication" is usually a white perspective where race is not adequately factored in—a factoring that might very well problematize some of the perspectives that are articulated. My aim here is not to devalue the political impulses informing feminist work in our discipline. The efforts that have been made by feminists to intervene in the male oriented structures of our discipline are truly commendable. I am only arguing for a greater attention to issues of race and marginalization (and, by extension, power and privilege) as we begin to develop feminist rhetorical and communication perspectives. Whose (and what) perspective is ultimately being articulated in the notion of a feminist rhetorical and communication perspective is something that we need to address and examine more carefully than we have.

12. This essay by Jameson has generated various debate and critiques. See specifically Ahmad's (1987) critique of Jameson's totalizing perspectives on "third world literature." See also Young's (1990) essay "The Jameson Raid" in his *White Mythologies*.

For another cogent critique of Jameson's postmodern perspectives on the third world, see Colas's (1992) discussion of the role of the third world in Jameson's (1991) *Postmodernism or the Cultural Logic of Late Capitalism*.

References

Ahmad, A. (1987). "Jameson's Rhetoric of Otherness and the National Allegory." *Social Text* 17: 3–25.

Anzaldua, G. (1987). *Borderlands/La Frontera: The New Mestiza*. San Francisco: Spinsters/Aunt Lute.

Anzaldua, G. (1994). "Del otro lado." In J. Ramos, ed., *Companeras: Latina Lesbians* (New York: Routledge), pp. 2–3.

Appadurai, A. (1990). "Disjuncture and Difference in the Global Cultural Economy." *Public Culture* 2(2): 1–24.

Appiah, K. A. (1991). "Is the 'Post-' in 'Postmodernism' the 'Post-' in 'Postcolonial'?" *Critical Inquiry* 17(2): 336–357.

Asante, M. K. (1987). *The Afrocentric Idea*. Philadelphia: Temple University Press.

Bhabha, H. (1990). "Interview with Homi Bhabha: The Third Space." In J. Rutherford, ed., *Identity: Community, Culture, Difference* (London: Lawrence & Wishart), pp. 207–221.

Bhabha, H. (1992). "Postcolonial Criticism." In S. Greenblatt and G. Gunn, eds., *Redrawing the Boundaries: The Transformation of English and American Literary Studies* (New York: MLA), pp. 437–465.

Biesecker, B. (1989). "Rethinking the Rhetorical Situation from within the Thematic of 'Difference.'" *Philosophy and Rhetoric* 22(2): 110–130.

Biesecker, B. (1992). "Coming to Terms with Recent Attempts to Write Women into the History of Rhetoric." *Philosophy and Rhetoric* 25(2): 140–161.

Biesecker, B. (1994, April). "Shifting Scenes: Rhetoric/Feminism/Postmodernism." Paper presented at the 64th annual meeting of the Southern States Communication Association, Norfolk, VA.

Breckenridge, C., and P. Van der Veer. (1993). "Orientalism and the Postcolonial Predicament." In C. Breckenridge and P. Van der Veer, eds., *Orientalism and the Postcolonial Predicament* (Philadelphia: University of Pennsylvania Press), pp. 1–19.

Campbell, K. (1973). "The Rhetoric of Woman's Liberation: An Oxymoron." *Quarterly Journal of Speech* 59: 74–86.

Campbell, K. (1986). "Style and Content in the Rhetoric of Early Afro-American Feminists." *Quarterly Journal of Speech* 72(4): 434–445.

Campbell, K. (1988). "What Really Distinguishes and/or Ought to Distinguish Feminist Scholarship in Communication Studies?" *Women's Studies in Communication* 11: 4–5.

Campbell, K. (1989). *Man Cannot Speak for Her.* 2 vols. New York: Praeger.

Colas, S. (1992). "The Third World in Jameson's *Postmodernism or the Cultural Logic of Late Capitalism.*" *Social Text* 31–32: 258–270.

Condit, C. (1988). "What Makes Our Scholarship Feminist? A Radical/ Liberal View." *Women's Studies in Communication* 11: 6–8.

Condit, C. (1993). "Rhetorical Criticism and Feminism." In S. P. Bowen and N. Wyatt, eds., *Transforming Visions: Feminist Critiques in Communication Studies* (Cresskill, NJ: Hampton Press), pp. 205–230.

Condit, C., and J. Lucaites. (1991). "The Rhetoric of Equality and the Expatriation of African-Americans, 1776–1826." *Communication Studies* 42(1): 1–21.

Condit, C., and J. Lucaites. (1993). *Crafting Equality: America's Anglo-African Word.* Chicago: University of Chicago Press.

Conquergood, D. (1991). "Rethinking Ethnography: Towards a Critical Cultural Politics." *Communication Monographs* 58(2): 179–194.

Dirlik, A. (1990). "Culturalism as Hegemonic Ideology and Liberating Practice." In A. JanMohamed and D. Lloyd, eds., *The Nature and Context of Minority Discourse* (New York: Oxford University Press), pp. 394–431.

Dobris, C. A. (1989). "In the Year of Big Sister: Toward a Rhetorical Theory Accounting for Gender." In K. Carter and C. Spitzack, eds., *Doing Research on Women's Communication: Perspectives on Theory and Method* (Norwood, NJ: Ablex), pp. 137–160.

Foss, K. (1989). "Feminist Scholarship in Speech Communication: Contributions and Obstacles." *Women's Studies in Communication* 12: 1–10.

Foss, K., and S. Foss. (1988). "What Distinguishes Feminist Scholarship in Communication Studies?" *Women's Studies in Communication* 11: 9–11.

Foss, K., and S. Foss. (1989). "Incorporating the Feminist Perspective in Communication Scholarship: A Research Commentary." In K. Carter and C. Spitzack, eds., *Doing Research on Women's Communication: Perspectives on Theory and Method* (Norwood, NJ: Ablex), pp. 65–91.

Foucault, M. (1980). *Power/Knowledge: Selected Interviews and Other Writings by Michel Foucault.* Edited by C. Gordon. Translated by C. Gordon, L. Marshall, J. Mepham, and K. Soper. New York: Pantheon Books.

Foucault, M. (1990). *The History of Sexuality, Vol. 2: The Uses of Pleasure.* Translated by R. Hurley. New York: Vintage Books.

Giddens, A. (1990). *The Consequences of Modernity.* Cambridge: Polity Press.

Giroux, H. A. (1992). "Postcolonial Ruptures and Democratic Possibilities: Multiculturalism as Anti-Racist Pedagogy." *Cultural Critique* 21: 5–39.

Grossberg, L. (1979). "Marxist Dialectics and Rhetorical Criticism." *Quarterly Journal of Speech* 65(3): 235–249.

Guha, R., ed. (1982–1987). *Subaltern Studies: Writings on South Asian History and Society.* 5 vols. Delhi, India: Oxford University Press.

Hall, S. (1994). "Cultural Identity and Diaspora." In P. Williams and L. Chrisman, eds., *Colonial Discourse and Postcolonial Theory: A Reader* (New York: Columbia University Press), pp. 392–403.

Jameson, F. (1986). "Third-World Literature in the Era of Multinational Capitalism." *Social Text* 15: 65–88.

Jameson, F. (1991). *Postmodernism or the Cultural Logic of Late Capitalism.* Durham, NC: Duke University Press.

JanMohamed, A. (1985). "The Economy of Manichean Allegory: The Function of Racial Difference in Colonialist Literature." *Critical Inquiry* 12: 59–87.

JanMohamed, A., and D. Lloyd. (1990). "Introduction: Toward a Theory of Minority Discourse: What Is to Be Done?" In A. JanMohamed and D. Lloyd, eds., *The Nature and Context of Minority Discourse* (New York: Oxford University Press), pp. 1–16.

Kaplan, C. (1994). "The Politics of Location as Transnational Feminist Practice." In I. Grewal and C. Kaplan, eds., *Scattered Hegemonies: Postmodernity and Transnational Feminist Practices* (Minneapolis: University of Minnesota Press), pp. 137–152.

Klumpp, J. F., and T. A. Hollihan. (1979). "Debunking the Resignation of Earl Butz: Sacrificing an Official Racist." *Quarterly Journal of Speech* 65: 1–11.

Logue, C. (1976). "Rhetorical Ridicule of Reconstruction Blacks." *Quarterly Journal of Speech* 62(4): 400–409.

Logue, C. (1981). "Transcending Coercion: The Communicative Strategies of Black Slaves on Antebellum Plantations." *Quarterly Journal of Speech* 67(1): 31–46.

Marquez, G. G. (1988). "The Solitude of Latin America" [Nobel Lecture, 1982]. In J. Ortega, ed., *Gabríel García Marquez and the Powers of Fiction* (Austin: University of Texas Press), pp. 87–91.

McCarthy, C. (1993). "After the Canon: Knowledge and Ideological Representation in the Multicultural Discourse on Curriculum Reform." In C. McCarthy and W. Crichlow, eds., *Race, Identity, and Representation in Education* (New York: Routledge), pp. 289–305.

McGee, M. (1975). "In Search of 'the People': A Rhetorical Alternative." *Quarterly Journal of Speech* 61(3): 235–249.

McGee, M. (1990). "Text, Context, and the Fragmentation of Contemporary Culture." *Western Journal of Communication* 54: 274–289.

McKerrow, R. (1989). "Critical Rhetoric: Theory and Praxis." *Communication Monographs* 56: 91–110.

McKerrow, R. (1991). "Critical Rhetoric in a Postmodern World." *Quarterly Journal of Speech* 77: 75–78.

McLaren, P. (1994). "Multiculturalism and the Postmodern Critique: Toward a Pedagogy of Resistance and Transformation." In H. A. Giroux and P. McLaren, eds., *Between Borders: Pedagogy and Politics of Cultural Studies* (New York: Routledge).

Mishra, V., and B. Hodge. (1994). "What Is Post(-)Colonialism?" In P. Williams and L. Chrisman, eds., *Colonial Discourse and Postcolonial Theory: A Reader* (New York: Columbia University Press), pp. 276–290.

Mohanty, C. (1989–1990). "On Race and Voice: Challenges for Liberal Education in the 1990s." *Cultural Critique* 14: 179–208.

Mohanty, C. (1991). "Under Western Eyes: Feminist Scholarship and Colonial Discourses." In C. Mohanty, A. Russo, and L. Torres, eds., *Third World Women and the Politics of Feminism* (Bloomington: Indiana University Press), pp. 51–80.

Nakagawa, G. (1990). "'What are we doing here with all these Japanese ?': Subject-Constitution and Strategies of Discursive Closure Represented in Stories of Japanese American Internment." *Communication Quarterly* 38(4): 388–402.

Nakayama, T. K., and R. L. Krizek. (1995). "White: A Strategic Rhetoric." *Quarterly Journal of Speech* 81(3): 291–309.

Natarajan, N. (1994). "Woman, Nation, and Narration in *Midnight's Children*." In I. Grewal and C. Kaplan, eds., *Scattered Hegemonies: Postmodernity and Transnational Feminist Practices* (Minneapolis: University of Minnesota), pp. 76–89.

Ono, K., and J. Sloop. (1992). "Commitment to *Telos*: A Sustained Critical Rhetoric." *Communication Monographs* 59(1): 48–60.

Pollock, D., and R. Cox. (1991). "Historicizing 'Reason': Critical Theory, Practice, and Postmodernity." *Communication Monographs* 58(2): 170–178.

Radhakrishnan, R. (1992). "Nationalism, Gender, and the Narrative of Identity." In A. Parker, M. Russo, D. Sommer, and P. Yaeger, eds., *Nationalisms and Sexualities* (New York: Routledge), pp. 77–95.

Radway, J. (1992). "In the Discussion Section of M. Wallace's *Towards a Black Feminist Cultural Criticism*." In L. Grossberg, P. Treichler, and C. Nelson, eds., *Cultural Studies* (New York: Routledge), pp. 664–671.

Rajan, R. (1993). *Real and Imagined Women: Gender, Culture, and Postcolonialism*. New York: Routledge.

Rakow, L. (1989). "Feminist Studies: The Next Stage." *Critical Studies in Mass Communication* 6(2): 209–215.

Said, E. (1976). "Interview." *Diacritics* 6: 30–47.

Said, E. (1978). *Orientalism*. New York: Random House.

Said, E. (1993). *Culture and Imperialism*. New York: Alfred Knopf.

Sangari, K., and S. Vaid, eds. (1990). *Recasting Women: Essays in Indian Colonial History*. New Brunswick, NJ: Rutgers University Press.

Spelman, E. (1988). *Inessential Woman: Problems of Exclusion in Feminist Thought*. Boston: Beacon Press.

Spitzack, C., and K. Carter. (1987). "Women in Communication Studies: A Typology for Revision." *Quarterly Journal of Speech* 73: 401–423.

Spitzack, C., and K. Carter. (1988). "Feminist Communication: Rethinking the Politics of Exclusion." *Women's Studies in Communication* 11: 32–36.

Spivak, G. (1988). *In Other Worlds: Essays in Cultural Politics*. New York: Routledge.

Spivak, G. (1990). *The Postcolonial Critic: Interviews Strategies, Dialogues*. Edited by S. Harasym. New York: Routledge.

Spivak, G. (1991). "Neocolonialism and the Secret Agent of Knowledge." *Oxford Literary Review* 13: 220–251.

Spivak, G. (1994). *Outside in the Teaching Machine*. New York: Routledge.

Spurr, D. (1993). *The Rhetoric of Empire: Colonial Discourse in Journalism, Travel Writing, and Imperial Administration*. Durham, NC: Duke University Press.

Stanback, M. H. (1988). "What Makes Scholarship about Black Women and Communication Feminist Communication Scholarship?" *Women Studies in Communication* 11: 28–31.

Stuckey, M. (1992). "Remembering the Future: Rhetorical Echoes of World War II and Vietnam in George Bush's Public Speech on the Gulf War." *Communication Studies* 43: 246–256.

Suleri, S. (1992). *The Rhetoric of English India*. Chicago: University of Chicago Press.

Tololyan, K. (1991). "The Nation-State and Its Others: In Lieu of a Preface." *Diaspora* 1(1): 3–7.

Van dijk, T. A. (1993). *Elite Discourse and Racism*. Newbury Park, CA: Sage.

Williams, P., and L. Chrisman. (1994). "Colonial Discourse and Postcolonial Theory: An Introduction." In P. Williams and L. Chrisman, eds., *Colonial Discourse and Postcolonial Theory: A Reader* (New York: Columbia University Press), pp. 1–20.

Young, R. (1990). *White Mythologies: Writing History and the West*. New York: Routledge.

Epilogue

Contributions from Rhetorical Theory

JOHN LOUIS LUCAITES
CELESTE MICHELLE CONDIT

The essays in this volume all exist within the discourse community identified as "contemporary rhetorical theory." Contemporary rhetorical theory, however, exists as just one set of voices within a large and varied academic community. The contributions that rhetorical studies have to make to this larger academic conversation arise from the unique situation and history of rhetorical studies in the discipline of communication.[1] As we indicated in the introductory essay, throughout its long history rhetorical studies has been sensitive to the discursive qualitites of context, of persuasiveness, and of the public space in which social and political interaction so frequently takes place. Consequently, we believe that a rhetorical perspective on the world opens the possibilities for constituting a distinctive alternative to the projects of modernism and postmodernism.

Modernism places its faith in the possibility of certainty, absolute truth, and universal objectivity. Modernist communities thus rely upon the efforts of elite experts—priests, philosophers, scientists, and so on—to obtain the knowledge of certain and universal truths, with the goal of translating these truths into normative social and political practices. In such a world, rhetoric is little more than the medium for disseminating these truth to nonexperts (i.e., "the masses") through various forms of "education." By contrast, postmodernism eschews the faith in certainty and absolute or universal knowledge as woefully mistaken or a deceit.[2] Public statements that are claimed as true in any absolute or univeral sense are characterized as the efforts of elites to deceive the less powerful into serving the interests of those with the power and capacity to speak the public will. Whereas modernism focuses on truth-seeking, postmodernism excels at unmasking false truths, revealing that the so-called certainties of science, philosophy, and religion as inherently mutable—a mutability that is a function of both their history and their future. Modernism sees itself as constructing a permanent edifice of truth and goodness, while postmodernism characerizes itself as "deconstructive," destroying the false monuments of modernism.

Each of these views has its comforts. Modernism offers a supremely powerful feeling of security and certainty that presumably extend everywhere and forever in space and time. Postmodernism offers the joy of unmasking authoritative pieties and the possibility of escaping otherwise inexorable, oppressive traps. Each view, however, also has imporant flaws. Modernism fails because societies do change and all of their knowledge eventually changes with them. Plato's *Republic* does not specify appropriate applications of *in vitro* fertilization or proper governing systems for the colonization of Mars (colonization of Mars requires both local governance and international economic alliances, and the communication difficulties in such a transaction are not addressed in the Platonic dialogues). Moreover, what counts as the ideal "public good" varies across time and space based upon one's role or position in the society.

Postmodernism's critique of modernism is thus well taken; unfortunately, postmodernism does not offer a viable independent alternative to modernism. As a perspective founded primarily in critique and opposition, postmodernism is always parasitic on that which it critiques. In presenting a world where public discourse is nothing but deceit, postmodernism precludes the possibility of any community whatsoever. The postmodern alternative to life as a citizen in a community is the "nomadic subject," an anomic body that wanders globally from place to place through time. Such a way of life may be necessary to those inhabiting the marginal positions of an oppressive society, and it may even be appealing to those who are young, who are single, and who have significant material resources. However, the life of the nomad is not inherently desirable for everyone, offering little comfort and many problems for those concerned with raising children, the serenity of old age, and the construction and maintenance of a social order that can provide for the safety, comfort, and care of its people. Just as contemporary nomads are parasitic on the existence of the modern society, so too is the postmodern value of "fragmentation" dependent on the existence of something to fragment. In the context of a unified global totality, fragmentation is a worthy instrumental value. However, "fragmentation" as a basic social goal leads to an undifferentiated mass of no particular characteristics whatsoever.

Rhetoric provides a third alternative to being-in-the-world. Instead of living inside the absolute totality of modernism, or living outside modernism in perpetual critique, the rhetorical perspective describes a *relatively* stable and *relatively* fluid community that eschews any clear distinction(s) between inside and outside. The rhetorical perspective enables such a worldview because it encourages us to employ the experience and understanding of a highly diverse citizenry as the most important component of communal decision making, not the presumed knowledge of timeless truths. The truth produced by rhetoric is always provisional, good enough for daily use, but also open to challenge when necessary. We describe such knowledge as "substantive," having a material consistency somewhere between the bedrock certainty of absolute and timeless truths and the total fluidity of permanent critique. In the rhetorical community it is the people, not the powerful elite, who judge the substance of such social knowledge.

Of course, when we talk of "the people," we are not focusing on isolated individuals or anomic groups, but rather on persons who play the role of "citizen." Such people certainly strive for their own interests and their own good, but their "own good" is interpreted through their particular identity as members of a community. They are neither mere individuals, nor mere undifferentiated pawns in the community, but specific role-players within the rhetorical vision that constitutes the community.

The rhetorical perspective thus opens the possibility of a middling orientation between modernism and postmodernism. Oriented as such, the people are concerned to "get things right," but that does not mean that they can wait for certain truths to be delivered to them by the priests of truth and knowledge. Instead, they act on their shared and compromised visions of the most probable course of action, based on what they believe they know, here and now. This more fluid, process-oriented perspective is made possible by replacing the idealist, philosophical notion of "foundations" as universal and permanent truths, with a rhetorical conception of foundations as constituted by and within communities that publicly contest their principles and priorities in free and open debate and discussion. Such rhetorical communities legitimize specific rights, norms, and entitlements (including the distribution of property) so that the history of the community's experience and knowledge forms substantive anchors against totalitarianism (whether fueled by monarchical will, the tyranny of the majority, or solipsistic individualism). Such rights, norms, and entitlements are always open to question, however, since the malleability and mutability of such anchors is self-evident from the fact that the community itself was the source of their substance. The rhetorical community's authority is thus never permanent or unquestionable. It exists in a context of contingency and situatedness, and exists for audiences and publics that are often differentially empowered and who must work to create coalitions in order to negotiate for their desired ends. On a rhetorical view, then, social and political arrangements are seldom rooted on firm and unmoveable bedrock; nevertheless, even though significant social and political change can be expected, it never comes easily, and when it does occur it requires substantial justification and rationale.

Because it makes possible this third fundamental alternative, the rhetorical perspective offers distinctive approaches to particular questions in social theory. One of the primary critiques made about many contemporary, poststructuralist and postmodernist approaches to discourse theory is that they favor a negative or deconstructive attitude that shows little or no concern for the affirmative, reconstructive potential in any given sociopolitical situation.[3] Rhetorical theorists who engage the problems and possibilities of discourse in the contemporary world tend to push the deconstructive critiques of poststructuralism and postmodernism forward, but they do so with an eye toward the pragmatic, emancipatory possibilities in any given situation. The concept of "strategic liberation" illustrates this possibility.

From a rhetorical perspective, "strategic liberation" is the possibility of improving life within one's community in temporary and incomplete, but nonetheless meaningful, ways. This perspective stands in contrast to philosophical or religious conceptions of social change that presume the perfection of human organization based on universal truths and moral precepts. By employing the rhetorical alternative of "strategic liberation," we mean to draw upon classical rhetoric's understanding of contingency to describe the manner in which individuals and groups seek to improve their local situation without presuming that such improvements are permanent, universal, or ideal solutions to particular problems.

The rhetorical theories represented in this volume similarly provide useful insights into the debate over the concept and phenomenon of "agency." In this debate, postmodernists have tended to discount the agency of individuals as message constructors or decoders by pointing to the ways in which an actor's beliefs and attitudes are prestructured by his or her placement in society as a function of gender, race, class, and the like. Modernists and those with a more traditional humanistic focus respond by pointing out the empirical experience of agency—there is at least the appearance that individual's and groups can affect the world in which they live—and its importance in theorizing the possibility of acting to make meaningful social and personal change. Contemporary rhetorical theories can help to resolve the disparity between social structure and lived experience by reconstituting our understanding of agency as a function of complex speaker–audience interactions. Such a view denies neither the materiality nor the significance of the agency of speaker or audience, but it does contextualize the agency of all parties to a social interaction as bound in relationship, rather than as the solitary product of some sort of determinism (be it economic or biological) or autonomous free will.

A third problem in social theory that can be profitably addressed from a rhetorical perspective is that of the status of science. Scientific studies are being conducted in almost every academic discipline, and it would be impossible to summarize the variety of issues and positions that have been taken about the status and role of science. However, again, the dialectic of modernism and postmodernism provides a defining trope for many of those discussions. On the modernist account, scientists search for permanent and absolute truths. They contribute to a lattice structure, or at least a stockpile of knowledge that will thereafter be permanently available for use. The postmodernist critique replies that this is patently untrue on its face. All of the scientific pronouncements of the past have been overturned or at least significantly modified through time, and the location and relations of various pieces of information are also constantly in flux. Moreover, the findings of science in various epochs bear a decided bias of conformity to the overarching worldviews of the societies from which they arise. Thus, the claim that science produces permanent and objective knowledge is obviously not only untrue, but, worse, an illusion that fosters the power of various ruling elites in history.

The rhetorical approach again allows us an alternative perspective, which understands that as a particular discourse community, science neither produces absolute and unchanging truths, nor is it merely a fantasy or farce that reproduces a dominant ideology. Rather, a rhetorical approach reminds us that scientific knowledge is "substantive" in precisely the same way that "social knowledge" is subtantive. The specific character of that knowledge, however, depends on the characteristics of the particular scientific community under consideration. Scientific knowledge does indeed change over time, but in science these changes do not obliterate previous knowledge or understandings. The discovery of Einsteinian relativity did not negate the utility of Newtonian mechanics: it simply circumscribed it. Moreover, within the discourse of science, Einstein's theory is understood as historically dependent upon Newton, and Copernicus, and perhaps even upon Democritus. Similarly, the arrival of theories of punctuated equilibrium, and the many other modifications to Darwin's original theories, are not understood as eliminating the insights of Darwin, but as circumscribing and redeploying them.

On the rhetorical account, science is simply a community with a very long memory, and one in which the role of past formulas in creating present formulations is honored, even though those past formulations may no longer have practical or daily use. Though scientists do not always recognize it, each previous scientific truth is almost always understood as having been reached through a staircase of previous truths, and each prior truth is honored as part of this staircase, even if the scientists of the day no longer stand upon that step, and even if the step is seen as decayed and defective. Moreover, the staircase of science is not one that leads in a single direction, so that various parts of the staircase are seen as under construction at various moments in time.

Given our view of science as a unique rhetorical community, it is not surprising that the steps erected by the scientific community also often tend to serve particular and different interest groups. Because science is "substantive," it builds its understandings out of the real material of social and physical life, but what it builds is inevitably influenced by its character as a community as well. Each step in science has a provisional kind of truth: it is the best truth that the community can make at the moment, given the rules, tools, and objectives with which it is operating. Within science, not all opinions are equal, and what counts as the intersubjective consensus is a rule-governed social enterprise determined by the community as it is constituted in any particular historical epoch. As such, scientific findings are "true," where that means that they are the best that can be described at the moment by the scientific community. Thus, scientific knowledge, on a rhetorical account, is neither *merely* a deceit nor a subjective opinion; rather, it is a provisional truth. The scientific community is distinctive because it places a relatively high value on the highest accuracy that is allowed by the available tools, rather than prioritizing rapidity or efficiency or immediate economic value. This ranking of values, however, is a matter of degree, rather than an absolute difference from other communities, and such value preferences may themselves be somewhat transient.

We hope these three examples indicate that the rhetorical construction and reconstruction of human social action have broad implications. By emphasizing both individual agency and human collectivities as the products of material performances of discourse, rather than as abstract ideals, we can begin to open possibilities for resolving the *aporia*—the apparent unknowability or undecidability—raised in the debates between classical philosophy and rhetoric. Contemporary rhetorical studies thus harbors exciting possibilities for the affirmative reconstruction of collective life in an increasingly multicultural, polyglot, liberal-democratic culture such as our own. It is to forward this agenda that we offer the essays in this volume and the general possibilities posed by the development of a critical and productive rhetorical theory for your use and consideration.

Notes

1. In indicating that rhetoric has a "distinctive" contribution to make, we do not mean to say that this is a unique contribution made by no one else in any other field. The study of rhetoric is so pervasive in the modern academy that any position we might outline has undoubtedly been taken by someone somewhere. The rhetorical perspective, unlike the scientific or philosophical perspective, does not give priority to "origins" (i.e., who discovered it first). The best rhetorician is not the one who espouses an idea first, but rather one who articulates it most effectively at a particular moment in time. To say that rhetorical study constitutes the possibility for distinctive contributions, then, is not to say that these contributions cannot be developed elsewhere, but rather to say that rhetorical theory offers a productive site at which contributions can be effectively mined and elaborated because of a broad and sustained interest in the power of language-in-use.

2. There are many different postmodernisms and our use of the singular "postmodernism" is not intended to suggest a totalizing philosophical or conceptual framework. Rather our use of the word "postmodern" refers to the range of conceptual and philosophical oppositions to "modernist" thinking that have emerged in the wake of the cultural, social, political, and economic conditions of modernity. Put somewhat differently, postmodernism refers to the many and numerous attempts to break out of the demands of philosophical modernism as means of understanding the conidtions of postmodernity, i.e., that which has come *after* modernity.

3. See, e.g., James Arnt Aune, "Rhetoric after Deconstruction," in Richard A. Cherwitz, ed., *Rhetoric and Philosophy* (Hillsdale, NJ: Erlbaum, 1990), pp. 253–274; and Thomas B. Farrell, *Norms of Rhetorical Culture* (New Haven, CT: Yale University Press, 1993).

INDEX

About the Editors

JOHN LOUIS LUCAITES (PhD, University of Iowa, 1984) is associate professor in the Department of Communication and Culture, adjunct associate professor in American Studies at Indiana University. He is also a Fellow at the Poynter Center for the Study of Ethics at Indiana University. He teaches courses in rhetorical theory and the relationship between rhetoric and social theory. His current research focuses on the critique of liberalism and democratic culture. He is the coauthor with Celeste Michelle Condit of *Crafting Equality: American's Anglo-African Word* (Marie Hochmuth Nichols Award for Outstanding Scholarship, National Communication Association, 1993).

CELESTE MICHELLE CONDIT (PhD, University of Iowa, 1982) is Professor of Speech Communication at the University of Georgia. She is coediting *Women's Studies in Communication*. Her books include *Decoding Abortion Rhetoric: The Communication of Social Change* (University of Illinois, 1990) and *Crafting Equality: America's Anglo-African Word* (University of Chicago, 1993; coauthored with John Louis Lucaites). She was the corecipient of the Marie Hocmuth Nichols Award and the Golden Monograph Award and the recipient of the Douglas Ehninger Award.

SALLY A. CAUDILL (PhD, University of Georgia, 1998) is a Visiting Assistant Professor in the Department of Communication Studies at Macalester College. She has published several essays on women's roles in reproductive technologies and public speaking. At present, her research interests include multicultural communication and the rhetoric of resistance. She has won numerous teaching awards and served as a student representative to the Women's Caucus of the National Communication Association.